WITH THE COMPLIMENTS OF

Dorothy Saintsbury

PROMOTION | DIRECTOR

THE DRYDEN PRESS BUILDING · 31 WEST 54th STREET · NEW YORK 19, N. Y.

PUBLIC OPINION AND PROPAGANDA

PUBLIC OPINION
and PROPAGANDA

A BOOK OF READINGS

EDITED FOR THE

Society for the Psychological Study
of Social Issues

DANIEL KATZ (Chairman)

Professor of Psychology, University of Michigan

DORWIN CARTWRIGHT

Director, Research Center for Group Dynamics, University of Michigan

SAMUEL ELDERSVELD

Associate Professor of Political Science, University of Michigan

ALFRED McCLUNG LEE

Chairman, Department of Sociology, Brooklyn College

THE DRYDEN PRESS · PUBLISHERS · NEW YORK

First printing, March 1954

Foreword

In 1947, the Society for the Psychological Study of Social Issues initiated the activities which led to the present book. Previously, the Society had undertaken, among other activities, the articulation of some of the perspectives of social science in a series of yearbooks: *Industrial Conflict, Civilian Morale, Human Nature and Enduring Peace.* A major contribution to the teaching of social psychology had been made by the preparation of a book of readings. In its tradition of identifying significant areas of social concern the analysis of which called for cooperative inquiry by social scientists, SPSSI then turned to the study of public opinion.

Committed as the Society is to a democratic value system, few things seemed more important than to contribute to increased clarification to this end. It was felt, however, that the findings to date were not sufficient to serve as a basis for a systematic exposition. As a first step, a collection of readings seemed a promising device to promote further understanding of the complexity of the problem, to highlight the multiplicity of approaches and emphases, and to contribute toward the improvement of work in the field.

On the basis of previous experience, the formula for a good book of readings seemed to consist of (1) a small, responsible editorial committee, working with (2) a larger advisory committee, with (3) both committees composed of experts in public opinion study who (4) were drawn from the several social sciences that have concerned themselves with the problem. Further, the necessary operating principles seemed to be: (1) the book was to be organized within a frame of reference valid for all of the disciplines involved; (2) it had to establish criteria of quality compatible with those accepted in

the fields it represented; (3) an appropriate balance between theory, method of study, and application was to be maintained; (4) it could not ignore the major controversies, philosophical, theoretical, or methodological, that revolved about the issues current in the field; (5) disagreements were to be resolved, whenever possible, by synthesis rather than by compromise or majority vote; and (6) finally, it must not be so long as to be unusable. It was not always possible to adhere to these principles.

In accordance with the Society's procedures, when the contents were finally decided upon, two qualified members who had not been involved in the preparation of the volume were asked to review it and to report on it to the Council of the Society. Dr. Herbert E. Krugman and Dr. Gerhart D. Wiebe accepted this task. At its Winter meeting in 1954, after reviewing the selections to be included and considering some of the major compromises that had been made, the Council endorsed the final table of contents.

Now, after seven years, the book is ready. Perhaps none of those concerned with its development regards it as precisely what he would have developed had he alone been responsible for it. Few, however, feel that it is not better for the divergence of the points of view that had to be considered in its creation.

The Society is enormously grateful to all who contributed to the production of this volume. We think it is a good book, and we have high hopes that it will contribute to improved understanding, to better and more significant research, and to the vitalizing of theoretical formulations in the area of public opinion analysis. To the extent that it achieves its aim, this volume will hasten its own obsolescence.

The City College of New York
March 1954

Eugene L. Hartley, President
Society for the Psychological
Study of Social Issues

List of Contributors

BEVERLY ALLINSMITH

WESLEY ALLINSMITH

FLOYD H. ALLPORT

GORDON W. ALLPORT

RUDOLF ARNHEIM

S. K. BAILEY

F. C. BARTLETT

BERNARD BERELSON

W. E. BINKLEY

HERBERT BLUMER

JEROME S. BRUNER

JAMES BRYCE

BUCHANAN COMMITTEE

JOHN C. CALHOUN

ANGUS CAMPBELL

CHARLES F. CANNELL

DORWIN CARTWRIGHT

RICHARD CENTERS

EUNICE COOPER

HELEN M. CROSSLEY

SEBASTIAN DE GRAZIA

RICHARD W. DODGE

LEONARD W. DOOB

CLIFFORD JUDKINS DURR

EMILY L. EHLE

SAMUEL J. ELDERSVELD

SEYMOUR FESHBACH

ELSE FRENKEL-BRUNSWIK

ARTHUR I. GLADSTONE

DAVID B. GLEICHER

CHARLES Y. GLOCK

RAYMOND L. GORDEN

GERALD GURIN

NORBERT GUTERMAN

LOUIS GUTTMAN

MORRIS H. HANSEN

PHILIP M. HAUSER

MARTIN F. HERZ

ERNEST R. HILGARD

CARL I. HOVLAND

HERBERT H. HYMAN

ALEX INKELES

MARIE JAHODA

IRVING L. JANIS

MORRIS JANOWITZ

ROBERT L. KAHN

of the Selections

ABRAHAM KAPLAN

DANIEL KATZ

ESTES KEFAUVER

PATRICIA L. KENDALL

ALICE S. KITT

JOSEPH T. KLAPPER

SHELDON J. KORCHIN

HAROLD LASSWELL

PAUL F. LAZARSFELD

ALFRED McCLUNG LEE

JACK LEVIN

WALTER LIPPMANN

S. M. LIPSET

A. LAWRENCE LOWELL

LEO LOWENTHAL

ARTHUR A. LUMSDAINE

CHARLES McCLINTOCK

MARGARET MEAD

CHARLES A. METZNER

MUNGO MILLER

WARREN A. MILLER

MARTIN MILLSPAUGH

M. C. MOOS

WARREN MOSCOW

NATIONAL RESOURCES COMMITTEE

THEODORE M. NEWCOMB

HUGH J. PARRY

STANLEY L. PAYNE

LEONARD I. PEARLIN

LEO J. POSTMAN

IRA DE A. REID

MORRIS ROSENBERG

FILLMORE H. SANFORD

IRVING SARNOFF

RICHARD L. SCHANCK

PAUL B. SHEATSLEY

EDWARD A. SHILS

M. BREWSTER SMITH

ULRICH STRAUSS

EDWARD A. SUCHMAN

DAVID B. TRUMAN

JULIUS TURNER

WALTER WEISS

G. D. WIEBE

ELIZABETH C. WINSHIP

KIMBALL YOUNG

Preface

In an age during which political and economic controls are mediated through symbols and sentiments and the functioning of society itself is dependent upon the mass communication of meaning, the field of public opinion and propaganda becomes a central area for scientist and citizen alike. Its basic understanding calls for rigorous analysis by the theoretician, and its practical control demands the enlightened interest of all members of the public.

For social science, this field of public opinion is of peculiar concern, for it is one of the few areas which has defied the specialization of the modern academic world. In accordance with the standardization of specialized functions in an industrial society, we have fractionated the sciences dealing with social behavior. But, fortunately, we have not been able to carry through this specialization in dealing with problems of public opinion and propaganda. Somehow the problems here have resisted division into arbitrary fragments. And social scientists from many disciplines have not only become interested in these problems; they have also worked cooperatively toward their solution. *The Public Opinion Quarterly,* to cite one instance, has not only had an audience which has cut across the behavioral disciplines, but its editors and contributors represent political science, history, anthropology, sociology, economics, and psychology.

It has been popular to preach an interdisciplinary approach but to practice a competitive division of specialized professional labor. The formal attempts to produce integration of the behavioral sciences by fiat have underestimated the importance of the on-going social structure. No matter what his ideal preoccupation, the scholar and scientist is subject to the social system in which he operates; positions and promotions are found in specific departments, which represent the intellectual climate as well as the vested interest of a given discipline.

The break in the institutional barriers has resulted less from good intention and formal resolution and more from significant problems common to scientists in different fields, as is the case in the study of public opinion. There are important aspects of such problems which concern specialists in a number of fields and, moreover, the solution of the over-all problem requires contributions from the many specialized disciplines.

From its inception, the Society for the Psychological Study of Social Issues has had as one of its objectives the encouragement of an interdisciplinary approach to the social sciences. Many of its earlier volumes, as well as its organ, the *Journal of Social Issues,* have represented cooperative efforts of various behavioral scientists on problems of interdisciplinary interest.

A book of readings in public opinion and propaganda became an agenda item for the Society several years ago, and an editorial committee was set up to include political science, sociology, and social psychology, with an even broader-gauged advisory board. The reason for the inclusion of many social disciplines is obvious. Political science by definition includes the dynamics of political change; sociology and anthropology are concerned with social control, with the social determination of public opinion, and with the relation between social structure and opinion; social psychology is interested in the individual dynamics and the group reinforcement of values, aspirations, and beliefs basic to opinion; and all of these disciplines would claim leadership, communication, and the influence process as a legitimate part of their subject matter.

In the development of this volume, the editors have accordingly followed an interdisciplinary approach and have presented readings which would show the societal context, the political structure, and the social dynamics of opinion formation. The point of view presented in this book, however, reflects more than the belief in the necessity of an interdisciplinary approach. The editors believe that the area of public opinion and propaganda is amenable to a scientific approach in the sense that the data of human behavior can be gathered under controlled conditions, that variables can be quantified, and that experimentation can be employed. Accordingly, empirical and research studies are included not necessarily because they are definitive but because they illustrate how the research method can be applied to problems often regarded as the exclusive property of the wisdom distilled from random impressions. Often the research studies are exploratory and incomplete, but if they leave us with only the beginnings of a structure, they also leave us with the challenge of significant and absorbing discoveries to come. And it should be remembered that science is always in an incomplete and unfinished state.

Because the field of public opinion is at present so unstructured, we have attempted a wide coverage of points of view, of types of studies, and of practical and theoretical problems. Without attempting to be representative of the vast literature in the field, we have tried to present the major positions on debated issues and to give the student familiarity with both classical concepts and recent empirical advances.

This book is designed for use in courses in public opinion and in propaganda on the assumption that just as the course is given in different departments in various institutions, its character, no matter where it is given, is interdisciplinary. The materials included in the present volume are there because they contribute to the field and not because they have been originally prepared by a specialist bearing a given label.

In the preparation of this book, we have had the benefit of the experience and counsel of the members of an advisory board of social scientists. They are responsible in good measure for whatever merit this volume has, but they are not to be held in any sense responsible for its defects. We are grateful, too, for the preliminary work of the first editorial SPSSI committee—consisting of Angus Campbell, chairman, Jerome S. Bruner, Louis Hartz, and Alfred McClung Lee—without which our task would have been more difficult. And, in the usual inadequate way, we call attention to the unsung editorial assistants who carry the brunt of the detailed work in producing a book. Phyllis Jackson ably assisted in the planning stages; Anne Naymik was a resourceful aid in manuscript preparation; and Mary Lee Baisch, as chief editorial assistant, was the mainstay of the editors—for everything from the smallest details to important decisions on which they needed advice.

We are grateful, too, to the authors who gave permission for the use of their articles and to the following journals and publishers, who graciously gave consent to the reprinting of their materials: the *Public Opinion Quarterly;* the *Journal of Abnormal and Social Psychology;* the *American Political Science Review;* the *American Sociological Review; Human Relations;* the *Journal of International Opinion and Attitude Research;* the *Journal of Psychology;* the *Journal of Social Psychology;* the *National Marketing Review;* the *Scientific American;* the

American Marketing Association; the American Psychological Association; the American Sociological Society; the Institute for Social Research of the University of Michigan; the National Council for Social Studies; the New York Academy of Sciences; the Social Science Research Council; Alfred A. Knopf, Inc.; Appleton-Century-Crofts, Inc.; Cambridge University Press; Duell, Sloane, & Pearce, Inc.; The Free Press; Harper and Brothers; Harvard University Press; Johns Hopkins Press; The Journal Press; Longmans, Green and Co., Inc.; Row, Peterson and Co.; Princeton University Press; and Yale University Press.

March 3, 1954

DANIEL KATZ
DORWIN CARTWRIGHT
SAMUEL J. ELDERSVELD
ALFRED McCLUNG LEE

Contents—An Overview

(For complete table contents of this book, see pp. xiii–xx)

PART ONE · THE NATURE AND FUNCTION OF PUBLIC OPINION

1·The Role of Public Opinion in a Democracy

2·Definitions of Public Opinion and the Public

PART TWO · THE SOCIAL AND POLITICAL CONTEXT OF PUBLIC OPINION

3·Cultural Background, Social Organization, and Economic Structure

4·Governmental Structure and Process: Political Parties, Pressure Groups

5·Mass Media

PART THREE · SOCIAL-PSYCHOLOGICAL PROCESSES BASIC TO PUBLIC OPINION

6·The Psychological Basis of Opinion and Attitude

7·Group Processes: Interaction, Communication and Influence, Social Reinforcement

PART FOUR · DYNAMICS OF OPINION FORMATION AND CHANGE

8·The Nature of Propaganda and the Propagandist

9·Propaganda Strategies and Techniques and Their Effects

10·Formation and Determination of Public Opinion

PART FIVE · THE IDENTIFICATION AND MEASUREMENT OF PUBLIC OPINION AND PROPAGANDA

11·Problems of Data Collection in the Measurement of Public Opinion: Sampling, Interviewing, Questionnaire Construction

12·Analysis and Interpretation of Data

Table of Contents

PART ONE

The Nature and Function of Public Opinion

CHAPTER 1 · THE ROLE OF PUBLIC OPINION IN A DEMOCRACY 2

The Nature of Public Opinion, 3 –
  JAMES BRYCE

Public Opinion and Majority Government, 11
  A. LAWRENCE LOWELL

Disquisition on Government, 15 –
  JOHN C. CALHOUN

The Multi-Group Nature of the State, 24
  W. E. BINKLEY AND M. C. MOOS

The Image of Democracy, 27
  WALTER LIPPMANN

The Current Status of American Public Opinion, 33
  HERBERT H. HYMAN AND PAUL B. SHEATSLEY

CHAPTER 2 · DEFINITIONS OF PUBLIC OPINION AND THE PUBLIC 49

Some Definitions of Public Opinion, 50
    (Compiled by ULRICH STRAUSS)

Toward a Science of Public Opinion, 51
  FLOYD H. ALLPORT

Comments on the Nature of "Public" and "Public Opinion," 62
    KIMBALL YOUNG

Publics, Public Opinion, and General Interests, 66
    HAROLD LASSWELL AND ABRAHAM KAPLAN

Public Opinion and Public Opinion Polling, 70
    HERBERT BLUMER

PART TWO

The Social and Political Context of Public Opinion

CHAPTER 3 · CULTURAL BACKGROUND, SOCIAL ORGANIZATION, AND ECONOMIC STRUCTURE   86

Public Opinion Mechanisms Among Primitive Peoples, 87
    MARGARET MEAD

Social Determinants of Public Opinions, 94
    ALFRED McCLUNG LEE

Trial by Newspaper, 105
    JOSEPH T. KLAPPER AND CHARLES Y. GLOCK

Trial by Mass Media?, 113
    MARTIN MILLSPAUGH

The Structure of Controls, 114
    NATIONAL RESOURCES COMMITTEE

Attitude and Belief in Relation to Occupational Stratification, 132
    RICHARD CENTERS

Religious Affiliation and Politico-Economic Attitude: A Study of Eight Major
    U. S. Religious Groups, 151
    WESLEY AND BEVERLY ALLINSMITH

CHAPTER 4 · GOVERNMENTAL STRUCTURE AND PROCESS: POLITICAL PARTIES, PRESSURE GROUPS   159

The Dynamics of Access in the Legislative Process, 160
  DAVID B. TRUMAN

Conference and Compromise, 176
  S. K. BAILEY

Representative Government Through the House of Representatives, 185
  JULIUS TURNER

The Machines, 194
  WARREN MOSCOW

General Interim Report of the House Select Committee on Lobbying
  Activities, 206
  (THE BUCHANAN COMMITTEE)

Letters that Really Count, 220
  ESTES KEFAUVER AND JACK LEVIN

Public Opinion Polls and Democratic Leadership, 226
  DORWIN CARTWRIGHT

CHAPTER 5 · MASS MEDIA   234

Books, Libraries, and Other Media of Communication, 235
  ANGUS CAMPBELL AND CHARLES A. METZNER

The World of the Daytime Serial, 243
  RUDOLF ARNHEIM

What "Missing the Newspaper" Means, 263
  BERNARD BERELSON

Do Rosy Headlines Sell Newspapers?, 271
  ELIZABETH C. WINSHIP AND GORDON W. ALLPORT

Freedom of the Press, 275
  ALFRED MCCLUNG LEE

Freedom of Speech for Whom?, 278
  CLIFFORD JUDKINS DURR

Television and the Election, 287 ✓
  ANGUS CAMPBELL, GERALD GURIN AND WARREN E. MILLER

PART THREE

Social-Psychological Processes Basic to Public Opinion

CHAPTER 6 · THE PSYCHOLOGICAL BASIS OF OPINION AND ATTITUDE

294

The Personal Setting of Public Opinions: A Study of Attitudes Toward Russia, 295
 M. BREWSTER SMITH

Attitude-Change Procedures and Motivating Patterns, 305
 IRVING SARNOFF, DANIEL KATZ, AND CHARLES MCCLINTOCK

The Evasion of Propaganda: How Prejudiced People Respond to Anti-Prejudice Propaganda, 313
 EUNICE COOPER AND MARIE JAHODA

Effects of Fear-Arousing Communications, 320
 IRVING L. JANIS AND SEYMOUR FESHBACH

The Influence of Source Credibility on Communication Effectiveness, 337
 CARL I. HOVLAND AND WALTER WEISS

✓ Effects of Preparatory Communications on Reactions to a Subsequent News Event, 347
 IRVING L. JANIS, ARTHUR A. LUMSDAINE AND ARTHUR I. GLADSTONE

Interaction of Psychological and Sociological Factors in Political Behavior, 363
 ELSE FRENKEL-BRUNSWIK

CHAPTER 7 · GROUP PROCESSES: INTERACTION, COMMUNICATION AND INFLUENCE, SOCIAL REINFORCEMENT

381

Some Principles of Mass Persuasion, Selected Findings of Research on the Sale of United States War Bonds, 382
 DORWIN CARTWRIGHT

The Basic Psychology of Rumor, 394

    GORDON W. ALLPORT AND LEO J. POSTMAN

The Bolshevik Agitator, 404

    ALEX INKELES

Determinants of Voting Behavior, A Progress Report on the Elmira
Election Study, 413

    ALICE S. KITT AND DAVID B. GLEICHER

Interaction between Attitude and the Definition of the Situation in the
Expression of Opinion, 425

    RAYMOND L. GORDEN

Some Patterned Consequences of Membership in a College Community, 435

    THEODORE M. NEWCOMB

Leadership Selection in Urban Locality Areas, 446

    IRA DE A. REID AND EMILY L. EHLE

PART FOUR

Dynamics of Opinion Formation and Change

CHAPTER 8 · THE NATURE OF PROPAGANDA AND THE PROPAGANDIST

462

The Aims of Political Propaganda, 463

    F. C. BARTLETT

Portrait of the American Agitator, 470

    LEO LOWENTHAL AND NORBERT GUTERMAN

Propaganda Techniques in Institutional Advertising, 478

    LEONARD I. PEARLIN AND MORRIS ROSENBERG

The Dimensions of Propaganda: German Short-Wave Broadcasts
to America, 491

    JEROME S. BRUNER

CHAPTER 9 · PROPAGANDA STRATEGIES AND TECHNIQUES AND THEIR EFFECTS   507

Goebbels' Principles of Propaganda, 508
    LEONARD W. DOOB

Some Reasons Why Information Campaigns Fail, 522
    HERBERT H. HYMAN AND PAUL B. SHEATSLEY

Personal Contact or Mail Propaganda? An Experiment in Voting Turnout and Attitude Change, 532
    SAMUEL J. ELDERSVELD AND RICHARD W. DODGE

Some Psychological Lessons from Leaflet Propaganda in World War II, 543
    MARTIN F. HERZ

Cohesion and Disintegration in the Wehrmacht in World War II, 553
    EDWARD A. SHILS AND MORRIS JANOWITZ

CHAPTER 10 · FORMATION AND DETERMINATION OF PUBLIC OPINION   583

Opinion Formation in a Crisis Situation, 584
    S. M. LIPSET

Test-Tube for Public Opinion: A Rural Community, 598
    RICHARD L. SCHANCK

The Boss and the Vote: A Case Study in City Politics, 602
    JEROME S. BRUNER AND SHELDON J. KORCHIN

Responses to the Televised Kefauver Hearings: Some Social Psychological Implications, 616
    G. D. WIEBE

Political Issues and the Vote: November, 1952, 623
    ANGUS CAMPBELL, GERALD GURIN AND WARREN E. MILLER

The Interaction of Motivating Factors, 641
    ANGUS CAMPBELL, GERALD GURIN AND WARREN E. MILLER

PART FIVE

The Identification and Measurement of Public Opinion and Propaganda

CHAPTER 11 · PROBLEMS OF DATA COLLECTION IN THE MEASUREMENT OF PUBLIC OPINION: SAMPLING, INTERVIEWING, QUESTIONNAIRE CONSTRUCTION   **650**

Area Sampling—Some Principles of Sample Design, 651
MORRIS H. HANSEN AND PHILIP M. HAUSER

Those Not at Home: Riddle for Pollsters, 657
ERNEST R. HILGARD AND STANLEY L. PAYNE

The Formulation of the Research Design, 662
DANIEL KATZ

Dual Purpose of the Questionnaire, 664
CHARLES F. CANNELL AND ROBERT L. KAHN

The General Problem of Questionnaire Design, 665
HERBERT H. HYMAN

The Art of Asking Why, Three Principles Underlying the Formulation of Questionnaires, 675
PAUL F. LAZARSFELD

The Controversy over Detailed Interviews—An Offer for Negotiation, 687
PAUL F. LAZARSFELD

The Use of a Projective Device in Attitude Surveying, 701
FILLMORE H. SANFORD

CHAPTER 12 · ANALYSIS AND INTERPRETATION OF DATA   **711**

Detecting Collaboration in Propaganda, 712
BERNARD BERELSON AND SEBASTIAN DE GRAZIA

Problems of Survey Analysis, 718
　　　PATRICIA L. KENDALL AND PAUL F. LAZARSFELD

A Solution to the Problem of Question "Bias," 729
　　　EDWARD A. SUCHMAN AND LOUIS GUTTMAN

Validity of Responses to Survey Questions, 738
　　　HUGH J. PARRY AND HELEN M. CROSSLEY

The Waukegan Study of Voter Turnout Prediction, 751
　　　MUNGO MILLER

INDEX　　　　　　　　　　　　　　　　　　　　　　　　**761**

PART ONE

The Nature and Function
of Public Opinion

·1·

The Role of Public Opinion

in a Democracy

◡

THE NATURE OF PUBLIC OPINION

PUBLIC OPINION AND MAJORITY GOVERNMENT

DISQUISITION ON GOVERNMENT

THE MULTI-GROUP NATURE OF THE STATE

THE IMAGE OF DEMOCRACY

THE CURRENT STATUS OF AMERICAN PUBLIC OPINION

THE NATURE OF PUBLIC OPINION

JAMES BRYCE

What do we mean by public opinion? The difficulties which occur in discussing its action mostly arise from confounding opinion itself with the organs whence people try to gather it, and from using the term to denote, sometimes everybody's views, —that is, the aggregate of all that is thought and said on a subject,—sometimes merely the views of the majority, the particular type of thought and speech which prevails over other types.

The simplest form in which public opinion presents itself is when a sentiment spontaneously rises in the mind and flows from the lips of the average man upon his seeing or hearing something done or said. Homer presents this with his usual vivid directness in the line which frequently recurs in the Iliad when the effect produced by a speech or event is to be conveyed: "And thus any one was saying as he looked at his neighbor." This phrase describes what may be called the rudimentary stage of opinion. It is the prevalent impression of the moment. It is what any man (not every man) says, *i.e.*, it is the natural and the general thought or wish which an occurrence evokes. But before opinion begins to tell upon government, it has to go through several other stages. These stages are various in different ages and countries. Let us try to note what they are in England or

America at the present time, and how each stage grows out of the other.

A business man reads in his newspaper at breakfast the events of the preceding day. He reads that Prince Bismarck has announced a policy of protection for German industry, or that Mr. Henry George has been nominated for the mayoralty of New York. These statements arouse in his mind sentiments of approval or disapproval, which may be strong or weak according to his previous predilection for or against protection or Mr. Henry George, and of course according to his personal interest in the matter. They rouse also an expectation of certain consequences likely to follow. Neither the sentiment nor the expectation is based on processes of conscious reasoning—our business man has not time to reason at breakfast—they are merely impressions formed on the spur of the moment. He turns to the leading article in the newspaper, and his sentiments and expectations are confirmed or weakened according as he finds that they are or are not shared by the newspaper writer. He goes down to his office in the train, talks there to two or three acquaintances, and perceives that they agree or do not agree with his own still faint impressions. In his business office he finds his partner and a bundle of other newspapers which he

From *The American Commonwealth* (New York: The Macmillan Company, 1916 edition), Volume II, pp. 251-266. Reprinted by permission of the publisher.

glances at; their words further affect him, and thus by the afternoon his mind is beginning to settle down into a definite view, which approves or condemns Prince Bismarck's declaration or the nomination of Mr. George. Meanwhile a similar process has been going on in the minds of others, and particularly of the journalists whose business it is to discover what people are thinking. The evening paper has collected the opinions of the morning papers, and is rather more positive in its forecast of results. Next day the leading journals have articles still more definite and positive in approval or condemnation and in prediction of consequences to follow; and the opinion of ordinary minds, hitherto fluid and undetermined, has begun to crystallize into a solid mass. This is the second stage. Then debate and controversy begin. The men and the newspapers who approve Mr. George's nomination argue with those who do not; they find out who are friends and who opponents. The effect of controversy is to drive the partisans on either side from some of their arguments, which are shown to be weak; to confirm them in others, which they think strong; and to make them take up a definite position on one side. This is the third stage. The fourth is reached when action becomes necessary. When a citizen has to give a vote, he votes as a member of a party, his party prepossessions and party allegiance lay hold on him, and generally stifle any doubts or repulsions he may feel. Bringing men up to the polls is like passing a steam roller over stones newly laid on a road; the angularities are pressed down, and an appearance of smooth and even uniformity is given which did not exist before. When a man has voted, he is committed; he has thereafter an interest in backing the view which he has sought to make prevail. Moreover, opinion, which may have been manifold till the polling, is thereafter generally twofold only. There is a view which has triumphed and a view which has been vanquished.

In examining the process by which opinion is formed, we cannot fail to note how small a part of the view which the average man entertains when he goes to vote is really of his own making. His original impression was faint and perhaps shapeless: its present definiteness and strength are mainly due to what he has heard and read. He has been told what to think, and why to think it. Arguments have been supplied to him from without, and controversy has embedded them in his mind. Although he supposes his view to be his own, he holds it rather because his acquaintances do the like. Each man believes and repeats certain phrases, because he thinks that everybody else on his side believes them, and of what each believes only a small part is his own original impression, the far larger part being the result of the commingling and mutual action and reaction of the impressions of a multitude of individuals, in which the element of pure personal conviction, based on individual thinking, is but small.

. . . When some important event happens, which calls for the formation of a view, pre-existing habits, dogmas, affinities, help to determine the impression which each man experiences, and so far are factors in the view he forms. But they operate chiefly in determining the first impression, and they operate over many minds at once. They do not produce variety and independence: they are soon overlaid by the influences which each man derives from his fellows, from his leaders, from the press.

Orthodox democratic theory assumes that every citizen has, or ought to have, thought out for himself certain opinions, *i.e.*, ought to have a definite view, defensible by arguments, of what the country needs, of what principles ought to be applied in governing it, of the men to whose hands the government ought to be entrusted . . . But one need only try the experiment of talking to that representative of public opinion, whom the Americans call "the man in the cars," to realize how uniform opinion is among all classes of people,

how little there is in the ideas of each individual of that individuality, which they
would have if he had formed them for himself, how little solidity and substance there
is in the political or social beliefs of nineteen persons out of every twenty. These
beliefs, when examined, mostly resolve
themselves into two or three prejudices and
aversions, two or three prepossessions for
a particular leader or party or section of
a party, two or three phrases or catchwords
suggesting or embodying arguments which
the man who repeats them has not analyzed.
It is not that these nineteen persons are incapable of appreciating good arguments,
or are unwilling to receive them. On the
contrary, and this is especially true of the
working classes, an audience is pleased when
solid arguments are addressed to it, and
men read with most relish the articles or
leaflets, supposing them to be smartly written, which contain the most carefully sifted
facts and the most exact thought. But to
the great mass of mankind in all places,
public questions come in the third or
fourth rank among the interests of life, and
obtain less than a third or fourth of the
leisure available for thinking. It is therefore rather sentiment than thought that
the mass can contribute, a sentiment
grounded on a few broad considerations
and simple trains of reasoning; and the
soundness and elevation of their sentiment
will have more to do with their taking their
stand on the side of justice, honour, and
peace, than any reasoning they can apply
to the sifting of the multifarious facts
thrown before them, and to the drawing of
the legitimate inferences therefrom.

It may be suggested that this analysis, if
true of the half-educated, is not true of the
educated classes. It is less true of that
small class which in Europe specially occupies itself with politics; which, whether
it reasons well or ill, does no doubt reason.
But it is substantially no less applicable to
the commercial and professional classes
than to the working classes; for in the former, as well as in the latter, one finds few
persons who take the pains, or have the

leisure, or indeed possess the knowledge, to
enable them to form an independent judgment. The chief difference between the so-
called upper, or wealthier, and the humbler
strata of society is, that the former are less
influenced by sentiment and possibly more
influenced by notions, often erroneous, of
their own interest. Having something to
lose, they imagine dangers to their property or their class ascendency. Moving in
a more artificial society, their sympathies
are less readily excited, and they more frequently indulge the tendency to cynicism
natural to those who lead a life full of un-
reality and conventionalisms.

The apparent paradox that where the
humbler classes have differed in opinion
from the higher, they have often been proved
by the event to have been right and their so-
called betters wrong (a fact sufficiently illustrated by the experience of many European countries during the last half-century),
may perhaps be explained by considering
that the historical and scientific data on
which the solution of a difficult political
problem depends are really just as little
known to the wealthy as to the poor. Ordinary education, even the sort of education
which is represented by a university degree,
does not fit a man to handle these questions, and it sometimes fills him with a vain
conceit of his own competence which closes
his mind to argument and to the accumulating evidence of facts. Education ought, no
doubt, to enlighten a man; but the educated classes, speaking generally, are the
property-holding classes, and the possession
of property does more to make a man timid
than education does to make him hopeful.
He is apt to underrate the power as well as
the worth of sentiment; he overvalues the
restraints which existing institutions impose; he has a faint appreciation of the
curative power of freedom, and of the tendency which brings things right when men
have been left to their own devices, and
have learnt from failure how to attain success. In the less-educated man a certain
simplicity and openness of mind go some
way to compensate for the lack of knowl-

edge. He is more apt to be influenced by the authority of leaders; but as, at least in England and America, he is generally shrewd enough to discern between a great man and a demagogue, this is more a gain than a loss.

. . . Nearly all great political and social causes have made their way first among the middle or humbler classes. The original impulse which has set the cause in motion, the inspiring ideas that have drawn men to it, have come from lofty and piercing minds, and minds generally belonging to the cultivated class. But the principles and precepts these minds have delivered have waxed strong because the common people received them gladly, while the wealthy and educated classes have frowned on or persecuted them. The most striking instance of all this is to be found in the early history of Christianity.

The analysis, however, which I have sought to give of opinion applies only to the nineteen men out of twenty, and not to the twentieth. It applies to what may be called passive opinion—the opinion of those who have no special interest in politics, or concern with them beyond that of voting, of those who receive or propagate, but do not originate, views on public matters. Or, to put the same thing in different words, we have been considering how public opinion grows and spreads, as it were, spontaneously and naturally. But opinion does not merely grow; it is also made. There is not merely the passive class of persons; there is the active class, who occupy themselves primarily with public affairs, who aspire to create and lead opinion. The process which these guides follow are too well known to need description. There are, however, one or two points which must be noted, in order to appreciate the reflex action of the passive upon the active class.

The man who tries to lead public opinion, be he statesman, journalist, or lecturer, finds in himself, when he has to form a judgment upon any current event, a larger measure of individual prepossession, and of what may be called political theory and

doctrine, than belongs to the average citizen. His view is therefore likely to have more individuality, as well as more intellectual value. On the other hand, he has also a stronger motive than the average citizen for keeping in agreement with his friends and his party, because if he stands aloof and advocates a view of his own, he may lose his influence and his position. He has a past, and is prevented, by the fear of seeming inconsistent, from departing from what he has previously said. He has a future, and dreads to injure it by severing himself ever so little from his party. He is accordingly driven to make the same sort of compromise between his individual tendencies and the general tendency which the average citizen makes. But he makes it more consciously, realizing far more distinctly the difference between what he would think, say, and do, if left to himself, and what he says and does as a politician, who can be useful and prosperous only as a member of a body of persons acting together and professing to think alike.

Accordingly, though the largest part of the work of forming opinion is done by these men,—whom I do not call professional politicians, because in Europe many of them are not solely occupied with politics, while in America the name of professionals must be reserved for another class,—we must not forget the reaction constantly exercised upon them by the passive majority. Sometimes a leading statesman or journalist takes a line to which he finds that the mass of those who usually agree with him are not responsive. He perceives that they will not follow him, and that he must choose between isolation and a modification of his own views. A statesman may sometimes venture on the former course, and in very rare cases succeed in imposing his own will and judgment on his party. A journalist, however, is obliged to hark back if he has inadvertently taken up a position disagreeable to his *clientele*, because the proprietors of the paper have their circulation to consider. To avoid so disagreeable a choice, a statesman or a journalist is usually on the alert to sound the general opinion before he commits himself on a new issue. He tries to feel the pulse of the mass of average citizens; and as the mass, on the other hand, look to him for initiative, this is a delicate process. In European countries it is generally the view of the leaders which prevails, but it is modified by the reception which the mass give it; it becomes accentuated in the points which they appreciate; while those parts of it, or those ways of stating it, which have failed to find popular favour, fall back into the shade.

This mutual action and reaction of the makers or leaders of opinion upon the mass, and of the mass upon them, is the most curious part of the whole process by which opinion is produced. It is also that part in which there is the greatest difference between one free country and another. In some countries, the leaders count for, say, three-fourths of the product, and the mass for one-fourth only. In others these proportions are reversed. In some countries the mass of the voters are not only markedly inferior in education to the few who lead, but also diffident, more disposed to look up to their betters. In others the difference of intellectual level between those who busy themselves with politics and the average voter is far smaller. Perhaps the leader is not so well instructed a man as in the countries first referred to; perhaps the average voter is better instructed and more self-confident. Where both of these phenomena coincide, so that the difference of level is inconsiderable, public opinion will evidently be a different thing from what it is in countries where, though the Constitution has become democratic, the habits of the nations are still aristocratic. This is the difference between America and the countries of Western Europe.

GOVERNMENT BY PUBLIC OPINION

We talk of public opinion as a new force in the world, conspicuous only since governments began to be popular. Statesmen, even so lately as two generations ago, looked on it with some distrust or dislike. Sir Robert Peel, for instance, in a letter written in 1820 speaks, with the air of a discoverer, of "that great compound of folly, weakness, prejudice, wrong feeling, right feeling, obstinacy, and newspaper paragraphs, which is called public opinion."

Yet opinion has really been the chief and ultimate power in nearly all nations at nearly all times. I do not mean merely the opinion of the class to which the rulers belong. Obviously the small oligarchy of Venice was influenced by the opinion of Venetian nobility, as an absolute Czar is influenced by the opinion of his court and his army. I mean the opinion, unspoken, unconscious, but not the less real and potent, of the masses of people. Governments have always rested and, special cases apart, must rest if not on the affection then on the reverence or awe, if not on the active approval then on the silent acquiescence, of the numerical majority. It is only by rare exception that a monarch or an oligarchy has maintained authority against the will of the people. The despotisms of the East, although they usually began in conquest, did not stand by military force but by popular assent. So did the feudal kingdoms of mediaeval Europe. So do the monarchies of the Sultan (so far, at least, as regards his Mussulman subjects), of the Shah, and of the Chinese Emperor. The cases to the contrary are chiefly those of military tyrannies, such as existed in many of the Greek cities of antiquity, and in some of the Italian cities of the Renaissance, and such as now exist in some of the so-called republics of Central and South America. That even the Roman Empire, that eldest child of war and conquest, did not rest on force but on the consent and good-will of its subjects, is shown by the smallness of its standing armies, nearly the whole of which were employed against frontier enemies, because there was rarely any internal revolt or disturbance to be feared. Belief in authority, and the love of established order, are among the strongest forces in human nature, and therefore in politics.

The first supports the governments *de jure*, the latter governments *de facto*. They combine to support a government which is *de jure* as well as *de facto*. Where the subjects are displeased, their discontent may appear perhaps in the epigrams which tempered the despotism of Louis XV. in France, perhaps in the sympathy given to bandits like Robin Hood, perhaps in occasional insurrections like those of Constantinople under Eastern Emperors. Of course, where there is no habit of combining to resist, discontent may remain for some time without this third means of expressing itself. But, even when the occupant of the throne is unpopular, the throne as an institution is in no danger so long as it can command the respect of the multitude and show itself equal to its duties.

In the earlier or simpler forms of political society public opinion is passive. It acquiesces in, rather than supports, the authority which exists, whatever its faults, because it knows of nothing better, because it sees no way to improvement, probably also because it is overawed by some kind of religious sanction. Human nature must have something to reverence, and the sovereign, because remote and potent and surrounded by pomp and splendor, seems to it mysterious and half divine. Worse administrations than those of Asiatic Turkey and Persia in the nineteenth century can hardly be imagined, yet the Mohammedan population showed no signs of disaffection. The subjects of Darius and the subjects of Theebaw obeyed, as a matter of course. They did not ask why they obeyed, for the habit of obedience was sufficient. They could, however, if disaffected, have at any moment overturned the throne, which had only, in both cases, an insignificant force of guards to protect it. During long ages the human mind did not ask itself—in many parts of the world does not even now ask itself—questions which seem to us the most obvious. Custom, as Pindar said, is king over all mortals and immortals, and custom prescribed obedience. When in any society opinion becomes self-conscious, when it be-

gins to realize its force and question the rights of its rulers, that society is already progressing, and soon finds means of organizing resistance and compelling reform.

The difference, therefore, between despotically governed and free countries does not consist, in the fact that the latter are ruled by opinion and the former by force, for both are generally ruled by opinion. It consists rather in this, that in the former the people instinctively obey a power which they do not know to be really of their own creation, and to stand by their own permission; whereas in the latter the people feel their supremacy, and consciously treat their rulers as their agents, while the rulers obey a power which they admit to have made and to be able to unmake them,—the popular will. In both cases force is seldom necessary, or is needed only against small groups, because the habit of obedience replaces it. Conflicts and revolutions belong to the intermediate stage, when the people are awakening to the sense that they are truly the supreme power in the State, but when the rulers have not yet become aware that their authority is merely delegated. When superstition and the habit of submission have vanished from the whilom subjects, when the rulers, recognizing that they are no more than agents for the citizens, have in turn formed the habit of obedience, public opinion has become the active and controlling director of a business in which it was before the sleeping and generally forgotten partner. But even when this stage has been reached, as has now happened in most civilized States, there are differences in the degree and mode in and by which public opinion asserts itself. In some countries the habit of obeying rulers and officials is so strong that the people, once they have chosen the legislature or executive head by whom officials are appointed, allow these officials almost as wide a range of authority as in the old days of despotism. Such people have a profound respect for government as government, and a reluctance, due either to theory or to mere laziness, perhaps to both, to interfere with its action. They say, "That is a matter for the Administration; we have nothing to do with it"; and stand as much aside or submit as humbly as if the government did not spring from their own will. Perhaps they practically leave themselves, as did the Germans of Bismarck's day, in the hands of a venerated monarch or a forceful minister, giving these rulers a free hand so long as their policy moves in accord with the sentiment of the nation, and maintains its glory. Perhaps while frequently changing their ministries, they nevertheless yield to each ministry and to its executive subordinates all over the country, an authority great while it lasts, and largely controlling the action of the individual citizen. This seems to be still true of France. There are other countries in which, though the sphere of government is strictly limited by law, and the private citizen is little inclined to bow before an official, the habit has been to check the ministry chiefly through the legislature, and to review the conduct of both ministry and legislature only at long intervals, when an election of the legislature takes place. This has been, and to some extent is still, the case in Britain. Although the people rule, they rule not directly, but through the House of Commons, which they choose only once in four or five years, and which may, at any given moment, represent rather the past than the present will of the nation.

I make these observations for the sake of indicating another form which the rule of the people may assume. We have distinguished three stages in the evolution of opinion from its unconscious and passive into its conscious and active condition. In the first it acquiesces in the will of the ruler whom it has been accustomed to obey. In the second conflicts arise between the ruling person or class, backed by those who are still disposed to obedience, on the one hand and the more independent or progressive spirits on the other; and these conflicts are decided by arms. In the third stage the whilom ruler has submitted, and disputes are referred to the sovereign multitude, whose will is expressed at certain intervals upon slips of paper deposited in boxes, and is carried out by the minister or legislature to whom the popular mandate is entrusted. A fourth stage would be reached, if the will of the majority of the citizens were to become ascertainable at all times, and without the need of its passing through a body of representatives, possibly even without the need of voting machinery at all. In such a state of things the sway of public opinion would have become more complete, because more continuous, than it is in those European countries which, like France, Italy, and Britain, look chiefly to parliaments as exponents of national sentiment. The authority would seem to remain all the while in the mass of the citizens. Popular government would have been pushed so far as almost to dispense with, or at any rate to anticipate, the legal modes in which the majority speaks its will at the polling booths; and this informal but direct control of the multitude would dwarf, it it did not supersede, the importance of those formal but occasional deliverances made at the elections of representatives. To such a condition of things the phrase, "Rule of public opinion," might be most properly applied, for public opinion would not only reign but govern.

The mechanical difficulties, as one may call them, of working such a method of government are obvious . . . But what I desire to point out is that even where the machinery for weighing or measuring the popular will from week to week or month to month has not been, and is not likely to be, invented, there may nevertheless be a disposition on the part of the rulers, whether ministers or legislators, to act as if it existed; that is to say, to look incessantly for manifestations of current popular opinion, and to shape their course in accordance with their reading of those manifestations. Such a disposition will be accompanied by a constant oversight of public affairs by the mass of the citizens, and by a sense on their part that they are the true governors, and that their agents, executive and legislative, are rather servants than agents: Where this is the attitude of the people on the one hand and of the persons who do the actual work of governing on the other, it may fairly be said that there exists a kind of government materially, if not formally, different from the representative system as it presented itself to European thinkers and statesmen of the last generation. And it is to this kind of government that democratic nations seem to be tending.

. . . The excellence of popular government lies not so much in its wisdom—for it is as apt to err as other kinds of government —as in its strength. It has been compared, ever since Sir William Temple, to a pyramid, the firmest based of all buildings. Nobody can be blamed for obeying it. There is no appeal from its decisions. Once the principle that the will of the majority honestly ascertained must prevail, has soaked into the mind and formed the habits of a nation, that nation acquires not only stability, but immense effective force. It has no need to fear discussion and agitation. It can bend all its resources to the accomplishment of its collective ends. The friction that exists in countries where the laws or institutions handed down from former generations are incompatible with the feelings and wishes of the people has disappeared. A key has been found that will unlock every door.

On the other hand, such a government is exposed to two dangers. One, the smaller one, yet sometimes troublesome, is the difficulty of ascertaining the will of the majority. I do not mean the difficulty of getting all citizens to vote, because it must be taken that those who do not vote leave their will in the hands of those who do, but the difficulty of obtaining by any machinery yet devised a quite honest record of the results of voting. Where the issues are weighty, involving immense interests of individual men or groups of men, the danger of bribery, of force, and still more of fraud in taking and counting votes is a serious one.

. . . The other danger is that minorities may not sufficiently assert themselves. Where a majority has erred, the only remedy against the prolongation or repetition of its error is in the continued protests and agitation of the minority, an agitation which ought to be conducted peaceably, by voice and pen, but which must be vehement enough to rouse the people and deliver them from the consequences of their blunders. But the more complete the sway of majorities is, so much the less disposed is a minority to maintain the contest. It loses faith in its cause and in itself, and allows its voice to be silenced by the triumphant cries of its opponents. How are men to acquiesce promptly and loyally in the decision of a majority, and yet to go on arguing against it? how can they be at once submissive and aggressive? That conceit of his own goodness and greatness which intoxicates an absolute monarch besets a sovereign people also, and the slavishness with which his ministers approach an Oriental despot may reappear in the politicians of a Western democracy. The duty, therefore, of a patriotic statesman in a country where public opinion rules, would seem to be rather to resist and correct than to encourage the dominant sentiment. He will not be content with trying to form and mould and lead it, but he will confront it, lecture it, remind it that it is fallible, rouse it out of its self-complacency. Unfortunately, courage and independence are plants which a soil impregnated with the belief in the wisdom of numbers does not tend to produce: nor is there any art known to statesmen whereby their growth can be fostered.

Experience has, however, suggested plans for lessening the risks incident to the dominance of one particular set of opinions. One plan is for the people themselves to limit their powers, i.e. to surround their own action and the action of their agents with restrictions of time and method which compel delay. Another is for them so to parcel out functions among many agents that no single one chosen indiscreetly, or obeying his mandate overzealously, can do much mischief, and that out of the multiplicity of agents differences of view may spring which will catch the attention of the citizens.

The temper and character of a people may supply more valuable safeguards. The country which has worked out for itself a truly free government must have done so in virtue of the vigorous individuality of its children. Such an individuality does not soon yield even to the pressure of democratic conditions. In a nation with a keen moral sense and a capacity for strong emotions, opinion based on a love of what is deemed just or good will resist the multitude when bent on evil; and if there be a great variety of social conditions, of modes of life, of religious beliefs, these will prove centres of resistance to a dominant tendency, like rocks standing up in a river, at which he whom the current sweeps downwards may clutch. Instances might be cited even from countries where the majority has had every source of strength at its command—physical force, tradition, the all but universal persuasions and prejudices of the lower as well as of the higher classes —in which small minorities have triumphed, first by startling and then by leavening and convincing the majority. This they have done in virtue of that intensity of belief which is oftenest found in a small sect or group, not because it is small, but because if its belief were not intense it would not venture to hold out at all against the adverse mass. The energy of each individual in the minority makes it in the long run a match for a majority huger but less instinct with vitality. In a free country more especially, ten men who care are a match for a hundred who do not.

Such natural compensations as this occur in the physical as well as in the spiritual and moral world, and preserve both. But they are compensations on which the practical statesman cannot safely rely, for they are partial, they are uncertain, and they probably tend to diminish with the progress of democracy. The longer public opinion has ruled, the more absolute is the authority of the majority likely to become, the less likely are energetic minorities to arise, the more are politicians likely to occupy themselves, not in forming opinion, but in discovering and hastening to obey it.

PUBLIC OPINION AND MAJORITY GOVERNMENT

A. LAWRENCE LOWELL

In his *Contrat Social* Rousseau attempts to prove that in becoming a member of a state the natural man may remain perfectly free and continue to obey only his own will. He tells us that in forming a state men desire to enforce the common will of all the members; and he takes as the basis of all political action this common will, which is

From *Public Opinion and Popular Government*, (New York: Longmans, Green and Co., 1926), pp. 8-15. Reprinted by permission of the publisher.

nearly akin to our idea of public opinion. Now, in order to reconcile the absolute freedom of every citizen to obey only his own volition, with the passing of laws in every civilized state against opposition, he says that when the assembled people are consulted on any measure, their votes express, not their personal wishes upon the subject, but their opinions in regard to the common will, and thus the defeated minority have not had their desires thwarted, but have simply been mistaken in their views about the common will. All men, he insists, want to give effect to this common will, which becomes, therefore, the universal will of everyone.

PUBLIC OPINION AND UNIVERSAL CONSENT

Though stated in a somewhat fanciful way, the theory contains a highly important truth, which may be clothed in a more modern dress. A body of men are politically capable of a public opinion only so far as they are agreed upon the ends and aims of government and upon the principles by which those ends shall be attained. They must be united, also, about the means whereby the action of the government is to be determined, in a conviction, for example, that the views of a majority—or it may be some other portion of their numbers— ought to prevail; and a political community as a whole is capable of public opinion only when this is true of the great bulk of the citizens. Such an assumption was implied, though usually not expressed, in all theories of the Social Compact; and, indeed, it is involved in all theories that base rightful government upon the consent of the governed, for the consent required is not a universal approval by all the people of every measure enacted, but a consensus in regard to the legitimate character of the ruling authority and its right to decide the questions that arise.

The power of the courts in America to hold statutes unconstitutional furnishes an illustration of this doctrine. It rests upon a distinction between those things that may be done by ordinary legislative procedure and those that may not; the theory being that in the case of the former the people have consented to abide by the decision of the majority as expressed by their representatives, whereas in the case of matters not placed by the constitution within the competence of the legislature, the people as a whole have given no such consent. With regard to these they have agreed to abide only by a decree uttered in more solemn forms, or by the determination of something greater than a mere majority. The court, therefore, in holding a statute unconstitutional, is in effect deciding that it is not within the range of acts to which the whole people have given their consent; so that while the opinion in favor of the act may be an opinion of the majority of the voters, it is not a public opinion of the community, because it is not one where the people as a whole are united in a conviction that the views of the majority, at least as expressed through the ordinary channels, ought to prevail.

CONSENT AND FORCE

We have seen that in some countries the population has contained, and for that matter still contains, distinct elements which are sharply at odds upon the vital political questions of the day. In such a case the discordant forces may be violent enough to preclude a general consent that the opinion of the majority ought to prevail; but this is not always true. If they are not, the assumption which lies at the foundation of popular government remains unimpaired. If they are, the forms of democracy may still be in operation, although their meaning is essentially altered. It may be worth while to dwell on this contrast a moment because it makes clear the difference between true public opinion and the opinion of a majority.

Leaving out of account those doctrines whereby political authority is traced to a direct supernatural origin, government among men is commonly based in theory either on consent or on force, and in fact each of these factors plays a larger or smaller part in every civilized country. So far as the preponderating opinion is one which the minority does not share, but which it feels ought, as the opinion of the majority, to be carried out, the government is conducted by a true public opinion or by consent. So far as the preponderating opinion is one the execution of which the minority would resist by force if it could do so successfully, the government is based upon force. At times it may be necessary to give effect to an opinion of the majority against the violent resistance, or through the reluctant submission, of the minority. A violent resistance may involve the suppression of an armed insurrection or civil war. But even when there is no resort to actual force it remains true that in any case where the minority does not concede the right of the majority to decide, submission is yielded only to obviously superior strength; and obedience is the result of compulsion, not of public opinion. The power to carry out its will under such conditions must to some extent be inherent in every government. Habitual criminals are held in check by force everywhere. But in many nations at the present day there are great masses of well-intentioned citizens who do not admit the right of the majority to rule. These persons and the political parties in which they group themselves are termed irreconcilable, and when we speak of public opinion in that country we cannot include them. So far as they are concerned there can be no general or public opinion.

Let us be perfectly clear upon this point. The presence of irreconcilables does not mean that the government is illegitimate, or that it is not justified in enforcing its will upon the reluctant minority. That will depend upon other considerations. The use of force may be unavoidable if any settled government is to be upheld, if civic order is to be maintained. But it does mean that the fundamental assumption of popular government, the control of political affairs

by an opinion which is truly public, is set aside. Florence may, or may not, have been justified in disfranchising her noble families, but Freeman was certainly right in his opinion that by so doing she lost her right to be called a democracy,—that is, a government by all the people,—and it makes little difference for this purpose whether a part of the body politic is formally excluded from any share in public affairs or overawed by force into submission.

NUMBERS AND INTENSITY IN OPINION

One more remark must be made before quitting the subject of the relation of public opinion to the opinion of the majority. The late Gabriel Tarde, with his habitual keen insight, insisted on the importance of the intensity of belief as a factor in the spread of opinions. There is a common impression that public opinion depends upon and is measured by the mere number of persons to be found on each side of a question; but this is far from accurate. If forty-nine per cent of a community feel very strongly on one side, and fifty-one per cent are lukewarmly on the other, the former opinion has the greater public force behind it and is certain to prevail ultimately if it does not at once. The ideas of people who possess the greatest knowledge of a subject are also of more weight than those of an equal number of ignorant persons. If, for example, all the physicians, backed by all other educated men, are confident that an impure water supply causes typhoid fever, while the rest of the people are mildly incredulous, it can hardly be said that public opinion is opposed to that notion. One man who holds his belief tenaciously counts for as much as several men who hold theirs weakly, because he is more aggressive, and thereby compels and overawes others into apparent agreement with him, or at least into silence and inaction. This is, perhaps, especially true of moral questions. It is not improbable that a large part of the accepted moral code is maintained by the earnestness of a minority, while more than half of the community is indifferent or unconvinced. In short, public opinion is not strictly the opinion of the numerical majority, and no form of its expression measures the mere majority, for individual views are always to some extent weighed as well as counted. Without attempting to consider how the weight attaching to intensity and intelligence can be accurately gauged, it is enough for our purpose to point out that when we speak of the opinion of a majority we mean, not the numerical, but the effective majority.

No doubt differences in the intensity of belief explain some sudden transformations in politics and in ethical standards, many people holding their views with so little conviction that they are ready to follow in the wake of any strong leader in thought or action. On the other hand they explain in part also cases where a law is enacted readily but enforced with difficulty; for the law may be carried through by a comparatively small body of very earnest men, who produce a disproportionate effect by the heat of their conviction; while the bulk of the people are apathetic and unwilling to support the effort required to overcome a steady passive resistance to the enforcement of the law.

The problem of intensity of belief is connected, moreover, with the fact that different ways of ascertaining the popular will may give different results, in ac-cordance with the larger or smaller proportion of the indifferent who are gathered in to vote. But this is a matter that belongs properly to a later discussion of the methods of expressing public opinion. We are dealing here only with its essential nature.

CONCLUSION

To sum up what has been said in this chapter: public opinion to be worthy of the name, to be the proper motive force in a democracy, must be really public; and popular government is based upon the assumption of a public opinion of that kind. In order that it may be public a majority is not enough, and unanimity is not required, but the opinion must be such that while the minority may not share it, they feel bound, by conviction not by fear, to accept it; and if democracy is complete the submission of the minority must be given ungrudgingly. An essential difference between government by public opinion as thus defined and by the bare will of a selfish majority has been well expressed by President Hadley. After saying that laws imposed by a majority on a reluctant minority are commonly inoperative, he adds, "It cannot be too often repeated that those opinions which a man is prepared to maintain at another's cost, but not at his own, count for little in forming the general sentiment of a community, or in producing any effective public movement."

DISQUISITION ON GOVERNMENT

JOHN C. CALHOUN

But that constitution of our nature which makes us feel more intensely what affects us directly than what affects us indirectly through others, necessarily leads to conflict between individuals. Each, in consequence, has a greater regard for his own safety or happiness, than for the safety or happiness of others: and, where these come in opposition, is ready to sacrifice the interests of others to his own. And hence, the tendency to a universal state of conflict, between individual and individual; accompanied by the connected passions of suspicion, jealousy, anger and revenge,—followed by insolence, fraud and cruelty; and, if not prevented by some controlling power, ending in a state of universal discord and confusion, destructive of the social state and the ends for which it is ordained. This controlling power, wherever vested, or by whomsoever exercised, is GOVERNMENT.

It follows, then, that man is so constituted, that government is necessary to the existence of society, and society to his existence, and the perfection of his faculties. It follows, also, that government has its origin in this twofold constitution of his nature; the sympathetic or social feelings constituting the remote,—and the individual or direct, the proximate cause.

If man had been differently constituted in either particular;—if, instead of being social in his nature, he had been created

without sympathy for his kind, and independent of others for his safety and existence; or if, on the other hand, he had been so created, as to feel more intensely what affected others than what affected himself, (if that were possible,) or, even, had this supposed interest been equal,—it is manifest that, in either case, there would have been no necessity for government, and that none would ever have existed. But, although society and government are thus intimately connected with and dependent on each other,—of the two society is the greater. It is the first in the order of things, and in the dignity of its object; that of society being primary—to preserve and perfect our race; and that of government secondary and subordinate, to preserve and perfect society. Both are, however, necessary to the existence and well-being of our race, and equally of Divine ordination . . .

But government, although intended to protect and preserve society, has itself a strong tendency to disorder and abuse of its powers, as all experience and almost every page of history testify. The cause is to be found in the same constitution of our nature which makes government indispensable. The powers which it is necessary for government to possess, in order to repress violence and preserve order, cannot execute themselves. They must be administered by men in whom, like others,

From Richard K. Cralle, ed., *The Works of John C. Calhoun.* (New York: D. Appleton, 1845), Volume I, pp. 1-70 *passim*. Reprinted by permission of the publisher.

the individual are stronger than the social feelings. And hence, the powers vested in them to prevent injustice and oppression on the part of others, will, if left unguarded, be by them converted into instruments to oppress the rest of the community. That, by which this is prevented, by whatever name called, is what is meant by CONSTI-TUTION, in its most comprehensive sense, when applied to GOVERNMENT.

Having its origin in the same principle of our nature, *constitution* stands to *government,* as *government* stands to *society;* and, as the end for which society is ordained, would be defeated without government, so that for which government is ordained would, in a great measure, be defeated without constitution. But they differ in this striking particular. There is no difficulty in forming government. It is not even a matter of choice, whether there shall be one or not. Like breathing, it is not permitted to depend on our volition. Necessity will force it on all communities in some one form or another. Very different is the case as to constitution. Instead of a matter of necessity, it is one of the most difficult tasks imposed on man to form a constitution worthy of the name; while, to form a perfect one, —one that would completely counteract the tendency of government to oppression and abuse, and hold it strictly to the great ends for which it is ordained,—has thus far exceeded human wisdom, and possibly ever will. From this, another striking difference results. Constitution is the contrivance of man, while government is of Divine ordination. Man is left to perfect what the wisdom of the Infinite ordained, as necessary to preserve the race.

With these remarks, I proceed to the consideration of the important and difficult question: How is this tendency of government to be counteracted? Or, to express it more fully,—How can those who are invested with the powers of government be prevented from employing them, as the means of aggrandizing themselves, instead of using them to protect and preserve society? It cannot be done by instituting a higher power to control the government, and those who administer it. This would be but to change the seat of authority, and to make this higher power, in reality, the government; with the same tendency, on the part of those who might control its powers, to pervert them into instruments of aggrandizement. Nor can it be done by limiting the powers of government, so as to make it too feeble to be made an instrument of abuse; for, passing by the difficulty of so limiting its powers, without creating a power higher than the government itself to enforce the observance of the limitations, it is a sufficient objection that it would, if practicable, defeat the end for which government is ordained, by making it too feeble to protect and preserve society. The powers necessary for this purpose will ever prove sufficient to aggrandize those who control it, at the expense of the rest of the community.

In estimating what amount of power would be requisite to secure the objects of government, we must take into the reckoning, what would be necessary to defend the community against external, as well as internal dangers. . . .

Self-preservation is the supreme law, as well with communities as individuals. And hence the danger of withholding from government the full command of the power and resources of the state; and the great difficulty of limiting its powers consistently with the protection and preservation of the community. And hence the question recurs,—By what means can government, without being divested of the full command of the resources of the community, be prevented from abusing its powers? . . .

There is but one way in which this can possibly be done; and that is, by such an organism as will furnish the ruled with the means of resisting successfully this tendency on the part of the rulers to oppression and abuse. Power can only be resisted by power,—and tendency by tendency. Those who exercise power and those subject to its exercise,—the rulers and the ruled,— stand in antagonistic relations to each other.

The same constitution of our nature which leads rulers to oppress the ruled,—regardless of the object for which government is ordained,—will, with equal strength, lead the ruled to resist, when possessed of the means of making peaceable and effective resistance. Such an organism, then, as will furnish the means by which resistance may be systematically and peaceably made on the part of the ruled, to oppression and abuse of power on the part of the rulers, is the first and indispensable step towards *forming* a constitutional government. And as this can only be effected by or through the right of suffrage,—(the right on the part of the ruled to choose their rulers at proper intervals, and to hold them thereby responsible for their conduct),—the responsibility of the rulers to the ruled, through the right of suffrage, is the indispensable and primary principle in the *foundation* of a constitutional government. . . .

I call the right of suffrage the indispensable and primary principle; for it would be a great and dangerous mistake to suppose, as many do, that it is, of itself, sufficient to form constitutional governments . . .

The right of suffrage, of itself, can do no more than give complete control to those who elect, over the conduct of those they have elected. In doing this, it accomplishes all it possibly can accomplish. This is its aim,—and when this is attained, its end is fulfilled. It can do no more, however enlightened the people, or however widely extended or well guarded the right may be. The sum total, then, of its effects, when most successful, is, to make those elected, the true and faithful representatives of those who elected them,—instead of irresponsible rulers,—as they would be without it; and thus, by converting it into an agency, and the rulers into agents, to divest government of all claims to sovereignty, and to retain it unimpaired to the community. But it is manifest that the right of suffrage, in making these changes, transfers, in reality, the actual control over the government, from those who make and execute the laws, to the body of the community; and, thereby, places the powers of the government as fully in the mass of the community, as they would be if they, in fact, had assembled, made, and executed the laws themselves, without the intervention of representatives or agents. The more perfectly it does this, the more perfectly it accomplishes its ends; but in doing so, it only changes the seat of authority, without counteracting in the least, the tendency of the government to oppression and abuse of its powers.

If the whole community had the same interests, so that the interests of each and every portion would be so affected by the action of the government, that the laws which oppressed or impoverished one portion, would necessarily oppress and impoverish all others,—or the reverse,—then the right of suffrage, of itself, would be all-sufficient to counteract the tendency of the government to oppression and abuse of its powers; and, of course, would form, of itself, a perfect constitutional government. The interest of all being the same, by supposition, as far as the action of the government was concerned, all would have like interests as to what laws should be made, and how they should be executed. All strife and struggle would cease as to who should be elected to make and execute them. The only question would be, who was most fit; who the wisest and most capable of understanding the common interest of the whole. This decided, the election would pass off quietly, and without party discord; as no one portion could advance its own peculiar interest without regard to the rest, by electing a favorite candidate.

But such is not the case. On the contrary, nothing is more difficult than to equalize the action of the government, in reference to the various and diversified interests of the community; and nothing more easy than to pervert its powers into instruments to aggrandize and enrich one or more interests by oppressing and impoverishing the others; and this too, under the operation of laws, couched in general terms;—and which, on their face, appear fair and equal. Nor is this the case in some particular communities only. It is so in all; the small and the great,—the poor and the rich,—irrespective of pursuits, productions, or degrees of civilization;—with, however, this difference, that the more extensive and populous the country, the more diversified the condition and pursuits of its population, and the richer, more luxurious, and dissimilar the people, the more difficult is it to equalize the action of the government,—and the more easy for one portion of the community to pervert its powers to oppress and plunder the other.

Such being the case, it necessarily results, that the right of suffrage, by placing the control of the government in the community must, from the same constitution of our nature which makes government necessary to preserve society, lead to conflict among its different interests,—each striving to obtain possession of its powers, as the means of protecting itself against the others;—or of advancing its respective interests, regardless of the interests of others. For this purpose, a struggle will take place between the various interests to obtain a majority, in order to control the government. If no one interest be strong enough, of itself, to obtain it, a combination will be formed between those whose interests are most alike,—each conceding something to the others, until a sufficient number is obtained to make a majority. The process may be slow, and much time may be required before a compact, organized majority can be thus formed; but formed it will be in time, even without preconcert or design, by the sure workings of that principle or constitution of our nature in which government itself originates. When once formed, the community will be divided into two great parties,—a major and minor,—between which there will be incessant struggles on the one side to retain, and on the other to obtain the majority,—and, thereby, the control of the government and the advantages it confers. . . .

As, then, the right of suffrage, without some other provision, cannot counteract this tendency of government, the next question for consideration is—What is that other provision? . . .

From what has been said, it is manifest, that this provision must be of a character calculated to prevent any one interest, or combination of interests, from using the powers of government to aggrandize itself at the expense of the others. Here lies the evil: and just in proportion as it shall prevent, or fail to prevent it, in the same degree it will effect or fail to effect the end intended to be accomplished. There is but one certain mode in which this result can be secured; and that is, by the adoption of some restriction or limitation, which shall so effectually prevent any one interest, or combination of interests, from obtaining the exclusive control of the government, as to render hopeless all attempts directed to that end. There is, again, but one mode in which this can be effected; and that is, by taking the sense of each interest or portion of the community, which may be unequally and injuriously affected by the action of the government, separately, through its own majority, or in some other way by which its voice may be fairly expressed; and to require the consent of each interest, either to put or to keep the government in action. This, too, can be accomplished only in one way,—and that is, by such an organism of the government, —and, if necessary for the purpose, of the community also,—as will, by dividing and distributing the powers of government, give to each division or interest, through its appropriate organ, either a concurrent voice in making and executing the laws, or a veto on their execution. It is only by such an organism, that the assent of each can be made necessary to put the government in motion; or the power made effectual to arrest its action, when put in motion;—and it is only by the one or the other that the different interests, orders, classes, or portions, into which the community may be divided, can be protected, and all conflict and struggle between them prevented—by rendering it impossible to put or to keep it in action, without the concurrent consent of all.

Such an organism as this, combined with the right of suffrage, constitutes, in fact, the elements of constitutional government. The one, by rendering those who make and execute the laws responsible to those on whom they operate, prevents the rulers from oppressing the ruled; and the other, by making it impossible for any one interest or combination of interests or class, or order, or portion of the community, to obtain exclusive control, prevents any one of them from oppressing the other. It is clear, that oppression and abuse of power must come, if at all, from the one or the other quarter. From no other can they come. It follows, that the two, suffrage and proper organism combined, are sufficient to counteract the tendency of government to oppression and abuse of power; and to restrict it to the fulfilment of the great ends for which it is ordained . . .

It may be readily inferred, from what has been stated, that the effect of organism is neither to supersede nor diminish the importance of the right of suffrage; but to aid and perfect it. The object of the latter is, to collect the sense of the community. The more fully and perfectly it accomplishes this, the more fully and perfectly it fulfils its end. But the most it can do, of itself, is to collect the sense of the greater number; that is, of the stronger interests, or combination of interests; and to assume this to be the sense of the community. It is only when aided by a proper organism, that it can collect the sense of the entire community,—of each and all its interests; of each, through its appropriate organ, and of the whole, through all of them united. This would truly be the sense of the entire community; for whatever diversity each interest might have within itself,—as all would have the same interest in reference to the action of the government, the individuals composing each would be fully and truly represented by its own majority or appropriate organ, regarded in reference to the other interests. In brief, every individual of every interest might trust, with confidence, its

majority or appropriate organ, against that of every other interest.

It results, from what has been said, that there are two different modes in which the sense of the community may be taken; one, simply by the right of suffrage, unaided; the other, by the right through a proper organism. Each collects the majority. But one regards numbers only, and considers the whole community as a unit, having but one common interest throughout; and collects the sense of the greater number of the whole, as that of the community. The other, on the contrary, regards interests as well as numbers;—considering the community as made up of different and conflicting interests, as far as the action of the government is concerned; and takes the sense of each, through its majority or appropriate organ, and the united sense of all, as the sense of the entire community. The former of these I shall call the numerical, or absolute majority; and the latter, the concurrent, or constitutional majority. I call it the constitutional majority, because it is an essential element in every constitutional government,—be its form what it may. So great is the difference, politically speaking, between the two majorities, that they cannot be confounded, without leading to great and fatal errors; and yet the distinction between them has been so entirely overlooked, that when the term *majority* is used in political discussions, it is applied exclusively to designate the numerical,—as if there were no other. Until this distinction is recognized, and better understood, there will continue to be great liability to error in properly constructing constitutional governments, especially of the popular form, and of preserving them when properly constructed. Until then, the latter will have a strong tendency to slide, first, into the government of the numerical majority, and, finally, into the absolute government of some other form. To show that such must be the case, and at the same time to mark more strongly the difference between the two, in order to guard against the danger of overlooking it, I propose to consider the subject more at length.

The first and leading error which naturally arises from overlooking the distinction referred to, is, to confound the numerical majority with the people; and this so completely as to regard them as identical. This is a consequence that necessarily results from considering the numerical as the only majority. All admit, that a popular government, or democracy, is the government of the people; for the terms imply this. A perfect government of the kind would be one which would embrace the consent of every citizen or member of the community; but as this is impracticable, in the opinion of those who regard the numerical as the only majority, and who can perceive no other way by which the sense of the people can be taken,—they are compelled to adopt this as the only true basis of popular government, in contradistinction to governments of the aristocratical or monarchical form. Being thus constrained, they are, in the next place, forced to regard the numerical majority, as, in effect, the entire people; that is, the greater part as the whole; and the government of the greater part as the government of the whole. It is thus the two come to be confounded, and a part made identical with the whole. And it is thus, also, that all the rights, powers, and immunities of the whole people come to be attributed to the numerical majority; and, among others, the supreme, sovereign authority of establishing and abolishing governments at pleasure.

This radical error, the consequence of confounding the two, and of regarding the numerical as the only majority, has contributed more than any other cause, to prevent the formation of popular constitutional governments,—and to destroy them even when they have been formed. It leads to the conclusion that, in their formation and establishment nothing more is necessary than the right of suffrage,—and the allotment to each division of the community a representation in the government, in proportion to numbers. If the numerical majority were really the people; and if, to take its

sense truly, were to take the sense of the people truly, a government so constituted would be a true and perfect model of a popular constitutional government; and every departure from it would detract from its excellence. But, as such is not the case, —as the numerical majority, instead of being the people, is only a portion of them, —such a government, instead of being a true and perfect model of the people's government, that is, a people self-governed, is but the government of a part, over a part, —the major over the minor portion.

But this misconception of the true elements of constitutional government does not stop here. It leads to others equally false and fatal, in reference to the best means of preserving and perpetuating them, when, from some fortunate combination of circumstances, they are correctly formed. For they who fall into these errors regard the restrictions which organism imposes on the will of the numerical majority as restrictions on the will of the people, and, therefore, as not only useless, but wrongful and mischievous. And hence they endeavor to destroy organism, under the delusive hope of making government more democratic. . . .

There is another error, of a kindred character, whose influence contributes much to the same results: I refer to the prevalent opinion, that a written constitution, containing suitable restrictions on the powers of government, is sufficient, of itself, without the aid of any organism,—except such as is necessary to separate its several departments, and render them independent of each other,—to counteract the tendency of the numerical majority to oppression and the abuse of power.

A written constitution certainly has many and considerable advantages; but it is a great mistake to suppose, that the mere insertion of provisions to restrict and limit the powers of the government, without investing those for whose protection they are inserted with the means of enforcing their observance, will be sufficient to prevent the major and dominant party from abusing its powers. Being the party in possession of the government, they will, from the same constitution of man which makes government necessary to protect society, be in favor of the powers granted by the constitution, and opposed to the restrictions intended to limit them. As the major and dominant party, they will have no need of these restrictions for their protection. The ballot-box, of itself, would be ample protection to them. Needing no other, they would come, in time, to regard these limitations as unnecessary and improper restraints;—and endeavor to elude them, with the view of increasing their power and influence.

The minor, or weaker party, on the contrary, would take the opposite direction;—and regard them as essential to their protection against the dominant party. And, hence, they would endeavor to defend and enlarge the restrictions, and to limit and contract the powers. But where there are no means by which they could compel the major party to observe the restrictions, the only resort left them would be, a strict construction of the constitution,—that is, a constitution which would confine these powers to the narrowest limits which the meaning of the words used in the grant would admit.

To this the major party would oppose a liberal construction,—one which would give to the words of the grant the broadest meaning of which they were susceptible. It would then be construction against construction; the one to contract, and the other enlarge the powers of the government to the utmost. But of what possible avail could the strict construction of the minor party be, against the liberal interpretation of the major, when the one would have all the powers of the government to carry its construction into effect,—and the other be deprived of all means of enforcing its construction? In a contest so unequal, the result would not be doubtful. The party in favor of the restrictions would be overpowered. . . .

Nor would the division of government into separate, and, as it regards each other, independent departments, prevent this result. Such a division may do much to facili-tate its operations, and to secure to its administration greater caution and deliberation; but as each and all the departments, —and, of course, the entire government,— would be under the control of the numerical majority, it is too clear to require explanation, that a mere distribution of its powers among its agents or representatives, could do little or nothing to counteract its tendency to oppression and abuse of power. To effect this, it would be necessary to go one step further, and make the several departments the organs of the distinct interests or portions of the community; and to clothe each with a negative on the others. But the effect of this would be to change the government from the numerical into the concurrent majority. . . .

The necessary consequence of taking the sense of the community by the concurrent majority is, as has been explained, to give to each interest or portion of the community a negative on the others. It is this mutual negative among its various conflicting interests, which invests each with the power of protecting itself;—and places the rights and safety of each, where only they can be securely placed, under its own guardianship. . . . It is, indeed, the negative power which makes the constitution,—and the positive which makes the government. The one is the power of acting;—and the other the power of preventing or arresting action. The two, combined, make constitutional governments.

But, as there can be no constitution without the negative power, and no negative power without the concurrent majority;— it follows, necessarily, that where the numerical majority has the sole control of the government, there can be no constitution; as constitution implies limitation or restriction,—and, of course, is inconsistent with the idea of sole or exclusive power. And hence, the numerical, unmixed with the concurrent majority, necessarily forms, in all cases, absolute government.

It is, indeed, the single, or *one power*, which excludes the negative, and constitutes absolute government; and not the *number* in whom the power is vested. The numerical majority is as truly a *single power*, and excludes the negative as completely as the absolute government of one, or of the few. The former is as much the absolute government of the democratic, or popular form, as the latter of the monarchical or aristocratical. It has, accordingly, in common with them, the same tendency to oppression and abuse of power.

Constitutional governments, of whatever form, are, indeed, much more similar to each other, in their structure and character, than they are, respectively, to the absolute governments, even of their own class. All constitutional governments, of whatever class they may be, take the sense of the community by its parts,—each through its appropriate organ; and regard the sense of all its parts, as the sense of the whole. They all rest on the right of suffrage, and the responsibility of ruler, directly or indirectly. On the contrary, all absolute governments, of whatever form, concentrate power in one uncontrolled and irresponsible individual or body, whose will is regarded as the sense of the community. And, hence, the great and broad distinction between governments is,—not that of the one, the few, or the many,—but of the constitutional and the absolute.

From this there results another distinction, which, although secondary in its character, very strongly marks the difference between these forms of government. I refer to their respective conservative principle;—that is, the principle by which they are upheld and preserved. This principle, in constitutional governments, is *compromise*; —and in absolute governments, is force;—as will be next explained.

It has been already shown, that the same constitution of man which leads those who govern to oppress the governed,—if not prevented,—will, with equal force and uncertainty, lead the latter to resist oppression, when possessed of the means of doing so peaceably and successfully. But absolute governments, of all forms, exclude all other means of resistance to their authority, than that of force; and, of course, leave no other

alternative to the governed, but to acquiesce in oppression, however great it may be, or to resort to force to put down the government. But the dread of such a resort must necessarily lead the government to prepare to meet force in order to protect itself; and hence, of necessity, force becomes the conservative principle of all such governments.

On the contrary, the government of the concurrent majority, where the organism is perfect, excludes the possibility of oppression, by giving to each interest, or portion, or order,—where there are established classes,—the means of protecting itself, by its negative, against all measures calculated to advance the peculiar interests of others at its expense. Its effect, then, is to cause the different interests, portions, or orders,— as the case may be,—to desist from attempting to adopt any measure calculated to promote the prosperity of one, or more, by sacrificing that of others; and thus to force them to unite in such measures only as would promote the prosperity of all, as the only means to prevent the suspension of the action of the government;—and, thereby, to avoid anarchy, the greatest of all evils. It is by means of such authorized and effectual resistance, that oppression is prevented, and the necessity of resorting to force superseded, in governments of the concurrent majority;—and, hence, compromise, instead of force, becomes their conservative principle. . . .

The concurrent majority, then, is better suited to enlarge and secure the bonds of liberty, because it is better suited to prevent government from passing beyond its proper limits, and to restrict it to its primary end, —the protection of the community. . . . The tendency of government to pass beyond its proper limits is what exposes liberty to danger, and renders it insecure; and it is the strong counteraction of governments of the concurrent majority to this tendency which makes them so favorable to liberty. . . .

Such are the many and striking advantages of the concurrent over the numerical majority. Against the former but two objections can be made. The one is, that it is difficult of construction . . . and the other, that it would be impracticable to obtain the concurrence of conflicting interests, where they were numerous and diversified; or, if not, that the process for this purpose, would be too tardy to meet, with sufficient promptness, the many and dangerous emergencies, to which all communities are exposed. This objection is plausible; and deserves a fuller notice than it has yet received.

The diversity of opinion is usually so great, on almost all questions of policy, that it is not surprising, on a slight view of the subject, it should be thought impracticable to bring the various conflicting interests of a community to unite on any one line of policy;—or, that a government, founded on such a principle, would be too slow in its movements and too weak in its foundation to succeed in practice. But, plausible as it may seem at the first glance, a more deliberate view will show, that this opinion is erroneous. It is true, that, when there is no urgent necessity, it is difficult to bring those who differ, to agree on any one line of action. Each will naturally insist on taking the course he may think best;—and, from pride of opinion, will be unwilling to yield to others. But the case is different when there is an urgent necessity to unite on some common course of action; as reason and experience both prove. When something *must* be done,—and when it can be done only by the united consent of all,—the necessity of the case will force to a compromise;—be the cause of that necessity what it may. On all questions of acting, necessity where it exists, is the overruling motive; and where, in such cases, compromise among the parties is an indispensable condition to acting, it exerts an overruling influence in predisposing them to acquiesce in some one opinion or course of action. . . .

But to form a juster estimate of the full force of this impulse to compromise, there must be added that, in governments of the concurrent majority, each portion, in order to advance its own peculiar interests, would have to conciliate all others, by showing a disposition to advance theirs; and, for this purpose, each would select those to represent it, whose wisdom, patriotism, and weight of character, would command the confidence of the others. Under its influence, —and with representatives so well qualified to accomplish the object for which they were selected,—the prevailing desire would be, to promote the common interests of the whole; and, hence, the competition would be, not which should yield the least to promote the common good but which should yield the most. It is thus, that concession would cease to be considered a sacrifice,— would become a free-will offering on the altar of the country, and lose the name of compromise. And herein is to be found the feature, which distinguishes governments of the concurrent majority so strikingly from those of the numerical. In the latter, each faction, in the struggle to obtain the control of the government, elevates to power the designing, the artful, and unscrupulous, who, in their devotion to party,—instead of aiming at the good of the whole,—aim exclusively at securing the ascendency of the party. . . .

To this, also, may be referred the greater solidity of foundation on which governments of the concurrent majority repose. Both, ultimately, rest on necessity; for force, by which those of the numerical majority are upheld, is only acquiesced in from necessity; a necessity not more imperious, however, than that which compels the different portions, in governments of the concurrent majority, to acquiesce in compromise. There is, however, a great difference in the motive, the feeling, the aid, which characterize the act in the two cases. In the one, it is done with that reluctance and hostility ever incident to enforced submission to what is regarded as injustice and oppression; accompanied by the desire and purpose to seize on the first favorable opportunity for resistance:—but in the other, willingly and cheerfully, under the impulse of an exalted patriotism, impelling all to acquiesce in whatever the common good requires . . .

THE MULTI-GROUP NATURE OF THE STATE

W. E. BINKLEY AND M. C. MOOS

The late William James is said to have observed that democracy is a system in which the government does something and waits to see who "hollers"! Then it does something else in order to relieve the "hollering" as best it can and waits to see who "hollers" at the adjustment.[1] No one who has ever been a public official will dismiss this as merely a humorous remark, for actually it strips away the whole elaborate system of fictions with which the realities of government have long been obscured and epitomizes the experience of self-governing peoples.

For example, a municipal council is confronted with what appears to be a public demand that the prevailing diagonal system of parking automobiles on business streets be changed to parallel parking. Characteristically the council decides to proceed cautiously by enacting an ordinance that leaves parking as it has been on one side of the street but changes to parallel parking on the other side. No sooner does the ordinance go into effect than protests arise from the merchants who have parallel parking on their side of the street because the number of automobiles able to park near their businesses has been reduced. At the next meeting of the municipal council the ordinance is repealed, diagonal parking is restored, and the tumult subsides.

[1] T. V. Smith: *The Promise of American Politics* (New York, 1936), pp. 199-200.

By the middle of the 1930's a strong demand for Federal legislation to protect the collective bargaining rights of labor led to the enactment of the Wagner Labor Relations Act. Employers, in all cases where the flow of interstate commerce would be affected, were forbidden to interfere with workers' self-organization and collective bargaining, to dominate a company union, to discharge an employee or discriminate against him because of union activity, or refuse to bargain collectively with the proper representative of the workers. During the next dozen years the growing resentment of management against the irksome restrictions placed upon it by the Wagner Act culminated in the passage of the Taft-Hartley Labor Relations Act which restricted some and abolished other labor prerogatives. The closed shop was outlawed and the union shop permitted only if the union represented a majority of the workers. A "cooling off" period was required before termination of a contract or the start of a strike. Organized labor promptly denounced the act and organized for political action in the next congressional election so effectively that of the members of the House who failed to be re-elected, all but four had voted to override the President's veto of the act. The next Congress was expected to make a further adjustment and then, as William James would put it, wait to see who complained about that.

Reprinted from pp. 3-8 of *A Grammar of Politics: The National, State and Local Governments,* by Wilfred E. Binkley and Malcolm C. Moos, by permission of the publisher, Alfred A. Knopf, Inc. and the authors. Copyright 1949, 1952, by Alfred A. Knopf, Inc.

No problem perplexes the legislator more than taxes. "Pluck the goose with as little squawking as possible" is a cynical principle of taxation but, as the late Frank W. Taussig remarked: "A great deal of legislation rests upon it." For example many of our taxes are not progressive in their rates but are, instead, regressive, which means that the poorer the taxpayer the greater the percentage of his income paid as tax. Competent authorities on local, state, and Federal taxes comment that "it is necessary to admit that taxation on the whole in the United States is regressive in operation and does not conform satisfactorily to the principle of ability to pay." Fortunately the income taxes levied by the Federal government are progressive and the electorate will not tolerate tampering with this principle. It roared at the proposal in the Eightieth Congress of a "twenty per cent reduction across the board" because this would have meant slight dollar reductions of taxes in the lower income brackets and heavy dollar reductions for the wealthy. Even a tax bill with graduated reductions was vetoed by President Truman on the ground that it still relieved the rich rather than the poor and every representative who was defeated in the next election had voted to override the President's veto. The most perplexing problem of the legislator is how to get the taxes levied and still leave the electorate good-humored enough to re-elect him for another term.

THE STATE

By the term "state" is meant the political society whose personnel or membership consists of its citizens. The citizens of a state include all those persons who owe the state allegiance and have the rights and privileges of citizenship. So important is the state that it has been called "The Great Society." Aristotle declared it to be "a common life for a noble end." We know now that the state was not originally a deliberate creation but emerged naturally out of men's social needs and is therefore a product of social experience. Its point of origin appears to

have been the primitive family and tribe. Vestigial relics of the primitive patriarchal system persist in our speech today in such terms as the "elders," "city fathers," "seniority," and "the Senate"—literally, the old men. At any rate, the family is where the child first encounters law and government —that of his parents.

The state is, of course, but one of the several forms of social control by which human beings prevent confusion and maintain orderly social life. But so accustomed are we to the state that we take it for granted and sometimes assign to it a mystical existence. So accustomed have we become to the legalistic and consequently artificial conception of the state that we fail to see that, as in the case of all human institutions, it consists of patterns of attitudes and behavior of its citizens. These patterns of collective behavior serve to protect the citizens from external foes and from internal disorder, and to furnish the means for providing such services as schools and highways. In brief, the way of life that constitutes the state provides for achieving collectively either what could not be done so well or could not be done at all by the individual. With the insight of the sociologist the late Franklin H. Giddings devised the term "stateways" to designate the rules of conduct that are legally enforced. However, it would be erroneous to assume that coercion constitutes the main activity of the state. It may seem so to law-breakers upon whom the state has "cracked down," but their experience is exceptional among the great body of citizens. Most citizens habitually observe the "stateways." By and large the state as an institution consists of habitual ways the citizens act under a particular form of social control. The state, then, is one of several ways of life that serve to maintain an orderly society where confusion would otherwise prevail.

THE MULTI-GROUP NATURE OF THE STATE

The basic concept needed for an understanding of the dynamics of government is the multi-group nature of modern society or the modern state. The feudal society of Western Europe was characterized by a cultural and religious homogeneity whose disintegration marked the dawn of modern times. Contributing to the breakup of the medieval social structure was the religious strife following the Protestant Revolt and the formation of new economic groups as the industrial revolution, accompanied by technological changes, proceeded. The framers of the American Constitution understood the multi-group structure of society, and Madison gave classic expression to their conception in the tenth article of the *Federalist*. The late Charles A. Beard gave a modern version of Madison's interpretation in the following apt paraphrase: "A landed interest, a transport interest, a railway interest, a shipping interest, an engineering interest, a manufacturing interest, with many lesser interests, grow up of necessity in all great societies and divide them into different classes actuated by different sentiments and views. The regulation of these various and interfering interests . . . constitutes the principal task of modern statesmen and involves the spirit of party in the necessary and ordinary operation of the government."

THE DYNAMICS OF PUBLIC OPINION

Democratic government is presumed to be controlled only by public opinion. In a democratic system public policy slowly and hesitatingly emerges from innumerable planned conferences and unplanned conversations. Pressure groups, the press, radio commentators, and all other agencies of communication utilized by a free people contribute to the formulation of public opinion. In a multi-group society public opinion tends to become a resultant of the competing influences of the various groups. With respect to a specific issue one might conceive of progressive forces pushing forward, conservatives thrusting to the right, and radicals to the left, and reactionary forces shoving back. The resultant movement of public opinion depends upon the relative strength of the several forces. Sometimes one, sometimes another, is strongest. Professor H. L. Childs conceives the process to be analogous to the play of mechanical forces: "Were it possible to plot pressure groups objectively as parallelograms of forces and compute the resultant, significant predictions might be made not only as to what party platforms are likely to be, which parties will win, but also as to significant trends in public policy."[2]

Democracy often provides the opportunity for competing groups to coordinate their aims in programs they can all support. This is done through institutional means for discovering common ground, as through legislatures, the chief organ for giving formal or legal expression to ultimate agreement. The policies thus declared "tend to become a series of compromises along lines of least resistance."[3] Over a century ago one of the keenest of American philosophers observed that "what is called public opinion, instead of being the united opinion of the whole community is usually nothing more than the voice of the strongest interest or combination of interests; and not infrequently of a small but energetic and active portion of the people."[4] Certainly that part of the public which ignores public affairs, or keeps its opinions concerning them to itself, or expresses them feebly, makes no contribution to the formation of public opinion. As John Dickinson expressed it: "The larger number of members of any political society have no will on nearly all matters on which government acts. The only opinion, the only will which exists is the opinion, the will of special groups."[5]

[2] H. L. Childs: "Pressure Groups and Propaganda," in *The American Political Scene*, edited by E. B. Logan (New York, 1936), p. 225.

[3] R. M. MacIver: *The Web of Government* (New York, 1946), p. 298.

[4] John C. Calhoun: "A Disquisition on Government," in Benjamin F. Wright: *Source Book of American Political Theory* (New York, 1929), p. 537.

[5] John Dickinson: "Democratic Realities and Democratic Dogmas." *American Political Science Review* (1930), 24:29.

THE IMAGE OF DEMOCRACY

WALTER LIPPMANN

THE SELF-CENTERED MAN

Since Public Opinion is supposed to be the prime mover in democracies, one might reasonably expect to find a vast literature. One does not find it. There are excellent books on government and parties, that is, on the machinery which in theory registers public opinions after they are formed. But on the sources from which these public opinions arise, on the processes by which they are derived, there is relatively little. The existence of a force called Public Opinion is in the main taken for granted, and American political writers have been most interested either in finding out how to make government express the common will, or in how to prevent the common will from subverting the purposes for which they believe the government exists. According to their traditions they have wished either to tame opinion or to obey it. Thus the editor of a notable series of text-books writes that "the most difficult and the most momentous question of government (is) how to transmit the force of individual opinion into public action."[1]

But surely there is a still more momentous question, the question of how to validate our private versions of the political scene. There is, as I shall try to indicate further on, the prospect of radical improvement by the development of principles already in operation. But this development will depend on how well we learn to use knowledge of the way opinions are put together to watch over our own opinions when they are being put together. For casual opinion, being the product of partial contact, of tradition, and personal interests, cannot in the nature of things take kindly to a method of political thought which is based on exact record, measurement, analysis and comparison. Just those qualities of the mind which determine what shall seem interesting, important, familiar, personal, and dramatic, are the qualities which in the first instance realistic opinion frustrates. Therefore, unless there is in the community at large a growing conviction that prejudice and intuition are not enough, the working out of realistic opinion, which takes time, money, labor, conscious effort, patience and equanimity, will not find enough support. That conviction grows as self-criticism increases, and makes us conscious of buncombe, contemptuous of ourselves when we employ it, and on guard to detect it. Without an ingrained habit of analyzing opinion when we read, talk, and decide, most of us would hardly suspect the need of better ideas, nor be interested in them when they appear, nor be able to prevent the new technic of political intelligence from being manipulated.

[1] Albert Bushnell Hart in the Introductory Note to A. Lawrence Lowell's *Public Opinion and Popular Government*.

From *Public Opinion* (New York: The Macmillan Co., 1922), pp. 253-275 *passim*. Reprinted by permission of the author and the publisher.

Yet democracies, if we are to judge by the oldest and most powerful of them, have made a mystery out of public opinion. There have been skilled organizers of opinion who understood the mystery well enough to create majorities on election day. But these organizers have been regarded by political science as low fellows or as "problems," not as possessors of the most effective knowledge there was on how to create and operate public opinion. The tendency of the people who have voiced the ideas of democracy, even when they have not managed its action, the tendency of students, orators, editors, has been to look upon Public Opinion as men in other societies looked upon the uncanny forces to which they ascribed the last word in the direction of events.

For in almost every political theory there is an inscrutable element which in the heyday of that theory goes unexamined. Behind the appearances there is a Fate, there are Guardian Spirits, or Mandates to a Chosen People, a Divine Monarchy, a Vice-Regent of Heaven, or a Class of the Better Born. The more obvious angels, demons, and kings are gone out of democratic thinking, but the need for believing that there are reserve powers of guidance persists. It persisted for those thinkers of the Eighteenth Century who designed the matrix of democracy. They had a pale god, but warm hearts, and in the doctrine of popular sovereignty they found the answer to their need of an infallible origin for the new social order. There was the mystery, and only enemies of the people touched it with profane and curious hands.

* * *

So the early democrats insisted that a reasoned righteousness welled up spontaneously out of the mass of men. All of them hoped that it would, many of them believed that it did, although the cleverest, like Thomas Jefferson, had all sorts of private reservations. But one thing was certain: if public opinion did not come forth spontaneously, nobody in that age believed it would come forth at all. For in one fundamental respect the political science on which democracy was based was the same science that Aristotle formulated. It was the same science for democrat and aristocrat, royalist and republican, in that its major premise assumed the art of government to be a natural endowment. Men differed radically when they tried to name the men so endowed; but they agreed in thinking that the greatest question of all was to find those in whom political wisdom was innate. Royalists were sure that kings were born to govern. Alexander Hamilton thought that while "there are strong minds in every walk of life . . . the representative body, with too few exceptions to have any influence on the spirit of the government, will be composed of landholders, merchants, and men of the learned professions."[2] Jefferson thought the political faculties were deposited by God in farmers and planters, and sometimes spoke as if they were found in all the people. The main premise was the same: to govern was an instinct that appeared, according to your social preferences, in one man or a chosen few, in all males, or only in males who were white and twenty-one, perhaps even in all men and all women.

In deciding who was most fit to govern, knowledge of the world was taken for granted. The aristocrat believed that those who dealt with large affairs possessed the instinct, the democrats asserted that all men possessed the instinct and could therefore deal with large affairs. It was no part of political science in either case to think out how knowledge of the world could be brought to the ruler. If you were for the people you did not try to work out the question of how to keep the voter informed. By the age of twenty-one he had his political faculties. What counted was a good heart, a reasoning mind, a balanced judgment. These would ripen with age, but it was not necessary to consider how to in-

[2] *The Federalist*, Nos. 35, 36. *Cf.* comment by Henry Jones Ford in his *Rise and Growth of American Politics*. Ch. V.

form the heart and feed the reason. Men took in their facts as they took in their breath.

* * *

THE SELF-CONTAINED COMMUNITY

That groups of self-centered people would engage in a struggle for existence if they rubbed against each other has always been evident. This much truth there is at any rate in that famous passage in the Leviathan where Hobbes says that "though there had never been any time wherein particular men were in a condition of war one against another, yet at all times kings and *persons* of *sovereign authority because* of their *independency*, are in continual jealousies and in the state and posture of gladiators, having their weapons pointing, and their eyes fixed on one another . . ."[3]

To circumvent this conclusion one great branch of human thought, which had and has many schools, proceeded in this fashion: it conceived an ideally just pattern of human relations in which each person had well defined functions and rights. If he conscientiously filled the role allotted to him, it did not matter whether his opinions were right or wrong. He did his duty, the next man did his, and all the dutiful people together made a harmonious world. Every caste system illustrates this principle; you find it in Plato's Republic and in Aristotle, in the feudal ideal, in the circles of Dante's Paradise, in the bureaucratic type of socialism, and in laissez-faire, to an amazing degree in syndicalism, guild socialism, anarchism, and in the system of international law idealized by Mr. Robert Lansing. All of them assume a pre-established harmony, inspired, imposed, or innate, by which the self-opinionated person, class, or community is orchestrated with the rest of mankind. The more authoritarian imagine a conductor for the symphony who sees to it that each man plays his part; the anarchistic are

inclined to think that a more divine concord would be heard if each player improvised as he went along.

But there have also been philosophers who were bored by these schemes of rights and duties, took conflict for granted, and tried to see how their side might come out on top. They have always seemed more realistic, even when they seemed alarming, because all they had to do was to generalize the experience that nobody could escape. Machiavelli is the classic of this school, a man most mercilessly maligned, because he happened to be the first naturalist who used plain language in a field hitherto preempted by supernaturalists. He has a worse name and more disciples than any political thinker who ever lived. He truly described the technic of existence for the self-contained state. That is why he has the disciples. He has the bad name chiefly because he cocked his eye at the Medici family, dreamed in his study at night where he wore his "noble court dress" that Machiavelli was himself the Prince, and turned a pungent description of the way things are done into an eulogy on that way of doing them.

In his most infamous chapter[4] he wrote that "a prince ought to take care that he never lets anything slip from his lips that is not replete with the above-named five qualities, that he may appear to him who hears and sees him altogether merciful, faithful, humane, upright, and religious. There is nothing more necessary to appear to have than this last quality, inasmuch as men judge generally more by the eye than by the hand, because it belongs to everybody to see you, to few to come in touch with you. Everyone sees what you appear to be, few really know what you are, and those few dare not oppose themselves to the opinion of the many, who have the majesty of the state to defend them; and in the actions of all men, and especially of princes, which it is not prudent to challenge, one judges

---

[3] *Leviathan*, Ch. XIII. Of the Natural Condition of Mankind as concerning their Felicity and Misery.

[4] *The Prince*, Ch. XVIII. "Concerning the way in which Princes should keep faith." Translation by W. K. Marriott.

by the result. . . . One prince of the present time, whom it is not well to name, never preaches anything else but peace and good faith, and to both he is most hostile, and either, if he had kept it, would have deprived him of reputation and kingdom many a time."

That is cynical. But it is the cynicism of a man who saw truly without knowing quite why he saw what he saw. Machiavelli is thinking of the run of men and princes "who judge generally more by the eye than by the hand," which is his way of saying that their judgments are subjective. He was too close to earth to pretend that the Italians of his day saw the world steadily and saw it whole. He would not indulge in fantasies, and he had not the materials for imagining a race of men that had learned how to correct their vision.

The world, as he found it, was composed of people whose vision could rarely be corrected, and Machiavelli knew that such people, since they see all public relations in a private way, are involved in perpetual strife. What they see is their own personal, class, dynastic, or municipal version of affairs that in reality extend far beyond the boundaries of their vision. They see their aspect. They see it as right. But they cross other people who are similarly self-centered. Then their very existence is endangered, or at least what they, for unsuspected private reasons, regard as their existence and take to be a danger. The end, which is impregnably based on a real though private experience justifies the means. They will sacrifice any one of these ideals to save all of them, . . . "one judges by the result . . ."

* * *

The democratic ideal, as Jefferson moulded it, consisting of an ideal environment and a selected class, did not conflict with the political science of his time. It did conflict with the realities. And when the ideal was stated in absolute terms, partly through exuberance and partly for campaign purposes, it was soon forgotten that the theory was originally devised for very special conditions. It became the political gospel, and supplied the stereotypes through which Americans of all parties have looked at politics.

That gospel was fixed by the necessity that in Jefferson's time no one could have conceived public opinions that were not spontaneous and subjective. The democratic tradition is therefore always trying to see a world where people are exclusively concerned with affairs of which the causes and effects all operate within the region they inhabit. Never has democratic theory been able to conceive itself in the context of a wide and unpredictable environment. The mirror is concave. And although democrats recognize that they are in contact with external affairs, they see quite surely that every contact outside that self-contained group is a threat to democracy as originally conceived. That is a wise fear. If democracy is to be spontaneous, the interest of democracy must remain simple, intelligible, and easily managed. Conditions must approximate those of the isolated rural township if the supply of information is to be left to casual experience. The environment must be confined within the range of every man's direct and certain knowledge.

The democrat has understood what an analysis of public opinion seems to demonstrate: that in dealing with an unseen environment decisions "are manifestly settled at haphazard, which clearly they ought not to be."[5] So he has always tried in one way or another to minimize the importance of that unseen environment. He feared foreign trade because trade involves foreign connections; he distrusted manufactures because they produced big cities and collected crowds; if he had nevertheless to have manufactures, he wanted protection in the interest of self-sufficiency. When he could not find these conditions in the real world, he went passionately into the wilderness, and founded utopian communities far from foreign contacts. His slogans reveal his prejudice. He is for Self-Government, Self-Determination, Independence. Not one of

[5] Aristotle, *Politics*, Bk. VII, Ch. IV.

these ideas carries with it any notion of consent or community beyond the frontiers of the self-governing groups. The field of democratic action is a circumscribed area. Within protected boundaries the aim has been to achieve self-sufficiency and avoid entanglement. This rule is not confined to foreign policy, but it is plainly evident there, because life outside the national boundaries is more distinctly alien than life within. And as history shows, democracies in their foreign policy have had generally to choose between splendid isolation and a diplomacy that violated their ideals. The most successful democracies, in fact, Switzerland, Denmark, Australia, New Zealand, and America until recently, have had no foreign policy in the European sense of that phrase. Even a rule like the Monroe Doctrine arose from the desire to supplement the two oceans by a glacis of states that were sufficiently republican to have no foreign policy.

Whereas danger is a great, perhaps an indispensable condition of autocracy, security was seen to be a necessity if democracy was to work. There must be as little disturbance as possible of the premise of a self-contained community. Insecurity involves surprises. It means that there are people acting upon your life, over whom you have no control, with whom you cannot consult. It means that forces are at large which disturb the familiar routine, and present novel problems about which quick and unusual decisions are required. Every democrat feels in his bones that dangerous crises are incompatible with democracy, because he knows that the inertia of the masses is such that to act quickly a very few must decide and the rest follow rather blindly. This has not made non-resistants out of democrats, but it has resulted in all democratic wars being fought for pacifist aims. Even when the wars are in fact wars of conquest, they are sincerely believed to be wars in defense of civilization.

These various attempts to enclose a part of the earth's surface were not inspired by cowardice, apathy, or, what one of Jefferson's critics called a willingness to live under monkish discipline. The democrats had caught sight of a dazzling possibility, that every human being should rise to his full stature, freed from man-made limitations. With what they knew of the art of government, they could, no more than Aristotle before them, conceive a society of autonomous individuals, except an enclosed and simple one. They could, then, select no other premise if they were to reach the conclusion that all the people could spontaneously manage their public affairs.

Having adopted the premise because it was necessary to their keenest hope, they drew other conclusions as well. Since in order to have spontaneous self-government, you had to have a simple self-contained community, they took it for granted that one man was as competent as the next to manage these simple and self-contained affairs. Where the wish is father to the thought such logic is convincing. Moreover, the doctrine of the omnicompetent citizen is for most practical purposes true in the rural township. Everybody in the village sooner or later tries his hand at everything the village does. There is rotation in office by men who are jacks of all trades. There was no serious trouble with the doctrine of the omnicompetent citizen until the democratic stereotype was universally applied, so that men looked at a complicated civilization and saw an enclosed village.

Not only was the individual citizen fitted to deal with all public affairs, but he was consistently public-spirited and endowed with unflagging interest. He was public-spirited enough in the township, where he knew everybody and was interested in everybody's business. The idea of enough for the township turned easily into the idea of enough for any purpose, for as we have noted, quantitative thinking does not suit a stereotype. But there was another turn to the circle. Since everybody was assumed to be interested enough in important affairs, only those affairs came to seem important in which everybody was interested.

This meant that men formed their picture of the world outside from the unchallenged pictures in their heads. These pictures came to them well stereotyped by their parents and teachers, and were little corrected by their own experience. Only a few men had affairs that took them across state lines. Even fewer had reason to go abroad. Most voters lived their whole lives in one environment, and with nothing but a few feeble newspapers, some pamphlets, political speeches, their religious training, and rumor to go on, they had to conceive that larger environment of commerce and finance, of war and peace. The number of public opinions based on any objective report was very small in proportion to those based on casual fancy.

And so for many different reasons, self-sufficiency was a spiritual ideal in the formative period. The physical isolation of the township, the loneliness of the pioneer, the theory of democracy, the Protestant tradition, and the limitations of political science all converged to make men believe that out of their own consciences they must extricate political wisdom. It is not strange that the deduction of laws from absolute principles should have usurped so much of their free energy. The American political mind had to live on its capital. In legalism it found a tested body of rules from which new rules could be spun without the labor of learning new truths from experience. The formulae became so curiously sacred that every good foreign observer has been amazed at the contrast between the dynamic practical energy of the American people and the static theorism of their public life. That steadfast love of fixed principles was simply the only way known of achieving self-sufficiency. But it meant that the public opinions of any one community about the outer world consisted chiefly of a few stereotyped images arranged in a pattern deduced from their legal and their moral codes, and animated by the feeling aroused by local experiences.

Thus democratic theory, starting from its fine vision of ultimate human dignity, was forced by lack of the instruments of knowledge for reporting its environment, to fall back upon the wisdom and experience which happened to have accumulated in the voter. God had, in the words of Jefferson, made men's breasts "His peculiar deposit for substantial and genuine virtue." These chosen people in their self-contained environment had all the facts before them. The environment was so familiar that one could take it for granted that men were talking about substantially the same things. The only real disagreements, therefore, would be in judgments about the same facts. There was no need to guarantee the sources of information. They were obvious, and equally accessible to all men. Nor was there need to trouble about the ultimate criteria. In the self-contained community one could assume, or at least did assume, a homogeneous code of morals. The only place, therefore, for differences of opinion was in the logical application of accepted standards to accepted facts. And since the reasoning faculty was also well standardized, an error in reasoning would be quickly exposed in a free discussion. It followed that truth could be obtained by liberty within these limits. The community could take its supply of information for granted; its codes it passed on through school, church, and family, and the power to draw deductions from a premise, rather than the ability to find the premise, was regarded as the chief end of intellectual training.

THE CURRENT STATUS OF AMERICAN
PUBLIC OPINION

HERBERT H. HYMAN AND PAUL B. SHEATSLEY

Twenty years ago an assessment of the status of American public opinion would have been dependent entirely upon the limited or biased viewpoint of the particular person making the appraisal. He would have had to infer, from what he could observe of the public's behavior, what information, attitudes, and beliefs lay behind that behavior, and he would have had no effective means of doing this. It would have been impossible to say with any authority to what extent the American public measured up to the ideal set forth in chapter one.

During the course of the last two decades, however, techniques of measuring public opinion through cross-section surveys have been rapidly developed and refined. The nationwide polls (as their experience in the last presidential election showed) are still unable infallibly to predict public behavior on the basis of the public's expressed attitudes, but they have nevertheless developed a high degree of skill in discovering what the public knows, what it thinks, and what it has done in the past. Their work has been supplemented by contributions from the academic world: mathematicians have improved sampling procedures; psychologists have devised better interviewing methods; and sociologists have contributed to an un-

derstanding of the dynamics of public opinion. The government provided a tremendous impetus to survey research during the war, when it relied upon sampling surveys to assess public information, morale, attitudes, and wants.

As a result of all this research, a vast body of survey data has accumulated, so vast that a mere reporting of the over-all results of the major nationwide polls in this country over a period of ten years has required two years of staff time at the Office of Public Opinion Research in Princeton and will fill several thousand closely written pages. The great bulk of these survey findings refer, of course, to public opinion on issues that, though important, are ephemeral. Yet, buried in this mass of survey results are occasional data which reveal the underlying characteristics and nature of American public opinion, and it is also possible to discern, within the fluctuating "votes" on particular issues, some of the basic beliefs and ideals of the people.

The major problem is one of assessment. No one has ever set out systematically to use this new tool of social research, the public opinion survey, to discover just how far short public opinion is of the stated goals. Instead, the various polling agencies have understandably concentrated on current is-

From the *National Council for Social Studies Yearbook,* 1950, Vol. 21, pp. 11-34. Reprinted by permission of the publisher and the authors.

sues and have asked whatever questions seemed best to them for their purposes at the time. Thus, we have a variety of different agencies asking a variety of different questions, sometimes with apparently contradictory results. We have a vast fund of information on some areas and no information at all on others.

Yet, fully aware of the inadequacies of the materials and the difficulties involved in interpreting it, we turn to the public opinion survey for the most accurate information we have on that phenomenon, "public opinion." The findings reported in this chapter have been obtained and confirmed by objective researchers who have used the best methods available to them at the time. All results, unless otherwise specified, represent the answers of a representative cross section of the adult population of the United States to questions addressed to them personally by experienced interviewers.[1] The precise interpretation to be placed upon the findings may be disputed, but it may be regarded as certain that if the entire population, rather than just a sample of it, had been confronted by the same question at the same time, the results would not have varied by more than a few percentage points.

A few words of caution are perhaps required before we attempt to sum up what the polls show in relation to public opinion. First, we deal here only with adult opinions. Persons under 21 are excluded from the samples obtained by most of the nationwide polls on the ground of their ineligibility to vote. Thus, these findings do not apply to the younger generation which is still in school.

Secondly, these findings do not always represent the "effective" public opinion. It might be argued that the opinion of nonvoters should be excluded from a discus-

[1] We are indebted to the American Institute of Public Opinion (Gallup Poll), the National Opinion Research Center, Elmo Roper (Fortune Poll), the American Jewish Committee, and the Bureau of Applied Social Research at Columbia University for the bulk of the survey data reported in this chapter.

sion of American public opinion, since they do nothing to implement their opinions at the polling booth. Or it might be argued that only those who are interested in the issue should be considered when defining public opinion. It is obvious that the will of the majority, sometimes rightly and sometimes wrongly, is not invariably the controlling factor in our political life. But we accept here the premise that American society is based on political equality, and it is the total American citizenry with whom we are concerned when we talk about popular education.

Thirdly, the figures we report should be taken as approximations rather than as precise measurements. Most of them are subject to a possible sampling variation of up to six or seven percentage points in either direction, but beyond that they furnish only a gross picture of public opinion and frequently obscure large differences among various population groups. Age, sex, education, geographical region, political preference—such factors as these, as well as amount of information about the issue and degree of interest in it, sometimes affect attitudes strongly, and the figures we present are mere averages of all the different individual and group opinions.

Lastly, if we seem to place undue stress upon the inadequacies of American public opinion and to lay insufficient emphasis upon its effectiveness, we do so for what seem to us two good reasons. In the first place, our poll results always tend slightly to overemphasize the public's knowledge, concern, and intelligence. In part, this is due to the inherent difficulty of interviewing illiterates, foreign-speaking peoples, and other types who are likely to be below the national level in certain respects. In part, it is due to the natural desire of the person being interviewed to "seem smart" and to try to impress the interviewer by exaggerating his opinions. In part it is due to the fact that the usual type of poll question sums up the issue for the person and merely asks him to choose whichever alternative comes closest to his opinion; confronted with such a ready-made choice the apathetic, uninformed individual is able to appear more discerning than he may actually be. In stressing the inadequacies of public opinion, therefore, we discount these factors to a certain extent.

But our major reason for emphasizing the ways in which public opinion falls short of the desired goals is that we feel this is the more constructive approach. After all, in areas where public opinion meets or surpasses the goals, we need have few fears. The more urgent task is to define the problems ahead of us so that we may analyze and attack them, and to do this effectively we must concentrate on the weaknesses and shortcomings, while seeming to ignore what are real gains and accomplishments.

We discuss the current status of American public opinion under the following main headings:

1. The interest and concern of the public regarding matters outside the realm of their immediate activities.
2. The extent of individual participation in the political process.
3. The role of critical thought and analysis in determining public opinion.
4. Public attitudes toward political leaders and institutions.
5. The extent of public adherence to the basic ideals of democracy.
6. Attitudes toward censorship of information.
7. Willingness to accept necessary or desirable changes, and readiness to resist undesirable changes.
8. Some fundamental American values.

THE AREA OF INTEREST
AND CONCERN

One of the two general goals for education has been stated as encouraging persons to participate effectively in increasingly larger areas. This demands an enlargement in the public's area of thinking to include not only the basic problems of security in this country but a healthy concern about seemingly remote events which take place far from our shores. It is clear that the impact of two world wars and the tremendous strides taken in the fields of transportation and communication have forced radical changes in the traditional isolationism of American thinking. Today, in spite of a still remaining core of isolationists who would have the United States withdraw entirely from world affairs, there is overwhelming public support of American policies which a generation ago would have been unthinkable. Surveys have consistently shown large majorities in favor of American participation in the United Nations, of maintaining troops in the defeated Axis nations, of spending billions on European recovery and relief, and of scores of other policies which have only an indirect, though important, effect on the average American.

Indeed, when asked how much interest they take in a series of issues, the public claims almost as much interest in such international problems as our relations with Russia and control of the atom bomb as they do in such personal worries as the cost of living. When asked what are the most important problems facing the United States today, majorities mention international problems as well as domestic, and at certain times when this question has been asked of national samples, the first problem mentioned has been one in the field of foreign affairs or world peace.

Yet there is an abundance of survey evidence that this interest in and concern about more distant problems is not based on any universal awareness that the interests of America are now global in character. It appears to reflect instead a mere desire to prevent war and a natural concern regarding the more obvious problems which threaten the fulfillment of that desire. Certainly the majority of Americans are not interested in foreign affairs as such, and they appear to take an interest only when those problems clearly affect their own interests.

Only small minorities, ranging from 10 percent to 30 percent of the population, for example, express any great interest in what has been happening in China, Palestine, Spain, or Korea.[2] These areas are regarded

[2] This chapter was written prior to the outbreak of hostilities in Korea.

as remote from any American interest, and questions about our policies there reveal large groups with no opinions, little information, and little concern. Similarly, most Americans appear to regard the impingement of foreign affairs on their thinking as a necessary evil. When asked whether the radio is giving them enough news about other countries, a sizable majority answered "Yes," and an additional 16 percent volunteered the opinion that there was "too much" foreign news on the radio. Again, when asked what particular questions in the field of foreign affairs they would like to know more about, exactly half of a national sample were unable to think of a single matter on which they wanted additional information.

On virtually every survey since the end of the war in which the public has been asked to name the most pressing problem facing them and their families, majorities have concentrated on such immediate domestic concerns as high prices, housing, taxes, depression, and unemployment. When asked shortly after election day what problem the new Truman administration should take up first, the great majority concentrated on the cost of living and better housing, and only about one person in five spoke of any foreign problem. And when the public is confronted directly with the choice between spending money on foreign affairs or on domestic needs, only about a third would give precedence to foreign affairs. Finally, surveys consistently reveal a minority of from 20 percent to 25 percent of the population who are concerned *only* with immediate domestic issues and who express little interest even in the most pressing problems of foreign affairs.

THE ROLE OF CRITICAL THINKING

The second general goal for education has been described as the encouragement of individuals to make increasingly finer discriminations. One of the basic characteristics of the ideal citizen is his use of reflective or critical thinking in arriving at his decisions on public issues. This naturally requires an awareness of the relevant facts, a recognition of his own interests and the interests of others in any public question, a critical weighing of the available evidence, and a resistance to appeals based on emotion rather than reason. We have seen that, although a majority of the American public recognize their immediate interests and are generally willing to make whatever apparent sacrifices are necessary to promote them, they find it hard to recognize their interests in problems which appear remote from their daily lives.

Parallel to this lack of interest in peripheral problems is a generally low level of information—in spite of the fact that nine Americans out of ten own a radio and read a daily paper. At the height of the 1948 Presidential campaign, for example, 12 Americans out of every hundred were unaware that Dewey was the Republican nominee, and nine out of a hundred did not know that Truman was running on the Democratic ticket; only about half the population could identify the vice-presidential nominees of either party, and one out of three did not know that Henry Wallace was running for president. Three years after the establishment of the United Nations and after several plenary meetings had been held in this country, one American out of every four either admitted he had never heard of the organization or could not even vaguely define its purpose. Awareness of any particular issue, proposal, or event is generally likely to be much lower, with the proportion ranging all the way from 20 percent to a maximum of 80 percent, depending upon the importance of the event, the amount of attention given to it by the press, and the length of time it has been before the public. In almost every instance where the polls have tested public information, at least 20 percent of the population have revealed complete ignorance.

Despite this, Americans are an articulate people and they express opinions on virtually every conceivable issue. Although tests of information invariably show at least 20 percent of the public totally uninformed (and usually the figure is closer to 40 percent), the "no opinion" vote on any poll question seldom exceeds 15 percent, and is often much lower. Mere lack of knowledge does not stop the public from offering opinions, a fact that is also revealed by the consistent finding that upwards of 10 percent of those expressing a given attitude will answer "don't know" when the interviewer asks them why they feel that way. In the absence of information, the public would be expected to have little competence for rational decisions and to fall easy prey to emotional symbols, and to a great extent this is true. A perpetual problem for those who seek to measure public opinion is to arrive at "unbiased" question wordings and to avoid "loading" the issue in any direction, for it is well known that, where knowledge is low and attitudes lightly held, people can be pushed into adopting almost any point of view, depending on the arguments put to them. Thus, it was often found that when a question stated that "President Roosevelt has proposed . . .," approval of the program was significantly higher than when the issue was presented without reference to the President's position.

Yet, when the particular issue is one on which the public feels strongly, absence of information seldom results in a submission to symbols. For example, a large part of the general public has little information about labor unions. Approximately a third can name neither any "good thing" that unions do nor any "bad thing" they do. Yet when two poll questions dealing with a specific aspect of labor relations were experimentally "loaded," one in favor of unions and one against unions, the results were the same. A similar finding was revealed at the time of the San Francisco conference when about a third of the public was not aware that the organization meetings of the United Nations were taking place. Yet, when two equivalent samples of the adult population were presented with questions which were purposely biased, in one case for and in the other against, the principle of world organization, the overwhelming majority of Americans endorsed the principle in both cases. These findings suggest that, although there is no critical weighing of evidence based on information, the public hardly may be said to arrive at their decisions quixotically or by chance.

It is in the political area that absence of one type of critical thinking can best be demonstrated. About three-fourths of the American public consider themselves members of one of the two major political parties; only about one person in five denies any party preference and describes himself as an "independent," one who "votes for the man." Yet, when asked whether it would make any difference to them personally which party were in office, 71 percent of a national sample answered "No." Similarly, only 20 percent felt that one of the two major parties was better able than the other to handle such important problems as the cost of living. When voters in three of the most populous states were asked what they liked and disliked about the major political parties, one person in three either could not name a single thing or else explained that he had always supported or opposed that party, without mentioning any reason. Another fifth of the sample merely said their party had better men or better policies or was more honest, without naming any specific political or ideological reason for their support.

Again, between 60 percent and 70 percent reported that they had no knowledge of what was in their party platforms during the 1948 presidential campaign, and when asked in the spring of that year to identify the position held by President Truman on six major issues, the average citizen could state only three of the six correctly; one person in five knew where Truman stood on only one or on none of them. Furthermore, it has consistently been found that people hear about and remember those things which fit their prior attitudes and tend to ignore or forget others. Thus, Republicans were well informed about Truman's position when it opposed theirs but were less aware of his support of some of the programs they themselves favored; similarly, Democrats tended to be aware of things they approved of in Truman's record and to be ignorant of the things in which they opposed him. Finally, there is an abundance of evidence to show that the voting preference of about three-fourths of the population is fixed, in terms of party loyalty, habit, and tradition, long in advance of the actual campaign. The campaign itself is critically followed by only a small minority who base their vote upon a rational consideration of the opposing appeals, and its main function is to get out the latent vote that already exists rather than to convince the supporters of the opposing party.

This is not to say that people do not somehow recognize their interests in a political campaign. Surveys consistently show that labor, for example, conceives of the Democratic party as identified with its interests, whereas business has faith in the Republicans, and all groups tend to vote in accordance with their conception of where their interests lie. These conceptions, however, seem chiefly to be based on tradition rather than on information and critical analysis, and they are not easily subject to change. As noted above, political preferences have been shown to be little affected by party campaigns, and panel studies, in which the same people are interviewed several times over a period of months, reveal a striking rigidity in the attitudes of most people. For instance, such a study in the city of Cincinnati revealed an almost complete failure to change basic attitudes toward foreign affairs as the result of a six-months' intensive information effort on behalf of the United Nations. Studies of the American population before and after the Bikini atom bomb tests showed no important change in public knowledge, beliefs, or opinions about atomic energy.

Thus, opinions are not formed capriciously and they do have some organized character. As a matter of fact, surveys show that attitudes are highly generalized, that it is frequently possible to predict a person's opinion on specific issues by reference to his attitude or belief regarding some broad basic question. There is little tendency toward a discrete examination of the facts in each case, but a reliance instead on certain underlying beliefs. Whether this represents a healthy stability of opinion or an unhealthy lack of responsiveness to new facts is difficult to say. But it does not appear to represent the type of critical analysis which is stated as the goal.

ACTION AND PARTICIPATION

The ideal citizen does not stop at having an opinion. He acts, individually or in a group, to implement his decision, and he is on guard against feelings of apathy, against the attitude that one man can do nothing. When the public is shown precisely what it can do to implement its desires (a difficult task, in view of the data on information levels and interest previously shown), there is a general willingness to act, even if the action calls for some sacrifice.

The performance of the American people during the recent war documents this assertion, and a wealth of data from wartime surveys offers specific points of evidence. Only 7 percent of the public, for example, could not explain what the United States was fighting for in the war, and 80 percent said they had a clear idea of what things they, as individuals, could do to help win it. Periodic checks on public cooperation with wartime appeals consistently showed up to 97 percent awareness of what was required and from 65 percent to 85 percent participation in such programs as buying bonds, planting victory gardens, or turning in waste fats and scrap metal. Majorities throughout the war expressed approval of whatever sacrifices they were called upon to make: gasoline rationing, food rationing, the draft, as well as other more drastic programs which were never put into effect: strict wage control and universal manpower mobilization, for example.

Yet, except in such extreme situations as wartime, when the public is united in its purpose and can see the relationship between individual action and the achievement of that purpose, there is in general a lack of American participation in political affairs, a feeling of futility about the role the individual can play and a tendency to leave the actual implementation of decisions to "the government" or "the experts." Simple election statistics show, for example, that only about half the eligible voters in the country turn out to exercise their franchise, even in crucial presidential elections. Surveys have shown that a majority of the public regard voting as "a duty rather than a right," and about a third of the public readily admit that it would not make much difference to them if they were prevented from voting in a presidential election.

In the realm of nonvoting action, the feeling of futility is even more apparent. Over half the population, for example, answered "I don't know" or "I can't do anything" to a question which asked them what things they as individuals could do to support or to change the government's current policy toward Russia. When asked, "Can you think of anything that you personally can do that would help prevent another war?" only 6 percent could name anything at all, and the other 64 percent answered "No." In a large midwestern city, over half of this urban population could think of nothing which they as individuals could do to help make the United Nations more successful. This pessimism about the individual's effectiveness in the face of such vast problems extends even to a lack of faith in group effectiveness. Half the population, for example, can think of nothing that "clubs or groups" could do to prevent wars, and a slightly larger number has no faith that "groups of scientists" can do anything to prevent wars. Indeed, as far as prevention of war is concerned, a majority feel that the United States as a nation can do nothing to prevent war, and that the United Nations, too, has no real chance for effectiveness in this realm.

Suggestions on the part of those who feel the individual is not entirely helpless range from such vague answers as "Just support the government," to such indirect actions as "Read the papers more," or "Pray." The three most frequently mentioned, however, are (a) writing to Congressmen or other officials and expressing your views; (b) voting, putting the right men into office; and (c) joining groups and working through them for the desired goals. At least two surveys have documented the finding that no more than 15 percent of the public has ever written a letter or sent a telegram to any official of the federal government, and a sizeable minority believe that government officials "go right ahead without regard to what most people think" anyway. We have already noted that only about half the eligible voters actually turn out even for presidential elections. The score is similarly bad as far as participation in groups is concerned. Only about 15 percent of the people claim membership in any group that discusses national or international problems, and many of the groups which are mentioned have only a peripheral concern with such matters.

It would seem that in this realm of individual effectiveness, American public opinion shows up least well. Yet as the wartime experience showed, Americans are not incapable of translating their opinions into effective action. If they can be shown how individual action on their part can help implement their decisions and satisfy their wants, no compulsion is necessary.

ATTITUDES TOWARD POLITICAL LEADERSHIP

In the abstract the public has high regard for the qualities which ideally fit a man for public office: experience, efficiency, honesty. When asked some months before the 1948 presidential nominations to name the one person in public life who had the best qualities for president, and then to explain what qualities that man had which influenced their choice, only about one person in four mentioned their man's policies or ideology. The great majority explained their preference in terms of his personal character: he was experienced, level-headed, practical, honest, fair, sincere, energetic, firm, decisive. Yet it would be easy to demonstrate that in their actual voting behavior, Americans quite often ignore such traits and make their choice instead on extraneous or purely selfish considerations.

Thus, an examination of the 1945 mayoralty election in Detroit revealed that appeals to racial hatred played a substantial part in the election of the winner. In that same year, the voters of Boston swept into office a man who was at the time under federal indictment for fraud in connection with solicitation of war contracts and who was convicted three months after his election. These charges were well known to Boston voters during the campaign, but surveys at the time of the election revealed that the man's supporters regarded him as a sort of Robin Hood character who robbed the rich to help the poor, a politician who always looked out for "the little man," and a person who was able to "get things done." Thus, the public managed to rationalize the candidate's dishonesty, and to vote for him in clear conscience in spite of an acknowledged trait which they unanimously opposed in the abstract.

On an abstract basis, too, Americans recognize the prestige of public office, regard public service as an honorable calling, and grant the value of faithful public servants. In a nationwide study of the "prestige" of approximately 90 different occupations, for instance, public office ranked near the top. Not only do such office holders as "Justice of the Supreme Court" rate extremely high in terms of prestige, but the same general finding holds right down the line: "mayor of a large city," "cabinet official," "Congressman," "county judge" and "administrative officer in a state government" all rank well above the average. Yet when asked a series of concrete questions about their attitudes toward politics, the public reveals a fundamental cynicism which seems far removed from the view that public service is an honorable career.

To the question of whether or not they would like to see their own son go into politics, two-thirds of a national sample flatly said "No," and the fact that the same results were obtained when the question was repeated after an interval of two years indicates that this sentiment is quite rigid. In reply to another question on the same survey, approximately half of the public took the stand that it was "almost impossible" for a man to go into politics without becoming dishonest. This same reason, incidentally, was advanced by about half of the group who would not like to see their sons enter politics: public service is essentially dishonest and corrupting. Many among those who would favor a political career for their sons explain their attitude by saying that politics is corrupt now and honest men are needed to reform it. Yet, when asked whether or not they are satisfied with the way most office holders in their state are handling their jobs, about half the population indicate satisfaction.

Ambivalent attitudes toward the government are routinely turned up by public opinion surveys on all sorts of issues. Such findings as the following appear to reveal a generalized distrust of government office-holders: 59 percent of the public say that the government is "holding back on a lot of information that the people ought to have," but only a fraction of this group can mention even vaguely the sort of information that is being concealed. A minority of the population criticize almost any government agency they are asked about, often expressing the belief that all public officials are grafters, bunglers, or worse. Yet on another level these same Americans will express great pride in their office-holders and their institutions, and will complain that other Americans do not support the government. A variety of surveys also show that the public tends to resent and oppose any suggestion of government "interference" with business; yet, when faced with such problems as high prices, unemployment, or lack of housing, they overwhelmingly turn to "the government" to do something about it.

An ideal public would certainly be familiar with the names and the duties of its office-holders and would be well informed about their actions. We have already seen that only about half the population could name the vice-presidential candidates of either party at the height of the 1948 campaign, and that about one person in ten did not even know who was running for president. On the local level, surveys have shown that upwards of 90 percent of the voters cannot name the men who hold such elective offices as county clerk, collector, or treasurer. We have also seen that only about one person in four explains his choice of a presidential candidate in terms of the man's policies, record, or ideology, and that fewer than half explain their preference for a particular political party in these terms.

Judged against the ideal of an educated public, current American attitudes toward political leaders and public office appear to leave much to be desired. Yet we have seen that various groups in the population do identify their real interests with the appropriate candidate, and thus on some deeper level they seem to weigh the candidates and issues rationally. Perhaps the explanation of the apparent inconsistencies of survey findings in this area lies in the fact that the public combines a deep respect for American institutions and offices with a healthy skepticism about the men who fill them.

THE BASIC IDEALS OF DEMOCRACY

An essential feature of an enlightened democratic public opinion is as stated in chapter one, a loyalty to the basic ideals of democracy, an acceptance of its responsibilities, and a recognition of its implications. The overwhelming majority of Americans are aware that they constitute a democracy and they are intensely proud of the fact. Eighty-eight percent of them, according to one survey, consider the United States a democratic country; curiously, only 60 percent consider Great Britain a democracy and even fewer believe that France is one. Furthermore, democracy is regarded as the only suitable type of government by the vast majority of Americans. They usually react strongly against any proposal which is described as "socialist," and they regard "dictatorship," "communism," and "fascism" as utterly antipathetic to their interests.

When one dips slightly below these symbols, however, the overwhelming majorities start to melt away. Nevertheless, when asked what democracy is, what there is about democratic countries that distinguishes them from others, four Americans out of five can still come up with a good answer. The two chief features, each of them mentioned by substantial proportions of the public, are (a) freedom: political, economic, and religious; and (b) popular rule; free elections and a voice in the government. (It is noteworthy that around 20 percent of the population are unable to give any definition of democracy at all.) Many educators were astounded a few years ago when one survey showed that 31 percent of all adult Americans said they had never heard of the Bill of Rights, an additional 36 percent said they had heard of it but could not identify it, and still another 12 percent gave incorrect versions of what it was. Yet, in spite of this superficial ignorance, the great majority of the public reveal a strong devotion, on a broad or abstract level, to the basic principles of liberty and equality.

When asked to choose, for example, between a government whose chief purpose would be to provide economic security and one whose chief purpose would be to insure political freedom, more than four out of five cast their vote for freedom. When asked what they regard as the greatest advantage of our type of government, almost two-thirds spontaneously mention various types of civil liberties. Only 1 percent of a national sample answered "No" when asked directly, "Do you believe in freedom of speech?" and on a variety of surveys an almost unanimous lip service has been paid to the fundamental democratic principles of liberty and equality. But again, when we drop to the level of specifics, the majorities fall off. Repeated surveys have shown that one American in every four would not permit the Socialist party to publish newspapers, and one in three would not allow newspapers to criticize our form of government. Even the minority who could successfully explain what the Bill of Rights is was not unanimous in upholding its guarantees: one-fifth of this group would deny to Socialists the right to publish newspapers.

In the realm of equality, there are again disturbing findings when the survey questions are put in terms of concrete situations. Three out of every ten men, for instance, affirm that any man who can fill a job satisfactorily should be given preference over all women for the position. *After* the recent war, only 59 percent of a cross section were willing to grant *loyal* Japanese who are American *citizens* the same chance as other people to get any kind of job. On at least two occasions, survey results demonstrated that only half the white population favored job equality for Negroes; half of them "wouldn't like" being treated by a Negro nurse if they were sick in a hospital; 42 percent think Negroes "should be required" to occupy separate parts of a train or bus when traveling from one state to another. Half of the white Christian population of a large city bordering the South expressed the opinion in a local survey that Jews should not be allowed to hold high political office; one in five felt the same way about Catholics; and one in three thought it would be a good idea if more business concerns refused to hire Jews. In a national survey, only 68 percent gave an unqualified answer of "Yes" to the question, "Would you be willing to work at your job alongside someone of a different color, race, or religion?"

The majority of Americans appear to deny still another traditional feature of democracy, that of offering political asylum and refuge to homeless and oppressed peoples. Faced with the simple proposition of whether or not to admit a certain number of displaced persons from Europe, less than one person in four approved. And these attitudes are not very susceptible to change. Even when it is suggested that other countries, too, would take some of these people, that they would be admitted only gradually, in small numbers, and that they are persons who fear to return to their old homes in Russian controlled territory, the majority

still disapprove of opening our doors. These latter attitudes, though they undoubtedly reflect the public's concern about housing shortages and possible unemployment, perhaps relate also to American feelings of superiority over "foreigners," which have been revealed by some surveys. On one occasion, for example, when a cross section of the public was handed a list of 17 different nationalities and asked to compare them with us, *only five* of the 17 peoples were admitted by a majority of Americans to be "as good as we are in all important respects": Canadians, Englishmen, Dutch, Scandinavians, and Irish. The remainder were judged "not quite as good as we are in important respects," or "definitely inferior." At the bottom of the list were Chinese, Spaniards, Italians, Mexicans, and Japanese.

It is, of course, encouraging to look at the positive side of such figures as we have presented. In most cases, the majority of Americans uphold the democratic ideals not only in theory but also in practice. Although minorities ranging from 20 percent to 40 percent would deny civil liberties and economic equality to certain peoples in certain instances, it is seldom that such discriminatory practices receive the sanction of the majority.

FREEDOM OF INFORMATION AND CENSORSHIP

Although sizable groups of Americans would favor censorship or suppression of unpopular political views, we have seen that the majority of the public generally line up in favor of the principles of free speech, even when it comes to specific issues which test those principles. On the other hand, they are far from endorsing complete license in this realm, and appear to show some caution toward allowing the unfettered expression of undemocratic or irresponsible utterances.

Thus, although 63 percent endorse the principle that "people in this country should be allowed to say anything they want to in a public speech," the minority who oppose the proposition or who are doubtful about it explain that "anything they want to" is a little too broad. They would object, for instance, to slander or obscenity, to appeals to group prejudice, to incitement to riot, to attacks on the form of our government. In reply to another question, more than three Americans out of four answer "No" to the question, "Do you think anyone in the United States should be allowed to make speeches against certain races in this country?"

Similarly, in time of war, the public recognizes the need for censorship of information. When, during the first week of the war, a complete blackout of information was thrown around our losses at Pearl Harbor, only 15 percent thought this withholding of important news was not justified. Periodic wartime surveys consistently turned up such findings as: only one person in ten thought censorship was too strict, 20 percent felt it was not strict enough; two-thirds of the people throughout the war agreed that they were being told as much as possible and denied the proposition that "the government *could* give us more information about the fighting in this war without helping the enemy."

The public furthermore appears to exercise wise judgment in its attitude toward the flow of news in peacetime. In a series of questions about the radio, for example, nine out of ten favored some controls to insure the accuracy of news broadcasts and to insure the equal right of both sides to a public controversy to express their views publicly. Two-thirds of the people believe that radio commentators should express their own opinions, rather than those of the station owner or the sponsor. Yet in deciding who should exercise the desired control over irresponsible broadcasting, the public does not see government ownership or censorship as a solution. Only 9 percent think the people would be better off if the government ran the radio stations, and only 6 percent favor government ownership of newspapers. The great majority who favor

control over the accuracy of news broadcasts and the ability of all sides to get a fair hearing on the radio, prefer self-regulation by the radio industry over government intervention by a ratio of two to one.

There is incidental evidence from other surveys that the public is not easily victimized by ancient tabus in the realm of information, but rather welcomes public discussion of important facts, regardless of their nature. A Gallup Poll in 1936, for instance, questioned people regarding their willingness to see a government bureau set up clinics and distribute information about venereal disease. This was at a time when the mass media of information studiously avoided any mention of the subject, and when there was a tacit assumption that "nice" people did not talk about syphilis. With fear and trembling the Gallup interviewers asked their questions, and were astounded to find not the slightest embarrassment or resentment, but a general desire to bring the subject out in the open and talk about it. Publication in 1948 of the famed Kinsey report on sexual behavior provided another opportunity for polls to measure public reactions to such information: only 11 percent expressed a belief that it was "a bad thing" to have this report available. Finally, it might be noted that the Office of War Information was surprised, in 1943, to find that a plurality of the American people *approved* of printing news stories and pictures "showing how American soldiers are suffering and dying"—although it had been previously assumed that publication of such graphic information would adversely affect morale.

In the area of international freedom of information, the public overwhelmingly endorses the principle of free and full exchange. For example, seven Americans out of ten approve, without qualification, the proposition that *all* newspaper reporters should be free to report *everything* they see going on in foreign countries, and that governments should exercise no censorship over them. About a third of the public say that the most important cause of war is the lack of understanding between nations owing to different languages, customs, and beliefs, and upwards of two-thirds express the opinion that a free flow of news all over the world is *very* important to world peace. Two persons out of three similarly believe that unrestricted freedom of information between the United States and Russia would make for better, rather than worse, understanding between the two countries, and the same proportion favor U.S. financial support of a United Nations broadcasting station which would beam news programs to people all over the world.

Yet, as we saw in our discussion of attitudes toward civil liberties, when these broad principles are brought down to specific issues, public support of the free exchange of news falls off sharply. Thus, large majorities say that American publishers should have the right to send magazines and newspapers into Russia without fear of Russian restrictions or censorship, and that American reporters should be free to travel around Russia and report what they find; indeed, there appear to be strong feelings on this point. But when asked whether Russian reporters should be allowed to travel around this country and report back to Russia what *they* find, the public is quite evenly divided, with only a bare majority accepting the reciprocal of the freedom they desire for the U.S. It is interesting that when the question about American reporters is experimentally asked *first* and the public is overwhelmingly on record in favor of "freedom," about 70 percent subsequently approve of granting freedom to Russian reporters. But when queried first about allowing *Russian* reporters freedom over here, only about 35 percent, express approval. The implication is that the public is aware that reciprocity should apply, but that they tend to vote against the specific application of the general principle unless the reciprocal feature is dramatically brought to their attention.

There are similar reservations about the disclosure of military information. The public has always been jealous of the atomic bomb and, from the first, steadfastly expressed disapproval of sharing "the secret" except under strict guarantees of control. When questioned in detail about the official American plan for international control of atomic energy, majorities of the public went along with the idea of international inspection and control of atomic plants, but they drew the line at "giving the international agency all the information it needs about atomic energy."

STABILITY *VS.* CHANGE

It has been stated that the ideal public is ready to accept whatever changes are required by new conditions and new times, but maintains a conservative attitude toward proposed changes which are based on mere expediency or which threaten the underlying structure of the democracy. Survey results present a rather mixed picture of the national character in this respect. It would be possible to cite innumerable instances in which the people have demanded change, but these could quite easily be countered by other instances where they have resisted it. Fundamentally, however, Americans appear to have a cautious attitude toward novel or radical proposals. Broad, general questions designed to measure the over-all temper of the public normally reveal what seems to be an underlying conservatism.

For example, when asked during the spring of 1945: "After the war, would you like to see many changes or reforms made in the United States, or would you rather have the country remain pretty much the way it was before the war?" 52 percent voted for keeping things about as they were. An additional 7 percent who had expressed a desire for "many changes" should also be included in this conservative group, for the nature of the changes they demanded was "a return to the Constitution and less government control." An equivalent finding is available from another question, which asked: "Do you think President Truman should go more to the right by following the views of business and conservative groups; go more to the left by following more of the views of labor and other liberal groups; or follow a policy half-way between the two?" The majority voted for a middle-of-the-road policy, with one person in five calling for greater liberalism and another 20 percent pressing for more conservatism. These results are partially explained by survey data which show that when asked whether they regard themselves as members of the "upper," "middle," or "lower" class, over eight Americans in every ten identify with "the middle class." Similarly, when asked to define their politics in terms of "liberal," "conservative," or "middle-of-the-road," the greater number claim the neutral position. Indeed, one survey found that 54 percent of a national cross section answered "No" when asked, "Do you think the Constitution of the United States should ever be changed in any way?"

This cautious attitude toward change is desirable in that it usually results in majority disapproval of proposals which, though they appear plausible, actually represent mere expedients or tend to violate traditional democratic concepts. As we saw in our discussion of attitudes toward civil liberties, though sizable minorities may often support undemocratic procedures and viewpoints, most Americans draw back from any suggestion which would involve a radical departure from traditional American practices. Thus, even at a time when there was considerable public resentment of post-war strikes, only a minority expressed approval of a law which would take away from labor the right to strike; at a time when the Townsend Plan for old-age pensions was reputed to be sweeping the country, a Gallup Poll found that less than 5 percent of the public actually supported the idea; in spite of the universal dislike of paying taxes, the majority have opposed tax reductions if it meant further unbalancing the budget; proposals for a preventive war against Russia before that country could develop the atom bomb received scant support from the overwhelming majority of Americans.

There is considerable evidence to show, however, that even when the public is lukewarm toward a proposed measure, or actually opposed to it, they are inclined to accept the change after the fact. For example, when President Truman first recommended a program of military aid to Greece and Turkey, only a little over a third of the people approved of the idea of sending arms to these countries. Yet, a year later, when the program had been put into effect and the public was asked whether or not it should be continued, only one person in four expressed opposition. Similarly, a tremendous majority of 82 percent expressed the view, during the spring of 1946, that price controls should be continued "during the next year"; but when most controls were lifted that fall, approximately half of the public nevertheless expressed approval of the decision. This tendency to accept the *fait accompli* has long been noted by the polls when they ask people how they voted in the previous presidential election. Though the losing candidate in the elections of 1940, 1944, and 1948 never received less than 45 percent of the popular vote, post-election polls have often found fewer than 30 percent of the public claiming that they voted for the loser.

But it would be wrong to assume that Americans are die-hard reactionaries who resist every new idea, and who accept changes only after they have been put into effect. As a matter of fact, Dr. Gallup in numerous articles has made out a good case for the proposition that the public, on many important issues, is ready to welcome new programs long before the elected representatives of the people are willing to put them into effect. He cites, for example, the 1935-1940 period when Congress opposed most efforts toward military preparedness, in the belief that the country was essentially pacifist and would find them guilty of "warmongering." Throughout that period, Gallup found overwhelming majorities in favor of a larger army, navy, and air force, even if this meant increased taxes. Similarly, polls showed popular majorities in favor of wartime rationing and price control, broadening of the income tax base, embargos on prewar shipments to Japan, selective military service, and a variety of other measures, from three months to a year before these laws were actually enacted by Congress. More recent polls have also documented the fact that the public is not antagonistic toward changes if they believe those changes are desirable and not in violation of democratic principles. Thus, in spite of the fact that some of the government's social welfare measures have been labeled "un-American" and "socialistic," the majority of the public has nevertheless expressed approval of such ideas as federal aid to states for education, government subsidies of low-cost housing, and programs for increased medical care.

It is possible to point, therefore, to both strengths and weaknesses in the American attitude toward change. Although, in general, there appears to be a healthy balance between steadfast adherence to basic democratic principles and readiness to accept necessary innovations, we have seen that there are strong minorities of various sizes who offer potential support to anti-democratic movements, and there is perhaps a dangerous tendency on the part of the public to accept whatever their government does as long as no immediate ill effects make themselves apparent.

FUNDAMENTAL VALUES

A number of the attributes of an enlightened public opinion have been stated in terms of fundamental values. Thus, the citizen opposes brutality, shuns the unnecessary use of force, avoids attitudes of cynicism and complacency, values loyalty, trust, and helpfulness. There are many gaps in the survey data relating to this area, since the polls have largely concerned themselves with attitudes toward current and transitory issues, rather than seeking to measure the underlying bases of those attitudes in terms of American character structure and values. Nevertheless, certain pertinent information can be found amid the welter of superficial poll findings.

Humanitarian values, for example, appear to pervade much of American political opinion. Surveys consistently found that the major reason for the widespread support of the Marshall Plan was sympathy with the needs of impoverished people, rather than the political and strategic implications of the program. A fundamental moral value seems at work here. It turns up again when we find about two-thirds of the population expressing a willingness, after the end of the war, to *return* to the rationing of meat and butter in order to feed needy countries who had been our allies. Indeed, a majority thought we ought to help "those who really need it, even if their present governments are unfriendly to us."

Yet there is a certain ambivalence about these humanitarian motives. A consistent minority of about 20 percent oppose any foreign aid and believe we should instead "help people here at home," and one detects throughout an undertone of the "Uncle Sucker" complex. We remarked in another context the public's unwillingness to admit any displaced persons from Europe, and surveys make it clear that the purpose of the aid we send abroad is to "help those countries get back on their own feet." Though the public continues to support these foreign aid programs, a majority consistently express the view that Europe "depends too much on us" and Europeans are not "working as hard as they should." And despite the fact that, even during the war, a majority of the American people always denied that they "hated" the German or Japanese people, they did not favor humanitarian aid to our former enemies after the recent war. Shortly after V-J Day, when the public was asked whether we should send free food to starving Germans and Japanese, or sell them food, or send them none at all, about half wanted only to sell the food and approximately another 15 percent would not send them anything at all.

It was notorious that Fascist leaders in Germany could weep over the plight of a broken twig while condoning the most shocking brutality to humans (Hermann Goering was head of the German equivalent of the American Society for the Prevention of Cruelty to Animals), but there is little evidence that the fundamental humanitarianism of Americans has proceeded to perverted levels of sentimentality. In a recent large national survey devoted to public attitudes toward animal vivisection, the overwhelming majority of the public favored the use of live animals for purposes of medical research, and they maintained this attitude in the face of a series of questions testing the strength of their opinion.

In a survey of the "prestige value" of some 90 different occupations, cited previously in another connection, the public was asked why they regarded certain of these jobs as rating high in prestige. Second only to "it pays well" on the list of reasons was the factor of "service to humanity." Similarly, in a study among youth of college age, "social usefulness" was mentioned by one-third of them as one of the three most important factors in choosing a job. While it is true that such answers might be given conventionally or even insincerely (with *baser* values actually in mind), they still show that Americans regard such factors as important.

Americans are basically trustful of one another. When asked bluntly, "Do you think most people can be trusted?" 66 percent answered "Yes." But this attitude does not always extend to foreign countries or to minority groups. Less than half the people in one large midwestern city answered "Yes" to this question: "Do you think most foreign countries can be trusted to meet us half-way in working out problems together?" During the war, one-third of the people expressed the belief that England would "try to boss us" after the war, and postwar surveys show about the same proportion who believe that England cannot be trusted to cooperate with us now. Even larger groups, of course, distrust other countries with which the U.S. has less close relations.

Though Americans in general are generous, trusting, and strongly impelled by humanitarian instincts, we find in certain surveys a high value placed on such concepts as discipline and punishment which research studies have shown to be often associated with an authoritarian or undemocratic character structure. Data in this realm are available only from samples of two large cities, but the striking similarity between the two in spite of the 1100 miles between them indicates that these beliefs are not an isolated phenomenon. Scattered throughout a series of agree-disagree propositions, items like the following produced a high level of agreement: three-quarters of the population of both cities agreed that the most important thing to teach children is absolute obedience to their parents; two-thirds in both cities agreed that any leader should be strict with the people under him to gain their respect; two-thirds agreed that young people have too much freedom nowadays (this item asked only in one of the cities); a sizable minority ranging from 35 percent to virtually half the population agreed that "prison is too good for sex criminals; they should be publicly whipped or worse."

It is unfortunate that more data in this area are not available from national surveys; to our knowledge, no comparable questions have ever been put to a representative cross section of all Americans. There are, however, one or two bits of evidence which support this picture of an underlying authoritarianism. When asked what they thought was the main fault in the way parents bring up their children these days, just about half of a national sample said parents are too lenient, do not exercise enough discipline. And the chief reason given by those who are dissatisfied with present-day education is the alleged lack of discipline in the schools. Moreover, when asked whether divorce laws are too strict, 35 percent of the population said they are not strict enough, 31 percent said they are about right, and only 9 percent felt the laws are too severe.

CONCLUSION

It is clear that this profile of American public opinion reveals many contradictions and inconsistencies. People often express approval of two ideas which are quite incompatible with one another and they frequently uphold a general principle while denying its specific application. But to a great extent, such inconsistency is natural and not surprising. When the determinants of opinions, beliefs, and values are so complex, it would be naïve to expect each of us to have a thoroughly integrated, logical structure of attitudes.

Let it be remembered, too, that the picture we have described is not that of an individual, but a collective statistical portrait. Thus, Mr. Jones himself may be a pretty consistent individual, but when his beliefs and attitudes are added to those of Smith and Brown (who differ with each other and with Jones on some matters and think alike on others), the picture becomes much less clear. Actually, when one looks beneath the aggregate "national totals," it is possible to discern a considerably more integrated pattern. The attitudes we have described are not distributed at random throughout the population; information and the lack of it are not characteristic of this person today and that person tomorrow; isolationist attitudes are not held by one group on this issue and by another group on another issue. Instead these beliefs, attitudes, and knowledge tend to be generalized. The apathetic person is likely to be apathetic toward all public issues, not just to some; the isolationist will express such opinions consistently; the uninformed person tends to be generally uninformed.

This greater internal consistency not only helps explain the over-all picture, but it has implications for the educator. It makes his job more difficult, because the integrated structure of these attitudes makes them harder to change; each separate belief and opinion supports the others, and to change one attitude often means tearing down a whole edifice. But in another sense, the fact that attitudes are generalized makes the educator's job an easier one. For it is not necessary to attack each opinion and belief separately in order to work an improvement. By focusing on those individuals and groups who fall short of the goals all along the line, by reorienting the pattern of their thinking along more desirable lines, it is possible to overcome, not just one, but a whole cluster of the inadequacies we have reported.

We have described the facts of American public opinion as well as we can assess them, but the problem of over-all evaluation remains. Should we be pleased that the public comes as close as it does to the ideal, or should we be discouraged that it falls short at so many points? Our own suggestion is that the stated set of goals be regarded as a long-term level of aspiration, rather than as a yardstick which may also be used to beat the public if it does not measure up.

Interviewers who gather public opinion are accustomed to hearing the expression of apathetic, narrow, uninformed viewpoints, but it is significant that many who take up the work in a crusading spirit gradually tend toward sympathy for persons of this type. They talk so often with families who are weighed down by a pressing burden of personal problems, with women who wear themselves out daily with the care of large families in substandard living quarters; they encounter abject poverty, crushing illness. And it sometimes appears ridiculous that this "clay" should be expected to react sensitively and to evaluate critically the complex political and economic questions which are presumed to be their responsibility. We should not be too critical, nor too impatient. And it would be well to realize that the remedy does not always and necessarily lie in the realm of mere information and education. Sometimes the task is only to free people from their pressing concern with personal problems so that they may have occasional opportunities to look out to broader horizons.

·2·

Definitions of Public Opinion

and the Public

~

SOME DEFINITIONS OF PUBLIC OPINION

TOWARD A SCIENCE OF PUBLIC OPINION

COMMENTS ON THE NATURE OF "PUBLIC" AND "PUBLIC OPINION"

PUBLICS, PUBLIC OPINION, AND GENERAL INTERESTS

PUBLIC OPINION AND PUBLIC OPINION POLLING

SOME DEFINITIONS OF PUBLIC OPINION

(COMPILED BY ULRICH STRAUSS)

JOHN STUART MILL—*ON LIBERTY*

The likings and dislikings of society, or some powerful portion of it, are thus the main thing which has practically determined the rules laid down for general observance, under the penalties of law or opinion. (p. 10)

MACHIAVELLI—*DISCOURSES*

We may infer, I think, too, that a wise man will not ignore public opinion in regard to particular matters, such as the distribution of offices and preferment; for here the populace, when left to itself, does not make mistakes, or if sometimes it does its mistakes are rare in comparison with those that would occur if the few had to make such a distribution. (p. 320, 1950 ed.)

BLUNTSCHLI—*THEORY OF THE STATE*

This general will exists in germ among a people as naturally as the tendency to union and organization, which we call the political tendency. This common will, in manifesting itself, becomes the will of the state, whereas mere individual will remains individual even if two individuals make a contract between them. (p. 282)

W. W. WILLOUGHBY—*NATURE OF THE STATE*

If, then, we would speak of the Sovereignty of the people, we can mean nothing more than the Sovereignty of Public Opinion —that power which Lieber (Political Ethics) defines as "the sense and sentiment of the community necessarily irresistible, showing its power everywhere," and the power which "gives sense to the letter and life of the law; without which the written law is a mere husk." Sovereignty is thus, as Professor Woodrow Wilson forcibly puts it, reduced to a "catalogue of influences" (An Old Master and Other Essays, p. 78). (p. 286)

Public Opinion, with no governmental organs through which its powers may be enforced, is certainly not, strictly speaking, a civil power. (p. 287)

BRYCE—*MODERN DEMOCRACIES*

Public opinion . . . is commonly used to denote the aggregate of views men hold regarding matters that affect or interest the community. . . . It is a congeries of all sorts of discrepant notions, beliefs, fancies, prejudices, aspirations. It is confused, incoherent, amorphous, varying from day to day and week to week. (Vol. I, p. 153)

DAVID HUME—*ESSAYS* Vol. I

As force is always on the side of the governed, the governors have nothing to support them but opinion. It is therefore, on opinion only that government is founded; and this maxim extends to the most despotic and most military governments as well as to the most free and most popular. The Soldan of Egypt, or the Emperor of Rome, might drive his harmless subjects, like brute beasts, against their sentiments and inclinations; but he must, at least, have led his mamelukes, or praetorian bands, like men, by their opinion. (p. 110)

Though men be much governed by interest, yet even interest itself, and all human affairs, are entirely governed by opinion. (p. 125)

A. V. DICEY—*LAW AND PUBLIC OPINION IN ENGLAND*

This term (Public Opinion) when used in reference to legislation, is merely a short way of describing the belief or conviction prevalent in a given society that particular laws are beneficial, and therefore, ought to be maintained, or that they are harmful, and therefore ought to be modified or repealed. (p. 3)

There exists at any given time a body of beliefs, convictions, sentiments, accepted principles, or firmly-rooted prejudices, which, taken together, make up the public opinion of a particular era, or what we may call the reigning or predominating current of opinion. (p. 19)

TOWARD A SCIENCE OF PUBLIC OPINION

FLOYD H. ALLPORT

Literature and popular usage with reference to public opinion contain many conceptions which impede clear thinking. These notions are drawn from analogies, personifications, and other figures of speech and are employed for journalistic terseness, for the purpose of arousing vivid imagery, or to conceal the emotional bias of the particular writer. They are so widespread in their use and are regarded with so much respect, even in textbooks of political and social science, that their reexamination is necessary as a first step in formulating a workable, scientific approach.

FICTIONS AND BLIND ALLEYS

1. *The Personification of Public Opinion*

Public opinion, according to this fiction, is thought of as some kind of being which dwells in or above the group, and there expresses its view upon various issues as they arise. The "voice of public opinion," or the "public conscience," are metaphors of this sort. The fiction arises through thinking of an expression given by a "group" at one time and another expression given by the same group at another time, and then assuming a continuity of some sort of soul

From the *Public Opinion Quarterly*, 1937, 1, 7-23. Reprinted by permission of the author and the publisher.

principle between the two expressions. It might be said, for example, that public opinion in 1830 favored slavery, but in 1930 opposed it; and the *daemon* of the group is thus thought of as changing its mind. When viewed from the descriptive standpoint of science, this fiction, of course, disappears, and we find only groupings of specific individuals with a certain common agreement among them at one time and a different sort of agreement at another time. Though misleading from the standpoint of research, this fiction may have arisen partly from a wholly genuine situation. A certain psychological continuity does exist in the fact that there are established in individuals, over a period of time, a number of habitual ideas, traditions, customs, and formulations of past experience, in short, a "reservoir" of accepted beliefs and practices, upon the basis of which many current issues are decided. The error, however, consists in thinking that these habitual, neural dispositions in individuals make up collectively a soul or being called "public opinion," which contemplates and decides upon public issues as they appear.

2. *The Personification of the Public*

A related fiction is one in which the notion of a collective, super-organic being is applied not to the opinion process itself, but to the public which "holds it." A personified "Public" is spoken of as turning its gaze, now this way, now that, as deciding, and as uttering its opinion. One of the effects of this loose, journalistic manner of writing is that, since "the public" is here not an explicitly denotable reality, but a metaphor, any kind of opinion may be attributed to it without the possibility of checking the assertion.

3. *The Group Fallacy of the Public*

Somewhat less mystical, but equally uncritical, is the usage of those who renounce the idea of a collective entity or group mind, holding that when they say "the public" they mean *individuals*; but who, nevertheless, go on employing such phrases as "the public

wants so and so," or "the country voted dry." Whether we personify the notion of the public or not, we are likely to commit a fallacy when we use a collective term as the subject of a verb denoting action. For the statement which the verb implies will often be true only of a part of the aggregate concerned. By this sort of terminology, which has also been called the "part-for-the-whole fallacy," one conceals facts concerning minorities which it is the business of research to uncover.

4. *The Fallacy of Partial Inclusion in the Use of the Term "Public"*

Applying the foregoing criticism more specifically the question arises, "What do we mean by a *public*?" Is it a population defined by geographical, community, political jurisdiction, or other limits; or is it merely the collection of people, within such an area, who have a common interest? In the first instance the term is *totally inclusive*, that is, it is employed to include *all* of *each* individual in the area, his body, his physiological processes and needs, as well as his various opinions and reactions. This usage, however, is not common because it is too complete; it includes so much that the categories of social scientists and leaders cannot be intelligently used in dealing with it. We cannot speak of *the* opinion of this public, because it includes too many alignments of opinion, many of which may be irrelevant or even contradictory.

The second meaning of the term public is usually, therefore, the one intended. This meaning is made up, not of entire individuals, but of an abstraction of a specific interest (or set of interests) common to a certain number within the population. Those who have such a common interest are said to constitute a *"public."* We may call this usage of the term public one of *partial inclusion*. Now let us suppose that the individuals having this particular interest (that is, comprising a public from the partially inclusive standpoint) are not also members of some other partially inclusive public. That is, let us suppose their public does not overlap with any other public. If we conceive opinion to go with interest, as is likely on important issues, this public becomes coterminous with the spread of an opinion upon certain issues. The public, in other words, would be defined as the number of people holding a certain opinion, and the people holding that opinion would be identified as those belonging to that public. The definition of the term public would thus be circular. The term public, as a partially inclusive phenomenon, would thus be found superfluous for the purpose of research, and the problem would be reduced directly to the task of discovering where and in what degree these alignments of individuals having similar opinions exist among the population concerned.

Now let us suppose, on the other hand, that the publics overlap, that is, that an individual may belong simultaneously in two or more groupings because of different opinions or interests he possesses on different issues. In such a case if we try to state, or discover by a canvass, the opinion of a certain partially inclusive grouping (a "public"), we might not know where a certain individual should be placed. Since he is in two groupings, he may have attitudes which tend to contradict each other on certain questions. One of these attitudes must be suppressed in favor of the other. If we place him arbitrarily in one of the publics we may be misjudging which attitude is dominant, thus producing a false result. If we place him in *both*, we count him twice, or perhaps have him cancelling himself, both of which consequences are absurd. With terminology such as this it becomes impossible to define our problem, or to discover our empirical units of study. Opinions are reactions of individuals; they cannot be allocated to publics without becoming ambiguous and unintelligible for research.

5. The Fiction of an Ideational Entity

Another non-scientific way of speaking about public opinion, sometimes encountered in popular usage and even in the literature, represents the opinion content as a kind of essence which, like a Platonic "idea," is distributed into the minds of all those who endorse it. The expression that a certain opinion is "public" illustrates this usage.

6. The Group-Product, or "Emergent," Theory

We now come to formulations which refer not to personifications or agencies, but to results. Public opinion in this sense is regarded as a new product emerging from integrated discussion in a group, a product of concerted individual thinking which is different both from an average or consensus of views and from the opinion of any particular individual. A variant of this definition is that which describes public opinion as "a step on the way toward social decision, a sort of gathering point of the social will in its organization toward action." This fiction will be discussed in connection with the one following.

7. The Eulogistic Theory

Those who are inclined to regard public opinion as the emergent result of group discussion usually carry the implications of their theory farther, viewing this result not only as different from the products of minds working individually, but as superior in character. In the process of interaction errors are thought to be weeded out so that the opinion of the more enlightened, improved by discussion, will in the end prevail. Public opinion is thus considered not as a segment of behavior common to the many, but as a single ideational product of interacting and creative personalities.

The criticism of the emergent and eulogistic theories calls for some careful distinctions. It is granted at the outset that when one individual enters into a discussion with others he often reaches conclusions which are different from any conclusion he would have arrived at through solitary reflection. The assumption which we should guard against, as unworkable in scientific methodology, is that this emergent product is something floating out, as it were, in space, and belongs to a group mind rather than to individuals' reactions. Argument A must be related to argument B and argument C in a particular individual's thinking. A cannot be in one individual's mind, B in another's, and so on, and produce any emergent that can be known to human intelligence. The emergent product must be expressed by some *individuals* or we cannot know it at all; and if it *is* expressed by some individual, it becomes difficult to show just how much the influence of integrated discussion has helped to form it. For no matter what common result individuals have reached through discussion with others, when they put that conclusion forward in overt action, in voting, for example, they are expressing not only what they *think*, but what they *want*. So-called "group thinking" may have taken place in individuals, as we have shown; but in the arena of practical affairs it is *individuals* who do things and not the integrated product of group thought. It may be that the individuals are acting *in accordance with* group thinking; but in large alignments of opinion this may be difficult to establish since it is so difficult to know what the content of this emergent opinion is.

We must realize, of course, that the questions which make up the content of public-opinion phenomena are usually not questions of ascertainable fact, but of *opinion*. There is, in such instances, no way of knowing whether the product of the interaction of individuals is of a higher or a lower order so far as truth, or even value, is concerned. Such interaction does bring out the issues more definitely, and it shows more clearly how the individuals are aligning upon different sides. In other words, it gives a clearer picture of what the individuals *want*. This result, however, does not necessarily constitute an intelligent solution of the problem. Such a solution can be known to have been reached only when time and experiment have given us some basis upon which to judge; when, in other words, the issue has become to some extent a question of fact. When this time arrives it is probable

that the emergent product will be the result not of group deliberation alone, but of a considerable amount of overt experimentation as well.

We are not denying the possibility that a superior product of group interaction may exist. We are merely saying that, if there is such an emergent product, we do not know where it is, how it can be discovered, identified or tested, or what the standards are by which its value may be judged. Though not discredited in the realm of possible abstract truth, theories of this sort seem to be blind alleys so far as a scientific treatment of the problem is concerned. Writers who have stressed them have perhaps been thinking of small, totally inclusive rural or pioneer communities where adjustment to nature and to one's fellow men is direct, and where the common, integrated opinion is practically synonymous with the common life; or else they may have been thinking of discussion groups in which a deliberate attempt is made to reach a result satisfactory to the wishes and judgment of all participating. In our modern vast and growing urban populations, complex in composition and organization, where face-to-face contacts of whole personalities are giving way to occupational and other groupings, it is doubtful how much real integrative effect does take place in an individual's ideas through discussion with others. Some occurs, no doubt; but it is probably mingled with the effects of emotional conditioning, with susceptibility to stereotypes, symbols, and "straddle-terms" of political leaders, as well as an undeviating regard for one's own individual interests. In any case the view that public opinion is a product of group thinking superior to the thinking of individuals and effective as a kind of super-individual group will or judgment is a scientifically sterile notion. This theory, like the others we have discussed, may be motivated by the desire of publicists for the support of a kind of "social providence" for their acts. Though comfortably optimistic, the emergent and eulogistic theories may lull us into a sense of false security in which the need for research and for facts regarding attitudes and control processes is in danger of being forgotten.

8. *The Confusion of Public Opinion with the Public Presentation of Opinion. (The Journalistic Fallacy)*

The preceding discussion has dealt with theories of the nature of public opinion itself. There should be added to these a common fallacy concerning the criterion by which a given opinion content should be regarded as "public" (that is, as widely accepted). This is the illusion that the item which one sees represented in print as "public opinion," or which one hears in speeches or radio broadcasts as "public information" or "public sentiment," really has this character of widespread importance and endorsement. This naive error has been fostered by review and digest journals, and by surveys urging popular or legislative action, in which evidence presented concerning "public opinion" has consisted of news-item and editorial clippings from different sections of the country. The lack of statistical foundation, or of studies relating this material to the actual lay of attitudes in the population, is so obvious that further comment is unnecessary.

COMMON AGREEMENTS AND SOME PROPOSED DISTINCTIONS

Notwithstanding these many futile characterizations of public opinion, there appear certain points of common agreement in the work of various scholars which may prove useful in guiding us past the blind alleys and setting us upon the proper road. These points of agreement the writer ventures to restate in his own way and to add a few other distinctions which, he believes, have value for research. The phenomena to be studied under the term public opinion are essentially *instances of behavior* of which the following conditions are true.

a. They are behaviors of human *individuals*.

b. They involve *verbalization*.

c. They are performed (or the words are expressed) by *many* individuals.

d. They are stimulated by and directed toward some *universally known object* or *situation*.

e. The object or situation they are concerned with is *important to many*.

f. They represent *action* or *readiness for action* in the nature of *approval* or *disapproval* of the common object.

g. They are frequently performed with an *awareness* that *others are reacting to the same situation* in a similar manner.

h. The attitudes or opinions they involve are *expressed* or, at least, individuals are in readiness to express them.

i. The individuals performing these behaviors, or set to perform them, may or may not be in one another's presence. (Public-opinion situation in relation to crowd.)

j. They may involve verbal contents of both *permanent* and *transitory* character, constituting "genetic groundwork material" and "*present* alignment," respectively.

k. They are in the nature of *present efforts to oppose or accomplish something*, rather than long-standing conformities of behavior. (Public opinion phenomena contrasted with law and custom.)

l. Being efforts toward common objectives, they frequently *have the character of conflict* between individuals aligned *upon opposing sides*.

m. They are sufficiently strong and numerous, as common behaviors, to give rise to the *probability that they may be effective* in attaining their objective.

These points of common agreement require some comment. Item (*a*), stating that the content of the phenomenon must be conceived as related to the actual *behavior of individuals*, is self-evident. It cannot be merely an invention, for example, of a journalist purporting to represent actual behaviors of acceptance. As for item (c), "many individuals," the specific number or proportion necessary cannot be stated, since it will vary with the situation. The number required to produce an effect toward the objective (m) must be considered in this connection.

(b) *Verbalization.* The common stimulating object or situation must be something that can be expressed in words; it must be capable of being immediately and clearly named. There can be no such thing as opinion without stating the content of the opinion in language form. The *response* of individuals to this common stimulating situation may be either verbal or non-verbal. It may, for example, be a grimace, gesture, or emotional expression. This reaction, however, must be *capable* of being readily translated into words, such, for example, as expressions of agreement or approval.

(d) *Common Stimulating Object.* The object or situation toward which the individuals' responses are directed must be clearly understood, and within the experience of all. It must be sufficiently limited to be related to a definite proposal for action. It could not be, for example, the general subject of taxation; but it might be the proposal of some particular tax law. Properly speaking, public opinion does not exist about the nature of the deity, though it might well exist with regard to spoken violations of accepted theological creeds.

(e) The common stimulating situation must not only be well known; it must be a *matter of universal importance.* Mere interest is not enough; the situation must touch upon fundamental needs or desires. The hazards of a man ascending in a stratosphere balloon arouse widespread interest, but they could not ordinarily be called matters of public opinion, since they are not important to many. A government policy of building military aircraft for "national defense," however, might well become a matter of public opinion.

(f) *Readiness for Approval or Disapproval.* The responses aroused or prepared in the individuals must be in the nature of active liking or disliking, of support or opposition. For example, the common knowledge of the various methods by which the sale of alcoholic liquors may be controlled, and of the relative advantages of these methods, does not belong in the category of public opinion unless such knowledge is connected with the widespread favoring or opposing of some particular method.

(g) *Awareness of Others Reacting.* A number of writers have maintained that public-opinion phenomena involve a "consciousness of kind" in the individuals holding or expressing the accepted view. It may make a considerable difference in one's behavior, in supporting or opposing a particular measure, if he is aware, or even if he imagines, that others are reacting in the same manner. Although this "impression of universality" is an important part of the opinion process, it is perhaps best not to require it as an essential element in every opinion alignment to be studied. Otherwise important phases of the problem may be overlooked, such, for example, as the distribution of opinions existing at the first moment the common proposal or stimulating object appears, and before people have had a chance to become aware of, or concerned about, the reactions of others.

(h) *Opinions Expressed.* If item (g), the effect of the opinions of others, be accepted as an important phase of public-opinion phenomena, the corollary follows that the individual's opinions must be outwardly expressed, or at least capable of being readily elicited. As shown by the work of Dr. Richard Schanck, it makes a decided difference in how one feels or thinks, whether the opinion is one that the individual readily expresses or acknowledges to others, or is his own personal and private view. Dr. Schanck has called these two types of reaction "public" and "private attitudes," respectively. To a publicist, the unexpressed opinion is usually unimportant since it does not represent a recognizable alignment. It is not his concern what the reasons of different personalities for holding or not holding certain common opinions may be. The fact of common acceptance or rejection is alone significant. From the scientific standpoint, however, although we recognize that a public-opinion phenomenon requires expression of opinions, we cannot neglect the field of private attitudes. In the long run, the existence of a widespread similarity of unexpressed private attitudes may be highly important, and should be discovered and measured by our techniques. Consider, for example, the potential importance of the opinion which great numbers of Germans or Italians may have about their rulers, but do not dare reveal.

(*i*) *Relation to Presence or Absence of Others.* A number of writers have discussed the difference between a public and a crowd. They seem in general to agree, however, that the phenomena which we call public opinion can occur in either situation. The condition of partial inclusion which we have previously cited as characteristic of the usual definition of a public is recognized by implication in the general agreement that an individual can be in a number of publics at one time, but in only one crowd. Another way to state the matter is to recognize that in either case we have a situation comprising many individuals reacting to a common object or situation, but under different conditions of association, proximity, stimulation, and response. Where individuals are separated, for example, in their own homes, there is not the possibility of visual, touch, and olfactory sensations from the other individuals which obtains in a crowd situation. Modern radio, however, has brought *auditory* stimulation from others into this segregated domain, as when we "listen in" to the applause of an audience in a political address. This limitation of sensory modes probably has an effect in the lessening of facilitation, or reenforcement, of the responses characteristic of the crowd situation; but it probably does not abolish such reenforcement. In the main, where individuals are reacting in one another's presence, motor responses often have the possibility of being more expressive, overt, vigorous, and direct in their action. In cases where

the individuals are separated, the reactions are likely to be more implicit, and can usually become effective only through some symbolic or representative mechanism, or indirect political process, such as voting. For the most part, however, the distinction between crowd-action and public-opinion phenomena seems to be one of degree rather than one of kind.

(*j*) *Transitory and Permanent Aspects.* In the treatment of public-opinion phenomena writers of one school have stressed the stable and rational character of the content and the aspect of its universal acceptance, while other writers have represented the opinion content as unstable, emotional, opportunistic, subject to propaganda, and divided upon controversial issues. This disagreement can be resolved if we view the phenomenon as a process with a time dimension, in which the older content becomes the stabilized and universal portion, while the more recent content represents the present ever-shifting alignment. We have referred above to what we have figuratively called a "reservoir" of common beliefs, attitudes, and knowledge, which forms a part of the sociologists' "culture pattern." More specifically, these mores of thinking and feeling are merely reactions that can be predicted to occur with greater certainty, both now and in the future, than can other types of reactions. Some of these long-standing behaviors may be of a rational character; or they may be the product of trial-and-error experience on a large scale, as, for example, the doctrine of American isolation or the avoidance of inflation. Others may be equally long-standing and predictable, but more emotional in character, such, for instance, as race prejudices. Now in the process of forming the new alignments, publicity agents employ these universal and long-standing attitudes to secure their immediate ends, their method being that of transferring the old reaction to a new stimulus by the familiar method of the conditioned response. The old response of approaching, withdrawing, rejecting, or struggling is evoked by the old stimulus term, and while it is occurring the new stimulus to which it is desired to transfer it is introduced. The result is the association of the old response, in the future, with the new stimulus.

We now have the suggestion of a solution of the disagreement regarding public-opinion content. The old responses, stable and universally accepted as following upon their original and "rightful" stimuli, still exist in the background. They are the universal, tried, and stable aspect of the opinion. But the fact of their transfer by conditioning *to a new stimulus* is something new, unstable, opportunistic, and effective among certain portions of the population (who are more biased, more gullible, or more heavily propagandized) but not among others. Hence we have here an explanation of the shifting, irrational, and divided aspect of the public-opinion process.

To take an example of the conditioning process above described, let us consider the doctrine that "All men are created equal." This idea has long been accepted as a part of American mores. Now such an established attitude alone does not satisfy our criteria for public-opinion phenomena, since it does not, of itself, suggest definitive action toward some objective. Nevertheless, it is one of the psychological foundations upon which opinion alignments, which do satisfy our criteria, can be built. In 1776 support for the war against George III was elicited by conditioning the responses of approval aroused by this formula to the proposals for revolutionary action. Thus the older maxim of individual equality was the stable, enduring, and unanimously accepted phase of the phenomenon. Its transfer to the revolutionary cause was the new, opportunistic, and, at first, highly controversial aspect. Between 1830 and 1861 the same reaction of individual equality and liberty was increasingly connected with the argument against slavery; and after the Civil War the reaction against slavery also became a part of the basic mores. In later years the same doctrine (with aversion to slavery added) has been employed to help align individuals toward abolishing compulsory prostitution (white slavery), child labor (child slavery), and undesirable working conditions (wage slavery). In a similar manner (to take another example) a nation-wide inveterate pride in race and culture, combined with a long-standing prejudice against Jews, are being employed by Hitler as an instrument with which to unify his followers in support of the measures of the Nazi regime.

We may call this body of long-standing, common attitudes which are conditioned to newer situations the *genetic groundwork responses* of public opinion; and in contradistinction we may speak of the consensus of many individuals, induced by transferring these earlier reactions to new stimuli, as the *present alignment*. One of the important problems of research is to discover the groundwork materials of real or potential importance for opinion in a population, and to determine their relation to alignments existing at present or in the process of formation.

(k) Action toward Present Objective. The distinction between genetic groundwork and present alignment suggests a further contrast between public-opinion phenomena and another set of long-standing behaviors, namely, those which constitute laws, customs, and traditions. These latter phenomena are perhaps special cases of the genetic groundwork upon which opinion alignments may be built. They differ, however, from the other groundwork in the existence of a steeper mode of conformity resulting from the more vigorous coercion of punishment and public disapproval for those who fail to conform. Usually, however, the opinion phenomenon does not represent a conditioning of the legalized response to a new stimulus, but is a widespread struggle reaction against individuals or proposals which go against the customary or legally prescribed practice. Thus we do not say that a law requiring a householder to shovel the snow from his sidewalk is itself a part of a public-opinion phenomenon, so long as

everyone obeys it. It is simply a common and expected practice of citizens. If, however certain individuals in a neighborhood persistently fail to remove snow from their sidewalks, causing inconvenience and danger to their neighbors, there may arise an alignment of expressed opinion against them. In order to make such an alignment effective the existence of the common practice expected and prescribed as law is likely to be cited. Laws protecting property are not, in themselves, public-opinion situations; but should numerous unpunished burglaries occur in a community within a short time, a condition fulfilling all the criteria of public opinion might speedily arise. Public-opinion phenomena arise when non-conformists openly refuse to treat the national flag with respect, to wear clothes, or to conform with other customs. With regard to laws not established but in prospect, the situation is reversed. It is not now a case of public-opinion phenomena arising against those who violate expected or legal practice, but of the new law being championed or opposed according as it conforms or does violence to previously existing groundwork (or can be made to appear to do so). An example of this relationship is afforded by the passing of legislation to prohibit Negroes from teaching in white schools in localities where they were likely to be appointed. Here the genetic groundwork of race prejudice was the response to which the newly proposed law became the conditioning stimulus.

(*l*) *Relation to Issue and Conflict.* Public-opinion phenomena, as we have seen, are those which involve readiness for action toward some present unattained objective. The common stimulating situation toward which the responses are directed is a plan or policy through which many individuals are trying to get what they want. This being true, situations will often arise in which the individuals are aligned in special-interest groups, members of each side trying to get what they want in opposition to individuals aligned in an opposing group. Opinions upon the two sides in this case are only aspects or symptoms of a more profound and general struggle. They may be only a rationalization of this struggle to secure favor with neutrals or stronger loyalty from adherents in the drive toward the real objective, which is often more biological or prepotent than the formulated opinions of its supporters would suggest. The Doctrine of States' Rights, for example, has been used as a rallying symbol for individuals with strong economic interests of various sorts.

We enter here the field of public opinion in relation to pressure politics, class and labor struggles, and social conflicts of every type. It becomes necessary here to transcend the view of the publicist who is usually interested only in one side of the controversy; for the alignment, or piling up in a J-curve of attitude distribution upon one side, is intelligible only in the light of a corresponding steepening upon the other side. In a two-party system of politics each party alignment has its full significance only in view of the opposing party alignment. The entire distribution becomes U-shaped. Strong communistic developments are contemporaneous with strong capitalistic and fascistic alignments; and the one grouping seems to derive its meaning in contrast with the other. The popular notion that these various "isms" arise as political philosophies gaining momentum through indoctrination as they spread is inadequate. These philosophies represent rationalizations of the more powerful factors which lie beneath. They are the verbal aspects of the total concerted struggle behaviors of individuals aligned upon the two sides. They are the verbal part of the techniques which the individuals are using to get what they want in the struggle. In international conflicts, similarly, we should take our public-opinion field as broader than the limits of one country alone. We should think of a U-shaped distribution of the population of both countries combined; for the shifts of attitude distribution in one of the countries bears a definite, predictable relationship to the shift in the other.

(*m*) *Probability of Effect.* Our final criterion, that of a probable degree of effectiveness is, from the standpoint of control, the most important of all. In the entire field of the population sampled there will probably be found consensuses of individuals favoring or disfavoring all sorts of common objects, in all ranges of number, intensity of conviction, and effort put forth. A thorough program of research would include the charting of all these consensuses. From a more practical standpoint, however, we shall probably have to choose from all this array the particular alignments in which we are most interested. And in this choice the criterion of selecting those which promise to be in some degree *effective* will probably be found the most useful and natural to employ. In making such a choice the mistake is sometimes made of selecting the alignment which seems to be the largest from the standpoint of numbers of adherents. A careful consideration of the probable effect of a given alignment, in which other factors besides number are taken into account, will help us to make a better selection. There may be many cases in which a large proportion of the people favor some action, but that does not necessarily argue the highest probability of that action being taken. The variable of *intensity*, that is the *degree of feeling,* or the *strenuousness of the effort* which individuals will make toward the common objective, must also be considered. For example, a recent nationwide sample poll on birth control has revealed that a substantial majority of the people are in favor of it. Yet legislative action supporting it has not been generally forthcoming, probably because the desire for it was not sufficiently intense. That is, the need and desire for contraceptive information and help that cannot now be gained by the individual himself is not felt acutely enough by the members of this majority to press for organized action in opposition to a minority who have a very intense feeling upon the other side. Collective results are brought about by enough people holding and expressing opinions, and by their expressing them strongly enough, or acting upon them. The situation must ensure that enough people are intensely enough affected.

Other influences must, of course, be recognized in predicting or understanding the production of effects. The existence of some type of organization for bringing collective action about, and the facility of using such organization are important. The presence of individuals of outstanding influence and ability to direct the undertaking is another factor. A third factor is the degree of reenforcement received by each individual through feeling that others have the same attitude as he; and this, in turn, depends upon the ease, quickness, and freedom of communication among the individuals. The channels through which citizens can make known their wishes to authorities must also be taken into account. We must remember also that the process through which the alignment becomes effective is complicated by a circularity of reenforcement. When, for example, an editor pretends in his columns that he is expressing "public opinion," he thereby influences authorities on the one hand and strengthens the alignment among the people on the other. The latter influence increases the popular manifestation of the attitude, with the effect of still further increasing the editor's confidence and aggressiveness in putting forth his editorials as "public opinion."

It is true that these various factors are at present difficult to isolate and measure. To separate them and study the contribution of each to the total effect is one of the problems of the new science of public opinion. For the present we must rely, in the absence of more definite knowledge, upon a practical familiarity with these complex situations. In applying the criterion of effectiveness it is, however, unnecessary to wait until the effect has already been produced. If we waited until that point, we should miss important aspects of the phenomenon as they were taking place. Nor is it necessary to be *certain* that the effect will occur, and that the opinion-alignment we are considering will play a definite part in producing it. It is sufficient that, when we survey the whole situation, there seems to be a probability above chance that this will occur. This, in fact, is the very method which political leaders use in gauging the potential importance for their programs of current opinion-movements in their communities. And although they have only this subjective weighing of the probabilities to count on, nevertheless, if they accept a certain opinion-alignment and act as if it were *going to be* effective, the responses of citizens adhering to that alignment will probably *tend to become* effective or more effective than they were before. Important as the original lay of attitude of individuals may be, we must consider also the *entire control situation,* with the numerous influencing factors we have cited, as a configuration in a multi-individual field. This phase of the problem cannot be overlooked if we are to be able to predict or even to understand effects. In the language of the new topological psychology we seem to be dealing here with vectors of force operating in a social field.

DEFINING THE "PUBLIC-OPINION SITUATION"

Our discussion of the fictions and blind alleys of method have shown us where the major futilities lie. When we try to find an object corresponding to the term public opinion, that is, when we regard it as an entity or a content to be discovered and then studied or analyzed, our efforts will meet with scant success. But when we distinguish by this term a multi-individual situation, or some of the relationships in such a situation, and then enter this situation and begin to study the explicit materials

which it affords, some valuable results may be gained.

The question now arises as to the nature of this "public-opinion situation" and how its characteristic relationships may be recognized. And the answer to this question is to be found in the points of common agreement which we have previously discussed. We are to deal with situations involving word reactions or reactions *to* words on the part of many individuals, which are directed toward common stimulating situations important to many, these reactions showing readiness to act favorably or unfavorably toward the situation, to be influenced by the awareness of others reacting, to associate older attitudes with present issues, to be directed toward an objective different from the *status quo,* to be frequently related to concerted conflict, and to suggest the likelihood of being effective. Through the use of these criteria we thus find reality and use for the notion of public opinion, while discarding those earlier attempts at formulation which led us off upon the wrong track. We have retained and identified public-opinion phenomena, while at the same time keeping our hands upon the explicitly denotable realities before us, upon behaviors of individuals which can be measured and recorded in the form of statistical distributions. The whole argument may be summarized by the following condensed and somewhat formal statement:

The term public opinion is given its meaning with reference to a multi-individual situation in which individuals are expressing themselves, or can be called upon to express themselves, as favoring or supporting (or else disfavoring or opposing) some definite condition, person, or proposal of widespread importance, in such a proportion of number, intensity, and constancy, as to give rise to the probability of affecting action, directly or indirectly, toward the object concerned.

COMMENTS ON THE NATURE OF "PUBLIC" AND "PUBLIC OPINION"

KIMBALL YOUNG

I

As a substantive, a public may designate any loose association of individuals held together by common interests, a common cultural base and various mechanical means of communication. It is generally agreed that there is no one public but rather publics. Some of these are, of course, large in scope and membership as in the case of a political public during a presidential campaign in the United States. Others may be narrow in aim and involve relatively small numbers of people as in the case of a public interested in a new form of art. As an association of individuals a public lacks formal institutionalization. One would not confuse a public with a secret fraternal order, a religious body, or a close-knit political party. In terms of stability and degree of institutionalization, then, a public is a transitory, amorphous, and relatively unstructured association of individuals with certain interests in common.

Some other features of a public may be seen by comparing it with a crowd. A crowd is also a transitory and relatively unorganized grouping of individuals. A limiting case of this would be a fleeting street crowd, passively watching workmen putting up a display sign. A more dynamic, persistent, and somewhat more organized crowd would

be a lynching mob. Perhaps at the other end of such a continuum one might consider an audience as a more or less institutionalized crowd. But in any case, a crowd, unlike a public, must have a definite locus in space. Its members are in physical contiguity with each other. Moreover, a crowd has certain typical spatial patterning: shoulder-to-shoulder rather than face-to-face contact and a focus or nucleus of interest and action, surrounded by a fringe or periphery of less active members. In a crowd there is direct motor interaction, supported by various perceptual elements: seeing, hearing, and tactile, kinesthetic and other less obvious sensory processes. Moreover, the crowd itself acts as a facilitating agent to perpetuate itself.

In contrast, members of a public need not, and often are not, in direct physical relationship with each other. Such an association is held together by the fact of a stimulus and interest, assumed to be common with others. A newspaper-reading public is such a case. The assumption of a common stimulus and mutual identification rests on memory and imagination rather than on direct perception of others looking, hearing, and moving toward a common focus of attention as is the case in a contiguous crowd. But again such tenuous relations of

From the *International Journal of Opinion and Attitude Research*, 1948, 2, 385-392. Reprinted by permission of author and publisher.

members of a public represent the limiting case.

However, members of a public may and do get together. Individuals may talk over what they have read in the newspaper or what they have heard on the radio. This, in turn, may influence their subsequent reading or listening. Furthermore, under stimulation of a leader or an organization, a public may come together to form a crowd or audience. This contingency is one of the most important, but often neglected aspects of the activities of publics. Loosely conjoined publics really do not become effective in action until they do come together as audiences or become tied up to other groupings of more institutionalized sort. Thus, a political party, a pressure group, or other more formal group may try to manipulate the more amorphous public to some particular end. For example, the public may be interested in watching the struggle for power between management and organized labor in a particular situation. Both sides of such a controversy may propagandize the "spectator" public in an effort to enlist members of the same into active participation on their side. Such participation may be marked by contributing to funds, refusal to pass through a picket line, or actually by joining up with one group or the other as a member. But once an individual has done that, he has changed the character of his membership in a public. From that of a somewhat passive observer he has become identified with a more structured group with a definite aim.

This is not to say that the individual can not and may not continue as a member of a public concerned with an issue. But certainly his role with respect to this public will change. He becomes an advocate not a spectator, and as such may, in time, serve to influence other members of such a public in one direction or another.

In short, while the concept public continues to be used as an association of individuals who are in tenuous and unstructured relations to each other, the effectiveness of any public—as an action body—rests upon its relationship to more formal

and institutionalized groupings. And it is this fact that makes it important in the formation of what is called public opinion.

II

To get at the meaning of public opinion, let us first examine each of the terms separately. As an adjective, the term public refers to topics, interests, or concerns more or less common to all adult members of a community or a nation. In this sense it stands in contrast to things considered private, that is either strictly personal, or involving a group whose affairs are not published or known to members of other groups, small or large. To make public means to communicate particular symbolic matter so widely that all who wish may learn about it.[1]

Opinion means a belief or conviction more verifiable and stronger in intensity than a mere hunch or impression but less valid and strong than truly verifiable or positive knowledge. We thus distinguish between a fact and an opinion. The term opinion is also used in a more narrow sense as in the law when a judge's opinion gives the rationale for a particular decision, or when an expert gives his opinion on technical matters.

Bearing the meaning of these two terms in mind, public opinion may be defined as beliefs, convictions, or views of individuals on matters or issues of widespread or public interest and concern. Public opinion may be studied cross-sectionally, that is, in terms of the convictions on public issues at a given point in time. Or it may be viewed dynamically in terms of the interactional processes involved in the formation of a consensus or common opinion. (See below.) It is also important to point out that public opinion is not equivalent to the opinions of publics as the latter

[1] Also, the term public is sometimes used to refer to acts of a government, as in public law. Or it may be used to qualify a place, conveyance, or form of activity in a community, as in public carrier, a public house, or public entertainment. We do not use the term in these senses.

were defined above.[2] Failure to make this clear leads to some confusion. True, students of public opinion are concerned with the opinions of a public or publics. But they may also be interested in the views or convictions of members of highly institutionalized groups, such as the adherents of a religious denomination, of an employers' or employees' association, and the like.

In other words, the loosely conjoined groups we call publics are not the sole makers of public opinion. Quite the contrary they are probably far less important in this matter than are more highly organized and purposeful groups.

In this connection, however, comment must be made about the use of the concepts public and public opinion by certain political scientists. Some of them would restrict the use of the term public, both as a noun and as an adjective, to the field of politics.[3] Some justify this on the ground that originally public had to do with political matters touching adults in a given community. This view, in turn, rests partly on the history of governmental forms in ancient Greece where the city-state and the society-community were practically identical. Today, most political and sociological theorists, at least those of the Anglo-American tradition, distinguish between society—in sense of national society—and state. The former is viewed as being the much larger over-all concept.

While much of present-day study of public opinion has centered on the words and actions of political publics and other political groupings, it would seem unwise to restrict the concepts to the political arena only. If we do, we shall simply have to invent other concepts to designate nonpolitical groupings of individuals and to indicate widely spread and communicated views or beliefs of the members of such groups. It seems unwise to add more con-

cepts to social psychology to satisfy a few critics from political science.

Let us now examine more closely the static and the dynamic features of public opinion. For cross-sectional description and analysis we note that public opinion has four basic dimensions: directionality, scope, strength or intensity, and depth.[4] Directionality has to do with the individual's being for or against, favorable or unfavorable, with respect to a given opinion. Scope has to do with narrowness or breadth of the public issues involved at a given time. Intensity is related to strength which, in turn, reflects the emotional-attitudinal aspects of verbal opinion. Depth has to do with the underpinning of opinion in the sentiments, moral codes, and values of the individual. In actuality we seldom get at this foundation of opinion except in terms of action itself or by a prolonged analysis of the roots of one's opinions, attitudes, and acts.

The inclusion of the elements of intensity and depth, however, are important to present-day studies in public opinion. Older views of the nature of public opinion held that it represented, at the static, descriptive level, a common consensus arrived at by rational and intelligent discussion of the public issues. This rationalist view has been much undermined by our present knowledge of the place of deep but usually unconscious motivations, emotions, and wishful thinking. Today none but the die-hards of an earlier rationalism and intellectualism hold this older view. Most workers in the field recognize that public opinion consists of verbalisms compounded of reasonable analysis and discussion resting on a foundation of hidden motivation and rationalization. This view, of course, constitutes a challenge to the earlier democratic theory and practice of public opinion formation. At best those of liberal views press for as rational a discussion as possible based on sound facts as well as opinions. In line with this point let us now

[2] This view represents a shift from my earlier position. See my *Social Psychology*, 2nd ed., 1944, p. 431.

[3] See, for example, Sait, E. M., *Political Institutions*, 1938, for a strong defense of this view.

[4] Obviously this is but a slight modification of Hadley Cantril's four dimensions: direction, breadth, intensity, and depth. See his *Gauging Public Opinion*, 1944, pp. 229-230.

look at the nature of public opinion formation, especially as it has developed under representative democracies.

A treatment of the dynamics of public opinion formation must concern itself with at least three major phases: (1) the rise of the issue; (2) the discussion about the issue and proposed solutions pro and con; and, (3) the arrival at consensus. Public opinion has its inception in the rise of a public problem. So long as matters continue in customary and habitual channels, a general agreement as found in the law, mores, and consensus continues. But once a public issue emerges the processes of opinion formation get under way. For purposes of analysis the discussional phase of opinion formation may be broken down into three important features. There is usually a preliminary phase of discussion, often consisting of little more than an attempt to define the issue and verbalize the hope for a solution. Later, as the discussion goes on, those concerned propose various and often divergent solutions. As to the means of solving the issue, sharp differences may and usually do arise. It is in this phase that the factors of disagreement as well as of agreement become most evident. In time we pass into a third phase of the discussion. People begin to take sides and we say that opinion is crystallizing. Sometimes the divergences over possible solutions are sharpened. Sometimes a merger or a compromise plan is proposed which draws on two or more alternate plans previously put forth. But in any case the discussion gives way to some expression of consensus, that is, evidence of degree of agreement or disagreement. The straw vote or public opinion poll is perhaps the most striking of the non-official measures of consensus. Other informal expressions of consensus are found in letters, petitions, and memorials to legislative bodies, executives, and others. Still others are in "Letters to the Editor" in newspapers. In political matters, of course, formal legalized voting is the acceptable measure of consensus.

These phases of the process of opinion formation represent but the barest essentials.

There are many variations in terms of historically differentiated culture patterns. In the primary community of the colonial period and earlier rural United States, public opinion centered largely around local issues. Consensus as to measures to be taken, and officials to be elected to carry them out, were handled through such institutions as the town meeting. This pattern has carried over today into our urbanized society but the political party and the mass media of communication have taken over most of the functions of the simpler democratic public discussion. Moreover, today the citizen is expected to have opinions about complicated issues far beyond his local ken. This includes matters of utmost importance both nationally and internationally.

It is in connection with this extensive range of public issues that students of political behavior have raised many important problems about the future of democratic public opinion formation. There is evergrowing need for the expert with his facts and interpretations of facts regarding far-flung problems and equally wide-ranging solutions. But, one asks: Who is the expert? And are we to trust his judgment as to policy as well as to fact? So, too, it is here that the pressure group and the propagandist get in their most effective work. Seldom can issues be produced by the propagandist, but as they emerge he may define them in his own way. And, what is more important, he may propose solutions and at the same time aim at securing the power to put these solutions into effect. Because the battle of propaganda sometimes becomes intense and prolonged, it is well to bear in mind that propaganda does not of itself induce consensus. Rather it may make for further frustration and confusion which in the end may undermine the very faith and practices of democratic discussion.[5] Certainly to continue to be effective, democratic societies

[5] H. D. Lasswell has ably discussed this in "The person: subject and object of propaganda," *Annals*, May, 1935, Vol. 179, pp. 187-193.

must provide for the widest use of facts and information as well as of opinions and proposed solutions. Moreover, public discussion of issues must be coupled with the moral responsibility of the participants who will agree to play the game of politics within the rules of democratic order. To make use of the devices of democratic opinion formation, only in the end, to destroy the political system which rests on public discussion has been a frequent method of the totalitarian revolutionists.

Finally, one may ask: Is there a public opinion in societies under modern authoritarian and totalitarian governments? So far as the discussion and solution of issues vital to such a country, these are obviously restricted to the ruling élite at the top of the power pyramid. This small group, however, very likely operates in terms of an issue, a discussion, and arrival at consensus. Obviously the right to define an issue, discuss it, and propose a solution may be differentially distributed among members of such an élite. None the less, there must be some elements of discussion of issue and proposals to solve the same, even under highly dictatorial patterns.

As to the masses of people underneath the ruling class, their views and sentiments may variously influence the élite. We know that shrewd dictators do have means of detecting the direction and force of popular ground swells of feeling and idea. But, controlling as they do all means of mass communication, dictatorial governments can direct the flow of fact and fancy to the masses in such a way as to influence the views and values of the latter. In other words by a combination of fairly steady employment and showmanship in propaganda and organization, there is no reason why authoritarian patterns of control may not continue for long periods of time. Thus, while public opinion must always be studied against the cultural background of the time and place, there is no reason to assume that the disappearance of one culture system, such as democracy, would completely eliminate the potential or actual influence of mass opinion of publics and other groupings on public policy and action.

PUBLICS, PUBLIC OPINION, AND GENERAL INTERESTS

HAROLD LASSWELL AND ABRAHAM KAPLAN

DF. [definition] A *group* is an organized aggregate. An *association* is a highly organized group, a *demigroup* one with a lower degree of organization.

From *Power and Society* (New Haven: Yale Univ. Press, 1950), pp. 31-33, 38-42. Reprinted by permission of the authors and the publisher.

An aggregate of persons mechanically cooperating with one another does not constitute a group, nor is a group constituted merely by the sharing of reciprocal perspectives. Even mutual identification among the members of an aggregate does not constitute a group as here defined if there are no diversified and integrated patterns of action. Skilled workers may identify themselves as such, but do not form a group unless their acts are integrated with one another on the basis of the identification.

Groups may, of course, exhibit varying amounts of solidarity and cooperation, provided both are present to some degree. There may be loose organization with respect to a wide range of shared interests, faiths, and loyalties; or the group may be highly organized for the satisfaction of a narrow demand. The terms "association" and "demigroup" are introduced to take account of the varying degrees in which the group characteristic may be present. Where the diversification, integration of operations, and solidarity are all considerable we speak of an association: the members of an association participate in a relatively complex and rigid division of labor in which both the operations and perspectives of each person are smoothly integrated with those of the others. In a demigroup, either cooperation or solidarity or both are relatively slight. Rather than an inclusive identification symbol for the whole group, there may be only over-lapping partial identification symbols —as in the case of a state where patriotic or nationalist perspectives are minimal. Or the division of labor may be of low degree or extent, the integrated operations perhaps consisting of little more than participation in an occasional ceremonial observance, exemplified by an aggregate of coreligionists without an organized church, or a very temporary pattern of loosely integrated action, as in the case of a lynch mob. In short, we do not distinguish absolutely between groups and nongroups, but focus attention on the extent and complexity of the interpersonal relations among the members of specified aggregates.

The importance of the group concept for political science need not be enlarged upon. Beard's emphatic statement (1934, 67) is scarcely an exaggeration: "This great fact stands out clearly, that through the centuries—down until our own day—group interests were recognized as forming the very essence of politics both in theory and practice." Yet, regardless of the importance which groups empirically do have, the concept is not to be taken as logically fundamental, in the sense that political phenomena are to be defined exclusively in terms of groups. We are interested in neither groups nor individuals as "social atoms," but in interpersonal relations, which under specified conditions exhibit organization of varying kinds and degrees.

* * *

DF. An *opinion* in a group is a demand or expectation controvertible in the group; a *consensus*, noncontrovertible.

That a demand or expectation is controvertible in a group means that disagreement with it does not forfeit group membership or evoke other equally severe sanctions. A perspective is a matter of consensus rather than opinion when disagreement with it is not countenanced. Usually disagreement is visited by severe sanctions; and at any rate, it does violence to the sentiments and expectations of the group—it is shocking and astonishing.

Opinion is not passive or quiescent but involves, in general, a phase of expression in which it is made effective to some degree or other. Stress toward completion of the act of "holding" an opinion characterizes the *intensity* of the opinion. Explicit and detailed symbolization of the perspectives and operations respectively determining and determined by the opinion may be called the *symbolic* and *operational elaboration* of the opinion. The former is a presentation of the purported ground for the opinion, the latter a specification of the action called for by the opinion. In terms of its symbolic elaboration, opinion may be characterized as "informed" or not, sentimentalized to various degrees, and so on.

PROP. [proposition] An opinion aggregate is the more likely to attain solidarity the more highly controversial the opinion, and the more the aggregate is in a minority.

Intense conflict with other opinions enhances mutual identification of those sharing the given opinion. The perspective of each person gives support to its maintenance by the others: demands can be made in the name of a self transcending the individual ego, expectations can claim warrant by being shared.

The smaller the minority, the more important is solidarity to make its opinion effective. And a minority is more favorably predisposed to solidarity because the need for justification of the perspective by other egos is more intensely felt. (There is, of course, a lower limit to the minority status beyond which solidarity is no longer likely; it is perhaps that below which the minority is too small to be either effective or subjected to attack.) The formation of blocs in legislative bodies and factions in political parties exemplifies the hypothesis.

DF. A *public* consists of the persons in the group who have or expect to have an opinion. *Public opinion* is the distribution of opinion in a public.

A public is defined in relation to a group so as to provide that divergencies of opinion within a public be superimposed on a basic consensus. Where such consensus is lacking, we have not one but several publics.

Note that the public is narrower in scope than the attention aggregate. To be a member of the public it is necessary to expect that one can have some effect on the formation of policy. On some questions a person may be undecided; he does not drop out of the public until he ceases to expect to participate at some time or on some questions. The degree of participation may change from issue to issue even though the public does not. Indices of the public include such acts as speaking, writing, canvassing, contributing to parties and causes.

(The expectations of the inactive can only be determined by intensive methods of observation.)

Public opinion comprises all of the opinions maintained by various parts of the public in question, as well as a specification of the parts having no opinion. When "public opinion" is spoken of in the singular, some one dominant opinion is referred to. The indices by which dominance has been determined must be specified. The *dominant opinion* is not necessarily the *majority opinion*; the opinion of an influential minority may be that which is actually effective.

DF. A *crowd* consists of the persons in a group who are expressing a consensus.

As a reaction against Le Bon's overgeneralization of the crowd concept, both "crowd" and "public" received sharper definition (consult Robert E. Park, *Masse und Publikum,* Buchdruckerei Lack & Granau, 1904). When a group is making nondebatable demands, it is acting as a crowd. (A crowd in action is a *mob.*) When the bounds of identification disappear and the person is concerned for his own ego, we have *panic.* In a crowd there is *psychic contagion,* a maximum of sincere, unreflective, excited dissemination of symbols.

DF. An *interest group* is an interest aggregate organized for the satisfaction of the interest.

All groups might be regarded as interest groups, since they all involve demands (preferences if not determinations) and expectations. But we may distinguish among various patterns of group activity those concerned with the satisfaction of interests—rather than, say, propagation of faiths or evocation of loyalties—and characterize the group as an interest group with regard to these patterns.

DF. A *special interest group* is one such that in fact or on its own expectation the satisfaction of its interest significantly exceeds that of the interests of those outside the group. A *general interest group* is one having, to a significant degree, other than special interests.

If a trade association or pressure group is "out to smash" another organization, it is—in terms of its own expectations—a special interest group. However, the nongratification of other groups is not always involved; indeed, advantages may accrue to outsiders, as when insurance companies combine to reduce accident rates by public education. What is in question are the comparative advantages to the group and to outsiders.

By the characterization "in fact" we refer to scientific and impartial estimates. We recognize that the self-estimates by group leaders (and members) *may* coincide with that of qualified scientists. Often, however, self-appraisals are false (even without hypocrisy); and those who think they serve the general interest are blinded to important advantages to themselves.

Every group has *some* special interests— for instance, those in its own existence and activity *as* a group. But not all special interests are necessarily in conflict; they may be compatible or even in some cases facilitative of one another. And in changing circumstances, special interests may come to be in the general interest: the special interests of the military become general interests in time of war. Of course, changes may equally take place in the opposite direction: an army brought into being for national defense may become the organ of national tyranny.

A difficulty in the classification of a particular aggregate as a general or special interest group is the number of interests that may be deliberately pursued, or actively affected, by a group. Consequences, furthermore, are often not visible over short periods of time. Professional associations are frequently given the benefit of the assumption that they serve the general interest; yet, as Graham Wallas (*Our Social Heritage,* Yale University Press, 1921) showed so well, the adjustment of professions to the common good is no simple matter. A difficulty in the classification of a particular aggregate as a general or special interest group is the number of interests that may be deliberately pursued, or actively affected, by a group. Consequences, furthermore, are often not visible over short periods of time.

PROP. The accommodation by and circulation of an interest group vary with the degree to which it is concerned with general rather than special interests.

The hypothesis is simply that the more general the interest, in the present sense of wide dispersion of the benefits of the satisfaction of the interest, the less intense the interested activity. On the whole, greater perseverance characterizes the pursuit of special advantages than of general improvement. Moreover, a general interest group is more permeable, requiring only a perspective of "public spiritedness" rather than adherence to some special interest. And with the lesser intensity of such perspectives, frequent shifts in membership are to be expected as obstacles are encountered.

PUBLIC OPINION AND PUBLIC OPINION POLLING

HERBERT BLUMER

This paper presents some observations on public opinion and on public opinion polling as currently performed. It is hoped that these observations will provoke the discussion for which, I understand, this meeting has been arranged. The observations are not along the line of what seems to be the chief preoccupation of students of public opinion polling, to wit, the internal improvement of their technique. Instead, the observations are designed to invite attention to whether public opinion polling actually deals with public opinion.

The first observations which I wish to make are in the nature of a prelude. They come from a mere logical scrutiny of public opinion polling as an alleged form of scientific investigation. What I note is the inability of public opinion polling to isolate "public opinion" as an abstract or generic concept which could thereby become the focal point for the formation of a system of propositions. It would seem needless to point out that in an avowed scientific enterprise seeking to study a class of empirical items and to develop a series of generalizations about that class it is necessary to identify the class. Such identification enables discrimination between the instances which fall within the class and those which do not. In this manner, the generic character of the object of study becomes delineated. When the generic object of study is distinguishable, it becomes possible to focus study on that object and thus to learn progressively more about that object. In this way the ground is prepared for cumulative generalizations or propositions relative to the generic object of investigation.

As far as I can judge, the current study of public opinion by polling ignores the simple logical point which has just been made. This can be seen through three observations. First, there is no effort, seemingly, to try to identify or to isolate public opinion as an object; we are not given any criteria which characterize or distinguish public opinion and thus we are not able to say that a given empirical instance falls within the class of public opinion and some other empirical instance falls outside of the class of public opinion. Second, there is an absence, as far as I can determine, of using specific studies to test a general proposition about public opinion; this suggests that the students are not studying a generic object. This suggestion is supported by the third observation—a paucity, if not a complete absence, of generalizations about public opinion despite the voluminous amount of polling studies of public opinion. It must be concluded, in my judgment, that current public opinion polling has not succeeded in isolating public opinion as a generic object of study.

Paper read before the annual meeting of the American Sociological Society held in New York City, December 28-30, 1947. From the *American Sociological Review*, 1948, 13, 542-554. Reprinted by the permission of the author and the publisher.

It may be argued that the isolation of a generic object, especially in the realm of human behavior, is a goal rather than an initial point of departure—and that consequently the present inability to identify public opinion as a generic object is not damning to current public opinion polling. This should be admitted. However, what impresses me is the apparent absence of effort or sincere interest on the part of students of public opinion polling to move in the direction of identifying the object which they are supposedly seeking to study, to record, and to measure. I believe it is fair to say that those trying to study public opinion by polling are so wedded to their technique and so preoccupied with the improvement of their technique that they shunt aside the vital question of whether their technique is suited to the study of what they are ostensibly seeking to study. Their work is largely merely making application of their technique. They are not concerned with independent analysis of the nature of public opinion in order to judge whether the application of their technique fits that nature.

A few words are in order here on an approach that consciously excuses itself from any consideration of such a problem. I refer to the narrow operationalist position that public opinion consists of what public opinion polls poll. Here, curiously, the findings resulting from an operation, or use of an instrument, are regarded as constituting the object of study instead of being some contributory addition to knowledge of the object of study. The operation ceases to be a guided procedure on behalf of an object of inquiry; instead the operation determines intrinsically its own objective. I do not care to consider here the profound logical and psychological difficulties that attend the effort to develop systematic knowledge through a procedure which is not a form of directed inquiry. All that I wish to note is that the results of narrow operationalism, as above specified, merely leave or raise the question of what the results mean. Not having a conceptual point of reference the results are merely disparate findings. It is logically possible, of course, to

use such findings to develop a conceptualization. I fail to see anything being done in this direction by those who subscribe to the narrow operationalist position in the use of public opinion polls. What is logically unpardonable on the part of those who take the narrow operationalist position is for them to hold either wittingly or unwittingly that their investigations are a study of public opinion as this term is conceived in our ordinary discourse. Having rejected as unnecessary the task of characterizing the object of inquiry for the purpose of seeing whether the enquiry is suited to the object of inquiry, it is gratuitous and unwarranted to presume that after all the inquiry is a study of the object which one refuses to characterize. Such a form of trying to eat one's cake and have it too needs no further comment.

The foregoing series of logical observations has been made merely to stress the absence of consideration of a generic object by those engaged in public opinion polling. Apparently, it is by virtue of this absence of consideration that they are obtuse to the functional nature of public opinion in our society and to questions of whether their technique is suited to this functional nature. In this paper I intend to judge the suitability of public opinion polling as a means of studying public opinion. This shall be done from the standpoint of what we know of public opinion in our society.

Admittedly, we do not know a great deal about public opinion. However, we know something. We know enough about public opinion from empirical observations to form a few reasonably reliable judgments about its nature and mode of functioning. In addition, we can make some reasonably secure inferences about the structure and functioning of our society and about collective behavior within our society. This combined body of knowledge derived partly from direct empirical observation and partly from reasonable inference can serve appropriately as means of judging and assessing current public opinion polling as a device for studying public opinion.

Indeed, the features that I wish to note

about public opinion and its setting are so obvious and commonplace that I almost blush to call them to the attention of this audience. I would not do so were it not painfully clear that the students of current public opinion polling ignore them either wittingly or unwittingly in their whole research procedure. I shall indicate by number the features to be noted.

1.) Public opinion must obviously be recognized as having its setting in a society and as being a function of that society in operation. This means, patently, that public opinion gets its form from the social framework in which it moves, and from the social processes in play in that framework; also that the function and role of public opinion is determined by the part it plays in the operation of the society. If public opinion is to be studied in any realistic sense its depiction must be faithful to its empirical character. I do not wish to be redundant but I find it necessary to say that the empirical character of public opinion is represented by its composition and manner of functioning as a part of a society in operation.

2.) As every sociologist ought to know and as every intelligent layman does know, a society has an organization. It is not a mere aggregation of disparate individuals. A human society is composed of diverse kinds of functional groups. In our American society illustrative instances of functional groups are a corporation, a trade association, a labor union, an ethnic group, a farmers' organization. To a major extent our total collective life is made up of the actions and acts of such groups. These groups are oriented in different directions because of special interests. These groups differ in terms of their strategic position in the society and in terms of opportunities to act. Accordingly, they differ in terms of prestige and power. As functional groups, that is to say as groups acting individually in some corporate or unitary sense, such groups necessarily have to have some organization—some leadership, some policy makers, some individuals who speak on behalf of the group, and some individuals who take the initiative in acting on behalf of the group.

3.) Such functional groups, when they act, have to act through the channels which are available in the society. If the fate of the proposed acts depends on the decisions of individuals or groups who are located at strategic points in the channels of action, then influence and pressure is brought to bear directly or indirectly on such individuals or groups who make the decisions. I take it that this realistic feature of the operation of our American society requires little explication. If an action embodying the interests of a functional group such as a farmers' organization depends for its realization on decisions of Congressmen or a bureau or a set of administrators, then efforts on behalf of that action will seek to influence such Congressmen, bureau, or administrators. Since in every society to some degree, and in our American society to a large degree, there are individuals, committees, boards, legislators, administrators, and executives who have to make the decisions affecting the outcome of the actions of functional groups, such key people become the object of direct and indirect influence or pressure.

4.) The key individuals referred to who have to make the crucial decisions are almost inevitably confronted with the necessity of *assessing* the various influences, claims, demands, urgings, and pressures that are brought to bear on them. Insofar as they are responsive and responsible they are bound to make such an assessment in the process of arriving at their decisions. Here I want to make the trite remark that in making their assessments these key individuals take into account what they judge to be worthy of being taken into account.

5.) The above points give a crude but essentially realistic picture of certain important ways in which our society operates. The fifth feature I wish to note is that public opinion is formed and expressed in large measure through these ways of societal operation. This point requires a little elaboration. The formation of public opinion occurs as a function of a society in operation. I state the matter in that way to stress that the formation of public opinion does not occur through an interaction of disparate individuals who share equally in the process. Instead the formation of public opinion reflects the functional composition and organization of society. The formation of public opinion occurs in large measure through the interaction of groups. I mean nothing esoteric by this last remark. I merely refer to the common occurrence of the leaders or officials of a functional group taking a stand on behalf of the group with reference to an issue and voicing explicitly or implicitly this stand on behalf of the group. Much of the interaction through which public opinion is formed is through the clash of these group views and positions. In no sense does such a group view imply that it is held in equal manner and in equal degree by all of the members of the group. Many of the members of the group may subscribe to the view without understanding it, many may be indifferent about it, many may share the view only in part, and many may actually not share the view but still not rebel against the representatives of the group who express the view. Nevertheless the view, as indicated, may be introduced into the forum of discussion as the view of the group and may be reacted to as such. To bring out this point in another way, one need merely note that in the more outstanding expressions of view on an issue, the individuals almost always speak either explicitly or implicitly as representatives of groups. I would repeat that in any realistic sense the diversified interaction which gives rise to public opinion is in large measure between functional groups and not merely between disparate individuals.

I think that it is also very clear that in the process of forming public opinion, individuals are not alike in influence nor are groups that are equal numerically in membership alike in influence. This is so evident as not to require elaboration. It is enough merely to point out that differences in prestige, position, and influence that characterize groups and individuals in the functional organizations of a society are brought into play in the formation of public opinion.

The picture of a series of groups and individuals of significantly different influence interacting in the formation of public opinion

holds true equally well with reference to the expression of public opinion. By expression of public opinion I mean bringing the public opinion to bear on those who have to act in response to public opinion. This expression is not in the form of a parade or array of the views of disparate individuals, in an open forum. Where the views are voiced in open forum they are likely, as has been indicated, to be in one way or another the expression of group views. But in addition to the voicing of views in the open forum, the expression of public opinion is in the form of direct influence on those who are to act in response to public opinion. Through such means as letters, telegrams, petitions, resolutions, lobbies, delegations, and personal meetings interested groups and individuals bring their views and positions to bear on the key persons who have to make the decisions. I am not concerned with whether such forms of expressing public opinion should occur; I merely wish to emphasize that in any realistic consideration of public opinion it must be recognized that such means of expressing public opinion do occur. A society which has to act will use the channels of action that it has in its structure.

6.) The last feature of public opinion that I wish to note is that in *any realistic sense* public opinion consists of the pattern of the diverse views and positions on the issue *that come to the individuals who have to act in response to the public opinion.* Public opinion which was a mere display, or which was terminal in its very expression, or which never came to the attention of those who have to act on public opinion would be impotent and meaningless as far as affecting the action or operation of society is concerned. Insofar as public opinion is *effective* on societal action it becomes so only by entering into the purview of whoever, like legislators, executives, administrators, and policy makers, have to act on public opinion. To me this proposition is self-evident. If it be granted, the character of public opinion in terms of meaningful operation must be sought in the array of views and positions which enter into the consideration of those who have to take action on public opinion.

It is important to note that the individual who has to act on public opinion has to *assess* the public opinion as it comes to his attention, because of the very fact that this public opinion comes to him in the form of diverse views and usually opposed views. Insofar as he is responsive to public opinion he has to weigh the respective views. How this assessment is made is an obscure matter. But one generalization even though trite, can be made safely, to wit, that the individual takes into account different views only to the extent to which such views count. And views count pretty much on the basis of how the individual judges the "backing" of the views and the implication of the backing. It is in this sense, again, that the organization of the society with its differentiation of prestige and power, enters into the character of public opinion. As was explained above, the key person who has to act on public opinion is usually subject to a variety of presentations, importunities, demands, criticisms, and suggestions that come to him through the various channels in the communicative structure of society. Unless one wishes to conjure in his imagination a very fanciful society he must admit that the servant of public opinion is forced to make an assessment of the expressions of public opinion that come to his attention and that in this assessment consideration is given to expressions only to the extent to which they are judged to "count."

The foregoing six features are, I believe, trite but faithful points about public opinion as it functions in our society. They may serve as a background for the examination of public opinion polling. I may state here that in this discussion I am not concerning myself with the problem of whether the individual opinions one gets through the polling interview are reasonably valid. My discussion, instead, is concerned with the question of the value of poll findings even if one makes the dubious assumption that the individual opinions that are secured are valid.

In my judgment the inherent deficiency of public opinion polling, certainly as currently done, is contained in its sampling procedure. Its current sampling procedure forces a treatment of society as if society were only an aggregation of disparate individuals. Public opinion, in turn, is regarded as being a quantitative distribution of individual opinions. This way of treating society and this way of viewing public opinion must be regarded as markedly unrealistic. The best way I can bring this out is by making continuous reference to the common sense empirical observations of public opinion that were noted previously. We do not know at all whether individuals in the sample represent that portion of structured society that is participating in the formation of public opinion on a given issue. That the sample will catch a number of them, or even a larger number of them, is very likely. But, as far as I am able to determine, there is no way in current public opinion polling to know much about this. Certainly the mere fact that the interviewee either gives or does not give an opinion does not tell you whether he is participating in the formation of public opinion as it is being built up functionally in the society. More important, assuming that the sample catches the individuals who are participating in the formation of the given public opinion, no information is given of their part in this process. One cannot identify from the sample or from the replies of those constituting the sample the social niche of the individual in that portion of the social structure in which the public opinion is being formed. Such information is not given in the conventional items of age, sex, occupation, economic status, educational attainment or class status. These are rarely the marks of significant functional position in the formation of public opinion on a given issue. We do not know from the conventional kind of sample or from the responses of the interviewee what influence, if any, he has in the formation or expression of public opinion. We do not know whether he has a following or whether he doesn't. We do not know whether or not he is speaking on behalf of a group or groups or whether he even belongs to functional groups interested in the issue. If he does, perchance, express the views of some such functional group, we don't know whether or not that group is busily at work in the channels of society to give vigorous expression to their point of view. We do not even know whether he, as an individual, is translating his opinion into what I have termed previously "effective public opinion."

In short, we know essentially nothing of the individual in the sample with reference to the significance of him or of his opinion in the public opinion that is being built up or which is expressing itself functionally in the operation of society. We do not know whether the individual has the position of an archbishop or an itinerant laborer; whether he belongs to a powerful group taking a vigorous stand on the issue or whether he is a detached recluse with no membership in a functional group; whether he is bringing his opinion to bear in some fashion at strategic points in the operation of society or whether it is isolated and socially impotent. We do not know what role, if any, any individual in the sample plays in the formation of the public opinion on which he is questioned, and we do not know what part, if any, his opinion as given has in the functional public opinion which exists with reference to the issue.

What has just been said with reference to the individual component of the public opinion poll applies collectively to the total findings. The collective findings have no assurance of depicting public opinion on a given issue because these findings ignore the framework and the functional operation of the public opinion. If this is not clear from what has already been said, I would like to point out the enormous difficulty that occurs when one seeks to assess the findings of a public opinion poll in terms of the organization of society with which an administrator, legislator, executive, or similarly placed person has to contend. As I have stated earlier such an individual who is presumably responsive to public opinion has to assess public opinion as it comes to his attention in terms of the functional organization of society to which he is responsive. He has to view that society in terms of groups of divergent influence; in terms of organizations with different degrees

of power; in terms of individuals with followings; in terms of indifferent people—all, in other words, in terms of what and who counts in his part of the social world. This type of assessment which is called for in the instance of an organized society in operation is well-nigh impossible to make in the case of the findings of public opinion polls. We are unable to answer such questions as the following: how much power and influence is possessed by those who have the favorable opinion or the unfavorable opinion; who are these people who have the opinion; whom do they represent; how well organized are they; what groups do they belong to that are stirring around on the scene and that are likely to continue to do so; are those people who have the given opinion very much concerned about their opinion; are they going to get busy and do something about it; are they going to get vociferous, militant, and troublesome; are they in the position to influence powerful groups and individuals *who are known*; does the opinion represent a studied policy of significant organizations which will persist and who are likely to remember; is the opinion an ephemeral or momentary view which people will quickly forget? These sample questions show how markedly difficult it is to assess the results of public opinion polling from the standpoint of the things that have to be taken into account in working in an organized society. This difficulty, in turn, signifies that current public opinion polling gives an inaccurate and unrealistic picture of public opinion because of the failure to catch opinions as they are organized and as they operate in a functioning society.

What I have said will appear to many as distinctly invalid on the ground that public opinion polling has *demonstrated* that it can and does detect public opinion faithfully, by virtue of its marked success in predicting election returns. This contention needs to be investigated carefully, particularly since in most circles polling, wherever applied, is regarded as intrinsically valid because of its rather spectacular success in predicting elections. What I think needs to be noted is that the casting of ballots is distinctly an action of separate individuals wherein a ballot cast by one individual has exactly the same weight as a ballot cast by another individual. In this proper sense, and in the sense of real action, voters constitute a population of disparate individuals, each of whom has equal weight to the others. Consequently, the sampling procedure which is based on a population of disparate individuals is eminently suited to securing a picture of what the voting is likely to be. However, to regard the successful use of polling in this area as proof of its automatic validity when applied to an area where people do not act as equally weighted disparate individuals begs the very question under consideration. I would repeat that the formation and expression of public opinion giving rise to effective public opinion is not an action of a population of disparate individuals having equal weight but is a function of a structured society, differentiated into a network of different kinds of groups and individuals having differential weight and influence and occupying different strategic positions. Accordingly, to my mind, the success attending polling in the prediction of elections gives no validity to the method as a means of studying, recording or measuring public opinion as it forms and functions in our society.

There is a very important contention in this connection which has to be considered. The contention can be stated as follows:

An election by public ballot is in itself an expression of public opinion—and, furthermore, it is effective and decisive expression of public opinion. It is, in fact, the ultimate expression of public opinion and thus it represents the proper norm of the expression of public opinion. In the election by ballot each voter, in accordance with the basic principles of democracy, has his say as a citizen and has equal worth to every other citizen in casting his ballot. If election by ballot be recognized as the genuine referendum in which true public opinion comes to expression, then the preeminence of current public opinion polling as the device for recording and measuring public opinion is established. For, public opinion polling with its current form of sampling has demonstrated that it can predict reliably and effectively the results of the election. Accordingly, public opinion polling, in itself, can be used as a type of referendum to record and measure the true opinion of the public on issues in the instances of which the public does not go to the election polls. Thus, public opinion polling yields a more reliable and accurate picture of public opinion than is represented by the confused, indefinite, slanted, and favor-ridden expressions of opinion that come ordinarily to the legislator, administrator, or executive who has to act on public opinion. The public opinion poll tells us where people stand. It gives us the *vox populi*.

My remarks with reference to this contention will be brief. It should be evident on analysis that the contention is actually a normative plea and not a defense of polling as a method of study of public opinion as such public opinion functions in our society. The contention proposes that public opinion be construed in a particular way, to wit, that public opinion *ought to be* an aggregation of the opinions of a cross section of the population rather than what it is in the actual functioning of society. To my mind it is highly questionable whether in the day by day operation of our society public opinion ought to be of the nature posited by the public opinion poll. Many appropriate questions could be raised about how and to what extent public opinion is expressed at the election polls, and, more important, whether it would be possible or even advisable for public opinion, in the form of an aggregation of equally weighted individual opinions, to function meaningfully in a society with a diversified organization. However, such questions need not be raised here. It is sufficient to note that if one seeks to justify polling as a method of studying public opinion on the ground that the composition of public opinion *ought to be* different than what it is, he is not establishing the validity of the method for the study of the empirical world as it is. Instead, he is hanging on the coat-tails of a dubious proposal for social reform.[1]

[1] I refer to such a program as dubious because I believe the much needed improvement of public opinion in our society should be in the process by which public opinion organically functions, i.e., by arousing, organizing, and effectively directing the opinion of people who appreciate that they have an interest in a given

In this paper I have presented criticisms of "public opinion polling" as a method for the recording and measurement of public opinion. These criticisms have centered around the distortion that stems from the use of a sample in the form of an aggregation of disparate individuals having equal weight. These criticisms should not be misinterpreted to mean that such a sampling procedure is invalid wherever applied or that wherever polling makes use of such a sampling procedure such polling is intrinsically invalid. Clearly, the criticism applies when such a sampling procedure is used to study a matter whose composition is an organization of interacting parts instead of being merely an aggregation of individuals. Where the matter which one is studying is an aggregation of individual units then the application of the sampling procedure spoken of is clearly in order. I make this banal statement only to call attention to the fact that there are obviously many matters about human beings and their conduct that have just this character of being an aggregation of individuals or a congeries of individual actions. Many demographic matters are of this nature. Also, many actions of human beings in a society are of this nature —such as casting ballots, purchasing tooth paste, going to motion picture shows, and reading newspapers. Such actions, which I like to think of as mass actions of individuals in contrast to organized actions of groups, lend themselves readily to the type of sampling that we have in current public opinion polling. In fact, it is the existence of such mass actions of individuals which explains, in my judgment, the successful use in consumer research of sampling such as is employed in public opinion polling. What I find questionable, and what this paper criticizes, is the use

issue. A reliance, instead, on a mere "referendum" by an undifferentiated mass, having great segments of indifference and non-participation, is unlikely to offer a desirable public opinion. At the best, in my judgment, such a "referendum" could operate as a corrective supplement and not as a substitute. The important question concerning the directions in which public opinion might secure its much needed improvement is, of course, outside of the scope of this paper.

of such sampling with its implicit imagery and logic in the study of a matter which, like the process of public opinion, functions as a moving organization of interconnected parts.

The last item I wish to consider briefly refers to the interesting and seemingly baffling question of how one should or can sample an object matter which is a complicated system of interacting parts, having differential influence in the total operation. Perhaps the question in itself is absurd. At various times I have asked different experts in sampling how one would sample an organic structure. With a single exception these individuals looked at me askance as if the question were idiotic. But the problem, I think, remains even though I find it difficult to state. In human society, particularly in modern society, we are confronted with intricate complexes of moving relations which are roughly recognizable as systems, even though loose systems. Such a loose system is too complicated, too encumbered in detail and too fast moving to be described in any one of its given "cycles" of operation adequately and faithfully. Yet unless we merely want to speculate about it we have to dip into it in some manner in order to understand what is happening in the given cycle of operation in which we are interested. Thus using the public opinion process in our society as an illustration we are able to make a rough characterization as to how it functions in the case, let us say of a national issue. However, if we want to know how it functions in the case of a *given* national issue, we are at a loss to make an adequate description because of the complexity and quick movement of the cycle of its operation. So, to know what is going on, particularly to know what is likely to go on in the latter stages, we have to dip in here and there. The problems of where to dip in, how to dip in, and how far to dip in are what I have in mind in speaking of sampling an organic structure.

I suppose, as one of my friends has pointed out, that the answer to the problem requires the formulation of a model. We have no such model in the instance of public opinion as it operates in our society. My own hunch is that such a model should be constructed, if it can be at all, by working backwards instead of by working forward. That is, we ought to begin with those who have to act on public opinion and move backwards along the lines of the various expressions of public opinion that come to their attention, tracing these expressions backward through their own various channels and in doing so, noting the chief channels, the key points of importance, and the way in which any given expression has come to develop and pick up an organized backing out of what initially must have been a relatively amorphous condition. Perhaps, such a model, if it could be worked out, would allow the development of a realistic method of sampling in place of what seems to me to be the highly artificial method of sampling used in current public opinion polling.

DISCUSSION

Theodore M. Newcomb
University of Michigan

Professor Blumer has long been known as a formidable critic, and I am sure there are many others who shared with me the anticipation of seeing him turn his battery of high-powered guns upon the practitioners of "public opinion." In my judgment, his guns in this instance have misfired. This is not to say that those who study attitudes by sampling methods are beyond criticism; even a lesser critic than Professor Blumer could point to many shortcomings on their part. It may truly be said of all of them, probably, that in one way or another they have done what they ought not to have done and that they have not done what they ought to have done, and in some of them there is little health indeed. His target was thus an easy one, and I want to raise the question of why it is that he has nevertheless, in my judgment, missed it.

The first reason, I think, is that he was not quite selective enough in his aim. I

wish he had not tried to direct his fire toward all the people who, to use his phrase, use polling as a device, all at once. The most conscientious of them differ so much from those who are less so that I can hardly think of what it is that they have in common. Perhaps it is that they all ask questions, and that they all do some sort of selecting of the individuals whom they question. But I had supposed that it is quite as important to "identify the class" of people one is criticizing as to do so for concepts one is discussing. If Professor Blumer had aimed at a sharply defined segment instead of the entire spectrum, I suspect he might have hit it. Some of those who use "polling" devices are, as he says, preoccupied with techniques. A good many of them reveal "an absence of using specific studies to test a general proposition." Some of them, I suppose, do not even know whether their respondents are archbishops or intinerant laborers. The shotgun approach is bound to hit somebody, but there are so many whom it does not touch that the shot must be called a miss. No one in this audience, at least, will feel that the shot could fairly be aimed at him.

Secondly, I wish Professor Blumer's major target had been a real one instead of an illusory one. I just don't know of anyone who is trying to study by "polling" methods what he described as public opinion. Let me restate his very specific definition of what public opinion "in *any realistic sense*" is: "the pattern of the diverse views and positions on the issue *that come to the individuals who have to act in response*" to that pattern (Blumer's italics). This is one of many possible "identifications as a class" of phenomena. There have been many other identifications of the class which goes by the same name in various times and in various places. But it is not the kind of "generic object" which American "pollers" have in mind during the 1940's. In fact, I see nothing in common between Professor Blumer's "generic object" and that of any "pollers" whom I know, except that the words "public opinion" are involved. In short, I think this shot was aimed at the phantom of a word and not at any real target at all. I think, further, that when he judges that "polling" is unable "to isolate 'public opinion' as an abstract or generic concept," he really means that he prefers his own formulation of the concept to that of others. For this he is scarcely to be blamed; I too prefer my own formulations to those of others. But this is not to say that others do not have them. This shot went wild, I think, because the target just wasn't there to be shot at. Nobody in this audience, again, is trying to do the things which "they" are criticized for doing badly.

Another of his shots went astray, in my judgment, because it was aimed at two targets blurred together in his finder, and so both were missed. "The inherent deficiency of public opinion polling," he says, "is contained in its sampling procedure." And yet his comments under this heading have largely to do with the kind of questions asked by those who use sampling procedures. I wish he had shown some inherent connection between sampling and failure to obtain adequate information.

All investigators necessarily sample. Some of them are systematic enough about it so that they know what universe their sample represents, and within what margin of probable error, and some are not. As Professor Blumer himself says, "we have to dip in here and there." Careful investigators, since they cannot ask everything of everyone, plan selectively as to what they will ask of whom, so that the one will be relevant to the other. It is quite as necessary for Professor Blumer to sample when he studies his version of public opinion as it is for anyone else. Since you sample, I sample, Professor Blumer samples and we all sample, it behooves all of us to do three things: to know what universe our population represents with what degree of certainty; to make sure that our questions are relevant to that universe; and to get all the relevant information that we can.

I know of no reasons why relevant and adequate information cannot be obtained from individuals systematically selected by sampling methods quite as well as from unsystematically selected samples. Professor Blumer would like to know "whether individuals in the sample represent that portion of a structured society that is participating in the formation of public opinion on a given issue." Very well. There are many avenues of investigation open to him, all of which will involve sampling. He may, e.g., hypothesize that certain sorts of individuals, or members of certain sorts of groups, do "participate in the formation of public opinion on a given issue," while others do not. Let him then sample both universes, obtain the relevant information, and either confirm or discard his hypothesis. Or, alternatively, let him sample the total adult population, obtain the relevant information—as to individual characteristics, group memberships, activities which bring pressure upon policy makers, etc., etc.—and again confirm or reject the hypothesis. Or he may draw up a hypothesis about the ways in which leaders, policy makers and representatives "assess the public opinion as it comes to their attention." If so, let him draw a sample of such individuals, obtain the relevant information from them, and test his hypothesis.

Very few investigators of "public opinion," I agree, have put such hypotheses to the test. But I fail to see the slightest incompatibility between sampling (whether professional or amateur) and the obtaining of relevant information. If Professor Blumer is not "able to determine [that there is any] way in current public opinion polling" to obtain the relevant information, I think he has simply not turned his abilities in this direction. I will not say that he prefers not to see any way in which this can be done, but I do think he shows a curious reluctance to try.

Society, I agree, is in many ways like a biological organism. It functions, as Professor Blumer says, not as an aggregation of interchangeable parts but as a dynamic configuration of member parts related by gradients, nodes of influence, etc. We must study not only the parts but also their modes of interdependence. But these interdependent processes and functions do not occur independently of human beings. We know about them only by observing people, not just as discrete individuals but as members of interrelated groups. We must observe them in order to answer our questions, but we cannot observe all of them. Both our record-taking and our sampling will be better if they are systematic than if they are not. But systematic sampling and systematic record-taking do not preclude the possibility of choosing relevant groups to sample nor of obtaining information relevant to functioning in a dynamic society. The two targets—sampling and relevant information—are so unrelated that they cannot serve simultaneously as a single target.

Finally, I think Professor Blumer's shots went wild because his guns were badly mounted. He has chosen as a foundation the method of first "isolating the generic object" following which propositions "could" be formed and, presumably, be tested. I think that he has put the cinders on top of the concrete, and that you don't get a firm foundation that way. I wish he had done it the other way around. The issue on which we disagree is one about which scientists have never been completely agreed. I happen to believe that Professor Blumer's stand is one which delays scientific progress. But it is a reasonable stand, and even his mistreatments of fact about the limitations of "polling" do not weaken it.

The issue in its broadest form is that of just how theory and research most effectively contribute to each other. In the more specific form in which he has posed it, it is the issue of how concepts and verified facts mutually support each other. At the one extreme in regard to this issue are those who believe that you must first think out a master theory and then find ways to test it. At the other extreme are those who believe in gathering mountains of verified facts which somehow will eventually fit themselves into a master theory. I do not accuse Professor Blumer

of belonging with the first group of extremists, but I think his position as outlined in this paper is too close to that extreme to result either in good theory or in good research.

None of our older-brother sciences has developed any body of useful theory except by setting itself manageable problems—i.e., hypotheses limited enough to be tested by systematic observation. Physicists never succeeded in "isolating generic objects" of importance to them (if, indeed, they have yet done so) except as they set themselves limited problems, e.g., concerning falling bodies under specified conditions. Geneticists did not first sit down and dream up the concept of the gene before entering their laboratories. The history of science is studded with concepts which are wrong or half wrong, useless or half useless. This is no argument against concepts—quite the reverse. It is an argument in behalf of constant refinement of concepts in the crucible of laboratory and field investigation. Concepts which are "isolated" *a priori* are of unknown usefulness until they are put to work, until it is shown that more fruitful hypotheses are successfully tested with them than without them. To assert that one kind of concept is more right or more "realistic" than another, before it has been put to this kind of test, is to remain at the level of dogmatic assertion.

Let me develop this point one short step further. Concepts may be developed either at the phenotypical or at the genotypical level. That is, "a class of empirical items" may be "identified" either on the basis of apparent similarities or on the basis of necessarily interdependent factors. For example, schizophrenic insanity may be genotypically like "normal introversion" though phenotypically more like manic-depressive insanity. Sadism and masochism, psychiatrists tell us, are genotypically similar, though phenotypically at opposite poles. By and large, genotypical concepts have proven more useful than phenotypical ones. *One kind of concept can be distinguished from the other only by empirical research*. By all means let us "isolate our generic concepts." The question is, How? . . .

DISCUSSION

JULIAN WOODWARD

I must confess to some feeling of disappointment after hearing Blumer's paper. I had hoped to hear an impartial and evaluative review of the present state of research in the vastly important field of mass communications and public opinion, a field that presents important problems both of research technique and of social policy. Blumer is one of the best qualified men in the country to provide such a review and to make suggestions for promising lines of attack on the existing problems.

But he has not chosen to do this. Instead what we have had is a forty minute argument in favor of a particular definition of the term "public opinion." In effect Blumer does three things:

1) He takes the pollsters to task for not formally defining their field of study.
2) He states that the implicit definition on which they have been working is sociologically incorrect because it assumes that public opinion is adequately measured by an unweighted count of individual opinions; and
3) He suggests that pollsters should be studying a kind of public opinion that weights individual opinion in terms of their actual impact on the people who make social decisions.

I would like to comment on these three points in reverse order.

Beginning with number three, let us agree that it would be a good thing, a very good thing, to measure opinions times impact in addition to just opinions alone. Clyde Hart, and other pollsters, have been pleading for this sort of approach for some time. The problem, as Blumer admits, is how to do it.

I would not, however, want to make the obvious difficulty of the task an excuse for not having done more than has been done to measure opinions in relation to impact. The political scientists have made some progress in describing the workings of pressure groups and the public opinion survey people might have taken more advantage of this work than they have so far. If we waive the important question of who is going to pay for such research there are several things that the public opinion researchers could do now that would start them down the road toward measuring public opinion as it actually functions. I will list some of them.

1) Surveys could measure the intensity with which opinions are held. Pollsters are virtually unanimous in proclaiming the desirability of intensity measures but so far, possibly for economic reasons, they have not done very much of it on a regular and systematic basis. There are also some methodological problems that are not yet solved but we know enough to do much more than we have. And an intensity weighting would be a step in the Blumer direction, for there is undoubtedly some correlation between strength of feeling and the exerting of political pressure.
2) Surveys could get factual data on people's affiliation with organized groups and make a beginning at analysis in terms of these breakdowns instead of the usual demographic ones.
3) Organizations like NORC and the Survey Research Center and also the public opinion research set-ups at Columbia, Princeton, Cornell, Harvard, Williams, and the University of Washington could be encouraged to use the now voluminous data of the polls in an attempt to study correlations between group memberships, personal statuses, and basic attitudes on the one hand and public opinions on the other. Findings from such research might provide a basis for more meaningful sample stratifica-

tions and a more functional opinion analysis.

4) Surveys can do a lot more than they have to measure the leadership factor in public opinion. It would not be difficult to set up an "oomph" index for public figures and measure the rise and fall of their potency with different groups in the population.

Yes, we might do these four things, along with many others that the discussants to follow me on the program are probably going to suggest. Thus a start might be made on the program Blumer advocates.

In our preoccupation with this new and needed approach I would not, however, want to minimize the importance of what public opinion surveys are now doing with the kind of one citizen, one vote sample that Blumer criticizes. After all political democracy is still based on the ultimate appeal to the ballot box—where votes are unweighted, and I do not think I am "hanging on the coat-tails of a dubious proposal for social reform" when I reaffirm the importance of this basic principle of democratic theory. The public opinion survey performs the tremendously important function of an auxiliary ballot box—a ballot box far more flexible than the one found in the polls on infrequent election days. Sooner or later the opinion poll is going to be used by government as a day-to-day public opinion audit. As such it will be a means of holding pressure groups in check and forcing them to put their alleged popular support in evidence. When they do have to do this, and it is already beginning to happen to some extent, the whole pattern of political decision in response to pressure will be modified. It will still be true that group pressure will be more important than a count of individual opinions, but it will be less true, because the politician will know when he is running counter to mass opinion on an issue, even though a pressure group tells him otherwise. He may still yield to minority pressures, probably will do so in a majority of instances, but not as often or

as easily as he once did. The pollsters believe this is a desirable change to be brought about.

There is another issue here that needs to be clarified so far as polling is concerned. Blumer is speaking as a sociologist to a meeting of sociologists and he is naturally concerned with the possibility of sociological generalizations that may come out of polling. He goes much too far, however, in implying as strongly as he does that the polls should be conducted so as to provide those generalizations. Some polls run by universities may be operated in the interests of pure science but the ones to whom Blumer refers are primarily public service institutions, or, if you prefer, they are businesses well on the way to becoming public utilities. As such they operate in the field of applied science, and pure scientific generalizations are incidental by-products, not the basic reasons for their existence as Blumer apparently would like them to be. It is not fair, therefore, to criticize the polls for something they have no business to be doing.

I reiterate that I believe the polls are profoundly right in sticking to their present type of unweighted sample for their basic reporting of opinions on public issues, although they would do well to experiment with types of weighting as an added service. I remember arguing at the Williamstown Conference on Public Opinion Research in favor of a poll in which opinions would be weighted by evidence of the respondent's interest in and information about the issue on which his opinion was being taken. I got sat on by some of my fellow pollsters, and rightly so, when I inadvertently gave the impression that I thought this was a substitute for, instead of a supplement to, the conventional opinion survey. I'm not sure but what Blumer isn't making the same error. I can't believe that he really wants to abandon the ballot concept entirely in the public opinion poll.

Now, finally, I'd like to go back to Blumer's first point, the failure of pollsters to "isolate 'public opinion' as an abstract or generic concept which could thereby become the focal point for the formation of a system of propositions." Stripped of academic gobbledegook, Blumer is saying that public opinion survey people have failed to define what they are after.

I'm not disposed to argue that definition of a field of investigation is a bad thing, or a useless thing. Of course it is both good and useful. But I *am* disturbed at the enormous emphasis Blumer gives it because I think that it illustrates a habit of thought that is all too common among us sociologists. Blumer, when asked to comment on the exciting new field of public opinion research and on a methodology that Stuart Chase reports social scientists to rate second only to comparative culture analysis as the most significant development in twentieth century social science; Blumer asked to do this, devotes a third of his paper to telling people in the field that they should get busy and define their "generic object" if they want salvation. Unhappily this is exactly what people outside the academic world, and not a few in the other disciplines inside it, have come to expect of the sociologist. They expect him to argue about definitions and to elaborate categories with $64 labels, instead of actually putting the available research tools to work on someone's problems.

This is not altogether fair to Blumer, who along with a good many other sociologists had the salutary experience during the war of having to make sociological techniques useful, and the results of research understandable, to busy administrators with immediate problems. Blumer can be just as lucid and practical as the next man on occasion, and I am using his paper today only as an excuse to point a moral that he would be the first to agree with. For in a meeting on mass Communication and Public Opinion it is perhaps permissible to call attention to the need that we sociologists pay attention to our own problem of mass communication and our own impact on public opinion. Fortunately very few of the practicing pollsters are here today—this is a family party of sociologists—but it is perhaps worth noting that if they *were* present, these public opinion survey people, who so far owe very little to the sociologists in the development of the art they practice, would hardly go away from the meeting convinced that they would owe much more in the future. I am afraid Blumer's paper would increase, rather than narrow, the distance between practitioner and professor and modify the former's practices very little. This is too bad, because Blumer could say things from which the practitioners could benefit greatly.

REJOINDER

In replying to the statements of Professors Woodward and Newcomb I wish to confine myself to a single point. The crucial difference between their views and mine lies in a methodological matter—whether a procedure like public opinion polling is to gain its justification through its adherence to a technique or, instead, through a realistic analysis of what it proposes to study.

As far as I can ascertain Professors Woodward and Newcomb regard current public opinion polling as operating with a conception of public opinion that is as tenable as any alternative conception. Thus, they seem to regard my criticism as having no value in that it is merely the application of a different conception of public opinion—a conception which has no preferential status. To my mind, however, the problem is precisely one of whether one proposes to study public opinion with a conception that is true to its empirical character or whether one proposes to study it with a conception which is patently unrealistic. I submit that current public opinion polling necessarily operates with a conception of public opinion that is a gross distortion. By virtue of its sampling procedure, current public opinion polling is forced to regard public opinion as an aggregate of equally weighted opinions of disparate individuals. To any one who has the slightest realistic knowledge of our society or the barest acquaintance with empirical instances of public opinion such a conception must appear as an untenable fiction. In calling attention to the fact that public opinion is organic and not an aggregate of equally weighted individual opinions I have no thought of advancing a pet definition but only of stressing the obvious empirical nature of public opinion. If it be granted that public opinion as it functions in society is organic, then public opinion polling as currently practised cannot yield a faithful or even a meaningful account of public opinion.

In my judgment there is no scientific virtue in a study which blinds itself to the obvious character of what it proposes to study.

HERBERT BLUMER

PART TWO

The Social and Political Context
of Public Opinion

·3·

Cultural Background, Social Organization,

and Economic Structure

PUBLIC OPINION MECHANISMS AMONG PRIMITIVE PEOPLES

SOCIAL DETERMINANTS OF PUBLIC OPINIONS

TRIAL BY NEWSPAPER

TRIAL BY MASS MEDIA?

THE STRUCTURE OF CONTROLS

ATTITUDE AND BELIEF IN RELATION TO OCCUPATIONAL STRATIFICATION

RELIGIOUS AFFILIATION AND POLITICO-ECONOMIC ATTITUDE

PUBLIC OPINION MECHANISMS AMONG PRIMITIVE PEOPLES

MARGARET MEAD

Students of primitive societies claim that they can make contributions to the social sciences which are primarily concerned with the analysis of social processes within our society. This claim has various theoretical bases: (1) The assumption that primitive societies are representative of simpler social forms, ancestral to our own, and therefore throw light upon the probable history of an institution, and the further assumption that the history of an institution throws significant light upon its functioning; (2) The coherency of the material; the fact that the social system of a small primitive group is sufficiently simple to be grasped in all its aspects by one investigator; and (3) The importance of cross-cultural comparisons in helping to clarify, sharpen, limit, and enlarge the instrumental concepts which are being used in the analysis of our own society. It is from this third point of view that the findings from primitive society should have most interest for students of public opinion. The theoretical claims of (1) are somewhat dubious, and also it is not of great importance for students of the operation of public opinion at the present day to consider hints as to how our Stone Age ancestors may be supposed to have manipulated the opinions of the group. Consideration (2), the coherency of the material, gives the data a special claim to consideration because it is from the analysis of whole societies that we can attempt the cross-cultural clarification of concepts.

In making cross-cultural comparisons various courses are open to us. We may take a hypothesis which has been developed from study of our own culture and subject it to negative criticism, showing how the premises upon which the hypothesis is based are invalidated by such and such facts obtaining in this or that primitive tribe. Such criticism requires the social scientist to redefine his concepts in the light of the non-agreement of these facts from other societies.

This approach leaves the student of our society holding the bag. The ethnologist says: "Here are instances from other functioning social systems for which your theory is not adequate. What are you going to do about it?" In group discussions where the ethnologist plays this role, his major contribution is to meet every generalization with: "Yes, but . . ."

But it should also be possible for the ethnologist to make positive contributions: to analyze the social forms of primitive society and to present them in sufficiently compact and intelligible terms so as to enrich the working concepts of other disciplines. In so vast and so slightly delimited

From the *Public Opinion Quarterly*, 1937, 1, No. 3, 5-16. Reprinted by permission of the author and the publisher.

a field as that of public opinion, the focus must be narrowed to make comparative comment of any value at all. I shall confine my discussion to the relationship between political functioning and public opinion. I shall refer to only a few selected primitive societies of which I have first-hand knowledge, or upon which I have access to first-rate written and oral materials.

THREE TYPES OF EMPHASIS

Among these few societies I have found it possible to distinguish three types of emphasis in the relationship between political organization and public opinion. These types are: (I) Those societies which depend for impetus or inhibition of community action upon the continuing response of individuals in public opinion situations, in the manner defined by Professor Allport; (II) Those which depend upon the operation of formal alignments of individuals, who react not in terms of their personal opinions concerning the given issue, but in terms of their defined positions in the formal structure; (III) Those societies which do not depend for their functioning on public opinion at all—in Professor Allport's sense of the term—but which function by invoking the purely formal participation in and respect for an impersonal pattern or code.

In our mixed and heterogeneous society all of these types of emphases appear, no one in a pure form, whereas in the greater coherence and simpler integration of primitive societies, the operation of each form can be found virtually unconfused by the presence of the others. Before discussing these extreme forms, however, it may be well to illustrate from our own society. When a group of individuals, as in a lynching mob or in a popular and spontaneous uprising demanding better working conditions, react immediately to a situation, each in terms of his own feeling on the subject, and without referring his action to considerations of party membership, church affiliations, or the relationship between his action and the forms of his society, and their action

is politically effective, this constitutes a situation which is typical of societies of Type I. Type II is found when individuals meet an issue, not by responding to the issue itself, but primarily in terms of party membership. As an example let us take an issue which is fortuitously present in the platform of one political party and is not a coherent part of the party program, and let us say that the individual whom we are considering is a member of his political party purely because his father was. Still he is strongly enough involved to support fiercely all moves of his own party and to condemn and execrate roundly all moves of the opposite party. The issue itself is subsidiary to its place in a scheme of opposition, in which, if the Democrat votes Yes, the Republican votes No. Type III is in a sense the most difficult to illustrate from our own society because our tradition of emotional involvement in every type of issue from the Revision of the Constitution to Daylight Saving Time is so strong. It is necessary to picture a society in which issues as vital as migration or war are settled as formally, from the standpoint of any effective expression of public opinion, as is the date of Thanksgiving Day. Here, although the behavior of the entire population is altered for a day by the yearly Proclamation, there is no issue involving public opinion. Similarly with the vagaries of the date of Easter Sunday. Although the date on which Easter falls each year is of great importance to large numbers of people whose commercial interests are involved in the seasonableness of the event, the date of Easter, arbitrarily fixed according to an outmoded method of calculation, remains outside the field of effective public opinion. With these preliminary illustrations in mind, we can look at primitive societies which exemplify these types.

TYPE I: THE ARAPESH

The Arapesh are a Papuan-speaking people of New Guinea, who occupy a mountainous country stretching between the sea coast and an inland plain. They are without any institutionalized political forms; they have no chiefs, priests, sanctioned soothsayers, or hereditary leaders. They live in small communities in which residence is exceedingly shifting, and are loosely classified for ceremonial purposes into geographical districts. Between the hamlets of each district, and between adjacent hamlets of different districts, there are numerous interrelationships based on present and past marriages, trade friendships, economic cooperation, etc. Any communal work is done by temporary constellations of affiliated persons based on the various ties of blood relationship, marriage, and residence. No man's allegiance to any group—his patrilineal kin, his patrilineal clan, his hereditary hamlet, his district, his ceremonial feasting division —is either fixed enough over time, or binding enough at any given moment, to prevent his following his own immediate impulses of helpfulness or of hostility, his tendency to avoid trouble or to plunge into it when occasion offers. The smallest event—the slaughter of a pig, the presence of a festering sore on the foot of some unimportant person, the death of an infant, the elopement of a woman—may become a political issue, and may lead to the formation of new alliances or to the declaration of new animosities. Both alliances and hostilities, however, are equally short-lived because, owing to the lack of political organization, they cannot be maintained over time; a new issue will realign everyone tomorrow.

Let us take the instance of the trespass of a pig owned by a resident in one hamlet on the gardens of a member of another hamlet. There is in existence a mode of procedure in such cases. The man whose garden has been trespassed upon kills the pig, and—if he feels friendly toward the owner of the pig, or is a quiet man and anxious to avoid trouble—sends word to the owner to come and get his pig. This results in a minimum of bad feeling as the meat can still be used to discharge debts among a meat-hungry people. If, however, the owner of the land is angered by the

trespass and his feeling of outrage is not assuaged by killing the pig, he not only kills the pig but he eats it. But such an act may lead to hostilities from the pig's owner and is therefore an act of political significance upon which he will not venture without first sounding out public opinion. While the pig continues to root in his garden, or while it lies freshly bleeding from his spear, he consults his nearest age-mates and immediate associates, his brother, his brother-in-law, his cousin. If they are against eating the pig, the matter goes no further. But if they approve, the matter is carried to a slightly higher authority, the fathers and uncles who happen to be in the immediate vicinity. Finally, to clinch the matter, a Big Man, a man who has shown some rather reluctant ability to take responsibility in the organization of social life, is consulted. If he says yes also, the pig is cut up and all who have given their consent to the venture share in eating the pig, and thus affirm their willingness to share in any unpleasant consequences —an immediate scrap, a longer battle of black magic, or the severance of existing peaceful feasting relationships with the pig-owner's group. This situation fulfils, it seems to me, Professor Allport's definition, and is the crux of all Arapesh political action. An Arapesh has an opinion *for* or *against* every course of action proposed, and upon the nature of these expressed opinions, who is *for* and who is *against*, depends the fate of the issue. Such a society may, perhaps, be said to represent the political importance of public opinion at its maximum, a society which depends upon personal attitudes and relies upon aggregations of emotionally involved persons to produce action.

Among other societies in which the immediate expressed responses of individuals are of maximum importance may be mentioned the Andamanese, the Ojibwa, and the Eskimo.

TYPE II: THE IATMUL

Societies of Type II are more highly organized and contain cultural forms which result in individuals acting together in groups in regard to an immediate issue, not because they have an *opinion* about the issue, but because they have an emotional allegiance to a formal group. Such societies are commonly organized upon a dual basis. This duality may be based upon differences as simple as that between the people born in winter and those born in summer, or between those who are forbidden to eat hawk and those forbidden to eat parrot, or between those who live south of the cemetery or those who live north of it. But upon such a simple and formal base, ideas of social opposition may be built which are sufficiently well organized to become the structural principle of action within a society. When membership in a group which is by definition opposed to another group has become of prime importance, any political issue instead of raising the question: "How do I personally feel about it?" raises the question: "What does my Group A think about this? Have they taken up a position in favor of it? If so, I, as one of the Group A, support it against Group B who will of course oppose it." In such societies the success of any attempt to influence the group toward action depends not upon the personal opinion of individuals, but upon the functioning of these formal antagonisms.

The Iatmul people of New Guinea are a tribe of head-hunters who live in large, independent villages on the Middle Sepik River in New Guinea. Without any form of chieftainship or centralized authority, they are able to integrate for peaceful community living and action against outsiders as many as a thousand people—the Arapesh district seldom included more than two hundred persons, a hamlet averaged about forty. Iatmuls depend upon a system of cross-cutting groups in terms of which individuals act as members of patrilineal clans, as members of matrilineal groups, as members of opposed age grades, as members of one of two opposed totemic moieties. Considerations of inter-group relationships, of defending one's mother's clan against all others, or of always meeting a challenge from the

opposing age grade, supersede the merits of actual issues. The communities are held together only by the fact that these various loyalties overlap and contradict each other so that the man who is one's formal foe today—*qua* group membership—is one's formal ally tomorrow.

Let us consider, then, examples of the functioning of public opinion among the Iatmul, in the play of group attitudes. The elder age grade of Moiety A were initiating the novices from Moiety B. Initiation ceremonies among the Iatmul are marked by a series of irresponsibly executed brutalities. On this particular occasion, an innovator, a member of the elder group of Moiety A, proposed that one bullying episode should be omitted from the series. This was an occasion upon which public opinion could be expressed. A member of the elder age grade of Moiety B, the group which would presently initiate the novices of Moiety A, immediately turned the proposal into an occasion for ceremonial hostility, completely ignoring the issue at hand, and accusing Moiety A of being afraid of what *his* moiety, B, would do later when they had to initiate the A novices. Moiety A, in response to this taunt, carried out the rite with particular cruelty. The fact that the proposed change would have softened the fate of their own children was ignored by Moiety B in favor of the chance to make a point of ceremonial hostility.

Here it is necessary to recognize a peculiarity of Iatmul culture. Any rite once neglected is regarded as gone forever. If the proposed omission had been carried through, the initiatory system would have been impoverished by one episode. Had the member of Moiety B been interested in preserving an item of ceremonial he could have chosen no more effective method than to invoke the rivalry feeling between the two groups. So a Iatmul who wished to organize a head-hunting raid in which other people were not yet interested, might start a proposal for the raid with a taunt to the other side about the paucity of heads which they had taken in the past year. This taunt would be flung back with interest, and in the end the jealous pride of each moiety would be involved in going on the same raid.

Thus in societies so organized the impetus to action is given not by an appeal to the direct opinion of individuals on an issue, but directly through the invocation of group loyalties and group rivalries. Where an individual is a member of a series of concentric groups—so that, as a member of his family, of his household, his clan, his village, his dual organization, his district, he is consistently associated with the same people—there is danger of these group attitudes hardening into hostilities which will split the society. Unless there is a central authority at the head to which all are bound, this danger is especially great if opinions become organized instead of fortuitous. This condition hardly obtains among the Iatmul because the cross-cutting of loyalties prevents the formation of permanent antithetical attitudes within the community.

TYPE III: THE BALINESE

In the third type of society the individual is not emotionally involved with the immediate issue, or in his loyalty to a group or to series of groups with overlapping and cross-cutting memberships. The community is not composed of political individuals, but of a certain number of house sites, seats in the council houses, recurrent duties to the temple. Into these cubbyholes in a spatially and calendrically defined social organization individuals are fitted as occasion dictates. Their whole dependence is on the preservation of the impersonal pattern.

In a Balinese mountain village, all able-bodied men are members of the village council and progress in turn toward greater and greater official importance until at last they are superannuated and replaced. In this scheme each human unit is a cipher; he fits into a cubbyhole which is successively filled by a series of human beings, each one of whom has been trained from childhood to feel that his whole safety depends upon the continuance of the pattern. Whereas in societies of Type I, the question is: "How do I feel about it?" and "How do A, B, and C feel about it?" and in societies of Type II the question is "Does my group support this?" or "Does the opposite group oppose it?", and the issue itself becomes irrelevant except to a few individuals who may consciously or unconsciously exploit these loyalties to produce results, in societies of Type III the question is only: "What is the place of this new proposal in our pattern of decreed and traditional behavior?" This question is asked as seriously and as self-consciously as the constitutionality of a proposed act of Congress might be discussed by a professor of jurisprudence. The process of rejection or acceptance, however, is as colorless as the placing of a name in a decreed alphabetical order.

For example, a new form of incest is committed in a village; a man marries his first cousin twice removed, his classificatory grandmother. In this village it is not permitted to marry a first cousin. In other villages of which the people have heard, it is forbidden to marry a person reckoned as two generations removed. The council meets and deliberates. The head men hesitate and demur; they do not know the answer. Relatives of the girl and of the boy are called before them and say merely: "We will follow whatever decision is made." The village law about first-cousin incest is that both persons shall be expelled from the village and placed on "Land of Punishment" to the south of it, and forbidden to participate in village land or worship other than the Gods of Death. No one pleads the cause of the boy or the girl. No one speaks of the outrage. Neither family attempts to gather adherents and form a party. The calendrical expert who is the greatest authority on village law points out: (1) that they might consider whether a first cousin twice removed is nearer than a plain second cousin, with whom marriage is permitted; and (2) that if the couple are expelled the village will have to undergo a taboo period of forty-two days and that such and such of the various feasts which are scheduled will have to be postponed and such and such feasts will have to be omitted entirely. The day drags on. Occasionally someone points out to the head man: "You are the heads. It is your business to decide what the law is." Finally it is decided that, no matter how far removed, a first cousin is a *first* cousin, and the law of the village is clear. The villagers are apportioned and half are sent to each house to lift the house and set it outside the village. The relatives of the girl worry about the cost of the purification ceremonies; the relatives of the boy weep a little quietly at home. No one takes sides; they follow the law, and for forty-two days no one may pray to the gods or consult a soothsayer about his illness. In Professor Allport's sense there is no public opinion situation. No one can be said to "favor or support" or to "disfavor or oppose" "some definite condition, person, or proposal of widespread importance." The only political feeling the people possess is in favor of the preservation of the pattern. Not *How do I feel*? or *How does my group feel*?, but *How does this issue fit in*? That is the only question.

It is as if the body politic to which a new issue had to be referred in each of the three types of society might be likened to three types of officials to whom one applied for some relaxation of a regulation. The first type would act as he felt, according to whether he liked or disliked the applicant, whether he wished to appear to be a jolly good fellow, whether he feared the consequences in terms of a rebuke from a superior, etc. The second type would refer his behavior to such considerations as that he and the applicant were both Masons or both Catholics or to a difference of race, nationality, or class. The third type of official merely looks up the code book to find whether or not the law which he is administering permits the granting of the request, and quite impersonally and coolly he replies that it can or cannot be done. He is involved in neither permission nor refusal; he merely administers the law.

INNOVATION IN THE THREE TYPES

An innovator or importer among the Arapesh must suit the new item to the feeling of the people. There is no body of law to which an innovation may be referred. The people are so easy-going that they are quite ready to accept as already customary an act which has occurred twice. There is no group sufficiently powerful and organized to defend an innovation, or to impose it on the community. There is no group pride which can be invoked to support an innovation otherwise unsupported. There is nothing whatsoever to determine the issue except the congruence of the proposed innovation with the feeling of the individual Arapesh who are immediately concerned.

For example, a new ceremony was being purchased by an Arapesh village, a ceremony which had been brought from afar. It contained new masks, new songs, new dances, new styles of clothing, and bits of associated magic. One of these bits of magic provided that the owners would become so desirable that all the women within many miles would run away to them. Now the village of Kobelen had paid a great deal for the ceremony, straining its resources to the utmost. But this last observance they rejected; they refused even to hear this charm. The idea of being pursued by strange and amorous women was thoroughly discordant with the mild, highly domesticated love ideals of the Arapesh. They said: "You may keep that spell. It would only bring us trouble."

An examination of Arapesh importations from surrounding cultures shows that this is typical; every importation is pruned and toned down until it is congruent—not with the articulate form of the culture, but with the feeling of individuals.

On the other hand, in the Iatmul village of Komindimbit, a strange wooden mask was introduced into the initiatory ritual. A group of men from that village had found it resting as a trophy of war in a foreign village and had stolen it and taken it home with them. They decided to make it into one more symbol in terms of which they could score off the other moiety. At the next initiation, the mask was duly treated as a mystery, housed in a special house, the novices of the other moiety were all whipped before they could see it. After this it was duly entrenched as part of the initiatory system.

As a third contrast, consider this problem arising in a Balinese mountain village: Can the village priestess wear black and white striped velvet? She is a sacred person, surrounded with taboos concerning what she may dare to wear, eat, carry, whom she may safely visit, under what type of roof she may safely sleep. It is a good piece of cloth, but can she wear it? The matter is referred to those who are wise in the law, and their decision takes into account (a) all black cloth is forbidden to religious functionaries in that village; (b) silk is forbidden; (c) this cloth is neither all black nor exactly silk. Can she wear it? Once the problem is settled, legalistically, in terms of how much black makes a piece of cloth black, how much softness may be assumed to be analogous to silk, she is still free to wear it or not. But if the decision is incorrect, she herself—not the village, not her kin, but she herself—will be punished by the Gods, and in any case no one else will be interested. The slightest break in the pattern must be viewed with great caution, and if adopted must be rationalized.

It may be objected that these instances are curiously incomparable; in one case I describe the rejection of an imponderable bit of magic, in the second case the incorporation of an alien religious object, and in the third a decision about wearing a piece of cloth. But I can plead, in extenuation, that I am following here the facts as I know them. Societies like the Arapesh which depend upon the emotional organization of their members to integrate their institutions can afford to risk the importation of whole institutions, whereas more tightly organized societies have to find a formal place for the importation, while the Balinese habitually deal with items of culture in small discrete bits.

Although I have, for purposes of clearer exposition, distinguished these three types, it must not be supposed that the classifications are mutually exclusive or that they exhaust the possibilities. The society of Zuni may be said to lie between that of Iatmul and Bali; they possess a series of cross-cutting and overlapping groups, as do the Iatmul, but their emotional involvement in any group is much less, and they rely a great deal, as do the Balinese, upon devotion to an impersonal pattern. But unlike the Balinese, the judgment of one man upon his neighbor is continually invoked—among the Zuni—as a socially regulating mechanism, and so public opinion is a constantly present negative sanction, slowing down and preventing action. But the terms in which a judgment is rendered in Zuni are reminiscent of the impersonal legalism of Bali. For example, a Zuni family murdered a Navajo guest. This was articulately condemned because the man who committed the murder did not have the ceremonial right to kill people.

CONCLUSION

This brief consideration of divergent social systems suggests that each of the different types of appeal to public opinion or ignoring of public opinion which we find in modern society presupposes a different relationship between the character formation of the citizen and the political system of which he is a unit. Each appeal: "How do *you* personally feel about this?" "Every member of X group will of course support . . ." or "The Y group are supporting this, therefore you, as a member of the opposed X group, must oppose!" "The proposed change will introduce such and such discrepancies in the legal structure upon which our society is based"—each of these designates the recipient of the appeal as a different sort of political animal. In an integrated primitive society, one type of appeal is reiterated until it becomes a factor in further integrating the individuals. In our diverse and disintegrate society, the incommensurability of these types of appeal may possibly stimulate some individuals to critical thought which transcends any of them. But it is even more possible that a continued exposure to such incomparable assumptions may be an important influence in the fragmentation and disintegration of the average citizen.

SOCIAL DETERMINANTS OF PUBLIC OPINIONS

ALFRED McCLUNG LEE

Two sharply contrasting views of economic developments, flaunting the terms "free enterprise" and "collectivism," constantly clash in political and economic debates in the United States. They are typified by these quotations:

"The reasons the big boys are hollering so much for free enterprise is because it means they will have freedom to exploit the workers."

"New Deal politicians spearheaded the collectivist drive for the first ten years; this task is now being taken over by the CIO [Congress of Industrial Organizations]— with no small degree of help from the present [Truman, Federal] Administration."

These statements sample the propagandas in one of the basic power struggles of our times in the United States of America and in the rest of the industrialized world. The first is from an Indiana factory worker in a talk with an industrial investigator. The second is from a speech by the vice-president in charge of public relations of the National Association of Manufacturers, the country's "peak" industrial trade association.

The manufacturers and other business men advocate "free enterprise" or "a competitive economy," and they represent themselves as identified with public welfare. They are accused of working toward an integrated national and international cartel system, a dictatorship of monopoly capitalists.

Trade union leaders and sympathetic politicians advocate "cooperative enterprise" or "economic as well as political democracy," and they represent themselves as identified with public welfare. They are accused, as above, of working toward a collectivized state, toward a political dictatorship which would control "everything."

And then there are other spokesmen somewhere between the leaders of these warring giants who look with fear alike on big business, big unions, and big government. In a world of pressure groups of increasingly vast proportions, this unorganized and dwindling middle class is of chief significance as a mass of potential supporters coveted alike by management and unionists but traditionally identified with management, or at least with the large property owners.

From the *International Journal of Opinion and Attitude Research*, 1947, 1, 12-29. Reprinted by permission of the author and the publisher.

The merits of these propaganda "lines" are not to be discussed in this paper. The concern here is with how such contrasting and embattled viewpoints can grow in the minds of vast numbers of people who presumably share a common culture. They are not the mere creations of clever propagandists for industrial, union, and middle-class power seekers, even though great energy and talent go into their formulation. The "lines" are rooted deeply in the common attitudes and sentiments which serve as the energy-allocation-patterns so fundamental to all accumulations of social power.

What is the setting and the mechanism in which such contrasting and yet deeply held viewpoints have developed? In a general way, it is referred to as the "climate of opinion" by politicians and political scientists and as "culture" by sociologists and anthropologists. But what do we mean in more detail by these terms?

Culture is at once a relatively simple and a highly complex conception. It is a collective term for all behavior patterns socially acquired and socially transmitted. It is the background for the fact that people in a given group or society tend to react similarly to similar stimuli. But those are merely a few starting points for an adequate conception of culture as the immediate aggregate of social determinants for public opinions. Each group, class, or caste has cultural and hence opinion characteristics somewhat different from each other group, class, or caste, and in addition there is the problem of personal deviations from such norms of behavior. Let us illustrate the character of these group and personal variations in culture as follows:

The religious morals recognized by public leaders in the United States are broad and general. They define the minimum essentials of religion in such terms as belief in God, in the efficacy of prayer, in the need for churchgoing, in some sort of personal immortality to be achieved through adherence to the church (any "recognized" church) and its tenets, and in the power of theology's compulsions to promote private and public respectability. The various ecclesiastical organizations—Jewish, Roman Catholic, Protestant, and other—accept, if they are "recognized" socially, the broad general agreements and then furnish their own versions of a society's religious morals from their own traditional beliefs and practices. Each version is presented, of course, as the one true version.

How does a rank-and-file member react to the Methodist (Wesleyan) version of his society's religious morals which he was reared to remember, venerate, and live by? Let us assume that he is also a steelworker, labor union member, husband, father, bowler, pigeon fancier, pianist of a modest sort, war veteran (World War II), and poker player. He is mildly disturbed at times by the way his minister attempts to spread a vague moral sanction over the peaceful actions of both employers and union members and a mild plague on both camps for actions disturbing to public tranquility. He has heard discussions by labor leaders of the rarity of pro-union clerics in any denomination. He has listened to talks at meetings of pigeon fanciers concerning how Charles Darwin used pigeon breeding records as part of the evidence behind the theory of organic evolution, a conception his clergyman traces more directly to Satan. Since ministers come and go, he did not wonder that his church's current "supply" opposed all wars before December 7, 1941, and then decided that the bombing of Pearl Harbor had made World War II "different." He knows that Methodists officially abhor poker and other gambling games even though some of his best and most trusted friends play poker with him once a week.

But our rank-and-file Methodist seldom wonders long if at all about these contradictions and others his group memberships might suggest to an objective student. In a personal crisis—estrangement from his wife, military service, prolonged unemployment, criminal involvement, a physical breakdown—these contradictions might exaggerate his insecurity and anxiety and make a lapse into a neurotic state more of a possibility. But in "normal" times, he is a "well-adjusted" fellow who has automatically repressed awareness of any such contradictions and has fitted gradually into the patchwork culture of his society. He just functions as do most people in a complex culture. He adheres to some of the values he has habitually found in Methodism and in churchgoing, and he also continues to fight for the union to the extent that the boys in the union think necessary, to accept some Darwinian ideas on organic variation and selection without labeling them Darwinian, to believe that he helped save Christian democratic civilization as a soldier in World War II, and to play poker. He also continues to adhere to the segmented subcultures of a great many other groups not mentioned. When a contradiction becomes obvious and disturbing to him for some reason, he has guilt feelings about it until he is able to repress it by falling back on some such cliche of one of his groups as "There's no use in my being a Boy Scout [i.e., boyishly idealistic] about it all my life," or "The minister is probably a regular guy with his pals at conventions even though at home he just has to put up a front to keep his job."

The illustration differs in no important manner from ones that might be given of individuals drawn from a great range of other religious groups. It not only suggests the ways in which groups departmentalize personality, but it also points to the vastly complex web of culture, subcultures, and social organization to which individuals must adjust and in terms of which persons must function in modern society.

Let us attempt to pick out the types of culture operative in the foregoing illustration. They are apparently four, as follows:

1. *Societal:* the general religious *opinions of the public*, other *conventions*, and *morals* and the versions of them evolved by such extensive societal divisions as the adherents to a general section of a societal institution (for example, a religious denomination).

2. *Group:* the religious *opinions of a public*, other *folkways*, and *mores* of the various groups to which our rank-and-file Methodist belongs.

3. *Personal:* the religious *personal opinions*, other *practices*, and *sentiments* he exhibits in his family life, at church, and elsewhere which are personal. They may or may not deviate from societal and group patterns; they are regarded as representative or typical of himself.

4. *Self:* the conscious and the repressed or subconscious *attitudes* and *sentiments* he holds concerning religious and religion-related matters.

Patterns dealing with a given area of interest, such as the religious, on these levels of culture bear definite relationships in a kind of societal relativity to those on all the other levels and also to those in other areas of interest. The societal patterns, especially the moral ones, have a compelling influence of a formal or ritualistic kind upon the others; groups and persons are under compulsion to rationalize their folkways and mores, personal opinions and other practices, and even attitudes and sentiments with societal conventions and especially morals. When these rationalizations—albeit traditional and in the culture—become too tenuous, the symbols of the morals may remain the same, but the morals as formulas of thought and action are likely to be due for adaptive redefinition. The terms of the formulas take on new or modified referents or values. Church history furnishes many examples of this sort of automatic societal adaptation.

Some writers give the impression of culture as being made up in part of free-floating elements from among which members of a society as a whole may make their own selections. The fact of differentiation is acknowledged, but to what extent do such differentiations within a culture offer the individual an actual range of choice as to practice patterns? Immoral mores and immoretic morals figure in the patchwork culture which jerry-builds our segmented personalities, but to suggest any great degree of rational choice of culture elements by persons in their maturation processes has little support in life-history documents. Once subcultural patterns are seen as the phenomena of groups, the possibility of "cultural alternatives" in any sense of free and frequent rational choices grows dim.

But before defining further the characteristics of culture on the societal and group levels of social organization and relating them to personal and self patterns, it is necessary to discuss briefly the term, group, and the related terms, class and caste.

"Group," it should be noted, is not regarded as such a categorical and truncated a conception as its employment to this point may have suggested. A group is any aggregate of two or more people who have some similar interest or interests and who thus, in this more or less narrowly defined aspect of their lives, participate in what amounts to a common area of social interaction on equal or on otherwise understood terms. In general, as the interests served are less immediately physiological (less immediately associated with basic maintenance and reproduction problems) or as the group members have fewer opportunities for face-to-face participation, the character of the social interaction becomes more tenuous, and the group folkways and mores are correspondingly more vaguely defined. In tiny groups, the folkways and mores resemble more closely the opinions and other practices of the persons involved. In large groups, the traits resemble or have more the characteristics of conventions and morals. In such vast groups as social classes, castes, and the divisions represented by major religious denominations, as we have seen, the group patterns take on more the character of class, caste, and divisional versions of societal conventions and morals.

A few more comments on social classes and castes are necessary. W. Lloyd Warner and Paul S. Lunt, in *The Social Life of a Modern Community*, define social classes as "two or more orders of people who are believed to be, and are accordingly ranked by the members of the community, in socially superior and inferior positions. Members of a class tend to marry within their own order, but the values of the society permit marriage up and down. A class system also provides that children are born into the same status as their parents. A class system distributes rights and privileges, duties and obligations, unequally among its inferior and superior grades." They found some six such social classes in "Yankee City."

Castes draw lines of demarcation more sharply than classes. Castes have a taboo on marriage outside of caste lines, and they have other patterns held by their members and reciprocated in by members of the other caste or castes which are in general more compulsive and make for greater cohesiveness than those of class. In the United States, caste lines are defined by criteria of identification with the white and the Negro castes which stress labeling far more than actual color or other racial traits.

Classes, castes, and major institutional divisions have as one of their functions the provision of a traditional orientation of the conventions and morals of society. Certain more class-conscious groups (for example, devout Communists and devout right-wing Republicans) also have folkways and mores which they identify with "class objectives," but which are typical of their groups rather than of their classes.

The significant familial, vocational, local church, and neighborhood groups are types to which the "group level" most obviously applies, types that contrast with the "societal level" and the "personal level." It is recognized and insisted that only arbitrary distinctions can be drawn between personal and small group phenomena, as overtly manifested, and between large group and societal phenomena. As in describing and conceptualizing other social and societal features, one deals here with phenomena that may be arranged in continua and for which usefully representative types may be selected, types with recognized relationships to the continua or other universes of data. Some may regard this sort of analysis as clumsy, despite its close approximation to sense observations, but categorical analyses become even more obstructive to the determination of significant relationships.

With these understandings about groups in mind, let us turn to the patterns which societies and groups evolve as parts of their cultures—conventions, and morals, folkways and mores—and out of which public opinions emerge.

1. SOCIETAL LEVEL

The cultural traits to be found characteristically on this level, *conventions*, are traditional patterns (verbal and other) which are accepted in a society as the proper modes of conduct for the man-as-he-should-be, with correspondingly disapproved conventions for the man-as-he-should-*not*-be. They include the societal types of public opinions, the *opinions of the public*.

Conventions are ideal types of thought and behavior derived over long periods of time through processes of generalization and rationalization from the patterns esteemed and idealized by the various groups, classes, castes, and other divisions of society. They are presented in an allegedly dogmatic guise, but they are characterized by being sufficiently general and glittering in both symbol and conception and sufficiently indefinite in referent to permit rationalistic avoidances within broad limits of apparent opposition and contradiction.

Conventions provide norms for group folkways, personal practices, and self-attitudes. The general language of a country, the "dictionary language" of a small abridged dictionary, not including colloquialisms and other special words, terms, meanings, and pronunciations, is a large section of a society's conventions. The members of no group talk precisely that way, but the people of all groups use words in ways somewhat resembling such "diction-ary language," resembling it enough to be recognizable as "the same language."

Morals are conventions to which have been given a judgment of societal welfare. They are the central, integrating conventions which provide a degree of ideological organization to the societal level of a culture. In other words, they are the traditional generalities concerning right, wrong, duties, rights, and taboos on societally important matters handed down through many generations and frequently formalized into sets of commandments, codes of ethics, or canons of ethical principles. They contain large elements of asceticism, humanitarianism, and formalism or ritualism. They dominate the teachings of societal surrogates—parents, ministers, teachers, governmental spokesmen—even though they are frequently at odds with the group mores of such surrogates and of the groups served by them: "Do as I say, not as I do!" Morals represent crystallizations of a society's traditional aspirations.

Morals are chiefly significant (1) in shaping the superegos of the young and thus the core of the superegos which function formally throughout life, (2) in describing the societal façades of institutions, associations (the localized and specific instances of institutions), and the roles of such institutional functionaries as physicians, mothers, fathers, labor leaders, scientists, business men, and government executives, and (3) in providing the main staples for propagandists—glittering virtue and name-calling generalities, righteous justifications and condemnations suitably and variously interpreted to advance or hinder persons, organizations, and courses of action. Morals have no necessary congruity with the mores of a society's constituent groups or with the sentiments held by people themselves. Such subjects as theology, ethics, economics, and traditional—but not scientific—"social science" concern themselves in great measure with working out rationalizations between morals, mores, and sentiments.

Moral role and institution definitions are

the societal versions of what roles and institutions ought to be. They are glittering façades of societal expectations with which human organizations and functionaries are commonly covered. It is upon the basis of such façades, by and large, that young people are attracted to professions and other callings. If their transition from moral to moretic comprehension is not handled gradually and carefully, disillusionment and even revulsion may result. As we shall see, men live in their societies more as the mores rather than as the morals prescribe, even though the morals have a large place in social control through their role in human rationalizations, justifications, and dramatizations of behavior. It sometimes takes a deal of patient albeit conscious casuistry, or, more effectively and automatically, some obscuring social distances, to give group mores the "proper" societal rationalizations, the "proper" relationships to societal morals. In other words, so far as social distances are concerned, what the public does not know about the mores of newspaper editors or physicians or professional cooks is presumed "not to hurt them" and certainly not to be "their business." The public ordinarily knows more about the societal façades or cloaks of these worthies than about their actual behavior.

Social distance, a big factor in maintaining these contradictions, results from group exclusiveness and a lack of awareness of many things stimulated by the ruts of established routines. It is social ignorance. It is what leads such a candid and accurate observer of society as Lincoln Steffens to say, "I saw that the Legislature wasn't what my father, my teachers, and the grown-ups thought; it wasn't even what my histories and the other books said. . . . Nothing was what it was supposed to be. . . . What troubled me most, however, was that they none of them had any strong feeling about the conflict of the two pictures." Faced with other evidences of social distance, Max Beerbohm spoke of the "mild, miasmal air" of Oxford University and told how, "enfolding and enfeebling," it keeps one "careless of the sharp, harsh, exigent realities of the outer world." William I. Nichols, then managing editor of *This Week*, warned publicists how, "to the very extent that you climb up in your job, you tend to leave behind you the people on whom all power, influence, and success depend. . . . If you are not careful you will forget those plain people . . . lose the wave length that goes into their lives and thoughts. And if that happens, then all the tricks, all the reader surveys, all the typographical devices in the world will be of no avail."

Morals, the central ideas or integrating conventions of the societal level of culture, are seen by members of a society as the broad major premises of discussions and actions on a societal level. In terms of them, spokesmen attempt to utter statements which will strike as large a share of the people as possible as being "just what I was thinking." Such a major moral premise of our society as the Commandment, "Thou shalt not kill," becomes in peacetime the center of a whole configuration of moral idealizations and other conventions, but in wartime the vagueness of morality and the expedient considerations embedded in the mores of powerful groups permit many professional moralists to sanction the necessity of killing. This does not, however, prevent superegos of service men from aggravating many a case for psychiatrists. Similar illustrations are abundant in the fields of race relations, education, democracy, international relations, and elsewhere throughout our society's morals.

2. GROUP LEVEL

On this level, folkways and mores (singular *mos,* adjectival form *moretic*) are the terms which correspond to conventions and morals on the societal plane. The folkways include *opinions of* a *public,* just as conventions include opinions of *the* public.

A *folkway* is a type of behavior trait common and traditional in a group. It is a summarizing abstraction, a social construct or patterned typification, derived from the relatively similar behavior (verbal and other) exhibited in the presence of similar stimuli by members of a group. It may or may not resemble folkways in other groups in the same society. It is likely to differ chiefly in detail from societal conventions, as in the case of group language peculiarities (slang, special terms, dialects). The *opinion of a public* is a verbal folkway, the view expressed typically in a group with regard to a situation, question, person, or course of action.

Certain folkways become vested with "an opinion that a usage is favorable to welfare." These folkways William Graham Sumner in his *Folkways* (1907), called *mores*. In other words, folkways become mores "when they include a judgment that they are conducive to societal welfare, and then they exert a coercion on the individual to conform to them, although they are not coordinated by any authority." To emphasize the compulsive nature of mores, Sumner adds that the "mores are social ritual in which we all participate unconsciously. . . . For the great mass of mankind as to all things, and for all of us for a great many things, the rule to do as all do suffices." Or, as Robert E. Park and E. W. Burgess stated it in their *Introduction to Science of Sociology*, "Under the influence of the mores men act typically, and so representatively, not as individuals but as members of a group." This recalls the discussion above of the manner in which personalities become departmentalized, in which a given person may in turn act in terms of societal, group, and personal patterns.

Mores are practical, expedient, and compelling. Their contrasts with society's morals are measures of what is popularly labeled as group hypocrisy. Mores and other folkways are so inclusive that an adult member of several groups finds himself equipped to handle most problems involving social relationships in terms of the patterns of the groups to which he belongs rather than through reference to more rational procedures. Somewhat of the process

of "becoming mature" in a society consists of a person accommodating his moral superego to the requirements of moretic group structures and personal desires and needs. Only in times of critical maladjustment in society do the folkways fail to furnish folkways-molded persons with rather automatic guidance in social relationships, with definitions of the "common sense" things for the man-as-he-has-to-be to do. At times of crisis, the resulting bewilderment emphasizes the all-embracing character of such traditional guides, despite inconsistencies between group mores and societal morals, and the trauma occasioned by being forced to face trying social problems without preconceived and socially tested formulas.

In terms of the institutional and role configurations in which culture predominantly presents itself to individuals, the folkways-mores patterns define the "internal" characteristics of such aggregates. Behind the cultural façade provided by morals-oriented societal expectations of the proper, right, or "necessary" characteristics of an institution and its associated roles, the folkways-mores patterns define the formulas upon which an institution and its associated roles "really work." These patterns, which in a professional field conflict sharply with the textbook idealisms dictated by societal expectations (conventions-morals), are the practical and expedient understandings and techniques, the customary ways of exercising power, cutting corners on the morals, handling aggressiveness, exploiting submissiveness, and making the best of public relations, industrial personnel, and other social action situations.

¹ The folkways and mores are largely unwritten, except in novels and in non-fiction works about peoples and groups other than those addressed. In discussing Niccolo Machiavelli's *The Prince* and *The Discourses*, Max Lerner notes that the Florentine "had adumbrated the methods of the benevolent despots"—had described their folkways and mores—"only too well." His offense had been only to unmask them,

to lay bare to the world the mechanisms of power which were behind the authority of the ruler." So far as most folkways are concerned, this exaggerates the situation, but it gives some suggestion of why folkways in general are accumulated by persons largely as a result of "practical experience—not book learning." Folkways and mores fall into role configurations of considerable precision and, for a given time and place, of rather great rigidity. An individualistic research physicist or attorney may fuss to himself about what he "has to do," but he will usually have to conform if he is to "get ahead" in his profession.

Folkways and mores also set the relations between an institution's functionaries and the "outside world" and between practical viewpoints and procedures and the institution's moral pretensions, as defined for it by society. Such clashes as those between the "practical men of affairs" and the "professors" can be interpreted in part in terms of the former being mores-molded and the latter being predominantly morals-shaped as they function in those roles. Only in avowed trades schools under industrial and professional domination, such as those of engineering, business administration, law, journalism, and medicine, do idealistic societal expectations (morals) give way to professional group mores during the formal training procedures. Medical professors note that, with few exceptions, only their younger students interest themselves in constructive critical analyses of the private practice of medicine as a social service. Morals-oriented English and sociology professors are supplemented by mores-oriented journalism and social work professors so that universities can produce more "practical"—more trade-conscious, less broadly social-conscious—reporters and fixers of social welfare problems.

To summarize, the group level of culture is typified by folkways, which include opinions of a public. Folkways are the modes of behavior of the man-as-he-has-to-be in terms of group operating criteria.

They are the characteristic traits common and traditional to a group. Mores are the central and integrating folkways, the folkways to which a judgment of social welfare and necessity has been attached. Folkways and mores fit into the cultural relativity of a society by resembling conventions and morals, by being rationalized with conventions and morals, or by being withheld from scrutiny through the operations of social distance (clannishness, professional discreetness, secrecy, lack of contact, ignorance, the pathos of prestige, the social blinders of prejudice or routine). In considering such relationships, the societal, group, and personal levels can be regarded as three levels of cultural generalizations from discrete behavior instances, with the time-factor lengthening the vagueness increasing as one proceeds from the personal to the societal levels. While conventions and morals define institutions-as-they-should-be (cultural façades), folkways and mores define institutions-as-they-have-to-be in an operating sense. They furnish the formulas for institutional routines and policies which institutional functionaries typically regard as right, proper, and necessary.

3. PERSONAL LEVEL

By the personal level of culture, reference is made to the external evidences a person gives of his personality characteristics, his habitual practices and sentiments. These practices, including personal opinions, fall into roles of men-as-they-appear-to-be and related configurations. Except for permissible mannerisms, as for example personal variants in speech, the personal versions of traits and roles resemble quite closely the group and societal trait and role types the supposed audience of the person supposedly anticipates. The number of short stories and novels written about the theme of the tyranny of social roles, especially by unadjusted writers in such periods of flux as that following World War I, testifies to a fact not usually bothersome or even recognized—the tyranny of social roles over our personal behavior. It takes a maladjusted or unadjusted person to detect this tyranny. Frequently what deviations exist in a person's behavior are explained or excused, quite accurately, in terms of the person's past or present membership in some group with such peculiarities. Certain group patterns, too, come to play central roles in the integration of a personality, and these tend to color the person's behavior in other social areas. This is dramatically apparent in the behavior of a banker or real estate salesman, however devout, during his activities as a church trustee.

By *practices*, a label is given to behavior patterns socially exemplified by persons who have derived them chiefly from the social models of the conventions and folkways, modified or supplemented by individual experiences and deviant inferences. Certain practices, because they are verbal and apply to specific referents, may be called *personal opinions*. Just as traits on the societal and group levels are integrated about certain emphasized central patterns, the morals and the mores, so practices are also organized about corresponding central patterns, the *sentiments*. Since sentiments are only vaguely behavioristic, with a knowledge of them derived by others largely inferentially from personal practices by comparison and analysis, their definition more appropriately falls into the discussion of the self level. At this point, it may merely be pointed out in a preliminary way that the sentiments are the internalizations of morals and mores. They are partly conscious and partly subconscious. Freudians bulk them and call them the superego. They have a strong emotional component.

As Leo W. Simmons has concluded in his *Sun Chief*, such a person as his Hopi subject is not only a creature, an occasional creator, and a carrier (transmitter) of culture but also a manipulator of it. His Hopi "is a *creature* of his culture in the sense that his behavior—his acts, thoughts, and feeling tones or sentiments—are largely molded by it." To an extent, the person is also "a *creator* of his culture in that he can never quite perfectly match up to the idealized standards, and may occasionally even initiate a variation—by accident, invention, or borrowing—and see it imitated by others until it has become a folkway or *mos*." The individual's function as a slightly imperfect *carrier* of culture to others is clear enough not to require elaboration. As a *manipulator*, a prime concern in opinion formation and propaganda, he may have the luck or ingenuity to "utilize the mores [and morals] to his own advantage," to "marshal them to strengthen his position or to coerce associates into fulfillment of his requirements; or he may even inspire other persons to make sacrifices. If he finds himself in situations of compromise, he may flaunt folkways, ignore mores, and take refuge in 'higher principles' [morals], arguments of expediency [probably derived from mores of a dominant group], or supernatural endorsements [furnished or suggested by the religious morals]."

The conclusions of Simmons are presented at some length because of their pertinence to a discussion of the personal and self-levels of cultural organization. In many ways, the present discussion of the social determinants of public opinions has as its central problem and theme the ways in which persons as the slightly imperfect creatures and carriers of culture can be manipulated through the use of cultural elements on the societal and group levels, in part through culture creation, in part through coercion or plausible rationalization, and in part through more effective culture transmission.

4. SELF LEVEL

During the maturational processes through which a newborn polymorphous-perverse primate grows into an astute insurance salesman or a tidy housewife, a physiological phenomenon gradually internalizes sufficient societal and group culture traits to become a socialized person. For "better or worse," as Gardner and Lois B. Murphy and T. M. Newcomb observe in their *Experimental Social Psychology*, the child thus achieves "much of his 'continuity,' his 'variability' and most of his 'consistency'—as well as most of his 'inconsistency.' " In this evolution of personality, both the behavioristic person of our personal level and the internal self of our self level grow and adjust to externalities and also to internal experiences and fantasies.

Charles Horton Cooley concluded that the self is always a social self, a "looking-glass self," and in his *Human Nature and the Social Order* he assigned it "three principal elements: the imagination of our appearance to the other person; the imagination of his judgment of that appearance; and some sort of self-feeling, such as pride or mortification." George H. Mead, in his posthumous *Mind, Self and Society*, concluded that self-consciousness arises through "taking the role of the other" and attributed the effectiveness of the social compulsions behind morals and especially mores to the psychological function of the "generalized other," a conception resembling Sigmund Freud's superego. Both Cooley and Freud recognized that the self contains elements which are conscious and others which are repressed or subconscious, what Cooley called "a cave swarming with strange forms of life, most of them unconscious and un-illuminated" and Freud called the "id." Here are elements of the superego, past experiences, old fears, submerged temporarily or permanently beneath the level of consciousness but still operative in motivation.

The self may be thought of as consisting of attitudes which are organized about certain central attitudes or sentiments and which define the customary thinking processes of a person, of a man-as-he-is. To sum up a definition briefly, an *attitude* is a state of accustomed mental readiness, patterned largely after societal conventions and group folkways, which offers a formula or a channel for drive, motivation, or reaction by a person to classes of objects, situations, objectives. It differs from societal and group norms to the extent to which the individual self is an imperfect creature and carrier of culture because of deviant faculties and experiences, fantasies, and inferences.

A central attitude or *sentiment* has a function on the personal and self levels corresponding to that of morals and mores on the societal and group levels, and a sentiment is a product predominantly of the internalization of a moral or a mos. Joseph K. Folsom calls a sentiment-attitude or sentiment an attitude that "involves potential *emotional* reactions centered about some object." A sentiment is one of the more enduring, integrating, and consistent aspects of personality. Sentiments are fairly stable but more emotional and less organized than corresponding societal and group norms. People do not like to reveal their sentiments when they are at all deviant or delicate, and, to a marked extent, do not actually put them into words or even understand the nature of these basic guides of their thought, feelings, and action. Psychiatrists have discovered that the people's sentiments are often apparently contradictory but that they are not so regarded by their owners, that sentiments change very slowly, and that they are difficult to ferret out, characterize, and measure. Psychiatrists know that our sentiments towards others frequently contain both affection and hate, sympathy and detestation.

Adequate illustrations for this integration of psychological and sociological theory would require a vast amount of space. All that can be done further in the present brief article, however, is merely to summarize the foregoing in tabular form as a "Resume of Social Determinants of Public Opinions." It is hoped that the theoretical synthesis is sufficiently clear, accurate, and usable to suggest illustrations to those working in the field.

RESUMÉ OF SOCIAL DETERMINANTS OF PUBLIC OPINIONS

Level of Social Organization	Patterns or Traits	Central Patterns	Role types	Institutional Function
Societal	Conventions— including Opinions of *the* Public	Morals	Man-as-he-should-be (Cultural Cloak)	Institution-as-it-should-be (Cultural Facade)
Group	Folkways— including Opinions of *a* Public	Mores	Man-as-he-has-to-be (operating Folkways and Mores)	Institution-as-it-has to-be (operating Folkways and Mores)
Personal	Practices— including Personal Opinions	[Sentiments]	Man-as-he-appears-to-be	Creature, Carrier, Creator, and Manipulator
Self	Attitudes	Sentiments	Man-as-he-is	Adaptations to Self's Needs, Understandings, Aspirations

Each term in the table naturally needs to carry with it the definitions and qualifications ascribed to it in the lengthier discussion. It should especially be borne in mind that the four "levels" are not discrete categories nor are the types of patterns, central patterns, roles, and institutional functions listed opposite them. One is dealing here with social types and type situations which are describable but changing in their relationships to the fluxing and fundamentally noncategorizable phenomena of human behavior and thought.

The applications of the foregoing theories to public opinion surveys throw poll interpretations into a much different light than has by now become traditional. The interviews for typical polls are, for example, in terms of a wide range of types of rapport. Although they are conducted presumably for the purpose of predicting behavior, they are conducted in terms of glittering stereotypes (societal morals). This may or may not alter their utility in predicting the outcome of elections, but it suggests especially the pressing need for other types of polling to be placed in a more adequate theoretical perspective. Public opinions can only be understood in terms of their societal, social, and psychic relationships.

TRIAL BY NEWSPAPER

JOSEPH T. KLAPPER AND CHARLES Y. GLOCK

On March 2, 1948, a subcommittee of the House Committee on Un-American Activities denounced Edward U. Condon, Director of the National Bureau of Standards, through the medium of the U. S. press. The subcommittee asserted that Dr. Condon "appears" to be "one of the weakest links in our atomic security." Its report, quoted in part by various newspapers, presented 27 paragraphs of "information . . . in substantiation of this statement." Part of this information consisted of excerpts from a letter written by FBI chief J. Edgar Hoover to Secretary of Commerce W. Averell Harriman.

Simultaneously the Department of Commerce, under which the Bureau of Standards operates, announced that Dr. Condon had been unanimously cleared by the Department Loyalty Board five days previously. Dr. Condon himself at once denied the subcommittee's allegations, asserted his loyalty and reliability, and shortly thereafter expressed his eagerness for a public hearing by the Committee—an eagerness which he had expressed several times previously in response to similar accusations made by its chairman, Representative J. Parnell Thomas, in magazine articles published a year before.

During the succeeding four and one-half months the "Condon Case" became a *cause celebre*. At least three Congressional committees, the Federal Bureau of Investigation, the Atomic Energy Commission, two executive departments and President Truman himself played speaking roles in the drama. Numerous learned, scientific and juristic societies, as well as various individuals, eminent and otherwise, issued statements. In the course of the controversy, the Administration's refusal to surrender the FBI letter to Congress led to extraordinary Congressional repercussions, including an attempt to write into law certain provisions regarding the retention and release of data to Congressional bodies. The Condon case itself for a time became only an incident in this argument. It was revived on various occasions, however, by additional attacks on Dr. Condon and by statements in his support. From time to time the Committee promised to grant Dr. Condon a public hearing, but the hearing never took place. The case continued to be argued in the press, albeit less frequently, even after the Atomic Energy Commission announced on July 15 that "on the basis of the voluminous record before it, the members of the Commission" were fully satisfied as to "Dr. Condon's loyalty to the United States" and considered his clearance for access to restricted data to be "in the best interests of the atomic energy program."

The Committee on Un-American Activities itself has made no formal determination of its charges against Condon. The case has been conducted largely in the press. Many citizens have become concerned about the affair as a striking example of what has sometimes been called trial by newspaper.

From *Scientific American*, 1949, 180, 16-21. Reprinted by permission of authors and publisher.

They believe that the Condon case poses the question of the responsibilities of modern organs of mass communication toward the liberties and reputations of individuals. As a result of this interest, the Bureau of Applied Social Research of Columbia University was asked by *Scientific American* and six eminent scientists to conduct a study of the press treatment of the Condon case. The scientists were: Harrison Brown and Harold C. Urey of the University of Chicago; Philip M. Morse of the Massachusetts Institute of Technology; George B. Pegram, Dean of the Columbia University Graduate Faculties; Charles Lauritsen of the California Institute of Technology, and John C. Warner of the Carnegie Institute of Technology.

The study that was undertaken is known in communications research as a "content analysis." In general terms this means a detailed examination of verbal or pictorial material for the purpose of providing an objective description of the material. For example, a literary critic who analyzes the novels of a given century to determine their political tenor is, in a sense, performing a content analysis. Students of mass communications, however, use the term in a narrower sense. They mean by it a study in which the material is classified according to objective criteria and thus rendered susceptible of statistical description.

The term itself, and the conscious practice of this discipline, are relatively new in social science, as is the whole field of communications research. It is only during the last 30 years that such giants of communication as the modern press, the radio and the screen have come to address and to influence whole populations at once. And it is only in the last decade or two that social psychologists have taken systematic note of these forces of opinion. Content analysis is one of several techniques they have developed for the objective study of the media of communication.

Content analysis has already been successfully employed in a number of complex inquiries. The treatment of minority groups in popular fiction, for example, has been examined through a content analysis of magazine stories. During the war content analysis was used with some success by Government agencies to predict enemy actions. Certain characteristic modes of speech were observed to have increased in frequency during enemy propaganda campaigns preceding surprise invasions. By observing the frequency of such modes of speech in current propaganda, U. S. analysts were able to note when a new invasion move appeared to be imminent.

THE METHOD

The Bureau of Applied Social Research and the sponsors of the analysis agreed at the outset that the study would be directed entirely to the press treatment of the Condon case, as distinguished from the case itself. Neither the Bureau nor the sponsors considered themselves qualified to evaluate or analyze the activities and statements of the various agencies and individuals involved. No attempt has been made, for example, to assess the truth or falsity of the charges brought against Dr. Condon. We have been content with noting in detail what charges against Dr. Condon were reported in the press, what support for these charges was there offered, and the like.

It was soon found that to analyze the material on the Condon case in a representative cross section of the whole U. S. press would be a huge task; even to determine what papers would constitute such a cross section would involve a research project of no mean dimensions. It was therefore decided to focus the study on the press of a single large city. Because of the number and variety of its dailies, the New York City press was selected. Material was drawn from all of the nine general daily papers of that city, *viz.*, the *Times*, the *Herald Tribune*, the *Daily News*, the *Daily Mirror*, *PM* and its successor the *Star*, all morning papers; and the *Sun*, the *World-Telegram*, the *Post Home News* and the *Journal-American*, all evening papers, some of them with week-end editions. The period studied was from March

1, 1948, to October 31, 1948, inclusive, *i.e.*, from the issuance of the subcommittee report to a date three and a half months after the Atomic Energy Commission had cleared Dr. Condon.

The Bureau set out to approximate as closely as possible a complete coverage of all news articles on the Condon case in all issues of the nine New York newspapers during the given period. This coverage was sought by two independent means. All the papers were asked for a list of the dates on which articles mentioning Dr. Condon were published (replies were received from every paper except the *Mirror*). Library editions of all papers were then searched for the articles published on those dates. In addition, a press clipping service was retained to make an independent search of all available editions of the nine papers for the entire period covered. Despite the precautions taken, it is quite possible that some articles or references may have been missed. There may be variations in completeness of coverage from paper to paper. Any misses that occurred may be considered random, however; the missing material, if any, would not significantly affect the findings, which are almost always stated in terms of ratios or percentages.

All the relevant material in each news article was divided into "statements," each statement consisting of a single complete idea, *e.g.*, "Dr. Condon was denounced by the Thomas Committee." A statement might be a sentence or a single word; for example, "The martyred Dr. Condon will be called to testify" contains two statements: one that Dr. Condon will be called to testify, the other that he is martyred. The total number of statements in the 306 news articles examined was 4,589. Of these, 680 neutral statements of identification (*e.g.*, "Dr. Condon is director of the National Bureau of Standards") were eliminated, since analysis of them seemed purposeless. This left 3,909 for analysis.

The statements were then classified in various categories known as "dimensions," such as the identity of the person or group to whom the statement referred (called the "referent dimension"), the paper in which it appeared, the theme of the statement, the person or group who made it, the basis offered for the statement, and so on. There were 23 such dimensions. The crucial part of this process was the classification of the theme of the statement. To make this as objective as possible, the themes were subdivided at the outset into numerous specific categories, so that the classifiers or coders were not asked to decide whether a given statement was "favorable" or "unfavorable" to the referent (*e.g.*, Dr. Condon), but to describe it in terms of what it actually said. For example, a statement such as, "Dr. Condon is alleged to have associated with a Soviet spy" was classified under the theme: "Association with person in Soviet or Soviet-satellite circles who is allegedly subversive or an espionage agent." These various specific categories were later grouped under more general classifications to furnish the basis for analysis. Thus the statement quoted above became part of a group headed: "Association with allegedly questionable persons." This group of statements in turn eventually was placed in the general category of statements unfavorable to Dr. Condon.

The statements were all coded on the basis of the original specific criteria. As a check on objectivity, each statement was coded by at least two different individuals, and discrepancies were submitted to several independent checks by supervisors. Thus every coded statement was the end product of a process involving the detailed breakdown of an article, the isolation of the statement, its classification by two different coders in 23 dimensions, comparison of the two codings, and final approval for the next operation.

After they were coded, the statements were recorded on International Business Machine (Hollerith) cards. It thus became possible to determine quickly, by means of IBM sorters, precisely what "dimension combinations" existed, and in what degree. If it seemed desirable to know, for example, how many times the *Sun* reported a demand upon President Truman for release of the FBI letter, the machine was merely set to pick out the cards punched ⅛ (column 1— hole 8: *Sun*), 18/5 (referent: Truman), 33/7 (demand for release of FBI letter). The results of the various machine "runs," taken individually or compared with one another, comprise the findings.

Despite the pains taken to ensure the highest possible degree of consistency, accuracy and objectivity, it must be remembered that we are here dealing not with the relatively stable phenomena of the physics laboratory but with the subjective phenomenon of language, which is as variable as human thought. Some degree of flexibility and interpretive inconsistency is therefore inevitable. While this margin of error is believed by the Bureau to be at the very minimum consistent with the nature of the task, one must lean backward in the interpretation of the findings. A very small percentage difference in two contrasted types of press treatment may not be significant in some cases; a notable percentage difference, however, can safely be regarded as significant.

The problem of the present study was to determine the nature of the "trial by newspaper" that Dr. Condon had received in the New York press. This involved a statistical measurement of the extent to which the newspapers treated him favorably or unfavorably. To that end the objective description of the press content on the case was analyzed as to the number of statements critical of Dr. Condon and those sympathetic to him; the number reporting demands for the FBI letter and those reporting refusals, and a miscellaneous category of statements that may be classified as neutral to Dr. Condon.

A statement was classed as unfavorable to Dr. Condon if it criticized him directly or reflected on him indirectly by supporting the Un-American Activities Committee's treatment of the case. An example of the first type of statement is: "Dr. Edward U. Condon . . . accused by a Thomas subcommittee . . . of associations with Soviet spies." An example of the second type:

"McDowell insisted that the Committee's previous labeling of Condon stands as an 'almost perfect description.' " Similarly, a statement was classed as favorable to Dr. Condon if it supported him directly (*e.g.*, "Dr. Condon . . . whose integrity and patriotism have been fully recognized by his scientific peers"), or criticized the Committee (*e.g.*, "The . . . Committee's attack on Dr. Edward U. Condon was condemned today as 'irresponsible' by 200 leading scientists").

Thus the statements on each side could be broken down into two categories: 1) anti-Condon and pro-Committee, 2) pro-Condon and anti-Committee. As will be seen, such a breakdown produced some interesting findings.

Analyses were made of the emphasis given to the respective statements and of the way in which they were presented. It must be kept in mind that this is not a study of the editorial statements made by the papers themselves but of their news coverage of the story; that is, of the statements made in the news columns by reporters and their sources. Obviously what a newspaper reports about an event is shaped to a large extent by the event itself. When a paper reported an event unfavorable to Dr. Condon it was under no obligation to create an event sympathetic to him to furnish a balance. Thus the fact that a paper may have reported more unfavorable than favorable events is not in itself necessarily a sign of bias. Bias may be shown, however, in the manner in which a paper reports an event and in its selection of which events to report and which to omit. An outside observer, lacking the newspapers' access to the events on which they based their reporting, can only judge their treatment of the Condon case by comparing the way in which the various newspapers dealt with the same events.

WHAT WAS SAID

The first general finding is that in the New York press taken as a whole there was a preponderance of statements favorable to

Dr. Condon. Of the 3,909 analyzed statements, 745 or 19 per cent were unsympathetic to Condon, and 971 or 25 per cent were sympathetic. These proportions, applying as they do to the total coverage by the entire New York press, are not particularly meaningful: few persons would consistently have read all nine papers and been exposed to this comprehensive coverage. More significant are the differences among the papers. The range of these differences is indicated in the percentages of pro-Condon and anti-Condon statements in the individual newspapers.

	Pro	Con
Times	65	35
Herald Tribune	64	36
Star	63	37
Post	57	43
World-Telegram	50	50
News	49	51
Mirror	47	53
Sun	43	57
Journal-American	18	82

(Because the *Journal-American* published relatively little on the Condon case, the findings for this paper may be less meaningful than for the others.)

Most of the pro-Condon statements were contributed by the first four papers—*Times, Tribune, Star* and *Post*—which accounted for nearly two thirds of the total New York coverage of the story in terms of number of statements. In the four papers taken as a group, statements sympathetic to Dr. Condon outnumbered unsympathetic ones in a ratio of 17 to 10. In the other five papers, which have a much larger total circulation than the first group, statements unsympathetic to Dr. Condon predominated in a ratio of 13 to 10 for the group as a whole.

Analysis of the two categories of statements on each side of the case—*i.e.*, those relating directly to Dr. Condon and those relating to the Committee—revealed another interesting difference in the handling of the case by the two groups of papers. There were few statements in praise of the Committee's treatment of the case: of the total of the anti-Condon statements in all the papers fewer than one in 13 supported the Committee itself. When it came to the pro-Condon statements, however, there were contrasting results in the amount of criticism of the Committee in the two newspaper groups. In the *Times, Tribune, Star* and *Post*, more than one third of the statements on Dr. Condon's side consisted of criticisms of the Committee's procedure. In the other five papers, this proportion was nearer one fourth. In other words, the second group published a substantially smaller proportion of statements criticizing the Committee than did the first group.

The statements favorable and unfavorable to Dr. Condon taken together accounted for 44 per cent of the 3,909 on the case. Of the rest, a surprisingly large group—some 15 per cent of all statements—concerned the struggle between Republican Congressmen and the Administration over the release of the FBI letter. The remaining 41 per cent of the statements in the case were classified as descriptive background of a neutral character.

A further breakdown showing how the treatment of Dr. Condon fluctuated during the progress of the case also yields significant information. In April, when the battle over the FBI letter reached its peak, the reflections of this event were markedly different in the two groups of newspapers. The *Times, Tribune, Star* and *Post* continued to give greater attention to the Condon case itself and to publish more pro-Condon than anti-Condon statements, although the ratio for the group fell to 12 to 10. In the other five papers, however, statements about the letter actually outnumbered statements about the Condon case proper, and the ratio of statements unsympathetic to Condon rose 23 to 10. When the Atomic Energy Commission cleared him in July, the *Times, Tribune, Star* and *Post* presented a 14-to-10 ratio of statements favorable to him, but the other five papers, in spite of his clearance, remained on the other side of the fence; in that month they printed an average of 11 anti-Condon statements for every 10 pro-Condon. Thereafter there was relatively little press activity on the Condon case, but in September, when the Un-American Activities Committee promised new "shocking revelations," the statements published in the group of five papers were 26 to 10 anti-Condon. In other words, two months after his AEC exoneration, the five papers were still presenting a predominantly unsympathetic picture.

These are simply objective data revealed by the analysis. Whether they show that the New York press was fair or unfair in its coverage of the case is a matter of interpretation, which is beyond the scope of this analysis. The interpretation will depend on the standards applied by the observer. Some may consider that justice would have been served by a perfect balance of pro- and anti-Condon statements in a paper's reporting. On this point, however, the analysis developed certain other pertinent data.

The data had to do with the sources, character and repetition of statements on the case. Because this analysis dealt with statements concerning Dr. Condon himself, the findings from this point will include only statements directly pro- and anti-Condon; *i.e.*, they exclude the statements for and against the Committee. Of the statements against Dr. Condon, 88 per cent were made by members of the Un-American Activities Committee directly or in excerpts that they quoted from the FBI letter. The accusations against Dr. Condon were virtually a monopoly of the Committee, for some of the remaining 12 per cent of anti-Condon statements were made by Dr. Condon himself or by his defenders in reviewing what the Committee had said about him.

On the other hand, the sources of the pro-Condon statements were legion. They included two departments of the executive branch of the government, the Commerce Department Loyalty Board, the Atomic Energy Commission, entire departments of leading universities, and dozens of scientists and scientific societies. Analysis of the weight given by the various papers to the sources of these statements yielded significant differences. The *Times, Tribune, Star* and *Post* gave considerably more attention to the width of Dr. Condon's support than did the other papers; 21 per cent of their pro-Condon statements were attributed to scientists and scientific societies, while in the other five papers only 4 per cent of the statements favoring Condon came from these sources. Indeed, it appears that those five dailies all but ignored the multitude of meetings, letters and statements in defense of Condon by reputable scientists and institutions. As a result, 77 per cent of the case for Dr. Condon as presented to the readers of those papers came from Dr. Condon himself, from representatives of the Administration, or from unnamed sources.

A similar analysis was made of the bases of the anti-Condon and pro-Condon statements and the relative weight given to them. The case against Dr. Condon was made up almost entirely of three charges: 1) that he associated with suspected persons, 2) that he was lax in regard to U. S. security, 3) that he was unfit in some other unspecified way.

Of the statements making the first charge, 89 per cent identified Dr. Condon's associates only in vague terms or did not identify them at all. His associates were generally described as persons "alleged" or "known" to be espionage agents, or as Soviet or Soviet-satellite diplomats, or as persons suspected of being subversive, without any specification as to why they were under suspicion or any evidence that Condon knew that his associates were under this vague cloud. Only eight per cent of the statements regarding association actually named his associates, and in most of these cases the charges were equally vague. With regard to Dr. Condon's "laxity," nearly all of the statements were simply assertions, most of them being repetitions of the phrase "the weakest link"; there was little or no specific indication as to how he may actually have endangered national security. In the third category, the allegations were even more vague. Indeed, whatever impression may have been produced on casual readers, the content analysis indicates that the case against Dr. Condon as presented in the newspapers may well have raised a question in careful readers' minds as to whether there was any case at all.

The case *for* Dr. Condon contains a substantial amount of specific material. About a quarter of the pro-Condon statements rest on the fact that he was cleared by official investigations. Other favorable statements are based on "two exhaustive FBI investigations" and several documents, still others on testimonials to Dr. Condon's loyalty and competence from a variety of sources. Yet in comparison with the case against Condon these facts were lightly treated by a majority of the New York papers, which throughout the case gave far heavier emphasis to the allegations by the Un-American Activities Committee than to the support of Dr. Condon from various sources.

HOW IT WAS SAID

A description of what the press said and what it omitted can give only a relatively superficial picture of its coverage. Equally important is the nature of the treatment, and the manner in which newspaper techniques affected the picture presented to the reader. These factors are difficult to analyze in any objective fashion, but the Bureau approached the problem from several new angles and obtained some fruitful results.

One approach was a test of the material by the criterion of the repetition of statements. In any continuing news story, it is to be expected that a newspaper will frequently find it necessary to review past events as background. In making the selection of what background information to print, the newspaper obviously exercises more selective judgment than it can with respect to the new material, for the background provides many more items from which to choose. If, for example, the un-American Activities Committee announced that it intended to hold a hearing on the Condon case, the "news" was pretty well restricted to that fact, but in injecting background into the report a paper could choose from among a number of statements, such as that Dr. Condon had been accused of as-

sociating with spies, that he had been cleared by the Loyalty Board, and so on. Thus it is of considerable interest to see what the papers chose to include as background in their reports as the news developed.

In the analysis of this phase of the newspapers' coverage, all statements printed within two days after an occurrence were classified as "new" and all others as "old." The general finding that resulted from this analysis was that in eight of the nine dailies the "old" or repeated statements built up the case against Dr. Condon more than the case for him. About 57 per cent of the case against him in the papers consisted of revivals of the original charges. On the other hand, criticisms of the Un-American Activities Committee were seldom repeated; only 11 per cent of the statements in this category were revivals.

In every category of statements on the case except the one that covered criticisms of Condon, new statements outnumbered the old. The newspapers repeated general denunciations of him six times as often as they repeated general statements in his support. If they had published no "old" statements at all, the score for statements directly naming Condon would have been 416 pro to 301 anti, instead of 695 to 631 the other way.

There is no reason to believe that this result was deliberate. But the fact remains that the reporting techniques employed by the papers served to inflate the case against Condon far beyond its native size.

Another significant finding concerns the newspapers' handling of the Committee's promises of a hearing to Dr. Condon, and of the breach of that promise. All the papers reported the promises much more often than the breach. Here again, however, there were substantial differences between the two groups of papers. The *Times, Tribune, Star* and *Post* published 14 statements on the Committee's promises for every 10 statements on its failure to keep the promise. In the other five papers as a group the ratio was about eight to one.

SUMMARY

Thus the content analysis produced these principal findings: the nine New York papers showed wide variations in their news treatment of the case, although all were reporting the same story. Some presented a picture predominantly favorable to Dr. Condon, some predominantly unfavorable. As reported in all the papers, the charges against Dr. Condon were vague. The width of the support of Dr. Condon received substantial attention in the *Times, Tribune, Star,* and *Post* but very little attention in the other five papers. The background material revived for use in the running news stories had the effect of building up the case against Dr. Condon but did not build up his defense to anywhere near the same degree. All the papers reported the Committee's promise to give Dr. Condon a hearing far more often than they reported its failure to do so.

Such are the objective findings. The writers have attempted to avoid judgments, or have labeled them clearly when they seemed unavoidable. How or why the press treatments here described took the form that they did, and whether the papers should be commended or condemned are questions to be considered by interested students of the press.

Case for and against Condon as presented in the New York press as a whole is summed up in this table showing the percentages of statements in various pro and con categories. Charges against him were invariably vague.

Analysis of sources of statements shows that anti-Condon case consisted largely of assertions by Thomas Committee. Scientists' defense of Condon got much less attention. "Newspapers" means no source specified.

TABLE 1

Per Cent	Pro
27	Cleared by AEC or Commerce Department
25	General Praise or Support
14	Denials of Specific Charges
9	Denials of Charges in General
5	Praise of Scientific Ability
5	Cooperative During Investigation
5	Specific Instances of Discretion
10	Other

Per Cent	Con
37	Guilt by Association
25	Lax as to Security
20	General Criticism or Demand for Dismissal
6	General Suspicion
3	Not Cleared by AEC or Commerce Department
9	Other

TABLE 2

Per Cent	Pro
23	Executive Department
19	Newspapers
16	Scientists or Scientific Societies
9	Atomic Energy Commission
4	FBI Report
10	Other

Per Cent	Con
78	Un-American Activities Committee
10	FBI Report as Quoted by Un-American Activities Committee
6	No Source Specified
6	Other

Revived statements represent repetition of old material in news stories. The newspapers repeated charges against Condon much more often than they did his exoneration, thus building up attack more than defense.

Per Cent	Pro		Per Cent	Con
66	New		43	New
34	Revived		57	Revived

TRIAL BY MASS MEDIA?

MARTIN MILLSPAUGH

When Judge John B. Gray of the Baltimore Supreme Bench convicted three radio stations of contempt in obstructing the administration of justice,[1] he stated that the function of a jury is to ". . . bring to the case public opinion in the community. . . ." Under this Court's controversial Rule #904, he judged that broadcasts on the arrest and charging of Eugene James for the knife murder of little Marsha Brill ". . . must have had an indelible effect on the public mind." James, a Negro, was deemed to have been deprived of his right to a jury trial when his lawyer was forced to request the substitution of a panel of judges because of publicity given the case.

Judge Gray ruled that the right to due process could take precedence over the guarantee of Press freedom in the First Amendment. The legal point will probably have to be solved by the Supreme Court, but the crucial nature of this case to the communications industry is shown by the activity of both the American Newspaper Publishers' Association and the American Society of Newspaper Editors in behalf of the stations' defense. The prosecution was supported by the Maryland Bar, which favored the rule.

PROS AND CONS IN THE BALTIMORE PRESS

Since the press executives themselves have recognized their interest in the matter, it

[1] Baltimore *Sun,* January 28, 1949, pp. 4, 22.

should be interesting to discover how the Baltimore newspapers, which were not held in contempt, handled the James case. An analysis was made of the way the four important papers (the morning and evening *Sunpapers,* Hearst's *News-Post,* and the Negro *Afro-American*) reported developments during the eight days which passed between the murder and setting of the date for James's trial. There was no doubt that he had killed the little girl, but the defense was later conducted on the question of his sanity: whether he was criminally responsible and liable for a first degree murder conviction.

The defendant's background, mental condition, home life, etc., were therefore items which might have had material bearing on the case. There were a number of pertinent facts along that line: he had never gone beyond the third grade; he had been hospitalized for a head injury; his family always lived in extreme poverty; and all three of the psychiatrists who examined him agreed that he had schizophrenic tendencies, at least. But the three large dailies gave little attention to these factors, devoting most of their space to accounts of the horror of the crime, the personality of the little girl, and in general contributing to the stereotype of James as an enemy of society.

DISTRIBUTION OF SPACE

In the analysis the "neutral" facts of the crime itself and of the manhunt were sepa-

From the *Public Opinion Quarterly,* 1949, 13, 328-29. Reprinted by permission of the author and the publisher.

rated from material which supported either the first degree murder prosecution or the defense, and a count was made of the column centimeters devoted to each side. It immediately became apparent that there was only one side of the case as far as the white dailies were concerned. The nine fact-points favorable to the prosecution were reported 21 times, and the seven points in favor of the defense were mentioned six times. Only the *Afro-American*, seeking to compensate for this imbalance, gave the bulk of its space to the points in James's favor. The column centimeters of space given to the crime in each paper are as follows (headlines, text, and pictures were included):

In effect, then, the stimulus which the three dailies presented to potential white jurors was not calculated to bring an impartial public opinion to bear on the trial. That the newspapers were not alone in this position will be indicated by the fact that Governor Lane himself congratulated the Baltimore police on the successful completion of the case before James had come to trial. The lawyers for both the prosecution and the defense, however, agreed that the story was reported to the defendant's disadvantage.

	Morning Sun	Evening Sun	News-Post	Afro
Neutral	332.1 cm.	255.8 cm.	778.6 cm.	20.2 cm.
Destructive to James's case	173.6	203.9	209.3	2.6
Helpful to James's case	0.0	49.9	59.8	80.9

THE STRUCTURE OF CONTROLS

NATURAL RESOURCES COMMITTEE

In this chapter an attempt will be made to examine the nonmarket controls through which economic activity is influenced and to show how the innumerable threads of control build up into a structure of controls which is quite as important as the structure of prices in determining the use which is made of national resources.

The major elements of control which are significant for the structure of the American economy are to be found in the great operating corporations, in the big financial institutions, in the trade and business associations, in the labor unions, in the farm organizations, in consumer organizations, and finally in the State and Federal governments. If the economic controls associated with these organizations could be clearly delineated,

Reprinted with minor adaptations from National Resources Committee, *The Structure of the American Economy* (Washington, D.C.: United States Government Printing Office, 1939), pp. 153-170.

the results would yield the main essentials in the structure of controls. . . .

Because the term "controls" involves a relatively new economic concept, it is important to give it the greatest possible clarity. It is used here to refer to the ability of one individual or group to influence the policies in respect to the use of resources which are adopted by another individual or group. Thus, if a person can influence the production policy of a particular farmer by offering to buy his product at a price, by threatening to foreclose his mortgage, or by some other means so that the farmer raises one crop rather than another, to that extent the person is in a position to exercise some measure of control over the farmer's activity. Likewise, a factory superintendent is usually in a position to exercise a considerable measure of control over the activities of the workers in the factory during working hours. The management of a corporation similarly exercises a measure of control over the activities of subordinates, while the directors and the security-holders may, in turn, exercise varying degrees of control over the policies adopted by the management. Other groups, such as important buyers of a company's products, suppliers of raw material, financing agencies, labor unions, and government agencies, may exercise a considerable influence over the policies of an enterprise and to that extent share in its control. In each case, policies are developed with respect to the use of the resources available to the individual, or enterprise, or agency, and each of the persons or groups who influenced these policies may be said to have exercised some measure of control over them.

It is possible to conceive of a highly complex pattern of threads of control running between all the individuals and groups in a society much as the physicist conceives of lines of attraction connecting all the stars and planets in the universe. In outlining the structure of controls, however, only certain major controls need to be considered.

Many of the threads of control exercised by individuals or groups are summarized in market phenomena. The influence which millions of bread consumers exercise over wheat farmers operates almost entirely through the influence of their demand on price and is thus summarized in the price of wheat. . . .

However, in practice, market controls only partly determine the use of resources. In many producing units there is a wide latitude of choice in price policy, and economic controls not operating through the market are in effect. The extent of these nonmarket controls is suggested by the prevalence of insensitive administered prices already noted and by the absence of free market prices in a large part of the American economy. Where policies with respect to the use of resources are only limited and not dominated by market controls, the nonmarket controls become a significant factor making for more or less effective use of resources. . . . The present outline of the structure of controls is concerned only with these major nonmarket controls.

Nonmarket controls may be said to be of major importance when policies affecting a very large number of persons can be significantly influenced. The major policies developed in large administrative organizations, such as an army or a large business corporation, usually are subject to a very considerable measure of nonmarket control and influence the actions of so many people in their use of resources as to be of significance to the functioning of the whole economy. The nonmarket controls exercised by financial institutions through the handling of investment funds, and the nonmarket controls exercised by the government through the regulation of business enterprises, through its fiscal policies, through the protection of property and enforcement of contracts, and through other major policies, likewise influence the activities of millions of people and are important to the structure of controls. Persons or groups in a position to influence policies at these points are, for this reason, in a position to influence to a corresponding extent the effectiveness with which the national resources are employed.

The nonmarket controls over policy are seldom sharply defined. Often the threads of nonmarket control build up in such a way as to result in many different foci of control, each focus having to do with some particular phase of activity. Thus, in a big corporation, while the main threads of control over operating policy may come to a focus in the hands of the corporation president, some threads of control are likely to rest with other groups; controls over financial policy may be partly focused in a special finance committee of the board of directors and partly focused in some bank or financial house to which the corporation is under obligation; the threads of control over labor policy may be divided between the corporation and a labor union, some threads focusing in the corporate management and some in the union officials; threads of control over some aspects of policy may rest with the government bodies, as in the case of minimum working standards or public utility regulation; still other threads may rest with some dominant buyer whose orders are so important that he can, within limits, dictate the internal policy of the corporation, say with respect to its policy toward labor organization; or a supplier of raw materials or of services may hold sufficient threads of control to influence or dominate corporate policy in particular respects. Thus, in any concrete situation, there is likely to be a complex network of controls, and a series of foci of varying degrees of importance, each concerned with some particular phase of activity.

The controls which come together at these different foci are sometimes direct and immediate, as in the case of a soldier and his immediate superior officer, or the worker and his shop foreman, but as often they are indirect and intangible. Sometimes they may operate simply through establishing a climate of opinion within which policies are developed. More often they impinge directly on the process of policy formation. The controls which a banker can exercise over a business enterprise may be only indirectly related to the process of borrowing. The controls

exercised by Government through its monetary and fiscal policies often go largely unnoticed. The controls which a corporation exercises over public opinion through its institutional advertising are far from direct. The whole structure of controls is thus made up of some elements of control which are easily traced and other elements so indirect that their existence can only be surmised.

The actual threads of control may be entirely informal or may be accompanied by a formal setting. For a business enterprise an organization chart may indicate the lines of control and responsibility with respect to its major policies. The corporate charter must set forth in some detail the formal division of controls between different groups of security holders and between security holders and the management. Sometimes the formal lines of control and the actual lines may differ. In many corporations a majority of the stockholders are, as a matter of form, in a position to control the corporate enterprise, while, as a matter of fact, they are not in position to exercise actual control. Since the formal controls are often more easily ascertained than the actual controls, there is always danger of arriving at a false impression as to the locus of controls in any concrete situation. Only gradually as the concept of controls is further clarified through discussion and as actual economic activity is more closely analyzed will it be possible to give clear definition to the structure of controls.

In the conduct of economic activity the controls exercised by individuals or groups arise from three main sources: possession of one or more of the factors of production, possession of liquid assets, and position in relation to a functioning organization.

Controls arising out of possession of the factors of production are relatively simple and direct. The farmer possessing land, tools, and seed is to this extent free of outside controls. The manufacturer possessing a factory can limit its use, usually determining when it shall be run and when it shall be closed. A strategically located worker may exercise some control over production through his freedom to quit work. Possession of one or another factor of production is thus one basis of control.

Possession of liquid assets, particularly the possession of salable securities and money, is a second source of economic controls. The possessor of liquid assets is in a position to buy action by others. Sometimes the mere possession of liquid assets without their actual expenditure can influence the action of others, though, for the most part, the controls derived from liquid assets depend on the expenditure of the liquid assets in the market.

The third and, for present purposes, the most important form of the economic controls exercised by individuals or groups arises from their position in relation to some functioning organization. The management of a large corporation may be able to exercise a significant degree of control over the use which is made of resources without itself owning any significant volume of assets. Because of its position in the corporate organization, the management shares in the controls arising from the assets of the corporation and the institutional relationships which develop out of its operations as a going organization. The leaders in a labor organization can exercise some control over production policy as a result of their position in an organization whose influence is based upon the labor factor of production. The leaders in a trade association similarly derive some measure of influence over the use of resources as a result of the organized relationship of its members. A government administrator is in a position to influence the use of resources as a result of his position in the governmental organization. The individuals in such positions do not exercise controls as a result of their own possession of assets but as a result of their organizational position.

The major importance of organizational controls is due, first, to the fact that the most significant nonmarket controls arise from organizations, and second, to the greater relative growth of such organizational controls. The great shift from a dominantly agricultural to a dominantly industrial economy during the last century has tended to expand organizational controls. The increased concentration of production into large corporate units, expansion of government functions, increased financial concentration, and growth of both labor organizations and trade associations all work in this direction. The expansion in the role of organization has reduced the relative importance of market controls and increased that of nonmarket controls to such an extent that market controls no longer dominate economic activity. Nonmarket controls have ceased to be isolated as incidental occurrences and have developed into an interrelated system of controls which is quite as important as the system of interrelated prices in determining the use to which resources are put. It is this system of nonmarket controls and its structure with which the remainder of this chapter is concerned.

The main essentials in the interrelated structure of controls have to do, first, with the large producing units, their major policies, and the controls over these policies, and, second, with the controls over aspects of the policies of smaller producing units such as can be exercised by government agencies, financial institutions, trade associations, labor unions, and similar organizations. The nonmarket controls which influence the use of resources made by these separate producers constitute a significant part of the structure of controls and will be examined below in some detail. For smaller producing units, the nonmarket controls are less likely to be significant, except where a number of separate units are subject to the same controls in respect to some phase of their policy as, for instance, where a trade association influences the terms of trade or a labor union influences the terms of work. In such cases it is the controls exercised by the organization influencing some particular aspect of policy for many producers which are important. The nonmarket controls influencing only the policy of the specific small producer can be disregarded because of the relatively minor role played by any one such producer in the national economy. In the following pages an attempt will be made to outline the main elements in the structure of controls, taking up, first, the controls exercised over the large corporations, giving particular emphasis to the controls exercised by the more important organizations of economic-interest groupings outside of the larger corporations; and finally, the controls exercised by government.

A clear indication of the controls exercised over the larger corporations can be obtained by examining the 200 largest nonfinancial corporations and the larger financial corporations. What persons or groups are in a position to influence the policies of these large corporations? What are the most important nonmarket controls?

In an examination of the controls exercised over the larger corporations, first consideration must be given to ownership. It has long been customary to regard the stockholders of a corporation not only as the owners of the corporation but also as the main source of control over its activity. Yet, in practice, ownership of most of the larger corporations has become so dispersed that the stockholders have ceased to be able to exercise a very significant degree of control over corporate policy. Sometimes legal devices such as nonvoting stock and pyramided holding companies have been adopted to divest stockholders of effective control over corporate policy and personnel. On the whole, ownership and control have become separated in the larger corporations.

The inability of stockholders to exercise major control over corporate policies can be suggested by an examination of the stock ownership of the country's largest nonfinancial corporation, the American Telephone and Telegraph Co. At the end of 1935 there were 659,000 stockholders on the books of the corporation, a number almost equal to the number of potential voters living in the five smallest States. The holdings of different sized blocks of stock are indicated in Table 1.

The 43 largest stockholders, each owning 10,000 shares or more, together owned only 5.2 per cent of the total stock, while the 700 holding 1,000 or more shares together held only 16.6 per cent. In this largest of all corporations, stock ownership is so widely dispersed that no one person or small group is in a position to dominate the corporation as a result of stock ownership. Neither are stockholders as a group in a position to

TABLE 1

DISTRIBUTION OF STOCK OWNERSHIP, AMERICAN TELEPHONE AND TELEGRAPH Co., 1935

Number of shares held	Number of holders	Per Cent of stockholders	Per Cent of total number of shares
1-5	..	36.8	3.8
6-10	..	20.7	6.1
11-25	..	22.5	13.2
26-99	..	15.9	26.4
100-999	..	5.0	33.9
1,000-9,999	..	.1	11.4
10,000 and over	43	...	5.2

SOURCE: Annual Report of the American Telegraph and Telephone Co. for 1935.

exercise significant control over corporate policy through majority vote. The policies of the corporation have seldom been presented to the stockholders for a vote before adoption, and even in the usual vote for corporate directors the proxy machinery usually eliminates any significant control by stockholders. As a result, control over the policies of the American Telephone and Telegraph Co. lies only to a minor extent with its stockholders.

While the dispersion of ownership and the corresponding separation of ownership and control has developed to a high degree in the case of this largest of corporations, it has carried to a considerable degree in most of the larger corporations. In the study of large corporations by Berle and Means, it was shown that of the 200 largest nonfinancial corporations in 1929, only 11 per cent were clearly controlled on the basis of majority stock ownership, while in the case of 65 per cent of the 200 corporations representing 80 per cent of their combined assets, the ownership of stock was so widely dispersed or so shorn of powers through some legal device that stockholders were not in a position to influence corporate policy to a major degree.

The same indication of a high degree of separation of ownership from control is disclosed in a more recent study based on information filed with the Securities and Exchange Commission. Many corporations are required to file with the Commission information on the total stockholdings of their officers and directors and the stockholdings of other individuals and corporations holding 10 per cent or more of any of their voting issues. This information was available at the end of the year 1935 for 155 of the 200 large corporations listed by Berle and Means. A compilation based on these data is given in Table 2.

TABLE 2

STOCKHOLDINGS OF CONTROLLING GROUPS. [Distribution of 155 large corporations according to proportion of voting stock owned by officers, management, and control group.]

NUMBER OF COMPANIES

Proportion of stock outstanding (per cent)	All officers	Management (all officers and directors)	Control group (officers, directors and stockholders with 10 per cent of any voting stock issued)[1]
0-1	96	61 ⎫	
1-3	25	30 ⎬	73
3-5	10	21 ⎭	
5-10	15	16 ⎱	24
10-15	3	11 ⎰	
15-50	4	14	43
50 and over	2	2	15
	155	155	155
Median holding as per cent power of voting power	.40	1.74	5.40

1 Includes both stockholdings by other corporations and by individuals. A large proportion of the stockholders holding 10 per cent or more at any voting stock issue were other corporations.

For nearly half of these 155 big companies no one stockholder owned more than 10 per cent of the voting stock, and the officers and directors together owned less than 5 per cent of the outstanding stock. In only 15 companies did the officers, directors, and large stockholders appear to own 50 per cent or more of the voting stock, and in several of these cases the large stockholders were other corporations. For the 155 corporations as a whole the control groups owned approximately 12.4 per cent of the voting stock. Since this figure includes substantial stockholding by other corporations, the stockholdings by individuals in a position to exercise dominant control over these corporations must have been appreciably less than 12.4 per cent of the total voting stock outstanding. No corresponding information is provided on the remaining 45 corporations; 21 of them had dissolved, merged or gone into receivership, 16 did not have to file such information with the Commission because their stocks were not listed on any public exchange, and eight were not included in the compilation for miscellaneous reasons. Presumably, the stocks of the 16 corporations not listed on any exchange were closely held and largely subject to control by their owners, while in the case of the 15 companies in receivership, control over policy was almost completely taken away from the owners by court action.

It is clear, therefore, that for most of the largest corporations ownership and control have become largely separated. This condition appears to be particularly characteristic of the corporations which have travelled furthest along the road of corporate development, such as the railroads and others of the older corporations. The lack of significant stockholder control over corporate policies may be regarded as the typical condition toward which the large corporate units have been tending. The main controls must be looked for elsewhere.

Since the owners of the larger corporations do not in most cases exercise a significant degree of control over corporate policy, attention must be shifted to the management which is at the center of the forces influencing policy formation. The officers and directors of a corporation are responsible for the development of policies and their execution. Together, the officers and directors are usually in a position to exercise a large measure of control over corporate affairs.

The separate roles of directors and of officers in policy formation vary from corporation to corporation and have been too little studied to make possible any precise distinction between their respective roles. The process of policy formation is a highly complex one in which many persons and groups may take part. To what extent the directors as a group usually act as a body of review for the policy proposals developed by the officers of a corporation, and to what extent they initiate policies is not clear and presumably varies from corporation to corporation. It is sufficient for this outline of the structure of controls to recognize that policy formation for most of the large corporations centers in the management, consisting of both officers and directors. Once this is recognized, it is possible to treat each producing unit as a going organization in which policy is continuously being formed and efforts made to carry it out. The management at the center of this process influences policy to a major extent as a result of its position in the organization, while a variety of both market and non-market controls limits the controls which the management itself is in a position to exercise.

The more important nonmarket controls impinging on corporate managements can roughly be grouped into three categories, (1) the corporate community, (2) other organized interest groups, and (3) government.

If each corporate management were quite independent of every other corporate management and subject only to market controls in its development of policy, the structure of nonmarket controls might be of only secondary importance. In fact, however, there is a great deal of interrelationship between corporate managements. Partly through interlocking directorates, partly through the activities of the major financial institutions, partly through particular interest groupings, partly through firms rendering legal, accounting, and similar services to the larger corporations, and partly through intercorporate stockholdings, the managements of most of the larger corporations are loosely brought together in what might be called the corporate community.

The formal interrelationships between the larger corporations brought about through interlocking directorates can be seen by examining the directorates of the 200 largest nonfinancial corporations and the 50 largest financial corporations. . . . In 1935 only 25 of these corporations had no director in common with at least one other corporation on the list. One corporation, the Western Union Telegraph Co., interlocked with 35 other corporations on the list. . . .

All together there were 3,544 directorships on the boards of these 250 corporations in 1935, and these positions were held by 2,725 individual directors. The distribution of the directorships, among individuals, is shown in Table 3. Between them, 400 men held nearly a third of these directorships; 1,000 men held over half.

The extent of this interlocking and the magnitude of the assets involved are indicated in Table 4. Out of the 250 corporations, 151 companies, whose assets amounted to nearly three-quarters of the combined assets of the 250, were interlocked with at least three other companies in the group. There can thus be no question of the very extensive formal interlocking of the large corporations.

Just how important for policy formation these interlocks may be is a much more difficult matter to determine. It would be easy to overestimate their importance, since many directors are relatively inactive. On the other hand, it might be equally easy to underrate the influence on policy which results from the climate of opinion developed in part through these interlocks. That the

TABLE 3

NUMBER OF DIRECTORS AND THEIR HOLD-
INGS OF DIRECTORSHIPS IN 200 LARGEST
NONFINANCIAL AND 50 LARGEST FINAN-
CIAL CORPORATIONS, 1935

Number of directorships held by a single individual	Total number of directors	Total number of director-ships held	CUMULATIVE NUMBER	
			Directors	Director-ships
9	1	9	1	9
8	3	24	4	33
7	6	42	10	75
6	6	36	16	111
5	19	95	35	206
4	48	192	83	398
3	102	306	185	704
2	303	606	488	1,310
1	2,234	2,234	2,722	3,544
Total	2,722	3,544	...	...

interlocks are not primarily brought about through inactive directors is suggested by the fact that 59 of the 83 directors holding 4 or more directorates in this group of corporations were in an active position in at least one of the corporations they served, being chairman of one of the boards, a member of an executive or finance committee or an executive officer of the corporation. Such men are likely to take a responsible share in the development of policy in any corporation in which they hold a responsible position. But until more study has been given to the process of policy formation, the actual role of interlocking directorates cannot be clearly determined.

A second influence tying together many of the large corporations results from extensive intercorporate stockholdings. In the case of at least 30 of the 250 large corporations, 10 per cent or more of the voting power derived from stock ownership was held directly or indirectly by another corporation in the group or by one of the 9 financial or holding companies not included in the list of 250 corporations but clearly part of the corporate community. In all but one of these cases, the corporate stock-

holders were the only stockholders with 10 per cent or more of the voting power. . . .

It is clear that while none of these corporations are legally controlled by another corporation, they are not entirely independent of each other. Often, a corporation holding 10 per cent or more of the stock of another corporation can influence the policies of the latter to a significant extent and in many cases even determine its management. Such large intercorporate stockholdings and the many smaller holdings of a similar character help to build up the interrelationships between the big corporations which form the basis of the corporate community.

A third factor binding the larger corporation into a corporate community derives from the activity of the firms which provide these large corporations with financial, legal, accounting, and similar services. Of these services, the financial are undoubtedly the most important. In the single year, 1935, 175 of the 200 largest nonfinancial corporations issued new securities. This meant that in most cases they had to call on one or more of the financial or investment firms to underwrite and distribute these issues. Most of such financing is handled by a very small number of firms. According to figures obtained from the Securities and Exchange Commission, 56 per cent of all the corporate underwriting in 1935 was initiated by only 10 firms. As an almost necessary result of such activity, each of the more important investment firms is drawn ultimately into the affairs of a number of the big corporations.

The more important accounting firms also act, though presumably to a lesser extent, as a binding force in the corporate community. The ten largest accounting firms certified 52 per cent of the accounts of all the accounting firms (754 in number).

In the same way, the leading legal firms, advertising firms, engineering firms, public relations counsellors, and espionage firms are apt to have a score or more of the larger corporations as their clients and come into intimate contact with one or another phase of their major policy problems.

All of these firms rendering special services to the big corporations necessarily deal with some important phase of corporate policy for each of the corporations which they serve. Almost inevitably they contribute in conferences and individual discussions to that climate of opinion within which corporate policies are formed, carrying from one corporation to another some degree of common background and temper of thought which adds a measure of unity to the corporate community.

larger corporations which are owned by the larger banks and insurance companies or the extent to which the leading financial institutions have provided funds to the larger corporations on the basis of short-term loans. Both sums must be of considerable magnitude and the basis of very real influence over corporate policies. Some controls are likely to arise at the time debts are being incurred, but most particularly they arise when difficulty is met with in the repayment of debts. Banks or insurance companies

TABLE 4

CORPORATIONS INTERLOCKING WITH ONE OR MORE OTHER CORPORATIONS AMONG 200 LARGEST NONFINANCIAL AND 50 LARGEST FINANCIAL CORPORATIONS, 1935

Type of Corporation	ALL CORPORATIONS		CORPORATIONS INTERLOCKING WITH ONE OR MORE OTHER COMPANIES		
	Number	Total Assets	Number	Assets	Per Cent of Total Assets
Industrial	107	$ 25,140.6	91	$ 23,022.3	91.6
Utilities	54	25,232.6	46	22,886.3	90.7
Railroads	39	23,874.0	38	23,705.9	99.3
Banks	30	20,707.6	30	20.707.6	100.0
Other financial	20	19,959.4	20	19,959.4	100.0
All Corporations	250	114,914.2	225	110,281.5	96.0

	CORPORATIONS INTERLOCKING WITH TWO OF MORE OTHER COMPANIES			CORPORATIONS INTERLOCKING WITH THREE OR MORE OTHER COMPANIES		
	Number	Assets	Per Cent of Total Assets	Number	Assets	Per Cent of Total Assets
Industrial	71	$16,261.9	64.7	60	$14,645.5	58.3
Utilities	34	20,153.2	79.9	26	16,049.6	63.6
Railroads	36	22,796.2	95.5	31	20,146.1	84.4
Banks	28	20,223.5	97.7	22	16,921.3	81.7
Other financial	18	19,045.8	95.4	12	16,095.1	80.6
All corporations	187	98,480.6	85.7	151	83,857.6	73.0

A fourth factor making for interrelationship among the larger corporations results from the activities of the larger financial corporations in the use which they make of the investment funds at their disposal. In 1935, banks, insurance companies, and similar financial corporations owned approximately a quarter of all the outstanding bonds of American corporations. No figures are available on either the bonds of the

once having loaned funds to a corporation, or having purchased its bonds, must keep in close touch with its activities. If the corporation gets into financial difficulties, they are directly concerned in keeping it solvent or with its reorganization. Because of the magnitude of the funds for which they are responsible, the financial institutions are often able to exercise a major influence in such proceedings and, after reorganization, to occupy a strategic position in relation to the reorganized corporation. Thus, as a result of the investment funds which they control and the opportunities which arise in connection with their use, the relatively small number of large financial institutions tends to increase the interrelationship in the corporate community.

When the interrelationships between the larger corporations are carefully examined, company by company, groupings of more closely related companies emerge. Sometimes several corporations are closely bound together, as in the case of the Electric Bond and Share Corporation and the three major systems in which it owns a large minority interest and which it manages on a contractual basis. Sometimes corporations have several directors in common as in the case of the United States Steel Corporation and the American Telephone and Telegraph Co. with four common directors, and Pullman, Inc. whose directorate of 14 included in 1935 two partners of J. P. Morgan and Co. and four representatives of the First National Bank of New York. Such a large number of common directors combined with other evidences of close association is taken to be sufficient grounds, not for classifying the corporation as subject to the same control, but as subject to some measure of common influence and properly classed as belonging to a common interest group. More often the basis for grouping corporations together is less concrete and grows out of an examination of the historical background of each corporation, as well as its current position. Interlocking directorates alone are not sufficient evidence of a close interrelationship between corporations. Neither is the possession of a minority stock interest alone evidence of close association. Nor is a single instance of the underwriting of a corporation's securities by a particular investment house evidence of a close association between the two. But when a corporation was initially promoted by a particular investment firm, when all its new security issues are handled by that firm, when the two have directors in common, and when other

evidence of a less precise nature points to a close association between the companies, it seems appropriate to treat them as part of a single interest group. . . .

In addition to the informal but none-the-less significant groupings of controls which center in the corporate community, there are certain economic-interest groupings operating through formal organizations, which have a significant impact on the policies adopted by specific producing units. The most important of the economic interests formally organized are those of business, labor, farmer, and consumer. In each of these fields of economic interest, there are national organizations which aim to protect the special economic interests of their members. Associated with these national organizations or independent of them are smaller economic-interest groupings organized on a regional or functional basis which aim to further the particular economic interest with which they are concerned. These organizations function partly through the collection and dissemination of information to their members, partly through measures aimed to influence public thinking, partly through their impact on the process of government policy formation, and partly through the development of common policies which their separate members are encouraged to adopt. The importance of these organizations in influencing directly or indirectly the policies of producing units varies so from organization to organization that no simple analysis can indicate the role they play in the structure of controls. The most that can be done is to indicate some of the more important organizations, the scope of their membership, and examples of the kind of controls they are in a position to exercise. This can most easily be done by taking up separately the organizations built around each of the four major economic interests.

The many organizations built on business interests do not fit into any simple pattern of activity. Some organizations like the American Bankers Association, the Association of American Railroads, the Edison Electric Institute, the National Manufacturers Association, and the American Iron and Steel Institute, represent to a very considerable degree an extension of the corporate community, being made up of, or to a significant extent dominated by, the larger companies. Other organizations, like the National Retail Dry Goods Association and the Association of Retail Druggists, are made up for the most part of relatively small enterprises. Between these extremes lie many trade associations which are neither an integral part of the corporate community nor yet mainly outside it. Likewise, the functions performed by such associations vary in the widest degree.

In 1937 there were, in addition to the finance, railroad, and utility associations, over 2,400 national and interstate trade associations, each tying together, loosely or more closely, separate enterprises in particular industries. To these must be added the 4,100 State and local trade associations whose importance is primarily local, and the 5,400 local chambers of commerce.

Not all of these associations have the same significance for the structure of controls. Those which are primarily loose organizations, largely fraternal and promotional in their activity, presumably have little influence on policies adopted with respect to the use of resources. On the other hand, closely-knit associations which present a united front for an industry in dealing with labor, in disciplining recalcitrant members, in developing practices affecting prices and production, in influencing public thinking, and in affecting government policy may exercise a very considerable measure of influence over the policies developed in the use of resources. Some business associations concentrate on one particular type of activity, such as trade relationships or government policy, while others carry on a more diverse activity. The significance of particular business associations for the structure of controls thus varies from association to association. Similarly, the character of its membership affects the significance of a particular association. An association in an industry made up of a few large corpora-

tions may add little to the structure of controls, being simply an additional avenue through which the large corporations exercise their controls. On the other hand, in an industry in which the individual producers are weak, the combination brought about through the trade association may represent a very considerable increase in the nonmarket controls which are exercised within the industry. Only as the wide variety of roles played by business associations are recognized can their place in the structure of controls be clearly seen.

Probably the five most important business associations are the national associations in the fields of finance, railroads, utilities, manufacturing, and all business. The American Bankers Association has a membership which in 1938 accounted for over 90 per cent of the banking assets of the country. The Association of American Railroads represents within its membership practically the whole of the railway mileage of the country. The Edison Electric Institute covered through its membership approximately 90 per cent of the country's electrical generating capacity. The National Association of Manufacturers included manufacturing enterprises employing roughly a third of the workers in manufacturing industries. The Chamber of Commerce of the United States has not specialized but brings into a single organization 1,000 local chambers of commerce, 500 trade and other business associations, and 10,000 separate corporations and individuals carrying on all types of activities.

With the possible exception of the United States Chamber of Commerce, these national associations appear to be more or less closely tied into the corporate community. Six of the 31 officers and directors of American Bankers Association are officers or directors of six of the country's 30 largest banks. The railroad and utility associations are almost entirely composed of the corporations listed among the 200 largest, and their directorates are for the most part made up of representatives of these large enterprises. The Chairman of the Board and six others of the 18 officers of the National Association of Manufacturers are responsible executives of the 106 largest industrial corporations, while 12 of the 70 directorates of the association were drawn from these largest corporations, and others of the largest corporations are represented on the association's more important policy committees. Even in the case of the United States Chamber of Commerce, there is an important interlocking with the large corporations, 16 directors and officers out of 57 being associated with the management of 28 of the 250 larger corporations.

The important role which such organizations aim to play in the American economy is suggested in their published literature. In one of its bulletins, the National Association of Manufacturers states that it is "the medium through which American industry is able to voice a united opinion on vital national questions" and that it is "the only organization exclusively representing the interests of American industry." The United States Chamber of Commerce indicates that its primary function is "to obtain the matured judgment of business upon national questions, and to present and interpret those views to the agencies of government and to the public."

While the functions actually performed by these associations are varied and complex, there is a certain similarity in the character of their activities. Each of them acts as a center for the gathering of information and its dissemination to members. Each of them facilitates the development of common standards and policies within its particular sphere of productive activity. Each of them acts to develop agreement among its members with respect to governmental policies, and campaigns are carried on to prevent the adoption by government of policies believed to be harmful to their interests and to encourage the adoption of favorable policies. Finally, each of these business associations makes it a part of its program to try to influence public attitudes with respect to the activities and aims of its members and public policies likely to affect

their interests. All of these association activities are aimed to influence, directly or indirectly, the policies adopted in the use of resources and constitute a more or less significant part of the structure of controls.

In addition to the five major associations listed above, there are the numerous more specialized trade and business associations. These associations play varying roles in separate industries, some being concerned particularly with labor relations, while others emphasize trade or pricing problems, government policies, public attitudes, or lines of activity less significant for the structure of controls.

The activity of these associations in relation to labor has varied all the way from attack on labor organization to the active acceptance of collective bargaining with representatives of labor. The National Metal Trades Association, for example, has made a regular practice of furnishing its members with operatives for industrial espionage, guards for struck plants, and strikebreakers up to 70 per cent of the total employees in a plant. When this association undertakes to support one of its members in a strike situation, it assumes full control over the conduct of the strike, and any member who settles a strike on terms other than those laid down by the association is liable to suspension or expulsion from the association. An employer who enters a closed-shop agreement with the union is ineligible for membership in the association. The American Iron and Steel Institute, without going to the extreme of the Metal Trades Association, has, in the past, acted for the industry in opposing the organization of workers, as is evidenced by the full-page advertisements published by the Institute in 1936 in 375 leading American newspapers, stating the position of the steel industry in opposition to the organizing campaign of the Steel Workers Organizing Committee. On the other hand, labor organization has come to be accepted as a normal part of the organization of many industries, and regional or national collective bargaining agreements are developed between the trade associations and labor unions, as in the case of clothing and coal. Whichever type of policy is adopted by a trade association, the controls it exercises are a part of the structure of controls which influence economic policies.

In the field of price problems, the activities of trade associations are not clearly defined. The antitrust laws make direct price controls illegal except as specific types of control, such as resale price maintenance, are specifically legalized. At the same time, many trade associations do carry on price reporting and similar services which have an effect on price behavior without directly controlling prices. In particular industries their activity undoubtedly facilitates price collusion among members of the industry or the maintenance of a system of price leadership. No attempt can be made here to appraise the significance of such controls. All that can be said is that they constitute an integral, though often minor, part of the structure of controls.

The activities of business associations in the fields of government policy and of public thinking are very much less direct in their effects on the use of resources, but are, nevertheless, significant for the structure of controls. Government policies can affect to a greater or less degree, not only the operations of the national economy, but also the structure of controls itself, while public attitudes are basic to the maintenance or modification of any given structure. Both of these will be discussed after the other major economic-interest groups have been considered.

Paralleling the large corporations and business associations are the organizations of labor, which occupy an increasingly important place in the structure of controls. Labor organizations exercise a measure of direct control over the use of resources both via the market, as they affect the relative bargaining strength of the parties and thereby the characteristics of the bargain in the labor market, and also administratively, to the extent that conditions of industrial operation are laid down by labor organizations or arrived at jointly by the

representatives of labor and the representatives of business. In addition, labor organizations, like business organizations, affect the use of resources indirectly through their influence on government policy and on public thinking. . . . For the present purpose it is sufficient to point to the scope of membership in labor organizations, to the scope and character of the two large national federations of labor unions, and to the character of the activities of the separate labor unions, whether members of the federations or independent of them.

No completely reliable figures are available as to the membership in labor unions, but figures of membership made public by the national federations and the more important independent unions together amounted to approximately 8,000,000 in 1938. This is approximately 55 per cent more membership than was reported in 1920, the previous peak of union membership, and nearly two and a half times the membership reported in 1929. Altogether, this reported membership in unions in 1938 represents approximately a quarter of the total employee population.

The great bulk of labor union membership is in unions which are affiliated with one or the other of the two major union federations, the American Federation of Labor and the Congress of Industrial Organizations. The total reported membership in 1938 affiliated with these organizations and unaffiliated is given below:

Membership of unions:
Affiliated with the American Federation of Labor   [1]3,600,000
Affiliated with the Congress of Industrial Organizations   [1]3,800,000
Unaffiliated trade unions   [2]750,000
Total   8,150,000

[1] Official figures of the American Federation of Labor and the Congress of Industrial Organizations.
[2] Estimated from the 1937 figures.

These two major labor organizations are primarily concerned with the servicing and strengthening of their constituent unions in their collective bargaining activity, with the encouragement of governmental policies favorable to their interests and the defeat of government policies believed to be harmful to them, and with influencing public attitudes respecting the activities and aims of their members and public policies likely to affect their interests. All of these activities are aimed at influencing more or less directly the policies adopted in the use of resources and the two national federations constitute a significant part of the structure of controls.

The separate labor unions affiliated with the two major labor organizations or independent of them have as their primary functions the influencing of industrial policies through collective bargaining. Their influence on industrial policy ranges all the way from participation in such industrial problems as the settlement of the grievances of individual workers, through collective bargaining as to the terms of employment, to participation with management in developing the broad policies of an industry. Some activities like the settlement of grievances, though important to the individual worker, are of only secondary importance to the structure of controls. But labor-union participation in determining wage rates and hours of work, and union participation in the development of other elements of industrial policy, are of prime importance to the structure of controls.

Some impression of labor-union participation in policy formation can be obtained by an examination of the trade agreements entered into between organized workers and managements. These agreements, which record the results of collective bargaining or negotiation between representatives of workers and of their employers, range from very brief and simple statements of wages, hours, and other conditions of work to highly developed and elaborate regulation of many details of industrial relationships. They range from local agreements between unions and individual employers or local associations of employers to national agreements which set standards for a whole industry and are negotiated by national collective bargaining machinery. The custom-ary form of local building or printing trades agreements is representative of activities local in scope, while the national agreement in the men's clothing industry, first negotiated in 1937 between the Amalgamated Clothing and the National Trade Association, is an outstanding example of an agreement on a national scale, affecting 135,000 union members and covering virtually the entire industry.

Agreements in the bituminous-coal industry cover broad districts, but not the entire market. However, the Appalachian agreement, negotiated by representatives of the United Mine Workers and the operators from some eight States, is customarily worked out prior to the agreements for other parts of the country, and this agreement sets standards which influence all other agreements in the industry. The type of agreement which is becoming of increasing importance is that which involves a labor union and a single great corporation, the agreement being negotiated between the leading officers of the union and executives of the corporation. Such agreement typically covers many plants, often in several States. In industries dominated by a few large corporations, the agreement with one company tends to set the pattern for others. . . . In such agreements, the more important subjects covered usually include union recognition, physical conditions and working time, wages and labor supply, employment policies, and job protection. Since strikes, lockouts, or stoppages of any sort are usually outlawed during the life of the agreement, they customarily provide machinery for the enforcement of the agreement and the settlement of disputes during its life. In various degrees, such agreements reflect the participation of labor unions in the development of the industrial policies most immediately affecting labor.

In some industries, labor unions have gone beyond the immediate problems of wages, hours, and working conditions to participate in the development of broader elements of industrial policy. In the clothing industries, for example, both the Amalgamated Clothing Workers and the International Ladies' Garment Workers Union have long records of working with the employers for stabilization of competitive conditions and efficient operation. Under the agreements in the full-fashioned-hosiery industry, the union and the employers have attempted to deal with a difficult competitive situation arising from the introduction of new machinery in certain sections of the industry. In the bituminous coal industry, a joint Mechanized Mining Commission has been established for the study of problems arising from mechanization. These and similar activities reflect the interest of labor organizations in the broader phases of industrial policy.

In addition to their activity in connection with collective bargaining and the development of broader industrial policies, individual trade-unions, like the two federations of labor, parallel the activity of business associations by seeking through appeals to public opinion and through direct pressure on government to secure the adoption of policies which are in the interest of their members. Union representatives appear frequently at national and state legislative hearings on measures dealing with wages, hours, social security, relief, public works, labor relations, and other matters of economic importance to workers.

The participation of labor organizations in the development of industrial policy and their influence on public policy make such organizations an integral part of the structure of controls. A consideration of their full significance in American society lies outside the scope of this report. As the structure of the economy becomes increasingly a matter of organized relationships and administrative controls, labor organizations take their place as major structural elements in the economy.

Organizations of farmers constitute a third type of economic-interest grouping which is of importance to the structure of controls. Though less closely organized than either business or labor groupings, the many farm organizations, particularly the marketing and purchasing cooperatives, play a significant role in the field of agriculture and in reflecting the farm interest in the development of Government policy and in public discussion.

In terms of strictly economic activity, the most important farm organizations are the marketing and purchasing associations. In the marketing season of 1937-38 there were over 10,900 marketing or purchasing associations controlled by farmers with a combined membership of 3,400,000 and doing approximately $2,400,000,000 worth of business.

Some of the farm cooperatives, particularly milk cooperatives, play much the same collective bargaining role for farmers as is played for labor by its unions. Thus a milk cooperative may carry on negotiations with the big milk distributors as to the wholesale price of milk. Other cooperatives supervise the flow of farm products to market, as in the case of the larger fruit growers' cooperatives. For most basic farm products the cooperatives are not in a position to influence significantly price or the flow of products to market except as they reduce the purchasing or marketing margin. Other farm cooperatives purchase farm products as well as market them. Through these farmer-controlled associations, the farmers extend their influence into many activities closely related to farm production.

In addition to the farmer-controlled cooperative associations there are the National Grange, the Farmers Union, and the Farm Bureau. The membership of these organizations for 1938 is given below:

	Membership[1]
National Grange	800,000
Farm Bureau	400,000
Farmers Union	92,000

[1] Furnished by the offices of the respective organizations in Washington.

While these national farm organizations have little to do directly with the use of resources, their influence on governmental policy where it impinges on the interests of farmers is significant. Like business and labor organizations, these farm organizations, though less closely unified, constitute an important element in the structure of controls.

The fourth major economic-interest group, that of consumers, is relatively little organized. The leading national organization, the Cooperative League of the United States, is primarily a league of consumer-controlled producing enterprises affiliating 1,770 local cooperative enterprises in 1938 with a total membership of 965,000. Other specific consumer interests, such as health and education, are reflected in national organizations, but there is no major national organization representing the consumer interest as a whole and apart from producing cooperatives.

Government units, Federal, State and local, provide the third set of nonmarket controls which, together with the market controls, constitute the essentials of the control structure. Because Government units are the primary organizations in the American economy through which the individuals and groups in the community are built into a social unity, they have powers and responsibilities which transcend those of any other type of organization, and the policies they adopt can vitally affect the use to which resources are put.

The controls which Government units can exercise arise primarily from organization, from the authority placed by society in the hands of government. To some extent they rest on the possession of the instruments of production, particularly public buildings and the public domain. Under certain circumstances they arise from the command over purchasing power. But in the main, the controls exercised by government rest on the complex social relationships which give government its special character.

Certain of the controls exercised by government are directly concerned with Government production. The operation of the Post Office, the Army and Navy, the highway and educational systems, health and fire protection, all represent activities which in many ways parallel the productive activity of private enterprises but in which there are special advantages in Government operation. In certain areas the Government, through its productive activity, exercises controls beyond the boundaries of the particular administrative unit, influencing the market, as in the case of its handling of parcel post and in the operation of certain utility systems on a yardstick basis. But in the main, the productive activities carried on by Government units are aimed primarily at supplying specific products or services. Such activity differs in one important particular from business production, namely that of financing. Government units can charge the cost of production either directly to the individuals receiving the products or services as a business has to do, or it can spread the costs of production more widely through taxation. The latter is the procedure employed in the case of public education, fire protection, health protection, and many other services which benefit not only the immediate recipient but others as well and for which the community as a whole is taxed. In spite of this significant difference in financing, however, the controls exercised by Government units through their productive activity are essentially the same in nature as those exercised by other big administrative units. They involve administrative rather than market coordination within the administrative units and, to that extent, narrow the coordinating role of the market in much the same manner as the large corporate enterprise.

The second major type of control exercised by government is through laws, rules, and regulations and this type of activity is difficult to measure and equally difficult to grasp. In 1935 there were 175,000 separate political jurisdictions and, except perhaps in the case of school districts, the bulk of these exercised some controls of a canalizing character—police and fire regulations, building regulations, property protection, health protection, traffic regulation, and a host of other controls essential to the complicated activity of everyday living.

The basic importance of these types of controls to the structure of the national economy can be seen by examining a few of the more important. Fundamental to the conduct of present-day business activity are four sets of canalizing rules set up by government—the protection of property, the enforcement of contracts, the rules for bankruptcy and the laws which make possible the development of corporations and their exercise of legal powers. Without these canalizing controls exercised by government, modern business, as it is known today, would be impossible. Parallel to the protection of property is the protection of collective bargaining, each being essential to protect the basic interests of the suppliers of one of the factors of production.

In addition to the establishment of the basic rules of the game, Government units canalize specific lines of activity through the development of special regulations and regulatory bodies. The regulation of trade practices and the canalizing of industrial policies are partly the concern of State and local governments but have increasingly become a concern of the Federal Government, as business enterprises increasingly affect interstate commerce. This latter development is reflected in the creation of the Interstate Commerce Commission, the Federal Trade Commission, the Federal Communications Commission, the Federal Power Commission, the Securities and Exchange Commission, and other lesser regulatory commissions and agencies. It is not possible here to appraise the extent or effect of the canalizing and sometimes administrative controls exercised through these agencies, yet it is clear that they constitute a significant element in the structure of controls.

In the field of business-labor relations, Government units have increasingly developed rules of conduct comparable to the already well-developed rules covering the relations between business units. Many State laws and the interpretations of the State courts have determined the rights of organized labor to engage in such activities as strikes, picketing, and certain types of boycotting to strengthen their bargaining position, just as the right of business to lock out its employees has long been recognized. Federal legislation and the Federal courts have further defined the activities permitted to employers and organized workers in specific respects. The importing of strikebreakers across State lines and the use of the yellow-dog contract by employers have been curbed, while the sit-down strike and secondary boycotts have similarly been outlawed. The National Labor Relations Act has brought the regulation of labor relations in industries operating in interstate commerce primarily within the sphere of the Federal Government. Under the terms of the act, the National Labor Relations Board is responsible for the protection of collective bargaining in the sphere of interstate trade and is building up a code governing business-labor relationships comparable to the code governing property relationship developed through the courts. It thereby provides a framework within which the balance of controls between employers and workers is being worked out. In areas subject to particular Federal intervention, namely the railroads and more recently the maritime industry, the Federal Government has gone farther in providing, through the National Mediation Board and the Maritime Labor Board, the specific machinery for settlement of business-labor disputes.

These various types of facilitating and regulatory activities involve the relation of local, State, and Federal Governments to all or most types of industries. As has been noted, they are not administrative in character but rather provide the framework of rules within which the activities of individuals are carried on.

A third type of control exercised by government units arises when a government agency directly participates in the development of industrial policies. This is the type of control exercised in the railroad and public utility fields in which rates are developed through the interaction of regulatory commissions, the utility enterprises, and the courts; in the shipping industry where government subsidies are given to induce an expansion in the American Merchant Marine; and in the field of agriculture in which subsidies are given to build up the soil and to limit the production of soil-depleting crops. How far public utility regulation and other controls over industrial policy on the part of government have been successful in facilitating the effective use of resources it is not the function of this report to consider. But it is clear that they constitute a significant element in the structure of controls.

The fourth main type of controls exercised by government which is significant to the national economy is that exercised through its fiscal policies. In this field it is primarily the fiscal policies of the Federal Government which are important. The Federal Government's responsibility for the money medium, its power to establish tariffs, and its great taxing, borrowing, and spending powers all place it in an outstanding position to influence the money flows which stimulate or dampen economic activity. Through its fiscal policies the Federal Government can, to a significant extent, convert current savings by one part of the community into current expenditures by another part, shift buying power from one group to another, and direct savings into capital formation. Whatever fiscal policies it adopts, the fiscal activity of the Federal Government is so important in relation to the whole economy that it must significantly affect its functioning.

In outlining the major controls exercised by Government units, the latter have been treated as if they were relatively independent units. But it has already been pointed out that many of the controls exercised

by the organized interest groups operate through government. Similarly, some of the controls exercised by the corporate community operate through government. As a result, the policies adopted by Government units and the controls they exercise reflect to a considerable degree the balance of controls in the whole community. Government thus represents more than any other single organization, the meeting ground of both the common and the conflicting interests of different economic groups and individuals and constitutes the major focus of the structure of controls.

. . . In this chapter an attempt has been made to sketch the structure of the nonmarket controls which significantly affect the use of resources. The three main elements in this control structure have been outlined —the corporate community with its many ramifications and its climate of opinion; the major organizations representing the economic interests of business, labor, farmer, and consumer; and, finally, the Government units through which the conflicting interests of different economic groups are developed into a more or less effective working compromise. These three sets of nonmarket controls combined with the market controls already discussed appear to constitute the main essentials of the control structure.

In this outline of the structure of controls, the focus has been on the character and locus of the major nonmarket controls. No attempt has been made to show how the nonmarket controls actually affect the policies adopted in the use of resources or how they interoperate with the market controls. The operating effect on the use of resources of the combined market and nonmarket controls is a subject requiring intensive analysis but lying beyond the scope of this report on the structure of the American economy.

ATTITUDE AND BELIEF IN RELATION TO
OCCUPATIONAL STRATIFICATION

RICHARD CENTERS

A. INTRODUCTION

Several psychologists and social scientists have recently stressed the need for an assessment of the psychological aspects of socioeconomic stratification (1, 6, 8, 11). William H. Form, in a recent article (4) has called attention to the looseness of generalization and conceptual formulation that exist in the prior efforts in this direction, based as these are, in the main, upon "crude insight rather than on empirical methods." Form's stricture may be over-severe, for the sociologists, social anthropologists, and psychologists who have broken ground in this area have not remained entirely armchair in procedure. Yet the typical study has not improved greatly upon the technique of intensive interview in single small communities and the statement of results in non-quantitative and over-general terms as exemplified by the Lynds (9, 10), Warner and associates (12, 2), Dollard (3), etc.

For example, as a result of such studies as the Lynds' *Middletown* and *Middletown in Transition,* one, if not eternally vigilant, is likely to gain an essentially stereotyped view of the American ideology and culture. Thus "the American" is said to believe in being successful, or "Middletown believes in being honest," or "the Business Class believes in

being loyal," etc. Valuable though such insights are, it is time that this sort of characterization gave way to more accurate portrayal of the situation. We need to know what proportion of Americans believe what and how many of a given social stratum do so before practical and theoretical understanding of cultural homogeneity and cultural heterogeneity can be truly gained.

The writer is in complete agreement with Form that more objective and statistical enquiry is needed, and further with Form's suggestion that such study should have national scope. The present paper represents an attempt in this direction.

B. PROBLEM

The present enquiry is perforce limited in range, and it has singled out as areas for exploration topics where cultural homogeneity has been often presumed to be large.

The Lynds' *Middletown in Transition* includes an interesting and provocative sketch of the "Middletown (and presumably the typical American) Spirit."

> By and large Middletown believes . . . that progress is the law of life, . . . that character, honesty and ability will tell, . . . that hard work is the key to success, . . . that if a man does not get on it is his own fault . . . that Negroes are inferior, . . . that individual Jews may be all

From the *Journal of Social Psychology*, 1938, 27, 159-185. Reprinted by permission of the author and the publisher.

right but as a race one doesn't care to mix too much with them, ... that the poor-boy-to-president way is the American way to get ahead, ... that "any man who is willing to work hard and to be thrifty and improve his spare time can get to the top," ... that the rich are, by and large, more intelligent and industrious than the poor, ... that a married woman's place is first of all in the home, and any other activities should be secondary to "making a good home for her husband and children," ... that America will always be the land of opportunity, ... that nobody would want to live in a community without churches and everybody should, therefore, support the churches, ... that churchgoing is sometimes a kind of nuisance, one of the things you do as a duty, but the habit of churchgoing is a good thing and makes people better (10, p. 403 ff.).

The study reported here had two aims, first, to discover the extent of uniformity of views such as these, and second, to determine what differences of view, if any, existed in virtue of the differing positions in society in which individuals were placed. Because of the great differences that obtain in the life experiences of persons of differing socioeconomic strata, and because of the dynamic influences encountered by occupancy of a certain position and rôle in life, it was the writer's hypothesis that differences in points of view would be by no means negligible.

C. METHOD

In July, 1945, a person-to-person interview of a representative cross-section of the adult white male population[1] included the following questions:

Do you think woman's place should be in the home, or do you think women should be free to take jobs outside the home if they want them?

Would you say that on the whole people take

[1] The survey was carried out through the facilities of the Office of Public Opinion Research of the Department of Psychology of Princeton University while the writer was a graduate student there. The Office, of which Dr. Hadley Cantril is director, had its own staff of trained and experienced interviewers in the field at that time.

religion too seriously, or that they don't take it seriously enough?

Do you think all the modern scientific inventions of new machines and materials will result in a better standard of living for all of us, or do you think that these things have been over-rated?

Do you think most people who are successful are successful because of ability, luck, pull, or the better opportunities they have had?

Why do you think some people have been able to get rich, because of ability, luck, pull, their better opportunities, or something else?

Why do you think some of the people are always poor?

Would you say that your children had just as good a chance, a poorer, or a better chance to rise in the world as anybody else?

Respondents were also interrogated regarding their attitude toward the pay of various occupational groups and with respect to their opinions of the Negroes and Jews. These questions are described more completely later in the report to avoid duplication of effort and as a matter of convenience because they are somewhat more complex in technique.

Each question included had been pretested in the field by the writer to insure that it could be understood by the general public, though the actual interviewing was, of course, carried out by others. In addition to the questions of opinion, interviewers also ascertained the occupation, age, national origin, education, and other background data for each respondent.

In the description of the results nine more or less distinct occupational categories are employed, namely: Large Business, Professional, Small Business, White Collar (clerks, salesmen, draftsmen, etc.), Skilled Manual (including foremen), Semi-Skilled, Unskilled, Farm Owners and Managers, and Farm Tenants and Laborers. Because some of the groups listed are of somewhat small size, figures are also cited for the two more inclusive categories of urban workers consisting of (a) All Business, Professional and White Collar persons and (b) All Manual workers. The figures for the national cross-section which appear in each table include a few persons whose occupation was either unclassified or unascertained.

D. RESULTS

1. *The Rôle of Women*

It is true that a majority of American men believe that woman's place is in the home. The majority is, however, only a slender one—53.8 per cent (Table 1). Large differences exist between occupational strata. For example, whereas 61.5 per cent of skilled manual workers declare woman's place to be in the home, only 37.5 per cent of professional men hold such a view. As a general trend, the lower the occupational status of the person the more likely he is to hold the "in the home" opinion. Among urban groups it is the skilled and semi-skilled who most often would restrict women to the home. Such a finding is not wholly surprising when it is recalled that recently women have in considerable numbers invaded industries and jobs that have long been the stronghold of the male. It is probable that women represent a more serious competitive threat here than elsewhere.

Numbers of manual workers gave as a reason for their opinion, "so men will have jobs." It might also be that manual workers are less "enlightened" and liberal with respect to the rôle of women in society because their educations are quite generally poorer, but the negligible difference between the white collar workers and the unskilled argues against this interpretation. White collar workers are quite generally better educated than the unskilled, but they are not appreciably more liberal with regard to women.

Both rural strata show comparatively large percentages of persons who take a conservative stand on this issue. Since their women, because of the conditions of life that prevail on the farm, play such an active economic rôle *at home* this is not difficult to account for. Not all of the orientation on this issue can be seen as an obvious function of such economic factors, of course. One would certainly be hard put to attempt to find such an interpretation for the views

TABLE 1

ATTITUDES OF OCCUPATIONAL STRATA: THE ROLE OF WOMEN

Q. Do you think woman's place should be in the home, or do you think women should be free to take jobs outside the home if they want them?

	N	% In the home	% Outside	% Qualified	% Don't know	For In the home: Differences are significant between:
National	1,092	53.8	29.3	14.9	2.0	
Urban						
A. All Business, Professional and White Collar	427	44.3	37.9	16.6	1.2	A & B
B. All Manual Workers	412	59.0	24.0	15.5	1.5	B & A
1. Large Business	54	44.4	38.9	14.8	1.9	1 & 5, 6
2. Professional	72	37.5	51.4	11.8	0.0	2 & 5, 6
3. Small Business	131	40.5	43.5	15.3	0.7	3 & 5, 6
4. White Collar	170	50.0	27.6	20.6	1.8	4 & 5
5. Skilled Manual	161	61.5	21.7	16.1	0.7	5 & 1, 2, 3, 4
6. Semi-Skilled Manual	174	59.8	23.6	15.5	1.1	6 & 1, 2, 3
7. Unskilled Manual	77	51.9	29.9	14.3	3.9	
Rural						
C. Farm Owners and Managers	153	64.1	22.9	11.1	1.9	
D. Farm Tenants and Laborers	69	59.4	20.3	11.6	8.7	

of large business people. It is probable that much of the "in the home" sentiment represents a survival of tradition and little more. It is a tradition, however, that is far weaker than formerly supposed.

2. Religion

In order to gain some insight into people's attitudes with respect to religion we asked them, "Would you say that on the whole people take religion too seriously, or that they don't take it seriously enough?"

Over 75 per cent of the public in general thinks that people do not take religion seriously enough (Table 2). Only about 8 per cent say that people take religion too seriously. Within the urban population it appears to make little or no difference what one's occupational position is; the belief that people don't take religion seriously enough is everywhere much the same. Rural strata differ slightly more in comparison with urban persons than they do between themselves. Not a single farm tenant or laborer thinks that people take religion too

seriously, and 88 per cent of them believe that people don't take it seriously enough.

When one inquires, however, into the people's approval of religion as it might be manifested by affiliation to some church, a different picture is presented (Table 3). Occupational strata differ. Whereas nearly four-fifths of business, professional, and white collar people belong to a church, only about two-thirds of manual workers do. Further, a difference of over 17 per cent exists between the two rural strata in this respect. Church affiliation is greatest in the upper stratum there also.

3. Confidence in Technological Progress

When people are asked, "Do you think that all the modern scientific inventions of new machines and materials will result in a better standard of living for all of us, or do you think that these things have been overrated?," the attitude varies (Table 4). While approximately 78 per cent of business, professional, and white collar people think that new inventions of machines and materials

TABLE 2

ATTITUDES OF OCCUPATIONAL STRATA: RELIGION

	N	% Too seriously	% Not seriously enough	% Qualified	% Don't know
National	1,085	8.2	76.1	7.0	8.7
Urban					
A. All Business, Professional and White Collar	425	10.2	75.5	7.5	6.8
B. All Manual Workers	409	8.8	73.1	8.1	10.0
1. Large Business	53	3.8	79.2	5.7	11.3
2. Professional	72	15.3	75.0	6.9	2.8
3. Small Business	131	8.4	72.5	9.9	9.2
4. White Collar	169	11.2	76.7	6.5	5.4
5. Skilled	159	8.2	72.3	9.4	10.1
6. Semi-Skilled	174	8.0	75.4	8.0	8.6
7. Unskilled	76	11.8	69.7	5.3	13.2
Rural					
C. Farm Owners and Managers	151	4.0	82.1	6.6	7.3
D. Farm Tenants and Laborers	69	0.0	88.4	1.4	10.2

TABLE 3

RELIGIOUS AFFILIATIONS OF OCCUPATIONAL STRATA: CHURCH MEMBERSHIP

	N	% Protes- tant	% Catholic	% Jewish	% Total Church	% Non- Church	For total church: differences are signifi- cant between:
Urban							
A. All Business, Profes- sional and White Collar	428	58.2	15.9	4.4	78.5	21.5	A & B
B. All Manual Workers	413	40.7	23.7	1.7	66.1	33.9	B & A
1. Large Business	54	64.8	16.7	5.6	87.1	12.9	1 & 5, 6, 7
2. Professional	73	68.5	9.6	5.5	83.6	16.4	2 & 5, 6, 7
3. Small Business	130	56.9	15.4	6.2	78.5	21.5	3 & 6
4. White Collar	171	52.6	18.7	2.3	73.6	26.4	
5. Skilled	162	43.2	24.1	1.2	68.5	31.5	5 & 1, 2
6. Semi-Skilled	174	42.0	19.5	2.9	64.4	35.6	6 & 1, 2, 3
7. Unskilled	77	32.5	32.5	0.0	65.0	35.0	7 & 1, 2
Rural							
C. Farm Owners and Managers	152	65.2	7.2	0.0	72.4	27.6	C & D
D. Farm Tenants and Laborers	69	46.4	8.7	0.0	55.1	44.9	D & C

will be a good thing, only about 65 per cent of manual workers think so. The approval drops sharply as one reads down the occupational levels. Approximately 85 per cent of large business owners and managers say "better standard of living." Only 58 per cent of unskilled workers say so. A clue as to why is provided in the considerable percentage of this latter group who said that "machines create unemployment." None of the large business people replied in such vein. Since no such response was solicited and yet spontaneously appears in increasing quantity among the lower occupational groups, it may be that the feeling is considerably stronger than our data attest. Still, people in general apparently do not want to say that "these things have been overrated," and the doubtful responses that increase in the lower occupational groups suggest that, though fear is present, it is manifested in doubt rather than outright disapproval. In the rural population approval or confidence in technological progress is comparatively high and there is only a negligible difference between strata.

4. Why People Succeed

It is one of the oldest traditions of American culture that one who works hard and saves his money will surely succeed, or at least such is the sort of thing one hears from childhood up, with our legends of poor boys who rose to wealth and fame, our Lincolns, our Fords, our Rockefellers. There are signs, however, that such a faith is dying. Lynd, listing some of the "outstanding assumptions of American Life" says (in paraphrasing the average man):

Hard work and thrift are signs of character and the way to get ahead.
But: No shrewd person tries to get ahead nowadays by just working hard, and nobody gets rich nowadays by pinching nickels. It is important to know the right people (8, p. 61).

We asked our cross-section: "Do you think that most people who are successful are successful because of ability, luck, pull,

TABLE 4

ATTITUDE DIFFERENCES OF OCCUPATIONAL STRATA: CONFIDENCE IN
MODERN TECHNOLOGY

	N	Better standard of living %	Overrated %	Machines create unemployment %	Other answers %	Don't know %	For Better Standard of Living: Differences are significant between:
National	1,092	72.5	17.9	1.6	1.9	6.1	
Urban							
A. All Business, Professional and White Collar	429	78.1	15.9	1.2	2.3	2.5	A & B
B. All Manual Workers	410	64.9	19.8	2.9	1.7	10.7	B & A
1. Large Business	53	84.9	13.2	0.0	1.9	0.0	1 & 5, 6, 7
2. Professional	73	76.7	15.1	1.4	5.4	1.4	2 & 6, 7
3. Small Business	131	75.6	17.6	0.8	2.3	3.7	3 & 6, 7
4. White Collar	172	78.5	15.7	1.7	1.2	2.9	4 & 6, 7
5. Skilled	161	69.6	18.0	1.2	1.9	9.3	5 & 1
6. Semi-Skilled	172	63.4	20.9	2.9	2.3	10.5	6 & 1, 2, 3, 4
7. Unskilled	77	58.4	20.8	6.5	0.0	14.3	7 & 1, 2, 3, 4
Rural							
C. Farm Owners and Managers	153	73.9	20.3	0.0	1.3	4.5	
D. Farm Tenants and Laborers	69	78.3	16.0	0.0	1.4	4.3	

or the better opportunities they have had?"

Nearly half the people (45.1 per cent) said unqualifiedly "ability," and an additional 14 per cent said ability plus luck or pull or opportunity. But there are large differences between occupational strata in this belief that people succeed because of ability (Table 5).

Whereas 62 per cent of large business men said ability without qualification, only about 26 per cent of unskilled workers gave such an answer. From top occupational groups to bottom there are ever diminishing numbers who say either ability alone or ability plus, and more and more of those who say "luck" or "pull," "the better opportunities they have had," or who simply don't know. Apparently people at the top like to believe that it was their ability that got them there—as it might certainly have been—but

people who occupy the lower occupational ranks don't appear willing in very large numbers to concede that such was the case. Sixteen and nine-tenths per cent of unskilled workers say luck; another 15.6 per cent say pull. In contrast, not a single person in the large business category admits that either factor plays a rôle in success.

5. Why Some People Are Rich

We asked people again, "Why do you think some people have been able to get rich, because of ability, luck, pull, their better opportunities, or something else?"

Again people in general said, more than anything else, "ability," but this time there were more qualifications, and many more said "their better opportunities." They gave a host of other answers as well (Table 6).

The picture is not vastly different from

TABLE 5

ATTITUDES OF OCCUPATIONAL STRATA: WHY PEOPLE SUCCEED

	N	Ability %	Ability plus other factors %	Luck %	Pull %	Better opportunities %	Combination of luck, pull & opportunity %	Don't know %	For Ability Differences are significant between:
National	1,092	45.1	14.4	6.1	7.5	20.3	2.8	3.8	
Urban									
A. All Business, Professional and White Collar	426	52.1	19.2	2.6	6.2	16.4	2.1	1.4	A & B
B. All Manual Workers	413	35.8	12.2	9.4	11.9	21.0	4.1	5.6	B & A
1. Large Business	54	62.3	20.8	0.0	0.0	16.9	0.0	0.0	1 & 5, 6, 7
2. Professional	73	46.6	31.5	2.7	5.5	11.0	2.7	0.0	2 & 7
3. Small Business	129	51.9	20.2	3.1	6.2	14.7	1.6	2.3	3 & 6, 7
4. White Collar	171	51.5	12.9	2.9	8.2	19.9	2.9	1.7	4 & 6, 7
5. Skilled Manual	162	41.9	14.8	6.8	10.5	19.1	2.5	4.4	5 & 1, 7
6. Semi-Skilled Manual	174	34.5	10.9	8.6	11.5	23.6	5.7	5.2	6 & 1, 3, 4
7. Unskilled Manual	77	25.9	9.1	16.9	15.6	19.5	3.9	9.1	7 & 1, 2, 3, 4, 5
Rural									
C. Farm Owners and Managers	153	56.2	9.2	5.9	3.3	21.6	1.3	2.5	C & D
D. Farm Tenants and Laborers	69	31.9	8.7	11.6	2.9	36.2	1.4	7.3	D & C

TABLE 6

ATTITUDES OF OCCUPATIONAL STRATA: RATIONALE FOR THE RICH

Per cent saying:	National	All bus., prof.,& white collar	All manual workers	Large business	Profes- sional	Small business	White collar	Skilled	Semi- skilled	Un- skilled	Farm owners & mgrs.	Farm tenants & labor
Ability	41.2	49.6	33.3	61.1	54.8	48.1	44.8	42.3	31.0	19.5	46.4	26.1
Luck	29.9	27.4	34.8	14.8	32.9	30.5	26.7	34.4	32.2	41.6	25.5	31.9
Pull	17.2	15.3	19.6	7.4	17.8	13.7	18.0	17.8	22.9	15.6	20.3	11.6
Better Opportunities	36.6	41.6	35.7	40.5	46.6	38.9	41.9	36.2	33.9	38.9	26.1	31.9
Inheritance	6.3	5.3	7.2	3.7	8.2	3.0	6.4	9.2	6.9	3.9	5.9	8.7
Education	0.2	0.2	—	—	—	0.8	—	—	—	—	0.7	—
Hard work, diligence, aggressiveness, nerve	1.9	3.1	1.1	1.9	5.5	2.3	3.0	0.6	1.7	1.3	2.6	—
Thrift, good management	1.4	1.2	1.5	3.8	—	—	1.8	3.1	0.6	—	2.7	—
Cunning, shrewdness, etc.	1.2	1.4	1.2	1.9	0.8	0.8	2.4	1.2	0.6	2.6	0.7	1.4
Selfishness, greed, etc.	0.3	0.4	0.2	—	1.4	—	—	0.6	—	—	—	—
Speculation, War Profiteering, Destructive Competition, Exploiting Workers	1.3	1.6	1.2	—	1.4	0.8	3.0	1.2	1.2	—	1.3	—
Unscrupulousness, Graft, Dishonesty	4.6	3.5	5.1	1.9	2.7	2.3	5.2	4.9	6.9	2.6	5.9	4.3
No opinion	4.2	2.8	4.3	3.7	1.4	3.0	2.9	4.3	4.0	5.2	3.9	11.6
N*	1,097	430	414	54	73	131	172	163	174	77	153	69

* Figures add to more than 100 per cent. Many respondents gave more than one answer.

TABLE 7

ATTITUDES OF OCCUPATIONAL STRATA: RATIONALE FOR THE POOR

Per cent saying:	National	All bus., prof., & white collar	All manual workers	Large business	Professional	Small business	White collar	Skilled manual	Semi-skilled manual	Un-skilled manual	Farm owners & mgrs.	Farm tenants & labor
Poor management	26.4	23.3	22.7	31.5	20.4	21.4	23.3	26.4	21.3	18.2	41.2	42.0
Laziness	15.0	14.9	16.2	18.5	10.9	16.0	14.5	19.0	16.1	10.4	14.4	11.6
Lack of opportunity	13.4	11.9	15.9	9.3	16.4	12.2	10.5	13.5	16.7	19.5	6.5	20.3
Lack of ambition	13.2	17.9	9.4	18.5	24.7	16.0	16.3	11.7	7.5	9.1	11.8	10.1
Lack of ability	12.4	14.9	10.1	12.9	23.3	12.9	13.4	12.3	10.9	3.9	11.8	10.1
Lack of thrift	11.3	11.4	12.8	7.4	12.3	11.5	12.2	11.7	14.9	10.4	12.4	2.9
Bad luck	9.7	8.1	10.9	9.3	4.1	7.6	9.9	11.7	13.2	3.9	8.5	13.0
Lack of education	8.6	10.9	5.3	12.9	8.2	11.5	11.0	4.3	5.7	6.4	7.8	11.6
Ill health	5.1	4.0	6.8	11.1	2.7	3.1	2.9	6.1	6.9	7.8	3.9	4.3
Economic system, Exploitation, Unemployment	4.3	3.7	5.5	—	5.5	0.8	6.4	4.3	6.3	6.4	2.0	1.4
Lack of initiative	3.8	5.6	3.1	3.7	9.6	5.4	4.7	4.3	2.3	2.6	2.0	—
Lack of planning	3.1	3.7	3.1	7.4	5.5	1.5	3.5	3.1	4.0	1.3	3.3	—
"They don't take advantage of their opportunities"	2.6	3.7	2.4	1.9	—	3.8	5.8	4.3	1.2	1.3	0.7	1.4
Lack of intelligence	2.5	3.0	2.7	5.6	1.4	0.8	4.7	4.3	—	5.2	1.3	—
Lack of judgment	2.5	3.0	2.7	1.9	4.1	3.8	2.3	2.5	2.9	2.6	1.3	—
Poor character*	2.1	2.1	2.7	1.9	4.1	—	2.9	3.1	1.7	3.9	0.7	2.9
Drink	1.9	0.9	3.1	—	1.4	0.8	1.2	2.5	2.3	6.4	2.0	—
Natural orders of things, destiny, fate, etc.**	1.6	1.6	1.4	—	1.4	0.8	2.9	1.2	1.7	1.3	2.6	1.4
Poor wages, wrong job	1.5	0.7	3.1	—	—	0.8	1.2	1.8	3.4	5.2	—	—
Too many children	1.2	.2	2.2	—	—	—	0.6	2.5	2.9	—	0.7	1.4
Fear, inferiority complex, too cautious	.9	1.2	1.0	1.9	—	2.3	0.6	0.6	1.7	—	—	—
Lack of pull	.7	1.2	0.7	—	—	2.3	0.6	0.6	0.6	1.3	0.7	1.4
Demoralized by charity	.4	0.2	0.2	—	—	0.8	—	—	0.6	—	0.7	—
No opinion	4.6	2.8	6.5	1.9	5.4	1.4	1.7	6.7	4.6	10.4	9.2	8.7
N†	1,097	430	414	54	73	131	172	163	174	77	153	69

† Figures add to more than 100 per cent. Many respondents gave two or more answers.

* Includes three people who said "sin."

** Including "The poor ye have with ye always."

that for the previous question. There is again less emphasis on ability and more on luck and pull with lower occupational ranks. Approximately 40 per cent of the unskilled believed that people get rich because of luck (among other things of course, since people named more than one reason in the main), and nearly another 40 per cent believed that the better opportunities the rich had had (among other things) was an important cause. Only minorities in each occupational category thought that unscrupulous practices or dishonesty was a factor. The semi-skilled, with approximately 7 per cent, are the most outstanding in this emphasis.

6. Why People Are Poor

When persons are asked why some of the people are always poor, the most frequent reply is that it is because of their poor management (Table 7). Moreover it makes no great difference what the respondent's occupational position is in this. Nearly every stratum gives poor management as its most characteristic response. It is an especially popular view among the rural population. Only professional people give responses that outnumber it. One quarter of these say it is because "they lack ambition," almost another quarter say "they lack ability." Laziness, lack of opportunity, lack of ambition, lack of ability, lack of thrift, bad luck, lack of education, and ill health are the next most popular reasons for poverty after "poor management." Those responses such as "lack of opportunity," "lack of education," "poor wages," "economic system," "exploitation," and "unemployment" that might be interpreted as indictments of the existing order of things, while not numerically negligible, are in the minority with every group.

People seem to believe that poverty is something that one brings on oneself more often than not. Surprising numbers give such replies as "poor character" and "drink." *Three people said, "sin"!*

7. Opportunity to Rise

It has long been believed by social theorists that one of the most potent factors

productive of inter-stratum harmony and operating against the formation of stratum and class solidarity of interest and action was the existence of considerable opportunities for vertical social mobility. Why should people, after all, form antagonisms to the social and economic system in which they live if they believe that the system permits them to rise in the social scale, and even to join the ranks of the dominant class? Certainly one might at least suppose that such a factor would operate to retard ideological cleavages in the population. Does such a poor-boy-to-president mentality exist?

As can be seen from inspection of Table 8, everywhere, in all strata, belief is strong to the effect that one's children have as good a chance or a better chance to rise in the world as anybody else's. Still there are differences. Decreasing numbers in the lower occupational brackets hold to this belief in opportunity for their children, and whereas 100 per cent of large business and professional people state "as good" or "better," only 79 per cent of unskilled workers think their children have "as good" or "better" opportunities. A difference exists also between the two rural levels. More farm tenants and laborers than any other group think that their children have poorer chances.

It is pertinent to inquire here whether such widespread convictions that one's children can get ahead have any foundation in fact. A glance at Table 9 will assure one that it has, for considerable proportions of urban people[2] have a higher occupational ranking than their fathers. Such upward mobility is balanced, however, by considerable downward movement, for many urban people of urban origin have occupational positions lower than those of their fathers.

Such generalizations are drawn, of course, in consideration of the data in terms of mobility as manifested by *any* improvement

[2] Farmers are not included in these comparisons because data as to whether their fathers were owners, managers, tenants, laborers, etc., was not obtained, and thus it could not be ascertained whether persons of rural origin manifested "vertical" or merely "horizontal" mobility.

TABLE 8

ATTITUDES OF OCCUPATIONAL STRATA: OPPORTUNITIES FOR CHILDREN

Q. Would you say that your children had just as good a chance, a poorer, or a better chance to rise in the world as anybody else's?

	N	% As good or better	% Poorer	% Don't know	For As good or better Differences are significant between:
National	1,027	89	7	4	
Urban					
A. All Business, Professional & White Collar	411	95	3	2	A & B
B. All Manual Workers	392	83	11	6	B & A
1. Large Business	53	100	0	0	1 & 5, 6, 7
2. Professional	73	100	0	0	2 & 5, 6, 7
3. Small Business	124	96	3	1	3 & 5, 6, 7
4. White Collar	161	89	5	6	
5. Skilled	156	84	10	6	5 & 1, 2, 3
6. Semi-skilled	164	84	12	4	6 & 1, 2, 3
7. Unskilled	72	79	10	11	7 & 1, 2, 3
Rural					
C. Farm owners and Managers	137	91	7	2	
D. Farm Tenants and Laborers	59	81	14	5	

or worsening of the subject's position with respect to that of his father, without reference to *how far* up the individual has come. While the tendency is for persons in given occupations to have come from parents in the same or adjacent occupational strata, it is obvious that many persons have moved several rungs up or down the ladder. Comparatively large numbers in the business, professional, and white collar groups have been drawn from parents whose occupation was manual (most often skilled labor). Considered as a whole, almost one-third of business, professional, and white collar people came from parents whose occupation was manual. In contrast only 17 per cent

TABLE 9

OCCUPATIONAL MOBILITY: ORIGINS OF URBAN OCCUPATIONAL STRATA OF URBAN PARENTAGE IN TERMS OF THE OCCUPATIONS OF THEIR FATHERS

	N	% from large business	% from professional	% from small business	% from white collar	% from skilled manual	% from semi-skilled manual	% from un-skilled manual
All Urban	605	3	6	23	12	30	20	6
A. All Business, Professional and White Collar	319	5	9	35	18	23	8	2
B. All Manual workers	286	—	3	9	5	38	34	11
1. Large Business	46	17	13	30	13	24	3	—
2. Professional	57	5	23	28	12	22	5	5
3. Small Business	86	1	9	53	9	17	9	2
4. White Collar	130	3	3	37	27	26	11	3
5. Skilled Manual	116	—	4	10	5	50	24	7
6. Semi-Skilled	122	—	2	11	4	31	45	7
7. Unskilled	48	—	2	2	8	29	28	31

of persons who are now manual workers came from parents who were in the higher stratum (i.e., Business, Professional, and White Collar).

On the whole it would appear that people do have some grounds for their belief in the opportunity to rise, for in their own experience it has been done.

8. Sympathies and Antipathies

How do people in various positions in the social and economic structure feel about others in that structure? What do they think about their rewards and privations, privileges and disfranchisements? In an attempt to gain some insight into such feelings we asked people some questions relating to them.

A. WHO GETS TOO MUCH PAY? Several prior studies have illuminated to some extent the envies people have and the invidious comparisons people make among themselves. Warner and Lunt (12), Davis and the Gardners (2), and others have touched upon the problem in a descriptive way. Kornhauser studied the situation in a more quantitative way in his 1937 Chicago Attitude Survey (6). In order to bring to light the situation prevailing at the time of our survey, we asked people, after handing them a card on which were listed the 11 occupational categories shown below, "Are there any on that list that you think get too much pay?"

A. Big business owners and executives.
B. Small business owners and operators.
C. Factory workers.
D. Office workers.
E. Doctors and lawyers.
F. Servants.
G. Farmers.
H. Laborers such as miners, truck drivers, and shopworkers.
I. Store and factory managers.
J. Waiters and bartenders.
K. Salesmen.

Approximately 60 per cent of the people think that big business owners and executives are overpaid. Nearly 35 per cent think that doctors and lawyers get more than they should. Relatively few of the people considered as a whole think that any other groups get too much pay. Nineteen per cent think that no one is paid too much (Table 10). Although there are differences among occupational strata, they are for the most part fairly small. They show up best in the detailed list of urban occupational groups. It is notable that more professional people than any other occupational group think that big businessmen are overpaid. When it is remembered that big and large business people are about their only social and economic superiors, and that they are, in a sense, rivals of this group for social prestige and esteem, the figure obtained here becomes understandable as a symptom of the sort of envy they must feel with respect to the superior rewards and remunerations of this group. The nearly 22 per cent of professionals who think that doctors and lawyers are overpaid probably reflects the sentiment of persons in professions other than these, who themselves get less.

The attitudes of the "large business" group also deserve comment. Nearly 41 per cent of them think that big business owners and executives get too much pay. They themselves have large incomes in the main, but the economic status of people classified as large business here is not uniformly the highest. Thirty per cent of them were rated by our interviewers as only "average," though the other 70 per cent were rated either "wealthy" or "average plus." Many of them obviously have very good reason to envy persons with better incomes than their own, and they very probably don't have persons just like themselves in mind when they say big business owners and executives get too much.

The rather general feeling that doctors and lawyers are overpaid is surprisingly consistent from one occupational stratum to another. Numbers of every occupational group, second only to those who think big businessmen get too much, believe doctors and lawyers are over-rewarded. The figure increases rather consistently from the top to the bottom of the occupational scale. Nearly 47 per cent of unskilled workers

TABLE 10

ATTITUDES OF OCCUPATIONAL STRATA: WHO GETS TOO MUCH PAY?

	N*	Big business owners & exec. %	Doctors & lawyers %	Small business owners & operators %	Store & factory mgrs. %	Salesmen %	Office workers %	Farmers %	Factory workers %	Laborers, etc. %	Waiters & bartenders %	Servants %	None %	No opinion %
National	1,097	60.3	34.8	3.3	4.6	2.6	2.1	1.0	4.2	1.4	1.5	2.1	19.0	8.5
Urban														
A. All Business, Professional & White Collar	430	61.2	25.1	2.3	1.4	2.1	0.9	0.7	4.7	2.3	1.9	2.8	24.4	4.7
B. All Manual Workers	414	58.9	43.2	4.4	8.0	3.1	2.7	1.9	1.9	0.5	1.2	1.7	16.7	10.6
1. Large Business	54	40.7	16.7	5.6	—	2.7	—		9.3		1.9	1.9	40.7	3.7
2. Professional	73	67.1	21.9	2.7				1.4	4.1	5.5	4.1	5.5	20.5	2.7
3. Small Business	131	61.1	30.5	0.8	0.8	1.5		0.8	4.6	1.5	2.3	3.1	25.2	3.1
4. White Collar	172	65.1	25.0	2.3	2.9	2.9	2.3	0.6	3.5	2.3	0.6	1.7	20.3	6.9
5. Skilled Manual	163	55.2	40.5	3.7	6.7	1.8	1.2	1.2	1.8	0.6		2.5	19.6	9.8
6. Semi-Skilled	174	61.5	44.3	5.2	7.5	3.4	2.9	2.9	2.9	0.6	1.7	1.7	14.9	9.8
7. Unskilled	77	61.0	46.8	3.9	11.7	5.2	5.2	1.3		0.6	2.6		14.3	14.3
Rural														
C. Farm Owners & Managers	153	58.2	39.2	3.3	3.9	2.6	1.3	——	7.2	2.0	1.3	2.0	15.0	11.8
D. Farm Tenants & Laborers	69	62.3	37.7	2.9	2.9	2.9	5.6	——	8.7		2.9	1.4	14.5	11.6

* Figures add to more than 100 per cent. The question was designed to obtain more than one name as a response.

think doctors and lawyers get too much pay.

b. WHO DOESN'T GET ENOUGH? It doesn't follow necessarily, of course, that people who don't get too much therefore are believed to get too little. We asked people again, "Are there any of those who don't get enough pay?" (Table 11).

Only one person in nearly 1,100 thinks that big business owners and executives don't get enough pay. Nor do very large numbers think that doctors and lawyers, small business owners and operators, store and factory managers and salesmen are underpaid. In terms of the opinions of the general public, it is most commonly farmers, office workers, laborers, servants, factory workers, waiters and bartenders, in sum, the dependent employed, producing and serving population, that is thought to be insufficiently rewarded. The people who think so are most often those who occupy these or similar positions themselves, as might be expected. While considerable proportions of business and professional people manifest some sympathy towards these lower groups, such sympathy is only to a minor extent reciprocated, for relatively few in these white collar, farming, and manual strata think that people in the top three (i.e., the business and professional groups) are underpaid. Indeed, the latter don't appear in any great numbers to think so themselves.

Another tendency that is sufficiently clear to deserve comment is that for persons in a given occupational stratum to say, more than persons in other strata do, that it is their own or a similar occupational stratum that is underpaid. It is, of course, more or less what might be expected.

9. Racial and Ethnic Prejudices

It has been supposed, by some writers, that race prejudice had economic bases. Klineberg says:

Prejudice exists because there is something to be gained by it. This gain is usually directly economic, in that it eliminates the competition of members of the minority group and makes it easier for those of the dominant group to obtain jobs or advancement. It may also serve as an instrument in the hands of those in authority to persuade the people that a minority group is responsible for all their misfortunes. It may similarly be the means of restoring feelings of security and self-confidence to those who have suffered defeat and failure, by providing a group to whom they may feel superior and of whom they may take advantage with impunity (7, 395 ff.).

Now if such were the actual bases of prejudice, one might expect to find considerably more expression of anti-Negro prejudice among the lower occupational strata of society, who are more in direct competition with Negroes than are the upper strata, and who conceivably have more economic misfortunes (e.g., they suffer more from unemployment than upper strata), and who occupy inferior positions, have suffered defeat and failure most often, and thus are in greater need of a scapegoat.

However, if this hypothesis concerning the bases of prejudice were valid with respect to the Jew, one might expect not only the representatives of lower level occupations to be strongly prejudiced, but also those in the business and professional strata, for they, though suffering less economic hardships, and less in need of a scapegoat for wounded egos (for they are, after all, fairly *successful* strata), are more in direct economic competition with Jews than any other. The Klinebergian hypothesis thus leads to no real prediction as to what sort of differences in anti-Jewish prejudice one might expect between strata, since all would be expected to be prejudiced for some reason or other. There might be differences and there might not; one can only look and see.

In an attempt to measure anti-Negro prejudice a multiple choice question containing four alternatives was employed. Our respondents were handed a card with the alternatives arranged as shown below.

Now I'd like you to pick out from the statements on this card the one that best describes the way you feel about Negroes.
A. I believe Negroes should have more opportunities than they do now.
B. Because Negroes are so different from white people as a race, I believe they should

TABLE 11

ATTITUDES OF OCCUPATIONAL STRATA: WHO DOESN'T GET ENOUGH PAY?

	N*	Big business owners & exec. %	Doctors & lawyers %	Small business owners & operators %	Store & factory mgrs. %	Salesmen %	Office workers %	Farmers %	Factory workers %	Laborers, etc. %	Waiters & bartenders %	Servants %	None %	No opinion %
National	1.097	0.1	1.3	8.7	4.3	5.8	32.2	36.8	22.1	28.6	13.7	26.9	11.5	8.9
Urban														
A. All Business, Professional and White Collar	430	0.2	2.3	10.5	5.3	7.0	42.1	28.8	16.5	24.4	12.3	25.1	13.7	6.0
B. All Manual Workers	414	—	1.0	7.0	4.6	7.0	30.2	37.2	35.3	40.1	18.1	31.9	7.0	10.1
1. Large Business	54	—	3.7	7.4	3.7	1.9	33.3	24.1	9.3	16.7	11.1	14.8	27.8	5.6
2. Professional	73	1.4	4.1	6.9	2.7	5.5	57.5	30.1	23.3	30.1	16.4	38.4	4.1	5.5
3. Small Business	131	—	1.5	12.9	6.9	64.6	32.8	26.7	10.9	16.8	10.9	18.3	19.1	8.4
4. White Collar	172	—	1.7	11.0	5.8	11.0	45.3	31.4	20.3	30.2	12.2	27.9	9.3	4.7
5. Skilled Manual	163	—	1.2	10.4	4.9	6.1	31.9	33.1	29.4	36.8	16.6	25.2	10.4	12.3
6. Semi-Skilled	174	—	—	5.2	4.6	6.9	28.2	43.1	39.7	39.7	18.4	35.1	4.6	6.3
7. Unskilled	77	—	2.6	3.9	3.9	9.1	31.2	32.5	37.7	48.1	20.8	38.9	5.2	14.3
Rural														
C. Farm Owners & Mgrs.	153	—	—	9.2	3.3	7.2	20.3	52.3	7.8	11.8	17.0	21.6	2.6	10.5
D. Farm Tenants & Laborers	69	—	—	8.7	—	7.2	5.8	49.3	5.8	14.5	17.4	20.3	—	18.8

* Figures add to more than 100 per cent. The question was designed to obtain more than one name as a response.

not be allowed to mix with whites in any way.

C. Although Negroes should not be mistreated by whites, the white race should always keep its superior position.

D. I believe Negroes should have the same privileges and opportunities as white people.

Results are summarized in Table 12. Most people, it is clear, are prejudiced against Negroes. Only modest support exists for an economic interpretation of prejudice, however, for, though those occupational groups that are in most direct competition with Negroes are somewhat more prejudiced, the differences are much smaller than those to be anticipated in terms of the Klinebergian hypothesis. It may well account for some prejudice, but surely the large numbers of prejudiced persons in the large business stratum have little to fear in the way of competition from Negroes. Nor would it seem reasonable to suppose that they have any truly great need of a scapegoat. Obviously other factors must be searched for.

It is notable in Table 12 that professional persons are the least prejudiced of all the groups listed. True, they are not in economic competition with Negroes, but neither, it was noted, are large business people, and the latter are distinctly more prejudiced. Since it is known that large business people have an even higher economic status than professional persons in general, one must look elsewhere for a difference in situation or experience that would account for the difference in attitude. A scrutiny of Table 13, where the educational achievements of the respective occupational strata are shown, provides the suggestion that a difference in education may be the significant factor, for our least prejudiced category, professional persons, are distinctly the best educated. As a glance at Table 14 will prove, prejudice and education are inversely related—the more education the less prejudice, so an educational interpretation of racial antipathy has point. Obviously, however, lack of education cannot, any more than economic conflict, be the sole interpretation of prejudice, for a majority even of college educated persons display an unfavorable attitude. It would be enlightening, perhaps, to compare persons of different educational backgrounds *within* each occupational category, since this might prove one or another of the two factors to be more important, but our sample of each occupational grouping is much too small to make this additional breakdown. At present, the expectation would be that both would be important variables, but that even both in combination would not completely account for the prejudice shown.

When we examine the data with respect to anti-Jewish feeling it becomes apparent that there is prejudice all up and down the occupational scale (Table 15). A statistically reliable difference exists between the two major urban groups, but the percentage of "don't know" responses is so large as to make interpretation of the difference of dubious value. Again, as in the case of anti-Negro attitudes it is the professional group that shows the least prejudice. And, again, the suspicion arises that the difference may be an educational one. As before, we are confronted with technical difficulties that prevent the determination of whether or not this is really the case. The large percentages of "don't know" on this question may mean that people are prejudiced and don't want to say so, but it would be unwise to assume that such is the case, and conclusions other than to the effect that nearly every occupational stratum shows extensive prejudice are hazardous.

E. SUMMARY

The aim of the present study was stated as an exploration of the attitude differences of occupational strata with respect to certain cultural norms, fundamental rationalizations, and stereotyped beliefs commonly supposed to be held rather uniformly throughout the American population. As a result of standardized interviews with persons representing a cross-section of the adult white male population the following facts were disclosed.

1. Somewhat over half of American

TABLE 12
ATTITUDES OF OCCUPATIONAL STRATA: ANTI-NEGRO PREJUDICE

	N	% Same opportunity (D)	% More opportunity than now (A)	% White supremacy (C)	% Strict segregation (B)	% Don't know	% for B & C combined	For B and C Combined differences are significant between:
National	1,065	18.2	14.3	44.8	20.6	2.1	65.4	
Urban								
A. All Business, Professional & White Collar	427	21.3	17.6	45.7	13.6	1.8	59.3	A & B
B. All Manual	408	16.9	13.0	40.9	27.0	2.2	67.9	B & A
1. Large Business	52	26.9	7.7	51.9	11.5	2.0	63.4	1 & 2
2. Professional	73	32.9	23.3	39.7	2.7	1.4	42.4	2 & 1, 3, 4, 5, 6, 7
3. Small Business	131	18.3	19.1	41.2	19.1	2.3	60.3	3 & 2
4. White Collar	171	16.9	16.9	49.7	14.6	1.9	64.3	4 & 2
5. Skilled Manual	160	17.5	14.4	43.1	21.9	3.1	65.0	5 & 2
6. Semi-Skilled Manual	173	17.3	10.4	40.5	30.6	1.2	71.1	6 & 2
7. Unskilled Manual	75	14.7	16.0	37.3	29.3	2.7	66.6	7 & 2
Rural								
C. Farm Owners & Managers	150	16.7	7.3	56.0	18.7	1.3	74.7	
D. Farm Tenants & Laborers	67	7.5	14.9	43.3	29.9	4.4	73.2	

TABLE 13

EDUCATIONAL LEVELS OF OCCUPATIONAL STRATA

	N	%† College	%‡ High School	%* Grade School
Urban				
A. All Business, Professional and White Collar	428	47	40	13
B. All Manual Workers	410	5	41	54
1. Large Business	54	57	32	11
2. Professional	72	100	—	—
3. Small Business	131	30	49	21
4. White Collar	171	36	51	13
5. Skilled Manual	161	11	48	41
6. Semi-Skilled	173	1	41	58
7. Unskilled	76	—	28	72
C. Farm Owners & Managers	153	20	47	33
D. Farm Tenants & Laborers	69	6	29	65

† Includes both graduates and non-graduates.
‡ Includes both graduates and non-graduates.
* Eighth grade or less.

TABLE 14

EDUCATIONAL LEVEL AND ANTI-NEGRO PREJUDICE

Educational level	N	Percentage who answer Favorable*	Un- favorable	No opinion	For Favorable differences are signifi- cant between:
1. College	258	44	55	1	1 & 2, 3
2. High School	448	32	66	2	2 & 1, 3
3. Grade School	373	25	71	4	3 & 1, 2

* Favorable statements are *A* and *D* and unfavorable statements are *B* and *C* on pages 145, 147.

men believe that woman's place is in the home, but considerable differences exist between occupational strata. The higher occupational groups manifest a definitely more liberal attitude toward women than lower occupational groups. The latter appear to fear the competition of women for jobs.

2. There is little difference shown in the attitudes of occupational strata with respect to the support of religion as indicated by a question of opinion. Majorities of all groups say that people in general do not take religion seriously enough. But support of religious institutions as indicated by frequency of actual church membership is quite defi-

nitely greater among the upper occupational groups as compared to the lower.

3. Confidence in modern machine and material technology is characteristically more common among the upper occupational groups. Manual workers are frequently doubtful as to the benefits of machines and often express fear of them by such remarks as "machines create unemployment." It is notable that unskilled workers give such a response more frequently than any other group.

4. People in higher occupational groups express the view that success and the accumulation of wealth are due to the ability

TABLE 15

ATTITUDES OF OCCUPATIONAL STRATA: ANTI-JEWISH PREJUDICE

Q. Do you think the Jews have too much power and influence in this country?

	N†	% Yes	% No	% Don't know	For No differ- ences are signifi- cant between:
National	1,054	67	23	10	
Urban					
A. All Business, Professional and White Collar	407	64	31	5	A & B*
B. All Manual	404	69	19	12	B & A*
1. Large Business	51	63	29	8	
2. Professional	68	53	41	6	2 & 5, 6, 7
3. Small Business	121	68	29	3	
4. White Collar	167	65	29	6	4 & 5, 6
5. Skilled Manual	157	70	18	12	5 & 2, 4
6. Semi-Skilled	170	72	18	10	6 & 2, 4
7. Unskilled	77	60	22	18	7 & 2
Rural					
C. Farm Owners and Managers	149	72	14	14	
D. Farm Tenants and Laborers	66	68	18	14	

† Excludes all persons who said they were of Jewish religion.
* The difference on Don't Know is also statistically significant.

of individuals much more frequently than do persons of lower occupational status. Large proportions of the latter reply that luck, pull, and superior opportunities are the factors involved.

5. There are no important differences among occupational strata with respect to the rationale for poverty in America. Persons of all strata appear to believe that being poor is the fault of the individual.

6. Small but statistically significant differences exist among occupational groups with regard to belief in the opportunities for their children to rise in the world. The upper two occupational groups are unanimously of the belief that their children's opportunities are as good as or better than those of others. The lower occupational groups express this belief much less frequently.

7. Lower occupational strata differ from higher groups in their beliefs about the pay of certain higher groups, namely doctors and lawyers. More of the former believe doctors and lawyers to be overpaid than do persons in higher occupational categories.

8. Differences of view with respect to what occupational groups are underpaid are small, but there is a clearly apparent tendency for persons of a given occupational stratum to say, more frequently than persons of other strata do, that it is their own or a similar occupational stratum that is underpaid.

9. There are small but statistically significant differences among occupational strata as concerns anti-Negro prejudice. The lowest occupational categories, more frequently than the higher, express views unfavorable to this group.

10. There are rather small but statistically significant differences among occupational levels in the frequency of expression of anti-Jewish prejudice. The differences are so large as regards the frequency of "don't know" replies, however, as to render any

conclusion on this question unwise. It *is* true beyond question that every occupational stratum contains a large number of persons who are prejudiced against the Jews.

11. Our findings with regard to prejudice tend only in a general way to agree with the theories of Otto Klineberg, which account for prejudice on the supposition that there is something, usually economic, to be gained by it, or hold that it is due to the need for a scapegoat on the part of persons who are economically disadvantaged. Caution is advised with respect to this interpretation because of the large differences in prejudice that are found between groups of persons of different educational levels, and which make it appear that prejudice is to a considerable extent a function of lack of education.

REFERENCES

1. CENTERS, R., & CANTRIL, H.   Income satisfaction and income aspiration. *J. Abn. & Soc. Psychol.*, 1946, 41, 64-69.
2. DAVIS, A., GARDNER, B. B., & GARDNER, M. R. *Deep South.* Chicago: Univ. Chicago Press, 1941.
3. DOLLARD, J.   Caste and Class in a Southern Town. New Haven: Yale Univ. Press, 1937.
4. FORM, W. H.   Toward an occupational social psychology. *J. Soc. Psychol.*, 1946, 24, 85-99.
5. HINSHAW, R. P.   The relationship of information and opinion to age. Unpublished Ph.D. thesis, Princeton University, 1944.
6. KORNHAUSER, A. W.   Analysis of "class" structure in contemporary American society —psychological bases of class divisions. Chap. 11 in *Industrial Conflict: A Psychological Interpretation.* (Ed. by G. W. Hartmann and T. Newcomb.) New York: Cordon, 1939.
7. KLINEBERG, O.   Social Psychology. New York: Holt, 1940.
8. LYND, R. S.   Knowledge for What? Princeton: Princeton Univ. Press, 1939.
9. LYND, R. S., & LYND, H. M.   Middletown. New York: Harcourt Brace, 1929.
10. ———.   Middletown in Transition. New York: Harcourt Brace, 1937.
11. PEAR, T. H.   Psychological aspects of English social stratification. *Bull. John Rylands Lib.*, 1942, 26, 1-27.
12. WARNER, W. L., & LUNT, P. S.   The Social Life of a Modern Community. New Haven: Yale Univ. Press, 1941.

RELIGIOUS AFFILIATION AND POLITICO-ECONOMIC ATTITUDE:
A STUDY OF EIGHT MAJOR U.S. RELIGIOUS GROUPS

WESLEY AND BEVERLY ALLINSMITH

Survey data provide the immediately interesting possibility of studying politico-economic differences among religious groups in this country. They also provide more permanently important possibilities of discovering determinants of such differences and

From the *Public Opinion Quarterly*, 1948, 12, 377-389. Reprinted by permission of the authors and the publisher.

thus of predicting such differences in the future. This article will both indicate politico-economic differences among religious groups and present evidence on the question: Is the chief determinant of these differences religious affiliation . . . or is it something else?[1]

In order to segregate politico-economic information according to religious affiliation, breakdowns were made of six post-war ballots, each comprising an American Institute of Public Opinion national cross-section of about 3000 cases.[2] These six ballots were selected because religious denomination of respondents had been recorded as background information, and because there was some duplication of opinion questions. Respondents were divided into 17 religious denominational categories, and these groups were broken on a variety of items, among them educational, economic, and occupational status, union membership, geographical distribution, vote in the 1944 national election, and questions measuring opinion. Findings from ballot to ballot were consistent, and so it was possible to combine ballots in certain cases to increase the N's of the various denominational samples.

Only the more pertinent of the breakdowns made for this project can be reported here, and the discussion will be restricted to the eight major denominational categories of the 17 actually studied.[3]

In the summer of 1945, Richard Centers

accomplished a public attitude survey designed to study the socio- and politico-economic orientations, and the subjective class identifications, of occupational and other strata within the United States.[4] Dr. Centers found his data to support an "economic interest group" theory of class structure. The results of the present study can be interpreted as a test of the following hypotheses inferred from Centers' findings, namely that the politico-economic orientation of a religious group can be predicted from the group's occupational status (or from parallel information); and that politico-economic differences *within* a group are again a function of occupational status.

With a qualification, these hypotheses are borne out.

The qualification concerns one group for which these principles do not appear to hold. This group is the Jewish group, comprising about 4 per cent of the U.S. population.

RELIGIOUS GROUPS CLASSIFIED BY POLITICO-ECONOMIC ATTITUDE

In Centers' study, the following question was asked:

Which of these statements do you most agree with?
1. The most important job for the government is to make it certain that there are good opportunities for each person to get ahead on his own.
2. The most important job for the government is to guarantee every person a decent and steady job and standard of living.

Centers found this question in general to differentiate urban manual workers from business, professional, and white collar workers. He also found the question to differentiate Roosevelt supporters from Dewey supporters in the 1944 election; and to differentiate people who consider themselves of the working class from people who think of themselves as middle class. Responses to this question correlated .68 (tetra-

---

[1] This research was carried out in the Office of Public Opinion Research, Princeton University, and was sponsored by the Federal Council of the Churches of Christ in America. The authors are greatly indebted to Dr. Hadley Cantril, Director of OPOR, and to his staff, for generous help, and for making available the material from which this report was derived and the facilities for the work it entailed.

[2] Four of these ballots, dated November 1945, December 1945, March 1946, and June 1946, represent "voting" samples of the nation. The remaining two ballots, dated June 1946 and August 1946, represent "social" samples. The chief difference between these samples is that Southern Negroes are included in the latter.

[3] For a report of additional data (on all 17 denominations) see the May 15, 1948 issue of *Information Service*, a weekly publication of the Department of Research and Education of

the Federal Council of the Churches of Christ in America (297 Fourth Avenue, New York 10, N.Y.).

[4] Cf. Centers, R., *The Psychology of Social Classes*, Princeton University Press, 1949.

choric *r*) with viewpoint toward nationalization of industry.

In our study this same question was asked. For convenience we shall refer to a person who prefers to be "on his own" as favoring "individualism" and to a respondent taking the second view as favoring "guaranteed economic security."

How do we find that religious groups stand on this issue of individualism versus security?

They stand according to the proportion of the group which is made up of urban manual workers. (See Table 1.) Urban manual workers are composed of skilled, semi-skilled, and unskilled workers, and of service workers such as firemen, barbers, and domestic servants. They are thus to be distinguished from business, professional, and white collar groups, and from farmers.[5]

The Christian groups on this Table show a perfect rank order correlation between occupational status and opinion. The Jewish group, on the other hand, while nearly *the highest* in its stand for guaranteed economic security, is *the lowest* group in per cent of urban manual workers.

The Jewish respondents are like Presbyterians and Congregationalists in per cent of urban manual workers, yet they resemble Baptists and Catholics in their view on guaranteed economic security.

WHAT ABOUT EPISCOPALIANS WHO ARE URBAN WORKERS?

We have thus shown, for the major Christian groups, a one-to-one correspondence between an indicator of politico-economic orientation (i.e., view on guaranteed economic security) and an indicator of socio-economic status (i.e., per cent of urban manual workers).

But of course a correlation between two variables is not necessarily evidence of a

[5] In determining occupational status, the respondent's occupation, if he is a student or housewife, is taken as that of the person who provides his livelihood. If the respondent is retired, or is unemployed, his former occupation is recorded.

TABLE 1

Denominational Groups	Number on which per cent to right is based	Per cent urban manual workers in denomination	Per cent of denomination for guaranteed economic security per cent to left	Number on which is based
National	11,671	44	44	5,932
Catholic	2,332	55	58	1,084
Baptist	1,344	51	51	964
Lutheran	720	43	40	362
Methodist	2,053	39	38	1,141
Episcopalian	571	36	33	248
Presbyterian	923	31	31	418
Congregational	362	28	26	155
Jewish	515	27	56	197

causal relationship between them. Many people might still be tempted to say that the fact that Episcopalians, for instance, when taken as a group, are heavily for individualism is related to the fact that they are Episcopalian in religion.

Our hypothesis on the other hand is that Episcopalians, taken as a group, favor individualism not because they are Episcopalian, but because such a small proportion of Episcopalians are urban manual workers. If this hypothesis is correct, if religion is not the major determinant, then Episcopalians will not tend all to think alike on this issue. Rather, Episcopalians will vary in their viewpoints in accordance with their variation in socio-economic status.

Do contrasting occupational groups within the Episcopalians stand as we should expect? How do Episcopalian urban manual workers compare with Episcopalian business, professional, and white collar workers on individualism versus security?[6] Here we

[6] Farmers are not included in this graph because, in the coding for the ballots broken in this study, farm owners and managers were lumped with farm tenants and laborers with the result that the farmer data are ambiguous. Cf. Centers (reference in footnote 4) for a demonstration of politico-economic differences between the two farm strata.

Congregationalists are not represented in this graph because there were too few of them in the sample to give significant results on this breakdown.

see that only 39 per cent of Episcopalian urban manual (skilled, semi-skilled, unskilled, and service) workers prefer individualism, compared with 69 per cent of Episcopalian white collar workers and 81 per cent of Episcopalian business and professional workers. The same trend is evident for the other Protestant groups, and for the Catholics.

One finds, then (the Jewish group again being exceptional), that business, professional, and white collar workers are more for individualism, *regardless of denomination,* and that manual workers, *regardless of denomination,* are more for security.

Here is a clear demonstration that economic role rather than religious affiliation is the important determinant of this politico-economic opinion. It is not a case of all Episcopalians thinking one way and all Baptists another. Business and professional Baptists tend to think like business and professional Episcopalians, and so on, differences *within* a denomination being a function of occupational differences. The fact that one denomination taken as a group differs from another in politico-economic orientation is not due to religious differences but to differences *between* the groups in socio-economic makeup.

Once more, however, the Jewish group is unlike the other groups; it is consistent from occupation category to occupation category, favoring security regardless.

OTHER CRITERIA OF POLITICO-ECONOMIC ORIENTATION SHOW SAME RELATIONSHIP

So far we have shown certain meaningful relationships to exist. But we have shown them on the basis of only one item of background information and one opinion item. Can we back up these findings with other data?

Hypothesizing affirmatively, we predict that additional criteria of politico-economic orientation will bear the same relation to socio-economic status, for any given group, as we have already found for our original criteria.

When we investigate, we find that this prediction is upheld. We find that we can back up occupational status with two other items of socio-economic information, and that we can back up the guaranteed economic security question with two other measures of politico-economic import. (See Table 2.) The third column from the left in Table 2, and the third from the right, represent our two original criteria—occupational status and view on guaranteed economic security. To the left are two other criteria of socio-economic status. Educational status is measured on the basis of what per cent of a group continued in school at least through high school graduation. The Congregationalists have the largest proportion who finished high school, while the Baptists have the smallest proportion (71 per cent compared to 35 per cent). So the Congregationalists are placed at the high status end of the scale, and the Baptists at the low end. The other groups fall between according to their percentage rank.

The second new criterion of socio-economic status is the interviewers' estimates of economic level. Respondents were classified into one of the six economic categories: Wealthy, Average Plus, Average, Poor, Old Age Assistance, On Relief. Again Congregationalists stand at the top, and Baptists are lowest. (Thirty-four per cent of the Congregationalists are rated as being of the lower economic level—Poor, Old Age Assistance, or On Relief—compared to 68 per cent of Baptists.)

Then at the extreme right we have two new criteria of politico-economic orientation. With regard to vote in 1944, less than a third of the Congregational major-party vote went to Roosevelt, compared to 92 per cent of the Jewish vote. So we place the Congregationalists at the "conservative" end of the scale, and the Jewish group at the "liberal" end. Finally we have another opinion question (also used by Centers, and which was also found capable of distinguishing Roosevelt supporters from Dewey supporters, etc.).

TABLE 2

RELATIONSHIP OF POLITICO-ECONOMIC ORIENTATION TO SOCIO-ECONOMIC
STATUS FOR MAJOR U.S. RELIGIOUS DENOMINATIONAL GROUPS

3 CRITERIA OF SOCIO-ECONOMIC STATUS					3 CRITERIA OF POLITICO-ECONOMIC OPINIONS AND ATTITUDES		
1	*2*	*3*			*1*	*2*	*3*
Educational Status	*Economic Status*	*Occupational Status*	HIGH STATUS	CONSERVATISM	*View on Guaranteed Economic Security*	*View on More Power for Working People*	*How Voted in 1944*
(Rank)	*(Rank)*	*(Rank)*	↑ Jewish	↑	*(Rank)*	*(Rank)*	*(Rank)*
Cong. Epis. Jew. Pres.	Cong. Pres. Epis. Jew.	Jew. Cong. Pres. Epis.	Congregational Presbyterian Episcopalian }	{ Congregational Presbyterian Episcopalian	Cong. Pres. Epis.	Cong. Epis. Pres.	Cong. Pres. Epis.
Meth.	Meth.	Meth.	Methodist }	{ Methodist	Meth.	Luth.	Luth.
Luth.	Luth.	Luth.	Lutheran }	{ Lutheran	Luth.	Meth.	Meth.
Cath.	Cath.	Bapt.	Baptist }	{ Baptist	Bapt.	Cath.	Bapt.
Bapt.	Bapt.	Cath.	Catholic }	{ Catholic	Jew.	Bapt.	Cath.
			↓	Jewish ↓	Cath.	Jew.	Jew.
			LOW STATUS	LIBERALISM			

Would you agree that everybody would be happier, more secure and more prosperous if working people were given more power and influence in government, or would you say we would all be better off if the working people had no more power than they have now?
Congregationalists are least strongly in favor of more power for working people; the Jewish group most strongly for it. The range is from 31 per cent to 58 per cent. Congregationalists again are, as a group, more conservative, and the Jewish group is again more liberal.

We have four groups which are relatively high in socio-economic status, two which are medium, and two which are relatively low. There is no overlap between the high groups and the medium and between the medium and low; bracketing in Table 2 was based on this fact.

What happens to the rank of these groups when we consider their politico-economic orientation rather than their socio-economic status? *They keep the same rank.* The high status groups are conservative in their opin-

TABLE 3
SUPPORTING DATA*

GROUP	(Voting Sample) EDUCATIONAL STATUS — High School Grad. or more	(Voting Sample) ECONOMIC STATUS — Lower Economic Level	(Voting Sample) OCCUP. STATUS — Urban Manual Workers	(Social Sample) POLITICO-ECONOMIC OPINION — For Guaranteed Economic Security	(Social Sample) POLITICO-ECONOMIC OPINION — For More Power for Working People	(Voting Sample) POLITICO-ECONOMIC BEHAVIOR — Major Party Vote for FDR in 1944	(Social Sample) BUSINESS AND PROFESSIONAL WORKERS — For Individualism	(Social Sample) WHITE COLLAR WORKERS — For Individualism	(Social Sample) SKILLED SEMI-SKILLED, UNSKILLED, & SERVICE WORKERS — For Individualism	(Social Sample) NON-ECONOMIC (INTERCLASS) OPINION — Relatively Friendly toward Russia
NATIONAL	48.1% 12,241	56.2% 12,019	43.9% 11,671	44.1% 5932	48.5% 5933	57.1% 9181	70.2% 1059	58.9% 978	36.7% 2342	63.7% 5933
Cath.	43.0% 2427	66.6% 2390	54.7% 2332	57.7% 1084	54.2% 1085	72.8% 1803	68.1% 144	49.6% 232	26.3% 559	58.4% 1086
Bapt.	35.4 1414	68.0 1381	51.4 1344	51.1 964	55.7 961	63.6 944	75.0 96	61.4 114	31.4 423	55.1 967
Luth.	43.7 762	53.0 723	42.5 720	40.3 362	41.4 362	45.4 586	80.8 52	50.0 56	39.1 138	66.7 360
Meth.	50.6 2162	51.7 2100	39.1 2053	37.9 1141	45.1 1140	49.6 1634	72.1 190	66.1 180	40.0 395	66.9 1137
Epis.	64.7 595	42.2 590	35.8 571	33.1 248	34.7 248	44.6 478	80.5 82	69.1 55	38.5 65	73.6 250
Pres.	62.9 974	38.1 961	31.4 923	31.1 418	37.1 418	39.9 782	78.9 114	64.6 79	52.6 114	71.8 418
Cong.	71.1 381	33.5 376	28.2 362	25.8 155	31.0 155	31.4 318	(See footnote 6)			76.0 154
Jewish	63.1 537	46.2 537	26.8 515	55.8 197	58.4 197	92.1 441	46.2 91	46.2 52	36.7 49	83.8 197

* "National" figures are those for the entire sample of seventeen denominational categories. Number of cases on which percentages are based is indicated below and to the right of each percentage.

ions and voting behavior; the low status groups are liberal.[7] Complete figures on

[7] A convincing distinction between two varieties of liberalism has been made by George Horsley Smith (in *The Journal of Educational Psychology*, February 1948, pp. 65-81). He found that "'liberals' as defined by non-economic or interclass values (e.g., endorsement of civil liberties and internationalism, opposition to prohibition)" tended to be economically well-off and better-educated people, while "'liberals' as defined by approval of certain politico-economic proposals (e.g., more power for labor in the government, government ownership of the banks, increased unemployment compensation)" tended to be less educated and economically poorer. In the present study we are concerned with this second group, the "politico-economic liberals," represented most heavily in our low status groups.

Assuming that Dr. Smith's distinction between politico-economic and non-economic liberals is valid, one might hypothesize that *high status* religious groups, rather than low status ones, *will be more liberal* on non-economic issues. This turns out to be the case. Dr. Smith analyzed the responses to the following question (asked in June and August 1946):

Which one of these four statements do you come closest to agreeing with?
1. It is very important to keep on friendly terms with Russia, and we should make every effort to do so.
2. It is important for the U.S. to be on friendly terms with Russia, but not so important that we should make too many concessions to her.
3. If Russia wants to keep on friendly terms with us, we shouldn't discourage her, but there is no reason why we should make any special effort to be friendly.
4. We shall be better off if we have just as little as possible to do with Russia.

Regarding the first two choices as the "liberal" answers, Dr. Smith interpreted this to be a non-economic or interclass issue and found that the better-off and better-educated people were more friendly toward Russia.

When religious groups are broken on this question, Congregationalists, Episcopalians, and Presbyterians (the groups which are most conservative on politico-economic issues) are more liberal than Methodists and Lutherans, who in turn are more liberal than Catholics and Baptists. Members of the Jewish group, well-educated and well-off, are, as expected, liberal on this non-economic issue. They are the only high-income group, however, who are also liberal on politico-economic issues. (See Table 3.)

which these ranks have been calculated are found in Table 3.

The Jewish group, as we predicted from the earlier data, is an exception. It is a high status group, yet its members are liberal in orientation.

RELIGIOUS IDENTIFICATION AS A CROSS-PRESSURE

In attempting to explain this apparent contradiction, we would make the obvious suggestion that economic interest is not the only interest which can cause group coherence. For Jewish people the cross-pressure of identification with other Jewish people seems to outweigh economic interest. For Christian groups such a powerful cross-pressure appears to be lacking, and economic interest is the basis for common viewpoints.[8]

To reconcile the Jewish data with that for the various Christian groups is not at all difficult if we accept the idea that religious affiliation, when considered from a politico-economic viewpoint, operates as a sort of latent cross-pressure which at times exerts little force but which suitable circumstances can activate. For instance, in specific localities Catholics may tend to vote as an outgroup. In Erie County, Ohio in 1940[9]

[8] One may speculate as to why members of this group feel it to their interest to be liberal, regardless of their economic position. This study can contribute no new evidence. Perhaps they want guaranteed economic security because of a generalized need for security; they may tend to desire a change in the present order because the status quo does not assure them the security it does for other high-income groups. And perhaps being only partially accepted by the latter forces them to associate with others in a like position, with the result that they are exposed to anti-status quo values. They might develop in this way a tendency to identify with outgroups, or to side with low status groups in general. It seems very likely that they saw in Roosevelt a champion of minority rights and supported him heavily for that reason.

[9] Cf. Lazarsfeld, P. F., Berelson, B., & Gaudet, Hazel, *The People's Choice,* New York: Duell, Sloan and Pearce, 1944.

Catholics of all economic levels voted predominantly Democratic (although each stratum was less Democratic than the one below it). The influence of religious affiliation in non-Jewish groups is not always merely local: Al Smith's Catholicism is reputed to have had in 1928 a nation-wide effect in attracting Catholic votes and provoking Protestant opposition.

If there is ever an indication that Protestants are likely to act together as a group (as they may have tended to do in the 1928 election cited just above), it would certainly be sensible to consider them as a single inclusive group. The present data suggest, however, that the Protestants are a very diverse lot and that *ordinarily*, at least on politico-economic issues, the trichotomy "Protestants, Catholics, and Jews" represents a meaningless oversimplification. Differences can be shown between major Protestant denominational groups which are as great as differences between such groups and non-Protestant groups. Thus differences between Congregationalists (taken as a group) and Catholics (as a group) are in general no greater than differences between Congregationalists and Baptists. Whenever possible, therefore, comparisons of religious groups, particularly when being made in socio- and politico-economic terms, ought to respect the distinctiveness of each of the major Protestant denominations.

SUMMARY AND CONCLUSIONS

Post-war survey data have been analyzed to study politico-economic orientation and its correlates for each of eight major U.S. religious denominational groups. This analysis has shown four things:

1) that there are differences in socio-economic status and economic role among these groups.
2) that correlated with these differences are differences among the groups in politico-economic opinions and behavior.
3) that politico-economic differences *within* a denominational group are associated with the socio-economic stratification within the group.

Thus differences *between* groups appear to be due primarily to differences in socio-economic makeup. For the major Christian groups, religious affiliation evidently is not the chief determinant of politico-economic attitudes, but is instead a "latent cross-pressure," exerting only minor influence at the national level; yet remaining (particularly for the Catholics, who in some circumstances are an outgroup) a *potential* basis for common viewpoints.

4) that the Jewish group, responding presumably to overwhelming cross-pressure, is a marked exception to these relationships between economic role and attitudes.

·4·

Governmental Structure and Process:

Political Parties, Pressure Groups

THE DYNAMICS OF ACCESS IN THE LEGISLATIVE PROCESS

CONFERENCE AND COMPROMISE

REPRESENTATIVE GOVERNMENT THROUGH THE HOUSE OF REPRESENTATIVES

THE MACHINES

GENERAL INTERIM REPORT OF THE HOUSE SELECT COMMITTEE

ON LOBBYING ACTIVITIES

LETTERS THAT REALLY COUNT

PUBLIC OPINION POLLS AND DEMOCRATIC LEADERSHIP

THE DYNAMICS OF ACCESS IN THE
LEGISLATIVE PROCESS

DAVID B. TRUMAN

"Every opinion," Mr. Justice Holmes observed in one of his great dissents, "tends to become a law." In thus adumbrating his conception of the legislative process Holmes pointed to a distinctive feature of modern representative government. Especially in the United States, the legislature, far more than the judiciary or the executive, has been the primary means of effecting changes in the law of the land. In consequence, the legislature traditionally has been the major focus of attention for political interest groups. Though this interest in legislation has not been an exclusive preoccupation, the established importance of group activities in legislatures is reflected in a popular synonym for the political interest group, the word *lobby*. Though for tactical reasons many groups profess slight or no concern with lobbying, legislative activity has been for the layman the distinguishing feature of the political interest group.

It follows that access to the legislature is of crucial importance at one time or another to virtually all such groups. Some groups are far more successful in this pursuit than others. Moreover, access is not a homogeneous commodity. In some forms it provides little more than a chance to be heard; in others it practically assures favorable action.

Some groups achieve highly effective access almost automatically, whereas it is denied to others in spite of their most vigorous efforts.

It will be appropriate, therefore, to begin an exploration of the role of groups in the legislative process by examining some of the factors that affect the kind of access that various groups are able to achieve. For the sake of convenience these may be divided into two types: first, a set of formal, structural factors whose importance will be readily apparent; second, a set of informal determinants whose effect is somewhat more subtle but of at least equal significance.

GOVERNMENTAL STRUCTURE AND DIFFERENTIAL ACCESS

The formal institutions of government in the United States do not prescribe all the meanderings of the stream of politics. They do mark some of its limits, however, and designate certain points through which it must flow whatever uncharted courses it may follow between these limits. Such is the character of formal organization in any setting. Although the effect of formal structural arrangements is not always what its de-

Reprinted from *The Governmental Process: Political Interests and Public Opinion*, by David B. Truman, by permission of the publisher, Alfred A. Knopf, Inc. Copyright 1951 by Alfred A. Knopf, Inc. (pp. 321-351).

signers intended, these formalities are rarely neutral. They handicap some efforts and favor others. . . .

Access is one of the advantages unequally distributed by such arrangements; that is, in consequence of the structural peculiarities of our government some groups have better and more varied opportunities to influence key points of decision than do others. Take as an example the provision for equal representation of States in the Senate of the United States. This has allowed agricultural interest groups that are predominant in many thinly populated States more points of access in the Senate than urban groups whose members are concentrated in a few populous States. Thus, were it not for this structural provision, the United States would not have been so solicitous for the sugar beet or silvermining interests as it has been over the years. It is obvious, moreover, that a group such as the American Farm Bureau Federation, which can cover a great many rural States, can gain readier access than urban groups concerning any matter on which it can achieve a satisfactory measure of cohesion. It is less obvious, but equally important, that an urban group whose interests are such that it can ally with the Farm Bureau derives an advantage in access over another urban group whose claims are such that it cannot effect an alliance of this sort. The National Association of Manufacturers and various trade associations, among others, have been the beneficiaries of such combinations.

Similar advantages, gained from the way in which the boundaries of legislative districts are drawn whether by legislatures or by constitutions, can be observed throughout the governmental system. They are clearly observable in the House of Representatives, many of whose districts, even in relatively urban States like Illinois, are defined by State legislatures in which rural groups predominate. The State legislatures, of course, show similar patterns.

The existence of the federal system itself is a source of unequal advantage in access. Groups that would be rather obscure or weak under a unitary arrangement may hold advantageous positions in the State governments and will be vigorous in their insistence upon the existing distribution of powers between States and nation. As the advantage of access shifts through time, moreover, groups shift from defenders to critics of the existing balance. At the turn of the century, for example, the insurance companies were active in Washington to get the Federal Government to take over the regulation of insurance, despite the obstacle of an adverse Supreme Court decision handed down shortly after the Civil War. Since the Court in 1944 altered the prevailing doctrine, the insurance companies have been equally vigorous in the opposite direction, at least in so far as they have tried to gain exemption from the Sherman Antitrust Act. A somewhat complicated symptom of a similar state of affairs is suggested by the contrast between argument and behavior in connection with the Tydings-Miller Act of 1937. This legislation, sponsored principally by the National Association of Retail Druggists, exempted from the provisions of the Sherman Act contracts fixing resale prices on goods sold in interstate commerce, provided that they were resold in a State which permitted such contracts. Proponents of the measure argued that it was simply a means of permitting the individual States to regulate their own affairs. When the law was passed, however, the N.A.R.D. set up an unofficial *national* board through which uniform contracts between manufacturers and retailers could be approved and administered. The policy was a national one, but the druggists' access to the States was more effective once the Federal antitrust hurdle was eliminated.

The separation of powers, especially between the legislature and the executive, and the accompanying system of checks and balances mean that effective access to one part of the government, such as the Congress, does not assure access to another, such as the presidency. For the effective constituencies of the executive and the members of the legislature are not necessarily the same, even when both are represented by men nominally of the same party. These constituencies are different, not simply because the president is elected from the whole country rather than from a particular State or congressional district although this fact has significance under a system characterized by loose party discipline, but rather because within any State or district, for various reasons, the organized, active elements responsible for the election of a senator or representative are not necessarily the same as those which give the State's or district's support to a candidate for president. This situation is accentuated at the national level by the staggered terms of senators, representatives, and president. A senator elected at the same time as a president must face re-election in an "off" year, and vice versa; a representative must "go it alone" at least every four years. In consequence, as Herring has put it, "Most congressmen are still independent political entrepreneurs." The representative, the senator, and the president each must give ear to groups that one or both of the others frequently can ignore.

An admirable illustration of this situation is the fact that four successive presidents—Harding, Coolidge, Hoover, and Franklin Roosevelt—found it possible to veto veterans' bonus legislation passed by the Congress, although on each occasion approximately four fifths of the House of Representatives chose to override the veto. Somewhat the same circumstance is indicated by the periodic group demands that reciprocal trade agreements should be submitted to the Senate for ratification as treaties. Such requests imply less effective access to the executive than to the maximum of thirty-three senators sufficient to reject a treaty.

As the preceding paragraphs suggest, access to points of decision in the government is significantly affected by the structure and cohesion of the political parties considered not just as electioneering devices, but as instruments of governing within the legislature. A single party organization that regularly succeeds in electing an executive and a majority in the legislature will produce one pattern of access to the government. The channels will be predominantly those within the party leadership, and the pattern will be relatively stable and orderly. A quite different pattern will be produced if the party is merely an abstract term referring to an aggregation of relatively independent factions. Then the channels of access will be numerous, and the patterns of influence within the legislature will be diverse, constantly shifting, and more openly in conflict. Party discipline provides the power to govern because it permits stable control of access to the points of policy determination.

It is no novelty to observe that in the United States political parties, particularly on the national scene, correspond more closely to the diffused than to the disciplined type of structure. Because the legislator's tenure in office depends on no overarching party organization, he is accessible to whatever influences are outstanding in his local constituency almost regardless of more inclusive claims. Whether he carries the label of the majority or the minority party, he finds himself now in the majority and now in the minority on legislative votes. Majorities rarely are composed of the same persons in votes on successive measures. They are likely to be bipartisan or, more accurately, nonpartisan.

The dominant character of access and of influence under the American system is well stated in the remark of a Texas Representative in response to a query concerning his motives in advocating the repeal of Federal taxes on oleo margarine: "If I were from the South and were not interested in a market for my people, I would indeed be unworthy to represent my people. Of course I am interested in the right of the cotton farmer to sell his seed. . . ." Diffusion of access has its ramifications as well. During the struggle over the McNary-Haugen farm "relief" bill from 1924 through 1928 President Coolidge was hostile both to the measure and to its principal group sponsor, the American Farm Bureau Federation. Vice-President Dawes, however, gave "support and assistance," to quote the words of the group's president, that were "of the utmost importance."

Advantages of access are likely to go to the group that can accentuate and exploit the local preoccupations of the legislator. Many corporations and trade associations have long made use of this tactic although the exact forms have been various. Railroad companies have worked through lawyers and doctors retained in the States and counties in which they practice to reach influential supporters of State and national legislators, as have other corporate enterprises. The Association of Railway Executives, predecessor of the Association of American Railroads, organized such a device in a rather complete form. As outlined by one of its officials:

I had it in mind putting into effect a plan whereby we would be advised as to who are the influential men behind the several Congressmen, and the further thought that we might be able through personal contact or by the careful distribution of literature to influence in a perfectly proper way the judgment of the men upon whom the several Congressmen rely for support and advice.

Such a system has never been more completely organized than it has been by the Iowa Farm Bureau Federation. Although the group does not openly endorse candidates for election, after the election it sets up committees of five members in each legislative district, whose function it is to capitalize upon local support. The qualifications of the members of these committees, according to Kile, are four in number: (1) they must be "willing to put Farm Bureau policies ahead of any personal interest"; (2) they must be from the same party as the successful candidate; (3) they must be men who "individually helped get the candidate elected"; and (4) they must be "politically potent in the district." A very similar plan of organization to exert local influence has been employed by, among others, the National Association of Retail Druggists. The Federal Trade Commission has described it as "the most important device" used by the association in its efforts to secure passage of desired legislation.

Such is the effect of our disintegrated na-tional party structure upon access. Although this structure may be in process of gradual change in the direction of greater integration and central control, as some competent observers believe, conclusive evidence of this shift is not at hand. We can be sure, however, that an altered party structure will be reflected in an altered pattern of group access to the Congress.

The effects of party structure upon group access to many of the State legislatures are similar to its effects upon access to Congress. The channels of approach for various groups are numerous and varied, as in Congress, except in those cases where an individual party leader or faction has been able to impose a high degree of discipline upon the rank and file. In the heyday of Boss Platt, access to the legislature of New York was available primarily through him, usually at a price. When in 1935 the Governor of Florida established temporary dominance over the State legislature, the Association of Life Insurance Presidents found that it could not even gain admission to legislative committee hearings until it had persuaded the Governor of its point of view. Other States, such as New York and New Jersey, have quite consistently shown a pattern of party government quite different from that at the national level. Where the party structure is integrated and the legislators are under discipline, access is channeled and is more available to those groups upon which the party as a whole, rather than the individual legislator, is dependent.

Once it has established access, by whatever means, a group will exert tremendous efforts to retain the structural arrangements that have given it advantage. An illustration is afforded by the struggle over the adoption of the Twenty-first Amendment appealing the Eighteenth. When the prohibition amendment was submitted, the Anti-Saloon League favored the method of ratification by the State legislatures, since it had built up its access to most of those bodies and could be sure that the weapons at its disposal would assure favorable action by the required number of States. When the repeal proposal was passed by the Congress in 1933, however, the method of ratification by conventions called especially for the purpose was specified for the first time in the history of amendments to the Federal Constitution. This means was employed in order to get around the established access of the league.

All the factors of a structural character that result in the unequal distribution of access among interest groups operating upon a legislature need not be discussed in detail. We must, however, even in this rough sketch, discuss one additional type, closely related to the structure of the party system—the structure of the legislature itself, including legislative procedure and the committee system. Legislative structure and rules of procedure are by no means neutral factors in respect to access. . . .

No legislative assembly of whatever size can, of course, carry on its activities without some internal division of labor, without methods of setting the order of business, or without means of regulating the process of deliberation. The procedures for selecting those to whom the leadership of an assembly is entrusted, for example, have a direct bearing upon the kind of access to the legislature that various groups may be able to achieve. Thus the practice in Congress and most of the States of assigning committee memberships and designating their chairmen on the basis of seniority gives a special advantage to groups having access to members from "safe" constituencies who are likely to look with hostility on the demands of the less established groups. Organizations whose membership is concentrated in "close" districts, where the incidence of change and the consequent demands for adjustment are high, are less easily able to establish access to committee chairmen.

Whoever sets the timetable of a legislature and determines how long debate on a measure shall continue has a significant control upon access. This power, of course, is one of the principal means by which the British Cabinet leads the House of Commons. In American State legislatures a unified party leadership, both legislative and executive, may enjoy similar dominance, and in that case effective access will be through such leadership. In the Congress, and at times in all of the State legislatures, control of the timetable lies with a loosely integrated collection of men belonging to the majority party, sometimes acting in consultation with the minority leaders. In the Senate, this scheduling function is performed by the floor leader, his aides, and the chairmen of the standing committees. The party Steering Committee and its Policy Committee are nominally a part of this machinery, but their importance is slight. In the House the timetable is set by the Rules Committee, the floor leader, the Speaker, and the chairmen of standing committees. The Steering Committee is of as little functional significance as in the Senate. Depending on the nature of the legislation to be considered and on the skill of the leadership, the legislators who determine the schedule may work in concert, or they may operate at cross purposes. In the latter case the legislative timetable is a compromise or emerges from a test of strength among these various points of power, a process in which the president, if he is of the same party, may play a significant role. Groups with access to parts of this machinery have a privileged influence upon the legislative program, especially if their objective is to obstruct rather than to promote a particular bill.

Both the power to limit debate and the practice of permitting unlimited debate on a measure have significance for the degree of access that various groups achieve. In the House of Representatives, where limitation on debate is customary, it usually takes the form of adopting a special rule reported by the Rules Committee. Practically all major legislation in the House is handled under this sort of procedure, which sets both the terms and the duration of debate. The Committee is thus in a position either to block or to expedite action on a bill, and access to its membership is a crucial advantage. Such access is likely to go disproportionately to established groups dominant in "safe" constituencies, since the seniority of all members of this committee is high. For example, in the Seventy-seventh Congress, elected in 1940, no member of the Rules Committee had had less than four consecutive terms of service, and the average number of such terms represented on the Committee was just under seven. Thus most of the members came from districts that had made no change in their representation since before the onset of the New Deal. A similar advantage accrues in the Senate to any defensive group that has access to even a small bloc of members. Under that body's practice of unlimited debate, such a minority can "talk a bill to death" through the filibuster, effectively preventing action by the Senate as a whole. In some cases this result has been achieved by one member alone. Although the Senate has had since 1917 a rule permitting closure of debate, it is rarely applied, and the effective veto power of a Senate minority remains virtually unchallenged.

Finally, the enormously complicated and technical rules under which debate is carried on in legislative chambers have an important influence upon relative access. In the first place, the rules themselves are not neutral; witness the heat frequently generated by an attempt to change them. At the beginning of the Eighty-first Congress in January, 1949, a successful effort was made to modify the House rules so that committee chairmen could call up bills that the Rules Committee failed to report out. The significance of such a modification was indicated both by the activity in the House and by the attention given the amendment in the press. But groups gain advantages in access not just from the substance of such procedural regulations. They may derive tremendous advantage if their representatives, whether in or out of the legislative halls, have a mastery of the ins and outs of parliamentary procedure. Like the technicalities of legal procedure in courts of law, procedural arrangements may be used as often to delay and obstruct action as to facilitate it. Thus the ability to command the services of a skillful parliamentary tactician may be the key to effective access to a legislature.

Reference has already been made to legislative committees. At this point it is necessary, however, to indicate that the place of committees in a legislative body has important effects upon the degree of access that various groups can achieve. It is as accurate today as it was nearly three quarters of a century ago when Woodrow Wilson published his little classic, *Congressional Government*, to say that, although the Congress as a whole formally legislates, the real policy determination takes place in the standing committees. Both because of the volume and the complexity of the problems coming before a modern legislature and because of the size of such bodies, they have had to leave the most important part of the examination, if not the preparation, of legislation to smaller units. Under the British system this function is performed primarily by the Cabinet, which is strictly speaking a committee of the legislature. Relatively minor use is made of other standing committees. In the Congress of the United States the sifting of legislative projects is pre-eminently the function of the committees, primarily the standing committees. Neither house, with rare exceptions, considers any measure that has not first been acted upon by one of these nominally subordinate bodies. Refusal to report a bill from a committee usually dooms the proposal. But perhaps the most significant feature of the system is that, although many major measures are altered by the Senate or the House after a committee has reported, both houses usually follow closely the recommendations of their committees. Few bills are passed in a form substantially different from that given them at the committee stage.

The effect that this system of committees has upon access stems not only from the relative finality of their actions but also from the comparative independence that they enjoy. These bodies are subject to little or no coordinating influence from any source. A committee majority, or even its chairman alone, effectively constitutes a little legislature, especially in so far as it blocks action on a proposal. Therefore access to a committee majority or even to a chairman may give a group effective advantage in the legislature itself, to the virtual exclusion of its competitors.

The role of committees in the State legislatures varies widely. In some their place is roughly similar to that of the congressional committee, whereas in others it is sharply different. One general difference is that, since State legislative sessions are shorter and less frequent and since many State legislators perform their duties on a part-time basis, there is usually less opportunity for prolonged committee consideration in the States. In some States, New Jersey, for instance, the committees are of no significance, except as graveyards for bills, since control by the party leaders is pervasive. Access to the committee under such circumstances is almost meaningless. In other States the committee function appears to be quite similar to that in Congress. Thus a study of several legislative sessions in Maryland and Pennsylvania shows that well over 80 per cent of the committee reports were accepted outright by these legislatures.

This evidence would suggest that committees in Maryland and Pennsylvania were indeed "little legislatures" and that access to them was crucial. Although such undoubtedly was the case in some instances, in these same two States there were other regularities that lay behind the acceptance of committee reports. The legislators followed the committees, to be sure, but the latter were dominated by chairmen who in turn co-operated closely with the governors and other legislative leaders. Similar evidence on the New York legislature indicates that State legislative committees and their chairmen enjoy much less freedom of action than their congressional counterparts. Political management by an informal conference of legislative leaders determines the content of major bills, not the individual committees

operating independently. Under such circumstances access to the legislature is not assured merely by establishing relationships with individual committeemen or chairmen. Lines of access tend to be integrated rather than diffused; consequently, the tactics of groups and relative advantage among them can be expected to show a pattern quite different from that characteristic of the Congress.

Aspects of formal structure, therefore, are significant determinants of the channels of access to legislatures, national and State. They afford advantages to some groups and impose handicaps upon the efforts of others to achieve influence in the legislature. Formal structure both reflects and sustains differences in power. It is never neutral.

THE ROLE OF KNOWLEDGE AND THE EFFECTS OF OVERLAPPING MEMBERSHIP

Governmental structure is not the only factor creating advantages in access to the key points of decision in the legislature. It is the most obvious, but perhaps not the most important. The politician-legislator is not equivalent to the steel ball in a pinball game, bumping passively from post to post down an inclined plane. He is a human being involved in a variety of relationships with other human beings. In his role as legislator his accessibility to various groups is affected by the whole series of relationships that define him as a person. Most of these relationships, however, cannot be identified by viewing the legislator as a creature of the statute book. We need not go into the complicated area of motives to account more fully for differences in accessibility by observing such continuing relationships, remembering that their stability is as important an element in the equilibrium of the individual legislator as are predictable relationships in the well-being of any other human.

One important factor among the informal determinants of access is created by the legislator-politician's need of information and the ability of a group to supply it. Any politician, whether legislator, administrator, or judge, whether elected or appointed, is obliged to make decisions that are guided in part by the relevant knowledge that is available to him. In this deciding, however, the politician is in a position analogous to the late Lord Keyne's stock-exchange investor, whose knowledge of the factors that will govern the future yield of an investment is necessarily partial or even negligible. The politician also must rely on somewhat conventionalized assessments of trends, corrected by new information about the relevant facts.

The politician is in continuous need of current information because he is at the mercy of the changes as they occur. Like a college president, a politician, especially an elected politician, is expected to have a judgment on all matters ranging from the causes of an outbreak of Bang's disease among the local livestock to the latest strategy of the Kremlin. He must make decisions on many of these questions, decisions on the content of his public statements, on the causes and persons he will champion, on how he will vote on a roll call.

The penalty for numerous or conspicuous decisions made in ignorance or in neglect of relevant available knowledge is disturbance in the politician's established relationships. The disturbance may be minor and temporary or serious and lasting. It may be reflected in a diminution of "reputation" or in a threat to his leadership position in party, faction, or other group. Finally, it may lead to defeat at the polls, a penalty that no elected official can be expected to welcome. Forced to make choices of consequence and to minimize serious disturbances in his established relationships, the legislator is constantly in need of relevant information. Access is likely to be available to groups somewhat in proportion to their ability to meet this need.

For purposes of discussion the knowledge required by the politician may be divided into two types: technical knowledge that defines the content of a policy issue; and

political knowledge of the relative strength of competing claims and of the consequences of alternative decisions on a policy issue. Any group may be in a position directly or indirectly to supply information of either type.

Representative of the first sort of knowledge is the specialized information about industry conditions that a trade association can provide for the politician, whether legislator or administrator. Almost any group is likely to regard knowledge of this sort as a major part of its stock-in-trade. Those who are preoccupied with moral judgments of group politics, in fact, normally treat the supplying of such information as a "legitimate" group activity. A measure of access almost inevitably accompanies the ability to provide this type of information. Where competing claims are not present, and where available knowledge of the likely political consequences suggests that the legislator will be little affected whatever decision he makes, technical information may control his decision. The politician who comes from a "safe" district, confronted with an issue of no moment in his constituency, is in a position to act upon what he regards as the "merits" of an issue, to act like what the ward heeler calls a "statesman." Especially where official sources of information are deficient, command of technical knowledge may provide access for groups that can supply the deficiency, especially if other influences are operating in their favor. Thus McKean noted that the absence of a legislative reference library, the impossibility of retaining technical staff on a legislator's salary, and the failure of the State government to provide such services as information on the progress of pending bills, gave privileged access to groups in New Jersey prepared to perform such functions.

The second type, political information, is of at least equal importance. Many familiar expressions, such as "keeping one's ear to the ground" and "mending fences," testify to this fact. The legislator, as anyone knows who has had even an amateur's brush with politics, can never know enough in this sphere. Who are behind this measure? How well unified are they? What dormant elements in the constituency will be stirred up if the proponents' claims are acceded to? Will there be a later opportunity to pacify them? For questions such as these there is rarely a final answer, but the legislator often must act as if there were. Where the situation remains obscure, his behavior may be ambiguous. Thus he may vote to kill a bill by sending it back to committee, but when that motion is lost, he may change his position and vote for the measure's passage. It may be easier to defend such apparent vacillation than to face the consequences of an unequivocal stand.

In politically ambiguous circumstances, and they are common, a group that can give the legislator an indication of the consequences of supporting or opposing a measure is likely to win his ear at least in some degree. Such "information," of course, is rarely taken at face value, since most groups find it expedient to exaggerate their influence and the cohesion of the rank and file. It is up to the legislator to apply a discount rate that seems appropriate. In some instances his knowledge of his constituency is such that he knows immediately how to evaluate such claims. In others he must be aided by trusted advisers, who may themselves, in consequence, become the objects of petitions from various interest groups. The evaluation of group claims may itself be a puzzling task, although a politician of any skill can often see through assertions that are largely pretense. Yet because pretense and exaggeration are common, a group may gain advantage in access if it is presented by agents who have a reputation for candor and realism. Few elected politicians are in a position requiring no reliable political knowledge.

The desire for information may not be the only informal factor leading the legislator to make himself accessible to particular interest groups. He is not simply a machine for calculating odds and acting on the most favorable ones. When he assumes office he does not cut himself off from all previous connections and divest himself of the attitudes he has acquired up to that time. The prevailing myths may hold that he does so or should do so, but to accept such folklore literally is to fall victim to the institutional fallacy, to look at formalities and to ignore relationships. . . . Such was essentially the point argued by Madison in the following passage from *The Federalist, No. 10:*

No man is allowed to be a judge in his own cause, because his interest would certainly bias his judgment, and, not improbably, corrupt his integrity. With equal, nay with greater reason, a body of men are unfit to be both judges and parties at the same time; yet what are many of the most important acts of legislation, but so many judicial determinations, not indeed concerning the rights of single persons, but concerning the rights of large bodies of citizens? And *what are the different classes of legislators but advocates and parties to the causes which they* determine? (Italics added.)

Madison concluded that legislators must inevitably have interest affiliations, and not infrequently we find evidence that members of Congress also assume so. Thus in 1929 the Senate committee investigating tariff lobbying criticized the head of a series of "paper" associations for pretending to an influence that he did not have. After commenting on his lack of technical qualifications, the committee added as further evidence of his fraudulent position: "He is on terms of intimacy with no Member of Congress so far as your committee has been able to learn."

Since an elected representative cannot give up his already existing attitudes and relationships, the legislature and various political interest groups inevitably overlap in membership. Any of the latter that can claim members in the legislature will thus enjoy a measure of privileged access. Other influences aside, the value of this means of access will vary with the number of such members and with the importance that they attach to such affiliation. It is well known, for instance, that the organized bar has had advantages in access to State and national legislatures in consequence of the number of lawyers elected to those bodies.

The American Legion usually can list among its membership one third to one half the members of Congress, in addition to Cabinet members and even the President. Not all of these are equally accessible to the Legion, but at least a portion of them are likely to be readily so. Similarly the Chamber of Commerce of the United States constitutes, as one author has put it, "an unofficial functional constituency of the federal legislature" in consequence of having several of its members in the Congress.

Where the claims of a group are or can be made sufficiently central for its members in the legislature, the latter can be formed into a "bloc" that is expected to act as a unit on as many as possible of the issues of concern to the group. At its height such was the "farm bloc" of 1921-2, which included a quarter of the Senators (14 Republicans and 10 Democrats) and a similar but less well defined segment of the House. Though a minority of both houses, it held a balance of power for the better part of four years.

The National Rivers and Harbors Congress, whose membership overlaps with that of a variety of other groups, including Congress, has acquired almost as much influence in the area of its claims. It is made up of contractors and State and local officials, members of Congress, and, ex-officio, officers of the Army Corps of Engineers. The loyalties uniting this group have demonstrated their strength on many occasions. When the Rivers and Harbors Congress announces its opposition to the recommendation of the Hoover Commission that the flood control and rivers and harbors activities of the Corps of Engineers be transferred to the Department of the Interior, it is in effect announcing the opposition of a "bloc" to any effort to implement the suggestion. When Representative William M. Whittington of Mississippi testified in 1945 before a Senate committee in opposition to a proposal to establish a Missouri Valley Authority, he spoke not only as a member of Congress and as chairman of the Flood Control Committee of the House, but as vice-president of the National Rivers and Harbors Congress and vice-president of the related Mississippi Valley Flood Control Association.

The variety of uses to which such multiple memberships can be put is almost infinite. The legislator who is a "member" of an active political interest group may, better than anyone outside the legislature, observe and report on developments within the legislative body and its committees; he may act as the group's spokesman on the floor; he may attempt to persuade key committee members; he may save the group postage by allowing it the use of his franking privilege; and so on. A few examples will suggest the range of relationships. When the retail druggists and their allies were attempting in the 1930's to secure passage of price-maintenance laws, full use was made of retailer-legislators, according to the manual on the subject issued by the National Association of Retail Druggists. In Iowa the druggists who were members of the legislature met as a group and selected the persons who were to sponsor the measure. In the State of Washington the bill was introduced by a collection of legislators, "several of whom were or had been in the retail business and knew the meaning of predatory price cutting. Such men needed no prodding when it came to arguing the bill on its own merits." Much the same procedures are followed by the veterans' organizations. The Legion distributes among its members in the Congress the responsibility for sponsoring its measures, and it supervises the tactics they employ. During the bonus drive of the 1930's the key member of the Veterans of Foreign Wars in Congress was Representative Wright Patman of Texas. He spearheaded the V. F. W.'s effort to secure immediate cash payment of the bonus. When the tariff revision of 1929-30 was in process, Senator Bingham of Connecticut placed on the payroll of the Senate the assistant to the president of the Connecticut Manufacturers Association. The latter not only advised Senator Bingham, but accompanied him to the meetings of the Senate Finance Committee, which prepared the measure, as an "expert" on tariff matters.

An important possibility to bear in mind in connection with the effect of a legislator's group memberships upon his accessibility is that the willingness to aid a group's claims need not involve any overt act on the part of the group, any "pressure" on the legislator, and it need not involve formal membership in the group. A legislator-politician no less than any other man has, lived his life in a series of environments, largely group-defined. These have given him attitudes, frames of reference, points of view, which make him more receptive to some proposals than to others. As a specialist in politics he may be in possession of information that obliges him to choose between his preferences as a successful upper-middle-class lawyer and the demands of a group of militant workers in his constituency. But in the absence of such conflicts, and even in the face of them, he is likely to be most accessible to groups or proposals that stem from sources comparable to those from which his own attitudes have been derived. Many, if not all, such legislators will insist in all sincerity that they vote as their own consciences dictate. They may even resent any effort from an otherwise acceptable group to force a particular decision from them. This is true, however, whether they are "liberals" or "conservatives," urbanites or country boys, their "consciences" are creatures of the particular environments in which they have lived and of the group affiliations they have formed.

Under such circumstances the notion of group "pressure" has limited value. Bailey makes this point extremely well in his discussion of the attitudes of those members of Congress who were on the joint conference committee that produced the Employment Act of 1946 in its final form. In accounting for the strongly hostile position of Senator Buck of Delaware, Bailey refers to Buck's close connections with the Du Pont family, including his marriage to the daughter of T. Coleman Du Pont. No overt group act was necessary to secure Buck's vote against the measure, for as Bailey observes, "It was not the pressure of Du Pont

on Buck but the pressure of Du Pont *in* Buck which was at work." Similarly it is scarcely necessary for an organized interest group to take overt action among members of Congress from the South in order to secure their votes against F.E.P.C. legislation and the like. Access for this point of view is assured in most cases by the attitudes which Southern legislators hold without prompting.

We encounter here again the fact that interest groups operate in a hierarchy of prestige. Some groups, as we have seen previously, enjoy a prestige which makes it unnecessary for them to participate actively in elections. Such high status groups are likely to acquire favorable access to the legislature for the same reasons. A politician need not himself be a member of the Chamber of Commerce of the United States to listen with respect to the testimony of a business leader who is pleading its case. Among the attitudes he is likely to have acquired in the average constituency are ones involving deference toward those groups that enjoy high prestige in the country as a whole. In the legislative process, as in other aspects of politics, groups are affected by their position or status in the society.

In this connection some reference should be made to what is widely referred to as the "social lobby." An informal influence upon access, it provides material for the more lurid exposes of legislative life and lends itself to treatment in eye-catching headlines. Popular impressions to the contrary, there is no reason to revise Herring's judgment that the influence of this device is "decidedly secondary." If the minor importance of the "social lobby" is not forgotten, however, examination of the phenomenon will provide instructive illustrations of the informal determinants of relative access.

The "social lobby," a technique rather than a type of group, is a device to create a feeling of obligation on the part of the legislator toward individuals who have established sociable relations with him through entertaining him and his family. It uses social intercourse to develop multiple memberships, on the not unwarranted assumption that in a conflict situation the face-to-face relations of the "social lobby" will be dominant. It is harder to refuse someone who has been kind to you than to turn away a more or less complete stranger.

If the attempted seduction is successful, it probably works best with the new legislator who is just taking up residence in a strange community. Having been a fairly large frog in a comparatively small pond, he suddenly finds the situation reversed. He may be disturbed by the abrupt interruption of his accustomed social relationships and feel the need for adequate substitutes. . . . The implied penalty for sharp political disagreement is ostracism from the friendly group, and the legislator may quite unconsciously find himself avoiding this penalty by conforming. Reinforcement in this direction may come from the legislator's wife and daughters. They too need satisfactory personal relationships in the new community; once established these may involve none of the conflicts which the legislator himself feels, and the sanction then becomes the more unpleasant. Especially if the ladies are "socially ambitious," exclusion from "important" social functions may be acutely painful. The rationale of the device is suggested by the Georgia representatives of the Association of Life Insurance Presidents in a report on the 1933 session of the State legislature. Accounting for their expenditures, they say in part: "This money has been spent in invitations to those of whom we wished to make friends, and seeing that their wives and daughters were looked after properly and courteously. . . ."

Normally the technique is more subtle, along the lines of the following statement by a former State legislator:

The legislator who remains aloof will find himself, if not quite ostracized, at least not "one of the gang," and will constantly be surprised at an unexpected solidarity on the part of a majority of his colleagues for or against a pending measure. His surprise will be dissipated when he learns that the night before the "gang" were at an entertainment at a downtown hotel, where probably the subject of legislation was not even mentioned, but in some subtle way an understanding was reached as to what was expected of those present as all around "good fellows."

Part of the subtlety in this case, of course, depended upon the clique structure within the legislature itself, to which we shall turn shortly.

Although the "social lobby" illustrates a type of informal overlapping membership, the reasons for its comparative unimportance are fairly obvious. In the first place, the successful politician, like other leaders, is likely to be a person whose pattern of interpersonal relations is fairly flexible and thus not readily subject to the sanction of ostracism. Secondly, since positions of power within the legislature customarily are occupied by experienced legislators rather than by newcomers, the seductive technique must operate in a limited field. The old hand does not need the flattery of the "social lobby" for his personal happiness; he may, in fact, favor a gathering by his presence rather than be favored by an invitation to it. Excepting, therefore, the occasional newcomer and the rare legislator who is undisturbed by bribery, the "social lobby" is at most a means of reinforcing the preferences already held by various members of the legislative body. Even among these it may not prevail over other devices in a legislative situation where opposing influences are present.

An important implication of the various multiple memberships of legislators is that their interactions with interest groups are not just one-way relationships. The popular view is that the political interest group uses the legislator to its ends, induces him to function as its spokesman and to vote as it wishes. As we have already seen, this is not an inaccurate view. But it is incomplete. In most of the examples discussed above the legislators were not subject to overt "pressure." They did not necessarily act in anticipation of group demands but rather behaved as persons in official position whose views of the pending legislation for various reasons approximated those of organized and potential interest groups. When a legislator arouses organized groups in connection with a proposal that he knows will involve them or when he solicits their support for a measure which he is promoting, the relationship becomes reciprocal. Even in connection with the development of a single bill from conception to enactment, the initiative may lie alternately with legislator and with group, including other outside influences.

The Employment Act of 1946 furnishes a good example of such reciprocal relationships, as Bailey's study indicates. Perhaps because this legislation involved few concrete deprivations or indulgences and is, therefore, not entirely typical of many controversial measures, it highlights the use that members of Congress may make of a variety of interest groups. The impetus for the bill came in part, to be sure, from the National Farmers Union. Much of the drive behind the measure, however, was supplied by the most important of the Senate and House sponsors and their aides. These solicited the support of a diversity of groups and welded them into what Bailey dubs the "Lib-Lab Lobby." Some of these interest groups in turn attempted to win over other members of Congress and officials of the executive branch, so that it became difficult to determine who was influencing whom. Certainly, however, it was no simple, one-way pattern of group demands upon legislators. On the opposition side as well, moreover, testimony against the measure was solicited by members of Congress. In particular, Representative Carter Manasco of Alabama, chairman of the House Committee on Expenditures in the Executive Departments, to which the bill was referred, took the initiative in mobilizing opposition witnesses.

Overlapping memberships of legislators, therefore, give privileged access to the interest groups involved, whether the membership is formal or of the "fellow-traveler" variety. Such membership does not mean simply that the legislator is "used" by the groups in a one-way, condition-response relationship. As "parties to the causes which they determine," legislators may equally function as leaders of the interest groups with which they identify.

THE GROUP LIFE OF THE LEGISLATURE

We have seen that formal governmental structure and various informal group-legislator relationships give some groups advantages over others in achieving access to the legislature. These factors are productive of patterns of interaction that affect legislative decisions. A third factor that also regulates access is the pattern of relationships within the legislature itself. We are concerned here more than in the earlier paragraphs with access not merely to the individual legislator, but to the legislature as a unit. Such a body is not properly conceived of as a collection of individual men, unorganized and without internal cohesion. Nor is it any better accounted for exclusively in terms of the formal, legal structure of the legislature. A legislative body has its own group life, sometimes as a unit, perhaps more often as a collection of subgroups or cliques. It has its own operating structure, which may approximate or differ sharply from the formal organization of the chamber. When a man first joins such a body, he enters a new group. Like others, it has its standards and conventions, its largely unwritten system of obligations and privileges. To these the neophyte must conform, at least in some measure, if he hopes to make effective use of his position. The claims and imperatives of his other group attachments must be accommodated and adjusted to those of a new one. This conformity is facilitated by the fact that the new group commands some of the means of satisfying the demands of the outside groups with which the new legislator identifies himself; the adjustment is also strengthened by the morale, the *esprit*, in the legislative body.

The morale of legislative groups is often marked, even when mutual confidence of the members is not productive of the most widely approved results. As one discriminating student of the legislative process has put it: "In general, the *esprit de corps* displayed by legislative bodies, especially the smaller ones, is probably not rivaled by any other formally organized, self-governing body. There seem to be factors inherent in the legislative process which are conducive to the production of good morale." The factors productive of legislative morale are rooted in the continuing interpersonal relationships among the members, which are initially grounded in the common experiences they have had in reaching and holding elective office. Politicians of quite different opinions and of at least nominally opposed political party are likely nevertheless to understand and respect a colleague's fears and triumphs. Like old veterans of a military campaign or like the alumni of a college athletic team, they speak a language which the uninitiated can never quite understand; they have had roughly parallel experiences that set them a little apart from those whose struggles have been of a different order. These commonalities help to support the conforming influences of the legislative group. "Smoke-filled cloakrooms and bars where one can rub elbows with his colleagues who have shared experiences with him and who know what he has been through to get there and stay there, are assimilating and conditioning grounds." The relationships of a legislator with his fellow legislators do much to moderate the conflicts inherent in the legislative process and to facilitate the adjustments without which the process could not go on. Skill in handling such relationships, moreover, generates influence that is reflected in leader-follower patterns within the chamber. Legislative skill, usually acquired only after considerable experience in the law-making body, creates its own following; less experienced or overly busy members will often be guided by the skilled veteran when a vote is called for and in a fashion that cannot be explained simply in terms of party loyalty or of the trading of votes.

The pattern of interpersonal relationships in the legislature may closely approximate the formal structure of floor leaders, whips, and committee chairmen. Whether it does or does not, however, the tyro who reaches the capitol breathing fire after a vigorous campaign soon finds that he can accomplish nothing until he learns how to get along with his colleagues. The acknowledged leaders of the body, whether they are the formal ones or not, can help the newcomer to advance himself and his projects at a modest price in conformity and recognition of reciprocal obligations. The conformity and recognition of obligations, moreover, involve some acceptance of the notion that the ramifications of some of the claims he espouses will, if the claims are unmodified, reach beyond the groups for which the new legislator speaks. The consequences of the demands he voices may affect his colleagues and the legislature as a group. He becomes more or less conscious of the need not to "upset the apple cart." Failure to learn the ways of the legislative group, to "play ball" with his colleagues, is almost certain, especially in a large body like the U. S. House of Representatives, to handicap the proposals in which the freshman legislator is interested and to frustrate his ambitions for personal preferment. The group life of the legislature thus may temper the claims of an interest group, since the legislator-spokesman must reconcile such demands with his role within the chamber. Even the established and skillful legislative leader rarely rides roughshod over his colleagues.

The political interest group whose spokesman "belongs" to the legislative group, who is "one of the boys," enjoys an obvious advantage in access to the legislature, especially if the representative is one of the acknowledged leaders of the chamber. Correspondingly, a group is handicapped if its only connections are with a maverick or a newcomer. It is not enough for the legislator to be a member, in some sense, of the interest group or even to be in a position of formal power. He must "belong" within the legislature as well.

Although the pattern of relationships

within the legislature thus affects the access of interest groups, it is important not to assume that these interactions produce an integrated, hierarchical structure. They may, but the life of the legislative group as of others may as easily involve a loosely allied collection of cliques. Where a measure of integration is achieved in one chamber, moreover, it may not extend to the other. The group life of a legislature may bear little or no likeness to cohesive party government. As Woodrow Wilson said of the power of the Rules Committee and the Speaker of the House of Representatives before the 1911 revolt: "It integrates the House alone . . .; does not unite the two houses in policy. . . . It has only a very remote and partial resemblance to genuine party leadership." Party government is a form of legislative group life, but it is not the only or the most common form in the United States.

THE INFLUENCE OF OFFICE

The influences we have discussed thus far come close to accounting for the relative access of interest groups to the legislature, but they are not complete. Formal structural aspects of government, the legislators' various group "memberships," and what we have called the group life of the legislature do not tell the whole story. In addition to these, the fact of holding public office is itself a significant influence upon the relative access of the groups. Not unrelated to the group life of the legislature, the influence of office is of sufficient importance to deserve separate and extended treatment.

We have had something to say about the positions or statuses that an individual occupies in his society and about norms of perception and behavior that he derives from his experiences in the society. These concepts were treated as determinants of the ways in which an individual knows, interprets, and behaves in his society. Looking more closely at these statuses, we can conceive of a whole society as a system of interrelated positions that people occupy, each individual normally filling a great many. For each recognized status in a society there are norms that prescribe more or less definitely how the occupant is to behave toward persons in related statuses. These prescribed ways of behaving are known as roles. . . .

Public office, including that of a legislator, is such a status. It hardly should be necessary to make this point were it not that its implications are so easily overlooked. When a man enters a legislative position he takes on a new role that is prescribed for him by the society. His success as a legislator depends in large part upon how well he performs that role.

* * *

The norms that define a role do not specify all the things that the occupant of a particular status shall do. They require some behaviors and forbid others; still others are a matter of the officeholder's discretion; that is, they are permitted under appropriate conditions but are not essential. These required and forbidden behaviors, it is important to bear in mind, are defined by norms that are socially determined; one might call them the standardized expectations of those who are aware of the particular status. Some of these behaviors are, of course, specified in legal enactments, such as corrupt practices legislation and the constitutional right of petition.

As the existence of these formal, legal definitions suggests, these behavioral norms are not neutral. Whether or not they are embodied in statutes and constitutions, they are activities about which many people in society feel very strongly; that is, these norms are associated with values the violation of which will cause disturbances of varying degrees of seriousness and will be punished in various ways—by impeachment, imprisonment, execution, ridicule, defeat at the polls, insult, lynching, and so on.

Not all behavioral norms are unambiguous. The legislator does not always "know what is expected of him" in a given situation, because in his constituency, unless it is remarkably homogeneous in every respect, various groups—organized and potential—will interpret his behavior in different ways. What is important to one segment may be irrelevant to another; what is bribery to one may be charity to another; some may be able to distinguish between "honest and dishonest graft" and others not; some may be sufficiently organized and cohesive to "remember" his actions for a long time, whereas others are not. Especially if the legislator aspires to move from a smaller to a larger and more heterogeneous constituency—from State legislator to governor, from Representative to United States Senator—what an existing constituency regards as a proper concern for one's supporters may appear to voters in the larger area as narrow parochialism. Hence is derived the importance of the forms and sources of knowledge that we discussed earlier in the chapter.

But many of the norms defining the legislator's role are relatively unambiguous, and these are the ones in which we are primarily interested here. The legislator is expected to avoid open partiality to the contested claims of a small minority; he must at least appear to be solicitous for the vocal needs of his constituents, but he is expected in some measure to look beyond his constituency; he must defend the orderly procedures of political settlement; he must support the political and civil freedoms involved in a fair trial, in petition, in speech, press, and assembly. These, along with many others, not only define his role but represent the substance of prevailing values without which the political system could not exist. . . .

It is, of course, obvious that the "rules of the game" are not invariably adhered to, that they are not accepted universally or with unvarying vigor in all parts of the society at all times. But it does not follow that they are not powerful. The protests of those who denounce "the government" for lapses and deviations, in fact, testify to the power of "the rules." The ability of a small group, speaking in defense of such values, to exercise influence out of all proportion to the size of its paid-up membership has the same significance. These norms, values, expectations, "rules of the game,"—call them what you will—largely define the institution of government along with other institutions of the society. For the legislator they set the approximate limits within which his discretionary behavior may take place.

* * *

CONCLUSIONS

The degree of access to the legislature that a particular group enjoys at a given moment is the result of a composite of influences. These determining factors will include the peculiarities of formal governmental structure and of the political party as a legislative instrument, such informal influences as the knowledge-supplying functions of the group and the character of the legislator's group affiliations, the formal and informal structure of the legislative body, and the influence of the standardized expectations in the community concerning the behavior of a legislator. Depending on the circumstances and the relative importance of these factors in a given situation, some groups will enjoy comparatively effective access, and others will find difficulty in securing even perfunctory treatment. As conditions change, as some of these influences become more and others less potent, the fortunes of group claims upon the legislature will rise or decline.

The most important implication of this multiple-factor conception of the dynamics of access is that the legislature is not just a sounding board or passive registering device for the demands of organized political interest groups. The legislature as a part of the institution of government embodies, albeit incompletely, the expectations, understandings, and values prevailing in the society concerning how the government should operate. These expectations may cover now a wide and now a relatively narrow range of behavior; they may be fairly explicit or highly ambiguous. Although the legislator's role is in part defined by limited expectations and norms prevailing in his constituency and in the interest groups with which he identifies himself, it is also the creation of the norms more widely recognized in the society. Partly because his role as a legislator inevitably gives him a specialized kind of experience from which he learns the limits of his behavior, partly because he has learned some of these norms as a member of the society, he cannot behave simply and completely as a vehicle for organized group demands.

It does not follow from the argument in this chapter that the widespread expectations about the legislature alone account for differences in ease of access or for all features of the legislative product. It is easy enough to identify cases in which the standardized expectations are ignored. The norms of official behavior inevitably partake of the quality of myth, of professed values. On the other hand, they are also operating values that affect all legislative behavior in some measure and that place limits upon both the methods and the content of group demands upon the legislature. In a stable political system the competing demands of organized interest groups are meaningless unless they are viewed in the context of these limiting and defining norms.

A second implication of this conception of the dynamics of access is that "pressure," conceived as bribery or coercion in various forms, is scarcely the distinguishing feature of interest groups in the legislative process. Such coercion is frequently attempted, of course, and it often has an observable effect. "Pressure" of group upon legislator, however, is at most one aspect of technique, one among many different kinds of relationships that exist within the lawmaking body. As indicated by the evidence we have examined, the belief that the relationship between groups and legislators is a one-way, coercive relationship simply does not explain the observed behaviors. The institution of government is not so passive and cannot be understood in such oversimplified terms.

CONFERENCE AND COMPROMISE

S. K. BAILEY

The institution of the conference committee is one of long standing. By the middle of the nineteenth century, according to Ada McCown,

the custom of presenting identical reports from the committees of conference in both houses, of granting high privilege to these conference reports, of voting upon the conference report as a whole and permitting no amendment of it, of keeping secret the discussions carried on in the meetings of the conference committee, had become established in American parliamentary practice.[1]

[1] Ada C. McCown, *The Congressional Conference Committee* (1927), pp. 254-255, quoted in George Galloway, *Congress at the Crossroads* (New York, 1946), p. 98.

From S. K. Bailey, *Congress Makes a Law* (New York: Columbia University Press, 1950), pp. 220-240. Reprinted by permission of author and publisher.

After the House of Representatives had passed its version of H. R. 2202 [Full Employment Bill] on December 14, 1945, the next step in the policy-making process was the appointment, in both Houses, of conference managers to whom was given the task of attempting to work out some compromise between the Senate-passed bill and the House substitute. Technically, the task of naming managers is the responsibility of the presiding officer in each house. Actually, the respective standing committee chairmen usually make recommendations which are automatically followed.[2] As we have noted, the Senate managers were Barkley, Murdock, Taylor, and Radcliffe, Democrats; and Tobey, Taft, and Buck, Republicans. The House managers were Manasco, Cochran, and Whittington, Democrats; and Bender and Hoffman, Republicans. Senator Wagner was initially appointed to chair the conference, but he was taken sick early in January, and Senator Barkley was prevailed upon to take the New York Senator's place.

PRE-CONFERENCE MANEUVERS

The Joint Conference Committee meetings began on January 22, 1946, just a year after the introduction of the Senate bill. Between December 14, 1945, and the Conference sessions, however, the issue of the fate of S.380 was by no means dormant. Immediately after the House vote, the liberal House sponsors went to Robert Hannegan with a passionate plea for the Democratic Party chairman to put pressure on President Truman. The feeling of the sponsors was that Truman had let them down in the House struggle, that the party had lost popular prestige among its liberal supporters as a result, and that the only way the President could recoup his lost prestige would be for him to insist that the Conference Committee report out a strong and progressive full employment bill.

Simultaneously, the Continuations Group of the Lib[eral]-Lab[or] lobby submitted to Truman a statement signed by all its members, memorializing the President to veto any Conference bill which did not measure up to liberal standards.[3]

As a result of these pressures, Truman on December 20, 1945, sent identical letters to Wagner and Manasco stating, ". . . no bill which provides substantially less than the Senate version can efficiently accomplish the purposes intended."[4] On January 3, 1946, Truman followed this up with a radio speech in which he made a "blunt request for real full employment legislation . . . urging voters to let their representatives know their sentiments."[5] Finally in his Message to Congress of January 21, 1946, Truman restated his desire that "a satisfactory Full Employment Bill such as the Senate bill now in conference between the Senate and the House" be passed.[6] The Message to Congress, which had been prepared in part by the Budget Bureau, had a number of references to the need for strong full employment legislation,[7] and altogether represented the strongest Presidential pressure for a liberal bill which came from the White House during the entire course of the struggle over S.380.

These general pressures, however, were not supported by any concrete proposals to the conferees from the Executive Branch —and thereby hangs a tale. It was the intention of Secretary of the Treasury Fred Vinson to work out a compromise version of the Full Employment Bill which might, with the weight of the President behind it, be accepted in part or as a whole by the Congressional conferees. Vinson and his assistants produced such a draft which provided, among other things, for a Cabinet committee under the directorship of the Secretary of the Treasury to replace the

[2] See J. P. Chamberlain, *Legislative Processes* (New York, 1936), pp. 244-245.

[3] Union for Democratic Action, "News Flash on Full Employment," No. 7 (Washington, Jan. 8, 1946).

[4] *Congressional Record,* 79th Cong., 2d Sess., Feb. 6, 1946, p. 1000.

[5] U.D.A., "News Flash."

[6] *Message of the President on the State of the Union and Transmitting the Budget for 1947* (Washington, 1946), p. xxii.

[7] *Ibid.,* see pp. vi, x, xxii, xxiv, xxvii, xxxvii, and lvi.

House-proposed Council of Economic Advisers. Vinson submitted his draft to Truman, who, in turn, referred it to John Snyder for comment. Snyder, for reasons best known to himself, pigeon-holed the Vinson draft, with the result that the Conference Committee had to proceed without the benefit of an administration-endorsed substitute. It is impossible to say whether or not an administration draft would have had much influence on the conferees, but the friction between Snyder and Vinson was certainly no help to the liberal cause. For a solid month, unified administration pressures were precluded by an internecine feud between two of the President's most powerful subordinates.

In the meantime, the key Congressional sponsors of the original Full Employment Bill were not idle. They recognized the fight ahead in the conference, and they attempted to develop a flexible strategy. Roughly speaking, they were bent on preserving as much of the language and substance of the Senate bill as possible, but in line with their decision about the Hatch amendment back in September, they were also concerned with establishing a series of positions to which they might retreat without losing the major battle. What these positions were will become apparent when we proceed to the story of the Conference Committee in action.

THE CONFERENCE COMMITTEE IN ACTION

Conference action began on January 22 and ended on February 2. The sessions were held in Senator Barkley's office in the Capitol, and were fairly well attended. Barkley, Taft, Murdock, Tobey, Cochran, Whittington, and Manasco were the most faithful members, although Buck and Hoffman appeared often enough to let their colleagues know that, in the words of an early Marx brothers song, "whatever it is, we're against it."

The struggle in the conference was between Barkley and Cochran on the one

hand, and Congressman Will Whittington, author of the House bill, on the other. Bertram Gross, as Wagner's special representative, was present at every meeting, as were Middleton Beaman of the House Office of Legislative Counsel and Charles Boots of the Senate Office of Legislative Counsel. A few minutes before each conference session, Gross buttonholed Barkley or Cochran or both, discussed with them the strategy of the day, gave them draft proposals—some purely for bargaining purposes—and in the case of Barkley, filled in the gaps in the busy Majority Leader's knowledge about the history and meaning of the various sections of the bill.

Beaman and Boots tried to keep track of the various agreements and disagreements in order that they might be of maximum assistance in preparing, with the aid of the respective managers, working drafts for each new conference session.

Stalemate

During the first two conference sessions, the possibility of any agreement between the House managers and the Senate managers seemed remote. Whittington outlined in detail the House objections to the Senate version of S.380, and made it quite clear that the House managers would not accept any compromise bill which contained the words "full employment" or "the right to work," or which suggested any government guarantee of employment, or which placed the ultimate emphasis upon federal spending. Barkley, for the Senate managers, on the other hand, issued a blast against the House substitute and reminded the conferees of the President's warning that only something close to the Senate version would be acceptable to him. Basing his remarks on an analysis of the House substitute prepared by Gross, Barkley outlined both the omissions and the "weaknesses" of each section of the House bill. Granted the adamant attitude of both sides, it was obvious that someone would have to retreat if the conference were to proceed.

The Struggle over the Declaration of Policy

The deadlock was broken on the third and fourth days of the conference when Gross worked out for Barkley a series of alternative policy declarations, none of which contained the term "full employment" but all of which contained the phrase "conditions under which there will be afforded useful and remunerative employment opportunities, including self-employment, for all Americans who are willing to work and are seeking work." The nature of the first concession on the part of the Senate sponsors is important, for it illustrates the technique used by Gross all the way through the conference debate. If the House managers objected to a particular phrase, Gross went to a thesaurus and juggled words around until he hit on a verbal equivalent. The fact that both sides were ultimately satisfied with most of the compromises made during the conference struggle cannot be understood without an appreciation of this technique. The House managers believed that real Senate concessions were being made with every change in language; the Senate sponsors were satisfied that a rose by any other name smells as sweet.

Perhaps the crowning example of this battle of the thesauruses was the fate of the "spending" provisions. S.380 as passed by the Senate had included the following words in the declaration of policy:

Sec. 2 (d) . . . the Federal Government shall . . . develop and pursue a consistent and carefully planned economic program . . . Such program shall among other things. . . .
(4) to the extent that continuing full employment cannot otherwise be attained, provide, consistent with the needs and obligations of the Federal Government and other essential considerations of national policy, such volume of Federal investment and expenditure as may be needed . . . to achieve the objective of continuing full employment.[8]

This provision had been attacked by almost every conservative spokesman, and it was one of the sections of the bill which the House managers in the conference insisted would have to come out. By the time

[8] S.380, 79th Cong., 1st Sess., Oct. 1, 1945.

the Conference Committee met, Gross and the leading Congressional sponsors of the bill had already come to the conclusion that special reliance on spending was both disadvantageous politically and naive programmatically. Although for bargaining purposes, they opposed Whittington's insistence that the spending provisions would have to come out, it is interesting to note that on January 18, three days *before* the conference, Gross had drafted a substitute policy statement which made no reference to government spending. What finally emerged in place of the spending clauses was a broad statement, part of which Gross had lifted from President Roosevelt's declaration of war against Germany in 1941:

Sec. 2. The Congress hereby declares that it is the continuing policy and responsibility of the Federal Government to use all practicable means . . . *to coordinate and utilize all its plans, functions and resources* for the purpose of maintaining conditions under which . . . . [Emphasis supplied.][9]

Since part of the "resources" of the federal government are its instrumentalities for spending and investment, and since the phrase finally accepted read "all . . . resources," the Senate sponsors felt, not without reason, that the conference phraseology was stronger than that in the original bill or in the Senate version. The House managers felt equally certain that dropping any specific mention of federal spending was a victory for their side. Conceivably they were both right.

The debate on the opening declaration of policy consumed the better part of five conference sessions. Every attempt by Whittington to dilute the policy declaration beyond a point acceptable to the Senate managers was countered by an attempt on the part of the latter to reintroduce the phrase "full employment." "Full employment" had been a point of contention from the very beginning of the bill's long history. Almost impossible of unambiguous definition, the phrase had been challenged

[9] Public Law 304, 79th Cong., 2d Sess., approved Feb. 20, 1946.

by Taft and Radcliffe in the Senate, and had been completely deleted from the House substitute. In conference, Whittington made it clear that under no circumstances would the phrase be admitted, and although the Senate managers had made an initial concession by deleting the phrase, they attempted for bargaining purposes to reintroduce it. At long last, Senator Tobey came through with "maximum" to replace "full," and everyone seemed satisfied. Tobey was also responsible for adding the phrase "and the general welfare" after "free competitive enterprise" in the statement of the government's obligation to "foster and promote."

The Abortive Strategy

Mention of Tobey's contributions to the conference brings to mind a carefully conceived strategy which was developed by certain people in the Executive branch. Towards the end of the conference, Tobey was approached by an administration friend of the original bill and was given the following sales talk. The original bill, of which Tobey was a co-sponsor, was being cut to pieces, not by Republicans, but by Southern Democrats. The year 1946 was an election year. If Tobey in conference could press for a liberal version of S.380, the Republican Party could take the credit for saving the Full Employment Bill. Tobey was impressed, and agreed to present a strong bill to the conference on February 2. The strategist then went to Whittington and informed him that a rumor was abroad to the effect that Tobey was going to put the Democratic Party on the spot, and that unless the Democrats in the conference succeeded on their own initiative in bringing out a liberal bill, the Republicans could make a successful campaign issue out of the situation. Whether or not this news impressed Whittington will never be known, for on February 2, the Edwin Pauley affair broke,[10] Tobey raced off to the new fray,

and failed to appear at the conference session on S.380.

The Final Agreement

Once agreement had been reached on the Declaration of Policy, the rest of the discussion went rapidly. The section dealing with the Economic Report of the President was a condensation and clarification of the House substitute on this issue. Written by Gross and introduced by Cochran, this revised section was adopted with almost no opposition.

The provisions for the Council of Economic Advisers as outlined in the House substitute were taken over almost intact, although certain important modifications were made, and at one point Whittington startled the conferees by introducing a brand new proposal. The big issue, of course, was the relationship of the Council to the President and to Congress. The Senate managers insisted that any provision which in any way served to make ambiguous the relation of the Council to the President would be unacceptable. The House bill, it will be remembered, carried the statement, "The President is requested to make available to the Joint Committee on the Economic Report, if it desires, the various studies, reports, and recommendations of the Council which have been submitted to the President."[11] The Senate managers forced the House managers to delete this section, but just when agreement seemed to be reached, Whittington came up with a completely new proposal, authored by the U. S. Chamber of Commerce and calling for the establishment of an "independent agency, an Economic Commission." After a hot debate on January 31, Whittington finally backed down, and agreement was reached.

With the general sanction of all concerned, the membership on the proposed

---

[10] Truman submitted Pauley's name for confirmation to the post of Undersecretary of the Navy. Pauley's background in oil and Demo-

cratic Party politics turned many Senators against him and his name was finally withdrawn.

[11] S.380, 79th Cong., 1st Sess., Dec. 5, 1945, p. 19.

Joint Committee on the Economic Report was cut to seven representatives from each House. Any larger number was felt to be unwieldy. Little debate developed on the issue of appropriations for the Council and for the Joint Committee.

A rapid survey of the work of the conference gives no real indication of the human side of the proceedings. Major credit for keeping the discussion moving must go to Senator Alben Barkley. Whenever discussions became tense and acrimonious, Barkley, as chairman, relieved the tension with a joke or a gentle whim. He performed what John Chamberlain has called the function of the "master broker"[12]—the classic job of the statesman-politician: the discovery of areas of agreement. This was not always easy in the Full Employment conference. Ideological conflicts were mixed up with personality conflicts. Senator Taylor was angry with Senator Taft when the latter dismissed the old-age pension provisions of the Senate bill as "window dressing"; Senator Tobey took such a personal dislike to Representative Carter Manasco that he had to force himself to sit in the same room with him; on the rare occasions when Clare Hoffman appeared, tempers rose noticeably; Whittington had to exercise considerable tact in getting Manasco to agree to a number of the compromises.

But on February 2, 1946, the job was done. The long legislative battle was all but completed. . . .

HOUSE AND SENATE APPROVAL

On February 6, 1946, the House listened to a number of schools of opinion about the meaning and value of the Employment Act of 1946.[13] Whittington and Manasco reported that the Act was acceptable to them, that the Senate managers had given in at every important point, and that the conference bill was, to all intents and purposes, the House substitute. Cochran and

Patman backed the conference bill as one which the liberals could support with good conscience. Some of the strong phrases were missing, they admitted, but the meat of the original bill was still there. Bender claimed that the conference bill was a fake, that it was not a full employment bill, but that he would support it reluctantly as a move in the right direction. Hoffman and Church also called the bill a fake, but vehemently protested its passage on the grounds that it represented unnecessary duplication of existing powers, and would lead to nothing constructive. After outlining the steps provided for by the Act, Hoffman characterized the whole procedure as chasing "the devil of unemployment around the stump, never quite catching him."[14]

On one thing almost everyone was agreed: that the question of Presidential appointments to the Council was of vital importance. The conservatives wanted men "of business ability."[15] The liberals wanted men who were "wholeheartedly devoted to the principles of the bill."[16]

The Employment Act of 1946 was finally passed in the House by a vote of 320 to 84. Two days later, on February 8, with the endorsement of both Senator Murray and Senator Taft, the conference bill went through the Senate without opposition. It was signed by President Truman and became law on February 20, 1946.

And what of the reaction of the interested pressure groups and the press? The Continuations Group, after being assured by Senator Murray and Bertram Gross that the Act was a worthy result of their labors, dutifully submitted a memorandum to Truman asking that he sign the conference bill. Many liberals felt secretly, however, that the conference bill was a weak and meaningless wraith. Some members of the C.I.O. were particularly bitter. Most conservatives rejoiced that the teeth had been removed from the original bill, and in general the

---

[12] *The American Stakes* (New York, 1940).
[13] *Congressional Record,* 79th Cong., 2d Sess., pp. 999-1009.

[14] *Ibid.,* p. 1001.
[15] *Ibid.,* p. 1000.
[16] *Congressional Record,* 79th Cong., 2d Sess., Feb. 8, 1946, p. 1170.

press gave it short shrift as a watered-down version of S.380. A few, and as time went on, a growing number of people, felt that whatever the hopes and fears of those responsible for the final Act, S.380 as passed was an important step in the direction of coordinated and responsible economic planning in the federal government.

CONCLUSIONS AND HYPOTHESES

With the President's approval of Public Law 304, we come to the end of our story, although by no means do we come to the end of the politics of the Employment Act of 1946. In the selection of top personnel for the Council of Economic Advisers, President Truman was subjected to a barrage of pressures;[17] the composition and activities of the Joint Committee on the Economic Report have reflected political decisions; the attempt of the Economic Council during the past three years to establish itself in the Executive hierarchy, to define the scope of its responsibilities and to develop a working philosophy, can only be understood in the context of American political processes broadly conceived. Already the Employment Act has been amended by another piece of legislation: the Legislative Reorganization Act of 1946, which revised the time schedule for the submission and consideration of the Economic Report. As time goes on, it is inevitable that further changes will take place in the scope of responsibilities of the President's Council and of the Joint Committee on the Economic Report, and it is certain that America is experiencing one of the first, rather than one of the last, experiments in economic planning and coordination.

Whether the Employment Act of 1946

[17] The choice of Edwin G. Nourse, former vice president of the Brookings Institution; John D. Clark, businessman and former dean of the College of Business Administration of the University of Nebraska; and Leon Keyserling, a New Deal lawyer and economist, indicates that the President wanted to antagonize as few interests as possible.

was a "good thing" or a "bad thing" is, in the context of this book, beside the point. The real question posed by the story of S.380 is what it suggests about the Congressional formulation of important social and economic policies in the middle of the twentieth century.

Certainly one generalization is that the process is almost unbelievably complex. Legislative policy-making appears to be the result of a confluence of factors streaming from an almost endless number of tributaries: national experience, the contributions of social theorists, the clash of powerful economic interests, the quality of Presidential leadership, other institutional and personal ambitions and administrative arrangements in the Executive Branch, the initiative, effort, and ambitions of individual legislators and their governmental and nongovernmental staffs, the policy commitments of political parties, and the predominant culture symbols in the minds both of leaders and followers in the Congress.

Most of these forces appear to be involved at every important stage in the policy-making process, and they act only within the most general limits of popular concern about a specific issue.

In the absence of a widely recognized crisis, legislative policy-making tends to be fought out at the level of largely irresponsible personal and group stratagems and compromises based upon temporary power coalitions of political, administrative, and non-governmental interests.

This type of policy-making is in part responsible for, and is certainly aided and abetted by, the rules, structures, and procedures of the Congress, and by a widely shared folklore of American Constitutional theory which is uncritically accepted by the great majority of our national legislators— the sanctity of Congressional prerogatives and the desirability of competing power systems in the federal government.

Put in its baldest form, the story of S.380 adds up to the fact that majority sentiment expressed in popular elections for a particular economic policy can be, and frequently is, almost hopelessly splintered by the power struggles of competing political, administrative, and private interests, and is finally pieced together, if at all, only by the most laborious, complicated, and frequently covert coalition strategies.

Granted that basic to the drafting of a full employment bill in the United States was a public awareness that the recurrence of widespread unemployment was a frightening possibility in the postwar years, the fact remains that the American voter could not and cannot hold any recognizable group, interest, or individual responsible for the Employment Act of 1946.

Certainly President Truman cannot be held responsible. It is true that he attempted to provide political leadership through his messages to Congress, his radio appeals to the public, the testimony of members of his Cabinet before the Senate and House committees, his conversations with key Congressional leaders, and his appointment of a Cabinet committee under Fred Vinson to press for passage of a strong bill. It is true also that he signed the final compromise Act. But the forces which shaped and modified the legislation were far beyond his control, and it is almost certain that if he had vetoed the conference bill he would have got nothing in its place.

The political parties cannot be held responsible, except in the negative sense that their weakness made irresponsibility inevitable. Both the Democratic and Republican Party platforms in 1944 paid their respects to the issue of full or high level employment, and both Presidential candidates as party leaders endorsed the principle of federal responsibility for providing "jobs for all." But during the legislative struggle over S.380, with the exception of the division on the two Hickenlooper amendments in the Senate, there was little indication that party affiliation was an important determinant of voting behavior. Neither Republicans nor Democrats were able to present an even reasonably solid

phalanx for or against the bill at the crucial stage of House consideration. Party lines were crossed with impunity. In short, so complicated were the interparty alignments that it is literally impossible for the voter to hold either party separately, or both parties together, responsible for the Employment Act of 1946.

Can responsibility be placed on the pressure groups? Not in any meaningful political sense. The National Farmers Union authored the proposal which in turn stimulated the drafting of S.380. The Lib-Lab lobby, under the leadership of the Continuations Group, worked diligently for a strong bill. But what of the Committee for Economic Development, the United States Chamber of Commerce, and the Machinery and Allied Products Institute which were of great importance in shaping the substance of the final bill? And what of the more uncompromising pressures from the "right" which opened the hole through which the more moderate conservative spokesmen ran? Even if there were mechanisms, which there are not, for identifying the various pressure-group influences and their respective impacts upon the policy-making process, how could the voting public hold them accountable?

Who remains? The individual Senators and Congressmen? But what control does a national popular majority have over a Will Whittington of Mississippi or a Clare Hoffman of Michigan or a John Cochran of St. Louis? These men were not representatives of national political parties based upon national programs. They were representatives of the dominant interests and culture symbols of tiny geographical areas which, even if taken in the aggregate, do not give a fair quantitative weighting to the sentiments and expectations of a national popular majority. Furthermore, the committee system in Congress means that key representatives may have an inordinate amount of individual power in the shaping of national destinies, even when those key representatives are effectively accountable only to a tiny economic and political junta in one Congressional District.

These are some of the facts of our political life. Their seriousness in terms of the future of American democracy are discounted both by those who fear majority rule and by those who have a sanguine faith that the American genius for unity in times of dire emergency will somehow continue to save "Pauline" as she dangles from the edge of the cliff.

The American democracy is built upon a number of unwritten propositions. One of the basic tenets is that political mechanisms are creatures of human intelligence and human will; that they are subject to change as human needs and expectations change. In an age when national problems require national answers and when democratic expectations have reached a point of no return in the direction of governmental responsibility for protecting citizens from the ravages of economic forces beyond their separate control, is it not time that intelligence was reapplied to our basic political institutions? Whether the American system can long endure depends upon a number of factors, but surely one of the most important ingredients of survival is a responsible political system which will reflect the will of the majority and which will enable the citizens to hold identifiable rulers accountable for policy decisions.

I fail to see how this can be done except by strengthening the only two instruments in our political life which have an inherent responsibility to the nation as nation: the President and the national political parties. This does not suggest a sudden adoption of the British system, a change which is out of the question. Nor does it imply the development of rigid class and ideological divisions in our society. In anything as huge as the American continent, economic and cultural diversity is as inevitable as it is desirable. The strengthening of Presidential leadership and party cohesion as rational instruments of majority rule would not mean that pressure groups and regional needs would suddenly be exorcised ruthlessly from any influence in decision-making at the national level. It would mean that after those forces had contributed their points of view and their respective energies in the formulation of national policies, the public could hold an identifiable institutional leadership responsible for final decisions.

Furthermore, the strengthening of party cohesion in Congress would unquestionably enhance the collective power and prestige of that vital institution. The present splintering of decision-making leads to inevitable confusion and frustration among our national legislators, and in some cases, such as in filibusters, to a travesty of democratic processes. Congress must have the continuing right of introducing, revising, and enacting legislation, but these functions should be carried on in such a way that the public can pin responsibility unequivocally.

In the absence of a responsible political system we run the grave risk of public cynicism and frustration, and of neglecting policies which could anticipate and to some extent preclude serious economic crises.

The story of the Employment Act of 1946 suggests a need for more responsible policy-making in our national legislature. It also suggests that until we move in that direction, national economic policies will continue to be formulated by a kaleidoscopic and largely irresponsible interplay of ideas, interests, institutions, and individuals.

REPRESENTATIVE GOVERNMENT THROUGH THE HOUSE OF REPRESENTATIVES

JULIUS TURNER

The effective coordination of representative government with democratic ideology provokes, perhaps necessarily, some contradictions which confuse our understanding of the American governmental system. Americans set forth as a principal demand upon their legislators that they be "independent" in their actions in government. The candidate is rash who will not announce that he is "fearless," that he has made "no promises to special groups," that he will "follow the President when he is right," but will remain free to "vote his convictions." American political mythology is crammed with the sagas of representatives who defied the demands of party and constituency in order to do what the representative believed to be right.[1]

[1] See, for example, Claudius O. Johnson, *Borah of Idaho* (New York, 1936); George W. Norris, *Fighting Liberal* (New York, 1945); Joseph B. Bishop, *Theodore Roosevelt and His Time* (2 vols., New York, 1920); Kenneth W. Hechler, *Insurgency* (New York, 1940). For the effects of this indoctrination on the public, see Virginia Moorehead Mannon, "What Kind of Congressmen Do We Need in Wartime?" *National Municipal Review* (July, 1942), XXXI, 376-378. Miss Mannon found in a survey of League of Women Voters members the following attitudes toward attributes of congressmen: Favorable—Intellectual integrity, Determination to subordinate party interest to

Against this goal of representative independence Americans set up the conflicting goal of representative responsibility. We demand that our rulers periodically return to be judged by the electorate as to the wisdom of their actions in office. While the independence of the representative may bring him support in the election from some of his constituents, he will find, if he has been "fearless" in his actions, that his independence has cost him the support of groups important to his re-election. He has failed to support farm parity: his district's farmers will not vote for him. The appropriations have been cut for the naval base in his district: the shipworkers will not vote for him and the owners are contributing to his opponent's campaign. He bolted his party on five measures which the President wanted passed for the national campaign; national party leaders are sending speakers and money to help his opponent in the primary, and the vacant postmastership in the representative's home town has been filled without his knowledge by a man he does not know.

national, Independent judgment, Broad background in civic affairs, Political sagacity; Opposed—Party regularity, Follower of individual, rather than party platforms, One who promises desired public projects for district.

From Julius Turner, *Party and Constituency: Pressures on Congress.* The Johns Hopkins University Studies in Historical and Political Science. Series LXIX, 1951, 1, 164-179. Reprinted by permission of the publisher.

The conflict between the ideal of independence and the reality of the demand for responsibility has resulted in a curious situation. The ideal of independence is often upheld by representatives in their speeches, and perhaps in their unrecorded activities in government, but their responsibility to the groups which can bring about their election is maintained in the votes of the great majority of congressmen. The number of congressmen is very small who over a large number of roll calls can successfully resist the pressures of constituency and party. And those who do resist these pressures are eliminated from office more quickly than other representatives.

Of course there are many congressmen who are caught between conflicting pressures, whose party and constituency, or whose groups within the constituency, disagree as to what the congressman should do. Such congressmen are beset with a greater problem than those whose party and all constituent groups urge them to vote for the same legislation. Representatives subject to conflicting pressures must be able to balance these pressures, decide which ones are more important, or attempt to please all by casting conflicting votes on a succession of roll calls. In some cases, on the other hand, a congressman with conflicting pressures may be more free than others to exercise both support and opposition, he may be able to depend to a greater extent on his own feelings in the matter.

The extent to which congressmen follow the pressures of party and some of the pressures of the constituency (metropolitan-rural, foreign-native, and section) has been shown in preceding chapters. Each of these pressures has been shown to be important on some issues in both parties in all years studied, although the pressure of party was much more important than any of the constituent pressures. Even in the case of party, however, we have found at least a few men on almost every roll call who have ignored party pressure and voted with the other party. This revolt on the part of some congressmen against the pressure of party might be termed "independence." In many cases, however, we discover that when a representative bolts his party he is not voting his conscience, but answering the more insistent pressure of groups in his constituency which disagree with the party. A very large number of congressional votes, therefore, may be accounted for as reflections of the pressure of either party or constituency.

Effect of Combined Pressures

The great extent to which congressmen follow the combined pressures of party and group can be discovered by examining the voting records of congressmen whose party and district groups were in substantial agreement as to what the congressman should vote for. When group and party agree, the failure of the representative to vote with party and group is an indication of independent action on the part of the congressman.

The year 1944 provides a good basis for the study of the combined influence of party and group on congressional voting behavior. In that year, it will be recalled from preceding chapters, the pressures of districts in the North and on the Coast, and of metropolitan and foreign constituencies[2] were such as to force representatives from these areas to be loyal to the program of the majority of Democrats, and to be insurgent as far as the Republican majority program was concerned. The pressures of the South, Interior, rural and native constituencies, on the other hand, were directed toward insurgency in the Democratic party and loyalty to the Republican party. If the pressures we have named were the only ones affecting Congress, and if congressmen exercised no independent judgment, we would expect all Northern metropolitan foreign Democrats to support the Democratic majority's program without dissent, and all Interior rural native Republicans to oppose

[2] The South included all Democratic districts in states which seceded in the Civil War, plus Oklahoma; the Coast included all Republican districts in states bordering on the Atlantic or Pacific.

the Democratic majority with the same unanimity.

As can be seen in Table 1, groups subject to the pressure we have described do not fall far short of the behavior which would be expected if the factors studied were the only ones on which congressmen depended in deciding their votes. When the loyalty to the Democratic majority program of the 59 Democrats who came from Northern metropolitan foreign districts is compared with the loyalty to the Democratic program of the 68 Republicans from Interior rural native districts, their behavior differs almost completely. Three-quarters of the Democrats were in the range of greatest loyalty to the party, 90.1-100 per cent loyal, and three-fifths of the Republicans were in the range least loyal to the Democratic majority, 0.0-10.0. Of the 59 Northern metropolitan foreign Democrats, eighteen had perfect loyalty records, voting with party and group on every roll call. Of the 68 Interior rural native Republicans, seven disagreed with the Democratic majority on every single vote. Only three Northern metropolitan foreign Democrats were less than 80.1 per cent loyal to the party, and only two Interior rural native Republicans

voted more than 20.0 per cent of the time with the majority of Democrats.

Combining the figures for the two parties, we can say that 25 of the 128 congressmen, or about one-fifth, voted according to the dictates of party and group on every roll call; 85, or about two-thirds, followed party and group on 90 per cent or more of the roll calls; only five, less than one in 25, opposed party and group on more than 20 per cent of the roll calls, and none opposed party and group more than 35 per cent of the time.[3]

Thus it appears that independent action on the part of a congressman when the pressures of party and group coincided was a rare event, an action which was indulged in on less than one-tenth of the votes of two-thirds of the representatives. The figures become even more impressive when it is recalled that the group pressures which we have measured make up only a part of the pressures on Congress. Those instances in which we find evidence of congressional opposition to party and other measured

[3] The record of greatest opposition to party and group in 1944 was achieved by H. Streett Baldwin, of Baltimore, who voted with the Democratic majority 65.2 per cent of the time.

TABLE 1

EFFECT OF COMBINED PRESSURES: FREQUENCY DISTRIBUTION OF NORTH-
ERN METROPOLITAN FOREIGN DEMOCRATS AND INTERIOR RURAL
NATIVE REPUBLICANS IN INDEX OF LOYALTY TO
DEMOCRATIC MAJORITY, 1944

Index of Loyalty to Democrats	Democratic North Metropolitan Foreign		Republican Interior Rural Native	
	Number	Per Cent	Number	Per Cent
10.1–20.0	0	0.0	41	60.3
0.0–10.0	0	0.0	25	36.8
20.1–30.0	0	0.0	2	2.9
30.1–40.0	0	0.0	0	0.0
40.1–50.0	0	0.0	0	0.0
50.1–60.0	0	0.0	0	0.0
60.1–70.0	1	1.7	0	0.0
70.1–80.0	2	3.4	0	0.0
80.1–90.0	12	20.3	0	0.0
90.1–100.0	44	74.6	0	0.0
Total	59	100.0	68	100.0

groups may reflect the pressure of un-measured factors, rather than the inde-pendent judgment of the representative.[4]

EFFECT OF CONFLICTING PRESSURES: DEMOCRATS

The majority of congressmen were not fortunate enough to represent areas where the pressures of party and all other important groups coincided. In 1944, 91 Democrats and 46 Republicans represented districts all of whose measured groups tended to oppose the program of the party of their representa-tive. Nearly 300 congressmen represented districts in which at least one factor ran counter to party. When such conflicts arose, the congressman usually reflected the con-flict in a roll call record midway between the extremes established by the members whose party and constituent groups agreed. Thus the Northern metropolitan *native*[5] Democrats had two factors in their con-stituencies favorable to loyalty to the Demo-cratic party; the fact that the constituencies were in the North, and that they were metro-politan. These constituencies, however, were *native*, a factor which would tend to lessen the loyalty of Democrats representing them. As shown in Table 3, Northern metropoli-tan *native* Democrats tended to be less loyal than Northern metropolitan foreign Demo-crats, although the loyalty of both groups was high. A majority of the seventeen Northern metropolitan *native* Democrats were above an index of 90.0, but three were less than 70.1.

In the Northern *rural native* and *Southern* metropolitan *native* districts, where two measured factors worked against Democratic

[4] Introductory experiments with congres-sional dichotomies based on the religious affilia-tion and occupation of constituents indicate that these attributes are probably as important as the group factors already selected as deter-minants of congressional voting behavior. Neither religion nor occupation, however, is nearly so important as party as a determinant of voting behavior.

[5] Hereafter factors which forced representa-tives to oppose the party majority will be italicized in the text and tables.

TABLE 2

COINCIDENCE OF FACTORS FAVORABLE TO PARTY LOYALTY: NUMBER OF REPUBLI-CANS AND DEMOCRATS REPRESENTING DIS-TRICTS WITH VARIOUS ATTRIBUTES AFFECTING PARTY LOYALTY, 1944

Attributes of Districts[a]	Number of Representatives	Number of Factors Opposing Party
DEMOCRATS		
Metropolitan Foreign North	59	None
Metropolitan *Native* North	17	1
Rural Foreign North	5	1
Rural Native North	25	2
Metropolitan *Native South*	17	2
Rural Native South	91	3
REPUBLICANS		
Interior Rural Native	68	None
Interior Rural *Foreign*	19	1
Interior *Metropolitan* Native	19	1
Coast Rural Native	19	1
Interior *Metropolitan Foreign*	10	2
Coast Rural *Foreign*	5	2
Coast Metropolitan Native	15	2
Coast Metropolitan Foreign	46	3

[a] Factors opposed to party are italicized thus: Metro-politan *Native* North. There are no foreign districts in the South.

loyalty, there was a greater tendency toward disloyalty to the party than in Northern metropolitan districts. Only 9 of the 25 *rural native* Northerners were above 90.0 in loyalty, and 5 were below 70.1. Only 4 of the 17 metropolitan *native Southerners* were above 90.0, and 4 were below 70.1.

The most marked insurgency among Dem-ocrats, however, was in representatives of *Southern rural native* constituencies, where all measured factors of the constituency worked against party loyalty. Only 5 of the 91 rural Southerners were above 90.0, and 47, or over half, were below 70.1. It should be noted, nevertheless, that the power of party was usually great enough to offset the other factors, for only thirteen of the 91 *Southern rural native* Democrats voted more than half the time for the Republican

TABLE 3

EFFECT OF CONFLICTING PRESSURES ON DEMOCRATIC LOYALTY:
FREQUENCY DISTRIBUTION IN INDEX OF LOYALTY OF DEMOCRATS
WITH DIFFERENT ATTRIBUTES IN CONSTITUENCIES, 1944[a]

Range of Index of Loyalty	Native Metrop. Foreign	North Metrop. Native	North Rural Native	South Metrop. Native	South Rural Native
Below 65.1	0	2	4	3	36
65.1–70.0	1	1	1	1	11
70.1–75.0	0	0	1	1	14
75.1–80.0	2	1	3	3	11
80.1–85.0	2	1	3	2	8
85.1–90.0	10	2	4	3	6
90.1–95.0	13	5	7	2	3
95.1–100.0	31	5	2	2	2
Total	59	17	25	17	91

[a] Includes all Democrats except five Northern *rural* foreign. There were no Southern foreign districts.

program, toward which the pressures of the groups in their constituencies directed them.

EFFECT OF CONFLICTING PRESSURES: REPUBLICANS

The tendency for the conflict of group with party to lower the congressman's party loyalty in proportion to the number of groups in his constituency opposing party is found in Republican ranks as well as in the Democratic. Interior rural *foreign*, Interior *metropolitan* native, and *Coastal* rural native Republicans, all of whom had only one measured factor in the constituency working against loyalty to the party, were more loyal than most other Republicans. These groups, nevertheless, fell behind the party regularity of Interior rural native Republicans, who had no measured factors in the constituency to deter votes with the party. Over half the Interior rural native Republicans were over 90.0 in loyalty, compared with only 6 of the 19 Interior rural *foreign*, 4 of the 19 Interior *metropolitan* native, and 12 of the 29 *Coastal* rural native Republicans. None of the 68 Interior rural native Republicans, all of whose measured attributes favored party loyalty, were below 70.1, but 5 of the 66 Republicans with

one factor opposing loyalty were below 70.1.

In the Interior *metropolitan foreign* and *Coastal metropolitan* native groups there were two factors in the constituencies which would tend to make the members bolt the party. These groups were more insurgent than any other Republicans except the *Coastal metropolitan foreign*, all of whose measured attributes worked against party loyalty. Seven of the 25 Republicans with two factors opposing the party majority were above an index of 90.1; only 4 of the 46 Republicans with all measured factors opposing party were above 90.1. Half of the *Coastal metropolitan foreign* group was below 80.1, but only one of these, Richard J. Welch of San Francisco, voted more often with the Democrats than with the Republicans. All Republicans except Welch voted with their party against the pressures of constituency a majority of the time.

Personal Characteristics of Representatives

The above figures on congressional voting behavior yield conclusions which conflict with some previous studies of roll calls. In Chapter I we cited Gleeck's study of congressional voting motivation, in which both congressmen and newspapermen and congressional secretaries testified that the con-

TABLE 4

EFFECT OF CONFLICTING PRESSURES ON REPUBLICAN LOYALTY:
FREQUENCY DISTRIBUTION IN INDEX OF LOYALTY OF
REPUBLICANS WITH VARYING ATTRIBUTES IN
CONSTITUENCIES, 1944[a]

Range of Index of Loyalty	Interior Rural Native	Interior Rural *Foreign*	Interior *Metrop.* Native	*Coast* Rural Native	Interior *Metrop.* *Foreign*	*Coast* *Metrop.* Native	*Coast* *Metro.* *Foreign*
Below 70.1	0	1	2	2	1	4	5
70.1–75.0	0	2	1	3	1	2	11
75.1–80.0	2	1	0	2	2	0	7
80.1–85.0	5	2	6	4	2	2	8
85.1–90.0	24	7	6	6	0	4	11
90.1–95.0	17	2	3	6	1	3	4
95.1–100.0	20	4	1	6	3	0	0
Total	68	19	19	29	10	15	46

[a] Includes all Republicans except five *Coastal* rural *foreign*.

gressman's personal opinion was the principal determinant of his vote.[6] Stuart Rice has studied the voting behavior of farmers, workers, and other party members in the New York legislature, concluding that these groups, selected according to the personal characteristics of the legislators, differed in their behavior.[7] Recently a liberal Catholic journal surveyed the voting records of Catholic members of Congress, concluding that Catholic representatives, as a group, were much more liberal than other members of Congress.[8]

The conflict between the findings of these other studies and the findings of this chapter lies in the conclusions, and not in the facts. Because farmers are usually elected from rural districts, and because Catholics are elected from districts where the proportion of Catholics in the population is high, it would not be difficult to discover spurious differences between farmers and workers or Catholics and Protestants in Congress. It appears, however, that these differences

[6] Gleeck, *Public Opinion Quarterly* (March, 1940), IV, 3-24.

[7] *Quantitative Methods in Politics*, pp. 211-216.

[8] Dale Francis, "Voting Record of Catholics in Congress," *Commonweal* (January 14, 1949), XLIX, 342-345. Francis notes the possibility that it was the constituency which accounted for liberal votes by Catholics in Congress.

are much more closely connected with differences in the constituencies than with differences in the personal characteristics of congressmen. We have found, for example, that the North-South conflict was an important factor in the behavior of Democratic congressmen. Yet Democrat Harry Sheppard of California, who was raised in Mobile, Alabama, voted like a Northern Democrat, even on issues concerning the Negro; the same "Northern" behavior was found in Compton I. White of Idaho, who was born in Louisiana and educated in Mississippi. We have found significant differences, furthermore, between representatives of foreign and native districts; yet most "foreign" districts were represented by native-born congressmen who had to trace back at least two generations to discover a foreign-born ancestor. The small number of farmers in Congress tended to vote alike, but they also voted like the lawyers, bankers, businessmen, and schoolteachers who happened to represent rural native districts. And lawyers, bankers, businessmen and schoolteachers differed in their voting behavior not along lines of occupation, but according to the party and districts they represented. Businessman Jay LeFevre, politician Hamilton Fish, and lawyer Daniel C. Reed, all Republicans from rural native districts in 1944, had very similar voting records; they agreed on nearly every issue on which Republicans disagreed with Democrats. But businessman Charles A. Buckley, politician Andrew L. Somers, and lawyer Donald L. O'Toole, who represented foreign metropolitan New York City districts, voted together for the Democratic party line, opposing the Republicans on over 95 per cent of the roll calls. The personal attitudes of a congressman, unless they happened to coincide with the attitudes of his party and district, were not usually found in his voting behavior.[9]

There was a minority of congressmen, however, whose voting records were quite different from what we might expect from our knowledge of their districts. There was, for example, one Northern metropolitan foreign Democrat in 1944 who voted less than two-thirds of the time with his party. This representative, H. Streett Baldwin of Baltimore and Baltimore County, had an index of 65.2. There were four other Northern metropolitan foreign Democrats who voted less than 85 per cent of the time with their party, and, as we have noted, only 18 who voted with the party on every occasion. In the cases of Northern metropolitan foreign Democrats like Representative Baldwin, all of the measured factors of

the constituency worked for loyalty to the party, so that it is quite likely that political independence was exhibited in their votes.

INDEPENDENCE AND ELECTORAL SUCCESS: DEMOCRATS

Representatives who are independent[10] of their constituencies and especially of their parties, however, are not treated kindly by the American electorate. The longevity in office of representatives who defied party and constituency appears to have been much less than the longevity of congressmen who yielded to the major pressures. The establishment of this fact, the high mortality of political independents, goes far to explain the means by which parties and groups apply pressure on Congress, and to explain the reason for the small number of political independents who remain in Washington.

The combined effect of party and constituency on electoral success is shown in Table 5, in which the continuity in office of Democratic insurgents in 1944 is compared with the continuity of Democrats as a whole. "Continuity" is here defined as a congressman's ability to remain in office

[9] The above is not to say that personal characteristics are of little importance in the other activities of a congressman. His work in committee, in writing and pushing action on legislation, and in rounding up support on a roll call may depend very much on his personal attitudes.

[10] Hereafter the word "independent" will be used to describe a congressman who fails to follow the pressure of either his party or his constituency; "insurgent" will be used to describe a congressman who fails to follow his party, although insurgents may in some cases follow the pressures of their constituencies.

TABLE 5

CONTINUITY IN OFFICE OF DEMOCRATIC INSURGENTS: PROPORTION OF ALL
DEMOCRATS, AND OF DEMOCRATS WHOSE LOYALTY WAS BELOW
70.1 IN 1944, WHO SURVIVED TWO ELECTIONS

Attributes of Districts	All Democrats			Insurgents (Below 70.1)		
	Number in 1944	Remained 1948 Number	Per Cent	Number in 1944	Remained 1948 Number	Per Cent
Nor-Met-For	59	33	55.9	1	0	0.0
Nor-Met-*Nat*	17	7	41.2	3	1	33.3
Nor-*Rur*-For	5	3	60.0	.	.	.
Nor-*Rur*-Nat	25	15	60.0	5	3	60.0
South-Met-Nat	17	9	52.9	4	1	25.0
South-Rur-Nat	91	62	68.1	47	30	63.8
Total	214	129	60.3	60	35	58.3

through two successive elections[11] after his roll call record is established. The congressman's ability to return to office in successive elections is a good index of the degree to which he has satisfied his party and constituents. If his over-all record has not been satisfactory to these groups, he will very likely be defeated in a primary or general election, or will be forced to resign without trying for re-election.

Not all failures to return to office, to be sure, indicate failures on the part of congressmen to satisfy party and constituents. Congressmen may leave office by way of death or resignation, as well as by defeat in an election. It seems to be a fair assumption, however, that death, and resignations not forced by party or constituency, occur with about the same frequency for all kinds of congressmen, regular or insurgent, and in all kinds of districts. Differences in the ratio of congressmen returned to office in groups with different voting behavior, therefore, reflect differences in political support given to the two groups.

The amount of political support given to all Democratic insurgents[12] in 1944 did not differ very much from the amount of support given to Democrats in general. About three-fifths of both insurgents and regulars were successful in the two elections, although the percentage of successful insurgents was slightly lower than the percentage for the party as a whole (58.3 per cent to 60.3). It would appear, therefore, that party bolters in the Democratic party had no reason to fear reprisals at the polls.

When, however, the figures are broken down according to the kinds of districts which the insurgents represented, a different pattern appears. In those districts where the pressures of the constituency worked against party loyalty, insurgents, who were following the constituency, were returned to office about as often as regulars. But in those districts where the pressures of the constituency favored party loyalty, insurgent Democrats were less likely to return to office than regulars.

The Northern and *Southern rural native* insurgents, who had several district pressures against party loyalty, were about as successful as regulars from such districts in returning to office. Three-fifths of both insurgent and regular Northern *rural native* Democrats were returned,[13] and 63.8 per cent of *Southern rural native* Democrats were returned, compared with 68.1 per cent of all Democrats from such districts.

In metropolitan districts, on the other hand, insurgent Democrats were much less successful than regulars. The single Northern metropolitan foreign insurgent was eliminated in 1946, although a majority of Democrats from such districts were successful in the two elections. Only one of the three Northern metropolitan *native* insurgents was successful, compared with six of the fourteen regulars. Only one of the four *Southern* metropolitan insurgents remained after two elections, although over half of all the members from these districts were returned.

The small number of foreign insurgents in the Democratic party in 1944 prevents speculation on the political sanctions of foreign constituencies. The cases are too few, furthermore, for final conclusions on the effectiveness of metropolitan constituencies in defeating Democrats who defied party and group, but the available evidence indicates that Democrats who opposed both metropolis and party were eliminated more quickly than those who obeyed these pressures. It is particularly significant that the Southern metropolitan areas should get rid of their Democratic insurgents at so high

---

[11] The successive elections were those of 1944, at the end of the 1944 session, and 1946. The test is extended over two elections because the single election of 1944, a Democratic landslide, did not appear to be a fair test of the ability of individual Republicans and Democrats to return to office. The Republicans won in 1946.

[12] Members are considered insurgent in this comparison if their party loyalty was 70.0 or less.

[13] The relative success of Northern rural native insurgents may have been caused by the fact that the three successful insurgents had received bipartisan support in the elections. All came from California, and had won both parties' nominations under the California cross-filing law.

a rate. The Southern one-party system is apparently not always sufficient to insulate the representative from party and group pressures.

INDEPENDENCE AND ELECTORAL SUCCESS: REPUBLICANS

The Republican party in 1944-46 was much more effective than the Democratic in punishing insurgent members. While over 70 per cent of all Republicans were successful in the two elections, only six of the sixteen insurgents, 37.5 per cent, managed to return over the same period. Republican discipline appeared to be effective, furthermore, in every kind of district where insurgency arose, for the proportion of successful insurgent Republicans was less than the proportion of successful regulars in every kind of district, regardless of the number of factors in the district working against loyalty to the party.

As in the case of the Democrats, however, Republican insurgents with characteristics in their districts contrary to the party line were relatively successful in returning to office. *Coastal metropolitan foreign* and native Republican insurgents, of whom 50.0 and 40.0 per cent were re-elected, respectively, were nearly as successful as all Republicans from such districts, of whom slightly more than half were re-elected. Four of the six re-elected insurgents came from these districts. Another came from an Interior *metropolitan* native district, and one from a rural *Coastal* native area.

It is perhaps significant that in the Republican party insurgents from foreign districts were relatively unsuccessful in returning to office. In the case of the Democrats we were unable to draw conclusions about foreign-native election reprisals because of the small number of insurgent Democrats from foreign districts. While the numbers were also small in the case of the Republicans, it is significant that *Coastal metropolitan foreign* insurgents were less successful than native insurgents from the same area, and that Interior *metropolitan foreign* insurgents were likewise less success-

ful than Interior *metropolitan* native. In Chapter V we found that the foreign factor tended to make Democrats loyal and Republicans insurgent in 1944, and, if foreign groups were politically effective, we would accordingly expect them to reward Republican insurgents with re-election. Since a contrary trend is discovered, we may surmise that foreign groups in Republican districts still have not gained political effectiveness. While foreign Republican districts failed to return insurgents to office, metropolitan and Coastal Republican insurgents received high degrees of support.

Of the 24 Republican or Democratic insurgents with one or more factors in the constituency favoring party in 1944, 9 survived the two subsequent elections of 1944 and 1946. Of those who did not survive, one died, two retired, five were defeated in the general election, and seven were defeated in primaries. The proportion defeated in primary elections is especially significant. Few members are ordinarily beaten in primaries,[14] but almost a third of the independents were defeated in this way. The party and constituent groups wield great electoral power over those who do not yield to pressure.

CONCLUSION

One central conclusion is to be drawn from this chapter and from the preceding chapters on congressional voting behavior. That conclusion is that the representative process as practised in twentieth-century America involves, insofar as voting behavior is concerned, the attempt of the representative to mirror the political desires of those groups which can bring about his election or defeat. There are, to be sure, a few representatives who ignore political pressure and go down to defeat, and there are a few others who are fortunate to represent districts where the electoral process is not sufficiently

[14] In 1946, a year in which labor and other groups were very active in primary elections, only 25 of the 435 incumbents were defeated in primary elections. See *Union for Democratic Action Congressional Newsletter*, No. 78, September 26, 1946, Washington, D.C.

TABLE 6

CONTINUITY IN OFFICE OF REPUBLICAN INSURGENTS: PROPORTION OF ALL
REPUBLICANS, AND OF REPUBLICANS WHOSE LOYALTY WAS
BELOW 70.1 IN 1944, WHO SURVIVED TWO ELECTIONS

Attributes of Districts	All Republicans			Insurgents (Below 70.1)		
	Number in 1944	Remained 1948 Number	Per Cent	Number in 1944	Remained 1948 Number	Per Cent
Int-Rur-Nat	68	58	85.3	.	.	.
Int-Rur-*For*	19	16	84.2	1	0	0.0
Int-*Met*-Nat	19	11	57.9	2	1	50.0
Coast-Rur-Nat	29	23	79.3	2	1	50.0
Int-*Met-For*	10	5	50.0	1	0	0.0
Coast-Rur-*For*	5	2	40.0	1	0	0.0
Coast-Met-Nat	15	8	53.3	4	2	50.0
Coast-Met-For	46	25	54.3	5	2	40.0
Total	211	148	70.1	16	6	37.5

developed for pressure groups and parties to arrange reprisals at the polls.[15] The great

[15] See the remarks of Mr. Williams of Mississippi, *Congressional Record*, Vol. 93 (80th Cong., 1st sess., February 20, 1947), p. 1227. "I did not come here as a Democrat necessarily, because we have only an insignificant number of Republicans in my district, so I do not have to vote along partisan lines. I vote as my conscience tells me to vote and I do not intend to go into this thing blindfolded."

majority of congressmen, nevertheless, yield to the pressures from their constituencies, and especially to the pressures of party, in casting their votes. This picture of American representative government may not perhaps conform to the ideal of good government which some men may propose. The American Congress, is, nevertheless, a mirror of political pressure.

THE MACHINES

WARREN MOSCOW

The last time an election was stolen in New York City was in 1933, when Tammany, fighting a losing battle to save its power and prestige, elected a Borough President and a District Attorney by a margin of about 12,000 votes, all fraudulent. Those were the only offices it managed to salvage that year out of the anti-machine landslide that elected

From *Politics in The Empire State*, by Warren Moscow, by permission of the publisher, Alfred A. Knopf, Inc. Copyright 1948 by Alfred A. Knopf, Inc. (pp. 120-147).

Fiorello La Guardia as Mayor for the first time. In the long run Tammany, known nation-wide as the prototype of machine politics, would have been better off if it had not stolen the prosecutor's office. Its District Attorney was picked by men interested in protecting rather than prosecuting the underworld, and the state-sponsored Dewey investigation two years later was the inevitable result.

The theft of an election, like that of 1933, probably won't happen again, or not for a long time. Tammany was desperate, but still strong, because it had the racket mobs and the police department was under its control. Squads of mobster "storm troopers," trade-marked for their own purposes by identical pearl-gray fedoras, marched in on polling place after polling place south of Fourteenth Street in Manhattan and took over the voting machinery.

* * *

From start to finish it was just a show of force and, because of that, was limited in its application to the sections of the county where lived the poorer and less educated voters—where such tactics had the most chance of success without interference.

Interference was tried. Fiorello La Guardia's campaign manager, William M. Chadbourne, raised his bull-like voice in protest, but was arrested for disorderly conduct and marched off to the hoosegow. Things really were rough that day.

But all this was the adrenalin-inspired struggle of a dying political machine, the Tammany Hall whose name had been synonymous with power and corruption in municipal politics. And even for the limited success it achieved, it needed the connivance of a police department whose members had grown used to the system, the theory of political action that permitted the underworld to get away with murder.

It would take many years of municipal decay—and the trend is not noticeably that way—to bring back the 1933 conditions to New York City. Now the police are held personally responsible for conditions in polling places; the entire machinery of the city, state, and national governments is geared to prevent election frauds. The check on possible major-party collusion has been greater because of the existence of the organized minor parties, entitled to polls watchers and capable of manning each booth with experienced people.

Tammany could never have stolen enough votes, even under 1933 conditions, to carry the mayoralty election that year. Tammany and similar machines in the other counties had not depended on stolen votes to win elections in New York for many years. Excepting the time at the turn of the century when ballot-boxes containing votes for William Randolph Hearst for mayor were found floating in the East River the day after election, the machines did not steal on a scale large enough to affect a city-wide election. Men in a position to know definitely estimate that since the days of voting machines there never have been cast more than 40,000 fraudulent votes in a city-wide election, and of these probably 30,000 were cast in Manhattan.

* * *

It is still possible to steal a primary election, where paper ballots are used and where the public interest is not focused on the result. But in a general election, not only has it become impossible, but the will to do it no longer exists. There are few these days in any political organization, the Communists excepted, who are willing to go to jail, or risk going, for a political cause.

* * *

Immigration built the political machines in New York City, starting 'way back with the flood of the Irish, and the machines were struck a death blow when the nation embarked, after World War I, on a policy of restricted immigration through the quota system. The machines did not show the effects until much later, but the cutting off of large-scale immigration deprived them of most of their annual crop of prospective voters, people whom they could help become citizens, people in a strange country, having to learn a new language. These people needed the helping hand extended by Tammany and its allies and were in return willing, even eager, to hand over their family bloc of votes. The second generation in those families, born here, better educated, better off financially, usually grew away from the dependence their parents had had on the district leader and his leg-man, the election district or precinct captain. But up to the cutting off of immigration, there was always a new group of arrivals to be taken into the fold.

The second most important factor in the decline of the machines was the social-welfare program put into effect under the New Deal. It is a political paradox that the machines all over the country turned in their greatest majorities for and under Franklin D. Roosevelt, implementing the social program that was cutting their own throats.

In the old days—in fact, up to 1931—it was against the law in New York State for public funds to be used for the support of anyone outside a public institution. To be fed or housed, you had to go to the poorhouse as far as any agency of government was concerned. This meant that the man who was temporarily down and out got his aid from his local political machine. The leader had a ready two bucks in his pocket —in days when two bucks meant something—and his card, with a scribbled notation, was always good for a job shoveling snow for the city or digging a ditch for the gas company. The Christmas and Thanksgiving baskets meant holiday cheer for those who otherwise would not have had the means to celebrate; the annual outing of the Umteenth Democratic Club meant a neighborhood picnic for those in whose lives picnics were rare.

The Roosevelt program produced home relief and unemployment relief, which kept families together; it brought aid to widows and dependent children—aid they got as a matter of right from government and not as a favor from a political machine. It is true that the people on WPA and home relief voted for Roosevelt en masse in the 1936 election, but in New York at least, they did it as a matter of economics, or in gratitude, not as the result of compulsion.

Which leads to the basic and fundamental fact about the political machines of today. It is that even when a machine wins and wins overwhelmingly, it does so without actually controlling the vote cast.

The people vote for machine candidates when they want to, not because they have to. There is no personal obligation to the machine for money, food, or jobs. The old intimate contact between ward captain and voter does not exist. It was a long time before political observers noted this trend. It was well hidden because during the period when the decay was eating at the vitals of the machines, they happened to have in New York City and state, a remarkable series of vote-getting candidates at the top of their tickets who attracted the electorate.

In New York City there is an apparently irreducible minimum of about 700,000 voters who will vote for anyone on the Democratic ticket, and slightly more than 300,000 who will vote for anyone on the Republican ticket. These are bed-rock figures and fall short, by hundreds of thousands of votes, of being enough to elect a candidate to major office. But to the Democratic minimums Smith, Jimmy Walker, Roosevelt, and Lehman added so much strength in their own right that the machine leaders could point with pride to the enormous majorities their organizations rolled up in the machine counties. Some even kidded themselves into thinking they and their boys were responsible.

* * *

NEW YORK COUNTY

The basic trouble with Tammany is that the present members still look back to the days when it was the dominant organization in the city. They have tried to keep their machine geared to the old ratio of power and patronage, to maintain that higher standard of political living which was theirs when they ran the city, and no longer can be kept up on the purse of a single county organization.

Tammany had so much, in the old days, that it suffered far more than any of the other county organizations when it lost control of City Hall in 1933, with the election of La Guardia. The others had lived off their county patronage, plus the bits Tammany let them have from the city trough. It is probable that Tammany could have survived one or two terms of La Guardia as Mayor, still possessing, as it did for a while, control of the magistrates' courts and the county offices. But before La Guardia was through, county offices and county government had been wiped out, or placed on a civil-service merit basis. And magistrates serve only ten-year terms.

By the time the Little Flower left City Hall, at the end of twelve years of independent, anti-machine rule, there was not—there could not be—a single person outside of the state and county courts who owed his job and therefore his primary allegiance to Tammany rather than to La Guardia.

The organization went bankrupt in more ways than one. Its new Wigwam on Seventeenth street, built to order in prosperous days, was sold out from under it by the bank that held the mortgage. The International Ladies Garment Workers Union, the "pantspressers in politics," took it over as headquarters. Tammany was reduced to a political scavenger status. Judgeship-selling became more prevalent. There were reports that even appointments as secretaries and court attendants had "for sale" tags on them. Still later the ruling clique in the Hall was reduced to the ignominy of the alliance with Marcantonio referred to elsewhere. Tammany, which once had run the city, had to get its favors and its protection second-hand.

It would be pleasant to report that Tammany had shown some signs of either reforming, or recovering its leadership since 1933. Curry, the very fine district leader whose obstinacy made him the worst county leader, went out in 1934, to be followed by a whole series of leaders who did not fill the

bill. Jim Dooling had the capacity, but was ill, and a sick man can not function in a job that requires sometimes the tact of an ambassador and at others the brass of a burglar. . . .

Through all those years and county leaderships Tammany's individual district leaders seemed to show little sign of understanding that times had changed. The caliber of their candidates for office was not improved. I recall checking one election eve in a La Guardia campaign with one of the most important and quickest-witted members of the Hall. What did he think was going to happen in the mayoralty race to be settled the next day?

"I think the best man will win," said the political light, and both he and I knew exactly whom he meant.

* * *

As a factor in New York County, Tammany has its importance. It has maintained its old-time substantial lead in enrollment, as the figures for the last presidential, mayoralty, and gubernatorial election years show:

Election	Democratic	Republican	ALP
1944	450,577	193,354	41,395
1945	308,837	93,388	49,499
1946	338,042	181,613	57,751

The election results are often different, however. In New York County, as elsewhere, enrolled Democrats have been inclined to vote under the American Labor or Liberal party emblems, pulling the Democratic vote consistently under the party's enrollment. The figures for the same three elections follow:

Election	Democratic	Republican	ALP	Liberal
1944	350,750	258,516	96,511	62,559
1945*	189,917	76,802	63,554	21,617
1946	212,718	264,990	80,995	32,175

* The 1945 mayoralty election was the only one of the three in which the Democratic, American Labor, and Liberal party votes were not cast for the same head of the ticket. In that year, it must be remembered, O'Dwyer received the Democratic and ALP nomination, Goldstein the Republican and Liberal; and Newbold Morris ran independently, getting more than 400,000 votes in the city at large.

In weighing Tammany's position, one must remember that the votes it once controlled are no longer there, even if Tammany could control them. Manhattan, for twenty years, has been in the process of being transformed into a business and management terminal, with no room for low-rent slums. A single improvement like the Holland Tunnel wiped out six blocks of tenements for its plaza, and the voters never came back. . . . With the loss of people, it has also lost congressional and legislative representation and the prestige that goes with large blocs of votes. If Tammany ever regains the ascendency in the city and state that it had in the days of Charles F. Murphy, it will be as the result of many years of careful rebuilding of political fences. Such a program is not clearly in sight.

Among New York County's Republicans, the organization trend is upward rather than down, but the GOP still has a long way to go to attain any rank. The party's plight goes back to the days of Sam Koenig, ousted as leader in 1933. In most of the twenty-two years that Koenig tried to keep his machine operating, his party's stands on state and national issues were contrary to the thinking of the majority of the people, and therefore he couldn't win an election. Koenig was a man of character and integrity, but his district leaders lived all during national prohibition on the pickings they got from dry-law corruption, plus a little federal patronage. Koenig took the rap, in the public's mind, and in the political ferment of 1933 the "old man" was beaten in a primary fight.

After an interim Kenneth F. Simpson took over, in 1935, and under his ebullient leadership the party perked up considerably, but it never had much patronage to grease its wheels until Tom Dewey became Governor and his personal lieutenant, Tom Curran, became county chairman. Its lack of a definite hold on the voters is best illustrated by the figures for the 1945 mayoralty election. Goldstein, the mayoralty nominee picked by Curran, Dewey, and the Liberal Party, got 76,802 votes on the Republican ticket, while Newbold Morris, La Guardia's candidate, received 100,064 votes

in the county, nearly all of them from Republicans.

But the New York County Republicans have received a very substantial share of state patronage, and, on the county-wide basis, by dealing with the ALP or the Democrats, they have been able occasionally to elect a judge or a county officeholder. Formerly its ability to get a candidate into office had been limited to the confines of the silk-stocking congressional and senatorial district dominated by upper Fifth, Madison, and Park avenues. The Republican organization is more alive and alert than it was, but if the GOP should lose the Governorship and not get any federal patronage, its position would not be good.

BROOKLYN

Back in the last century, the Democratic boss of Coney Island, John Y. McKane, stole enough votes for his party's ticket to swing the state and the presidential election to Grover Cleveland. Apart from that, the Brooklyn Democratic crowd has always operated on a reasonably conservative basis. In the early part of the current century Brooklyn went Republican as often as not, but as the tomato fields and potato patches gave way to two-family dwellings, inhabited by refugees from Manhattan's crowded streets, the borough became more and more Democratic in its voting tendencies. In 1927 the organization, then headed by John H. McCooey, scored its first clean sweep, electing every alderman, assemblyman, and county officeholder.

McCooey was a fat, ruddy-faced little man who could have posed without make-up as Santa Claus in any Fulton Street department store. And he was Santa Claus to the Kings County Democrats, bringing them to the top of the world politically. Smith and Roosevelt helped with their vote-getting power, of course.

There is the story of the candidate for a minor judgeship, who was expected to win easily in Roosevelt's first campaign for the Presidency. But he developed an acute case of candidatitis—he hadn't seen his name mentioned in the papers and he was sure he was going to be licked. He stood in Mc-Cooey's receiving line one Monday morning, intending to unburden himself on the county boss. But his local district leader saw him first, knew what was on his mind, and yanked him by the ear over to a corner.

The leader said: "Look. You've seen a ferryboat pull into a slip. When it pulls in, it pulls a lot of garbage in with it. Stop worrying. Roosevelt is a ferryboat."

McCooey, in his dotage, hooked up too closely with Curry's leadership of Tammany Hall, and the two managed to drag their organizations down into friendless defeat. "Uncle John" died a year later, in 1934, and he was succeeded by an even defter man, Frank V. Kelly, who took an organization that had been hit hard, that was ready for strife and dissension, and he kept it toeing the mark for another dozen years. Kelly was independent financially, with a substantial income from an insurance business. He kept the machine clean and he consistently followed the policies of Roosevelt and Lehman, which was all he really needed to do. He never could defeat La Guardia in the county, but neither was anyone else successful in doing so in New Deal territory when La Guardia had the Roosevelt blessing.

The enrollment figures for the borough are impressive for the Democrats:

Election	Democratic	Republican	ALP
1944	715,904	256,158	83,244
1945	513,468	105,120	89,782
1946	563,915	207,902	102,961

The election figures for the same years:

Election	Democratic	Republican	ALP	Liberal
1944	475,866	396,866	155,544	132,195
1945*	293,515	104,750	92,816	53,452
1946	311,516	353,846	140,817	67,890

* Morris received 136,632 votes for mayor.

It is interesting to note that Democratic party strength was so low everywhere in 1946 that even in Brooklyn it took the margins furnished by the American Labor and Liberal parties to give Mead, the party's gubernatorial nominee, a majority in the county. This compares with the 366,739 majority Roosevelt received in 1944, roughly 50,000 more than his total margin in the state.

Kelly died before the 1946 election, and John Cashmore, the Borough President, was elected leader. The influence of Mayor O'Dwyer—who declared for Cashmore while the district leaders were still debating the choice—and that of members of the judiciary who had been Kelly's closest advisers, put him in. Tradition of long standing was broken when Cashmore was picked, since he was a Protestant coming after an unbroken line of Irish-Catholic leaders.

Cashmore, affable, and with a good record in government, remained faced, after he assumed the leadership, with substantial opposition within his party. . . .

Despite this, and the possibility of trouble ahead, the Brooklyn organization has continued to look good when compared with Tammany. It has behind it the largest bloc of voters of Democratic tendencies anywhere in the East. It has put a succession of reasonably good men into public office and has given the public little to complain about, except for a brief period when the county prosecutor's office was in poor hands and racketeers ran wild.

In the opposite corner has been a Brooklyn Republican organization that never amounted to much. For years its leaders were only figureheads, with little to give in the way of patronage or to contribute to party policies. In 1934 the last of these figureheads, Frederick J. H. Kracke, whose chief claim to fame was that for more than forty years he had never been off the payroll of some public treasury—a feat remarkable for anyone and particularly notable for a Republican—gave up the job to keep a payroll post under La Guardia. John R. Crews, a former pugilist, assumed the leadership and retains it at this writing. Crews turned out to be a much better than average practical politician. He is a plugger. With the help of state patronage from the Dewey administration, to which he has always been loyal, he has put the organization in better condition than ever before.

But the party in Brooklyn has no real solid foundation, and it seems destined to remain in a minority for years to come.

THE BRONX

The best political machine in the city has been run since 1922 by Edward J. Flynn, the polished and urbane lawyer who is the Bronx County Democratic chairman and Democratic national committeeman from New York, and who was Democratic national chairman as well during the 1940 campaign, when Jim Farley dropped the reins in the third-term Roosevelt race. Flynn's national status was ruined by the "paving-block scandal" mentioned earlier. President Roosevelt withdrew his nomination as minister to Australia at Flynn's request because of the hubbub, but no one has ever successfully questioned his leadership of the Bronx Democrats.

Flynn's leadership is unique in that he runs the organization the way a good business executive, risen through the ranks, would direct a large corporation. He set up a smooth-working system, picked trustworthy deputies, and has not bothered himself with details. He is not the boss who sits patiently at the head of a receiving line in county headquarters every Monday to pass personally on hundreds of requests. He is seldom there, nor is he continually being consulted by his lieutenants at his prosperous midtown Manhattan law office.

Flynn and Franklin D. Roosevelt were close friends, socially as well as equals around the fireplace in the Roosevelt home or in the White House, highball in hand. Flynn benefited in state and national prestige from this association—an association he had earned by his loyalty and his daring in one of three major political gambles Flynn took in the course of his career.

The first of these gambles was when in the pre-Roosevelt days he supported Al Smith in Smith's successful effort to get rid of John F. Hylan as Mayor. Walker, who succeeded Hylan, thereafter recognized Flynn as a leader in his own right, instead of as merely a vassal of Tammany Hall, which had ruled the Bronx directly when the Bronx was a part of New York County.

The second gamble directly concerned Roosevelt. Flynn had been named Secretary of State by Roosevelt in New York State when Roosevelt was Governor. Roosevelt made the move so that he would not have to reappoint to the post Robert Moses, then closely associated with Smith. Flynn had obligations to Smith, however, and when it became evident that Roosevelt was gunning for the Presidency, Flynn went to Smith and asked him if Smith himself, defeated in 1928, was going to seek the nomination again in 1932. Smith assured him he would not, he was through. Flynn plumped for Roosevelt, and stuck with him even after Smith changed his mind and became a candidate for the nomination. Bronx organization sentiment was for Smith, but Flynn stood by his guns. He never suffered for having done so.

His third gamble came when, knowing that the Democratic city ticket picked by Tammany in 1933 was destined to get a terrific shellacking, he put into the race a third city-wide ticket headed by Joseph V. McKee. The McKee ticket finished second to La Guardia's and its presence in the contest saved Flynn from losing his county offices. All three gambles required imagination and courage.

In addition, Flynn had the background and personal tolerance to keep peace in an organization run by the Irish, but dependent largely on the Jewish and Italian overflow from Manhattan for its votes. He built up local confidence in himself and his nominees by close scrutiny of prosecuting officers and the judiciary in his county. Justice could not be bought or sold there, and the public came to know it. Flynn himself recalls that a noted racketeer who lived in Westchester County and had business offices in Manhattan could get home daily only by crossing the Hudson River via the Holland Tunnel to New Jersey and recrossing it via the Bear Mountain Bridge many miles to the north. Had he entered the Bronx, he would have been clapped into the hoosegow.

The registration and election figures for the Bronx tell part of the story. The registration figures:

Year	Democratic	Republican	ALP
1944	408,959	121,794	55,700
1945	300,794	50,573	65,035
1946	331,655	106,603	71,750

The vote:

Year	Democratic	Republican	ALP	Liberal
1944	265,591	211,158	98,926	86,008
1945*	161,499	56,812	66,321	36,612
1946	181,904	192,459	99,632	48,492

* The Morris vote for mayor was 88,464.

Despite the 1946 vote, the Bronx Republican organization is a decrepit group, really no menace at all to the Democrats. Flynn's Republican vis-à-vis, John J. Knewitz, holds an appointive public job under Democratic judges, which has led to the charge that, politically speaking, he is on Flynn's payroll. . . .

SUBURBIA

Just as the Democratic machines dominate New York City, their Republican counterparts run the suburbs, Westchester on the north and Nassau, with more rural Suffolk, occupying all of Long Island east of the city line.

For purposes of political computation, the suburban counties have always been lumped as "up-state," along with the 54 other counties outside New York City proper. But there is a vast difference between the Westchester and Nassau population and politics and the rest of the up-state territory.

Governmentally Westchester and Nassau operate under county charters that are new and distinctive; politically they represent a

constantly increasing percentage of the voting power of the state while the balance of "up-state" decreases in importance. The two counties have grown tremendously in population every decade, and the current one will probably show the greatest growth of all. The additional population comes largely from New York City, where there is no room for people who want trees and grass or a back yard in which Junior may romp. Most of the migrants have been Democrats, and this may affect the voting trends in the next few years, since persons of more modest incomes have been driven out of New York City by the housing shortage there. But up to the present the conservatism that attaches itself usually to suburban living has dominated the politics of these counties.

In Westchester the figures are:

ENROLLMENT

Year	Democratic	Republican	ALP
1944	67,617	170,418	2,340
1946	45,887	160,836	3,220

THE VOTE

Year	Democratic	Republican	ALP	Liberal
1944	91,461	174,635	10,353	5,778
1946	48,826	173,225	7,667	2,755

In Nassau the comparable figures are:

ENROLLMENT

Year	Democratic	Republican	ALP
1944	44,171	164,656	1,384
1946	28,284	150,119	1,530

THE VOTE

Year	Democratic	Republican	ALP	Liberal
1944	68,137	159,713	5,616	4,759
1946	33,812	152,650	4,840	1,995

Westchester and Nassau contain whole cities plus villages within the old established town lines, all grown together or growing together. Attempts to run them with separate governments along traditional lines collapsed a decade ago. A new system was put in, combining city and county government features. A county executive rules the county just as does the mayor of a city, and the County Board of Supervisors serves as the governing body under him. The plan has served to integrate governmental functions as well as political rule.

In Nassau the county boss, J. Russel Sprague, became county executive as soon as the job was created. Sprague is of the newer generation of leaders, smooth, efficient, unostentatious. He succeeded Kenneth F. Simpson as national committeeman from the state, and for years was closest of all the county leaders to Thomas E. Dewey. The mutual endearment lessened a trifle, and in the spring of 1948 Sprague was hoping eventually to retire and spend his time to better advantage on his deep-sea fishing boat. The Nassau machine he ran was always a tight one, with no revolt ever seriously threatened. It was a particularly neat combination of city machine and county organization, smart enough to keep the people happy and bury its own dead.

Westchester, to the north, once was run by William L. Ward, a prosperous manufacturer and close-mouthed boss, willing to help run the state organization or fight it as he chose. In the early thirties, when the Legislature was attempting the probe of New York City that was to become known as the Seabury investigation, Ward blocked the move for months by ordering his Westchester legislative contingent to oppose it. It took a call from the White House, from Herbert Hoover in person, to get Ward to release his people. Whatever Ward's reasons were for opposing the investigation, no one ever questioned his authority. Things are different in the county now.

* * *

There is a boss in Suffolk, the third of the suburban counties, in the person of W. Kingsland Macy, the former state chairman who battled the public-utility control of the Republican Party years ago. Macy, famous for his starched wing collars as well, is now a Representative in Congress, yearning for the United States Senatorship.

But he never let his personal ambitions interfere with the party welfare, and the majorities he turned in for the ticket were impressive. In 1944 Suffolk added about 34,000 majority to the 168,000 majority Dewey had over Roosevelt in Nassau and Westchester; in 1946 it added 46,000 to Dewey's majority of 235,000 in the other two counties. Nowhere in suburbia is there a Democratic organization capable of challenging the Republicans, outside of individual cities like Yonkers in Westchester and Long Beach in Nassau, two Democratic islands of poor governmental repute.

UP-STATE CITIES

The O'Connell machine in Albany is probably closest to the ideal of the practical politician. It more nearly resembles the old-type Tammany organization, of Murphy's day, than any other extant. It is a prototype of the Irish-Democratic organizations so familiar in the cities of the north, but is much better than most now in existence. It has the vices of entrenched paternalism and plenty of the practical virtues as well. But, good or bad, the people of Albany like it, and the machine has been able to beat off direct attacks on it by the Dewey administration. So strongly was it entrenched that Dewey, directing the warfare from the State Capitol across the park from the O'Connell City Hall, finally gave up. Even the infiltration of Republican officeholders, brought to Albany by GOP state patronage, has not been able to reduce the O'Connell machine majorities.

At one point in the Dewey battle to break the O'Connells, the Governor ordered the seizure of the city records, and state accountants took physical possession of City Hall, on the pretext that a "shortage" existed in the Albany city accounts. The shortage did not exist, and the hope of the Governor's office that some evidence of other scandal could be uncovered while the Governor's men were on the job never materialized.

The O'Connell organization has been accused of most of the high political crimes, and it has been guilty of some of them, like high-pressuring the sale of the product of the family-owned brewery, or finagling with real-estate assessments, lowering them for friends and raising them for foes. The organization has also made some money from poolrooms and from other privileges more legitimately licensed by the city. Tapped telephone conversations have revealed that it would even try to influence a judge in a political case before him.

But, on the plus side, it cleaned up organized vice in Albany at the request of Al Smith when he was Governor. It has never sold a political job, has kept promotion in the organization on a merit basis, and lastly and most important it has given Albany a succession of good local administrations. John Boyd Thacher and Erastus Corning, 2nd, the last two Mayors, were excellent representatives of the old Dutch families still important in the city's life. City services are better than average and not too expensive.

The O'Connell ability to deliver the vote is phenomenal. In 1936, when Roosevelt was at the height of his drawing power, the Albany machine gave him a majority of 18,000. Four years later, with Willkie buttons to be seen all over Albany's main streets, and a major revolt apparently in progress, the Roosevelt majority in the county was still 18,000.

In the last two elections, when the Dewey power was at its greatest, the Albany situation was as follows:

ENROLLMENT

Year	Democratic	Republican	ALP
1944	37,373	10,821	241
1946	45,532	10,157	526

THE VOTE

Year	Democratic	Republican	ALP	Liberal
1944	43,784	30,887	3,106	399
1946	43,646	29,370	4,263	914

In mayoralty elections the Republican opposition to the O'Connell organization falls off to nothing at all, and a Democratic landslide of 40,000 has occurred once or twice.

The O'Connell organization has been kept going partly on the basis of personal loyalty to the family. The head of the clan at this writing is Dan, brother of the founder, Ed, who died half a dozen years ago. And there is no better example of its smart leadership than in its dealings with the American Labor Party, which in Albany was under left-wing control for years. Finally the O'Connells got bored with the trouble the Reds caused, and enrolled enough of their own henchmen as American Labor Party members to take over party control in the primaries. There is not another Democratic organization in the state with the disciplined membership to accomplish that feat.

Nor would another leadership spare that many faithful adherents from its own party ranks, for fear it might need them to quash a primary revolt at some time. There are no primary fights in Albany in the Democratic ranks, and just for an additional margin of safety the Albany machine runs satellite organizations in Green Island and Cohoes, which balance GOP majorities in the rest of the county and leave the Albany city margin the majority in the county as well.

The Albany County Republican organization is unimportant. It lived for years on crumbs given it by the O'Connells, plus hopes for a bigger share. It has fared well under the Dewey state administration and the county chairman, Kenneth S. MacAffer, has prospered in his dual role as local patronage-dispenser and lobbyist for important interests before the Legislature.

Syracuse, one hundred and fifty miles west of Albany on the barge-canal route, is another city where politics and whisky are taken straight—only it is the Republicans who are in control. A decade ago there was an Assemblyman, Horace Stone, who was a thorn in the side of that party. He was also the law partner of the Mayor and county chairman, rough-and-tumble "Rolly" Marvin. Marvin persuaded Stone to run for the state Senate, a somewhat tougher race, and then his own party organization proceeded to give Stone the works and retire him from politics.

Years later Marvin, out as Mayor and trying for a comeback, ran for the state Senate himself and was slaughtered by his own party, ending Marvin's long period as political boss. Marvin had made the error of backing Wendell L. Willkie against Tom Dewey for president in 1940 and compounded it by sticking to Willkie during the years that followed. Dewey set up an opposing state patronage-dispenser in the city and soon lifted Marvin's political scalp.

Party control passed then into the hands of a group of lawyers—Syracuse law firms have been famous in the state—whose members have always furnished advice and money-raising talents for the party. They may compete for legal business, but they unite when their party is in danger. Charles A. McNett is titular county chairman.

Organized labor, though strong in the railroads of which Syracuse is a center, has not been able to cut down too much the old-time Republican majorities in Onondaga County, which includes Syracuse, because there is a big rural vote outside the city.

As noted elsewhere, it is a manifestation of a good Democratic year when that party carries the cities in the industrial belt west of Albany. It takes an exceptional year, however, for the Democrats to carry the counties in which those cities are located. Roosevelt carried Syracuse by 2,000 in 1944, but lost the county by some 7,000, net. The figures for Onondaga County are:

ENROLLMENT

Year	Democratic	Republican	ALP
1944	35,068	100,096	840
1946	22,929	94,043	918

THE VOTE

Year	Democratic	Republican	ALP	Liberal
1944	64,729	80,507	7,922	911
1946	37,204	82,641	3,575	560

The Democratic organization in Onondaga County is about on a par with the Republican organization in the Bronx.

Still farther west is Rochester, one of the busiest, most attractive cities of its size in the nation. Politically, it is the product of a well-established big-business paternalism.

The late George Eastman, Kodak magnate, took over the running of the city more than three decades ago, when it was news for a big businessman to interest himself actively in civic affairs. Eastman licked the established political machines, but today the big-business interests that he headed work in close co-operation with the Republican machine—they have a larger voice in the city's affairs than anywhere else in the state.

Tom Broderick, the Monroe County Republican chairman, is pretty openly the representative of big business. Decisions of the Rochester city administration are made, not in City Hall, but in the bank building a few hundred feet away, if important enough to be considered by the real powers. The University of Rochester is one of the most heavily endowed in the nation—third heaviest a few years ago. The leading morning and evening newspapers are both owned by Frank E. Gannett, about whose conservatism there can be no doubt. The Gannett newspapers print large quantities of national and world news in a much more objective fashion than most of the newspapers of the nation, but on local affairs they restrict themselves to a straight diet of sweetness and light. Eastman Kodak and Bausch & Lomb, the great optical-instrument makers, remained open-shop for years, and the only substantial organized labor force in the city was the Amalgamated Clothing Workers, employed in the city's renowned tailoring industry. The Democratic Party perks up in state and national campaign years, but plays dead the rest of the time.

The figures for Monroe County, including Rochester, are as follows:

ENROLLMENT

Year	Democratic	Republican	ALP
1944	51,162	154,678	3,844
1946	32,680	140,408	5,860

THE VOTE

Year	Demo-cratic	Repub-lican	ALP	Liberal
1944	108,973	111,725	9,584	1,116
1946	56,787	116,772	8,720	751

As can be seen, Roosevelt carried the county in 1944, with the help of the ALP and Liberal votes. His majority in the city of Rochester was approximately 20,000, but the enrollment figures, heavily weighted in favor of the Republicans, are a better guide to the vote on local candidates.

* * *

THE COUNTRY COUSINS

* * *

The country vote is cast, in the main, by people who are citizens, whose grandfathers and great-grandfathers were citizens. It is the backbone of the Republican Party. The farm population dwindles with the years, and more and more of the up-state vote comes from the villages and the towns. But it remains Republican. A Democrat in many an up-state community is about as socially acceptable as a Republican in Mississippi.

There are good Republican organizations all over this section, and few in the Democratic ranks that count at all. In Binghamton, William H. Hill, an old-time leader, is the directing force of the party in the group of ten "southern tier" counties that lie along the Pennsylvania border. Hill's counties are good for a combined Republican majority of from 65,000 to 80,000 in any state-wide election.

And in the north country, the counties bordering on the St. Lawrence, whence comes much of the state's milk and dairy supplies, there is the Watertown organization that once ran the Republican Party in the state. It is to this day the most independent in its thinking of all the up-state organizations, principally on the issues of milk and water-power. Democratic candidates known to be on the side of the dairy farmer, as against the big milk companies, and for the development of the St. Lawrence seaway and power project, run well ahead of their ticket in this area.

The Hudson River Valley counties seem to be above any such issues. They just vote Republican. Orange, Ulster, and Dutchess are places where the party's up-state majorities are nurtured. Franklin Roosevelt, born and bred in Dutchess, managed to carry the city of Poughkeepsie in one state landslide, but otherwise his neighbors voted against the man who was the county's chief claim to national fame. All gossip to the contrary, they would have voted just as solidly *for* him had he been a Republican.

One fact stands out in any study of the state, locality by locality. It is that the minority party's enrollment is always substantially smaller than its vote, while the majority-party enrollment is always larger than the vote it gets for its ticket. One obvious reason for this—but not the only reason—is that enrollment is a matter of public record, but the ballot is secret, and there are places all over the state where it pays to be known as a member of the majority party, whether one votes for its candidates or not.

GENERAL INTERIM REPORT OF THE HOUSE SELECT COMMITTEE ON LOBBYING ACTIVITIES

(THE BUCHANAN COMMITTEE)

(E) TECHNIQUES OF LOBBYING

Lobbying is as natural to our kind of government as breathing is to the human organism, and it is almost equally complex. Part of this complexity springs from the fact that there are no significant interests in our society—economic, social, or ideological—which do not in one way or another seek something from government. With so many conflicting voices clamoring to be heard, the only means of securing a full hearing has been to constantly find new techniques by which your views can be presented more effectively than your competitor's. The demands of vigorous competition have thus made lobbying an exacting and an ever-evolving profession. The encyclopedia of lobbying practices needs frequent supplements to keep it up to date.

, And they had best be cumulative supplements; for while lobbying techniques are continually being streamlined, the old standbys of pressure tactics are only slowly relinquished. New methods are added but old ones are not dropped. For example, direct contacting of legislators, the critical component of any traditional definition of lobbying, is still a common practice. Individuals and groups very properly seek to apprise legislators directly of their views on public

issues. The variations on this old practice are, of course, endless.

Some groups make their views known by letters, telegrams, and phone calls. Others depend largely on personal contact with Members of Congress, and still others think that they can best serve their cause by organizing delegations for marches on the Capitol. The Civil Rights Congress has often used this last approach and has on numerous occasions sponsored mass train trips to Washington for the purpose of what its officers call "speaking on . . . legislation."[53]

Members of Congress are used to being sought out in their offices, in their homes, in the corridors of the office buildings and of the Capitol, in the cloakrooms and restaurants, on the floor of the Chamber itself. They expect and welcome letters, telegrams, and telephone calls from constituents and from those outside their districts as well. In an age where the actions of Congress directly affect the lives of so many, legislators depend on these communications in a very real and immediate way. They are both the pipelines and the lifelines of our kind of representative government.

But such statements and comments are not always as spontaneous, original, or

[53] Hearings, pt. 9, Civil Rights Congress, p. 12.

From House Report No. 3138, Union Calendar No. 1085, 81st Congress, 2nd Session, created pursuant to H. Res. 298, United States Government Printing Office: Washington: 1950, pp. 23-43.

genuine as they appear. Some tend to degrade the right of petition into a solemn-cynical game of blind man's buff, a test of wits between the lobbyist and the legislator. Representative Clarence Brown remarked jocularly during an early hearing that he could smell such inspired pressure letters without opening the envelopes; but it is not always easy to separate the real expression of opinion from the contrived one. Consider, for example, the following letter sent by the National Association of Real Estate Boards to realtors throughout the Nation:

Suggested paragraphs for use in letter to Congressman (Note.—Be sure to change form and ideas into your own words, rearrange, omit some parts, and add personal experiences):
Dear _____: We have both heard a lot of complaint about rent control and OPA generally. . . .
Recently I met with some of our good friends, including _____ _____, and we discussed what best should be done to correct the injustices being practiced in the name of controlling rents.
Our decision was to start here in (city) _____ a movement to force the OPA Administrator to allow adjustment in rents of at least 15 per cent. This should be done this fall in order to give all of us plenty of time to arrange the adjustments. I am taking this up with (name of friend) _____ of (another city) _____ also and may discuss it with others to see whether we might spread the movement over the country.
Before doing that, however, I want to ask you if you will (sponsor) (support) such an amendment to the price-control law. If you will do so, I will try to get such a movement started in other sections immediately.
Here are some of the reasons why I think this should be done—and they apply only to rents:
(State in your own words some of the "15 facts" which you think will appeal to him most.)
I am asking others of the group to write you about this, and I will telephone you later, as we are anxious to start the movement with your help.
(Signed) _____ _____ [54]

Most other lobby groups also encourage their members to contact Members of Congress on pending legislation, and suggestions

on what to say and how to say it are frequently provided. But usually time is too short for detailed planning of this kind. The group that is pressed for time can only ask its supporters to make themselves heard. This statement in a letter of June 7, 1948, from Nathan E. Cowan, legislative director of the CIO, to the presidents of all CIO international unions and to State industrial councils, is typical of this approach:

Telegraph or, if possible, telephone your Congressman urging that he be on hand if the bill comes out for a vote. Demand that no weakening amendments be added during debate.[55]

The National Association of Real Estate Boards, however, has systematized all means of direct contact between its members and legislators more completely than any other group appearing before this committee. This group conducts letter and telegram campaigns. It also prepares, sometimes on request, specific letters which local members transmit to their Senators and Representatives. The association has developed through its local member boards remarkably extensive lists of congressional "contacts," persons who are expected to wield particular influence with the Representative or Senator from the district or State concerned. There is, among others, a list of "special contacts" for the House Banking and Currency Committee; another for the Senate Banking and Currency Committee; a third for the House Rules Committee; and a fourth which is labeled "Key Senate Phone Contacts."[56] When a pressure campaign reaches the critical stage, when a final ounce of effort may be the margin between success or failure, the "contact" swings into action. The expectation is, of course, that the "contact's" political, business, or personal acquaintance with the Member of Congress—and it is on this basis that he is selected as contact—will enable him to make a de-

[54] Hearings, pt. 2, Housing Lobby, appendix, exhibit 359-C, p. 964.

[55] Hearings, pt. 2, Housing Lobby, appendix, exhibit 473, pp. 1097-1098.
[56] Hearings, pt. 2, Housing Lobby, appendix, exhibits 262-303, 350-457, pp. 822-860, 954-1083.

cisive impression on the Member's thinking. Six to seven hundred of these contacts make up the membership of what the National Association of Real Estate Boards calls the enlarged committee of the Realtors' Washington Committee, which handles and directs much of the lobbying for the association. Herbert U. Nelson, National Association of Real Estate Boards executive vice president, describes the work of the enlarged committee as follows:

The specific objective and activity of the enlarged committee, when called upon, is to wire or write their Senators or Representatives regarding any critical matters which may arise from time to time that seriously affect the real-estate industry and where quick action is required. Only those who have shown a willingness or desire to render support in this manner, or who are closely acquainted or have personal contact with Members of Congress, have been appointed on the enlarged committee.[57]

There is, of course, nothing essentially new in this approach except the degree of careful organization and planning which the National Association of Real Estate Boards applies to it. Every pressure group worthy of the name has recognized since at least 1910 that the sheer volume of letters and wires from home is apt to have some influence on congressional decisions. They have also recognized, however, that volume alone is apt to raise congressional suspicion. Hence, the National Association of Real Estate Board's careful selection of contacts, usually men of substance within their communities, men whose views are likely to command maximum respect. For example in a letter dated April 10, 1947, the executive secretary of the Dayton Real Estate Board wrote to Calvin K. Snyder of the Realtors' Washington Committee:

Dear Mr. Snyder: Reference is made to your letter of April 3, 1947, relative to realtors in Dayton who might carry weight with Senator Taft.

Some of these are as follows:

Sidney Eisenberger, prominent in town, has entree with Taft. Address: 729 Grand Avenue, Dayton 6, Ohio.

Ernest Steiner, former State senator, prominent Republican, Shriner, realtor, 607 Winters Building, Dayton 2, Ohio.

Allen Becher, well known realtor; experienced in legislative matters, 1107 U. B. Building, Dayton 2, Ohio.

Paul Schenck; real estate board president; president of the board of education, 709, Gas and Electric Building, Dayton 2, Ohio.

Please let this office know whenever we may be of service to your committee.

Sincerely yours,
THE DAYTON REAL ESTATE BOARD
JAMES J. SPATZ, Executive Secretary[58]

The following letter to Lee F. Johnson, executive vice president of the National Housing Conference, from a Florida member shows that other groups also operate on much the same basis:

THE HOUSING AUTHORITY OF
THE CITY OF LAKELAND,
Lakeland, Fla., June 21, 1949

Mr. Lee F. Johnson,

Executive vice president,
National Housing Conference, Inc.,
Washington, D. C.

DEAR MR. JOHNSON: You will be interested to know that I have secured strong telegrams each of which was addressed to Hon. J. Hardin Peterson, Congressman from First Florida District urging him to support H. R. 4009. As I told you in Washington when there a few weeks ago I had the assurance of Congressman Peterson that he would support this measure but just wanted him to know that the leading citizens of Lakeland, his home town, were in favor of this measure. For your information I am giving you the names of the people sending telegrams as well as their vocation and avocation.

E. B. (Smokie) Sutton, mayor commissioner, city of Lakeland, general contractor.

George J. Tolson, commissioner, city of Lakeland, railroad union leader.

L. Guerry Dobbins, commissioner, city of Lakeland, gasoline and oil dealer.

C. V. McClurg, president, Peoples Savings Bank, large property owner and civic leader.

J. W. Cordell, president, Florida National Bank.

Thomas W. Bryant, attorney and large property owner, Florida State representative (former).

Judge A. R. Carver, attorney, large property owner and civic leader.

[57] Hearings, pt. 2, Housing Lobby, appendix, exhibit 353-A, p. 958.

[58] Hearings, pt. 2, Housing Lobby, exhibit 262-H, p. 825.

Fred T. Benford, merchant, director, First Federal Savings and Loan.

Homer E. Hooks, president, junior chamber commerce, advertising executive.

Levie D. Smith, president, Lakeland Chamber of Commerce; past president, Lakeland Board Realtors, realtor and property owner.

Tom R. Marler, president, Lakeland Board Realtors, realtor and civic leader.

Dr. Herman Watson, outstanding physician and surgeon, owner, Watson Clinic, large property owner.

John Templin, lumberman, general contractor and builder, director, chamber of commerce.

I feel that these 12 men are probably the most outstanding men in Lakeland, and each of them is definitely in favor of slum clearance and additional public housing for Lakeland.

I trust this information will be of some value to you and with very best wishes, I am,

Cordially yours,

Earle M. Willis.[59]

Such support for any measure could understandably exert some influence. Quality as well as quantity pays in pressure politics.

In the days when lobbying meant little more than unabashed bribery, committees of Congress were the favorite focus of the old lobby barons. Then as now, crucial decisions were made in committee, and men having entree to them could quietly make the necessary arrangements. The committees are even more important in the modern legislative process, but with the institution in 1911 of open hearings on all major legislation the possibilities of easy influence diminished. The lobbyist who appears formally before committees today is generally obliged to argue on the merits. Despite public scrutiny and the watchfulness of competitors, however, some misrepresentation is still possible. In a letter dated January 17, 1949, to Herbert U. Nelson, of the National Association of Real Estate Boards, Art Barrett of Detroit had an interesting suggestion along these lines:

My thinking is simply this: I believe our case opposing the extension of rent control would be helped tremendously if we could parade in a few small property owners from around the country, a little bedraggled and run-down-at-

the-heels-looking, who could get their story over to Congress that the small man who owns a little property is taking one hell of a beating. . . .[60]

This sort of stagecraft fully developed could turn the congressional process into a masquerade ball.

Although the techniques of direct contact with Members and committees are as old as lobbying itself, they can still be of service to the modern pressure group in the presentation of its point of view. New twists have to be added to keep the old methods useful, but they continue to be of importance in the overall lobbying picture. Not only do these techniques allow groups and individuals to present their views but they also provide the means by which valuable and perhaps otherwise unavailable information can be brought to the Congress' attention. This intelligence function of lobbying is likewise not new, but it does assume special importance in an era of complex and wide-ranging legislation. The pressure group is, of course, quite likely to exaggerate its research and informational activities. The National Association of Manufacturers typically maintains, for instance, that at least 80 percent of its operations are of this character. Although such claims bear close scrutiny, it is nevertheless true that most well-established pressure bodies take their informational work quite seriously.

Facts are seldom presented for their own sake, or without having been carefully selected for maximum impact. But where a full hearing is available for all interested groups, we can rely on competitive watchfulness and public scrutiny as partial safeguards against misrepresentation of the facts by any one group.

The service function in lobbying takes many forms. When representatives of organized groups appear before committees of Congress, for example, they are not only presenting their own case but they are also providing Members of Congress with one of the essential raw materials of legislative

[59] Hearings, pt. 2, Housing Lobby, appendix, exhibit N-6, p. 1341.

[60] Hearings, pt. 2, Housing Lobby, appendix, exhibit 22, p. 543.

action. By the same token, the drafting of bills and amendments to bills, the preparation of speeches and other materials for Members, the submission to Members of detailed memoranda on bill-handling tactics —all of these are means by which lobby groups service the legislative process and at the same time further their own ends.

In addition to these services rendered to Members of Congress in their official capacities, lobbying organizations often perform favors of a more personal sort. Three generations ago, when standards of congressional morality were less exacting than they are today, the lobbyist could favor the Member in ways which strike the modern mind as crude. The lobbyist of the 1880's was a bountiful host, a social guide, a financial confidant, and a free-handed companion at the gaming table. But times change, and, while the theme of personal attentiveness still runs through modern pressure tactics, the forms which it takes have changed. Formal dinners for Members of Congress and, in addition to these, more casual and intimate gatherings, remain part of the lobby group's stock in trade. But apart from these vestiges of the old "social lobby," the personal service aspects of lobbying have been considerably revamped. Today, the resourceful pressure group may seek to serve themselves as well as Members of Congress by arranging remunerative speaking or writing engagements for them, or by such friendly acts as helping the new Member to secure housing in Washington.[61]

The relationships between Members of Congress and groups interested in legislation are infinitely varied. Many Members have spoken before such groups, frequently for no remuneration whatsoever. In other cases, Members have arranged for groups to reproduce their writings on public issues. One Member, for example, has regularly written a weekly Washington column which has been distributed by a group filing reports under the Lobbying Act. He has received no pay for this writing, but he has received "research expenses" which have

ranged from $250 to $500 per month.[62] Obviously, those groups which cannot work on equally close terms with Members are left at a considerable disadvantage.

There is a final long-standing lobbying technique which, without any modernization at all, has become increasingly prevalent during the past 40 years. We refer to the use of the franking privilege for mass mailings of printed matter.

It is unlawful for Congressmen or Government officials to lend the frank or "permit its use by any committee, organization, or association. . . ." [63] Furthermore the Criminal Code provides for a fine of $300 in the case of any person who "makes use of any official envelope . . . to avoid the payment of postage. . . ."[64] Yet the Committee for Constitutional Government obtains mass distribution of various materials through the use of congressional franks in the following manner. A Member inserts in the Congressional Record an article or speech that may or may not have been furnished him by the committee. It is reproduced by the Government Printing Office much less expensively than at commercial rates. The printing is paid for by the Member, who in turn is reimbursed by E. A. Rumely's group. The matter is mailed in bulk, sometimes already stuffed and sealed in franked envelopes, to the Committee for Constitutional Government in New York, where it is stored. At the moment deemed most timely and convenient for the committee, the individual envelopes are addressed and mailed postage-free under the congressional frank.

The advantages of this arrangement for the lobby group were pointed out by E. A. Rumely in a letter dated December 29, 1948 to the president of the Anderson Co., of Gary, Ind.:

Our problem at the present time is finances to distribute the material that must go out on Federal education, socialized medicine, public-housing. We want to repeat our effort in the court fight and get out millions of copies. Franked material travels to its destination at

[61] Hearings, pt. 2, Housing Lobby, pp. 54-55, 291-294.

[62] Hearings, pt. 5, Committee for Constitutional Government, pp. 155-156.
[63] 39 U. S. C., sec. 335.
[64] 18 U. S. C., sec. 1719.

about a total cost of one-half cent per copy; nothing equals this in effectiveness, per dollar spent.[65]

Some Members have not used their best judgment in allowing the employment of their frank by lobbying organizations.[66] We think that franked mailings to a Member's constituency, by himself and for himself, are useful and entirely proper. But some Members in allowing the extraordinary if not indiscriminate use of their frank by lobby groups, have failed to abide by this or any comparable standard. When one organization, the Committee for Constitutional Government, admits to having distributed 8 to 10 million franked releases in the past 4 years, it is assuming a privileged status to which it is not entitled.[67] The frank is not properly used as a veiled subsidy to any group, whatever its views may be. Close to 2½ million pieces of franked material of one Member of Congress were obtained by this one organization alone in a single year for distribution postage-free at the taxpayers' expense.[68] This same organization publicly advocates Government economy.

(F) LOBBYING AND GRASS-ROOTS PRESSURE

If lobbying consisted of nothing more than the well-established methods of direct contact, there would have been relatively little need for our investigation. These methods may lack finesse, but they generally have the virtue of directness. At least the effort to influence runs straight-line from the individual or group to the Member of Congress. Although the process may be sleeked up occasionally, it is essentially uncomplicated and straightforward.

Ever since President Wilson's first administration, however, the ever-growing army of pressure groups has recognized that the power of government ultimately rests on the power of public opinion. This simple discovery lies at the root of the evolution of lobbying techniques since 1913. The extensive use of franked releases antagonistic to the chief items of the Underwood tariff bill of that year was probably the first large-scale effort to bring public opinion to bear on legislation. In this sense, the use of highly charged franked releases as an instrument of pressure was the bridge between the old lobbying and the new. It opened the way to the development of entirely new dimensions in the theory and practice of lobbying. Today, the long-run objective of every significant pressure group in the country is and must inevitably be the creation and control of public opinion; for, without the support of an articulate public, the most carefully planned direct lobbying is likely to be ineffective, except on small or narrow issues.

If a descriptive label is needed, this new emphasis in pressure tactics might best be called "lobbying at the grass roots." What it amounts to is this: Rather than attempt to influence legislation directly, the pressure group seeks to create an appearance of broad public support for its aims, support which can be mobilized when the legislative situation demands it. The general premise underlying this effort is that if people are made to feel deeply enough about an issue they will translate their feelings into action which will affect that issue's resolution by the Congress. This expression of public opinion may be genuine in the sense that the views expressed are expressed spontaneously and with conviction. Or, on the other hand, such expression may be artificial and contrived. In either case, the process is one which has been deliberately and specifically instigated by one group or another having a particular stake in legislative issues. This process may bear little resemblance to the lobbying of 1880, but the intent behind it and the end results are unquestionably the same; namely to influence the determination of legislative policy. As Representative Halleck succinctly observed:

The committee has pretty well discovered, I think, that one of the very effective ways to

[65] Hearings, pt. 5, Committee for Constitutional Government, p. 104.

[66] Hearings, pt. 2, Housing Lobby, pp. 223-226; 292; 661-663.

[67] Hearings, pt. 5, Committee for Constitutional Government, pp. 99-101.

[68] Hearings, pt. 5, Committee for Constitutional Government, p. 100.

influence legislation is to operate out at the grass roots and possibly to deal in public opinion.[69]

The suggestion that efforts to influence public opinion might, under certain circumstances, be classified as "lobbying" met with considerable resistance from numerous witnesses appearing before us. They usually described themselves as "educators" or "publishers" or, in one case, "educator-publisher." As such, a number of them claimed that they had never lobbied in their lives. Although we have reason to suspect these protestations of injured innocence, they do raise important questions of policy. Where, for example, is the line to be drawn between "lobbying at the grass roots" and publishing or education, which may also be concerned with the creation of opinion? So far as stimulating people to exert pressure on their Congressmen is concerned, is it not true that "every idea is an incitement," as Justice Holmes once said?

The answers to these questions are closer at hand than the protestors care to admit. Those who are reticent to make public disclosure of their activities and sources of financial support enjoy their self-made confusion. The all-pervading purpose and intent of the Lobbying Act was to bring into the open activities intended to influence legislation, directly and indirectly, and to provide full public disclosure of the financing and expenditures involved in these activities. Lobbying at the grass roots is no hazy myth; it is a basic reality of modern efforts to influence legislation. We have already stated our position on the question of full disclosure: A group's own allegations that it is exempt from the Lobbying Act are plainly self-serving. Where doubt exists, sound public policy calls for full disclosure of the facts.[70]

Unfortunately, many people attach sinister significance to the word "lobbying." The present statute on the subject does not contain the word "lobbying" anywhere in its substantive provisions. Except in the title, the statute speaks only of attempts to influence legislation, directly and indirectly.

What persons and groups should be required to file reports under the Lobbying Act? We suggested earlier that the only practical gauges of lobbying activity are intent and some substantial effort to influence legislation. We believe that these criteria apply to most of those who have protested that their efforts to influence or educate public opinion do not constitute lobbying. All receipts or expenditures to influence legislation, directly or indirectly, should be reported to Congress and the public, if they are substantial enough in size so that the legal maxim of de minimis non curat lex (the law is not concerned with trifles) would not apply.[71] In a separate report we shall deal more fully with the provisions of the present Lobbying Act and suggested amendments.

Naturally, there will be borderline cases demanding careful analysis and judgment, but we have no hesitation in saying that doubts should always be resolved in favor of full public disclosure of the facts. Two examples drawn from our investigation illustrate particularly cogently the types of problems which are involved.

The Committee for Constitutional Government, a nonprofit organization incorporated under the laws of the District of Columbia, has filed statements pursuant to section 305 of the Lobbying Act, but it has done so under protest, maintaining both that its activities do not constitute lobbying and that, in any case, the Lobbying Act is void. Moreover, the statements filed by the Committee for Constitutional Government have consistently failed to disclose all facts relative to its receipts for the distribution of books and pamphlets on legislative issues. The group's three major activities appear

[69] Hearings, pt. 10, Legislative Activities of Executive Agencies, p. 353.

[70] See p. 36, p. 2, Rept. No. 1 of the Special Committee to Investigate Senatorial Campaign Expenditures (1946) for an interesting parallel.

[71] For a more complete analysis of this aspect of the question, see Futor, An Analysis of the Federal Lobbying Act, 10 Federal Bar Journal 366 (1949).

to be raising money, stimulating letter and telegram campaigns on pending legislation, and distributing books, pamphlets and other printed matter to Members of Congress, State legislators, other public officials, and private institutions, organizations, and individual citizens.[72] The Committee for Constitutional Government denies that it is in lobbying at all. Indeed, in a booklet entitled "Needed Now—Capacity for Leadership, Courage to Lead," published in 1944, the committee deprecated the value of the older lobbying techniques under which delegations "buttonhole legislators" as "stunts which attract some popular attention but persuade no Congressmen." Said the committee: "The place to persuade Congressmen is back home."[73]

In keeping with this homely maxim, the Committee for Constitutional Government sent out between 1937 and 1944:

Eighty-two million pieces of literature—booklets, pamphlets, reprints of editorials and articles, specially addressed letters and 760,000 books.

More than 10,000 transcriptions, carrying 15-minute radio talks on national issues, besides frequent national hook-ups for representatives of the committee.

Three hundred and fifty thousand telegrams to citizens to arouse them to action on great issues.

Many thousands of releases to daily and weekly newspapers—full pay advertisements in 536 different newspapers with a combined circulation of nearly 20,000,000.[74]

To these figures, the booklet adds an extraordinary footnote "Throughout its 7 years, the committee has not spent one dollar for lobbying."[75]

Furthermore, the activities of the Committee for Constitutional Government have been greatly expanded since 1944. In the distribution of books and pamphlets, for example, E. A. Rumely, executive secretary

of the Committee, testified that his organization had distributed "close to 700,000" copies of The Road Ahead since the book's publication in 1949.[76] The Committee has also widely distributed copies of numerous other publications such as Why the Taft-Hartley Act?, Labor Monopolies or Freedom, and Compulsory Medical Care and the Welfare State. These facts and figures are certainly more than enough to establish that the Committee for Constitutional Government exerts "substantial effort" in connection with national issues. What of "intent to influence legislation?" We submit that any fair-minded person who has the time and patience to read a substantial part of the publications distributed by the Committee for Constitutional Government can reach no reasonable conclusion but that such intent is present in overwhelming abundance. In both books and pamphlets, frequent reference is made to specific legislation pending before Congress. John T. Flynn's The Road Ahead, for example, includes sharply critical analyses of the proposed Columbia Valley Authority, of national health insurance, the Spence bill, the Brannan plan. Melchior Palyi's Compulsory Medical Care and the Welfare State is also concerned with health insurance legislation. The reader of these and other Committee for Constitutional Government materials is exhorted again and again to write his Congressman, to send a copy of the book or pamphlet to the Congressman, and to distribute the material as widely as possible. The reader is not only urged to accept a point of view, but to act as well.

This sort of material clearly indicates intent to influence legislation. But Mr. Rumely does not so concede; to do so would be to admit that the reports under the Lobbying Act filed by the Committee for Constitutional Government should show the full details of its financial support. The reports as filed tell only a fraction of the facts.

One of the reasons Rumely advanced for

[72] Hearings, pt. 5, Committee for Constitutional Government, p. 380.

[73] Needed Now—Capacity for Leadership, Courage To Lead (New York, 1944), pp. 5-6.

[74] Ibid., p. 30.

[75] Ibid., p. 31.

[76] Hearings, pt. 5, Committee for Constitutional Government, p. 109.

incomplete reporting is his claim that his organization is a commercial publisher. Any attempt by Government to obtain any information about commercial publishers he brands as a violation of the constitutional guarantees of freedom of the press. As to this contention, Representative Doyle stated:

A commercial publisher takes the normal risks of operating a private business. It does not beg the public for money to help it carry on. A commercial publisher expects to pay income tax on his receipts. It does not seek tax exemption, as does this lobbying committee. A commercial publisher is in business for profit; it is not primarily an advocate. A commercial publisher does not constantly grind out pamphlets, leaflets, books, etc., which present only one side of the subject. I appraise the pamphlets and books which this committee has put out as presenting one side of the subject.

A commercial publisher does not couple his publishing activities with incessant appeals to the citizenry to bring pressure to bear on members of Congress in order to influence legislation.

The ordinary publishers of the United States are not governed by the Federal Lobbying Act in any way, and need not file reports under it. The ordinary publisher is not attempting to influence legislation; it is attempting to make money.

The issue should not be confused by attempts of out-and-out lobbying organizations to conceal their objectives or to keep the public from being fully familiar with all their activities, including where they get their money and how they spend it.[77]

The content of the publications concerned is, of course, important in determining whether or not the distributor may lawfully be required to disclose his sources of support—either before this committee or pursuant to the Lobbying Act. As Representative Brown told Mr. Rumely:

If you have any booklets . . . in which you have set forth the reasons why certain legislative proposals should be enacted, or certain legislative proposals should be defeated, and you have sent these out over the country wholesale, either as gifts or through other organizations, then I think this committee has an absolute right to demand information on them.

Mr. Rumely replied:

[77] Hearings, pt. 5, Committee for Constitutional Government, p. 136.

We have issued no such books.[78]

This flat denial overlooks literally dozens of plain references to specific measures in publications distributed by the Committee for Constitutional Government. There appears on page 140 of The Road Ahead, to cite but one example:

What can one say now as one reads the plans that have been laid before Congress for the revival of something infinitely more fantastic than the NRA, plans which can be described as nothing less than weird.

One of these proposals relates chiefly to industry and is known as the Spence Act [sic]. The other relates to the farm and is known as the Brannan plan.

The Spence bill is specifically identified in a footnote as "H. R. 2756, introduced February 15, 1949." The Brannan plan is similarly identified as being "embodied in Senate bills 1971 and 1882" (p. 43). And in a special appendix to the Committee for Constitutional Government's edition of The Road Ahead, the following appears:

In our opinion, sane farm leaders and business leaders especially had better bestir themselves. If they let the Brannan plan campaign go by default, they and all of us will rue the day (p. 183).

Yet Mr. Rumely says: "We have issued no such books." Under these circumstances, Mr. Rumely's claim that the first amendment grants him absolute immunity from any inquiry is wanting in substance and must yield to the rights of the public and the Congress. Not the freedom of the press but simple honesty is at stake here.

The program of the Committee for Constitutional Government illustrates the extent to which lobbying at the grass roots has become a major effort in modern pressure politics. It also illustrates some of the difficulties which are apt to be met in making the principle of full disclosure effective. An organization like the Committee for Constitutional Government will call itself educational or a publisher, or both if the occasion demands, and then claim immunity from

[78] Hearings, pt. 4, National Economic Council, Inc., p. 27.

full disclosure. Or, to take another extreme case, the Civil Rights Congress will insist that it is "a defense organization and not a lobbying organization" in order to claim privileged status—this notwithstanding the facts that the group has registered under the Lobbying Act and has organized delegations to come to Washington for the admitted purpose of influencing legislation.

More substantial questions are raised by groups such as the Foundation for Economic Education. This organization has been granted tax exemption as an organization "operated exclusively for educational purposes," and donations to it are deductible by the donor in determining his net income. We have already commented in detail on the foundation's financial support.

The foundation as such has little direct contact with Members of Congress. Its major function is, rather, the preparation of pamphlets, booklets, and articles presenting one side of public issues. The foundation has distributed almost 4,000,000 booklets and pamphlets in the 4-year period since 1946, and it has records indicating that 389 newspapers and magazines have in some way used its articles. Furthermore, its president estimates that many times that number have actually used this material. Some of the articles are quite general in nature, but many others take definite stands on specific legislative issues. Will Dollars Save the World was sharply critical of the Marshall plan. Illusions of Point Four is self-explanatory. So You Believe in Rent Controls? was clearly intended to undermine any such belief. Roofs or Ceilings, another anti-rent-control pamphlet, was deemed so effective that the National Association of Real Estate Boards bought and distributed 500,000 copies.

It is difficult to avoid the conclusion that the Foundation for Economic Education exerts, or at least expects to exert a considerable influence on national legislative policy. The difficult questions are: "To what extent, and how directly?" Foundation for Economic Education literature contains little of the specific exhortation to action which is so much a part of the publications distributed by the Committee for Constitutional Government. It frequently deals with current legislative issues, but it deals with them in terms of generalities rather than by giving detailed arguments for or against specific measures. To what extent does this literature demonstrate intent by the Foundation for Economic Education to influence legislative policy, directly or otherwise?

The content and distribution of each booklet have considerable bearing on these questions. For example, a group may distribute, as the Foundation for Economic Education has, studies of rent control in European countries—which present dozens of examples which might well lead people to believe that rent controls of any kind anywhere are unjust and unsound. Although these studies never mentioned the United States, their distribution would, we believe, constitute an attempt by the sender to influence legislation directly if they were sent to Members of Congress, as they have been, while a rent-control law was in effect or under consideration. Similarly, their distribution would constitute an attempt to influence legislation indirectly if they were sent to educators, editors, clergymen, and other community opinion leaders, as they have been, while such a law was in effect or under consideration. Is it the intent of the Foundation that its publications should have no such influence whatsoever? If so, it is difficult to understand why these publications all relate to what Mr. Read, president of the Foundation, calls "subjects high in current interest and discussion." It is equally difficult to imagine that the Nation's largest corporations would subsidize the entire venture if they did not anticipate that it would pay solid, long-range legislative dividends.

The situation is complicated by the fact that the Foundation for Economic Education regards itself as an organization devoted exclusively to educational purposes, and has secured legal recognition of this status through a Treasury tax exemption. As Mr. Read put it—

In my opinion, no primary or secondary school, no college or university or other institution of learning in this country is more genuinely, and with any more uncompromising honesty, dedicated to the search for truth in economics, political science and related subjects than is the foundation.[79]

Mr. Read conceded that there were differences between the foundation and other educational institutions, but these, he thought, "enhance rather than detract from the educational character of our operation." With all due respect to Mr. Read, it is necessary to point out that there is one such difference which he does not mention, and it is a difference which seriously detracts from the educational character of his "operation." That difference is this: The true educational institution does not sponsor one point of view to the exclusion of all others. The true educational institution has no pattern to which the teacher must make his views conform, consciously or otherwise. Mr. Read cannot honestly claim that these criteria govern the Foundation for Economic Education, nor does he attempt to do so.

Our point in presenting this detailed analysis of the foundation's activities is to suggest the problems which lobbying at the grass-roots presents relative to full disclosure under the principles of the Lobbying Act. Upon careful consideration of these problems, we endorse the views expressed by Representative Albert in his statement to Mr. Read:

However, I do feel sure that unless organizations as effective as yours in influencing legislation can be covered by a lobbying act, that the Lobbying Act is not worth the paper it is written on.[80]

Both the Foundation for Economic Education and the Committee for Constitutional Government have as their major function the distribution of printed matter bearing on public issues, and this is probably the most important component in what we have called lobbying at the grass roots. Every group active in this area, however, has a different tone, a different clientele, a different technique of distributing its materials. The Committee for Constitutional Government promotes its products vigorously, seeking the widest possible market for them. It is currently striving to place a copy of The Road Ahead in every fifth home in the Nation. On June 28, 1950, Mr. Rumely testified that up to that date his committee had sent 3½ million separate post-card advertisements for the book, the first million of which sold 175,000 copies.[81] The Foundation for Economic Education, on the other hand, contends that its publications are sent only upon request and that no deliberate efforts are made to sell them in bulk. Where the Committee for Constitutional Government strives to saturate the thinking of the community, the Foundation for Economic Education is content with a carefully placed sprinkling. The Foundation for Economic Education has, in fact, distributed a pamphlet called On Distributing Literature, in which it suggests how materials can best be placed:

In offering literature to others, whether employees or friends, any semblance of the offering as a "must" activity is not good. Such an attitude creates an unnecessary resistance. Rather, keep the effort in the realm of a voluntary opportunity. "It is yours if you like it."[82]

These instructions are, of course, for the benefit of those persons, firms, and schools that purchase foundation literature for secondary distribution. Such sales have accounted for a substantial part of the more than 4,000,000 pamphlets which the foundation has printed since 1946.

Secondary distribution is simpler for some groups than for others. The National Association of Real Estate Boards, for example, has ready-made outlets for its material in the many member boards and individual

[79] Hearings, pt. 8, Foundation for Economic Education, p. 9.

[80] Hearings, pt. 8, Foundation for Economic Education, p. 112.

[81] Hearings, pt. 5, Committee for Constitutional Government, p. 109.

[82] Hearings, pt. 8, Foundation for Economic Education, p. 82.

realtors throughout the Nation. Thus the 500,000 copies of "Roofs or Ceilings" which the National Association of Real Estate Boards purchased from the Foundation for Economic Education were distributed through local member boards. This arrangement combines the advantages of central purchasing with the greater impact of local sponsorship.

Although groups like the National Association of Real Estate Boards have a natural advantage in secondary distribution of materials, other groups without comparable Nation-wide organizations have achieved similar results by a careful focussing of efforts. As organizations like the Committee for Constitutional Government, the National Economic Council, and the Foundation for Economic Education draw their major financial support from relatively narrow and well-defined sources, so, too, are their materials directed at those persons and groups, which are expected to have an important influence on opinion within their communities. True, the pressure group seeks maximum distribution for its product, but it seeks this distribution in terms of status and position first and in terms of ordinary people last. Mr. Rumely of the Committee for Constitutional Government gave us this illustration:

Mr. Rumely. . . . For example, this book Compulsory Medical Care, we have one donor who has paid to send 15,500 libraries a copy of that book.

Mr. Fitzgerald. Who was that?

Mr. Rumely. I won't tell you.

Mr. Fitzgerald. You refuse?

Mr. Rumely. Certainly, I refuse to tell you. Let me finish. I am looking around now for another donor to send a copy to 15,000 editors, because we wish that book to hit the editors on the same day that the library gets it, because the editor may be moved to say something about it and build up interest in it.

Therefore, I am holding back the distribution of 15,500 to the libraries until I can find some generous, public-spirited organization or person to pay for the distribution to the newspapers.[83]

[83] Hearings, pt. 5, Committee for Constitutional Government, p. 120.

Even more revealing is the special offer which the Committee for Constitutional Government has appended to its paperbound edition of The Road Ahead:

Buy 2, 5, 10, 25, or as many more copies as you can afford, and place them in circulation among clergymen, businessmen, large and small, heads of service groups, farm leaders, editors and publishers, public officials, judges, governors, and particularly, regardless of party, Members of Congress—Senators and Representatives. This book should go to everyone in a position to disseminate ideas; to foremen, supervisors, salesmen, insurance agents and, when these have been reached, to housewives and industrial employees. So that, if possible, every family in the Nation may have a copy.

The Committee for Constitutional Government has set its sights on the distribution of 2½ million copies of The Road Ahead, to what it calls the "opinion-molding leadership individuals of the Nation who wield the greatest influence and who will buy in large quantities and distribute in their respective circle."[84]

This sort of distribution reflects accurately what most of the other mass pamphleteering groups are also trying to do. They are trying to stimulate grass-roots pressure, and they are concentrating their efforts on the strongest of the roots. Whatever one may think of their views, it is obvious that these organizations have a bold and, in some respects, ruthless conception of what makes a typical American community tick.

Mass distribution of books and pamphlets is only one of the means by which the pressure groups have sought to influence

[84] The Committee for Constitutional Government labels this effort a "non-partisan educational effort." The Reader's Digest billed its condensation as a digest of what it claimed the New York Times had called one of the two "most important books about the contemporary scene that we will have this year." What the Times actually said was that "The Road Ahead" was one of the two most important books of the year because it was one of "the latest and most extreme manifestations of an endemic hysteria currently affecting a considerable segment of our population." In a later issue, the Reader's Digest stated that its use of the fractured quotation was inadvertent.

legislation through the creation and exploitation of a charged public opinion. Wherever public opinion is made, the pressure group is likely to be found. The variations are endless, but a few examples will serve to indicate the general outlines of this approach.

Many pressure groups recognize the importance of educational institutions as molders of public opinion, and a particular effort is made to reach and to utilize these institutions and their personnel to the fullest extent. There are many different approaches. The National Association of Real Estate Boards, for example, has induced colleges and universities to set up special courses in which its general point of view was taught. It has also stimulated the writing of text books on real estate, home building and management, and real estate economics, which it estimates are currently used by 127 colleges and universities.[85] Other groups like the Foundation for Economic Education include prominent educators among their officers. This is particularly useful in selling the group's activities as nonpartisan and educational. The foundation also operates a "college-business exchange program," under which college teachers spend the summer months with industrial and financial organizations, which finance the "fellowships."[86] In countless other ways the pressure groups have recognized the importance of the educational process. They do not necessarily pervert this process, but they make every effort to exploit it.[87]

The pressure groups have long been aware of the power of the press and have sought to harness this power for their ends. One of the prime conditions of successful public relations is anonymity of the source; thus it is not surprising that the effort to use the Nation's newspapers and periodicals as instruments of pressure politics has been concentrated on gaining access to editorial and news columns. One way in which this can be done is discussed in the following exchange between Representative Doyle and Mr. Rumely:

Mr. Doyle. One other question: I noticed, in many California papers, what I would call standard editorials, of exactly the same text. In your processes, do you send out stereotyped editorials?

Mr. Rumely. No; we do not send out canned editorials. We send out informative information which we hope the papers will print. In a fight like this one, we picked out about 20 editorials that told our side, and sent them to all newspapers in the United States.[88]

Labelling this process is less important than ascertaining its results. In this case, Mr. Rumely's material apparently proved attractive to the several dozen editors, in California and elsewhere, who printed it verbatim. The purposes which underlie activities of this kind and the means by which they are carried on are illustrated by a release sent on May 5, 1949, by the public-relations department of the National Association of Home Builders to the presidents and secretaries of local associations:

As the fight to defeat the huge public housing program goes into its last stages, it is important that you get as much local publicity in your newspapers and on the radio as possible, pointing out the evils and the faults of public housing.

Congressmen read their home-town papers carefully. They follow trends as reported in the press. If your Congressman sees stories in his papers emphasizing the failures of public housing, he will be more inclined to vote against the pending measure.

There are many ways in which you can secure publicity. Remember, however, that publicity in the press and on the radio is always founded on action. If you take action, you will get attention. Opinion alone is not sufficient. Here are some suggestions that have proven effective to obtain action and the kind of publicity you want:

Editorials

In many communities newspapers will use editorials if they are presented to them. Four

[85] Hearings, pt. 2, Housing Lobby, pp. 57-58.
[86] Hearings, pt. 8, Foundation for Economic Education, exhibit D-9, p. 132.
[87] That they may pervert it has been demonstrated again and again, however. For a classic example, see pts. 71a and 81a of the Federal Trade Commission's reports entitled "Utility Corporations" 70th Cong., 1st sess. S. Doc. 92.

[88] Hearings, pt. 5, Committee for Constitutional Government, p. 117.

suggested editorials are included. Perhaps your papers will use them or rewrite them.

If prepared editorials are not used by your newspapers, each of these can be used in another way. They can be addressed to the "mail bag" column of your newspaper as a signed letter from one of your officers. If you would prefer to use them in this way, do so. Simply have them copied as a letter addressed to the editor of your paper and have one of your officers sign it.

Fact Sheet

Because the pending housing legislation is so complex, a fact sheet is always helpful to newspaper editors, reporters, and radio commentators. One is enclosed. If you want additional copies, let us know. Distribute these to anyone who is in a position to influence public opinion.[89]

An even bolder example of stereotyped materials is provided by the "Sylvester Says" series of the National Retail Lumber Dealers Association. These quarter column releases, many of which take stands on legislative issues, are distributed in mats to 1,400 newspapers by Western Newspaper Union, a nationwide syndicated news service. The source is indicated on the mat, but not in the individual releases. In this way, the lumber dealers have presented their views to at least 4,000,000 readers who had no inkling of the material's source. The association's publicity director declared:

If it were paid for at an advertising rate of $500 per page (Washington Post rate is $658.80 on contract) the free space occupied by the Sylvester feature would have cost the retail lumber dealers $272,500.[90]

Accurate figures as to the number of readers which releases of this kind are likely to reach are extremely difficult to compile. Mr. Leonard Read, of the Foundation for Economic Education, could not tell us how many newspapers and magazines had reprinted any of his organization's material, but he was certain that the number was "many times more" than the 389 which had been counted by the committee staff. He did, however, hazard the guess that the Foundation's recent Clipping No. 26 had a "reprinting in magazines, journals, and newspapers in America that would exceed 100,000,000."[91] That one group can secure such widespread use of its materials suggests the tremendous potentialities of this approach.

* * *

(G) PRESSURE ON MANY FRONTS AT ONCE

The pressure group cannot be satisfied. If it fails to achieve its aim at once, it keeps fighting to achieve it. If it gets what it wants, then with very few exceptions it wants something more. This is part of what was meant by the earlier reference to lobbying as inherently expansive. One-shot organizations, groups which fight for specific objectives and fold up shop when they have won them, are relatively few in number. There is an institutional momentum which tends to limit pressure group mortality.

But lobbying is inherently expansive in an even more significant sense. We refer to the fact that modern pressure politics is not and cannot be confined to legislative policy alone. One of the oldest textbook truisms about lobbying is that it is non-political in the sense that pressure groups are interested only in issues and not in men. We think, however, that our investigation provides evidence to the contrary; a majority of the groups which we investigated were in some degree engaged in influencing the outcome of elections. This is not said in condemnation, express or implied, but simply as a statement of the facts.

[89] Hearings, pt. 2, Housing Lobby, exhibit H-260, p. 351.
[90] Hearings, pt. 2, Housing Lobby, pp. 484-501.

[91] Hearings, pt. 8, Foundation for Economic Education, p. 127.

LETTERS THAT REALLY COUNT

ESTES KEFAUVER AND JACK LEVIN

The third article in the famous Bill of Rights says: "Congress shall make no law . . . abridging . . . the right of the people . . . to petition the Government for a redress of grievances." Thus did the Founding Fathers recognize the fundamental right of the citizen to express his opinion to Congress, and protect in the Constitution the privilege of writing to one's senator or congressman.

That is how congressional mail started. This Capitol Hill mail has now reached the stupendous average volume of more than 100,000 pieces daily. More than eighty employees are required to man the Capitol post offices in normal periods. When floods of mail result from controversies such as that over "packing" the Supreme Court, the fight to regulate utilities, and, more recently, the battles over the OPA and regulation of labor unions, the normal figure often doubles. In fact, it seems almost odd today that a constitutional amendment once was thought necessary to protect the citizens. No member of Congress would remain in office beyond the next election if he disregarded the petitions and letters he gets from constituents.

When the author first came to Washington from Tennessee in 1939, he followed the pleasant custom of paying his respects to the Speaker of the House, who at that time was Representative Will Bankhead of Alabama. During the course of conversation this question was asked: "What is the secret of long tenure? How do members get reelected term after term without substantial opposition?"

Speaker Bankhead replied without hesitation: "It is a simple one. Give close and prompt attention to your mail. Your votes and speeches may make you well known and give you a reputation, but it's the way you handle your mail that determines your reelection." In the intervening years the solid truth of his answer has become evident. Members who desire to make Congress their career follow the advice given by Speaker Bankhead.

Senator Kenneth McKellar of Tennessee, a veteran of more than thirty-two years in Congress, has a rigid office rule that requires every communication received to be answered on the same day. It may be a simple form letter that says the matter referred to is being investigated and that further information will follow, but the constituent is impressed. Senator McKellar credits to this practice much of the success of his long career at the Capitol.

Mail is the most practicable way of maintaining a close relationship between Congress and the people. In the past few years when sessions have been almost continuous, members have had little time to visit their home states and districts. When they can get away from Washington, their time is

Estes Kefauver and Jack Levin, *A Twentieth-Century Congress,* (New York: Duell, Sloan and Pearce, 1947), pp. 170-184. Reprinted by permission of the authors and the publisher.

consumed largely by people with specific and usually personal problems. There is little opportunity to take soundings on reaction to legislation that may be pending. In the author's particular district not more than one in a thousand constituents visits the office in any single year. Hence, the chief reliance in "feeling the pulse of the people" must be placed on mail.

In the early days of the Republic, mail, of course, was scant. It did not become a great physical burden until recently. Until the turn of this century, national legislation touched the daily lives of Americans only briefly, if at all, except in time of war. As late as the 1920's, President Calvin Coolidge said the federal government could cease to operate and the average citizen wouldn't know the difference for three months.

All that is changed today. With the great strides in education, the wide dissemination of news by radio, daily newspapers, and magazines, and the growth of huge organizations whose programs are affected by the federal government, has come a vast expansion in government itself. Add to these facts the modern facilities for personal communication such as the typewriter, telephone, mimeograph, improved telegraph, and speedier printing, and one has the answer to those millions of letters that arrive annually at the Capitol.

A predecessor from the Third Tennessee District, Representative John A. Moon, had a single secretary who penned replies on the bottom or back of the letter sent in by the constituent. Former Senator Burton K. Wheeler of Montana can recall when 20 letters in one day was "big" mail. A survey of several congressional offices indicates that the average member now receives more than 100 communications daily. Of course, it runs unevenly. The more controversial bills a member sponsors, the more mail he gets. The size and type of district naturally affects the volume too. A Western senator, the storm center of one great debate, received as many as 7000 letters in a single day. Most members now have three secretaries devoting the greater part of their time to the bundles of mail delivered to each office four times a day.

The public should understand how this mail is evaluated, how it is handled, and how much of it really influences legislation. Which are the letters that really count?

Thousands of letters arrive every day asking personal favors and assistance with no direct bearing on the legislative duties of the members. This might be called "constituent service" mail. Its range is infinite. A citizen doesn't know the head of the Veterans Administration, or the Secretary of the Treasury, and he has business with their departments. So he writes his senator or congressman. Some requests are ludicrous. Former Representative Joe Byrns, Jr., of Tennessee tells of a letter asking him to go to the Patent Office and ascertain what hadn't been patented so the writer could make a patent application therefor. Constituent service isn't confined to mail. They come in person. Visitors are seldom interested in legislation, but they take time from legislative work.

Then there is a good run of requests for information about pending bills, for copies of hearings or reports, for explanations of amendments or of a rule proposed by a bureau. They are answered carefully and promptly, and form a part of the index to public interest in given issues.

Now come the petitions, chain telegrams, form letters, post cards, pamphlets, brochures, and individual letters, all aimed directly at influencing votes. This is the "pressure mail." Let us consider petitions first. They have been used longer and have an official status. They vary from a dozen names on a single post card to huge rolls measured in hundreds of yards and delivered to the Capitol by truck.

Petitions may come from patrons on a small rural mail route or they may be lists containing thousands of signatures gathered in every state in the union by a national organization. In the House those for or against a pending bill are "dropped in the hopper." This is a small wooden box attached to the side of the Clerk's desk on the House floor. The same receptacle is used for filing bills. The next day the *Congressional Record* carries under a regular subhead, "Petitions, Etc.," insertions like this:

Under Clause 1 of Rule XXII of the House, petitions and papers were laid on the Clerk's desk, and referred as follows:

581 by Mr. Mahon: Petition of about 175 farmers and business men of Scurry County, Texas; urging parity prices for farm commodities, etc.; to the Committee on Agriculture.

Petitions, memorials, and resolutions go to the committees having jurisdiction of the subject matter and normally they are never heard of again. No one reads them. They gather dust in Capitol files until finally carried away. They seldom influence legislation.

Legislators know it is possible to get many people to sign a petition for almost any cause, worthy or otherwise. Some time ago in Knoxville, Tennessee, booths were placed on the main street. Bells were rung to attract the attention of passersby. In this manner thousands of names were secured on a petition asking presidential aid for Earl McFarland, an escaped convict from the Washington, D.C., jail who was under death sentence.

The author once received a petition signed by 170 patrons of the post office at Daylight, Tennessee, protesting the proposed removal of that office to another location three miles distant. The signatures were obtained by a businessman whose store was near the old site. A few weeks later there arrived another petition signed by a number of constituents saying the new location would be in the public interest. *Many patrons signed both lists!*

In 1945 a House judiciary subcommittee headed by Representative Sam Hobbs of Alabama was holding hearings on the Bryson bill to outlaw the sale of intoxicating beverages near Army camps. Petitions asking favorable action began arriving by the ton. One side of Judge Hobbs' spacious reception room was piled ceiling high with these documents. Representative Emanuel Celler of New York and others opposing the measure became alarmed at the weight of the "pros" and told the opposition to get busy. In a short time truckloads of petitions against the bill were received. And so it goes, but regardless of length or weight, petitions are of little value as a persuasive force.

Equally ineffective are the chain telegrams. Dozens are received each week. Individuals, corporations, and organizations seem to think they are the best way to impress a member with the urgency of a cause. Actually, many such telegrams have the opposite effect. Unless the message is in fact urgent, a letter may be more useful. It is easy for an executive, well supplied with secretaries and finances, to dictate a telegram to one member and direct that the same wire be sent to the entire congressional delegation from his state, or even to every member of Congress.

Some groups drumming up pressure collect the cost of a chain telegram from their members at a meeting and get permission to send it over their names. This is a popular pressure tactic but largely ineffectual. When the same telegram is sent to several congressmen, the text is run off on a duplicating machine and the individual names of members inserted. The senators and congressmen know they are being circularized. When a large number of telegrams on the same subject is received, they usually get the treatment they merit—a mimeographed acknowledgement.

Here are some typical chain telegrams:

CONGRESSMAN ESTES KEFAUVER HOUSE OFFICE BLDG WASHDC. THE JOHN DOE LEAGUE REPRESENTS THOUSANDS OF INVESTERS THROUGHOUT THE COUNTRY. WE STRONGLY ENDORSE HR 6259 AND URGE THAT THIS ANTI-ROYALTY MEASURE BE REPORTED FAVORABLY.

JOHN DOE LEAGUE INC.

HON ESTES KEFAUVER HOUSE OFFICE BLDG WASHDC PERSONAL SUBJECT EXTENSIONS OF SELECTIVE SERVICE. YOU KNOW THAT THE EYES OF THE OVERWHELMING MAJORITY OF PARENTS AND SONS OF THIS NATION ARE FOCUSED UPON YOU WITH THE EARNEST HOPE THAT YOU WILL GIVE BACK TO THE KIDS OF THE NATION THEIR IN-

HERENT RIGHTS AND FREEDOMS. MAY I PROPOSE THE FOLLOWING AMENDMENTS. DRAFT AGE TO BE 20 OR 21. ALL SCIENTIFIC STUDENTS IN COLLEGES OR UNIVERSITIES SHOULD BE EXEMPTED. DRAFT SHOULD BE SUSPENDED MAY 15TH TO DETERMINE WHETHER WITH INCREASED SALARIES VOLUNTARY ENLISTMENTS WILL PROVIDE NECESSARY REPLACEMENTS. RESPECTFULLY YOURS.

JOHN DOE

While the author does not question for a moment the privilege of such petitioners, he does advise them that the chain wire is not going to have much effect on his vote.

The next items in the pressure-tactic catalogue are form letters and chain post cards. Organizations sometimes send their members cards which are to be signed and forwarded to Washington. They arrive in batches, as many as a hundred at a time, and when this occurs it is obvious that someone is pumping the pressure bellows. Frequently, of course, the pumping is done for a worthy cause or a piece of constructive legislation. Here are samples picked at random, with the spaces for signature left blank:

Hon. Estes Kefauver,
House of Representatives,
Washington, D.C.

Sir:

There is now pending a bill for mobile libraries, introduced by Senator Lister Hill and Representative Emily Taft Douglas, and this letter conveys to you our earnest desire that you support this worthy measure. In our State it is estimated that more than one million persons would profit from this bookmobile service. During the war traveling libraries were successfully used for the armed forces stationed in inaccessible localities.

In rural areas, those now without library facilities in schools and in the home would, for four years at least, be enabled to have book culture, if there is a yearly federal grant of $25,000 to each state. Individual states would provide up to a maximum of $50,000 annually.

In Tennessee 40% of the population has no access to library facilities. Over the nation, 35,-000,000 adults and school age boys and girls are denied the blessing of books. We pray that you do your utmost in behalf of these underprivileged people.

Respectfully,
Club Name _____
_____
Secretary
Number of members _____

May 20, 1946

Honorable Sir:

Beer, the beverage of moderation, is the drink of the working man.

Why this curtailment?

No wheat is used in its production.

Thousands of brewery workers are idle. Thousands of retailers and wholesalers are needlessly affected.

Labor connected with distribution of beer is idle.

Business investments of huge amounts are endangered.

Our State and Federal Treasuries will show a loss of millions of dollars.

Again, why this curtailment?

Name_____ Address_____
City_____ State_____

Dear Congressman:

Stockings are important to health as well as appearance. I need hosiery desperately and our stores have none.

Won't you help?

Please urge the Civilian Production Administration to allocate rayon yarns to hosiery mills until nylon stockings are available in adequate quantities.

Thank you for your interest and attention.

Name_____
Address_____

The letter concerning stockings arrived along with 260 others. All were addressed to "Estes T. Kefauver, M.C." The author's middle initial *not* being "T," this was a dead giveaway of the common origin of the pressure. The drumbeater had been grossly careless in not even checking the name of the man whose assistance was solicited.

The masterminds behind these mass-production mail campaigns devote much time and skill to composing such congressional form letters. They use the latest duplicating devices in attempts to make the letters look like individually written communications. With some excellent multigraph work one has to look twice before realizing it is a form epistle.

The form letter strategy is varied. Members of Congress frequently receive a number of letters on a particular subject. The language is different in each, but all convey substantially the same message and make the same request. In May of 1946 the author received sixty letters in one week from industrial firms. The thought expressed by all was the necessity for balancing the federal budget and reducing bureau expenditures. They were well written and began to look impressive.

However, one member of this particular industry was apparently short of secretarial assistance. He just sent on the bulletin from his trade organization and asked that it be given consideration. The bulletin gave the organization members instructions, suggesting that each write his congressman to urge reduction in federal spending, express alarm at the rising national debt, and demand that government costs be reduced. The bulletin was careful to advise each member to write in his own language and *not to mention that his letter had been suggested by the association.*

Tactics of this nature do not rate very high in influencing a member of Congress.

Finally, comes the pamphlet—in many forms. It may be a hurried job run off in fine type on cheap paper, or it may be an expensively printed brochure in attractive colors and well illustrated with charts and pictures. Many of these are valuable for reference, but should be digested and used only with care to keep in mind the special interest of the person or group that spent the money to prepare and distribute them.

Senators and congressmen aren't often fooled by these various types of pressure mail. They do not judge the sentiment of their constituency entirely by the preponderance of inspired letters or telegrams. Some time ago, former Representative Clare Luce of Connecticut remarked that she had received twenty pounds of mail against a pending proposal and twenty-four pounds for it. She added quickly that the poundage did not necessarily determine the sentiment of her district or the validity of the pro and con arguments. In short, letters that count aren't measured on a postage scale.

It would, however, be inaccurate to say that petitions, form letters, chain telegrams, and other forms of mass propaganda are discounted entirely. Pressure mail forces a member to find out what the legislation is about, to give it some study, and to inform himself on both sides of the issue. And by study of the forces behind a pressure campaign, he may get considerable light on the real purposes of the legislation. We do not imply that all propaganda tactics are used for selfish interests. However, an alert member will do his own investigating.

Petitions and mass letters sometimes have another value. If a member has decided to vote a certain way on a bill, or to recommend a certain person for a postmaster job, a bundle of communications favoring his decisions can be used effectively to buttress the position he has taken, or to defend himself against protests of angry constituents. On one occasion the author recommended the appointment of a rural carrier. It proved to be an unpopular selection. However, in the office was a petition signed by practically every patron on the mail route involved. Several who protested the recommendation had signed this petition. Faced with this fact, they made excuses, but could not complain too bitterly of the choice that had been made.

When one's vote on a national issue is challenged, it is somewhat comforting to be able to tell disgruntled constituents that "I had twenty letters sustaining my vote to every one I received against it." By and large, however, members know that pressure groups often produce such extreme disproportions through an outpouring that may represent only a relatively small minority of the people in a state or district. Members usually know their people, their prejudices, virtues, and weaknesses, and how certain groups among their constituencies react to various philosophies of government. When they lose this knowledge, they usually become ex-members.

What, then, are the letters that really count? To oversimplify a moment, they are those from people who count. They come from people who are known to the member as taking a national viewpoint. He has friends who are interested in his record and his future. Letters from these friends are valued. Messages from students of government and economics are helpful. For example, Dr. Frank Prescott, head of Chattanooga University's School of Government, writes the author frequently and at length. His knowledge is respected and his opinion valued.

A member of Congress usually has several key men and women in each county of his constituency. When he needs information about applicants for a job or the effect of some legislation on that county or area, he writes to them and their replies count. Frequently these people will be asked to give their opinion of the public reaction in their respective communities to national issues being debated in Congress. They "feel out" the sentiment and advise the member. Letters from schoolchildren often have a freshness and display original thinking that is valuable.

Congressmen want details and not generalities. Letters from an individual which give the facts of how a particular proposal would affect him as an individual, a farmer, a worker, or a businessman, always are welcomed. A candy concern that simply protests generally against reducing the sugar quota doesn't make much impression. If that firm advises that the reduction will decrease its operation by forty per cent and cause one hundred twenty people to lose their jobs, then sugar legislation is going to get special attention.

Two congressmen stressed this point in discussing effective mail. Former Representative George Outland of California, writing in *The Reader's Digest*, said: "When possible, make your letter apply to the local situation. Tell your Representative how a national issue affects your community, your business or your family. Be specific, frank, factual, natural." Representative Brooks Hays of Arkansas in the *Congressional Record* suggests that, to be effective, letters should "give reasons for your position. You may have some ideas about the application of measures to local and particular situations that have not occurred to others." One penciled page from a respected farmer or businessman in this category will outweigh in influence a hundred form letters inspired by a pressure drive.

Expressions from individuals and groups that have studied a problem are most helpful. Organizations such as the League of Women Voters, the American Association of University Women, the Federation of Women's Clubs, the National Planning Association, and the American Bar Association devote much time to analyzing measures before Congress. They have no special axes to grind and their well-reasoned communications are always beneficial.

Another type of letter that counts heavily is somewhat hard to define. Its outstanding feature is its utter sincerity. A rural citizen may write in crude hand on a sheet of school tablet paper or even on brown wrapping stock. One can see that the writer has erased one word to substitute another. The congressman knows that this citizen has pondered the subject matter for a long time and that he means what he writes.

A word about the letters that don't come. Anyone with a personal or selfish interest in a proposal will write freely and get as many others as possible to support him, and where possible enlist the aid of political leaders. The new member of Congress may think these communications reflect public opinion in his bailiwick. Actually, it may be just the opposite. The average citizen who does not have any peculiar interest in a measure is not apt to be vocal. The people who do not write expect their senator or congressman to "do the right thing," and it doesn't occur to them to lend a helping hand with an encouraging letter.

At one point in the 1946 OPA fight, congressional mail was running eighty per cent *against* OPA extension, yet a Gallup poll showed the public was more than seventy per cent *in favor of* extension. Proposals for extension of Selective Service brought a ten to one ratio of opposition mail, yet all polls showed a majority of the people felt that the draft should be continued.

It is not unusual to hear a congressman in Washington say something like this: "I've got to get out of town for a few days. When

I sit in my office and read complaints, criticism, and threats, day after day, and get no encouragement, I begin to think the country is going to the dogs." It is true that ninety per cent of the mail asks for something or predicts extinction at the polls if a member does not do so and so. The rare letter of appreciation is like a rainbow in a storm-clouded sky. The average legislator is trying to do his best, and a little written encouragement gives his morale a terrific boost.

When that happens, he is a more useful member of Congress.

The purpose of this book is to show how Congress can do its work more effectively and how its members can do a better, more efficient job. More "letters that really count" will be a real public contribution toward achieving this goal. And letters that tell members to complete the job of congressional reorganization will contribute to the effective government which this age demands.

PUBLIC OPINION POLLS AND DEMOCRATIC LEADERSHIP

DORWIN CARTWRIGHT

The great potentialities of sample surveys in serving both the legislative and administrative branches of the Government are now well established. Through an extremely rapid growth of the science of sampling it has become possible to obtain relatively quickly and with moderate expense an accurate miniature of the total population. Thus, in a sense, it is possible to convene the entire population of the country and to get an expression of opinions and desires with an ease and efficiency never dreamed of by the framers of the Constitution.

The Founding Fathers, not knowing of the science of sampling, could, of course, make no provision for public opinion research in the democratic process of government. Their method for keeping control in the hands of the people was that of assuring free elections in which *leaders* were chosen to represent the people. While a voter might have some notion of how his representative would vote on specific issues, he would have to take his chances that his spokesman would actually follow his wishes. The democratic control, and the very essence of democracy, lay in the fact that elected leaders would have to stand before the people periodically for re-election. In the years that have followed, this control has proved to be quite limited; on many issues the will of the people has been but weakly exercised.

In the executive branch of the government democratic control was made even more indirect. Activities and policies of the administrative agencies were to be deter-

From the *Journal of Social Issues*, 1946, Volume II, Number 2, pp. 23-32. Reprinted by permission of the author and the publisher.

mined by elected representatives, the President and the Congress; not by popular vote. Had the founders of our government foreseen the tremendous growth of bureaucracy which has taken place since their day and had they been able to imagine the intimate way in which the executive agencies would come to touch the lives of all our citizens, it is possible that they would have devised some more direct method of control over this branch of government. Had they known of public opinion research, they might have made provision in the Constitution for its regular use.

Pressure groups constitute a most impressive symptom of the illness of our democratic functioning. Much has been written about them but, like ghosts, one has to see them to believe in them. A visit to Washington on any day chosen at random will reveal that not only the offices of Congressmen, but also the corridors of the administrative buildings, are frequented by special pleaders claiming to represent the wishes of one group or another. Techniques of lobbying have become so highly developed that persons with a professional reputation in the field are avidly sought by groups able to pay well to have their wishes felt in Washington.

Against such a barrage the conscientious public servant has little defense. What can he do to determine the true wishes of the public? He can read editorials (known to be unrepresentative); he can have his mail tabulated (hardly more trustworthy); he can take a field trip and search out the opinions of "typical" people (but don't ask him to prove they are typical); he can even follow the procedure employed by the O.P.A. and bring into Washington an "average housewife." Surely, the citizen who doesn't belong to a strong organization with a lobby in Washington or who doesn't know a Congressman's wife has little chance of influencing governmental policies and procedures except through rare visits to the voting booth.

Looking at the government through the eyes of those who shape policies, there is need to keep in touch with the public for yet another reason. It is not enough to know

whether or not the public is in favor of some broadly defined program; let us say, inflation control. Even though its objectives receive overwhelming approval, a program may fail because its detailed operation does not correctly take into account the "human element" inherent in any public action. There is every indication that the public fully supported a government program of keeping prices down during the war, and yet a war bond program based solely upon an anti-inflationary appeal would not have sold enough bonds because the public did not generally see the connection between buying bonds and the prices of commodities. Nor would any program composed solely of advertising have done the trick. Intensive research for the Treasury showed that large-scale organization for face-to-face selling was required in spite of the fact that the War Bond program was one of the most popular of the Government's wartime activities.

It is clear, of course, that an experienced administrator will know a good deal about the "human element" in public administration even without the aid of public opinion research. The Treasury, for example, by enlisting the full support of the advertising industry and the aid of its best men in selling bonds, tapped a vast wealth of such experience. And yet these experts insisted that facilities be made available for keeping them closely in touch with the thinking of the public. They knew all too well that hunches and intuitive principles could lead them far astray. They had found that business survival demanded the type of knowledge provided by "market research."

Considering only briefly, then, some of the barriers to effective democratic government under modern conditions, the potential contributions of sample surveys appear to be truly great. Isn't it self-evident that legislators and administrators should employ public opinion research at every opportunity? Yet, even if this be granted, certain cautions need to be exercised. Consideration of the proper function of leadership in a democracy and facts about the actual present-day operation of public opinion research should restrain a bit the enthusiasm of the extremists. Let us examine a little more closely what the ideal relation between the people and their leaders might be.

What do we want of our leaders in a democracy? What should they do for us? Certainly they should represent the will of the majority; we all agree to that. But they should do more. We want men who will lead as well as follow the public will; we want experts who know more about the subject than anyone else; we want men of vision who can invent new solutions to our problems. No doubt a poll of the American people would reveal support of each of these propositions. If the public really accepts these functions of the leader, however, it then follows that leaders should by no means always abide by the results of the polls. There are certain circumstances under which they are obligated to disregard them.

PUBLIC INFORMATION AND THE EXPERT

Although the educational level of this country is high and media of information reach every segment of the population daily, popular knowledge of public affairs is meager. Many examples could be cited showing how little people know about these matters. For instance, at the height of discussion of the Little Steel Formula, April, 1945, only 52 percent of those approached by Gallup interviewers asserted that they had heard of it, and only 30 percent could give a reasonably accurate indication of what it was intended to do. It has been found on several occasions that less than half of the population can give correctly such items of information as the number of years for which a member of the House of Representatives is elected. Perhaps more revealing is the finding of the *Fortune* Poll in August, 1944, that 46 percent of the population thought that John L. Lewis was president of the C.I.O. while nearly one percent mentioned Eric Johnston and another Beardsley Ruml. In May, 1945, Gallup reported that only 41 percent of the adult population knew what the T.V.A. is, and in June of the same year he found that only 31 percent knew what the O.W.I. did. Even if public awareness were increased ten-fold, it is doubtful that the "average man" would have sufficient knowledge of most governmental problems to be able to make intelligent decisions without special information and study.

One may ask what special significance for polling this lack of information has. Isn't it simply a problem of the democratic form of government, and doesn't it imply only that public education needs extending? Probably it is not that simple. The kind of government established by our Constitution did not envision going to the public for the solution of the thousands of problems which arise each year. It was intended that these problems would be solved by leaders and experts selected by the people. Public opinion polls which go to the people and ask them to choose among specific proposals for the solution of these detailed problems actually force many people to make pronouncements upon matters about which they know little. To expect government leaders to follow these choices as a mandate from the people is to substitute mediocrity for expertness.

Let us consider a specific example. In a survey conducted in April, 1944, by the Division of Program Surveys of the Department of Agriculture, less than 60 percent of the population could give an explanation of what makes prices rise in time of war that showed any substantial understanding of the causes accepted by economists. Since it was clear that the public wanted prices held down, government officials had the responsibility to try to keep them under control, but it is doubtful that officials could have best accomplished this goal by asking the public to choose the details of an inflation control program. Had they conducted a poll for this purpose and followed the advice of the public rather than that of economics experts, it is likely that they would not have been reelected to office, for the public was certainly more interested in keeping prices down than in seeing some one vaguely conceived program of price control put into operation.

It seems to be equally inappropriate to ask the public what the income tax rate should be for the different income brackets. The fact that polling organizations have repeatedly found that people choose tax rates for the upper brackets far below present levels carries no obligation to Congress to lower these rates. It simply indicates how hard it is for people to imagine anyone else paying more in taxes than they themselves earn. Although the case is not so clear, the question of the sales tax is of the same kind. Economists agree that it is "regressive", placing a heavier burden on those least able to pay. That the little man does not recognize this fact and is for some reason enticed into supporting the tax in a poll seems poor reason to impose it upon him. *Leaders* who represent the little man and who know the facts about the sales tax will be unimpressed by a survey that has forced the unsophisticated laymen to make a pronouncement on economic policy.

A serious defect in the average public opinion poll is that by posing "issues" to a person it is possible to get him to select among proposals about which he has little knowledge and little conviction. Under these circumstances, "overwhelming" support of a proposal, in the sense that a large number of people select it, does not necessarily mean at all that the public is intensely anxious to have the proposal adopted. It may mean that most people know little or nothing about the details of the proposal but see it as being related to some value which they do accept. For example, during the war most people felt that winning the war was the most important consideration that should apply to any public question. Holding this belief and not knowing much about the details of government operation and economic functioning, what could they do but approve almost any specific proposal presented to them as a means of winning the war?

From analysis of many questions put to the American people during the war, Gallup has concluded that the people were, in general, ahead of the Congress in approval of vigorous and even restrictive measures for winning the war. That the people were willing to make necessary sacrifices there can be no doubt. But it is extremely doubtful that people actually felt a need for all the specific proposals they endorsed when put to them by enterprising pollsters. Consider the following questions asked by the Gallup Poll:

"Do you approve or disapprove of the proposal to draft nurses to serve with the Army and Navy?" (February, 1945)

"Government and Army officials say it is absolutely necessary to have more men to work in munitions plants and war industries. Do you think Congress should pass a law to permit local draft boards to draft civilians between ages of 21 and 45 who are able to work for these industries?" (February, 1945)

"Do you think Congress should reduce income taxes this year, or should this wait until after Japan is defeated?" (June, 1945)

In each instance a clear majority favored the "tougher" policy; in two of them approximately three-fourths of the population agreed. Were people angered that their "will" had been ignored when Congress failed to follow all of these and other proposals tested by the pollsters? There is very little indication that they were.

The crucial fact is that a specific proposal about which the public has little information will be judged in terms of the values to which it seems to be related. Mutually contradictory proposals will then be approved if they are seen as related to approved values and if the contradiction is not made too obvious in the questionnaire. Similarly, when information is meager, minor variations in the wording of the question can produce widely different answers. Surely, an administrator can be seriously misled if he follows uncritically the majority opinion registered in a poll without knowing the level of information and strength of conviction associated with that opinion.

In the area of international affairs this problem is particularly acute. Public thinking about these matters is limited, but values and stereotypes abound. "Overwhelming" support of proposals not clearly conceived nor firmly held can be readily found in a public opinion poll. The desire for peace is so strong that specific proposals presented as contributing to the attainment of peace have a good chance of being approved if the pollster on the doorstep insists on an answer. Compare the following two questions and the answers to each.

"After the war, would you like to see the United States join some kind of world organization, or would you like to see us stay out?" (National Opinion Research Center, January, 1945)

Join 64%
Stay out 26%
Undecided 10%

"Do you think the United States should join a world organization with police power to maintain world peace?" (American Institute of Public Opinion, April, 1945)

Yes 81%
No 11%
No opinion 8%

The difference between 64 and 81 percent is considerable and could have strikingly different practical consequences. Unless the busy administrator realizes the magical quality of the phrase "to maintain world peace," he might be misguided through reliance upon the findings of a given poll.

A particularly dangerous error is sometimes made in the use of public opinion findings—especially in the area of thinking about international affairs. Questions like the ones just mentioned refer to a vague area of thought perhaps best labelled as "friendly cooperation for world peace." While it is important to recognize that the American public has swung sharply since the beginning of the war toward accepting this general philosophy, it would be a serious mistake to assume that the public has much understanding or ready support for proposals for world organization which do not automatically appear to be related to these values. Take the loan to Britain for instance. Those who had been impressed by the new era of world cooperation as heralded by the polls were rudely awakened when the polls got around to the British loan. Although roughly two-thirds of the population favor American participation in a world organization, only one-third approve of the loan to Britain. While the public will approve many specific proposals which are seen by them as being a part of a program of friendly cooperation, they will reject others which experts feel to be equally essential to such a program simply because these proposals call into play other sets of values. Public opinion research which doesn't get at the full story can seriously mislead those who try to follow it.

In summary, then, it is clear that the public does not have sufficient knowledge about most governmental problems to pass intelligent judgment upon them. This is not at all to say that the public is negligent of its duties in a democracy. Modern government has become so extensive and so complicated that even experts must specialize on certain types of problems. The danger of applying public opinion polls to these areas lies in the fact that people can be induced to express an opinion in a poll on matters about which they know little. They often do so without any intention that their opinions should result in government action. By asking policymakers to follow the results of such polls we are substituting poorer knowledge for better. Only when a problem has become subject to extensive public discussion and issues clearly drawn should a government leader seriously consider polling results as a mandate. Even then, he may feel compelled to follow his own judgment of what is best for the country.

Technical problems associated with polling about matters of little public knowledge strengthen this conclusion. Questions which give fixed alternatives to the respondent may badly mislead a policymaker in that large percentages of approval need not indicate at all conviction of intensity of feeling. Moreover, they tend to conceal lack of knowledge and understanding. It is doubtful that such questions by themselves should ever be taken by a government leader as a demand for action. Fortunately, techniques have been developed which go far toward solving these difficulties. The use of "open" interviews and of new techniques for measuring intensity of feeling can minimize greatly the dangers involved in traditional polling. Research on public thinking can contribute greatly to the democratic process, but failure to recognize and overcome these technical problems can vitiate entirely the values of such research.

LEADERSHIP AND INVENTION

Social progress, like technological progress, depends upon the widespread adoption of new procedures which have been developed by a relatively small number of people. As much as we might wish it, the average man is neither an inventor nor an innovator. It is hard for him to imagine conditions or states of affairs which differ much from the familiar. The public stereotype of the inventor as something of an eccentric reflects this fact that the creative thinker is different from the average run of man. If you ask the average man to solve some problem, he tends to rely upon familiar methods; his thinking is confined to customary ways of viewing the matter. Were this not the case, each of us could be inventors.

In another way the inventor differs from the rest of us. He is a restless soul who is never satisfied with the present condition of things. He is constantly looking for improvements, for better procedures. But only when our needs are seriously thwarted do we common mortals search out new practices. If the horse will get us where we want to go, we are happy—until the automobile leaves us in its dust. We are quick to adopt a new and better creation after we have seen it work, but we are slow to perceive its need and to invent it.

Applied to government this means that our institutional procedure should provide adequately for social inventiveness on the part of specialists rather than rely upon the masses for social innovations. We recognize that the truly great leader is the man who

can see the possibilities for improvement in an imagined new state of affairs. The successful leader is the man who can get the public to adopt these new social inventions. To the extent that we desire social progress, we must seek leaders who can surpass the rest of us in finding new and better solutions to our social problems.

There is evident at the present time a tendency to make use of public opinion research in a way that would destroy this function of leadership. In the guise of being democratic and of giving the average man a greater voice in social affairs, public opinion research can be used to impede progress through misplacing the function of invention in our society. By asking the public to invent solutions to social problems and by interpreting the absence of new solutions as a desire for the *status quo*, public opinion polls are sometimes employed to bring pressure to bear against innovation and change.

Consider an example in government. From the establishment of the federal income tax in 1913 until 1943 our system of tax collection was complicated, confusing, and inconvenient to the person with moderate income. Yet, complaints about the method of collection were few just because that was the way things were done. Suppose, then, in 1941 a poll had been conducted in which taxpayers were asked whether they could think of any better way of collecting taxes. There is little reason to believe the suggestions would have been numerous, and the Treasury Department might well have decided that nothing new was needed. In 1943, however, just as soon as a withholding tax was inaugurated in the form of the Victory Tax, there was overwhelming approval in the polls of having all income taxes deducted from pay. From this reaction, it is clear that it would have been wrong to assume from the poll in 1941 that the public was wedded to the *status quo* in tax collection.

The situation is basically the same in any poll which asks the public to suggest solutions to social problems. What should be done to solve the unemployment problem in the future? What should our policy be toward Germany? What should be done about a probable surplus of wheat production within a few years? Unless some new solution to such problems has been widely publicized, people will tend to think only of techniques which they have already experienced. Take the question of surplus wheat as an example. In public opinion interviews wheat farmers propose solutions to this problem which constitute essentially the old A.A.A. program that social inventor Wallace got farmers to adopt during the depression. A public opinion survey in 1929, however, would not have yielded many suggestions for this type of program. Only after farmers had become familiar with its workings, could they apply its approach to future problems. But now the situation has changed again, and many agricultural economists believe that the A.A.A. type of program is no longer appropriate, that it can be viewed only as emergency patchwork, and that a basically new orientation is needed. If government leaders take the findings of the current polls as evidence that the public demands continuation of the A.A.A. kind of program, the same creative influences which originally produced the A.A.A. will be hampered in bringing about further improvement in our agricultural economy.

The use of public opinion research to justify the *status quo* in any area of public life deserves the same criticism. Radio programming provides a particularly interesting illustration. People are no more inclined to have suggestions for changing their radio service than they are for changing any other part of their world. Vested interests which wish to maintain present programming in radio can easily collect public opinion data to show how few people have any suggestions for basic changes in their radio service. Experience has shown, however, that new types of programs, once created, may become extremely popular over night. Had a survey been conducted a few years ago asking for suggested changes in radio programs, probably no one would have suggested "a new type of program in which someone asks people questions." But today quiz programs rate high in listener appeal. By the same token it is unjustified to take current polling results that over half of the population have no suggestions for improving radio service as a reason for satisfaction with present standards of radio programming.

From quite a different area of life comes a most dramatic example of how far wrong one can go in predicting future behavior on the basis of polling questions which ask people to construct new situations. The British Institute of Public Opinion asked the British public in March of 1945 the following question:

"Who would you like to see leading the new government after the war?"

Note that the question was asked before V-E day, but only a few months before the actual election. In view of the election results, the answers to the polling question would seem almost unbelievable. Yet it must be kept in mind that this question is one which asked people to imagine a state of affairs that is quite different from the one in which they found themselves at the time. Accordingly, we should expect the results of the poll to reflect wartime thinking more closely than postwar behavior. Actually, the polling results did just that. The answers were as follows:

Eden	31%
Churchill	20%
Cripps	6%
Attlee	4%
Bevin	3%
Morrison	3%
Sinclair	1%
Shinwell	1%

Had one interpreted this finding as a strong wish for maintenance of the *status quo* in British political leadership after the war, the subsequent election would have come as quite a shock.

From this discussion it would be incorrect to conclude that public opinion research can make no contribution to invention and progress in government. On the contrary, it is just this area of public life where it can be of the greatest assistance. Properly designed and executed research on public needs can give social inventors goals to aim at. As the previous article has indicated, studies of the efficiency and effectiveness of existing governmental procedures can give leads for further improvements. Sample surveys can be very useful in determining whether a program that is sound from an economics point-of-view will be at all satisfactory when the "human element" is considered.

SUMMARY

Modern democratic government needs public opinion research to make it function more smoothly and more democratically. The many possible contributions of sample surveys have been enumerated here and elsewhere in this issue. But unrestrained enthusiasm would be out of order. The promiscuous application of public opinion polls to all matters of government would be inadvisable and actually dangerous for it would take away from our leaders important functions which they alone can adequately perform. As a result of enthusiasm for a new and useful device, we must not ask our leaders to give up their proper roles of leadership. Polls must not divest them of their duties as experts and inventors.

It would be a display of shortsightedness, however, if for the reason that polls can be misused, we were to fail to use them at all. With care and with earnest avoidance of misapplication we can greatly improve our methods of self-government through public opinion research. Our choice is not whether to use sample surveys or to abandon them. We must use them now that we know how. Let us only be sure that we use them properly.

·5·

Mass Media

BOOKS, LIBRARIES AND OTHER MEDIA OF COMMUNICATION

THE WORLD OF THE DAYTIME SERIAL

WHAT "MISSING THE NEWSPAPER" MEANS

DO ROSY HEADLINES SELL NEWSPAPERS?

FREEDOM OF THE PRESS

FREEDOM OF SPEECH FOR WHOM?

TELEVISION AND THE ELECTION

BOOKS, LIBRARIES, AND OTHER MEDIA
OF COMMUNICATION

ANGUS CAMPBELL AND CHARLES A. METZNER

More than half of the adults of the nation live within a mile of a public library. Yet only a fifth of them visited a public library during the year preceding this survey, and only a tenth averaged as much as a visit a month. Most adults, particularly in the larger cities, have used public libraries at some time in their lives. The fact that so many neglect their advantages now, in spite of their closeness to library facilities, raises the questions: How much do American adults read? and Where do they get their reading matter?

THE BOOK-READING PUBLIC

Most of the book reading is done by a small minority of the people

About half of the nation's adults read no books at all during the year preceding the survey, and many others read only a few. A small percentage read a very large number of books. In fact the ten percent of the population that read the most accounted for more than two-thirds of all the book reading done during the year. When asked by the interviewers "Did you read any books last year, including small 25 cent books?" and then "About how many did you read?", the people answered as follows:

TABLE 1.

NUMBER OF BOOKS REPORTED
READ DURING THE PRECEDING
YEAR

	All Adults
Read no books	48%
Read 1 to 4 books	18
5 to 9 books	7
10 to 49 books	18
50 books or more	7
Number read not ascertained	2
	100%

In short, book reading is a highly concentrated activity—a few people read a very great deal, some do a moderate amount of book reading, and a large majority read very few books or none at all. On the average, women read more books than do men and young people more than their elders. As might be expected, the extent of book-reading is highly related to both education and income. Book-reading is somewhat more common in the larger communities than in small towns or rural areas although the differences are not large.

Many people expressed uncertainty as to the precise number of books they had read in the previous year, especially those who had read a good many books. They were more sure of the number of books they had

From *Public Use of the Library*, Survey Research Center, University of Michigan, pp. 1-14.
Reprinted by permission of the authors and the publisher.

read in the previous month. The number of books reported read in a single month is not inconsistent, however, with the number reported read in a year.

Most book readers prefer fiction

Three-fourths of the adults who read at least one book during the year read fiction, either exclusively or for the most part. Women tended to concentrate more highly on fiction than did men. Nearly a third of the men readers read all or mainly non-fiction, but only one in seven of the women readers did so.

TABLE 2.

"WERE THEY MAINLY FICTION OR STORIES, OR WHAT WERE THEY?"*

	Men readers	Women readers	All readers
All fiction	46%	57%	52%
Mainly fiction	19	24	22
Mainly non-fiction	19	8	13
All non-fiction	12	6	8
Only the Bible	3	4	4
Not ascertained	1	1	1
	100%	100%	100%

* This table is based upon those who read at least one book during the year preceding the interview. Those who said they read mainly fiction in answer to the above question were also asked, "Did you read any books that weren't stories or fiction?"

As would be expected, people with different amounts of schooling differ in the kind of reading they do. As formal education increases, the proportion of non-fiction reading increases. The amount of reading people do is also related to the type of reading done. Those who read both fiction and non-fiction read a much larger total number of books than do those who confine themselves solely to either fiction or non-fiction.

USE OF OTHER CHANNELS OF COMMUNICATION

Book reading, of course, is not the only kind of reading done. Many people who never look at a book get information from newspapers and magazines. Nor is reading the only source of information available

to the public. The mass media of radio, movies, and speeches reach tremendous numbers of people.

Books, and consequently public library service, are but one part of the vast network of mass communication in the modern world. How many and what kind of people use these other avenues of information, and how do they compare with those who also read books and use libraries?

Newspaper and magazine reading are very widespread

Most American adults read a newspaper every day. Although 50 percent of the nation's adult population say they read no books during the year, 80 percent are not without their daily paper. Men and women read newspapers about equally often. College people are not much more likely to read a newspaper every day than are those who have finished only grammar school, but they are much more apt to read more than one paper a day. There is, however, among the people who did not complete grammar school a sizeable group (about a third) who never see a paper, or who read one only occasionally.

"Reading" a newspaper is, of course, a variable matter—some people merely glance at the headlines, others read nearly everything in the paper. About a fifth of the readers look only at the main news, the sports and the funnies. An almost equal number say they read almost everything in the paper. The well-educated on the whole cover the paper more thoroughly, and men and women show some newspaper reading differences. Men more commonly read the editorials and financial pages than do women while women are more likely to read the women's section and the society news.

Magazine readership is less widespread than newspaper reading. The survey used a very free definition of magazine reading. The questions asked were "Are there any magazines you read regularly?" and, if Yes, "What magazines are they?" All manner of weekly and monthly publications, other than newspapers, were recorded, including church publications, technical journals, and other periodicals of interest to special groups. Seven out of ten adults report reading at least one magazine regularly. The relationship to education is very pronounced. In the group with the least education over half do not read any magazines, while among the high school and college group it is common to find people who read several magazines regularly.

Government pamphlets are read widely

About half the adults of the country have read at least one government bulletin at some time, and the proportion is even larger among those who live in rural areas and small towns. College educated people are twice as apt to have read them as those with little education and women read them more than do men. Part of the reason for the difference between small town and rural use of government pamphlets as contrasted with that of larger towns may lie in the popularity of agricultural bulletins. Among men, the most popular government bulletins are those dealing with agriculture and reclamation of land. Among women, they are the bulletins on health, cooking, and child care.

Most adults listen to the radio every day

About eight out of ten people listen to the radio at least an hour a day. Some, particularly among women, have their radios on almost continually. Radio listening is very widespread among all educational groups; the largest proportion of heavy listeners (over six hours a day) is found among high school graduates.

There are, of course, many types of radio listening. Some people prefer only entertainment programs, some listen to educational broadcasts, and for those whose radios are on from six to twelve hours a day we may even question how much they really listen at all. Educational programs play an important part in radio listening, however. When asked "Aside from news broadcasts, do you ever listen to talks and discussions on the radio?" 55 percent of the people in-

terviewed said they listened to such programs once a week or more, others listened less often, and only 25 percent said they never listened to them at all.

The fact that radio programs provide information is of major importance to many listeners. When people were asked what type of program they would miss most if their radios were out of order 42 percent indicated they would miss information or news most, 45 percent said they would miss entertainment the most, and nine percent would miss both equally. Indicative of the importance of radio in the lives of the American public is the fact that only one percent said they wouldn't miss either type of program much. Among the educational groups it is the high school graduates, those who listen to the radio most, who would miss the entertainment programs most and the educational least.

Fewer people attend public speeches

Though over half the nation's adults listen to talks on the radio, only about a fifth attended any type of public speech during the year. This channel of communication reaches the fewest people of all the mass media considered in the survey. It is also the one most highly related to educational level. Only about one-seventh of those with less than grade school education attended speeches during the year, compared with nearly half the college people. Speeches given at PTA meetings, civic organizations and women's clubs are the most frequently reported heard; rather than public lectures or mass meetings. The influence of membership in local groups appears to be a significant factor in determining the audience reached through this medium.

A majority attend the movies at least once a month

About two-thirds of the adults in this country go to the movies at least once a month and half of them go at least twice a month. Those who never go to the movies are a much smaller percentage (21 percent) than those who go once a week or more

(31 percent). Movie going varies greatly with age. Young people go to the movies much more frequently than older people. Forty percent of those over 60 years of age don't go to the movies at all, while 50 percent of those between 21 and 29 go at least once a week.

FIGURE I

PROPORTION OF ADULT POPULATION
USING VARIOUS MEDIA OF
COMMUNICATION

82%

Read one or more newspapers a day.

79%

Listen to radio one or more hours a day.

69%

Read one or more magazines regularly.

63%

Attend one or more movies a month.

50%

Read one or more books a year.

21%

Hear one or more speeches a year.

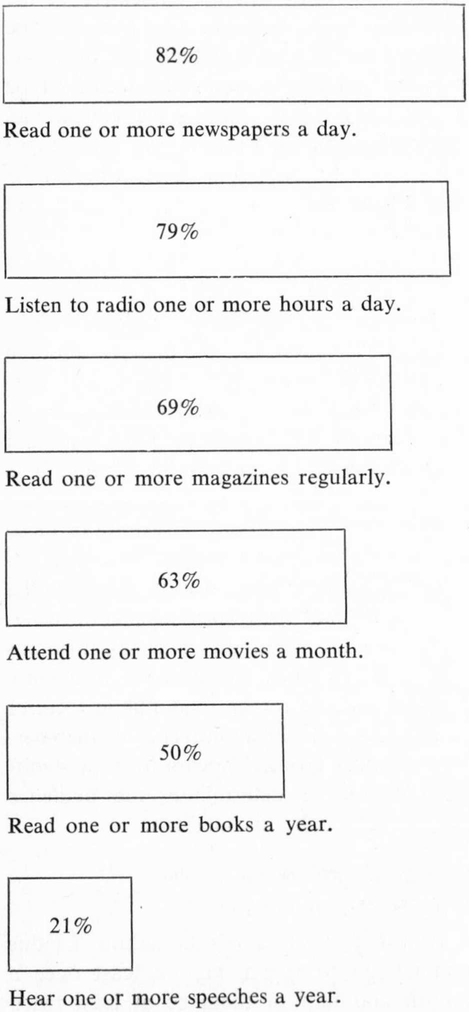

Higher income and increased schooling also stimulate movie going. Movie attendance is highest among the high school graduate and college groups, much higher than among those who did not finish grammar school. Among people with annual incomes of $3,000 or over, no appreciable differences are found between people who finished high school and those who did not. Quite a striking difference is seen, however, between these two educational groups among people with income of less than $3,000. The combination of low income and relatively little schooling seems to predispose strongly against movie attendance. Age is a factor here, as many of those with little schooling are older persons who grew up in a period when high school education was not so widespread. People with income of less than $2,000 attend movies relatively infrequently, 42 percent stating that they never go. How many of these are rural dwellers, whose money income is low and who live considerable distances from motion picture houses, is not known, but the pattern of movie attendance is no doubt affected by such factors.

It is seen that the different channels of communication, of which book reading is but one, reach the American public in rather widely differing degrees. Of all these media, books are, with the exception of public speeches, the least extensively used by the adults in this country (Figure I).

Have books given way to the radio? It is seen that books are far down the list in the frequency of exposure of the American public. We might well ask: Are the movies a substitute for reading? Do people with the "reading habit" tend to gravitate toward books or periodicals, one being preferred at the expense of the other? Are books in competition with other media of communication for the time and attention of the American public? These questions cannot perhaps be answered directly, but the survey offers some indications of the extent to which book readers are also users of other media and how library users and non-users compare in such activities as movie going and radio listening.

BOOK READING, LIBRARY USE, AND OTHER COMMUNICATION MEDIA

*Book readers are heavy users
of other communication media*

Book readers do not by any means confine their attention to this one medium of communication and information. From the point of view of time alone it might be thought that people who read books, particularly those who read quite a number during the year, would not devote as much time to radio, newspapers, and movies as those who spend no time in book reading. But the book reading public appears to be one intensely interested in all forms and avenues of communication—they not only read more, but they listen more and they see more.

However radio may have affected the nation's reading habits, the effect does not show up in a comparison of the radio listening of people who read many books with that of people who read no books. Taken as a group the people who read as many as 15 books during the year listened to the radio as much, if not more, than did those who read few books or none at all. Some people, of course, may read and listen to the radio at the same time. About two-thirds of the adults in this country report listening to the radio from one to six hours a day, regardless of whether they do any book reading or not.[1]

People who read books, and particularly the heavy consumers of books, are more

[1] Some other correlates of the use of a variety of media of communication have been explored in a recent Survey Research Center study, "Interest, Information, and Attitudes in the Field of World Affairs", November, 1949. It is found in this study that the greater the number of communication activities people engage in, the more likely they are (1) to have more knowledge of world affairs, (2) to have a high interest in this area, and (3) to have travelled extensively. These and other interrelations support the hypothesis that there is a general "activity pattern", that high rank in one sphere of activity tends to be related to high rank in another, within limits.

likely to read both newspapers and magazines than those who read no books. Eight out of ten adults read a paper almost every day, although only five out of ten read as much as one book during the entire year. This means, of course, that many people who never read a book read their newspapers faithfully. Nevertheless, there is a definite relation between newspaper reading and book reading. Those who never read a newspaper are confined almost entirely to the group who do little or no book reading, and those who read two or more papers a day are to be found mainly among the heavier book readers.

Like newspaper reading, magazine reading is much more widespread than the reading of books, and some people who seldom or never read books report reading four or five magazines, or even more, regularly. But

TABLE 3

RELATION OF FREQUENCY OF USE OF COMMUNICATION MEDIA TO NUMBER OF BOOKS READ DURING THE YEAR

	BOOKS READ DURING THE YEAR**			
	None	*1-4*	*5-14*	*15 or more*
Radio listening				
None	4%	3%	4%	4%
Less than 1 hour a day	6	11	4	7
1-6 hours a day	68	60	66	66
More than 6 hours a day	10	12	22	18
Newspaper reading				
None	10	6	1	*
1-5 a week	13	12	4	4
Every day	67	71	73	69
Twice a day or more	7	10	21	26
Magazine reading				
None	46	23	14	14
1-3	34	45	38	36
4 or more	12	23	39	45
Movie attendance				
None	29	18	6	14
Less than 1 a month	14	21	13	15
1-4 a month	43	51	63	48
More than 4 a month	13	10	18	23

* Less than one percent.
** The "Not ascertained" and "Don't know" cases have been omitted from this table.

on the whole, book readers are by far the greatest consumers of periodicals. And the heaviest readers, those who read fifteen or more books a year, read the greatest number of magazines by quite a wide margin.

Movie going, unlike much radio listening, competes for the time which might be devoted to reading. We might expect that those who read a good deal do not find time to go to the movies as often as those who read little or not at all. The facts brought out in this study partially support this supposition although the picture is complicated by correlated factors. For example, those who read no books at all go to shows less often than those who average better than a book a month, a fact undoubtedly associated with their low financial status. The heaviest movie going is found among the moderate readers of books—81 percent of the adults who read between five and 14 books a year go to the movies at least once a month. Among the heavy readers (15 or more books a year) there is a decline in this high average attendance rate and a notable increase in the number who typically go to no movies during an average month.

Undoubtedly those factors, such as education, income, and occupation, which contribute to increased use of one channel of communication, operate in the case of all types of mass media. There seems to be no segregation into groups who tend to use one medium rather exclusively. People who read a great deal also use all the forms of mass communication to a great degree.

Library use is highly related to use of other avenues of communication

The public library functions in the community as a center where information is available to the public. As such, it is part of the whole system of channels through which information is disseminated, and the relation of the library to these other channels is of interest. The question arises, how do library users differ from non-users in their use of other media of mass communication? Library user for the purpose of this study has been defined as anyone who has used the public library at least once during the preceding year.

People who use libraries virtually all read newspapers. The segment of the population which reads no newspapers is almost entirely confined to the group which has never visited a public library. Between those who visit the library relatively often and those who visit it only infrequently there is not much difference in newspaper reading.

Magazine reading is very highly related to library use. Among those who go to the library frequently, almost half read from four to six or more magazines regularly. This is very similar to the pattern found for readers and non-readers of books. People who read many books also consume other types of reading matter heavily. As might be expected, they also make up a very large part of the library clientele. Those who use the library do much more reading in general, and those who use the library most read most. Almost three-fourths of those who had never used the library had not read a book in the previous year.

Radio seems to be the avenue of communication least related to either book reading or library use. There is moderate to heavy radio listening by both those who use the public libraries and those who do not. Movie going, on the other hand, is highly correlated with library use. A fourth of the frequent users of the library go to the movies oftener than once a week. Only five percent never go. But 35 percent of those who never have used the library never go to the movies. The fact that movie attendance is more highly related to library use than it is to book reading suggests that library use, in addition to the motives and habits of reading, is a more active pattern requiring special habits. Library users are not only heavy readers but are apparently a relatively mobile group. Corroboration for this hypothesis is found in the later discussions of age and library use and the reasons given for not using the library.

In general, readers of books and library users exhibit a similar pattern in the amount of exposure to other mass means of com-

TABLE 4

RELATION OF PUBLIC LIBRARY USE TO
FREQUENCY OF USE OF OTHER
COMMUNICATION MEDIA

| | NUMBER OF VISITS TO LIBRARY DURING YEAR** | | | |
	Never used	None in last year	1-9 times	10 or more times
Radio listening				
None	4%	3%	6%	6%
Less than 1 hour a day	6	7	8	7
1-6 hours a day	66	65	66	67
More than 6 hours a day	7	19	17	15
Newspaper reading				
None	13	2	*	*
1-5 a week	16	5	1	6
Every day	63	71	82	79
Twice a day or more	5	21	14	15
Magazine reading				
None	49	20	11	13
1-3	33	44	36	28
4 or more	10	28	45	48
Movie attendance				
None	35	15	8	5
Less than 1 a month	15	14	15	17
1-4 a month	41	55	60	51
More than 4 a month	8	16	17	27
Books read				
None	72	41	14	12
1-4 during year	18	19	26	2
5-9	2	11	13	11
10-49	6	20	38	44
50 or more	1	7	8	29
Proportion of total sample***	37%	44%	9%	9%

* Less than one percent.
** For purposes of simplification, all "Don't know" and "Not ascertained" cases have been omitted. For this reason some of the columns do not total 100 percent.
*** This information was not obtained from one percent of the sample.

munication. They are people who take full advantage of all avenues of information. They are heavy readers of newspapers and periodicals, they listen to the radio at least as much as others do, and they see a great many more movies.

It is possible to think of the audiences reached by the major media of printed communication as a series of concentric circles. Newspaper readers are the largest group and include virtually everyone who is reached by any of the printed media. Magazine readers are the next largest group and enclosed almost entirely within this group are the book readers. The library draws its limited clientele for the most part from this inner circle of book readers. Radio covers all of these groups and is used by them all in amounts that do not vary greatly. Movie going is also common among all these groups and tends to vary with the use of the printed media although this relationship is an imperfect one.

WHERE DO PEOPLE GO WHEN THEY WANT INFORMATION?

We have seen that a large proportion of the nation's people are exposed to the information contained in newspapers, magazines, radio broadcasts, government bulletins, and motion pictures. However, the frequency of exposure to a medium of information may not be indicative of the degree to which people rely on this medium to provide the information which they require. The question is, when specific problems arise and information is needed, where do people seek this information? To what extent do they think spontaneously of the public library as the place to go to find out what they want to know?

Where do people go for specific information?

There is obviously an almost infinite number of topics on which people might seek information. The survey could include specific questions on only a few. In the survey, people were asked where they would go for information on four specific topics: (1) home decoration, (2) nutrition, (3) foreign countries, and (4) rearing of children. While these topics cannot necessarily be regarded as representative of all the topics on which information might be wanted, they were chosen for inclusion in the survey because they are of broad interest and because they cover a fairly wide range of subject matter. The questions regarding the choice of sources of these different types of information were asked at the beginning of the interview, before any specific questions were raised concerning libraries, books, or any other particular source of information.

On the whole the study found a very high reliance on experts as a source of information, particularly when people are seeking the answer to a fairly practical question. When asked, "Suppose you wanted to find out something about how to paint or fix up your house (apartment) yourself. How would you go about it?", these were the major sources given:

56% would consult a professional source (painter, decorator, etc.)
14% would rely on their own experience
13% would ask friends
9% would consult magazines
6% would consult books
2% would consult the library*

* The "Not ascertained" and "Don't know" cases have been omitted from this and the following tables.

The sources that would be sought out for information on nutrition were not appreciably different, although books ranked higher on the list. The question was asked as follows: "Now suppose you wanted to find out something about what foods are good for a person, that is, what vitamins they have. How would you go about getting information about that?" The following answers were most frequently obtained:

56% would consult a professional source
18% would look it up in a book
9% would ask a family member or friend
8% would consult a magazine
1% would consult the library

Undoubtedly many who stated that they would look for this information in a book would get their books from the public

library, but they did not say so until asked, "Where would you get the book?" Only one percent spontaneously mentioned the public library as the place they would go to find out something about nutrition.

For information about a foreign country, people think less often of seeking out expert persons and more often of institutional sources of information. In this connection the library was mentioned spontaneously by about one-tenth of the people, but no doubt a high percentage of the books consulted would come from a library. The interviewers asked, "If a friend wrote you that he was in a foreign country that you had never heard of, how would you go about finding out something about the place?"

31% would get a book on the subject
13% would ask a service club
11% would consult the library
10% would consult maps
10% would consult friends
9% would consult federal government agencies

In considering possible sources of information on problems of raising children, people most commonly think of individuals whose opinion they respect. Doctors are most frequently mentioned, although other types of experienced people are also referred to. Some people (20 percent) feel that their own experience is sufficient to meet such problems and an equal number refer to books as a special source. The following were the most frequently mentioned sources of information when the interviewers asked, "If someone asked you how he could find out something about bringing up children, how would you tell him to go about it?"

31% would consult a professional person
21% would consult a book
20% would rely on their own experience
15% would consult family member or friend
4% would consult a magazine
3% would ask the public library

THE WORLD OF THE DAYTIME SERIAL

RUDOLF ARNHEIM

INTRODUCTION

Within a span of a dozen years, radio daytime serials, an American invention, have become an intimate feature of this country's daily life. What kind of mental food, healthy or noxious, do they offer? What makes them so appealing? What kind of a picture of private and social life do they represent? Which attitudes are condemned, which recommended?

The nickname "soap opera" indicates not only the symbiosis of drama and soap, but also its consequences for the cultural level of the programs. The effects of commercial control are well known from what motion picture producers and pulp writers offer to their customers. Any admissible means to exercise a strong appeal is welcome, and since generally the strongest and widest appeal can be secured by the crudest means, commercial art production tends towards lowering the cultural level.

The producers of radio serials take no chances in trying to meet the taste of their customers. Letters in which the listeners express approbation or protest are carefully studied. Telephone surveys determine the approximate size of the audience of each serial. On the basis of such data, and with a good deal of flair for what suits the purpose, the plots, the characters, the settings of the serials are made to order. That is

why a content analysis of the serials can be expected to yield not only something about the programs, but also something about the listeners. These stories are likely to offer a picture of the world such as a particular social group would wish it to be.

The "streamlined" methods of radio serial production also justify a statistical approach. An attempt to describe, let us say, the European novel of the 19th century by discovering how often a few easily definable features can be found in a sample of fifty novels written during the period, would be inadequate. Such features, even where they referred to essential characteristics of the single work, would be misleading by their isolation from the individual context. Radio serials, however, are produced by a small group of advertising agencies which have specialized in this field. What the programs have in common outweighs individual particularities to such an extent that wherever a serial author undertakes to accomplish his task in a personal way, the result stands out as an obvious exception to the rule.

In order to avoid misunderstandings it should be added that whenever in this study we speak about the "tendencies" of the serial authors or producers we do not mean to prejudge the question of to what extent these authors and producers consciously follow certain trends or realize their socio-

From P. F. Lazarsfeld and F. N. Stanton (eds.), *Radio Research 1942-43* (New York: Duell, Sloan and Pearce, 1944), pp. 43-81. Reprinted by permission of the author and the publisher.

logical and psychological implications. Undoubtedly a considerable number of "rules of thumb" is deliberately used. But on the whole, the content analyst is in a position somewhat similar to that of the psychoanalyst who by interpreting the dreams of a patient, reveals the mechanism and the meaning of strivings of whose existence the patient is unaware or which he even wishes to contest.

THE DATA

In order to get data for a content analysis, either the actual broadcast, or records from the broadcasts, or the scripts could be used. Records and scripts together would provide an ideal basis for a thorough study. However, as the present study was designed mainly to gather some preliminary information and to work out suitable methods of interpretation, a more expedient procedure was applied. Forty-seven students, 39 female and 8 male, each listened to one radio serial for three weeks, in the period from March 17 to April 7, 1941. For each daily installment listened to, a report sheet was filled out.

The serials were chosen at random among those available to New York radio listeners between 8 A. M. and 6 P. M. The choice had, to some extent, to be adapted to the timetable of the students. As a result, some of the better-known serials have not been covered, while duplicate reports were received on three others. The following 43 serials were covered by the survey.

1. Against the Storm
2. Arnold Grimm's Daughter
3. Backstage Wife
4. Betty and Bob
5. David Harum
6. Edith Adams' Future
7. Ellen Randolph
8. Girl Alone
9. Government Girl
10. Guiding Light
11. Helen Trent
12. Hilltop House (Bess Johnson)
13. Home of the Brave
14. John's Other Wife
15. Joyce Jordan
16. Julia Blake, The Heart of
17. Just Plain Bill
18. Kate Hopkins
19. Kitty Keane
20. Life Can Be Beautiful (three listeners)
21. Lone Journey
22. Lorenzo Jones
23. Ma Perkins
24. Mary Marlin
25. Midstream
26. Mother O'Mine
27. Myrt and Marge
28. O'Neills (two listeners)
29. Our Gal Sunday
30. Pepper Young's Family
31. Portia Faces Life
32. Right to Happiness
33. Road of Life
34. Scattergood Baines (two listeners)
35. Stella Dallas
36. Valiant Lady
37. Vic and Sade
38. We Are Always Young
39. We, the Abbotts
40. When a Girl Marries
41. Woman in White
42. Young Widder Brown
43. Young Dr. Malone

Normally, radio serials go on the air for fifteen minutes at a time every weekday, with the exception of Saturday. Within our test period, 16 installments of each serial could have been listened to. For various reasons, however, this aim was reached only approximately. On the average, 12.7 installments were listened to (average deviation: 2.7). The total number of installments covered was 596.

Most of the reports which we obtained proved to be quite sufficient for the analysis intended. It was possible then to extract from them (1) all passages referring to the single conflicts or "problems" that form the plots of the serials; (2) all references to actions and reactions of the single characters and all evaluations of the characters given or implied during the program; (3) all references to specific topics, such as politics, learning, newspapers, the function of women, etc.

THE SOCIAL MILIEU

Locale

Do radio serials choose the large centers of modern life as settings for the adventures of their characters, or do they prefer small towns or the village? Do they have their heroes escaping from civil community to solitude and the wilderness? A rough classification of the settings is given in Table 1. As two types of settings appeared in 5 of our samples, we present the results in terms of the number of serials and of settings.

TABLE 1

LOCALE OF THE SERIALS

Locale	Number of serials	Number of settings
Large cities	8	13
Middle or small towns	16	20
Rural communities	4	5
Combinations	5	—
Doubtful (either large or middle town)	5	5
Other cases	5	5
Total	48	48

Middle or small towns predominate over large cities, such as New York or Chicago. In only 10 per cent of all cases is the serial laid in a rural community. The preference for middle towns may reflect an intention of catering to listeners who belong to just that social setting. In this case, we would have to note that these listeners are believed to prefer plays which, at least outwardly, reproduce the framework of their own life rather than permitting access to the higher sphere of metropolitan life.

But whether a large or a small place is chosen as a setting, there is certainly no tendency toward fleeing regular life in a community. Even the five "other" cases mentioned in Table 1 refer to fragments of this normal life rather than to exotic or fantastic backgrounds. These took place in the "most expensive sanitarium of the country," at a country college, in two cases on the estates of wealthy people, and on a pleasure cruise near Havana. With the exception of the latter, the episodes were all set in the United States. This again indicates that listeners are believed to enjoy a familiar environment rather than one which permits or demands that they imagine what may happen elsewhere.

Social Status of Main Characters

What are the social backgrounds of the people presented in the radio serials? Are they rich or poor? Are they individuals distinguished by social prestige and influence or are they representatives of the common folk? Table 2 shows the occupation of the central, plot-sustaining group of characters. Most of the categories in this table are self-explanatory. "Society people" comprise those characters whose status was described exclusively by their belonging to "society" (society matrons, the son of a millionaire, etc.).

TABLE 2

OCCUPATIONAL STATUS OF MAIN CHARACTERS
(Proportion of 48 Settings in Which the Different Occupations Appear)

Occupational status	Number of settings	Per cent of all settings
Society people	9	19
High officials	10	21
Big business	16	33
Professionals	35	73
Housewives	31	65
Small business	15	31
Wage earners	9	19
Destitute people	3	6

If we accept the order of the categories as a rough social scale we find that the status of the main characters clusters at about the middle of the scale with professionals and housewives being most frequent. The frequent appearance of housewives can be explained by their predominance in the audience. The preference for the professionals seems less easy to explain. The physicians, lawyers, college teachers, artists, etc., who comprise this group are probably on a higher social level than the average listener, but they are not the highest class available for wish-dreams. Society people, high officials, and big businessmen do not appear more frequently than small business people and employees whose status can be supposed to correspond most closely to the average listener's. One might speculate that physicians and lawyers are indispensable in the troubles which are characteristic of the plots. In fact, the serials afford sufficient opportunity to lawyers for keeping busy. But there is not enough illness in serials to explain the large number of physicians.

And quite often the lawyers and doctors appear mainly as husbands, friends, etc., rather than in the exercise of their professions. Can this result be explained by the attitude of lower middle class people towards other social classes? Do they consider the class of learned or artistically gifted men, who give help and advice or produce enjoyment and who live on a higher economic level, the object of admiration and aspiration; and does resentment dominate their attitude towards still higher social groups?

The complete absence of the working class proper is striking. The characters of serials include small shopkeepers, business employees, a taxi driver, even one garage mechanic, and then there is a jump to a small group of destitute outcasts: an ex-convict, a family of unemployed migrant workers, a senator reduced to vagabondage by amnesia. *There is no case of a factory worker, a miner, a skilled or unskilled laborer, playing an important role in any of the 43 serial samples.* Here again, social attitudes of the listeners, and possibly the policy of advertisers, might give an explanation.

Apart from the occupational scale, we examined how often people appeared who were equipped with the *splendor of wealth*: people who possess large houses and servants, who visit nightclubs, charter private planes, send orchids by wire, etc. This happened in 24 out of 48 settings; i.e., in 50 per cent, and specifically in 85 per cent of the large town settings; 30 per cent of the middle and small town settings; and 20 per cent of the rural settings. The occupational groups who contributed to this feature were the "society people," businessmen, and, among the high officials, mainly senators, but also some of the doctors, lawyers, and artists.

About the relations between high-class and low-class people it can be said that while popular fiction of the European tradition often introduces the reader into the company of rich noblemen, the radio serials, an American product, present their heroes as illuminated by the upper sphere, but not necessarily identified with it. On the contrary, in many of the cases in which wealthy and socially highly situated people appear, they are shown paying courtship to the attractiveness or efficiency, or both, of the middleclass people. This may be an attempt to compensate the listener for her lack of social prestige and power in real life. Personal qualities, which are independent of the distribution of benefits in the community and therefore equally accessible to all are chosen to counteract social inequality.

The fiction of mutual intercourse on an equal level is stressed, e.g., in the case of a famous Broadway actor who consumes his time and nervous energy in helping the humble middle-class family next door. Marriage with a member of the upper-class conveys honor on the just plain people. There is the spectacular career of the "orphan girl who was reared by two miners and who in young womanhood married England's wealthiest, most handsome lord." Ma Perkins, an elderly housewife and lumberyard owner in the country, has her daughter married to a brilliant young congressman in Washington. Mrs. Stella Dallas, who is a lower middle-class woman and wants to remain one, was married to a diplomatic attache in the Capital, and her daughter "went out of her mother's life" by marrying a man who is prominent in Washington society. At the same time, proud self-assertion and a certain resentment against people who draw high prestige from wealth or a professional position is often clearly expressed. A rich businessman's marriage proposal is rejected. A bankrupt real estate agent protests against his daughter's desire to marry an attractive young millionaire. The elegant and rich physician courting a simple "government girl" is a "heel" who well deserves to be murdered by an equally rich "glamour girl." A taxicab driver wrote a symphony worth $25,000 and receives but scarcely appreciates the attentions of an unscrupulous wealthy wangler and his elegant wife.

Leaders

Great importance is attributed to the quality of "leadership." In *30 out of 48 settings, i.e., in 62.5 per cent, such "leaders" were found among the central characters.*

Table 3 shows the number of leaders in communities of different sizes, the "leaders" being broken down into those who excel by their professional position and those who do so by their personal qualities, such as intelligence, helpfulness, initiative. These "personal leaders" are further divided according to leadership in the whole community or in their private group (family, friends, etc.).

Leadership is due to personal qualities about as often as it is to a professional position. The leaders by personal merit exert their influence within their private group twice as often as in the whole community. In the large cities the professional leaders prevail. Most of them are people of a nationwide reputation, e.g., a president of the United States, senators, famous actors, a number 1 debutante. In the middle or small towns this group of leaders is still predominant: a superintendent of schools, a city manager, a parson, an influential journalist of the local paper, etc. In the rural setting, personal efficiency and helpfulness enable individuals to become leaders in their community, although they are a barber, a garage mechanic, a small store owner, etc.

An examination of the plots shows that often individuals of relatively low social standing, but great personal merits, are described as being more efficient leaders than those on whom society has conferred the prestige of official leadership.

David Harum, who is the owner of a small store, but first of all a "country philosopher," appears absorbed in a community garden project. Garage mechanic Lorenzo Jones is organizing a charity dance. The "leave-it-to-me" man, storekeeper Scattergood Baines, convicts the respected president of the local school of a grave professional error. Ma Perkins, the country woman, provides a senatorial committee with the decisive clues for the disclosure of a large scandal, and the owner of a small second-hand book store at the lower East Side of New York, an old Jew, gives philosophical advice to a famous physician, to his son, and to last year's number 1 debutante, who, excited by their troubles, rather foolishly buzz among the book shelves.

THE PROBLEMS

The Role of the Problems

The narrative content of our samples consists almost entirely of problems created and solved by the characters. These problems stem from disturbances of static life situations, rather than from obstacles to the accomplishment of goals. One could imagine plays in which the characters were bent on achieving certain positive aims such as educating children, fighting for a social reform, solving a scientific problem. Then the "problems" would consist in conquering the forces opposed to the realization of the aim. The typical radio serial situation, instead, cannot be compared to a stream hampered by a dam, but rather to a stagnant lake which is troubled by a stone thrown into it. The attitude of the serial characters is essentially passive and conservative, possibly a reflection of the role which the average serial listener plays in the community.

Human existence is pictured as being continuously threatened by catastrophe. There is not just one problem which has

TABLE 3

LEADERS IN COMMUNITIES OF DIFFERENT SIZE

Type of leadership	Large cities	Middle or small towns	Rural communities	Others	Total Number
		Locale			
Professional	6	9	1	3	19
Personal	1	5	6	6	18
In community	—	1	5	—	6
In private group	1	4	1	6	12
Total	7	14	7	9	37*

* 37 cases are given instead of the 30 indicated above because in seven settings two of the three leader categories were present.

to be faced by a character or a group of characters, but an uninterrupted chain of more or less severe nuisances. A total number of 142 problems was traced in 596 installments. *The average number of problems per serial was 3.3 (average deviation: 1.6) for the test period, which comprised an average of only 12.7 fifteen-minute installments.* Roughly speaking, there was one problem for every four installments.

Literature may seem to offer something similar in the great epics such as the Odyssey or in the Bible story of Job. But in these epics the succession of the episodes is as rigidly regular as the recurring design of a frieze. The stylized composition and the unrealistic content of the stories are the reasons why the succession of disastrous episodes appears not as a true-to-life picture, but as a symbol for a high degree of suffering, intensity being expressed through repetition. Radio serials, instead, do their best to create the impression that they present "real life." They interlace the episodes in an irregular, more "lifelike" manner. In the realm of such "realism," the wave-after-wave attacks of evil cannot but have an unintended humorous effect on the more discriminating listener. An unsophisticated serial listener who accepts these programs as convincing and true must carry away the impression that human life is a series of attacks to be warded off by the victims and their helpers.

Due to the briefness of the test period, no distinction was possible between problems of major or minor weight. In order to get an idea of the general structure of the serials, one would have to examine them over a longer period. Roughly, two types of serial "composition" were distinguishable. In one, a leader, generally by personal qualities, guides the other characters through their personal troubles. The "conflict-carriers" as well as the type of conflict involved may vary from episode to episode. In other cases, there is a group of people, generally a family, to whom disaster after disaster occurs. If the family is large enough and has a fringe of fiances and friends, the

victims of new troubles are never lacking. In some cases also a constant setting helps to maintain the unity of the serial.

The Content of the Problems

What kinds of problems trouble the serial characters? An examination of the data suggested the nine content categories listed in Table 4. The table shows in how many of the total 43 serials each type of problem occurred. It also shows how the total number of problems which were traced during the test period is distributed among the nine categories.

TABLE 4

DISTRIBUTION OF KINDS OF PROBLEMS
(Proportion of serials in which each type occurred and per cent distribution of types of problems)

Kind of problem	Per cent of 43 serials*	Per cent of all 159 problems**
Personal relations	91	47
Courtship	49	16
Marriage	44	18
Family	33	10
Friends	12	3
Economic and professional	47	22
Crime	30	9
Illness, accidents	29	9
Public Affairs	26	10
Others	9	3

* In 91 per cent of all 43 serials studied a problem pertaining to personal relationships occurred. However, as one serial might contain different types of problems of personal relationships, the proportions for the subgroup "personal relations" adds up to more than 91 per cent. Percentages in the second column of the table add up to 100 because here the base is not the total number of serials, but the total number of problems.
** The increase from 142 problems to 159 is explained by the fact that some problems had to be brought under more than one category.

Problems in the realm of "personal relations," i.e., problems occurring between lovers, marriage partners, in the family or among friends, account for 47 per cent of all problems. One or more of them occurred in 91 per cent of all 43 serials studied for a three weeks' period. Most of the cases listed as economic, professional, crime, or illness problems, and even some of the public affairs problems could be classified under another master category, namely as "problems endangering the individual." This is obvious in the case of illness and accidents, but economic threats and crime might concern the community as a whole, and in the realm of public affairs one would certainly expect it to be so. Instead, the economic and professional problems deal mostly with the job or money difficulties of individuals, crimes are committed against individuals, and even the corrupt officials who dominate the public affairs group are shown mainly as damaging single persons—ambitious district attorneys trying to convict innocents, or a senator wanting to expose a colleague. This second master category of problems, related to the economic or professional standing, the physical integrity, and the reputation of the individual, is almost as large as the group devoted to "personal relations." Both of these categories together account for nearly all the problems traced during the test period. The world of the serials is thus quite clearly a "private" world in which the interests of the community fade into insignificance.

What Causes the Problems?

Do people create trouble for themselves or are other people to blame? What role is played by non-personal forces such as natural powers or economic and political conditions? The distribution of the different causes is shown in Table 5.

Trouble is somewhat more often created by the very people who have to suffer from it ("sufferers") than by other persons. In only 24 cases out of 159 (15 per cent), non-personal forces rather than individuals are described as creators of trouble.

Disturbances of a "personal relationship" are created by members of the group concerned almost three times as often as by other people outside the group, while the situation is reversed where the individual is endangered by crime, a professional problem, or a public affair. Non-personal forces are decisive in the illness and accident cases, but for the rest, have some importance only in the economic category.

The problems of life are presented largely as caused by individuals, by their shortcomings or corruption, rather than by any general social, economical, or political conditions.

An examination of the plots shows that more than half of the "getting a job"-problems, for instance, dealt with being offered a job which the person did not care to accept rather than with the difficulties of finding work. Sons did not want to enter their fathers' business. A college professor refused a position in New York because country life suited him better. Intriguing women also caused difficulties in getting a job. As far as "losing a job" was concerned, two people wanted to get rid of their present occupation. Personal shortcomings, jealousy, professional rivalry, and political blackmailing furnished threats to people's employment. There were some instances of dis-

TABLE 5

CAUSES OF THE DIFFERENT KINDS OF PROBLEMS

Kind of problem	CAUSED BY				
	People themselves	Others	Non-personal forces	Doubtful	Total number
Personal relations	52	19	1	3	75
Courtship	19	5	1	1	26
Marriage	24	3	—	1	28
Family	8	7	—	1	16
Friends	1	4	—	—	5
Economic and professional	8	16	7	4	35
Crime	2	10	—	3	15
Illness, accidents	1	—	13	—	14
Public Affairs	2	11	2	1	16
Others	2	1	1	—	4
Total	67	57	24	11	159

honest professional behavior. There was a profiteering landowner. A crooked businessman tried to profit by the sale of a symphony at the expense of the poor composer. A man was swindled into buying a manganese mine. And a dishonest renting agent intrigued against the appointment of an administrator who would reveal his frauds. In only two cases economic reasons for job problems were given: a man needed a job because he needed the money, and another one did not get a promised job because "business was bad." Other "non-personal forces" to interfere with business were an inundation, illness, an accident, etc.

Troubles in public administration were likewise attributed to the shortcomings of individuals. Senators tried to sell the government bad land for an army camp. District attorneys worked for their personal careers rather than for justice. High municipal officials were involved in intrigue, blackmailing and fraud. And the president of a community garden was tempted to cheat. National Defense was used as a pretext to present private problems very loosely connected with public issues; a private, through carelessness, provoked an accident which a woman-friend of his was accused of; another private, on leave, visited a girl who fell ill with measles, and was prevented by quarantine from being back at the camp in time.

Crimes were rarely committed and by very bad people only. In 12 out of 15 total crime cases, innocent and virtuous people were accused of having committed murder or adultery; having embezzled the property of a bus company; having taken somebody's car, etc. This feature may be designed pleasantly to nourish the listener's feeling that she is often the victim of accusations which she does not deserve.

MORAL EVALUATION

Three Types of Characters

A significant relationship seems to exist between the kind of "problem" presented and the moral evaluation of the characters involved.

There is little difficulty in finding out for many of the leading characters whether they are meant to be good or bad people. The announcer, whose comments are to be considered as authoritative, often attributes to them precise traits which imply equally precise ethical evaluations. He will talk about "the kindly man walking down the stairs" or refer to "that half-gangster" who is trying to obtain the heroine's favor. Just

as outspoken about their fellow-characters are the characters themselves. Especially the "reliable" people (present in almost every serial as a moral framework from which to judge the happenings) express the opinion of the authors. Besides, the actors generally do their best to distinguish, by the inflexions of their voices, the tough scoundrel or the suave intriguer from the considerate friend or the nervously lamenting victim of passion, fate, or villainy.

In addition to the "bad" and the "good" people we find a third group of characters, almost as neatly defined as those of the two other groups. They excel in unpleasant qualities such as jealousy, vindictiveness, lack of balance, deceitfulness, selfishness, but it is clearly stated that these defects do not spring from an evil nature, but are weaknesses resulting from bad experiences or lack of control. It is suggested that they may eventually be brought back to their better selves. For the sake of brevity we shall call this third type the "weak" people.

One might have expected a clear-cut black-and-white method of moral evaluation in radio serials. Instead, as is shown in Table 6, the "weak" people are most frequent among the creators of trouble. A further remarkable result is given by the large proportion of "good" people among the trouble makers.

TABLE 6

MORAL EVALUATION OF CHARACTERS WHO CREATE TROUBLES

Troubles created for:	MORAL EVALUATION OF CHARACTERS				
	Good	Bad	Weak	Doubt-ful	Total Number
Themselves	18	8	34	2	62
Others	5	30	12	6	53
Total	23	38	46	8	115*

* To the 115 total problems caused by persons, 20 have to be added which were caused by non-personal forces and 9 in which the cause was undecidable. This leads to a total of 144 problems. The increase from 142 to 144 problems is explained by the fact that in two cases good as well as weak creators of trouble were traced.

Good people create trouble, e.g., by deceiving others for their own good: a wife "gives hope" to a blind husband by making him believe she is expecting a child; an actor plays the role of a blind girl's brother to save her from knowing that the brother is in prison under a murder charge; another actor offers his services to make a neglecting husband jealous. A "good" man may fall in love with somebody else's wife or, being married himself, to another woman, but such a love relation is never "consummated," and generally the third person's faultiness tends to justify the slip. Good people also accuse themselves of crimes in order to shield others.

There is a clear difference between the moral evaluation of those who create trouble and those who do it to others. Weak characters prevail in the former group and good ones too are frequent. Those who create problems for others are mainly bad, sometimes weak, and good only in a few cases.

As far as the "sufferers" are concerned, Table 6 gives information only about those who create trouble to themselves. If *all* the sufferers are considered—those who create trouble to themselves as well as those who have to suffer from others—the good people are shown as doing most of the suffering (Table 7). Bad people are hardly ever the

TABLE 7

MORAL EVALUATION OF ALL SUFFERERS

Moral evaluation	Number of sufferers
Good	103
Bad	8
Weak	46
Doubtful	9
Total	166*

* The Increase of 142 to 166 sufferers is again explained by the number of cases which had to be classified under more than one category.

victims of trouble. To the 166 cases of Table 7, six are to be added in which the community is described as the sufferer—which low number shows again the privacy of the world of daytime serials.

The Characterization of Men and Women

As the serials cater mainly to a female audience it seemed worth while to look for differences in the presentation of men and women.

Table 8 shows that men appear considerably more often as trouble-makers than

TABLE 8

MORAL EVALUATION OF MEN AND WOMEN WHO CREATE TROUBLE

| | TROUBLES CREATED FOR | | | | | |
| Moral evaluation | Themselves | | Others | | Total number* | |
	M	W	M	W	M	W
Good	11	9	4	3	15	12
Bad	4	4	23	8	27	12
Weak	20	17	9	3	29	20
Doubtful	1	2	3	3	4	5
Total	36	32	39	17	75	49

* The increase from a total of 115 in Table 6 to 124 (75 men and 49 women) in Table 8 is explained by the fact that e.g., the bad troublemaker in a problem-situation may actually be more than one person, sometimes a man and a woman. The same condition holds good for the sufferers in Table 9.

women do. This refers particularly to the cases in which trouble is created for others. (A breakdown according to the kinds of trouble listed in Table 4 shows that men surpass women in doing harm to other people especially in the realm of public affairs, crime and economic problems.) The male troublemakers are almost as often bad as they are weak and are considerably less often good. Among the women, the weak characters are almost twice as frequent as the good or the bad ones. Thus the difference in the sex distribution is most striking for the bad people: bad troublemakers are more than twice as often men as women.

The distribution and moral evaluation of men and women among *all* the sufferers is shown in Table 9. It can be seen that men and women are about equally often the

TABLE 9

MORAL EVALUATION OF ALL MEN AND WOMEN WHO SUFFER FROM PROBLEMS

Moral evaluation	Men	Women
Good	59	65
Bad	5	4
Weak	33	19
Doubtful	3	6
Total*	100	94

* See footnote to Table 8.

victim of trouble-situations. Among the weak sufferers, men predominate.

Moral evaluation goes in favor of the women. Men create trouble more often than women, especially to other people. They are mostly weak and bad, the latter considerably more often than women. Among the people who have to suffer men excel clearly in the group of the weak.

A few examples of marriage problems may show how this tendency comes out in the plots. Marriage disturbances through unfaithfulness are presented rarely and handled with care. The presentation goes in favor of the wife. In no case does a wife fall in love with another man. In three cases, husbands had a girl friend: two of these husbands were described as "selfish, suspicious, jealous" and "unstable, unbalanced"; the third succumbed to a "petty, selfish, quarrelsome, jealous" woman. Where the marriage was imperiled by the shortcomings of one of the partners, there was usually something wrong with the husband. He was a tyrant or neglected his wife, or disgusted her by his laziness, or his being involved in political intrigues, etc. There were only two cases of thoroughly bad wives— one who defamed a colleague of her husband out of professional rivalry, and another whose husband, a plastic surgeon, refused after an accident to restore her "wickedly beautiful face through which she did every bad thing in her life." This latter was the only case of a man who wanted to get rid of any unsympathetic wife, and it seemed significant that her guilt was stated as springing from what is a woman's most desired asset—beauty.

The Solutions of the Problems

It has often been observed that in popular narrative art (novels, plays, movies) trouble-situations are solved according to conventional ethical standards. The stories are governed by perfect justice, thus providing the audience with reassurance and pleasant compensation. The same holds good for radio serials.

Plans apt to create trouble to other people or to the trouble-makers themselves are permitted to develop, but hardly ever to be consummated. In a sample of 73 solutions, only about 12 per cent of the trouble-creating plans were carried through; all others were thwarted. The relatively largest measure of success was granted to the "good" troublemakers.

It seems interesting that while all the motives ascribed to good people were considered excusable or even praiseworthy, there was still a distinction—presumably also based on moral evaluation—as to whether the plans were allowed to succeed; they were *not* in cases in which they interfered with an institution like marriage, family, or the administration of justice. "Good" people were allowed: to leave a woman for the time being because of faithfulness to an insane wife; to refuse a better job because of preference for country life; to choose neither of two suitors; and to help a blind husband over a crisis by making him believe he would have a son. But they were prevented from such things as withholding an adopted child from her real mother, making love to an honest girl while married to a disagreeable wife, or seducing an honest wife neglected by her husband; or accepting punishment for a murder committed by somebody else.

Earlier in this chapter it was stated that good people prevail among the sufferers and that the bad are hardly ever the victims of trouble. While this is characteristic for the initial set-up of the problems, the solutions show that perfect justice is provided. No definitive harm is done to the victims; many of them are agreeably indemnified for what they had to suffer. No good troublemakers are punished, their motives being virtuous. But all the bad ones are. And as the weak troublemakers did wrong but are eligible for reform, about one half of them is punished, the rest not.

It may be added that the perfect justice which rules the serials is of a curious type. There is a reason for its existence, but it has no sufficient cause. Whether a person is punished or rewarded is explained by the sort of ethical evaluation of his or her deeds which may be expected from the average listener. But there is no indication in the serials of a principle which brings justice about. Virtuous and efficient persons are shown to help innocent sufferers and to fight malefactors. But who provides these helpers, who assists them in succeeding, who makes the honest invalids recover, who sends a paralytic stroke to the villain? God might be this principle, but he is hardly ever mentioned. There is no causal explanation for the high correlation between what people deserve and what they get. Radio serials procure the satisfaction created by a rule of ideal justice, but do not bother about explaining to whom we are indebted for such a perfect state of affairs.

A PSYCHOLOGICAL FORMULA OF SOAP OPERA

The Object of Identification

The listener's evaluation of the plot and the characters involved will largely depend on whom she identifies herself with. If she is presented, for instance, with the story of a woman who cheats her best friend, everything depends on whether the center of attention is the malefactor, the circumstances which led the woman to do what she should not have done and perhaps did not wish to do, her struggles of conscience, her repentance, and so on; or whether the plot is given the perspective of the victim. In the first case, the play reminds one of human imperfection. By eliciting identification with the sinner it warns that all people are sinners. It creates an attitude of melancholy humility, but at the same time enlightens by clarifying the mechanism that pushes people into guilt. In the second case it appeals to the Pharisee in man. It shows that decent people are treated badly even by those whom they have every reason to trust. It evokes the satisfaction of being good oneself while others, unfortunately, are bad. Instead of opening the road towards humble self-knowledge it nourishes the cheap pleasure of self-complacency.

Identification is invited in the radio serials by various means, most of which belong to the common technique of narrative art—novel drama, film. The central position of a character invites the listener to perceive and to evaluate the plot situation from the point of view of this person. Identification is furthered by the sheer quantity of time devoted to a character and by the amount of insight given into what the person thinks and feels. Physical, intellectual and ethical perfection, social power and prestige must also promote identification very strongly.

Furthermore, there is the factor of resemblance: a middle-aged housewife will identify herself more readily with a middle-aged housewife, etc.

On the basis of these criteria, the objects of identification were sought. The crude and oversimplifying technique of characterization used by the average radio serial author made this task much more easy and reliable in practice than it might seem in theory. *For 118 out of 121 cases on whom there was sufficient detail, there was no doubt about the object of identification intended.* Twenty-one cases had to be omitted because of poor reports.

Identification tends towards a surprisingly uniform type. Moral perfection is the most constant feature of the group of symptoms which was used for establishing the "object of identification." With no exception these characters are spotlessly virtuous, good-hearted, helpful. They are intelligent, often physically attractive. They are the "leaders by personal qualities," whose frequent appearance was discussed above. *In 101 out of 118 cases, the object of identification was a woman.* As to her main function in the plot, the "ideal woman" was presented as

An eligible woman	in 23 cases
A wife	21
A mother	16
A professional woman	14
A friend	13
A daughter	2
Unspecified	12
	101

The Psychological Structure of Radio Serials

We are now equipped to suggest a psychological formula which seems to underlie the outwardly varied plots of radio serials and which expresses itself in many of the previously discussed features characteristic of the serials. Three types of characters with significantly different roles sustain this psychological structure. They are suggested by and roughly correlated with the three types of moral evaluation which we were able to distinguish. The function of these

Moral evaluation	Role in plot	Listener's attitude
Weak	Helpless trouble-maker, guilty sufferer, reformable	Resonance to portrait
Good	Helpful leader, innocent sufferer	Identification with ideal
Bad	Outside-cause of trouble, personification of hostile forces, unreformable	Hatred towards enemy

three types can be described in the following way.

I. The *"weak"* characters have a large share of guilt in the uninterrupted series of catastrophes which—according to radio serials—form human life. But they are not bad by nature. The trouble they create though often directed against others makes them suffer themselves because they disturb the harmony of the private group to which they belong. They are selfish, jealous, vindictive, deceitful and need other people's help to get out of the conflict situations which they create. It is this type which may be expected to furnish an unvarnished *portrait of the average listener* herself. *Resonance* is the probable reaction provoked by the weak character, who faithfully mirrors the listener's own feelings and experiences. It is the presence of this type which we may expect to attract the listener to the radio serials as something which concerns herself.

II. However, the portrait offered by the "weak" characters is an unpleasant one. So if the listener is to enjoy the resonance which it provokes in her, she must be given the means of detaching herself from it. The second type, represented by the *good* people, fulfills this function. It keeps identification away from the weak type. It provides a safe platform from which to look down on the weak character's unfortunate adventures in an attitude of aloofness and complacency. It adds the embodiment of an *ideal* to the representation of the true-to-life portrait. It allows the listener to *identify* herself with a woman who is always good and right, recommended by her virtue, energy, helpfulness, leader qualities and by the outstanding position which is granted to her in the structure of the play and by her fellow-characters. She appears mostly as an "eligible" woman desired by desirable suitors, or as a wife, but quite often also as a mother, a friend, a professional woman. The weak character is the object of her helpful activity. The object of identification provides reparation for the essentially passive and subordinate role which in real life the listener plays as a housewife and as a member of the underprivileged classes. She assumes government in a world of individuals in which the power and the function of the community are eliminated. An examination of the plots shows that she steers the destinies of afflicted people more often than she is herself involved in conflict. But if she is involved, then she appears prevalently as the innocently suffering victim of other people's failures, thus offering to the listener the opportunity to pity herself. If she creates trouble herself she does so as a praiseworthy person for praiseworthy reasons.

III. The third type is formed by the thoroughly *bad* people. They come from outside to threaten the security of the characters to whom the listener is linked by resonance and identification. Whereas for the good woman the weak character is an object of help, the bad one is the *enemy* against whom she has to defend others and herself. And it must be remembered that the bad people are mostly men. In a world of individuals, the villains represent not only personal adversaries like a girl rival but also the anonymous forces of politics and economics which in real life constantly afflict the listener's existence. No community is admitted between the bad people and the listener, no understanding for their motives exists or is desired. They are evil per se: they provoke nothing but resentment and fear. They attack the innocent victim—as symbolized in so many court trial episodes of the serials. By lending human shape to the outside forces of disturbance and by painting these disturbers in solid black, radio serials provide a confirmation of the listener's attitude towards what she considers her enemies. Only in the case of physical illness or accidents are impersonal forces recognized and allowed to join the ranks of the enemy.

Our *psychological formula* could then be stated in about the following terms. Radio serials attract the listener by offering her a portrait of her own shortcomings, which lead to constant trouble, and of her inability to help herself. In spite of the unpleasantness of this picture, resonance can be enjoyed because identification is drawn away from it and transferred to an ideal type of the perfect, efficient woman who possesses power and prestige and who has to suffer not by her own fault but by the fault of others. This enables the listener to view (and to criticize) her own personal shortcomings, which lead to trouble, as occurring in "other," less perfect creatures. Still, these shortcomings, being her own after all, are presented as springing from mere weakness of character; reform is possible and often achieved. No such tolerance is needed for the outside-causes of the listener's suffering. Her resentment against them is confirmed and nourished by the introduction of the villain-type, who also personifies and assumes responsibility for any detrimental effects of non-personal forces (in whose immunity the listener is interested), such as the institutions of society.

The psychological scheme presented here is a hypothesis based on the evidence of our content analysis. It would be desirable to test it by investigating the reactions of listeners.

SOME SPECIFIC FEATURES

The following paragraphs are designed to illustrate in a more detailed way some of the features which were brought to light by our foregoing analysis.

Women

The importance of the woman as a leader in the family, in the circle of her friends, and even in the large community of the nation is constantly emphasized. Not even the president of the United States can do his job without the help of his mother. In *Mary Marlin*, the mother of Rufus Kain, president of the USA, is severely ill. In a delirious vision, her dead husband appears to her and tells her that she cannot join him yet because "her work with Rufus is not finished." The serial world presents the picture of a matriarchy which, in a more or less hidden way, underlies a society nominally dominated by the man. There is a preference for situations in which the wife gets an opportunity to seize the reins. . . .

The reform of a "weak" husband is expected to be brought about by the wife. A striking example of this was offered by the announcer of *Valiant Lady* who addressed Mrs. Tubby Scott in the following way: "Your change in Tubby is not deep enough—you have to start over again!"

Husbands are fully conscious of their wives' importance. Tubby turns in despair to thoughts of Joan, who can help him in everything: "Everything begins and ends with Joan." The women are equally aware of the situation. "You men are all alike," says "Granny" in *John's Other Wife*, "I don't know what you'd do without us women." In *Stella Dallas*, when a farmer is removed to a hospital with a broken leg, the doctor has to call the man's wife to tell her that Gus can't sleep because he is lonesome, he really needs her. The doctor suggests that Minnie come to Boston. Translated into humor, the motif produces, for instance, an elderly storekeeper who is very unwillingly nagged into buying "a smart stylish suit" by a female friend, although he protests he can do all right by himself (*The O'Neills*). One the other hand, lawyer Portia Blake, when a man offers his help, in a facetious tone remarks that she is not a maiden in distress and can take care of herself.

Constant efforts are made by the serial authors to prove that a middle-aged woman still has her full share in life. So important is this subject that it is sometimes used as the leitmotif of the daily introduction to the serial. Helen Trent, for example, is presented as "the woman who proves, what so many want to prove, that romance can come to middle life and even beyond." Or, on another day: "When life seemed finished she can recapture romance even at thirty-five and beyond." Or: "The romance of Helen Trent who, when life mocks her, dashes her against the rocks of despair, fights back bravely, successfully to prove that romance can begin at thirty-five." . . .

There is a preference for mother and daughter appearing as comrades or competitors, almost as members of a twin couple with equal chances and equal experiences (e.g., *Myrt and Marge*). In *Right to Happiness*, a man is badly punished by a young rival, by divorce, and malaria for having courted the mother, but married the daughter. When Ma Perkins' daughter marries, everybody comes with invitations and pies. Ma says she will not be considered an invalid and doesn't like all this help. She says: "If anyone tells me I am not as young as I used to be I shall scream." . . .

Experts

There is a general tendency to show that plain, intelligent people are able to do almost anything better than trained specialists who enjoy the prestige of being experts in their field. The serials indemnify the "little fellow" (both sexes) for living in a society which, for every branch of life, makes him the passive object of somebody who is supposed to know better because he has had an opportunity to specialize on that job. A doctor says that Just Plain Bill can "help cure human hearts better than any doctor." This does not sound very professional, but in *We, the Abbotts*, Hilda, a middle-aged maid, overtakes Dr. Fisher to suggest a physician in New York who cures by a "foreign protein reaction." Dr. Fisher becomes angry about having this suggestion made, but when he again goes up to see the patient he comes rushing down the stairs to tell Hilda to send for the New York doctor.

That private individuals are better detectives than the police is a well-established tradition of crime literature. Mother Morrison (who once saved a man from a death sentence) somehow finds the clue to the villain's whereabouts and induces the neighbor to drive her to a secluded river bank on the outskirts of the town. Here she discovers the villain threatening to drown Sam Benson. . . .

Learning

If the average serial listener lacks higher education and if, for this reason, she feels inferior socially, she will welcome any devaluation of learning. So learning is presented quite often as a whimsical hobby-horse—as something in contrast to what makes the real qualities of a man or a woman. When in *Scattergood Baines*, fun is made of the school president who accused the wrong boy of cheating and afterward has to stand up before the whole school to exonerate him, his use of learned words makes part of the comical effect: a man who says things like "impugning my veracity" was wrong where storekeeper Scattergood was right! On the rural level, the hero or heroine proves outstanding human qualities in spite, or maybe because, of wrong English (Ma Perkins) or bad spelling (Lorenzo Jones). On the upper level, we have lawyer Portia Blake returning to her cottage to find Cathie, the reporter, in her living room glaring at a typewriter. Cathie is not sure how to spell "principal," and Portia spells it out for her. The spelling problem in question is so simple, that many a listener is probably able to do better than Miss Cathie, the professional writer. In a similar way, the listener may feel superior when, in *Life Can Be Beautiful*, somebody inquires whether Romeo and Juliet "live in Long Island, too."

Subordinate people are presented as showing off with bits of higher education in a humorous way. In *When a Girl Marries*, the maid made a deep impression on her friends, at a social meeting, by using two long words supplied by her employer, lawyer Harry, the evening before. And in *Lone Journey*, a young farm hand, Enor, is presented as hopelessly struggling with philosophy and difficult words while he shows warm insight and understanding as soon as he relies on his inborn simple wisdom. So it is not learning that counts, and when, in *Vic and Sade*, the heroine indignantly opposes a motion to the effect that members of the Sewing Club should study Portuguese, she can be sure of the support of the listener.

Neighbors

A person or a family may have friendly relations to others, but this is then a relationship between individuals. There is little indication of a healthy attitude of the individual towards the community as a whole. Generally, the community does not enter into the picture at all: the walls of the heroine's house are the borders of the world. But when it does, it seems safe to say, that the community, and specifically the neighborhood, is mostly described as an enemy, a hostile block of people who want to know, but should not know what is wrong in your private affairs. Where life is nothing but a sequence of private "problems," the community is identical with the threat of scandal. Scattergood Baines' wife meets a woman in the street who tells her that the whole town is talking about her, Mrs. Baines', absence from the Ladies' Club—obviously because there is some difficulty with her daughter Barbara's marriage plans. She is trying to pry out more information, but she fails. In *Mother o' Mine*, a little girl is found in tears because of the way her playmates have been treating her since the suspicion of murder has been cast upon her Aunt Judy.

Newspapers

The fear of publicity determines the role attributed to newspapers in the serials. Quite often, reporters and newspapers are presented as a menace to social prestige. When a reporter rings the doorbell, the average serial character feels like a delinquent on whom the executioner

calls. The resentment against the man who comes to find out for the "neighbors" about the shameful things going on in the heroine's or hero's house, is reflected in the unfriendly descriptions of the reporter's personality and ethical standard. In *Stella Dallas*, Mimie bursts in breathlessly, saying that Jerry Madison, the newspaper reporter, is there. This unnerves Stella, who has feared publicity. She cannot bear to think that he will learn of her present plight and publicize it in the Washington papers, where her beloved daughter Lolly and her socially prominent son-in-law, Richard Grosvenor, will see it. This would wreck the happiness of these two people, she feels. During her conversation with Jerry, in which she appeals to his decency and better nature, Sheila comes in, and from the latter's conversation with Stella, Jerry finds out about the present story. Immediately, he is like a hound on the trail. Nothing matters to that news hound but the story. And the only way out is for somebody to take a plane for Washington to bribe the editor of the paper not to print the story.

A hardly more pleasant picture results where the press is described as a powerful tool in politics. Mr. Abbott is told by an editor that he cannot write for the paper because he is playing ball with the wrong group of politicians. Lucas, a gangster of the worst kind, should be the man for John to play up to. In *Ma Perkins*, corrupt politicians use a newspaper to brand farmers as unpatriotic should they try to oppose the construction of an army camp on the unsuitable land owned by the villians. In *David Harum*, the editor of the Homeville paper tries to bribe the president of a community garden project, to make the project fail. Occasional exceptions such as the pleasant (female!) reporter, in *Portia Faces Life*, who writes a series of articles on food in national defense, are neither frequent nor prominent enough to change the picture essentially. Where the newspaperman appears as a "good" person his function in the play is generally not determined by his profession but by his personal qualities as a friend or similarly.

Politics

References to domestic or foreign events of general importance were rare at the time of our test. When radio serials talk politics they generally mean individual corruption in Congress and municipal administration, and the picture they exhibit on such occasions could hardly be more horrible. At a first glance, one might be inclined to evaluate the polemical descriptions as courageous political reform work. This may be true to some extent, but as political corruption is shown mostly as caused by individual villains or by the "collective villainy" of politicians in general, such procedures

must be expected to nourish an already existing resentment against people and organized community-life rather than furthering insight into the political and economic mechanisms of society.

It is hard to say which of the two prevalent types of soap opera politicians produces the most repugnant effect: the reckless gangster who fights for power and wealth by killing, stealing, lying, ruining other people's happiness, prestige, career, and position, or the basically honest, but weak type who, after he has slipped once, is forced by the villians to go on doing their dirty work. In *We, the Abbotts*, evil Mr. Lucas has obtained the position of a superintendent of schools, formerly held by John Abbott. Not satisfied with having Abbott chased out of his job, Lucas blackmails him by preventing him from getting a new job. Lucas wants evidence from John about another politician, Campbell, who is in his way. When John delivers a lecture on music, Lucas has several people booing and yelling him off the stage intimating that he is a grafter and scoundrel. The atmosphere of the serial is characterized by remarks of the following type: "In order to live these days it is necessary to get along with the political rats. You must eat humble political pie to keep a job." When Mrs. Abbott calls on Lucas, he threatens to punish her husband even more and says he will even go so far as to injure her children. In fact, he smears the children by accusing them of theft and "scandalous association" and sets fire to John's car. With ruthless methods, Lucas sets up a citizens' committee with two thousand members. The committee is meant to overthrow the mayor of the town, who "is connected with the gambling machine." In a conversation between John and his son, political fatalism and lack of insight are expressed very clearly. They are discussing why they should be unemployed while a grafter like Lucas is hoarding money. Jack is indignant, but his father consoles him by telling him: "Things happen and we don't know why—we can see only a small portion of the universe." He cites the example of a huge painting covered by curtains in such a way that only a small part is showing. "It would be impossible to conceive the whole composition." Episodes of this kind seem to confirm the thesis that radio serials are politically aggressive, but conservative.

In some cases it is difficult to decide whether the serial authors realize that they are giving a discouraging picture or whether they simply take unpleasant things for granted. In a breakfast-table conversation between a newly wedded congressman and his wife, in *Ma Perkins*, Fay says she feels a wife should take an interest, and asks whether her husband ever wants to vote differently from the way the party wishes him to vote. He says, not often—and if he did not follow the party he would be left to paddle his own canoe in the next election. Later on, the young wife asks an elderly, experienced congressman whether it is true that many important things are settled behind scenes. He says many people think ability and merit are the only prerequisites of success, but it is no longer true. However, he goes on, America is a rock rising above cruelty and snobbery, founded deeply on the proposition that all men are brothers. He feels that the Washington Monument, simple, straight, and tall, is a symbol of that integrity.

FACING THE ISSUE

Are Problems Adequately Presented?

If radio serials are to be of any cultural value their function cannot be fulfilled by providing thrilling entertainment through the stirring up of emotions and pleasant compensation for the inconveniences of life. Interviewers with listeners have shown that many women go to the serials for advice as to suitable behavior or attitudes in different situations. Therefore, it seems necessary to examine whether the serials deal with problems adequately. A comparison between the serials and real life can hardly go beyond elementary social and psychological facts. But it seems even more important to find out whether the set-up and development of the problems is such as to allow valid insight.

A work of narrative art has the task of describing typical life situations through individual cases. The fact that not just "this case" but "such a case" is presented creates the basis for a possible general interest in the story. Generalization from experience is a common method for learning about the types of things and happenings that constitute the world. It follows that if a radio serial presents the marriage troubles of Henry and Edith Adams, the performance is received as a bit of information on marriage in general and that it is meant to be received in this way. Is the picture adequate? Are there attempts to expose properly the problems involved and their possible solutions? If not, of what kind are the deviations and distortions? Do they spring from tendencies to present life situations in a certain way, to pass over certain aspects, to protect some things and to proscribe others? Which are these tendencies, and what means are used to serve them?

Atypical Causes

Atypical causes of trouble are frequently used for business problems. Much more often than by economic conditions, business or professional troubles are caused by other people who want to damage the "sufferer" for personal reasons which have nothing to do with the business situation. Arline asks her father, a banker, to dismiss his female lawyer, Portia Blake, because her husband fell in love with the lawyer. A girl wants to prevent Bess Johnson from becoming Dean of a school, because the woman thwarted the girl's attempt to marry against her father's wishes. In both cases the connection between the business situation and the private situation is purely accidental. Gordon is unemployed —why? Are jobs scarce in his field? No, he is an artist who became blind and therefore had to give up his job. An individual case is chosen in which illness instead of the economic situation causes the trouble.

Generalization on the basis of such cases must lead to a wrong picture of the world. Why is such a tendency, consciously or unconsciously, active in the serial authors? Political conservatism would tend to detract attention from any drawbacks of the general economic situation and rather blame other factors. It is probable that such a presentation fits in perfectly with the outlook of the average serial listener. Personal causes like the jealousy of a woman and natural catastrophes such as illness create a more immediate emotional response than an abstract economic mechanism.

Similarly, atypical causes are used to show up marriage problems, without casting a shadow on the institution itself. To admit that the marriage situation as such may lead to trouble is unwelcome to the listener. There is, e.g., the threat of infidelity. In order to avoid unpleasant insight, a specific type of case is constructed in which the triangle pattern is maintained but in which the "institutional" situation is suitably modified: affection to a missing, insane, or dead husband, wife or fiance prevents a new marriage. In these cases, the disturbing force, inherent in an exemplary person, does not tend any longer towards an adulterous relationship, but on the contrary, springs from loyalty to a marriage relation which was dissolved by fate and therefore ceased to be a moral obligation. And the disturbing affection does not threaten to break up an existing marriage but only to hamper the bringing about of a marriage which does not yet exist.

Ambiguous Motivation

The combination of two conflicts prevents a clear insight into the relationship of cause and effect. Jonathan Hobson wants to get a full-time job, although he will have to give up his dreams of writing poetry. He thinks that working on the Defense Program is a duty and important. This noble struggle between helping the community and fulfilling a personal vocation is, however, blurred by the fact that Jonathan is part of a family of completely destitute migrant workers, his father having just been sent to the hospital severely ill. He needs the money, and thus it is not possible to state how the young man would have behaved if confronted with only one of the two problems. In another serial, Edith Adams, although engaged to a decent lawyer, still feels herself bound to her vicious ex-husband. He falls dangerously ill, and she feels she should help him. Pity and helpfulness superimposed on affection confuse the issue.

Villains as Substitutes for General Problems

"Bad" people should not be introduced into a situation capable of provoking conflict by itself, because their personality is such as to cause trouble. This is, however, what the radio serial authors do by preference. They use a bad character in order to discharge certain types of situations of their trouble-provoking qualities by shifting the responsibility from the situation to the character. Furthermore, the bad type or villain is characterized as untouched by any interior conflict. He is nothing but the vehicle of a disturbing desire; the struggle is fought out not within him, but by exterior forces accidentally connected with the conflict-carriers. The reaction to such a bad troublemaker is likely to depend on the listener's attitude towards the category of people represented by the character. A "selfish, domineering" mother-in-law may appear as an exception which does not prove anything or which even leads to the conclusion—which does not follow from what was presented—that everything is all right; if only the mother-in-law is a good woman. If, in turn, the listener thinks unfavorably of the category of people in question, he may readily accept the individual bad person as typical of the lot. In this way, the idea of "collective villainy" is nurtured, according to which certain groups of people, mothers-in-law, husbands, lawyers, or whatever they may be, are bad. Corrupt politicians, conniving officials, ambitious district attorneys, are preferably presented in this way. No attempt is made to explain the situation which may lead to misdeeds and which is or may be open to reform. The problem comes down to the existence of a group of bad people who have to be endured or eliminated.

Mr. Brill, a bad plantation owner, takes advantage of the shortage of housing caused by defense work to profiteer from some empty cottages he possesses. Mr. Carleton offers $3,000 to a poor composer for a symphony which he hopes to resell for the fantastic sum of $25,000. Any attempt to connect these cases with the problem of profit as such, is cut short by the fact that Mr. Carleton is described as a "villain" and that Mr. Brill is referred to as "a devil with the pitchfork." The personal villainy of these two people or the "collective villainy" of businessmen in general is made to account for the damage they inflict upon others. A senator tries to sell some bad land he possesses to the government for the construction of an army camp. There is a detailed description of how his connection with the terrain in question is hidden by means of several holding companies. The listener has the choice of considering the man either an exception among the honorable company of congressman or a representative of collective political villainy. Attempts to render the bad man harmless are described in detail, but there was no hint at the general question whether or not a combination of administrative position and business tended to provoke conflict. Similarly, newspaper reporters are described as people, who, out of personal savagery, enjoy exposing private affairs to the public. The general problem which may lie in making money out of sensational news is not touched.

Thirst for freedom in conflict with need of discipline could provide an excellent subject for a serial episode which takes place against the background of an orphanage. But again the opportunity is missed by choosing a type of headmistress who is not the person to make the best case for school discipline. Mrs. Seabrook is a "sour, dominating, fussy, petty, egoistic, rigid" woman. Her orders are severe, her punishments for little mistakes are exaggerated. She pays one of the children to spy on the others. Thus, when the children revolt, it is not against discipline, but against Mrs. Seabrook. The underlying problem remains untouched.

Extrinsic Solutions Through Accidental Power

Bill Cameron's wife has fallen in love with Dwight Cramer, one of her husband's business partners. Cameron wants Cramer to be dismissed. There is no conflict in him as to whether he should sacrifice an efficient member of the firm to his own comfort. The issue is decided, through extrinsic power, by the head of the firm who refuses to dismiss Dwight, because he is a bright fellow and because Dwight's father

is a valuable client. In another case, a young student, Barbara Bartlett, tries to elope with a friend, against her father's will. Again there is no conflict in the girl: the solution does not come from her decision between her father's wishes and her own, but from the intervention of an outsider.

Often the plot is simply of a "fact-finding" character, especially in criminal investigations or court trials. Myrt and Marge, a mother and daughter, accuse themselves of murder in order to shield each other. Neither of them seems to care about whether it is admissible to lie in court for the purpose of saving a beloved person. The solution depends on the judge's being able to identify the guilty person. Where an innocent person is defended against a crime charge, the one character who should be in the center because the conflict should be fought out in his or her own bosom (the guilty person who lets an innocent one be accused), generally holds a secondary position.

Providing a Happy End

As the solutions of the problems are controlled by "justice" rather than by inner necessity, care is taken to prevent unpleasant things happening to decent people. This means that the classical dramatic situation is avoided where incompatible forces throw excellent people into a catastrophe. There is no objection to the "happy end" if it develops logically from the given conflict situation. But often it is obtained by the trick of simply removing, acccidentally, one of the factors which produced trouble. Caroline Benton, a spoiled problem child, does not want her widowed father to marry Ellen Brown. After much heated discussion, Mrs. Brown reveals that she does not really care for Mr. Benton, and leaves. In another case, a farmer is asked to yield his land to the government for the construction of an army camp. Mr. Martin wants the army to have camps, he is a good American, but he needs his land. Here the conflict between the requirements of the community and those of the individual is neatly set up. Unfortunately, Mr. Martin's land turns out to be of no use to the government. In a third case, Elaine, in order to give her blind husband something to live for, has made him believe she is expecting a child. She will have to confess sometime, and she is afraid that he may lose faith also in her assertion that he is likely to get his eyesight back. But before the problem comes up, he sees flashes of light. His recovery will make it easier for him to cope with his wife's "merciful deception." An event, which is possible but which contradicts the requirements of the problem, allows an evasion and recommends the dangerously unintelligent behavior of a woman by pretending that it proved to be successful.

A conflict is easy to solve if it does not exist. Suspicion, misunderanding, lies and intrigues make it possible to describe all the suffering provoked by a real conflict and still have everything settled after a while. Composer Gary believes that his sweetheart has a love affair with Dwight, a music critic, whereas honest Dawn visited the critic only to interest him in Gary's symphony. An intriguing woman makes her friend, Helen Trent, believe that lawyer Gil cultivates a morbid affection for his dead wife which will prevent him from ever loving another woman. In literature, the non-existent conflict is sometimes used to show the tragic consequences of human ignorance. Generally it happens only in comedy that the real situation is revealed in time. Radio serials use the comedy trick to avoid the sad consequences of a dramatic conflict.

Surreptitious Causality

A particularly significant artifice consists in using the *post hoc, ergo propter hoc* to demonstrate that bad deeds do not pay. The general tendency of the human mind to establish causal connections between happenings contiguous in time and space is used in the radio serials to give the appearance of a causal connection to cases of pure coincidence.

Bad Henry Adams who betrays his wife with a girl friend has a paralytic stroke. Bill Walker courted Mrs. Doris Cameron, then married her daughter. The marriage goes wrong for reasons independent of the previous happenings, but the listener is informed that Bill "got what he deserved." Christy Allen is worried about her husband's relations with his former wife. She was engaged to Mark Scott, but ran away with his best friend, Phil, and she feels that her marriage troubles are in some way the punishment for what they did to Mark. In this way it is suggested that the purely accidental punishments introduced into the plot for the triumph of justice, were caused by some unmentioned principle, in consequence of the bad deeds that preceded them.

CONCLUSIONS AND PROPOSALS

Potential Effects of Daytime Serials

This content analysis yields no information on the influence which radio serials actually exert on the listeners. But it suggests the directions in which these influences, if any, are likely to go.

Do radio serials invite *self-knowledge* and *self-criticism*? Our analysis suggests that they make the listener feel at home by offering her a world which outwardly resembles her own and in which people make themselves and others suffer by committing familiar mistakes and by displaying familiar shortcomings of character. Although this presents to the listener a rather unvarnished portrait of herself, it cannot be expected to lead her to self-knowledge and self-criticism. Her identification is deflected to an ideal type of perfect, innocently suffering woman. She is encouraged to view failures as happening only to other people, and is confirmed in her belief that her suffering is caused not by herself, but by the imperfection and villainy of others.

There is little effort to make the listener aware of her *prejudices and resentments*; rather, she is carefully flattered. Men are shown to be inferior to women, the working class is ignored, learning is deprecated. The egocentric and individualistic concept of a world in which the community appears mainly as a threat from outside is supported —hyenas howling around the campfire, with the law of the jungle as the only resort. Only private problems exist. Events are shown to be caused not so much by people expending their energies on fulfilling their tasks in spite of all obstacles, but rather by their desperate defense of a status quo the value of which is not clearly demonstrated by the serials. Even the primitive strife for love and companionship is eclipsed by an essentially negative fight against forces which endanger established relationships. While this may mirror the fact that the listener fails to see values in her own life, it certainly does not encourage her to discover or create them. *Dissatisfaction* with her own achievements and with the state of affairs in the world around her, which could serve as a spur towards striving for improvement, *is drained off by substitute gratification.* Identification with the "ideal woman," a fiction which cannot serve as a model which the listener could try to live up to, endows her with an efficiency she does not possess and assurance that the assistance which she ought to seek in her own energies will be forthcoming from the outside. Suitable adjustment to the problems of the climacteric may be hampered where wish-fulfillment dreams are presented as reality: the middle-aged woman appears as youthful, attractive, ardently courted by desirable suitors. A reign of perfect justice, without any hint of how it is obtained, offers a gratuitous solution for problems of social life. Similarly, daily removal to a daytime serial world of violent passion and suspense may well weaken the listener's sensitiveness to the less thrilling opportunities of real life to practice affection, faithfulness, pity; to render unselfish service, to find pleasure in modest tasks and unpretentious beauty.

Service and Progress

This survey indicates that radio serials maintain a firm grip on so many millions of American women because they satisfy their psychological needs the easy way, by devices which are known from the psychiatric analysis of wish-dreams. The sociologist would have to tell us whether changing conditions have led children and husbands to live their lives so much outside the home that it no longer offers the wife and mother enough scope for the expression of her capacities and affections—that it can no longer give her the feeling that she is needed, esteemed, and loved. Is the woman left behind as little more than a passive object of supply for the mechanism of production—a consumer, deprived of the creative tasks to which her natural gifts and strivings entitle her, left alone with a talking box as the only source of satisfaction?

If this is so, radio programs by themselves do not have the power to bring about a change in the social situation of women confined to an unsatisfactory kind of home life. But they are able to contribute something by creating an appropriate psychological attitude. They hold almost a monopoly on the mental life of so many women. Thus they are to some extent responsible for whether the forces created by the needs of these women are diverted to a substitute-satisfaction or are instead directed towards understanding and improving reality.

Producers of radio serials take pride in asserting that they give their audience exactly what it wants to get. The commercial maxim of offering what the largest possible number of customers is likely to buy is interpreted as a practical application of democratic principles: self-government, control of community life by the people. But it seems evident that such government and control presupposes an ability to judge. In the field of medicine, for instance, hardly anybody would venture to assert that it would be democratic to promote the most popular remedies rather than those which are scientifically proved to be the best. It is democratic to strive for popular consent to progress. To what extent such an attitude of social responsibility can be obtained while radio serials are produced as a commercial vehicle, we will make no attempt to decide. But it seems that the wartime situation offers an opportunity for progress in this field. In times of war, the extraordinary effort to be made by the nation requires the physical and moral support of all individuals. Therefore the government takes steps to promote understanding, good will, collaboration. A series of radio programs for instance, has been presented for the purpose of making the citizen realize that what the whole community does is done for him and cannot be done without him. This principle should hold good in times of peace as well. Still many a citizen is accustomed to consider the community a conglomeration of individuals, each of whom minds his own business, reluctantly pays his taxes, and takes it for granted that there are clean, well-lit streets to walk, bridges to pass, and parks to relax in. Genuine team-spirit as it is needed for the war-effort cannot be obtained by

propaganda limited to what the citizen is asked to do for the war. Such appeals must rely on a substructure of community-consciousness: unless the individual deeply realizes that, in times of peace or war, the natural and most profitable way of living consists in acting as a member of a whole in the interest of common aims, he cannot be expected to contribute wholeheartedly to his country's defense.

This is where radio serials ought to come in. They are particularly suited to show the mutual dependence of community and individual from the point of view of the home situation. In addition to creating a substructure for wartime morale, such enlightenment might well prove to be valuable for future times in which battle-fields, war-bonds, and night-shifts in munition factories will once again have become legendary, whereas the problems of political and economic organization will be even more alive than they were before.

WHAT "MISSING THE NEWSPAPER" MEANS

BERNARD BERELSON

I. INTRODUCTION

In the late afternoon of Saturday, June 30, 1945, the deliverymen of eight major New York City newspapers went on strike. They remained on strike for over two weeks,

and during that period most New Yorkers were effectively deprived of their regular newspaper reading. They were able to buy the newspaper PM and a few minor and specialized papers at newsstands, and they could buy copies over the counter at cen-

From P. F. Lazarsfeld and F. N. Stanton, (eds.), *Communications Research, 1948-49* (New York: Harper and Brothers, 1949), pp. 111-129. Reprinted by permission of the author and the publisher.

tral offices of some newspapers. But the favorite papers of most readers were simply inaccessible to them for seventeen days.

These unusual circumstances presented a good opportunity for various interested parties—advertisers, newspaper publishers, radio executives, social scientists—to gauge public attitudes toward the newspaper, and at least three general polls of opinion were independently conducted during the strike. Some if not all findings of two polls have been made public, one by the Elmo Roper agency and the other by Fact Finders Associates, Inc. This article is a report on the third, an exploratory survey conducted for the Bureau of Applied Social Research, Columbia University.

According to the published findings, the Roper and Fact Finder organizations directed their efforts to determining what people had done in order to keep up with the news, what parts of the newspaper they particularly missed, and how much they missed the newspapers as the strike went on. On no specific question are their results strictly comparable, but in three ways they aimed at the same general attitudes or behavior, although in quite different ways. Both agencies attempted to get at the nature of the substitute for the newspaper, and in both cases respondents stressed that they listened to news broadcasts over the radio. Both attempted, in quite different ways, to discover what parts of the newspaper were particularly missed, and in both cases respondents stressed news (national, local, and war news) and advertising. Finally, both attempted to get at the degree to which the newspapers were actually missed, and in both cases respondents indicated that they missed the papers intensely.

Because the questions used by the two polling agencies differed greatly, the results are not strictly comparable. Furthermore, neither poll is able to interpret its data, which consist altogether of "surface facts" relevant only to the specific question at hand. Saying that one "misses the newspaper," or a part of it, can cover a variety of psychological reactions. What does "missing the newspaper" mean? Why do people miss it? Do they really miss the parts they claim, to the extent they claim? Why do they miss one part as against another? The Roper and Fact Finders polls bring little or nothing to bear on such questions, which are at the core of the basic problem, namely, to understand the function of the modern newspaper for its readers. Neither poll succeeds in getting at the more complex attitudinal matters operating in the situation.

It was to attack this problem that the present study was conducted. At the end of the first week of the strike, the Bureau of Applied Social Research of Columbia University sponsored a quite different kind of study of people's reactions to the loss of their newspapers. Where the Roper and Fact Finders surveys were extensive, the Bureau's was intensive, designed to secure psychological insight in order to determine just what not having the newspaper meant to people. It is an axiom in social research, of course, that such studies can most readily be done during a crisis period like that represented by the newspaper strike. People are not only more conscious of what the newspaper means to them during such a "shock" period than they are under normal conditions, but they also find it easier to be articulate about such matters.

Accordingly, the Bureau conducted a small number (60) of intensive interviews. The sample, stratified by rental areas in Manhattan, provided a good distribution by economic status although it was high in education. No attempt was made to secure statistically reliable data on poll questions of the Roper or Fact Finders sort (although for a few similar questions, such as what was missed in the papers, the results are the same as those from the Roper survey). Instead, the Bureau's interviews were designed to supply so-called qualitative data on the role of the newspaper for its readers, as that became evident at such a time. The results are not offered as scientific proof, but rather as a set of useful hypotheses.

In brief, then, the two polls on the subject present certain "surface facts," without knowing just what they mean. This study tries to suggest what "missing the newspaper" really means. Let us start with people's stereotyped responses to questions about missing the newspaper.

II. THE ROLE OF THE NEWSPAPER: WHAT PEOPLE SAY

Because of people's inclination to produce accepted slogans in answer to certain poll questions, there is always the danger that verbal response and actual behavior may not correspond. This danger was confirmed here. Intensive follow-up interviewing of the respondents demonstrated that practically everyone *pays tribute* to the value of the newspaper as a source of "serious" information about and interpretation of the world of public affairs, although not everyone uses it in that way. During the interview our respondents were asked whether they thought "it is very important that people read the newspapers or not." Almost everyone answered with a strong "Yes," and went on to specify that the importance of the newspaper lay in its informational and educational aspects. For most of the respondents, this specification referred to the newspaper as a source of news, narrowly defined, on public affairs.

However, not nearly so many people use the newspaper for this approved purpose, as several previous reading and information studies have shown. The general tribute without supporting behavior was evident in this study as well. When the respondents were given the opportunity to say spontaneously why they missed reading their regular newspapers, only a very few named a specific "serious" news event of the period (such as the Far Eastern war or the British elections) whereas many more answered with some variant of the "to-keep-informed" cliche or named another characteristic of the newspaper (e.g., its departmental features).

At another point in the interview, respondents were asked directly, "What news stories or events which happened last week (i.e., before the strike) did you particularly miss not being able to follow up?" Almost half the respondents were unable to name any such story or event whereas others named such non-"serious" news stories as the then-current Stevens murder case. About a third of the respondents did cite a "serious" news event, most of them the Far Eastern war. Furthermore, directly following this question, the respondents were asked which of a list of six front-page stories of the week before they had missed "not being able to follow up in your regular paper." Here, too, only a little more than a third of the respondents said that they had missed reading about the average serious event in this list. Thus, although almost all of the respondents speak highly of the newspaper's value as a channel of "serious" information, only about a third of them seemed to miss it for that purpose.

In brief, there seems to be an important difference between the respondents' *general* protestations of interest in the newspaper's "serious" purposes and their *specific* desires and practices in newspaper reading. The respondents' feeling that the newspaper "keeps me informed about the world" seems to be rather diffuse and amorphous, and not often attached to concrete news events of a "serious" nature. Again, for example, take the answer to our question, "Now that you don't read your regular newspaper, do you feel you know what's going on in the world?" Fully two-thirds of the respondents felt that they did not know what was going on although, as we have seen, only about half that many had any notion of what in the world they wanted more information about. To miss the newspaper for its "serious" news value seems to be the accepted if not the automatic thing to say.

But this does not mean that the newspapers were not genuinely missed by their readers. There were many spontaneous mentions of the intensity with which the respondents missed their papers, and several of those who missed them a good deal at the beginning of the strike felt even more strongly about it as the week wore on. The question is, *why* did people miss the newspaper so keenly. However, let us first review the several uses to which readers typically put the newspaper. This is the next step in our effort to put content into a check mark on a poll questionnaire by suggesting what "missing the newspaper" really means.

III. THE USES OF THE NEWSPAPER

The modern newspaper plays several roles for its readers. From the analysis of our intensive interviews, we have attempted to construct a typology of such roles, or functions, of the newspaper. Obviously the types enumerated here, while discrete, are not necessarily mutually exclusive for any one newspaper reader. Undoubtedly, different people read different parts of the newspaper for different reasons at different times. The major problem is to determine the conditions under which the newspaper fulfills such functions as those developed here—and perhaps others—for different kinds of people. In this connection, the special value of a small group of detailed interviews lies in the identification of hypotheses which can then be tested, one way or the other, by less intensive methods. In other words, such "qualitative" interviews suggest the proper questions which can then be asked, in lesser detail, for "quantitative" verification.

In this section we shall mention briefly several immediate uses of the newspaper which we found in the interviews. The illustrative quotations are typical of those appearing in the interviews. Some of these uses correspond to acknowledged purposes of the newspaper, others do not.

For Information About and Interpretation of Public Affairs

There is a core of readers who find the newspaper indispensable as a source of information about and interpretation of the "serious" world of public affairs. It is important to stress, in this connection, that this interest is not limited simply to the provision of full information about news events.

Many people are also concerned with commentaries on current events from both editorials and columnists, which they use as a touchstone for their own opinions. For example:

I don't have the details now, I just have the result. It's almost like reading the headlines of the newspaper without following up the story. I miss the detail and the explanation of events leading up to the news. I like to get the story behind and the development leading up to—it's more penetrating . . . I like to analyze for myself why things do happen and after getting the writers' opinions of it from the various newspapers, in which each one portrays the story in a different manner, I have a broader view and a more detailed view when I formulate my own opinion.

As a Tool for Daily Living

For some people the newspaper was missed because it was used as direct aid in everyday life. The respondents were asked, "Since you haven't been able to get your regular newspaper, have you found some things that you can't do as well without it?" Fully half of them indicated that they had been handicapped in some way. Many people found it difficult if not impossible to follow radio programs without the radio log published in the newspaper. Others who might have gone to a motion picture did not like the bother of phoning or walking around to find out what was on. A few business people missed / such merchandising comments as the arrival of buyers; others were concerned about financial and stock exchange information. Several women interested in shopping were handicapped by the lack of advertisements. A few close relatives of returning soldiers were afraid they would miss details of embarkation news. A couple of women who regularly followed the obituary notices were afraid that acquaintances might die without their knowing it.

Finally, there were scattered mentions of recipes and fashion notes and even the daily weather forecast in this connection. In short, there are many ways in which people use the newspaper as a daily instrument or guide and it was missed accordingly.

For Respite

Reading has respite value whenever it provides a vacation from personal care by transporting the reader outside his own immediate world. There is no question but that many newspaper stories with which people readily identify supply this "escape" function satisfactorily for large numbers of people. Exhibit A in this connection is the comics, which people report liking for their story and suspense value. Beyond this, however, the newspaper is able to refresh readers in other ways, by supplying them with appropriate psychological relaxation. The newspaper is particularly effective in fulfilling this need for relief from the boredom and dullness of everyday life not only because of the variety and richness of its "human interest" content or because of its inexpensive accessibility. In addition, the newspaper is a good vehicle for this purpose because it satisfies this need without much cost to the reader's conscience; the prestige value of the newspaper as an institution for "enlightening the citizenry" carries over to buttress this and other uses of the newspapers.

When you read it takes your mind off other things.

It [the strike] gave me nothing to do in between my work except to crochet, which does not take my mind off myself as much as reading.

I didn't know what to do with myself. I was depressed. There was nothing to read and pass the time. I got a paper on Wednesday and felt a whole lot better.

For Social Prestige

Another group of readers seem to use the newspaper because it enables them to appear informed in social gatherings. Thus the newspaper has conversational value. Readers not only can learn what has happened and then report it to their associates but can also find opinions and interpretations for use in discussions on public affairs. It is obvious how this use of the newspaper serves to increase the reader's prestige among his fellows. It is not that the newspapers' content is good

in itself but rather that it is good *for* something—and that something is putting up an impressive front to one's associates.

You have to read in order to keep up a conversation with other people. It is embarrassing not to know if you are in company who discuss the news.

Not that I am uneasy about what's happening but I like to know about the country so when people ask you questions you don't feel so dumb and silly.

It makes me furious, absolutely furious, because I don't know what's going on and all my friends who are getting the papers do know.

For Social Contact

The newspaper's human interest stories, personal advice column, gossip columns, and the like provide some readers with more than relief from their own cares and routine. They also supply guides to the prevailing morality, insight into private lives as well as opportunity for vicarious participation in them, and indirect "personal" contact with distinguished people.

One explanation of the role of the human interest story is that it provides a basis of common experience against which urban readers can check their own moral judgments and behavior (the "ethicizing" effect). The requirements for such stories are that they shall be understandable in terms of the reader's own experience and that they shall be "interesting." (One respondent who read the tabloids although he disliked them remarked that "the *Times* isn't written interestingly enough" and that "*PM* is the most honest paper but should have more interesting stuff like the *Journal-American*.") From the comments of a few respondents, it appears that the human interest stories and the gossip columnists do serve something of this purpose. In fact, a few respondents indicated that they missed the newspapers because, so to speak, some of their friends resided in its pages. A few women who read the gossip columnists and the society pages intensively seemed to take an intimate personal interest in their favorite newspaper characters and to think of them in congenial terms.

I miss Doris Blake's column [advice to the lovelorn]. You get the opinions in Doris Blake of the girls and boys and I find that exciting. It's like true life—a girl expressing her life. It's like everyday happenings.

I always used to condemn the mud-slinging in the *News* and *Mirror*, and many times I swore I'd never buy them if it weren't for the features I like. But just the other day I said to a friend of mine that I'd never, never talk like that about the papers again, because now I know what it is to be without them.

I missed them [favorite columnists] for their information, their news, their interviews with various people, their interaction with people. It is interesting to know people's reactions. If you read the background of individuals, you can analyze them a little better.

I like the *Daily News*. It's called the "scandal sheet" but I like it. It was the first paper that I bought when I came to New York. When you live in a small town and read the papers you know everybody who's mentioned in the papers. The *News* is the closest thing to them. The pictures are interesting and it makes up for the lack of knowing people . . . You get used to certain people; they become part of your family, like Dorothy Kilgallen. That lost feeling of being without papers increases as the days go on. You see, I don't socialize much. There's no place that you can get Dorothy Kilgallen—chitchat and gossip and Louella Parsons with Hollywood news.

IV. THE DESIRABILITY OF READING

This brief review of some uses to which readers typically put the modern newspaper serves to introduce the following sections, in which we shall try to elaborate other (nonconscious) psychological reasons for the genuine interest in newspaper reading. Here again, we shall use material from our intensive interviews as illustrations.

There is some evidence in our interviews to indicate that *reading itself* regardless of content is a strongly and pleasurably motivated act in urban society. The major substitute followed during the period ordinarily given to the reading of the newspaper was some *other* form of reading, of a non-"news" character. For the most part, the content of such substitute reading seemed to be quite

immaterial to the respondents, so long as "at least it was something to read":

I read some old magazines I had.

I read whatever came to hand—books and magazines.

I read up on all the old magazines around the house.

I read whatever was lying around and others I hadn't had a chance to read before.

I went back to older magazines and read some parts I didn't usually read.

From such quotations one gets an impression that reading itself, rather than *what* is read, provides an important gratification for the respondents. The fact is, of course, that the act of reading carries a prestige component in American life which has not been completely countered by the rise of "propaganditis." After all, important childhood rewards, from both parent and teacher, are occasioned by success in reading and thus the act has extremely pleasant associations. Not only do the people of this country support libraries to promote the practice of reading; they also give considerable deference to the "well-read" man. In fact, the act of reading is connected with such approved symbols as "education," "good literature," "the full man," "intellectuality," and thus takes on its own aura of respectability and value. And largely because of this aura, it is "better" to read something, anything, than to do nothing. For example, an elderly salesman told us:

Life is more monotonous without the paper. I didn't know what to do with myself. There was nothing to do to pass the time. It just doesn't work, nothing to pass the time.

One might speculate that in addition to the apparent desire of such people not to be left alone with their thoughts—in itself another gratification of reading to which we shall return—the Puritan ethic is at work in such cases. That is, such people may feel that it is somehow immoral to "waste" time and that this does not occur if one reads something, because of the "worthwhileness" of reading. In short, in explaining why people missed their regular newspapers, one must start by noting that the act of reading itself provides certain basic satisfaction, *without primary regard for the content of the reading matter.*

V. ANOTHER USE OF THE NEWSPAPER

Within this context, what of the newspaper? Of the major sources of reading matter, the newspaper is the most accessible. It is also cheap and its contents can be conveniently taken in capsules (unlike the lengthier reading units in magazines and books). All in all, the newspaper is the most readily available and most easily consumed source of whatever gratifications derive from reading itself. In addition, there are some other general bases for the *intensity* with which people missed the newspaper.

References by several people to "not knowing what's going on" and to "feeling completely lost" illustrate the sort of *insecurity* of the respondent which was intensified by the loss of the newspaper:

I am like a fish out of water . . . I am lost and nervous. I'm ashamed to admit it.

I feel awfully lost. I like the feeling of being in touch with the world at large.

If I don't know what's going on next door, it hurts me. It's like being in jail not to have a paper.

You feel put out and isolated from the rest of the world.

It practically means isolation. We're at a loss without our paper.

In some way, apparently, the newspaper represented something like a safeguard and gave the respondents an assurance with which to counter the feelings of insecurity and anomie pervasive in modern society.

This need for the newspaper is further documented by references to the *ritualistic and near-compulsive character* of newspaper

reading. Many people read their newspapers at a particular time of the day and as a secondary activity, while they are engaged in doing something else, such as eating, traveling to work, etc. Being deprived of the time-filler made the void especially noticeable and especially effective. At least half the respondents referred to the habit nature of the newspaper: "It's a habit . . . when you're used to something, you miss it . . . I had gotten used to read it at certain times . . . It's been a habit of mine for several years . . . You can't understand it not being there any more because you took it for granted . . . The habit's so strong . . . It's just a habit and it's hard to break it . . ." Some respondents used even stronger terms:

Something is missing in my life.
I am suffering! Seriously! I could not sleep, I missed it so.

There's a place in anyone's life for that, whether they're busy or not.

I sat around in the subway, staring, feeling out of place.

The strength of this near-compulsion to read the newspaper was illustrated in other ways. Such diverse newspapers as the tabloid *News* and the *Times* sold thousands of copies daily over the counter at their central offices. One respondent "went from stand to stand until I decided that it was just no use trying to get one." Another walked ten blocks looking for a paper; another went to her newsstand every night during the first week of the strike, hoping to get a paper. One young man reread out-of-date newspapers more thoroughly, "as a resort." Still other respondents admitted to reading the paper regularly even though they believed that they could spend their time more profitably:

It replaces good literature.

I usually spend my spare time reading the papers and put off reading books and studying languages or something that would be better for me . . . [Most of the paper] is just escape trash, except possibly the classified ads and I'm beginning to waste time reading them now, too, when there's no reason for it, just habit.

In this connection, the notion that knowledge is power sometimes appears. One man reported that he felt uneasy "because I don't know what I am missing—and when I don't know I worry." A few people even seemed to suggest that their being informed about the world had something to do with the control of it. A private secretary, for example, recognizing that she was "just a little cog in the wheel," remarked sadly that she "felt cut off" but that "things go on whether you know about it or not." Presumably, the regular contact with the world through the columns of the newspaper gave this person the feeling that she was participating in the running of the world. But when the newspaper was withdrawn, she realized that her little contribution was not being missed.

This sort of analysis throws a new light on the fact that about twice as many people missed the newspaper *more* as this week went on than missed it less. For such people, the absence of the daily ritual was only intensified as the week wore on. Something that had filled a place in their lives was gone, and the adjustment to the new state of affairs was difficult to make. They missed the newspaper in the same sense that they would have missed any other instrument around which they had built a daily routine.

Only a few respondents gave an affirmative answer to our question, "Are there any reasons why you were relieved at not having a newspaper?" But even they revealed the near-compulsive nature of newspaper reading. In some cases the fascinating attraction of "illicit" content seemed to constitute the compelling factor, e.g., in the case of the middle-aged housewife who reported:

It was rather a relief not to have my nerves upset by stories of murders, rape, divorce, and the war . . . I think I'd go out more [without the newspapers] which would be good for me. Papers and their news can upset my attitude for the whole day—one gruesome tale after the other. My nerves would be better without the paper.

The typical scrupulousness of the compulsive character is apparent in this case of a middle-aged waiter who went out of his way to read political comment with which he strongly disagreed:

I hate the policy of the *Mirror* [his only newspaper] . . . the editorial writer and also the columnist DeCasseres. It's a pleasure not to read him. . . . I didn't have an opportunity of disagreeing with Winchell.

In still other cases, the compulsion resembled an atonement for guilt feelings about nonparticipation in the war; the comments of two women respondents suggest that they had forced themselves to read the war news, as the least they could do in prosecuting the war:

Under the stress and strain of wartime conditions, my health was beginning to fail and I enjoyed being able to relax a little.

I've been reading war news so much, I've had enough of it.

A young housewife felt that it was her duty to follow the developments of the war "for the boys—the spirit of it." And such respondents were gratified at the newspaper strike because it provided them with a morally acceptable justification for not reading the newspaper, as they felt compelled to do. Once the matter was taken out of their hands they felt relieved.

VI. SUMMARY AND CONCLUSION

In this article we have attempted to elaborate and "deepen" the answers to typical poll questions applied to a complex set of acts and feelings. We have tried to go beyond the general protestations of the newspaper's indispensability and seek out some basic reader-gratifications which the newspaper supplies. In doing so, we have noted certain typical uses of the modern newspaper—both "rational" (like the provision of news and information) and non-"rational" (like the provision of social contacts and, indirectly, social prestige). In addition, however, we have hypothesized that reading has value per se in our society, value in which the newspaper shares as the most convenient supplier of reading matter. In addition, the newspaper is missed because it serves as a (non-"rational") source of security in a disturbing world and, finally, because the reading of the newspaper has become a ceremonial or ritualistic or near-compulsive act for many people. In this way, we have progressively tried to define, in psychological and sociological terms, what missing the newspaper really means.

DO ROSY HEADLINES SELL NEWSPAPERS?

ELIZABETH C. WINSHIP AND GORDON W. ALLPORT

In spite of the many limitations imposed on editors during time of war, they still wield a vast amount of psychological power. Through the headlines they write they create the picture of the world-scene that their public carries in mind for an entire day. Should the picture be rosy or should it be drab? The headline writer is usually free to make the decision.

In three important respects, indeed, headline writers are free agents: they select the communique from which to draw their head; they choose the aspect of the communique they wish to feature; and they fashion the final wording with all its subtle connotations. A glance at the newsstand will show that editors do not always select the same communique, nor choose the same aspect for emphasis, and no two ever have identically the same wording. The varied versions have strikingly different psychological effects.

OPTIMISM AND PESSIMISM: NEWSPAPER PRACTICE

What type of headline is most favored by newsmen? In a period when news is neither very good nor very bad, which will appear more frequently—optimistic or pessimistic headlines? Seeking an answer to this question, we have classified the heads and subheads of twelve representative papers for the period extending from August 17 to November 17, 1942—an interval during which defeats and discouragements were intermingled with successes. The papers are: the *Chicago Sun, Chicago Tribune, Chicago Daily News, Dallas Morning News, Philadelphia Inquirer, Los Angeles Times, Washington Post, Boston Daily Record, Boston Evening Globe, Christian Science Monitor, Albany Knickerbocker News,* and *New York Daily News.* The headlines, totaling 3226 in number, were rated according to the following instructions:

(1) Optimistic (O): all good news and optimistic interpretations; i.e., calculated to give the average reader an optimistic impression, regardless of justifiability. Example: U.S. NAVY WINS BATTLE IN SOLOMONS.

(2) Pessimistic (P): all bad news and pessimistic interpretations; i.e., calculated to give the average reader a pessimistic im-

From the *Public Opinion Quarterly*, 1943, 7, 205-209. Reprinted by permission of the authors and the publisher.

pression. Example: F.D.R. HINTS AT MEATLESS DAYS.

(3) Neutral (N): all headlines that are neutral, ambiguous, questionable, or unclassifiable. Example: TELLS CONVOY STORY. All domestic political news was classed as N.

Judgments were made without reference to the subsequent text of the story.

In Table 1 the preponderance of optimistic headlines is clearly shown.[1] There were more than three times as many optimistic headlines as neutral during this period, and nearly three times as many as pessimistic. Approximately one-quarter of the news concerned national and local affairs not closely related to the progress of the fighting armies. As most of this news was political, it was classed as N. The bulk of the optimistic and pessimistic headlines therefore concerns news of actual combat, and, as the table shows, the tendency in treating this news is to emphasize optimism to a marked degree.

Did the historical tide of events justify all this optimism? It is not possible to answer this question in wholly objective

[1] To gain some indication of the reliability of this classification the results of two separate analyses of the *Chicago Tribune* were compared. Ninety-three per cent of all items were judged identically. The comparatively low reliability in judging N items, 78 per cent, is partially explained by the fact that in several cases items in a compound headline were marked O and P by one analyst, whereas they were lumped together and marked N by the other.

terms. True, the invasion of North Africa occurred in this period, but only during the final week. The eleven previous weeks contained plenty of grim communiques from the Solomons, from the Stalingrad front, and from the submarine zone. Few editors, we feel, would defend their cheery headlines on the grounds of the preponderance of happy events during the period under discussion. Some might argue that optimistic headlines make people feel gayer, raise morale. About this point we will have more to say later. Perhaps the hard-headed editor may say simply that the Pollyanna headline is "good business," and there let the matter rest. Let us see whether the hard-headed editor is correct.

DO OPTIMISTIC HEADLINES INCREASE SALES?

Certainly the newspaper world thinks he is. Just to confirm our impression, we asked ten newspaper men in responsible positions about this point. Nine agreed that happy headlines sell papers. To bring this sacred cow to test, the day-by-day circulation figures of seven newspapers were checked against the headlines to see whether there was a consistent increase in circulation with any one type. The papers were the *Chicago Sun, Chicago Tribune, Chicago Daily News,* the *Boston Globe,* the *Washington Post,* the *Albany Knickerbocker News,* and the *Dallas Morning News.* The figures used were the total net paid circulation of each paper,

TABLE 1

CLASSIFICATION OF ALL HEADLINES AND SUBHEADLINES IN 12 NEWSPAPERS
(August 17—November 17, 1942)

Class	Description	Number of Headlines and Subheadlines	Per Cent of Total
O	All good news and optimistic interpretations	1918	59
P	All bad news and pessimistic interpretations	703	22
N	All neutral, ambiguous, questionable and unclassifiable headlines	605	19
Total		3226	100

TABLE 2

ANALYSIS OF THE CIRCULATION OF THE *Chicago Sun*
FROM AUGUST 17 TO NOVEMBER 17, 1942
(Parentheses indicate number of days)

PER CENT OF DAILY CIRCULATION FOR EACH WEEKDAY ON:

Day	The average day		O days		P days	
Monday	(14)	100	(9)	100.724	(0)	......
Tuesday	(14)	100	(8)	100.119	(4)	101.265
Wednesday	(13)	100	(4)	96.310	(4)	103.833
Thursday	(13)	100	(8)	96.495	(3)	110.390
Friday	(13)	100	(7)	100.679	(4)	99.568
Saturday	(13)	100	(9)	101.027	(3)	96.718
Average	(80)	100	(45)	99.225	(18)	102.354

each day, from August 17 to November 17, 1942, *and were not confined to street sales alone.* Since circulation varies consistently during the week—for example, sales are usually smaller on Saturdays than on any other day—the analysis of circulation was carried out on a day-by-day basis. Mondays were compared only with other Mondays, Tuesdays with other Tuesdays, and so on.

The average circulation for each day in the week is given a "par value" of 100. On any day a paper's circulation might be above par, below par, or right on the line. The question is this: are circulation figures consistently above par when headlines are optimistic? The answer for two of the papers, the *Chicago Sun* and the *Chicago Tribune*, is contained in Tables 2 and 3. In these tables, figures indicate the per cent of circulation above or below par for days with optimistic headlines and pessimistic headlines. For example, 110 means that circulation is 10 per cent above average, 90 that it is 10 per cent below.

Certainly the figures in these tables contain no compelling proof of the value of rosy headlines as circulation-builders. Where the *Chicago Sun* is concerned, pessimistic headlines seem to be the better drawing card; the reverse holds for the *Chicago Tribune.* These two papers are at the extremes, with the other papers falling between. They are listed below. The figure after each paper indicates the per cent difference in circulation between optimistic and pessimistic days. Plus two, for example, means that circulation is two per cent higher on optimistic days than on pessimistic days; minus two the reverse.

1. Chicago Tribune	+2.93%
2. Chicago Daily News	+ .87%
3. Dallas Morning News	+ .84%
4. Washington Post	+ .80%
5. Boston Evening Globe	− .02%
6. Albany Knickerbocker News	− .05%
7. Chicago Sun	−3.13%
The average difference for all these papers is	+ .32%

Are these differences statistically significant? To test significance, the largest among them (for the *Chicago Sun*) was examined. The entry of −3.13% signifies that for the 80 days under consideration the average circulation of the *Sun* was approximately three per cent less on optimistic days than on pessimistic days. Applying the customary formula for the statistical significance of differences, we find that there is a 50-50 chance of getting a difference in circulation of 8.38% between one Monday and another Monday, one Tuesday and another Tuesday, etc. What these chance factors are, we don't know. Certain it is that the optimism or pessimism of headlines is far less important than the total of chance circumstances. For the difference in circulation attributable to style of headline (3.13%) to be statistically reliable, it would have to be at least two and a half times as great as the variation in circulation due to chance. Actually it is

TABLE 3

ANALYSIS OF THE CIRCULATION OF THE *Chicago Tribune*
FROM AUGUST 17 TO NOVEMBER 17, 1942

(Parentheses indicate number of days)

PER CENT OF DAILY CIRCULATION FOR EACH WEEKDAY ON:

Day	The average day		O days		P days	
Monday	(14)	100	(6)	98.580	(0)	......
Tuesday	(14)	100	(5)	112.940	(7)	99.225
Wednesday	(13)	100	(5)	100.972	(1)	99.799
Thursday	(13)	100	(4)	100.371	(2)	99.326
Friday	(13)	100	(8)	100.045	(3)	99.520
Saturday	(13)	100	(1)	98.461	(2)	96.888
Average	(80)	100	(29)	101.894	(15)	98.951

not even half the size of chance circulation variation. If this is true for the *Chicago Sun,* which shows the greatest difference in circulation resulting from the nature of its headlines, it is even truer for the other papers examined.[2]

And thus for the sacred cow! Our evidence fails to confirm the common opinion of newspaper men. Sales vary widely, yes, but the reasons do not seem to include the optimistic or pessimistic coloring of the headlines.[3] It is true that our data are derived from net paid circulation figures, and not street sales alone. Yet if street sales are significantly affected by the mood of

[2] The standard deviation of circulation for the *Sun* on optimistic days was 6.59%, on pessimistic days 10.53%. The probable error of the difference between mean circulation on optimistic and pessimistic days was 8.38%. With the difference between the mean circulation for optimistic and pessimistic days amounting to only 3.12%, the chance of this difference being other than randomly determined is very small.

[3] Neither, apparently, do they include the weather. A further study, carried on with three of the papers above and checked against daily weather reports, resulted in a difference of .54 per cent between rainy days and fair days— negligible and not statistically significant.

the headlines, the influence of this effect upon total circulation is too slight to be taken seriously.

Having demonstrated the questionable circulation value of optimistic headlines, we take it the next question is this: what specifically do headlines do to people's desire to participate in war activities? In short, how do headlines affect active morale? A piece in *Time* (May 24, 1943) hints that optimistic headlines may not do much good in stimulating citizens to worthy war deeds.

Since the North African victory, some blood donors are failing to keep appointments at Red Cross donor centers. The Red Cross has noticed such defaults always increase after good news.

Should this prove to be the case generally, the taste of the newspaper community for rosy headlines may be a more serious matter than we figured. If the matter is serious, this article has shown very clearly that there is no financial barrier in the way of remedying the situation. Cheering headlines do not sell more papers. Why, then, should cheering headlines, possibly harmful to morale, be *à la mode?*

FREEDOM OF THE PRESS

ALFRED McCLUNG LEE

What press freedom any civilized country has or has had may be regarded as a temporary by-product of the continuous struggle by economic, political, and religious interests for control of the press. Then, too, as Alexander Hamilton[1] asked in 1788, "What is the liberty of the press? Who can give it any definition which would not leave the utmost latitude for evasion?" He contended "that its security, whatever fine declarations may be inserted in any constitution respecting it, must altogether depend on public opinion, and on the general spirit of the people and of the government." Press freedom, in other words, to the extent that it corresponds to actual conditions, is defined by the mores of a time and place. Frequently students of Freedom of the Press[2] start with the assumption that some ideal version of the doctrine is the yardstick against which press freedom in practice can or should be graded. Sometimes they even go so far as to claim that Freedom of the Press, as described, is the ideal "towards which we *must* strive." . . .

Such legally sanctioned catch phrases as Freedom of the Press, then, inevitably produce a conflict in interpretation between those who would cling to the "real meaning" of the fetish words of the constitutional heroes and those whose interests are better served by a "practical definition" in terms of present needs.[3] In periods of rapid change in life conditions, when popular acceptance of new rationalizations lags perceptibly, the gulf between these two viewpoints widens and tends to call forth efforts at sharper definition, at a reassessment of both the ideal and the practical in terms of realities. Popular doctrines, however, "are always vague; it would ruin a doctrine to define it, because then it could be analyzed, tested, criticized, and verified."[4]

* * *

While legislators and judges, during the nineteenth and early twentieth centuries,

[1] "The Federalist, No. LXXXIV," *The Federalist*, ed. by E. G. Bourne, New York: M. W. Dunne, 1901, pp. 156-157.

[2] Throughout this paper, "Freedom of the Press" refers to the catch phrase of social discourse and struggle; "press freedom" refers to the actual social phenomenon as measured by the access of differing, competing, and even conflicting group spokesmen to press media of communication.

[3] For a further description of such differences, see the author's "Levels of Culture as Levels of Social Generalization," *American Sociological Review, 10,* (1945): 485-495, and "Social Determinants of Public Opinions," *International Journal of Opinion and Attitude Research, 1*: 1 (March, 1947): 12-29.

[4] W. G. Sumner, *War and Other Essays*, ed. by A. G. Keller, New Haven: Yale University Press, 1911, p. 36.

Revised from "Freedom of the Press: Services of a Catch Phrase," in G. P. Murdock (ed.), *Studies in the Science of Society* (New Haven: Yale University Press, 1937), pp. 355-375, pp. 357, 364, 366-369, and 375 quoted. Used by permission of the author and the publisher.

were working out a definition of Freedom of the Press from a political standpoint, publishers were utilizing changing life conditions, mechanical and economic developments, and cultural tendencies to evolve, from an economic standpoint, a more "respectable" connotation for the Press. In a formal statement, Colonel Robert R. McCormick,[5] publisher of the *Chicago Tribune* and chairman of the Freedom of the Press Committee of the American Newspaper Publishers' Association, sums up the political rights of "decent" daily newspapers as he believes they are implied by the doctrine of Freedom of the Press: "The right of freedom of the press is a 'right which shall not be abridged by any law of congress.' The freedom of the press would be abridged by any law passed by congress which, by the exercise of a code or otherwise, would do any of the following things: First, unreasonably raise the cost of production . . . second, unreasonably decrease the return from publishing . . . third, interfere with the transmission of news by telegraph or otherwise. . . . And, finally, anything that would unreasonably interfere with the freedom of the press in any way which may ever be invented." . . .

The story of the manner in which daily newspaper properties have been stabilized is long and complicated. It includes the development of monopolistic cooperative and other newsgathering memberships and franchises,[6] of monopolistic feature rights,[7] of efficient newspaper distributing organizations with which a newcomer can compete only with the greatest difficulty,[8] of advertising rates which yield no profit to new and even established small papers, of advertising contracts that effectively exclude or at least hamper "outsiders" and new papers,[9] and

of buying arrangements available only to those able to purchase huge quantities of supplies.[10] Despite these and other changes, however, it should not be forgotten that it is still *possible* to start a daily in New York City with approximately the same capital as was employed a century or more ago—a daily of the same sort as those successful then. But it would not satisfy the current expectations of potential subscribers. Our folkways relating to newspaper reading, including the price we are willing to pay indirectly by purchasing advertised goods, contribute strongly to the stability of the relatively few dailies by which we are now served. We demand that our papers purchase costly features and run columns and columns of expensive cabled stories about the love affairs of royalty.

Such a brief summary of the factors restricting or prohibiting the entrance of new units into any field monopolized by established dailies inevitably oversimplifies an extremely complicated situation. A more extensive survey of the facts than is here possible, however, merely modifies and refines the impression, and does not fundamentally alter the conclusions, which may be stated in a fashion paraphrasing the generalizations of McCormick. The industry has raised the cost of production to a point prohibiting most newcomers.[11] It has decreased the return from publishing for the unestablished to an extent not accomplished politically in this country since long before the Revolution. And it has interfered with the transmission of news by telegraph and otherwise, through promoting the necessity of huge outlays for wire news as well as through monopolistic arrangements. . . .

---

[5] "The Freedom of the Press Still Furnishes That Check upon Government Which No Constitution Has Ever Been Able to Provide," Chicago: The Tribune Co., 1934, pp. 33-34.
[6] See A. M. Lee, *Daily Newspaper in America*, New York: Macmillan Co., 1937, Chaps. 13 and 14.
[7] *Ibid.*, Chap. 15.
[8] *Ibid.*, Chap. 9.
[9] *Ibid.*, Chap. 10.

[10] *Ibid.*, Chaps. 7 and 8.
[11] See Marshall Field, *Freedom Is More Than a Word*, Chicago: University of Chicago Press, 1945, part 3, and A. M. Lee, affidavits dated May 10, 20, and 22, 1943, in U. S. Dept. of Justice, *Affidavits Filed in Support of Plaintiff's Motion for Summary Judgment* (U. S. A. v. A. P. *et al.*, Civil Action No. 19—163, Dist. Court of the U. S. for the Southern Dist. of N. Y.), filed and served May 25, 1943, pp. 76-170, for statistical evidence.

Perhaps, despite the rapid technological, economic, and social adjustments in modern civilization, the kind of press freedom now covered in practice by Freedom of the Press as a doctrine will endure and prove "retrospectively rational." The facts cited and others referred to, however, suggest that the pathos surrounding this doctrine is cracking, and that its new adjustment, now formulating, will not meet with the full approval of the interests who have come to control most daily newspapers.

DIMINISHING COMPETITION AMONG DAILY NEWSPAPERS IN THE 25 LARGEST CITIES: 1900-1950*

Year	Population	Morning newspapers		Evening newspapers		Average morning circulation	Average evening circulation	Total no.	No. of ownerships
		No.	Circulation	No.	Circulation				
1900	12,576,438	69	....	84	....	......	......	153	...
1910	16,647,384	66	....	86	....	......	......	152	...
1920	20,696,355	49	6,014,331	76	8,418,687	125,299	116,926	125	104
1930	25,477,606	43	9,116,889	69	11,358,463	217,069	164,617	112	96
1935	....	39	9,004,188	62	9,981,351	236,952	160,990	101	86
1940	26,745,522	37	10,044,196	57	10,747,547	271,465	191,921	94	79
1945	....	37	12,605,579	53	11,871,442	340,691	223,989	90	76**
1950	29,292,742	35	11,995,590	51	13,146,912	342,731	257,783	86	72**

* Adapted from Alfred McClung Lee, affidavit dated May 10, 1943, pp. 76-93, in U. S. Dept. of Justice, *Affidavits Filed in Support of Plaintiff's Motion for Summary Judgment* (U. S. A. v. A. P. *et al.*, Civil Action No. 19-163, Dist. Court of the U. S. for the Southern Dist. of N. Y.), May 25, 1943, p. 85. The 1945 and 1950 figures have been added. Tabulated from lists in N. W. Ayer and Son, *American Newspaper Annual: 1901* and *American Newspaper Annual and Directory: 1911*, and the "International Year Book Numbers" of *Editor and Publisher* for 1920-21, 1931, 1936, 1941, 1946, and 1951. Only newspapers with a circulation of 1 percent or more of the population of the city of publication were counted. This limitation was adopted to exclude trade and other special-interest papers and thus to confine the tabulation to newspapers of general circulation. All foreign-language papers were also excluded. Pp. 86-92 of the affidavit give details for each city for the 1900-1942 period.

** The further elimination of duplication due to newspaper "chains" extending to two and more cities reduces this total in 1945 to no more than 53 ownerships, in 1950 to no more than 46.

DIMINISHING DAILY NEWSPAPER COMPETITION IN THE UNITED STATES: 1920-1950*

Year	Cities with dailies	Cities with only one daily newspaper		Cities with only dailies under common control		Cities with competing dailies	
		Number	Per cent of total	Number	Per cent of total	Number	Per cent of total
1920	1292	724	56.0	743	57.5	549	42.5
1930	1402	1002	71.5	1114	79.5	288	20.5
1940	1426	1092	76.6	1245	87.3	181	12.7
1945	1388	1107	79.8	1273	91.7	115	8.3
1950	1410	1124	79.7	1314	93.2	96	6.8

* Adapted from Alfred McClung Lee, affidavit dated May 10, 1943, pp. 76-93, in U. S. Dept. of Justice. *Affidavits Filed in Support of Plaintiff's Motion for Summary Judgment* (U. S. A. v. A. P. *et al.*, Civil Action No. 19-163, Dist. Court of the U. S. for the Southern Dist. of N. Y.), May 25, 1943, p. 92. The 1945 and 1950 figures have been added. Tabulated from the lists of English-language daily newspapers in *Editor and Publisher* "International Year Book Numbers" for 1920-21, 1931, 1941, and 1951. The only papers eliminated were those outside of the geographical area of the 48 states and the District of Columbia and also certain special-interest trade and collegiate dailies which were included only in the 1946 and 1951 lists but which had been specifically excluded from previous lists by *Editor and Publisher*. Morning and evening papers were treated as competing units when under separate control.

FREEDOM OF SPEECH FOR WHOM?

CLIFFORD JUDKINS DURR

In this country it is difficult to start a good argument on the desirability of freedom of speech. No one is willing to take the opposing side. We are all for it—or at least unwilling to admit we are not—just as we are for "freedom" generally, and "liberty," and "justice," and all the other noble words we have been taught from our infancy to respect. Unfortunately, however, when we begin to apply the principle of freedom to specific cases, unanimity ends. The champions of the principle align themselves into opposing groups, each claiming to be freedom's true defender, each declaring that all others would betray it. Then we have the confusing spectacle of opposing armies clashing head-on in vicious combat, each rallying around an identical banner and each shouting an identical battle cry. The onlooker may quite naturally ask: "What is this freedom that is being fought over? Freedom from what? Freedom for whom? Is there enough freedom for all, or is the quantity so limited that it may be entrusted only to the care of the most deserving?"

In the fight over "freedom of speech" radio broadcasting is a particularly active battlefront at the present time. The "incident" which set off this fight was the adoption by the Federal Communications Commission, in 1941, of regulations dealing with the relationship of broadcasting stations to the networks. The new rules were designed to remove certain contractual restraints upon the free flow of programs, and to give to the stations a little more control over their own time. The networks—or at least the two biggest national networks—did not like these regulations. In an effort to have them set aside, they resorted to the courts, claiming that the FCC was not only interfering with their business practices but was stifling their freedom of speech. The litigation was finally brought to an end by decision of the United States Supreme Court upholding the validity of the regulations. Now the two networks, joined by the National Association of Broadcasters, have appealed to Congress. Their battle cry of "freedom of speech" is ringing through the halls of Congress and the Congressional committee rooms, in the press, and over the air.

We are being warned that the rights guaranteed to us by the First Amendment to the Constitution are about to be snatched away by despotic "bureaucrats," aided and abetted by the Supreme Court itself. Freedom of speech over the air will be gone forever, we are told, unless Congress forthwith limits all government supervision over the public domain of the radio spectrum to the mere engineering job of protecting the broadcasters from interfering radio signals of their fellows. Safety lies only in placing in the hands of the broadcasters the unregulated authority to decide what shall be said over

From the *Public Opinion Quarterly*, 1944, 8, 391-406. Reprinted by permission of the author and the publisher.

the air and who shall say it. Columbia Broadcasting System, Inc., one of the mightiest champions of free speech, solemnly warned its stockholders in its Annual Report for the fiscal year ended January 1, 1944:

The question squarely before Congress . . . is whether the American people want the Government to have the power to tell them what they can or cannot hear on the air. The proposed legislation is receiving the diligent attention of your company's officers in cooperation with the National Association of Broadcasters. With America approaching the time when more than ten million of her sons and daughters will be in the uniform of their country in a war for freedom, it is vital that a free radio, the essential agency of a free people, be preserved.

As one of the "bureaucrats" involved and therefore an admitted partisan in this fight, I would like to point out that there may be limitations upon freedom of speech other than political limitations; that constitutional guarantees do not protect against economic restraints; and that with the tremendous economic concentration which has already taken place in this country and which is still increasing at a constantly accelerating pace, our actions may be as effectively limited and directed by a system of economic rewards and punishments as by duly enacted laws. In addition, there is no more effective way of distracting attention from economic controls and restraints than by appealing to our traditional suspicion of and hostility to political restraints. We are warranted in asking whether or not the freedom *from* control over broadcasting which is being so vigorously urged carries with it freedom *to* control.

In his testimony before the Senate Committee on Interstate Commerce in December, 1943, in connection with hearings on a proposed bill to limit governmental supervision over radio channels in accordance with the specifications mentioned above, Mr. Niles Trammell, President of the National Broadcasting Company, stated:

The argument is now advanced that business control of broadcasting operations has nothing to do with program control. This is to forget that "He who controls the pocketbook controls the man." Business control means complete control, and there is no use arguing to the contrary.

His argument was directed against any type of government regulation over contracts between the national networks and their affiliated broadcasting stations. But if we accept his view of the effectiveness of pocketbook control—and he should be in an excellent position to observe its operations in the field of broadcasting—then freedom of the air in this country is subject to dangers far more serious and far more immediate than any present threats from government.

RADIO CONTROL REVIEWED

In the twenty-five years which have elapsed since the last war, radio has grown up. It has developed from a plaything for mechanically minded teen-age boys to a tremendous instrument of power capable of pouring information and ideas as well as entertainment and advertising plugs, at practically any hour of the day or night, into 32,000,000 American homes. It has also grown into a major business enterprise in its own right. In 1927, the gross time sales of all broadcasters in this country, including the networks, was less than $5,000,000. Five years later in 1932, this figure had increased to nearly $62,000,000, and in 1937, to over $144,000,000. In 1943 the figure had reached an all-time high of over $307,000,000, and there is no reason to believe this is anywhere near the ceiling. In only one year, 1933, the turning point of the depression, have radio time sales failed to show a substantial increase over those of the preceding year.

At the beginning, broadcasting in this country might have taken any one of a number of turns. It might have been operated by manufacturers of radio receiving sets and equipment as a means of providing a market for their product. It came close to being an adjunct of the telephone company which established the first network and proposed to lease the programming rights on a toll basis. It might have been taken over by educational institutions or by non-profit organizations, which may or may not have been concerned with the promotion of particular philosophies. Or it might have been taken over and operated by the government, as has happened in many other countries. Instead, we sought to steer a middle course between private commercial exploitation and governmental operation. Title to the radio channels was reserved to the people; the operation of broadcasting stations was placed in the hands of private individuals and groups licensed by the government for limited periods, charged by law with the responsibility of using the public-owned channels in the "public interest," and subject to loss of their licenses if they failed so to operate. Diversification in the presentation of news, opinion, and entertainment was sought through diversification in the control of the radio outlets. Monopolization either by private groups or by the government was repudiated.

Subject only to the general requirement that their operations be "in the public interest," to the general libel and slander laws, and to statutory restrictions against profane and obscene language and discrimination among political candidates during political campaigns, responsibility for determining what shall or shall not go out over the air is placed in the hands of the broadcasting licensees. In clear statutory language the Federal Communications Commission, the government agency which issues the broadcasting licenses and whose responsibility it is to see to it that the broadcasters operate in conformity with the law and public interest, is denied any right of censorship. Section 326 of the Federal Communications Act expressly provides:

Nothing in this Act shall be understood or construed to give the Commission the power of censorship over the radio communications or signals transmitted by any radio station, and no regulation or condition shall be promulgated or fixed by the Commission which shall interfere with the right of free speech by means of radio communication.

Thus the Federal Communications Commission is forbidden in explicit terms to censor or interfere in any way with the right of free speech. But no similar restraint on censorship on interference with freedom of speech is imposed upon those who daily determine the content of American broadcasting—the station licenses, the networks, the advertisers, and the advertising agencies.

DIVERSIFICATION CHECKMATED

Inasmuch as there are today approximately nine hundred standard broadcast stations on the air, it would seem that this number should afford the diversification we have sought. In the field of ideas it is only to be expected that there will be some limits to the range with which this diversification operates; all commercial stations operate under the same general business principles and consequently can be expected to have some common hostility to economic or political theories inconsistent with their way of doing business. With this large number of stations on the air, however, the balancing out of the prejudices, predilections, and mistakes of judgment in one direction against those in another should be expected to afford a fairly balanced presentation of opinion as well as of news and entertainment.

But what happens to the diversification we have sought when the broadcasters contract away their responsibility or enter into voluntary understandings among themselves as to what shall or shall not go out over the air?

Nearly six hundred of the nine hundred standard broadcast stations are affiliated with one or more of the four national networks. These six hundred stations together utilize 95 per cent of the nighttime broadcasting power of the entire country, and over 53 percent of their total broadcasting time is devoted to national network programs.

Approximately 40 per cent of the entire revenue of the affiliated stations comes from the national networks. In addition to this, the wide listening audience which an affiliated station is able to build up through the use of popular network programs, and the consequent increase in the effectiveness of the station as an advertising medium, results in a substantial increase in the salability of non-network time. The value of network affiliation is strikingly illustrated by the fact that in 1942, the last year for which complete figures are available, the net income (before Federal income taxes) of the average network-affiliated station was more than fifteen times the net income of the average unaffiliated station. It is apparent that an affiliation contract is the biggest economic asset a station can have. Many of them could not survive without network affiliation, and few of them could prosper without it. In addition to the direct utilization of more than half of the broadcasting hours of their affiliated stations, therefore, the networks, with this power of economic life and death in their hands, are in a position to influence strongly, if not to direct, the general program policies of the affiliated station even with respect to non-network time.

FROM DIVERSIFICATION TO CONCENTRATION

But a further examination of the situation shows that the networks themselves are far from being free agents. They are dependent upon their advertisers.

The newspaper publisher desiring independence in his news and editorial policies seeks it in the maximum of revenue from his subscribers, his want-ad columns, and a multiplicity of advertising accounts. He would not be too happy if the financial success of his paper should depend upon the accounts of one or two or even a half-dozen advertisers.

About 70 per cent of all newspaper advertising revenue comes from local business concerns and only 30 per cent from national and regional advertisers. In the case of radio broadcasting, the opposite is true: in 1943, over 70 per cent of the advertising revenue of all broadcasting stations, affiliated and unaffiliated, came from national and regional advertisers. Broadcasting is thus predomi-

nantly an instrument of nationwide business concerns rather than of local merchants. National network advertising is, by its very nature, exclusively national advertising. Moreover, the cost, which runs as high as $25,000 for a single hour of full network coverage, is beyond the reach of any but the wealthiest national concerns.

Of the hundreds of thousands of business concerns in this country, only a select few reach the national networks. In 1943, 144 advertisers provided 97.2 per cent of the national networks' business.

One-eighth of NBC's entire advertising business came from one advertiser, and two advertisers provided almost one-fourth. Ten advertisers accounted for nearly 60 per cent of its business. One-seventh of Blue's advertising business came from one advertiser, and two provided approximately one-fourth. Over 60 per cent of its business came from ten advertisers. To a slightly less degree, the same situation prevails in the case of CBS and Mutual.

Concentration is even greater with respect to the advertising agencies. Nearly 60 per cent of CBS's business came from ten agencies, with nineteen agencies providing over 80 per cent. More than 66 per cent of Blue's business came from ten agencies; over 90 per cent was concentrated in the hands of twenty-three agencies. In the case of Mutual, 65 per cent of the business came from ten agencies, and twenty-three agencies provided nearly 85 per cent of the business. Although no figures are available for NBC, as that network does not publish information showing the agencies with which it does business, there is no reason to believe that its advertising is less concentrated.

That the economic interests of business concerns engaged in the same line of business are not dissimilar is a reasonable assumption; their differences in point of view are not likely to go very much beyond differences as to the merits of their respective products. It is therefore even more disturbing when we look at the figures by industries to find that of the estimated total billings of all four national networks, amounting for 1943 to $152,000,000, over 74 per cent was concentrated in four industry groups. These groups are as follows:

1. Food, beverages, confections $40,441,486 26.5%
2. Drugs   31,253,091 20.5%
3. Soaps, cleansers, etc.   22,267,340 14.6%
4. Tobacco   19,070,522 12.5%

Thus, we move from diversification to concentration. To summarize: We start out with nine hundred "independent" stations; about six hundred of these, together using 95 per cent of the nighttime broadcasting power of the entire country, bind themselves by contract to four national networks; the four national networks receive over 74 per cent of their revenue from four national industries. Is this our road to freedom of the air?

THE NAB CODE IN PRINCIPLE AND IN ACTION

The operation of the Code of the National Association of Broadcasters is an illustration of what may happen to diversification when broadcasting station licensees, or a substantial number of them, reach a common understanding with reference to program practices and policies. The Code is a voluntary one; unlike an affiliation contract between a network and a station, it has no legally binding effect upon its subscribers. The purpose of the Code, as stated in its foreword, is "to formulate basic standards" for the guidance of broadcasters in dealing with the "social side" of broadcasting. It lays down some excellent principles with which few can find cause for disagreement, but the interpretation and application of those principles sometimes lead to rather questionable results. To mention two of them will suffice here.

First, the Code provides that no time shall be sold for the presentation of public controversial issues. Instead, as part of their public duty, the broadcasters shall bring such discussions to their audiences without regard to the willingness or ability of an advocate of a particular point of view to pay for the privilege of advocating it. An exception is made in case of political broadcasts and the public-forum type of programs; the latter may be commercially sponsored "when control of the fairness of the program rests wholly with the broadcasting station or network."

Second, solicitation of memberships in organizations, whether on paid or free time, is deemed unacceptable except for charitable organizations such as the American Red Cross and "except where such memberships are incidental to the rendering of commercial services such as an insurance plan either in respect to casualty, to life or property."

As a matter of first impression, both of these rules appear salutary. When a listener turns on his radio for news or entertainment, he does not like to be panhandled for contributions or exhorted to join organizations. Moreover, the refusal to sell time for controversial discussions should promote a better-balanced presentation of points of view—*provided* that this refusal is applied with complete impartiality to all groups and points of view, and *provided* that time of a sufficient quantity and quality is kept free for a well-rounded discussion by competent spokesmen of all responsible points of view.

The operation of these two rules is not, unfortunately, so simple or so impartial as their wording. First of all, there is the necessity of deciding the very controversial question as to what subjects are controversial. The NAB Code Manual, issued by the NAB Code Compliance Committee, offers its guidance in meeting this problem. "Discussion (or dramatization) of labor problems on the air," it says, "is almost always of a controversial nature. Even the so-called 'facts' about labor, such as the American Federation of Labor's audited membership figures, are usually challenged." A complex problem is thus solved very simply by holding that labor unions are controversial *per se*. Labor unions being controversial *per se*, it naturally follows that any program paid for by a labor union is likewise controversial *per se,* and hence in violation of the Code. Even a broadcast of a symphony orchestra, according to the testimony of a network president, becomes controversial if a labor union pays for it.

The Code Manual finds nothing controversial, however, whether in the realm of "fact" or opinion, about business problems. Hence the remarks of a commentator sponsored by a business concern become purged of controversiality by virtue of such sponsorship, even though he may be expressing his opinion (an opinion which his sponsor may, by happy coincidence, often share) on such subjects as rationing, price control, taxation, international affairs, or even labor problems. There was nothing controversial about the remarks of Mr. W. J. Cameron when he was sponsored by Ford Motor Company. Yet the symphony program which was interrupted by his five-minute homily would have immediately become controversial if sponsored by the American Federation of Labor or the Congress of Industrial Organizations.

According to the same network president, the function of radio is to sell goods and services. As he put it:

We are selling time for one specific reason, and that is to sell goods manufactured by American manufacturers, to the public.

If an idea happens to be thrown in for good measure, along with the merchandise-selling job, that, of course, is all right. Moreover, it is all right to sell time to a sponsor in order that he may sell his "good-will," either in connection with or apart from the sale of goods, provided the sponsor is in the business of selling goods. For example, the subject of monopolies and cartels would seem to the uninitiated to lie within the realm of public controversy. But apparently no controversy is raised when the announcer for a manufacturing concern which is being sued for violating the anti-trust laws departs from his customary advertising spiel and sets his listeners right by explaining the benefits the public has received from the manufacturer's agreement with foreign business concerns. In addition, a manufacturing concern which has nothing to sell to the public because it is engaged exclusively in the manufacture of airplanes for the Army and Navy, may buy time to incur good will and tell the public how it is helping to win the war by making excellent airplanes. A union representing the employees who work for the same manufacturer, on the other hand, cannot buy time to incur good will and tell the public how its members are helping to win the war by making the same airplanes, for that would be controversial.

Mutual insurance companies, although membership organizations, are exempt from the ban against the use of radio for the solicitation of memberships, because their memberships are "incidental to the rendering of commercial services." Yet a consumer's cooperative whose memberships are incidental to the sale of goods or the rendering of services is in an entirely different category and, under the provisions of the Code, would be denied all access to the air, whether on free or sponsored time. As a result of complaints made by the Cooperative League of the U. S. A. a year and a half ago, which resulted in some very strong protests on the floor of Congress, the NAB Code Committee has now devised a formula under which consumers' cooperatives may buy time provided they carefully avoid saying anything critical about any other system of distribution.

The NAB Code Manual, in further discussing the subject of labor unions and controversial issues, warns NAB members:

The situation is further complicated by the fact that employers, as a rule, won't discuss their labor problems on the air and are *inclined to frown on those stations, especially in smaller communities, which open their facilities to labor unions.* (Italics supplied)

It is possible, of course, that this attitude on the part of the employers, who may also happen to be advertisers, has little bearing on the amount of free time made available to labor unions for the discussion of their problems or with the policy against the sale of time for such purposes. It is also possible that the attitude of the large advertisers has nothing to do with the policy relating to consumers' cooperatives. But I think we are warranted in leaving the burden of proof where it logically falls.

The NAB Code, as pointed out above, is voluntary and without legally binding effect. But the disapproval of one's business associates can be unpleasant, and the only ethical alternative to compliance with the rules of an association is to get out. There is, furthermore, more than one way of skinning a cat. Another way was pointed out by a past chairman of the NAB Code Committee, who testified before the Senate Interstate Commerce Committee last year:

. . . There are powerful committees in the various communities that will implement the removal from the air of such "negative broadcasters." They will bring such influence to bear that such broadcasters will naturally feel they will have to go off the air unless they do something to remedy the situation. *When such influence is brought to bear upon stations that are guilty they will not be able to operate, because they certainly cannot operate without funds.* (Italics supplied)

Before we leave the subject of the NAB, a few figures with reference to that organization may be interesting. The total NAB membership dues for 1943 amounted to $345,110. Of this amount, $50,400 was contributed by CBS and $41,700 by NBC. Stations affiliated with these two networks contributed $152,280. Thus, these two networks and their affiliated stations provided over two-thirds of the entire dues of the NAB. It is difficult to believe that NBC and CBS do not exercise an influence on NAB policies at least commensurate with their contributions. In fact, if would be very difficult to find one important instance in which the NAB has adopted any policy inconsistent with the policies and interests of these two networks.

UNSOLD TIME—A MIRAGE

The NAB Code requirement that controversial issues shall be discussed on the air only during unsold time assumes that sufficient unsold time is available for the purpose. This assumption, unfortunately, no longer holds true.

The increasing popularity of broadcasting stations as an advertising medium has meant a corresponding decrease in the amount of unsold time available for public service programs. After all, broadcasters are in business to make money, and they make money by selling time. So far as the national networks are concerned, we have just about arrived at the point where there is "standing room only" on the air. In 1943, such outstanding public service programs as "Wake Up, America!" and "Adventures in Science" were dropped from the networks in favor of commercially sponsored programs; in addition, the networks were seeking commercial sponsors for other programs of the round table and town meeting type. Since then, the pressure of commercial advertising has increased still more. For the first two months of 1944, according to *Variety*, the estimated time sales of the four national networks increased 40 per cent over the comparable months in 1943; thus, the "standing room only" sign may soon be replaced by "waiting in the foyer."

The squeeze on public service programs is particularly acute during the evening hours from 7:00 to 11:00 p.m., when the largest audiences are available. An examination of the network programs for a recent week shows that of the twenty-eight hours between 7:00 p.m. and 11:00 p.m., CBS had commercial sponsors for all except one hour and forty-five minutes, while NBC had commercial sponsors for all except an hour and a half—and there is no assurance that even these few remaining hours will not soon be sold. Blue and Mutual are not as yet in quite so prosperous a situation. Blue had six hours still unsold, Mutual fourteen and a half hours. Blue's estimated gross time sales for the first two months of 1944, however, increased 45 per cent over the first two months of 1943, whereas Mutual's increased 82 per cent. Neither of them should be very long in catching up with the procession.

The only barriers to the complete occupation of the air by advertisers, and the consequent total elimination of public service programs, are self-restraint on the part of the broadcasters and networks themselves—somewhat fortified, perhaps, by the complaints of their listeners—and the public-interest provision of the Communications Act, which the networks and the NAB are so earnestly urging Congress to narrow.

Even if we should assume that advertisers are concerned only with the sale of their goods and not with the sale of their ideas, what will be the effect on our thinking, on our very culture, if we receive our information and ideas as a mere by-product of the advertising business? Can we be as serious as we should be about this war when the news about it comes to us by the courtesy of a laxative or hair tonic? Will we rise to the challenge of the tremendous post-war problems facing us, both at home and abroad, when the discussion of these problems is associated in our minds with the merits of a particular brand of cigars or gasoline? Can our deepest emotions about our country and the things it stands for remain unimpaired in the face of a constant identification of patriotism with the purchase of a particular brand of merchandise?

THE SOAP OPERA, BOON TO ADVERTISERS

Advertising concentration limits diversity even in the field of entertainment. An illustration is the "soap opera," about which we have recently heard a great deal.

Soap operas, of course, are not operas; neither are they devoted solely to the sale of soap. They may be used equally well as a means of selling breakfast foods. "A continuing serial in dramatic form in which an understanding of today's episode is dependent upon previous listening"—so runs the definition. No good purpose would be served here in a discussion of their vices or virtues. In hearings before the Senate

Committee on Interstate Commerce, the President of the National Broadcasting Company defended them as good, healthy entertainment, presenting in support of his contention extracts from a report prepared at NBC's request by a committee of experts consisting of an eminent neurologist, a well-known psychiatrist, and the editor of the *Journal of the American Medical Association*. The report found that:

They [soap operas] seem to fill a real demand for a public of considerable size and their shortcomings are heavily outweighed by their virtues.

On the other hand, another eminent psychiatrist whose views were likewise included in the record of the Senate hearings stated that:

. . . the authors have screened the emotional sewers, drained the emotional swamps for much of their material

and that

to use the hearts and minds of millions of women without regard to their mental or emotional welfare to sell any product is little short of treason in a nation at war.

The reader may either take his choice between these points of view or listen to the soap operas and reach his own conclusions. The only question presented here is whether or not they take up too much precious broadcasting time, a portion of which, at least, might well be devoted to other types of programs.

In January, 1940, there were a total of fifty-nine and a half daytime hours of commercially sponsored time between ten a.m. and six p.m., Monday through Friday, on the four national networks. Of these fifty-nine and a half hours, fifty-five were devoted to soap operas. By April, 1941, soap opera time had increased to an all-time high of sixty-four hours per week. Since then, although the amount of time devoted to soap operas has declined, it still ranges from forty-eight to fifty hours per week. It is no wonder that a poll of housewives showed that thirty-six thought there were too many soap operas for every one who thought there were too few. Fifty soap-opera hours per week—which means forty soap operas per day—is a pretty sizeable dose.

In view of the attitude of the housewives themselves, the loyalty of the two biggest national networks to the soap-opera type of program is difficult to explain. The networks have some very excellent programming talent on their staffs; it would seem that if they were primarily concerned with listeners rather than with advertisers, they would not devote so overwhelming a proportion of their daytime broadcasting to one particular type of program, however good it might be. Possibly the explanation lies in the sixty-odd million dollars of billings to the food and soap industries, the chief sponsors of soap-opera programs. The sponsors' loyalty to a type of program which appeals to a comparatively narrow audience can perhaps be explained on the theory that a limited listening audience which can be reached repeatedly and in a concentrated way will provide more buyers than a wider audience that gets its message in a less concentrated dosage. After all, it is hard for the addict to keep away from the radio on Wednesday when Tuesday's installment left the heroine securely locked in the burning house.

WILL FM GIVE US OUR SECOND CHANCE?

By many advocates of a "free radio" it is suggested that all of our problems of diversity in broadcasting are on the threshold of solution by the scientists and engineers; that with the expansion in the use of frequency modulation (FM) which will follow the war and the development of new frequencies for television and other broadcasting uses, there will be plenty of outlets on the air for all kinds of programs and for everyone with a worthwhile idea. The forty channels set aside for FM will alone provide room for many more additional stations than the total number which can now operate in the standard broadcasting band.

In short, the scientists and engineers are now offering us a renewed opportunity—another chance of deciding whether radio broadcasting shall become the instrumentality of public service it was originally intended to be or whether it will continue its present trend of becoming merely the most effective commercial advertising medium. After the war, when radio equipment becomes freely available again, we will start off with an almost clean slate in the field of FM broadcasting.

But the mere opportunity the engineers and scientists are offering us does not guarantee that we will use that opportunity wisely. The kind of public service a broadcasting station renders cannot rise above the motives, interests, and abilities of those who operate it. It is inevitable that this new method of broadcasting will drift under the control of the commercial groups who now dominate our present system unless newcomers are willing to enter the field— individuals and groups who are interested first in the job to be done in the field of news, entertainment, education, and free discussion, and who are interested in advertising revenue, if at all, only as a method of supporting an instrumentality of public service. If individuals and groups willing to accept this challenge do not arise, the increase in the number of stations made possible by our scientists and engineers will mean merely that substantially the same programs we now have will be listened to over more frequencies and more receiving sets.

The Federal Communications Commission, having reserved five of the forty FM radio channels exclusively for educational use, has thus expressly invited educational institutions to enter the field. These five channels will provide room for hundreds of educational stations throughout the nation. Such stations need not limit themselves to classroom instruction; the regulations governing FM educational stations recognize that education neither ends with a high-school diploma or a college degree nor is embraced exclusively within the covers of textbooks.

The earmarking of such channels for educational use does not mean that the remaining channels must all be devoted to commercial operations. They are open to commercial and non-commercial applicants alike, on the basis of their qualifications and their showing that they will serve the public interest better than competing applicants.

In thinking of radio, we are too much inclined to think in terms of what radio can bring to the people—a one-way pipeline of news, ideas, and entertainment—and too little in terms of its value as an outlet through which the people may express themselves. Democracy thrives more on participation at its base than upon instruction from the top. FM, and particularly educational FM, offers an opportunity for community participation. Roundtable discussion of local problems by local people, and town meetings in which local people participate, may be as exciting and as important as similar types of programs on national and international affairs participated in by authorities of national or international reputation. Moreover, while programs by the local music society, the college department of music, the policeman's band, or the local little theatre

may not reach the technical perfection of similar performances by a national symphony orchestra or Hollywood professionals, they bring to the community a sense of participation and an awareness of cultural values that can never be piped in from studios in New York or Hollywood.

The world is now in the midst of a major crisis, greater than any that has heretofore occurred in its history. Following the war, when tremendous economic, political, and cultural adjustments will have to be made, the pattern of the future will depend upon our ability to make these adjustments in the right way. In this country, we are dedicated to the principles of democracy. If the pattern of the future is to be a democratic pattern, it cannot be imposed from the top; it must be based upon the desires, beliefs, and feelings of the people themselves. Democracy can function only in an atmosphere of full information and frank discussion. In determining the course of the future, radio can play its part for good or evil, depending upon whether it is the voice of the few or an outlet for full information and free expression, as uncurbed by commercial as by political restraints.

TELEVISION AND THE ELECTION

ANGUS CAMPBELL, GERALD GURIN, AND WARREN E. MILLER

The Presidential campaign of 1952 was the first in which television played a major part. How much did this new medium influence the election? No one really knows, because no specific studies were made to measure the impact of TV on the thinking of the

From *Scientific American*, 1953, 188, 46-48. Reprinted by permission of the authors and publisher.

electorate. But we do know something about how television compared with the other media of information in bringing the campaign to the public, and what groups in the population were most exposed to, or affected by, the television campaign.

As part of a two-year study of political behavior financed by the Carnegie Corporation, the Survey Research Center of the University of Michigan last fall made an intensive analysis of the factors affecting the decision of citizens to vote. In the course of this we asked a sample of the U. S. population in November a few questions about the media (newspapers, radio, television and magazines) through which they had "paid attention to the campaign," and requested them to say which they considered had been most important to them. Our sample, 1,714 citizens of voting age, was selected in such a way that there is only one chance in 20 that its representation of the country at large is in error by more than four percentage points. Its representation of specific regions of the country or of classes of the population is subject to a somewhat larger margin of error.

The first noteworthy fact is that the public went out of its way to watch the campaign on television. Only about 40 per cent of the homes in the U. S. have television sets, but some 53 per cent of the population saw TV programs on the campaign—a reflection of "television visiting." On the other hand, the campaign news and material in newspapers, magazines and on the radio did not reach all of their respective audiences: more than 80 per cent of the population take daily newspapers and have radios and more than 60 per cent regularly read magazines, but in each case the number following the campaign in these media was smaller than the total audience.

	North-east	Mid-west	South	Far West	Total
Television	71	57	31	57	53
Radio	60	72	74	72	69
Newspapers	80	87	66	83	79
Magazines	35	43	36	52	40

PERCENTAGE OF PEOPLE in various parts of the U. S. who "paid attention to the campaign" through each medium is given in this chart.

	North-east	Mid-west	South	Far West	Total
Television	48	33	13	33	31
Radio	13	27	39	28	27
Newspapers	21	24	21	22	22
Magazines	4	6	5	5	5
More than one medium	9	7	10	8	9
None of the four	5	3	12	4	6

SOURCE OF MOST INFORMATION about the campaign is also given in per cent. Here the differences among the media are much more striking.

	Tele-vision	Radio	News-papers	Maga-zines
Voted for Eisenhower	43	40	44	54
Voted for Stevenson	38	25	33	22
Did not vote	19	35	23	24

INFLUENCE OF MEDIA was difficult to assess. Percentages give behavior of each group which rated one medium their most important source.

There are several points of interest in the geographical picture given by this table. The relatively poor showing of radio in the Northeast indicates that television is supplanting radio in that region. In the South radio leads all other media because that predominantly rural region has relatively few TV sets and a smaller proportion of newspaper readership than other parts of the country.

When people were asked which medium had given them the most information about the campaign, the impact of television became even more striking. In the nation as a whole television, though available to only a minority of the people, led the other media in the number of persons who rated it most informative. Of those who actually watched the campaign on TV (nearly all of whom are exposed to other media), 59 per cent considered television their most important information source. In contrast, among those who followed the campaign in newspapers, which takes in 79 per cent of the population, only 28 per cent rated newspapers as the medium from which they got most of their information. Again there were marked regional differences: the Northeast relied most heavily on television, the South on radio, and the Midwest and West were almost identical in pattern, with television in the lead.

To what sections of the population did television appeal most? The situation is summarized in the table at the top of the next page, which breaks down the responses into population categories. To begin with, the ability to buy a set obviously is an important selective factor: the proportion of people who followed the campaign on television was much smaller in the lowest income group (under $3,000) than in the higher-income groups. (We know that ownership of sets rises with income.) In general the attraction, or availability, of television was highest in metropolitan areas and among the better paid groups—professional and business men, white-collar workers and skilled workers. The rural, low-income and unskilled groups relied mainly on radio. But it seems certain that among these people also television will supplant radio as TV sets, and broadcasting stations, become available to them. Where income and facilities allow, people of all groups tend to turn from radio to television.

When it comes to newspaper and magazine reading, the differences among the occupational and income groups are not so wide. But there are substantial differences according to education: the better educated people were, the more they read about the campaign. And by the same token, the less they valued television as the source of information. The income factor masks this, as well-educated people are more likely to have high incomes and therefore to own television sets. When we separated education from income status, however, we found that people with college degrees or some college education rated television markedly lower than did those with less schooling. This is shown in the table on page 291.

Among people in the higher-income groups, who can afford television sets, the campaign on TV seems to have made a significantly greater impact on those with only a grammar or high school education than on college people. It got its highest rating from people with an income of $5,000 or more who never went to high school. A third of the college group considered TV the most important single source of information on the campaign, but reading played a proportionately larger part in their information-getting than it did for those with less education. This simply bears out the truism that higher education tends to create active rather than passive habits of obtaining information.

Television as a campaign medium has made its main inroads into radio. On the whole the newspapers and magazines so far seem to have held their ground, for their importance was rated as high in the Northeast, where TV sets are most common, as in other regions. But as television expands its coverage and develops techniques for appealing to the various kinds of audiences, it will undoubtedly offer more and more competition for the attention of the voters.

As to how television affected the voting itself, we have no clear evidence. Those who rated television their most important source of information voted for Eisenhower in about the same proportion as those who relied mainly on radio or newspapers [see table on page 288]. Magazine readers were considerably more Republican. Stevenson did somewhat better among the television devotees than among those who preferred radio or newspapers, but these differences may not be very significant, as geographical and other factors also entered into the situation.

We cannot tell from our studies whether television had a distinctive impact on voters. It may be that television, radio and the

	TELEVISION		RADIO		NEWSPAPERS		MAGAZINES	
	Watched Campaign	*Most Important Source*	*Listened to Campaign*	*Most Important Source*	*Read about Campaign*	*Most Important Source*	*Read about Campaign*	*Most Important Source*
Sex of Respondent								
Men	56	31	72	23	83	27	42	6
Women	51	31	68	31	76	18	39	4
Place of Residence								
Metropolitan	76	49	62	14	82	22	35	4
Towns or Cities	47	27	71	30	81	23	43	5
Open Country	36	16	76	41	67	19	38	7
Family Income in 1952								
Under $3000	34	17	73	38	66	20	27	4
$3000 to $4999	60	37	68	23	84	25	40	4
$5000 or above	70	42	67	19	91	22	58	7
Occupation of Head of Household								
Professional people	63	22	80	19	97	30	67	15
Businessmen, managers, officials	69	43	70	21	92	21	60	7
Clerical, sales, office workers	61	38	67	18	89	25	46	7
Skilled workers	61	43	63	20	79	22	32	2
Unskilled workers	36	22	68	39	63	17	22	3
Farmers	33	14	78	42	72	21	53	6
Education of Respondent								
Grammar School	40	25	67	33	65	21	23	2
High School	63	38	69	25	86	21	45	5
College	60	28	80	20	95	28	75	11

SECTIONS OF THE POPULATION who either "paid attention to the campaign" through one or more media, or rated one medium their most important source of information about the campaign, are given in per cent by this table. A selective factor emphasized by the breakdown is the ability to purchase a television set.

newspapers were all equally partisan (or nonpartisan) in covering the campaign and thus had similar effects on their followers. On the other hand, it is also possible that television did have a more potent effect on the individuals who viewed the campaign, but that the degree of its influence is con-cealed by selective factors which were not controlled in our analysis. To measure the comparative effects of the various media it will be necessary to track down these other factors and make allowances for them.

In the 1956 election there will be an opportunity to analyze the effects specifically and precisely, and it is to be hoped that such studies will be undertaken. By then television probably will have expanded its coverage of the nation so greatly that the sociological pattern of its audience, and of the other media audiences, will be substantially different from what it was in the 1952 campaign. The direction of these changes will itself be revealing as to the nature of television's impact.

Another word of caution should be added. The 1952 data apply only to the audiences for political broadcasting and reporting. It cannot be assumed that the same pattern of media preferences would be found in other areas of information or entertainment.

	LESS THAN $3000			$3000 TO $4999			$5000 OR OVER		
	Grammar School	*High School*	*College*	*Grammar School*	*High School*	*College*	*Grammar School*	*High School*	*College*
Television	13	27	10	37	40	29	49	45	33
Radio	40	37	27	26	22	20	14	20	19
Newspapers	20	15	43	25	25	28	18	20	25
Magazines	2	6	7	2	5	7	4	5	13
More than one medium	9	9	10	6	6	15	10	7	9
None of the four	16	6	3	4	2	1	5	3	1

LEVEL OF EDUCATION influenced the choice of the medium which was the most important source of information about the campaign. In general the better educated the respondent to the questionnaire, the more he relied on reading and the less he relied on television. The proportions are given in per cent.

PART THREE

Social-Psychological Processes
Basic to Public Opinion

·6·

The Psychological Basis of Opinion and Attitude

THE PERSONAL SETTING OF PUBLIC OPINIONS: A STUDY
OF ATTITUDES TOWARD RUSSIA

ATTITUDE-CHANGE PROCEDURES AND MOTIVATIONAL PATTERNS

THE EVASION OF PROPAGANDA: HOW PREJUDICED PEOPLE
RESPOND TO ANTI-PREJUDICE PROPAGANDA

EFFECTS OF FEAR-AROUSING COMMUNICATIONS

THE INFLUENCE OF SOURCE CREDIBILITY ON COMMUNICATION
EFFECTIVENESS

EFFECTS OF PREPARATORY COMMUNICATIONS ON REACTIONS
TO A SUBSEQUENT NEWS EVENT

INTERACTION OF PSYCHOLOGICAL AND SOCIOLOGICAL FACTORS
IN POLITICAL BEHAVIOR

THE PERSONAL SETTING OF PUBLIC OPINIONS:
A STUDY OF ATTITUDES TOWARD RUSSIA

M. BREWSTER SMITH

Underlying the rapid growth of public opinion research in the last decade has been the fruitful conception of public opinion as a sum or resultant of the opinions of individual members of the public. Such a conception leads immediately to the question, "What are Smith, Jones, Brown, and all the other members of the public actually thinking on a given subject?"—a question to which the techniques of the sampling survey are providing increasingly adequate answers. When our interest extends to the formative and directing influences on public opinion, the same approach leads us to ask, "Why do Smith, Jones, etc. think as they do?" "Depth interviewing" and its modifications have been developed to press this attack. If we are to take seriously the productive assumption that public opinion is most effectively studied on the individual level, an important source of insights into the dynamics of opinion should be found in the study of opinions as they reflect the personalities of the individuals who hold them. The relatively few studies that have made forays into this area have not attempted a systematic formulation of the ways in which opinions are grounded in the personality.

To develop and test such a coherent psychological approach to public opinion, the intensive methods of clinical personality study and the broader but shallower methods of the polling survey were brought to a focus in a cooperative study of attitudes toward Russia.[1] The study as a whole will be reported elsewhere. Here some of the main findings of a part of the project—a panel survey of attitudes toward Russia among a cross-section of adult men in a New England community—will be described with two ends in view: first, to illustrate the main lines of an attempt to formulate systematically the nature of opinion and its relation to personality factors, and second, to throw some incidental light on the important problem of American attitudes toward Russia.

The initial formulations underlying the opinion surveys emerged from the related clinical study of a small number of individuals, whose personalities and opinions were investigated in the course of over thirty hours of individual interviewing and testing. Our objective in the opinion surveys was to refine and test the generality of formulations that had proved important in understanding the opinions of the individual cases studied by intensive methods.

A "panel" representing adult men in the community was interviewed personally at

[1] This study was made possible by support from the Harvard Laboratory of Social Relations. The writer is particularly indebted to Dr. J. S. Bruner for his participation and guidance in the planning and analysis of the survey phase of the project.

From the *Public Opinion Quarterly*, 1947, 11, 507–523. Reprinted by permission of the author and the publisher.

the men's homes, first in March and then in May, 1947.[2] The first series of interviews, which systematically explored the men's attitudes toward Russia, comprised 319 men. Of these, 250 were re-interviewed in order to obtain information about their personalities. The smaller group taking part in both interviews did not differ markedly in demographic characteristics from the initial group.

Two general approaches were employed in the design of the interviews and in their analysis. The first of these sought to provide a systematic *descriptive analysis* of attitudes toward Russia. Here the attempt was made to delineate an "anatomy" of attitudes that would provide an adequate basis for the "physiology" of a subsequent *functional analysis*. The latter was concerned with the interplay of opinions and other manifestations of the personality.

PRINCIPAL CONCEPTS OF A DESCRIPTIVE ANALYSIS

Descriptively we may fruitfully distinguish how a respondent *feels* about Russia—the *affective* aspect of his attitudes, and what he *thinks* about it—their *cognitive* aspect. On the affective side, there are the familiar factors of *direction*, defined in terms of his approval or disapproval of Russia as a whole or of such features as he may differentiate, and *intensity*, his degree of concern. On the cognitive side, the *informational context* of his attitudes may be distinguished as the structure of his beliefs and knowledge that affect his opinions, and their *time perspective* as his expectations concerning future developments in regard to Russia.

Both the cognitive and affective elements of a person's attitudes patently have much to do with what he wants to *have done* about Russia. The latter aspect we singled out as the individual's *policy orientation*: the measures toward Russia that he supports

and opposes. Policy orientation has the most direct political relevance of the various descriptive categories, but is probably bound more closely than the others to the issues of the moment. All of these categories seem necessary for an adequate description of the attitudes comprising public opinion. A brief consideration of some of our findings may serve to indicate the utility of this scheme, as well as to introduce some necessary elaborations.

Direction, Intensity, and Organization

Probably the first problem to be faced in a description of public opinion toward Russia is its direction: are people favorable or unfavorable? As one might expect, the direction of opinion was found to vary according to the aspect of the problem in question. Direction was therefore studied in terms of the lines along which attitudes toward Russia were commonly differentiated. In most respects, unfavorable opinions prevailed. The extent of disapproval showed marked variation, however, and in regard to Russia's part in World War II, the proportion of respondents who indicated unqualified approval considerably exceeded the disapproving group.

Aspect of Russia	Per Cent Indicating Approval
Russia's part in World War II[3]	46%
Russia's international role[4]	14
Russian system of government[5]	6

One need not rest, however, with the statement that attitudes are predominantly

[2] We are indebted to Dr. Alvin Zander and Dr. Seth Arsenian for their kind coperation in facilitating the field work. Mrs. Betty Lopez, Mr. David Schneider, Mr. Henry Riecken, and the author trained the interviewers, and Mrs. Lopez supervised the interviewing.

[3] The question was: "Looking back on it now, what would you say about Russia's part in the war?" Data are for respondents indicating unqualified approval.

[4] Based on the card question: "Now, about Russia's part in the world today—do you think it has been mostly good, more good than bad, about half good and half bad, more bad than good, or mostly bad?" Data are for respondents giving the first two answers.

[5] Based on the question: "How do you feel about the Russian system of government? What is good and what is bad about it?" Data are for respondents giving favorable answers, with or without qualification. All three questions were asked in the March, 1947, survey.

favorable in some respects and unfavorable in others. The different aspects of Russia involved in the men's attitudes had different weight in determining their over-all evaluation of Russia and their policy orientation. Table 1 shows, for example, that when the respondents were asked to pick out what was most important (among 12 things listed) in making them feel about Russia the way they did, only 9 per cent cited "the part Russia played in World War II," as compared with 23 per cent who selected "Russia's part in spreading world Communism" and 21 per cent who mentioned "the lack of freedom and democracy inside Russia."

Attitudes toward Russia can therefore be conceived as hierarchically *organized*. The aspects in regard to which Russia was likely to be viewed with relative favor turn out only rarely to have had determinative importance for the respondents. This finding suggests the danger of looking to poll results from single questions for an assessment of the over-all direction of opinion. It is vital to know whether direction of opinion in regard to a given aspect is consequential or trivial in the organization of the respondent's attitudes. The conception of the hierarchical organization of a person's attitudes makes it possible to speak consistently of his being favorable to Russia in some respects and unfavorable in others, at the same time that we ascribe to him a generally favorable—or unfavorable—attitude toward Russia.

It is not enough to know the direction of attitudes toward Russia; we must also know their intensity. It seems likely, in fact, that the just-considered hierarchical organization of a person's over-all attitude depends directly on the intensity of his component attitudes. Thus, those features of Russia about which he feels most strongly determine his over-all evaluation of Russia and have most to do with his policy orientation toward the country. Support for this plausible view is found in the survey data. When asked which things were most important and which next most important in making them feel as they did about Russia, some respond-

TABLE 1

RELATIVE IMPORTANCE ATTRIBUTED BY RESPONDENTS TO VARIOUS ASPECTS OF RUSSIA*

Aspects of Russian Foreign Relations		52%
Russia's part in spreading world Communism	23%	
The possibility of war with Russia	11	
The part Russia played in World War II	9	
Russia's treatment of small countries	9	
Aspects of Russian Internal Affairs		46
The lack of freedom and democracy inside Russia	21	
The lack of free enterprise inside Russia	12	
Russia's treatment of the church and religion	7	
Russia's concern for the welfare of her people	5	
The equality given all races and minority groups in Russia	1	
Russian planning and efficiency	**	
Russian backwardness and inefficiency	**	
Russia's point of view on morality and the family	0	
No opinion		2
Total		100%
Number of respondents		250

* The question, asked in May, 1947, was: "As you know, we're interested in the way people look at Russia, what they see in her. I wonder if you could tell me which of these things you think is most important in making you feel about Russia the way you do?" [Show card.]
** Less than 0.5 per cent.

ents indicated two aspects both of which could be classed under "Russian foreign relations" (see Table 1 for the classification), while others named aspects both in the area of "Russian internal affairs." When these extreme groups are compared in respect to the intensity of their attitudes toward Russia's international role, 75 per cent of the former group as against 56 per cent of the latter are found to have said that they were at least "quite a lot" concerned.[6] In this case, then, intensity of opinion was higher with respect to the dominant area

[6] The question, asked in the May survey, was: "How concerned are you about Russia's part in the world today—a great deal, quite a lot, not so much, or none at all?" There were 71 and 59 respondents in the two groups, respectively.

in the organization of the respondents' attitudes. If we want to find the keystones of opinion on a topic, according to this view, we should look for the areas in which the intensity of opinion is highest.

Time Perspective

A study limited to the affective side of opinion—its direction and intensity—would give at best an incomplete understanding of opinion phenomena. The person's beliefs and expectations form the premises for his evaluation and policy orientation. In this regard, the complex pattern of expectations that constitutes the time perspective of a person's attitudes is of major importance. For some, the meaningful future extends little beyond the practical concerns of tomorrow. The opinions of such persons with narrow time perspective surely take form under different influences and have different meaning from those of persons whose broad time perspective includes a careful balancing of future possibilities. Another important distinction is between "short run" and "long run" perspectives. In the long run perspective, the constraint of reality may be more lax than in the short run, while the implications of threat or benefit to the individual are less immediate. Discrepancies between the two views may therefore be expected.

Results from our survey seem to require this distinction between the short and long run. When the respondents were asked,

"Do you think the United States and Russia will get along together better, worse, or about the same in the next few years?",

44 per cent said relations would get "better," while only 15 per cent indicated that they would get "worse." These optimistic findings must be contrasted with the results for the following question:

"Do you expect the United States to fight in another war within the next 50 years? [If 'yes,' 'perhaps,' or 'don't know'] Are there any particular countries that you think we might fight against?"

Here 51 per cent of the sample said they definitely expected another war, and named

Russia as the probable enemy, while an additional 13 per cent thought that if there were to be another war it would be with Russia.

Rather than providing a relatively unbiased assessment of expectations in regard to possible war with Russia, this question appears to have tapped the stereotyped assumption of the inevitability of future wars, a belief that entails little personal threat when held in the relatively remote time perspective of the long run. The high proportion who mentioned Russia as the probable enemy did not necessarily foresee war with Russia; rather, they expected another war eventually and regarded the country with which American relations were most problematic as the most likely candidate. In the short run, nearly half of the respondents expected improvement in relations between the countries at the time of the survey.

Informational Context

Time perspective is only a part of the important cognitive aspect of attitudes. There remains to be considered their informational context—the entire complex of beliefs and knowledge that bears on a person's opinions. At the core of the informational context of our respondents' attitudes toward Russia lay the picture of Russia that they had formed for themselves. The degree of factually correct information—or *informational level*—is only one aspect of the informational context, and not the most important one.

Several questions revealed the prevalent stereotype of Russia among our respondents as one of a dictatorship engaged in spreading world Communism for purposes of self-aggrandizement. The economic aspect of Communism took a relatively secondary place, while considerations of social welfare figured scarcely at all. Beliefs concerning moral and religious practices were marginal to the stereotype, but those that prevailed were still mostly unfavorable in purport. The picture of Russia formed by our respondents was of course intimately related to the direction and policy orientation of their attitudes.

In regard to informational *level*, however, as estimated from scores on a series of seven "fact questions" on Russia, there was practically no relation to the direction of their opinions about Russia's international role nor to their policy orientation. On the other hand, the better informed men were distinctly more optimistic in their time perspective in regard to relations with Russia. They were less likely to pick Russia as a probable enemy in a future war, and, as Table 2 illustrates, they were more likely to expect United States-Soviet relations to improve.

TABLE 2

EXPECTATIONS ABOUT UNITED STATES-
SOVIET RELATIONS, IN RELATION TO
INFORMATIONAL LEVEL

Question: "Do you think the United States and Russia will get along together better, worse, or about the same in the next few years?"

	Well Informed Respondents	Poorly Informed Respondents
Relations will get *better*	53%	35%
Relations will stay the *same*	28	36
Relations will get *worse*	14	16
No opinion	5	13
Total	100%	100%
Number of respondents	155	164

Results such as these call into question the conclusion of Walsh in 1944 that "the decisive factor in American opinion toward Russia appears to be neither class, nor religion, nor political preference, but information."[7] If we re-examine the data as summarized by Walsh, we find that it is again time perspective—expectations about post-war relations—that is related to informational level. It may have been that the extent of information about Russia was also related to the direction and policy orientation of opinion at that time, but the poll results that he quotes do not provide the necessary data. The present scheme has the merit of calling attention to distinguishable

[7] *Cf.* W. B. Walsh, "What the American People Think of Russia," *Public Opinion Quarterly, 8,* No. 4 (1944).

aspects of attitudes that warrant separate consideration.

Policy Orientation

The cognitive and affective aspects of attitudes both underlie their policy orientation, which we have defined as the measures, in this case toward Russia, that the respondent supports and opposes. From the standpoint of the individual as well as from that of political relevance, policy orientation represents in a very real sense the point or focus of his attitudes. Behind the persistent tendency of most people to evaluate the salient features of their world is the need to know where one *stands*, to know in at least a rudimentary way the course of action one would take if the occasion should demand it. In the case of political attitudes on topics of public concern, policy orientation consists for the most part in alignment in terms of publicly defined issues.

At the time of our first survey (just before the President's "Truman Doctrine" speech), the following question provided the principal information on our respondents' policy orientation:

"Some people say that the United States should try to do everything possible to cooperate with Russia and others say that we've got to be tough with Russia. Which do you agree with most?"

Fully 53 per cent said that the United States should be "tough" with Russia, while only a third (33 per cent) favored a policy of "cooperation." In itself, such a finding is not too informative. Further questions revealed, for example, that the majority could not further specify the policies they would favor, while many of those favoring "cooperation" appeared to have had relatively stern policies in mind. In addition, the supporters of a "tough" policy proved to be less easily dislodged from their position, and were more likely to indicate that policy toward Russia would make a difference in their vote for a presidential candidate. Such matters of lability and passivity of policy orientation need investigation to give meaning to the bare proportions found in support of different policies.

Illustrative Relationships

The descriptive features of attitudes that have been distinguished cannot of course be conceived in isolation. The study of their relationships is itself informative, and raises significant problems for functional interpretation. Two examples may serve to emphasize the complexity of the processes involved.

Intensity of concern about Russia was found to be associated with a high level of information about Russia. Among the relatively well-informed respondents, 71 per cent said they were at least "quite a lot" concerned about Russia's part in the world today, in comparison to 52 per cent among the poorly-informed group. The respondents who were higher in intensity were found to have had more frequent and adequate contact with the press, radio, and magazines. Presumably the relationship is a reciprocal one: knowledge leads to concern, while concern leads to receptivity to information. This reciprocal relation between intensity and informational level has an important consequence: holders of the most narrowly stereotyped unfavorable views were not particularly likely to show the intensity that their beliefs might be supposed to warrant. The ignorance underlying their unfavorable stereotypes was part of a complex interaction that also involved their relative lack of concern about Russia.

Another close relationship held between the direction of a person's opinions and the nature of the beliefs forming his informational context. There is good evidence that the interplay here was also reciprocal. The influence of beliefs on the direction of opinion needs no special supporting evidence. The reverse influence is neatly documented by Table 3. There it may be seen that respondents who were relatively favorable toward Russia were more likely than unfavorable respondents to decide erroneously that Russia declared war on Japan shortly before the first atomic bomb. In this case it

seems quite clear that the direction of opinion was causally prior to the belief. It is unlikely that many of the respondents had heard or read the erroneous assertion as a fact, while virtually all of the respondents must have been aware of the true succession of events when they were occurring. In all likelihood, those who answered the question incorrectly had no belief on the matter prior

TABLE 3

BELIEFS CONCERNING RUSSIAN ENTRY INTO THE WAR AGAINST JAPAN, IN RELATION TO DIRECTION OF OPINION TOWARD RUSSIA

Belief	Favorable Respondents*	Unfavorable Respondents*
Russia declared war in 1941	4%	4%
Russia declared war shortly before the first atomic bomb was dropped	49	35
Russia declared war shortly after the first atomic bomb was dropped	38	45
Russia never declared war	4	9
Don't know	5	7
Total	100%	100%
Number of respondents	45	109

* The question, asked in March, 1947, was, "Now about Russia's part in the world today—do you think it has been mostly good; more good than bad, about half good and half bad; more bad than good, or mostly bad?" Data for the first two and the last two categories are compared here.

to the asking of the question, and created on the spur of the moment a belief consistent with the direction of their attitudes.

FUNCTIONAL ASPECTS OF ATTITUDES TOWARD RUSSIA

One cannot pursue the study of attitudes far, however, without inquiring about their function in personality. The correspondence, for example, between the informational context and direction of an attitude can only be understood in terms of the values activating the individual's over-all view of Russia. That is to say, the correspondence between the conception of Russia as a dictatorship and unfavorable attitudes is only "natural" in a public sharing democratic values to which dictatorship is repugnant. Several ways in which attitudes are enmeshed with personality factors emerged from the study. They may reflect or express the person's central values (their *value* function). They may show consistency with his characteristic ways of reacting (their *consistency* function), or perhaps gratify indirectly his basic needs (their *gratification* function). They may form part of his attempt to construct for himself a stable and meaningful world within which he can order his life (their *meaning* function). Finally, they may serve to express his identification with and promote his acceptance by his favored social groups (their *conformity* function).

Personal Values and Attitudes toward Russia

The nature of a person's central values was found to be important for his attitudes toward Russia in several respects. In the first place, the scope of his interests is of primary importance in determining the intensity of his attitudes toward Russia. Secondly, the particular values that he holds dear sensitize him to corresponding aspects of Russia and provide him with standards of judgment. Finally—a consequence of the second point—the nature of his value system has much to do with the hierarchical organization of his attitudes toward Russia.

As might be expected, men with broader interests were much more likely than others to show a relatively high level of intensity in their concern about Russia. We took as one rough index of breadth of interests whether a respondent said that he usually preferred "to be with people who are quite a lot concerned about what is going on in the world, or with people who are mostly interested in their homes and families." Men who gave the former response were also more likely than others to place high value on participation in community affairs and on taking an interest in national and world affairs. As Table 4 shows, 80 per cent of the men with broader interests said that they were at least "quite a lot" concerned about Russia's part in the world. Only 51 per cent of the group with narrower interests, on the other hand,

TABLE 4

INTENSITY OF ATTITUDES TOWARD RUSSIA, IN RELATION TO BREADTH OF INTERESTS

Question: "How concerned are you about Russia's part in the world today? . . ."	*Respondents with Broad Interests**	*Respondents with Narrow Interests**
. . . a great deal	40%	23%
. . . quite a lot	40	28
. . . not so much	19	43
. . . none at all	1	4
No opinion	0	2
Total	100%	100%
Number of respondents	73	110

* The question, asked in May, 1947, was: "By and large, do you usually prefer to be with people who are quite a lot concerned about what is going on in the world, or with people who are mostly interested in their homes and families?"

showed this level of intensity. Intensity of attitudes toward Russia thus formed part of a more general tendency to take an interest in the world beyond hearth and home. A respondent may have prided himself on a range of interests that involved concern about Russia; or, his broader range of interests may have led him to enrich his information about Russia to an extent that he saw its relevance to values that were important to him.

The part played by the person's central values in determining the hierarchical organization of his attitudes toward Russia may be illustrated by the case of the value of *liberty*. Respondents who gave a response classifiable under this value when asked what things in life were most important to them[8] (62 cases) were compared with all others (188 cases) in regard to the aspect of Russia that they said had most to do with their feelings. Of the group stressing liberty, 36

[8] The question was: "We've been talking about some of your present opinions. We are also interested in finding out what sorts of things people think are important in life. I have a question here about what you think is important in life. It's a little hard to put in words right off, I know, but from your experience, what would you say are the most important things to you? What sort of things mean the most to you?"

per cent selected "the lack of freedom and democracy inside Russia," compared with 17 per cent of the remaining respondents—and this was the only notable difference in the responses of the two groups. The degree to which a value is important to the individual can thus determine which aspect of Russia plays the key part in the organization of his attitudes.

The correspondence between a person's central values and the features of Russia around which his attitudes are organized is, however, by no means direct. Some values of greatest importance to him may fail entirely to *engage* with his conceptions of Russia. A good example of this was the value of economic security. The most frequent responses elicited by the open-ended question on personal values referred to economic security—matters like a steady job, good pay, etc. A naive application of the present approach might therefore lead one to expect that individual economic security as espoused by Russia would play an important part in the attitudes toward Russia formed by the men stressing this value. Actually, nothing of the kind was observed. There was no association between economic security as a value and emphasis on corresponding aspects of Russia.

Two facts that are probably sufficient to account for this finding have major implications for a general formulation of the relation between personal values and the organization of attitudes. In the first place, the information in terms of which the respondents might have seen the relevance of Russia to economic security was simply not available in the current media of communication. While it is probably true that the holding of a value sensitizes a person to perceive and digest information that pertains to it, there is a limit to the extent that he will actively seek out information that is not readily available. In this case, the resultant informational context furnished no basis for the *engagement* of the value. Secondly, the value of economic security was likely to entail a rather narrow scope of interests, in the form in which it was important to most

of our respondents. Men who cited it as a central value were likely to show relatively little interest in current events or community participation. Their interests tended to center more exclusively around the daily concerns of a minimal existence. There was therefore small occasion for them to apply the value of economic security in their judgments of Russia.

For a value to enter into a person's attitudes on a topic, then, there are at least two necessary conditions: the scope of the value must be broad enough to apply to the topic, and the information available to the person must contain at least some basis for engaging his value. Taking these limitations into consideration, we may tentatively extend our principle of the organization of attitudes. It was previously suggested that the hierarchical organization of a person's attitudes on a complex topic depends directly on their relative intensity. Now we may say that *intensity is a function of the extent to which a personal value is engaged and of the importance of this engaged value in the hierarchy of the person's central values.*

Other functional relationships to the personality doubtless also enter into the determination of intensity. Here it may be noted that the present statement goes far to clarify the reciprocal relationship found to exist between informational level and intensity. A more adequate informational context permits the person's values to engage more fully with Russia.

Personality Traits and Attitudes toward Russia

A person's attitudes are formed so as to be consistent with his characteristic modes of reaction, and may be pressed into service for the indirect gratification of underlying personality strivings. Although there is a serious limit to the kinds of personality data obtainable from door-to-door interviews, one can, nevertheless, get at some important personality factors in field interviewing. An illustration of the consistency of personality traits with attitudes toward Russia is a case in point.

People characteristically respond to a frustrating situation, according to Rosenzweig,[9] in one of three ways: they may turn aggressively on others ("extrapunitive reaction"), or on themselves ("intrapunitive reaction"), or they may ignore the frustration ("impunitive reaction"). It seemed likely that these characteristic types of reaction might carry over into their opinions. A rough indicator of the first two of these tendencies was provided by responses to the following question:

"When things go wrong, are you more likely to get sore at other people or to feel bad and blame yourself for the situation?"

Table 5 compares the men who said that they usually "get sore at" others with those who said they blamed themselves. It may be seen that those who blame others—the "ex-

TABLE 5

OPINIONS ABOUT RUSSIA, IN RELATION TO
REPORTED REACTION TO FRUSTRATION

Opinion	Tends to Blame Others	Tends to Blame Self
Blames Russia for U.S.-Soviet disagreement*	74%	63%
Expects U.S.-Soviet relations to stay the same or deteriorate	76	49
Favors "tough" U.S. policy toward Russia	67	57
Number of respondents	46	127

* The question, asked in May, 1947, was: "Do you think that the present disagreements between the United States and Russia are *entirely* Russia's fault, *mostly* Russia's fault, the fault of the *United States*, or do you think that *both* countries are equally to blame?" Data are for respondents giving the first two answers. The other questions have already been quoted.

trapunitive" group—were somewhat more likely than the "intrapunitive" respondents to blame Russia for United States-Soviet disagreements and to support a "tough" United States policy toward Russia. This is what one would expect if their attitudes were to be consistent with the rest of their personality tendencies. They were also considerably

[9] Cf. S. Rosenzweig, "Types of Reaction to Frustration," *Journal of Abnormal and Social Psychology*, 29, No. 3 (1934).

more likely to expect United States-Soviet relations to stay the same or deteriorate. The latter finding appears to have been an *indirect* consequence of the distinguishing personality characteristic. Perhaps a greater tendency to blame oneself and the groups with which one was closely identified required a defensive sanguineness from the intrapunitive group. Or, on the other hand, those who saw the United States as at least partly implicated in the blame may have been more likely to think the disagreements between the countries remediable.

Attitudes toward Russia as a Source of Meaning and Stability

On *a priori* grounds one might suppose that a person's attitudes toward any topic serve the important function of sorting out his world of experience into a predictable order that can provide the background for an orderly existence. It is necessary to postulate some such function in order to interpret the constraint that knowledge places on wishful thinking. The present data on attitudes toward Russia provide several illustrations of the tendency of a person's beliefs and expectations to conform to the direction of his attitude. But, not surprisingly, the more informed respondents were less likely to let their feelings enter into their beliefs. For example, of the well-informed group (155 cases), 55 per cent said that they expected the world to become more communistic, compared with 41 per cent of the poorly-informed group (164 cases). Here was an expectation that was surely distasteful to a large majority of the respondents but was accepted by a majority of the well-informed.

That knowledge imposes a constraint on wishful thinking is an obvious fact, but one which should not be neglected. This constraint would seem to depend on the likelihood that beliefs subject to contradiction in the normal course of experience may jeopardize the stability of one's world picture. It is possible to fend off some of the implications of experience, but the need for stability places limits on the development of one's private world.

This formulation leads to an hypothesis regarding the balance between differentiation and consistency in a person's attitudes. An undifferentiated attitude, depicting Russia as all black or all white, has the advantage of simplicity, posing fewer problems of decision than one compounded of shades of gray. But in order that a person's picture of the world may seem trustworthy and have the stability desirable in a map from which he takes his bearings, it must also take into account the situation as he understands it. The extent that a person's attitudes are differentiated, then, may represent the compromise between the need for simplicity and the need for adequacy that best fulfills his requirement of a stable and meaningful conception of his world.

Social Conformity and Attitudes toward Russia

The functional relationships thus far illustrated propose relatively basic relations between the structure and content of attitudes and personality factors. But the content of a person's attitudes may also be taken over more or less bodily from his associates or from prestigeful persons as a way of expressing identification with them and facilitating their acceptance. This pressure toward conformity is rooted in the person's basic needs for acceptance and approval. It is not, however, the sole or perhaps even the principal source of influence promoting relative uniformity of opinion within face-to-face groups. In addition there is the fact that members of such groups are likely to have common informational contexts on a topic, both because they share similar sources of information and because members of the group are themselves major sources of information for one another. Furthermore, they are also likely to have acquired from one another and from similar life experiences a relatively similar value outlook.

The survey findings were in keeping with the supposition that conformity plays an important role in the determination of a person's attitudes. Our data also suggest the interesting possibility that the need for conformity may favor *shifts* in the total distribution of opinion. A simple comparison of the men's own opinions with those that they ascribe to their friends reveals a tendency for the friends to be considered slightly more anti-Russian:[10]

Evaluation of Russia's International Role	Own Opinions	Estimate of Friends' Opinions
Mostly good or More good than bad	11%	7%
About half good and half bad	29	21
More bad than good or Mostly bad	59	66
No opinion	1	6
Total	100%	100%
Number of respondents	250	250

Such a finding may be characteristic of a state of affairs in which the "anti" position is more strongly and vociferously held than the "pro"—as our data indicate was certainly the case in regard to Russia at the time of the survey. To the extent that the need for approval creates real pressure toward conformity, conformity must be toward the opinions of others *as the person understands them*. When one direction of opinion has relatively higher "audibility" than the other, conformity may be expected to lead not merely toward uniformity but toward uniformity in the direction of the more audible opinion.

CONCLUSION

While the individual attitudes underlying public opinion on any topic are indeed complex, their complexity need not preclude systematic analysis. All too often, investigations of public opinion have proceeded to devise questions about this or that aspect of a public issue on a hit-or-miss basis. A framework for the description of attitudes is clearly needed.

The descriptive scheme that has been

[10] Data are for the May, 1947, survey.

developed here in connection with attitudes toward Russia should prove generally useful. Cognitive and affective elements as well as policy orientation can be fruitfully distinguished in most political attitudes. A systematic approach of this sort throws into perspective important relationships among attitudinal features from which a more adequate understanding of opinion processes may be attained.

Such an adequate understanding, however, requires insight into the functions that opinions serve in the psychological economy of the person who holds them—the ways in which opinions are embedded in personality. We have illustrated in connection with attitudes toward Russia a first approximation toward an analysis of these functions. Further investigations embodying a functional approach should add to the understanding of the dynamics of opinion on particular topics and in different publics, and be a promising source of advance in the theory of public opinion.

ATTITUDE-CHANGE PROCEDURES AND MOTIVATING PATTERNS

IRVING SARNOFF, DANIEL KATZ, AND CHARLES McCLINTOCK

A major difficulty in the field of attitude research has been the oversimplification of problems in terms of a narrow theory of motivation. The perceptual model of the Gestalt school sees the situation as one in which people strive toward a more inclusive and stable organization of the psychological field; thus the individual tries to reconcile conflicting impressions, seeks to know what the world is like, and to make sense of it. According to this model, individuals will change their attitude in rational fashion if they are presented with facts and reasons which accord with their own beliefs and assumptions. Another motivational model has followed the reward-punishment pattern and has seen attitudes as part of an adaptive response to the social world. Group norms become of first importance since the individual must have acceptance and support from his group. Finally, the personality theorist and clinician emphasize the internal dynamics underlying attitudes in which the individual's need to preserve his self-image and self-integrity become more important than external reward and punishment.

The Rational Model: The Search for Meaning

This approach emphasizes the fact that people seek to understand their world and to achieve a consistent picture of its complexities. They attempt to deal with the realities of the matter which are within the

Revised for this volume from "The Motivational Basis of Attitude Change," *Journal of Abnormal and Social Psychology*, 1954, 49.

framework of their own experiences and to deal with these realities in an understanding fashion. The blind emotionalism and the stupid irrationalities of a person are not necessarily as blind or as irrational if we took the trouble to understand his particular set of experiences and his frame of reference. "Emotional processes are as a rule under the direction of cognitive factors, and are controlled by a trend to find relevant relations." (2, p. 275)

It is assumed that every person has a need to explore, to know about the external world. This need may be observed in the meanderings of naive children, as well as in the controlled experiments of trained scientists. Often this quest for information seems to be a curiosity which is entirely self-contained. At other times, it appears to be in the service of other motives, such as survival or the desire to master the environment.

Considered in this light, attitudes may sometimes be a function of the range of information which has been accessible to the individual in regard to certain target objects. Let us assume, for example, that a curious child has heard of the word *Negro* for the first time. He goes to his parents for information and is told, among other things, that Negroes are bad people, stupid, dirty, animal-like. Assuming that he has heard no information to the contrary, that he has had no actual experience with Negroes, and that his parents have always supplied him with reliable facts about things, it follows that he will be inclined to accept this statement about Negroes. Even if the child is entirely free of other motivational needs to maintain this attitude, it is likely to persist until his contact with Negroes indicates to him that not all of them are stupid or until he is confronted by contrary information which he considers to be more reliable than that which his parents gave him.

Reward and punishment

Some of the principles of learning theory may be applied to certain types of attitude formation. Specifically, these principles are involved when attitudes are adopted as a consequence of externally applied rewards and punishments. A white youngster in rural Mississippi may begin life on very favorable terms with his Negro playmates. Still, as he matures, his adjustment to and acceptance by the white community depend in some measure upon the extent to which he has come to share the prevalent anti-Negro biases. If he rejected these biases, he might be vulnerable to social ostracism and even more severe manifestations of disapproval.

Ego defense

In his social relationships every individual attempts to gratify his basic physiological needs and the socially acquired ones. Some individuals, because of the strength, maturity, and integration of their egos, are able to perceive and tolerate the existence of their inner drives, including those which may be socially taboo. Such a person can, in terms of a realistic assessment of the social situation, decide which impulses to express and which ones to suppress. It is possible for him to approach others in a straightforward manner; to react to them in terms of how they, as unique individuals, actually fulfill or frustrate his needs. His social attitudes are likely to be appropriate since he is able to differentiate clearly between what is going on inside him and what is emanating from others.

At the other end of the scale of ego strength there are persons who are obliged to use devious means of gratifying their impulses. In an attempt to resolve inner conflict, they minimize or obliterate certain aspects of their emotional life. This deflection of impulse from conscious awareness does not destroy it. On the contrary, it continues to press for overt expression and requires the individual to expend considerable energy in keeping it below the threshold of consciousness. Despite the most strenuous counter measures (repression and other mechanisms of defense), the impulse tends to attain at least partial expression and gratification. This expression is achieved by means of symptom formation, a device which, however incapacitating it may be, serves a dual and somewhat paradoxical function:

1. It permits expression of the unconscious impulse.

2. It prevents the individual from becoming aware of the existence of the unconscious impulse.

Attitudes may thus function as ego defenses, and may be viewed as symptoms. For example, the type of bigot described in the California studies is one who cannot accept his own hostile impulses. (1) By projecting them onto others, he gains gratification of his impulses while maintaining the fiction that these impulses originate in others rather than in himself.

Rather than attempting to elaborate any one of these three models to take account of all psychological phenomena concerned with attitudes, it seemed wiser to us to accept their essential contributions and to specify the conditions under which one or another of the theories best accounts for the phenomena under investigation. We feel that all people develop and alter their attitudes in terms of all three motivational contexts. Certain types of people, however, will be more likely to acquire attitudes on the basis of one kind of motivational pattern than will other people. Moreover, attitudes formed in the service of a given type of motivation will tend to show different characteristics than attitudes acquired in the interests of other motivational sources. In general, to take one important example, the dimension of the appropriateness or inappropriateness of an attitude, i.e., the amount of gross distortion of the target or referent of the attitude, will be related to the third type of motivation, ego defensiveness. Since the attitude has the function of protecting the individual from facing his internal conflicts, it will not be referred to the external world for reality testing. Moreover, any prediction of change or any attempts to modify attitudes must take account of these different motivational bases: (1) attitudes may be acquired in the interest of rationally structuring the individual's world and of testing what the world is like; (2) they may be

formed as an adaptation to rewards and punishments imposed by the social situation; and (3) the attitude may be a function of the ego defensive needs of the individual. It follows that the processes which produce a change in the first type of attitudinal structure will not necessarily be operative for the second or third types of structure. Where the individual's attitude is based upon his search for meaning, his attitude can be changed by giving him more information about the cognitive object. Where the attitude is based, however, upon a motive like group approval or desire to advance in the group, additional information which opposed this attitude may have no impact. Where the attitude reflects the individual's manner of resolving his inner conflicts, he will resist changes which would be in his own self interest.

It should be noted, moreover, that attempts to change the ego defensive individual which are based upon the logic of the first two approaches may actually reinforce his old attitudes. These appeals really assume either (a) the individual is interested in a more accurate and more complete knowledge of the world, or (b) he is primarily concerned with maximizing the satisfaction of his conscious needs. If, however, he is primarily concerned with avoiding a direct facing of his own internal conflicts, then he will protect himself from such a possibility the moment he senses an attempt to make him change. The well-known phenomenon of resistance is an example in point. The resistance generated to protect the ego results in a blanket rejection of the change situation, a perceptual distortion of what it is like and an emotional reinforcement of the attitude. Though we recognize the importance of resistance in other contexts, we have slighted its role in attitude change. Hence, persuasion and propaganda can have negative rather than positive effects.

It is not our thesis, however, that ego defenses cannot be breached, but that different procedures are involved in dealing with these defenses than with non-conflicted motives.

ADAPTING CHANGE-PROCEDURES TO THE MOTIVATIONAL BASIS OF ATTITUDE

I. *Changing Attitudes Through Attacking the Cognitive Object and the Frame of Reference in Which It Is Perceived: The Rational Approach*

Inappropriate attitudes, though more characteristically acquired as ego defense, can also be acquired (a) in the interests of social rewards and punishments and (b) in the functioning of the perceptual-cognitive process itself. In the last mentioned instance, the assumption is that the individual acquires beliefs either out of intellectual curiosity, reality-testing, or a desire for cognitive structure in terms of having to know what his world is really like. The belief or attitude may be inappropriate because the individual comes into contact with only a limited aspect of reality. In practice, of course, a number of these processes occur simultaneously. The individual takes on certain attitudes because he wants to be accepted as a group member, but the beliefs he acquires must make sense to him with respect to being accurate pictures of the world he knows.

The theory would be that when new facts are presented they result in cognitive reorganization rather than exclusion or blocking. In addition, sophisticated cognitive theory assumes that perception occurs in a frame of reference which is the momentary product of a number of possible forces. Pressing internal needs or the objective nature of the situation may result in a temporary frame in which things are perceived in relation to that frame. Since people already possess definite standards for perceiving Negroes,[1] it is important, if we are to change their perceptions, to be sure that the dominant frame of reference at the time the materials are introduced is not the product of these old standards. Essentially, this calls for the activation of a "new" frame without any reference to the old standards. Once the "new" frame is operative, material bearing upon the old cognitive object can

[1] Attitudes toward Negroes were the dependent variable in our experimental program.

be introduced without the old standard operating as a censor. Specifically this can be accomplished through experimentation in the form of the creation of a frame of cultural relativity and cultural causation, and then the introduction of information about Negroes.

II. *Changing Attitudes Through the Application of Social Rewards and Punishments*

1. THE USE OF GROUP NORMS   One of the major reasons for attitude change is the desire to gain the social approval of others. It is natural that experiments in social psychology have concentrated heavily upon the manipulation of group norms. The desire for social approval is a broad term, however, covering both deep-lying affiliation needs and the immediate rewards of adapting to the group situation. We are concerned here primarily with this latter type of conformity, namely the acceptance of group standards because of their immediate reward character. For example, the individual who accepts the values of the group has increased his chances of being liked by his fellows, of moving up in the group structure or of sharing in the returns from group effort. In these terms, it would first be necessary to find out what the individual's relation to the group is and what types of satisfaction he derives from group membership. If we know these facts, then we are in a better position to predict changes in attitude as a result of a changed perception of group norms. Similarly we could predict those individuals who would tend to maintain their attitudinal position independent of the group. The assumption here is at the simple level that the more the rewards and the greater the sanctions the group has, the more effective will a changed perception of the group position be. In the persuasion pattern the attempt is made to achieve cognitive restructuring through making the individual see new possibilities in achieving his goals. In the use of group norms, the change is more external in that the group norm is changed and the individual merely moves with it.

2. RESTRUCTURING THE INDIVIDUAL'S VALUE

SYSTEMS The great bulk of the efforts to change attitudes in the world of affairs is through persuasion and argumentation, in which an appeal is made to existing value structures. Some value system, other than that to which the target object is ordinarily connected, is invoked, and the necessity of meeting its requirements is stressed. In inducing change in the manner described under the *rational* approach, the emphasis was placed upon the perceptual side of the process, in getting people to look at the old object in a new frame of reference. Thus subjects would have had to take the further step of restructuring their attitudes themselves. No direct attempt would be made to suggest that they should not pursue a discriminatory policy toward Negroes. In this second type of experiment, however, the attempt will be to restructure their attitudes for them through making the specific connections between the target object and a different set of values. This can be done (1) through exploiting a very powerful system, (2) through utilizing more different values for the change than existed for the old attitudinal structure, and (3) through showing how the values tied to the target are blocked by social reality and are not in fact being achieved. In practice, all three methods are combined to produce change. From the point of view of content, the persuasive technique frequently relies upon demonstration of a fusion between the individual's self interest and socially desirable goals. It further shows the feasibility of the alternative suggested, as contrasted to the impracticality of all other alternatives. These relationships have been systematically formulated and experimentally demonstrated by H. Peak and her colleagues (4, 5).

The theory implicit in these persuasive techniques is that the individual will restructure his psychological field to maximize the attainment of his goals and values. Personality theorists have suggested that this theory is correct within limitations, namely, that when ego needs are threatened, the individual will respond to persuasive efforts by blocking and resistance. The resistance may result in more strongly reinforced attitudes than was true before the attempted persuasion. Again, the prediction is that the change attempts will have differential effects, depending upon the personal needs of the subject. Moreover, since the appeal to values operates more at the motivational than the perceptual level, the prediction is that for non-ego defensive people there will be more change than in the first and second series of experiments. For the ego defensive people there will be less change because of the phenomenon of resistance.

III. *Changing Attitudes by Attacking Ego-Defensive Forces Through the Use of Catharsis and Direct Interpretation*

Two techniques widely employed in psychotherapy which have possible application to group situations are permissive catharsis and direct interpretation. The basic objective is to help the individual attain insight and to restructure his attitudes accordingly.

1. PERMISSIVE CATHARSIS The free ventilation of thought and feeling in an accepting interpersonal atmosphere is an integral part of virtually all schools of psychotherapy. It is generally assumed that this type of expression helps the patient to change in the following ways:

(a) It offers him relief from the tension of burdensome affects such as guilt and hostility. The very act of expressing these feelings is supposed to drain off energy which would necessitate the formation of various somatic and psychic symptoms.

(b) It permits him to verbalize and hence objectify his inner conflicts. Such objectification leads to clearer self-perception. This clarification in turn makes it possible for him to utilize his intellect more effectively in choosing among alternative means of resolving his conflicts.

2. DIRECT INTERPRETATION This technique uses a combination of logic and suggestion; patients are confronted with psychological explanations of their behavior. These explanations are supposed to give them immediate insight into the internal factors (motivations) which determine their overt behavior. The patient is then to bring the weight of his own common sense to bear

upon the proffered insight and to change his behavior in the light of this newly acquired knowledge. Thus, the lengthy process of uncovering is short-circuited and the patient is directly informed about the underlying motives of which he had previously been unaware. In employing this sort of approach, the therapist is generally obliged to rely upon the degree of authoritativeness with which the patient invests him and the sources (research findings, theory) on which he bases his interpretation.

It is granted, however, that these techniques will not be effective for all ego defensive people. In some cases resistances may still be too strong to be affected, either by catharsis or by direct interpretation. The assumption is made, therefore, that people who already have enough insight to be concerned about their own conflicts and to be dissatisfied with some of their own behavior will respond to these techniques. Just as individual therapy can make little headway with patients who do not want to be helped, so group procedures will affect only those group members who are dissatisfied with their self-image, even though they do not understand the basis of their conflict.

In this type of experiment the direct interpretation can consist of psychological explanations of the dynamics of scapegoating and of displaced and repressed hostility. The objective will be to give self insight. Individuals who are more insightful at the start will apply the interpretation to themselves more readily than individuals lacking insight. One advantage of the technique of direct interpretation is that it can be used in printed materials and is not confined to interpersonal communication.

SOME EXPERIMENTAL FINDINGS

A. *Rational Persuasion Compared with Authoritarian Suggestion*

An experiment was devised by M. Wagman to test the proposition that different personality types would respond differentially to various kinds of change procedure. (6) It was postulated that non-authoritarian people would be more affected by rational persuasion than would authoritarian people, whereas the authoritarian personality would be more responsive to suggestion from power figures than would the non-authoritarian person. It was predicted that even when the influence exerted was in the direction of greater tolerance for minority groups, the authoritarian type of individual would be moved more by suggestion coming from authoritative sources than by a reasoned presentation of facts and arguments.

The measure of authoritarianism was the F scale developed by Frenkel-Brunswik and her colleagues, an instrument designed to give degrees of authoritarian character structure. The authoritarian suggestion consisted of statements attributed to power figures, which emphasized institutional values of efficiency and orderliness for their own sake, rather than as means to ends. The rational persuasion consisted of materials presenting facts and reasons based upon scientific study and historical and anthropological considerations of racial differences.

The subjects, 250 University of Michigan undergraduates, were given pre-measures at the first session, the influence attempt at a second session, and post-measures at a third session. In the first session they were given not only the attitude scales, as measures of the dependent variable, but also the F scale and the Michigan completion test as measures of personality characteristics. In the second session, different influence treatments were used. Approximately 70 subjects received the authoritarian suggestion which was designed to move them in a less prejudiced direction; 70 subjects were given the rational persuasion materials, again directed toward movement toward less prejudice; a third group of 70 subjects was given the authoritarian suggestion designed to move them in a more prejudiced direction. Finally, 40 subjects served as a control group. In a third session, post-measures were taken which repeated the original attitude scales. The influence attempt was separated from the pre- and post-measures by the use of different experimenters and by structuring the situation as part of a different investigation.

The results of this experiment can be summarized as follows:

(1) The rational persuasion materials were more effective in producing more favorable attitudes toward Negroes for the non-authoritarian than for the authoritarian subjects.

(2) A number of the authoritarian subjects showed greater prejudice after the persuasion attempt than they had originally shown.

(3) The authoritarian suggestion, when used to produce more favorable attitudes toward Negroes, had greater success for authoritarian subjects than did the rational persuasion.

(4) The authoritarian suggestion, when used to produce less favorable attitudes, was more successful with the authoritarian than the non-authoritarian subjects.

(5) A number of non-authoritarian subjects reacted negatively to the authoritarian suggestion designed to move them away from a liberal position, i.e., they became even more liberal.

B. *Rational Persuasion Compared With Self-Insight*

The limitations of both prestige suggestion and rational persuasion are implied in the above experiment. These attempts are differentially effective and if used with certain types of people can actually have negative effects. Moreover, authoritarian suggestion in one direction may produce change only as long as counter suggestions do not occur. In a second experiment, rational persuasion was compared with the technique of direct interpretation.

The subjects were 300 women students at the Michigan State Normal College at Ypsilanti, divided into their own sorority and dormitory groupings. The experiment was in three stages. In stage one, all subjects took a battery of personality tests and filled out a number of measures designed to test their beliefs, feelings, and attitudes toward relations with minority groups. The per-

sonality measures consisted of: (1) The Bender Gestalt test, (2) the F scale of Authoritarian Character Structure, (3) the Michigan Completion Test, scored for patterns of ego defensiveness, (4) a specially constructed thematic apperception test designed to get at hostility toward Negroes, and (5) fairly direct questions about the nature and kind of felt internal conflict. The attitude measures consisted of stereotyped statements about Negro characteristics, a revised Bogardus Social Distance scale, and twelve specific action issues. In addition, the subjects indicated their perception of the group position on two of the issues. In the second session, influence-attempts to change attitudes were introduced and the attitude scales were repeated at the end of the session. In the third session some six weeks later, the attitude measures were administered at the start of the session, then different feed-back procedures were employed, and finally some of the attitude scales were repeated before the groups were dismissed.

The primary change manipulation took place during the second session. Two different experimental procedures were employed. One consisted of the rational persuasion materials, very similar in nature to the experiment already described in this section. The purpose here was to give the individual an opportunity to restructure his beliefs in relation to factual and logical materials. The second influence procedure used on comparable groups of subjects employed the technique of direct interpretation. A case study was presented of a girl who had never acquired insight into her own hostilities and inadequacies and who developed in consequence certain social prejudices. The case was presented sympathetically and with sufficient similarity of background to the subjects so that they would have little difficulty in identifying with her. They were asked specifically after reading the case story to indicate how relevant they thought this analysis was to the problem of prejudice in general. They were also asked whether they found themselves employing any of the psychological mechanisms which the girl in the story unconsciously utilized. The rationale for this procedure was that it might give some degree of insight to girls who already were not wholly satisfied with their own behavior. Thus, if they could see how all of us use defense mechanisms to buttress our own egos at the expense of other people, they might restructure some of their beliefs which have a defensive function.

The major purpose of the third session (some six weeks later) was to obtain a measure over time of stability of changes which had been produced in the second session. Since the girls had to be assembled for the taking of this test, their coming together was also used for trying different feed-back procedures to produce further change. The measures of the dependent variable (the attitude scales) were given at the very beginning of the meeting. Then some groups were merely given a reinforcement of the original procedure they had been subjected to. Other groups were influenced further through the use of three group variables: (1) presentation of group norms, (2) a discussion of the treatment of Negroes in relation to the value of national security, (3) a similar discussion carried to the point of commitment to specific propositions about the problem. In both the second and third sessions measures were taken of perception of group consensus.

Though the analysis of all the data in this experiment has not been completed, these findings can be reported:

(1) The interpretation materials produced more liberal attitudes toward Negroes than did the rational persuasion attempt.

(2) The changes produced by direct interpretation were more permanent than were the changes produced by rational persuasion. After the six-week period there was more of a tendency to move back toward original position for people subjected to

rational persuasion than for people subjected to direct interpretation.

(3) The subjects who originally saw themselves as very much like the group persisted in estimating the group as close to their own position during the whole change process. This confirms T. Newcomb's concept of a fairly constant tolerance by the individual for his own non-conformity. (7) People with a narrow limit either conform to changing group attitudes or autistically distort their perception of where the group is. And the most significant finding here is that this behavior during the attitude experiments was related to personality measures of conformity obtained from the Michigan Completion Test and the California F scale. (3)

REFERENCES

1. ADORNO, T. W., Frenkel-Brunswik, E., Levinson, D. J. & Sanford, R. N. *The Authoritarian Personality*. New York: Harper, 1950.

2. ASCH, S. E. "The Doctrine of Suggestion, Prestige, and Imitation in Social Psychology." *Psychol. Rev.*, 1948, 55, 250-276.

3. BARLOW, M. F. "Security and Group Approval as Value Systems Related to Attitude Change." Ph.D. Dissertation, University of Michigan, 1953.

4. CARLSON, E. R. "A Study of Attitude Change and Attitude Structure." Ph.D. Dissertation, University of Michigan, 1953.

5. ROSENBERG, M. J. "The Experimental Investigation of a Value Theory of Attitude Structure." Ph.D Dissertation, University of Michigan, 1953.

6. WAGMAN, M. "An Investigation of the Effectiveness of Authoritarian Suggestion and Non-Authoritarian Information as Methods of Changing the Prejudiced Attitudes of Relatively Authoritarian and Non-Authoritarian Personalities." Ph.D. Dissertation, University of Michigan, 1953.

7. WHITE, M. S. "Attitudes Change as Related to Perceived Group Consensus." Ph.D Dissertation, University of Michigan, 1953.

THE EVASION OF PROPAGANDA: HOW PREJUDICED PEOPLE RESPOND TO ANTI-PREJUDICE PROPAGANDA[1]

EUNICE COOPER AND MARIE JAHODA

A. PROPAGANDA EVASION AS A PROBLEM

Communication research points up the fact that it is difficult in general for a communication to reach people who are not already in favor of the view it presents. It is well-known that many people evade points of view which are at odds with their own by the simple expedient of not exposing themselves to such views. Those who most need to be influenced by certain communications are least likely to be reached by them (6, 7).

Thus, the bulk of the listeners to educational radio programs are among the better educated segment of the listening audience. A study of a radio program designed to promote friendship, coöperation, and mutual respect among various immigrant groups showed that a program about Italians was listened to chiefly by Italians, a program about Poles was listened to chiefly by Poles, and so on (5). In the same way, anti-prejudice propaganda is likely to reach or

affect a considerably smaller proportion of the prejudiced group in the population than of the non-prejudiced.

This is, of course, not a denial of the value of pro-democratic propaganda. The audience of such propaganda is composed of sympathizers, neutrals, and opponents. Although the opponents may be largely unaffected, the other two groups may still be influenced. Here, however, we are chiefly concerned with the reaction of the prejudiced person to anti-prejudice propaganda. What happens when in an experimental situation they are involuntarily confronted with it?

There are, theoretically, two possibilities: they may fight it or they may give in to it. But our research in this field has shown us that many people are unwilling to do either: they prefer not to face the implications of ideas opposed to their own so that they do not have to be forced either to defend themselves or to admit error. What they do is to evade the issue psychologically by *simply not understanding the message*.

It is true that understanding of communications is related to the amount of education of the audience. However, even among people on the same educational level, those who are prejudiced are more apt to

[1] One of the activities of the Department of Scientific Research of the American Jewish Committee is to test the potential effectiveness of anti-prejudice communications. This article is based upon a number of studies conducted by the Department.

From *The Journal of Psychology*, 1947, 23, 15-25. Reprinted by permission of the authors and the publisher.

misunderstand a message than the unprejudiced.[2]

This article deals with two aspects of the problem of propaganda evasion: its mechanisms and its cultural basis. The first part is drawn from evidence collected in about a dozen studies of the public's response to anti-prejudice propaganda; the second part is speculative and hypothetical. Considerably more research would be needed to verify our tentative ideas on the motivation of propaganda evasion.

B. THE MECHANISMS OF PROPAGANDA EVASION

The evidence for the techniques employed by a prejudiced respondent in order to avoid understanding is, of necessity, inferential. The process of evasion occurs in the respondent's mind some time between the presentation of a propaganda item and the respondent's "final" statement in answer to the interviewer's questions. The mechanisms involved in evasion, although they may be rather complicated and may appear to be deliberate, are in most cases probably unconscious. It is impossible to determine from even depth interview data at what level of consciousness the process occurs, that is, to what extent the respondent is aware of his evasion.

Evidence of the evasion process is often revealed in the course of the interview, if the interview is considered as an integrated whole and individual statements are not accepted in a disjointed, static fashion as isolated answers to isolated questions.

1. Identification Avoided—Understanding "Derailed"

An example of how a dynamic interpretation of the whole course of the interview reveals evidence of the process of evasion is provided by a recent study of a cartoon series. The cartoons lampoon a character dubbed Mr. Biggott.[3] To bring home the

satire of the cartoon, he is shown as a rather ridiculous prudish figure, with exaggerated anti-minority feelings.

What the producers of the cartoon intended was roughly this: The prejudiced reader would perceive that Mr. Biggott's ideas about minorities were similar to his own; that Mr. Biggott was an absurd character; that it was absurd to have such ideas —that to have such ideas made one as ridiculous as Mr. Biggott. He would, then, as the final stage in this process, presumably reject his own prejudice, in order to avoid identification with Mr. Biggott.

The study showed a very different result. Prejudiced respondents who understood the cartoon initially—that is, they went through the first three stages mentioned above—went to such lengths to extricate themselves from their identification with Mr. Biggott that in the end they *misunderstood the point of the cartoon*. To use the phrase of the writers of this report, there was a "derailment of understanding."

Here is an example of one of the ways in which the cartoons were misunderstood:[4] The respondent at first identified with Mr. Biggott, saying, among other things which indicated this identification, "I imagine he's a sour old bachelor—(laughing)—I'm an old bachelor myself." He also seemed to be aware of Mr. Biggott's prejudices. As the interview progressed, in order to differentiate himself from Mr. Biggott he concentrated on proving that Mr. Biggott's social status was inferior, that he was a *parvenu*. This led to a loss of focus on the real problems presented by the cartoons.

Sixth generation American blood. He don't want anything but sixth generation American blood! Ha! That's pretty good.

[2] There is evidence for this in a number of studies conducted by this Department and by the Bureau of Applied Social Research of Columbia University.

[3] Several Mr. Biggott studies were done. The one from which the following examples are drawn was conducted for the Department of Scientific Research of the American Jewish Committee by the Bureau of Applied Social Research of Columbia University.

[4] In the particular cartoon discussed, Mr. Biggott is shown lying in a hospital bed with a doctor in attendance, and saying that for his blood transfusion he wants only "sixth generation American blood."

At this point the man begins to focus on Mr. Biggott's social inferiority and his attention is deflected from the issue of prejudice more and more as the process continues:

Well, you know, *I'm eighth generation myself*, of English descent on both sides. My family settled up on Connecticut, C———, Connecticut, in 1631. A sixth generation American—he's a man of six generations himself. *Maybe less than that. . .* (What is the doctor thinking?) He's astonished, I guess. He thinks this man has an awful nerve. He looks like a crabby old man. *He may not be the best blood either.*

Mr. Biggott's prejudices have become snobbish pretensions and as the interview continues, the respondent regards him more and more as a "lower class" symbol:

(Do you know anyone like him?) *No, I have no interest in knowing anyone like that. I've known some like him* up in C———. This particular man was in the Congregational Church—*of course* that's the church to which my family belongs. . . . He made plenty of money as an undertaker too. You know, my father died a few years ago. The burial cost $180. He knew that at the time I didn't have any money. He trusted me, let me pay it gradually. But, you know, he charged me 6 per cent interest. Yes, *that's what he charged me. Even though he knew my family and all that. . . .*

By this time the issue of prejudice has been completely side-tracked. Biggott reminds the respondent only of an old acquaintance whom he considers rather crude. At the end the cartoons become for him only a kind of test for judging personality characteristics:

(What do you think is the purpose of these cartoons?) To get the viewpoint of anyone. From the viewpoint you can form some opinion of that person. You can get different answers—some agree and some say something else. You can compare them and draw some conclusions . . . (What is the artist trying to do?) To get the *viewpoint of people to see if they coincide with the artist's idea of character* and all. Some would, some would differ.

In the same study there were other variations in what might be called the path of the misunderstanding. Some people caricatured Mr. Biggott, made him a target of ridicule; others made him appear intellectually inferior; still others transformed him into a foreigner or a Jew. Regardless of the particular line developed, the process is essentially the same. Whether or not a respondent follows one of these lines rather than another is probably a matter of temperament and character.

Such complicated forms of arriving circuitously at misunderstanding when there is good evidence that spontaneous understanding was present at first are, of course, not the only form of evasion that the prejudiced person takes to escape facing the criticism implied in the message of a propaganda item; but they are the most revealing forms as to the influence of prejudice on comprehension. The conflict about having prejudices must be strong, and at the same time the prejudice must be deeply rooted in the character structure. Under the pressure of this psychological predisposition the respondent takes the roundabout way of first understanding the content of the propaganda item; then identifying with the prejudiced figure, perceiving the criticism of his own position involved in the item; inventing means of disidentification from the special instance of prejudice depicted by the propaganda item; and in the process losing the original understanding of the message. Apparently this process occurs frequently; the unconscious ingenuity of the respondent sets in mainly during the last two steps.

2. *The Message Made Invalid*

In other cases the process of disidentification leads to more rationalized argumentation. Understanding has been admitted too openly to permit distortion of the message. The respondent accepts the message on the surface but makes it invalid for himself in one of two ways. He may admit the general principle, but claim that in exceptions one is entitled to one's prejudices; or he may admit that the individual item is convincing in itself, but that it is not a correct picture of usual life situations involving the minority group discussed. There is evidence in our studies of both types.

The first type of distortion occurred as a common reaction to a protolerance propaganda booklet. This was presented in the form of a series of well-drawn comic cartoons exposing the absurdity of generalizations about various groups. It concluded with the Golden Rule, "Live and let live." Prejudiced persons frequently followed the whole story with interest and amusement to the end, accepting the Golden Rule, but added: "But it's the Jews that don't let you live; they put themselves outside the rule."

Perhaps even more frequent is the tendency to accept the isolated story presented in propaganda as "just a story." The need to maintain the attention value of a propaganda item through a human-interest appeal has led many propagandists to exemplify by one outstanding dramatic story the general principle for which they wish to enlist support. This technique was used in a broadcast dramatization, "The Belgian Village," presented on the CBS series, "We, the People." In the story, a Jewish couple in an occupied Belgian Village are saved by the loyal support of the villagers who hide them from the Gestapo. The dramatization was followed by a direct appeal, spoken by Kate Smith, for sympathy and tolerance toward the Jews. Considerably more of the apparently prejudiced respondents[5] than of the others in the test audience refused to admit the applicability of this dramatic story to other situations. They called it an "adventure story," a "war story," they discussed the dramatic highlights with great interest, but treated the explicit appeal attached to the incident either as if it had not occurred or as an unjustified artificial addition.

3. Changing the Frame of Reference

There remain to be discussed two other forms of misunderstanding by prejudiced persons. One of them is of greater interest than the other: in these cases the prejudiced person's perception is so colored by his prejudice that issues presented in a frame of reference different from his own are transformed so as to become compatible with his own views. Quite unaware of the violation of facts he commits, he imposes on a propaganda item his own frame of reference. This type of response was found in a study of a cartoon depicting a congressman who has native fascist, anti-minority views. The cartoon series seeks to expose and ridicule him so as to focus the readers' attention upon such native anti-democratic movements and to cause them to disapprove of these tendencies. For example, in one cartoon, the Congressman is shown interviewing an applicant in his office. The man has brought a letter of recommendation saying that he has been in jail, has started race riots, has smashed windows. The Congressman is pleased and says, "Of course I can use you in my new party."

One respondent commented: "It might be anything crooked . . . might be a new labor party. That shady character makes me think so, the one applying for a job."

Another, in response to the second picture in the series said: ". . . a bunch of men down in Congress that are more interested in keeping their jobs, interested in the votes rather than anything else . . . I never liked Senator Wagner. . . ."

Another: "It's about a strike . . . about trouble like strikes . . . He is starting a Communist party."

The type becomes clearest in the following reply: "It's a Jewish party that would help Jews get more power."

The only clue that these respondents took from the cartoon was the fact that it tried to show up a bad politician. The rest they supplied themselves by identifying the Congressman with whatever appeared to them to be "bad politics." Thus they imposed their own ideology on the cartoon and arrived at an interpretation satisfactory to them—an interpretation which, however, represented a complete misunderstanding of the cartoon's message.

4. The Message Is Too Difficult

The remaining type of misunderstanding can be dismissed quickly. This takes the

[5] They were rated "conservative" on political attitude questions which have a fairly high correlation with a negative attitude toward minorities.

same form as misunderstanding by unprejudiced people. Some respondents frankly admit that "they don't get the point." This is most frequently due to intellectual and educational limitations of these respondents or to defects in the propaganda.

These evasion processes have obvious implications for the producers of cartoons (and probably of propaganda in general). Given the tendency to evade opposition propaganda, evasion is facilitated by making the message subtle or satirical. However, simplifying the message may lessen its emotional impact. What seems to be indicated is that the more subtle—and therefore the more easily distorted and misunderstood—forms may be appropriate for neutrals and for inactive sympathizers of the anti-prejudice message: these people do not show evidence of this tendency to *evade* the message although they may misunderstand for other reasons; and the impact of the item may make stronger supporters of them. For the prejudiced person the research suggests that this approach is ineffective.

For a better understanding of the evasion mechanism we must turn to an examination of the motivation underlying it and its rôle in our culture.

C. EVASION—A CULTURAL PATTERN

A thorough examination of the motivation underlying evasion would require a much more extensive treatment than we can provide here. However, certain cultural features may be mentioned which seem to bear out in other areas the kind of evasion mechanism discussed above.

1. Fear of Isolation and the Threat to the Ego

The fear of isolation is a major force in our society, where the majority of people are dependent upon group membership not only for their physical well-being but also for psychological support. They rely upon group codes and group values as guides for their behavior and their ideals. Nearly everyone wants to "belong." At the same time this is complicated by the fact that assembly-line production and the general complexity of modern life tend to drive people into more and more atomistic contacts with their fellow men, thereby increasing the fear of losing identity with the group.

From a psychological point of view, the evasion of a propaganda message with which one disagrees functions as a defense mechanism. Such defense mechanisms come into play whenever an individual senses a danger to his ego structure—that is, whenever his self-confidence hangs in the balance. As we have seen, the steps involved in the evasion process are fairly complicated. However, these complications are obviously negligible compared to the discomfort that would be created by facing the message.

The printed propaganda items that attack prejudice are an attack on the ego of the prejudiced person. Moreover, they constitute an attack made with the authority of the printed word, thus presumably speaking for a large part of the world that disapproves of the respondent. He is confronted with a two-fold threat to his security: On the one hand he is an outsider in the world represented by the propaganda item; on the other hand, giving careful consideration to the validity of the propaganda and possibly accepting it threatens the individual's security in the group to which he feels he belongs and which supports his present ideas. The interviewing situation increases the threat to the security of the individual who feels attacked by anti-discrimination propaganda. Interviewers are trained to use an engaging, polite, and friendly manner when approaching a respondent; they are selected, not only for the skill they have acquired, but also for neatness and pleasantness of appearance in order to facilitate their contact with strangers. The respondent, who is on the defensive, probably links the person of the interviewer with that outside world which may disapprove of him. The interviewer's reluctance to voice his own opinion creates the suspicion that he, too, might disapprove of the respondent's attitude.

The emotional nature of prejudice has been well enough established to explain why the prejudiced respondent often does not trust his own capacity for logical argument on the subject. He feels himself attacked in spheres that actually transcend logic. So where possible, he evades the issue. Although there is insufficient evidence on this point, we venture the guess that the less a person has rationalized his prejudices, the greater will be his tendency to evade an attack on them. Those who are most advanced in the rationalization of prejudice will not feel the need for evasion to the same degree as their less ideologically developed supporters. Witness the pseudo-science on race questions developed by the Nazis and their followers in this country. Those however, who are infected without having made the decisive step over to the "lunatic fringe," and who are only dimly aware of the irrational basis of their particular attitude, will try to weasel out of their difficulty when confronted with the disconcerting anti-discrimination message.

2. *The Multiplicity of Value Systems*

Another dimension must be added to the phenomenon of propaganda evasion before it can be understood. This dimension is closely related to that part of our life experience which involves inconsistencies or contradictions. There exists in our society a culturally conditioned habit of evasion, a product of the fact that each individual is compelled to participate in many different groups, each of which has its own more or less well defined value systems. Often, these value systems are somewhat inconsistent with each other; sometimes they imply a different hierarchy of values.

Examples of simultaneous acceptance of inconsistent value systems abound. The obsequious bookkeeper who assumes a dominant rôle in political discussions with his barbershop cronies is a familiar figure in the modern literature of the western world. We are not surprised when a store owner who privately champions progressive causes, refuses to hire a Negro salesclerk on the grounds that his customers will object. The example of the bookkeeper illustrates the necessity for flexibly shifting from one social rôle to another. The storekeeper, too, is involved in a conflict between his public and private attitudes. He keeps the solution of this conflict in abeyance by setting up a special hierarchy of values for his business rôle: he knows that he is supported by the generally accepted view that taking care of one's profits takes precedence over other considerations.

Thus, two possible alternatives are available. These contradictions may either be recognized and resolved; or they may be evaded. Instead of looking squarely at the inconsistencies, one may divide one's life into so many little pockets in which behavior is determined by independent and even contradictory values; or one may realistically examine and compare the values involved in his various day-to-day rôles and then weigh their relative merits as behavior guides.

Evidence of this was found in a study of the impact of factory life on children who had just left school (4). The moral values they had been taught in school were confronted in the factory with an inflation of the importance of efficiency to the exclusion of morality. Nevertheless, the absorption of this new value system was achieved with incredible speed. But the two systems were not reconciled, nor was one abandoned for the other. They coexisted in strictly separate compartments of the personality; the issue of conflict was evaded by the departmentalizing of the personality.

3. *Other Cultural Factors in Evasion*

In this context the lack of spontaneity so characteristic of people living in our culture must be considered (1, 2, 3, 8). The public which comprises the audience for the mass media of communications is entertainment hungry. Many of them are lulled into boredom and fatigue by their jobs; outside their jobs they want to have fun. They want to be entertained without having to think. And they are encouraged to persist in this mental laziness by the stereotypy of these communications. Not only are they continually confronted with entertainment cast in the same mold; they are even told how to react to it. Everything is, as it were, pre-digested for them. They are informed by advertisements that a comedy will make them "laugh 'til their sides ache," that a sentimental love story will "wring their hearts," to mention only the most superficial appeals. As one writer has put it, "they march to their destiny by catch-words." Ideas are adopted, not as ideas, but as slogans. Where ideas infiltrate in the guise of entertainment the habitual shying away from effort comes to the rescue of the person who is the propaganda target and helps him to miss the point of the message. The only alternative would be to face the implications of the message and think about them, and this they neither want nor are habituated to do.

Also involved but probably less important in the complex of propaganda evasion is the factor of recognition-value. Audiences tend to prefer the things which are familiar to them. The best-liked music is the music one knows. What is new is a little suspect, requires more effort in listening, and has no pre-established associations which prescribe a pattern of response. Hence it is rejected (1). It is quite likely that a similar tendency makes itself felt in the consideration of new (and oppositional) ideas.

4. Why Evasion?

Why has evasion become so general? The answer lies partly in the difficulties the individual must face to achieve uniformity in the various areas of his everyday experience. To face the contradictions and try to resolve them would undoubtedly set up disturbing tensions which would in turn involve serious difficulties for most individuals. For example, consider the fact that most people agree with the ideas of their own social group; they are conditioned by the people with whom they live and, in turn, they choose to be with people whose attitudes are compatible with their own. Adopting a conflicting attitude would create antagonisms in inter-personal relationships, requiring considerable adjustment on the part of the individual. Even *considering* an opposing point of view may create great discomfort.

Thus evasion appears as a well-practised form of behavior, which receives encouragement from the social structure in which we live. In connection with response to anti-prejudice propaganda it serves as a defence against group attack. This may partly explain why persons with a poorly developed ego structure tend most frequently to take this easy way out.

REFERENCES

1. ADORNO, T. W. On popular music. *Stud. Philos. & Soc. Sci.* 1941, 9 17-48.
2. HORKHEIMER, M. Art and mass culture. *Stud. Philos. & Soc. Sci.*, 1941, 9, 293-304.
3. ———. The end of reason. *Stud. Philos. & Soc. Sci.*, 1941, 9, 366-388.
4. JAHODA, M. Some socio-psychological problems of factory life. *Brit. J. Psychol.*, 1941, 31, 191-206.
5. LAZARSFELD, P. F. (*Ed.*) Radio and the Printed Page. New York: Duell, Sloan & Pearce, 1944.
6. ———, BERELSON, B., & GAUDET, H. The People's Choice. New York: Duell, Sloan & Pearce, 1944.
7. ———, & MERTON, R. K. Studies in radio and film propaganda. *Trans. N. Y. Acad. Sci.*, 1943, 6, 58-79.
8. LOWENTHAL, L. Biographies in popular magazines. In *Radio Research*, 1942-1943. New York: Duell, Sloan & Pearce, 1944. (Pps. 507-548.)

EFFECTS OF FEAR-AROUSING COMMUNICATIONS

IRVING L. JANIS AND SEYMOUR FESHBACH

It is generally recognized that when beliefs and attitudes are modified, learning processes are involved in which motivational factors play a primary role. Symbols in mass communications can be manipulated in a variety of ways so as to arouse socially acquired motives such as need for achievement, group conformity, power-seeking, and the more emotion-laden drives arising from aggression, sympathy, guilt, and anxiety.

The present experiment was designed to study the effects of one particular type of motive-incentive variable in persuasive communications, namely, the arousal of fear or anxiety by depicting potential dangers to which the audience might be exposed.[1] Fear appeals of this sort are frequently used to

[1] This study was conducted at Yale University as part of a coordinated program of research on attitude and opinion change, financed by a grant from the Rockefeller Foundation. The attitude change research project is under the general direction of Professor Carl I. Hovland, to whom the authors wish to express their appreciation for many valuable suggestions concerning the design of the experiment. Special thanks are due to Dr. Isador Hirschfeld of New York City and Dr. Bert G. Anderson of the Yale Medical School for their helpful advice in connection with the preparation of the illustrated talks and dental hygiene. The authors also wish to thank Dr. S. Willard Price, Superintendent of Schools at Greenwich, Connecticut, and Mr. Andrew Bella, Principal of the Greenwich High School, for their generous cooperation.

influence attitudes and behavior. For example, medical authorities sometimes try to persuade people to visit cancer detection clinics by pointing to the dangerous consequences of failing to detect the early symptoms of cancer; various political groups play up the threat of war or totalitarianism in an attempt to motivate adherence to their political program. Our interest in such attempts is primarily that of determining the conditions under which the arousal of fear is effective or ineffective in eliciting changes in beliefs, practices, and attitudes.

Implicit in the use of fear appeals is the assumption that when emotional tension is aroused, the audience will become more highly motivated to accept the reassuring beliefs or recommendations advocated by the communicator. But the tendency to accept reassuring ideas about ways and means of warding off anticipated danger may not always be the dominant reaction to a fear-arousing communication. Under certain conditions, other types of defensive reactions may occur which could give rise to highly undesirable effects from the standpoint of the communicator.

Clinical studies based on patients' reactions to psychiatric treatment call attention to three main types of emotional interference which can prevent a person from being influenced by verbal communications which deal with anxiety-arousing topics.

From the *Journal of Abnormal and Social Psychology*, 1953, Vol. 48, no. 3, pp. 78-92.
Reprinted by permission of the authors and the publisher.

1. When a communication touches off intense feelings of anxiety, communicatees will sometimes fail to pay attention to what is being said. Inattentiveness may be a motivated effort to avoid thoughts which evoke incipient feelings of anxiety. This defensive tendency may be manifested by overt attempts to change the subject of conversation to a less disturbing topic. When such attempts fail and anxiety mounts to a very high level, attention disturbances may become much more severe, e.g., "inability to concentrate," "distractibility," or other symptoms of the cognitive disorganization temporarily produced by high emotional tension (4).

2. When exposed to an anxiety-arousing communication, communicatees will occasionally react to the unpleasant ("punishing") experience by becoming aggressive toward the communicator. If the communicator is perceived as being responsible for producing painful feelings, aggression is likely to take the form of rejecting his statements.

3. If a communication succeeds in arousing intense anxiety and if the communicatee's emotional tension is not readily reduced either by the reassurances contained in the communication or by self-delivered reassurances, the residual emotional tension may motivate defensive avoidances, i.e., attempts to ward off subsequent exposures to the anxiety-arousing content. The experience of being temporarily unable to terminate the disturbing affective state elicited by a discussion of a potential threat can give rise to a powerful incentive to avoid thinking or hearing about it again; this may ultimately result in failing to recall what the communicator said, losing interest in the topic, denying or minimizing the importance of the threat.

The above reaction tendencies, while formulated in general terms, take account of three specific types of behavior observed during psychoanalytic or psychotherapeutic sessions (1, 2, 3). The first two refer to immediate reactions that often occur when a therapist gives an interpretation which brings anxiety-laden thoughts or motives into the patient's focus of awareness: (a) attention disturbances, blocking of associations, mishearing, evasiveness, and similar forms of "resistance"; and (b) argumentativeness, defiance, contempt, and other manifestations of reactive hostility directed toward the therapist. The third refers to certain types of subsequent "resistance," displayed during the later course of treatment, as a carry-over effect of the therapist's disturbing comments or interpretations.

Although the three types of defensive behavior have been observed primarily in clinical studies of psychoneurotic patients (whose anxiety reactions are generally linked with unconscious conflicts), it seems probable that similar reactions may occur among normal persons during or after exposure to communications which make them acutely aware of severe threats of external danger. Nevertheless, it remains an open question whether such sources of emotional interference play any significant role in determining the net effectiveness of fear-arousing material in mass communications, especially when the communications are presented in an impersonal social setting where emotional responses of the audience are likely to be greatly attenuated.

The present experiment was designed to investigate the consequences of using fear appeals in persuasive communications that are presented in an impersonal group situation. One of the main purposes was to explore the potentially adverse effects which might result from defensive reactions of the sort previously noted in the more restricted situation of psychotherapy.

METHOD

The experiment was designed so as to provide measures of the effects of three different intensities of "fear appeal" in a standard communication on dental hygiene, presented to high school students. The influence of the fear-arousing material was investigated by means of a series of questionnaires which provided data on emotional reactions to the communication and on changes in dental hygiene beliefs, practices, and attitudes.

The Three Forms of Communication

A 15-minute illustrated lecture was prepared in three different forms, all of which contained the same essential information about causes of tooth decay and the same series of recommendations concerning oral hygiene practices. The three (recorded) lectures were of approximately equal length and were delivered in a standard manner by the same speaker. Each recording was supplemented by about 20 slides, which were shown on the screen in a pre-arranged sequence, to illustrate various points made by the speaker.

The three forms of the illustrated talk differed only with respect to the amount of fear-arousing material presented. Form 1 contained a strong fear appeal, emphasizing the painful consequences of tooth decay, diseased gums, and other dangers that can result from improper dental hygiene. Form 2 presented a moderate appeal in which the dangers were described in a milder and more factual manner. Form 3 presented a minimal appeal which rarely alluded to the consequences of tooth neglect. In Form 3, most of the fear-arousing material was replaced by relatively neutral information dealing with the growth and functions of the teeth. In all other respects, however, Form 3 was identical with Forms 1 and 2.

The fear appeals were designed to represent typical characteristics of mass communications which attempt to stimulate emotional reactions in order to motivate the audience to conform to a set of recommendations. The main technique was that of calling attention to the potential dangers that can ensue from nonconformity. For example, the Strong appeal contained such statements as the following:

> If you ever develop an infection of this kind from improper care of your teeth, it will be an extremely serious matter because these infections are really dangerous. They can spread to your eyes, or your heart, or your joints and cause secondary infections which may lead to diseases such as arthritic paralysis, kidney damage, or total blindness.

One of the main characteristics of the Strong appeal was the use of personalized threat-references explicitly directed to the audience, i. e., statements to the effect that "this can happen to you." The Moderate appeal, on the other hand, described the dangerous consequences of improper oral hygiene in a more factual way, using impersonal language. In the Minimal appeal, the limited discussion of unfavorable consequences also used a purely factual style.

The major differences in content are summarized in Table 1, which is based on a systematic content analysis of the three recorded lectures. The data in this table show how often each type of "threat" was mentioned. It is apparent that the main difference between the Strong appeal and the Moderate appeal was not so much in the total frequency of threat references as in the variety and types of threats that were emphasized. The Minimal appeal, however, differed markedly from the other two in that it contained relatively few threat references, almost all of which were restricted to "cavities" or "tooth decay."

TABLE 1

CONTENT ANALYSIS OF THE THREE FORMS OF THE COMMUNICATION: REFERENCES TO CONSEQUENCES OF IMPROPER CARE OF THE TEETH

Type of Reference	Form 1 (Strong Appeal)	Form 2 (Moderate Appeal)	Form 3 (Minimal Appeal)
Pain from toothaches	11	1	0
Cancer, paralysis, blindness or other secondary diseases	6	0	0
Having teeth pulled, cavities drilled, or other painful dental work	9	1	0
Having cavities filled or having to go to the dentist	0	5	1
Mouth infections: sore, swollen, inflamed gums	18	16	2
Ugly or discolored teeth	4	2	0
"Decayed" teeth	14	12	6
"Cavities"	9	12	9
Total references to unfavorable consequences	71	49	18

One of the reasons for selecting dental hygiene as a suitable topic for investigating the influence of fear appeals was precisely because discussions of this topic readily lend themselves to quantitative and qualitative variations of the sort shown in Table 1. Moreover, because of the nature of the potential dangers that are referred to, one could reasonably expect the audience to be fairly responsive to such variations in content—the teeth and gums probably represent an important component in the average person's body image, and, according to psychoanalytic observations, the threat of damage to the teeth and gums can sometimes evoke deep-seated anxieties concerning body integrity. In any case, by playing up the threat of pain, disease, and body damage, the material introduced in Form 1 is probably representative of the more extreme forms of fear appeals currently to be found in persuasive communica-

TABLE 2

FEELINGS OF WORRY OR CONCERN EVOKED DURING THE COMMUNICATION

Questionnaire Responses	Strong Group (N=50)	Moderate Group (N=50)	Minimal Group (N=50)
Felt worried—a "few times" or "many times"—about own mouth condition	74%	60%	48%
Felt "somewhat" or "very" worried about improper care of own teeth	66%	36%	34%
Thought about condition of own teeth "most of the time"	42%	34%	22%

tions presented via the press, radio, television, and other mass media.

The fear appeals did not rely exclusively upon verbal material to convey the threatening consequences of nonconformity. In Form 1, the slides used to illustrate the lecture included a series of eleven highly realistic photographs which vividly portrayed tooth decay and mouth infections. Form 2, the Moderate appeal, included nine photographs which were milder examples of oral pathology than those used in Form 1. In Form 3, however, no realistic photographs of this kind were presented: X-ray pictures, diagrams of cavities, and photographs of completely healthy teeth were substituted for the photographs of oral pathology.

Subjects

The entire freshman class of a large Connecticut high school was divided into four groups on a random basis. Each of the three forms of the communication was given to a separate experimental group; the fourth group was used as a control group and was exposed to a similar communication on a completely different topic (the structure and functioning of the human eye). All together there were 200 students in the experiment, with 50 in each group.

The four groups were well equated with respect to age, sex, educational level, and IQ. The mean age for each group was approximately 15 years and there were roughly equal numbers of boys and girls in each group. The mean and standard deviation of IQ scores, as measured by the Otis group test, were almost identical in all four groups.

Administration of the Questionnaires

The first questionnaire, given one week before the communication, was represented to the students as a general health survey of high school students. The key questions dealing with

dental hygiene were interspersed among questions dealing with many other aspects of health and hygiene.

One week later the illustrated talks were given as part of the school's hygiene program. Immediately after the end of the communication, the students in each group were asked to fill out a short questionnaire designed to provide data on immediate effects of the communication, such as the amount of information acquired, attitudes toward the communication, and emotional reactions. A follow-up questionnaire was given one week later in order to ascertain the carry-over effects of the different forms of the communication.

RESULTS

Affective Reactions

Evidence that the three forms of the illustrated talk differed with respect to the amount of emotional tension evoked during the communication is presented in Table 2. Immediately after exposure to the communication, the students were asked three questions concerning the feelings they had just experienced "while the illustrated talk was being given." Their responses indicate that the fear stimuli were successful in arousing affective reactions. On each of the three questionnaire items shown in the table, the difference between the Strong group and the Minimal group is reliable at beyond the .05 confidence level.[2] The Moderate group consistently falls in an intermediate position but

[2] All probability values reported in this paper are based on one tail of the theoretical distribution, since the results were used to test specific hypotheses which predict the direction of the differences.

does not, in most instances, differ significantly from the other two groups.

Further evidence of the effectiveness of the fear-arousing material was obtained from responses to the following two questions, each of which had a checklist of five answer categories ranging from "Very worried" to "Not at all worried":

1. When you think about the possibility that you might develop diseased gums, how concerned or worried do you feel about it?

2. When you think about the possibility that you might develop decayed teeth, how concerned or worried do you feel about it? Since these questions made no reference to

group. The difference between the Moderate and the Minimal groups, however, is insignificant.

In order to obtain an over-all estimate of the relative degree of emotional arousal evoked by the three forms of the communication, a total score was computed for each individual in each experimental group, based on answers to all five questions: two points credit was given to each response specified in Tables 2 and 3 as indicative of high disturbance; one point credit was given to intermediate responses on the checklist; zero credit was given for the last two response categories in each checklist, which uniformly designated a relative absence of

TABLE 3

PERCENTAGE OF EACH GROUP WHO REPORTED FEELING SOMEWHAT OR VERY
WORRIED ABOUT DECAYED TEETH AND DISEASED GUMS

	Strong Group (N=50)	Moderate Group (N=50)	Minimal Group (N=50)	Control Group (N=50)
One week before the communication	34	24	22	30
Immediately after the communication	76	50	46	38
Change	+42%	+26%	+24%	+ 8%

	RELIABILITY OF DIFFERENCE*	
Group	CR	*p*
Strong vs. Control	3.06	<.01
Strong vs. Minimal	1.59	.06
Strong vs. Moderate	1.37	.09
Moderate vs. Control	1.54	.06
Moderate vs. Minimal	0.17	.43
Minimal vs. Control	1.43	.08

* The statistical test used was the critical ratio for reliability of differences in amount of change between two independent samples, as described by Hovland, Lumsdaine, and Sheffield (5, p. 321).

the illustrated talk, it was feasible to include them in the pre- and postcommunication questionnaires given to all four groups.

Systematic comparisons were made in terms of the percentage in each group who reported relatively high disturbance (i.e., "somewhat" or "very worried") in response to both questions. The results, presented in Table 3, show a marked increase in affective disturbance among each of the three experimental groups, as compared with the control group. Paralleling the results in Table 2, the greatest increase is found in the Strong

worry or concern. Hence individual scores ranged from zero to ten. The mean scores for the Strong, Moderate and Minimal groups were 7.8, 6.6, and 5.9 respectively. The Strong group differs reliably at the one per cent confidence level from each of the other two groups ($t=2.3$ and 3.6). The difference between the moderate and Minimal groups approaches reliability at the .08 confidence level ($t=1.4$).

In general, the foregoing evidence indicates that after exposure to the communications, the Strong group felt more worried about the condition of their teeth than did the other two groups; the Moderate group, in turn, tended to feel more worried than the Minimal group.

Information Acquired

Immediately after exposure to the illustrated talk, each experimental group was given an information test consisting of 23 separate items. The test was based on the factual assertions common to all three forms of the communication, including topics such as the anatomical structure of the teeth, the causes of cavities and of gum disease, the "correct" technique of toothbrushing, and the type of toothbrush recommended by dental authorities. No significant differences were found among the three experimental groups with respect to information test scores. Comparisons with the Control group show that the three forms of the dental hygiene communication were equally effective in teaching the factual material.

Attitude Toward the Communication

The questionnaire given immediately after exposure to the illustrated talk included a series of seven items concerning the students' appraisals of the communication. From the results shown in Table 4, it is apparent that the Strong group responded more favorably than the other two groups.[3]

These findings imply that interest in the communication and acceptance of its educational value were heightened by the Strong appeal. But this conclusion applies only to relatively impersonal, objective ratings of the communication. Additional evidence presented in Table 5, based on questions which elicited evaluations of a more subjective character, reveals a markedly different attitude toward the communication among those exposed to the Strong appeal.

One of the additional questions was the following: "Was there anything in the illus-

[3] The Strong group differs significantly ($p<.05$) from the Minimal group on five of the seven items and from the Moderate group on three items; the Moderate group does *not* differ reliably from the Minimal group on any of the items.

trated talk on dental hygiene that you disliked? "Unfavorable ("dislike") answers were given by a reliably higher percentage of students in the Strong group than in the Moderate or Minimal groups (first row of Table 5). A tabulation was also made of the total number of students in each group who gave complaints in their answers to either of two open-end questions which asked for criticisms of the illustrated talk. The results on complaints about the unpleasant character of the slides are shown in row two of Table 5; the difference between the Strong group and each of the other two groups is reliable at the .01 confidence level. Similarly, a reliably higher percentage of the Strong group complained about insufficient material on ways and means of preventing tooth and gum disease (row three of Table 5).[4] The latter type of criticism often was accompanied by the suggestion that some of the disturbing material should be eliminated, as is illustrated by the following comments from two students in the Strong group: "Leave out the slides that show the rottiness of the teeth and have more in about how to brush your teeth"; "I don't think you should have shown so many gory pictures without showing more to prevent it." Comments of this sort, together with the data presented in Table 5, provide additional evidence of residual emotional tension. They imply that the Strong appeal created a need for reassurance which persisted after the communication was over, despite the fact that the communication contained a large number of reassuring recommendations.

[4] In row three of Table 5, the difference between the Strong and Moderate groups is reliable at the .01 confidence level, and the difference between the Strong and Minimal groups is significant at the .08 level. Other types of criticisms, in addition to those shown in Table 5, were also tabulated. Most of these involved minor aspects of the presentation (e.g., "a movie would have been better than slides") and were given by approximately equal percentages of the three groups. The vast majority of students in the Moderate and Minimal groups expressed approval of the illustrated talk or stated that they had no criticisms.

TABLE 4

PERCENTAGE OF EACH GROUP WHO EXPRESSED STRONGLY FAVORABLE APPRAISALS
OF THE COMMUNICATION

Appraisal Response	Strong Group (N=50)	Moderate Group (N=50)	Minimal Group (N=50)
The illustrated talk does a very good teaching job.	62	50	40
Most or all of it was interesting.	80	68	64
It was very easy to pay attention to what the speaker was saying.	74	36	50
My mind practically never wandered.	58	46	42
The slides do a very good job.	52	20	22
The speaker's voice was very good.	66	56	58
The illustrated talk definitely should be given to all Connecticut high schools.	74	58	70

The apparent inconsistency between the results in Tables 4 and 5 suggests that the Strong appeal evoked a more mixed or ambivalent attitude toward the communication than did the Moderate or Minimal appeals. Some of the comments, particularly about the slides, help to illuminate the differentiation between the individual's *objective* evaluation of the communication and his *subjective* response to it. The following illustrative excerpts from the Strong group were selected from the answers given to the open-end question which asked for criticisms and suggestions:

I did not care for the "gory" illustrations of decayed teeth and diseased mouths but I really think that it did make me feel sure that I did not want this to happen to me.

Some of the pictures went to the extremes but they probably had an effect on most of the people who wouldn't want their teeth to look like that.

I think it is good because it scares people when they see the awful things that can happen.

Such comments not only attest to the motivational impact of the Strong appeal, but also suggest one of the ways in which the discrepancy between subjective and objective evaluations may have been reconciled. In such cases, the ambivalence seems to have been resolved by adopting an attitude to the effect that "this is disagreeable medicine, but it is good for us."

Conformity to Dental Hygiene Recommendations

The immediate effects of the illustrated talks described above show the type of affective reactions evoked by the fear-arousing material but provide little information bearing directly on attitude changes. The questionnaire administered one week later, however, was designed to measure some of the major carry-over effects of fear appeals, particularly with respect to changes in dental hygiene practices, beliefs, and preferences. The results provide an empirical basis for

TABLE 5

PERCENTAGE OF EACH GROUP WHO EXPRESSED COMPLAINTS ABOUT
THE COMMUNICATION

Type of Complaint	Strong Group (N=50)	Moderate Group (N=50)	Minimal Group (N=50)
Disliked something in the illustrated talk.	28	8	2
The slides were too unpleasant ("horrible," "gory," "disgusting," etc.).	34	2	0
There was not enough material on prevention.	20	2	8

estimating the degree to which such communications succeed in modifying attitudes.

Personal practices were investigated by asking the students to describe the way they were currently brushing their teeth: the type of stroke used, the amount of surface area cleansed, the amount of force applied, the length of time spent on brushing the teeth, and the time of day that the teeth were brushed. The same five questions were asked one week before the communication and again one week after. These questions covered practices about which the following specific recommendations were made in all three forms of the illustrated talk: (a) the teeth should be brushed with an up-and-down (vertical) stroke; (b) the inner surface of the teeth should be brushed as well as the outer surface; (c) the teeth should be brushed gently, using only a slight amount of force; (d) in order to cleanse the teeth adequately, one should spend about three minutes on each brushing; (e) in the morning, the teeth should be brushed after breakfast (rather than before).

Each student was given a score, ranging from zero to five, which represented the number of recommended practices on which he conformed. Before exposure to the communication, the majority of students in all four groups had very low scores and the group differences were insignificant. By comparing the score that each individual attained one week after the communication with that attained two weeks earlier, it was possible to determine for each group the percentage who changed in the direction of increased or decreased conformity.

The results, shown in Table 6, reveal that the greatest amount of conformity was produced by the communication which contained the least amount of fear-arousing material. The Strong group showed reliably less change than the Minimal group; in fact, the Strong group failed to differ significantly from the Control group, whereas the Minimal group showed a highly reliable increase in conformity as compared with the Control group. The Moderate group falls in an intermediate position, but does not differ reliably from the Strong or Minimal groups. Although there is some ambiguity with respect to the relative effectiveness of the Moderate appeal, the data in Table 6 show a fairly consistent trend which suggests that as the amount of fear-arousing material is increased, conformity tends to decrease. In contrast to the marked increase in conformity produced by the Minimal appeal and the fairly sizable increase produced by the Moderate appeal, the Strong appeal failed to achieve any significant effect whatsoever.

TABLE 6

EFFECT OF THE ILLUSTRATED TALK ON CONFORMITY TO DENTAL HYGIENE RECOMMENDATIONS

Type of Change	Strong Group (N=50)	Moderate Group (N=50)	Minimal Group (N=50)	Control Group (N=50)
Increased conformity	28%	44%	50%	22%
Decreased conformity	20%	22%	14%	22%
No change	52%	34%	36%	56%
Net change in conformity	+ 8%	+ 22%	+ 36%	0%

RELIABILITY OF DIFFERENCE

Group	CR	p
Control vs. Minimal	2.54	< .01
Control vs. Moderate	1.50	.07
Control vs. Strong	0.59	.28
Strong vs. Moderate	0.95	.17
Strong vs. Minimal	1.96	.03
Moderate vs. Minimal	0.93	.18

One cannot be certain, of course, that the findings represent changes in overt behavioral conformity, since the observations are based on the Ss' own verbal reports. What remains problematical, however, is whether the verbal responses reflect *only* "lip-service" to the recommendations or whether they also reflect internalized attitudes that were actually carried out in action. The results, nevertheless, demonstrate that the Strong appeal was markedly less effective than the Minimal appeal, at least with respect to eliciting verbal conformity.

Further evidence in support of the same conclusion comes from responses pertinent to a different type of dental hygiene behavior which had also been recommended in the illustrated talk.[5] The students were asked to give the approximate date on which they had last gone to a dentist. The percentage in each group whose answers indicated that they had gone to the dentist during the week following exposure to the illustrated talk were as follows: 10 per cent of the Strong group, 14 per cent of the Moderate group, 18 per cent of the Minimal group, and 4 per cent of the Control group. The percentage difference between the Minimal group and the Control group was found to be statistically reliable at the .04 confidence level; none of the other comparisons yielded reliable differences. Although not conclusive evidence, these findings are in line with those in Table 6: the Minimal appeal again appears to have been superior with respect to eliciting conformity to a recommended practice.

Beliefs Concerning the "Proper" Type of Toothbrush

The illustrated talk presented an extensive discussion of the "proper" type of toothbrush recommended by dental authorities.

[5] In all three forms of the illustrated talk, an explicit recommendation was made concerning the desirability of obtaining advice from a dentist about one's own toothbrushing technique. In addition, several references were made to the importance of going to a dentist for prompt treatment of cavities, before the decay spreads to the inner layers of the tooth.

Four main characteristics were emphasized: (*a*) the bristles should be of medium hardness, (*b*) the brush should have three rows of bristles, (*c*) the handle should be completely straight, and (*d*) the brushing surface should be completely straight. Personal beliefs concerning the desirability of these four characteristics were measured by four questions which were included in the pre-communication questionnaire as well as in the questionnaire given one week after the communication. The main finding was that all three experimental groups, as compared with the Control group, showed a significant change in the direction of accepting the conclusions presented in the communication. Among the three experimental groups, there were no significant differences with respect to net changes. Nevertheless, as will be seen in the next section, the fear-arousing material appears to have had a considerable effect on the degree to which the students adhered to such beliefs in the face of counteracting propaganda.

Resistance to Counteracting Propaganda

In addition to describing the four essential characteristics of the "proper" toothbrush, the illustrated talk contained numerous comments and illustrations to explain the need for avoiding the "wrong" kind of toothbrush. Much of the material on cavities and other unpleasant consequences of tooth neglect was presented in this context. *The importance of using the proper kind of toothbrush* was the theme that was most heavily emphasized throughout the entire communication.

The key questionnaire item, designed to determine initial attitudes before exposure to the communication, was the following:

Please read the following statement carefully and decide whether you believe it is true or false.

It does not matter what kind of toothbrush a person uses. *Any sort of toothbrush* that is sold in a drugstore will keep your teeth clean and healthy—if you use it regularly.

Do you think that this statement is true or false? (Check one.)

TABLE 7

EFFECT OF THE ILLUSTRATED TALK ON REACTIONS TO SUBSEQUENT COUNTER-
PROPAGANDA: NET PERCENTAGE OF EACH GROUP WHO CHANGED IN THE
DIRECTION OF AGREEING WITH THE STATEMENT THAT "IT DOES NOT
MATTER WHAT KIND OF TOOTHBRUSH A PERSON USES"

Type of Change	Strong Group (N=50)	Moderate Group (N=50)	Minimal Group (N=50)	Control Group (N=50)
More agreement	30	28	14	44
Less agreement	38	42	54	24
No change	32	30	32	32
Net change	−8	−14	−40	+20
Net effect of exposure to the illustrated talk	−28	−34	−60	

RELIABILITY OF THE DIFFERENCES IN NET CHANGE

Group	CR	p
Control vs. Minimal	3.66	< .001
Control vs. Moderate	2.05	.02
Control vs. Strong	1.71	.05
Strong vs. Moderate	0.36	.36
Strong vs. Minimal	2.03	.02
Moderate vs. Minimal	1.66	.05

One week after exposure to the communications, the question was asked again, in essentially the same form, with the same checklist of five answer categories (ranging from "Feel certain that it is true" to "Feel certain that it is false"). But in the post-communication questionnaire, the question was preceded by the following propaganda material which contradicted the dominant theme of the illustrated talk:

A well-known dentist recently made the following statement:

Some dentists, including a number of so-called "experts" on dental hygiene, claim it is important to use a special type of toothbrush in order to clean the teeth properly. But from my own experience, I believe that there is no sound basis for that idea. My honest opinion, as a dentist, is that it does not matter what kind of toothbrush a person uses. Any sort of toothbrush that is sold in a drugstore will keep your teeth clean and healthy—if you use it regularly.

That this propaganda exposure had a pronounced effect is revealed by the attitude changes shown by the Control group. A statistically reliable change in the direction

of more agreement with the counterpropaganda was found in the Control group.[6]

How effective were the three forms of the illustrated talk in preventing students from accepting the propaganda to which they were exposed one week later? Did the fear appeals augment or diminish the students' resistance to the counteracting propaganda? A fairly definite answer emerges from the results in Table 7, which shows the percentage of each group who changed in the direction of agreement or disagreement with the counterpropaganda statement.

Before exposure to the illustrated talk, the

[6] In the Control group, the percentage who disagreed with the statement dropped from 54 to 34. This change proved to be significant at below the .02 confidence level, according to the formula described by Hovland, Lumsdaine, and Sheffield (5, p. 319). The control group did not show any significant change on other questions dealing with dental hygiene beliefs, preferences or practices, all of which were presented in the final questionnaire before the propaganda material was introduced. Consequently, it seems fairly safe to conclude that the propaganda exposure was responsible for the significant change displayed by the Control group.

group differences were negligible: approximately 50 per cent of the students in each of the four groups agreed with the statement that "it does not matter what kind of toothbrush a person uses." But two weeks later (immediately after exposure to the counterpropaganda) there were marked and statistically reliable differences which indicate that although all three forms of the illustrated talk had some influence, the Minimal appeal was most effective in producing resistance to the counterpropaganda. Thus, the results suggest that under conditions where people will be exposed to competing communications dealing with the same issues, the use of a strong fear appeal will tend to be less effective than a minimal appeal in producing stable and persistent attitude changes.

Some clues to mediating processes were detected in the students' responses to an open-end question which asked them to "give the reason" for their answers to the key attitude item on which the results in Table 7 are based. A systematic analysis was made of the write-in answers given by those students who had disagreed with the counterpropaganda. In their refutations, some of the students made use of material that had been presented one week earlier, either by referring to the illustrated talk as an authoritative source or by citing one of the main arguments presented in the illustrated talk. From the results presented in the first two rows of Table 8, it is apparent that such refutations were given more frequently by the Minimal group than by the other experimental groups. The comparatively low frequency of such answers in the Strong and Moderate groups was not compensated for by an increase in any other type of specific reasons, as indicated by the results in the last row of the table.[7]

Although the group differences are not uniformly reliable, they reveal a consistent trend which suggests an "avoidance" tendency among the students who had been exposed to the fear appeals. Apparently, even those who resisted the counterpropaganda were inclined to avoid recalling the content of the fear-arousing communication.

DISCUSSION

The results in the preceding sections indicate that the Minimal appeal was the most

[7] On the first type of reason (reference to the illustrated talk), the only difference large enough to approach statistical reliability was that between the Minimal group and the Control group ($p=.08$). On the second type of reason (arguments cited from the illustrated talk), the difference between the Minimal group and the Control group was found to be highly reliable ($p=.03$) while the difference between the Minimal and Moderate groups approached statistical reliability ($p=.08$). The Control group differed reliably from each of the experimental groups (at beyond the .10 confidence level) with respect to giving arguments which contradicted those contained in the illustrated talk (row three of the table). None of the other percentage differences in Table 8 were large enough to be significant at the .10 confidence level. (In some columns, the percentages add up to more than 100 per cent because a few students gave more than one type of refutation.)

TABLE 8

TYPES OF REFUTATION GIVEN BY STUDENTS WHO DISAGREED WITH THE COUNTERPROPAGANDA

Type of Refutation	Strong Group (N=30)	Moderate Group (N=29)	Minimal Group (N=39)	Control Group (N=18)
Explicit reference to the illustrated talk as an authoritative source for the opposite conclusion	7%	14%	18%	0%
One or more arguments cited that had been presented in the illustrated talk	43%	38%	59%	28%
One or more arguments cited that contradicted the content of the illustrated talk	0%	0%	0%	22%
No answer or no specific reason given	50%	52%	36%	50%

effective form of the communication in that it elicited (*a*) more resistance to subsequent counterpropaganda and (*b*) a higher incidence of verbal adherence, and perhaps a greater degree of behavioral conformity, to a set of recommended practices. The absence of any significant differences on other indicators of preferences and beliefs implies that the Moderate and Strong appeals had no unique positive effects that would compensate for the observed detrimental effects.

Thus, the findings consistently indicate that inclusion of the fear-arousing material not only failed to increase the effectiveness of the communication, but actually interfered with its over-all success.

The outcome of the present experiment by no means precludes the possibility that, under certain conditions, fear appeals may prove to be highly successful. For instance, the Strong appeal was found to be maximally effective in arousing interest and in eliciting a high degree of emotional tension. The evocation of such reactions might augment the effectiveness of mass communications which are designed to instigate prompt audience action, such as donating money or volunteering to perform a group task. But if the communication is intended to create more sustained preferences or attitudes, the achievement of positive effects probably depends upon a number of different factors. Our experimental results suggest that in the latter case, a relatively low degree of fear arousal is likely to be the optimal level, that an appeal which is too strong will tend to evoke some form of interference which reduces the effectiveness of the communication. The findings definitely contradict the assumption that as the dosage of fear-arousing stimuli (in a mass communication) is increased, the audience will become more highly motivated to accept the reassuring recommendations contained in the communication. Beneficial motivating effects probably occur when a relatively slight amount of fear-arousing material is inserted; but for communications of the sort used in the present experiment, the optimal dosage appears to be far below the level of the strongest fear appeals that a communicator could use if he chose to do so.

Before examining the implications of the findings in more detail, it is necessary to take account of the problems of generalizing from the findings of the present study. The present experiment shows the effects of only one type of communication, presented in an educational setting to a student audience. Until replications are carried out—using other media, topics, and fear-eliciting stimuli, in a variety of communication settings, with different audiences, etc.—one cannot be certain that the conclusions hold true for other situations. The results from a single experiment are obviously not sufficient for drawing broad generalizations concerning the entire range of fear-arousing communications which are currently being brought to the focus of public attention. Nor can unreplicated results be relied upon for extracting dependable rubrics that could be applied by educators, editors, public relations experts, propagandists, or other communication specialists who face the practical problems of selecting appropriate appeals for motivating mass audiences.

Nevertheless, the present experiment helps to elucidate the potentially unfavorable effects that may result from mass communications which play up ominous threats, alarming contingencies, or signs of impending danger. For instance, the findings tend to bear out some of the points raised concerning the need for careful pretesting and for other cautions when warnings about the dangers of atomic bombing are presented in civilian defense communications that are intended to prepare the public for coping with wartime emergencies (6). Moreover, despite our inability to specify the range of communications to which our conclusions would apply, we can derive tentative inferences that may have important theoretical implications with respect to the dynamics of "normal" fear reactions.

We turn now to a central question posed by the experimental findings: Why is it that the fear-arousing stimuli resulted in less adherence to recommended practices and less resistance to counterpropaganda? Although our experiment cannot give a definitive answer, it provides some suggestive leads concerning potential sources of emotional interference.

In the introduction, we have described three forms of "resistance" frequently observed in psychotherapy that might also occur among normal personalities exposed to mass communications which evoke strong fear or anxiety: (a) inattentiveness during the communication session, (b) rejection of the communicator's statements motivated by reactive aggression, and (c) subsequent defensive avoidance motivated by residual emotional tension. We shall discuss briefly the pertinent findings from the present experiment with a view to making a preliminary assessment of the importance of each of the three types of interfering reactions.

1. Our results provide no evidence that a strong fear appeal produces inattentiveness or any form of distraction that would interfere with learning efficiency during the communication session. The three forms of the communication were found to be equally effective in teaching the factual material on dental hygiene, as measured by a comprehensive information test given immediately after exposure to the communication. Beliefs concerning the desirable characteristics of the "proper" type of toothbrush were also acquired equally well. One might even surmise (from the results in Table 4) that the Strong appeal may have had a beneficial effect on attention, because a significantly higher percentage of the Strong group reported that (a) it was very easy to pay atention to what the speaker was saying and (b) they experienced very little "mind-wandering."

The absence of any observable reduction of learning efficiency is consistent with numerous clinical observations which imply that normal personalities can ordinarily tolerate unpleasant information concerning potential threats to the self without manifesting any marked impairment of "ego" functions. Our findings definitely suggest that the use of fear-arousing material of the sort presented in the illustrated talks would rarely give rise to any interference with the audience's ability to learn the content of the communication.

It is necessary to bear in mind, however, that in the present experiment the communication was given to a "captive" classroom audience. When people are at home listening to the radio, or in any situation where they feel free to choose whether or not to terminate the communication exposure, the use of strong emotional appeals might often have drastic effects on sustained attention. Consequently, the tentative generalization concerning the low probability of inattentiveness would be expected to apply primarily to those fear-arousing communications which are presented under conditions where social norms or situational constraints prevent the audience from directing attention elsewhere.

Even with a "captive" audience, it is quite possible that under certain extreme conditions a strong fear appeal might interfere with learning efficiency. For instance, the same sort of temporary cognitive impairment that is sometimes observed when verbal stimuli happen to touch off unconscious personal conflicts or emotional "complexes" might also occur when a mass communication elicits sharp awareness of unexpected danger, particularly when the audience immediately perceives the threat to be imminent and inescapable. Hence, the inferences from our experimental findings probably should be restricted to fear appeals which deal with remote threats or with relatively familiar dangers that are perceived to be avoidable.

2. The fact that the Strong group expressed the greatest amount of subjective dislike of the illustrated talk and made the most complaints about its content could be construed as suggesting a potentially aggressive attitude. But if the aggressive reactions aroused by the use of the Strong fear appeal were intense enough to motivate rejection of the conclusions, one would not expect to find this group giving the most favorable appraisals of the interest value of the illus-

trated talk, of the quality of its presentation, and of its over-all educational success. Thus, although the possibility of suppressed aggression cannot be precluded, it seems unlikely that this factor was a major source of emotional interference. In drawing this tentative conclusion, however, we do not intend to minimize the importance of aggression as a potential source of interference. In the present experiment, the communication was administered as an official part of the school's hygiene program and contained recommendations that were obviously intended to be beneficial to the audience. Under markedly different conditions, where the auspices and intent of the communication are perceived to be less benign, the audience would probably be less disposed to suppress or control aggressive reactions. The low level of verbalized aggression observed in the present study, however, suggests that in the absence of cues which arouse the audience's suspicions, some factor other than reactive hostility may be a much more important source of interference.

3. Subsequent defensive avoidance arising from residual emotional tension seems to be the most likely explanation of the outcome of the present study. We have seen, from the data on immediate affective reactions, that the disturbing feelings which had been aroused during the illustrated talk tended to persist after the communication had ended, despite the reassuring recommendations which had been presented. The analysis of complaints made by the three experimental groups (Table 5) provides additional evidence that the need for reassurance persisted primarily among the students who had been exposed to the Strong appeal. Such findings support the following hypothesis: *When a mass communication is designed to influence an audience to adopt specific ways and means of averting a threat, the use of a strong fear appeal, as against a milder one, increases the likelihood that the audience will be left in a state of emotional tension which is not fully relieved by rehearsing the reassuring recommendations contained in the communication.* This hypothesis is

compatible with the general assumption that when a person is exposed to signs of "threat," the greater the intensity of the fear reaction evoked, the greater the likelihood that his emotional tension will persist after the external stimulus has terminated.

Whether or not the above hypothesis is correct, the fact remains that "unreduced" emotional tension was manifested immediately after the communication predominantly by the group exposed to the Strong appeal. Our findings on subsequent reactions provide some suggestive evidence concerning the consequences of experiencing this type of residual tension. In general, the evidence appears to be consistent with the following hypothesis: *When fear is strongly aroused but is not fully relieved by the reassurances contained in a mass communication, the audience will become motivated to ignore or to minimize the importance of the threat.* This hypothesis could be regarded as a special case of the following general proposition which pertains to the effects of human exposure to any fear-producing stimulus: other things being equal, the more persistent the fear reaction, the greater will be the (acquired) motivation to avoid subsequent exposures to internal and external cues which were present at the time the fear reaction was aroused. This proposition is based on the postulate that fear is a stimulus-producing response which has the functional properties of a drive (2, 7).[8]

[8] In the sphere of human communication, the key theoretical assumption could be formulated as follows: If rehearsal of the reassuring statements contained in a communication fails to alleviate the emotional tension elicited by the use of a fear appeal, the audience will be motivated to continue trying out other (symbolic or overt) responses until one occurs which succeeds in reducing fear to a tolerable level. Thus, a strong fear appeal which is intended to motivate the audience to take account of a realistic threat of danger could have the paradoxical effect of motivating the audience to ignore the threat or to adopt "magical," "wishful" or other types of reassuring beliefs that are antithetical to the communicator's intentions. Moreover, according to the same theoretical assumption, when a communication produces a high degree of persistent fear, the audience

In the context of the present experiment, one would predict that the group displaying the greatest degree of residual fear would be most strongly motivated to ward off those internal symbolic cues—such as anticipations of the threatening consequences of improper dental hygiene—which were salient during and immediately after the communication. This prediction seems to be fairly well borne out by the evidence on carry-over effects, particularly by the finding that the greatest degree of resistance to the subsequent counterpropaganda was shown by the group which had been least motivated by fear. The use of the Strong appeal, as against the Minimal one, evidently resulted in less rejection of a subsequent communication which discounted and contradicted what was said in the original communication. In effect, the second communication asserted that one could ignore the alleged consequences of using the wrong type of toothbrush, and, in that sense, minimized the dangers which previously had been heavily emphasized by the fear-arousing communication.

The results obtained from the students' reports on their dental hygiene practices could be interpreted as supporting another prediction from the same hypothesis. It would be expected that those students who changed their practices, after having heard and seen one of the three forms of the illustrated talk, were motivated to do so because they recalled some of the verbal material which had been given in support of the recommendations, most of which referred

to the unfavorable consequences of continuing to do the "wrong" thing. In theoretical terms, one might say that their conformity to the recommendations was mediated by symbolic responses which had been learned during the communication. The mediating responses (anticipations, thoughts, or images) acquired from any one of the three forms of the illustrated talk would frequently have, as their content, some reference to unpleasant consequences for the self, and consequently would cue off a resolution or an overt action that would be accompanied by anticipated success in warding off the threat. But defensive avoidance of the mediating responses would reduce the amount of conformity to whatever protective action is recommended by the fear-arousing communication. Hence the prediction would be that when rehearsal of statements concerning potential danger is accompanied by strong emotional tension during and after the communication, the audience will become motivated to avoid recalling those statements on later occasions when appropriate action could ordinarily be carried out. An inhibiting motivation of this kind acquired from the illustrated talk would tend to prevent the students from adopting the recommended changes in their toothbrushing habits because they would fail to think about the unpleasant consequences of improper dental hygiene at times when they subsequently perform the act of brushing their teeth.

Much more direct evidence in support of the "defensive avoidance" hypothesis comes from the analysis of spontaneous write-in answers in which the students explained why they disagreed with the counterpropaganda (Table 8). Those who had been exposed to the least amount of fear-arousing material were the ones who were most likely to refer to the illustrated talk as an authoritative source and to make use of its arguments. The relative absence of such references in the spontaneous answers given by those who had been exposed to the Moderate and Strong appeals implies a tendency to avoid

---

will be motivated to engage in overt escape activities, some of which may prove to be incompatible with the protective actions recommended by the communicator. Unintended effects of this kind can be regarded as spontaneous "defensive" reactions which are motivated by residual emotional tension. In the present experiment, it would be expected that, in addition to the tendency to avoid thinking about the threat, other defensive reactions would also occur. For example, following exposure to the Strong appeal, some of the students may have succeeded in alleviating their residual emotional tension through spontaneous interpersonal communication with fellow students.

recalling the content of the fear-arousing communication.

Although the various pieces of evidence discussed above seem to fit together, they cannot be regarded as a conclusive demonstration of the defensive avoidance hypothesis. What our findings clearly show is that a strong fear appeal can be markedly less effective than a minimal appeal, at least under the limited conditions represented in our experiment. Exactly which conditions and which mediating mechanisms are responsible for this outcome will remain problematical until further investigations are carried out. Nevertheless, so far as the present findings go, they consistently support the conclusion that the use of a strong fear appeal will tend to reduce the over-all success of a persuasive communication, if it evokes a high degree of emotional tension without adequately satisfying the need for reassurance.

SUMMARY AND CONCLUSIONS

The experiment was designed to investigate the effects of persuasive communications which attempt to motivate people to conform with a set of recommendations by stimulating fear reactions. An illustrated lecture on dental hygiene was prepared in three different forms, representing three different intensities of fear appeal: the Strong appeal emphasized and graphically illustrated the threat of pain, disease, and body damage; the Moderate appeal described the same dangers in a milder and more factual manner; the Minimal appeal rarely referred to the unpleasant consequences of improper dental hygiene. Although differing in the amount of fear-arousing material presented, the three forms of the communication contained the same essential information and the same set of recommendations.

Equivalent groups of high school students were exposed to the three different forms of the communication as part of the school's hygiene program. In addition, the experiment included an equated control group which was not exposed to the dental hygiene communication but was given a similar communication on an irrelevant topic. Altogether there were 200 students in the experiment, with 50 in each group. A questionnaire containing a series of items on dental hygiene beliefs, practices, and attitudes was administered to all four groups one week before the communications were presented. In order to observe the changes produced by the illustrated talk, postcommunication questionnaires were given immediately after exposure and again one week later.

1. The fear appeals were successful in arousing affective reactions. Immediately after the communication, the group exposed to the Strong appeal reported feeling more worried about the condition of their teeth than did the other groups. The Moderate appeal, in turn, evoked a higher incidence of "worry" reactions than did the Minimal appeal.

2. The three forms of the illustrated talk were equally effective with respect to (a) teaching the factual content of the communication, as assessed by an information test and (b) modifying beliefs concerning four specific characteristics of the "proper" type of toothbrush. The evidence indicates that the emotional reactions aroused by the Strong appeal did not produce inattentiveness or reduce learning efficiency.

3. As compared with the other two forms of the communication, the Strong appeal evoked a more mixed or ambivalent attitude toward the communication. The students exposed to the Strong appeal were more likely than the others to give favorable appraisals concerning the interest value and the quality of the presentation. Nevertheless, they showed the greatest amount of subjective dislike of the communication and made more complaints about the content.

4. From an analysis of the changes in each individual's reports about his current toothbrushing practices, it was found that the greatest amount of conformity to the communicator's recommendations was produced by the Minimal appeal. The Strong appeal

failed to produce any significant change in dental hygiene practices, whereas the Minimal appeal resulted in a reliable increase in conformity, as compared with the Control group. Similar findings also emerged from an analysis of responses which indicated whether the students had gone to a dentist during the week following exposure to the illustrated talk, reflecting conformity to another recommendation made by the communicator. The evidence strongly suggests that as the amount of fear-arousing material is increased, conformity to recommended (protective) actions tends to decrease.

5. One week after the illustrated talk had been presented, exposure to counterpropaganda (which contradicted the main theme of the original communication) produced a greater effect on attitudes in the Control group than in the three experimental groups. The Minimal appeal, however, proved to be the most effective form of the illustrated talk with respect to producing resistance to the counterpropaganda. The results tend to support the conclusion that under conditions where people are exposed to competing communications dealing with the same issues, the use of a strong fear appeal is less successful than a minimal appeal in producing stable and persistent attitude changes.

6. The main conclusion which emerges from the entire set of findings is that the over-all effectiveness of a persuasive communication will tend to be reduced by the use of a strong fear appeal, if it evokes a high degree of emotional tension without adequately satisfying the need for reassurance. The evidence from the present experiment appears to be consistent with the following two explanatory hypotheses:

a. When a mass communication is designed to influence an audience to adopt specific ways and means of averting a threat, the use of a strong fear appeal, as against a milder one, increases the likelihood that the audience will be left in a state of emotional tension which is not fully relieved by rehearsing the reassuring recommendations contained in the communication.

b. When fear is strongly aroused but is not fully relieved by the reassurances contained in a mass communication, the audience will become motivated to ignore or to minimize the importance of the threat.

REFERENCES

1. ALEXANDER, F., & FRENCH, T. M. *Psychoanalytic therapy*. New York: Ronald, 1946.
2. DOLLARD, J., & MILLER, N. E. *Personality and psychotherapy*. New York: McGraw-Hill, 1950.
3. FENICHEL, O. *Problems of Psychoanalytic technique*. New York: Psychoanalytic Quarterly, 1941.
4. HANFMANN, EUGENIA. Psychological approaches to the study of anxiety. In P. H. Hoch and J. Zubin (Eds.), *Anxiety*. New York: Grune & Stratton, 1950. Pp. 51-69.
5. HOVLAND, C. I., LUMSDAINE, A. A., & SHEFFIELD, F. D. *Experiments on mass communication*. Princeton: Princeton Univer. Press, 1949.
6. JANIS, I. L. *Air war and emotional stress.* New York: McGraw-Hill, 1951.
7. MOWRER, O. H. *Learning theory and personality dynamics: Selected papers.* New York: Ronald, 1950.

THE INFLUENCE OF SOURCE CREDIBILITY ON COMMUNICATION EFFECTIVENESS*

CARL I. HOVLAND AND WALTER WEISS

An important but little-studied factor in the effectiveness of communication is the attitude of the audience toward the communicator. Indirect data on this problem come from studies of "prestige" in which subjects are asked to indicate their agreement or disagreement with statements which are attributed to different individuals.[1] The extent of agreement is usually higher when the statements are attributed to "high prestige" sources. There are few studies in which an identical communication is presented by different communicators and the relative effects on opinion subsequently measured without explicit reference to the position taken by the communicator. Yet the

latter research setting may be a closer approximation of the real-life situation to which the results of research are to be applied.

In one of the studies reported by Hovland, Lumsdaine and Sheffield, the effects of a communication were studied without reference to the source of the items comprising the opinion questionnaire. They found that opinion changes following the showing of an Army orientation film were smaller among the members of the audience who believed the purpose of the film was "propagandistic" than among those who believed its purpose "informational."[2] But such a study does not rule out the possibility that the results could be explained by general predispositional factors; that is, individuals who are "suspicious" of mass-media sources may be generally less responsive to such communications. The present study was designed to minimize the aforementioned methodological difficulties by experimentally controlling the source and by checking the effects of the source in a situation in which the subject's own opinion was obtained without reference to the source.

A second objective of the present study was to investigate the extent to which opin-

* This study was done as part of a coordinated research project on factors influencing changes in attitude and opinion being conducted at Yale University under a grant from the Rockefeller Foundation. (See Hovland, C. I., "Changes in Attitude Through Communication," *Journal of Abnormal and Social Psychology*, Vol. 46 (1951), pp. 424-437.) The writers wish to thank Prof. Ralph E. Turner for making his class available for the study.

[1] See e.g. Sherif, M., "An Experimental Study of Stereotypes," *Journal of Abnormal and Social Psychology*, Vol. 29 (1935), pp. 371-375; Lewis, H. B., "Studies in the Principles of Judgments and Attitudes": IV. The Operation of "Prestige Suggestion." *Journal of Social Psychology*, Vol. 14 (1941), pp. 229-256; Asch, S. E., "The Doctrine of Suggestion, Prestige, and Imitation in Social Psychology." *Psychological Review*, Vol. 55 (1948), pp. 250-276.

[2] Hovland, C. I., A. A. Lumsdaine and F. D. Sheffield, *Experiments on Mass Communication*. Princeton: Princeton University Press, 1949, pp. 101f.

From the *Public Opinion Quarterly*, 1952, 15, 635-650. Reprinted by permission of the authors and publisher.

ions derived from high and low credibility sources are maintained over a period of time. Hovland, Lumsdaine and Sheffield showed that some opinion changes in the direction of the communicator's position are larger after a lapse of time than immediately after the communication. This they refer to as the "sleeper effect." One hypothesis which they advanced for their results is that individuals may be suspicious of the motives of the communicator and initially discount his position, and thus may evidence little or no immediate change in opinion. With the passage of time, however, they may remember and accept *what* was communicated but not remember *who* communicated it. As a result, they may then be more inclined to agree with the position which had been presented by the communicator. In the study referred to, only a single source was used, so no test was available of the differential effects when the source was suspected of having a propagandistic motive and when it was not. The present experiment was designed to test differences in the retention, as well as the acquisition, of identical communications when presented by "trustworthy" and by "untrustworthy" sources.

PROCEDURE

The overall design of the study was to present an identical communication to two groups, one in which a communicator of a generally "trustworthy" character was used, and the other in which the communicator was generally regarded as "untrustworthy." Opinion questionnaires were administered before the communication, immediately after the communication, and a month after the communication.

Because of the possibility of specific factors affecting the relationship between communicator and content on a single topic, four different topics (with eight different communicators) were used. On each topic two alternative versions were prepared, one presenting the "affirmative" and one the "negative" position on the issue. For each version one "trustworthy" and one "untrustworthy" source was used. The topics chosen were of current interest and of a controversial type so that a fairly even division of opinion among members of the audience was obtained.

The four topics and the communicators chosen to represent "high credibility" and "low credibility" sources were as follows:

	"High Credibility" Source	*"Low Credibility"* Source
A. *Anti-Histamine Drugs*: Should the anti-histamine drugs continue to be sold without a doctor's prescription?	*New England Journal of Biology and Medicine*	Magazine A* [A mass circulation monthly pictorial magazine]
B. *Atomic Submarines*: Can a practicable atomic-powered-submarine be built at the present time?	Robert J. Oppenheimer	*Pravda*
C. *The Steel Shortage*: Is the steel industry to blame for the current shortage of steel?	*Bulletin of National Resources Planning Board*	Writer A* [A widely syndicated anti-labor, anti-New Deal, "rightist" newspaper columnist]
D. *The Future of Movie Theaters*: As a result of TV, will there be a decrease in the number of movie theaters in operation by 1955?	*Fortune* magazine	Writer B* [An extensively syndicated woman movie-gossip columnist]

* The names of one of the magazines and two of the writers used in the study have to be withheld to avoid any possible embarrassment to them. These sources will be referred to hereafter only by the later designations given.

In some cases the sources were individual writers and in others periodical publications, and some were fictitious (but plausible) and others actual authors or publications.

The "affirmative" and "negative" versions of each article presented an equal number of facts on the topic and made use of essentially the same material. They differed in the emphasis given the material and in the conclusion drawn from the facts. Since there were two versions for each topic and these were prepared in such a way that either of the sources might have written either version, four possible combinations of content and source were available on each topic.

The communication consisted of a booklet containing one article on each of the four different topics, with the name of the author or periodical given at the end of each article. The order of the topics within the booklets was kept constant. Two trustworthy and two untrustworthy sources were included in each booklet. Twenty-four different booklets covered the various combinations used. An example of one such booklet-combination would be:

Topic	Version	Source
The Future of Movie Theaters	Affirmative	Fortune
Atomic Submarines	Negative	Pravda
The Steel Shortage	Affirmative	Writer A
Anti-Histamine Drugs	Negative	New England Journal of Biology and Medicine

The questionnaires were designed to obtain data on the amount of factual information acquired from the communication and the extent to which opinion was changed in the direction of the position advocated by the communicator. Information was also obtained on the subject's evaluation of the general trustworthiness of each source, and, in the after-questionnaires, on the recall of the author of each article.

The subjects were college students in an advanced undergraduate course in History at Yale University. The first questionnaire, given five days before the communication, was represented to the students as a general opinion survey being conducted by a "National Opinion Survey Council." The key opinions bearing on the topics selected for the communication were scattered through many other unrelated ones. There were also questions asking for the subjects' evaluations of the general trustworthiness of a long list of sources, which included the critical ones used in the communications. This evaluation was based on a 5-point scale ranging from "very trustworthy" to "very untrustworthy."

Since it was desired that the subjects not associate the experiment with the "before" questionnaire, the following arrangement was devised: The senior experimenter was invited to give a guest lecture to the class during the absence of the regular instructor, five days after the initial questionnaire. His remarks constituted the instructions for the experiment:

Several weeks ago Professor [the regular instructor] asked me to meet with you this morning to discuss some phase of Contemporary Problems. He suggested that one interesting topic would be The Psychology of Communications. This is certainly an important problem, since so many of our attitudes and opinions are based not on direct experience but on what we hear over the radio or read in the newspaper. I finally agreed to take this topic but on the condition that I have some interesting live data on which to base my comments. We therefore agreed to use this period to make a survey of the role of newspaper and magazine reading as a vehicle of communication and then to report on the results and discuss their implications at a later session.

Today, therefore, I am asking you to read a number of excerpts from recent magazine and newspaper articles on controversial topics. The authors have attempted to summarize the best information available, duly taking into account the various sides of the issues. I have chosen up-to-date issues which are currently being widely discussed and ones which are being studied by Gallup, Roper and others interested in public opinion.

Will you please read each article carefully the way you would if you were reading it in your favorite newspaper and magazine. When you finish each article write your name in the lower right hand corner to indicate that you have read it through and then go on to the next. When you finish there will be a short quiz on your reaction to the readings.

Any questions before we begin?

The second questionnaire, handed out immediately after the booklets were collected, differed completely in format from the earlier one. It contained a series of general questions on the subjects' reactions to the articles, gradually moving toward opinion questions bearing on the content discussed in the articles. At the end of the questionnaire there was a series of fact-quiz items. Sixteen multiple choice questions, four on each content area, were used together with a question calling for the recall of the author of each of the articles.

An identical questionnaire was administered four weeks after the communication. At no prior time had the subjects been forewarned that they would be given this second post-test questionnaire.

A total of 223 subjects provided information which was used in some phase of the analysis. Attendance in the history course was not mandatory and there was considerable shrinkage in the number of students present at all three time periods. For the portions of the analysis requiring before-and-after information, the data derived from 61 students who were present on all three occasions were used. Thus for the main analysis a sample of 244 communications (four for each student) was available. Since different analyses permitted the use of differing numbers of cases, the exact number of instances used in each phase of the analysis is given in each table.

RESULTS

Before proceeding to the main analyses it is important to state the extent to which the sources selected on *a priori* grounds by the experimenters as being of differing credibility were actually reacted to in this manner by the subjects. One item on the questionnaire given before the communication asked the subjects to rate the trustworthiness of each of a series of authors and publications. Figure 1 gives the percentages of subjects who rated each of the sources "trustworthy."

The first source named under each topic

had been picked by the experimenters as being of high credibility and the second of low. It will be observed that there is a clear differentiation of the credibility in the direction of the initial selection by the experimenters. The differences between members of each pair are all highly significant (t's range from 13 to 20). The results in Figure 1 are based on all of the subjects present when the preliminary questionnaire was administered. The percentages for the smaller sample of subjects present at all three sessions do not differ significantly from those for the group as a whole.

Differences in perception of communication of various audience sub-groups

Following the communication, subjects were asked their opinion about the fairness of the presentation of each topic and the extent to which each communicator was justified in his conclusion. Although the communications being judged were *identical*, there was a marked difference in the way the subjects responded to the "high credibility" and "low credibility" sources. Their evaluations were also affected by their personal opinions on the topic before the communication was ever presented. Audience evaluations of the four communications are presented in Table 1. In 14 of the 16 possible comparisons the "low-credibility" sources are considered less fair or less justified than the corresponding high credibility sources. The differences for the low credibility sources for the individuals initially holding an opinion different from that advocated by the communicator and those for the high credibility sources for individuals who initially held the same position as that advocated by the communicator are significant at less than the .004 level.[3]

[3] The probability values given in the table, while adequately significant, are calculated conservatively. The two-tailed test of significance is used throughout, even though in the case of some of the tables it could be contended that the direction of the differences is in line with theoretical predictions, and hence might justify the use of the one-tail test. When analysis is made of *changes*, the significance test takes into

FIGURE 1

CREDIBILITY OF SOURCES

Topic	Source	N	Percent Rating Source as Trustworthy
Anti-Histamines	New Engl. J. Biol. & Med.	208	94.7%
	Magazine A	222	←5.9%
Atomic Submarines	Oppenheimer	221	93.7%
	Pravda	223	←1.3%
Steel Shortage	Bull. Nat. Res. Plan. Bd.	220	80.9%
	Writer A	223	←17.0%
Future of Movies	Fortune	222	89.2%
	Writer B	222	←21.2%

EFFECT OF CREDIBILITY OF SOURCE ON ACQUISITION OF INFORMATION AND ON CHANGE IN OPINION

Information

There is no significant difference in the amount of factual information acquired by the subjects when the material is attributed to a high credibility source as compared to the amount learned when the same material is attributed to a low credibility source. Table 2 shows the mean number of items correct on the information quiz when material is presented by "high credibility" and "low credibility" sources.

Opinion

Significant differences were obtained in the extent to which opinion on an issue was changed by the attribution of the material to different sources. These results are presented in Table 3. Subjects changed their opinion in the direction advocated by the communicator in a significantly greater number of cases when the material was attributed to a "high credibility" source than when attributed to a "low credibility" source. The difference is significant at less than the .01 level.

From Figure 1 it will be recalled that less than 100 per cent of the subjects were

account the internal correlation (Hovland, Sheffield and Lumsdaine, op. cit., pp. 318 ff.), but the analyses of cases of post-communication agreement and disagreement are calculated on the conservative assumption of independence of the separate communications.

in agreement with the group consensus concerning the trustworthiness of each source. The results presented in Table 3 were reanalyzed using the individual subject's own evaluation of the source as the independent variable. The effects on opinion were studied for those instances where the source was rated as "very trustworthy" or "moderately trustworthy" and for those where it was rated as "untrustworthy" or "inconsistently trustworthy." Results from this analysis are given in Table 4. The results, using the subject's own evaluation of the trustworthiness of the source, are substantially the same as those obtained when analyzed in terms of the experimenters' a priori classification (presented in Table 3). Only minor shifts were obtained. It appears that while the variable is made somewhat "purer" with this analysis this advantage is offset by possible increased variability attributable to unreliability in making individual judgments of the trustworthiness of the source.

RETENTION OF INFORMATION AND OPINION IN RELATION TO SOURCE

Information

As was the case with the immediate post-communication results (Table 2), there is no difference between the retention of factual information after four weeks when presented by high credibility sources and low credibility sources. Results in Table 5 show the mean retention scores for each of the four topics four weeks after the communication.

TABLE 1

EVALUATION OF "FAIRNESS" AND "JUSTIFIABILITY" OF IDENTICAL COMMUNICATIONS
WHEN PRESENTED BY "HIGH CREDIBILITY" AND "LOW CREDIBILITY" SOURCES
AMONG INDIVIDUALS WHO INITIALLY AGREED AND INDIVIDUALS WHO INITIALLY
DISAGREED WITH POSITION ADVOCATED BY COMMUNICATOR

A. PER CENT CONSIDERING AUTHOR "FAIR" IN HIS PRESENTATION*

Topic	High Credibility Source		Low Credibility Source	
	Initially Agree	Initially Disagree (or Don't Know)	Initially Agree	Initially Disagree (or Don't Know)
Anti-Histamines	76.5%	50.0%	64.3%	62.5%
Atomic Submarines	100.0	93.7	75.0	66.7
Steel Shortage	44.4	15.4	12.5	22.2
Future of Movies	90.9	90.0	77.8	52.4
Mean	78.3%	57.9%	60.5%	51.9%
N=	46	76	43	79

B. PER CENT CONSIDERING AUTHOR'S CONCLUSION "JUSTIFIED" BY THE FACTS**

Topic	High Credibility Source		Low Credibility Source	
	Initially Agree	Initially Disagree (or Don't Know)	Initially Agree	Initially Disagree (or Don't Know)
Anti-Histamines	82.4%	57.1%	57.1%	50.0%
Atomic Submarines	77.8	81.2	50.0	41.2
Steel Shortage	55.6	23.1	37.5	22.2
Future of Movies	63.6	55.0	55.6	33.3
Mean	71.7%	50.0%	51.2%	36.7%
N=	46	76	43	79

* Question: Do you think that the author of each article was fair in his presentation of the facts on both sides of the question or did he write a one-sided report?
** Question: Do you think that the opinion expressed by the author in his conclusion *was* justified by the facts he presented or do you think his opinion *was not* justified by the facts?

Opinion

Extremely interesting results were obtained for the retention of opinion changes. Table 6 shows the changes in opinion from immediately after the communication to those obtained after the four-week interval. It will be seen that compared with the changes immediately after the communica-

tion, there is a *decrease* in the extent of agreement with the high credibility source, but an *increase* in the case of the low credibility source. This result, then, is similar to the "sleeper effect" found by Hovland, Lumsdaine and Sheffield.[4] The results derived from Tables 3 and 6 are compared in

[4] *Op. cit.*

TABLE 2

MEAN NUMBER OF ITEMS CORRECT ON FOUR-ITEM INFORMATION QUIZZES ON EACH OF
FOUR TOPICS WHEN PRESENTED BY "HIGH CREDIBILITY" AND "LOW CREDIBILITY"
SOURCES. (TEST IMMEDIATELY AFTER COMMUNICATION)

Topic	Mean Number of Items Correct			
	High Credibility Source		Low Credibility Source	
Anti-Histamines	(N=31)	3.42	(N=30)	3.17
Atomic Submarines	(N=25)	3.48	(N=36)	3.72
Steel Shortage	(N=35)	3.34	(N=26)	2.73
Future of Movies	(N=31)	3.23	(N=30)	3.27
Average	(N=122)	3.36	(N=122)	3.26
Per cent of items correct		84.0		81.5
^{p}diff. M.			.35	

TABLE 3

NET CHANGES OF OPINION IN DIRECTION OF COMMUNICATION FOR SOURCES CLASSIFIED BY EXPERIMENTERS AS "HIGH CREDIBILITY" OR "LOW CREDIBILITY" SOURCES*

Topic	*Net percentage of cases in which subjects changed opinion in direction of communication*			
	High Credibility Sources		*Low Credibility Sources*	
Anti-Histamines	(N=31)	22.6%	(N=30)	13.3%
Atomic Submarines	(N=25)	36.0	(N=36)	0.0
Steel Shortage	(N=35)	22.9	(N=26)	−3.8
Future of Movies	(N=31)	12.9	(N=30)	16.7
Average	(N=122)	23.0%	(N=122)	6.6%
Diff.		16.4%		
^{p}diff.		<.01		

* Net changes = positive changes *minus* negative changes.

TABLE 4

NET CHANGES OF OPINION IN DIRECTION OF COMMUNICATION FOR SOURCES JUDGED "TRUSTWORTHY" OR "UNTRUSTWORTHY" BY INDIVIDUAL SUBJECTS

Topic	*Net percentage of cases in which subjects changed opinion in direction of communication*			
	"Trustworthy" Sources		*"Untrustworthy" Sources*	
Anti-Histamines	(N=31)	25.5%	(N=27)	11.1%
Atomic Submarines	(N=25)	36.0	(N=36)	0.0
Steel Shortage	(N=33)	18.2	(N=27)	7.4
Future of Movies	(N=31)	12.9	(N=29)	17.2
Average	(N=120)	22.5%	(N=119)	8.4%
Diff.		14.1%		
^{p}diff.		<.03		

TABLE 5

MEAN NUMBER OF ITEMS CORRECT ON FOUR-ITEM INFORMATION QUIZZES ON EACH OF FOUR TOPICS WHEN PRESENTED BY "HIGH CREDIBILITY" AND "LOW CREDIBILITY" SOURCES (RECALL FOUR WEEKS AFTER COMMUNICATION)

Topic	*Mean Number of Items Correct*			
	High Credibility Source		*Low Credibility Source*	
Anti-Histamines	(N=31)	2.32	(N=30)	2.90
Atomic Submarines	(N=25)	3.08	(N=36)	3.06
Steel Shortage	(N=35)	2.51	(N=26)	2.27
Future of Movies	(N=31)	2.52	(N=30)	2.33
Average	(N=122)	2.58	(N=122)	2.67
Per cent of items correct		64.5		66.7
^{p}diff.			.46	

Figure 2, which shows the changes in opinion from before the communication to immediately afterwards and from before to four weeks afterwards.

The loss with the "trustworthy" source and the gain with the "untrustworthy" source are clearly indicated. A parallel analysis using the individual's own evaluation of the source credibility (similar to the method of Table 4) showed substantially the same results.

Retention of name of source

One hypothesis advanced for the "sleeper effect" involved the assumption that forgetting of the source would be more rapid than that of the content. This is a most difficult point to test experimentally because

TABLE 6

NET CHANGES OF OPINION FROM IMMEDIATELY AFTER COMMUNICATION TO FOUR WEEKS LATER IN DIRECTION OF "HIGH CREDIBILITY" AND "LOW CREDIBILITY" SOURCES

Topic	High Credibility Source (A)	Low Credibility Source (B)	Difference (B-A)
Anti-Histamines	(N=31) −6.5%	(N=30) +6.7%	+13.2%
Atomic Submarines	(N=25) −16.0	(N=36) +13.9	+29.9
Steel Shortage	(N=35) −11.4	(N=26) +15.4	+26.8
Future of Movies	(N=31) −9.7	(N=30) −6.7	+3.0
Average	(N=122) −10.7%	(N=122) +7.4%	+18.1%
$p$diff.			.001

it is almost impossible to equate retention tests for source and for content. It is, however, possible to make a comparison of the retention of the name of the source where the subjects initially agreed with the source's position and considered the communicator a "trustworthy" source, and those where they disagreed and considered the source "untrustworthy." Data on this point are presented in Table 7.

No clear differences are obtained immediately after the communication, indicating comparable initial learning of the names of the different sources. At the time of the delayed test, however, there appears to be a clear difference in the retention of the names of "untrustworthy" sources for the group initially agreeing with the communicator's position as compared with that for the group disagreeing with the communicator's position ($p=.02$). Since the "sleeper effect" occurs among the group which initially disagrees with an unreliable source (but subsequently comes to agree with it), it is

FIGURE 2

"RETENTION" OF OPINION. CHANGES IN EXTENT OF AGREEMENT WITH POSITION ADVOCATED BY "HIGH CREDIBILITY" AND "LOW CREDIBILITY" SOURCES

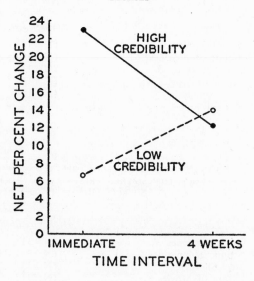

TABLE 7

RECALL OF SOURCE IMMEDIATELY AFTER COMMUNICATION AND AFTER FOUR WEEKS

Recall	Trustworthy Source		Untrustworthy Source	
	Individuals initially holding position advocated by communicator	Individuals not initially holding position advocated by communicator	Individuals initially holding position advocated by communicator	Individuals not initially holding position advocated by communicator
Immediately after communication	93.0% (N=43)	85.7% (N=77)	93.0% (N=43)	93.4% (N=76)
Four weeks after communication	60.5 (N=43)	63.6 (N=77)	76.7 (N=43)	55.3 (N=76)

interesting to note that among this group the retention of the source name is poorest of all. Too few subjects were available to check whether retention was poorer among the very subjects who showed the "sleeper effect," but no clear-cut difference could be seen from the analysis of the small sample.

DISCUSSION

Under the conditions of this experiment, neither the acquisition nor the retention of factual information appears to be affected by the trustworthiness of the source. But changes in opinion are significantly related to the trustworthiness of the source used in the communication. This difference is in line with the results of Hovland, Lumsdaine and Sheffield, who found a clear distinction between the effects of films on information and opinion.[5] In the case of factual information they found that differences in acquisition and retention were primarily related to differences in learning ability. But in the case of opinion, the most important factor was the degree of "acceptance" of the material. In the present experiment, this variable was probably involved as a consequent of the variation in source credibility.

The present results add considerable detail to the Hovland-Lumsdaine-Sheffield findings concerning the nature of the "sleeper effect." While they were forced to make inferences concerning possible suspicion of the source, this factor was under experimental control in the present experiment and was shown to be a significant determinant of subsequent changes in opinion. In terms of their distinction between "learning" and "acceptance," one could explain the present results by saying that the content of the communication (premises, arguments, etc.) is learned and forgotten to the same extent regardless of the communicator. But the extent of opinion change is influenced by both learning and acceptance, and the effect of an untrustworthy communicator is to interfere with the acceptance of the material ("I know what he

[5] Ibid.

is saying, but I don't believe it"). The aforementioned authors suggest that this interference is decreased with the passage of time, and at a more rapid rate than the forgetting of the content which provides the basis for the opinion. This could result in substantially the same extent of agreement with the position advocated by trustworthy and by untrustworthy sources at the time of the second post-test questionnaire. In the case of the trustworthy source, the forgetting of the content would be the main factor in the decrease in the extent of opinion change. But with an untrustworthy source the reduction due to forgetting would be more than offset by the removal of the interference associated with "non-acceptance." The net effect would be an increase in the extent of agreement with the position advocated by the source at the time of the second post-communication questionnaire. The present results are in complete agreement with this hypothesis; there is a large difference in extent of agreement with trustworthy and untrustworthy sources immediately after the communication, but the extent of agreement with the two types of source is almost identical four weeks later.

The Hovland-Lumsdaine-Sheffield formulation makes forgetting of the source a critical condition for the "sleeper" phenomenon. In the present analysis the critical requirement is a decreased tendency over time to reject the material presented by an untrustworthy source.[6] This may or may not require that the source be forgotten. But the individual must be less likely with the passage of time to associate spontaneously the content with the source. Thus the passage of time serves to remove recall of the source

[6] In the present analysis the difference in effects of trustworthy and untrustworthy sources is attributed primarily to the *negative* effects of rejection of the untrustworthy source. On the other hand, in prestige studies the effects are usually attributed to the *positive* enhancement of effects by a high prestige source. In both types of study only a difference in effect of the two kinds of influence is obtained. Future research must establish an effective "neutral" baseline to answer the question as to the absolute direction of the effects.

as a mediating cue that leads to rejection.[7]

It is in this connection that the methodological distinction mentioned earlier between the procedure used in this experiment and that customarily employed in "prestige" studies becomes of significance. In the present analysis, the untrustworthy source is regarded as a cue which is reacted to by rejection. When an individual is asked for his opinion at the later time he may not spontaneously remember the position held by the source. Hence the source does not then constitute a cue producing rejection of his position. In the usual "prestige" technique, the attachment of the name of the source to the statement would serve to reinstate the source as a cue; consequently the differential effects obtained with the present design would not be expected to obtain. An experiment is now under way to determine whether the "sleeper effect" disappears when the source cue is reinstated by the experimenter at the time of the delayed test of opinion change.

Finally, the question of the generalizability of the results should be discussed briefly. In the present study the subjects were all college students. Other groups of subjects varying in age and in education will be needed in future research. Four topics and eight different sources were used to increase the generality of the "source" variable. No attempt, however, was made to analyze the differences in effects for different topics. Throughout, the effects of the "Atomic Submarine" and "Steel Shortage" communications were larger and more closely related to the trustworthiness of source variable than those of the "Future of Movies" topic. An analysis of the factors responsible for the differential effects con-stitutes an interesting problem for future research. A repetition of the study with a single after-test for each time interval rather than double testing after the communication would be desirable, although this variation is probably much less significant with opinion than with information questions. The generality of the present results is limited to the situation where individuals are experimentally exposed to the communication; i.e. a "captive audience" situation. An interesting further research problem would be a repetition of the experiment under naturalistic conditions where the individual himself controls his exposure to communications. Finally for the present study it was important to use sources which could plausibly advocate either side of an issue. There are other combinations of position and source where the communicator and his stand are so intimately associated that one spontaneously recalls the source when he thinks about the issue. Under these conditions, the forgetting of the source may not occur and consequently no "sleeper effect" would be obtained.

SUMMARY

1. The effects of credibility of source on acquisition and retention of communication material were studied by presenting identical content but attributing the material to sources considered by the audience to be of "high trustworthiness" or of "low trustworthiness." The effects of source on factual information and on opinion were measured by the use of questionnaires administered before, immediately after, and four weeks after the communication.

2. The immediate reaction to the "fairness" of the presentation and the "justifiability" of the conclusions drawn by the communication is significantly affected by both the subject's initial position on the issue and by his evaluation of the trustworthiness of the source. Identical communications were regarded as being "justified" in their conclusions in 71.7 per cent of the cases when presented by a high credibility

[7] In rare instances there may also occur a change with time in the attitude toward the source, such that one remembers the source but no longer has such a strong tendency to discount and reject the material. No evidence for the operation of this factor in the present experiment was obtained; our data indicate no significant changes in the evaluation of the trustworthiness of the sources from before to after the communication.

source to subjects who initially held the same opinion as advocated by the communicator, but were considered "justified" in only 36.7 per cent of the cases when presented by a low credibility source to subjects who initially held an opinion at variance with that advocated by the communicator.

3. No difference was found in the amount of factual information learned from the "high credibility" and "low credibility" sources, and none in the amount retained over a four week period.

4. Opinions were changed immediately after the communication in the direction advocated by the communicator to a significantly greater degree when the material was presented by a trustworthy source than when presented by an untrustworthy source.

5. There was a *decrease* after a time interval in the extent to which subjects agreed with the position advocated by the communication when the material was presented by trustworthy sources, but an *increase* when it was presented by untrustworthy sources.

6. Forgetting the name of the source is less rapid among individuals who initially agreed with the untrustworthy source than among those who disagreed with it.

7. Theoretical implications of the results are discussed. The data on post-communication changes in opinion (the "sleeper effect") can be explained by assuming equal *learning* of the content whether presented by a trustworthy or an untrustworthy source, but an initial resistance to the *acceptance* of the material presented by an untrustworthy source. If this resistance to acceptance diminishes with time while the content which itself provides the basis for the opinion is forgotten more slowly, there will be an increase after the communication in the extent of agreement with an untrustworthy source.

EFFECTS OF PREPARATORY COMMUNICATIONS ON REACTIONS TO A SUBSEQUENT NEWS EVENT

IRVING L. JANIS, ARTHUR A. LUMSDAINE, AND ARTHUR I. GLADSTONE

The present study is focused on the effects of preparatory communications in relation to opinion reactions evoked by news events.[1]

This relationship is closely tied up with a more general problem: How do prior communications that result in changed beliefs

[1] This study was conducted at the Institute of Human Relations, Yale University, as part of a coordinated program of research on attitude and opinion formation, financed by a grant from the Rockefeller Foundation. The attitude-change research project is under the general direction of Professor Carl I. Hovland, to whom the authors are indebted for valuable suggestions and criticisms. The authors also wish to express their appreciation to Joseph A. Foran, Superintendent of Schools at Milford, Connecticut, and to the faculty of the Milford High School.

From the *Public Opinion Quarterly*, 1951, Vol. 15, No. 3, pp. 488-518. Reprinted by permission of the authors and the publisher.

predispose the individual to react to subsequent experiences?

It is generally recognized that a single news event can produce gross changes in public opinion. Such changes have often been observed following an authoritative announcement that is released via the press, the radio, and other mass media—especially if the announcement concerns a new state of affairs of great political, military, or social importance.

During the past decade public opinion surveys have provided fairly clear-cut data affording quantitative indices of gross shifts in expectations following or accompanying the announcement of major military events. Several instances are to be found in reports by Cantril and his associates.[2] For example, at the time of the invasion of the low countries in May 1940, the American public became far less confident that the Allies would defeat Germany; a month later, with the fall of France, came a drop in the proportion of the public expecting that America would get into the war.[3] One limitation of such findings, however, lies in the fact that so many critical events were being reported so frequently that it is difficult to discern which specific events were the main cause of the shift.

Regardless of the precision with which the precipitating event can be identified, it seems clear that such changes in public opinion are likely to involve more than simply believing in the truth of the news announcement itself. In addition, *inferences* are made from the reported event. Outstanding events that come to the focus of public attention tend to create new expectations about the future and provide grounds for modifying beliefs about other, related issues.

Many policy-makers, political leaders, and public relations experts are keenly aware of the potential changes in public opinion

that may be precipitated by impending events. And often, when a momentous event is anticipated, an attempt is made to control its effects by releasing mass communications designed to "prepare" the audience in advance. Such communications may be referred to as "preparatory propaganda" or "preparatory communications."

One clear-cut instance of "preparatory propaganda" occurred during the latter part of World War II, when United States government leaders recognized that the impending collapse of Germany might markedly increase optimism about the ease of defeating Japan. Early in 1945, attempts were made to diminish this effect by issuing mass communications designed to prevent over-optimistic reactions. Whether or not the intended effect was actually achieved remains an open question; no data are available on the effectiveness of the preparatory communications in altering the opinion-impact of the subsequent event. Other attempts to prepare a public in advance for the purpose of modifying reactions to later events have been described in the social science literature; but again no systematic study of the effects has been reported.

That preparatory communications can have at least *immediate* effects of considerable magnitude is documented by evidence of the sort presented by Hovland, Lumsdaine, and Sheffield.[4] For example, radio transcriptions used early in 1945 (as part of the publicity campaign designed to diminish "over-optimism" about a quick end to the war) were found to be highly successful in modifying the opinions of a large proportion of the audience and, in addition, some experimental evidence was obtained concerning the kinds of arguments that were most effective under various conditions. But very little is known as yet about the conditions under which such communications diminish or augment the opinion-impact of *later* events. Not only is there no evidence

[2] Cantril, H., F. Mosteller, D. Rugg, J. Harding, F. Williams, D. Katz, J. S. Stock, *et al., Gauging Public Opinion*, Princeton: Princeton University Press, 1940.

[3] Cantril, H., "America faces the war: a study in public opinion," *Public Opinion Quarterly*, 1940, Vol. 4 (1940), pp. 387-407.

[4] Hovland, C. I., A. A. Lunsdaine, and F. D. Sheffield, *Experiments on Mass Communication*, Princeton: Princeton University Press, 1949, 345 pp.

on the relative effectiveness of alternative ways of producing such effects; it has not even been demonstrated experimentally that communications can produce *any* change in the impact of a subsequent major event. The present study provides evidence bearing on both aspects of the problem.

CONDITIONS REQUIRED FOR AN
EXPERIMENTAL INVESTIGATION
OF THE PROBLEM

The conditions necessary for investigating the effectiveness of preparatory communications are not easy to arrange. The difficulties of conducting a clear-cut experiment arise not only from the inherent complexities of studying mass reactions to significant news events, but also from the requirement that relevant propaganda must have been presented prior to the occurrence of a critical event. Insofar as psychological interest centers upon events which are unexpected or which create some degree of surprise, it would seem that the experimenter would need to have "inside" information about the impending event in advance, so that he could present the preparatory communication well before the event. In the absence of such foreknowledge, however, the investigator may occasionally take advantage of relevant propaganda which happens to have preceded, by a suitable interval, some unforeseen event. This was the situation in the experiment reported here.

Precise information bearing on the problem can generally be obtained only when the opportunity arises to study a situation which has the following features:

a. A major news event occurs which produces gross changes in expectations or beliefs that are inferred from the event, and circumstances permit reliable measurement of the changes produced.

b. Some time prior to the event there has been exposure to one or more *effective* communications relevant to the beliefs to be investigated. If a preparatory communication was given but was not attended to, or was very "poor" propaganda, successful carry-over effects would seem to be much less likely. Consequently, one should be able to demonstrate that at the time the communication was given, it was sufficiently influential to produce at least some temporary changes in the relevant beliefs.

c. Suitable opinion-measures must be obtained for two equivalent groups with differential exposure to the preparatory communication.[5] The group with little (or no) exposure serves as a control group and is needed in order to draw sound conclusions about the ultimate effects of the communication.

During 1949 the opportunity arose to study a situation which possessed the features just listed. These necessary conditions for an experiment on preparatory communications came about unexpectedly in the course of carrying out another experiment on a completely different problem. The experiment provides us with opinion measures that were obtained one week before and one week after an "optimistic" radio program on Russian A-bomb developments, given in early June of 1949. This "optimistic" communication emphasized that Russia would *not* be able to produce a stockpile of atomic bombs for a long time to come. In addition, follow-up measures were obtained three months later from experimental and control groups—after the official announcement that Russia had exploded an atomic bomb. The opportune circumstances thus made it possible to observe the effectiveness of a preparatory communication in altering subsequent reactions to a major news event.

The present findings are derived from the study of reactions to one particular type of communication and one particular event, and are based on relatively small samples of one particular type of audience. Nevertheless, the data provide some basis for an

[5] The term "equivalent" used to characterize the two groups is intended to imply the necessity for an *experimental* set-up, in which exposure or non-exposure is determined at the will of the experimenter rather than by the choice of the subjects. This condition is required in order to avoid the so-called self-selection fallacy: a voluntarily exposed group is likely to differ from a voluntarily non-exposed group in terms of original opinion, susceptibility to opinion change, etc.

evaluation of alternative hypotheses concerning the effects of preparatory communications.

HYPOTHESES

On the basis of different theoretical assumptions about the dominant psychological factors affecting carry-over effects, different outcomes would be predicted. Interest will be focused initially on two main kinds of hypotheses. The first assumes that an optimistic preparatory communication will produce "interference"—creating, in effect, a diminution or "softening" of the tendency for "pessimistic" opinion-changes to result from the subsequent event. The opposite outcome would be predicted by an hypothesis which assumes that when part or all of the preparatory communication is subsequently falsified by the event, there will be a tendency to *overcompensate*, resulting in augmentation of the opinion-impact of the event.

An "interference" hypothesis may be formulated as follows: *Once a belief is modified by a communication, the newly acquired opinion responses will tend to interfere with the subsequent acquisition of any incompatible opinion responses.* According to this hypothesis, people who have been influenced by optimistic propaganda will show some degree of "resistance" to the opinion-changes evoked by a subsequent "pessimistic" event. This type of hypothesis may be derived from learning principles, on the assumption that beliefs and their supporting arguments are symbolic habits which follow basic laws of learning. A more detailed discussion of the theoretical bases for the "proactive inhibition" predicated by this "interference" hypothesis will be given after the experimental findings have been presented.[6]

[6] The terms "resistance" and "proactive inhibition" are regarded as equivalent terms. They are used throughout this paper in a purely descriptive sense to refer to the *decrement* in opinion change due to exposure to an antecedent communication. A group that has received a preparatory communication is said to show

The second type of hypothesis predicts that after a person has been "misled" by a prior communication, any interference tendency will be subordinated to a tendency to overcompensate. More specifically, such an "overcompensation" hypothesis would assert that *a person's beliefs are more likely to be influenced by an event if he has been previously influenced by propaganda which is falsified by the event.* The "over-compensation" outcome would appear to be plausible for several reasons. If people recall the falsified propaganda, they may dismiss all of the propagandist's conclusions, along with his supporting arguments, as untrustworthy, suspect, or false. Moreover, if a person feels that he had been "taken in" by erroneous propaganda, he may tend to discharge his annoyance or anger by shifting to the opposite position.

Increased sensitivity to the implications of the event or a heightened disposition to change might, of course, also arise on the basis of other motivational factors. The preparatory communication may have the effect of increasing the *discrepancy* between pre-event beliefs and new expectations created by an irrefutable event. This might produce a temporary loss of self-esteem and some degree of insecurity about one's ability to anticipate the future correctly. Even a temporary, mild emotional disturbance of this kind might be sufficient to create an added incentive to avoid the former erroneous belief by switching to the opposite extreme. Thus the operation of any one of several possible mechanisms might lead to the prediction of a heightened tendency to change beliefs in the direction suggested by the event.

Similarly, the opposite prediction of "resistance" could be based on grounds other than the postulated mechanism of "inter-

"proactive inhibition" or "resistance" to the opinion-impact of the news event if it shows *significantly less change* than the control group. The way the control group responds to the news event is assumed to represent the changes that would occur in the normal course of events if there had been no antecedent communication.

ference" from incompatible responses. A likely alternative, for example, is that resistance could arise solely from increased familiarity with the issue or from similar "sophistication" effects produced by a preparatory communication which evokes forethought about a controversial topic. This "sophistication" hypothesis would agree with the "interference" hypothesis in predicting that the optimistic preparatory communication will produce "resistance" to the pessimistic impact of the event, but it would involve the further assumption that the same effect could be achieved by *any* antecedent communication that poses the issue—regardless of whether the communication presents optimistic or pessimistic conclusions. "Sophistication" effects will be discussed later in connection with some supplementary experimental observations.

For the present, attention will be focused on testing the *contrasting predictions* derived from the two main kinds of hypotheses stated above, without reference to the underlying psychological mechanisms postulated. The alternative predictions merely state that an effective preparatory communication which is at least partially contradicted by a subsequent event will produce either (a) a net decrease or (b) a net increase in the amount of opinion-shift evoked by the event.

THE EXPERIMENT

In the spring of 1949, experimental tests were conducted among the students of a high school in a small Connecticut town located in a heavily industrialized region. The town has a local newspaper but there is a wide readership of metropolitan newspapers, including several from New York City.

There were 55 students in the main experimental group (exposed to the preparatory communication) and 55 in the control group. The proportions of freshman, sophomore, junior, and senior students were approximately equal in the two groups, so that there was no essential difference in

educational level. Nor was there any appreciable age difference: the mean age in each group was approximately 15.5 years. There were small but non-significant differences in I.Q., as measured by the Otis group intelligence test. For example, 30 students in the experimental group (54½ per cent) and 34 students in the control group (62 per cent) had an I.Q. of over 100.[7]

In the middle of May 1949, an initial questionnaire was administered to 19 classes in the high school. This "before" questionnaire contained opinion items dealing with a variety of current events. It included several questions concerning atomic developments in Russia, but also included questions on other topics and was generally designed to avoid calling special attention to the A-bomb topic.

Early in June, a 20 minute radio program, recorded on sound-tape, was played in certain of the classrooms. This program had been specially prepared for purposes of the experiment. At the beginning, a radio announcer gave the name of the program and then introduced the commentator as an expert on the subject. The commentator took the position that Russia will *not* be able to produce A-bombs in large quantities *at least for the next five years*. Typical arguments or themes used to support this conclusion were the following:

1. We know that Russia does not now (June, 1949) have the bomb, because scientists in this country would have been able to detect an atomic explosion with their sensitive instruments.

2. There is good reason to believe that Russian scientists have not yet solved the technical problems necessary to make even one successful A-bomb.

3. There is no single "secret" of the bomb but rather a host of technical and engineering secrets of "know-how" required

---

[7] Statistical analysis of I.Q. subgroups indicates that the experimental findings reported below could not be attributed to the slight disparity in the I.Q. distributions for the two groups.

to convert atomic theory into an actual bomb.

4. The Russians cannot learn all of the secrets through espionage, but will have to work out many of them for themselves. Newspaper spy stories have been greatly exaggerated; most attempts to steal secrets from us have been thwarted.

5. Russia does not have nearly as many top-flight atomic scientists as we do, and those she has cannot hope to match our rate of progress in atomic development.

6. Even after the Russians have all the "know-how," a tremendous industrial effort will be needed to make even one bomb; after they finally make one bomb, it will still be a long time before they can produce large numbers.

7. Russia cannot devote her full industrial effort to atomic development because of other pressing production needs.

8. Russia has a critical shortage of uranium, which is the essential material needed to produce A-bombs in quantity.

This program will be referred to as the "optimistic" communication. It was given in classrooms where social science subjects were being taught and where the use of similar recordings was not an unusual occurrence. The recording was presented as an educational program on a controversial topic, which the high school teacher thought would be of interest to students studying current history or related subjects.

The classrooms were divided into two main groups on a purely random basis. Some of the classrooms—the experimental group—were given the radio program, while the others—the control group—were given a similar kind of radio transcription on a completely different topic (social changes in post-war Italy).

One week later, all of the students were given a second questionnaire (the June Questionnaire), which included the critical items concerning atomic developments in Russia. Both the control group and the main experimental group were given this questionnaire, without any further experimental treatment.[8]

In September 1949, four days after President Truman announced that Russia had exploded an A-bomb, a third questionnaire was administered to all of the students. The purpose of this post-event questionnaire was, of course, to ascertain the changes produced by the announcement. By comparing the experimental group with the control group it was then possible to study reactions to the news event as a function of exposure to the preparatory communication which had been presented several months earlier. The basic design of the main experiment is summarized in Table 1.

[8] In addition, there was a supplementary experimental group of 55 students who had also been exposed to the preparatory communication a week earlier. But immediately before the June questionnaire was administered, the supplementary group was exposed to an additional radio program which was designed to counteract the arguments and conclusions of the first. The results obtained from this third group of subjects do not enter into the main experiment but will be discussed later in connection with the "sophistication" hypothesis. As will be seen, the supplementary results permit investigation of alternative explanations of the main findings.

TABLE 1

DESIGN OF THE MAIN EXPERIMENT

Step	Date (1949)	Experimental Group (N=55)	Control Group (N=55)
1.	May	1st questionnaire	1st questionnaire
2.	Early June	"Optimistic" preparatory communication (presented in 8 classrooms)	Irrelevant radio program (presented in 5 class-rooms)
3.	Late June	2nd questionnaire	2nd questionnaire
4.	September	Announcement of the event	Announcement of the event
5.	September	3rd questionnaire	3rd questionnaire

EXPECTATIONS CONCERNING ATOMIC DEVELOPMENTS IN RUSSIA

a. *Immediate effects of the radio program*

The key opinion item in the present experiment was the following, which will be referred to as Question "A":

About how long from now do you think it will be before the Russians are really producing *large numbers* of atomic bombs?
Answer: About_____from now.
(If you think they are already producing large numbers of atom bombs, just put a check mark here_____.)

Changes from May to June in the responses given to Question "A" reveal that the preparatory communication had a considerable immediate effect. Before the program was presented the two groups showed little difference in their responses; answers of five years or longer were given by about three-fifths of the students in both groups (cf. the May results in Table 2). In June, one week after exposure to the program, almost everyone in the experimental group (94 per cent) gave estimates of five years or longer. Over the same time period the control group remained relatively unchanged (67 per cent gave estimates of five years or longer in June).[9]

Thus, there is clear-cut evidence that several months before the event the experi-

[9] The difference between the two groups in June—as computed by the conventional test for significance of a difference between two percentages from different samples—is statistically reliable at below the one per cent confidence level. (This and other probability values given in this article are based on one-tail of the probability distribution.) It should be mentioned that the powerful immediate effect of the radio program is even more sharply revealed when the two groups are compared with respect to the proportion giving extremely high estimates in June. For example, only 16 per cent of the control group gave estimates of more than 10 years, whereas 56 per cent of the experimental group did so. A detailed analysis of the changes in the estimates given by each individual in each group also confirms the conclusion that the preparatory communication had a significant effect in June 1949.

mental group had become much more "optimistic" (giving significantly longer estimates) as a result of exposure to the radio program.

b. *Effects of the news event*

The news event in September, which settled the closely related issue of Russia's ability to produce its *first* A-bomb, also had a marked effect on responses to the key item quoted above (Question "A"). In the September questionnaire, the vast majority of students in both groups *decreased* their time estimates with respect to Russia's ability to produce large numbers of A-bombs. Thus, the belief that is measured by Question "A" had been markedly influenced in the positive (optimistic) direction by the radio program and was subsequently influenced in the opposite (pessimistic) direction by the news event. Accordingly, this opinion item meets the essential requirements for testing alternative hypotheses concerning the carry-over effect of preparatory propaganda.[10] By comparing the post-

[10] The change from May to September within the control group and within the experimental group was statistically significant at below the one per cent confidence level. The significance of the before-after change was computed by the formula: $C.R. = \dfrac{A-D}{\sqrt{A+D}}$ (cf. Hovland, Lumsdaine and Sheffield, *op. cit.*, p. 319).

The appropriate interval for studying the changes produced by a preparatory communication is from: a) the period *before the communication was given*, to b) the period *after the event has occurred*. Accordingly, in the present experiment, "resistance" to the opinion-impact of the event is observed by comparing the changes from May to September shown by the experimental group with the corresponding changes shown by the control group. For the purposes of detecting the resistance due to the preparatory communication, it does not matter what estimates the students gave during the period between the communication and the event. Consequently, responses to the June (immediate post-communication) questionnaire do not enter into the measurement of resistance to the opinion-impact of the event. It should be borne in mind that "resistance" is measured by the *relative* amount of change attributable to the experimental treatment rather than the absolute amount of change induced by the event.

TABLE 2

EFFECT OF THE PREPARATORY COMMUNICATION ON REACTIONS TO THE ANNOUNCEMENT
OF RUSSIA'S ATOMIC EXPLOSION

Question "A": "About how long from now do you think it will be before the Russians are really producing *large numbers* of atomic bombs?"

Initial and Final Estimates on Question "A"

	Pre-Communication Responses (May, 1949)		Post-Event Responses (September, 1949)	
Responses	Experimental Group (N=55)	Control Group (N=55)	Experimental Group (N=55)	Control Group (N=55)
15 or more years	18% ⎫	14½% ⎫	0 % ⎫	0 % ⎫
10–14 years	4 ⎪ 56%	14½ ⎪ 60%	9 ⎪ 34½%	4 ⎪ 18½%
6–9 years	12 ⎪	20 ⎪	11 ⎪	5½ ⎪
5 years	22 ⎭	11 ⎭	14½ ⎭	9 ⎭
3–4 years	22	18	27	18
0–2 years	20	20	34½	58
No Answer	2	2	4	5½
Total	100%	100%	100%	100%

event changes of the experimental and control groups, we are able to observe the way in which the preparatory communication altered the opinion-impact of the subsequent event.

The essential results are summarized in Table 2, which shows the initial and final responses given by the two groups. Before the radio program was administered (May, 1949) the differences between the two groups were very small and non-significant. After the September event, however, there were large and statistically significant differences. The estimates of the experimental group, although showing a net decline, were nevertheless consistently *longer* than those of the control group, thus deviating in the direction that had been favored by the preparatory communication.

Responses of five years or more represent relatively "optimistic" expectations. The proportion of the control group giving such responses declined by nearly 42 per cent (from 60 per cent in May to 18½ per cent in September); whereas the corresponding decline for the experimental group was only 22 per cent. The effect of the preparatory communication is also revealed by the relatively pessimistic responses of *two years or less*; in September, the control group showed an increase of 38 per cent whereas

the experimental group showed an increase of only 14½ per cent. (The second order difference of 23½ per cent between experimental and control changes is statistically reliable at below the two per cent level of confidence.)[11]

* * *

A convenient statistic to represent the net shift in terms of both increased and decreased estimates is provided by an index of net change, as suggested by Hovland, Lumsdaine and Sheffield.[13] This measure summarizes individual shifts all along the response continuum, but takes into account only the proportions changing their estimates in one *direction* or the other without reference to the *size* of the individual shifts. The "net shift," or net proportion of decreased estimates . . . is equal to the percentage of decreased estimates minus the percentage of increased estimates, or 32½ per cent for the experimental group and 54½ per cent for the control group. The net effect is taken as 54½ minus 32½, or 22 per cent. The standard error of this net

[11] The test used to determine the reliability of the second order difference was the critical ratio for comparing changes between an experimental and a control group, presented on page 321 in Hovland, Lumsdaine, and Sheffield, *op. cit.*

[13] *Op. cit.*, p. 211.

effect is 15 per cent, giving a probablity value of .07. A comparable analysis based on increased and decreased estimates of *more than three years* shows a net effect of 20½ per cent and a standard error of 11 per cent, giving a probability value of below .04.

The above results indicate that, while both groups lowered their estimates following the event, there was significantly *less* net change among those who had received the preparatory communication (the experimental group) than among those who had not (the control group).[14] Since the two groups of high school students were similar with respect to background characteristics and did not differ materially in their initial beliefs, the post-event differences can be attributed to the change induced by the preparatory communication. Thus we conclude that the radio program which had been presented three months earlier had an observable carry-over effect, producing a significant degree of *resistance* to the opinion-impact of the event. In other words,

[14] In the above-presented statistical tests for assessing the significance of the differences found between experimental and control groups, the conventional practice of basing the number of degrees of freedom on the *number of individuals* tested has been employed. This practice, however, ignores the fact that, since sampling and administration of the experiment was done in terms of pre-formed classroom groups, the observations for individuals within a classroom cannot strictly be considered as independent measures. A more rigorous set of significance tests would be based on classroom-group measures as the basic observations, with degrees of freedom based on the *number of classroom units*. As a check against the possibility that selective factors associated with unit sampling might vitiate the present findings, such tests were made for the present data in addition to those employing the conventional assumptions. For these supplementary unit-sampling tests, error estimates were based on class-to-class variability for five class room units in the experimental group and five in the control group, as well as for five units in the supplementary experimental group discussed later. The tests for comparing any two groups were thus based on only eight degrees of freedom (5+5−2). These tests are summarized in footnote 19, below.

the "optimistic" radio program had the effect of *reducing* the amount of "pessimism" evoked by the subsequent event. This finding can be interpreted as providing support for the "interference" hypothesis described on page 491.

c. *Additional evidence*

Confirmatory evidence is provided by the results obtained from another questionnaire item which also deals with Russia's future A-bomb supply:

Question "B" was: "About how many atomic bombs would you guess *Russia* will have made by five years from now?
They will have made about_____atomic bombs by then."

Although the changes for this item are not as pronounced as for Question "A," they closely parallel those already described. Initially (in May) there was only a slight and non-significant difference between the estimated number of bombs given by the two groups in answer to Question "B." But one week after exposure to the radio program (in June), the experimental group showed a significant change in the expected direction while the control group remained relatively unchanged; and subsequently, after the event (in September), the former group continued to give smaller estimates than the latter.

A statistically significant difference was also found when the individual score changes (May to September) were analyzed for Question "B." As is shown in Table 3, lower (more "optimistic") estimates in September were given by 36 per cent of the experimental group but by only 18 per cent of the control group. The difference of 18 per cent is significant at below the five per cent level of confidence.[15]

This finding again indicates that the preparatory communication, which had the im-

[15] In terms of the index of net change, the net percentage increasing their estimates in the experimental group minus the corresponding percentage in the control group was 31 per cent. The standard error of this net effect was 16½ per cent, giving a probability value of .03.

TABLE 3

CHANGES IN ESTIMATED NUMBER OF ATOMIC
BOMBS RUSSIA WILL HAVE IN FIVE YEARS
(QUESTION "B")

Change in Estimate from May to Sept.	Experimental Group (N=55)	Control Group (N=55)
Increased	51%	64%
Decreased	36	18
No Change	0	9
No answer (on one or both questionnaires)	13	9
Total	100%	100%
Net change	+15%	+46%

mediate effect of evoking more optimistic (smaller) estimates of Russia's future A-bomb supply, gave rise to a significant degree of *resistance* to the opinion-impact of the subsequent news event. Thus the second questionnaire item provides a replication of the first and therefore contributes additional evidence in support of the "interference" type of hypothesis.

EXPECTATIONS CONCERNING THE OUTBREAK OF ANOTHER WORLD WAR

Ever since the end of World War II, public discussions about the chances that Russia will provoke a war with the United States have repeatedly emphasized our superiority in atomic weapons as a major deterrent. Since the preparatory communication as well as the news event elicited marked changes in expectations concerning Russia's ability to produce A-bombs, it might be expected that parallel changes would occur in expectations concerning the outbreak of another world war. As will be seen, the data indicate that such changes did in fact occur. Consequently, we have the opportunity to observe the effect of the preparatory communication on another inferred belief that was also influenced by the subsequent event. The data are based on the following item, which was included in the June and September questionnaires:

Question "C": "If we do fight another war, when do you think it will probably start—how long from now? (Just make the best guess you can.)
    About_____years from now."

One week after exposure to the "optimistic" radio program which had emphasized Russia's weakness in atomic weapons, the experimental group gave longer estimates in response to Question "C" than did the control group. For example, relatively optimistic estimates of *six years or more* were given by 54 per cent of the former group and by only 33 per cent of the latter; the 21 per cent difference between the two groups is reliable at below the five per cent level of confidence.

Since Question "C" had not been included in the May questionnaire, it was necessary to rely on the "after only" comparisons for determining the effects of the radio program. It seems fairly safe, however, to assume that the significant difference observed in June is attributable to the communication exposure, particularly since the two groups had been equated on background characteristics and showed no substantial differences on similar opinion items which were included in the May questionnaire.

Following the September news event, the estimates given by both groups were significantly shorter than in June, indicating that the official announcement of Russia's atomic explosion had the effect of producing more pessimistic expectations with respect to the imminence of war.[16] Nevertheless, the estimates of the experimental group remained

[16] Evidence of a statistically reliable change is provided by comparing the pre-event (June) and post-event (September) responses of the control group. For example, the proportion of those who gave estimates of *three years or less* increased from 16 per cent to 47 per cent. (A similar, but much less marked, increase was displayed by the experimental group.) It is conceivable, of course, that other events or communications which occurred during the period between June and September 1949 could have influenced this change. But although this possibility cannot be excluded, it appears to be improbable. A systematic check on newspapers and popular magazines during this period showed that there was relatively little discussion of the prospects of war. Certainly there was no other outstanding news event that would have been likely to produce the change.

consistently *higher* (more "optimistic") than those of the control group. For example, relatively pessimistic estimates of *three years or less* were given by 31 per cent of the experimental group and by 47 per cent of the control group; similarly, estimates of *less than five years* were given by 40 per cent of the experimental group and by 60 per cent of the control group. (These differences between the two groups are reliable at below the five per cent confidence level.)

To summarize: the longer estimates made in response to Question "C" by the experimental group in June indicate that the preparatory communication produced increased optimism concerning the outbreak of war. In September, the shorter estimates made by both groups indicate that the event evoked an increase in pessimism. The fact that there was, nevertheless, a significant difference (in the predicted direction) between experimental and control groups after the event provides additional support for the "interference" hypothesis. On the assumption that the two groups initially (in May) had approximately the same beliefs, these results again imply that the "optimistic" communication produced *resistance* to the pessimistic impact of the subsequent news event.

SKEPTICISM ABOUT THE ANNOUNCEMENT

The official announcement of Russia's atomic explosion was generally interpreted in news stories as meaning that Russia already had produced one or more A-bombs. That this interpretation was accepted by the vast majority of the students in our experiment is indicated by their responses to the following question (included only in the September questionnaire):

Question "D": "How many atom bombs do you think Russia has *right now*?
They have about_____atom bombs now."

The post-event responses of the two groups are shown in Table 4.

Although the experimental group tended to give slightly lower estimates than the control group, there were no marked differ-

TABLE 4

POST-EVENT RESPONSES TO QUESTION "D"

Estimated Number of A-bombs Russia has at present (Sept. 1949)	Experimental Group (N=55)	Control Group (N=55)
100 or more	7%	14%
6 to 99	22	22
3 to 5	27½	33
1 to 2	25½	22
0	11	7
Undecided	7	2
Total	100%	100%

ences. For example, 82 per cent of the experimental group and 91 per cent of the control group asserted that Russia has *at least one A-bomb*. The absence of any clear-cut differences on Question D suggests that the preparatory communication had a relatively slight effect, if any, with respect to the most *obvious* interpretation or implication of the news event. Evidently the official announcement had an overriding effect with respect to structuring the students' beliefs about Russia's *current* A-bomb supply. Thus, the findings in Table 4, when contrasted with those obtained for beliefs about Russia's *future* A-bomb supply (Table 2 and 3), suggest that the resistance produced by the kind of preparatory propaganda employed may tend to affect primarily those beliefs that are indirect or fairly problematical implications of the event.

CONCERN ABOUT THE A-BOMB THREAT

Two of the items included in the questionnaire provide some indication of the *emotional* impact of the September event:

Question "E": "Some people are worried about the possibility that their own city might be destroyed some day by an atomic bomb. Have you ever been concerned about this possibility? (Check one)
_____I have worried about it *quite often*
_____I have worried about it *at times*
_____I have only worried about it *once in a great while*
_____I have *never* worried about it at all"

Question "F": "If there is another big war, do you think any American cities will actually be destroyed by atomic bombs? (Check one)

_____Yes, probably *many* of our cities will be
destroyed.
_____Yes, probably *a few* of our cities will be
destroyed.
_____No, probably *none* of our cities would be
destroyed."

Concern about the possibility of A-bomb
attacks, as reflected by responses to Questions "E" and "F," was uninfluenced by the
preparatory communication in June but increased after the official announcement in
September.[17] On both items, the experimental group tended to be somewhat less
pessimistic than the control group, but the
differences were very slight and non-significant. For example, in the control group
the proportion of those who reported relatively high anxiety on Question E (worried
"quite often" or "at times") increased from
42 per cent in June to 58½ per cent in
September; in the experimental group there
was a parallel increase from 38 per cent in
June to 51 per cent in September.

The fact that the post-event responses of
the two groups did not differ significantly on
Questions "E" or "F" suggests that these
"emotional" responses—unlike the beliefs
measured by the more direct opinion items
—may not have been affected by the communication. In other words, the radio program apparently failed to produce any resistance to the *"emotional"* impact of the
event. In order to evaluate these negative
results in relation to the "interference"
hypothesis, it is necessary to take account
of the immediate effects of the preparatory
communication. In June, after exposure to
the radio program, the responses to Questions "E" and "F" given by the experimental
group did not differ significantly from those
given by the control group. This finding

[17] On both questions, the control group displayed a statistically significant change from
June (before the event) to September (after
the event). The percentage answering "worried
. . . quite often" or "worried . . . at times" in
response to Question "E" showed a net increase
of 16½ per cent (C.R.=1.87; probability-
value=.03). Similarly, the percentage answering
"Yes" to Question "F" showed a net increase
of 18 per cent (C.R.=2.5; probability-value
<.01).

indicates that the preparatory communication had no significant effect on responses
to the two "threat" items. Accordingly, no
differential response to the event would be
predicted by the "interference" hypothesis,
since this hypothesis specifies that preparatory propaganda will effectively reduce the
impact of a subsequent event only insofar
as it successfully builds up responses that
are *incompatible* with the responses evoked
by the event.

"INTERFERENCE" VS.
"SOPHISTICATION" EFFECTS

In general, the results of the main experiment reported in the preceding sections
provide a clear-cut basis for evaluating the
two main types of hypotheses specified in
the introductory section. The "over-compensation" type of hypothesis, which predicts an augmentation of the impact of the
event on previously held opinions, is definitely not confirmed by any of the six indices
used to observe the opinion changes elicited
by the news event. On the other hand, the
"interference" type of hypothesis, which
predicts *resistance* to opinions arising from
the event, is consistently supported by the
findings.

The post-communication results (in June
1949) reveal only two specific areas of
opinion that were influenced by the preparatory communication: expectations about
future atomic developments in Russia and
expectations about the imminence of war.
In both instances, a significant degree of
resistance to the opinion-impact of the event
was observed. In the case of the two items
dealing with the A-bomb threat to the
United States, however, the responses were
left intact by the preparatory communication and consequently no proactive inhibition
would be predicted by the "interference"
hypothesis. Thus, the latter negative findings
as well as the former positive findings are
consistent with the prediction that resistance
to the opinion-impact of an event will occur
due to the interference from incompatible

responses that have been built up by an ante-cedent communication.

The essential factor in the present experiment, according to the "interference" hypothesis, is the conflict between the optimistic beliefs created by the preparatory communication and the pessimistic beliefs evoked by the news event. But the results could also be explained in quite a different way. The same outcome might have occurred as a result of cognitive changes produced by the antecedent communication, irrespective of the "optimistic" or "pessimistic" beliefs that it produced.

The critical carry-over effect of a preparatory communication might arise from the "sophistication" it creates with respect to the issue involved. There are two main ways that a preparatory communication might raise the level of sophistication in an audience, so as to minimize the tendency to "jump to conclusions" in a naïve, uncritical way when a dramatic news event occurs: (a) merely raising the issue may stimulate forethought, initiating a spontaneous effort to take account of the pros and cons; (b) irrespective of the communicator's conclusions, merely presenting a series of relevant arguments may familiarize the audience with the nature of the problem and call its attention to various factors that should be taken into account. Both the spontaneous forethought and the increased familiarity with the issue would create a more sophisticated frame of reference that might enable the audience to make a more critical (and perhaps a more rational) assessment of the implications of the event, weighed in the light of other relevant considerations. Subsequently, when an outstanding event occurs, the audience might be more likely to take account of its *limited* significance, rather than naïvely relying upon the single event, to the exclusion of all other considerations, for forming a new set of beliefs.

Applied to our present experiment, such a "sophistication" hypothesis could account fairly well for the results that have been reported so far. The experimental group was exposed to a preparatory communication which raised the issue beforehand and called attention to various factors—such as the amount of uranium available, the need for skilled manpower, etc.—relevant for drawing a "reasonable" conclusion about Russia's ability to produce a large stockpile of A-bombs. Because this specific issue was not under active discussion in the press or radio during the months preceding the announcement of Russia's atomic explosion, students in the control group were probably *not* exposed to communications that would tend to create a comparable degree of sophistication. Moreover, the readiness with which the students in the experimental group changed their beliefs in response to the commentator's talk suggests that the students had not previously acquired a well-structured, sophisticated point of view.

According to the sophistication hypothesis, resistance to the opinion-impact of the subsequent event would not be due to the particular beliefs fostered by the preparatory communication. Suppose that, instead of an optimistic communication, a pessimistic communication had been used (arguing that Russia could produce large numbers of A-bombs within a *short time*); the same effect could have been achieved, so far as raising the level of sophistication is concerned—provided that the same sort of factors (uranium, skilled manpower, etc.) were mentioned. Thus, the fact that the radio program argued in favor of a "long time" position and had the immediate effect of creating beliefs that were incompatible with those evoked by the subsequent event might be more or less inconsequential. If the critical carry-over effect is due to "sophistication," the same outcome would be predicted, irrespective of the particular position advocated by the preparatory communication.

In order to differentiate "sophistication" effects from "interference" effects, it would be necessary to have an experimental set-up specifically designed to isolate the two variables. Ideally, the experimental group which acquires interfering beliefs should be compared with a second experimental group that is exposed to a communication which creates a sophisticated frame of reference without producing any interfering beliefs. Relatively pure sophistication effects could probably be achieved by using a communication which takes the opposite position from that to which the "interference" group is exposed, or perhaps by presenting a strictly balanced discussion of the issue which merely describes the factors to be taken into account without offering any arguments pro or con. The "interference" group, on the other hand, might be given little opportunity to develop "sophistication" by using a communication which presents a minimum of factual arguments—for instance, by relying mainly on prestige suggestion for creating the interfering beliefs. Thus, it would be possible to have a relatively pure "interference" group in contrast to a relatively pure "sophistication" group. The two experimental groups could then be compared with each other and with the control group in order to determine whether resistance to the subsequent event is produced by "interference," by "sophistication," or by both.

SUPPLEMENTARY EXPERIMENT

The type of experimental design necessary for discriminating "interference" effects from "sophistication" effects is very crudely approximated in our present experiment if we make use of the data obtained from a supplementary experimental group. The orginal experiment carried out in the spring of 1949 had included, in addition to the control group and the main experimental group, a *third* equated group of 55 students. In early June, 1949, this supplementary experimental group was exposed to the same radio program as the regular experimental group; but one week later, immediately before the June questionnaire was administered, they were exposed to an additional radio transcription. This new communication dealt with exactly the same topic but was designed to serve as *counter-propaganda*. In this second program the commentator argued in favor of the position

that *Russia already had developed the A-bomb and within two years would be producing the bomb in large numbers.* The supplementary group (which we shall call the "double-communication" group) differed from the main experimental group only in that it was exposed to both of the communications rather than merely to the first one. Like the other two groups, this group was given the September questionnaire four days after the official announcement of Russia's atomic explosion.

In effect, the supplementary experimental group provides a partial experimental control on "sophistication" effects that makes it possible to investigate whether or not resistance to the opinion-impact of the news event was due, at least in part, to "interference" effects. The additional radio program to which the double-communication group was exposed contradicted specific arguments of the original communication but could not be expected to reduce sophistication effects in any way. On the contrary, it raised the issue a second time and pointed to the same factors as relevant ones to be considered in drawing a sound conclusion. Consequently, the students in the double-communication group had *more* opportunity than the original experimental group to develop a sophisticated frame of reference. Unlike the main experimental group, they had a chance to hear cogent arguments on both sides of the issue, as well as being stimulated a second time to think about the issue and to rehearse the relevant factors.

* * *

Two of the three indices (Questions "A" and "C") tend to bear out the "interference" hypothesis, since they show that the single-communication group displayed more resistance than the double-communication group. These findings imply that "sophistication" effects alone cannot account for the resistance shown by the single-communication group. But this conclusion is weakened by the finding that the double-communication group differed significantly from the control group on Question "B."

Considering all of the findings together, the evidence appears to be compatible with the supposition that both "sophistication" effects and "interference" effects may have been operative. The results considerably strengthen the plausibility of the hypothesis that "interference" effects did play at least some role in producing resistance to the opinion-impact of the event among the students who were exposed to the optimistic preparatory communication. The assumption that the "sophistication" effect was the *only* factor operating would be difficult to defend in the light of the results from Questions "A" and "C." But it is clear that the evidence should be regarded as suggestive, rather than conclusive, so far as differentiating between "interference" and "sophistication" effects is concerned.

THEORETICAL IMPLICATIONS

The main findings of the experiment show that the pessimistic opinion responses evoked by a major news event were minimized by prior exposure to an "optimistic" communication. Following the event, the group of students who received the communication consistently maintained more optimistic beliefs than those who had not. The supplementary findings presented in the preceding section suggest that this type of outcome probably cannot be explained solely in terms of "sophistication" effects. That is, it appears likely that the resistance to change is due, at least in part, to the fact that the beliefs created by the preparatory communication were incompatible with the opinion responses evoked by the event. This is in line with the effects predicted by an "interference" hypothesis, which specifies that the beliefs formed by a preparatory communication will tend to interfere with incompatible opinion responses evoked by a subsequent event.

The term "interference" effect is used to designate one particular source of resistance to the subsequent event—namely, that which is attributable to the interfering beliefs previously created by the preparatory communication. In its most general form, the "interference" hypothesis asserts that any communication which successfully modifies a person's beliefs will reduce the opinion-impact of any subsequent event or communication that tends to produce antithetical beliefs.

In this experiment only one particular historical situation was investigated. Nevertheless, the findings carry the general implication that one exposure to a brief communication is capable of producing a substantial carry-over effect that is sustained over a period of at least several months. If the entire experiment is viewed as a case study of opinion-change, proactive inhibition emerges as a tendency that seems to be sufficiently powerful to override the influence of other counteracting response tendencies.

* * *

The "proactive inhibition" revealed by the results of the experiment could readily be described in terms of perceptual, cognitive, or habit-interference constructs. For example, the way in which the "interference" hypothesis has been formulated is compatible with the view that when a communication succeeds in altering beliefs, it influences the way in which subsequent events are perceived or interpreted. One could say that a new or modified frame of reference is created by the preparatory communication which determines the way in which subsequent relevant experiences will be assimilated. On the other hand, in terms of a stimulus-response theory of learning, the formulation would state that the particular beliefs and supporting arguments acquired from the preparatory communication possess a certain degree of habit-strength and, as a consequence, will interfere with the acquisition of competing or antithetical belief-responses stimulated by the subsequent event. Such formulations obviously have heuristic value insofar as they suggest testable hypotheses which specify critical factors and mediating mechanisms. For example, the last formulation suggests that it may be fruitful to observe in what ways, if any, the proactive inhibition we observed is attributable to mutual interference between incompatible verbal responses. It is important to bear in mind, however, that this "learning" formulation, as well as alternative formulations carries the implication that whenever a preparatory communication evokes an opinion-change, it will tend to produce resistance to the opinion-impact of any subsequent event that evokes antithetical opinion responses.

In the discussion so far it has been assumed that the interference hypothesis would hold true under all conditions, whenever people are exposed to an influential communication. Obviously, however, the results of this single experiment cannot establish the generality of an hypothesis. The present findings merely increase the plausibility of the "interference" hypothesis, but leave open the possibility that certain qualifying conditions may have been responsible for the outcome. Until a series of replicating studies are carried out—with different sub-populations, with other types of opinions and events, employing various channels of communication, and a wide range of propaganda appeals, etc.—the generality of the findings will remain open to question.

Two specific features of the particular situation that was studied should be singled out as possible qualifying conditions:

First, proactive inhibition might occur only when the event carries "unpleasant" implications whereas the preparatory communication fosters beliefs that are consonant with the audience's needs or wishes. In the experiment, the preparatory communication fostered optimistic beliefs, while the event was essentially "bad news." The audience may have been motivated to develop satisfying, optimistic views with respect to Russia's inability to wage a destructive war against the U.S. and to minimize the unpleasant, anxiety-arousing implications of the news

that Russia possesses the A-bomb. Systematic investigation is required in order to determine whether proactive inhibition occurs only when optimistic or anxiety-reducing communications precede a pessimistic or anxiety-arousing event. When the optimism-pessimism sequence is reversed, or when emotionally neutral beliefs are involved, factors other than those which give rise to proactive inhibition might prove to be dominant.

Second, proactive inhibition following exposure to a preparatory communication might occur only for relatively impersonal, unstructured beliefs that elicit a relatively low degree of ego-involvement. The specific beliefs investigated in the present experiment involved expectations about events that were relatively remote in the future and that had only indirect personal implications. Conceivably, a different outcome might have been found if the communication and the event had involved expectations of more immediate and more personal significance for the audience (e.g. expectations concerning imminent mobilization of all able-bodied persons of high school age for civil defense or for military duty). Investigations of a variety of opinion topics might show that other factors, such as the tendency to discount antecedent propaganda, would play a far greater role when the belief entails a high degree of self-involvement.

The foregoing discussion has called attention to several hypotheses which require intensive investigation. At present so little is known about the dynamics of opinion-change that when one attempts to predict or explain the carry-over effects produced in any concrete social situation, it is hard to say which of the many possible psychological factors to take into account and, of those that are relevant, which ones to weight most heavily. The present experiment obviously provides only a preliminary assessment of the relative strength of certain classes of psychological factors.

INTERACTION OF PSYCHOLOGICAL AND SOCIOLOGICAL FACTORS IN POLITICAL BEHAVIOR*

ELSE FRENKEL-BRUNSWIK

The theoretical models developed to deal with the interaction of sociological and psychological factors in the formation of political behavior indicate a wide divergence of opinion. At one extreme are a group of scientists, mainly psychiatrists and anthropologists, who see most social phenomena as deriving from the subjective experiences of the individual. The specific traumata inherent in different methods of upbringing and in the resulting renunciations imposed upon the child are regarded by them as the formative basis for customs, religions, social attitudes, and so forth. Some specific examples of their point of view may be found in attempts to explain war as an expression of the destructive instincts, or capitalism as a manifestation of the anal syndrome. But at the other extreme are proponents of the view that the social structure is independent of the single individual and that individual behavior can be explained and predicted in terms of membership in classes and groups

as they have developed historically, mainly on the basis of mode of subsistence.

Failing to agree with either of these extreme points of view, one may argue that any speculation about the causal interrelation of sociological and psychological factors in the group and in the individual must recognize the fact that these factors have been artificially isolated and abstracted and that no exclusive factual primacy can be given to any of the aspects in a pattern so closely interwoven. An inquiry into the totality of the social process must consequently consider the structure of the social institutions as well as the different ways in which the economic and social organization is experienced by, and incorporated within, the individual.

A more fruitful question than that of factual primacy of factors is the one which inquires to what degree the conceptual tools of psychology and of sociology are equipped to describe the various phenomena in question. Accepting Parsons' assertion that social institutions and the standardized behavior derived from these institutions comprise the major content of sociology,[1] we shall deal

* This paper is a somewhat expanded version of one presented as part of the Symposium on Sociological and Psychological Problems Involved in the Study of Social Stratification and Politics, at the forty-seventh annual meeting of the American Political Science Association in San Francisco in August, 1951.

[1] See T. Parsons, *Essays in Sociological Theory: Pure and Applied* (Glencoe, Ill., 1948).

From the *American Political Science Review*, 1952, Vol. XLVI, No. 1, pp. 44-65. Reprinted by permission of the author and the publisher.

in this paper with the origin and change of institutional patterns with very little, if any reference to psychological concepts. On the other hand, when we turn our attention to the functioning of the institutions and their influence on man and his social behavior, psychology will be predominant.

Harold D. Lasswell's *Psychopathology and Politics*[2] was a pioneer study which tried to integrate psychological and political concepts, and Erich Fromm's *Escape from Freedom*[3] was another outstanding attempt at such a synthesis. (The influence of Fromm's work on the recent group study of *The Authoritarian Personality*[4] can be seen very clearly.) Other valuable attempts to synthesize psychological and sociological aspects have been made by Abram Kardiner,[5] Ralph Linton,[6] Clyde Kluckhohn,[7] and Margaret Mead.[8] In the present writer's previous studies,[9] she has stressed the importance of differentiating the motivational aspect of social behavior from its effects and adaptive value; and we shall take up this distinction, with its implications for political behavior, in the next section. Here we need only emphasize that both social behavior and personality structure are important links in the network of societal interaction, with sociology and psychology representing different levels of organization and of abstraction. As we proceed further, we shall en-

counter the necessity of differentiating sublevels within psychology as well as within sociology. In making, as we can and must, the distinction between the concepts of psychology and those of sociology, it is necessary to keep in mind that the study of individuals in their personality structures is but one of the many methods by which the social structure can be revealed. However, a deep and penetrating study of individuals may often tell us more about the themes of a contemporary society than will a surface description of the existing institutions.

It is intriguing to follow the reverberations of social patterns within the most intimate realms of individual life. We know a little, but not enough, of how social and technological changes play upon neurotic symptoms and how they find their way into the most bizarre delusions of psychotics whose very disturbance is their obvious remoteness from the social realities. And the findings of research on the "authoritarian personality"[10]—a pattern most relevant to the contemporary social scene—have revealed, among other things, such trends as self-alienation, mechanization, standardization, and stereotypy, piecemeal functioning, intolerance of ambiguity, lack of individuation and spontaneity, and a combination of irrationality with manipulative opportunism. These features, discerned in the psychological study of individuals, are closely akin to some of the features inherent in the process of industrial mass production and the machinery by which it operates; the functioning of social institutions seems clearly to be illuminated by studying how they are realized within the individual.

However, we cannot continue to develop concepts of mental health and integration without reference to the economic and social realities. This means that, in addition to the assessment of the rational and manifest purposes of social institutions, we must assess their irrationalities, inconsistencies,

[2] (Chicago, 1930)

[3] (New York, 1941).

[4] The studies for this book (New York, 1950), Vol. 5 of *Studies in Prejudice*, were carried out by T. W. Adorno, E. Frenkel-Brunswick, D. J. Levinson, and R. N. Sanford, and they are its joint authors.

[5] *The Individual and His Society* (New York, 1939).

[6] *The Cultural Background of Personality* (New York, 1945).

[7] *Mirror for Man* (New York, 1949).

[8] *And Keep Your Powder Dry* (New York, 1942).

[9] See especially "Psychoanalysis and Personality Research" in "Symposium on Psychoanalysis by Analyzed Experimental Psychologists," ed. G. W. Allport, *Journal of Abnormal Social Psychology*, Vol. 35, pp. 176-97 (1940), and *Motivation and Behavior*, Vol. 26, No. 3, of Genetic Psychology Monographs (1942).

[10] This and many subsequent references are to the material about and treatment of this concept in *The Authoritarian Personality*. However, also see below, n. 15.

and latent meanings in order to know what kind of behavior we may expect from individuals. The complete appraisal of an individual, the evaluation of his adjustment, his sanity or insanity, implies a knowledge of the social realities, whether these be rational or irrational. All therapeutic techniques and therapeutic goals must be in accord with these realities.

Thus we come to ask what kind and degree of integration of the internal "personality agencies" we may expect from individuals who live in a period of increasing division of labor and of part-functioning in the manufacturing process, from individuals increasingly controlled by outside forces which must remain opaque and unintelligible to them, with the value of the family challenged and many other traditional values in decay, with social changes too rapid to be genuinely assimilated, and with an emphasis on success and competition which compels the individual to a degree of externalization that is only too likely to interfere with internal integration. To make this picture even more complex, the rewards of competition and initiative are increasingly diminished as participation in, and belonging to, big organizations become more important.

On the other side of this picture are forces which counteract to a certain degree the threatened disintegration. The same individual who has to meet the challenges just listed is exposed to a great variety of strivings and attempts, the goal of which is penetration to the fundamentals behind the confusing and shifting surface, and which promise new kinds of stabilities and salvations. Furthermore, the rising number of choices offered the individual in the course of the progress of industrial society may compensate for the restrictions stemming from the same process.

While social institutions in this manner undoubtedly influence the reactions and orientations of individuals, political institutions, such as that of democracy, conversely must be formulated with reference to psychological realities. How should democratic values be made vital to men of various socio-economic and national backgrounds? What degree of rationality, of tolerance of the complexities and conflicts inherent in the democratic process, can be expected of them? How much need for absolutism and dogmatism do we find in the various countries? How can democratic values be stated so that misinterpretation both in the direction of totalitarian absolutism and in the direction of a too far-reaching relativism will be avoided? Some of these questions can be answered by considering the type of personality for whom totalitarian forms of government have special appeal. The political attitudes of this personality group can also serve as paradigms to illustrate the interaction of psychological and sociological variables. But first we must turn briefly to the psychological tools, conceptual and methodological, which are at our disposal in describing man in his society.

I. GENERAL CONSIDERATIONS IN A SCIENCE OF PERSONALITY

Interest in the dynamics of human behavior in its full complexity appeared on the scene of psychology rather suddenly, and chiefly through the influence of psychiatry and psychoanalysis. The suddenness was a result of the fact that those interested in personality as a unit became weary of waiting until academic psychology, using experimental and laboratory techniques, could proceed beyond the study of the relatively simple sensory or motor units with which it customarily dealt. Behaviorism in its earlier forms was not really open to questions of motivation, since it emphasized directly observable ("manifest" or "overt") responses to immediate stimuli, rather than the internal dynamics of personality or the broader context and background of behavior with its consequences that point beyond the momentary situation. In fact, however, the distinction between the manifest and the inferred motivational personality is of the utmost importance in studying our culture. In any advanced culture an individual's real motivations quite often have to be disguised or transformed in order to pass individual and social censorship. Nevertheless, as common observation itself bears witness, as a rule they do not cease to exist and to exert influence. (For example, it is well known that exaggerated friendliness may serve, or even be the direct result of, strong hostile tendencies.) For this reason, the shift of emphasis from the level of external, overt manifestation to the level of motivational dynamics, stemming from psychoanalysis, has opened the way to highly fruitful explanations and predictions, and ultimately to the establishment of a stratified psychology of personality as an exact science.

The concept of underlying motivation supplies us with an instrument which, because of its particular level of abstraction or depth, is helpful in uncovering hitherto unrecognized relationships and consistencies in the field of personality—under the provision, of course, that the relations between inferred drive and overt behavior have been analyzed and the meanings of the former specified in objective, "operational" terms. This type of analysis has been extended from the customary casuistic to the more useful statistical stage in a study on the interrelationships between motivation and behavior.[11] A group of adolescents, known to a group of observers over a period of many years, was rated by the latter on the basis of underlying motivation rather than on the usual one of displayed social techniques. The results supported the original assumption that such "intuitive" drive-ratings are of considerable advantage in organizing a great body of data consisting of descriptions of behavior, of so-called projective materials (such as perceptual responses to inkblots or stories told upon showing of a picture), of self reports, and of other surface material. In fact, by conceiving of seemingly diverse behavioral reactions as alternative manifestations of one and the same dynamic force, we are enabled to resolve successfully many apparent inconsistencies. Central motivations can be established and consistent themes in an individ-

ual's life can be uncovered. It often turns out, if we draw our inferences in this way from a great variety of manifestations (using gross as well as minimal cues) instead of taking verbalized statements or social techniques as directly valid, that we arrive at a more fruitful and unified interpretation of personality, and that such interpretations provide an improved basis for long-range predictions of the socially relevant aspects of behavior.

Having stressed the importance of the motivational approach, we must point out that this emphasis should not lead us to ignore the clear effects which behavior has upon society.[12] In a complete description of personality both aspects, the manifest and the motivational, must necessarily be included. Psychoanalysis and psychiatry cannot be entirely acquitted of the charge of having gone to the extreme of a one-sided emphasis on motivation. In the past, especially, it has very often appeared that a diagnosis of, say, underlying aggression was all that mattered, and the question of whether the underlying hostility led in a compensatory fashion to great achievement or to criminality seemed to be of little importance. In our discussion of political behavior we shall see the necessity of viewing behavior both from the motivational angle and from the angle of manifest appearance and observable results. This is a step which makes possible a great deal of differentiation because it connects human behavior not only to its internal sources but also to external realities. We shall see that, in order to understand fully the reactions of individuals to social issues, we must keep these differentiations in mind and must use this multilayer approach.

In our opinion, Freud's signal contributions to sociology and political science are his interpretation of human behavior from the angle of its latent, unconscious, irrational, and archaic aspect, and his emphasis on the formative influence of early childhood, of dreams and of fantasies. It was Freud who also first pointed out the inti-

[11] *Motivation and Behavior* (above, n. 9).

[12] See "Psychoanalysis and Personality Research" (above, n. 9).

mate interaction of biological and social facts in the individual although he has sometimes been accused of a too far-reaching biological orientation. Such processes as sucking, bowel movement, and masturbation, considered as purely biological phenomena before the advent of the dynamic approach to personality, have been woven by psychoanalysis into the fabric of social interaction. From the newer viewpoint, sucking appears not only as a means of getting food but also as a means of experiencing and expressing affection and aggression, and the process of bowel movement is seen as one which is utilized by the child in his struggle with his parents and with authority in general. We now realize that cultures in general, and individual parents and children in particular, use these biological processes as a medium to induce or to express such social attitudes as submission or stubbornness, generosity or retention, and so forth. Similarly, dreams, which were considered as private and meaningless before Freud, are now being used as a basis for a reconstruction of the most decisive and subtle aspects of interpersonal relationships.

The ways in which Freud deals with social problems, however, are undoubtedly insufficient. His direct writings on the origin and structure of society[13] have been justly criticized for their speculative and ahistoric nature. Indeed Freud, who introduced the historic aspect into the consideration of the individual, did not himself make use of this aspect in describing primitive societies, while, in addition, the close analogy which he draws between the maturational stages of the individual and the maturational stages of societies appears to a large extent unwarranted by fact. Social influences are seen as a series of traumata which bring to a halt and discontinue gratification and expression of instinctual strivings. Though this image of civilization as a pattern of forces chronically interfering with the individual and leaving him mutilated is not altogether without point, it certainly is too narrow. The concept of sublimation, adduced to

explain how the energies of the ungratified instincts are transferred to socially constructive goals, remains relatively sterile and vague in the writings of psychoanalysis, and very little has been said about the satisfactions which may be derived from successfully adopted social roles and identities. This omission indicates that the environment enters the scope of traditional psychoanalytic investigation mainly insofar as it permits a repetition of childhood reactions to father, mother and other persons in the past social environment of the child. Yet social attitudes and social techniques are at least as real as underlying motivation and early childhood, even though we may need to speculate on the latter in order to understand the former. For example, in our own studies, which were focused primarily on the subject's social attitudes,[14] our inquiry into his attitude toward, say, Roosevelt, was not undertaken in order to increase our understanding of his attitude toward his own father. But it is true that we probably would never have been able to understand the range and subtlety of our subject's attitudes toward Roosevelt had we not been guided by the accumulated and integrated findings of psychoanalysis on attitudes toward fathers, father-substitutes, and father-figures.

II. THE AUTHORITARIAN PERSONALITY: A DESCRIPTION ON FOUR LEVELS

The distinct personality pattern which emerged from two Berkeley studies[15] and

---

[13] *Totem and Taboo* (New York, 1918) and *Moses and Monotheism* (New York, 1939).

[14] *The Authoritarian Personality.*

[15] Adult subjects were used for the project which resulted in *The Authoritarian Personality.* Children are the subjects of a second project, now being carried out at the Institute of Child Welfare of the University of California by the present writer with several collaborators. For preliminary reports of the latter, see the writer's "A Study of Prejudice in Children," *Human Relations,* Vol. 1, pp. 295-306, and her "Intolerance of Ambiguity as an Emotional and Perceptual Personality Variable" in Pt. 1 of "Symposium on Interrelationships between Perception and Personality," *Journal of Personality,* Vol. 18, pp. 108-43 (1949).

which we have chosen to call "the authoritarian personality" will serve as a concrete example to illuminate in a more specific way the interaction of psychological and social factors. In our present description of this personality pattern, we shall first use the resources and language of clinical psychology. This approach alone will cover two levels, that of overt social behavior and that of underlying motivation; the discrepancy between the two has been shown to be one of the major characteristics of the authoritarian character. Our subsequent discussion, in this context, of the authoritarian's ways of perceiving and thinking will not introduce a really new level of description, since these matters may be classified with overt behavior as the directly observable reactions of the individual. A third level may be designated as social-psychological, since we shall deal here with attitudes toward social institutions and social roles. Finally, a fourth level of description will be from the sociological point of view, examining the authoritarian personality within the various social and occupational groups. Here some reference will be made to the political and social organization as historical background of the phenomena studied.

Totalitarianism as a political attitude held by individuals in America lends itself especially well to these four levels of description. Since the prevalent political organization in America is not a totalitarian one, such an attitude must be explained psychologically as well as sociologically. In countries where totalitarianism is a pervasive form of enforced organization, the importance of psychological factors involved in the choice of ideology is greatly reduced, for only when the existing institution leaves room for genuine preference do psychological and sociological factors become important.[16]

It is easy to anticipate that it will be impossible to give a pure psychological or a pure sociological description. We attempt here such an artificial isolation in order to demonstrate the relative contribution of the two types of conceptual organization. Naturally, the relatively lopsided descriptions which we have thus chosen to give will yield incomplete pictures. Only when taken together will they constitute an approximately comprehensive determination.

The material evidence of the two Berkeley projects mentioned above takes its start from questionnaire scales designed to elicit responses to a variety of slogans or statements involving social and political attitudes, with special emphasis on "ethnocentrism"—commonly known as racial or national prejudice—including attitudes toward parents, authority, conventional values, criminality, superstition, fellow men, fate, etc. Individuals found to be either extremely high or extremely low on ethnic prejudice were subjected to further study by intensive interviews and by the so-called projective techniques, such as the Thematic Apperception Test.[17] The interviews delved, among other matters, into the subjects' images of various social "outgroups," their spontaneous ideas and conceptions of major political and social events, of religion, of parents and childhood, of friends and of people in general, and of their experiences with, and expectations of, the other sex.

Intercombination and synopsis of results from the various methods employed show that intolerance toward one minority group correlates with intolerance toward other minority groups. This rejection of everything that is "different" goes hand in hand with an undue glorification of one's own group; it is for this reason that the term "ethnocentrism" was introduced. This attitude in turn is related to a broader sociopolitical outlook which can be described as a kind of pseudo-conservatism, since it combines rigid adherence to the *status quo* with readiness to use force for the restora-

[16] See the writer's "*Dynamic and Cognitive Categorization of Qualitative Material:* (1) General Problems and the Thematic Apperception Test, and (2) Interviews of the Ethnically Prejudiced," *Journal of Psychology*, Vol. 25, pp. 253-60 and 261-77 (1948).

[17] For a description of this test, see H. E. Murray and other workers at the Harvard Psychological Clinic, *Explorations in Personality* (New York, 1938), pp. 530-45.

tion of what is extolled as, say, "the true American way of life." Because these various attitudes are closely interrelated, such terms as "authoritarianism," "ethnocentrism," "prejudice," and "antidemocratic" attitude will be used interchangeably throughout this presentation. It should perhaps be noted that the studies, well under way before the end of the last war, concentrated mainly on the fascistic form of totalitarianism, then in the foreground of interest.

1. Clinical Description

The distinct personality syndromes of the two extreme groups, those "high" and those "low" on ethnocentrism, evolve in the main from the analysis of the interviews for which the present writer was mainly responsible. The method of evaluation represents a compromise between individual case studies and quantification.[18] As much as possible of the richness and intricacy of the material was encompassed by a number of specially instructed raters. A number of broadly conceived categories, such as submission to family and degree of aggression and repression, were set up on the basis of a preliminary survey of the interviews. Each subject was then rated on these categories by clinically trained persons who did not know whether the person in question had an authoritarian-ethnocentric or a democratic orientation; the diagnosis of attitudes toward family, sex, etc., thus was always a "blind" one.

The description which follows is a statistically substantiated composite picture; few, if any, single individuals exhibit at the same time and to a marked degree all of the traits listed under either of the two syndromes. From a psychological point of view, an overall summary of the authoritarian personality must first stress the great number of discrepancies and discontinuities —seldom conscious, to be sure—which can be found in this type of individual. The ethnocentric individual is less likely than

the ethnically unprejudiced to face within himself such emotional tendencies as ambivalence, passivity, fear, aggressive feelings against parents and authorities, and instinctual impulses which are considered "bad" or immoral. Because he usually fails to integrate these tendencies with the conscious image he has of himself, he rather tends to ascribe them to the outside world and to fight them there. Closely related to this tendency is his moralistic condemnation of other people. For him the world itself comes to appear as a dangerous and hostile place, to be viewed with distrust, suspicion, and cynicism. An undercurrent of panic is evident in his fear that food and other supplies may run short and that he may be left helpless in the face of danger, which he is all too ready to anticipate. Asked to retell a story in which aggressive as well as friendly characters were described, the prejudiced children as a group recalled a greater number of aggressive characters, whereas the unprejudiced children recalled a greater number of friendly characters, than had been mentioned in the story originally read to them. Moreover, the total distortion of reality—here the original story —was greater among the ethnocentric children.[19]

It is easy to understand that persons so fear-ridden will tend to be unusually manipulative and exploitive in their relations with others. Fellow men become, to borrow a term from Otto Fenichel, mainly "deliverers of goods."[20] Thus, along with the self-centered overpersonalization of the social scene, human relationships become depersonalized. The kind of material-magic dependency just described extends not only to people and authority but also to inanimate forces; ethnocentric subjects subscribe more often to superstitious beliefs. It seems to be important for them to use devices by which they can get evil and dangerous forces to join them on their side. Such support

[18] See the article in two parts cited above, n. 16.

[19] See "Intolerance of Ambiguity as a Personality Variable" (above, n. 15), pp. 123 ff.

[20] Psychoanalytic Theory of Neurosis (New York, 1945).

should be considered a substitute for an underdeveloped self-reliance; and it is apparently this same feeling of helplessness, together with underlying destructive impulses, which leads the ethnocentric subject to agree more often than others with questionnaire statements which describe or predict doom and catastrophe, the spread of contagious diseases, and so forth.

The prejudiced person's attitude toward work shows an externalization similar to that just noted in his attitude toward people and animistic forces. He is indifferent toward the content of work and lays emphasis upon work mainly as a means to success and power.

Prejudiced individuals also tend to create and adopt extreme and mutually exclusive pairs of values such as dominance-submission, cleanliness-dirtiness, badness-goodness, virtue-vice, masculinity-femininity, and so forth. They consider the absoluteness of such dichotomies to be natural and eternal and so exclude the possibility of any intermediate or overlapping position. Their adherence to these delineated norms is likely to be rigid, even though it may imply restrictions and disadvantages for their own group. Thus it is that not only the prejudiced men but also the prejudiced women favor restricting women to narrowly defined fields of activity which are considered to be "feminine."

In an attempt to understand these rigidities and dependencies, we may turn to the childhood situation of our authoritarian-minded subjects. Here we find a tendency toward rigid discipline on the part of the parents. They demand that their children learn quickly the external, rigid, and superficial values which they themselves have adopted but which are beyond the comprehension of children. This insistence may be explained by the fact that faithful execution of prescribed roles and the exchange of duties and obligations is, in the families of the prejudiced, often given preference over the exchange of free-flowing affection. In telling of their parents, ethnocentric children tend to think in the category of strict-

ness and harshness, whereas the unprejudiced tend to think primarily in terms of companionship. We are led to assume that an authoritarian home regime, which induces a relative lack of mutuality in the area of emotion and shifts emphasis onto the exchange of "goods" and of material benefits without adequate development of underlying self-reliance, forms the basis for the opportunistic type of dependence of children on their parents which is described here, and that the inherent general stereotypy is an outcome of this orientation.

However, it is of great importance that, although he tends to submit to the authority of his parents on the surface level, the authoritarian child harbors an underlying resentment against them. Along with conventional, stereotypical idealization of the parents, we find indications that the child feels, without being fully aware of it, that he has been victimized by them. Frequently ethnocentric children tend to begin, when speaking of their parents, somewhat vaguely and on a note of general admiration; but the praise will likely be followed by descriptions of specific episodes of neglect, unjust discipline and the like. Fear and dependency seem not only to discourage the child from conscious criticism of his parents but further to lead to an acceptance of punishment and to an identification with the punishing authority.

It is especially the male authoritarian who seems intimidated by a threatening father figure; and we may note here that our material shows the family of the ethnocentric individual to be more often father-dominated, whereas that of the unprejudiced is more frequently mother-centered. However, since in the prejudiced home the closeness of the parent-child relationship is based more on fear than on love, and since the punishments and rewards meted out must seem inconsistent to the child, no genuine identification with parents nor real internalization of values can be achieved.

The ambivalent submission to the parent of the same sex, especially that of the son to the father, and the ensuing latent homosexuality are often counteracted by a rigid display of the accepted characteristics of one's own sex and by repression in oneself of tendencies of the opposite sex. The prejudiced man tends to think of himself as active, determined, energetic, independent, tough, and successful in the competitive struggle. We may find here parallels to the well-known Nazi emphasis on virility. Of course, there is no room in this ego-ideal for passivity and softness, and strong defenses are accordingly erected against these attitudes in general, with the result that only their opposites are established in consciousness. Nonetheless, inclinations toward dependency and a far-reaching passivity— although they remain unaccepted and ego-alien—are evident. There is reason to speak of a sexual marginality of the ethnocentric man and to recall also the sexual deviations observed in the Nazi "elite."

In addition to the dichotomizing of sex roles *per se* by the prejudiced, we also find among them dichotomous sex attitudes in a broader sense of the term, such as the sharp opposition of "sex" versus "marriage," of "pure" versus "low" women, and so forth. This explains why the prejudiced woman clings to a self-image of "femininity" defined by subservience to, and adulation of, men at the same time that she shows evidence of an exploitive and hostile attitude toward men.

To summarize our description thus far, in our extremely ethnocentric subjects, both adults and children, we find surface conformity lacking integration and expressing itself in a stereotyped approach devoid of genuine affect in most areas of life. This tendency toward a conventional, externalized, shallow type of social relation has a generally pervasive character in the authoritarian personality. Even in the purely cognitive domain, as we shall see, ready-made clichés tend to take the place of spontaneous reactions.

2. Perception and Thinking

In the foregoing we have seen that the authoritarian personality tends to resort to black-white judgments and to unqualified and unambiguous overall acceptance or rejection of other people. In his descriptions, whether of ingroup or outgroup, of parents, or of a political leader, this individual displays both stereotypy and lack of differentiation—in short, an all-or-nothing approach. His opinions are "closed" and cannot be modified; new experiences are immediately viewed from the standpoint of the old set and are classified in the same way as the earlier ones.

The rigidity of the ethnocentric person which is implied in this presentation seems to a certain extent to be a generalized personality trait. Experiments on perception and thinking carried out with the children in our study show that stimuli which are unfamiliar, ambiguous, or subject to change are experienced by the prejudiced as strange, bewildering, and disturbing, much as they would be to a leader lacking in absolute determination.[21] Children in this group tend either to jump to premature conclusions or to hold on rigidly to a familiar stimulus and to ignore the changes that may prevail. In the retelling of the story mentioned above, the ethnocentric children reproduce literally some of the phrases but misrepresent the essence of the story more often than do the unprejudiced children. Clinging to a concrete, isolated detail of reality and over-generalizing are two alternative ways of avoiding complexity and of making things definite at the expense of the existing facts. Indeed, with the ethnocentric child, the intolerance of ambiguity seems to pervade the solving of problems ranging from those of parent-child relationship and sex roles to simple perceptual and intellectual tasks. In the course of these attempted solutions a subtle but profound distortion of reality must necessarily take place, since stereotypical categorizations can never do justice to all of the aspects of reality.

The implication of this intolerance of ambiguity and of complexity for political behavior cannot be stressed too much. It is

[21] See "Intolerance of Ambiguity as a Personality Factor," pp. 126 ff.

obvious that difficulties will be encountered in explaining democratic values to individuals who have the need for a definitely-structured social outlook and for organization in simple and clear-cut, hierarchical rather than equalitarian, terms which exclude the possibility of free and dynamic exchange of influences.

In this connection a German psychologist, E. R. Jaensch, perhaps the foremost exponent of Nazi ideology in psychology, praises precise, firm, regular reactions which are unambiguously tied to external stimulus configurations.[22] He refers to the physics of Einstein as a type of science "without consideration of reality" and with a tendency to "dissolve all reality into theory" and contrasts this type of approach with the more desirable "concretely-oriented German physics." Jaensch misses the point that more abstract attitudes, oriented toward overall principles, often are better able to penetrate to reality than is an exclusive attention to facts in their concreteness. In our experiments with authoritarian-minded children, we were able to demonstrate that an over-respect for the concrete did not do justice to the problems and principles inherent in the conceptual tasks with which our subjects had been confronted. As was pointed out above, an over-concrete attitude often turns into overgeneralization; and both are seen to be inferior approaches compared with the method of abstract thinking.

Our observations have led us to believe that the adjustment of the authoritarian person is confined to narrowly circumscribed conditions. It is precisely his extreme conformity, rigidity, and need to ascribe all his own weaknesses and shortcomings to a scapegoat which account for the restricted conditions of his functioning. In fact, Jaensch has considered adaptability and tolerance of tentativeness to be a sign of degeneration:

In the case of racial mixture, nature has to leave everything uncertain and in suspense; the individual at birth may be endowed with nothing fixed and certain but only with the uncertainty, indeterminability and changeability which would enable him to adjust to each of the various conditions of life. The opposite is true if an individual possesses only ancestors who from time immemorial have lived in the North German space and within its population. From the biological point of view, it is not only extremely probable but certain that such an individual will live under the same environmental conditions as his ancestors. The characteristics necessary for this, therefore, may be safely placed in his cradle as innate, fixed and univocally determined features.[23]

As with many contentions of Jaensch, this one too is far from being empirically verified. Though it is sometimes true that the ethnically marginal person is more adaptable, this position often leads to greater rigidity. But we shall have to say more about this point in the following sections.

Concerning the democratic-minded person, it may suffice here to emphasize that he is generally better able to face uncertainties and conflicts, as indeed he must in order to master the physical and social realities. Readiness to recognize, to accept, and to master diversities, conflicts, and differences in oneself and in others, as contrasted with the need to set off clear demarcation lines, was found to be one of the most basic distinguishing criteria of the two opposite patterns in our studies.

3. Social-Psychological Description

We may now turn back and interpret much of what we have said about the authoritarian personality pattern in the light of a further fact, that is, his rigid conformity to cultural clichés. It must be stressed that this conformity does not consist in a genuine identification with traditional values. Our evidence points to the fact that the authoritarian person has frequently lost his roots in tradition and has made an attempt to compensate for this loss by a rather nonfunctional, forced, and rigid conformity. This surface-conformity to externalized values can be observed in a variety of spheres of life. One of the earliest expres-

[22] See his *Der Gegentypus* (Leipzig, 1938).

[23] *Ibid.*, pp. 230 ff.

sions is to be found in his attitude toward parents. His conception of sex roles[24] is likewise highly conventionalized, with emphasis on activity, determination, toughness, and success in the masculine ideal, and on passivity and subservience in the feminine ideal; and in all personal relationships preference is given to restricted roles rather than to vaguely defined ones. Thinking in hierarchical terms—such as dominance versus submission, orientation toward power and success, dichotomizing of sex roles, and the like would have to be considered part of this conformity. In fact, most of the dichotomies which imply valuation, such as good and evil, strength and weakness, dirtiness and cleanliness, masculinity and femininity, can be seen as mirroring a conventional inventory of social clichés. The ethnocentric group, which desperately wants to "belong" and to be successful, acts as custodian of these distinctions, keeping them always in mind as the approved vehicles by which its most obsessively cherished goals may be reached.

The moralistic conventionalism of the authoritarian personality characterizes not only the more conservative type within this group but also the lunatic fringe and the psychopathic variety. A set of interviews with the highly ethnocentric among prison inmates has shown that on certain levels this group ardently identifies itself with the prevalent conventional values and condemns ethnic outgroups on the basis of their deviations from these values.[25] These interviews show widespread preoccupation with external social goals, a preoccupation constantly directed toward the narrow and steep ascent to a higher social status. Since the individuals so absorbed tend to identify themselves with a group which is socially and economically superior to their own, it follows that their sense of belonging to the

privileged groups is extremely tenuous. Their level of aspiration is often quite fantastic; in certain cases the intellectual and artistic aspirations have even less basis in reality than had those of some of the Nazi leaders. It is the discrepancy between the status aspired to and that achieved which leads to the feeling of social and economic marginality.

Because of their real or imagined marginality, some individuals feel persistently threatened with being degraded in one way or another. It is in defense against the possibility of being grouped with the underdog that identification with the privileged groups is so insistently asserted. Apparently the great number of conflicts and confusions concerning personal, sexual, and social roles are responsible for determined efforts to eliminate uncertainties in all contexts of life; yet our interview material furnishes ample evidence that chaos and violent destructiveness lurk behind the rigid surface, posing dangers to the very society to which there seems to be conformity.

The concept of social marginality includes both sociological and psychological aspects. Authoritarianism correlates less well with actual socio-economic status (as will be shown later) than with subjective dissatisfaction with one's status; and therefore, on the basis of our material, we must expand the concept of marginality to cover sexual and physical marginality as well. In passing, we may refer to the case of a boy in our study who, though from a liberal home, reveals attitudes of extreme ethnocentrism. The interview material points to a history of illness and ensuing feelings of physical inadequacy as probable reasons for his need to assert his superiority by designating the outgroups as inferior.

As mentioned above, external criteria, especially social status, are the yardsticks by which the ethnocentric individual tends to appraise people in general; these criteria furnish the grounds on which he either admires and accepts or rejects his fellow men. The ethnocentric person tends to take cognizance primarily of whether the be-

[24] For detailed exposition of the concept of "role," see Linton, *The Cultural Background of Personality*, and Parsons, *Essays in Sociological Theory*.

[25] The interviews, conducted by W. R. Morrow, are described in *The Authoritarian Personality*.

havior of individuals is appropriate to alleged social roles, and tends to ignore the intrinsic values of the individuals themselves. He takes social institutions so literally that his personal orientation and behavior reflect in many ways the basic structure of certain gross features of our civilization. The relative uniformity in the personality structure of individuals in the ethnocentric group is derived from this adoption of status and role values. However, this does not mean that the behavior and feelings of these individuals represent our social institutions in *all* of their essential aspects. We have evidence that, in their reactions to perception, thinking, and memory tasks, ethnocentric individuals show great fidelity with respect to concrete details but tend to miss the overall problem.[26] A similar quality can be discerned in their interpretations of social institutions. Among other distortions, they tend to simplify the meaning of these institutions and interpret the predominant values too homogeneously and too absolutely in the direction of status values, ignoring other trends in the civilization. In the final analysis, rigid adherence to conventional values turns out to be no more than a superstructure beneath which operate many tendencies which are self-destructive of the society to which superficial conformity has been achieved.

It was, to repeat, psychoanalysis which introduced the differentiation between manifest and latent content, a distinction which is seen to be especially important for an understanding of the authoritarian personality. In the tradition of a pre-Freudian social psychology, we would have to take exaggerated conformity at its face value and would thus overlook the fact that it stems from feelings of social insecurity and resentment and that it can switch dramatically into its opposite. Both conformity and its reverse, chaotic upheaval, are considered by the authoritarian person to be useful means for gaining power, and he will give preference to whichever appears more likely to succeed.

[26] See "Intolerance to Ambiguity as a Personality Variable," pp. 126. ff.

4. Sociological Considerations

In the preceding few pages we have begun to discuss some psychological findings in more nearly sociological language. It is now appropriate to inquire whether or not the feeling of social marginality which is so characteristic of the ethnocentric individual, is related to distinct socio-economic factors. In an attempt to determine the sociological factors in the background of the authoritarian personality, we used a variety of approaches.[27] A questionnaire was used to ascertain the political preferences, group memberships and incomes of our subjects. An analysis of the responses to questions on political party preference indicates that no relationship exists between ethnocentrism and preference for either the Democratic or Republican Party as such, but that New Deal Democrats and Willkie Republicans obtain significantly lower scores on ethnocentrism than do members of the traditional wings of the Democratic and Republican Parties. The correlation of .5, obtained with the groupings just described, shows, however, that there is considerable individual variability. Further analysis reveals that in the middle-class groups the relation between ethnocentrism and political preference is much closer than in working-class groups. Different individuals seem to support a given political group for different reasons, and inquiry into the basis of selection is as important as establishing group membership. There is, furthermore, a significant difference in degree of ethnocentrism between those individuals who agree with the politics of their parents and those who disagree. As we might expect from the psychological data, the subjects who disagree with their parents on politics are significantly lower on ethnocentrism than those who agree.

Economic and social stratification may to a certain degree determine party preference,

[27] The material of this and the following two paragraphs is based on Ch. 5 of *The Authoritarian Personality*, prepared and written by Levinson. The remainder of the present section is based on material, as yet unpublished, from the project on Social Discrimination in Children referred to above, n. 15.

but they seem to have little to do with such social and political attitudes as ethnic prejudice. We find that members of a CIO union had a slightly higher mean score on ethnocentrism than a Parent Teachers Association group composed largely of middle-class members of a relatively high educational level. Members of a women's club were substantially higher on ethnocentrism than were a group of members of the League of Women Voters. In the latter instance, neither actual class nor educational level differentiated the two groups; but such factors as upward economic mobility, pseudo-conservative values, and the like, did.

There is a slight tendency for the lowest and highest income groups to score higher than the middle-income group on ethnocentrism, while within the latter ethnocentrism seems to decrease as income increases. These relationships, however, are so tenuous as to support the hypothesis that economic factors as such are not closely related to ethnocentrism so far as individuals are concerned. These findings are in line with those of other observers to the effect that economic factors alone are insufficient to account for the occurrence of fascist movements.[28] We must view the economic and sociological factors in the light of their meaning to the individual and to society as a whole if we are to increase their predictive value.

Over a period of time the present writer was able to collect extended data on the socio-economic history of the families of extremely ethnocentric and of non-ethnocentric children. One of the chief purposes of obtaining this material was to see whether or not the feeling of marginality which is so important to ethnocentrism is determined by sudden changes in the socio-economic status of the families. The assumption in collecting such data was that loss of status might undermine an individual's social security and that gain in status might lead to all kinds of attempts to maintain the

gain. This hypothesis has been only partially confirmed in the sense that families with a long history of privileged socio-economic status seem to be on the whole less ethnocentric than families with unstable histories; but instability of status, *per se,* goes almost as often with tolerance as it does with ethnocentrism.

For the most part the families studied had been recruited from lower-middle-class and middle-class sectors of the population. As a group, the ethnocentric families do not differ to any marked degree from the more democratic-minded families in purely economic terms, i.e., difference in income, housing conditions, number of cars, radios, etc. However, within the group studied, the few individuals whose living conditions fell decidedly below middle-class standards were mostly ethnocentric and those whose conditions were definitely above them were mostly liberal. Since the neighborhood of the schools from which our subjects were drawn would indicate middle-class identification on the part of all the families studied, the differences in ethnocentrism which we observed may thus hinge upon the relation of level of status-aspiration to actual status rather than upon status *per se.*

Ethnocentrism also seems more closely related to the occupational affiliation of families than to purely economic factors. The parents and grandparents of unprejudiced children are significantly more often from professional fields, such as medicine, law, teaching, the ministry, etc., than are those of ethnocentric children. We may refer here to Daniel Lerner's finding that a certain proportion of the Nazi elite, especially the propagandists, were intellectuals, or, as he put it, more precisely "alienated intellectuals."[29] This is not as contradictory to our findings as it may seem at first glance. Some of our authoritarian subjects display intellectual, or rather pseudo-intellectual, and artistic ambitions which—according to their own report—they were unable to realize because they were cheated of their

---

[28] So, for example, reported Reinhard Bendix in "Social Stratification and Political Power," a paper read at the Symposium in which the present one was originally presented.

[29] In "Elites: The Psychosocial Elect in Politics," another of the papers read at the Symposium on Social Stratification and Politics.

opportunities. However, whereas in Germany this type of pseudo-intellectual possesses a certain accepted occupational status of his own, in America he is likely to turn to some kind of substitute occupation, such as working in a garage or being a waiter, and he is therefore often listed under occupational groups other than artistic or intellectual ones. In the relatively rare cases where the father or grandfather of our ethnocentric subjects comes from one of the professions, it is likely to be the engineering profession.

These results point to a certain relationship between education and freedom from prejudice. Information, and especially information along the lines of social science, is by no means directly related to economic factors, however. The crucial factor seems to be a certain psychological receptiveness accompanied by accessibility to facts. This is why experiments have shown that extensive information about minority groups does not markedly alter the beliefs of ethnocentric persons.

We find, furthermore, a higher percentage of non-ethnocentric families among the small merchants in our sample and a higher percentage of ethnocentric families among the workers. This circumstance may be an indication that the small merchant in America, in spite of the big monopolies, does not yet feel basically threatened. (In Germany, as we know, the small independent lower-middle-class groups contributed the greatest number of Nazi followers.) Among employees as a whole, we find an even distribution of ethnocentric and unprejudiced families. In particular, however, the salesmen, policemen, firemen, etc., are more frequently among the prejudiced, while bus drivers, accountants, and government workers are more frequently among the unprejudiced. Some of these relationships can perhaps be explained psychologically. Thus, choosing the occupation of salesman may indicate self-promoting tendencies and choosing that of policeman may reveal identification with authority and aggression, whereas choosing to be a bus driver may be related to enjoyment of this kind of activity as an end in itself.

In general, the ethnocentric individual tends toward a more unstable history of work than the non-ethnocentric. He seems to be less rooted in his daily task, and there is a greater discrepancy between aspiration level and performance. Another possible source of excessive status concern may be seen in the fact that the parents of our ethnocentric children report significantly more often than the others that their own parents were foreign born (especially Italian and German), indicating perhaps that they still see themselves as enmeshed in the process of assimilation.

While these socio-economic considerations throw some light on our problem, the fact remains that certain families or individuals accept their objective social marginality cheerfully while others develop rigid defenses against it; the latter apparently have to reject the "outgroups" in order to demonstrate that they themselves are not weak or different. Economic deprivation may be one differential factor, but there undoubtedly are others. Thus we found in our study that certain families are preoccupied with the maintenance of their middle-class status and of the social distance from ethnic minority groups who may live nearby, while other families of similar socio-economic level show no similar tendencies. At the same time the political attitudes of the two groups —similar in socio-economic history as they often are—range from extreme ethnocentrism to a stable liberalism. Perhaps the foregoing paragraphs may be illustrated by the following concrete examples, which describe the backgrounds of one of our most prejudiced and of one of our most unprejudiced children:

The socio-economic histories of the two families show great similarity. The father of the unprejudiced child, whom we shall call "Joan," had at the time of our interview just sold a small restaurant which he had come to consider a bad investment. His professional history includes managing a store, selling insurance, and working in a restaurant as waiter and cook. He is a college graduate as is his wife, a trained musician who is now a school teacher. Joan's maternal grandfather, according to his daughter, was first "a small town doctor where he was a dictator and patriarch to the population. He entered the army as a medical officer and liked the opportunity which it gave him for expressing authority." Joan's mother apparently received a great deal of warmth from her own mother, but she rebelled against her father. Joan's father was born in Yugoslavia, the son of a leader in a liberal party who was a pharmacist by profession and whose function in the community was similar to that of a doctor. Though the father's occupational history, especially as compared with that of his parents and that of the parents of his wife, could have led to a feeling of social marginality, this family actually does not seem to be dissatisfied with its present status; much of the time of its members is devoted to such pursuits as supporting the liberal causes of the community, participating in discussion groups, and so forth.

Very different are the psychological characteristics and social beliefs of another family with a similar socio-economic history. The father of "Karl," one of the most ethnocentric boys in our study, is a mechanic. Karl's mother was born in this country, and so was her father, while her mother was born in England. Karl's maternal grandfather was a doctor, as was the case with the unprejudiced Joan's maternal grandfather. But while the marriages of Joan's grandparents were stable on both sides, Karl's maternal grandmother had divorced her husband shortly after Karl's mother was born. In fact, Karl's mother had a succession of stepfathers of whom one, who was a combination of actor and coal miner, played the most important role for her. Karl's father and his own father were born in this country, whereas the child's paternal grandmother came from Germany. The paternal grandparents died when Karl's father was four years old, and his father was reared by grandparents "who were rich but not generous with their money." (They owned a large farm and a wholesale liquor store.) Both of Karl's parents had been exposed to strict discipline. Though Karl's father is a mechanic, he asserts that his occupation is only temporary since he is likely soon to make a big mechanical invention. This aspiration remains on a fantasy level since there is little evidence of any concrete work toward the goal. Similarly, Karl's mother, who works as a waitress, thinks that some day she will compose music or write a novel. She finished the eighth grade, whereas the father's education stopped even before he had reached this level. It would lead too far here to go into the details of the political beliefs of Karl and of his family; it

may suffice to say that they were definitely on the fascistic side.

Future publications will include further cases in which socio-economic background fails to account for political and ethnic attitudes, along with others which can readily be understood in such terms.

III. CONCLUSION

By way of summary, it has appeared inadvisable to attempt any far-reaching compartmentalization of sociological vs. psychological description. In our psychological description we found ourselves concerned with parental figures, with authority, with child-training, mating behavior, and so forth. All of these are concepts frequently referred to by sociologists. On the other hand, we had to stress the fact that the psychological, and in particular the psychoanalytic, approach enables us to catch certain subtle aspects of human behavior which are usually by-passed in purely sociological descriptions. For example, such a formal principle as that of the closeness of opposites, first observed by Freud in discussing the vicissitudes of instincts, has been shown to be a much more general characteristic of individual behavior than was originally anticipated; it is probably applicable to societies as well. Depth psychology has challenged the dominance of the phenotype in psychological thinking and has sharpened our eyes to the underlying dynamic patterns.

Thus we found in our ethnocentric men that stress on virility goes hand in hand with an underlying passivity and receptivity which leads to the wish to follow a strong leader and to be his lieutenant. A person of this kind demands approval of, and submission to, parents, teachers, and authority in general; at the same time his underlying resentment and even hatred of such authority is only thinly disguised in his protocols. His explicit emphasis on conventional values is paralleled by a leaning toward destruction and chaos. In fact, there seems to be a vacillation between a total adoption and a total negation of the prevalent values of society; in this sense, lack of distance and too much distance from cultural values seem closely related. The avoidance of ambiguity and the need for absolutes indicate a desperate attempt to counteract internal chaos and the lack of social and personal identity. Ramifications of the pattern can be found in the prevalence of premature reduction of ambiguous perceptual and cognitive patterns to certainty by clinging to the familiar or by superimposing one or many distorting clichés upon stimuli which are not manageable in a simple or stereotyped fashion. The same tendency toward oversimplification often leads to anti-intellectualism and to the feeling that individualism, with its emphasis on uniqueness and on responsibility, is too heavy a burden.

In a society in which alternative ideologies are offered, a prediction, from psychological data, of such social and political beliefs as liberalism or totalitarianism seems to offer good chances of success. Prediction of the ethnocentrism score on the basis of the clinical interview has been fairly successful in our studies. In addition to the features already mentioned, insight into one's own shortcomings, thinking in social and psychological terms, and equalitarianism in interpersonal relations seemed intimately connected with liberalism, while externalization of one's own problems and their projection into the environment and into the social scene, as well as excessive power-orientation, seemed intimately connected with ethnocentrism. Certain personality scales correlate as high as .8 with fascist ideology.

The correlations of authoritarian attitudes with socio-economic factors as such are much less pronounced. Some relations have been found to occupational categories, as well as to the fact of having a long history of American ancestry. Particularly important in this connection is the concept of social marginality. Since this concept is best defined in terms of the relation between aspired and achieved status, it is tied to both sociological and psychological factors;

and it has been extended to cover sexual and physical marginality as well. Any of these kinds of marginality will often—but by no means always—lead to overconformity and rigidity in the social, as well as in the cognitive, area.

All this is not to say that the frequency of the authoritarian personality within a given society will primarily determine whether totalitarianism as a political movement will or will not come to the fore in that society at a given time. It is not enough that a few people support such a movement; there must be mass support in the end. In our society the increasing mental standardization accompanying the processes of mass production, the increasing difficulty of genuine identification with society due to the anonymity of the big organizations and the ensuing isolation of the individual, the unintelligibility of political and social forces, the decline of the individual's ability to decide and master his life rationally and autonomously, and finally the power of propaganda machinery to manipulate—are among the most potent of the factors which might contribute to such mass support in the foreseeable future. The tradition of having a many-power system and the tradition of democracy, the readiness to criticize governmental as well as parental authorities, the resistance against oversystematization, the increased number of choices offered by technological progress, and the intensified attempt to understand the social and economic processes in their inconsistencies and irrationalities—are among the most potent preventive factors which justify an optimistic outlook.

Since every individual possesses features of the authoritarian as well as of the democratic personality, though in varying proportions, such objective factors as economic conditions and such psychological factors as feelings of dissatisfaction, helplessness, and isolation may decide the issue in a particular overall situation. Otherwise we could not understand the relatively abrupt increase of authoritarianism and ethnocentrism in Nazi Germany. We certainly cannot consider ethnocentrism, fascism, and communism as due solely to short-comings of backward and immature individuals; rather, we must see such mass movements as intrinsic in the totality of social organization. As we have stated before, it is especially the ethnocentric individual who seems to be responsive to trends within our society, to the extent that he seems culture-bound. Instead of showing individual faults, he seems to be the prototype of a member of a mass society. He has given up his personal identity and is ready to be moved by propaganda. Even his hate is mobile and can be directed from one object to another. Therefore, we overrate such an individual if we assume that his behavior is determined by self-interest, political, economic, or social. In effect, the Nazi elite acted against its own interest and in the direction of self-destruction; in this case, rational self-interest was overlaid by the need for self-glorification and for an over-estimation of the self's own strength, as well as by the corresponding need to deprecate the strength of the enemy and—characteristically—to see the enemy as effeminate.

Returning once more to the authoritarian individual in our society, we note that—strangely enough—it is this externally over-adjusted type of person who is internally much less adjusted than the democratic-minded individual. The relation of the latter to society can best be described as one of medium distance. It is true that the authoritarian character in a certain sense is a mirror of his society. Yet at the same time he over-simplifies and distorts the social and cultural realities which have shaped him, as he distorts the perceptual ones. He reacts to some of the clichés rather than to the underlying complexities of our society. For this reason his adjustments function under narrowly circumscribed conditions only. He is not adapted to change and thus lacks one of the most important requirements in all modern societies.

The individual whose relationship to society is more basic and more reliable, is at the same time one who can afford to be more critical and who can face more easily the external as well as the internal inconsistencies. So long as these inconsistencies can be faced, splitting of the personality can be avoided and a greater flexibility and integration is possible, even if this integration is achieved by nothing more than an awareness that one has to behave inconsistently. There is no way around the fact that in a democracy each citizen is called upon to accept many-sidedness, conflicts, uncertainties, differences, and complexities. But this necessity is compatible with, and even congenial to, the holding of strong beliefs in intrinsic principles of conduct, so long as these principles are broadly and flexibly conceived and alternative manifestations are permitted. Rigid adherence to an absolute dogma is a poor substitute for such intrinsic, and basically more consistent, principles; it constitutes an inadequate attempt to escape lurking chaos, cynicism, and unbridled relativism. It is for this reason that superpatriots and defenders of a rigid national code may abruptly turn to disbelief and even treachery.

Should the more individualized approach to other people and to themselves and the greater courage to be "different" which are found among democratic-minded persons be interpreted to mean that they are less interwoven with their culture than are ethnocentric individuals? We may perhaps say that the former are less rigidly culture-bound; but they are not any less determined by the general institutions of our culture than are the authoritarian personalities. Christian ethics with its emphasis on internalization, the American melting-pot ideal, the democratic tradition with its protective attitude toward the weak, the emphasis on individualism—all of these human institutions must certainly be called upon to help explain the democratic personality. Today as never before we witness a contrasting crystallization of the two patterns, although they may frequently be interwoven. Power-orientation, anti-intellectualism, externalization, hostile exclusion, rigid stereotyping, and dogmatism are on the one side; understanding, thoughtfulness, empathy, compassion, insight, flexibility, justice, reason, and scholarship are on the other.

One of the important questions facing us today is just how much ambiguity, uncertainty, and dissolution of traditional values individuals are able to face without being overcome by anxiety and by a wish to "escape from freedom," to use the term popularized by Fromm. New constructive solutions, free of recourse to oversimplica- tion and dogmatism, will have to be substituted for discarded ones if we are to avoid putting too great a burden upon the individual. Only if we succeed in this effort can we circumvent the tendency of certain individuals to compensate for their own personal impotence by erecting the image of an all-powerful leader and by attaching themselves to a doctrine which promises an absolute and all-embracing answer to their confusions.

·7·

Group Processes: Interaction, Communication and Influence, Social Reinforcement

SOME PRINCIPLES OF MASS PERSUASION

THE BASIC PSYCHOLOGY OF RUMOR

THE BOLSHEVIK AGITATOR

DETERMINANTS OF VOTING BEHAVIOR

INTERACTION BETWEEN ATTITUDE AND THE DEFINITION OF THE SITUATION IN THE EXPRESSION OF PUBLIC OPINION

SOME PATTERNED CONSEQUENCES OF MEMBERSHIP IN A COLLEGE COMMUNITY

LEADERSHIP SELECTION IN URBAN LOCALITY AREAS

SOME PRINCIPLES OF MASS PERSUASION

SELECTED FINDINGS OF RESEARCH ON THE
SALE OF UNITED STATES WAR BONDS

DORWIN CARTWRIGHT

Among the many technological advances of the past century that have produced changes in social organization, the development of the mass media of communication promises to be the most far-reaching. Techniques making possible the instantaneous transmission of visual and auditory messages around the world have greatly heightened the interdependence among ever larger numbers of people. It has now become possible from one source to influence the thinking and behavior of hundreds of millions of people. One person can now address at one time a major portion of the world's population to educate, entertain, incite, or allay fears. Only psychological and social factors make it impossible at the present time to assemble into a single audience virtually the entire population of the world.

This heightened interdependence of people means that the possibilities of mobilizing mass social action have been greatly increased. It is conceivable that one persuasive person could, through the use of mass media, bend the world's population to his will. Writers have described such a state of affairs, and demagogues have tried to create one, but nothing so drastic has yet even been approached.

Perhaps because of fears aroused by such a possibility, there has been a tendency to exaggerate both the possible evils of mass persuasion and its powers to influence behavior. An examination of the actual effectiveness of campaigns of mass persuasion may contribute to objective thinking.

In the course of a year in the United States alone, literally scores of organizations make use of a significant part of the mass media in order to carry on some campaign. Only the financial cost of using the media seems to limit their use for these purposes. One need mention but a few examples to suggest an almost endless list. The financing of social welfare agencies throughout the United States, for instance, is accomplished largely through annual campaigns designed to enlist contributions from the general public. Political campaigns are an essential part of any democratic political system. During the war the various governments relied upon campaigns to organize public behavior behind their national war efforts. And campaigns are currently under way to induce people to drive in such a way as to reduce traffic accidents, to eat the kinds of food that will create better standards of health, to take steps necessary to cure cancer, to contribute to the endowment of educational institutions, to participate in food production programs of the government, to support or oppose specific legislation, etc., etc. Most

From *Human Relations,* 1949, 2, 253-267. Reprinted by permission of the author and the publisher.

of the activities of businesses intended to promote the sale of goods by means of advertising should be included in this list.

Despite the great reliance placed upon campaigns by organizations of all types, it is none the less evident that campaigns do not necessarily succeed in inducing desired behavior among any substantial proportion of the population. As research techniques have become available to evaluate the actual effects of campaigns, it has become a rather common experience for organizations and agencies to spend substantial sums of money on such activities only to find from objective appraisals that little perceptible effect was accomplished. It is not yet possible on the basis of research to state exactly how large a campaign of what kind is required to produce a given amount of influence on mass behavior, but evidence is accumulating to indicate that significant changes in behavior as a result of campaigns are rather the exception than the rule.

During the recent war there arose an opportunity to collect some data relevant to this problem. The United States Government undertook, as a part of its inflation control program, to sell Savings Bonds to the population by means of campaigns. Regular research projects, undertaken to make these efforts as effective and efficient as possible, provide some data concerning the effects produced by campaigns of various kinds and magnitudes. Since the major part of the effort going into these campaigns was contributed voluntarily, it was not possible to get a precise measure of their magnitude even in terms of the money value of their costs, but fairly good estimates were possible. Some illustrative findings may be cited. During the Second War Loan it was estimated that slightly more than $12,000,-000 worth of measurable advertising was displayed through the various mass media. In addition to this there were countless rallies, meetings, editorials, feature articles, and the like. In other words, during a period of approximately two months there was developed an unusually concentrated campaign of social pressure to induce people to buy War Bonds. What were the measurable effects? A national survey conducted after the campaign found that 62 per cent of the adult population could recognize the name of the drive and that 20 per cent of those receiving income had bought bonds for the drive. Comparable figures for the Seventh War Loan provide an indication of the effects of an even larger effort. During this campaign over $42,000,000 worth of measurable advertising was displayed; now 94 per cent of the adult population could recognize the name of the drive and 40 per cent of the income receivers bought bonds for the drive.

There are of course many other effects of such campaigns in addition to those listed here, and comparable data are needed from campaigns of a different sort before safe generalizations can be made, but it is reasonable to conclude from these data that even the most efficiently conducted campaigns do not produce major effects upon mass behavior cheaply nor without considerable effort.

We may ask why it is that campaigns seem to require so much effort. One obvious variable influencing the outcome of campaigns is the relation between the behavior encouraged by the campaign and the behavior which the population desires. It is easier to get people to do something they want to do than something they oppose. But this seems to be only part of the story. Another reason that campaigns may fail to be fully influential is that the techniques for using the media are not always the most effective. Research on readership, listening behavior, and the like shows that some techniques, *qua* techniques, are better than others in attracting attention, creating favorable attitudes toward the media, etc. But again the evidence available indicates that the amount of improvement in the effectiveness of a medium that can be obtained by refinement of techniques is limited.

A more fruitful approach to this problem would seem to lie in an analysis of the psychological processes involved in the induction of behavior by an outside agent.

What happens psychologically when someone attempts to influence the behavior of another person? The answer, in broad outline, may be described as follows: To influence behavior, a chain of processes must be initiated within the person. These processes are complex and interrelated, but in broad terms they may be characterized as (i) creating a particular cognitive structure, (ii) creating a particular motivational structure, and (iii) creating a particular behavioral (action) structure. In other words, behavior is determined by the beliefs, opinions, and 'facts' a person possesses; by the needs, goals and values he has; and by the momentary control held over his behavior by given features of his cognitive and motivational structure. To influence behavior 'from the outside' requires the ability to influence these determinants in a particular way.

It seems to be a characteristic of most campaigns that they start strongly with the first process, do considerably less with the second, and only lightly touch upon the third. To the extent that the campaign is intended to influence behavior and not simply to 'educate,' the third process is essential.

Let us now elaborate these principles in more detail, calling upon the data concerning the sale of War Bonds to provide illustrations and documentation.

CREATING A PARTICULAR COGNITIVE STRUCTURE

It is considered a truism by virtually all psychologists that a person's behavior is guided by his perception of the world in which he lives. Action is taken on the basis of a person's view of the 'facts' of the situation. Alternatives are chosen according to beliefs about "what leads to what." The content and relationships among parts of a person's psychological world may be called his cognitive structure, and it may be stated that a person's behavior is a function of the nature of his cognitive structure. It follows from this formulation that one way to change a person's behavior is to modify his cognitive structure. Certain kinds of changes of behavior, moreover, seem to be

possible only if certain changes of cognitive structure take place. This principle applies to all efforts to influence behavior, whether in a face-to-face situation or by communication through a distance.

The modification of cognitive structure in individuals by means of the mass media has several prerequisites. These may be stated in the form of principles.

1. The 'message' (i.e., information, facts, etc.), must reach the sense organs of the persons who are to be influenced.

Stated in such a bald fashion this principle seems obvious enough. Yet it has practical consequences which are not so commonly recognized. Research upon readership and listenership has made it clear that putting a message on a national radio network or in a national periodical by no means assures that it will actually reach the sense organs of a significant proportion of the population. Only a fraction of the population listens to the radio at any given time, and quite small proportions see a given issue of a periodical. For the most part, people choose the media and thus the 'messages' which are to reach them at any given time. They decide whether they will listen to the radio, read a magazine, go to the movies, or attend a political rally. There is no guarantee, therefore, that providing the opportunity for mass stimulation of the entire population will result in the actual stimulation of any large segment of it.

1a. Total stimulus situations are selected or rejected on the basis of an impression of their general characteristics.

Although the factors determining the way people select stimulus situations are only partially known, there appear to be broad categories which people employ in characterizing stimulus situations, such as entertainment, news, politics, advertising, and the like. Whether or not a person will choose one or another stimulus situation seems to depend upon his reaction to the general category. An illustration of this process is provided by research on the War Bond program. Early in the war the Treasury Department distributed through the mail a pamphlet about bonds to every household in most parts of the country. As a test of its effectiveness a sample survey was conducted in Baltimore, Maryland, to determine how many people had read the pamphlet. Although this pamphlet had been placed in the mailbox of nearly every family in the city, it was found that 83 per cent of those interviewed did not remember having seen it, even after being shown a copy of the publication and being allowed to examine its contents. Of the 17 per cent who recalled having received a copy, about one-third reported that they had not looked through it at all and were able to recognize only the front cover. This means, then, that only about 11 per cent of the adult population had read any part of the pamphlet. In attempting to learn why so many people failed to read the pamphlet after receiving it, it was found that many people had confused the pamphlet with other publications of similar format, such as Sunday newspaper supplements or other advertising matter. A number of people asserted that they had thrown it away because they had thought it was a commercial advertising leaflet. Another group of people took it to be a children's publication and gave it to their children without reading it themselves. What happened, then, was that upon the basis of a first general impression people categorized the pamphlet as something they did not care to read and disposed of it without further scrutiny.

1b. The categories employed by a person in characterizing stimulus situations tend to protect him from unwanted changes in his cognitive structure.

Apparently one common consequence of this categorization of stimulus situations is the protection of the person from stimuli which might produce unwanted changes in his cognitive structure. Illustrative of this principle are the tendencies of people to read newspapers whose editorial policy tends to agree with their own and to listen predominantly to political candidates who belong to their own party. Further evidence

may be derived from the wartime research program for the Treasury. In the spring of 1944 Treasury Department officials were exploring the possibilities of using documentary movies in order to heighten citizen identification with the war effort. As an experiment to determine the effects of one particular movie, a week's showing was organized in a public auditorium in Bridgeport, Connecticut. Tickets were distributed widely throughout the population by labor unions, employers, civilian defense organizations, nationality groups, civic organizations, city employees, and many others. During the week approximately five percent of the adult population of Bridgeport came to the movie. As a part of the evaluation of the effects of the movie on people's interest in participating in voluntary civilian war activities, interviews were conducted with a random sample of those attending and with a control sample of people who did not attend the movie. One of the most striking findings of this study revealed that the people who attended the movie were the ones whose behavior was already closest to that encouraged by the movie. For example, approximately 40 per cent of those attending the movie had offered blood to the Red Cross while only 20 per cent of those not attending had done so. Other measures of activity in community affairs revealed similar differences, and there was evidence that those attending the movie came disproportionately from the upper income levels of the population. In other words, the way in which the appeal to attend the movie was categorized by the public made it less attractive to those very people whom the movie was designed to influence. Had the movie been shown in commercial theaters simply as 'entertainment' it might not have selected such a special group of people.

2. Having reached the sense organs, the 'message' must be accepted as a part of the person's cognitive structure.

Even after a 'message' reaches the sense organs of an individual there are many reasons that it may not be incorporated into his cognitive structure. Everyone knows that there is often a considerable difference between telling a person something and having him pay attention to it, remember it, or accept it as true. In general the same factors operate to facilitate or inhibit the acceptance of a given 'message' that influence the selection of stimulation from the media. We may therefore note the following principles.

2a. Once a given 'message' is received it will tend to be accepted or rejected on the basis of more general categories to which it appears to belong.

2b. The categories employed by a person in characterizing 'messages' tend to protect him from unwanted changes in his cognitive structure.

Anyone desiring to influence the behavior of others must keep constantly in mind a very simple and obvious fact, namely, that everyone, after the earliest stages of infancy, possesses a remarkably stable cognitive structure upon which he depends for a satisfactory adjustment to his environment. Any effort to change behavior through a modification of this cognitive structure must overcome the forces tending to maintain the present structure. Only when a given cognitive structure seems to the person to be unsatisfactory for his adjustment is he likely readily to receive influences designed to change that structure. It is instructive to examine what happens when an item is presented which is at variance with the cognitive structure. When such a situation occurs a disequilibrium is established which must be restored in some fashion. Characteristically one or more of three things seem to happen.

2c. When a 'message' is inconsistent with a person's prevailing cognitive structure it will either (a) be rejected, (b) be distorted so as to fit, or (c) produce changes in the cognitive structure.

Which of these outcomes will actually occur depends upon the relative strength of the forces maintaining the cognitive

structure and of those carried by the new 'message.' It will not be possible to explore here the factors determining the magnitude of these forces, but it may be indicated that the forces maintaining a cognitive structure are ordinarily of a very great magnitude. Evidence from the War Bond research may be cited to illustrate two points of relevance here. First, it will be seen that, despite continued efforts throughout the war to get people to understand some of the major purposes the Government had for its War Bond program, there was little actual change in people's beliefs. This is evidence of the stability of cognitive structure and its resistance to change. Second, it will be evident that this stability was maintained by people selecting from the great variety of promotional material developed for the campaigns those features which conformed to their existing cognitive structure and rejecting those which deviated.

After each of the War Loans a sample of the population was asked: "Why do you think the Government is anxious to get people to buy bonds?" The specific answers given by respondents to this question have been grouped under a few major headings in Table 1. It will be seen how little the answers changed over a period of thirty months of War Bond publicity.

The stability of the percentages in the table is most remarkable. With minor exceptions the variability does not exceed that expected simply from repeated samplings of a population with constant characteristics. Since the same individuals were not interviewed in the various studies it is not possible to determine with certainty that individuals were not shifting from one category to another from one time to the next, but the most likely hypothesis would seem to be that there was remarkably little change throughout the war in people's views as to why the Government was wanting to sell bonds.

This stability was maintained in the face of a tremendous barrage of promotion through all the media of communication. Examination of the content of this promotion makes

TABLE 1

REASONS ATTRIBUTED TO GOVERNMENT FOR WANTING TO SELL BONDS

Reasons	Second Loan April 1943	Third Loan Sept. 1943	Fourth Loan Jan. 1944	Fifth Loan June 1944	Sixth Loan Nov. 1944	Seventh Loan June 1945
	%	%	%	%	%	%
To finance the war, to win the war, to help soldiers	65	75	65	65	67	68
To prevent inflation	14	11	14	15	15	14
To get people to save	4	4	7	8	7	10
To provide postwar security	4	2	2	3	2	3
Other reasons	13	8	12	9	9	5
	100	100	100	100	100	100
Number of interviews	1,358	1,583	1,441	1,925	2,148	2,263

it clear that no single explanation of the Government's reasons was universally pushed, and it is reasonable to suppose that there was a rough correspondence between the percentage of the publicity devoted to any given reason and the number of people already holding that reason. But the remarkable fact remains that, with the great array of reasons being publicized, people seemed to keep the ones they arrived at in the very beginning of the war.

In the course of the research program considerable attention was given to the nature of popular thinking about the functioning of the economy and the role of War Bonds in the prevention of inflation. From this analysis it became clear, for example, why the promotion designed to explain the Government's interest in bond sales as a means of inflation control did not succeed in changing popular thinking. It became apparent that for many people war finance was seen simply as the collection of dollars by Uncle Sam which were then paid by him to manufacturers of war goods. If Uncle Sam sold the bonds, he could buy equipment; if he did not sell them, he could not get the supplies. Asked directly whether failure to sell enough bonds would cause a shortage of military equipment, 49 per cent of those interviewed after the Fourth Loan said that it would. With such a conception of the nature of the economy

is it not surprising that, when asked whether they thought buying bonds would help keep prices down, 54 per cent either asserted directly that bond purchases had no effect on prices or said that they could not see any relation between the two. Nor is it surprising that during the war there was a slight increase in this percentage since a number of people noted that even though bonds were being sold in large quantities prices were continuing to rise.

From this and similar evidence the conclusion seems warranted that people succeeded in maintaining an early established cognitive structure by selecting from the War Bond promotion those items which conformed to that structure and by ignoring items deviating from it.

Numerous examples of the distortion of 'messages' to make them agree with existing beliefs could be cited, but perhaps the most dramatic are those related to the conviction held by a minority of the population that the Government would not redeem the bonds. Whenever a change of procedure in the redemption of bonds was instituted, rumors cropped up among these people to the effect that the new change was a step toward 'freezing' bonds. At one point during the war a group of enthusiastic citizens (probably as a publicity stunt) conducted a bonfire in which they burned their bonds as a gesture to indicate their willingness to give money to the Government for the war. This event stimulated rumors among those distrusting the Government's intention to repay that the bonds were no good and that people were burning them because they were worthless.

To summarize the evidence presented up to this point, it is clear that changes in cognitive structure cannot be assured simply by guaranteeing wide coverage of the media of communication. By selecting the stimuli from the media which they will allow to reach their sense organs and by rejecting or distorting messages that deviate too much from existing cognitive structures, people manage to resist much of the effort made to change their thinking by techniques of mass persuasion. To the extent that changes in behavior are dependent upon changes of cognitive structure they, at the same time, resist efforts to modify their usual manner of behavior.

CREATING A PARTICULAR MOTIVATIONAL STRUCTURE

We have now explored some of the implications of the notion that behavior is guided by a person's cognitive structure. For a satisfactory analysis of the process of social induction of behavior, however, it is necessary to examine a bit further what it is that energizes behavior. As a general statement it may be said that personal needs provide the energy for behavior and express themselves through the setting up of goals in the person's cognitive structure. That is to say, certain activities (like eating, going to the movies, running for Congress, etc.) become attractive when corresponding needs are activated, and the amount of energy that will be devoted to these activities depends upon the strength of the need (i.e., the level of need tension). It should be noted further that goals have a location in the cognitive structure so that for a given individual some activities are seen as leading to the satisfaction of certain needs and others are seen as unrelated to such satisfaction or even leading away from it. Thus, for one person 'joining a union' may be seen as a path leading to economic security,

while for another 'being nice to the boss' may be seen as the path toward the same goal, with 'joining the union' being in exactly the opposite direction.

It follows from these general observations about the nature of human motivation that efforts to influence the behavior of another person must attempt either to modify needs (and goals) or to change the person's motivational structure as to which activities lead to which goals. This means that a person can be induced to do voluntarily something that he would otherwise not do only if a need can be established for which this action is a goal or if the action can be made to be seen as a path to an existing goal. Little is known at the present time about the establishment of needs, but it appears unlikely that any single campaign via the mass media can actually establish new needs. Whether or not this feat is possible, the following principle may nevertheless be stated.

3. *To induce a given action by mass persuasion, this action must be seen by the person as a path to some goal that he has.*

When people were asked during the war why they were buying bonds, they gave answers that could readily be interpreted in terms of the motivational principles outlined here. The most common reasons were related to the desire to win the war. People said, in essence, though they phrased it in many ways, "I want to help win the war, and buying War Bonds is one way I can help." Stated reasons of this type were the following: (percentages are given to indicate the proportion of the adult population giving them after the Seventh Loan.) (a) Because the country needs the money to pay for the war (64 per cent). (b) To help the boys, to bring them back (16 per cent). (c) To get the war over sooner (6 per cent).

Another goal for which buying bonds was seen as a path may be loosely defined as 'personal economic security.' People who gave reasons of this type said in essence, "I want to provide economic security for myself and family, and buying War Bonds is one way I can achieve this goal." The most common of these reasons given after the Seventh Loan were: (a) To save for some indefinite personal use in the future (44 per cent). (b) To have reserves in case of a post-war depression (5 per cent). (c) Because bonds are a good investment (24 per cent).

A third rather common type of goal was "wanting to be a good citizen." Reasons related to this goal tended to be stated in terms of the Government's needs or objectives. To the extent that the Government's objectives were seen as also providing satisfaction of personal financial needs these reasons could also be classified under the previous heading. The more frequent of these reasons were: (a) To help prevent inflation (14 per cent). (b) Because the Government wants people to save (10 per cent). (c) To prevent a post-war depression (1 per cent).

Undoubtedly many people had other personal goals for which buying bonds was seen as a path. It appears, for example, that some people saw the buying of bonds at public rallies as a means of gaining prestige. At first glance it would seem that the number of goals that could be made to appear attainable through the purchase of bonds would be almost limitless. Further scrutiny of the facts, however, indicates that there were actually severe limitations on the kinds of connections that could be established between bond-buying and personal goals. Unless people could see something in the nature of buying bonds that made this act appear reasonably a path to a given goal, all the power of mass persuasion that could be mobilized could not get the connection accepted.

3a. *A given action will be accepted as a path to a goal only if the connections 'fit' the person's larger cognitive structure.*

As documentation of this principle it is necessary only to refer again to the fact that, despite efforts to explain the relation between buying bonds and inflation con-

trol, over half of the population still denied that there was such a relationship because it did not fit into their general understanding of the nature of the economy. Similarly those people who believed that the Government would not repay the bonds could not be induced to believe that buying bonds would provide them with personal economic security after the war.

3b. *The more goals which are seen as attainable by a single path, the more likely it is that a person will take that path.*

It is, of course, possible for a given action to be seen as leading simultaneously to more than one goal. When such a situation exists, the forces directed toward these various goals will all assume the direction of the one action which is the path common to them all. It is to be expected, then, that making a given action appear as leading to several goals will increase the likelihood that that action will be chosen. In persuading people to buy War Bonds, this meant that the more reasons they could be led to see for buying the more likely they should be to buy. Evidence from the research program consistently supported this conclusion. Consider the findings of the survey after the Seventh Loan (Table 2). It is seen that people who saw more than one type of reason for buying bonds were much more likely to buy, whether solicited or not, than were those who had only one type of reason.

TABLE 2

THE RELATION OF THE NUMBER OF
REASONS MENTIONED TO BUYING
BONDS IN THE SEVENTH WAR LOAN

Types of Reasons Mentioned	Proportion buying for drive of those:	
	Personally asked to buy	Not asked to buy
	%	%
Patriotic, personal financial, and national financial	65	35
Patriotic and personal financial *or* Patriotic and national financial	57	22
Patriotic only	44	9
Number of interviews	1,232	1,104

In order to be certain that differences in income among those giving different numbers of reasons do not produce these results, it is necessary to conduct this analysis separately within restricted income ranges. When this procedure is followed, it is found that at every income level people who gave more than one type of reason were more likely to buy than were those who mentioned only one type.

3c. If an action is seen as not leading to a desired goal or as leading to an undesired end, it will not be chosen.

3d. If an action is seen as leading to a desired goal, it will tend not to be chosen to the extent that easier, cheaper, or otherwise more desirable actions are also seen as leading to the same goal.

These two principles are simply elaborations of the general motivational scheme already outlined. They point, however, to exceedingly important practical implications for anyone desiring to influence behavior by mass persuasion. Much of the 'psychological warfare' of competing propagandists or of competing advertising programs is concerned with these principles. In such competition much effort is devoted to the objective of showing how one's own proposed course of action leads to a desired goal while the action proposed by the competitor does not lead to a desired goal or actually leads to an undesired end. The efforts of dictators to monopolize the channels of communication stem largely from the realization that competitors may offer more acceptable paths to accepted goals.

Those people who during the war believed that the government would not repay the bonds may be cited to illustrate *Principle 3c*. For these people, 'buying bonds' was perceived as leading to 'losing my money.' Needless to say, it was found that these people resisted efforts to get them to buy bonds and were quite ready to redeem their bonds if they were induced to purchase them. In order to make willing bond buyers out of these people it was necessary to change their motivational structure in regard to the consequences seen to be connected with the act of buying bonds. Examples of the competition of paths to the same goal may also be found in the War Bond campaigns. People who chose to invest their money in something more profitable than bonds were choosing a path to economic gain which appeared to be better than bonds. The following list of the more common reasons given for not buying bonds will be seen to illustrate the operation of both of these principles: bonds may not be redeemed; other investments are safer; bonds aren't liquid enough; bonds give less return than other investments; bonds have too long a maturity period; bonds may be no good because we might lose the war; bonds will be worthless because of inflation; bonds are not necessary for victory; bonds prolong the war; savings should be kept in several forms; and, owning bonds gives the Government a record of my savings.

The analysis presented in this and the preceding sections specifies some of the requirements for campaigns designed to influence behavior. In brief, we have seen that a campaign must reach the sense organs with 'messages,' that these 'messages' must be of such a nature as to be accepted into existing cognitive structures, and that proposed courses of action must be seen as leading to desired goals. It might appear that, if these requirements were met, a campaign would succeed in inducing desired changes of behavior. The evidence indicates, however, that a further requirement exists.

CREATING A PARTICULAR BEHAVIORAL STRUCTURE

The phrase 'good intentions' suggests the nature of this further requirement. It is quite possible for a person to have a given cognitive and motivational structure for a long period of time without its ever actually gaining control of his behavior. There are certain motivational systems, like those of hunger or thirst, which gain control of a person's action periodically because of a heightened discomfort that arises and persists until action is taken. There are, however, other systems, much more commonly those with which campaigns of mass persuasion deal, which carry with them no insistent prod to action within any clear limitation of time. To the extent that a campaign attempts to induce action in regard to systems of this latter type it must be designed to deal specifically with this problem.

4. To induce a given action, an appropriate cognitive and motivational system must gain control of the person's behavior at a particular point in time.

Needless to say, a person's behavior is at all times under the control of some motivational system, and the problem of inducing a given action is that of getting a particular cognitive and motivational structure in control of behavior at some specific point in time. The competition among various structures for the control of behavior is often very great. When a person is asked why he has not actually done a particular thing that he seemingly had accepted as desirable, he may answer that he did not have the time, energy, or financial resources. Such a statement is equivalent to saying that other motivational systems have maintained control of his behavior to such an extent that they monopolized his time and resources.

In selling War Bonds this type of competition was most evident. Following each of the War Loan drives a sample of those not buying bonds were asked their reasons for not buying. From one-half to three-quarters of these people replied that they "could not afford to buy bonds during the drive." This answer was, of course, a socially acceptable way of excusing oneself for not having submitted to social pressure, but in most instances it also reflected the fact that other motivational systems (such as those related to the needs for food, shelter, recreation, social status, etc.), had remained in control of behavior throughout the period of the drive. Most of these people held quite favorable attitudes toward bonds, accepted the desirability of their owning bonds, and agreed that buying bonds was a patriotic act. The problem of getting them actually to buy during a campaign consisted, therefore, not so much of creating favorable cognitive and motivational structures as of getting those structures in control of behavior at some specific point in time during the drive.

4a. The more specifically defined the path of action to a goal (in an accepted motivational structure), the more likely it is that the structure will gain control of behavior.

4b. The more specifically a path of action is located in time, the more likely it is that the structure will gain control of behavior.

Examination of a number of campaigns of mass persuasion will reveal that quite commonly the course of action being encouraged is described in relatively general terms. It is rare that the proposed action is described in concrete detail or given a precise location in time. There are, of course, good reasons for couching the language of a campaign of mass persuasion in general terms: circumstances vary greatly among people in the general population, so that a specific statement may not apply realistically to all and, if a statement is made too specific, it can more easily be rejected. But despite these difficulties, the fact seems well documented that, unless a proposed action is defined quite specifically, it is probable that it will not actually be carried out in behavior, even though it has been accepted as desirable.

The experience of the Second War Loan is especially illuminating in this connection. As we have already seen, more than $12,-000,000 worth of promotion was put into this campaign. Analysis of its content, however, disclosed that the major appeal to action was expressed in the phrase, "Buy War Bonds." Interviews after the campaign revealed that this statement was sufficiently broad for people to accept the desirability of the action without feeling any pressure actually to buy bonds during the time of the campaign. In the interviews many people said in effect, "I agree completely that people should buy bonds; in fact I own quite a number myself." When asked why they had not bought during the drive, many people indicated their belief that they had conformed completely with the requests of the publicity "to buy bonds," even though they had not purchased any during the campaign.

As a result of this type of analysis of the Second Loan, Treasury officials developed quite a different campaign for the Third Loan. In this campaign the major appeal to action was phrased, "Buy an *extra* bond for the Third War Loan." In addition, an individual quota of a $100 bond was given emphasis, and other devices were used to make it clear that an extra purchase was being requested during a specified period of time. From the research following the Third Drive it became abundantly clear that the revised promotion had been much more effective. It was found, for example, that the number of people asserting that they had not bought "because I am doing my share" dropped from 19 per cent after the Second Loan to 6 per cent after the Third and that the number of people buying bonds rose from 20 to 39 per cent.

There were many ways in which the act of buying bonds could be specified in publicity. The major ways employed in the War Bond publicity were by indicating the amount to be purchased, the time for buying, and the place to buy. Thus, the campaigns said in effect, "Buy an extra $100 bond during the drive from the solicitor where you work." All available evidence indicates that this type of appeal was far more effective than those couched in more general terms.

4c. A given motivational structure may be set in control of behavior by placing the person in a situation requiring a decision to take, or not to take, a step of action that is a part of the structure.

If an action, like buying bonds, has become a part of a person's motivational structure, one way to bring that structure into control over the person's behavior is to place him in a situation where he must decide whether or not he will buy a bond at that moment. The necessity of making a decision in regard to a specific action requires that motivational structures of which this action is a part be brought to bear in determining the next step in action. When such a decision is required, the action will be taken if the resultant forces in all activated motivational structures are in the direction of that particular action. This means, of course, that forcing a decision will result in the desired action only if appropriate cognitive and motivational structures have been accepted by the person. By the same token, however, it means that the desired action will result if the appropriate structures do exist.

The technique of personal solicitation in selling War Bonds made use of this principle. When a person was solicited, he was asked to make a decision to buy, or not to buy, a bond at that time. A 'solicitor' might also take the occasion to try to create favorable cognitive and motivational structures, but the essential function of solicitation lay in the fact that it required the person to make a decision. From these considerations we may conclude that personal solicitation should precipitate bond buying among people whose motivational structure was favorable to buying bonds. In other words, a campaign of personal solicitation should greatly increase the number of people buying bonds if it follows an effective campaign of publicity and education. The more effective the publicity (in creating favorable cognitive and motivational structures) the greater should be the effect of solicitation.

The great mass of data collected after each of the War Loans supports these conclusions quite strongly. In Table 3 are presented only some of these findings,

TABLE 3

SOME RELATIONS BETWEEN PERSONAL SOLICITATION AND BUYING

	Second Loan April, 1943	Third Loan Sept., 1943	Fourth Loan Jan., 1944	Fifth Loan June, 1944
	%	%	%	%
Of all income receivers:				
Were personally solicited	25	50	51	58
Bought extra bonds	20	39	45	47
Of those not solicited:				
Bought extra bonds	12	18	25	22
Of those solicited:				
Bought extra bonds	47	59	63	66
Number of interviews	1,358	1,583	1,441	1,925

selected to illustrate the results under rather different conditions. It is seen that there is a close relation between the number of people solicited in a drive and the number of people actually buying bonds. Further, the percentage of people buying bonds is much greater among those solicited than among those not solicited. In all the data analyzed the same conclusion was reached: people who were personally asked to buy were always found to be more likely to buy —in every drive, in every income bracket, in every occupational group, in every section of the country.

The dependence of the outcome of solicitation upon the existence of favorable motivational structures can be seen in Table 2. Solicitation among people with more favorable structures was much more likely to precipitate buying than among those with less favorable structures (among those with three reasons for buying, 65 per cent; two reasons, 57 per cent; one reason, 44 per cent).

CONCLUSIONS

The principles presented here derive from a more extensive theory of human motivation. They are concerned with the particular motivational problem of inducing behavior

'from the outside.' To the extent that they are valid, they should apply to all inductions, whether through the mass media or in a face-to-face situation. They should also apply to inductions attempted for all types of purposes, whether to sell, to train, to supervise work, to produce therapy, and so on. In all such attempts the process of induction must be concerned with the establishment of cognitive, motivational, and behavioral structures. Only when conditions are proper in respect to all three of these, will the actual induction of behavior occur.

Applied to the field of mass persuasion, these principles may serve as a yardstick for evaluating the probable success of any proposed campaign. The principles are by no means exhaustive, nor do they give detailed guides for the creative aspects of the development of campaigns. They do, however, provide a list of essential requirements for the success of any campaign of mass persuasion. It can be seen, moreover, that, because of the inherent difficulties of meeting these requirements, campaigns are not likely to make basic changes in the behavior of large numbers of people unless there is a monopolization of the channels of communication or unless the changes being encouraged are in the same direction as those being stimulated by other influences.

THE BASIC PSYCHOLOGY OF RUMOR

GORDON W. ALLPORT AND LEO J. POSTMAN

RUMORS IN WARTIME

During the year 1942, rumor became a national problem of considerable urgency. Its first dangerous manifestation was felt soon after the initial shock of Pearl Harbor. This traumatic event dislocated our moral channels of communication by bringing into existence an unfamiliar and unwelcome, if at the same time a relatively mild censorship of news, and it simultaneously dictated the lives of millions of citizens whose futures abruptly became hostages to fortune.

This combination of circumstances created the most fertile of all possible soils for the propagation of rumor. We now know that *rumors concerning a given subject-matter will circulate within a group in proportion to the importance and the ambiguity of this subject-matter in the lives of individual members of the group.*

The affair of Pearl Harbor was fraught with both importance and ambiguity to nearly every citizen. The affair was important because of the potential danger it represented to all of us, and because its aftermath of mobilization affected every life. It was ambiguous because no one seemed quite certain of the extent of, reasons for, or consequences of the attack. Since the two conditions of rumor—importance and ambiguity—were at a maximum, we had an unprecedented flood of what became known

as "Pearl Harbor rumors." It was said that our fleet was "wiped out," that Washington didn't dare to tell the extent of the damage, that Hawaii was in the hands of the Japanese. So widespread and so demoralizing were these tales that, on February 23, 1942, President Roosevelt broadcast a speech devoted entirely to denying the harmful rumors and to reiterating the official report on the losses.

Did the solemn assurance of the Commander in Chief restore the confidence of the people and eliminate the tales of suspicion and fear? It so happens that a bit of objective evidence on this question became available to us almost by accident. On the twentieth of February, before the President's speech, we had asked approximately 200 college students whether they thought our losses at Pearl Harbor were "greater," "much greater," or "no greater" than the official Knox report had stated. Among these students 68 per cent had believed the demoralizing rumors in preference to the official report, and insisted that the losses were "greater," or "much greater" than Washington admitted. Then came the President's speech. On February 25 an equivalent group of college students were asked the same question. Among those who had not heard or read the speech the proportion of rumor-believers was still about two-thirds. But among those who were acquainted with the

From *Transactions of the New York Academy of Sciences*, Series II, 1945, VIII, 61-81.
Reprinted by permission of the authors and the publisher.

President's speech, the number of rumor-believers fell by 24 percent. It is important to note that, in spite of the utmost efforts of the highest authority to allay anxiety, approximately 44 percent of the college population studied were too profoundly affected by the event and by the resulting rumors to accept the reassurance.

The year 1942 was characterized by floods of similar fear-inspired tales. Shipping losses were fantastically exaggerated. Knapp records one instance where a collier was sunk through accident near the Cape Cod Canal. So great was the anxiety of the New England public that this incident became a fantastic tale of an American ship being torpedoed with the loss of thousands of nurses who were aboard her.

Such wild stories, as we have said, are due to the grave importance of the subject for the average citizen and to the ambiguity to him of the objective situation. This ambiguity may result from the failure of communications, or from a total lack of authentic news, a condition that often prevailed in war-torn countries or among isolated bands of troops who had few reliable sources of news. Again, the ambiguity may be due to the receipt of conflicting news stories, no one more credible than another; or it may be due (as in the case of the Pearl Harbor rumors) to the distrust of many people in the candor of the Administration and in the operation of wartime censorship. As the war progressed, a higher degree of confidence in our news service was rapidly achieved, and rumors concurrently subsided.

In addition to the fear-rumors of 1942, which persisted until the tide of victory commenced to turn, there was a still more numerous crop of hostility-rumors whose theme dealt always with the shortcomings, disloyalty, or inefficiency of some special group of cobelligerents. The Army, the Navy, the Administration, our allies, or American minority groups were the most frequent scapegoats in these rumors. We were told that the Army wasted whole sides of beef, that the Russians greased their guns with lend-lease butter, that Negroes were saving icepicks for a revolt, and that Jews were evading the draft.

These hostility rumors were the most numerous of all. An analysis of 1,000 rumors collected from all parts of the country in 1942 revealed that they could be classified fairly readily as:

Hostility (wedge-driving) rumors	= 66 per cent
Fear (bogey) rumors	= 25 per cent
Wish (pipe-dream) rumors	= 2 per cent
Unclassifiable rumors	= 7 per cent

To be sure, the proportion of fear and wish rumors soon altered. As victory approached, especially on the eve of V-E and V-J day, the whirlwind of rumors was almost wholly concerned with the cessation of hostilities, reflecting a goal-gradient phenomenon whereby rumor under special conditions hastens the completion of a desired event. But, throughout the war and continuing to the present, it is probably true that the majority of all rumors are of a more or less slanderous nature, expressing hostility against this group or that.

The principal reasons why rumor circulates can be briefly stated. It circulates because it *serves the twin function of explaining and relieving emotional tensions felt by individuals.*

The Pearl Harbor rumors, for example, helped to *explain* to the teller why he felt such distressing anxiety. Would his jitters not be justified if it were true that our protecting fleet was "wiped out" at Pearl Harbor? Something serious must have happened to account for his anxiety. Families deprived of sons, husbands, or fathers vaguely cast around for someone to blame for their privation. Well, the Jews, who were said to be evading the draft, were "obviously" not doing their share and thus the heavy burden falling on "good citizens" was explained. True, this draft-evasion charge did not last very long, owing, no doubt, to the inescapable evidence of heavy enlistments among Jews and of their heroic conduct in the war. But when shortages were felt, the traditional Jewish scapegoat was again trotted out as a convenient explanation of the privations suffered. Their operation of the black market "explained" our annoying experiences in the futile pursuit of an evening lamb chop.

To blame others verbally is not only a mode of explanation for one's emotional distress, but is at the same time a mode of relief. Everyone knows the reduction of tension that comes after administering a tongue lashing. It matters little whether the victim of the tongue lashing is guilty or not. Dressing down *anyone* to his face or behind his back has the strange property of temporarily reducing hatred felt against this person or, what is more remarkable, of reducing hatred felt against this person or thing. If you wish to deflate a taut inner tube you can unscrew the valve or you can make a puncture. Unscrewing the valve corresponds to directing our hostility toward the Nazis or Japanese, who were the cause of our suffering. Making a puncture corresponds to displacing the hostility upon innocent victims or scapegoats. In either case, the air will escape and relaxation follow. To blame Jews, Negroes, the Administration, brass hats, the OPA, or the politicians is to bring a certain relief from accumulated feelings of hostility, whatever their true cause. Relief, odd as it may seem, comes also from "bogey" rumors. To tell my neighbor that the Cape Cod Canal is choked with corpses is an easy manner of projecting into the outer world my own choking anxieties concerning my son or my friends in combat service. Having shared my anxiety with my friend by telling him exaggerated tales of losses or of atrocities, I no longer feel so much alone and helpless. Through my rumor-spreading, others, too are put "on the alert." I therefore feel reassured.

EXPERIMENTAL APPROACH

Leaving now the broader social setting of the problem, we ask ourselves what processes in the human mind account for the spectacular distortions and exaggerations that enter into the rumor-process, and lead to so much damage to the public intelligence and public conscience.

Since it is very difficult to trace in detail the course of a rumor in everyday life, we have endeavored by an experimental technique to study as many of the basic phenomena as possible under relatively well controlled laboratory conditions.

Our method is simple. A slide is thrown upon a screen. Ordinarily, a semidramatic picture is used containing a large number of related details. Six or seven subjects, who have not seen the picture, wait in an adjacent room. One of them enters and takes a position where he cannot see the screen. Someone in the audience (or the experimenter) describes the picture, giving about twenty details in the account. A second subject enters the room and stands beside the first subject who proceeds to tell him all he can about the picture. (All subjects are under instruction to report as "accurately as possible what you have heard.") The first subject then takes his seat, and a third enters to hear the story from the second subject. Each succeeding subject hears and repeats the story in the same way. Thus, the audience is able to watch the deterioration of the rumor by comparing the successive versions with the stimulus-picture which remains on the screen throughout the experiment.

This procedure has been used with over forty groups of subjects, including college undergraduates, Army trainees in ASTP, members of community forums, patients in an Army hospital, members of a Teachers' Round Table, and police officials in a training course. In addition to these adult subjects, children in a private school were used, in grades from the fourth through the ninth. In some experiments, Negro subjects took part along with whites, a fact which, as we shall see, had important consequences when the test-pictures depicted scenes with a "racial angle."

All of these experiments took place before an audience (20-300 spectators). By using volunteer subjects, one eliminates the danger of stage fright. There was, however,

FIG. 1. A sample of pictorial material employed in the experiments. Here is a typical terminal report (the last in a chain of reproductions): "This is a subway train in New York headed for Portland Street. There is a Jewish woman and a Negro who has a razor in his hand. The woman has a baby or a dog. The train is going to Deyer Street, and nothing much happened."

a social influence in all the audience situations. The magnitude of this influence was studied in a control group of experiments where no one was present in the room excepting the subject and the experimenter.

At the outset, it is necessary to admit that in five respects this experimental situation fails to reproduce accurately the conditions of rumor-spreading in everyday life. (1) The effect of an audience is considerable, tending to create caution and to shorten the report. Without an audience, subjects gave on the average twice as many details as with an audience. (2) The effect of the instructions is to maximize accuracy and induce caution. In ordinary rumor-spreading, there is no critical experimenter on hand to see whether the tale is rightly repeated. (3) There is no opportunity for subjects to ask questions of his informer. In ordinary rumor-spreading, the listener can chat with

his informer and, if he wishes, cross-examine him. (4) The lapse of time between hearing and telling in the experimental situation is very slight. In ordinary rumor spreading, it is much greater. (5) Most important of all, the conditions of motivation are quite different. In the experiment, the subject is striving for *accuracy*. His own fears, hates, wishes are not likely to be aroused under the experimental conditions. In short, he is not the spontaneous rumor-agent that he is in ordinary life. His stake in spreading the experimental rumor is neither personal nor deeply motivated.

It should be noted that all of these conditions, excepting the third, may be expected to enhance the accuracy of the report in the experimental situation, and to yield far less distortion and projection than in real-life rumor-spreading.

In spite of the fact that our experiment

does not completely reproduce the normal conditions for rumor, still we believe that all essential changes and distortions are represented in our results. "Indoor" rumors may not be as lively, as emotionally toned, or as extreme as "outdoor" rumors, and yet the same basic phenomena are demonstrable in both.

What happens in both real-life and laboratory rumors is a complex course of distortion in which three interrelated tendencies are clearly distinguishable.

LEVELING

As rumor travels, it tends to grow shorter, more concise, more easily grasped and told. In successive versions, fewer words are used and fewer details are mentioned.

The number of details *retained* declines most sharply at the beginning of the series of reproductions. The number continues to decline, more slowly, throughout the experiment. Figure 2 shows the percentage of the details initially given which are retained in each successive reproduction.

The number of items enumerated in the description from the screen constitutes the 100 percent level, and all subsequent percentages are calculated from that base. The curve, based on 11 experiments, shows that about 70 percent of the details are eliminated in the course of five or six mouth-to-mouth transmissions, even when virtually no time lapse intervenes.

The curve is like the famous Ebbinghaus curve for decline in individual retention, though in his experiments the interval between initial learning and successive reproductions was not as short as under the conditions of our experiment. Comparing the present curve with Ebbinghaus's, we conclude that *social memory accomplishes as much leveling within a few minutes as individual memory accomplishes in weeks of time.*

Leveling (in our experiments) never proceeds to the point of total obliteration. The stabilization of the last part of the curve is a finding of some consequence. It indi-

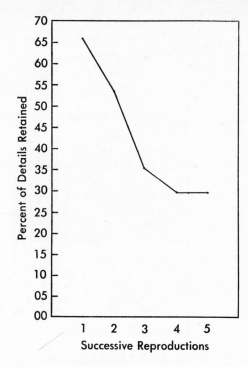

FIG. 2. Percentage of details originally given which are retained in each successive reproduction.

cates (1) that a short concise statement is likely to be faithfully reproduced; (2) that when the report has become short and concise, the subject has very little detail to select from and the possibilities of further distortion grow fewer; (3) that the assignment becomes so easy that a virtually rote memory serves to hold the material in mind. In all cases, the terminal and the anteterminal reports are more similar than any two preceding reports.

The reliance on rote is probably more conspicuous in our experiments than in ordinary rumor-spreading, where accuracy is not the aim, where time interval interferes with rote retention, and where strong interests prevent literal memory. There are, however, conditions where rote memory plays a part in ordinary rumor-spreading. If the individual is motivated by no stronger desire than to make conversation, he may find himself idly repeating what he has recently heard in the form in which he heard it. If a rumor has become so crisp and brief, so sloganized, that it requires no effort to retain it in the literal form in which it was heard, rote memory seems to be involved. For example:

The Jews are evading the draft;
The CIO is communist controlled;
The Russians are nationalizing their women.

We conclude that whenever verbal material is transmitted among a group of people whether as rumor, legend, or history, change will be in the direction of greater brevity and conciseness. Leveling, however, is not a random phenomenon. Our protocols show again and again that items which are of particular interest to the subjects, facts which confirm their expectations and help them to structure the story, are the last to be leveled out and often are retained to the final reproduction.

SHARPENING

We may define sharpening as the selective perception, retention, and reporting of a limited number of details from a larger context. Sharpening is inevitably the reciprocal of leveling. The one cannot exist without the other, for what little remains to a rumor after leveling has taken place is by contrast unavoidably featured.

Although sharpening occurs in every protocol, the same items are not always emphasized. Sometimes, a trifling detail such as a subway advertising card becomes the focus of attention and report. Around it the whole rumor becomes structured. But, in most experiments, this same detail drops out promptly, and is never heard of after the first reproduction.

One way in which sharpening seems to be determined is through the retention of odd, or attention-getting words which, having appeared early in the series, catch the attention of each successive listener and are often passed on in preference to other details intrinsically more important to the story. An instance of this effect is seen in a series of protocols where the statement, "there is a boy stealing and a man remonstrating with him" is transmitted throughout the entire series. The unusual word "remonstrate" somehow caught the attention of each successive listener and was passed on without change.

Sharpening may also take a *numerical* turn, as in the experiments where emphasized items become reduplicated in the telling. For example, in reports of a picture containing the figure of a Negro, whose size and unusual appearance invite emphasis, we find that the number of Negroes reported in the picture jumps from one to "four" or "several."

There is also *temporal* sharpening manifested in the tendency to describe events as occurring in the immediate present. What happens *here* and *now* is of greatest interest and importance to the perceiver. In most instances, to be sure, the story is started in the present tense, but even when the initial description is couched in the past tense, immediate reversal occurs and the scene is contemporized by the listener. Obviously, this effect cannot occur in rumors which deal specifically with some alleged past (or future) event. One cannot contemporize the rumor that "the *Queen Mary* sailed this morning (or will sail tomorrow) with 10,000 troops aboard." Yet it not infrequently happens that stories gain in sharpening by tying them to present conditions. For example, a statement that Mr. X bought a chicken in the black market last week and paid $1.50 a pound for it may be (and usually is) rendered, "I hear they *are* charging $1.50 a pound on the black market for chicken." People are more interested in today than in last week, and the temptation, therefore, is to adapt (assimilate) the time of occurrence, when possible, to this interest.

Sharpening often takes place when there is a clear implication of *movement*. The flying of airplanes and the bursting of bombs are frequently stressed in the telling. Similarly, the falling flower pot in one picture is often retained and accented. Indeed, the "falling motif" may be extended to other objects such as the cigar which a man in the picture is smoking. In one rumor, it is said to be falling (like the flower pot), though in reality it is quite securely held between his teeth.

Sometimes sharpening is achieved by ascribing movement to objects which are really stationary. Thus, a subway train, clearly at a standstill at a subway station, is frequently described as moving.

Relative size is also a primary determinant of attention. Objects that are prominent because of their size tend to be retained and sharpened. The first reporter calls attention to their prominence and each successive listener receives an impression of their largeness. He then proceeds to sharpen this impression in his memory. The large Negro may, in the telling, become "four Negroes," or may become "a gigantic statue of a Negro."

There are verbal as well as physical determinants of attention. Thus, there is a pronounced tendency for *labels* to persist, especially if they serve to set the stage for the story. One picture is usually introduced by some version of the statement, "This is a battle scene," and this label persists throughout the series of reproductions. Another story usually opens with the statement, "This is a picture of a race riot."

To explain this type of sharpening, we may invoke the desire of the subject to achieve some spatial and temporal schema for the story to come. Such orientation is essential in ordinary life and appears to constitute a strong need even when imaginal material is dealt with.

An additional factor making for preferential retention of spatial and temporal labels is the *primacy* effect. An item that comes first in a series is likely to be better remembered than subsequent items. Usually, the "label" indicating place and time comes at the beginning of a report and thus benefits by the primacy effect.

Sharpening also occurs in relation to familiar symbols. In one series of reports, a church and a cross are among the most frequently reported items, although they are relatively minor details in the original picture. These well-known symbols "pack" meaning and are familiar to all. The subject feels secure in reporting them because they have an accustomed concreteness that the other details in the picture lack. Retention of familiar symbols advances the process of conventionalization that is so prominent an aspect of rumor-embedding. In two of our pictures are a night stick, symbol of police authority, and a razor, stereotyped symbol of Negro violence. These symbols are always retained and sharpened.

Explanations added by the reporter to the description transmitted to him comprise a final form of sharpening. They represent a tendency to put "closure" upon a story which is felt to be otherwise incomplete. They illustrate the "effort after meaning" which customarily haunts the subject who finds himself in an unstructured situation. Such need for sharpening by explanation becomes especially strong when the story has been badly distorted and the report contains implausible and incompatible items. As an example, one subject who received a badly confused description of the subway scene (Fig. 1) inferred that there must have been "an accident." This explanation seemed plausible enough to successive listeners and so was not only accepted by them but sharpened in the telling.

In everyday rumors, sharpening through the introduction of specious explanations, is very apparent. Indeed, as we have said, one of the principal functions of a rumor is to explain personal tensions. To accept tales of Army waste or special privilege among OPA officials could "explain" food shortages and discomfort. Such stories, therefore, find wide credence.

Here, perhaps, is the place to take issue with the popular notion that rumors tend to expand like snowballs, become overelaborate, and verbose. Actually, the course of rumor is toward brevity, whether in the laboratory or in everyday life. Such exaggeration as exists is nearly always a sharpening of some feature resident in the original stimulus-situation. The distortion caused by sharpening is, of course, enormous in extent; but we do not find that we need the category of "elaboration" to account for the changes we observe.

ASSIMILATION

It is apparent that both leveling and sharpening are selective processes. But what is it that leads to the obliteration of some details and the pointing-up of others; and what accounts for all transpositions, importations, and other falsifications that mark the course of rumor? The answer is to be found in the process of *assimilation, which has to do with the powerful attractive force exerted upon rumor by habits, interests, and sentiments existing in the listener's mind.*

Assimilation to Principal Theme

It generally happens that items become sharpened or leveled to fit the leading motif of the story, and they become consistent with this motif in such a way as to make the resulting story more coherent, plausible, and well-rounded. Thus, in one series of rumors, the war theme is preserved and emphasized in all reports. In some experiments using the same picture, a chaplain is introduced, or people (in the plural) are reported as being killed; the ambulance becomes a Red Cross station; demolished buildings are multiplied in the telling; the extent of devastation is exaggerated. All these reports, false though they are, fit the principal theme—a battle incident. If the reported details were actually present in the picture, they would make a "better" *Gestalt*. Objects wholly extraneous to the theme are never introduced —no apple pies, no ballet dancers, no baseball players.

Besides importations, we find other falsifications in the interest of supporting the principal theme. The original picture shows that the Red Cross truck is loaded with explosives, but it is ordinarily reported as carrying medical supplies which is, of course, the way it "ought" to be.

The Negro in this same picture is nearly always described as a soldier, although his clothes might indicate that he is a civilian partisan. It is a "better" configuration to have a soldier in action on the battlefield than to have a civilian among regular soldiers.

Good Continuation

Other falsifications result from the attempt to complete incompleted pictures or to fill in gaps which exist in the stimulus field. The effort is again to make the resulting whole coherent, and meaningful. Thus, the sign, "Loew's Pa . . .," over a moving picture theatre is invariably read and reproduced as "Loew's Palace" and Gene *Antry* becomes Gene *Autry*. "Lucky Rakes" are reported as "Lucky Strikes."

All these, and many instances like them, are examples of what has been called, in *Gestalt* terms, "closures." Falsifications of perception and memory they are, but they occur in the interests of bringing about a more coherent, consistent mental configuration. Every detail is assimilated to the principal theme, and "good continuation" is sought, in order to round out meaning where it is lacking or incomplete.

Assimilation by Condensation

It sometimes seems as though memory tries to burden itself as little as possible. For instance, instead of remembering two items, it is more economical to fuse them into one. Instead of a series of subway cards, each of which has its own identity, reports sometimes refer only to "a billboard," or perhaps to a "lot of advertising" (Fig. 1). In another picture, it is more convenient to refer to "all kinds of fruit," rather than to enumerate all the different items on the vendor's cart. Again, the occupants of the car come to be described by some such summary phrase as "several people sitting and standing in the car." Their individuality is lost.

Assimilation to Expectation

Just as details are changed or imported to bear out the simplified theme that the listener has in mind, so also many items take a form that supports the agent's habits of thought. Things that are perceived and remembered the way they *usually* are. Thus a drugstore, in one stimulus-picture, is situated in the middle of a block; but, in the telling, it moves up to the corner of the two streets and becomes the familiar "corner drugstore." A Red Cross ambulance is said to carry medical supplies rather than explosives, because it "ought" to be carrying medical supplies. The kilometers on the signposts are changed into miles, since Americans are accustomed to having distances indicated in miles.

The most spectacular of all our assimilative distortions is the finding that, in more than half of our experiments, a razor moves (in the telling) from a white man's hand to a Negro's hand (Fig. 1). This result is a clear instance of assimilation to stereotyped expectancy. Black men are "supposed" to carry razors, white men not.

Assimilation to Linguistic Habits

Expectancy is often merely a matter of fitting perceived and remembered material to preexisting cliches, which exert a powerful influence in the conventionalization of rumors. Words often arouse compelling familiar images in the listener's mind and fix for him the categories in which he must think of the event and the value that he must attach to it. A "zoot-suit sharpie" packs much more meaning and carries more affect than more objective words, such as "a colored man with pegged trousers, wide-brimmed hat, etc." (Fig. 1). Rumors are commonly told in verbal stereotypes which imply prejudicial judgment, such as "draft dodger," "Japanese spy," "brass hat," "dumb Swede," "long-haired professor," and the like.

MORE HIGHLY MOTIVATED ASSIMILATION

Although the conditions of our experiment do not give full play to emotional tendencies underlying gossip, rumor, and scandal, such tendencies are so insistent that

they express themselves even under laboratory conditions.

Assimilation to Interest

It sometimes happens that a picture containing women's dresses, as a trifling detail in the original scene, becomes, in the telling, a story exclusively about dresses. This sharpening occurs when the rumor is told by groups of women, but never when told by men.

A picture involving police was employed with a group of police officers as subjects. In the resulting protocol, the entire reproduction centered around the police officer (with whom the subjects undoubtedly felt keen sympathy or "identification"). Furthermore, the nightstick, a symbol of his power, is greatly sharpened and becomes the main object of the controversy. The tale as a whole is protective of, and partial to, the policeman.

Assimilation to Prejudice

Hard as it is in an experimental situation to obtain distortions that arise from hatred, yet we have in our material a certain opportunity to trace the hostile complex of racial attitudes.

We have spoken of the picture which contained a white man holding a razor while arguing with a Negro. In over half of the experiments with this picture, the final report indicated that the Negro (instead of the white man) held the razor in his hand, and several times he was reported as "brandishing it widely" or as "threatening" the white man with it (Fig. 1).

Whether this ominous distortion reflects hatred and fear of Negroes we cannot definitely say. In some cases, these deeper emotions may be the assimilative factor at work. And yet the distortion may occur even in subjects who have no anti-Negro bias. It is an unthinking cultural stereotype that the Negro is hot tempered and addicted to the use of razors as weapons. The rumor, though mischievous, may reflect chiefly an assimilation of the story to verbal-cliches and conventional expectation. Distortion in this case may not mean assimilation to hostility. Much so-called prejudice is, of course, a mere matter of conforming to current folkways by accepting prevalent beliefs about an out-group.

Whether or not this razor-shift reflects deep hatred and fear on the part of white subjects, it is certain that the reports of our Negro subjects betray a motivated type of distortion. Because it was to their interest as members of the race to de-emphasize the racial caricature, Negro subjects almost invariably avoided mention of color. One of them hearing a rumor containing the phrase, "a Negro zoot-suiter," reported "There is a man wearing a zoot suit, *possibly* a Negro."

For one picture, a Negro reporter said that the colored man in the center of the picture "is being maltreated." Though this interpretation may be correct, it is likewise possible that he is a rioter about to be arrested by the police officer. White and Negro subjects are very likely to perceive, remember, and interpret this particular situation in quite opposite ways.

Thus, even under laboratory conditions, we find assimilation in terms of deep-lying emotional predispositions. Our rumors, like those of everyday life, tend to fit into, and support, the occupational interests, class or racial memberships, or personal prejudices of the reporter.

CONCLUSION: THE EMBEDDING PROCESS

Leveling, sharpening, and assimilation are not independent mechanisms. They function simultaneously, and reflect a singular subjectifying process that results in the autism and falsification which are so characteristic of rumor. If we were to attempt to summarize what happens in a few words we might say:

Whenever a stimulus field is of potential importance to an individual, but at the same time unclear, or susceptible of divergent interpretations, a subjective structuring process is started. Although the process is complex (involving, as it does, leveling, sharpening, and assimilation), *its essential nature can be characterized as an effort to reduce the stimulus to a simple and meaningful structure that has adaptive significance for the individual in terms of his own interests and experience. The process begins at the moment the ambiguous situation is perceived, but the effects are greatest if memory intervenes. The longer the time that elapses after the stimulus is perceived the greater the threefold change is likely to be. Also, the more people involved in a serial report, the greater the change is likely to be, until the rumor has reached an aphoristic brevity, and is repeated by rote.*

Now, this three-pronged process turns out to be characteristic not only of rumor but of the individual memory function as well. It has been uncovered and described in the experiments on individual retention conducted by Wulf, Gibson, Allport, and, in Bartlett's memory experiments carried out both on individuals and on groups.

Up to now, however, there has been no agreement on precisely the terminology to use, nor upon the adequacy of the three functions we here describe. We believe that our conceptualization of the three-fold course of change and decay is sufficient to account, not only for our own experimental findings and for the experiments of others in this area, but also for the distortions that everyday rumors undergo.

For lack of a better designation, we speak of the three-fold change as the *embedding* process. What seems to occur in all our experiments and in all related studies is that each subject finds the outer stimulus-world far too hard to grasp and retain in its objective character. For his own personal uses, it must be recast to fit not only his span of comprehension and his span of retention, but, likewise, his own personal needs and interests. What was outer becomes inner; what was objective becomes subjective. In telling a rumor, the kernel of objective information that he received has become so embedded into his own dynamic mental life that the product is chiefly one of projection.

Into the rumor, he projects the deficiencies of his retentive processes, as well as his own effort to engender meaning upon an ambiguous field, and the product reveals much of his own emotional needs, including his anxieties, hates, and wishes. When several rumor-agents have been involved in this embedding process, the net result of the serial reproduction reflects the lowest common denominator of cultural interest, of memory span, and of group sentiment and prejudice.

One may ask whether a rumor must always be false. We answer that, in virtually every case, the embedding process is so extensive that no credibility whatever should be ascribed to the product. If a report does turn out to be trustworthy, we usually find that secure standards of evidence have some-how been present to which successive agents could refer for purposes of validation. Perhaps the morning newspaper or the radio have held the rumor under control, but when such secure standards of verification are available, it is questionable whether we should speak of rumor at all.

There are, of course, border-line cases where we may not be able to say whether a given tidbit should or should not be called a rumor. But if we define rumor (and we herewith propose that we should), as *a proposition for belief of topical reference, without secure standards of evidence being present*—then it follows from the facts we have presented that rumor will suffer such serious distortion through the embedding process, that *it is never under any circumstances a valid guide for belief or conduct.*

THE BOLSHEVIK AGITATOR

ALEX INKELES

THE PERSISTENCE OF PERSONAL ORAL AGITATION

Although the mechanically unaided voice undoubtedly accounts for the bulk of all human communication, the mass media such as the newspaper, the radio, and the film have radically altered the whole pattern of public communication. The impact of these mass media on modern society has been so marked that students of public opinion have concentrated their attention on them almost exclusively. As a consequence of this concentration, the study of direct personal communication has been neglected, and there has been some tendency to undervalue its significance for the formation of opinions and attitudes.

In contrast, Bolshevik thought and practice continue to place the heaviest emphasis on daily face-to-face contact between the masses and representatives of the party, as a fundamental instrument of public communication and as a method of influencing

From Alex Inkeles, *Public Opinion in Soviet Russia*, (Cambridge: Harvard University Press, 1950), pp. 67-93 *passim*. Reprinted by permission of the author and the publisher.

opinions and shaping attitudes. In the U. S. S. R. such communication is referred to as "personal oral agitation." Agitation, as has been noted, is defined as the dissemination of a single simple idea to a large number of people. In that sense agitation may be printed in newspapers and magazines or on posters. Or it may be oral. In communist thought oral agitation is further differentiated. *Mass* oral agitation is conducted primarily by the radio, but speeches at mass meetings also fall in this category. There are two other important forms of oral agitation: that conducted with a few people in face-to-face contact, known as *group* agitation, and that involving only one person besides the agitator, known as *individual* agitation, referred to above collectively as "personal oral agitation."

. . . The extent of the party's interest and faith in personal agitation is probably best reflected in the size of the army of agitators it has mobilized and organized to carry its message to the people. Thus, at the time of the election campaign in February 1946, the party was able to draw on the services of approximately three million agitators. This figure does not represent the size of the regular corps of agitators, since at election times the party usually makes especially strenuous agitation efforts and many people are drawn into that work on a short-term basis. Evidence available on a large number of republics and regions of the U. S. S. R. indicates that the party regularly maintains a force of approximately two million agitators. Assuming a population of about two hundred million, this would yield a ratio of one agitator for each one hundred of population, or one agitator for every sixty-five persons over the age of fifteen.

This ratio is, of course, not uniformly maintained throughout the territory of the Soviet Union. The concentration is higher in the more densely settled and economically important areas. In the Ukrainian Republic in 1949, for example, there were 764,000 agitators, yielding a ratio of one agitator to approximately every fifty persons in the population. The concentration in the urban areas is also much greater than in rural areas. Thus, the capital city of Moscow, with a population of about five million, had 160,-000 agitators in 1946, or a ratio of one agitator for every thirty individuals in the population. In contrast, in some rural areas there are many collective farms, incorporating several hundred people, which do not boast a single agitator, and which may be visited by a district agitator only two or three times a year. These are the Soviet equivalent of the famous "deaf corners" of Tsarist Russia.

In the face of the great territory and population of the country, the formal media of communication in the Soviet Union are inadequate to the tasks set for them by the party. But whatever these inadequacies, they cannot serve as a satisfactory explanation of the continued emphasis that the party has placed on personal oral agitation. The expansion of the system of personal agitation has not only kept pace with the growth of the formal media, but has, if anything, exceeded the rate of growth of the press, radio, and film. For example, the *Agitator's Guidebook*, a semimonthly handbook of information, advice, and instruction for local agitators, increased in circulation by more than eighteen times between 1925 and 1939, and between 1935 and 1939 alone it increased sixfold. Its circulation of 650,000 copies in 1939 made it the largest magazine and journal of any type in the Soviet Union. The journal, furthermore, is printed only in Russian, and non-Russian speaking agitators are served by native language equivalents of the *Agitator's Guidebook*. There is one in each union republic and territory, in nine of the autonomous republics, and in thirty-six regions, with a combined circulation of 800,-000 copies per issue in 1947.

The party's continued emphasis on personal oral agitation is based on the assumption that this form has certain special qualities which particularly suit it to the party's needs and interests. The party may, of course, fulfill its self-assigned functions as a leader, teacher, and guide of the masses from a distance. But the party recognizes that the kind of effort and sacrifice which it expects and requires on the part of the population depends upon some intimate contact between it and the masses. The existence of any real gulfs between the party and the people renders ineffective the leadership principle. For this reason Lenin, Stalin, and other Bolshevik leaders have insisted that, at least in this respect, the party must make it an inalienable principle of its tactics to stay "close" to the masses. The party, in brief, cannot expect discipline and sacrifice from the masses unless it is itself a model of these virtues. This approach is characterized by the party's conception of "agitation by example," and it is indeed regarded as the first responsibility of the individual agitator that he set his group a shining example of effort, discipline, and sacrifice.

It is clear that personal oral agitation is much better suited to giving concrete meaning to the party's conception of "agitation by example" than are the radio or the press. In addition, group and individual agitation are ideally suited to the resolution of the party's ever-pressing problem of mobilizing the people for greater agricultural and industrial production. But the greatest importance of this type of agitation lies in the fact that it provides a direct channel of communication between the masses and the otherwise distant party leaders. For the Bolshevik agitator is in daily, intimate contact with small groups of people whose problems he knows at first hand and whom he meets in a relatively free atmosphere of discussion. He is thus able to provide the party officials at all levels with a constant flow of information on the state of popular thought. He can report the desires and interests of the people, and advise the party leaders of trends in public opinion which they may effectively exploit or which they must counteract.

The Bolshevik agitator is, in the last analysis, the figure on whom the success of the party's oral agitation depends. Of all the representatives of the party it is the agitator who has the most frequent, regular, and intimate contact with the industrial workers, the collective farmers, and the rest of the Soviet citizens. He is the individual through whom the party daily "talks things over with the people," as the writers for party journals are fond of putting it. Before or after the change of shift or in the rest period in the plants and on the farms, and even in the workers' dormitories or at their apartments, he meets with small groups to conduct his agitation. Whether he reads aloud some article from the daily press, describes some important recent decision of the party or government, leads a critical discussion of the work performance of his group, or exhorts them to greater effort, he speaks in each case as the voice of the party. He is a major link between the party leadership and the masses.

THE SELECTION AND TRAINING OF AGITATORS

Traditionally, every Communist has been expected actively to propagate the views of the party in his daily work and contacts, and a provision to this effect is embodied in the party rules as one of the first duties of a Bolshevik. The party is not inclined, however, to provide for so important an activity as agitation solely on the basis of a blanket responsibility of the total party membership. Consequently, the executive committees of primary party organizations are instructed to designate specific agitators from among the best party and Komsomol members and from among the non-party Bolsheviks (those sympathetic to the party's aims although not members). These agitators are selected from among the regular personnel in the industrial enterprises, collective farms, Machine-Tractor Stations, State Farms, and other establishments and institutions at which the primary party organizations are located.

This "designation" of certain individuals as agitators derives from the conditions of party membership. In addition to his regular occupation, every member is expected to perform some special work for the party. Service as an agitator is one of the most common and, from the point of view of the party, one of the most acceptable methods for the discharge of this obligation. Such service is officially regarded as the prime party responsibility of those performing it, and they are supposed to be freed of other party duties. Party members who prefer agitation to other party duties may volunteer for service as an agitator. Similarly, persons who are not members but are classified as party "sympathizers" may volunteer or may be invited to work as agitators. The proportion of such non-party agitators is not great. For example, less than one fourth of the agitators in Moscow during the 1947 election campaign were non-party, and generally during elections the number of such agitators is much higher than at other times.

The party member, having been selected or having volunteered for agitation work, and having been confirmed for the job by the local party executive committee, is usually assigned to a kind of agitators' seminar known as *agit-kollectiv*. The first agit-collectives were set up in 1923, following a decision of the Twelfth Party Congress which stressed the need for a specialized apparatus for instructing local agitators and working out the details of local campaigns. In the succeeding years the party issued instructions from time to time governing the operations of these groups, and in 1938 a formal set of "Model Rules for Agit-Collectives" was adopted. Those rules are apparently still in force.

Agit-collectives are established, and their work is supervised, by the primary party organizations at industrial establishments, governmental offices and institutions, collective farms and Machine-Tractor Stations, and so on. An agit-collective should number not less than fifteen and not more than thirty agitators. For this reason, major establishments and particularly large industrial plants, which may have as many as fifteen hundred agitators, will usually have several agit-collectives. There may be one for each shop in the plant, and the same shop may have a different collective for each of the shifts. In moderate-sized plants there will usually be only a few agit-collectives. At most small plants and establishments there will usually not be enough agitators to form a collective. This is especially true on collective farms and in Machine-Tractor Stations, and as late as 1940 it was reported that there were many collective farms that did not have a single agitator. In the case of such plants and farms the individual agitators will usually be enrolled in an agit-collective operating under the supervision of the district or county party organization.

The secretary of the local primary party organization is expected to serve as the chairman of the agit-collective, conducting the meetings and personally instructing the agitators in their duties. In larger plants where the primary party organization is broken down into shop committees, the agit-collective in each shop will be supervised by the head of the party shop committee. In such cases, the secretary of the parent primary party organization will direct a factory-wide agit-collective made up of the heads of the shop agit-collectives and of the more experienced or strategically located agitators. The party secretary, or the man he deputizes as director of the agit-collective, is expected to report back to the executive committee of his party organization at least twice monthly; he then gives an account of the work of his group of agitators and receives instructions for the future. The executive committee of the primary organization is, of course, itself subject to instructions from higher party authorities, in particular from the Department of Propaganda and Agitation of the Central Committee.

The agit-collective is expected to meet once every ten days. At these meetings a plan of work is drawn up to cover the next period, and this plan is supposed to be approved by the executive committee of the primary organization. The subjects discussed at these meetings include current events; major aspects of current party policy; mass political campaigns, such as those associated with forthcoming elections; questions of special interest to the workers at the local plant, such as the application of recent government decisions; and most important, the practical economic or political tasks facing the given plant, farm, or organization. The members are expected to review and discuss their experiences, obtain advice from the best agitators and the director, and learn not only what to agitate about but also how to approach each subject.

The immediate and chief purpose of the agit-collective is to prepare the agitator to carry on agitation on a specific subject of importance, such as reducing waste in the plant, during a specified campaign period. But the agit-collective is also supposed to improve his general qualifications as a representative of the party who goes before the workers. The agit-collective will, therefore, also discuss general subjects like geography, economics, and cultural or political questions. Through the collective, the party makes available to the agitator books, newspapers, maps, visual aids, and special literature of all kinds. The agitator is also served by the local *partkabinet* (party cabinet). At the *partkabinet* the agitator may consult individually or in groups with a party official about some question of theory or about the correct way to answer certain questions of the workers. The *partkabinet* also provides the agitators with analyses of important speeches and decrees, and prepares digests of the press for them on important political and economic problems in both internal and international affairs.

In addition, the party has from time to time ordered special short-term schools established for agitators at the district or county level. These courses usually last ten days or less, and are generally given in the evenings so that the agitator need not leave his regular job in the factory. On occasion, these courses will be on a special subject of particular importance at the time, such as foreign affairs. Most of them are general, however, and the student will divide his time between lectures and self-study or reading. The courses are designed to improve the general preparation of the agitator, and usually include lectures on Soviet and world geography, on "conditions" in capitalist countries, and on the economic

and political policies of the Soviet regime. They are not supposed to duplicate the services of either the regular schools for adult education or the regular party schools for Marxist training, but are expected to orient themselves specifically to the task of improving the effectiveness of the agitators as the voice of the party among the rank and file of the working population. . . .

THE SOCIAL ROLE OF THE BOLSHEVIK AGITATOR

The Bolshevik agitator is the most constant direct personal link between the party leaders and the mass of the people. It is said of him that he "fulfills the most important Party responsibility and is one of the most important figures of the proletarian revolutionary movement." But the lot of the agitator is not a happy one, buffeted as he is by the pressures from both above and below. It is the efforts of agitators to evolve for themselves a stable, satisfying, and satisfactory role in this total situation that must now be considered.

If one were to make a list of the specific tasks and functions which the party has assigned to its agitators, it would more than fill this page. These duties range from leading the workers to maintain a high level of cleanliness at their workbenches, to eliminating the remnants of capitalist thought in men's minds and inculcating a new "socialist consciousness." For the purposes of this study the responsibilities of the agitators may be regarded as divided into two related categories, the practical and the political. Both types of agitation have their roots deep in the Soviet system.

The practical tasks of the agitator are concentrated at the level of industrial and agricultural production, in the shop and the brigade. The success of the Plans, on which the success of the regime has largely rested, depends on extra-human effort, or, as Stalin put it, on the willingness of the people to work in the new way. The whole industrial order has been in an almost continuous state of flux, with millions of new workers entering industry from the rural areas, with new processes, techniques, and procedures being constantly introduced. In the midst of all this the Bolshevik agitator has been expected to be both a stabilizer and an innovator. He has been expected to introduce the new workers to the industrial order, and by his steadiness and personal achievement to act as a model for all. At the same time he has been expected to be first in every new movement, pushing the workers on to new goals, training them in new methods, urging them to combat waste or to increase productivity, criticizing their failures and deficiencies.

On the political side, the agitator has to carry "the word" of the party to the people. He must introduce and explain the new decrees, expound and justify the party's policy. He is expected to persuade and convince, to mobilize opinion in support of the party's leadership and its actions, to criticize those who are defined as enemies and praise those who are defined as friends. He must keep the "revolutionary spirit" alive among the masses, educate them in communism, rally them to the support of the party and the Soviet motherland.

The needs of the party are constant, and the pressure it exerts on the agitator is correspondingly regular. But the agitator must reckon not only with the party officials who instruct him, for he daily faces a live audience of people with whom he has other relations than that of agitator. If the agitator had only good news to bring the people, of course, his most serious problem would be limited to that of maintaining audience interest. But the practical and political tasks of the agitator are not always such as will arouse an enthusiastic response in his audience. Most of the time the content of the agitation is such that it places new demands on the people who listen—more production, less waste, greater cleanliness in the shop and in the living quarters, better work discipline.

The workers have questions to ask, furthermore, and frequently these queries are what are termed "difficult" or even "painful"; but the party insists that they be answered, and it is the agitator who must make the reply, lest they be answered by "hostile" elements who have their own answers, not those of the party. The agitator may be asked, for example, why it is still necessary to queue up at the stores despite the supposed improvement in consumers' services. Or he may be asked why the pay of directors is so much higher than that of some workers. And sometimes he must introduce measures, such as the increase in work norms or the lengthening of the work day, which arouse the "temporary displeasure" of particular groups of workers. Such problems are considered to be tests of the agitator's "Bolshevik tempering," and he is told: "Do not hide from a puzzling, trenchant, or even hostile question, but, on the contrary, give an answer that is straightforward and full of the stuff of the Party spirit." . . .

Such is the situation of the agitator as he is pressed forward by the party; yet he must reckon on the response of his audience with which he must live and work during the hours when he is not acting in the role of agitator. One possible resolution of the problem would be to have agitation conducted by professional agitators sent out from a central point to speak in some shop or on some farm and then to move on to their next assignment. Such a procedure would have the virtue of facilitating that type of direct control of agitation content to which press, radio, and film lend themselves quite naturally. But the party rejected this course. It did so not only because of the organizational, financial, and manpower burden it would have imposed, but also because it would have meant putting oral agitation on a mass basis rather than on a group and individual basis. For in the view of party officials, group and individual agitation have marked advantages over other forms of oral agitation, at least for the purposes and ends to which the party's oral agitation is primarily oriented.

Consequently, the average party member is likely to find himself, if he is selected to conduct agitation, assigned to agitate in his own shop or his own farm brigade. It is largely from this fact that there arise certain persistent difficulties for the agitator, which manifest themselves in two ways that are closely related.

In the first place, the socially defined role of the agitator involves inconsistent expectations which can easily produce a conflict situation for the men who agitate. The party emphasizes the selection of agitators from the rank and file of the workers because it knows that such an agitator will have the same general interests as his audience; indeed, his effectiveness as an agitator is presumed to depend in good part on this similarity. At the same time, the party expects these agitators to be spokesmen for other, different, interests which are passed on to the agitator from the higher reaches of the party hierarchy. These other interests may be broader, larger, national interests, but they are still different interests. And frequently these larger interests may not be perfectly coordinated with the immediate interests of the agitator, for example, when he must agitate for a speed-up system which national interest requires even though he personally may be lukewarm or even hostile to the idea of exerting still more "extra" effort. Thus, there is potential strain which is structured by the several conflicting expectations of the agitator's role, and which is in this sense internal to the role itself.

In the second place, a man's role as agitator may conflict with other roles which he plays as a member of society. In particular, it may conflict with the agitator's personal relations with his audience of fellow workers, personal relations toward which he has a real emotional commitment. Because the men who are his "audience" when he acts as agitator are often, during the rest of the day, simply his fellow workers, men with whom he eats in the factory lunchrooms, rides home on the trolley in the evening, and whom he perhaps sees socially and reckons as friends after working hours. And in some situations, in so far as the agitator consolidates his party position by fulfilling his agitation instructions, he may at the same time be disrupting his relations with his fellow workers.

Our problem, therefore, is to explore the alternatives which his situation presents to him, and to attempt to discover that form of the role of agitator which provides the fullest resolution of the difficulties inherent in the agitator's situation.

One solution of their dilemma which many agitators have apparently adopted has been to dodge their responsibility, in one way or another to get out of agitation. Certainly all of the turnover in the ranks of the agitators, and it appears to be considerable, cannot be attributed to the personal difficulties faced by the agitator, but a significant percentage of the total may safely be traced to this factor.

In one way or another virtually all of the various party decisions on agitation and innumerable articles and editorials in the *Agitator's Guidebook* have complained of the instability of the corps of agitators. The so-called "paper" agitators, carried on the roles but not actively conducting agitation, have been a continuous problem. In a Dnepropetrovsk plant in 1939, for example, agitators failed to hold twenty-three scheduled sessions in a short period; and in six election districts in the same city, of a total of 704 scheduled agitation sessions in September and October, 312 were not held owing to failure of the agitators to meet their obligations. . . .

To shirk his responsibilities as an agitator, although it might get him relieved of the duty, can hardly serve the party member in good stead so far as his party standing is concerned. There is a second, safer, alternative. It is the course of action which the party has often labeled the "routinization" of agitation, or "formalism," or "bureaucratic-clericalism" in agitation work. This is the charge leveled against those who stick to agitation "in general," who are alleged to avoid troublesome questions, who concentrate on the revolutionary dates and agitate according to the calendar, who wait for the people to come to them and who read pre-pared speeches instead of seeking out the people, who look the other way when they see shirkers on the job or hear hostile remarks made against the regime. These are the people, it is said, who distorted the 1935 party decision about the importance of using literary materials in agitation, and who thought that thereafter they could fulfill their agitation obligation solely by reading aloud from *War and Peace* and *Don Quixote*. These were the people accused of being interested only in the figures they could turn in to the party committee on the number of talks they had given and the number who attended, but whose agitation was hackneyed and had no real impact on the organization of the mass.

Although this kind of "routinization" of agitation solved some of the personal problems of the agitator, it could not be a permanent solution of either half of his dilemma. For he could not long hope to retain his audience if he kept his agitation work on a continuously abstract level, and in any event the party was unwilling to have its agitation turned into a simple adult-education program. These first two courses of action, dodging responsibility and "formalism," are not really resolutions of, but rather are unstable compromises with, the problem faced by the Bolshevik agitator. The crux of the problem lies in the defined role of the agitator. He must be capable of criticizing the work of his fellow workers, of introducing them to measures which they may find objectionable, and of defending the party and government against criticism. Yet he cannot escape at the end of the session, for he speaks to workers he knows and sees every day, frequently on intimate terms. The crucial problem becomes one of recruiting as agitators individuals of sufficient authority among the people to carry this off without later suffering such social ostracism or rebuff at the hands of their audiences as would reduce their effectiveness as agitators. Such authority can be based either on the personal qualities of the agitator or on his social status. . . .

The successful agitator is currently described as the man who knows not only how each person in his shop works, but also how he lives, what his family is like, what his living conditions are, and whether or not he needs advice on one or another personal problem. The agitator is told that "only in the event that the agitator stands in close contact with the people does he actually win for himself authority and respect." Again and again in descriptions of the experience of model agitators, there are examples of such personal contact between the agitator and the members of his group. Sometimes it is the case of an agitator who assisted some worker to improve his qualifications and his earnings. Another time he helps a man, whose work was poor because his quarters were inadequate, to find a room, or he helps another man with some difficulty he was having in collecting his pay. He may help the men who share his dormitory room with their reading and evening study, or he may help another man solve a family problem.

In every case, the fact of central importance is that the agitator is establishing a relationship of social solidarity with the members of his work group; or, as one man who had been given personal assistance by the agitator is reported to have put it, the agitator had developed the feeling that the shop and the working group in it was a sort of family, with close ties, and that each man had certain responsibilities toward it. . . .

Thus, one solution of the agitator's dilemma has been to develop agitators whose personal standing with their audiences has been very high. The party literature indicates that this type of relation, based on the social solidarity of agitator and audience, was developed independently by individual agitators who sought a satisfactory solution to the problem, and was also sanctioned and encouraged by the party. It was and remains, nevertheless, only a partial solution and an unstable compromise.

One of the difficult tasks of the group agitator is to exhort and constantly to urge the workers on to greater efforts. This he can do more effectively if he has the esteem and personal respect of his co-workers. Even more difficult, however, are his tasks of criticizing workers whose production records are poor or who violate labor discipline, and of introducing and carrying into effect new government measures such as increases in the work norms. These tasks he can also perform more effectively if he has close personal relations with his audience. But the very element that gives him this increased effectiveness also acts as a real limiting factor on that effectiveness. For at times when the agitator is being pressed most by the party for more intensive criticism of lagging workers, or when he has to introduce measures which meet the displeasure of the workers, his personal relations with those workers will then most induce him to temper his criticism or to soft-pedal the measures as much as it is within his power to do so. Furthermore, in so far as he behaves as a good party man at such times and carries out the instructions of the party to the letter, then he runs the risk of losing that close contact with his fellow workers which was the basis of his authority in the first place.

Thus, the personal standing of the agitator is clearly but one means of giving him the authority he requires to fulfill his function successfully. Another means is to select for agitation people of high social status, in particular the managerial personnel of the plant. . . .

Managerial personnel as agitators also have authority, but it is authority based on their social status, their standing in the hierarchy of positions in the productive process, and not on their purely personal relations with the audience. The foreman, shop director, engineer, or plant director are not like the traveling jack-of-all trades agitator of earlier years. They know the plant and its production problems, and they have regular contact with the workers whom they know and who know them to varying degrees. Since the agitator is supposed to criticize errors and to explain the reasons for new processes, the managerial personnel is clearly suited to carry on agitation. For the manager-agitator possesses the authority of technical competence, which, it may be assumed, would frequently enable criticism of a man's work with less resentment than might be aroused by such criticism coming from an agitator who is just another worker. At the same time, the managerial personnel is generally better trained and is frequently well educated and well informed, which adds to its general standing and to its qualifications for agitation.

Thus, pressing managerial personnel into agitation largely overcomes the two major sources of conflict that inhere in the situation of the agitator who is a rank-and-file worker. In the first place, the internal conflict of duties is not so apparent in the case of the manager-agitator, for very few of his interests are the same as those of the workers with whom he agitates. If the national interest demands extra effort for higher production, he can freely agitate for that goal, since it does not conflict with his immediate interests as a manager. Indeed, it is frequently very much to his interest in general to agitate for higher production and greater effort. In the second place, service as an agitator by the representative of management is less likely to involve conflict between different roles. For there is a secure social distance between him and his audience. Once having completed his agitation work, he is not obliged to continue on an intimate personal basis with his audience, working shoulder to shoulder with the other workers. He is free to withdraw, not only to his own special work, but to the company of other people of managerial rank. Since he has only limited cause to fear loss of the personal good will of his audience as a threat of real social deprivation, he is better suited to conduct agitation in those hard times when the need for the agitator is greatest. . . .

But there are also limits on the effectiveness of the managerial agitator, and again these limits arise from the very source of his strength. Despite official assertions that there is no antagonism between the managerial personnel and the workers in the

Soviet Union, and the conclusion of some serious scholars that such antagonism between managers and workers may indeed be less in the U. S. S. R. than in the industrial order in capitalist countries, it cannot be safely assumed that there is no longer a considerable gulf between the two groups, or that there is no longer any antagonism, resentment, or suspicion between the mass of workers and management. In so far as such social distance persists between the two groups, then the representative of management who comes forward in the role of agitator must expect his effectiveness as an agitator to be reduced by the feeling he generates as a representative of management. Furthermore, in so far as there is at all widespread among the workers a feeling that management receives a disproportionate share of the total plant income (witness the question about managers' salaries cited above), then the presentation of any demands by managerial agitators for higher production or new processes must become suspect in such a way as to reduce seriously the effectiveness of their agitation.

It may be anticipated, therefore, that in the future the party will continue to draw upon both the rank-and-file and the managerial groups for its agitators, seeking through their combined efforts to achieve that mobilization of the mind, will, and energy of the working masses which it finds necessary to its purposes.

DETERMINANTS OF VOTING BEHAVIOR

A PROGRESS REPORT ON THE ELMIRA ELECTION STUDY

ALICE S. KITT AND DAVID B. GLEICHER[1]

By and large, the analysis of the Elmira election study thus far completed has provided a demonstration of the major advantages accruing from the use of the panel technique. For one, we have estimated that our four waves of interviewing provided us

with approximately 360 pieces of information about each of our thousand-odd panel members. This information covers a wide range of topics, including the number of community organizations respondents belong to, how members of their families are going to vote, whether they tend to agree or disagree with their friends on political matters, how they voted in past elections, how they think various groups of their fellow citizens are going to vote, what their images of the candidates are, and what their views on various campaign issues are. In addition, the panel technique permits us to follow the shifts in the vote intention of our respondents

[1] It is particularly difficult in a cooperative study such as this one to isolate individual contributions made by members of the workshop team, but mention should be made at this point of those whose analyses have been directly utilized in the following report: namely, Stanley Friedman, Norman Kaplan, Elihu Katz, Alice Kitt and Allen Meyer. The writers of this report wish to thank Professor Paul F. Lazarsfeld for his guidance in selecting and organizing the material.

Reprinted from the *Public Opinion Quarterly*, 1950, 14, 393-412, by permission of the authors and the publisher.

during the course of the campaign. Since this method allows for the collection of data undistorted by memory lapses, we have a wealth of information on the *number* and the *direction* of shifts in respondents' vote intention, and thus we are able to conduct detailed analyses of both individual and group changes in opinion over time.

THE EFFECT OF PERSONAL CONTACTS ON INTEREST

One problem area which is illuminated by the use of the panel technique is that of the role played by local political parties during the campaign. It is the claim of practicing politicians that their efforts succeed in increasing the amount of interest people have in the election, and consequently lead to a greater turnout at the polls. Since one of the repeated questions used in the study was on how much interest people had in the presidential election, and since we also found out whether people were contacted by the political organizations, we can ascertain whether the politicians' efforts actually bear fruit. Respondents were asked in October,

In the last three or four weeks has anyone from any of the parties seen or phoned you in regard to the election campaign?

and

Did you receive any postcards, pamphlets or other literature about the election?

Some 158 respondents reported impersonal contact from the parties in the form of campaign literature, and 63 reported personal contact by party workers. While a check disclosed no significant differences in demographic factors between those contacted and those not contacted by the political parties, we did find one characteristic of the contacted group of respondents which distinguishes them from the not-contacted group. Among those reporting that they received campaign literature from the local party office, there is a far larger proportion of people who had on a previous interview showed a high level of interest in the campaign. Some 41 per cent of those who in October said

they had received campaign literature had a *high* level of interest in the campaign in June, in contrast to 29 per cent of those who did not receive campaign literature—a difference of 12 per cent. Since it seems unlikely that the use of mailing lists or neighborhood house-to-house distribution would involve any bias toward the more highly interested voter, we might well attribute this greater proportion of highly interested respondents among the contacted group to the fact that people very interested in the political campaign are more apt to 'notice' the political pamphlets, cards or notices they receive.

A similar relationship between interest and reported personal contact by workers from the political parties does not appear to exist. A personal visit or telephone call is more apt to be accurately recalled and reported. Thus there is but a 1 per cent difference in the proportion who had a *high* level of interest in the campaign between respondents who were contacted personally by party workers and those who were not so contacted.

Since there are approximately three times as many impersonal contacts as personal contacts, this tendency for party-contact to predominate among the high-interest respondents can be seen in Table 1. Comparing the ratio of the contacted to not-contacted groups, we see that it drops from approximately 1:2 among the *high* interest group, to 1:3 among the *medium* interest, and to 1:4 among those with a *low* level of interest.

But this interest differential is not a disturbing factor in our analysis precisely because the panel technique enables us to control it by classifying respondents according to the level of interest they expressed prior to the reported contact. By so doing, we can study the *direction* of interest shift *after* the contact within each interest group, and thus ascertain whether interest in the election campaign increases to any greater extent among those contacted by the local parties than among those who are not contacted. Table 1 reveals the interest shift which oc-

TABLE 1

THE COMBINED EFFECT OF PERSONAL AND IMPERSONAL PARTY
CONTACT UPON LEVEL OF INTEREST

INTEREST LEVEL IN AUGUST

Interest Level in October	High		Medium		Low	
	Contacted	Not Contacted	Contacted	Not Contacted	Contacted	Not Contacted
High	67%	58%	42%	25%	5%	8%
Medium	26	29	44	52	26	18
Low	7	13	14	23	69	74
	100%	100%	100%	100%	100%	100%
	(n=81)	(n=192)	(n=69)	(n=207)	(n=43)	(n=158)

curred between August and October among those contacted and those not contacted.

On each of the interest levels as they existed in August, there is a greater shift toward a higher level of interest by October among those respondents who report some contact by the political parties than among those who did not. For example, among those who expressed a *low* interest in August, 31 per cent of the individuals who had been contacted and only 26 per cent of those not contacted had shifted to either a *medium* or *high* level of interest by October. Among those with a *medium* level of interest in August who were contacted by the political parties, 42 per cent had shifted to *high* interest by October, in contrast to a shift of only 25 per cent among those who were not contacted by the party during this two-month period—a difference of 17 per cent. Party contact is thus seen to generate greater interest in the campaign. On the other hand, among those who showed a *high* level of interest in the interview prior to the party contact, the contact helped to forestall any downward shift in level of interest. Among those contacted, 67 per cent still showed a high level of interest in the October interview, in contrast to 58 per cent among those not contacted. In these cases party contact is seen to have the further function of preserving the interest level.

Indeed, it is only through the use of the panel technique that we are able to obtain this before-and-after picture of the effect of contact by the political organizations upon the level of interest which people have in the election. At best, the cross-sectional survey might show the level of interest which a group of respondents has *after* contact by the political organizations. But any analysis of the static picture obtained in this fashion would be fraught with ambiguities. It could not tell us the more dynamic story of a *change* in interest level or of the *direction* of that change in the striking manner which the use of a panel of respondents permits.

THE EFFECT OF PERSONAL ENVIRONMENT ON POLITICAL BEHAVIOR

In order to illustrate the way in which the panel technique can illuminate the role of factors which make for change of vote intention during the course of the campaign, we shall select two sub-areas in which considerable work has already been completed. Here again the panel technique brings out components of shifts in vote intention which a cross-sectional survey would not be able to trace. The areas are: (1) the personal environment of the voter—the effect of knowledge of the vote intention of other people with whom the respondent is in continual social contact upon the respondent's own vote inclination; and (2) the subsequent vote intentions of Republicans in the light of their pre-convention candidate preference as opposed to the actual candidate selected at the convention.

One of the central foci of the Elmira study is that of the effect of the political composition of the social groups within which people move upon their voting behavior. If the family of a respondent, or his closest friends, or the people with whom he works, are of the same political persuasion as himself, we consider his social environment to be relatively homogeneous. If, however, the respondent's family and friends differ with him on political questions, we consider his social environment to be relatively heterogeneous.

Respondents were asked in August:

Think of your three closest friends (outside of work). How is each of them going to vote?

On the basis of the responses to this question, we were able to divide our respondents into five groups: those whose three closest friends were either all Republicans or all Democrats; those who had either two Republican friends and one Democratic friend, or two Democratic friends and one Republican friend; and those who did not know how their closest friends were going to vote. Since we shall not discuss this last group, which comprised 27 per cent of the sample, we might note in passing that not knowing how one's three closest friends are going to vote may be taken as an indication of the relatively non-political nature of the personal social environment of these respondents, and

is thus indirect evidence of their lack of interest in politics. This interpretation was in fact substantiated by the finding that, of the five groups indicated above, this group of respondents who did not know how their friends would vote had the lowest proportion of people with a high level of interest in the 1948 election.

We might also note parenthetically that relatively few people move in a "mixed" environment as far as their friends' politics are concerned. Only 16 per cent of the respondents report that two of their friends are voting the same way (Republican or Democratic) and that the third friend is a maverick who is voting for the other party.

The extent to which these friendship groups are significant for the politics of the respondents themselves can be seen from Table 2. The index of vote inclination used in this table is based on the responses to questions on whether respondents intended to vote, for whom they intended to vote, and how strongly they felt about their choice. If they were uncertain as to how they would vote, or if they said they might not vote at all, they were asked to express a "leaning" toward one or the other party. These elements, combined into the index, give us a seven-point scale of the strength of the respondents' vote inclination.

In the table we see that if a man has three friends, all of whom intend to vote the same way, there is very little likelihood that he will vote in some other way.

TABLE 2

FRIENDS' VOTE INTENTION AND STRENGTH OF OWN VOTE INTENTION

vote inclination of respondent

Vote intention of three friends	Republican			Democratic			
	Very Strong	Strong	Weak	Very Strong	Strong	Weak	
RRR	55%	30%	8%	1%	4%	2%	100% (n=311)
RRD	34	31	3	8	15	9	100% (n=79)
DDR	22	18	10	18	25	7	100% (n=40)
DDD	2	9	8	34	37	10	100% (n=116)

Slightly more than 90 per cent of the respondents with three Republican friends, show some degree of Republican vote inclination themselves. As one might anticipate in a predominantly Republican community, this tendency is not as marked for the respondents with three Democratic friends; yet here as well about 80 per cent of these respondents express a Democratic vote inclination. But the most interesting contrast is that between the homogeneous and the mixed groups. If a respondent is a member of a mixed friendship group, we can observe two things. First he is less likely to feel very strongly about his vote inclination. For example, 34 per cent of those with two Republican and one Democratic friend have very strong Republican inclinations in contrast to 55 per cent of those who are in the homogeneous group and have three Republican friends. Second, the ratio of Democratic to Republican vote inclinations among respondents in mixed friendship groups is much less sharp than in the homogeneous friendship groups. We have noted that of those who have three Republican friends over 90 per cent have a Republican inclination, while among those who count a Democrat among their three closest friends, the proportion drops to about 68 per cent. Similarly, among those with three Democratic friends, 81 per cent have a Democratic vote inclination, while among those who have one Republican friend and two Democratic friends, the proportion drops to 50 per cent.

In effect, then, people intended to vote "with their friends," and felt most strongly about their own intention when there was political homogeneity in their friendship group.

The question of whether these friendship groups are significant for the *direction* in which a shift of vote inclination takes place during the course of the campaign is perhaps of even greater interest. Again using the index of vote inclination, we shall call a man a "shifter toward Republican" if between August and October he became a stronger Republican or a weaker Democrat, and we shall call a man who became a

stronger Democrat or a weaker Republican during this two-month period a "shifter toward Democratic." We can then check the expectation that shifts in the vote inclination of respondents will be in the direction of the political persuasion of their friends. Table 3 confirms this expectation. As this table shows, of the people who shifted and who had three Republican friends, a higher proportion (56 per cent) shifted toward the Republicans than toward the Democrats (44 per cent). Correlatively, a higher proportion of those with three Democratic friends shifted toward the Democrats. But those who were in a mixed political friendship group (two Republican friends and one Democratic friend, or two Democratic friends and one Republican—the RRD and DDR groups in the table) were just as likely to shift toward the Republicans as toward the Democrats.

TABLE 3

AUGUST TO OCTOBER SHIFTERS

Political Inclination of Three Closest Friends	Shifted toward Republicans	Shifted toward Democrats	Total
RRR	56%	44%	100% (n=106)
RRD } DDR }	49	51	100% (n=47)
DDD	39	61	100% (n=51)

Space does not permit a discussion of the effect of the vote intention of co-workers upon the intensity of vote inclination or the direction in which shifts in vote inclination take place. But we find that the same tendency which has been noted in the case of friends holds for co-workers as well, although in a less marked fashion, since the choice of co-workers is more restricted and the extent of social interaction between co-workers is more limited.

Since there is perhaps no other group of individuals with whom we have more continuous and close contacts than our own families, we might expect that the political persuasions of family members will play a significant role in our respondents' patterns of vote intention. Our panel members were therefore asked in June:

So far as you know, how are the people in your family living here going to vote in the Presidential election this year?

Respondents were then classified according to whether the vote intention they expressed in June was the same as that of all other members of their family, or different from all other members of their family, and their June vote intention was contrasted with their August vote intention. It was then possible to ascertain whether there was a higher proportion of Republican vote intentions in August among those who had previously indicated that both they and their families intended to vote Republican, than among those who indicated that they intended to vote Republican but that one or more members of their family intended to vote Democratic. Table 4 shows the striking differences which obtain between these groups. Among those respondents who intended to vote Republican in June, and whose family shared this vote intention, fully 90 per cent had the same Republican vote intention in August. If there was either partial or complete disagreement between the Republican respondent and his family, however, the proportion still intending to vote Republican in August drops to 77 per cent among those in partial disagreement and 56 per cent among those in complete disagreement with the members of their

family. The same pattern obtains among those with a Democratic vote intention. The proportion of respondents intending to vote Democratic in August drops only to 80 per cent among those who were in full accord with their family's vote intention in June, but to 65 per cent and 54 per cent among those in disagreement with their family.

It can be noted further that there are two major responses to a lack of political homogeneity between the respondent and his family. First, there may be a shift in vote intention to the party which the respondent's family supports. Thus, among those who in June intended to vote Republican but who were in disagreement with their family politically, there is an increased proportion of Democratic vote intentions by August— from 2 per cent to 12 per cent to 20 per cent among the *agree*, *partial*, and *disagree* groups respectively.

Second, there may be a retreat from the June vote-intention to an uncertain response category in August—either a "Don't Know," "Undecided," or "Do Not Intend to Vote" response. For example, among respondents who in June expected to vote for the Republican Party, and whose families shared their vote intention, only 8 per cent said that they were undecided how to vote or did not intend to vote. Among those who were in either partial or total disagreement with their family, however, 11 and 24 per cent respectively shifted to these responses during the two-month period.

Thus if we are to do an adequate job of

TABLE 4

HOMOGENEITY OF FAMILY AND RESPONDENT

Vote Intentions of Family and Respondent	Republican Vote Intention of Respondent in June				Democratic Vote Intention of Respondent in June			
	August Vote Intention:				August Vote Intention:			
	Rep.	D.K.	Dem.		Rep.	D.K.	Dem.	
Agree	90%	8%	2%	100% (n=271)	12%	8%	80%	100 (n=79)
Partial	77	11	12	100 (n=114)	10	24	65	100 (n=45)
Disagree	56	24	20	100 (n=25)	23	23	54	100 (n=22)

predicting the direction of shifts in vote intention during the course of political campaigns, we must add to our battery of significant variables data on how the people with whom our respondents have close and continual social contacts are expecting to vote.

PRE-CONVENTION PREFERENCES AND VOTING BEHAVIOR

We now turn to the problem of the relationships among respondents' preferences for the various Republican potential candidates (in June), the pattern of their vote intentions during the campaign, and the vote they eventually cast in November. For instance, if a man said in June that he believed Stassen would make the best Republican candidate, we would like to know how he reacts politically when the convention nominates Dewey. Will he continue to support the Republican Party but feel less intense about his vote intention? Or will he tend to bolt his party and support the Democrats? And will there be differences on these points between the Stassen-supporter and those who favored Taft, or Vandenberg, or the candidate himself—Dewey? This is a rather dramatic story, and can be told only through the use of the panel technique.

It is interesting to note that we had originally expected to find that factionalism would play a more significant role in the case of the Democratic party than in the Republican. It was felt that many Democrats had refused to accept Truman as a worthwhile candidate, preferring some other candidate—Eisenhower for example. Flowing from this, we had expected that our data would show that these non-Truman Democrats had rejected Truman all through the campaign, but that when the chips were down they came through and finally voted for him. In other words, we expected to find that many of the last-minute deciders were originally supporters of other pre-convention contenders for the Democratic nomination. The study reveals that in Elmira, at least, no such pattern existed among the Democrats. The voting behavior of the pre-convention supporters of both Truman and Eisenhower were to all intents practically alike, not only in November, but in August and October as well.

This was strikingly not the case among the supporters of various candidates on the Republican side of the fence.

As Table 5 shows, there are actually considerable differences in the final voting behavior of those with Republican vote intentions in June, depending upon which of the pre-convention contenders they had favored. As one would expect, fully 92 per cent of those who indicated Dewey as the best Republican candidate in June actually voted for him in November. Among those who did not get the candidate of their choice, however, there is a quite different story. The supporters of Stassen and Vandenberg finally turned in a considerable number of votes for Truman: 33 per cent of the Stassen and 23 per cent of the Vandenberg supporters eventually cast ballots for

TABLE 5

FINAL VOTE OF JUNE REPUBLICANS* BY
"BEST REPUBLICAN PRESIDENT"

Final Vote	Dewey	Taft	Stassen	Vandenberg
Dewey	92%	92%	67%	77%
Truman	8	8	33	23
	100%	100%	100%	100%
Per cent not voting	23	4	20	9
Total Cases	(293)	(26)	(75)	(43)

* June Republicans—those who expressed an intention to vote for the Republican Party in June, plus those who expressed no vote intention, but indicated a "leaning" toward the Republican Party.

the Democratic Party. The Taft Supporters on the other hand, proved to be "down-the-line" Republicans; they voted just as heavily for Dewey as did the Dewey supporters themselves.

It is of interest to note that these results were foreshadowed by the replies to a question asked in June, which read:

What if the candidates were Truman, Dewey, and Wallace—which of these three do you think you would vote for?

At this early date, 3 per cent of the Dewey supporters and 4 per cent of the Taft supporters said they would vote for Truman, whereas 35 per cent of the Stassen supporters, and 22 per cent of the Vandenberg supporters said they would vote for Truman if the candidates were Truman, Dewey and Wallace.

There is one additional factor worthy of mention which differentiates these four Republican groups. If we divide them according to the strength of their feelings about their Republican vote intention, we find that it is the Stassen and Vandenberg supporters who do not feel strongly about their Republican intention who eventually bolt their party and vote for Truman. In the case of the Dewey and Taft supporters, on the other hand, the intensity of their Republican vote intentions does not affect their final vote. Even should a Taft and Dewey supporter not feel strongly about his vote intention, he tends to vote for the Republican Party anyway.

The evidence thus appears to point to the conclusion that there are marked differences in subsequent voting behavior among the Republican pre-convention supporters of Dewey, Taft, Stassen and Vandenberg. A "Republican" is not always a Republican come hell or high water. He has rather definite preferences and may bolt if his demands are not met. The Republicans were divided in this way in June and this division remained. Many of the Republicans who did not want Dewey refused to accept him, and therein lies one of the reasons for the outcome of the November election.

TREND TOWARD TRUMAN STRONGEST AMONG UNION WORKERS

To this discussion of factors which make for a change in vote intention, we might append one item which constitutes a rather interesting exemplification of the trend toward Truman during the course of the campaign. Table 6 shows this trend for the sample as a whole, and for the following three occupational groups: (1) skilled, unskilled and service employees who are unionized—the "Union Workers" in the table; (2) skilled and unskilled workers who are not unionized—the "Non-union Workers" in the table; and (3) all employed white-collar, managerial and professional workers, including those who are self-employed. Here we can see the steady increase in the proportion of respondents who had Democratic vote intentions in each of the interviewing waves administered during the campaign, as well as the final vote cast in November. With the exception of a drop of some 3 per cent in the white-collar group between August and October, there is a steady increase in Truman supporters in the sample, the sharpest increase occurring between early October and Election Day itself. And since we are dealing with the same group of respondents at each interview wave, we need not be concerned about sampling error between interviews.

But of perhaps even greater interest are the differences in the trend toward Truman within the three occupational groups. In the white-collar group, for example, the proportion who finally voted for the Democratic Party in November was 25 per cent, only 3 per cent more than those who expressed this vote intention in June. Among the non-union workers, 37 per cent voted for the Democratic Party, in contrast to 25 per cent who had indicated a Democratic vote intention in June. But the strongest trend toward Truman is seen among union workers, whose final vote of 55 per cent for the Democratic Party was 16 per cent above

TABLE 6

TREND TOWARD TRUMAN AMONG OCCUPATIONAL GROUPS

Occupational Group	Proportion with Democratic Vote Intention Plus 'Leaning'			Proportion who Voted Democratic of Two-Party Vote
	June	August	October	November
Union Workers	39%	42%	48%	55%
Non-Union Workers	25	25	29	37
White Collar plus	22	24	21	25
Total Sample	28%	30%	33%	37%

the Democratic vote intention expressed in June.

FACTORS AFFECTING TURNOUT: SEX AND INTEREST

In general the data from the Elmira study corroborate the finding of the study of the 1940 election in Sandusky, Ohio, to the effect that with the exception of the sex of the respondents, non-voting was a function of the level of interest which respondents had in the election.[2] Table 7 indicates both these relationships. That is, (1) the less a group is interested in the election, the larger the proportion who say they do not intend to vote; and (2) on each interest level, women are more likely than are men to say they do not intend to vote. Thus, on the high interest level, only 7 per cent of the men say they do not intend to vote, in contrast to 12 per cent of the women. On the low level of interest, the proportion of those

[2] Cf. Lazarsfeld, Paul F., Bernard Berelson and Hazel Gaudet, The People's Choice, New York, 1948.

who do not intend to vote increases to 30 per cent of the men, and 46 per cent of the women. As the previous study indicated, men appear to be subject to greater social pressure to express interest in political affairs than are women. It appears to be this social pressure to express an intention to vote which leads to the marked difference between men and women on the low interest level, and to the observation that women appear to be "more reasoned" than men. If women are not interested in the election, they are less apt to say they intend to vote.

WOMEN MORE RELIABLE THAN MEN

But if we move now from these expressions of vote intention to the actual behavior of men and women on these various interest levels at the polls, we have evidence of a more elusive category of non-voters. It is at this point that the Elmira material enables us to gain further information about those who do not exercise their franchise. We may divide the non-voters into two groups: on the one hand, those who never

TABLE 7

PROPORTION OF MEN AND WOMEN WHO DID NOT INTEND TO VOTE; BY LEVEL OF INTEREST (OCTOBER)

	High Interest		Medium Interest		Low Interest	
	Men	Women	Men	Women	Men	Women
Do not intend to vote	7%	12%	13%	17%	30%	46%
Intend to vote	93	88	87	83	70	54
	100%	100%	100%	100%	100%	100%
Total cases	(121)	(153)	(125)	(148)	(110)	(152)

intended to vote and did not vote; and on the other hand, those who during the campaign said they intended to vote *but*, when Election Day arrived, *did not vote*. It should be noted that this group of vote-intenders but eventual non-voters can be isolated only through the use of the panel.

If we follow up the final vote behavior of those who said in October that they intended to vote, we find the following pattern— again controlling by sex and interest level. In Table 8, we can see that the vote intentions expressed by men are not nearly as reliable an indication of their eventual behavior as are those of the women. On each interest level, but more strikingly so on the *low* interest level, there is a larger proportion of men than of women who say they will vote but in fact do not vote. While the differences are slight on the high and medium interest levels, on the low interest level, 13 per cent of the men in contrast to 5 per cent of the women who had previously indicated a vote intention did not vote. Thus, to the earlier finding that the vote intentions of women follow more closely the amount of interest they have in political affairs, we can now add a second characteristic: if women say they intend to vote, they are more apt than men actually to do so.

NON-VOTERS WHO SAID THEY VOTED

Here we may remark parenthetically that about 9 per cent of the individuals who told

our interviewers that they had voted, had in fact not done so. This was established by referring to the Election Board records. Some had not registered and therefore could not vote; others, though registered, did not cast their ballots on Election Day. The number of respondents who were not honest in their responses was thus sufficiently small so as not to cause undue alarm, but the interesting finding is that certain of our panel members were more prone to prevarication than others. It turns out that the people who had previously expressed a *high* level of interest had a greater number of, to use an unequivocal term, "liars" than people who had a medium interest level or no interest at all. Among respondents who according to the Election Board records had not voted, 16 per cent of those with a *high* level of interest answered the question "Did you vote?" in the affirmative, in contrast to only 7 per cent of those with a *medium* level of interest, and none of those with *no* interest in the election.

Two possible interpretations are suggested as to why the highly interested group had not told the truth. There is the possibility that they actually had not been greatly interested in the election and never intended to vote, but that the same social pressure that led them to say they had great interest also led them to say they had voted. But perhaps a more psychologically convincing interpretation is that these individuals had been genuinely interested in the election, and had

TABLE 8

PROPORTION OF MEN AND WOMEN WHO DID NOT VOTE AMONG THOSE WHO
INTENDED TO VOTE; BY LEVEL OF INTEREST

(OCTOBER)

	High Interest		Medium Interest		Low Interest	
	Men	Women	Men	Women	Men	Women
Intended to vote and did not vote	7%	5%	8%	7%	13%	5%
Intended to vote and did vote	93	95	92	93	87	95
	100%	100%	100%	100%	100%	100%
	(n=112)	(n=133)	(n=107)	(n=121)	(n=77)	(n=79)

every intention to vote, but that something kept them from registering or from going to the polls and they were ashamed to admit it—with the result that they said that they voted, when in fact they did not.

ATTITUDE TOWARD COMMUNITY AS A RELEVANT VARIABLE

The Elmira material also touches upon an aspect of voting and non-voting which has not previously been considered germane to analyses of political behavior, except in the quiet of a theorist's study. Yet it concerns a characteristic of the non-voter which is both of considerable sociological interest and of some practical importance in the task of anticipating who will and who will not vote.

We approached this characteristic by asking whether a relationship could be established between an individual's political behavior and his attitude toward the community in which he lives. This was actually but an extension of our interest in the influence of family, friends and co-workers upon the political behavior of our respondents.

If we view the casting of a vote as an act of participation in the life of the community, then it might be of great importance to know how people feel about that community. We might expect that people who feel it is a very good place in which to live will be likely to participate in community affairs and thus will be more likely to vote than people who feel "out of things" and are not satisfied with their community.

A question was asked of respondents in June which enables us to investigate this hypothesis. People were asked:

In general, how do you feel about living in this community—would you say it's a very good community to live in, only fairly good, or not good at all?

If we take those who say it is a very good place to live as "satisfied" with their community or, as the sociologist might put it, "integrated" into the life of the community, and those who assess the community as only "fairly good" or "not good at all," as the "unintegrated" group, we find that these two groups have different proportions of non-voters. Socio-economic status is used as a control, since it is related to both non-voting and to community integration.

As we anticipated, those respondents who did not feel the community was a very good place in which to live were more apt to be non-voters than their counterparts, the integrated groups. Thus, on both SES levels, the integrated groups have a smaller proportion of non-voters. On the high SES level, 17 per cent of the integrated but 25 per cent of the unintegrated did not vote in the election; on the low SES level, 31 per cent of the integrated in contrast to 42 per cent of the unintegrated individuals, were non-voters.

CAN PEOPLE FORECAST HOW THEIR OWN GROUP WILL VOTE?

We could quite easily end our story here, with this account of the voter and the non-voter—but we would not like to conclude even this progress report without indicating a rather interesting and unexpected aspect of the Elmira material. And it is in this area of our work that we may have the beginnings of a substantial retort to those who after the 1948 election claimed that in the future they would place little or no faith in the findings of the polls, but would instead go out and secure data on how people will vote through personal contacts and informal discussions of politics.

This approach is based on the assumption that if we but know a group intimately enough we can tell how they will vote, and it is on this very point that the Elmira material sheds some light. Our data enable us to make a number of observations on how well people can estimate how other groups are going to vote. What we have here, then, is an attempt to study the predictive ability of people. This analysis was based on the responses to a series of questions asked in the June interviewing wave, which were of the following order:

Do you think most *poor people* around here would be most likely to vote for the Republican, Democratic or Wallace third party?

Similar questions were asked concerning the vote intention of factory workers, Communists, Catholics, Negroes, farmers, rich people, college people and Jews.

Our illustration will be confined to the question pertaining to how "poor people" were expected to vote but, first, two general results deserve mention. One is that people tend to "pull" the group whose vote is being estimated in the direction of their own vote intention, even though this is contrary to the way that group actually behaves politically. Whatever group is under discussion, Republican respondents will be more likely to expect it to vote Republican as compared with Democratic respondents. And, secondly, these guesses tend to become more distorted the more strongly the respondents feel about their own party choice. Thus, although an ethnic study conducted by the Cornell Field Research Office reveals that approximately 81 per cent of the Negroes in Elmira voted Democratic (of the two-party vote), 55 per cent of the Republican respondents who felt very strongly about their own party choice predicted that Negroes would vote Republican. In general the more strongly a respondent feels about his own party choice, the more will he misjudge the vote of the group he is questioned about.

Table 9 provides light on one further problem: Are respondents who are themselves most *like* the group of "poor people" (those on the low SES level) likely to be less affected by their own vote intentions in estimating how their group will vote than are people who are most *unlike* the "poor people" (those on the high SES level). The tables shows a somewhat surprising fact: people on the low SES level are *more*, not less, apt to bias their estimations of how poor people will vote in the direction of their own vote intentions. Because of this, on the low SES level, the difference between estimates of the Democratic and Republican vote is 42 per cent (65 per cent−23 per cent) in contrast to only an 18 per cent difference (68 per cent−50 per cent) on the high SES level. When we recall that only 16 per cent of our respondents had "mixed" friendship groups of both Democrats and Republicans, it becomes even more understandable that respondents not only project their own political persuasions upon the group whose vote they are forecasting, but are also prone to assume that the entire category of "poor people" have the same vote intention as does the smaller group of their family and friends. Since people move in relatively homogeneous political environments, this is an easy assumption for them to make. Among high SES level respondents the only bias to which they are subject is that of their own vote intention, and they therefore make fewer mistakes than those who are themselves members of the category whose vote they are estimating.

This same pattern, which is reflected in Table 9 on "poor people's" vote, is found when Protestants and Catholics are questioned about how Catholics will vote, etc.— all of which tends to support our conclusion that the closer the respondent is to the group

TABLE 9

FORECAST OF POOR PEOPLE'S VOTE BY INTENTION AND SES LEVEL

How most poor people will vote:	*Vote Intention of Respondent on Low SES Level:*		*Vote Intention of Respondent on High SES Level:*	
	Republican	*Democrat*	*Republican*	*Democrat*
Democratic	35%	77%	50%	68%
Republican	65	23	50	32
	100%	100%	100%	100%
Total Cases	(173)	(106)	(178)	(41)

whose vote is to be estimated, the greater is his tendency to believe that the group will behave in the same way that he intends to behave. On the basis of this finding, we believe there is good reason for our skepticism about the ability of journalists to serve as predictors of how the complex of groups with whom they have contacts will vote. In addition, the time may not be far off when we will be able to turn the spotlight of our polling techniques on these journalistic political analysts. We may be on the road to taking the journalist-turned-expert as the "object" of our research, and to predicting his predictions!

CONCLUDING COMMENT

We have covered but a small segment of a large range of problem areas now under analysis as a result of the Elmira study. We have every expectation that, as this analysis proceeds, we shall have more to say not only about the problem areas touched upon in this article, but also about several important problem areas in which work has only recently begun.

One of the most stimulating aspects of the analysis of the Elmira data has been the intimate and cumulative sense of the systematic progression from Sandusky to Elmira. The investigation in Ohio helped in two ways: it provided ideas for new questions to be included in the Elmira questionnaire; and it gave perspectives for the present analysis. It can already be seen that the Elmira study will have the same function for a study which the Campaign Research Committee hopes to organize for 1952. Only by linking up a whole series of studies of the same kind, undertaken under various conditions, can we hope to develop slowly a really comprehensive understanding of voting behavior.

INTERACTION BETWEEN ATTITUDE AND THE DEFINITION OF THE SITUATION IN THE EXPRESSION OF OPINION

RAYMOND L. GORDEN

The main purpose of this study is to explore the relationships between a person's *private opinion* and his *definition of the situation* and how they affect his expression of *public opinion* in a social situation.

The pursuit of this objective is divided into two phases. The first is an experimental study in which the only aspect of the individual's definition of the situation under consideration is his *estimate of the group opinion*. This part of the study describes the extent to which each individual alters his

From the *American Sociological Review*, 1952, 17, 50-58. Reprinted by permission of the author and the publisher.

private opinion to conform to his estimation of the group opinion when asked to express his opinion in that group. The second phase of the study uses case materials to gain insight into the reasons for the behavior of the extreme conformists and nonconformists. In this material, other aspects of each person's definition of the situation are considered in addition to his estimate of the group opinion.

In order to observe the dynamic interplay between each person's *private opinion* and his *definition of the situation* which interact to develop his expression of *public opinion,* it is necessary to study a group (a) in which there is a wide range of private opinions, (b) where the members of the group are so intimately acquainted as to have a clear definition of the situation with respect to the particular subject upon which they are asked to express themselves, and (c) where there is variation in the *definition of the situation* from person to person resulting from differences in each person's background, the nature of his connection with the group, and his role and status in the group.

DESCRIPTION OF THE GROUP STUDIED

The study began by participant observation of a group of 36 members of a cooperative living project. Because of turnover in membership and individuals taking vacations during some phase of the collection of data, complete data were collected on only 24 of the members.

About half of the members were students and the rest worked in a variety of professions, semi-professions, and vocations ranging from college instructor to waitress. All but one person had some college education. The ages ranged from 21 to 35 years. Half were males and half were females. These people lived in a large, single-family residence which had four floors and seven bathrooms.

The household tasks were shared and all the members ate the evening meal in the common dining room. According to another study by the writer, some of the more important forces bringing the people into the co-op were (a) a common interest in the cooperative movement, (b) economical housing, (c) a desire for primary association with other minority groups, (d) a desire to meet members of the opposite sex, and (e) a desire to be in an atmosphere where members of minority groups can relax and be treated as equals.

Although the group was composed of a wide variety of cultural backgrounds, there was one common denominator; namely, all the members belonged to a minority group. The group included seven Negroes, nine Jews, of whom only two attended religious services (Reformed), five members of Catholic background, of whom only two considered themselves in good standing with the church, and three pacifists. Of the three married couples living in the house, two were interracial marriages.

The political affiliation and beliefs in the group can best be characterized by the following categories: Democrats, 15; ex-Progressives, 14; Socialists, 4; Communist, 1; Republican, 1. The seven Negroes were all Democrats and were noticeably more conservative than the Caucasians. This is mainly because the Negroes were trying to achieve a higher status than their parents. The Caucasians, on the other hand, tended to be rebellious against the "bourgeois" standards of their parents.

In the opinion of the writer, this group is heterogeneous enough to offer wide variations in attitude toward Russia and, at the same time, the members are sufficiently identified with the group to be influenced by a rather clear conception of the norms of the group.

THE EXPERIMENTAL SITUATION

Opinion on Russia was chosen for this study because it is a subject with emotional content, a subject toward which this group holds a wide range of feelings, and a subject upon which the sanctioned range of expression of public opinion is narrowing.

The writer was a regular member of the co-op group for a period of months and was able to collect data from observation and nondirective interviewing before the experimental phase of the study was begun.

Three types of data relating to the experimental study were collected. First, each individual recorded his *private opinion* on Russia on a Likert-type attitude scale in a situation where the respondent was assured complete anonymity. Second, in a manner described in detail later, he was asked to express his opinion on each of these items in the presence of his fellow co-op members. These responses are referred to as his *public opinion*. Third, by a method also described later, he was asked to make an estimate of the opinion of the group on each of these same items. These responses are hereafter referred to as his *estimate of group opinion*, which is the only aspect of his *definition of the situation* which is obtained in the experimental situation. Other aspects of his definition are dealt with later in the case study material. Thus we have, from each individual, three types of responses to each of 12 items dealing with Russia. An item-for-item comparison of the three responses can thus be made for each individual, since the "anonymous" questionnaires were secretly identifiable.

For the experiment the 24 members were divided into two subgroups matched according to race, occupational status, sex, and rank order of the total score on their *private opinion*. The two groups were interviewed simultaneously in different rooms. The interviewers worked with each group. In one group both interviewers were co-op members. In the other group one was a co-op member and the other was an "outsider" representing a nationally known opinion research organization. This procedure was used in an effort to detect any effect the interviewer himself might have on the responses in the group situation. A comparison of the responses received by each

interviewer, and subsequent interviews with the respondents "after the study was completed," indicated that the respondents in general felt that all the interviewers were objective, neutral, and uncritical in comparison with the others who were listening to their responses.

The experiment had been proposed to the group as a scientific study of a new public opinion polling technique. At a regular house meeting, the group voted unanimously to cooperate with the writer in this study.

The following interviewing technique was used. The group was told that the interviewers would make a statement regarding Russia, and the respondent was to say to what extent he agreed or disagreed with the statement, using the five possible replies indicated on a card which was going to be handed to him. The group was also told that the members should listen to the replies of the others so that they could be prepared to estimate the group opinion.

At this point in the design of the study, an important question of methodology presented itself—When and how can each individual's most valid estimate of the group opinion be obtained? A pretest with another group seemed to indicate that an individual's awareness of the discrepancy between his private opinion and his conception of the opinions of a given group of people was not as acute at any time *before* actually making a statement on a controversial subject as it became when the physical act of speaking occurred. Some individuals reported a growing awareness *during* the utterance of their statements, which caused them to alter the wording in order to soften the impact on the group. Other individuals testified that, although they would change the wording of a statement which they had strongly endorsed before, they did not sense an acute emotional reaction until *after* the statement was finished.

Since it was impossible to interrupt the person during his statement in this experiment, it was decided that the respondent should give his estimate of the group opinion on each item, immediately *after* his statement on *each item*, by indicating on a check-chart his estimate of the group opinion. It was suggested in the directions to each respondent that this could be done most accurately by comparing the direction and degree of the feeling of the group in relation to his own feeling on that particular item and then quickly checking his first impression.

There were many indications of the effect of the group pressure on the individual other than his choice of response. After the directions were given to the group, there were definite symptoms of tension and awareness of the group pressure. It is the writer's belief that each one felt that it was a bit awkward to appear to be too interested in the opinions of the group and so made an effort to be busy, thus easing his own tension as well as that of the person being interviewed. This conviction is based on such observations as the following:

Case 2, a person who had the most anti-Russian score on both the anonymous response and the group response, came into the group, whispered to her husband, and left. He also left to set the table for dinner. After a while the interviewer went after him and told him it would only take a minute. He consented reluctantly because, he explained, he was busy. After his own interview, however, he had time to remain in the group until the last interview was completed.

Case 8 sat on one end of a couch with a Penguin Book in his hand, opened to page 38. Twenty-two minutes later he was on the same page.

Five of the respondents who usually speak in normal voices replied almost inaudibly to the interviewer, whose ear was approximately three feet from the respondent. In these cases the interviewer would pretend not to have heard, and in a clear, matter-of-fact voice audible to the rest of the group ask, "You said agree? Was that strongly or moderately? Strongly? Thank you."

In two cases where the person felt that the group strongly disagreed with his statement, the interviewer and the respondent had the following exchange.

Respondent: (in an almost inaudible voice) Agree strongly.

Interviewer: Did you say agree or disagree?
Respondent: Agree.
Interviewer: Was that strongly or moderately?
Respondent: Moderately.
Interviewer: Moderately? Thank you.

It appears that each thought better of his first response and changed from strongly to moderately, which was nearer to his conception of the group norms. The general atmosphere of the group had a lack of spontaneity and a stiff sort of nonchalance.

ANALYSIS OF DATA

There are some general relationships between the three scores, which are consistent for the group. Analysis of the relationship between *private opinion* and *estimate of group opinion* indicates a marked tendency for the individual to estimate correctly the *direction* of the median opinion of the group (as indicated by the aggregate private opinion) in relation to his own private opinion.

TABLE 13.1

DISTRIBUTION OF RESPONDENTS BY THEIR PRIVATE OPINIONS ON RUSSIA AND THE DIRECTION OF THEIR ESTIMATE OF THE GROUP OPINION IN RELATION TO THEIR OWN PRIVATE OPINIONS

Individual's Private Opinion	DIRECTION OF ESTIMATE OF GROUP OPINION		
	More Pro-Russian	More Anti-Russian	Total
Pro-Russian	2	10	12
Anti-Russian	10	2	12
Total	12	12	24

From Table 13.1 we see that those whose opinions were more pro-Russian on the *private opinion* scale tended correctly to estimate the group opinion as being more anti-Russian than their own. It can be said that 20 of the 24 people were correct in their estimate in regard to the general direction of the group opinion.

There is another general relationship found between the individual's *private opinion* and his *estimate of the group opinion*. Those who are pro-Russian on the private opinion scale tend to estimate the opinion of the group as being more pro-Russian than it actually is, and *vice versa*, as shown in Table 13.2. Thus, although the estimate of the direction of the group mean from the individual's private opinion is correct, the conception of the absolute position of the group appears to be influenced by the individual's own feeling, as well as by the actual group opinion.

TABLE 13.2

DISTRIBUTION OF RESPONDENTS BY THEIR
PRIVATE OPINIONS ON RUSSIA AND
THEIR ACCURACY IN ESTIMATING
MEAN OPINION OF THE GROUP

Individual's Private Opinion	ACCURACY OF ESTIMATE OF GROUP OPINION		
	Too Pro-Russian	*Too Anti-Russian*	*Total*
Pro-Russian	10	2	12
Anti-Russian	2	10	12
Total	12	12	24

It can be similarly demonstrated that there is a positive relationship between the anonymous opinion and the opinion expressed in the group, as may be seen from Table 13.3.

TABLE 13.3

DISTRIBUTION OF RESPONDENTS BY THEIR
PRIVATE OPINIONS ON RUSSIA AND
THEIR PUBLIC OPINIONS ON RUSSIA

Private Opinion	PUBLIC OPINION		
	Pro-Russian	*Anti-Russian*	*Total*
Pro-Russian	11	1	12
Anti-Russian	1	11	12
Total	12	12	24

Tables 13.1, 13.2 and 13.3 show that in general each person can correctly estimate whether the group is either more or less pro-Russian than himself, but he usually does not realize that the amount of this difference is as great as it is. Also, in general, there are no individuals who shift from the "pro" category on their *private* opinion

to the "anti" category on their *public* opinion or *vice versa*.

This rather crude analysis does not, however, demonstrate the shifts of lesser magnitude. In order to reveal these smaller changes we must compare each person's total score for the three types of responses. Since there are 12 items with five-point responses, the possible range of the total scores is from 12 to 60, with 60 representing the extreme pro-Russian score.

In 13 cases the expression of *public opinion*, as indicated by *total scores* in the group situation, more closely approximated the person's conception of the group norms than did his *private opinion*. In eight cases the expression in the group is further from their conception of group norms than is their expression in the anonymous situation. In three cases there was no change in the total score from the anonymous to the group situation.

This might suggest that in general the person's expression of opinion regarding Russia is influenced by his conception of how others regard Russia. This appears to be a plausible enough result, but the eight cases whose attitudes were counter to their conceptions of the group, and the three who indicated no influence by the group, must be studied in comparison with the 13 cases who conformed to the group.

It is necessary at this time to point out that the comparison of these three total scores for each person is used only for a rough group comparison, and that there are certain meaningful differences that are hidden in the total scores. For example, we shall compare the actual responses on the separate items by Case 2 with those by Case 23, which in terms of total scores appear very similar. Thus in Table 13.4 we see that, although in both cases the *total* score was practically the same in Columns II and III, there are a number of disagreements in the individual items (see items 4, 6, 8, and 10) in Case 2, and no discrepancy in Case 23.

In Case 2 the person resisted his conception of the group norms to the extent of six

TABLE 13.4

A COMPARISON OF THE RESPONSES OF TWO INDIVIDUALS ON
EACH ITEM IN THE THREE SCORES

	CASE NO. 2			CASE NO. 23		
	I	*II*	*III*	*I*	*II*	*III*
Item Number	*Private Opinion*	*Estimate of Group*	*Public Opinion*	*Private Opinion*	*Estimate of Group*	*Public Opinion*
1	1	2	2	1	2	2
2	2	1	1	3	1	1
3	4	4	4	3	3	3
4	2	4	2	2	2	2
5	2	1	1	2	4	4
6	4	1	5	3	4	4
7	2	5	5	1	2	2
8	1	5	1	2	2	2
9	3	2	2	4	4	4
10	4	2	4	4	4	4
11	2	4	4	4	4	4
12	5	5	5	4	5	5
Total	32	36	36	33	37	37

points in the pro-Russian direction (items 4 and 8), and also resisted to the extent of six points in the anti-Russian direction (items 6 and 10), making the total score the same. On the other hand, Case 23 on each item conformed to her conceptions of the group norms even though it meant becoming more pro-Russian on items 1, 5, 6, 7, and 12, and more anti-Russian on item 2. Thus we see the inadequacy of total scores for describing the individual variation in relationship to his conception of the group norm.

These two cases are discussed because they afford the most clear contrast with respect to the degree to which individual variations are concealed by total scores. In no other case was the inconsistency as great as in Case 2.

In order to avoid such deception and in order to sharpen our analysis, we shall use the following four terms to describe the possible relationships between the three types of responses:

Agreement will indicate the extent to which the person's private opinion coincides with his estimate of the group opinion.

Conformity will indicate the degree to which the person alters his private opinion to conform more closely to his conception of the group norms when speaking in the group.

Resistance will indicate the extent to which a person retains his original private opinion despite his conception of the group as being different.

Reaction will be used to describe the situation where a person in effect reverses the direction of his private opinion in order to be different from the group.

The frequency of each of these modes of adjustment for each individual is shown in Table 13.5. A comparison of column A with any of the other columns is not valid, because the figures in column A represent the number of *items* out of the 12 where the individual's responses indicated no differences between his private opinion and his conception of the group opinion. However, a comparison of columns B, C, and D is meaningful, since the figures in each of these columns represent the total number of *degrees* of a given type of response for the 12 items. Therefore, inspection of Table 13.5 allows us to compare individuals with respect to the *proportion* of conformity, resistance, or reaction. However, the total of columns B, C, and D for any one case is

TABLE 13.5

THE DEGREE OF AGREEMENT,
CONFORMITY, RESISTANCE, AND
REACTION BY INDIVIDUAL CASES

Case No.	A Agreement*	B Conformity**	C Resistance**	D Reaction**
1	2	4	6	0
2	2	9	8	1
3	1	0	8	9
4	1	11	1	3
5	3	5	2	4
6	5	2	6	2
7	7	4	2	2
8	8	5	2	0
9	3	7	1	2
10	0	6	7	2
11	2	9	4	1
12	0	7	3	6
13	0	5	5	2
14	1	10	8	6
15	3	5	1	3
16	2	5	1	4
17	3	3	5	2
18	4	2	6	8
19	5	13	0	0
20	6	7	0	0
21	3	8	2	1
22	2	5	3	3
23	6	8	0	0
24	1	3	2	6
Total	70	143	83	67

* These figures indicate the number of *items* out of the twelve where the person's private opinion agreed with his conception of the group norms.
** These figures represent the number of degrees of discrepancy on the five-point response.

limited by the number of items, indicated in column A, where there was agreement between the person's private opinion and his estimate of the group opinion. Only when the individual's private opinion differs from his estimate of the group opinion can we record the effect of his conception of the group opinion on his expression of public opinion. The totals of columns B, C, and D indicate that, for the group as a whole, conformity was the predominant mode of adjustment to the discrepancy between the person's private opinion and his estimate of the group opinion.

Since the reliability of these responses is unknown, no attempt is made to explain why each individual had a particular proportion of conformity, resistance, or reaction. Instead, it would seem more prudent to select only the extreme conformists and the extreme nonconformists and explore the case study materials in an attempt to explain these contrasting patterns of adjustment.

The degree of conformity was determined by the formula $B - (C + D)$, where the letters refer to the columns in Table 13.5. The conformists chosen were those with the two highest scores on this formula, and the nonconformists were the two lowest. Applying the formula to the cases in Table 13.5, we find Cases 19 and 23 to be the conformists and Cases 3 and 18 to be the nonconformists.

CASE STUDY MATERIALS

The writer does not claim that the evidence presented by the case study materials is conclusive, nor does he claim that it was collected in such a manner that the collection of this portion of the data could be precisely repeated and verified. However, the writer feels that after having an intimate acquaintance with the personalities, through living in close contact with them for more than a year and systematically gathering case materials for over three months, some significant insights have been gained.

Case 3 (nonconformist). Mr. W. is a 25-year-old part-time student who is working on a full-time job. He is highly intelligent. He is not closely identified with the cooperative living group, but belongs to a small gang of high school buddies with whom he plays cards and drinks. He mentioned that he craved recognition, which he found hard to get in the co-op group, but liked living there because he "hated to live alone, and besides I need someone around to kick me out of bed in the morning or to call the boss and tell him I'm sick and can't work."

The writer has observed Mr. W taking opposite sides on the same issue from time to time, and he admits "getting a kick" out of showing his knowledge and shocking people with his views. He also feels there is no great penalty for having contrary views: "No one gives a damn what you say or do as long as you get your work-job done. Everyone here is liberal, or at least thinks he is."

In this case we find three important factors which seem to account for Mr. W's nonconformity. First, he is more closely identified with his high school gang and does not depend heavily upon the co-op group for intimate response. Second, he admits craving recognition, "but I don't get it here at the co-op; I'm just a plain old Joe here, and a prize dope." Perhaps his apparent negativistic shifting of sides, to show off his knowledge and shock people, is an attempt to obtain this recognition. Third, he conceives the group sanctions to be mild and tolerant.

Case 18 (nonconformist). Miss X is a professional worker, 25 years of age, who has lived at the co-op house for about a year. She was born in Austria and spent a few years in England. According to her own testimony, most of her social contacts are in this group. "I came hoping that the informal atmosphere would help me get rid of some of my inhibitions and peculiar reactions to the opposite sex. I don't belong to any cliques outside of the co-op. I have always lived in some peculiar circumstances where I have never really become sociable."

She feels that the group is tolerant of deviations. She points out that although there is a wide range of opinions on vital matters, "they all get along pretty well because both sides are tolerant and want to 'live and let live.' "

Miss X is a socialist who in general seems to have a more moderate view of Russia than many. A statement which seems to represent her position is, "Even the U. S. A. is not very democratic, and Russia is less so. I think the Labor Party in England will do a better job of balancing both economic and political power."

Miss X, according to the observations of the writer, her friends, and her own testimony, has deep-seated negativistic reaction patterns: "If they (men) think I am a 'loose girl' I like to prove that I'm not; and if they think I am too prudish, I like to pretend that I really don't have any inhibitions but am just being coy. I'm not just trying to attract them, because as soon as they get interested then I change. Yet I don't want them to leave. I don't know why that is."

We see that both Mr. W and Miss X have personality traits which might increase the possibility of a negativistic reaction in the group. Both of them define the group as being tolerant. Both have superior intelligence and college degrees and no inferior feeling regarding personal appearance. Here the similarity ends. He is well integrated into an outside clique while she has her most intimate associations in the co-op group. However, her reaction to others is in many cases of a non-adjustive nature, and she is not well integrated into any social group. Perhaps her identification with the group is not great despite the fact that she does not have a greater degree of identification elsewhere.

Case 19 (conformist). Mr. Y is 20 years old and has not completed his high school education, which he is attempting to do on the G. I. Bill. He has been at the co-op house only two months. He is of Jewish background and is minority conscious. He is from a lower socioeconomic class and has aspirations for upward mobility via education. He has a strong identification with the co-op group. He says, "It is the first place that I have found since I came back from the army that made me feel at home. I don't have to worry about discrimination here and nobody is going to push me around. That's one reason why I want to get an education. . . . That's one reason I came to the co-op. There are lots of students here, and they are all smarter than I am. It is a good chance to learn a lot. . . . I don't know anything about Russia as it is today, even if my mother does tell me how things were when she was there forty years ago . . . and it sounds like a place where people get pushed around, but I don't know anything about it, so why should I show my ignorance?"

Mr. Y's dependence on the group is obvious. He likes the group and feels it is a privilege to mingle with those who are "smarter" than he is. He willingly and consciously conforms to a group who would "never push me around."

Case 23 (conformist). Miss Z is also a relatively new member in the house. She is 21 years old, attractive, Negro, and striving for upward social mobility by way of the teaching profession. She has finished college, dresses well, has "good manners," and considers tact and diplomacy a very desirable trait in herself. She is gregarious and finds the co-op a "haven of refuge" while waiting for a full-time teaching job. She expresses her attitude toward the group in the following manner:

"I was told before I came into the co-op that it didn't make any difference whether you were white, black, or something in between, and I've found that to be true. I have been so fed up on prejudice—even the Negroes are prejudiced against other Negroes and whites."

In an informal interview after the experimental situation, she explained that she wasn't sure whether her statements in the group were the group's opinions or her own. "I was left with no alternative but to assume or interpret what is meant by each statement without asking the interviewer, so I tried to interpret the meaning of each statement according to what I thought it meant to most of the other people in the house. . . . I know that there are some people in the house who are in political science and international relations who know a lot more about Russia than I do. I should know a lot more but I don't."

In both cases (19 and 23) there is a strong identification with the group in the sense that it fulfills certain needs for the individual. Also, both people feel that their opinion on the matter is inferior to the others'. In Mr. Y's case it seems that his conformity is more intentional, while in the case of Miss Z it takes the form of changed interpretation of the meaning of the questions in view of the probable meaning to others in the group. It is impossible to say why Mr. Y conformed more than Miss Z, but one factor is that Miss Z did not conceive of the group norms as being so far from her anonymous opinion as did Mr. Y. This fact places a limit upon the degree of conformity possible in her case.

In comparing the two most extreme conformists with the two most nonconformist members of this group, we find certain rather clear differences. First, the conformists had a number of factors which contributed to their need for security and acceptance into the group. Second, certain combinations of factors made them feel that their opinion was less important than their being accepted. And third, there was the implication that they could not deviate strongly from the group without jeopardizing their present or future status.

On the other hand, the nonconformists not only had certain personality factors which might predispose them toward a nega-tive reaction to the group norms, but also it appears that they did not have so much to lose nor did they seem to feel that they would lose anything by nonconformity in this particular group. The writer, after living with the group for three years, feels that as people remain in the group longer, they become aware of a wider range of values and find that there is even more tolerance of ideas than they suspected. Among the older members there is not only tolerance of different ideas, whether conservative or radical, but a certain prestige value in being different if the difference is sincere.

SUMMARY AND CONCLUSIONS

1. *Awareness of group pressure*

Both the symbolic responses of the members of the group and the more subtle non-symbolic interaction in the group clearly indicate an acute awareness of the presence of the other members of the group when they are asked to express their opinion. Confused efforts to appear nonchalant, efforts to escape the situation, and attempts to prevent others from hearing one's response are all telltale signs of the awareness of pressure.

2. *Accuracy of estimate of group opinion*

Although there was a considerable range in the accuracy of individuals' estimates of the group opinion, certain general relationships were found. (a) As indicated in Table 13.1, nearly everyone in the group correctly estimated the *direction* of the group opinion in relation to his own private opinion. (b) But, as indicated in Table 13.2, there was a strong tendency to underestimate the degree of this discrepancy. In 20 out of 24 cases those who were above the median score for the group estimated the group opinion to be higher than it was or *vice versa*.

Here it is important to note that there was no significant or consistent difference in the accuracy of individual estimates of group opinion which could be related to the order in which the person was interviewed. This was true despite the fact that those who were interviewed last had heard many more responses from the members of the group upon which they could base an objective estimate. There are some possible explanations which would merit further investigation: (a) They may not have accepted the expressions of public opinion in the group as representing the real attitudes of the individual, or (b) the total effect may have been too confusing and therefore the respondent used some modification of his preconceived image of the group in estimating the group opinion. (c) Each respondent may have been interested only in the reactions of certain individuals in the group.

Although from one point of view it is important to understand the various factors influencing the accuracy of the estimate of the group opinion, the significant factor which influences the person's behavior in the group is his subjective feeling and imagery with regard to the group norms, regardless of how accurately this feeling and imagery may reflect the "objective" situation.

3. *The effect of the definition of the situation*

We have already commented briefly upon the effect on the qualitative nonsymbolic interaction in the group, and will restrict the comments at this point to the effect upon the quantitative symbolic responses.

In general, the individuals tended to conform to their conception of the group norms when giving their public opinion. The typical pattern is for the individual to compromise between his private opinion and his conception of the group opinion when expressing his public opinion.

In addition to merely comparing the total scores, a more searching analysis of the data was made by making an item-by-item comparison of the three types of responses for each individual. This type of analysis indicated three types of adjustment to differences between the person's private opinion and his conception of the group norms. About 49% of these adjustments followed the conformity pattern, 28% followed the resistance pattern, and 22% followed the reaction pattern. Most of the individuals did not fall clearly into one of these adjustment patterns, but there was a wide variation in the proportion of each type of adjustment by each individual. However, there were three cases (see Cases 19, 20, and 23 in Table 13.5) who were pure conformists and one case (3) who showed no conformity in his adjustment pattern.

4. *Causes of the variation in adjustment patterns*

Since the reliability of the responses had not been established, only the two extreme conformists and the two extreme nonconformists were selected in an attempt to explain these apparently opposite types of adjustment. The following factors were felt by the writer to be significant in explaining the varying degrees of conformity and may serve as hypotheses for a more precise and controlled study: (a) the degree of the person's identification with the group, (b) his conception of the group's attitude toward nonconformity, (c) his conception of his own role in relation to the group, and (d) special personality traits such as negativism.

SOME PATTERNED CONSEQUENCES OF MEMBERSHIP IN A COLLEGE COMMUNITY

THEODORE M. NEWCOMB

Membership in established groups usually involves the taking on of whole patterns of interrelated behaviors. This was one of the hypotheses pursued in the study which is here reported in part. The group selected for study consisted of the entire student body at Bennington College between the years 1935 and 1939, a group consisting of about 250 women each year. The more than 600 individuals studied during this period did not all achieve equal degrees of membership in the community, however. Hence one of the problems to be investigated was that of the manner in which the patterning of behavior varied with different degrees of assimilation into the community.

The college is situated on a hilltop four miles from the Vermont village from which it takes its name. The year in which this study was begun was the fourth year of its existence, i.e., the first year in which there was a senior class. Its educational plan was somewhat novel, particularly its emphasis upon individual guidance and upon instruction individually and in very small groups. Most of the faculty lived on or near the campus; their relations with the students were characterized by informality, democracy, and *camaraderie*. Virtually all the

needs of modern community living were provided on the campus; both students and teachers spent most of their time living, working, and playing together as a community. To a very unusual degree the community was integrated, self-contained and self-conscious. No phrase was more constantly on the lips of its members than "the college community."

Becoming absorbed into such a community involves the taking on of many sorts of new behaviors, not all of which can be investigated in a single study. A single, though rather inclusive, area of adaptation to the college community was therefore selected for special study, namely, *attitudes toward public affairs*. There were two reasons for this selection: (1) methods of attitude measurement were readily available; and (2) there was an unusually high degree of concern, in this community at this time, over a rather wide range of public issues. This latter fact resulted partly from the fact that the college opened its doors during the darkest days of the depression of the 1930's, and its formative period occurred in the period of social change characterized by the phrase "the New Deal." This was also the period of gathering war clouds in Europe. Under-

A partial summary of the author's *Personality and Social Change* (New York: Dryden Press, 1943), and "The Influence of Attitude Climate upon Some Determinants of Information," *Journal of Abnormal and Social Psychology*, 1946, XLI, 291-302. Reprinted by permission of the author and the publishers.

lying both of these circumstances, however, was the conviction on the part of the faculty that one of the foremost duties of the college was to acquaint its somewhat over-sheltered students with the nature of their contemporary social world. The resulting interest on the part of students in contemporary public issues manifested itself as a *community-wide*, and not merely a classroom, phenomenon. There were constant lectures, discussions, movies, rallies, and money-raising activities which influenced classroom activities but were not limited to them, and in which students and faculty jointly participated. It became a mark of "the good Bennington citizen" to acquire an interest in such affairs. Partial evidence for this statement, and for other characteristics associated with membership in this community, is presented below.

An Inclusive Pattern of Declining Conservatism

Juniors and seniors may be presumed to have become community members in a fuller sense than have freshmen or sophomores. In Table 1 it is shown that the political

TABLE 1

PERCENT OF PREFERENCES BY STUDENTS FOR PRESIDENTIAL CANDIDATES IN 1936

Candidate	52 Fresh-men	40 Sopho-mores	52 Juniors-Seniors
Landon (Republican)	62	43	15
Roosevelt (Democrat)	29	43	54
Thomas + Browder (Socialist, Communist)	9	15	30

preferences of juniors and seniors in 1936 were far less conservative than those of freshmen and sophomores. (Similar polls in 1940 and in 1944 yielded almost identical results.) These differences are much more marked, though in the same direction, than those shown by similar polls in other American colleges.

As a more exact measure of attitudes to-ward domestic American issues, an attitude scale called "Political and Economic Progressivism" (PEP) was devised. It had to do primarily with issues made prominent by the New Deal, such as organized labor, public relief, and the role of corporate wealth. The scale was so devised that a high score indicates conservatism (defined in terms of these issues) and a low score nonconservatism. According to this measure, also, conservatism decreased steadily with each succeeding year in the community. During each of the four years covered by the study, mean senior scores were lower than those of juniors, which were lower than those of sophomores, which in turn were lower than those of freshmen. Mean score differences between adjacent classes were not always statistically significant, but during each of the four years freshman-senior differences were highly significant, their critical ratios ranging between 3.9 and 6.5. These differences were not the result of the withdrawal from college of certain students each year; differences of the same magnitude appear when scores of the same individuals as freshmen, as sophomores, as juniors and as seniors are compared. These differences were also found to be much greater than those shown by students either at Williams College or at Skidmore College, to whom the PEP attitude scales were also given. (The writer's original monograph provides evidence indicating that the respondents at both Williams and Skidmore are fairly representative of the entire student populations.) Tables 2 and 3 show the consistency with which PEP scores decline with each succeeding year, at Bennington, and how this decline compares with those at the other two colleges.

Altogether, eleven different attitude scales were employed during the four-year study, most of them only once. Four of them represented inclusive attitudes (PEP, internationalism, social distance, and dissatisfactions) and the others specific issues (Civil War in Spain, CIO, Supreme Court, Soviet Russia, American isolation, the Munich settlement, and the New Deal). Intercor-

TABLE 2

MEAN PEP SCORES, BENNINGTON

Year	Freshmen		Sophomores		Juniors		Seniors	
	N	Mn	N	Mn	N	Mn	N	Mn
1935-36 (fall)	88	74.5	74	66.5	47	68.6	45	65.8
1936-37 (fall)	69	75.8	55	68.5	37	62.3	27	60.1
1937-38[a]	64	71.9	85	69.1	50	63.7	37	59.9
1938-39[a]	55	75.9	62	70.0	58	68.5	45	62.7

[a] Fall scores for freshmen, spring scores for others.

TABLE 3

MEAN PEP SCORES, BENNINGTON, WILLIAMS AND SKIDMORE COLLEGES

College	Freshmen		Sophomores		Juniors		Seniors	
	N	Mn	N	Mn	N	Mn	N	Mn
Bennington[a]	276	74.2	241	69.4	166	65.9	155	62.4
Williams	95	76.1	114	69.4	74	70.7	36	71.2
Skidmore	83	79.9	53	78.1	70	77.0	46	74.1

[a] Totals for four years.

TABLE 4

SUMMARY OF INTERCORRELATIONS AMONG VARIOUS ATTITUDES

	Freshmen		Juniors-Seniors
	Fall term	Spring term	
Mean r	.35	.43	.48
Range of r's	.02. to .60	.10 to .71	.18 to .79
Number of r's	11	31	42
Number of reliable r's[a]	5	24	40

[a] Correlation coefficients equal to four times their probable errors, or more, are considered reliable.

relations were calculated between scores on all scales given during the same year. All intercorrelations were positive, without exception (high scores being consistently assigned to "conservative" attitudes, as the term was commonly applied to each issue at the time). For each college class 42 such intercorrelations were calculated; they are summarized in Table 4. Intercorrelations obtained for freshmen during their first term in the community are distinguished from those obtained during the second term, since second-term freshmen have already become assimilated into the community to a noticeable degree.

The inclusive pattern of attitude change may also be seen in the mean score differences between freshmen and juniors-

TABLE 5

CRITICAL RATIOS OF MEAN ATTITUDE DIFFERENCES BETWEEN FRESHMEN AND JUNIORS-SENIORS

Attitude toward	Critical ratios
PEP	3.9;6.5;4.6;4.6
Internationalism	3.2
Civil War in Spain	3.4
CIO	3.2
Supreme Court reform	4.3
New Deal	4.2
Dissatisfactions	3.3
American isolation	2.0
Munich settlement	2.1
Social distance	1.7
Soviet Russia	0.5

seniors, as shown in Table 5. For the eleven attitudes measured, juniors-seniors are reliably less conservative than freshmen in

TABLE 6

CORRELATIONS BETWEEN SCORES ON PUBLIC AFFAIRS TEST AND ATTITUDE
SCORES OF SAME INDIVIDUALS IN DIFFERENT YEARS

Attitude Measured	Years	As freshmen		As sophomores		As seniors	
		N	r	N	r	N	r
PEP	1936, 1937	55	−.03	55	−.39		
PEP	1937, 1938	48	−.11	48	−.36		
PEP	1935, 1939	42	+.11			42	−.43
Internationalism	1937, 1938	48	−.16	48	−.40		
Internationalism	1935, 1939	42	−.08			42	−.39

seven, unreliably less conservative in three and not at all in one. (Differences of three times their standard deviations are considered reliable.)

Information about Public Affairs

Accompanying many of the scales of attitudes toward various public issues were tests of information concerning those same issues. In addition, a Public Affairs test (published by the Cooperative Test Service, and widely used among American colleges) was routinely administered to all freshmen, all sophomores (with the exception of one class) and all seniors in the college. The following data will show that becoming assimilated into the community involves characteristic changes in information, as well as in attitudes.

Scores on the Public Affairs information test, dealing with a wide range of contemporary issues, show a consistent relationship to scores on two similarly inclusive attitude scales—the PEP scale and a scale of internationalist (vs. isolationist) attitudes, throughout the four years of the study, as shown in Table 6. This relationship is shown most clearly if earlier and later scores for the same individuals are used, rather than comparing coefficients based upon large freshmen groups with much smaller senior groups. None of the freshmen correlations is significant; those of the same individuals as sophomores or as seniors are highly so. As freshmen, conservatives are almost as likely to be well informed as nonconservatives; a year later the nonconservatives among the same group are a good deal more likely to be better informed than the conservatives.

The consistency with which Public Affairs information scores increased with declining PEP scores is shown in Table 7, in which mean information scores for the highest, middle and lowest thirds of each senior class, in respect to PEP scores, are shown. In spite of the very small numbers involved, the differences between the lowest and highest thirds, in Table 7, are statistically reliable in three or four cases; three of the critical ratios are greater than 3.0, and the fourth 2.4. The higher information scores on the

TABLE 7

MEAN PUBLIC AFFAIRS INFORMATION SCORES OF SENIORS,
CLASSIFIED BY SENIOR PEP SCORES

Seniors	Lowest third in PEP		Middle third in PEP		Highest third in PEP	
	N	Mn	N	Mn	N	Mn
Graduating in 1936	15	77.7	13	75.2	15	57.4
Graduating in 1937	13	75.4	13	64.9	13	54.6
Graduating in 1938	12	73.2	12	58.2	13	52.2
Graduating in 1939	16	73.3	15	68.1	16	54.5

part of the least conservative group are not associated with higher "intelligence" scores; scores on the Psychological Examination of the American Council on Education are not related to PEP scores, all correlations being consistently or near zero.

Information tests were given concerning various specific issues concerning which attitude scales were also administered. Data concerning only one of these, the Civil War in Spain (then in progress) are presented here. Care was taken to include information items of strictly neutral content, that is, such that knowledge of the correct answer would not dispose the individual toward either a favorable or unfavorable attitude. For the entire Bennington population the correlation between pro-Loyalist attitude and "neutral" information concerning the Spanish Civil War was .45. Since the Bennington climate had been distinctly pro-Loyalist (movies, speakers, and money-raising activities in behalf of the Loyalists had been frequent), it seemed desirable to use as controls a student community where the attitude climate was known to be anti-Loyalist, and another where it was more or less indifferent. A Roman Catholic university and Williams College, respectively, were chosen for this purpose. The differences among the three communities in respect to this issue may be seen in Tables 8 and 9.

Concerning this issue two other information tests were given in all three communities. One consisted of true-or-false items, the true answers to which were presumably disposing toward pro-Loyalist attitude (e.g., the statement, true at the time, that "General Franco's government has been recognized

TABLE 8

PERCENTAGE OF RESPONSES TO ATTITUDE STATEMENT: "I HOPE THE LOYALISTS WIN THE WAR."

Attitude	Bennington (N=174)	Williams (N=312)	Catholic (N=83)
Strongly agree	42	28	4
Agree	40	36	7
Uncertain	12	24	13
Disagree	4	9	26
Strongly disagree	2	3	50

TABLE 9

MEANS AND DISPERSIONS OF SCORES OF ATTITUDE TOWARD THE SPANISH CIVIL WAR (LOW SCORES PRO-LOYALIST)

	Bennington	Williams	Catholic
Mean	41.2	43.6	53.6
Standard deviation	7.2	9.8	6.8
Range	18–61	19–70	39–74

as the legitimate power in Spain only by governments which are overtly fascist, or near-fascist."). The other consisted of statements the true answers to which were presumably disposing toward anti-Loyalist attitude (e.g., the true statement that "Indisputable evidence has been adduced showing that some clergy have been executed and many persecuted by Loyalist sympathizers."). Results from these tests appear in Tables 10 and 11, which show that (1) responses to these two tests, though both are based upon "facts," are quite different in all three communities; and (2) that Bennington juniors and seniors distinguish much more clearly between the two tests than do freshmen.

The conspicuous differences between comparable correlations at Bennington and the Catholic university are explainable in terms of their opposite attitude climates in respect to this issue, as indicated by their enormously different mean attitude scores (critical ratio 13.1) and their small dispersions, compared to Williams. As a result of these attitude climates, students in either community found it easier to get one sort of information than the other; they were more likely to acquire and to retain that kind of information which supported their attitudes than the kind which undermined them; and both information and attitudes were simultaneously influenced by degree of concern over the issue. At Bennington those most concerned over the issue became most pro-Loyalist in attitude; they acquired and retained most information supporting the attitude; and they were least able to accept as "fact" such information as tended to undermine their attitudes. Those most concerned over the issue at the Catholic university became most anti-Loy-

TABLE 10

MEAN INFORMATION SCORES CONCERNING CIVIL WAR IN SPAIN

Type of Information	Bennington						Williams		Catholic	
	Freshmen		Juniors-Seniors		All classes					
	N	Mn	N	Mn	N	Mn	N	Mn	N	Mn
Neutral	45	5.5	41	8.3	139	7.4	312	7.0	83	4.1
Pro-Loyalist	48	8.2	67	12.0	174	9.8	312	10.1	83	1.7
Anti-Loyalist	48	3.2	67	1.9	174	2.7	312	1.2	83	7.2

TABLE 11

CORRELATIONS OF ATTITUDE AND INFORMATION SCORES CONCERNING THE SPANISH CIVIL WAR

Type of Information	Bennington						Williams		Catholic	
	Freshmen		Juniors-Seniors		All classes					
	N	r	N	r	N	r	N	r	N	r
Neutral	45	−.23	41	−.54	139	−.45	312	−.26	83	+.38
Pro-Loyalist	48	−.16	67	−.59	174	−.57	312	−.34	83	−.08
Anti-Loyalist	48	−.04	67	+.08	174	−.04	312	+.06	83	+.51

alist in attitude, and were most likely to retain and to reject, respectively, those kinds of information which supported or undermined their attitudes.

It is of particular significance that at Bennington attitudes and information were created community-wise, and not merely in relation to courses of study pursued. At Williams both pro-Loyalist attitude and neutral information scores were considerably higher on the part of students in Social Science courses than on the part of other students;

at Bennington no such difference appeared. Quite clearly it was the community climate, not courses of instruction, which led to the attitude-information pattern characteristic of Bennington students.

Individual Prestige Associated with Declining Conservatism

Frequency of choice as one of five students "most worthy to represent the College" at an intercollegiate gathering was used as a measure of individual prestige;

TABLE 12

MEAN PEP SCORES, CLASSIFIED ACCORDING TO FREQUENCY OF BEING CHOSEN AS REPRESENTATIVE (1938)

Frequency of Choice	Freshmen		Sophomores		Juniors-Seniors		Entire College	
	N	Mean	N	Mean	N	Mean	N	Mean
40–89	—	—	3	60.3	5	50.4	8	54.1
12–39	—	—	5	65.6	15	57.6	20	59.7
5–11	—	—	5	65.3	18	62.2	23	62.7
2–4	10	64.6	18	68.6	19	61.6	47	65.3
1	12	63.4	17	68.6	15	62.1	44	65.0
0	61	72.8	39	71.3	14	69.0	114	71.7
Total	83	70.9	87	68.8	86	62.1	256	67.1

nominations were submitted in sealed envelopes by 99 percent of the students in the spring of 1938 and again in 1939. The relationship between PEP non-conservatism and prestige, as thus measured, was almost identical in 1938 and 1939; results for the former year appear in Table 12. The nonconservatism of those with high prestige is not merely the result of the fact that juniors and seniors are characterized by both high prestige and nonconservatism; in each college class, those who have prestige are less conservative than those who have less prestige.

Reputation for Community Citizenship

Most students participated actively in community affairs, took a good deal of pride in the college, and manifested in various ways their general enthusiasm for it, but there were nevertheless individual differences in these respects. Reputation scores of various aspects of "community citizenship" were therefore obtained. "Guess-Who" ratings were made by a group of 24 students, carefully selected so as to represent every cross-section and grouping of importance within the college. Each of these 24 judges named three individuals from each class who were reputedly most extreme in each of 28 characteristics related to community citizenship. As indicated by the partial results reproduced in Table 13 there is

TABLE 13

MEAN PEP SCORES, ACCORDING TO
REPUTATION FOR IDENTIFICATION
WITH THE COMMUNITY

Reputation Score	N	Mean PEP Score
+15 or more	15	54.4
+5 to +14	23	60.6
+4 to −4	63	65.3
−5 to −14	32	67.9
−15 or less	10	68.2

a close relationship between reputation for identification with the community and nonconservatism, in spite of the fact that no reference whatever was made to the latter characteristic when the judges made their ratings. (The "reputation scores" in Table

13 are composite scores based upon the frequency with which individuals are named in five items dealing with "identification with the community" minus the number of times named in five other items dealing with "negative community attitude." Examples of the former items are "absorbed in college community affairs" and "influenced by community expectations regarding codes, standards, etc."; examples of the latter are "indifferent to activities of student committees" and "resistant to community expectations regarding codes, standards, etc.")

The fact that nonconservatism is associated with interest in public affairs is particularly well illustrated by reputation scores for the item "most absorbed in national and international public affairs." Among a group of 22 juniors and seniors whose PEP scores were extremely low, exactly half were named more than once as being extreme in this characteristic, and seven were named five times or more. Among another group of 22 juniors and seniors whose PEP scores were extremely high, only one was mentioned more than once as extreme in this characteristic, and none was named as many as five times. Marked interest in public affairs is associated with non-conservative attitude, in this community, and both are associated with prestige and "good citizenship."

Awareness of Community Attitude Climate

Several indices of "good citizenship" or "community assimilation" have been shown to be related to the acquiring of nonconservative attitudes. These indices are all based upon observed behaviors, either pencil-and-paper behavior or the kind of day-to-day behavior upon which reputations were judged. There is also reason to believe that the way in which the individual views the community is related to her manner of adaptation to it. Perceptual habits, as well as overt behaviors, should provide an index of community assimilation. More fully stated, her own perception of her relationship to the community is presumably a determinant of her behavior. This self-view of own relationship to the community we shall term "subjective role."

In order to obtain an index of subjective role, subjects were asked to respond in two ways to a number of attitude statements taken from the PEP scale: first, to indicate agreement or disagreement (for example, with the statement, "The budget should be balanced before the government spends any money on social security."); and secondly, to estimate what percent of freshmen, of juniors-seniors, and of faculty would agree with the statement. Table 14, in which own

TABLE 14

MEAN PERCENT ESTIMATES OF CONSERVA-
TIVE RESPONSE, BY THOSE RESPONDING
CONSERVATIVELY AND NONCON-
SERVATIVELY

Mean Estimate of Response

Estimates by	Freshmen	Juniors-Seniors	Faculty
30 seniors, concerning items answered conservatively	68	53	46
30 seniors, concerning items answered nonconservatively	59	25	15
34 freshmen, concerning items answered conservatively	63	58	54
34 freshmen, concerning items answered nonconservatively	47	35	30

responses to PEP items are compared with the same individual's estimates of conservative response by freshmen and by juniors-seniors to the same items, shows that (1) seniors estimate the difference between freshmen and juniors-seniors to be a good deal greater than do freshmen; and (2) conservatives, both freshmen and seniors, estimate differences between freshmen and juniors-seniors to be much less than do nonconservatives. Those who are in fact nonconservative regarding a given issue tend to think of freshmen as more conservative than themselves on that issue, but to think of juniors-seniors and faculty as much less so than freshmen. Those who are in fact conservative regarding a given issue

tend to think of all three groups as being also conservative, with only slight differences among the three groups. Both conservative and non-conservative seniors tend to think of themselves as agreeing with the majority of their class, but the conservatives have a less realistic view of the attitudes of their classmates than do the nonconservatives.

In Table 15 are combined the percent estimates of all subjects, regardless of

TABLE 15

ACTUAL AND ESTIMATED PERCENTAGES OF
CONSERVATIVE RESPONSE AT BENNINGTON
AND AT SKIDMORE

Percent Conservative Response By

	Freshmen	Juniors-Seniors	Faculty
Actual (Bennington)	34	20	10
As estimated by Bennington seniors	61	30	21
As estimated by Bennington freshmen	52	43	39
Actual (Skidmore)	47	36	—
As estimated by Skidmore seniors	52	48	42
As estimated by Skidmore freshmen	54	52	50

whether their own responses were conservative or not. Table 15 also includes comparable responses by 252 Skidmore students, from all four classes, together with the actual responses of the several groups at both colleges, for purposes of comparison with the estimated responses. These data show that (1) all Skidmore students, on the average, underestimate the degree to which juniors and seniors are less conservative than freshmen; (2) Bennington freshmen slightly underestimate this difference; and (3) Bennington seniors greatly overestimate it; most of this overestimation (as shown in Table 14) is attributable to the great majority of estimates by seniors on items which they themselves answered nonconservatively (80 percent of all items); estimates on these items greatly exaggerate the conservatism of freshmen. Freshmen are actually more conservative than juniors-seniors by a greater amount at Bennington than at Skidmore, but at Bennington the actual differences are commonly supposed to be a good deal greater than they are, particularly by seniors, by those who are themselves nonconservative and (as shown in Tables 12 and 13) by those who have prestige and reputation for "good citizenship." Assimilation into the Bennington community includes, for the average student, the acquiring of the subjective role of going along with the majority who are becoming less conservative.

Personality Patterns and Community Assimilation

The preceding data have to do with majority trends, and with the differences between those who become less and those who become more assimilated into the community. These data tell us nothing about individual exceptions to the generalizations, nor do they tell us much about the personality characteristics of the individuals from whom the quantitative data are drawn. Fortunately, a considerable body of personality data was available, and by assembling them it is possible to understand a good deal about the psychological processes by which students did or did not come to take on the characteristic community patterns, as described above.

Fairly intensive personality studies were made of a few subjects, rather than routine and hasty ones of all. Altogether 43 subjects were thus studied, chosen (1) as being from the classes entering in 1935 and 1936 (the two classes which had participated in the study as freshmen and for three or four years thereafter); and (2) as being roughly in the most or the least conservative quarter of their classes in 1939 (i.e., as having PEP scores of $+.5$ standard deviations or more, or $-.5$ standard deviations or less). One of the major sources of personality data was official college records —detailed reports from teachers, who included much information about personality characteristics as well as about academic performance; and from counselors, who worked individually with students, knew them extremely well, and twice each year

wrote careful statements about personality, community adjustment, and academic progress. The second major source was a series of detailed interviews by the investigator concerning each subject—with the student herself, as she neared graduation; with one or more of her counselors; and with the college psychiatrist, who provided a wealth of detailed information and professional understanding.

On the basis of such evidence, together with the quantitative data, comparable data were assembled for each of the 43 selected subjects; care was taken not to record any trait as applying to a given subject unless independently verified from two or more sources, not including the subject herself. A "hypothesis" was then drawn up concerning the dynamics of each subject's attitude development in the community; in most cases the subject herself contributed a good deal toward formulating this hypothesis.

The significant thing about these hypotheses was that they fell into a very few patterns. With only minor deviations, each of 19 conservative subjects fitted into one or another of four patterns, and each of 24 nonconservatives into one or another of four quite different patterns. These patterns, moreover, correspond to objective distinctions, as well as to more or less distinct groupings of personality data of less objective sort. The objective indices (which also correspond to personality differences) were those of reputation for community identification, and of own relationship to classmates, as self-perceived in terms of attitude similarities or differences.

Thus the four groups of conservatives were:

1. those reputedly negativistic toward the community, and aware of their own conservatism;
2. those reputedly negativistic toward the community, and not aware of their own conservatism;
3. those not reputedly negativistic toward the community, and aware of their own conservatism;

4. those not reputedly negativistic toward the community, and not aware of their own conservatism.

The four groups of nonconservatives were:

1. those reputedly active in community affairs, and aware of their own relative nonconservatism;
2. those reputedly active in community affairs, and not aware of their own relative nonconservatism;
3. those not reputedly active in community affairs, and aware of their own relative nonconservatism;
4. those not reputedly active in community affairs, and not aware of their own relative nonconservatism.

Take, for example, the two groups of negativistic conservatives. Those who are not aware of their own relative conservatism, i.e., who believe they are attitudinally typical, are found to be timid and socially insecure, to have small and limited groups of friends, and to come to college with almost no aspirations toward "social success." This latter characteristic is clearly related to their almost complete failure to achieve any sort of "social success" in precollege relationships. The negativistic conservatives who are aware of their own relative conservatism are markedly less retiring and less inhibited, are more socially facile; they do not, like the unawares, tend to belong to compact little friendship groups; unlike the unawares, they had achieved a considerable degree of precollege social success, and came to college with high hopes of continued success—hopes which were doomed to disappointment. In short, the unawares are insulated in tiny social groups; their negativism functions as a protective shell of indifference toward what they cannot cope with; hence their unawareness. The negativism of the awares is an aggressive reaction to the frustration of the ambitions which were at first directed at the total community; hence their awareness.

Among the nonnegativistic conservatives, the distinctions between the awares and the unawares are partly similar to and partly different from the preceding distinctions. The awares have markedly greater self-confidence and possess greater social skills; they are eager and enthusiastic, whereas the unawares tend to be plodding and conscientious. The awares have considerable prestige, the unawares almost none. Both groups show more than average attachment to and dependence upon parents, but the crucial distinction seems to be that the unawares were so absorbed by home and family conflicts and allegiances as to be scarcely at all susceptible to community-wide college influences, while the awares, equally "loyal" to parents, were capable of maintaining a divided allegiance; i.e., they yielded to all college community influences except those attitudinal ones which would have brought conflict with parents. The unawares, unable to cope with two worlds, participate only superficially in college community life; hence their unawareness. The awares are capable of participating in both worlds, but reject such college influences as would result in home conflict; hence their awareness.

The two groups of nonconservatives who are not reputedly community-active may be described as passively conforming rather than as negativistic, the unawares are considered dependent upon instructors, and anxious to please, while the awares are highly independent. The unawares are eager and enthusiastic, while the awares are not. The awares are more outstanding academically, and it is clear that they have set higher standards for themselves. The unawares believe that they would follow the majority attitude trend in a conservative college, while the awares would not. The unawares describe their major ambitions, on entering college, in terms of friendship rather than of prestige, while the reverse is true of the awares, for whom intellectual prestige is particularly important. Self-interpretations, finally, show the unawares tend to think of their own attitude change as just one aspect of being assimilated into the community; hence their unawareness of their own relative nonconservatism. The awares, however, tend to think of their attitude change as an intellectual achievement in respect to which they have outdistanced most students, and hence their awareness.

The two groups of community-active nonconservatives have much in common. Both are composed of "substantial citizens," hard-working and conscientious, though the unawares are considered more enthusiastic and the awares more persistent. Both groups are high in prestige; both groups had achieved considerable recognition before coming to college, though memories of pre-college "failures" are more acute on the part of the unawares. They differ primarily in the following respects: the unawares are more anxious to please, and need more guidance from instructors. The awares are much more commonly described as "meticulous" or "perfectionist," and are more apt to be intellectual leaders. The awares have come to reformulate their ambitions less in terms of personal success and more in terms of the success of "causes." In short, lack of awareness on the part of the one group represents loyal cooperation in respect to approved social attitudes; as "leaders" they must, of course, be slightly "ahead" of the majority, but not too far. The awares, on the other hand, are not only sufficiently secure that they can afford to go beyond the majority, but their awareness is a mark of the hard-won struggle by which they reached their nonconservative positions; hence, of course, they are aware.

In short, it may be said for each of the eight groups that the personality processes which appear to be essentially responsible for whatever attitude adaptation is made are also responsible for whatever degrees of awareness is shown. Those who are conservative because they have avoided the community could scarcely have an opportunity to discover that they are conservative. Those who are conservative because they aimed at leadership, failed, and repudiated whatever the community stood for could scarcely fail to be aware of their own conservatism. Those who have ac-quired more than the average degree of nonconservatism because they are anxious to conform cannot be aware of their own relative extremeness, else they would withdraw to a more moderate position. Those who are extremely nonconservative because they need to excel must be aware that they are somewhat extreme, etc.

There is no magic involved in the discovery that the different dynamic patterns by which individuals arrive at their attitudinal adjustments to the community correspond so closely to the objective classifications according to reputation (here referred to as objective role) and self-perceived relationship to classmates (here referred to as subjective role). Objective roles are assigned, with more or less correctness, by fellow community members on the basis of observable personality characteristics. Among those assigned similar objective roles, different subjective roles are self-assigned on the basis of other personality characteristics. Those for whom objective and subjective roles are similar, according to quantitative data, thus have many personality characteristics in common. These common personality characteristics, moreover, are directly related to the processes of personality adaptation by which attitudes are acquired in this particular community.

SUMMARY

Associated with the process of assimilation into this student community are found an inclusive pattern of attitudes of declining conservatism toward public issues; increasing information concerning them, in particular such kinds of information as serve to support the developing attitudes; increasing individual prestige; increasing reputation for active "good citizenship"; and increasing awareness of the decreasing conservatism of others. The average student is characterized by all these changes to a modest degree; the "typical" leader (whether senior or, more rarely, sophomore or freshman) shows all of them to a considerable degree; the "typical" unassimilated student, whether freshman or senior, is conspicuously lacking in all these characteristics.

Among those who most conspicuously adopt the prevailing norms in respect to attitudes toward public issues, several more or less distinct modes of personal adaptation to the community are found, and certain individuals are exceptions to the general findings concerning personal prestige, reputation for "good citizenship," and awareness of the community attitude trend. These exceptions are specifically related to the characteristic mode of personal adaptation, and both are accounted for in terms of the individual's objective and subjective roles in relation to the community.

Among those who most conspicuously fail to adopt the prevailing norms in respect to attitudes toward public issues, other more or less distinct modes of personal adaptation to the community are found, and again there are certain individual exceptions to the general findings. These exceptions, too, are specifically related to characteristic modes of personal adaptation, and both are accounted for in terms of objective and subjective roles, as measured by quantitative indices.

These findings are consistent with the point of view that a community is distinctive in terms of the objective roles which it recognizes, both approvingly and disapprovingly, and that the individual's adaptation to the community is understandable in terms of his subjective role, seen in relation to the objective roles.

LEADERSHIP SELECTION IN URBAN LOCALITY AREAS

IRA DeA. REID AND EMILY L. EHLE*

In the summer of 1948, the Institute for Research in Human Relations in Philadelphia undertook for the Office of Naval Research a project on "The Identification and Acceptance of Leadership in Urban Communities." The study was designed: (1) to determine the usefulness of the opinion survey as an instrument by which urban re-

spondents can identify by name and role the leaders whom they regard as influential in the community; (2) to gather descriptive data on the American ideology of political, economic, or social leadership in general; (3) to test the hypothesis that the individual's deep-lying insecurities expressed in the general variable recently receiving attention as "authoritarianism" have a bearing on his readiness to accept leadership; and (4) to explore the patterns of local leadership as

* John N. Patterson, Barney Korchin, Fillmore H. Sanford, and Doris M. Barnett were collaborators in the over-all project of which the material in this article is one aspect.

From the *Public Opinion Quarterly*, 1950, Vol. 14, 2, 262-284. Reprinted by permission of the authors and the publisher.

they exist in a large urban community. This article is primarily concerned with an aspect of the last-named problem—the patterns according to which local leaders are chosen.

The data presented below were drawn from a field study designed around 24 four-block areas chosen at random within census tracts representative of the city and county of Philadelphia. The four-block area, called here the "locality," or the "locality area," was the basic spatial unit employed in this study. Although seven types of socio-economic areas ranging from rhododendron-planted suburbia to the outside toilet blocks of South Philadelphia were included in the sample, on the assumption that differing neighborhood patterns could be expected to exist, the total sample matched the total population within at least 2 per cent on the basic characteristics of race, religion, education, economic class, occupation, sex, and age. In June and July 1949, an intensive 72-question schedule was administered, of which six items were projective type pictures.[1]

For the purposes of this study, a leader was defined as the person designated by the respondent as a leader in either advice or action situations. The resultant choices emerged principally in response to the following two questions in the schedule: "I prefer that the person I go to for advice be—————," and "In your opinion, who are the individuals in this neighborhood who have become the leaders and have been accepted as leaders by the people around here?"

Throughout this article, N=963 and the sub-totals for each neighborhood ($n_1\ n_2\ n_3$-n_{25}) =39 or 40.

GEOGRAPHICAL LOCATION AND LEADERSHIP NOMINATION

Is there any relationship between the geographical location of an area and the ability of its residents to nominate leaders?

One of the theories of modern urban com-

munity growth and organization is based upon the principle of zones structured and developed in concentric circles from the center of the city. The core of this theory is that land use and residency within the area tends to follow a given spatial pattern. By dividing Philadelphia into concentric circles based upon their mileage from center-city, nine areas are indicated. At the center of the city is the business district, or Zone I. Around this district is a zone in transition, or an area of social disorganization (Zone II). Zone III is an area of workingmen's homes, and Zone IV is the area of middle-class homes and apartment houses. The outer zones in this configuration represent various levels of "suburbia," commuters' zones of upper economic class residences. The pattern may vary by sections of the circles as well as within each circle, but all in all the so-called "natural areas" of use and residence in Philadelphia tend to conform to this pattern.

This patterning of urban residence is essentially related to the ability of an area's residents to pay a given rental. The central area seldom is used for living purposes; the relatively few inhabitants usually are persons in the higher income brackets who can afford to pay the rental or sale prices demanded. Thus, in Zone I we find an upper economic class area, the occupants of which have the highest educational level in the total sample but a period of occupancy below the average of all areas, and which in ability to nominate a leader ranks 16th in the 24 localities.

Zone II, the oldest residential area of the city (averaging nearly 12 years as compared with 8.4 years for the city as a whole) is of the type described by human ecologists as a zone in transition. All of the localities in this zone are of the lower economic order. The formal education of the residents, as measured by the percentage finishing high school, is one of the lowest. This zone, however, exceeds all others in its ability to nominate leaders, having a nomination index of 65.8 per cent as compared with 41.1 per cent for all areas.

The lowest economic class locality areas

[1] For some early notes on methodology, see Ehle, Emily L., "Techniques for Study of Leadership," *Public Opinion Quarterly*, Vol. 13, No. 2 (1949), pp. 235-240.

TABLE 1

CHARACTERISTICS OF AREA POPULATIONS

Zone	Distance From Center-City	Average Years of Residence	Economic Type*	Average Per Cent Finishing High School	Area Index of Ability to Nominate Leaders	Organization Participation Score	Authoritarian-Equalitarian Score†
I	Under 1 mile	6	U	95%	32.5	6.6	3.4
II	1–1.99 miles	10.2	L	53	65.8	4.0	4.5
III	2–2.99 "	9.5	U & L M	81	25.3	4.8	4.2
IV	3–3.99 "	8.8	L & L M	52	44.4	3.2	4.1
V	4–4.99 "	6.4	U & L M	63	42.6	3.9	4.0
VI	5–5.99 "	8.5	U & L M	74	56.3	5.0	3.7
VII	6–6.99 "	7.5	U & L M	75	26.3	3.4	3.8
VIII	7–7.99 "	9.7	U & L M	61	43.3	3.9	4.1
IX	8–8.99 "	7.5	L M	70	43.7	5.7	3.9
ALL AREAS:		8.4		69	41.1		

* Sample figures on economic classifications of respondent made by interviewer were based on the following descriptive instructions: "U" (Upper)—the wealthy and well-off; includes well-to-do merchants, executives, professional men and prosperous farmers. These people usually have all the luxuries they desire. "UM" (Upper Middle)—the upper middle class; have all the comforts of life common to their community, but not all the luxuries they desire. Occupation similar to the "U" group, but are not as well off. "LM" (Lower Middle)—the bulk of the middle class; work for all the comforts of life and have to save to buy some of the luxuries. Their occupations include minor white-collar jobs, proprietors of small local stores, the skilled trades, skilled factory work, etc. "L" (Lower)—the poor; those who have to struggle to get most of the necessities of life. Manual workers, unskilled workers, unemployed, etc.

† This score is based on a scale of 1-6 (Equalitarian-Authoritarian) developed from answers to eight schedule items designed to tap various aspects of the authoritarian personality. Discussion of the implications of authoritarianism for the acceptance of leadership will appear in psychological journals.

are located within the first four zones. From Zone V to the territorial limits of the city the locality areas reveal a strip layer pattern of upper-middle and lower-middle class economic areas, with characteristics that vary from class to class and from zone to zone. (See Table 1.)

An examination of the two measurements of individual behavior and attitudes as measured by the organization participation and the authoritarian-equalitarian scores shows no significant differences that may be causally related to the zone theory of population distribution. It may be noted, however, that Zone I, which has the highest educational level, has also the highest organization participation score and the lowest authoritarian-equalitarian score.

Throughout this study, incidentally, evidence was obtained to belie the stereotyped concept of the American as a "joiner." Seventy-eight per cent of the sample belong to no religious organization beyond general membership in a church, 85 per cent belong to no civic or charitable organization, 74 per cent report no affiliation with occupational groups (unions, business, or professional associations). Further examples of this low participation in group activity are to be found in a study of 1,154 female respondents made in the same city.[2] Of a representative sample of Philadelphia women, 55 per cent are found to belong to no organization of any kind.

MORE LEADERS MENTIONED IN POORER AREAS

Is there any relationship between the economic characteristics of a locality area and its ability to nominate leaders?

[2] "Leisure Time Patterns: Their Implications for the YWCA," survey conducted for the YWCA of Philadelphia by the Institute for Research in Human Relations, Philadelphia, 1949.

TABLE 2
LEADER NOMINATION AND RESIDENCE BY ECONOMIC TYPE OF AREA

		LEADER NOMINATIONS BY PER CENT OF RESPONDENTS			LEADER RESIDENCY BY PER CENT OF RESPONDENTS		
Economic Class	Locality Area Number*	None	One	Two	Within Four-Block Area	Within Four-Eight-Block Area	Beyond Eight-Block Area
Upper:	2	67.5%	20.0%	12.5%	43.0%	57.0%	—
Upper Middle:		63.3	18.7	18.7	41.4	46.9	5.4%
	3	77.5	15.0	7.5	45.5	54.5	—
	4	80.0	10.0	10.0	60.0	10.0	—
	10	30.0	25.0	45.0	23.0	54.0	15.0
	13	55.0	27.5	17.5	—	92.0	8.0
	22	60.0	20.0	20.0	56.0	44.0	—
	21	72.5	15.0	12.5	64.0	27.0	9.0
Lower Middle:		54.7	24.4	20.2	38.2	47.5	5.3
	6	77.0	18.0	5.0	37.5	50.0	12.5
	8	47.5	25.0	27.5	56.0	44.0	—
	11	62.5	17.5	20.0	47.0	40.0	—
	12	25.0	15.0	60.0	45.0	30.0	10.0
	14	57.5	25.0	17.5	19.0	50.0	6.0
	15	47.5	40.0	12.5	50.0	50.0	—
	17	65.0	20.0	12.5	67.0	33.0	—
	19	50.0	30.0	20.0	28.5	71.5	—
	20	70.0	25.0	5.0	14.0	36.0	21.0
	21	62.5	25.0	12.5	40.0	60.0	—
	23	37.5	32.5	30.0	16.5	58.0	9.0
Lower:		49.6	25.0	25.0	50.1	44.3	1.3
	1	52.5	37.5	10.0	44.0	56.0	—
	5	75.0	22.5	2.5	57.0	43.0	—
	7	67.5	17.5	12.5	67.0	33.0	—
	9	52.5	25.0	22.5	75.0	25.0	—
	16	37.5	25.0	37.5	41.0	59.0	—
	25	12.5	22.5	65.0	17.0	50.0	8.0
AVERAGE FOR ALL LOCALITY AREAS:	Upper	67.5	20.0	12.5	41.4	57.0	—
	Upper Middle	63.3	18.7	18.7	41.4	46.9	5.4
	Lower Middle	54.7	24.4	20.2	38.2	47.5	5.3
	Lower	49.6	25.0	25.0	50.1	44.3	1.3
ALL AREAS:		58.8	22.0	19.1	42.8	48.9	4.0

* One of the locality areas (No. 18) was discovered to be almost "rural" in configuration and was discarded from the city sample. The substitution of No. 25 explains the appearance of this number in a sample of only 24 four-block units.

When locality areas are grouped according to their general economic type, several significant clusters of characteristics become evident. (See Table 2.) In the first place, the higher the economic class of the area, the greater is the chance that there will be no area leader nominations. Conversely, the lower the area in economic wealth, the higher is the rate of leader nominations. We find that in the higher economic class area 67.5 per cent of the respondents were unable to nominate a leader, while in the lowest economic category the non-nominating persons formed only 48.4 per cent of the total. In the upper-middle class areas the percentage unable to nominate was 63.3, while the lower-middle class areas had a non-nominating rate of 54.7 per cent.

The economic class significance of leader nomination is also revealed by the fact that one-leader nominations are more typical of the upper-economic classes than of the lower one, despite the fact that the former group does not nominate leaders as frequently as the lower economic groups. Nominations of two or more leaders indicate the same general tendency. Furthermore, though the incidence of leadership residence within the four-block and the four- to eight-block areas was somewhat similar for the city as a whole (43.1 per cent for four-block areas and 49.4 per cent for four-eight block areas), unique variations were found when these areas were grouped according to their economic type. The general principle underlying these variations is that leader residence within the four-block area tends to be higher in lower and lower-middle locality areas than in upper-middle and upper ones. The significant variations from this conclusion noted in areas where 50 per cent or more of the leader-nominees reside within eight blocks rather than within the four-block locality area are related to such aspects of leader appeal as religion and race. These aspects are discussed in subsequent sections of this analysis.

THE OCCUPATIONAL ROLE OF LEADERS

A further characteristic of leader nomination is reflected in the occupational role of the persons nominated as leaders by the several areas. The upper economic class areas tend to nominate persons associated with some specific occupational function— the physician, the lawyer, the minister, the businessman.[3] Only two of the seven high

[3] Operators and owners of small locality or community shops and stores were separately identified in the tabulations and were not classified as businessmen in this study.

economic areas (upper and upper-middle) nominated a political leader as their first choice. In the 17 lower economic areas, however, 13 areas chose the political person as the leader, and one each chose a minister, a businessman, a welfare worker and a lawyer. The only nominees for first choice who received as many as half of the nominations (with one exception) were the political leaders (Table 3). It is important to note that these nominations were not made by persons who are themselves active in politics, for only 61 out of the 429 persons nominating leaders described themselves as politically active. (The three localities reporting the largest number of active participants in politics were 2, 10, and 1, in no one of which was the political leader the area's first choice of leader.)

In general, the action leader of the locality area in the modern community is the political person. Allowing weights of 5, 3, and 1 respectively for the first, second, and third most frequently mentioned leadership roles, the incidence of the roles selected reveals choices in the following rank-order:

Occupations	Choices
Politicians	92
Community Workers (Social)	27
Businessmen	24
Ministers, Priests, Rabbis	18
Lawyers	12
Physicians	8
Skilled Workers	5
Teachers	4
Others	9

For generalized leadership the political leader (in most instances the committeeman), the welfare leader (a community organization person, a settlement worker, or other social workers), and the businessman have the widest appeal. The religious leader is important only in the Jewish and Negro neighborhoods. Other professional persons seem important more because of personal characteristics than because of their occupational roles. The selection of the political role three times as often as any other role reveals the pervasive character of that leadership in the modern urban community.

TABLE 3

ROLES OF LEADERS NOMINATED BY ECONOMIC AREAS

Economic Area	Locality Area Number	First Choice	Per Cent	Second Choice	Per Cent	Third Choice	Per Cent
Upper:							
	2	Physician	21.4%	Political Role	21.4%	None	—
Upper Middle:							
	3	Lawyer	41.7	Political Role	21.4	—	—
	4	Political Role	62.5	NSR *	25.0	Teacher	17.5%
	10	Minister (Rabbi)	35.5	NSR *	29.0	Lawyer	9.7
	13	Political Role	73.7	Welfare Role	10.5	—	—
	22	Skilled Worker	31.3	Business Role	18.8	Minister (Rabbi)	18.8
	24	Business Role	36.4	Welfare Role	18.2	Lawyer	18.2
Lower Middle:							
	6	Political Role	41.7	—	—	—	—
	8	Political Role	43.5	Welfare Role	13.0	—	—
	11	Political Role	46.7	Physician	13.3	Business Role	13.3
	12	Minister	37.5	Political Role	28.1	Business Role	18.8
	14	Welfare Role	41.2	Business Role	29.4	Political Role	23.5
	15	Political Role	40.0	Welfare Role	20.0	—	—
	17	Political Role	80.0	Welfare Role	13.3	—	—
	19	Political Role	57.1	Welfare Role	14.3	—	—
	20	Political Role	18.2	Welfare Role	13.6	Minister	9.1
	21	Political Role	66.7	Teacher	11.1	—	—
	23	Business Role	59.8	Political Role	18.5	—	—
Lower:							
	1	Lawyer	30.0	Business Role	30.0	Political Role	20.0
	5	Political Role	58.8	Business Role	11.8	—	—
	7	Political Role	47.1	—	—	—	—
	9	Political Role	70.0	—	—	—	—
	16	Political Role	38.5	Minister	15.4	Welfare Role	11.5
	25	Political Role	74.3	Minister	14.3	—	—

* NSR—non-structured role.

WHOM TO SEE FOR ADVICE?

When respondents are asked to name a good person to go and see when in trouble, class differences again become apparent. An analysis of the professional roles that are important when one is in trouble reveals that lawyers are most relied upon in the highest and lowest economic groups. The middle income groups, while also relying heavily on the legal profession, indicate an affinity for leadership provided by the religious leader and the physician. The politician is most often sought by the lowest income groups, although his role as a source for advice is very minor compared with his importance for other types of leadership. (See Table 4.)

What are the reasons for selecting specific leaders for advice? Does the general category of economic class offer any general explanations? Some facts are quite evident. In all areas respondents weigh heavily the leader's capacity to be well liked, or the general admirable characteristics which he may have, such as kindness, understanding, or friendliness. The leader's ability to help his followers is also mentioned in nearly all areas. Next in general importance is the extent to which a leader reveals himself as a man of strength, but this specification varied widely among the areas and had little relevance to economic class. Respect for the position one had attained in the area or in the wider community showed similar variations, while general competence was of less importance than any other factor save that the leader be "a man of the people." Specific conclusions may be reached as to the choices of the lowest economic areas which have the highest nominating ability: they are only mildly concerned with the leader's "democracy" or his "character"; admiration is less important here than in any other economic class, but the leader must be strong, be respected for the position he has attained, and must help his followers (Table 5).

LENGTH OF RESIDENCE

When leadership nomination and selection are analyzed on the basis of residence within the area, the following characteristics are noted: (See Table 6.)

1. The ability to nominate leaders increases with the average length of residence within areas.
2. The longer the average residence within an area, the greater the likelihood of a single leader being nominated, rather than several individuals.

TABLE 4

PERSONS TO BE SEEN FOR ADVICE, BY ECONOMIC AREAS, ROLES, AND LOCALITY AREAS

Economic Area	Locality Area Number	Lawyer	Minister	Physician	Politician
Upper:					
	2	19.5%	7.3%	4.9%	—
Upper Middle:					
	3*	—	—	—	—
	4	24.4	29.3	7.3	2.4%
	10	27.5	—	15.0	—
	13	14.3	31.0	9.5	—
	22	20.0	14.3	17.1	5.7
	24	7.5	12.5	10.0	—
Lower Middle:					
	6	20.5	17.9	—	5.1
	8	20.5	25.6	2.6	—
	11	26.8	26.8	7.3	2.4
	12	34.4	18.8	—	—
	14	26.3	15.8	18.4	—
	15	13.9	8.3	19.4	—
	17	17.1	19.5	14.6	2.4
	19	10.3	17.9	15.4	5.1
	20*	—	—	—	—
	21*	—	—	—	—
	23	23.1	7.7	5.1	—
Lower:					
	1	27.8	22.2	11.1	5.6
	5	21.6	16.2	13.5	2.7
	7	31.6	7.9	15.8	10.5
	9	10.0	10.0	22.5	2.5
	16	38.9	8.3	2.8	2.8
	25	19.4	19.4	2.8	13.9
AVERAGE FOR ALL LOCALITY AREAS:	Upper	19.5	7.3	4.9	—
	Upper Middle	18.7	21.8	11.8	4.1
	Lower Middle	20.3	16.9	13.2	3.5
	Lower	27.9	15.4	9.2	6.5
ALL AREAS:		21.6	15.4	9.8	6.5

* Other roles chosen in these areas.

TABLE 5

MOST FREQUENTLY GIVEN REASONS FOR SELECTING ADVICE LEADERS
BY LOCALITY AREAS, GROUPED BY ECONOMIC TYPE

Economic Area	Locality Area Number	Does Things For Others	Helps Followers	General Admiration	Man of Character	Man of People	Man of Strength	Position He Has Attained	Competence
Upper:									
	2	—	5.9%	23.6%	23.6%	—	11.8%	5.9%	—
Upper Middle:									
	3	—	—	—	24.9	—	41.5	—	—
	4	—	—	40.0	10.0	10.0%	10.0	24.9	—
	10	4.8%	2.4	24.0	7.2	2.4	24.0	20.0	9.6%
	13	12.3	8.2	16.4	4.1	—	12.3	4.1	8.2
	22	—	—	12.9	4.3	8.6	8.6	12.9	8.6
	24	—	7.7	7.7	—	—	15.4	15.4	7.7
Lower Middle:									
	6	—	10.0	30.0	—	—	30.0	20.0	10.0
	8	—	7.6	41.8	—	—	15.2	—	—
	11	—	9.6	28.8	—	9.6	9.6	4.8	9.6
	12	—	19.8	10.8	—	5.4	10.8	12.6	16.2
	14	—	8.6	34.4	4.3	4.3	12.9	—	8.6
	15	—	8.0	16.0	32.0	8.0	12.0	—	8.6
	17	—	5.0	35.0	4.8	5.0	—	25.0	—
	19	—	9.6	43.2	4.8	—	9.6	4.8	4.8
	20	—	—	53.9	15.4	7.7	—	23.1	—
	21	5.0	35.0	20.0	—	—	10.0	—	—
	23	3.0	6.8	6.1	12.1	3.0	21.2	27.3	3.0
Lower:									
	1	—	20.5	12.3	28.7	8.2	12.3	8.2	4.1
	5	—	6.6	13.2	—	6.6	19.8	13.2	6.6
	7	—	11.8	17.7	5.9	—	23.6	17.7	5.9
	9	—	15.6	20.8	10.4	5.2	5.2	—	15.6
	16	5.2	13.0	15.6	2.6	—	18.2	23.4	2.6
	25	3.5	36.8	14.0	10.5	1.8	5.3	14.0	3.5

3. The longer the average residence within a locality area the greater the possibility that a leader will be a resident of the area.
4. The incidence of leadership being found beyond an eight-block limit is lowest (in fact, completely absent) in areas of brief and of lengthy residence.

· RELIGION

The assumption that religious identification may also be a factor in leadership nomination may be tested by the selection behavior indicated in eight locality areas having distinctive types of religious affiliation. Upper-middle and lower-middle class Jewish neighborhoods tend to nominate a leader more frequently than Catholic neighborhoods of the lowest economic groups, while Protestant localities reveal the city's highest incidence of nominations. However, if a Catholic locality nominates a single leader he is more likely to be a resident of that four-block area, than is the leader nominated in a Jewish area or a Protestant locality. Furthermore, in the Protestant locality one is more likely to find the leader operating in a political role than in either of the other religious groupings. (See Table 7.)

RACIAL CHARACTERISTICS

This religious classification is not a sufficient index to the selection behavior of an area. When locality areas are classified on

TABLE 6

DISTRIBUTION OF LEADERSHIP NOMINATION AND RESIDENCE BY AVERAGE LENGTH OF RESPONDENTS' RESIDENCE IN AREA

Locality Areas by Years of Residence	Per Cent of Respondents Nominating Leaders	Per Cent Nominations Residing:		
		Within Locality	Within 8 Blocks	Beyond 8 Blocks
Under Five Years:				
3	22.5%	45.5%	54.5%	—
Five to Nine Years:	44.6	34.7	48.3	6.0%
2	32.5	43.0	57.0	—
4	20.0	60.0	10.0	—
5	25.0	57.0	43.0	—
10	70.0	23.0	54.0	15.0
12	75.0	45.0	30.0	10.0
13	45.0	0.0	92.0	8.0
14	42.5	19.0	50.0	6.0
16	62.5	41.0	59.0	—
19	50.0	28.5	71.5	—
20	30.0	14.0	36.0	21.0
21	37.5	40.0	60.0	—
23	62.5	16.5	58.0	9.0
24	27.5	64.0	27.0	9.0
Ten to Fourteen Years:	47.6	40.5	44.3	6.8
6	23.0	37.5	50.0	12.5
17	32.5	67.0	33.0	—
25	87.5	17.0	50.0	8.0
Fifteen Years and Over:	49.2	56.0	44.0	—
1	47.5	44.0	56.0	—
9	47.5	75.0	25.0	—
15	52.5	50.0	50.0	—
ALL AREAS:	41.5	43.1	49.4	3.0

the basis of their dominant ethnic and/or racial characteristics, the following observations appear pertinent (Table 8):

1. Locality areas of mixed nationalities or of heavy foreign stock concentration and areas of native-white Gentile populations tend to nominate few leaders.
2. Areas of high leadership nomination are those areas having predominant Jewish, Negro, and Negro-white populations.
3. The general leadership pattern for these areas is political, the only variation being found in the areas of Jewish concentration.
4. There is the greatest acceptance of a generalized leadership or willingness to judge one man as "good" for a variety of situations in Negro and upper-middle class Jewish areas.

5. There is a general tendency for leaders to live beyond the four-block but within the four-eight block locality area. This fact is especially pertinent for areas of high Jewish, Negro and Negro-white residence.
6. With the exception of those areas having a high incidence of Jews in the population, all minority areas have a relatively high authoritarian-equalitarian score and a relatively low score of participation in social organizations.

PROXIMITY OF LEADERS TO FOLLOWERS

One other exploration may be made at this point. What selection behavior is indicated when areas are grouped on the basis of leader residence? Does the presence of

TABLE 7

LEADERSHIP NOMINATIONS BY RELIGIOUS AFFILIATION CHARACTERISTICS
OF SELECTED LOCALITY AREAS

Locality Areas by Dominant Religious Characteristics	Economic Type	Per Cent of Respondents Nominating Leader	Role of Person Nominated as Leader	Major Reason for Selection
Catholic:				
1	L	47.5%	Lawyer	Man of Character
5	L	25.0	Politician	Man of Strength
Jewish:				
10	UM	70.0	Rabbi	Man of Strength
23	LM	62.5	Businessman	Position Accomplished
Protestant:				
12	LM	75.0	Minister	Helps People
13	LM	45.0	Politician	General Admiration
16	L	62.5	Politician	Political Person
25	L	87.5	Politician	Political Person
ALL AREAS:	—	44.0	—	—

TABLE 8

LEADERSHIP NOMINATIONS BY ETHNIC-RACIAL CHARACTERISTICS OF SELECTED LOCALITY AREAS

Locality Area	Dominant Ethnic Racial Characteristic of Population	Per Cent of Respondents Nominating Leader	Per Cent of Leaders Nominated Living Within Area	Role of Person Nominated as Leader	Major Reason for Selection	A-E Score	Social Participation Score	Per Cent Having High School or More Education
	Native Born:							
17	White	35.0%	67.0%	Politician	General Admiration	4.2%	2.5%	37.0%
16	Negro	62.5	41.0	Politician	Position	4.3	4.7	72.0
25	White and Negro	87.5	17.0	Politician	Helps People	4.9	4.4	40.0
10	Jewish	70.0	23.0	Rabbi	Helps People	3.4	5.9	80.0
	Foreign and Native Born:							
7	White, Mixed	33.0	67.0	Politician	"Strength"	4.3	2.5	42.0
	Foreign Born:							
1	Italian	47.5	44.0	Lawyer	"Character"	4.4	3.0	48.0
5	Polish	25.0	57.0	Politician	"Strength"	3.9	4.0	60.0
11	Italian	37.5	47.0	Politician	General Admiration	4.3	3.4	68.0
23	Russian, Jewish	62.5	16.5	Businessman	Position	3.5	6.3	67.0

the leader within the locality seem to have any relationship to the ability to nominate a particular person or role?

It may be reasonably concluded from Table 9 that more than 90 per cent of the effective leadership in the average locality area can be found within an area of eight blocks, and that, except in unusual cases, effective area leadership is not found beyond that limit. It may also be concluded that the poorer the economic area the greater the number of leadership nominations, and the greater the leadership competition. In fact, in no one area can any leader claim to have the informal or unstructured support of a majority of people in that locality.

The ability to nominate a leader increases as the locality area is increased from four blocks to one of four to eight blocks. The nominations of one leader only, however, increase as the area is widened to eight blocks, but decrease beyond the limit. Finally, the larger the area, the greater the possibility of multiple nominations.

A clue to the nature of small locality area leadership selection is found in the choices of the several groupings. The four-block locality area tends to choose the political leader. The eight-block areas tend to be more diverse in their choices, selecting political leaders in six of the eleven areas. In the nine areas selecting leaders beyond the eight-block limit the political leader was chosen in four and other leaders—religious, professional and business—in the remaining five.

THE POLITICAL LEADER AS A COHESIVE FORCE

Certainly no final and ultimate conclusions are permitted by this exploratory and tentative analysis of the leadership nomination and acceptance behavior of people residing within given locality areas. We may be able to understand, however, some of the factors that permit the modern urban community to maintain some semblance of organic unity within the small locality areas, sometimes

called neighborhoods. The key to this understanding is found in determining what the urbanite John Doe does when he wants to get something done in his living area. To whom does he go? For what reasons? Are the steps he takes at such times related to his interpretation of who is a leader in his vicinity?

The "leader" as nominated provides a clue to the nature and reality of the "togetherness" of the modern city and its sub-areas. It is true that the facile functioning of the leadership process remains fugitive and fanciful from an analytical point of view. We know that leadership not only exists, but that to a greater extent than in any other person or role, it is the work of the politician, the political leader, the committeeman, that provides the over-all locality area unity. While it is not always certain that the urban person's need for action leadership can be met within the given locality area, the evidence consistently indicates that when and where such leadership is available the political person is likely to be the first choice of the area's residents. He gets done the things that people want done in ways that appeal to them as individuals. He is the city's foremost provincial. Furthermore, he is the choice not of a particular economic class but of all classes save those in the areas of highest education and highest economic attainment. And though one might expect such a situation to give rise to local "bossism" or monopolistic leadership, the data indicate that in none of the areas, regardless of the racial, religious, ethnic or social composition does the selection of the political leader as a first choice reveal a monopoly of the area's leadership control.

Equally as revealing is the heavy incidence of absentee-leadership in the small or four-block locality area. The impersonal nature of modern living is revealed by this fact and by the relatively low incidence of organizational membership among persons of all classes in all areas. Political leadership, asking no fees for its services, and no special activity from its recipients save at long-time

TABLE 9
LEADER NOMINATIONS BY LEADER RESIDENCE AND ROLE

Area	No Nomination	One Nomination	Two or More Nominations	Role of First Leader Choice	Role of Second Leader Choice	Economic Type of Area
Fifty per cent or more of leaders within locality area	65.6%	19.3%	14.3%			
4	80.0	10.0	10.0	Politician	NSR*	UM
24	72.0	15.0	12.5	Businessman	Welfare Worker	UM
8	47.5	25.0	27.5	Politician	Welfare Worker	LM
9	52.5	25.0	22.5	Politician	None	L
17	65.0	20.0	12.5	Politician	Welfare Worker	LM
5	75.0	22.5	2.5	Politician	Businessman	L
7	67.5	17.5	12.5	Politician	None	L
Fifty per cent or more of leaders within eight-block area	52.7	25.5	20.9			
2	67.5	20.0	12.5	Physician	Politician	U
3	77.5	65.0	7.5	Lawyer	Politician	UM
6	77.0	18.0	5.0	Politician	None	LM
14	57.5	25.0	17.5	Welfare Worker	Businessman	LM
15	47.5	40.0	12.5	Politician	Welfare Worker	LM
19	50.0	30.0	20.0	Politician	Welfare Worker	LM
21	62.5	25.0	12.5	Politician	Teacher	LM
23	37.5	32.5	30.0	Businessman	Politician	LM
1	52.5	37.5	10.0	Lawyer	Lawyer	L
16	37.5	25.0	37.5	Politician	Minister	L
25	12.5	22.5	65.0	Politician	Minister	L
Some leaders beyond eight-block area	48.6	22.8	28.6			
10	30.0	25.0	45.0	Rabbi	NSR	UM
13	55.0	27.5	17.5	Politician	Welfare Worker	UM
24	72.5	15.0	12.5	Businessman	Welfare Worker	UM
6	77.0	18.0	5.0	Politician	None	LM
12	25.0	15.0	60.0	Minister	Politician	LM
14	57.5	25.0	17.5	Welfare Worker	Businessman	LM
20	70.0	25.0	5.0	Politician	Welfare Worker	LM
23	37.5	32.5	30.0	Businessman	Politician	LM
25	12.5	22.5	65.0	Politician	Minister	L

* NSR—Non-structured role.

intervals, suggests a chain of symbolic if not actual "togetherness" which more than any other phenomenon seems to provide a substitute for the rapidly vanishing neighborhood spirit. As one respondent expressed the situation, "The committeeman can get us what we want and need when we want and need it. He'll ask few favors from you, charge you nothing and will keep his mouth shut." Urban dwellers seem to expect little more.

The obvious leadership nakedness of the small urban locality area coupled with the respondents' expressed desire for leadership of strength, position, competence and ability to "get things done," reveals a major weakness in the social organization of the modern urban community. Leaders are nominated most and known best in those areas where economic conditions are poorest and where the bonds of association appear to be closely identified with the group status that we currently label "the minorities." Further knowledge of the leader's role, his attitudes towards the followers, and the methods through which he exerts his influence appears necessary for an understanding of the ways in which cohesion and unity may be obtained and maintained in the modern community of nigh-dwellers.

SOME SOCIOLOGICAL IMPLICATIONS

Many theories and interpretations of modern community life have been based upon the assumption that the core of urban social organization was a loosely-defined and vaguely interpreted area called the neighborhood. Within each such area, however, is a sub-area of quantitative definition with well-defined boundaries where people live in close physical proximity. This is the block. A combination of four juxtaposed blocks, judgmentally selected, became, for this analysis, *a locality area*. The basic characteristics of the block and the locality area are (1) the propinquity or relative geographical nearness of its residents, and (2) the social distance or status position of the area's inhabitants in relation to one another, and in relation to other areas and their inhabitants.

These two characteristics and the actions and reactions which they induce are basic determinants of the organization and function of group behavior in the area. The question of nearness or nigh-dwelling is an important factor in the analysis of any communication process or the behavior attending it. The physical structure of the urban community and its residential accommodations tend to attract within specific block areas residents with specific types of social characteristics. These residents are most frequently persons who can afford the prices charged for ownership or rental of these properties. The ability to pay the prices charged is related to the income principle underlying economic status in our society. The economic class concerned is reputed to act in a particular set of ways, to have a particular type of need and desire, and to give a particular type of response to a specific situation.

For the purposes of this study the authors assumed that the leadership principle and leadership roles are related to the economic character of an urban area, its racial and/or ethnic composition, the length of residence of the area's inhabitants, and the general unstructured social and cultural traits of the residents. We also assumed that the leadership situation develops around certain values and interests which people hold dear, and that these values and interests are represented in part in the basic spatial structurings of the modern urban community. In this study, we associate leadership with the individual's adaptation to the local environment, assuming that the leaders are selected on rational grounds that may not always be revealed in or by the studies of organizations and office-holding in the locality. Our pivotal problem was that of discovering the factors which may be correlated with leadership nomination and acceptance, or which may enable a leader to emerge and to assemble a following in a given area.

We believe that the data presented here lend additional support to the thesis that the intimacy of the modern urban community as indicated in the human behavior of what we have uncritically called the "neighbor-hood" has been broken up by the growth of an intricate mesh of contacts wider than those of the family, play group, and small area activities. As a cohesive economic and social unit this "neighborhood" has declined greatly in importance, having succumbed to the wider spatial distribution of social relations.

In place of the close and congenial contacts which were the alleged characteristics of the neighborhood, there has developed a series of less intimate, less permanent and often more superficial relations which have increased the geographical and social range of the individual's life. With new and more choices, the urban person is no longer dependent on geographically near people with reference to work and play. Orientation in personal relations and social activities may take place more in terms of place of work than in block of residence. The shop steward, for example, may find his social rela-tions with his fellow workers in his shop, and his associational interests in terms of "the job" rather than in terms of "the house." In fact, this leadership may be more meaningful to the worker in the plant than the influence of any neighbor the worker might have. Furthermore, with the increase of residential mobility, transit facilities, and the variety of voluntary associations to which one may belong, the place and area of residence become one of night-sleeping-occupancy and the only relatively fixed point in the urban existence.

Gone are the emotional ties of the old neighborhood and its people. Gone too are the strong bonds knit by the corner grocer who gave credit, the teacher, the preacher, the physician who serviced the community needs. In place of a community of people once known as a neighborhood has arisen a free-floating mass of individuals having common residence, but lacking the over-all relationship that once was meaningful.

PART FOUR

Dynamics of Opinion Formation and Change

·8·

The Nature of Propaganda and the Propagandist

THE AIMS OF POLITICAL PROPAGANDA

PORTRAIT OF THE AMERICAN AGITATOR

PROPAGANDA TECHNIQUES IN INSTITUTIONAL ADVERTISING

THE DIMENSIONS OF PROPAGANDA: GERMAN SHORT-WAVE BROADCASTS
TO AMERICA

THE AIMS OF POLITICAL PROPAGANDA

F. C. BARTLETT

To-day propaganda is in the air and on it. There is no escaping from its insistent voice. Even were it only half as effective as it is often claimed to be its power would be enormous. It is said to be able to determine the behaviour of the most obscure citizen, and at the same time to settle the destinies of the great nations. It is at work to fashion the education of the child, the ambitions of youth, the activities of the prime of life, and it pursues the aged to the grave. It has no respect for times, or seasons, or topics.

It is not at all easy to be sure what this tremendous growth of propaganda in the contemporary world signifies, whether it is a passing phase or something deep and permanent. Sometimes it seems as if the august nations of the world have become for the time like little boys at school who make horrid faces at one another and shout resounding threats. Then again it seems as if behind all the tumult and the show there lies some obscure admission that the final forces which move the world of men are those powers which together make the human mind, powers which ambitious people, now more than ever, must know how to move to their own purposes, but which all the world is still strangely reluctant to study seriously.

Whatever the inordinately rapid growth of propaganda may signify, the main reasons for it are clear and certain enough. It springs fundamentally from those two closely related movements which are responsible for most of the perplexities of modern civilisation: the increasingly effective contact of social groups, and the rapid spread of popular education.

Only a short time ago social groups distant from one another in space had relatively clumsy and slow means of intercommunication. The leaders of one group could shape their internal policy with very little anxious and immediate consideration of the reactions which a change in that policy might produce in other groups. To-day it is not news only that flashes swiftly from end to end of the whole world. People, the elements of culture, the media of economic existence, ideas—all these can move with a freedom never before matched in history. And since it is contact with things that are different that is beyond anything else the stimulant for change in human affairs, it has become vitally necessary for the leaders of all the great groups somehow to try to get control of the chief means of expanding contact and to use these to further their own ambition.

For this great growth of rapid exchange between one social group and another modern applied science is primarily responsible. The development of swift and easy forms of locomotion, the rise of a popular Press, the invention and universal use of

Reprinted from F. C. Bartlett, *Political Propaganda*, pp. 1-22, by permission of the author and publisher. (Copyright, 1940, Cambridge University Press, London.)

the cinema, of wireless and of television, mean that no group can live to itself, or be left alone to die.

Perhaps more important still these and all the other inventions which facilitate swift and effective intercommunication are not merely toys or weapons for the favoured few. Most of them are already available to all, and more become available year by year. The enormous development of popular education in all the social groups of the modern world has increased beyond count the number of persons in every group who can and do take immediate advantage of the extending means of intercommunication. The barriers which the course of history and the ingenuity of man have built between group and group are threatened with destruction. A policy which formerly needed to be explained only to the few, and their assent gained before action, now must win the active support of the many. A precipitate action must now be explained and justified at once to the most distant peoples, because the news of it will spread and its repercussions will be as wide and almost as quick as the travel of the news.

Even were the growth of popular education uniform throughout the world, the social perplexities which would arise would be tremendous. When as is the case, the rising tide of education flows rapidly in one region, slowly in another, with all kinds of temporary set-backs and delays, and with occasional localised spectacular advances, it is no wonder that the complex difficulties produced often seem as if they must baffle all attempts at solution.

The rapid development of effective contact between different groups in contemporary society means that no important political, economic or other cultural change can take place anywhere which will not swiftly be treated as affecting the destinies of distant groups. The rise of popular education means that any major political, economic or other cultural change must be explained, or justified, to an ever-increasing number of people. These two movements together provide the setting and the fundamental conditions which have led to a terrific outburst of political propaganda.

Naturally they are not the only conditions. It so happens, for example, that just at a time when wide social contacts are more effective than ever before, and when more people than ever before are being trained to take an interest in and become vocal about social, political, and economic changes, the power to effect such changes has apparently, in several quarters, become concentrated in the hands of small groups, or of individuals. And it is these small dictator groups, or dictator individuals, who mainly have developed modern political propaganda. For there is this difference at least between the tyrant of the ancient world and the dictator of to-day, that the tyrant, in his relatively small and isolated group, could, within limits, do as he pleased and "damn the consequences." The modern dictator, holding the destinies of very large groups, and having to work in a most intricate pattern of threads of connexion between his own group and others, is forced to appeal for wide public approval and openly to try to justify what his private ambition prompts him to do. Nevertheless the basic conditions for the political propaganda of to-day, which give it its peculiar characteristics and make it a vital concern of every large State, no matter what its political constitution, are these two: the increasing contact of differently organised social groups, and the spread of popular education.

Practically everybody agrees that propaganda must be defined by reference to its aims. Those aims can, in fact, be stated simply. Propaganda is an attempt to influence opinion and conduct—especially social opinion and conduct—in such a manner that the persons who adopt the opinions and behavior indicated do so without themselves making any definite search for reasons. Although the spread of education is one of the primary conditions from which political propaganda has sprung, yet the aims of the latter are different from those of the former and may be sharply opposed to them.

Education also is an attempt to influence and control thinking and conduct, but to do so in such a manner that the persons who think and act are stimulated to seek to understand for themselves why they do what they do. It goes without saying that much of what appears in every public system of education takes a form more appropriate to the aims of propaganda. Indeed it must be so, because general actions have to be taken and opinions adopted before intelligence can be sufficiently developed to worry much about reasons. Whether in the case of the individual or of the social group, the early stages of education must come very near to the characteristic forms of propaganda. But there is a vital distinction between a propaganda which is designed to fix people forever at its own level, and a propaganda which is designed to lead those to whom it is directed through the necessary preliminary steps to education.

Apart from this, there are strong reasons why no modern State can afford to neglect political propaganda. As has been indicated already, however self-contained a State may set out to be as regards its internal policy, it cannot possibly escape external relations with other States more or less on a level with itself. The practical questions which arise as a result are often of extreme urgency, and cannot wait until the very large numbers of people who are naturally interested in them have had time to appreciate and weigh up the reasons for them. The leaders of a State are frequently forced somewhat hurriedly to adopt a policy which affects the interests of their own immediate followers and of the members of other States. They must justify this policy after the decision and must do so publicly. Actually the political propaganda of contemporary life is generally first developed by the State, within that State, for its own inhabitants. There is nothing surprising in this since, for reasons which will become clear later in the present discussion, internal propaganda is definitely easier than external, especially for highly self-contained States. Nevertheless external propaganda is probably of greater importance to every large group in modern society, and its neglect may run any such group into serious peril.

Whether propaganda is used as a first-aid to education in a relatively backward community, whether it takes the form of a suggestive statement of policy addressed to other groups of a similar level of culture, or whether it is an organised effort to produce uniformity of opinion and conduct throughout the membership of the group itself, it should be regarded as an episode, a temporary necessary expedient. If it develops into a hardened institution, contaminating the flow and usurping the place of genuine education, it does so because there are forces at work trying to keep the mass of the people addressed permanently in the position of infants in arms.

This is precisely what occurs whenever political propaganda becomes a weapon to be used by the single dominant Party in the totalitarian State. Within any such State, therefore, when propaganda develops vigorously, there is always a huge implied gap between those who control publicity, and those whom they attempt to control by its means. To a superficial view the gap may not appear at all, but it is there, a possible line of disastrous division. It is one of the curious things about human society that, where potentialities of division are very numerous, the possibility of serious splitting may be at a minimum, but where possible lines of division are few, the group may be in serious danger of radical deterioration. For when potentialities of division are numerous, if a split occurs it is likely to affect individuals or small groups of individuals only, leaving the general society not much upset. But where there are one or two simple lines of possible cleavage, any actual division works disaster to the whole group.

Political propaganda used by the single Party must address large masses of people and attempt to move them to uniformity of opinion and of action. Since the great aim is to get results, and not at all to promote or stimulate understanding of the results, the more whole-hearted and single-minded the propagandist is, the more his methods make it plain that he thinks that the individuals with whom he has to deal are a very poor lot, and especially that they are, and should stay, at a low level of intellectual development. It is true that one of the tricks of his procedure is to tell them that they are much better than other people. The fact remains that the whole implication of his method of appeal is that he arrogates to himself a superiority which he permanently and finally denies to others. He pretends that he alone can think constructively; that he has the finer feelings; that his is the responsibility of decision and others have only the right and obligation of acceptance. Between him and his public, wherever it may be and however it may be made up, there is a great gulf fixed, and the widest part of that gulf— it is implied—marks a difference of intelligence. This is the claim, sometimes loudly asserted, but always present.

Nobody needs to go far with psychology in order to learn that the people who make a great parade of their superiority very rarely are actually superior. They may be, but as a general rule the repeated assertion of superiority springs from a deep and only imperfectly realised suspicion that others are, in fact, better equipped, particularly in those very directions in which the greatest superiority is most emphatically claimed. Especially is this true when intelligence is the quality upon which stress is laid. The intelligent man and group are the first to recognise and to stimulate the intelligence of others. It is now clear enough that the distribution of intelligence is not markedly variable in any large group taken at random anywhere throughout the civilised world, and it is wildly improbable that any small group, not selected primarily and specifically for intelligence, should be, in fact, supreme in brain power. In particular there is so far no political directing group anywhere which has been selected chiefly on a basis of intelligence, and there probably never can be, since in such a group, other qualities, such as rapidity of decision, leadership, public spirit and a liking for responsibility, are at least equally important. If therefore propaganda is regarded as itself a final and complete activity, and not as a mere introduction to some public manner of training people to think, the assumption of superior intelligence inevitably made by its directors must sooner or later be discovered by others to be unfounded and a sham.

Lying behind all this, however, is an even more fundamental mistake. It is that social stability depends upon uniformity of thought and action. This is a vulgar and a vital error, though it is one which politicians of all times and places seem naturally prone to make. The modern director of single Party political propaganda adopts without reserve that old slogan, propounded in this country many years ago, in a period of great social upheaval, by Edmund Burke: Ability is the enemy of Stability. Both of them mean by this, ability in the mass of the people, not in themselves. They think that intelligence, restless and widespread, means equally widespread criticism, the weakening of loyalties and accumulating tendencies to social disintegration. But the modern propagandist in public affairs is far less honest about his slogan than was Burke, who made it perfectly plain that he wanted political direction to remain in the hands of the few, and was willing and anxious that these should be selected specifically for their intelligence. The typical modern director of political propaganda has to pretend that his aim is to combine all people in a concern for public affairs, and to secure their active co-operation. He is therefore forced to say "If we can get all people to act, think and feel alike then, and then only, will our group be stable, persistent in the face of shock, and permanent."

This contention is directly opposed to the very basis upon which the modern nation group is built. The integrity and power of every large contemporary social group are founded upon an increasing specialisation of function on the part of its members. It is true that society has got into all kinds of muddles, because it has adopted this principle of growth without any clear-sighted recognition of its implications, so that in all directions disastrous discrepancies are to be seen between actual abilities and the functions that are demanded of them. The fact remains that every step in the development of modern society demands yet finer, more informed, more balanced specialisation. That this is possible and necessary, while yet each large group is able to maintain and strengthen its own character, is due to two simple and incontrovertible psychological facts: first that human beings differ profoundly from one another in their psychological and sociological endowment, and second that these differences are complementary.

It could be urged, perhaps, that the specialisations which are the life-process of advancing civilisation all concern how people are to act and not how they are to think. They have to do with technical skills, with industrial processes and commercial activities, and not very much with ideas, beliefs, theories. Any such division of human functions is psychologically unsound. People cannot be forever urged to increasing specialisation in certain departments of life, and kept on a dull level of uniformity in others. This is especially impossible when ideas and beliefs about political and social affairs are concerned. The specialisation of technical and industrial skills, in the long run, both push up the general standard of life and increase the general leisure. Then nothing on earth, except the sternest repressive measures—and even these for a short time only—can prevent that diversity which is the key to progress in one realm from spreading also to others.

Any form of propaganda based, as most totalitarian propaganda is, upon a contemptuous idea of the common intelligence and upon a belief in the virtues of uniformity of ideas and feeling, is doomed to ultimate collapse, for it is opposed to the most fundamental of all the characteristics of human development.

The fact that political propaganda, as it has often been shaped, aims, either wittingly or unwittingly, at producing whole nation groups in which all individuals think, act and feel alike, has profound consequences. For this aim can be realised only in so far as the population concerned can be guarded from other influences. A successful propaganda of this type carries with it a dominant and stringent censorship. Further, since the demand is that people should adopt a uniform outlook, not for a short time only, but be fixed in it as permanently as possible, organised political propaganda must invade the proper field of education, and try to influence the young even more drastically than the middle-aged and the old.

Further, to produce the kind of uniformity required, the great bulk of the members of a group must be given an overwhelming confidence in their own social order, and far and away the easiest and most effective manner of doing this is to induce in them an antagonistically critical reaction to all other social orders. The directors of a rigid system of political propaganda do not often, save in their more incautious moments, admit that their aim is war. But the truth is that the more successful they are within their own community, the more nearly do they bring that community into the state in which war is practically inevitable.

All that has been said up to now has direct application to the greater part of political propaganda in the modern dictator State. But, for many reasons, the more democratic countries cannot afford to neglect political propaganda. The dictator State, being organised in the main by an unbridled desire for power, will not leave the democratic countries alone, and this demands various forms of counter-propaganda. Also any world that harbours dictators is a world that hurtles from crisis to crisis, each of which necessitates rapid decisions. Most political decisions are, in the nature of the case, simply forced to rush ahead of fully considered and analysed reasons, to adopt practices in advance of anything like complete evidence. The practices, nowadays, must be given an open and public justification. Moreover the public character of most modern propaganda means that in every democratic country there will be large numbers of people who will read and hear totalitarian propaganda, for they cannot be forcibly prevented from this, as they would be in the dictator State. Some public answer must then be organised. Finally, if the concealed, but nevertheless real, trend of single Party political propaganda becomes realised and war results, for all kinds of reasons which are too obvious to need stating, all the large groups of the world that are drawn in must use methods of public propaganda.

At the same time, it is equally true to say that at present political propaganda in all the democratic countries is in a relatively backward and undeveloped state. Nobody seems yet to have decided just what it should aim at, or how it should pursue its aims.

What is a democracy? To this question all kinds of answers can be given. From the present point of view, however, one consideration overrides all others. In the modern world, political propaganda may be said to have been adopted as a weapon of State, but very nearly everywhere it has been developed as the tool of a single political party within the State. This is precisely what cannot happen, except in an incomplete way, in a democratic country. A democracy differs from every other form of government in that it must always contain at least two main parties, each treating the other with a very considerable degree of tolerance. Although each party may develop its own political propaganda, neither can violently suppress that of the other without destroying the spirit of democracy itself.

If a period of very great and general public stress should develop—and the most extreme case of this is war—the party which is temporarily in power must organise centralised propaganda, and with this, inevitably, will go a kind of official censorship, though the precise form of a censorship that is consistent with a democracy is difficult to determine. At the same time, within the centralised form of propaganda the two party voices—usually nowadays

there are many more—will still be heard. There may be complete agreement as regards the main practical issues that are at stake, but there will still be differences in the direction of approach to the settlement of these issues, and these differences must continue to be more or less freely expressed in public.

Such a state of affairs passes the comprehension of the dictator propagandist and of his satellites, and appears to them to be mere weakness. For it demands both an intelligence and a power of forbearance in the general population which they do not desire and do not believe to be possible.

When there is no great state of public stress, a democratic country will look upon all forms of public propaganda, whether political or not, as chiefly a concern of sectional interests, of particular parties, or sects, of charitable organisations, of business and commercial enterprise. Also a democracy considers it normal not to live in a state of boiling public excitement, but in a totalitarian State constant public excitement is needed to help to prevent diversity of views.

The best way of seeing what propaganda can be in a democratic State is to look briefly at the character and aims of advertising. An advertiser, if he is to be successful, must recognise very fully that many other agencies will probably set to work at the same time as himself, using exactly the same methods as his, to induce just the same people to buy products different from those in which he is himself directly interested. Even when a virtual monopoly has been secured, the advertiser cannot go all the lengths of the single Party political propagandist, though he is likely to go as far as ever he can. He is cramped, not because his final aims are very different, but mainly because there still remain competing bodies whom he cannot crush out of existence by some method additional to that of his propaganda.

It would be extremely interesting to take the popular advertisements of twenty or thirty years ago and compare them with those of to-day. Current advertisements would probably be found to be much more dramatic, more pictorial, and more amusing, to match their wider appeal; and at the same time either more indirect, demanding for their interpretation a rather swift and alert intelligence, or, if they remain on a level of straight description, more technical, requiring a higher standard of specialised knowledge. Crude as they still are in many ways, on balance it seems certain that they are all the time becoming more intellectually interesting.

In fact, the general line of advertisement development could hardly be other than this. For what makes a man think for himself, in a critical kind of way, more than anything else, is that he should have a lot of different courses of action all thrust upon him at the same time, or in rapid succession, each of them being persuasively presented as the best, or the most desirable, or the most reasonable. Under such circumstances no doubt he can, if he likes, and if circumstances allow, try first one course and then another in a hit-or-miss kind of way. But that takes more time than most people can spare, and for a variety of reasons is not very satisfactory. Sooner or later the ordinary person is pretty well bound to try to look fairly at the different possible lines of action and then decide for himself. In deciding he can be swayed by various influences, but he is at least on the way to thinking things out independently. Thus, people who are concerned in an advertising campaign, meant to whip up the sales of any particular product, knowing well that it is extremely likely that other people will launch an overlapping campaign to whip up the sales of a competing product of the same general type, had better reflect that this is the kind of situation that is very liable to start people thinking for themselves. The thinking may be delayed for a long time, but it will be the eventual issue. In the long run this must powerfully shape the course and the content of advertising.

Now when a democratic group establishes central propaganda for political or social purposes, the director of the propaganda has to set himself to do what the advertiser does willy-nilly. He knows that other voices besides his own are going to be heard by the public, speaking on the same questions, but probably not to the same effect. He knows that if he is going to play according to the rules of the game, in his own State he cannot put a gag upon these other mouths, or that anyhow he cannot go very far in this direction. Therefore he must so shape his propaganda that people will take it, sift it, choose for themselves to follow his line, and all the while remain as intellectually alert as they are able.

Clearly this means that the contradiction which is inherent between propaganda and education is sharpest of all in a democracy, and that the democratic director of propaganda has a singularly difficult job. Many people ignore this and yet at the same time, by becoming violently critical, exemplify it. They do not bother to think how very simple and direct the aims of political propaganda in the dictator State are—the "submission of the masses."[1] They do not consider how complex and roundabout are the methods that a democracy must use in order to achieve, at one and the same time, individual initiative and social control. Beyond doubt every style of group government that has ever been tried has its own particular excellencies and failings. One method, however, need not become a better one if it imitates the excellencies of another; it may merely become different from what it was. Those people, for instance, who urge that England should learn from some dictator State, not only that propaganda ought to be organised, but also how it should be expressed, are not putting the case for a better or a more efficient England. They are demanding that in this respect England should simply cease to be England.

The problem must be fairly faced. Public propaganda does not change its character as it shifts its locality. Everywhere and

[1] From a statement by Dr. Goebbels, German Minister of Propaganda, quoted from Albig: *Public Opinion*, p. 316.

always it is an attempt to shape common opinion, feeling and action without regard for reasons. It may itself be so devised that it becomes an effort to establish final and irresistible barriers against even the eventual emergence of reasons, in so far as these must be set before, or considered by, the common man. Or, again, it may be so directed that it becomes one of the influences which are designed to lead to the eventual emergence of reasons, available for free consideration by the greatest possible number of people, and to be used consciously for the control and direction of decisions. In the former case propaganda is an enemy of education; in the latter it becomes one of the aids to education. If propaganda breaks down in the former case —and everybody who has any belief in the inescapable onward march of the human intelligence must be convinced that it will —it is most likely to be followed by a period of social anarchy. In the latter case it carries the seeds of its own decay, and must pass when the time has come. But it will pass easily and in an orderly manner. It is like the props and supports which the infant uses as he is learning to walk; but then, when his muscles have grown firmer and the nervous tissues and their connexions are ready, he discards his props and goes firmly by himself where he pleases.

PORTRAIT OF THE AMERICAN AGITATOR

LEO LOWENTHAL AND NORBERT GUTERMAN

The reformer or the revolutionary translates complaints into objective issues, presumably solvable by collective action. The agitator converts complaints not into an issue for action against one or another symbol of authority, but into a theme eliciting the destructive impulses of his public.

Nobody is thinking of agitators right now. The American agitator is not at present at the center of political attention. Some agitators have, however, occasionally come fairly close to the national political scene. Acting on the assumption that America was nearing a grave crisis, they have tried to build mass movements—with most notable success during the years of the New Deal and shortly before America's entry into the war. Charles E. Coughlin managed to draw several million radio listeners; Gerald L. K. Smith amassed over 100,000 votes. But by and large these have been the exceptions.

Far more numerous are those less conspicuous agitators who are active locally and who, far from evoking the image of a leader worshipped by masses of followers, rather suggest quack medicine salesmen. Their activity has many characteristics of a psychological racket: they play on vague fears or expectations of a radical change. Some of these agitators hardly seem to take their own ideas seriously, and it is likely that their aim is merely to make a living

From the *Public Opinion Quarterly*, 1948, 12, 417-429. Reprinted by permission of the authors and the publisher.

by publishing a paper or holding meetings. What they give their admission-paying audience is a kind of act—something between a tragic recital and a clownish pantomime—rather than a political speech. Discussion of political topics invariably serves them as an occasion for vague and violent vituperation and often seemingly irrelevant personal abuse. The line between the ambitious politician and the small-time peddler of discontent is hard to draw, for there are many intermediary types.

What is important, however, is that the American Fascist movement finds itself in a preliminary stage in which movement and racket may blend—much as was the case with Nazi agitators in the Germany of 1923 and 1924. Our purpose in this study, therefore, is to outline some of the distinguishing characteristics of the American agitator and then to examine the social and psychological factors which enable him to flourish.

WHO IS THE AGITATOR?

It is quite obvious that the agitator does not fit into the reformer type; his grievances are not circumscribed, but on the contrary take in every area of social life. Nor does he address himself to any distinct social group, as does the reformer; except for the small minority he brands as enemies, every American is his potential follower.

Yet he does not fit into the revolutionary group, either. While the discontent he articulates takes in all spheres of social life, he never suggests that in his view the causes of this discontent are inherent in and inseparable from the basic social set-up. He speaks of the violation or misappropriation of the present form of society, but he does not hold it ultimately responsible for social ills, as does the revolutionary. Indeed, the agitator is usually a defender of the status quo.

He points to enemies, groups or individuals held responsible for the bad situation, but he always suggests that what is necessary is the elimination of *people* rather than a change in political structures. Whatever political changes may be involved in

the process of getting rid of the enemy he sees as a means rather than an end. The enemy is represented as acting, so to speak, directly on his victims without the intermediary of an impersonal social form, such as capitalism is defined to be in socialist theory. For instance, although agitational literature contains frequent references to unemployment, one cannot find in it a discussion of the economic causes of unemployment. The agitator lays responsibility on an invariable set of enemies, whose evil character or sheer malice is at the bottom of social maladjustment.

Sometimes, these internationalists (a few international financiers) are not even interested in price or profit. They use their monopoly control to determine the living standards of peoples. They would rather see unemployment, closed factories and mines, and widespread poverty, if they might see the fulfillment of their own secret plans.

Unlike the reformer or revolutionary, the agitator makes no effort to trace this dissatisfaction to a clearly definable cause. The whole idea of objective cause tends to recede into the background, leaving only on one end the subjective feeling of dissatisfaction and on the other the personal enemy held responsible for it. As a result, his reference to an objective situation seems less the basis of a complaint than a pretext for a complaint rooted in other, less visible, causes.

This impression is confirmed when we observe with what facility the agitator picks up issues from current political discussions and uses them for his own purposes. Throughout the past fifteen years, despite the extraordinary changes he witnessed in American life, the agitator kept grumbling and vituperating in the same basic tone. When unemployment was of general concern, he grumbled about that; when the government instituted public works to relieve unemployment, he joined those who inveighed against boondoggling. Sensational news items supply him with occasions for branding the culprits whom he holds responsible for all social evils:

The death of General George S. Patton, Jr. remains a mystery. He was a careful driver. He admonished all who drove for him to drive carefully. He was known to be wise and cautious in traffic. He was killed by a truck that charged into him from a side road.

He opposed the Morgenthau Plan. He was against the liquidation of the German race merely because they were Germans. He refused to be dominated and bulldozed by revengeful Jews. He had promised to blow off the lid if he ever returned to the United States. Some people doubt if his death was an accident.

His imagination knows no restraint:

Do you remember a couple of years ago that a mysterious gas cloud of drifting death fell upon northern France and Belgium and floated across the channel and up the Thames even to London itself? . . .
Do you know that even in Free America at the present moment, stark and violent Death waits upon the footsteps of men who know such facts and give them effectively to the public?

While the propagandist molds existing audience predispositions into "predetermined" casts, the agitator appeals to predispositions which are still in flux; his function is to bring to flame the smoldering resentments of his listeners, to express loudly and brazenly what they whisper timidly, and to lend social sanction to actions that might otherwise seem dangerous temptations. He works, as it were, from inside the audience, stirring up what lies dormant there.

AGITATION AND SOCIAL CHANGE

Agitation may be viewed as a specific type of public activity and the agitator as a specific type of "advocate of social change" —a concept that will serve us as a convenient frame of reference.

An "advocate of social change" may be defined as follows:

The immediate cause of his activity is a social condition that a section of the population feels to be iniquitous or frustrating. This discontent he articulates by pointing out its presumed causes. He proposes to defeat the social groups held responsible for perpetuating the social condition that gives rise to discontent. Finally, he promotes a move-

ment capable of achieving this objective and he proposes himself as its leader.

When an investigator begins a study of any movement for social change, the first and most natural problem he confronts is to locate the cause of the movement in a specific condition of discontent. In most instances the solution of this problem presents no difficulties at all—in fact, the advocate of social change himself devotes a great part of his energy to articulating this cause. When we examine agitation, however, we face an entirely different situation. That the agitator wants to exploit existing discontent is obvious enough: he seems always to be addressing people who are smarting under the harshest injustice and whose patience has been strained to the breaking point. But whenever the investigator scans the texts of agitation and, on the basis of his experience in studying other kinds of social movements, tries to discover what is the discontent it articulates, he is consistently disappointed.

The difficulty is not that agitation fails to provide him with answers, but rather that it answers a question he did not ask: whenever he asks *"what,"* he is answered as if he had asked *"who."* He finds numerous vituperative and indignant references to enemies, but nowhere can he find a clearly defined objective condition from which the agitator's audience presumably suffers. At best, agitation provides the investigator with contradictory or inconsistent references to such alleged conditions. Unless we decide, as has often been done, that the agitator is simply a lunatic, we must assume that, although a sense of discontent exists, he, unlike other advocates of social change, is either unable or unwilling to state it explicitly. Hence, the agitation analyst faces the task of himself explicating the state of discontent to which the agitator refers.

A CATALOGUE OF GRIEVANCES

Even a cursory glance at agitational material shows that any attempt to analyze it by methods that help discover the purposes of the revolutionary or the reformer could lead only to an impasse. If we try to classify the agitator's complaints in terms of the simplest categories, we obtain approximately the following picture:

a) *Economic Grievances*

The agitator roams freely over every area of economic life, seeing in each the evil and iniquity he finds in all of modern existence. He may begin anywhere at all. Too much help is being extended to foreign nations: "If we have any money to offer for nothing, or to loan, or to give away, we had better give it to our own first. Of course, that is old-fashioned."

Not only are foreigners taking our money, they also threaten our jobs. "People born in America have to commit suicide because they have nothing to eat while refugees get their jobs."

Behind such injustices stand "The International Bankers, who devised and control our money system, [and] are guilty of giving us unsound money."

Such situations constitute a danger to the American way of life, for "what is more likely to follow many years of Nudeal communistic confiscatory taxation, wool-less, metal-less, auto-less regimentation and planned scarcities than our finally becoming stripped by necessity to Nudism?"

b) *Political Grievances*

International commitments by the U. S. government jeopardize political liberties. "Like Russia, the United States is suffering from the scourge of internationalism." The American people are warned: "Be not duped by the internationalists who dwell amongst us."

Of course it is only reasonable that "treaties and agreements . . . shall be reached with other nations, but . . . we want no world court and no world congress made up of a few Orientals and a few Russians and a few Europeans and a few British . . . to make laws for us to obey."

From within, this country is threatened by radicalism, which prepares strikes that are "dress rehearsals for a forthcoming general strike that is meant to paralyze the Nation."

We face both the danger of a "Soviet America where . . . an Austrian-born Felix Frankfurter presides over an unending 'Moscow trial' " and the rule of "tyrannical bureaucrats" who if they "could have their way completely" would institute a "dictatorship in America as merciless as anything on earth."

c) *Cultural Grievances*

The agitator is greatly disturbed because the media of public information are in the hands of the enemies of the nation. "The Hollywood motion picture industry is being exploited by Russian Jewish Communists determined to inject their materialistic propaganda into the fresh young minds of our children." Hollywood is "largely dominated by aliens who have appropriated to their own use the inventions and discoveries of native citizens and who now specialize in speculation, indecency and foreign propaganda."

"The American press will never be free" until control "is removed from racial, religious and economic pressure groups."

d) *Moral Grievances*

The enemies of the agitator are notoriously lax in morals: they engage in luxury consumption, this "crowd of Marxists, refugees, left-wing internationalists who enjoy the cream of the country and want the rest of us to go on milkless, butterless, cheeseless days while they guzzle champagne."

And what is most galling of all is that "we gentiles are suckers." For "while we were praying they had their hands in our pockets."

THE APPEAL TO EMOTIONS

The list of diffuse complaints in the above section could be lengthened indefinitely; it should be sufficient to indicate that the grievances the agitator voices do not refer to any clearly delineated material or moral condition. The only constant elements discernible in this mass of grievances are references to certain emotions or emotional complexes. These may roughly be divided as follows:

Distrust

The agitator plays on his audience's suspicions of all social phenomena impinging on its life in ways it does not understand. Foreign refugees cash in on the "gullibility" of Americans, whom he warns not to be "duped" by internationalists. Strewn through the output of the agitator are such words as *hoax, corrupt, duped, manipulate.*

Dependence

The agitator seems to assume that he is addressing people who suffer from a sense of helplessness and passivity. He plays on the ambivalent nature of this complex which on the one hand reflects a protest against manipulation and an impulse to independence and on the other hand a wish to be protected, to belong to a strong organization or be led by a strong leader.

Exclusion

The agitator suggests that there is an abundance of material and spiritual goods, but that we do not get what we are entitled to. The American taxpayer's money is used to help everyone but himself—"we feed foreigners," the agitator complains, while we neglect our own millions of unemployed.

Anxiety

This complex manifests itself in a general premonition of disasters to come, a prominent part of which seems to be the middle class' fear of a dislocation of its life by revolutionary action, and its suspicion that the moral mainstays of social life are being undermined. The agitator speaks of "the darkest hour in American history" and graphically describes a pervasive sense of fear and insecurity:

This afternoon America is caught in the throes of fear, apprehension and concern. Men are afraid . . . to vote, afraid not to vote. . . .

Our population has been caught by the ague and chills of uncertainty. Unless these uncertainties can be removed, unless these fears can be destroyed, we shall never have prosperity again.

Disillusionment

This complex, a tendency more than an actuality, is seen in such remarks as the agitator's characterization of politics as "make-believe, pretense, pretext, sham, fraud, deception, dishonesty, falsehood, hypocrisy." In fact, "whenever a legislative body meets, liberties of the people are endangered by subtle and active interests." Ideological slogans inspire resentment: "Democracy a Misnomer, A Trick Word Used by Jew and Communistic Internationalists to Confuse and Befuddle American Citizens . . ." Values and ideals are enemy weapons, covering up the machinations of sinister powers which, "taking advantage of the mass ignorance of our people, accomplish their purposes under the cloak of humanitarianism and justice."

THE MALAISE OF MODERN SOCIETY

The agitation analyst now faces the problem: are these merely fleeting, unsubstantial, purely accidental and personal emotions blown up by the agitator into genuine complaints or are they themselves a constant rooted in the social structure? The answer seems unavoidable: these feelings cannot be dismissed as either accidental or imposed; they are basic to modern society. Such feelings as distrust, dependence, exclusion, anxiety, and disillusionment blend together to form a fundamental condition of modern life: malaise.

When we define the discontent utilized by agitation as malaise, we are, so to speak, on our own for we cannot substantiate this definition by explicit references to agitational statements. It is an hypothesis, but it is a highly plausible one, because its only alternative would be to see the maze of agitational statements as a lunatic product beyond analysis. Moreover, it helps to account for certain recurrent characteristics of agitation: its diffuseness, its pseudo-spontaneity, its flexibility in utilizing a variety of grievances, and its substitution of a personal enemy for an objective condition.

For it should not be imagined that the agitator spins his grumblings out of thin air. The feelings to which he refers are rooted in social reality, and their existence can be ascertained in sources other than agitational material. The modern individual's sense of isolation, his so-called spiritual homelessness, his bewilderment in the face of the seemingly impersonal forces of which he feels himself a helpless victim, his weakening sense of values—all these supply the basic motifs of the greatest writers of our time. This malaise reflects the stresses imposed on the individual by the profound transformations taking place in our economic and social structure. Correlated with this phenomenon are such developments as the replacement of the class of small independent producers by gigantic bureaucracies, the decay of the patriarchal family, the breakdown of primary personal ties between individuals in an increasingly mechanized world, and the substitution of mass culture for traditional patterns.

These objective causes have been operating for a long time with gradually increasing intensity. They are ubiquitous and apparently permanent; yet they are difficult to grasp because they are only indirectly related to specific hardships or frustrations. Their accumulated psychological effect is something akin to a chronic disturbance, an habitual and not clearly defined malaise which seems to acquire a life of its own and which the victim cannot trace to any known source.

On the plane of immediate awareness, the malaise seems to originate in the individual's own depths and is experienced by him as an apparently isolated and purely psychic or spiritual crisis. It enhances his sense of antagonism to the rest of the world and seems to constitute for him a last defense position of his individuality. Those groups in society that at present are most susceptible to agitation seem to experience this malaise with particular acuteness—perhaps precisely because they do not confront social coercion in its more direct forms.

THE DOCTOR WHO PREVENTS THE CURE

Although malaise actually reflects social reality, it also veils and distorts it. Malaise is neither an illusion of the audience nor a mere imposition by the agitator; it is a psychological symptom of an oppressive situation. Because the agitator does not try to diagnose this symptom with regard to the underlying social situation, he makes it into a pseudo-explanation of his audience's discontent. In this way the agitator tricks his audience into accepting the very situation that produced its malaise. Under the guise of a protest against the oppressive situation, the agitator binds his audience to it. Since this pseudo-protest never produces a genuine solution, it merely leads the audience to seek permanent relief from a permanent predicament by means of irrational outbursts.

We have suggested that malaise is an alienated awareness of social reality. The element of alienation can be found in at least the following factors:

For those afflicted by the malaise, social reality is reflected in categories of individual experience; it ascribes social evil, not to an unjust or obsolete form of society or to a poor organization of an adequate society, but rather to cloudy ultimates of instinct. For the agitator these instincts function beyond and above history: Jews, for instance, are evil—a "fact" which the agitator simply takes for granted as an inherent condition that requires no explanation or development. In this sense, malaise is an attempt to reduce the maze of seemingly impersonal and immovable forces that control human destiny to a known group of people to whom certain traits can be attributed. Abstract intellectual theories do not seem to the masses in modern society as immediately "real" as their own emotional reactions. It is for this reason that the emotions expressed in agitation appear to function as an independent force—which exists prior to articulation of an issue, is expressed by this articulation, and continues to exist after it.

Malaise can be compared to a skin disease. The patient who suffers from such a disease has an instinctive urge to scratch his skin. If he follows the orders of a competent doctor, he will refrain from scratching and seek a cure for the cause of his itch. But if he succumbs to his unreflective reaction, he will scratch all the more vigorously. This irrational exercise of self-violence will give him a certain kind of relief, but it will at the same time increase his need to scratch and will in no way cure his disease. The agitator says: keep scratching.

THE ADVANTAGE OF VAGUENESS

The agitator voices the prevalent stereotyped expressions of this malaise and exploits them for his own purposes. He exploits not primarily the feelings generated by specific hardships or frustrations, but more fundamentally those diffuse feelings of malaise which pervade all modern life. The malaise which is experienced as an internal psychic condition cannot, however, be explained by the action of any definite cause, but only by the social process in its totality. Such an explanation—following the classical method of articulating causes of discontent in universal and verifiable terms and then proposing definite methods to remove them—is beyond the resources of the agitator. First, because it would require a serious intellectual effort of a sort which he does not relish; second, and more important, because any attempt to make his audience aware of the real causes of malaise, which reflects an obscure protest against the coercive power of society, would contradict his essential purposes.

Here the agitator turns to account what might appear his greatest disadvantage—his inability to relate the discontent to an obvious causal base. While most other political movements promise a cure for a specific, and therefore limited, social ailment, the modern agitator, because he himself indirectly voices the malaise, can give the impression that he aims to cure some chronic, ultimate condition. And so he insinuates that while others fumble with symptoms, he attacks the very roots of the disease in that he voices the totality of modern feeling.

Because the malaise is perceived as originating in the deepest layers of the individual psyche, it can be interpreted as an expression of frustrated spontaneity and essential spiritual needs. The agitator, implicitly working on this assumption, thus claims in effect that he represents the most general interests of society, while his opponents, who concern themselves with such limited, specific matters as housing or unemployment or wages, represent only selfish class interests. He can excoriate the others for their seemingly materialistic attitude, since he, on the contrary, has at heart only the nation and the race.

The agitator gravitates towards malaise like a fly to dung. He does not blink at its existence as so many liberals do; he finds no comfort in the illusion that this is the best of all possible worlds. On the contrary, he grovels in it, he relishes it, he distorts and deepens and exaggerates the malaise to the point where it becomes almost a paranoic relationship to the external world. For once the agitator's audience has been driven to this paranoic point, it is ripe for his ministrations.

THE AGITATOR AS A SYMPTOM OF SOCIAL DISORGANIZATION

The prevalence of malaise in recent decades is reflected in growing doubt as to the validity of the beliefs that bound western society together. Religion, the central chord of western society, is today often justified even by its most zealous defenders on grounds of expediency. Religion is proposed not as a transcendent revelation of the nature of man and the world, but as a means of weathering the storms of life, or of deepening one's spiritual experience, or of preserving social order, or of warding off anxiety. Its claim to acceptance is that it offers spiritual comfort. A similar development may be found in morality. There are today no commonly accepted—commonly as a matter of course and beyond the need for discussion—moral values. Such a pragmatic maxim as "honesty is the best policy" is itself striking evidence of the disintegration of moral axioms. And much the same is also true for economic concepts: the businessman still believes in fair competition, but in his "dream life . . . the sure fix is replacing the open market."

As a result, the old beliefs, even when preserved as ritualistic fetishes, have become so hollow that they cannot serve as spurs to conscience or internalized sources of authority. Now authority stands openly as a coercive force and against it is arrayed a phalanx of repressed impulses that storm the gates of the psyche seeking outlets of gratification.

When, for whatever reasons, direct expression of feelings is inhibited, they are projected through some apparently unrelated materials. We may accordingly assume that if the audience is not aware of the causes of the malaise, this is due not only to their inherent complexity, but chiefly to subconscious or unconscious inhibitions, which probably originate in a reluctance to direct hostile feelings toward power groups. By following the audience's spontaneous projections, the agitator appears to voice a protest against these groups while actually playing into their hands. He sanctions immediate resentments and seemingly paves the way for the relief of the malaise through discharge of the audience's aggressive impulses; but simultaneously he perpetuates the malaise by blocking the way toward real understanding of its cause and, resultantly, by further blurring reality.

All such utilizations of malaise are possible only on condition that the audience does not become aware of its roots in modern society. The malaise remains in the background of agitation, the raw material of which is supplied by the audience's stereotyped projection of the malaise. Instead of trying to go back to their sources, to treat them as symptoms of a bad condition, the agitator treats them as needs that he promises to satisfy. He is therefore not burdened with the task of correcting the audience's inadequate ideas; on the contrary, he can let himself be carried along by its "natural" current.

In the United States the tendency is to wave aside the agitator as a minor—although unpleasant—phenomenon. Only a few succumbed to him here, but in Europe millions did. Were there no other evidence at hand, this one fact would be sufficient to establish the conclusion that there are powerful psychological magnets within agitation that draw groups of people into the leader's orbit; that it is not necessarily a small-time, street-corner racket, but may become destructive of our western values on a large scale. The agitator is not to be dismissed as a lunatic, therefore, but rather deserves close attention as a symptom of underlying social disorganization.

PROPAGANDA TECHNIQUES IN
INSTITUTIONAL ADVERTISING

LEONARD I. PEARLIN AND MORRIS ROSENBERG

The overwhelming bulk of advertising in the American mass media is designed to promote the sale of products and services. But there is an area of advertising which, bordering closely on the sale of ideology, has developed and elaborated distinctively fascinating propaganda techniques. This is the area of "institutional advertising."[1] The purpose of this paper is to analyze the implicit devices used in the institutional advertising of three large corporations in their efforts to win "good will" from a potentially hostile public.

A selection of radio "commercials" broadcast by the United States Steel Corporation, the Standard Oil Company of California, and the Association of American Railroads was analyzed in order to determine the range of techniques employed.[2] The chief distinguishing characteristic of these commercials is that they did not urge the audience to buy any product. The apparent aim in presenting the high-priced programs of which the commercials were a part was to create a "favorable impression" on the American public. How was this done? Six devices may be distinguished: elaboration of latent consequences, humanization, denial and conversion, audience ego-involvement, status contagion or association, and omission of profane or divisive subjects.

ELABORATION OF LATENT CONSEQUENCES

In a society organically united through the division of labor, large scale commercial and industrial activities will have broad ramifications throughout the social structure. The positive ramifications are propagandistically exploited in institutional advertising. The most conspicuous propaganda technique utilized in institutional advertising is that of giving to incidental, accidental, or unavoidable company activity the quality of apparent intention or purpose. More technically expressed, it entails transforming a latent consequence into a manifest (or apparently intentional) function.[3] Each

[1] See Borden, Neil, *Economic Effects of Advertising* (Chicago: Richard Irwin, Inc., 1944), p. 98.

[2] Since this paper seeks to elucidate the range of devices utilized rather than the frequency of use, a representative sample was not used. Occasional references of "more" or "less" represent frankly impressionistic judgments. The time periods covered were: United States Steel (USS), *The Theatre Guild on the Air* and *Hour of Mystery*, September 9, 1945 to June 29, 1947; Standard Oil Company of California (SO), *The Standard Hour*, September 24, 1950, to December 31, 1950; and the Association of American Railroads (AAR), *The Railroad Hour* (Show Train), October 16, 1950 to January 22, 1951.

[3] An extensive and well-organized discussion of the principle of functionalism in sociology and anthropology may be found in Merton, Robert K., *Social Theory and Social Structure* (Glencoe: The Free Press, 1949), pp. 21-81.

From the *Public Opinion Quarterly,* 1952, 16, 5-26. Reprinted by permission of the authors and the publisher.

company is in business for one intentional purpose: to earn a profit. In the process of fulfilling this aim, however, it must perform a multitude of acts. It must build plants and machines, hire workers, pay wages and salaries, select foremen, purchase various goods and services, pay taxes, and so on. It will accept contracts; it will engage in extensive technological research to reduce costs and increase profits; it will promote safety in order to reduce accident insurance rates; it will seek to extend the range of uses for its products in order to enlarge its markets. Each of these steps is oriented toward the one manifest purpose of increasing and distributing profits for personal benefit. Though this may be its purpose, however, it has many other unintentional consequences which the advertisers stress as making functional contributions to various social units.

An analogy may clarify this point. A plant absorbs carbon dioxide which is expelled from human lungs and uses it to produce oxygen. The action of the plant is essential to the maintenance of human life. But this clearly does not mean that it is the intention of the plant to preserve human life; it is simply an accidental by-product of its normal functioning. Similarly, a company selects an economically strategic location for setting up its plant for the production of goods. Naturally, it hires employees and pays wages, thereby contributing to the prosperity of the community. Since this latter consequence was in no sense its intention, one would not ordinarily expect to grant the company credit or gratitude for its action. Nonetheless, this credit is consistently claimed by the institutional advertisers. The Standard Oil Company of California, in paying large taxes to the State of California, points out that this results in a lower tax rate for Californians. This may be the result of their tax payment, but certainly it reflects no altruistic intention.

Analysis of this technique resolves itself into the three elements contained in the question: "Who does what for whom?" In other words, we may distinguish the actor, the action and the beneficiary.

Actor

Three benefactors implicitly claim credit for the latent consequences of engaging in business: (1) the corporation, (2) the industry, and (3) the capitalist system. The actor most frequently referred to is the corporation.[4]

Action

Functionalism ordinarily assumes that the action of an institution is indispensable to the maintenance of society. These institutional "commercials" reveal three types of contributions made by the actor to the beneficiary. Credit is claimed by the actor for "making a contribution to," "establishing conditions for," or "proving indispensable to" the beneficiary.[5]

(1) "MAKING A CONTRIBUTION TO" Phrases of the following sort reveal the "contribution to" claim. "Steel *played a major part* . . ."; "through financial *assistance by* . . ."; "to *meet the needs of* . . ."; "large companies *contribute* to our national strength and to our individual lives . . ."; "how different *life* would be *without* . . ."; "*furnish* knowledge and machines."

(2) "ESTABLISHING CONDITIONS FOR" The second latent consequence claimed deals with behavior which makes possible certain ends without directly contributing to them. For example, a company might claim that establishing a plant in a local community had set the conditions for local talent to exercise initiative and get ahead. The company would not claim credit for this

[4] This impressionistic view is in agreement with Blackwood's view that the trend of institutional propaganda is toward the emphasis on the individual corporation and away from industrial groups. See Blackwood, George, "The Advertising of Ideas," *Labor and Nation*, Vol. 6 (Fall, 1950), p. 27.

[5] The following are quotes taken directly from the broadcasts. All italics in this paper, including those within quotes, are ours. They do not necessarily represent the emphases of the broadcasters, but are rather designed to sharpen the reader's focus on the propaganda technique employed. Hereafter, references give the sponsor and date of the broadcast. United States Steel is referred to as USS, Standard Oil as SO, and Association of American Railroads as AAR.

exercise of initiative, but would implicitly maintain that initiative could not have been exercised were it not for the company. This claim is reflected in such expressions as: we *"have made possible . . ."*; the company *"gives* employees *a chance* to . . ."; the firm *"provides opportunities for . . ."*; "their service *helps make possible . . ."*; *"make possible* the employment of hundreds of thousands. . . ."

(3) "PROVING INDISPENSABLE TO" This action is a key criterion of functionalism; it implies that the unit will not survive without the actor. It is reflected in such phrases as: ". . . America *depends on* the railroads . . ."; ". . . it is *because* of these *essential contributions* which the railroads make . . ."; playing a *"basic"* or *"vital"* part.

Beneficiary

In order to obtain the respect and good will of the audience, the institutional advertisers seek to indicate how the latent consequences of their business operations benefit (contribute to, set conditions for, prove indispensable to) the members of the audience themselves, or those institutions or norms valued by the audience. These latent consequences are shown to help: (1) the individual in the audience; (2) sub-groups of the population; (3) sacred social institutions and values; and (4) the society as a whole. An organization which produces such widespread social benefits will presumably obtain audience approval.

Benefits to the individual

Contributions to the individual are usually of a material sort. The companies suggest that the latent consequences of their business conduct are to contribute to the physical and economic gratifications of the listener; to promote his leisure, pleasure, ease and comfort; and to protect his physical survival.

(1) PHYSICAL GRATIFICATIONS ". . . the American railroads, the same railroads that bring you most of the food you eat, the clothes you wear, the fuel you burn, and all the other things you use in your daily life," is the recurrent theme of the Association of American Railroads. "Without railroads, you would not have your housing, your food, and countless other necessities and luxuries,"[6] says the same sponsor, sagely ignoring his own motivations. Standard Oil, emphasizing the multiple uses to which petroleum has been put, asks: "How do Petrochemicals affect you? They are the ingredients that help make possible your plastic alarm clock, nylon hosiery, the synthetic tile on your kitchen floor, work-saving 'soapless soaps' you use for dishwashing . . . , your rayon scarf, the germicide in your medicine chest, the gleaming synthetic enamel on your stove and refrigerator, the face lotion and perfume on your vanity, the insecticide sprays you use in your garden. The list could go on almost endlessly."[7]

(2) ECONOMIC GRATIFICATIONS This appeal points out to the listener how company activities contribute to his economic welfare. "The State of California alone, as title holder to the Sacramento River bed, has received from Standard some $6,700,000 in less than 10 years . . . *royalties pocketed by Californians in the form of lower taxes.*"[8] Or, again, we hear: "In other words, improvements in steel-making are the result of pooled resourcefulness, and this system of combined research activity will go on saving millions of dollars for you, the public, in peace just as it did for you during the war."[9] No mention is made, in the first case, that taxpaying is mandatory, or, in the second, that benefits accrue to the company.

(3) COMFORT AND PLEASURE A favorable picture of the steel industry is promoted by pointing out the leisure-pleasure benefits accruing to the audience. ". . . many of you are already planning your summer vacation. And this year such planning is mighty pleasant. . . .

"But whether you go by automobile, bus, train, plane, or boat, you'll travel faster and

[6] AAR, October 23, 1950.
[7] SO, December 10, 1950.
[8] SO, December 3, 1950.
[9] USS, October 7, 1945.

more economically because of steel, and you'll travel with far greater comfort and safety, too."[10] At another point, a glowing picture is painted: "Just think how different life would be without cars and planes and radios . . . without electric refrigerators and washing machines, vacuum cleaners and all the other modern appliances that reduce the drudgery of housework. . . . And in this picture of American progress, steel played a major part."[11]

(4) SAFETY An additional method of earning the gratitude of the average American is to point out how he is freed from potential dangers by the company product. Discussing the contributions of steel to safety, we are told by an authority: "In the first place, I'd put the steel framework used today in most schools, theatres, office buildings, factories and apartments which, when properly utilized, makes them fireproof. A close second would be the all-steel bodies on automobiles, railroad cars and street cars. These two uses of steel, alone, save thousands of lives every year, and prevent countless serious injuries. Of course, there are, in addition, an infinite number of other ways in which steel products contribute to safety . . . such as surgical instruments, decompression chambers and . . . steel toes. . . ."[12]

The clear-cut implication of these commercials is that the average listener leads a vastly happier personal life because of these companies. The fact that this happiness is incidental and, indeed, irrelevant to the manifest purpose of the business; namely, investment for profit—is beclouded by the ingenious emphasis placed on these latent consequences.

Benefits to population sub-groups

In addition to the various benefits accruing to all Americans as an incidental consequence of the business activities of these large companies, the commercials are careful to make specific appeals to particular population sub-groups. These population sub-groups, it may be noted, are not those most likely to favor the companies, such as big businessmen or conservatives generally, but rather those groups whose allegiance is more tenuous and who stand in potential opposition to the companies. Advantages to sub-groups of the following sort may be noted: farmers, workers, small businessmen, local communities, westerners, southerners. These groups, traditionally suspicious of what they regard as large Eastern capital, are cleverly wooed by convincing evidence of the benefits they obtain from these companies.

The farmers are seen to benefit in the following ways: "Yes, modern farm implements of steel have vastly increased the farmer's productive powers while they have lightened his labors and raised his standard of living. And, in addition, steel brings many comforts, many time and labor-saving conveniences to his home and family."[13]

The benefits of industry to workers are emphasized by pointing out that these companies provide jobs. Thus, a necessary step in the production process; namely, hiring labor—is converted into a windfall for workers: ". . . you've probably forgotten just what those raw materials are—and how their vast scale production and transportation *provide work* for thousands upon thousands all over America, not counting those actually employed in making steel—almost 300,000 of them by U. S. Steel alone. . . .

"Yes, these raw materials are . . . essential to thousands of different industries using steel and employing millions of our fellow citizens."[14] Reference is also made to the "better jobs" provided by new tools of production.

The traditional opposition of small business to big business is countered by pointing out the advantages accruing to small business as a result of the incidental, unintentional activities of the large firms. Standard Oil makes this point very explicit. "It is a company practice," they say, "to buy locally

[10] USS, February 24, 1946.
[11] USS, December 2, 1945.
[12] USS, January 20, 1946.

[13] USS, March 10, 1946.
[14] USS, December 9, 1945.

whenever practical. As a result, Standard is a big customer for some ten thousand different businesses throughout the West. Its shopping list exceeds 50 thousand items—goods and services like lumber, carpentry, shovels, paper, hose—everything it takes to keep a company like ours going. In totalling up the sales on these goods and services, the cash registers of thousands of local western business firms ring up more than 100 million dollars every year! These are facts that explode an old myth to the effect that big business makes it tough for small business."[15]

Local communities, which have sometimes resented the domination of the large company, are shown to benefit as well: "The more than 100 million dollars a year that Standard spends directly with local firms . . . plus its 110 million dollar payroll . . . plus the 19 million dollars in city, county, and state taxes it pays, all contribute substantially to the growth and prosperity of thousands of western communities."[16]

Finally, U. S. Steel's subsidiaries are shown to benefit westerners and southerners: "For, oddly enough, it was only by fencing in many fields and grazing lands that America's West was opened up. In this development, the American Steel and Wire Company played an important part."[17] Another subsidiary claims that it "will continue to serve the South."[18]

Promotion of cultural values

Institutional advertising does not simply emphasize the latent benefits derived by the individual listener or his membership group. A comparably effective device is to point out the (unintentional) contributions of the large firms to those fundamental values to which the audience is dedicated. The audience does not benefit directly, but is called upon to respect the benefactor of its values, just as we may admire a philanthropist for his donation without ourselves benefiting therefrom. Thus, the commercials implicitly and explicitly affirm the companies' functional con-

tributions toward the maintenance of culturally sacred values of the following sort: that every man should have the chance to get ahead, that the family is a sacred institution, that peace and brotherhood are high and noble aims, that America is the land of progress, that teamwork is the best and most effective type of action.[19] It should be noted how the manifest function of the behavior, namely, its contribution to the company welfare—is generally hidden and the latent functions stressed.

Getting ahead

A large factory bureaucracy operates on the principle of layers of hierarchically superposed authority. The more competent are those in the middle and upper echelon positions, the better coordinated will be the complex production process. A by-product of filling these higher positions with the best and most experienced men is to provide opportunities for success to a number of people. It is this by-product which is stressed in the commercials. One broadcast runs: "Yes, Bill Bancsi is one of the thousands of steelworkers who have *gone ahead* through U. S. Steel's outstandingly successful employee training and upgrading program . . . a program which provides job opportunities limited only by the capabilities of the individual. . . ."[20] Again we hear: "Among all the workers, United States Steel's training program has been continued vigorously, educating men to do better jobs, and fitting them for higher and more responsible positions."[21] The audience can only conclude that the company makes a positive contribution to the culturally sacred value of success.

The family

In various commercials, stress is placed upon what appear to be efforts of the com-

---

[15] SO, November 12, 1950.
[16] SO, November 12, 1950.
[17] USS, September 30, 1945.
[18] USS, January 27, 1947.

[19] Two outstanding contributions to the subject of American values, among others, are: Lynd, Robert S. and Helen M. Lynd, *Middletown in Transition* (New York: Harcourt Brace, 1937), Ch. XII, and Williams, Robin M., Jr. *American Society* (New York: Knopf, 1951), Ch. 11.
[20] USS, January 6, 1946.
[21] USS, March 30, 1947.

panies to maintain family unity, directly or indirectly. Standard Oil cites the case of an inducted employee whose military service income will be supplemented by the company to make up his normal civilian income so that ". . . his young family can continue to develop with the same economic advantages it had when the breadwinner was home."[22]

Peace and brotherhood

Western religions have emphasized these values for many centuries and they are firmly embedded in the ethical structure of the culture. One U. S. Steel subsidiary is shown to carry on its work with almost missionary zeal, seemingly unconcerned over its own interest in the matter: "In Alaska and the Andes, in the Uganda territory of Africa, the workers of the American and Virginia Bridge Companies are helping men carry on commerce, and are bringing them closer together in friendship and the ways of peace. America and Virginia Bridge have already resumed their job of building the structures which help join the peoples of the world in understanding and serving each other."[23]

Teamwork

In complex, multi-faceted industries, careful coordination of effort is essential. This characteristic, rooted in the very nature of contemporary capitalism, is transformed by the advertisers so as to promote the moral virtue of cooperation: "Yes, we're seeing plenty of teamwork these Fall days . . . teamwork on the gridiron and in the vitally important business of railroading which provides the dependable, efficient mass transportation service so essential to the economic well-being and military strength of our nation."[24]

Progress

The Lynds point out that Middletown believes in the advantages and inevitability of progress. Such progress is characteristically

of a material nature; it is, consequently, easy to understand why large production units stress their contribution to it. After describing "the progress America has made since the turn of the century" in terms of cars, planes, radios, washing machines, etc., one advertiser concludes: "And in this picture of American progress, steel played a major part."[25] We hear that the low cost of steel to a great extent "has made possible our modern world of machines and the miracles that flow from them. . . ."[26]

This incomplete catalogue of sacred institutions and values illustrates how institutional advertisers lay claim to important social contributions. The sociologist may see mirrored in such commercials an excellent reflection of the moral sentiments of a society.

Benefits to the total society

Institutional commercials not only stress the benefits accruing to the individual, to his membership groups and to many of his values, but indicate how the advertisers contribute to the maintenance and prosperity of the total society. These claims are most strongly pressed in periods of national emergency or under the threat of war, but even under conditions of peace the contribution to the general welfare is pointed up. By implication, the nation would face defeat or ruin without these contributions. Such statements as the following appear: ". . . *America* depends on the railroads."[27] "The result is a strong, efficient oil industry which can meet the big problems *we all* face today . . . when once again *our nation* needs the oil so vital for our security."[28] "And standing ready to move the great life stream of goods and food and fuel that keep *our country* sound and strong—are the American railroads."[29] As mentioned above, U. S. Steel refers to itself as the "Industrial Family that Serves the *Nation*." A large number of references to producing, powering or transport-

[22] SO, November 26, 1950.
[23] USS, September 23, 1945.
[24] AAR, October 30, 1950.

[25] USS, December 2, 1945.
[26] USS, December 2, 1945.
[27] AAR, November 6, 1950.
[28] SO, October 15, 1950.
[29] AAR, December 4, 1950.

ing military goods for the purpose of national defense and victory strengthen the idea that these contributions to the survival of the total society are substantial.

In those rare and intermittent periods of peace, the contribution to national welfare and prosperity is expressed in a number of ways. The large number of jobs provided; huge payrolls; new, better and more numerous goods produced and transported; recitations of technical progress—all reinforce the impression that a prosperous and secure America depends on the advertisers. "U. S. Steel . . . recognizes that U. S. Steel prospers only as *the nation* prospers,"[30] implies an identity of interest. The AAR points out ". . . how your railroads help to make possible and to maintain the high economic level in the United States."[31] Standard Oil, defending large companies, states that ". . . it takes these companies to do jobs like this to help improve *our* standard of living. . . ."[32] Accepting the implicit premise of latent consequences of normal activity, the conclusion is inescapable that the welfare and security of the total society depends on large companies.

HUMANIZATION

Humanization is a major device utilized by institutional advertisers to create warm, agreeable public pictures of themselves. The company images presented by these commercials include traits which are considered particularly admirable in an individual in the American culture. The company or the industry, objectively abstract institutions, are made to appear as pleasant, estimable people. If one accepts the message of the commercials, one obtains the following picture of the companies: they are friendly, personal, folksy; bountiful and generous; protective and solicitous; industrious, assiduous, hard-working; wholesomely patriotic. In addition to these emotionally appealing human personality traits, the companies are

[30] USS, March 30, 1947.
[31] AAR, October 23, 1950.
[32] SO, October 22, 1950.

also shown to have laudable intellectual characteristics: they are rational and scientific; they are ingenious and imaginative; despite their sparks of brilliance, however, they are cautious, sage, equipped with unusual insight. An individual possessing these personality and intellectual traits would be well-liked in his community, and this is the effect the companies seek to create through humanization.

Personality traits

To show themselves as friendly, personal, and human, Standard Oil tells the story of one of its employees who has been called to the service: "Now one of the tough things about being called to active duty is that frequently a man stands to take a big cut in pay when he goes into the service. But Jim's employer, the Standard Oil Company of California, has a plan of benefits for employees called to military service. Standard gave Jim one month's salary when he left and in addition they will pay him, every month, the difference between his military pay and his earnings as a mechanic with the Company. . . .

"In a sense, these benefits are Jim's dividends from our free economic system. But they also show one of the many ways in which Standard . . . and other companies . . . respond to the human, individual needs of their employees. They show how a company, with big resources, can and does act to preserve the *human* resources, of our nation—people like Jim and his family."[33]

In addition to its humanism, the above quotation also reflects a very generous nature. This is expressed even more clearly when U. S. Steel shows itself to be very liberal in paying wages, ignoring any pressures which have been imposed on it to do so and implying that its action is purely the reflection of a liberal and expansive spirit: "As for pay, the average hourly earnings of workers in other industries, shows that United States Steel's workers are among the highest paid in American industry. . . . The

[33] SO, November 26, 1950.

average hourly earnings of these U. S. Steel workers . . . were nineteen and a half per cent higher than the average hourly earnings of workers in all manufacturing industries."[34]

The companies are quick to show that their generosity is no mere hard-headed disbursement of funds, however; they indicate that they are deeply protective and solicitous of the welfare of those who "depend" upon them: "During the year, more than 1800 employees retired on pensions. Their average length of service with United States Steel was 36 years. And during the year, more than 85 per cent of all the employees were insured under the Employees' Group Life Insurance Plan for almost $700,000,000. . . .

"These . . . facts . . . indicate that United States Steel is doing its best to fulfill its responsibility to its employees."[35]

It is not to be imagined that a company equipped with the tenderer sentiments is lacking in the more rigorous personality characteristics of assiduity and perseverance. The company is shown to take great pains, to be unsparing in effort, much as the industrious craftsman of early capitalism. U. S. Steel speaks of ". . . the kind of *painstaking* research and development work which goes on constantly at United States Steel. . . ."[36] A statement with similar implications is the following: "United States Steel *worked hard* in 1946 to supply as much as possible of the steel and other products and services the nation needed so badly. . . . United States Steel has always *worked to the best of its ability* to meet the needs of our country."[37]

The institutional advertisers also have one other characteristic which endears them to the audience: they are extremely patriotic. They manifest this patriotism by working hard to supply the soldiers at the front, by hiring and helping veterans, and by associating themselves with national plans for victory.

Intellectual traits

In addition to their personal warmth, patriotism, and will-to-work, the institutional advertisers depict themselves as being equipped with the sagacity and slightly miraculous wisdom which an ideally intellectual person would possess. They are never silly, irrational, whimsical, shortsighted. Their rational, scientific orientation is expressed in such statements as the following: "Now, I won't try to tell you how steels are tested, for if I started I could talk for a week just about a few of the better-known testing techniques now being employed. These include testing by chemical analysis, high temperature, X-ray fluoroscope, electron microscope, radium rays, plus the most modern tension and fracture equipment."[38]

But this is no dull and unimaginative rationality; it is inspired, creative, ingenious: "These people do not realize what tremendous effort, technical inventiveness and bold administrative skill are required for the realization of a modern railroad network on which a nation's life depends."[39]

Intellectual maturity requires that creativity be tempered with caution. Foresight and wisdom are characteristic of the truly intellectual man. In this context, the railroads tell an interesting story: "Weeks ago, Post Office officials and railroad representatives met to lay *careful plans* for handling Christmas mail. Every phase of the plan was worked out . . . adequate car supply, plenty of locomotives and switch engines, sufficient manpower, location of cars in advance where they will be available when needed . . . and all other details required to move a mountain of mail in a short time."[40] And Standard Oil clings to its recurrent theme: "And I believe that my former friend's story demonstrates well another way in which Standard Oil Company of California *plans ahead* to serve you and the nation better."[41]

The personality and intellectual traits of

[34] USS, March 30, 1947.
[35] USS, March 30, 1947.
[36] USS, March 23, 1947.
[37] USS, April 6, 1947.

[38] USS, February 3, 1946.
[39] AAR, October 23, 1950.
[40] AAR, November 27, 1950.
[41] SO, December 3, 1950.

the institutional advertisers are shown to correspond to those individual human traits lauded in the culture. By developing a warm emotional feeling tone toward themselves, institutional advertisers hope to construct a bridge of loyalty to themselves, or at least to set up a solid barrier against attack.[42]

DENIAL AND CONVERSION

It is reasonable to suspect that the institutional advertisers' constant reiteration of personal nobility covers a lurking fear of wide-spread negative public opinion toward them. In point of fact, these companies seem to know just which elements in the American value system militate against them, and they take great pains to eradicate or nullify these features in their self-portraits. Two devices are used in this effort: denial and conversion.

Denial

By denial is simply meant the device whereby certain characteristics, frequently attributed to companies such as the institutional advertisers, are rejected as not being consistent with a commendable human characteristic. The nature of the denials implies the gist of the anticipated attacks. The companies want to destroy the idea that they are cold, impersonal organizations, that they are run by a small clique of rich and powerful men, that they are monopolistic and unfair, or that they are exploitative and power-hungry.

The charge of impersonality, for example, is countered in the illustration cited above in which personal interest is shown by Standard Oil in Jim and his family. "Standard and other large companies" . . . are shown to "respond to the human, individual needs of their employees" in an effort to "preserve the human resources of our nation." One public relations advantage of

small business over large organizations is that it carries a connotation of personal intercourse, sociability and intimacy. Hence, large companies seek to undermine the popular picture of their coldness and impersonality by characterizing themselves as warm and *gemeinschaftlich.*

The general fear of power concentration in America and the specific suspicion of the small and powerful clique has engendered considerable public hostility toward giant corporations. The joint stock company, which is the prevalent contemporary form of the large business association, has provided the companies with a powerful counter-argument, and they use it to the limit: "Now and then you hear it said that Standard . . . and other large companies . . . are monopolies. That they benefit a few rich people. But . . . if all the owners of Standard of California were gathered in one place, they would make up a good sized city. . . . More than 70 per cent of these people have less than 100 shares each."[43] Similarly we hear that: "Among these [225,000 U. S. Steel] stockholders may be your next-door neighbor, your grocer, your doctor or your insurance company."[44] The railroads refer to ". . . the million people who as small stockholders own the railroads. . . ."[45] Apparently, the easy confusion between ownership and control enables a few people with power to pose as the servants of the large masses of common people.

Allied with the fear of concentrated economic power is the traditional American abhorrence of monopoly. This is a sore spot which the large companies seek to heal with affirmations of the following sort: "Today there are 25,000 service stations in the West selling all brands of gasoline. They compete vigorously for your patronage. And this very rivalry has developed practically all the services you count on wherever you drive. . . .

"This is particularly important today,

---

[42] This is a version of the "strategy of propaganda" described in Harold Lasswell, "The Theory of Political Propaganda" in *Reader in Public Opinion and Communication*, Berelson, Bernard, and Morris Janowitz (Eds.) (Glencoe: The Free Press, 1950), p. 178.

[43] SO, October 1, 1950.
[44] USS, December 16, 1945.
[45] AAR, December 25, 1950.

when the oil industry in the West is being accused of lack of competition among its members. The fact is, it was the competitive spirit in all parts of the oil business that built an industry able to supply the petroleum our nation needed to win World War II."[46]

The companies must also deal with the cultural disapproval of excessive profit seeking. A culture emphasizing pecuniary success does not necessarily sanction all means of striving for it. People are encouraged to seek profits, but are maligned if they appear to be exploitive or profit-hungry. However, since a company could not be deemed oppressive if its employees honor it, U. S. Steel points out that ". . . the men and women who go to work for U. S. Steel are very apt to like their jobs and stay in them."[47] Nor are the companies obsessed with the desire for profit. Indeed, soldiers on leave were permitted to travel for only two cents a mile during the Christmas holidays,[48] indicating a higher concern for patriotism, the family and religion than for mere profit. It is clear that the big companies, according to their commercials, do not even make a large amount of profit: ". . . United States Steel earned a profit of only five and one-half per cent on its investment, or to put it another way, six cents on each sales dollar. This seems far from an excessive profit. . . ."[49] To small businessmen this is a convincing argument, since such a return on their investment would be quite meager. It is easy to ignore the tremendous capital outlay in the steel industry. Thus, the fact that the large companies implicitly deny the charges of impersonality, small clique control, monopoly, exploitation and profit greed indicates the widespread cultural distaste for these attributes.

Conversion

There are certain attacks which, difficult to deny, are converted. By the technique of conversion is meant the method by which

"profane" values are converted into "sacred" values. What is done is to take undesirable attributes often associated with company behavior and convert them to desirable features by presenting them in such a manner that they are perceived as beneficial to society. This technique, it will be seen, is not mutually exclusive of the utilization of latent consequences, as is the case with the other devices discussed. Although there is considerable overlap between the two, they can be distinguished by the propaganda intent with which they are used. That is, latent consequences are used to draw favorable relationships, while conversion (and denial) are used to eliminate unfavorable relationships, to reverse hostile attitudes. Thus, fearful of attack on the charge of inordinate profits and size, and unable to deny these charges, the advertisers transform these characteristics into virtues.

The profane attribute of profits is often converted by emphasizing the spending of earnings: "To meet the rising demands of our national rearmament . . . and to serve the essential transportation needs of our country . . . the railroads are enlarging and improving every part of their plant. This program has cost more than a billion dollars each year since the end of World War II."[50]

Similarly, the undesirable attributes of "bigness" are converted by pointing up the efficiency of large-scale production: "It's a big job, this exploring and developing and producing oil and gas. It involves enormous costs. It's a job that must be done by companies with great resources . . . companies with money to risk for the good of all of us."[51]

The emphasis is laid not on making of profits, but on spending profits in such a way as to contribute to social values. It goes without saying that this advantage could not be realized without profits to begin with, and so a justifiable claim is made for this profane value. The value of efficiency is used to defend business. The mammoth size of these companies allegedly works in favor of the

[46] SO, October 8, 1950.
[47] USS, April 6, 1947.
[48] AAR, December 11, 1950.
[49] USS, April 6, 1947.

[50] AAR, January 22, 1951.
[51] SO, December 3, 1950.

people, for no one could deny that a large company can do things only hoped for by a smaller business. It is because of big concerns that we are able to have such things as "new and more efficient products," and so on.

CREATION OF EGO-INVOLVEMENT

One of the very keenest institutional advertising devices is the attempt to cause the audience to identify with the company, industry, or social system in an ego-involved manner.[52] If such ego-involvement can be created, then any attack on the company would be perceived by the audience as an attack upon themselves. Such a device may produce powerful and active company allies.

The simplest and most obvious method in developing audience identification is to indicate that the fate of the audience is, for good or evil, bound up with the destiny of the company. This is illustrated in the following quotation: "People all over the country have invested their money in the ownership of the (U. S. Steel) Corporation. You yourself probably have an interest, either directly or because your insurance company, your hospital or your local college may well own stock in United States Steel."[53] Similarly, Standard Oil does not hesitate to acclaim that the theme of Oil Progress Week is: "Your own progress and oil progress go hand in hand."

A second identification device is to imply the notion that the audience and company form a common unit. For example, when Americans are told that the Mississippi River is one of the most magnificent in the world, the realization that this body of water is our very own enhances the ego. The following statement, delivered by a foreign visitor, undoubtedly created much ego gratification as he spoke to Americans of *their* magnificent railroads: "How welcome it was to receive the invitation . . . to come to the United States to study *your* railroads . . . to see how *you* handle *your* vast amount of transportation by railroads. . . .

"May *your* trains continue to run. . . ."[54]

Probably the most subtle identification device, however, is that of getting the audience interested in the problems, aspirations, and aims of the company—so interested that the listener tends to see these problems as his own. This is effectively accomplished by taking the audience "backstage" to the inner operations of the company, showing them what problems must be confronted and overcome. Hearing how steel is produced, how oil is drilled, how research is carried on, what the trials and tribulations of production are—all this is designed to give the audience a sense of sharing in the company. Each of the three identification devices discussed here are intended to develop in the public a sense of identification so that the enhancement or contraction of the company produces a corresponding influence on the ego of the listener.

ASSOCIATION OR STATUS CONTAGION

An interesting method of gaining respectability is to associate one's self with that which is respectable.[55] Such association does not necessarily imply a contribution to the valued object. It might simply involve taking a verbal stand in favor of the value or by some other device establishing an association between the company and the value held by the listener. Institutional advertisers seek to obtain an aura of sanctity by associating themselves with dominant cultural values. All America values the family, religion, veterans, science, American military forces, the American way of life, freedom, community spirit, and so on.

Methods of achieving the association between company and value are often highly

[52] See Sherif, Muzafer and Hadley Cantril, *The Psychology of Ego-Involvements* (New York: Wiley, 1947).

[53] USS, June 9, 1946.

[54] AAR, October 23, 1950.

[55] Benoit-Smullyan has called such association in the field of stratification "prestige contagion." See "Status, Status Types and Status Interrelations," *Amer. Sociological Rev.*, Vol. 9, 1944, pp. 151-161.

ingenious. We find U. S. Steel referring to itself as "The Industrial *Family* that Serves the Nation," and the railroads state: ". . . this Railroad Hour *family* says to you and your *family*. . . ."[56] On the same program we hear: "The heart of that seeking for peace and goodwill is in the family—an institution which foreshadows the family of mankind. So Christmas, the festival of peace, is the great family festival, celebrated in the homes where families gather."[57] This characterization of giant industrial aggregates as simply large families covers the picture of cold, impersonal industrial efficiency with a blanket of warm emotion. It is one of the most cunning public relations devices; its only drawback is that it may suffer from over-use.

Religion, as a sacred institution as well as a potentially divisive force, is handled gingerly. In one Christmas broadcast the story of the Nativity is told—simply, directly and without further comment.[58] There is no mention of steel, capitalism or other profane values. But the implication is clear that the company holds the same attitude of reverence toward religion as does the audience.

The advertisers seek to associate themselves with American grandeur. With reference to American strength, they speak of ". . . the most productive economy the world has ever seen."[59] The railroads state: "Throughout the world, our nation is known as the 'Arsenal of Democracy.' The rich, unequalled productive economy of a free people has made it so."[60] Moving one step further, they take a position in favor of the most all-encompassing of values, "the American way of life." ". . . may they [the railroads] continue to interconnect the multitude of things which make up the American way of life."[61] Or again, we hear: "Yes, men with faith in our American way of life made this country what it is . . . and its

future depends largely on what you and I and everybody does to strengthen our democratic form of government."[62] A related value, unequivocally accepted and integrated in the American value system, is freedom. We hear of ". . . the blessed American freedom we fought, worked and sacrificed to preserve. . . ."[63] "So during the days ahead—let's remember, 'Freedom is Everybody's Job.' "[64] Although in these cases the companies themselves claim no credit for the institutions or values, they seek to associate themselves with them. Similar associations are made to science, community life, democracy, and other values universally applauded in the society.

There is, however, one danger in this device of association with sacred values. It assumes that the audience will itself effect the psychological linkage between the value and the company. This is not necessarily the case. A broadcast by a company favoring the American way of life might simply reinforce people in their belief in the American way but not change their opinions of the company. This unreliable instrument, therefore, is used relatively sparingly; latent consequences are used much more frequently. The companies do not simply associate themselves with the family, although they do this too; rather, they show how they contribute to upholding the institution. They do not simply use their name and American defense in the same commercial; rather, they discuss the planes and guns that they have sent to the front. Leaving little to chance, the advertisers show that the latent consequences of their actions directly serve purposes dear to the hearts of Americans. They do not depend upon association or status contagion alone.

OMISSION

An important part of the technique of creating good will or a favorable impression is to avoid any references which might

[56] AAR, December 25, 1950.
[57] AAR, December 25, 1950.
[58] USS, December 23, 1945.
[59] AAR, December 4, 1950.
[60] AAR, December 4, 1950.
[61] AAR, October 23, 1950.

[62] AAR, December 25, 1950.
[63] USS, December 30, 1945.
[64] AAR, December 25, 1950.

have the opposite effect. Since the commercials deal with ideology and not with the innocuous superlatives of product advertising, an extraordinary amount of care is necessary to avoid statements which might alienate a substantial minority. The omissions are extremely instructive as to the cultural areas which may be a source of antagonism.

It is striking that certain institutions with which the audience is deeply concerned are either not mentioned at all or given only passing reference. The government and organized labor are two cases in point. Actually, these cases fit into a broader framework of the omission of any area which might imply conflict. The impression obtained is that, since either favorable or unfavorable statements would be resented by a substantial segment of the population, the most effective solution is to steer clear of the topic. The institutional advertiser is as anxious to lure pro-Administration and pro-organized labor listeners into its net as any others; hence, the natural business inclination to attack these groups must be stifled. Assuredly, it is not lack of interest or viewpoint which produces such reticence. In general, all potentially disruptive discussions are avoided. The advertisers wish to agree with everyone, alienate no one. Small business is mentioned but rarely, and then only for the purpose of indicating the benefits derived from big business. Class or status differences, racial, ethnic, national, regional, sexual differences are eschewed. These subjects are rarely discussed even from the viewpoint of the American creed, apparently for fear of alienating those who are prejudiced. Only concepts on which there is guaranteed agreement, such as freedom, democracy, and the American way of life, are extensively discussed.

The second set of omissions refer to latent dysfunctions. As much ingenuity can be exercised in pointing out the evil unintentional consequences of large business operations as the benefits derived. One might cite the dysfunctional effects of competition on brotherhood, of beltline production on human spontaneity, of bureaucracy on creativity, of monopoly on small business, of business cycles on social stability, and so on, ad infinitum. Analysis in terms of latent functions sets up conditions strongly favorable to card-stacking. Social elements are so intimately intertwined that the functional and dysfunctional consequences of large scale production appear to be bounded only by the ingenuity of the script writer and his courage in stretching a point referring to indirect functional consequences. Nevertheless, the utter failure to mention anything dysfunctional leaves the reputation of the large companies quite unbesmirched.

An important element in respectability lies in the avoidance of anything violating conventional aesthetic standards. Hence, vulgarity, obscenity and crudeness are avoided. Of course the grosser forms of "poor taste" are not permitted expression on the radio,[65] but the apparent sensitivity of the institutional advertisers to anything which might violate popular sentiments is instructive and meaningful.

Finally, we may note the conspicuous absence of any reference to profane values. Topics such as profit, money-making, self-seeking behavior—all behavior oriented toward the private ends of the company—are avoided, except where these profane values are themselves converted into sacred ones by the use of latent consequences. Only benefits to the social sub-group, individual or the total society are mentioned. Salaries of high company officials are avoided, profits rarely discussed. These subtle omissions thus enable the institutional advertisers to maintain untarnished the aura of sanctity created by their positive claims.

[65] See "National Association of Broadcasters: The Broadcasters' Creed; Standards of Practice" in Schramm, Wilbur (ed.), *Mass Communications* (Urbana: Univ. of Illinois, 1949).

THE DIMENSIONS OF PROPAGANDA: GERMAN SHORT-WAVE BROADCASTS TO AMERICA

JEROME S. BRUNER*

The present study is an attempt to order propaganda to psychologically significant dimensions of variation. As visual stimuli vary in brightness, hue, saturation, pleasantness, and so on, so does propaganda, a social stimulus situation, vary in specific dimensions: it may be, among other things, negative or positive, emotional or "cold," colloquial or highbrow. On the characteristics or dimensions of propaganda as a social stimulus field, little systematic research, up to now, has been done. By and large, investigators have been content to describe propaganda in simple, particularistic terms without providing common denominators in terms of which comparisons of different propagandas can be carried out. As a result, there are on record countless detailed descriptions of the propaganda campaigns of the past and present, many of them excellent historical documents. But the full value of such records cannot be realized until standardized categories of description have been developed, for the value of propaganda re-

search lies not in mere description but in the chance it affords for correlating propaganda with political trends and with changes in public opinion. And correlation is impossible without standard categories for representing variation—in this case, variation in propaganda.

Accordingly, two samples of German radio propaganda to the United States and one of British, included for comparative purposes, have been submitted to exhaustive analysis. From the results of this analysis were constructed what appeared to the writer as nine significant dimensions within which propaganda varies. In the present paper, German radio propaganda will be described in terms of these and, where possible, compared to British propaganda.

German broadcasts beamed to North America during the period from January 20 to August 10, 1940, constitute the first sample. Since the volume of German broadcasting to America during this period was too great to handle in a single investigation, only transmitted material explicitly related to America was selected for analysis. Seven hundred and seventy-eight fifteen-minute programs were combed for such references, and in this vast output, 272 were found. These references varied in length from full fifteen-minute broadcasts to a mere fifty

* Part of the research herein reported was carried out while the writer was a member of the research staff of the Princeton Listening Center, a project of the Rockefeller Foundation. He is indebted to Professors E. G. Boring and G. W. Allport, to Dr. I. L. Child, and to Katherine Frost Bruner for valuable advice.

From the *Journal of Abnormal and Social Psychology*, 1941, Vol. 36, No. 3, pp. 311-337. Reprinted by permission of the author and the publisher, The American Psychological Association.

words of comment on some American subject.[1]

In order to facilitate the examination of trends in German broadcasting to America, the period from January 20 to August 10 was divided into four intervals.

Period I (total references to America, 29): January 20 to February 19. The opening date of this period has no particular political significance. The closing date, February 19, falls right in the middle of the dispute over the seizure of the Altmark when Germany, by accusing Britain of designs on Norway, was giving the sign—had the world been able to read it—that she was preparing an invasion.

Period II (total references to America, 35): February 20 to April 9. April 9 is the date on which the Reichswehr carried out the "protective invasion" of Norway and Denmark. Period II is, therefore, a "pre-invasion" period in which the German General Staff must have been laying plans for action in Scandinavia.[2]

Period III (total references to America, 58): April 10 to June 23. This period is divisible into two sub-periods. The first of these, extending to May 10, the date on which the Low Countries were invaded, was characterized by a marked diminution of references to America on the German radio. The second sub-period, extending to the date on which the Armistice of Compiègne was signed, showed a fourfold increase of references to America over the first sub-period.

Period IV (total references to America, 150): June 24 to August 10. Representing a time of stalemate after the fall of France, the period terminated with the beginning of mass air raids on the British Isles.

The second sample consisted of all available material dealing with the Altmark case transmitted by the Overseas Service of the British Broadcasting Service and the North American Service of the *Deutsche Kurzwellensender* at Zeesen-Berlin between February 17 and March 1, 1940.[3] Sixty-seven programs fifteen to thirty minutes in length were examined for such material and 91 references to the Altmark obtained—fifty-four from Berlin, the remainder from London. References to the Altmark case, ranging from about 35 to 1400 words, for both German and British broadcasts averaged about 325 words in length.

Each sample was submitted to analysis in terms of a large number of categories of classification dealing with content, emotional appeal, propaganda devices, type of "pressure" exerted upon the audience, and so on. The exact nature of these categories will be made clear in the course of presenting the results. The writer, in addition, indulged his privilege of "free observation" in an effort to note such subtle propaganda characteristics as would not yield to the method of categorical classification. We may turn, then, without further ado to a consideration of German propaganda in terms of nine dimensions.

THE DISSOLVENT-UNIFYING DIMENSION

Propaganda may have as its characteristic the potentiality for creating faction or cohesion in a population. German radio propaganda to the United States cleaves to the former course.

Dissolvent propaganda[4]

Hitler himself has described the aim and methods of this type of propaganda. "Our strategy is to destroy the enemy from within, to conquer him through himself," he

---

[1] The material upon which this investigation is based was made available by the Princeton Listening Center.

[2] For an account of the close connection of German broadcasting and other governmental activities in Nazi Germany, see Dressler-Andress, H., German broadcasting, *Ann. Amer. Acad. pol. soc. Sci.*, 1935, 178, 7 et seq.

[3] Transcriptions of the broadcasts were supplied by the Princeton Listening Center, which recorded about 75 per cent of the non-entertainment broadcasts to America during this period.

[4] This section is based entirely on German broadcasts to America during the first half of 1940 and does not refer to the Altmark material.

confided to Hermann Rauschning. "Mental confusion, contradictions of feeling, indecisiveness, panic—these are our weapons." Or again, "Artillery preparation before an attack as during the World War will be replaced in the future war by the psychological dislocation of the adversary through revolutionary propaganda." And German broadcasts to America—particularly during Periods III and IV, after the active phase of warfare commenced—were ammunition for the new type of artillery barrage. The following devices were employed.

a. BREAKING FAITH IN THE CUSTOMARY SOURCES OF INFORMATION Propaganda which seeks to disunify a nation must first destroy or weaken the standards in terms of which people judge events. Such standards we adopt in large part from our social milieu. "Each of us," comments Walter Lippmann, "lives and works on a small part of the earth's surface, moves in a small circle, and of these acquaintances knows only a few intimately. Of any public event that has wide effects, we see at best only an aspect. . . . Inevitably, our opinions cover a bigger space . . . than we can directly observe. They have, therefore, to be pieced together out of what others have reported and what we can imagine."[5] On the whole, it is the newspaper and the radio in modern society which supply whatever security-giving stereotypes or standards we construct to "cover the spaces we cannot directly observe." Upon the former, Germany centered its attack.

Starting in the late winter of 1939-40, the German radio began its campaign against the predominantly pro-British American press. In an attempt to discredit it as inaccurate, biased, and venal, the attack was launched on four fronts. (1) The press was linked with already established negative stereotypes: "British plutocrats," "aliens," "Jews," and "Wall Street." (2) To disparage the accuracy of the American press, wishful news reports and editorial interpretation of prominent American papers were subjected to derisive scrutiny. A regular program

called "Listen and judge for yourself" was devoted entirely to that end. (3) International intrigue, always good for a thrill, was made the "nigger in the woodpile"; a "plot" for persuading the government to occupy South America, for example, was attributed to Arthur Hays Sulzberger of the New York Times. (4) Slyly they questioned, did the American press represent American opinion?

Had this campaign succeeded, and had no new sources of information been made available—and the Germans were certainly not trying to substitute any—acute confusion might well have reigned. And had it reigned, one weapon would have been added to the arsenal of dissolvent propaganda. That such confusion might readily predispose a nation toward severe social disorganization was understood dramatically in the panic following the "Martian invasion." One of the important conditions for that panic, as Cantril has shown, was the absence of adequate standards of judgment for interpreting the report that Martians were invading the United States.[6]

b. SETTING GROUP AGAINST GROUP To divide and conquer is the dictum of the new propaganda. Not only did the German radio attempt to drive a wedge between the United States and the Allies; it labored also to split group from group within the United States. The anti-Semitic appeal, as always, was the opening wedge. By constant assertion that Jews in America were attempting to run the Government against the desires of "the Gentile population who wish no traffic with Jews," the problem was exaggerated to crisis proportions. Such appeals served also as the hammer for other wedges. Said one speaker in the early spring of 1940:

Leslie Hore-Belisha may attract considerable attention in New York, but when he crosses the Hudson River to regions where the genteel and Gentile population lives, he will not . . .

Other groups too the German radio sought to pit against each other—political parties, economic classes, isolationists and interventionists, geographical regions.

[5] Lippmann, W. Public Opinion. New York: Macmillan, 1936, p. 79.

[6] Cantril, H. The invasion from Mars. Princeton: Princeton University Press, 1939.

c. SETTING THE PEOPLE AGAINST THEIR LEADERS A nation without leadership is anarchy. To break the faith of the American people in their leaders was the constant design of the German radio. "Who," asked one speaker as early as April, 1940, "is making the decisions in America—the people or the politicians?" And later, "The United States have their own problems, and when it came to the test, they proved unwilling to sacrifice for the democracies which Roosevelt cheered on so long as he could conceive the faintest hope of their not being defeated."

d. EXAGGERATING CRISIS SITUATIONS Because constant crisis leaves a people emotionally exhausted, it is a powerful ally of the dissolvent propagandist.[7] Even before the outbreak of active warfare in Europe, this device was put into service. Before they actually existed, crises were invented. In February, 1940, for example, a commentator confided to his audience that he had it "on good authority" it was but "a matter of weeks" before the United States would be drawn into the war by the conspiracy of British warmongers and their American satellites. When active warfare did commence in Europe, opportunity was taken to make every diplomatic and military event appear as a symptom of impending crisis—an episode in the drama of inexorable German advance.

e. STIMULATING FEELINGS OF GUILT Compulsive indecision is one price man pays for conflict over what he deems to be "right." When such a conflict is aggravated by a sense of guilt for related actions in the past, indecisiveness is heightened. All during the spring and summer of 1940 America was reminded of its behavior during the last war. Painful examples of the way in which America had been misled by British propaganda during World War I were dug up, along with detailed accounts of war hysteria. And all the time, announcers pointed to parallels —even to the extent of reading an alleged

letter of a sixteen-year-old boy in Tennessee retailing the manner in which anti-German persecutions had already begun in America. "Soon it will be time also," concluded the speaker, "for burning German textbooks and smashing German cameras and mouth organs. Patriotic mothers will refuse to send Mary and Johnny to Kindergarten. . . . Friends will not wave to each other on the street—the raised arm might be taken for a German salute. . . . And while we're about it, let's not forget to discharge professors and school teachers who, in an absent-minded moment, let slip a good word for German science and culture." Thus was the enthusiastic adoption of univocal anti-German or pro-British attitudes toward the war spiked.

f. AGGRAVATING THE FIFTH-COLUMN SCARE The fifth-column is a double-edged sword. As a weapon of military strategy, its effectiveness has already been realized.[8] As a means of fostering divisive suspicion, moreover, its potentialities have not been overlooked by German strategists. Said a speaker on August 1, 1940, "If my information is reliable, you are beginning to notice the first-line symptoms of this fever in your own country here and there."

Table 1 reveals that the peak of German discussions of the fifth column appeared during Period III, at the time when the reports of Leland Stowe and other American correspondents were creating such a sensation in America. It is important to note, however, that the Germans did not merely try to *defend* themselves against these charges; rather, by countercharges they tried to complicate the issue as much as possible. "There's much talk of fifth-column activity in the United States," said a speaker on July 13. "Well, it would seem that such activities are actually being carried on; and if the investigators look carefully, they'll probably find that the hatbands of the columnists have London labels." But rarely if ever did the Germans attempt to deny the

[7] On this point, see Edmond Taylor's report of the collapse of French morale. *The strategy of terror*. Boston: Houghton Mifflin, 1940.

[8] Donovan, W., and Mowrer, E. *Fifth column lessons for America*. Washington: American Council on Public Affairs, 1940.

charge that they themselves had employed fifth-column tactics in Europe.

So fantastic at times were the turns given to fifth-column stories that one doubts whether they were intended to be believed by the American audience or merely stated to create confusion and doubt about the fifth column in general. A melodramatic announcement, for example, was broadcast during the spring of 1940 to the effect that the combined British and French Secret Service were planning to blow up two ships repatriating Americans from abroad. The alleged intention of the act was to create an atrocity; and when the atrocity had been committed, the "network of British fifth-columnists in America," leveling an accusing finger at Berlin, would stampede the United States into the war. The act had not yet been committed, it was claimed, only because the conspirators had not decided what sort of "infernal machine" was to be used. Here we have the so-called "whopping lie," used so frequently by the Germans. It is probably not intended to be believed, but only to cast doubt on the claims of the other side. Apparently similar in aim were German claims against the British in the sinking of the Athenia, and likewise their claims that Norway had been "protectively" invaded.

TABLE 1

PERCENTAGES OF REFERENCES TO AMERICA IN EACH PERIOD CONTAINING DISCUSSIONS OF BRITISH PROPAGANDA AND FIFTH-COLUMN ACTIVITIES IN AMERICA

Period			
I	II	III	IV
Jan. 20 to Feb. 19	Feb. 20 to April 9	April 10 to June 22	June 23 to Aug. 10
17	23	31	20

g. STIMULATING FATALISM The nation convinced of the futility of resistance is ripe for the ravages of dissolvent propaganda. Ever since the outbreak of the war in September, 1939, Berlin broadcasts have tried to create an impression of the inevitability of German victory. When German military might became evident in fact as well as in promise, the campaign intensified. Constantly listeners were told of the calm assurance of the German people, of the invincibility of German arms, of the weakness and confusion of the enemies of the Reich in resisting the might of the *Reichswehr*. By July 1, German announcers were taking for granted a complete and imminent victory. Trade appeals after that date, for example, were made on the ground that Germany was "slated to play the dominant role on the continent of Europe." Britain "must" collapse, America was warned; it was fatal to be "the exponent of an out-moded system." "In a race where the stakes are so big," admonished one speaker, "it is sheer folly to put your money on the wrong horse."

h. "THE STRATEGY OF TERROR." That a cowed population is open to the depressing effects of fatalism has been demonstrated by Edmond Taylor in his study of the French collapse.[9] After the invasion of Scandinavia, the horror of war was a constant theme of Berlin speakers. The main stress of this material was the fruitlessness of resistance. In contrast to war and its horrors stood cooperation with Germany; samples were the peaceful affiliates of the Axis. Never in the period covered by the present survey was the United States directly threatened with an onslaught of German force. But in discussions of German activities against her enemies, it was made abundantly clear that resistance by any nation was hopeless.[10]

THE NEGATIVE-POSITIVE DIMENSION

Propaganda may criticize or justify, attack or defend. The variation between these two extremes is the negative-positive dimension. Hitler has indicated the place of German

[9] Taylor, E. *Op. cit.*

[10] Other branches of German propaganda have been active in this line. The German film, *Blitzkrieg in the West*, circulated without question to any group who will take it by the German Library of Information in New York, portrays the "inevitable" advance of German divisions in Flanders and France with constant emphasis on the futility of resistance.

propaganda in this continuum by the statement, "He defends himself best who personally attacks."[11]

Several methods have been used in the present study to isolate the negative and positive characteristics of our samples. A first, rather crude, attempt was to compute the number of references to America during the first half of 1940 containing criticism or praise of Germany, Great Britain, and the United States. Four categories were employed.

a. *Vilification of Britain in her relations with the United States.* Any reference which portrayed Great Britain, her colonies, or her dominions in a malevolent role with reference to the United States, whether culturally, economically, politically, or militarily is included here.

b. *Praise of Germany in her relations with the United States.* Included here are all items which portrayed Germany in a benign cultural, economic, political, or military role with reference to the United States.

c. *Praise of the United States, her traditions, citizens, institutions, or actions.*

d. *Criticism of the United States, her traditions, citizens, institutions, or actions.*

Table 2 contains the results. The thing for the reader to note here particularly is the emphasis on negativism. Later discussion will deal with these results further.

TABLE 2

PERCENTAGES OF BERLIN REFERENCES TO AMERICA CONTAINING CRITICISM AND PRAISE

Period

	I N=29	II N=35	III N=58	IV N=150
Vilifications of Britain	73	63	51	47
Pleasing Picture of Germany	24	34	32	33
Praise of America	31	43	26	19
Criticism of America	21	29	39	42

A second method approached the problem from a different angle. An attempt was made to delve into the actual content of the references in order to ascertain the kinds of positive and negative pressures which were being exerted on the listening audience. This second method of classification, consequently, took as its unit of analysis not the heterogeneous "reference to America," which might deal with several topics, but the actual "pressures" on the audience. By a pressure is meant the expression of a bias—criticizing or commending something. The expression of such "bias," the writer felt, might serve as a strong stimulus to the adoption of similar or opposite bias on the part of the listener; it should prove, therefore, a significant and meaningful unit upon which to base a quantitative analysis.

Accordingly, a set of "dimensions of bias" was constructed and German broadcasts during the first half of 1940 submitted to analysis in terms of it. The "dimensions" follow.

1. *Anti-environment pressures* ($-E$). These are divisible into two groups:

a. *Personal anti-environment pressures* (Pers $-E$). Statements which praise, criticize, or otherwise discuss the audience with respect to its response or attitude toward some aspect of the environment being criticized.[12] "The American people are to be praised for condemning the activities of certain Jews in their midst," is an example.

b. *Impersonal anti-environment pressures* (Impr $-E$). Criticisms of the environment which do not explicitly relate the audience to the aspect of the environment criticized.

2. *Pro-environment pressures* ($+E$). These too are divisible into types:

a. *Personal pro-environment pressures* (Pers $+E$). Statements which praise, criticize, or otherwise discuss the audience with respect to its response or attitude toward some aspect of the environment being praised. An example is, "The American people honor in Senator Borah the great traditions of their country."

[11] Hitler, A. *Mein Kampf.* New York: Reynal and Hitchcock, 1939, p. 746.

[12] *Environment* refers to traditions, institutions, leaders, policies, etc., which are said by the German radio to be parts of the American scene.

b. *Impersonal pro-environment pressures* (Impr +E). Commendations of the environment which do not explicitly relate the audience to the aspect of the environment commended.

3. *Anti-self pressures* (−S). Criticism of the audience for some attitude toward its environment or for some characteristic alleged to be exhibited by the audience.

4. *Pro-self pressures* (+S). Commendation of the audience for some attitude toward its environment or for some characteristic alleged to be exhibited by the audience.

5. *Types of environment* (E Am, E Br, and E Gr).

a. *British-linked environment* (E Br). Criticism or praise of some aspect of the American environment explicitly related by an announcer to the British—*e.g.*, criticism of the American press asserting it to be the pawn of the British Foreign Office. The linkage may be more or less direct: the statement that British politicians are pulling wires behind the American diplomatic scene is direct; pointing out an affinity between "Wall Street" and "British plutocracy" is relatively indirect.

b. *German-linked environment* (E Gr). Criticism or praise of some aspect of the American environment explicitly related to Germany. Praise of the American way of life which likens the chance for advancement there to the New Order in Germany is an example.

c. *Native American environment* (E Am). Discussions, either critical or commendatory, of aspects of the native American scene without explicit references to foreign influence or affinity.

6. *Personal pressures* (Pers). All discussions of the audience, either critical or commendatory, whether related to attitudes toward the environment or to audience characteristics as such.

7. *Impersonal pressures* (Impr). Criticism or praise of the environment without reference to the audience.[13]

[13] All categories are not mutually exclusive, although they form mutually exclusive pairs. Thus, anti-environment (−E) and pro-environ-

The results of this classification appear in Table 3. The negative tone of German broadcasting is quite apparent. At all times the anti-environment category (−E) led all others in frequency and was markedly higher than the pro-environment category (items 3, 4, 25, in Table 3). Further, an increasing tide of criticism of the United States (item 11) and a concomitant decrease of praise (item 13) was to be noted. As time went on, in short, the Berlin radio became more critical of America, shifting the brunt of criticism from Britain (item 12) to this country. This graded negative pressure will be discussed again in a later section.

With respect to praise and criticism of the audience, the same thing is to be noted: a gradual shift from praise to criticism (items 1, 2, 24). In addition, both praise and criticism of the environment became increasingly impersonal as time went on (items 5-8). The meaning of this depersonalization will become clearer shortly.

The same negativity can be seen in the analysis of the Altmark material. Here an opportunity is afforded for placing both British and German propaganda on the negative-positive dimension. Analysis provides many unambiguous examples of the relative negativity of German appeals. In Table 4 are presented comparisons of German and British broadcasts. The items contained there are ones which epitomize the option of attacking the adversary or justifying one's own cause. How often the British

ment (+E) pressures do not overlap; neither do anti-self (−S) and pro-self (+S) pressures, nor personal (Pers) and impersonal (Impr) pressures. Likewise, the three types of environment (E Br, E Gr, and E Am) are mutually exclusive. Pro-self (+S) and anti-self (−S) pressures are composed of all personal pro-environment pressures (Pers +E) and personal anti-environment pressures (Pers −E) which praise or criticize the audience respectively, plus all praise or criticism of the audience which is unrelated to the environment. The category treating personal pressures (Pers) comprises −S and +S, and all discussions of the environment which treat the audience neutrally. Impersonal pressures are the sum of Impr −E and Impr +E.

TABLE 3

PERCENTAGE OF NEGATIVE AND POSITIVE PRESSURES

Period

		I N=41	II N=53	III N=79	IV N=208
1.	−S	17	4	23	17
2.	+S	20	34	8	4
3.	−E	71	70	63	67
4.	+E	29	23	33	28
5.	Pers −E	44	42	27	21
6.	Impr −E	27	28	36	46
7.	Pers +E	15	10	10	7
8.	Impr +E	14	13	23	21
9.	Pers	59	59	37	30
10.	Impr	51	51	63	70
11.	−E Am	20	23	38	34
12.	−E Br	51	47	25	33
13.	+E Am	20	15	18	10
14.	+E Gr	9	8	15	18
15.	Pers −E Am	5	8	11	9
16.	Impr −E Am	15	15	27	25
17.	Pers −E Br	39	34	16	12
18.	Impr −E Br	12	13	9	21
19.	Pers +E Am	8	4	4	0
20.	Impr +E Am	12	11	14	10
21.	Pers +E Gr	7	6	6	7
22.	Impr +E Gr	2	2	9	11
23.	Pers: Impr Ratio	(1.2)	(1.2)	(.70)	(.63)
24.	+S:−S Ratio	(1.18)	(8.5)	(.35)	(.24)
25.	+E:−E Ratio	(.41)	(.33)	(.52)	(.42)

TABLE 4

PERCENTAGES OF REFERENCES TO THE ALTMARK CASE CONTAINING CRITICAL AND JUSTIFICATORY ITEMS

	British	German
Emphasizing own legal justification in case	57	26
Emphasizing enemy legal blame in case	51	70
Favorable treatment: own nation	89	60
Unfavorable treatment: enemy nation	81	91
Enemy violation of international law	54	72
Own respect for international law	41	26
Charging Altmark case involves enemy atrocity*	16	50

* Both sides had equal opportunity to make atrocity charges in the case; the British could concentrate on the treatment of the English captives on board the Altmark, the Germans on the violent behavior of the boarding party which seized the ship.

choose the latter and the Germans the former is a striking commentary on their divergent strategies.

Still another index of the intensity of the negative appeals is possible here: the type of emotional language used by Germany and Great Britain in their broadcasts on the Altmark. Table 5 contains the ratio of emo-

TABLE 5

RATIO OF EMOTIONALLY TONED TO NEUTRAL WORDS IN THE REPORTING OF THE ALTMARK CASE

	British	German
Ratio of emotionally toned to neutral words	1:60	1:36.5
Negatively emotionally toned words to neutral words	1:129	1:59
Positively emotionally toned words to neutral words	1:110	1:87

tionally toned to neutral words found in the transmissions of both powers. Not only were German broadcasts more emotional than British; they showed in addition a greater density of negatively toned than positively toned words.

The importance of negative propaganda as an adjunct to the strategy of demoralization is intrenched in the history of Europe prior to World War II. The German-Polish non-aggression pact of 1931, for example, contains explicit articles forbidding the use of negative propaganda by either signee against the other. The same provision is made in the League of Nations *Convention governing the use of radio in the cause of peace* (1937).[14] In an attempt to account for the alleged effectiveness of negative propaganda, F. C. Bartlett points to the fact that social thinking in general tends more often to be negative and critical than positive and constructive. Negative thinking, he says, since it requires less detachment from the social group, demands less effort on the part of the individual.

Parenthetically, Bartlett suggests that negative propaganda makes its appeal to "a lot of obscure motives . . . connected with antago-

[14] Grandin, T. The political use of the radio. *Geneva studies*, No. 10, 1939.

nism to established forms of control."[15] Psychoanalytic writers have made much of this point. As a result of inevitable frustration, according to them, latent aggression is built up in the course of social life. Thus, in times of crisis when frustration runs high, such latent aggression may become a particularly potent factor in determining social response. Negative propaganda, appealing to this fund of unexpressed aggressiveness, may in terms of this theory lead to two demoralizing consequences: either the individual will consciously adopt aggressive attitudes toward symbols of authority within the culture, or he will be overcome by anxiety lest the newly incited aggression prove too overwhelming an impulse for him to control. In either event, that much dissonance has been added to the harmony of social life; and thereby the aim of dissolvent propaganda, discussed in the preceding section, is furthered.[16]

THE TEMPORAL DIMENSION

A propaganda campaign takes place in time; with time, its characteristics change. It may start with a flourish, gradually peter out, flare up again, then die out completely. Such trends may characterize the campaign as a whole; they may also apply to parts thereof—for example, the amount of criticism. Two marked trend characteristics are featured in German short-wave propaganda.

a. The method of graded attack

In the preceding section the over-all characteristic of German propaganda was shown to be negative; criticism rather than justifi-

[15] Bartlett, F. C. Political propaganda. Cambridge: Cambridge University Press, 1940, p. 78 et seq.

[16] For psychoanalytic interpretations of the efficacy of negative propaganda, see French, T. M., Social conflict and psychic conflict, Amer. J. Sociol., 1938-39, 44, 922-931; and White, A. B., The new propaganda, London: Gollancz, 1939, esp. Chap. 9, "Anxiety, guilt, and hostility." The frustration-aggression hypothesis is discussed by Doob, L., Dollard, J., et al., Frustration and aggression, New Haven: Yale University Press, 1939.

cation could be considered its hallmark. But negativity developed gradually; its growth exemplified the method of graded attack. Evident not only in the general rise of criticism over the four periods, it was also apparent in specific campaigns carried out by Reichssender Berlin.

For example, in attacks on the American press the campaign got under way with criticisms of "some American newspapers," an arraignment with which few could take exception. No specific newspapers were mentioned. The next stage of the attack, somewhat allegorical, was carried in a weekly dramatic monologue "Hot off the wire." Gertie Hahn, who played the role of switchboard girl on the fictitious "Pittsburgh Tribune," in answering the calls for information, transmitted tales about the inner workings of the paper to her girl friend Nancy. Among the bits she let slip were condemnations of "Rosenbloom and Finklestein," the editors of her paper, allegedly so extremely pro-British as to twist around the wires sent from Berlin by the paper's German correspondent Joe, Gertie's boy friend. Having thus established two legendary scapegoats, the Berlin radio next revealed to its audience that ninety per cent of the foreign correspondents for American newspapers were British subjects. On the heels of this disclosure came charges that American papers were indulging in inspired "fortune-telling" rather than news-reporting; evidence was adduced in the program called "Listen and judge for yourself" and in the topical talks of "Mr. Okay." In the next phase, attacks were launched straight against two potent prestige symbols of American journalism— the New York Times and the New York Herald-Tribune. In due course these papers and others were charged with being "Jewish controlled," "alien affiliated," or corrupted by other "sinister influences." The culminating step was the blanket charge that the American press as a whole was "criminally stupid," the agent of "Jews, warmongers, and Wall Street."

Quantitatively, the method of graded attack can be expressed in terms of the fluctuations in praise and criticism through the four periods covered by this survey, as represented in Tables 2 and 3. Shifting the brunt of criticism gradually from the British-linked to the American environment was one token (items 11 and 12, Table 3). By this means the audience was first invited to whet its critical spirit on "foreign" symbols, and then gradually slipped a purely American set of symbols upon which to turn that criticism which formerly had been reserved for the British. There was, in fact, little difference in the negative stereotypes with which the British and then the Americans were labelled. Both were plutocrats or warmongers or Jewish-controlled. The amount of shift in criticism from Britain to America is presented in Table 6 (item 1).

At the same time that criticism was being directed increasingly upon purely native—hence ego-involved—aspects of the environment, certain other significant shifts appeared. A gradual decrease in the amount of "personal" as compared to "impersonal" praise devoted to the environment became apparent (item 2, Table 6). So extreme was this tendency in the case of praise of the purely American environment, that by Period IV the ratio dwindled almost to zero (item 3). Concomitant with the depersonalization of praise went a steady shift in the focus of praise, from the native American to the German-linked American environment (item 4). A similar downward trend is to be observed in the +S: −S ratio (item 24, Table 3).

TABLE 6

THE GRADED ATTACK AGAINST THE
UNITED STATES

	Period			
	I	II	III	IV
1. −E Am : −E Br	39	.49	1.52	1.03
2. Pers +E : Impr +E	1.07	.77	.44	.33
3. Pers +E Am : Impr +E Am		.66	.36	.29	.04
4. +E Am : +E Gr	2.20	1.87	1.20	.55

Two functions are served by the method of graded attack. In the first place, rapport with the audience may be effected in the more congenial phases of early contact. In the second place, through some obscure psychological mechanism, audiences will tolerate more criticism when that criticism is introduced gradually. And the Berlin radio could not afford to antagonize its listeners, for in radio propaganda, the listener is sovereign; one flip of the dial does the trick.

Concern for the audience may have been at the bottom of another gradual change of policy during the four periods covered in the present survey. As time went on, criticism of the environment grew less and less personal—and this in apparent contradiction to the tactic of increasing pressure described above. (Pers −E: Impr −E ratio: Period I, 1.63; II, 1.50; III, .75; IV, .46.) The writer sees in this decrease an attempt to avoid over-criticism. If a broadcaster would not offend his audience, there is a certain point of criticism beyond which he dare not go. As the German radio centered its criticism more and more squarely upon the purely American, and hence ego-involved aspects of the environment, and as praise dwindled, compensation had to be made in some other sphere. This demand, it appears to the writer, has been fulfilled by an impersonalization of criticism.

The significance of the step-by-step method in propaganda has been remarked by several writers. Doob, for example, designates this type of campaign as "delayed revealed."[17] Hitler too has commented on the efficacy of the method.[18] Probably the best empirical demonstration of its power is provided in the experiments of Lewin and his colleagues on overcoming undesirable food preferences in children.[19]

[17] Doob, L. *Propaganda: Its psychology and technique.* New York: Holt, 1935. He says, "In delayed revealed propaganda, the propagandist reveals his aim only after he has aroused related attitudes." *Cf.* p. 413.

[18] Hitler, A. *Mein Kampf.* New York: Reynal and Hitchcock, 1939, p. 850 *et seq.*

[19] Lewin, K. The conceptual representation and measurement of psychological forces. *Contributions to psychological theory*, 1938, I, No. 4, 117-119.

b. Policy pace-making

Another temporal characteristic of propaganda is the manner in which it is geared to contemporary diplomatic and military manoeuvers. In the sense of "softening" or preparing a population for future moves, German propaganda, as we have pointed out in preceding sections, precedes or sets the pace for policy. Several striking instances of the technic are revealed in the results of the present investigation.

"Unpreparing" the audience for the outbreak of active hostilities in Europe was one such instance. Period II, it will be remembered, comprises the weeks immediately preceding the German invasion of Scandinavia. Milder, more conciliatory, and less indicative of belligerent intentions than at any other time, Berlin broadcasts during that period gave no readable indication of the holocaust which was to follow. Discussions of Germany, on the contrary, pictured an amiable people, innocent of warlike designs—a "peace-loving nation" in contrast to Great Britain "with a navy on your very shores." Items 1, 2, and 24 in Table 3 depict the cordial tone adopted toward the American audience at that time. A further comparison of the congeniality of Period II with the negative tone of later periods is provided in item 11 of the same table and in Table 6. To a constant listener, the invasion which ended Period II must indeed have been a shock. For so mild had been the broadcasts that the *blitz* character of the German move northward could not but have been enhanced.

In addition, when the purpose served, the German radio carried material which *directly* foreshadowed future policies of the Reich. Weeks before Hitler delivered his "last appeal to reason" to the English on July 19, the German radio had been broadcasting similar exhortations. Again, the speech of Reichsminister of Economics Walther Funk on July 25 "offering" the United States economic collaboration with the "new" Europe, was foreshadowed as early as the end of June, when Berlin speakers appealed to American economic self-interest to trade with "the dominant power on the continent."

By providing advance justification for possible action against Norway, Germany in her treatment of the Altmark case again betrayed her hand to those few who had sat at the card table with her before. Constantly the world was told that Britain was the traditional violator of neutral rights—particularly Norwegian rights. Table 7 reveals how closely Germany linked her cause with the cause of Norway "against the depredations of the piratical British." By such ties Germany intimated that she might have to protect herself against the British threat to the north. Yet nothing specific was said about the measures Germany *would* take.

TABLE 7

PERCENTAGE OF REFERENCES TO THE ALTMARK CASE CONTAINING DISCUSSION OF NEUTRAL-BELLIGERENT RELATIONS

	British	German
Citing neutral public opinion unfavorable to enemy country	3	20
Pointing out danger to neutrals from enemy country	38	65
Picturing Norway as oppressed by enemy	41	74
Linking loss of Altmark with violation of Norwegian rights	0	57

PERSONAL-IMPERSONAL DIMENSION

How deep into the "inner man" does propaganda seek to pierce? There are innumerable ways of going beneath the skin. One may use emotional language (see Table 2). Or one may discourse on those things another holds dear; criticisms of a man's wife go deeper than diatribes against the policies of Madam Secretary Perkins. Or, for a third, one may play up dramatically the place of an individual in a context of events under discussion. "Cambridge has littered streets" is not so potent a charge as "You ought to be ashamed of the littered streets of Cambridge." The variation between the personally charged and the superficial appeal is what we refer to here as the personal-impersonal dimension.

Analysis of Table 2 shows us that, in terms of emotionality of language, German propaganda in the Altmark case went farther toward the personal pole of the dimension than did British. In other respects, this difference was not sustained (see Table 8).

TABLE 8

PERCENTAGE OF REFERENCES TO THE ALT-MARK CONTAINING "PERSONAL" APPROACH TO THE AUDIENCE

	British	German
"You-me" form of address	22	19
Analogizing events in terms of American scene	3	6
"Plain folks" device	46	19
Wit, sarcasm, and irony	16	17

Three out of the four indices chosen show equality between the British and the German. The fourth, however—the "plain folks" device, talking as one Little Man to another —evened up the score all around.

Some indication of the place of German references to America during the first half of 1940 on the personal-impersonal dimension is contained in the personal and impersonal categories of Table 3 (items 1, 2, 5-10, 15-23). Three things were noted there: (1) a gradual decline in the ratio of personal to impersonal discussions (item 23); (2) a sharp decrease in praise of the audience following Period II (item 2); (3) a steady depersonalization over the four periods of all praise and criticism of the American environment (items 5-8). The reader can find the absolute level of this personal and impersonal material by reference to Table 3.

STRATIFIED-HOMOGENEOUS DIMENSION

So long as there is organized society, there will be specialized groups with different needs and different interests; and so long as there are propagandists, they will make their appeal to these specialized groups. This method of stratified appeals is not new. It received its first intensive use in World War I.[20] To measure the stratification of propaganda directly is virtually impossible; there are occasions when a single propaganda appeal may mean all things to all people. Notwithstanding this fact, approximate indices can and should be constructed.

A check-list, of course, offers the simplest procedure. One might list specialized appeals to economic, cultural, geographical, racial, and occupational groups, to be checked appropriately. And since stratified appeals are so closely related to the strategy of divide and rule, one might also check whether the appeals constitute a wedge between groups or a plea for cooperation. No such method, unfortunately, was employed in the present investigation. But certain observations are relevant. For example, among divisive stratified appeals were attempts to turn the American people against their leaders, Gentiles against Jews, lower class against upper, the country against New York and Wall Street, America against Britain, the people against alien refugees, isolationists against interventionists, newspaper readers against the press. "Stratified" programs were instituted for housewives (Zeesen Women's Club), the intelligentsia (The College Hour), esthetes (topical talks), music lovers (music), business men (Economic Review), German-Americans (German-language transmissions), scandal-mongers (Charley's Cabaret and Mr. Okay), the upper classes (Constance Drexel, et al.), anti-Semites (The Jew in American History, etc.), white-collar workers (Gertie Hahn), automobile drivers (topical talk), midwesterners (Dear Harry and the Folks Back Home in Iowa), the unemployed (Jim and Johnny), patriots (British Disregard for American Rights, and Paul Revere Rides Again), New Yorkers (Mr. Okay). On the

[20] See Thimme, H., Weltkrieg ohne Waffen, Berlin and Stuttgart: Cotta, 1932; Bruntz, G. G., Allied propaganda and the collapse of the German empire in 1918, Stanford: Stanford University Press, 1938; "Hansi" et Tonnelat, E., A travers les lignes ennemies, Paris: Payot, 1922.

whole, appeals were not homogeneous, but highly stratified.

To the economic royalist, the financial interpretation of an event is more dramatic than a consideration of its place in the divine scheme. The Frère de Sacré Coeur may feel otherwise. Whatever interpretation is given, it will interest some and bore others. An index of interpretation, therefore, proves a valuable tool in predicting roughly the type of individual to whom propaganda is directed. A preliminary attempt to get at such an index was made in the investigation of the Altmark case; four types of interpretation of the case were recorded. The results appear in Table 9.

A better set of categories might have been Spranger's six value types: political, social, religious, economic, esthetic, and theoretical. That such classification may serve as a basis of prediction is suggested by the work of Woolbert. She found that persons rating high in a particular value on the Allport-Vernon Study of Values, when presented with a dummy newspaper composed of equal amounts of material judged by the experimenter to fall into the six types, tended to read and remember items of their same value type.[21] An analysis of references to America during the first half of 1940 would probably have revealed a fairly even spread over all six types, with peaks in the social and economic. "Value analysis," however, was not undertaken.

TABLE 9

PERCENTAGE OF REFERENCES CONTAINING
FOUR TYPES OF INTERPRETATION OF THE
ALTMARK CASE

	British	German
Moral interpretation	65	67
Legal interpretation	54	80*
Military interpretation	43	22
Economic interpretation	5	9

* Remember that in terms of conventional international law, the Germans had a better legal case than did the British (Britain violated Norwegian waters). Britain's saving graces were moral (freeing the suffering English captives) and military (the efficacy of the British blockade).

[21] Cantril, H., and Allport, G. W. Recent applications of the *Study of values.* This JOURNAL, 1933, 28, 259-273.

AUTHORITATIVE-CASUAL DIMENSION

Since prestige suggestion is probably one of the most important psychological factors in propaganda, a knowledge of "authoritativeness" becomes a "must." Are the Scriptures quoted? Government reports? Eye-witnesses? Famous aviators? What about the prestige of the medium? Is it a broadcast over C.B.S., B.B.C., *Reichssender Berlin*, or *Paris Mondial*? All the authoritative sources in the world would not shake the average American's suspicion of what can be heard over *Reichssender Berlin*. And who is speaking? The prestige of Lord Haw-Haw and Fred Kaltenbach on the German radio is a wisp compared to that of B.B.C. speakers: Harold Laski, J. B. Priestley, A. V. Alexander, Noel Coward, Leslie Howard, Vincent Sheean, and other luminaries.

It is impossible to say how much prestige the German radio and its speakers have in America. To assume that they have little is fairly safe. Although this fact abrogates prestige suggestion as a major device, the prestige technics used by the Berlin staff must not be overlooked. No systematic study on the subject has been carried out on the references to America during the first half of 1940; yet several authoritative devices were apparent. One is the use of the eye-witness report. E. D. Ward, for example, served the Berlin radio in the capacity of a roving eye-witness reporter covering the victorious wake of the German armies in Flanders and France. What he had to say was delivered with the assurance of the onlooker. H. V. Kaltenborn might have been his stylistic model—curt and "objective." Koischwitz's tony "College Hour" simulated the classroom procedure for its prestige effect. And frequent on other programs were citations of "official figures" on bombings, food conditions, the progress of the war. The use to which the contents of captured diplomatic archives and personal documents have been put, particularly in connection with "war guilt" and the Polish

TABLE 10

PERCENTAGE OF ALTMARK REFERENCES
CONTAINING PRESTIGE DEVICES

	British	German
Asserting universality of a view	38	47
Citing documentary evidence as proof	35	20
Citing a neutral authority as proof	24	21
Citing an historical precedent as proof	24	30

invasion, are familiar. "Mr. Okay" lifted his prestige by the shaky bootstrap of confiding to his audience that his information was "confidential." But the greatest boost of all was the prestige of German victories.

In the Altmark propaganda, a comparison of some British and German prestige devices was attempted. The results appear in Table 10. Although there is numerical equality in the use of prestige devices by both powers, we must repeat again that such equality may be nullified by the greater overall prestige of the British radio in America and the distrust of Germany. So long as one can invoke the proverb, "Beware the Devil quoting Scripture," mere statistical equivalence becomes irrelevant.

DIMENSION OF COLLOQUIALITY

One criterion of good propaganda upon which all writers agree is that it speak the language of the group to which it is directed. Taking full cognizance of this, the Berlin radio has made a special point of using speakers who know intimately the language and argot of the people under propaganda attack. To France went the voices of Obrecht and Ferdonnet, two renegade French journalists. England has been showered by the Etonian syllables of William Joyce, Lord Haw-Haw. The North American beam bears into the living rooms of this country the American voices of Fred Kaltenbach, Constance Drexel, E. D. Ward, and others. Whenever "foreigners" were used as announcers, they knew the American language—Otto Koischwitz, for one, erstwhile instructor at Hunter College in New York.

An attempt to measure what might be called "general colloquiality" in the Altmark propaganda by counting the number of slang expressions met with only lukewarm success. Nine percent of the German references, and eight per cent of the British contained some slang. But such a finding is relatively meaningless, for what is slang to one listener may be relatively stilted or unintelligible to another.

Colloquiality also comprises "style." Certain speakers favored the "objective" approach; among these was E. D. Ward, who on several occasions was introduced with a display of breath-taking candor—his views, the audience was assured, were "not necessarily those of this station." Fred Kaltenbach, on the other hand, was partial to a more or less "homespun" technic. Frequently referring to the United States as "we" or "our country" and to Germany as "they," he addressed his remarks to a "pal" back in Waterloo, Iowa, his "home town." His script was liberally peppered with *bons mots* and catch phrases such as "Roly Poly Windsy" for Churchill, the slogan "England borrows, France fights, and America pays," and highly colloquial remarks such as "Socker Berlin is sure to k.o. Kid London."

"Mr. Okay" (Otto Koischwitz, expert on Eugene O'Neill,[22] author of two intermediate German textbooks used by New York City high schools up to April, 1941,[23] and erstwhile instructor in German at Hunter College, New York) presented a news commentary which invariably began with the phrase, "Confidentially. . . ." In his role as confidential tipster and muckraker, he lambasted the American press as "Jewish-controlled," "alien-affiliated," or "criminally stupid," divulged the juicier morsels of anti-Semitism in New York, and reviled American leaders as "plutocratic," "corrupt," "stupid." A program given in his own name, titled "The College Hour," simulated an American classroom, replete with opening and closing bell, and Koischwitz playing

[22] Koischwitz, O. *Eugene O'Neill.* Berlin: Junker and Duenhaupt, 1938.

[23] New York *P. M.*, April 22, 1941, p. 13.

pedagogue. The aim was twofold: to show that learning and erudition were not dead in Germany and to present subtle National Socialist interpretations of such writers as Spranger, Strindberg, O'Neill, Spengler, Materlinck. Here his manner was rather condescending; he even stooped to spelling out difficult terms for his hearers.

Constance Drexel (announced as a "Philadelphia socialite and heiress" but, apparently to avoid litigation, spelled Drechsel in communications sent the writer by the German Library of Information in New York) affected the social chit-chat style; hers was the manner of Elsa Maxwell as she described the life of the American colony in Berlin and general cultural doings there. It was Miss Drexel who assured her audience in the spring of 1940 that the ideals of the New Germany "were those of ancient Greece: truth and beauty." Another woman announcer on the North American Service was Gertie Hahn, who conducted the dramatic monologue called "Hot Off the Wire," a program which has already been described. Her style, an unfortunate choice for imitation by a German, was that of the gum-chewing, flippant American switchboard operator in the Hollywood manner.

IMMEDIATE-REMOTE DIMENSION

Propaganda may deal with the press of contemporary issues or with more remote, general concerns. In so far as it concentrates on the former, it is exerting *direct* pressure on attitudes toward contemporary affairs. Although, of course, propaganda dealing with remote issues may also influence contemporary attitudes, such influence tends to be neither so direct nor so vivid. The stuff of which good propaganda is made, actually, seems to require a mixture, in proper proportions, of these two ingredients.

Both German and British propaganda in the Altmark case hewed to the line of contemporaneity. They did not, of course, resist the temptation of a sidewise glance at such remote concerns as "the glorious naval tradition" of Britain or the "piratical bombardment of Copenhagen" by the British in 1807.

Not more than five to ten per cent of the material, however, was thus concerned. In the case of German references to America in the first half of 1940, the material broke into about 70 per cent contemporary and 30 per cent remote.

DIMENSION OF REPETITIOUSNESS

Hitler, among propagandists, has made most of the need for repetition in propaganda. "Now the purpose of propaganda," he says, "is not continually to produce interesting changes for the few blasé little masters, but to convince; that is, to convince the masses. The masses, however, with their inertia, always need a certain time before they are ready even to notice a thing, and they will lend their memories only to the thousandfold repetition of the most simple ideas."[24]

In German broadcasts to America, Hitler's dictum has been put to good use. Aside from the recasting of content, there has been from time to time little change in the form of the arguments or the nature of the heroes lauded or the villains attacked. From May, 1940, to the time of writing, Berlin broadcasts have changed little. The attacks on the press, Jews, leadership, and institutions of America have continued unabated and only slightly changed; the inevitability of German victory and British defeat is still with us; the conception of the war as a Jewish-British-plutocratic plot against Germany and Adolf Hitler is pumped with as much enthusiasm today as in the spring of last year. The language of the broadcasters too has remained unchanged. "War-monger," "alien-affiliated," "Jewish-controlled," "plutocratic meddler," and other verbal weapons from the German arsenal have received their thousandfold repetition and more.

CONCLUSIONS

Little if anything is known about the effects of these broadcasts; there are even, indeed, no accurate figures on the number

[24] Hitler, A. *Mein Kampf.* New York: Reynal and Hitchcock, 1939, p. 239.

of people in America who listen. We do know that there are some 45,000,000 radio sets in the United States and that of these at least one-fifth are equipped with short-wave bands. Of these, however, probably more than half are too critically tuned to be of much use for intelligible foreign reception. That still leaves a considerable number of potential listeners to be accounted for. In addition to the "direct" audience, there is a vast "indirect" one. Many German-language newspapers in the United States carry in their columns short-wave material from Berlin; so does the semi-fascist press. C.B.S. and N.B.C. maintain expensive listening posts to supply news reporters and commentators with material sent from Germany and other countries. That the broadcasts we have been analyzing are important social stimuli there can, in short, be little doubt.

The purpose of the present paper has not been to predict the future effect of these social stimuli or to guess the past effect. Primarily, its aim was to describe systematically one set of such stimuli—those being carried to the United States on German transmitters. The importance of such systematic description in terms of dimensions of variation need not be discussed again at any great length. In order to correlate changes of opinion with changes in propaganda "pressure," systematic methods of expressing variation in propaganda must be developed and used. The determination of such correlations between propaganda and public opinion, affording as it does the basis for prediction of opinion shifts, is a central task of social psychology, particularly in times of crisis.

Analogous is the problem of the correlation of propaganda changes and political trends. Here again, correlation waits upon the elaboration of systematic dimensions of variation. The important goal, once more, is prediction.

A third need served by the elaboration of such dimensions is the comparison of divergent propagandas. Heretofore common denominators have been lacking. With the construction of adequate dimensions comes the opportunity for intelligible parallel study of campaigns as divergent as those of the German Propaganda Ministry and the corner grocery.

Finally, such a procedure provides a means whereby trends in propaganda can be represented over a period of time in systematic—even quantitative—fashion.

The dimensions proposed are, of course, tentative. To summarize, these are:

1. Dissolvent-unifying dimension
2. Negative-positive dimension
3. The temporal dimension
4. Personal-impersonal dimension
5. Stratified-homogeneous dimension
6. Authoritative-casual dimension
7. Dimension of colloquiality
8. Immediate-remote dimension
9. Dimension of repetitiousness.

The crux of the matter is the need for a dimensional procedure, whatever specific form it may ultimately take. If propaganda analysis is ever to transcend the realm of *belles lettres,* systematization is indispensable.

·9·

Propaganda Strategies and Techniques
and Their Effects

———

GOEBBELS' PRINCIPLES OF PROPAGANDA

SOME REASONS WHY INFORMATION CAMPAIGNS FAIL

PERSONAL CONTACT OR MAIL PROPAGANDA?

SOME PSYCHOLOGICAL LESSONS FROM LEAFLET PROPAGANDA IN WORLD WAR II

COHESION AND DISINTEGRATION IN THE WEHRMACHT IN WORLD WAR II

GOEBBELS' PRINCIPLES OF PROPAGANDA

LEONARD W. DOOB

Among the Nazi documents salvaged by American authorities in Berlin in 1945 are close to 6,800 pages of a manuscript ostensibly dictated by Propaganda Minister Goebbels as a diary which covers, with many gaps, the period from January 21, 1942 to December 9, 1943. The material was typed triple-spaced in large German-Gothic script and with wide margins upon heavy watermarked paper, with the result that the average page contained less than 100 words. About 30 per cent of this manuscript —the most interesting and generally the most important parts—has been very accurately and idiomatically translated by Louis P. Lochner.[1] The analysis in the present article is based upon careful examination of the entire document which is now in the Hoover Institute and Library on War, Peace, and Revolution at Stanford University.[2]

The material undoubtedly was dictated by Goebbels, but it is not necessarily an intimate or truthful account of his life as an

individual or propagandist. He was too crafty to pour forth his soul to a secretary. What he said must have been motivated by whatever public audience he imagined would eventually see his words; or—as Speier has pointed out[3]—the document may possibly represent parts of an authentic diary which were selected by him or someone else for some specific purpose. A section called "Yesterday—Military Situation," with which each day's entry began and which Lochner has sensibly omitted altogether, was definitely not written by Goebbels: the writing was most objective; often the same events mentioned therein were reported again and commented upon in other parts of the same day's entry; and infrequently a blank page appeared under the same heading with the notation "to be inserted later." In the manuscript we have, there are few personal details. Instead it appears that Goebbels wished to demonstrate an unswerving loyalty to Hitler; to expose the ineptitudes of the German military staffs; to boast about his own accomplishments, his respectability, and his devotion to the Nazi cause; and to place on the record criticisms of rival Nazis like Goering and Rosenberg.

The nature of the document would be a problem most germane to an examination of

[1] Lochner, Louis P. [Editor]. *The Goebbels Diaries*. New York: Doubleday & Company, 1948.

[2] The writer wishes to express his gratitude to Mr. Philip T. McLean of the Library for making arrangements to have the manuscript microfilmed; to the Yale Attitude Change Project for paying the costs of the microfilm; and to Professor Carl F. Schreiber of Yale University for aid in translating some of the more difficult words and phrases.

[3] Speier, Hans. Review of Lochner, *op. cit.*, *Public Opinion Quarterly*, Fall, 1948, pp. 500-505.

From the *Public Opinion Quarterly*, 1950, 14, 419-442. Reprinted by permission of the author and the publisher.

Goebbels' personality or the history of Nazidom, but these topics are not being discussed here. Attention has been focused only on the principles which appear to underlie the propaganda plans and decisions described in the manuscript. Spot checks suggest but do not prove that the words of the diary actually correspond to the activities of Goebbels' propaganda machine. One typical example of the correspondence must suffice. The entry in the diary for November 11, 1943, contained this observation: "There is no longer any talk in the English press of the possibility of a moral collapse of the Reich. On the contrary, we are credited with much greater military prowess than we enjoy at the moment. . . ." On the same day, the *Berliner Illustrierte Nachtausgabe* carried an editorial which asserted that the "jubilant illusions" of the British regarding a German collapse have "suddenly changed to deep pessimism; the enemy's strongest hopes are crushed." Two days later the headline of the leading article in the *Voelkischer Beobachter* was "War of Nerves Departs." On November 13 the diary stated that the English "have been imagining that exactly on this day [November 11] there would be in the Reich a morale breakdown which, however, has now been pushed by them into the invisible future." A day later a Nazi official spoke over the domestic radio: "The key-dates chosen by the enemy are now passed: our people have repulsed this general attack. . . ."

All that is being assumed, in short, is that the manuscript more or less faithfully reflects Goebbels' propaganda strategy and tactics: it is a convenient guide to his bulky propaganda materials. He always magnified the importance of his work, no doubt to indicate his own significance. The truth of what he dictated in this respect is also irrelevant, inasmuch as the effects of his efforts are not being scrutinized.

The analysis which follows, it must constantly be remembered, is based on a very limited period of Goebbels' stewardship, a period in which on the whole Germany was suffering military and political defeats such as the winter campaigns in Russia, the withdrawal from North Africa, and the capitulation of Italy. From time to time, nevertheless, events such as temporary military advances and the triumphs of Japan in Asia occurred; hence there are also suggestions as to how Goebbels functioned as a winner. The writer has checked primarily and secondary sources from 1925 through 1941 and after 1943, and is therefore at least privately confident that the principles are not limited to the diary.

In this analysis a principle is adduced—in an admittedly but unavoidably subjective manner—from the diary when a minimum of six scattered references therein suggests that Goebbels would have had to believe, consciously or unconsciously, in that generalization before he could dictate or behave as he did. To save space, however, only a few illustrations are given under each principle. Whenever possible, an illustration has been selected from the portion published by Lochner: the reader has readier access to that volume than to the manuscript at Stanford. The same procedure has been employed regarding references. A quoted phrase or sentence is followed by the number of the page being cited, either from the Lochner book (in which case a simple number is given in parentheses), or from the Stanford manuscript (in which case the number is preceded by the letter "M," and represents the Library's pagination). The concluding sentence of each paragraph, moreover, contains the one reference considered to be either the best or the most typical for the entire paragraph, again preferably from the Lochner book. The writer will gladly honor written requests for additional references.

These principles purport to summarize what made Goebbels tick or fail to tick. They may be thought of as his intellectual legacy. Whether the legacy has been reliably deduced is a methodological question. Whether it is valid is a psychological matter. Whether or when parts of it should be utilized in a democratic society are profound and disturbing problems of a political and ethical nature.

1. PROPAGANDISTS MUST HAVE ACCESS TO INTELLIGENCE CONCERNING EVENTS AND PUBLIC OPINION

In theory, Goebbels maintained that he and his associates could plan and execute propaganda only by constantly referring to existing intelligence. Otherwise the communication would not be adapted either to the event or the audience. As Germany's situation worsened, he permitted fewer and fewer officials to have access to all relevant intelligence. By May of 1943 he persuaded Himmler to supply unexpurgated reports only to himself (373).

The basic intelligence during a war concerns military events. Each day's entry began with a separate description of the current military situation. There is every indication that Goebbels was kept acquainted with Germany's own military plans (162).

Information about Germans was obtained most frequently from the reports of the *Sicherheits-Dienst* (SD) of the secret police. In addition, Goebbels depended upon his own Reich Propaganda Offices, German officials, and written or face-to-face contacts with individual German civilians or soldiers. As has been shown elsewhere,[4] little or none of this intelligence was ever gathered or analyzed systematically. Once Goebbels stated that the SD had conducted "a statistical investigation . . . in the manner of the Gallup Institute," but he said he did "not value such investigations because they are always undertaken with a deliberate purpose in mind" (M827). Goebbels, moreover, tended to trust his own common sense, intuition, or experience more than formal reports. He listened to his mother because, he said, "she knows the sentiments of the people better than most experts who judge

[4] United States Strategic Bombing Survey. *The Effects of Bombing on German Morale.* Washington, D. C.: U.S. Government Printing Office, 1947. Vol. I, p. 42.

from the ivory tower of scientific inquiry, as in her case the voice of people itself speaks" (56).

The SD as well as German officials supplied intelligence concerning occupied countries. Information about enemy, allied, and neutral nations was gathered from spies, monitored telephone conversations, and other classified sources; from the interrogation of prisoners as well as from the letters they received and sent; and from statements in or deductions from those nations' mass media of communication. Here, too, Goebbels often relied upon his own intuitive judgment, and he seldom hesitated to make far-reaching deductions from a thread of evidence. A direct reply by the enemy, for example, he unequivocally interpreted as a sign of his own effectiveness: "a wild attack on my last article" by the Russian news agency "shows that our anti-Bolshevik propaganda is slowly getting on Soviet nerves" (271).

2. PROPAGANDA MUST BE PLANNED AND EXECUTED BY ONLY ONE AUTHORITY

This principle was in line with the Nazi theory of centralizing authority and with Goebbels' own craving for power. In the diary he stressed the efficiency and consistency which could result from such a policy (M383). He felt that a single authority—himself—must perform three functions:

a. *It must issue all the propaganda directives*

Every bit of propaganda had to implement policy, and policy was made clear in directives. These directives referred to all phases of the war and to all events occurring inside and outside of Germany. They indicated when specific propaganda campaigns should be begun, augmented, diminished, and terminated. They suggested how an item should be interpreted and featured, or whether it should be ignored completely. Goebbels willingly yielded his authority for issuing directives only to Hitler, whose approval on very important matters was always sought. Sometimes gratification was expressed concerning the ways in which directives were implemented; but often there were complaints concerning how Goebbels' own people or others were executing a campaign. The Nazi propaganda machine, therefore, was constantly being reorganized (341).

b. *It must explain propaganda directives to important officials and maintain their morale*

Unless these officials who either formally or informally implemented directives were provided with an explanation of propaganda policy, they could not be expected to function effectively and willingly. Through his organizational machinery and also through personal contact, Goebbels sought to reveal the rationale of his propaganda to these subordinates and to improve their morale by taking them, ostensibly, into his confidence. The groups he met varied in size from an intimate gathering in his home to what must have been a mass meeting in the Kroll Opera House in Berlin (484).

c. *It must oversee other agencies' activities which have propaganda consequences*

"I believe," Goebbels told Hitler, "that when a propaganda ministry is created, all matters affecting propaganda, news, and culture within the Reich and within the occupied areas must be subordinated to it." Although Hitler allegedly "agreed with me absolutely and unreservedly," this high degree of unification was not achieved (476). Conflicts over propaganda plans and materials were recorded with the following German agencies: Ribbentrop's Foreign Office and its representatives in various countries; Rosenberg's Ministry for the Eastern Occupied Areas; the German Army, even including the officers stationed at Hitler's G.H.Q.; the Ministry of Justice; and Ley's Economic Ministry. Goebbels considered himself and his ministry troubleshooters: whenever and wherever German morale seemed poor—whether among submarine crews or the armies in the East—

he attempted to provide the necessary propaganda boost (204).

Goebbels' failure to achieve the goal of this principle and its corollaries is noteworthy. Apparently his self-proclaimed competency was not universally recognized: people whom he considered amateurs believed they could execute propaganda as effectively as he. In addition, even a totalitarian regime could not wipe out personal rivalries and animosities in the interests of efficiency (M3945).

3. THE PROPAGANDA CONSEQUENCES OF AN ACTION MUST BE CONSIDERED IN PLANNING THAT ACTION

Goebbels demanded that he rather than the German Ministry of Justice be placed in charge of a trial in France so that "everything will be seized and executed correctly from a psychological viewpoint" (M1747). He persuaded Hitler, he wrote, to conduct "air warfare against England . . . according to psychological rather than military principles" (313). It was more important for a propagandist to help plan an event than to rationalize one that had occurred (209).

4. PROPAGANDA MUST AFFECT THE ENEMY'S POLICY AND ACTION

Propaganda was considered an arm of warfare, although Goebbels never employed the phrase "psychological warfare" or "political warfare." Besides damaging enemy morale, he believed that propaganda could affect the policies and actions of enemy leaders in four ways:

a. *By suppressing propagandistically desirable material which can provide the enemy with useful intelligence*

Often Goebbels claimed that he refused to deny or refute enemy claims concerning air damage: "it is better," he said in April of 1942, "for the English to think that they have had great successes in the air war than for them actually to have achieved such victories" (M2057). For similar reasons he regretfully censored items concerning the poor quality of Soviet weapons, Germany's plans to employ secret weapons, and even favorable military news (272).

b. *By openly disseminating propaganda whose content or tone causes the enemy to draw the desired conclusions*

"I am also convinced," Goebbels stated in the spring of 1943, "that a firm attitude on our part [in propaganda] will somewhat spoil the appetite of the English for an invasion" (302). As the Battle of Tunisia drew to a close, therefore, the resistance of German troops there was used as an illustration of what would happen if the European continent were invaded. Perhaps, Goebbels must have reasoned, General Eisenhower's plans might be thus directly affected; British or American public opinion might exert influence upon SHAEF; or the morale of the armies in training for the invasion might be crippled (M4638).

c. *By goading the enemy into revealing vital information about himself*

At the end of the Battle of the Coral Sea Goebbels believed that the Japanese had scored a complete victory. The silence of American and British authorities was then attacked "with very precise questions: they will not be able to avoid for any length of time the responsibility of answering these questions" (M2743).

d. *By making no reference to a desired enemy activity when any reference would discredit that activity*

Goebbels did not wish to bestow a "kiss of death" on matters which met his approval. No use was made of news indicating unfriendly relations between two or more of the countries opposing Germany because— in Goebbels' own favorite, trite, and oft repeated words—"controversy between the Allies is a small plant which thrives best when it is left to its own natural growth" (M941). Likewise the Nazi propaganda apparatus was kept aloof from the Chicago *Tribune*, from a coal strike in the United States, and from anti-Communist or pro-fascist groups in England. Quarrels between Germany's enemies, however, were fully exploited when—as in the case of British-American clashes over Darlan—the conflict was both strong and overt (225).

5. DECLASSIFIED, OPERATIONAL INFORMATION MUST BE AVAILABLE TO IMPLEMENT A PROPAGANDA CAMPAIGN

A propaganda goal, regardless of its importance, required operational material that did not conflict with security regulations. The material could not be completely manufactured: it had to have some factual basis, no matter how slight. It was difficult to begin an anti-semitic campaign after the fall of Tunis because German journalists had been failing to collect anti-Jewish literature. Lack of material, however, never seems to have hindered a campaign for any length of time, since evidently some amount of digging could produce the necessary implementation. Journalists were dispatched to a crucial area to write feature stories; steps were taken to insure a supply of "authentic news from the United States" (92); a change in personnel was contemplated "to inject fresh blood into German journalism" and hence better writing (500); or, when necessary, the Protocols of Zion were resurrected (376).

Like any publicity agent, Goebbels also created "news" through action. To demonstrate Germany's friendship for Finland, for example, a group of ailing Finnish children was invited to Germany on a "health-restoring vacation" (M91). The funerals of prominent Nazis were made into newsworthy pageants; the same technique was applied to the French and Belgian victims of British air attacks. German and Nazi anniversaries were celebrated so routinely that the anniversary of the founding of the Three Power Pact was observed even after the downfall of the Italian member (M5859).

6. TO BE PERCEIVED, PROPAGANDA MUST
EVOKE THE INTEREST OF AN AUDIENCE AND
MUST BE TRANSMITTED THROUGH AN ATTEN-
TION-GETTING COMMUNICATIONS MEDIUM

Much energy was devoted to establishing
and maintaining communications media.
Motion picture theaters and newspapers were
controlled or purchased in neutral and
occupied countries. "It's a pity that we cannot reach the people of the Soviet Union by
radio propaganda," Goebbels stated, since
"the Kremlin has been clever enough to
exclude the Russian people from receiving
the great world broadcasts and to limit
them to their local stations" (453). The
schedule of many German radio programs
was adjusted when the British introduced
"double summer time." A dilemma existed
regarding receiving sets in occupied countries: if they were confiscated, people
would be cut off from Nazi as well as enemy
propaganda; if they were not, both brands
could be heard. Inside the Reich, machinery
was created to reopen motion picture
theaters as quickly as possible after heavy
air raids (M5621).

Some kind of bait was devised to attract
and hold an audience. What Goebbels called
"propaganda" over the radio, he believed,
tended after a while to repel an audience. By
1942 he concluded that Germans wanted
their radio to provide "not only instruction
but also entertainment and relaxation"
(M383), and that likewise straight news
rather than "talks" were more effective with
foreign audiences. Like any propagandist in
war time, he recognized that a radio program could draw enemy listeners by providing them with the names of war prisoners.
The best form of newspaper propaganda was
not "propaganda" (i.e., editorials and exhortation), but slanted news which appeared to
be straight (M4677).

Goebbels was especially attached to the
motion picture. At least three evenings a
week he previewed a feature film or newsreel not only to seek relaxation and the company of film people but also to offer what
he considered to be expert criticisms. Fea-

ture pictures, he stated, should provide
entertaining and absorbing plots which might
evoke and then resolve tension; simultaneously they should subtly affect the attentive
audience not through particular passages
but by the general atmosphere. Evidence
for Goebbels' belief in the supreme importance of newsreels comes from the fact
that he immediately provided his newsreel
company with emergency headquarters after
one of the heaviest air raids Berlin experienced toward the end of 1943. "It costs
much trouble to assemble the newsreel
correctly each week and to make it into an
effective propaganda weapon," he observed
on another occasion, "but the work is worthwhile: millions of people draw from the
newsreel their best insight into the war, its
causes, and its effects." He also believed that
newsreels provided "proof" for many of his
major propaganda contentions: visual images
—no matter how he himself manipulated
them before they were released—possessed
greater credibility than spoken or written
words (M335).

Goebbels never stated explicitly whether
or not in his opinion some media were better
suited to present particular propaganda
themes than others. Only stray observations
were made, such as that leaflets were ineffective when "opinions are too rigid and viewpoints too firm" (M2065). His one basic
assumption appears to have been that all
media must be employed simultaneously,
since one never knew what type of bait
would catch the variety of fish who were
Nazi targets (M828).

7. CREDIBILITY ALONE MUST DETERMINE
WHETHER PROPAGANDA OUTPUT SHOULD BE
TRUE OR FALSE

Goebbels' moral position in the diary was
straightforward: he told the truth, his
enemies told lies. Actually the question for
him was one of expediency and not morality.
Truth, he thought, should be used as frequently as possible; otherwise the enemy or
the facts themselves might expose falsehood,

and the credibility of his own output would suffer. Germans, he also stated, had grown more sophisticated since 1914: they could "read between the lines" and hence could not be easily deceived (M1808).

Lies, consequently, were useful when they could not be disproved. To induce Italians to leave the areas occupied by English and American forces and then to shanghai them into Germany as workers, Goebbels broadcast the claim that "the English and Americans will compel all men of draft age to enlist" (462). Even truth, however, might damage credibility. In the first place, some apparently true statements could later turn out to be false, such as specific claims concerning the damage inflicted by planes against enemy targets. Then, secondly, truth itself might appear untrue. Goebbels was afraid to inform the Germans that General Rommel had not been in Africa during the closing days of the campaign there: "everybody thinks he is in Africa; if we now come out with the truth when the catastrophe is so near, nobody will believe us" (352).

Similarly, every feature and device had to maintain its own credibility. A special communique or bulletin was employed, for example, to announce important events. Goebbels was afraid to resort to this device too frequently, lest it lose its unusual character, and hence he released some significant news through routine channels (M5799).

8. THE PURPOSE, CONTENT, AND EFFECTIVE-
NESS OF ENEMY PROPAGANDA; THE STRENGTH
AND EFFECTS OF AN EXPOSÉ; AND THE NA-
TURE OF CURRENT PROPAGANDA CAMPAIGNS
DETERMINE WHETHER ENEMY PROPAGANDA
SHOULD BE IGNORED OR REFUTED

Most of the time Goebbels seemed mortally afraid of enemy propaganda. Even though he had controlled all the mass media in Germany since 1933, he must have been convinced that Germans had not been completely converted to the Nazi cause, or at least that they might be corrupted by enemy efforts. He admitted in January of 1942 that "foreign broadcasts are again being listened to more extensively" even though death could be the penalty for doing so (44). Fourteen months later he noted with dismay that "the English and Americans have greatly expanded their radio broadcasts to the Axis countries and intend to step them up even more" (312).

Goebbels' first impulse was to reply to enemy propaganda. He wrote as though he were a member of a great International Debating Society and as if silence on his part would mean the loss of the argument and of his own prestige. Actually, however, he judiciously balanced a number of factors before he decided to ignore or refute enemy claims (M2593).

In the first place, he analyzed enemy propaganda. If it seemed that the goal of the propaganda was to elicit a reply, he was silent. "The English," he stated on February 6, 1942, "are now employing a new mode of propaganda: they commit General Rommel to objectives which at the moment he certainly cannot have, in order to be able to declare perhaps in eight or fourteen days that he has not reached these goals" (M423). A direct reply would have been equivalent to selling the German armies short. His practice was to expose such traps to his subordinates and then to have them maintain silence in the mass media (M4606).

On the other hand, a reply was made if it were felt that the enemy was transmitting blatant falsehoods. Since almost any enemy statement was considered false, Goebbels believed that only the blatant ones should be exposed. In this category he included claims that Germans had bombed Vatican City, that there had been "disturbances in Berlin" (M4664), that Stalin was adopting a more lenient policy toward religion, etc. (M4971).

Ineffective enemy claims required no reply, since a refutation would either give them more currency or else be a waste of propaganda energy. Enemy propaganda was very frequently branded as being ineffective, judgments which appear to have been either intuitive or rationalizations of an inability to reply. Effective enemy propaganda, however, demanded immediate action. The enemy, for example, was seldom permitted to acquire prestige; thus Goebbels attacked British boasts concerning a parachute landing at Le Havre, a raid on St. Nazaire, and the occupation of Madagascar. Sometimes it appears as though he instituted counter-proceedings not because the enemy was being successful but simply because he was able to do so. When the enemy was thought to be employing horoscopes and other occult propaganda against Germany, a reply in kind was immediately prepared. If the enemy seemed to be scoring an especially important propaganda triumph in its "war of nerves" —specifically at the beginning of the heavy British raids on German cities, after the downfall of Mussolini, or in the midst of strong pressure on Turkey by Britain in the late fall of 1943—the only really adequate reply was considered to be a speech by Hitler himself (251).

Then, secondly, Goebbels examined his own propaganda arsenal before he assayed a reply. He kept silent if he believed that his case, in the absence of facts or arguments, would appear too weak. He was so afraid of the German National Committee which the Russians formed in Moscow that he carried on no counter-propaganda against this group. Sometimes an enemy claim was disregarded and a counter-claim advanced. As Germany was attacked for her treatment of Jews, the policy of "complete silence" seemed unwise: "it is best to seize the offensive and to say something about English cruelty in India or the Near East" (M3064) and also to "intensify . . . our anti-Bolshevik propaganda" (M3225).

Goebbels tried, too, to estimate in advance the effectiveness of a rebuttal. If his own case as well as the enemy's appeared strong but if the enemy's might look stronger because of his attempts to refute it, he withheld his fire. It always seemed better to concentrate on the dissemination of a Hitler speech rather than to reply to foreign critics. Often, however, he believed that an exposé

could protect Germans or help immunize foreigners from an enemy campaign that was either about to be or actually had been launched. Peace appeals by the three allies were therefore anticipated, and his reply to the communique from the Teheran Conference was "biting and insolent; we empty buckets of irony and derision over the Conference" (545).

In the third place, Goebbels believed that his current propaganda had to be surveyed before enemy propaganda could be ignored or refuted. He attempted no reply when that reply might divert attention away from, or when it ran counter to more important propaganda themes. "There's no point in concerning oneself daily with new themes and rumors disseminated by the enemy," he stated, since it was essential to concentrate on the "central theme" of anti-Semitism (M4602). In March of 1943 he permitted "Bolshevik reports of victories . . . to go into the world unchallenged": he wanted Europe to "get the creeps," so that "all the sooner it will become sensible" and co-operate against the Russians (284).

9. CREDIBILITY, INTELLIGENCE, AND THE POSSIBLE EFFECTS OF COMMUNICATING DETERMINE WHETHER PROPAGANDA MATERIALS SHOULD BE CENSORED

Goebbels had no scruples whatsoever concerning the use of censorship. "News policy," he stated, "is a weapon of war; its purpose is to wage war and not to give out information" (210). His decision rested upon three pragmatic considerations (299).

Goebbels recognized, first, that often credibility might be impaired if an item were censored: "in excited and strained times the hunger for news must somehow be satisfied" (40). When the Foreign Office censored news which he considered important, he complained that "by that sort of policy we are fairly compelling the German public to listen to foreign and enemy broadcasts" (164). Again and again, therefore, he felt that he had to speak up, although he would have preferred to be silent. Toward the end of 1943, for example, he stated that the problem of evacuating people from the bombed areas "has become so serious that it must be discussed with the clarity it deserves" (M6435).

The usual policy was to suppress material which was deemed undesirable for German consumption, but simultaneously to employ it in foreign propaganda if it were suited thereto. Tales concerning alleged cannibalism by the Soviets were spread in foreign countries, but such material was banned inside Germany lest it terrify Germans whose relatives were fighting the Russians. Sometimes, however, undesirable material was not censored domestically in order to maintain its credibility abroad (M2699).

Censorship was invoked, in the second place, when intelligence concerning the outcome of a development was insufficient. Here Goebbels wished either to preserve credibility or to have more facts before formulating a directive. Military forecasts he considered especially risky, but he also avoided comments on political events outside the Reich until he could fairly definitely anticipate their effects upon Germany (M5036).

Then, finally, Goebbels estimated the possible effects of communicating the information. Censorship was pursued when it was thought that knowledge of the event would produce a reaction which was undesirable in itself or which, though desirable under some circumstances, was not in line with a current directive. Judged by the kind of news he suppressed, Goebbels was afraid that the following might damage German morale: discussions about religion; statements by officials in neutral or occupied countries that were hostile to Germany or by enemy officials that might evoke sympathy for them; enemy warnings that there would be raids before heavy ones began and—later—the extent of the damage inflicted by enemy planes; dangerous acts which included the assassination of officials, sabotage, and desertion; the unfortunate decisions or deeds of German officials; the belittling of German

strength by an occurrence like the escape of General Giraud from a German prison; an unnecessarily large increase in Germans' anxiety; and hints that Germany did not approve completely of her Axis partners (249).

10. MATERIAL FROM ENEMY PROPAGANDA MAY BE UTILIZED IN OPERATIONS WHEN IT HELPS DIMINISH THAT ENEMY'S PRESTIGE OR LENDS SUPPORT TO THE PROPAGANDIST'S OWN OBJECTIVE

Although his basic attitude toward enemy propaganda was one of contempt, Gobbels combed enemy broadcasts, newspapers, and official statements for operational items. Here he was not motivated by the somewhat defensive desire to reply to the enemy, but by offensive considerations: words of the enemy (Cf. Principle 8) could help him reach his propaganda goals. "In the morning we published in the German press a collection of previous Churchill lies and featured ten points; this collection is making a deep impression on the neutral press and shows Churchill to be, as it were, the Admiral of Incapability" (M202). In particular the enemy provided a basis for Goebbels' "strength-through-fear" campaign as indicated below in Principle 16. "This fellow Vansittart is really worth his weight in gold to our propaganda" (342), he wrote, and likewise he felt that any discussion in England or Russia concerning reparations or boundary questions after Germany's defeat "contributes significantly to the maintenance and strengthening of morale" inside the Reich (M765).

11. BLACK RATHER THAN WHITE PROPAGANDA MUST BE EMPLOYED WHEN THE LATTER IS LESS CREDIBLE OR PRODUCES UNDESIRABLE EFFECTS

By "black" propaganda is meant material whose source is concealed from the audience. Goebbels disguised his identity when he was convinced that the association of a white medium with himself or his machine would damage its credibility. At one time, for example, he wanted to induce the English to stop bombing Berlin by convincing them that they were wasting their bombs. He claimed that he used rumor-mongers to spread the idea there that the city "for all practical purposes is no longer capable of supporting life, *i.e.*, no longer exists" (M6654). Presumably the tale had a better chance of being believed if German authorities were not connected with it. A most elaborate plan was concocted to try to deceive the Russians regarding the section of the front at which the Germans in the summer of 1942 had planned their offensive. A German journalist, who had first been sent deliberately to the Eastern front, was then dispatched to Lisbon where he was to commit, ostensibly under the influence of liquor, what would appear to be indiscretions but which actually were deceptions. In addition, it was planned to plant "a camouflaged article . . . through middlemen either in the Turkish or the Portuguese press" (226), and the *Frankfurter Zeitung* was made to print an "unauthorized" article which was later "officially suppressed and denounced in a press conference" (221). Goebbels sought to increase the number of Soviet deserters by improving the prisoner-of-war camps in which they would be kept —this ancient psychological warfare device rested on the hope that news of the improvement would reach Soviet soldiers through informal channels. Otherwise, except for a security-conscious hint from time to time, the diary made no reference to black operations inside enemy countries (M4235).

Goebbels also utilized black means to combat undesirable rumors inside the Reich. An official denial through a white medium, he thought, might only give currency to the rumors, whereas what he called "word-of-mouth" propaganda against them could achieve the desired effects. This method was employed to offset German fears that "in case more serious raids were to occur, the government would be the first to run away"

from Berlin (421). At all times "citizens who are faithful to the state must be furnished with the necessary arguments for combatting defeatism during discussions at their places of work and on the streets" (401). Sometimes, however, rumors were officially attacked when, in Goebbels' opinion, all the facts were completely and unequivocally on his side (518).

12. PROPAGANDA MAY BE FACILITATED BY LEADERS WITH PRESTIGE

Such a principle is to be expected from Goebbels, whose Nazi ideology stressed the importance of leadership. Germans, it was hoped, would feel submissive toward propaganda containing the name of a prestigeful leader. Ostensibly Goebbels always anticipated momentous results from a Hitler statement especially during a crisis; he noted routinely that the communication had been received by Germans with complete enthusiasm or that it "has simply amazed the enemy" (506).

Leaders were useful only when they had prestige. Goebbels utilized propaganda to make heroes out of men like Field Marshal Rommel. In the privacy of his diary he savagely attacked German leaders whose public behavior was not exemplary, since they thus disrupted propaganda which urged ordinary Germans to make greater sacrifices and to have unswerving faith in their government. An incompetent Nazi official was not openly dismissed from office, lest his incompetence reflect upon "the National Socialist regime"; instead it was announced that he had been temporarily replaced because of illness (224).

13. PROPAGANDA MUST BE CAREFULLY TIMED

Goebbels always faced the tactical problem of timing his propaganda most effectively. Agility and plasticity were necessary, he thought, and propagandists must possess at all times the faculty of "calculating psychological effects in advance" (204). Three principles seemed to be operating:

a. *The communication must reach the audience ahead of competing propaganda*

"Whoever speaks the first word to the world is always right," Goebbels stated flatly (183). He sought constantly to speed up the release of news by his own organization. The loss of Kiev was admitted as quickly as possible "so that we would not limp behind the enemy announcement" (M6061).

b. *A propaganda campaign must begin at the optimum moment*

Goebbels never indicated explicitly or implicitly how he reached the decision that the time to begin a campaign or make an announcement was either ripe or right. He made statements like this: "we have held back for a very long time" in using an Indian leader, who as a German puppet committed his country to a war against England, "for the simple reason that things had not advanced far enough as yet in India" (107). At one point he stated that counter-propaganda against enemy claims should not be too long delayed: "one should not let such lying reports sink in too deeply" (M2430).

c. *A propaganda theme must be repeated, but not beyond some point of diminishing effectiveness*

On the one hand, Goebbels believed that propaganda must be repeated until it was thoroughly learned and that thereafter more repetition was necessary to reinforce the learning. Such repetition took place over time—the same theme was mentioned day after day—as well as in the output of a single day. An anti-Semitic campaign, for example, continued for weeks, during which time "about 70 to 80 per cent of our broadcasts are devoted to it" (366). On the other hand, repetition could be unnecessary or even undesirable. It was unnecessary when "the material thus far published has completely convinced the public" (386). It was undesirable when the theme became boring or unimpressive, as occurred in connection with announcements concerning German submarine successes. Sometimes, moreover, booming guns at the start of a campaign, though desirable psychologically, could make the propaganda too "striking" and consequently result in a loss of credibility (M6343).

14. PROPAGANDA MUST LABEL EVENTS AND PEOPLE WITH DISTINCTIVE PHRASES OR SLOGANS

Again and again Goebbels placed great stress upon phrases and slogans to characterize events. At the beginning of 1942, for example, he began a campaign whose purpose was to indicate economic, social, and political unrest in England. He very quickly adopted the phrase *"schleichende Krise"*—creeping crisis—to describe this state of affairs and then employed it "as widely as possible in German propaganda" both domestically and abroad (M762). His thinking was dominated by word-hunts: privately—or semi-privately—in his diary he summarized his own or enemy propaganda with a verbal cliché, even when he did not intend to employ the phrase in his output. He admitted that the experiencing of an event was likely to be more effective than a verbal description of it, but he also recognized that words could stand between people and events, and that their reaction to the latter could be potently affected by the former (M1385). To achieve such effects, phrases and slogans should possess the following characteristics:

a. *They must evoke desired responses which the audience previously possesses*

If the words could elicit such responses, then Goebbels' propaganda task consisted simply of linking those words to the event which thereafter would acquire their flavor. When the British raid on St. Nazaire in March of 1942 aborted, Goebbels decided to claim that it had been made to appease the Russians who had been demanding that their ally engage in military action. The raid was dubbed the "Maisky Offensive," after the Soviet envoy in London. Sometimes news could speak for itself in the sense that it elicited desired responses without the addition of a verbal label. A military victory was not interpreted for Germans when Goebbels wished them to feel gratified. Most news, however, was not self-explanatory: Goebbels had to attach thereto the responses he desired through the use of verbal symbols. The most regulated news and commentary, nevertheless, could produce undesirable and unintended actions; even a speech by Hitler was misinterpreted (M4677).

b. *They must be capable of being easily learned*

"It must make use of painting in black-and-white, since otherwise it cannot be convincing to people," Goebbels stated with reference to a film he was criticizing (M271). This principle of simplification he applied to all media in order to facilitate learning. The masses were important, not the intellectuals. All enemy "lies" were not beaten down, rather it was better to confine the counter-attack to a single "school example" (M2084). Propaganda could be aided, moreover, by a will to learn. Cripps' appeal to European workers under German domination to slow down on the job, for example, was ignored: "it is difficult to pose a counter-slogan to such a slogan, for the slogan of 'go slow' is always much more effective than that of 'work fast' " (107).

c. *They must be utilized again and again, but only in appropriate situations*

Here Goebbels wished to exploit learning which had occurred: the reactions people learned to verbal symbols he wished to transfer easily and efficiently to new events. He criticized English propaganda because "its slogans are changed on every occasion and hence it lacks real punch" (M1812). The context in which people's reactions occurred was also important. "I forbid using the word 'Fuehrer' in the German press when applied to Quisling," Goebbels declared, "I don't consider it right that the term *Fuehrer* be applied to any other person than the *Fuehrer* himself. There are certain terms that we must absolutely reserve for ourselves, among them also the word 'Reich' " (66).

d. *They must be boomerang-proof*

Goebbels became furious when he thought of the expression "Baedeker raids, which one of our people so stupidly coined during a foreign press conference" (M2435): it interfered with his own effort to call British raids wanton attacks on "cultural monuments and institutions of public welfare" (M2301). "There are certain words," he added, "from which we should shrink as the devil does from Holy Water; among these are, for instance, the words 'sabotage' and 'assassination' " (93).

15. PROPAGANDA TO THE HOME FRONT MUST PREVENT THE RAISING OF FALSE HOPES WHICH CAN BE BLASTED BY FUTURE EVENTS

It was clear to Goebbels that the anticipation of a German success along military or political lines could have certain immediate beneficial effects from his viewpoint. The confidence of Germans and the anxiety of the enemy could be increased. Such tactics, however, were much too risky: if the success turned out to be a failure, then Germans would feel deflated and the enemy elated. His own credibility, moreover, would suffer. For this reason he was wildly indignant when, after the German army withdrew, the enemy ascribed to him "premature reports of victories" at Salerno. Actually, he claimed, the announcements had come from German Generals (457).

Often the false hopes seemed to spring from the Germans themselves, a form of wishful thinking which occurred spontaneously as they contemplated the possibility of an offensive by the German armies, as they received news of a single victory, or as they imagined that the enemy could be defeated by political events. Goebbels, therefore, frequently issued warnings about "false illusions" and he prevented particular victories from being trumpeted too loudly. At other times enemy propaganda strategy was thought to be committing the German armies to military goals which they could not be expected to achieve (118).

16. PROPAGANDA TO THE HOME FRONT MUST CREATE AN OPTIMUM ANXIETY LEVEL

For Goebbels, anxiety was a double-edged sword: too much anxiety could produce panic and demoralization, too little could lead to complacency and inactivity. An attempt was constantly made, therefore, to achieve a balance between the two extremes. The strategy can be reduced to two principles (M6162).

a. *Propaganda must reinforce anxiety concerning the consequences of defeat*

Enemy war aims were the principal material employed to keep German anxiety at a high pitch. "The German people must remain convinced—as indeed the facts warrant—that this war strikes at their very lives and their national possibilities of development, and they must fight it with their entire strength" (147). Lest the campaign of "strength-through-fear" falter, no opportunity was missed to attack enemy peace terms which might appear mild. Anti-Bolshevik campaigns attempted not only to stiffen German resistance but also to enlist the cooperation of all neutral and occupied countries. On the one hand, Goebbels tried to convince himself in the diary that Germans would not be misled again—as they had been, according to his view, in World War I—by enemy peace terms: they "are quite accurately acquainted with their enemies and know what to expect if they were to give themselves up" (M6684). On the other hand, he felt very strongly that Germans were most vulnerable to peace propaganda. He feared, for example, that American propaganda might be directed "not . . . against the German people but against Nazism" (147) and "we can surely congratulate ourselves that our enemies have no Wilson Fourteen Points" (47).

Occasionally it became necessary to increase the anxiety level of Germans concerning a specific event. On February 24, 1942, after the first disastrous winter campaign in Russia, Goebbels "issued orders to the German press to handle the situation in the East favorably, but not too optimistically." He did not wish to raise false hopes but, perhaps more importantly, he did not want Germans to "cease to worry at all about the situation in the East" (99).

b. *Propaganda must diminish anxiety (other than that concerning the consequences of defeat) which is too high and which cannot be reduced by people themselves*

Air raids obviously raised German anxiety much too high, but they were a situation over which Goebbels could not exercise propaganda control. In other situations involving a demoralizing amount of anxiety he could be more active. "To see things in a realistic light" when the military situation in Tunisia became hopeless, German losses were portrayed as being "not of such a nature that as a result our chances for [ultimate] victory have been damaged" (M4542). In contrast, he attempted to use the same principle in reverse—the so-called "strategy of terror"—against his enemies. Leaflets were dropped on English cities "with pictures of the damage done by the English in Luebeck and Rostock, and under them the Fuehrer's announcement of his Reichstag speech that reprisal raids are coming" (193).

17. PROPAGANDA TO THE HOME FRONT MUST DIMINISH THE IMPACT OF FRUSTRATION

It was most important to prevent Germans from being frustrated, for example, by immunizing them against false hopes. If a frustration could not be avoided, Goebbels sought to diminish its impact by following two principles:

a. *Inevitable frustrations must be anticipated*

Goebbels' reasoning seems to have been that a frustration would be less frustrating if the element of surprise or shock were eliminated. A present loss was thus endured for the sake of a future gain. The German people were gradually given "some intimation that the end is in sight" as the fighting in Tunisia drew to a close (352). They likewise received advance hints whenever a reduction in food rations was contemplated; the actual announcement, nevertheless, always disturbed them (M1484).

b. *Inevitable frustrations must be placed in perspective*

Goebbels considered one of his principal functions to be that of giving the Germans what he called a *Kriegsüberblick*, a general survey of the war. Otherwise, he felt, they would lose confidence in their régime and in himself, and they would fail to appreciate why they were being compelled to make so many sacrifices (M4975).

18. PROPAGANDA MUST FACILITATE THE DISPLACEMENT OF AGGRESSION BY SPECIFYING THE TARGETS FOR HATRED

Goebbels had few positive gratifications to offer Germans during the period of adversity covered by the diary. He featured enemy losses, quite naturally, whenever he could and whenever Germans were not over-confident. Only once did he praise Germans for withstanding the enemy as long as they had. By and large, the principal technique seems to have been that of displacing German aggression on to some outgroup (M6220).

Favorite hate objects were "Bolsheviks" and Jews. Goebbels was disturbed by reports which indicated that "the fear of Bolshevism by the broad masses of European peoples has become somewhat weaker" (M4572) or that "certain groups of Germans, especially the intellectuals, express the idea that Bolshevism is not so bad as the Nazis represent it to be" (335). Anti-Semitic propaganda was usually combined with active measures against Jews in Germany or the occupied countries. German aggression was also directed against American and British pilots, but on the whole the United States and Great Britain did not stir

Goebbels' wrath, at least in the diary (147).

In enemy countries Goebbels had a strong penchant to engage in "wedge-driving": he sought to foment suspicion, distrust, and hatred between his enemies and between groups within a particular country. He thus assumed that the foundation for hostility between nations or within a nation already existed for historical reasons or as a result of the frustrations of war. His task was to direct the aggression along disruptive channels (46).

19. PROPAGANDA CANNOT IMMEDIATELY AFFECT STRONG COUNTER-TENDENCIES; INSTEAD IT MUST OFFER SOME FORM OF ACTION OR DIVERSION, OR BOTH

In almost all of his thinking about propaganda strategy and objectives, Goebbels adopted the distinction between what were called *Haltung* (bearing, conduct, observable behavior) and *Stimmung* (feeling, spirit, mood).[5] After a heavy raid on a German city, he generally claimed that the *Haltung* of the people was excellent but that their *Stimmung* was poor. He wished to have both of these components of morale as favorable as possible. *Stimmung* he considered much more volatile: it could easily be affected by propaganda and events; it might be improved simply by offering people some form of entertainment and relaxation. *Haltung* had to be maintained at all costs, for otherwise the Nazi régime would lose its support and people would be ready to surrender. Germans, in short, were compelled to preserve external appearances and to coöperate with the war effort, regardless of their internal feelings. As more and more defeats and raids were experienced, Goebbels became convinced that *Stimmung* had to be almost completely ignored (M6452).

Goebbels clearly recognized his own propaganda impotency in six situations. The basic drives of sex and hunger were

[5] Lochner has ignored the distinction and has generally translated both as "morale," a term which Goebbels likewise occasionally employed in an equally ambiguous manner.

not appreciably affected by propaganda. Air raids brought problems ranging from discomfort to death which could not be gainsaid. Propaganda could not significantly increase industrial production. The religious impulses of many Germans could not be altered, at least during the war. Overt opposition by individual Germans and by peoples in the occupied countries required forceful action, not clever words. Finally, Germany's unfavorable military situation became an undeniable fact. When propaganda and censorship could not be effective, Goebbels advocated action or, in one of his official positions (for example, as Gauleiter of Berlin), he himself produced the action. Diversionary propaganda he considered second-best (M3508).

Consider his propaganda with reference to military defeats. For a while he could describe them as "successful evacuations" (461). For a while he could even conceal their implications. Eventually, however, they were too apparent, especially after the heavy air raids began and the difficulties of fighting a two-front war increased. Then he was reduced not quite to silence but certainly to despair. At the end of the fighting in Tunisia he was forced to conclude that the following propaganda themes were not proving impressive: "our soldiers there have written a hymn of heroism that will be graven eternally on the pages of German history; they retarded developments for half a year, thereby enabling us to complete the construction of the Atlantic Wall and to prepare ourselves all over Europe so that an invasion is out of the question" (360). He tried to divert Germans through another anti-Bolshevik campaign, but this too was insufficient. What Germans really needed were "some victories in the East to publicize" (M4433). German losses in Russia, moreover, plagued Goebbels. Whenever possible, he tried to offset news of defeat in one section with reports of victories in others, but by 1943 he simply had no favorable news to employ as a distraction. *Stimmung* was doomed, and even *Haltung* worried him: "at the moment we cannot change very much through propaganda; we must once again gain a big victory somewhere" (M3253). Most fortunately, that victory and ultimate triumph never came.

SOME REASONS WHY INFORMATION CAMPAIGNS FAIL

HERBERT H. HYMAN AND PAUL B. SHEATSLEY

The Charter of the United Nations Educational, Scientific and Cultural Organization contains the following significant statement:

. . . the States parties to this Constitution . . . are agreed and determined to develop and to increase the means of communication between their peoples and to employ these means for

From the *Public Opinion Quarterly*, Fall 1947, 11, 412-423. Reprinted by permission of the authors and the publisher.

the purposes of mutual understanding and a truer and more perfect knowledge of each other's lives. To realize this purpose the Organization will . . . recommend such international agreements as may be necessary to promote the free flow of ideas by word and image.

As a preliminary step, the Preparatory Commission of UNESCO has instructed the Secretariat to survey the obstacles in the way of such a program.[1] These obstacles to be surveyed include such things as the breakdown and inadequacy of existing communication facilities in many parts of the world, and the political, commercial and economic restrictions which hamper the free exchange of information throughout the United Nations.

But even if all these *physical* barriers to communication were known and removed, there would remain many *psychological* barriers to the free flow of ideas. It is the purpose of this paper to demonstrate some of these psychological factors that impede communication and thereby to formulate certain principles and guides which must be considered in mass information campaigns. Existence of these psychological factors will be demonstrated by a variety of data gathered in recent surveys of the American public by the National Opinion Research Center, and one general truth is implied throughout the discussion:

The physical barriers to communication merely impede the *supply* of information. In order to increase public knowledge, not only is it necessary to *present* more information, but it is essential that the mass audience *be exposed to* and that it *absorb* the information. And in order to insure such exposure and absorption, *the psychological characteristics of human beings must be taken into account.*

To assume a perfect correspondence between the nature and amount of material presented in an information campaign and its absorption by the public, is to take a naive view, for the very nature and degree of public exposure to the material is determined to a large extent by certain psychological characteristics of the people themselves.[2] A number of these psychological characteristics are discussed below under the following topics:

The Chronic "Know-Nothing's" in Relation to Information Campaigns

The Role of Interest in Increasing Exposure

Selective Exposure Produced by Prior Attitudes

Selective Interpretation Following Exposure

Differential Changes in Attitudes After Exposure

THERE EXISTS A HARD CORE OF CHRONIC "KNOW-NOTHING'S"

All persons do not offer equal targets for information campaigns. Surveys consistently find that a certain proportion of the population is not familiar with any particular event. Offhand, it might be thought that information concerning that event was not distributed broadly enough to reach them, but that this group would still have an equal chance of exposure to other information. Yet, when the knowledge of this same group is measured with respect to a second event, they tend also to have little information in that area. And similarly, they will have little or no information concerning a third event.

If all persons provided equal targets for exposure, and the sole determinant of public knowledge were the magnitude of the given information, there would be no reason for the same individuals always to show a relative lack of knowledge. *Instead, there is something about the uninformed which makes them harder to reach, no matter what the level or nature of the information.*

Thus, in May 1946, NORC asked a question to determine public knowledge of the report of the Anglo-American Committee

---

[1] See "UNESCO's Program of Mass Communication: I," *Public Opinion Quarterly*, 10, No. 4 (1946).

[2] For a theoretical discussion of the problem see Daniel Katz, "Psychological Barriers to Communication," *The Annals*, March, 1947.

on Palestine which recommended the admission of 100,000 Jewish immigrants to that country. Only 28 per cent of the national sample expressed any awareness of this report. It might be assumed that the remaining 72 per cent were ready and willing to be exposed, but that there had been too little information about the report. Yet Table 1 shows that this unaware group consistently tended to have less awareness of other information about the international scene which had been much more widely reported.

The size of this generally uninformed group in the population may be indicated by computing an index of general knowledge based on all five information questions in the field of foreign affairs, which were asked on that particular survey. The five subjects covered by these questions were:

1. The Palestine report spoken of above [1][3]
2. The Acheson-Lilienthal report on atomic energy [2]
3. The Paris meeting of the Big Four Foreign Ministers, then in progress [3]
4. The proposed loan to England, then being debated in Congress [4]
5. The political status of Palestine, the fact that she is ruled by England [5]

TABLE 1

	Group Which is Not Aware of Palestine Report	Group Which is Aware of Palestine Report
Per cent Aware of:		
Acheson-Lilienthal report on atomic energy	32%	64%
Spring 1946 meeting of Foreign Ministers in Paris	39%	85%
Proposed loan to England	73%	96%
	N=931	N=358

Table 2 shows how the population divided in its awareness of these five items. As may be seen, roughly one person out of seven

[3] Figures in brackets refer to actual question-wordings which are reported in the note at the end of this article.

TABLE 2

Aware of:	Per cent of National Sample
No items	14%
One item	18
Two items	20
Three items	17
Four items	19
Five items	12
Total sample	100%
	N=1292

reported no awareness of *any* of the five items, and approximately one person in three had knowledge of no more than *one* of them. This generally uninformed group, therefore, is of considerable magnitude.[4] It is possible, of course, that the existence of this group may be related to external factors of accessibility to information media, and that if the information were somehow channelled into their vicinity, they would soon become exposed. For example, information on foreign affairs is probably less easily available to small-town residents than it is to city-dwellers, and we find a relationship, as shown in Table 3, between size of com-

TABLE 3

Size of Community	Mean Score on Knowledge Index Number of Items Known
Metropolitan Districts over one million	2.81
Metropolitan Districts under one million	2.45
Cities 2,500 to 50,000	2.38
Towns under 2,500	2.28
Farm	2.03

munity and awareness of our five items. These differences, however, are relatively small, in comparison with the psychological differences to be shown later in Table 4 and elsewhere. The next section discusses the

[4] If anything, the size of the group is under-represented, for two reasons: (1) The respondent's claim to awareness was accepted at face value, without any check on his actual knowledge; (2) Polls consistently tend to over-sample the more literate, higher socio-economic groups in the population.

effect of certain psychological factors on level of knowledge.

INTERESTED PEOPLE ACQUIRE THE MOST INFORMATION

The importance of *motivation* in achievement or learning, or in assimilating knowledge, has been consistently shown in academic studies. Yet this important factor is often ignored in information campaigns, amid all the talk of "increasing the flow of information." The widest possible dissemination of material may be ineffective if it is not geared to the public's interests.

It is well known that opinion polls can measure areas of knowledge and ignorance, but the complementary areas of apathy and interest have been more often overlooked. Yet they can be just as readily measured, and they are highly significant in understanding the factors behind a given level of knowledge.

NORC, in a poll taken in May 1946, measured the public's interest in eight different issues in the field of foreign affairs [6]. These issues were:

1. Our relations with Russia
2. The atomic bomb
3. Our policy toward Germany
4. The United Nations organization
5. The British loan
6. The meeting of Foreign Ministers in Paris
7. Our relations with Franco Spain
8. Our policy toward Palestine

Public interest varied widely in these eight issues, ranging from 77 per cent of the national sample which reported "considerable" or "great" interest in our relations with Russia to 28 per cent which reported "considerable" or "great" interest in our policy toward Palestine. Thus, it is clear that each specific information campaign does not start with the same handicap in terms of public apathy. Motivation is high on some issues, low on others.

Nevertheless, there is consistent evidence

that interest in foreign affairs tends to be *generalized*. Some people are interested in many or all of the issues; another large group is apathetic toward most or all of them. Intercorrelations (based on approximately 1290 cases) between interest in one issue and interest in each of the other seven, definitely establish this point. The 28 tetrachoric correlation coefficients range from .40 to .82, with a median r of .58. Table 4 shows how the population divides in its interest in these eight issues.

TABLE 4

	Per cent of Total Sample Expressing Considerable or Great Interest	
"High Interest"		37%
All eight issues	11%	
Seven issues	11	
Six issues	15	
"Medium Interest"		40
Five issues	15	
Four issues	14	
Three issues	11	
"Low Interest"		23
Two issues	7	
One issue	5	
None of them	11	
		100%
	N=1292	

It will be noticed that 11 per cent of the sample expressed little or no interest in any of the eight issues, and that another 12 per cent were interested in only one or two of them. Almost one-quarter of the population, therefore, reported interest in no more than two of the eight issues—a state of apathy all the more significant when it is remembered that the list included such overpowering subjects as the atomic bomb and our relations with Germany and Russia, and that the respondent's own estimate of his degree of interest, doubtless subject to prestige considerations, was accepted without question.

The close relationship between apathy on the one hand, and ignorance of information materials on the other, is shown in Table 5. It is a likely assumption that both the contrasted groups in the table had equal

TABLE 5

	Per cent Who Have Heard of Acheson Report on Atomic Energy	
Respondents with great or considerable interest in atomic bomb	48%	N=953
Respondents with little or no interest in atomic bomb	20	N=337

	Per cent Who Have Heard of Anglo-American Report on Palestine	
Respondents with great or considerable interest in Palestine policy	51%	N=365
Respondents with little or no interest in Palestine policy	19	N=921

TABLE 6

Interested in:	Mean Score on Knowledge Index
No items	.85
One item	1.42
Two items	1.12
Three items	1.89
Four items	2.37
Five items	2.64
Six items	3.15
Seven items	3.50
Eight items	3.81
	N=1292

This fact cannot be ignored by those in charge of information campaigns. Such groups constitute a special problem which cannot be solved simply by "increasing the flow of information." *Scientific surveys are needed to determine who these people are, why they lack interest, and what approach can best succeed in reaching them.*

PEOPLE SEEK INFORMATION CONGENIAL TO PRIOR ATTITUDES

Information campaigns, while they involve the presentation of *facts*, nevertheless present materials which may or may not be congenial with the attitudes of any given individual. Lazarsfeld,[6] in describing the exposure of a sample panel to political campaign propaganda, concludes that "People selected political material in accord with their own taste and bias. Even those who had not yet made a decision (on their vote) exposed themselves to propaganda which fit their not-yet-conscious political predispositions."

Our evidence from polling national samples in other information areas supports the view that people tend to expose themselves to information which is congenial with their prior attitudes, and to avoid exposure to information which is not congenial. Although it was not possible to administer before-and-after tests of attitudes, the following technique offers indirect evidence to support the argument of selective exposure.

opportunity to learn about the two reports. Yet the information reached approximately half of the interested group, and only about one-fifth of the disinterested.[5]

The relationship between interest and knowledge can be demonstrated in a different way, if we compare the scores of each of our interest groups on our knowledge index. As seen in Table 6, at each stage of increasing interest, knowledge rises correspondingly.

It can be argued, of course, that the exposed people became interested after they had been exposed to the information, and that the disinterested persons are apathetic only because they were not exposed. It is probable that the two factors *are* interdependent; as people learn more, their interest increases, and as their interest increases, they are impelled to learn more. Nevertheless, from the point of view of initiating a *specific* campaign at some point in time, it remains true that in the case even of outstanding public issues, large groups in the population admit "little or no interest" in the problem.

[5] Lazarsfeld reports a similar finding on the relationship of interest to exposure to political information. See Lazarsfeld, Berelson and Gaudet, *The People's Choice*, New York: Duell, Sloan and Pearce, 1944, p 79.

[6] *Op. cit.*, p. 80.

National samples were asked if they had heard or read anything about a given piece of information. The entire sample was then given the gist of the information in one or two sentences. (In the case of those who had admitted familiarity with the material, the description was prefaced by some such phrase as, "Well, as you remember . . .") Immediately following the description of the information, the entire sample was then asked some relevant attitude question.

We found in every case that the group who reported prior exposure to the information had a different attitudinal reaction from those without prior exposure. One could assume that this difference reflected the influence of the information on those previously exposed, except that, as described above, *both groups*, before being asked the attitude question, had been supplied with identical descriptions of the information in question.

Thus, in June 1946, a national sample of the adult population was asked whether they had heard or read about the Anglo-American Committee report on Palestine [1]. Every respondent was then either told or reminded of the essential provisions of the report, and was asked whether he favored United States assistance in keeping order in Palestine if 100,000 additional Jews were admitted to that country [7]. As seen in Table 7, those with prior knowledge of the report were significantly more favorable toward such assistance.

Similarly, in April 1946, a national sample was asked whether they had heard or read about the recent joint statement by England, France, and the United States which denounced the Franco government of Spain [8]. Included in the question was the gist of the statement: "the hope that General Franco's government in Spain would soon be followed by a more democratic one." The entire sample was then asked its attitude toward this country's Spanish policy [9]. Again, those who had prior knowledge of the three-power statement were significantly more hostile in their attitudes toward Franco. (See Table 7.)

TABLE 7

	Per cent of Those With Opinions Who Favor U.S. Aid in Keeping Order in Palestine	
Previous knowledge of Committee report	36%	N=339
No previous knowledge	30	N=805

	Per cent of Those With Opinions Who Favor Breaking Relations With Franco	
Previous knowledge of Three-Power statement	32%	N=657
No previous knowledge	21	N=268

It is true that those who learned about the report or statement for the first time during the interview were more inclined to offer no opinion when questioned on their attitudes, but the above table excludes the "No opinion" group, and comparisons are based only on those with definite opinions.

The differences reported, which are in all likelihood not due to chance, suggest the phenomenon of "selective exposure" to information. In both cases, every respondent was aware of the contents of the statement or report when he answered the question on policy. Yet in each case, those with *prior* knowledge of the information had significantly different attitudes. It would appear, therefore, that persons reached by the Palestine report were those who were more likely in the first place to favor United States assistance there, rather than that they favored U. S. assistance because they were familiar with the information contained in the report. Similarly, it would seem that the group which had prior knowledge of the statement on Spain was already more anti-Franco in their attitudes, rather than that they became more anti-Franco by virtue of exposure.

The fact that people tend to become exposed to information which is congenial with their prior attitudes is another factor which must be considered by those in charge of information campaigns. Merely "increasing the flow" is not enough, if the information continues to "flow" in the direction of those already on your side!

PEOPLE INTERPRET THE SAME INFORMATION DIFFERENTLY

It has just been shown that it is false to assume a perfect correspondence between public exposure to information and the amount of material distributed. It is equally false to assume that exposure, once achieved, results in a uniform interpretation and retention of the material.

In a series of experimental studies beginning with the work of Bartlett,[7] and carried on by a host of other investigators such as Margolies, Clark, Nadel, and Murphy,[8] it has been consistently demonstrated that a person's perception and memory of materials shown to him are often distorted by his wishes, motives, and attitudes. One demonstration of these general psychological findings in the area of international affairs is available in a recent NORC survey.

In September 1946, a national sample was asked whether they thought that the newspapers *they read* made Russia out to look better than she really is, worse than she really is, or whether they presented accurate information about Russia [10]. The same survey also asked a question to determine where the respondent put the blame for Russian-American disagreements [11]. When the sample was classified into two groups—those who blamed Russia entirely and those who put the responsibility on both countries or on the United States alone— there were revealed striking differences in

beliefs as to whether Russia was being presented fairly or unfairly in the newspapers they read (see Table 8). It is clear from this finding that people selectively discount the information they are exposed to, in the light of their prior attitudes.

TABLE 8

	Per cent Who Say Their Newspapers Make Russia Look Worse Than She Really Is	
Blame Russia entirely for Russian-American disagreements	41%	N=458
Blame United States entirely or blame both countries	54	N=168

The finding is all the more striking when one considers the fact that people tend to read the particular newspapers which are congenial to their own attitudes and beliefs. Thus, one would expect the anti-Russian group to be reading newspapers which, if studied by means of objective content analysis, would be found to slant their editorial content against Russia. Similarly, one would expect the pro-Russian group to read newspapers which, if measured objectively, would be found to emphasize favorable news about Russia. Despite this, the anti-Russian group is *less* likely to say *their* newspapers present Russia unfavorably, while the pro-Russian group is *more* likely to say *their* newspapers present Russia unfavorably.

Here, then, is another psychological problem that faces those responsible for information campaigns. Exposure in itself is not always sufficient. People will interpret the information in different ways, according to their prior attitudes.

---

[7] F. C. Bartlett, *Remembering,* New York: Macmillan Co., 1932.

[8] B. Margolies, unpublished M.A. thesis, Columbia University, New York City; K. Clark, "Some Factors Influencing the Remembering of Prose Material," *Archives of Psychology,* No. 253, 1940; S. F. Nadel, "A Field Experiment in Racial Psychology," *British Journal of Psychology,* 1937, Vol. 28, 195-211; and G. Murphy and J. M. Levine, "The Learning and Forgetting of Controversial Material," *Journal of Abnormal and Social Psychology,* 1943, Vol. 38, 507-518.

INFORMATION DOES NOT NECESSARILY CHANGE ATTITUDES

The principle behind all information campaigns is that the disseminated information will alter attitudes or conduct. There is abundant evidence in all fields, of course, that informed people actually do react differently to a problem than uninformed people do. But it is naive to suppose that information always affects attitudes, or that it affects all attitudes equally. The general principle needs serious qualification.

There is evidence, based on investigations made with academic samples, that individuals, once they are exposed to information, change their views *differentially*, each in the light of his own *prior* attitude. Data gathered by NORC in recent national surveys show that these academic findings are equally applicable to the entire adult population.

In a continuing study of attitudes toward the proposed British loan, conducted between December 1945 and February 1946, it was found that a significant factor influencing attitudes toward the loan was the belief that this country would or would not get something out of it economically [12]. As shown by Table 9, those who were of the opinion that the loan held advantages to this country were strongly in favor, while those of a contrary opinion, or doubtful, were overwhelmingly opposed to the loan.

TABLE 9

	Per Cent Who Approve Loan to England	
We will get advantages from the loan	66%	N=265
Don't know if advantages	29	N=291
We will not get advantages	20	N=294

Furthermore, 39 per cent of those who expressed approval of the loan mentioned some economic advantage as their reason, while 75 per cent of those opposed listed an economic argument. Under these circumstances, it was logical to suppose that attitudes could be changed toward approval of the loan, by informing the public of its economic advantages to the United States. It was not possible to conduct a before-and-after test of this thesis, but some interesting findings were revealed by a study of two equivalent samples which were polled simultaneously.

One of these samples was given the appropriate information before being questioned

on their attitude. They were told that England had agreed to pay the money back with interest over a period of years, and that England had further agreed to take definite steps to remove restrictions on their trade with us and to join us in promoting world trade in general.[9] They were then asked whether they approved or disapproved of lending England the specified amount [13]. This was the experimental sample. The control sample was simply asked whether they approved or disapproved of the proposed loan, on the basis of what they had heard about it, with no additional information supplied them [4].

The experiment proved that the given information did materially change attitudes toward the loan. The experimental sample registered a 14 per cent higher "Approve" vote than did the equivalent control sample which was not given the information. But this over-all comparison obscured the *differential* effect of the information.

For example, there was no difference between the two samples in the proportion of "Disapprovers" who gave an economic argument for their disapproval. Fifty-one per cent of those in the control group who were opposed gave as their reason that "England won't pay us back," and 50 per cent of those in the experimental group who were opposed offered the same argument—in spite of the fact that they had been specifically informed of England's agreement to return the money with interest. It was apparent that a large group of those opposed to the loan were rooted to their belief that the money would not be repaid, and the mere information that England had *agreed* to repay the loan was of no effect in changing their attitudes.

Table 10 shows another significant differential effect of the information. Among those who were already favorably disposed toward England, the information given to the experimental group was sufficient to sway a large proportion toward approval of

[9] This sample was also informed that President Truman had asked Congress to approve the loan, an additional prestige factor probably having some persuasive effect.

TABLE 10

Per cent Approving Loan Among Those Who:	Control Sample (Not Exposed to Information)		Experimental Sample (Exposed to Information)	
Trust England to cooperate with us	45%	N = 619	70%	N = 242
Do not trust England to cooperate	17	N = 231	18	N = 133

the loan [14]. Less than half of this group friendly to England favored the loan in the control sample, but in the experimental sample, which was given the information, the proportion rises to 70 per cent. But among those with hostile or suspicious attitudes toward England, the information had *no effect whatever*. This group was overwhelmingly opposed to the loan without the information, and they remained overwhelmingly opposed to it even when they were exposed to the information.

CONCLUSIONS

The above findings indicate clearly that those responsible for information campaigns cannot rely simply on "increasing the flow" to spread their information effectively. The psychological barriers we have pointed out create real problems for those charged with the task of informing the public, and in many cases public opinion surveys offer the only means by which these problems can be recognized, and thereby overcome.

Surveys are already widely used to provide the information director with scientific knowledge of the quantitative distribution of his material. They can tell him how many people have been reached by his information, and more important, which particular groups have not been reached. Surveys, too, can quite easily measure public interest in information materials and areas, thus providing him with accurate knowledge of the handicaps his program faces within various population groups.

But on a different and higher level, surveys can inform the information director

of the whole structure of attitudes on any public issue. They can tell him the major factors affecting public opinion on the issue, and the relative influence of these various factors in determining attitudes. They can tell to what extent information has reached the public and how far it has changed existing opinions. They can also tell what information is still needed and what aspects of it must be stressed in order to reach the unexposed or unsympathetic groups.

Psychological barriers to information campaigns are readily admitted by those who stop to consider the point, but they seem often to be overlooked in the general eagerness simply to distribute *more* information. The data we have cited in this paper are merely those which happen to be available from recent NORC surveys, but the kinds of barriers we have mentioned apply eternally to all types of public information. By documenting the very real effect that these psychological barriers have on public exposure to and interpretation of information materials, we hope we will encourage a proportionately greater attention to these intangible factors on the part of those who plan and carry out programs involving mass communication.

NOTE

QUESTIONS REFERRED TO IN
TEXT OF ARTICLE

1. Did you hear or read anything about the recent report by the Anglo-American Committee on Palestine?

2. Did you hear or read anything about the report on the control of atomic energy, which was published by the State Depart-

ment a few weeks ago? It's sometimes called the Acheson report.

3. Have you heard or read anything about the recent meeting in Paris where Secretary of State Byrnes has been talking with the foreign ministers of England, France, and Russia?

4. Have you heard about the recent proposals for a United States loan to England, and for other economic and financial agreements between the two countries? (*If "Yes"*) In general, do you approve or disapprove of these proposals?

5. As far as you know, is Palestine an independent country, or is she ruled by someone else? (*If "Someone else"*) Do you happen to know what country does rule her?

6. We'd like to know how much interest the public takes in some of these questions. For instance, how much interest do you take in news about (*each item below*)—a great deal of interest, a considerable amount, only a little, or none at all? (The United Nations, Our policy toward Palestine, The proposed loan to England, Our policy toward Germany, Our relations with Franco Spain, The atomic bomb, The recent meeting of foreign ministers in Paris, Our relations with Russia.)

7. (As you remember) The report recommends that 100,000 more Jewish refugees be admitted to Palestine in spite of protests by the Arabs there. President Truman has said he thinks this ought to be done. Now England says that the United States ought to help her keep order in Palestine if trouble breaks out between the Jews and the Arabs. Do you think we *should* help keep order there, or should we keep out of it?

8. Now about Spain. Have you heard about the recent statement, in which the United States joined with England and France to express the hope that General Franco's government in Spain would soon be followed by a more democratic one?

9. Which one of these three statements comes closest to *your* opinion about our government's policy toward Spain? (*Card handed to respondent*)

A. We should go even further in opposing Franco, and should break diplomatic relations with his government.

B. It was a good thing to speak out against Franco, but we have gone far enough for the present.

C. We have already gone too far in working against Franco, and are interfering in Spain's internal affairs.

10. Do you think the newspapers you read generally make Russia look better or worse than she really is?

11. In the disagreements between Russia and the United States, do you think one of the countries is entirely to blame, or do you think both countries have something to do with the misunderstanding?

12. Aside from getting paid interest on the loan, do you know whether the United States would be getting anything else out of the deal—that is, would *we* be getting any advantages or concessions? (*If "Yes"*) What?

13. Under these proposals, we would lend England nearly four billion dollars, which they have agreed to pay back with interest during the next fifty years. England has also agreed to take definite steps to remove restrictions on our trade with them, and to join us in promoting world trade in general. President Truman has now asked Congress to approve this plan. Do you think Congress should or should not approve it? (*Unless "Don't know"*) Why do you think so?

14. In general, do you think England can be trusted to cooperate with us in the future, or don't you think so?

PERSONAL CONTACT OR MAIL PROPAGANDA?
AN EXPERIMENT IN VOTING TURNOUT AND ATTITUDE CHANGE*

SAMUEL J. ELDERSVELD AND RICHARD W. DODGE

INTRODUCTION

The problem of stimulating a body of citizens toward greater participation in the political process or toward some desired expression of voting preference has not received sufficient attention from students of political behavior. There have been numerous studies, for example, which have increased our understanding of the social and economic factors which are related to voting participation and voting preference. But the important and significant problem of manufacturing consent through the manipulation of the means of communication has been largely neglected by political scientists. In spite of the increased reliance that political parties have placed on the mass media, little is known concerning the comparative effectiveness of the various media as instruments of persuasion. In the fields of market research and communications, for example, considerable attention has been paid to this problem;[1] that a similar effort is needed in the realm of politics requires no documentation. Gosnell's study[2] of an attempt to stimulate citizens to register and vote in two elections, one national and one local, in Chicago is a landmark in this area,

[1] See Paul F. Lazarsfeld and Frank Stanton (eds.), *Communications Research*, 1948-49, Harper, 1949.

[2] Harold F. Gosnell, *Getting Out the Vote*, University of Chicago Press, 1927.

but there have been few to follow his lead. The present study, on a considerably more modest scale than Gosnell's, involves the effect of using two different methods of urging citizens to vote favorably on a proposition regarding a general revision of a municipal charter.

This experiment differed in several important ways from that conducted by Gosnell. Basically, the latter was directed toward increasing the number of voters registered and toward securing a high turnout at the polls, while the effort reported here sought to influence selected individuals to vote for a ballot proposition. The by-product of this appeal may have been to increase voting participation, but it was not the central consideration. In the second place, the Chicago study dealt with *all* adult citizens in the 12 districts selected, whereas only persons who were either opposed to charter revision or apathetic on the matter were included in the present report. This group would be expected to offer greater resistance to pro-charter revision propaganda than would the population as a whole. Gosnell's experimental group was subjected to varying types of get-out-the-vote propaganda, all of which was sent through the mail. The study was designed to permit the measurement of the varying effects of factual and emotional appeals. The Ann Arbor study, on the other hand, involved the use of two

* This study is one of a series being conducted by the Political Behavior Project of the University of Michigan under a grant from the Ford Foundation.

different means of stimulating voter re-action—a personal interview as compared with literature sent through the mails. Further, the control and experimental groups in Gosnell's study were geographically distinct portions of the same precinct, whereas the three subdivisions of the Ann Arbor study were distributed randomly throughout the three wards.

To check on the performance of his group, Gosnell utilized official poll books and records, which, even with nonpartisan watchers present, were susceptible to fraud and corruption, as he admitted. In Ann Arbor, the respondents in the sample were given a post-election interview in which data were collected on their voting behavior and recall of subjection to several kinds of communication media. Such information was subject to the errors inherent in the survey technique.

There were two principal similarities between the studies. Both dealt with selected areas of the respective cities, which corresponded with political divisions rather than with the entire city. The conditions surrounding the aldermanic election in Chicago generally paralleled those for the Ann Arbor municipal election in that both were partisan in character and there was relatively less publicity about the candidates and issues than would be normal for a state or national election.

Fully as important as the findings in this study is the method in which it was executed. The entire project was carried on in conjunction with an undergraduate course in Pressure Groups and Public Opinion at the University of Michigan. Each member of the class participated directly in at least one phase of the study, with some voluntarily working on other aspects in addition to the one assigned. The course instructor was assisted by four advanced graduate students, each of whom was made responsible for one stage in the operation. These five persons acted as an overall planning group, holding weekly meetings to discuss methods of procedure and to iron out any complicating factors which might arise. A

more complete discussion of the methodology of the study has been reserved for a later section. This preliminary allusion serves to underline the authors' belief in the importance of this study as a pedagogical technique.

THE CONTEXT OF THE STUDY

Appearing on the ballot in the Ann Arbor municipal election of April 6, 1953 was a proposal asking the voters' approval or disapproval of a general revision of the city charter. If a majority of those voting on the proposition favored such a revision, a nine member charter study commission was to be elected from the city at large within 60 days. Upon completion of its work and submission of its recommendations the electorate would have 60 days to consider the proposals and then would be asked to accept or reject the plan as a whole.

This was the fourth attempt to secure a general revision of the 1889 charter, previous efforts in 1917, 1921 and 1939 having failed to win the necessary approval. Those in favor of Charter Revision cited a number of reasons for their stand, the chief among them being that the City Council is required to devote too much time to administration and not enough to policy making; lack of consistency with regard to duties, length of service and responsibility of boards and commissions; no direct line of administrative responsibility; and that the city lacks the basic home rule powers essential to running a modern city.

This movement for charter revision was supported by such representative civic organizations as the Rotary, Kiwanis and Lions Clubs—and by women's groups like the League of Women Voters and the American Association of University Women. The issue was also removed from the arena of partisan politics by specific pledges favoring charter revision inserted in the city platforms of both major parties. There was thus no organized campaign to secure votes against revision of the city charter, although undercover opposition was reported among businessmen, satisfied with the status quo, who feared that any modification of the governmental structure might result in some kind of economic deprivation like a higher tax rate.

The two groups most active in soliciting support for yes votes on the charter revision proposition were the League of Women Voters and the *ad hoc* Citizen's Committee for Charter Revision. Both organizations circularized voters, conducted house to house canvasses and made telephone calls in their efforts to arouse interest in the election. Thus, the voters, city-wide, were subjected to stimuli other than that applied in the course of our experiment. This is inevitable when one is dealing with this kind of social science experimentation and the assumption is made that the effect of these other stimuli was more or less randomly distributed among the respondents with whom we were concerned.[3]

Some use, too, was made of radio spot announcements and newspaper advertising by various charter revision proponents. In addition, the daily newspaper ran several editorials expressing strong support for the proposition.

The results of the municipal election, held on April 6, 1953, are shown in the following table. Figures for the three wards in which our sample was drawn are presented, as well as the totals for the entire city.

It is apparent from the table that 7 out of 10 persons who went to the polls voted on the charter revision proposition, a very respectable showing for such a measure.

[3] See the discussion in Gosnell, *op. cit.*, pp. 23ff. and Ch. 4.

The proposal itself was overwhelmingly approved by a 9 to 1 margin city wide. Even if those who failed to vote on the charter revision issue are considered as opposed to the measure, a dubious assumption at best, it still received a clearcut majority of the total vote cast. Therefore, the significant point for charter revision proponents was in getting out the vote, for nearly two out of every three persons who voted in the election expressed themselves as favorable to a general revision of the municipal charter.

METHOD

The first methodological problem was the identification of the subjects of the experiment. To be included within the study, persons had to be at least undecided on the advisability of charter reform or, preferably, opposed to it. Fortunately, there were data available on this particular problem in a study of political attitudes and affiliations of a random sample in three wards in Ann Arbor conducted in the spring of 1952. The interview schedule used in this early study included one question requesting the respondents' views on whether there should be a change in the city charter in the direction of setting up a city manager form of government.

The next step in setting up the 1953 study was to divide the total group of respondents, who were either opposed to or had no opinion on charter revision, into three sub-groups. One way of achieving this desired end is to use cross-sectional experimental design in which the various sub-

TABLE 1

VOTE IN MUNICIPAL ELECTION IN ANN ARBOR, APRIL 6, 1953

	Ward 2	Ward 4	Ward 6	Total City
Estimated eligible vote (67% of pop.)	5,215	3,946	5,990	32,328
Reg. vote as % of eligible vote	92.5	65.6	42.4	70.4
Vote on CR as % of reg. vote	18.3	15.2	32.1	22.5
Vote on CR as % of vote cast	70.4	59.2	76.1	69.4
% of favorable vote on CR	84.6	86.8	94.4	89.9

groups are matched on selected character-istics.[4] This can be accomplished either by identical matching of individual cases or, more commonly, by a comparison of fre-quency distributions on the selected traits. In our study the number of cases was too small to permit the employment of either of these techniques, since the probable shrinkage resulting from any controls would have involved too great a loss in our original sample. However, even if there were a sufficient number of cases, there would be some difficulty in deciding on what factors the matching process would be based. This stems from a lack of knowledge regarding the variables which are related to stimulating responses in situations like the one with which we are concerned here. Reliance was therefore placed on a completely random distribution of the total group among the three sub-groups.

One of these groups was then designated as the control group to which the two experimental groups could be compared at the conclusion of the study. The two-fold division of the experimental groups per-mitted the utilization of differing stimuli, thus allowing observation of any variations that might occur between them. The two experimental sub-groups were designated as mail propaganda and personal contact, respectively.

The next problem involved the specific means of applying the two kinds of stimuli. An attempt was made to obtain an inter-view with each of the persons in the per-sonal contact group. Members of the class did the bulk of this interviewing. As an aid in identifying the correct respondent from the previous year's study, the student can-vassers were supplied with such essential information as age, sex, education, religious preference, political affiliation, etc. They were instructed to introduce themselves as individuals who were working on behalf of the Citizen's Committee for Charter Revi-sion. Each student was provided with an

identification card signed by the Chairman of the Citizen's Committee. If asked whether they were University students, they were sup-posed to answer truthfully but under no cir-cumstances were they to reveal themselves as members of a Political Science class in public opinion. The members of the class who were engaged in canvassing were required to famil-iarize themselves with the literature on char-ter revision, distributed by such groups as the League of Women Voters and the Citizen's Committee. The canvassers were expected to argue the case for Charter Revision from three basic points of view—the archaic provisions of the charter, the absence of clear lines of responsibility and the conse-quent waste and inefficiency which this state of affairs induced. However, the students were advised to adapt their presentation to the needs of the particular situation with which they were confronted. Upon com-pletion of the personal contact, each student was asked to write a report of the interview. Reports were also required in those cases where contacts were attempted, but for one reason or another were not completed. These reports included information regard-ing the degree of certainty that the correct respondent was contacted, the specific cir-cumstance of the interview, the length of the interview, the main arguments stressed by the canvasser, a rating of the respondent's attitude toward charter revision at the start of the interview and whether his attitude changed, a rating of his interest in and information about city government and charter revision, etc. Of the original num-ber of 45, personal contacts were established with 30, which is a high rate of success, in view of the circumstances surrounding the study.

The second experimental group was sub-jected to a different set of stimuli. Four waves of charter revision propaganda were mailed to the individuals in this group. To facilitate this process, wherever possible, the names of the persons being contacted were either secured from the City Directory or, in a few cases, were obtained from the preceding year's interview schedule. There

[4] See F. Stuart Chapin, *Experimental Designs in Sociological Research*, Harper, 1947, pp. 34-39.

was considerable discussion concerning the type of appeal that this propaganda effort should make. It was decided that rather than concentrate on one level of appeal, an attempt should be made to duplicate an actual propaganda situation. Thus, we would be measuring the total impact of the propaganda on the individuals in our experimental group by utilizing a variety of appeals. The four waves were mailed out in the closing weeks of the campaign with about a week's interval between each mailing. The first piece of literature was a small folder setting forth in simple terms what approval of the charter revision proposition on the ballot entailed. Chief emphasis was placed on the need for having responsible and efficient government and how the present charter failed to permit this. The wide support which the proposition attracted from both political parties and from many civic groups was stressed. The second wave consisted of a two page mimeographed report prepared by the Citizen's Committee for Charter Revision. This report was a listing of defects in the present charter with a brief discussion of these points, illustrated with specific examples. There was no explicit exhortation to go to the polls beyond the recital of these defects. The students in the class designed a frankly emotional appeal for the next mailing. In a series of seven panels, the difficulty of fixing responsibility was graphically illustrated in cartoon form with the proprietor of a mythical market being confronted with buck-passing in his attempts to arouse the city government to repair a broken water-main. As a concluding measure to induce persons in this experimental group to go to the polls and vote for charter revision, a post-card reminder was mailed to arrive on the morning of election day. To achieve a more personal effect, the brief message was written in longhand.

The interviewing of the sample, as a follow up to the election, was accomplished exclusively by members of the class. With a few exceptions, each student took at least one interview, with some taking as many as 5 and 6. A number of interviewer training sessions were held to acquaint students with the intricacies of this crucial aspect of the survey technique. Demonstration interviews were held for the benefit of the students during these training sessions. Stress was laid on such important aspects of the interview situation as getting the respondent to answer the question when he tries to digress, the use of non-directive probes, the proper method of introduction, the art of being politely insistent, etc. Considerations of time necessitated elimination of a pretest of the interview schedule. Students were therefore urged to take a practice interview with a roommate or other friend. As in the personal contact interviews, the student interviewers were supplied with basic social and economic data plus the usual face sheet information to facilitate identification of the previous year's respondent. The students were instructed to present themselves as members of a Political Science class at the University of Michigan.

Mention should be made of the "mortality" from the original sample of 138 respondents. The large number of respondents who were "lost" in 1953 should not occasion surprise when the relevant facts of the survey and the nature of the community are recalled. It is inevitable when an entire year elapses between interviews that changes in the original sample will occur. People die, others move away, some are temporarily out of town or otherwise unavailable. Two of the three wards in this study border on the University and contain a sizeable number of graduate students and younger faculty members, a group which as a whole would be expected to be relatively transient in its housing accommodations. The respondents who for any reason were not interviewed in 1953 are approximately equally divided between each of the sub-groups. This is true for the reasons for non-interviews as well, except that five of the seven refusals are found in the control group.

FINDINGS

As a prelude to presenting some of the more significant results of this study, the principal limitations of the data will be reviewed briefly. The data refer to persons in three wards of the City of Ann Arbor and are therefore not representative of the entire city. The persons included in our study are those who were either apathetic, uninformed or opposed to a modification of the city charter in the direction of a city manager. Representing a group that is less receptive to municipal reform than the general population, these respondents offered a particularly attractive arena for an experiment in stimulating attitudes toward the advisability of such reform. We must recognize, too, that the way in which the original question in the 1952 study was phrased tended to structure responses around the city manager plan. Conceivably, persons who were favorable to charter revision in principle, but opposed to the introduction of a city manager, might be included in the present study on the basis of their answer to the question in the 1952 study. How many cases there were of this type is unfortunately not known, but it is felt that the data are not fundamentally impaired by this fact. The large number of respondents in the 1953 sample with whom interviews were not secured is to be expected in view of the 12 month interval between the initial and follow up interviews. It is assumed that this so called "sample mortality" was distributed randomly throughout all the respondents and therefore that the results are not basically altered from those which would have been obtained if it had been possible to take interviews with all the respondents. With these qualifications in mind, the findings may be presented as indicative of tendencies upon which more research must be performed before their validity is completely established.

Table 2 presents the figures on voting in the April 6 election for our three sample groups and is the basic table for our experiment. There is a perceptible trend toward greater approval of charter revision among the experimental groups. Thus, only slightly more than half of those in the control group who voted in the election also voted for the proposition. On the other hand, the comparable figures for the mail and personal contact respondents were 76.9% and 100% respectively. While the number favoring charter revision increased in all groups, it was proportionally greater in the two experimental groups.

Another significant finding is the contrast in the turnout at the polls. Where only one-third of the control group respondents voted in the election, nearly 60% of those contacted by mail and three-fourths of

TABLE 2*

VOTE IN ELECTION FOR CONTROL AND EXPERIMENTAL GROUPS

	Control Group	Mail Propaganda	Personal Contact	Total	
Voted in election and voted:					
for CR	4	10	15	29	
against CR	1	2	—	3	
other†	2	1	—	3	
Total voted in election	7 (33.3%)	13 (59.1%)	15 (75%)		35
Did not vote in election and favorable to CR	1	—	1	2	
opposed to CR	—	—	—	—	
stand on CR unknown 1953	13	9	4	26	
Total did not vote in election	14 (66.7%)	9 (40.9%)	5 (25%)		28
Total number of cases	21	22	20		63

* It was possible to examine the voting records at the City Clerk's office of those respondents who said they voted in the municipal election. However, the unreliability of the City Directory made it difficult to identify many of the respondents with certainty and, therefore, the results of this check are inconclusive.

† Refused to say how voted on CR, did not vote on CR, and not sure whether voted on CR.

those contacted personally exercised the franchise. It is impossible to ascertain precisely whether our charter revision propaganda was instrumental in changing attitudes toward charter revision as well as persuading people to go to the polls. In other words, we were unable to isolate other stimuli that impinged upon the electorate in order to observe our groups in a completely controlled situation. In the year that elapsed between the two surveys there may have been a gradual shift in sentiment toward the desirability of revision, spurred by increasing publicity and public discussion. Thus, by the time our experiment was conducted the opposition to, or apathy regarding, charter revision that we observed in the spring of 1952 may have largely disappeared. In that case, our experiment may have become one of getting out the vote, since as we saw in the official returns, nearly two out of every three voters who went to the polls voted for general charter revision.

Some support for the hypothesis that voters were stimulated by our propaganda to go to the polls, as much as persuaded to modify their views on charter reform, is provided by a breakdown of the vote cast by the mail group. When these respondents are divided into two groups on the basis of whether they recalled receiving any literature through the mails which dealt with charter revision, we find that two-thirds of those who admitted receiving mail voted in the election, while the proportion for the respondents who failed to recall receiving any such mail was less than 50%. In each group (voters plus non-voters), about the same proportion (7 out of 15 and 3 out of 7) were on record as voting for the proposal.

In the foregoing discussion, we have seen that the two experimental groups differ both in their voting participation and in the amount of support they gave to charter revision. Personal contact respondents scored higher on both counts. This finding is in line with all experience in the field of public opinion sampling in which it has

been amply demonstrated that a face-to-face interview is more informative and results in a higher rate of response than reliance on sending questionnaires through the mails. By approaching this matter from a slightly different angle, we can produce empirical evidence of the superiority of the personal interview in terms of the respondent's ability to recall whether or not he received the appropriate stimulus and, if so, the organization or group responsible for it. The following table presents data obtained

TABLE 3

RECALL OF SOURCE OF CONTACT BY EXPERIMENTAL GROUPS

Recalled appropriate stimulus from:	Mail Propaganda	Personal Contact
League of Women Voters	1	
Citizen's Committee		1
Junior Chamber of Commerce		2
Political Party		2
Other Group	14 (63.6%)	13 (65%)
Not Sure	1	1
Recalled no stimulus	6 (27.3%)	1 (5%)
Total	22	20

in the post-election interviews involving the recall, by persons in the two experimental groups, of subjection to either mail or personal contact, as the case might be. It is recognized that respondents in each group experienced other influences, some of which are revealed in the table. Also, all of those included in the "other group" category did not necessarily recall *our* stimulus. However, it is noteworthy that almost an identical proportion of each experimental group recalled the appropriate *type* of contact, depending upon the subgroup in which they were placed. Probably the most significant datum is the respective proportions who recalled no contact whatsoever—5% for the personal contact group but 27.3% for the mail recipients.

An attempt was made in the post-election interviews to discover the exposure of the respondents to three channels of opinion formulating media; i.e. radio, newspapers and handbills. There are several difficulties

icant aspects of the experiment. Clearly, much remains to be done in this area before any definite conclusions can be drawn on the effect of propaganda on individual voting decisions. Difficult though it is to determine the differential influence of various types of channels of communication in actual political situations, attempts should be made to control as many of the variables as is possible. The Ann Arbor data showed the greater effectiveness of a personal interview over sending literature through the mails. However, as was pointed out above, during the course of a political campaign the voters are subjected to a multiplicity of stimuli so that the task of discovering a pattern of stimuli and then ascertaining their effect is a formidable one. Lazarsfeld used a technique in determining the relative influence of newspapers and radio on respondents which relied on the specificity of the response as an index of the influence of the particular medium on voting decisions.[6] He found that in the context of the influence of these two media radio was more effective than newspapers. The Erie County study also demonstrated the potentiality of personal contact as a source of influence, particularly with regard to those persons who were generally untouched by the mass media. Our research has also adverted to the importance of this avenue of influence which suggests that a concerted attempt be made to study this phenomenon more intensively.

Gosnell as well as Hartmann[7] have both shown that voters react differently to alternate types of appeals, one to the emotions and one to the intellect. Although the types of appeal sent to the respondent in our mail experimental group vary, the study was not designed to permit the measurement of the differing impact of such appeals.

[6] Paul F. Lazarsfeld, Bernard Berelson and Hazel Gaudet, *The People's Choice*, p. 126.

[7] Gosnell, *op. cit.*; George W. Hartmann, "A Field Experiment on the Comparative Effectiveness of 'Emotional' and 'Rational' Political Leaflets in Determining Election Results," *The Journal of Abnormal and Social Psychology*, XXXI, (1936-1937), pp. 99-114.

In addition, the scope of such investigations should be widened geographically to include representative urban and rural areas throughout the country. It is equally important to study these phenomena in urban areas of different size in order to discover what distinguishing characteristics, if any, depend on city size.

In line with these suggestions, it is planned to continue experimentation in Ann Arbor on this problem of voter stimulation. With studies designed explicitly for the purpose at hand, many of the difficulties that inhered in the data from the 1952 study could be overcome. This process would also permit old techniques to be refined and improved and new ones to be tested. In this way, progress could be anticipated on both the methodological and substantive fronts.

Finally, a few concluding comments with regard to method, which, as has been suggested earlier, is of at least equal importance with the findings of this area. This experiment was conducted in conjunction with a course in public opinion with students participating in every phase. Although there are several drawbacks for this procedure, they would appear to be overborne by the advantage, from a pedagogical point of view, of involving students in the actual operation of a sample survey. Participation in the various steps of the process, and thereby confronting the problems which inevitably arise, will familiarize the student with the survey method in a more thorough and lasting way than comparable time spent in immersion in the literature of the field. This is not to deny the importance of the literature, but merely to assert the probable superiority of field experience in an undergraduate course in public opinion. The entire operation was facilitated by the assistance of four advanced graduate students, three in political science and one in sociology. They were able to shoulder some of the administrative burden and thus relieve the course instructor from attending to the details of each phase of study.

It should be admitted that utilization of students has its disadvantages, too. Tailoring the project for the needs of a one semester course requires adhering to a tight time schedule. Even though the preliminary selection of respondents was accomplished before the semester began, the later phases had to be speeded up more than was ideally suitable. It probably is impossible to complete the analysis stage within one semester, but every effort should be made to distribute a small report on some of the major findings or a collection of key tables to the students, so that they will appreciate the kinds of data that such a study can collect.

Considerations of time, when added to student inexperience, undoubtedly introduced bottlenecks and errors at various stages of the process. Further study should be given to the problem of proper allotment of time for the several phases of such an experiment. Depending on the type of operation being conducted, earlier stages might be telescoped in favor of more time for thorough training of interviewers and pretesting of the interview schedule. In any event, the experience with this survey indicates that it is entirely feasible to utilize field training in connection with an advanced undergraduate course. The major difficulties which arose can be largely removed by modifications in procedure as suggested by past experience.

In 1927, Gosnell raised two basic questions about get-out-the-vote campaigns; 1) what effect large scale efforts to get individuals to the polls had on increasing the turnout (or whether the latter were dependent upon other factors like the closeness of the election) and 2) what is the significance of such an attempt? (do we gain by securing a high turnout at the polls if the added increment does not exercise the franchise in an intelligent manner?) At the present time, we are not much further along toward knowing the answers than we were 27 years ago. However, the practical importance of the accumulation of basic data on this problem of stimulating the electorate can not be denied. With the increased reliance on the mass media which has characterized the American political scene in this country, and especially the introduction of television as a principal channel of political information, the study of the impact these media have on the population has become more necessary. This development will lead to more research in this area, if only because the tremendous expense involved will cause parties and sponsors to clamor for investigations of the audience reached in an effort to utilize such costly facilities in a more economical manner. Therefore, it would seem that this particular area of political behavior, long avoided by students, presents an especially rewarding opportunity to researchers to contribute both in a theoretical and a practical way to our knowledge of political processes.

SOME PSYCHOLOGICAL LESSONS FROM LEAFLET PROPAGANDA IN WORLD WAR II

MARTIN F. HERZ

The effectiveness of leaflets which were used in combat propaganda during the past war could be gauged to a much larger extent than was possible in the case of most other forms of propaganda. Continuous prisoner interrogation about the impact of combat leaflets, for instance, permitted the elaboration of certain principles, and their confirmation and subsequent refinement, whereas with respect to the effectiveness of strategic propaganda it has been possible to make only broad and very general observations. Our mistakes in combat propaganda were often readily apparent, while correct psychological judgments could be confirmed by observing the behavior of enemy troops. It is the purpose of this article to set forth some conclusions about leaflet writing and propaganda in general which resulted from this experience.

THE INSUFFICIENCY OF TRUTH

During the early days of combat leafleting, the psychological warfare field team with the Fifth Army in Italy was partially dependent on shipments of propaganda material from governmental agencies in Britain and the United States. One leaflet sent to Italy seemed a first-rate job. It described, with many pictures and a brief text, the life in "British, American and Canadian Pris-oner-of-War Camps." It showed, for instance, a Canadian base camp that had formerly been a hotel, a camp orchestra, a well-groomed prisoner (an officer) sitting in an overstuffed chair, and other prisoners playing billiards or sitting on a porch listening to the radio. Everything this leaflet said or depicted was true. It was thought best, however, to test it first on some of the prisoners in the Aversa P/W enclosure.

As a result of those tests, the entire shipment had to be discarded. The prisoners were by no means uncooperative—in fact, many of them stated that if only they had known that treatment would be as good as it was in Aversa, they would have surrendered earlier. Nevertheless, they simply refused to believe that conditions in P/W camps in America could be as shown on the leaflet.

Although it was true that prisoners in American P/W camps received eggs for breakfast, further testing showed us that this notion was so preposterous to the Germans on the other side of the firing line that they simply laughed at the idea. Since this discredited the balance of our message, it became another favorable truth which we learned to suppress. The same, incidentally, applied to an important strategic propaganda theme, that of war production. We had to refrain from telling the Germans that

From the *Public Opinion Quarterly*, Vol. 13, 1949, No. 3, 471-486. Reprinted by permission of the author and the publisher.

Henry Kaiser put ships together in five days. Although this spectacular fact was true, we had to stress the less spectacular and more general fact that we were building several times the tonnage sunk by the U-boats. Intelligence on what the Germans believed, and what they could be expected to believe, forced us to do this.

Eventually, as the result of extensive prisoner interrogations, a basic theme on P/W treatment was worked out, which found its widest application on the Western Front. Instead of picturing captivity in the U.S. as the outrageous idyll which it really was, we used the slogan: *"It's no fun being a prisoner-of-war!"* and went on to show that it was a grim but tolerable fate for anyone who had fought hard but who nevertheless had been unable to evade capture. We did point out, however, that being a prisoner had certain redeeming features. The punch line to this type of appeal was: *"Better Free Than a Prisoner-of War, Better a Prisoner-of-War Than Dead."* That line proved highly effective. Understatement, in this instance, was probably the only viable means of communicating with the enemy.

HOW CAN EFFECTIVENESS BE JUDGED?

At this point, the question may legitimately be asked just how it was known, during the last war, whether a combat leaflet was more, or less, successful. After all, the psychological warfare intelligence officer could only in the rarest instances observe the behavior in battle of those enemy units which had been subjected to a specific leaflet message. Since this question is important to consideration of the following case material, we will dwell on it briefly.

Evidence of effectiveness, or of lack of effectiveness, was obtained chiefly from the following sources: (a) quantity of leaflets found on the persons of prisoners; (b) recollection of leaflets by prisoners, and comments about them; (c) favorable mention, and detailed discussion by soldiers behind the German lines, as reported by co-operative prisoners; (d) detailed description of their surrender by prisoners; (e) preoccupation of German counter-propaganda with specific Allied leaflets, including plagiarism by German combat propagandists; (f) comments by the enemy command, as learned from captured documents on troop morale.

In some cases, where continued dissemination of one special leaflet was deemed desirable, prisoner reactions could even be used to sharpen its effectiveness, as in the case of the well-known SHAEF Safe-Conduct leaflet. The first edition of that leaflet, produced in the early days of the Normandy invasion, showed merely the seal of the U.S. and the British royal crest, together with a standard text in English and German which called upon the Allied front-line soldier to accord his prisoner good treatment. By the time the Safe-Conduct leaflet went into its sixth printing, the following changes had been made as the result of P/W interviews: (a) the German text had been placed above the English; (b) a note had been inserted, stating specifically that the English text was a translation of the German; (c) General Eisenhower's signature had been added; (d) his name had been spelled out, because it was learned that Germans did not recognize the written signature as Eisenhower's; (e) the leaflet was printed in red rather than in green, which made it more conspicuous on the ground; and (f) a note had been added under the word "Safe Conduct," pointing out that the document was valid for "one or several bearers." These improvements resulted from continuous testing of the leaflet's effectiveness.

In planning for propaganda exploitation of our landing at Anzio and Nettuno in January 1944, we provided for dissemination of a leaflet on the main (Cassino) front as soon as we knew that our troops were ashore. In this leaflet we committed the mistake of making specific predictions, speaking of the German retreat being blocked and of a "battle of encirclement" that would commence with the landing operation. When the beachhead was subsequently contained, the Germans were so elated about the falsity of our prediction that they disseminated replicas of our (German-language) leaflet to the American soldiers at the front, jeering at us and delighting in proving us wrong. It need hardly be pointed out that this was rather foolish on their part: our soldiers had never seen our German-language leaflet and did not care what it said. What the Germans might have done, but failed to do, was to disseminate the leaflet *to their own troops,* thus demonstrating the falsity of our propaganda.

THE HANDLING OF PROPAGANDA DEFEATS

The lesson to be learned from this experience would seem to be that it is highly risky to make predictions about a forthcoming operation, and also quite unnecessary. The argument was advanced during the planning stage before Anzio that we "owed it to our boys to assume that they would be successful," since "if they fail, the incidental propaganda defeat won't matter." In other words, it was contended that the propaganda risk was part of the major military risk. Experience proved this attitude to be wrong. While it is necessary to take military (and political) risks, it does not appear to be necessary to take propaganda risks. If facts go against us, we can still salvage some propaganda honor from them by admitting that the facts are against us. If we make false predictions, however, subsequent admissions have much less value because our whole credit has been undermined. Victories, after defeats in battle, may restore the enemy's fear of our weapons; but truth, after falsity, does not necessarily restore the belief in our truthfulness.

The second instance of an Allied propaganda defeat also contains food for thought. We had achieved considerable success with a leaflet which factually and in pictures described the first day in the life of German P/W's captured on the Cotentin peninsula.

The leaflet was widely disseminated all over the Western front. When we broke out of the beachhead and captured Paris, the last picture on the leaflet (which showed P/W's being embarked on an LST) was overprinted in red to show that henceforth prisoners would no longer be shipped to America but would remain in enclosures in Western France. This was a correct decision based on interrogations which showed that many Germans, feeling that the war was about to end, were fearful of being shipped to America, from where it would presumably take longer to get home after the armistice.

German counter-propaganda selected this widely disseminated leaflet to "prove" that since "prisoners are no longer sent to America"—they were being shipped to Siberia instead. The accusation was substantiated in no other way. It was very widely made, however, and eventually expanded into the general slogan *Sieg oder Sibirien!* (victory or Siberia) which tied in with Goebbels' brilliant "strength through fear" propaganda on the home front. This confronted us with the problem of how to meet a preposterous falsehood that apparently was having some success in bolstering German troop morale.

After careful discussion, it was decided not to respond directly, because (a) any reply could be picked up by the Germans as similarly spurious "proof" of the correctness of their contention; and (b) we did not wish to give additional currency to the idea of Siberia. It was assumed that every denial of a flagrant lie lends it a certain dignity that it did not possess before. The word "Siberia" was consequently never mentioned in our output, and the German campaign eventually died a natural death. During the entire period, we continued our regular output on P/W treatment, ignoring the question of shipment but playing up somewhat more heavily the guarantee, under the Geneva Convention, that prisoners would be returned home "as soon as possible after the war."

In general, to deny a lie disseminated by

the enemy is in most cases merely to give it additional circulation. (The Soviets are experts at picking up a denial and using it to revitalize the original falsehood.) Disputing a specific point with an opponent usually means descending to his level. When the enemy has scored, it is usually best to chalk up the score in his column and then to hit him somewhere else.[1] If we dispute a point with him, we meet him on ground which he has chosen and engage in defensive propaganda. Later it will be demonstrated that defensive propaganda is— at least in combat propaganda—a virtual impossibility. Propaganda is essentially an offensive weapon.

TARGET: THE MARGINAL MAN

The marginal man in propaganda is the man who does not believe everything we say, but who is interested in our message because he does not believe everything our opponents say either. In war, he is the man who distrusts us and has reasons for fighting, but who also has good reasons for not fighting. He is the *potential waverer*. (Real waverers are presumably already convinced, and thus are not strictly marginal targets.) In our combat propaganda we always tried to address ourselves to potential waverers, to the men who despaired of victory but were reluctant to draw the consequences, the men who were still willing to fight but who fought without determination, who would "never surrender" but who might submit to capture "if the situation were hopeless." To address the out-and-out fanatics would have been a waste of time, and would have harmed us with our other listeners and friends. On the other hand, to address directly the defeatists and those waiting to desert harmed us with the potential waverers.

The concept of the marginal propaganda man may be a useful one for peacetime

[1] In certain cases, of course, denial of an enemy falsehood cannot be avoided. In such instances, the denial will be best made by implication, and without reference to the original lie.

propaganda also. Too much output may be addressed to persons who already agree with us. With battle lines fairly clearly drawn, communications which meet the approval of completely pro-American elements are less important than those which appeal to potential waverers on both sides of the ideological front (i.e., we must not forget potential waverers in our own democratic ranks). That is why public opinion polling on the effectiveness of our peacetime propaganda, if it does not weight its samples in favor of the critical strata of the population, may be misleading. If, for instance, a theme of ours elicits exceptional enthusiasm on the part of extreme rightist elements abroad, while intensifying doubts about us on the part of potential waverers among the democratic left, then such a theme has done us more harm than good.

The reasoning behind this conclusion is similar to that which made us forego outright appeals to the German soldier to desert, on the assumption that the desertion-minded would in any event receive our message warmly, whereas a blunt appeal for desertion would have harmed us with the potential waverers. For the potential waverer needs more than "just one little push" to make him topple. To address him with overly partisan, overly direct, overly anti-enemy propaganda might sour him on us completely. Similarly, if propaganda favoring American "rugged individualism" is directed to potential waverers abroad who are convinced that they want economic security most, but who are not yet convinced that it is worthwhile to surrender freedom for it, equally adverse results might be expected.

NECESSITY OF CONCENTRATING PROPAGANDA FIRE

During the war, demands were continuously made upon our propagandists to "tell the enemy" a large number of things, to attack him on a variety of fronts and to undermine his credit in numerous ways. These demands tended to lead to output which devoted a small amount of attention to a large number of subjects.

The dispersion of themes in some of our combat propaganda may also have been caused in part by the advertising and journalism background of many of our propagandists. Yet combat propaganda and other propaganda addressed to enemy populations in wartime posed quite different problems than domestic advertising. The advertising man need only imagine that he is charged with publicizing *Fleetfoot* automobiles in publications which contain anti-*Fleetfoot* material, both editorial and advertising, in about twenty-five times the lineage that he has at his disposal. Let him imagine that the publications on which he must rely to communicate with his public will contain material such as the following:

A news item describing how a certain individual sat down at the wheel of his *Fleetfoot*, switched on the ignition, stepped on the starter, and was blown to smithereens by gasoline fumes which had accumulated under the hood, due to imperfections of the carburetor. . . . Pictures of the man's funeral. . . . Resolutions of the bereaved of other families similarly stricken to boycott *Fleetfoots*. . . . A news item about another *Fleetfoot* driver who dizzily careened down a steep incline when his brakes failed to function, and a picture of the resulting smashup and carnage. . . . Reports of protest meetings against the slipshod manufacturing methods and repressive labor policies of *Fleetfoot*. . . . Pictures of disorders at the *Fleetfoot* plant, and articles describing the disorganization of the production line, which resulted in rejected parts being inadvertently built into cars on the assembly line. . . . Stories about the cost-cutting policies of the *Fleetfoot* management which brought the elimination of many safety features ordinarily present in other cars. . . . Statistics proving the falling-off of *Fleetfoot* sales and production, and the increase in complaints and fatalities. . . .

To appreciate the situation of the wartime propagandist one need only imagine such items appearing in all newspapers and other media of a country, in a volume many times that of any message that the *Fleetfoot* advertiser can bring to bear. For in a totalitarian country, the mass and insistence of domestic propaganda is altogether out of proportion to what the enemy can offer. Only an occasional leaflet and snatches of radio programs, and often only messages passed on at second hand, can be brought to the attention of the average enemy target. Under such circumstances, it would be idle to speak of the beauty, low price, popularity, engineering advances, etc. of the latest model—as one would do in domestic advertising. There is only one thing, under such circumstances, that can and should be pounded home: namely, that *Fleetfoots work*.

In peacetime, preparatory to possible hostilities, the basic desideratum of propaganda addressed to potential enemy populations is that it should contain proof of our veracity. Praising the excellence of our product is not only secondary but rather beside the point. As we have seen, it would be difficult to sell the beauty and stylishness and engineering advances of *Fleetfoots* to potential customers who are day in, day out, told that *Fleetfoots* are a danger and a menace.

During the last war, many well-meaning critics of our propaganda effort thought that we should have re-educated the Germans while trying to make them surrender. To this day there are some who do not understand why our propaganda to German soldiers did not characterize Hitler as the villain he indubitably was. To convince German soldiers of the iniquity of the Nazi system, however, would have been a task infinitely more difficult and time-consuming than merely to convince them *that they were being defeated and that it was sensible to give up*. Re-education is not a task of psychological warfare, but of postwar reconstruction. Many men surrendered during the last war who had been convinced by our combat propaganda that to fight on was hopeless and that they would be well treated if they gave up. To convince them of the falsity of Nazism and of Hitler's iniquity might have taken many months and perhaps years longer.

The correctness of this finding is well demonstrated by the failures of Soviet Russia's initial combat propaganda effort against Germany during the last war.

MAKING EXCESSIVE DEMANDS UPON THE ENEMY

All through the bitter winter of 1941 in front of Moscow, when the Soviets might have had an excellent opportunity to appeal to the frustrated attacking troops, German morale was perceptibly stiffened by injudicious, doctrinaire Soviet propaganda. Conversations with Austrian Communists who participated in that propaganda effort reveal that a bitter fight raged between

IF YOU WANT TO SAVE GERMANY, THEN OVERTHROW HITLER![2]

German soldiers! On May 26, 1942 the Soviet-British treaty of alliance was concluded. On June 11, 1942, the Soviet-American agreement was signed.

These treaties mean that all of Hitler's plans to sow disunity among the anti-Hitler coalition have FAILED.

That means a firm military alliance of the three greatest powers in the world and shows their unshakable will to carry the war to a complete victory over Hitler.

Among the USA, England, and the Soviet Union complete agreement was reached concerning the opening of a second front this very year, 1942.

HITLER'S FATE IS SEALED: HITLER'S DEFEAT IS UNAVOIDABLE!

It is up to you, German soldiers, to see that Hitler's defeat is not Germany's defeat also.

Soviet propagandists and political officers, with the latter insisting that Soviet combat propaganda be "revolutionary." Soviet leaflets thus initially called upon German soldiers in the front-line to "overthrow Hitler in order to save Germany."

It is a well-established principle of psychology that if pressure is put on a person to perform an act of which he is incapable, serious internal strains and disturbances are set up which may even culminate in hostility toward the person who is making the demands. To call on people who are completely incapable of "overthrowing Hitler" to do so in order to attain their salvation, only means

[2] Translation of a Russian leaflet.

that such people will either despair of their salvation or will turn their backs altogether on the message and its source.

The Soviets eventually learned their lesson and strictly divorced their ideological propaganda from their combat propaganda, but only after caricatures of Hitler, messages exalting the bravery of the Soviet Army and denouncing fascism, etc., had done them immeasurable harm. Even after the break had been made, however, the spilling-over of Communist concepts and nomenclature (including occasional domestic propaganda caricatures and words such as "bankruptcy," "lackeys," "cliques") continued to give their propaganda an outlandish flavor, in spite of their brilliant use of captured German generals for combat psychological warfare purposes. It is an axiom of all propaganda of the written word, of course, that the language must be truly that of the recipient—and that any queerness of idiom severely detracts from the effectiveness of the message. This is so obvious that we may forego the pleasure of offering Japanese exhibits which convincingly demonstrate the point.

"EXPORTING" DOMESTIC PROPAGANDA

Generally speaking, it can be said that domestic propaganda and propaganda addressed to the enemy simply do not mix. It follows that exceptional loathing and hatred of the enemy, perhaps derived from personal humiliation, persecution, and other on-the-spot experiences, do not by any means constitute good qualifications for combat propagandists. Thus persons who returned from Germany and Japan shortly before the war, and considered their primary mission to be spreading knowledge in America about the iniquity and menace of the systems there, found it extremely difficult to achieve the necessary adjustments that would make them useful for propaganda directed toward the enemy civilian populations. Similarly, in combat propaganda, the propagandist's exultation over the enemy's discomfitures should not be too apparent in his output.

Leaflets gleefully pointing at weaknesses and absurdities of the enemy, jibing and jeering at his travails, (the "We hear you have a one-legged man in your company" type) generally proved unsuccessful during the last war.[3] It was difficult to prevent the production and dissemination of such material, however, since intelligence officers, for whom propaganda inevitably means capitalizing on all weaknesses and mistakes of the enemy, frequently pressed very strongly for leaflets of this type.

The above point is by no means as obvious as it seems, for while in theory many might agree, in practice it seemed unreasonable to some that we did not fight "ideologically" in our combat propaganda. To clinch this point, therefore, it is well to observe the effect on ourselves of enemy propaganda which incorporated domestic propaganda elements.

One example may be found in German anti-Semitic propaganda. The Nazis, to whom it seemed obvious that the Jews were behind America's entry into the war, found it impossible to contain themselves on that score. As a result, leaflets and radio programs which otherwise might have had a measure of success became even queerer and stranger to the American soldiers—for instance, the Axis-Sally programs with their reference to the "Jewnited States," or leaflets about wartime profiteers which pictured a character named Sam Levy who had been helped up the ladder to fame and fortune by Mr. Mordecai Ezekiel. To the Nazis, the name of the real-life figure such as Mr. Ezekiel seemed a God-given propaganda asset which the propagandist simply could not pass up. After all, did not that name clearly convey the idea of an untrustworthy, scheming and grasping individual? To Germans who had been steeped in Nazi anti-Semitic propaganda it undoubtedly had such a connotation. To American GI's, however, such leaflets looked more like "propaganda" than they would have otherwise, and the entire

venture acquired a fatally alien and unreasonable quality.

A second example is afforded by German and Japanese anti-Roosevelt propaganda. Let it not be said that the average American was more loyal to his President or more convinced of Roosevelt's essential honesty than the average German was of Hitler's. Many a German who considered the war a mistake, and perhaps even a crime, nevertheless resented slurs on Hitler, especially when made by the enemy. The same, *mutatis mutandis,* was true of many American soldiers. . . .

The third, and most recent, example may be taken from the propaganda now being directed to Europe. In this the Soviets, whose propagandists appear to have their hands tied by directives, have without question sinned and failed the most: in Austria, for instance, the Soviet newspaper *Oesterreichische Zeitung,* with its alien make-up, its queer wording ("over-fulfilled the norm," "miasmas of capitalism," etc.) and its preponderance of outlandish news items, has lost nearly all reader interest—although the Austrian Communist paper, which is written by Austrians, is quite another story. War films of all nations, in which enemy soldiers are shown, have met with unfavorable receptions in ex-enemy territory. Plays, such as the eminently successful "Watch on the Rhine," which packed them in on Broadway, elicited general astonishment and dismay over what German and Austrian theatergoers (including violent anti-Nazis) considered to be inaccuracies and "patent propaganda."

DOCTRINE OF LIMITED AGREEMENT

Thus it can be said that in combat propaganda it would be fatal to expect the enemy to identify himself with our side. Totalitarian enemies do not revolt because they cannot, and they do not change sides because they rarely understand the truth until it is too late. Consequently, we cannot expect an individual enemy to agree with us on more than one point at a time.

In order to find any common ground at all, to find a point of departure for the

---

[3] There are some exceptions, however, especially in the case of unusually low-morale enemy formations.

psychological manipulation of the enemy, it may even be necessary to select a point of his own creed on which to register agreement. During the last war, the elements of the German propaganda position which we used as such "points of departure" were (a) the belief in the excellence of the soldierly qualities of the German infantryman; and (b) the belief that he was being crushed by Allied superiority of materiel, rather than out-fought man for man. No propaganda to enemy targets can be successful unless some such common ground which can be used as a point of departure for the message is found.

As an example of the validity of this doctrine, there is featured what was probably the most successful combat leaflet of the last war. This leaflet is usually passed over by chroniclers of our combat propaganda record because of its seeming lack of originality or insidiousness. Yet it was again and again adjudged the most successful venture of this type (next to the SHAEF Safe-Conduct leaflet). It was found in large numbers on the persons of prisoners, was republished in many variants at various stages of the campaign in the West, and was also reprinted and used with good success by combat propagandists in the Mediterranean Theater. It salved the feelings of the enemy by crediting him, by implication, with great soldierly virtue; it accommodated his alibi of material inferiority; it described him in soldierly (non-political) terms, avoiding any political arguments; it did not overly praise captivity; and it "left the decision to the reader," seemingly not urging him to desert. Also, on its reverse side, along with a dry, curt summary of the essential facts about captivity, it spelled out the behavior necessary to effect surrender.

Propaganda to non-enemy targets is governed by the opposite considerations. In addressing ourselves to an enemy-occupied country, for instance, the audience's identification with our side must obviously be *taken for granted*—even if it does not completely obtain. It must always be assumed that citizens of occupied countries will greet us as liberators when we redeem them. (This assumption also immeasurably lightens the task of consolidation and post-war reorientation propaganda in occupied territories.) To make concessions to the Quisling point-of-view in any particular would be quite out of place.

WEDGE-DRIVING AND APPEALS TO THE UNCONSCIOUS

To "widen the gulf" between two enemy nations, to "drive a wedge" between officers and enlisted men, or to "exploit the cleavage" between elite troops and combat infantry, or "between the party and the people," are ever-cherished objectives of the propaganda directive writer. As objectives they are of course entirely sound. Implementation may, however, involve so many psychological difficulties that more harm than good is done. For sometimes it will suffice for a latent dissatisfaction to be brought out into the open by the enemy, for it to disappear.

Witness the German propaganda at the Anzio beachhead in February 1944, which reasoned quite correctly that British troops, who had borne the heaviest brunt of the German offensive at Aprilia (Carroceto), were apt to grumble about the seemingly less dangerous role played by the Americans. Several wedge-driving leaflets along such lines were disseminated, including some titillating ones showing British girls being undressed and fondled by Americans. The German approach, however, was so lacking in subtlety that according to British officers on the beachhead the comradeship-in-arms between British and Americans there was enhanced rather than diminished by the Nazi propaganda effort. Also—possibly through the projection of a theme that was vexing and frustrating to the reader without his being able to do anything about it— anti-German sentiment among British troops may even have increased.

The Japanese combat leaflet writers also attempted to capitalize on the known sex-frustration of American soldiers in the jungles of the South Pacific, but again the result was so crass and clumsy that if it lowered the morale of any American soldier reading such a leaflet, at the same time it quite likely made him want to vent his pent-up feelings upon the enemy. Although there were some abler attempts in the same direction, all suffered from the directness of the appeal: it simply is not for the enemy to remind us of our desire for women, or, for that matter, of our desire to get out of the battle alive. What goes for sex goes even more for cowardice. Enemy media can hardly appeal plainly and directly to the individual's unsoldierly, un-heroic desire for self-preservation. Perhaps it could if he were alone, but since powerful group pressures work upon him, and feelings of duty, comradeship, fear and patriotism intervene, the overt appeal cannot run directly counter to them. German appeals to our GI's, slogans such as "Take it easy, you'll last longer," fall into this category.

DANGERS OF BLACK PROPAGANDA

It may be said, in view of the above—and there are many other examples—that to bring out and nourish any subconscious feelings of resentment on the part of the enemy soldier may be beyond the capabilities of "white" propaganda (the source of which is admitted) and instead is a fitting subject for "black" or "gray" propaganda (ostensibly produced by dissident elements within the enemy population, or mentioning no source at all.) The difficulty there, however, is that detection of the origin of such propaganda will not only result in heightened hatred against the actual originator for having thus invaded the most private recesses of the enemy's mind, but it will also redound emphatically to the detriment of all "white" propaganda from the same source.

As a good example of this danger, mention might be made of an Allied "black" or "gray" leaflet of the last war that was designed to fan the sex-starved German soldier's resentment against the alleged increased latitude given foreign laborers in Germany. The leaflet in question showed a swarthy foreign worker shamelessly disporting himself with a naked Teutonic maiden, and was decidedly apt to arouse the passions of a front-line soldier. Had it been possible to conceal the source completely, beyond the shadow of a doubt, this leaflet might well have been a smashing success in undermining German troop morale. As it was, however—and this is a criticism of most of our naive "black" and "gray" activity of the last war—the enemy could easily see from the elaborateness of the leaflet (which in this case was printed in four colors) that this was Allied propaganda. Even though he might agree with the message, he would resent it since it was painful to him. Moreover, since at the same time all our "white" media were laboring hard and patiently to establish the essential honesty and forthrightness of our propaganda, some harm was probably done to the credit of our white media.

No nation can talk out of two sides of its mouth at the same time: we cannot on the one hand speak nothing but the truth and then, with a changed voice and pretending to be someone else—but quite obviously still ourselves—say things which we don't dare to say straight out. Black propaganda must be like the voice of a master ventriloquist which really appears to come out of the mouth of an entirely different individual. In the case of the "gray" leaflet under discussion, the general make-up of the message and especially the elaborateness of its presentation, made it quite obvious that it was not the product of a clandestine printing press in Germany. Had it been possible to create such an impression, however, or had it been possible to make it seem an inadvertent German disclosure, it might have been the important adjunct to our overt program which it was originally intended to be.[4]

[4] There are a few cases on record where black propaganda did succeed in "driving wedges"—notably the case of a counterfeit instruction to German officers to "save themselves (run away) in hopeless situations," an order which in any event succeeded in fooling a number of American intelligence officers.

ON THREATS AND "TOUGHNESS" IN PROPAGANDA

There does not appear to be a single case on record in the last war when an ultimatum resulted in surrender of a surrounded enemy unit. On the other hand, we know of many cases when, in the face of a hopeless situation, commanders sent or received emissaries to discuss surrender. Because, in a sense, a totalitarian country at bay resembles a beleaguered fortress, the question of collective surrenders in the face of collective threats is all-important. First of all, it must be said that the threat of force is only effective if immediately followed by force—nothing is more damning than an empty propaganda threat. Second, a message written from the strength of one's position cannot be hedged or qualified, or couched in a defensive tone, and should not attempt to answer imaginary counter-arguments. The German appeal to the American forces in Bastogne, in fact, might have been written by an American fifth columnist in the ranks of a German combat propaganda company, or by American black operators attempting to raise the morale of the defenders. Instead of emphasizing all factors of German strength, the writer attempted to answer all imaginable counter-arguments and thus practically created the impression that the Germans at Bastogne were the beleaguered ones and that the Americans "really had no reason to be as self-confident" as he imagined them to be. This is an excellent example of the general proposition that defensiveness has no place in combat propaganda and little place in any propaganda.

Threats, however, do occasionally have a place in propaganda. In order to describe the conditions under which they may have a salutary effect, it is necessary to differentiate among four basic situations: (a) the situation of the enemy soldier—if he can do something about getting out of the fight, and (b) if he can do nothing about getting out of the fight; similarly (c) the situation of the civilian who is in a position to act, and (d) that of the civilian who can do nothing about the war. If these differentiations are not borne in mind, the effects of propaganda may be diametrically opposed to those which have been intended.

As to the enemy soldier, if he is in any position to surrender, a threat followed up with a display of strength (e.g., overwhelming artillery superiority) may make him ripe at least for capture. If he is in no position to surrender, however—and most members of beleaguered garrisons belong in this category —he is quite likely to be galvanized into especially fanatical resistance by the threat, because of the psychological mechanism of frustration which has been mentioned above.

As to civilians, those who are in no position to do anything about the war—and these constitute the overwhelming majority of the population of all totalitarian countries—will quite likely be embittered by threatening propaganda. Occasionally, however, such bitterness can be exploited for tactical purposes. The Germans are said to have used terror propaganda during their Blitzkrieg in 1940 specifically in order to create panic and encourage civilians to take flight and thus clog the roads. They also attempted to use scare tactics during their Ardennes offensive, when they cynically advised unfortunate French civilians in the Strasbourg-Mulhouse area (where they had temporarily recrossed the Rhine) to "save yourself—for we will treat you just as well as we have treated your comrades during the last four years!" The Western Allies also used such tactics when, at the behest of Prime Minister Churchill, they unfolded a propaganda effort early in 1945 which was designed to start large numbers of Germans trekking from certain specified "danger areas." These are the only known instances in the last war when threatening propaganda to civilians had the intended effect.

THE "HELPLESS CIVILIAN" TARGET

By far the most important category of targets, however—in point of numbers, at least—is the civilian population (category "d") that can do nothing to end the war, consisting as it does of persons who cannot even remove themselves from the impact of bombing attacks. To threaten them—however gratifying it may be to the enemy-hating propagandist—is psychologically unsound. Rather, the propagandist must seek, by continuous analysis of the patterns of life in the enemy country, to discover those actions which the enemy civilian can reasonably take in his own interest, and where his own interest coincides with ours. To find such actions may afford the key to propaganda to enemy civilians. In the absence of that key, most propaganda directed to enemy civilians will have little concrete effect on the course of a war. In fact, when it is considered that military defeats in any event constitute psychological blows of the first magnitude against the enemy civilian, it would seem that, prior to the time when mutual-interest situations begin to obtain, little can be gained from propaganda directed toward enemy civilians in wartime, except by way of building up credibility. Thus our enormous leaflet output which was dropped on Germany during the war, on which so little evidence of effectiveness has been obtained, can really be judged only in terms of whether it built up belief in our essential honesty. This confidence was needed in the final months of the war when we were in a position to exploit mutual-interest situations.

This—the seeking of mutual-interest situations—constituted by far the most difficult and delicate psychological warfare research project of the last war. Whereas at the beginning of the war, "tough" propaganda from the West was received with derisiveness; whereas during the invasion period it produced sullenness and frustration; at the end of the war our propaganda was all too often greeted by German civilians with the remark: *"I agree with everything you say, but what am I to do?"* . . . In a war against a different country, entirely different mutual-interest situations may obtain. The important lesson is that the earlier such instructions can be formulated and the better they can be presented as being of mutual interest and as being *feasible*, the more successful will propaganda against enemy civilians be.

COHESION AND DISINTEGRATION IN THE WEHRMACHT IN WORLD WAR II

EDWARD A. SHILS AND MORRIS JANOWITZ

I. THE ARMY AS A SOCIAL GROUP

This study is an attempt to analyze the relative influence of primary and secondary group situations on the high degree of stability of the German Army in World War II. It also seeks to evaluate the impact of the

From the *Public Opinion Quarterly*, Vol. 12, 1948, No. 2, 280-315. Reprinted by permission of the authors and the publisher.

Western Allies' propaganda on the German Army's fighting effectiveness.[1]

Although distinctly outnumbered and in a strategic sense quantitatively inferior in equipment, the German Army, on all fronts, maintained a high degree of organizational integrity and fighting effectiveness through a series of almost unbroken retreats over a period of several years. In the final phase, the German armies were broken into unconnected segments, and the remnants were overrun as the major lines of communication and command were broken. Nevertheless, resistance which was more than token resistance on the part of most divisions continued until they were overpowered or overrun in a way which, by breaking communication lines, prevented individual battalions and companies from operating in a coherent fashion. Disintegration through desertion was insignificant, while active surrender, individually or in groups, remained extremely limited throughout the entire Western campaign.

In one sense the German High Command effected as complete a defense of the "European Fortress" as its own leadership qualities and the technical means at its disposal permitted. Official military analyses, including General Eisenhower's report, have shown that lack of manpower, equipment, and transportation, as well as certain strategical errors, were the limiting factors.[2] There was neither complete collapse nor internally organized effort to terminate hostilities, such as signalized the end of the first world war.

This extraordinary tenacity of the German Army has frequently been attributed to the strong National Socialist political convictions of the German soldiers. It is the main hypothesis of this paper, however, that the unity of the German Army was in fact sustained only to a very slight extent by the National Socialist political convic-

tions of its members, and that more important in the motivation of the determined resistance of the German soldier was the steady satisfaction of certain *primary* personality demands afforded by the social organization of the army.

This basic hypothesis may be elaborated in the following terms.

1. It appears that a soldier's ability to resist is a function of the capacity of his immediate primary group (his squad or section) to avoid social disintegration. When the individual's immediate group, and its supporting formations, met his basic organic needs, offered him affection and esteem from both officers and comrades, supplied him with a sense of power and adequately regulated his relations with authority, the element of self-concern in battle, which would lead to disruption of the effective functioning of his primary group, was minimized.

2. The capacity of the primary group to resist disintegration was dependent on the acceptance of political, ideological, and cultural symbols (all secondary symbols) only to the extent that these secondary symbols became directly associated with primary gratifications.

3. Once disruption of primary group life resulted through separation, breaks in communications, loss of leadership, depletion of personnel, or major and prolonged breaks in the supply of food and medical care, such an ascendancy of preoccupation with physical survival developed that there was very little "last-ditch" resistance.

4. Finally, as long as the primary group structure of the component units of the Wehrmacht persisted, attempts by the Allies to cause disaffection by the invocation of secondary and political symbols (e.g., about the ethical wrongfulness of the National Socialist system) were mainly unsuccessful. By contrast, where Allied propaganda dealt with primary and personal values, particularly physical survival, it was more likely to be effective.

Long before D-Day in Western France, research was undertaken in the United

---

[1] For a further treatment of these problems see Dicks, Henry V., *Love, Money and War*, London: Keegan Paul Rutledge (forthcoming).

[2] Report by the Supreme Commander on operations in Europe by the Allied Expeditionary Force, June 6, 1944 to May 8, 1945.

Kingdom and North Africa on these social psychological aspects of the enemy's forces. These studies were continued after D-Day by the Intelligence Section of the Psychological Warfare Division of SHAEF. Although of course they are subject to many scientific strictures, they provide a groundwork for the evaluation of the experiences of the German soldier and for the analysis of the social organization of the German Army. Methods of collecting data included front line interrogation of prisoners of war (Ps/W) and intensive psychological interviews in rear areas. Captured enemy documents, statements of recaptured Allied military personnel, and the reports of combat observers were also studied. A monthly opinion poll of random samples of large numbers of Ps/W was also undertaken. This paper is based on a review of all these data.

Modes of Disintegration

Preliminary to the analysis of the function of the primary group in the maintenance of cohesion in the German Army, it is necessary to classify the modes of social disintegration found in any modern army:

1. Desertion (deliberately going over to the enemy lines)
    a) by individual action
        (1) after discussion with comrades
        (2) without prior discussion with others
    b) by groups acting in concert
2. Active surrender (deliberate decision to give up to the enemy as he approaches and taking steps to facilitate capture, e.g., by sending emissaries, by calling out, by signalling, etc.)
    a) by single individuals
    b) by group as a unit
        (1) by mutual agreement
        (2) by order of or with approval of NCO or officer
    c) by plurality of uncoordinated individuals
3. Passive surrender
    a) by individuals acting alone

(1) non-resistance (allowing oneself to be taken prisoner without taking effective steps to facilitate or obstruct capture; passivity may be a means of facilitating surrender)
(2) token resistance (allowing oneself to be taken prisoner with nominal face-saving gestures of obstruction to capture)
    b) by plurality of uncoordinated individuals

4. Routine resistance: rote or mechanical, but effective execution of orders as given from above with discontinuance when the enemy becomes overwhelmingly powerful and aggressive
5. "Last-ditch" resistance which ends only with the exhaustion of fighting equipment and subsequent surrender or death. (This type of soldier is greatly underrepresented in studies of samples of Ps/W. Therefore the study of Ps/W alone does not give an adequate picture of the resistive qualities of the German soldier.)

A more detailed description of each of the above classes will be useful in the following analysis:

Desertion involved positive and deliberate action by the German soldier to deliver himself to Allied soldiers for capture by crossing the lines, e.g., by planfully "losing himself" while on patrol and "blundering" into the enemy's area of control or by deliberately remaining behind during a withdrawal from a given position so that when the Allied troops came up they could take him.

In *active surrender* by the group as a unit, the positive act of moving across to enemy lines was absent but there was an element common with desertion in the deliberate attempt to withdraw from further combat. Like many cases of desertion, the decision to surrender as a group was arrived at as a result of group discussion and mutual agreement. The dividing line between active surrender and desertion brought about by lagging behind was shadowy. There were other forms of group surrender which were clearly different from desertion, e.g., the sending of an emissary to arrange terms with the enemy, the refusal to carry out aggressive orders, or to fight a way out of encirclement.

In *passive surrender*, the intention of a soldier to remove himself from the battle was often not clear even to himself. The soldier who was taken prisoner by passive surrender might have been immobilized or apathetic due to anxiety; he might have been in a state of bewildered isolation and not have thought of passive surrender until the perception of an opportunity brought it to his mind. Non-resistant passive surrender frequently occurred in the case of soldiers who lay in their foxholes or hid in the cellars or barns, sometimes self-narcotized by fear, or sometimes deliberately waiting to be overrun. In both cases, they made only the most limited external gestures of resistance when the enemy approached. In the second type of passive surrender—token resistance—the surrendering soldier desired to avoid all the stigma of desertion or surrender but nevertheless showed reluctance to undertake aggressive or defensive actions which might have interfered with his survival.

An examination of the basic social organization of the German Army, in terms of its primary group structure and the factors which strengthened and weakened its component primary groups, is first required in order to account for the stability and cohesion of resistance, and in order to evaluate the impact of Allied propaganda.

II. THE FUNCTION OF THE PRIMARY GROUP[3]

The company is the only truly existent community. This community allows neither time nor rest for a personal life. It forces us into its circle, for life is at stake. Obviously com-

promises must be made and claims be surrendered. . . . Therefore the idea of fighting, living, and dying for the fatherland, for the cultural possessions of the fatherland, is but a relatively distant thought. At least it does not play a great role in the practical motivations of the individual.[4]

Thus wrote an idealistic German student in the first world war. A German sergeant, captured toward the end of the second world war, was asked by his interrogators about the political opinions of his men. In reply, he laughed and said, "When you ask such a question, I realize well that you have no idea of what makes a soldier fight. The soldiers lie in their holes and are happy if they live through the next day. If we think at all, it's about the end of the war and then home."

The fighting effectiveness of the vast majority of soldiers in combat depends only to a small extent on their preoccupation with the major political values which might be affected by the outcome of the war and which are the object of concern to statesmen and publicists. There are of course soldiers in whom such motivations are important. Volunteer armies recruited on the basis of ethical or political loyalties, such as the International Brigade in the Spanish Civil War, are affected by their degree of orientation toward major political goals. In the German Army, the "hard core" of National Socialists were similarly motivated.

But in a conscript army, the criterion of recruitment is much less specialized and the army is more representative of the total

which 'we' is the natural expression. One lives in the feeling of the whole and finds the chief aims of his will in that feeling" (p. 23). . . . "The most important spheres of this intimate association and cooperation—though by no means the only ones—are the family, the play group of children, and the neighborhood or community group of elders" (p. 24). . . . "the only essential thing being a certain intimacy and fusion of personalities." (p. 26)

Cooley, Charles Horton, *Social Organization*, New York, 1909.

[4] *Kriegsbriefe gefallener Studenten*, 1928, pp. 167-172. Quoted by William K. Pfeiler, *War and the German Mind*, New York, 1941, p. 77.

[3] "By primary groups I mean those characterized by intimate face-to-face association and cooperation . . . it is a 'we'; it involves the sort of sympathy and mutual identification for

population liable to conscription. Therefore the values involved in political and social systems or ethical schemes do not have much impact on the determination of a soldier to fight to the best of his ability and to hold out as long as possible. For the ordinary German soldier the decisive fact was that he was a member of a squad or section which maintained its structural integrity and which coincided roughly with the *social* unit which satisfied some of his major primary needs.[5] He was likely to go on fighting, provided he had the necessary weapons, as long as the group possessed leadership with which he could identify himself, and as long as he gave affection to and received affection from the other members of his squad and platoon. In other words, as long as he felt himself to be a member of his primary group and therefore bound by the expectations and demands of its other members, his soldierly achievement was likely to be good.

Modern social research has shown that the primary group is not merely the chief source of affection and accordingly the major factor in personality formation in infancy and childhood. The primary group continues to be the major source of social and psychological sustenance through adulthood.[6] In the army, when isolated from civilian primary groups, the individual soldier comes to depend more and more on his military primary group. His spontaneous loyalties are to its immediate members whom he sees daily and with whom he

develops a high degree of intimacy. For the German soldier in particular, the demands of his group, reinforced by officially prescribed rules, had the effect of an external authority. It held his aggressiveness in check; it provided discipline, protection, and freedom from autonomous decision.[7]

Army units with a high degree of primary group integrity suffered little from desertions or from individually contrived surrenders. In the Wehrmacht, desertions and surrenders were most frequent in groups of heterogeneous ethnic composition in which Austrians, Czechs, and Poles were randomly intermixed with each other. In such groups the difficulties of linguistic communication, the large amount of individual resentment and aggressiveness about coercion into German service, the weakened support of leadership due to their inability to identify with German officers—all these factors hampered the formation of cohesive groups.

Sample interviews with Wehrmacht deserters made in North Africa in 1943 and in France and Germany in 1944 and 1945 showed an overwhelmingly disproportionate representation of elements which could not be assimilated into primary groups. A total of 443 Wehrmacht Ps/W captured toward the end of the North African campaign, consisting of 180 Germans, 200 Austrians and 63 others (Czechs, Poles, Yugoslavs, etc.), had very markedly different tendencies towards desertion: 29 per cent of the Germans were deserters or potential deserters; 55 per cent of the Austrians fell into these two classes, as did 78 per cent of the Czechs, Poles, and Yugoslavs. Of the 53 German deserters, only one declared that he had "political" motives for desertion. In the Western European campaign, the bulk of the deserters came from among the "Volksdeutsche,"[8] Austrians, Poles, and Russians who had

[5] On the relations between the *technical* group and *social* group cf. Whitehead, T. N., *Leadership in a Free Society*, Cambridge, Mass., 1936, Ch. IV.

[6] Cooley, *op. cit.*, Part I, pp. 3-57; Freud S., *Group Psychology and the Analysis of the Ego*, Ch. IV; Mayo, Elton, *The Human Problems of an Industrial Civilization*, New York, 1933; Wilson, A. T. M., "The Service Man Comes Home," *Pilot Papers: Social Essays and Documents*, Vol. 1, No. 2 (Apr. 1946), pp. 9-28; Grinker, R. R. and Spiegel, J. P., *Men Under Stress*, Philadelphia, 1945, Ch. 3; Whitehead, T. N., *op. cit.*, Ch. I, X, VII; also Lindsay, A. D., *The Essentials of Democracy*, Oxford, 1935, 2nd ed., pp. 78-81.

[7] German combat soldiers almost always stressed the high level of comradeliness in their units. They frequently referred to their units as "one big family."

[8] Individuals of German extraction residing outside the boundaries of Germany.

been coerced into German military service. It was clear that in view of the apolitical character of most of the deserters, the grounds for their desertion were to be sought among those variables which prevented the formation of close primary group bonds, the chief of which were insuperable language differences, bitter resentment against their coerced condition, and the unfriendliness of the Germans in their units.

Among German deserters, who remained few until the close of the war, the failure to assimilate into the primary group life of the Wehrmacht was the most important factor, more important indeed than political dissidence. Deserters were on the whole men who had difficulty in personal adjustment, e.g., in the acceptance of affection or in the giving of affection. They were men who had shown these same difficulties in civilian life, having had difficulties with friends, work associates, and their own families, or having had criminal records. Political dissidents on the other hand, when captured, justified their failure to desert by invoking their sense of solidarity with their comrades and expressed the feeling that had they deserted when given a post of responsibility their comrades would have interpreted it as a breach of solidarity. For the political dissident, the verbal expression of political dissent was as much anti-authoritarianism as he could afford, and submission to his group was the price which he had to pay for it.

The persistent strength of primary group controls was manifested even in the last month of the war, when many deserters felt that they would not have been able to have taken the initial step in their desertion unless they had discussed the matter with their comrades and received some kind of legitimation for the action, such as a statement of approval.[9] And, on the other hand,

the same ongoing efficacy of primary group sentiment was evident in the statements of would-be deserters who declared they had never been able to cross the threshold because they had been told by their officers that the comrades who remained behind (i.e., the comrades of the men who had deserted) would be shot. Hence, one of the chief forms of disintegration which occurred in the last stages of the war took the form of group surrender in which, after ample discussion within the unit, the authorization of the leading personalities and often of the NCO's had been granted for the offering of token resistance to facilitate capture, or even for outright group surrender.

Factors Strengthening Primary Group Solidarity

THE NAZI NUCLEUS OF THE PRIMARY GROUP: THE "HARD CORE." The stability and military effectiveness of the military primary group were in large measure a function of the "hard core," who approximated about ten to fifteen per cent of the total of enlisted men; the percentage was higher for noncommissioned officers and was very much higher among the junior officers.[10] These were, on the whole, young men between 24 and 28 years of age who had had a gratifying adolescence in the most rewarding period of National Socialism. They were imbued with the ideology of *Gemeinschaft* (community solidarity),[11] were enthusiasts for the military life, had definite homo-erotic tendencies and accordingly placed a very high value on "toughness," manly comradeliness, and group solidarity.[12] The presence of a few such men in the group, zealous, energetic, and unsparing of themselves,

[9] Approval of desertion by a married man with a large family or with heavy familial obligations was often noted near the war's end. For such men, the stronger ties to the family prevented the growth of insuperably strong ties to the army unit.

[10] The "hard core" corresponds to opinion leaders, as the term is currently used in opinion research.

[11] Schmalenbach, Hermann, "Die soziologische Kategorien des Bundes," *Die Dioskuren*, Vol. I, München, 1922, pp. 35-105; and Plessner, Hellmuth, *Grenzen der Gemeinschaft*, Bonn, 1924.

[12] Bluher, Hans, *Die Rolle der Erotik in der männlichen Gesellschaft*. Jena, 1921, Vol. II, Part II especially, pp. 91-109; pp. 154-177.

provided models for weaker men, and facilitated the process of identification. For those for whom their charisma did not suffice and who were accordingly difficult to incorporate fully into the intimate primary group, frowns, harsh words, and threats served as a check on divisive tendencies. The fact that the elite SS divisions and paratroop divisions had a larger "hard core" than other divisions of the army—so large as to embrace almost the entire group membership during most of the war—accounted for their greater fighting effectiveness. And the fact that such a "hard core" was almost entirely lacking from certain *Volksgrenadier* divisions helped to a considerable extent to account for the military inferiority of these units.

One of the functions of the "hard core" was to minimize the probability of divisive political discussions. There was, of course, little inclination to discuss political matters or even strategic aspects of the war among German soldiers. For this reason widespread defeatism concerning the outcome of the war had little consequence in affecting behavior (until the spring of 1945) because of the near impossibility—objective as well as subjective—of discussing or carrying out alternative plans of action.

In contrast with the "hard core," which was a disproportionately large strengthening factor in the integrity of the military primary group, the "soft core" was a source of infection which was by no means comparable in effectiveness. Unlike the first world war experience in which anti-war attitudes were often vigorously expressed and eagerly listened to by men who were "good comrades," in the second world war the political anti-militarist or anti-Nazi who expressed his views with frequency and vigor was also in the main not a "good comrade." There was a complete absence of soldiers' committees and organized opposition, even in March and April 1945 (except for the Bavarian Freiheitsaktion which was constituted by rear-echelon troops). On isolated occasions, the Western Allies were able to exploit a man who had been a "good comrade" and

who, after having been captured, expressed his defeatism and willingness to help end the war; he was thereupon sent back into the German line to talk his comrades into going over with him to the Allied lines. Here the "soft core" man exploited his comradely solidarity and it was only on that basis that he was able to remove some of the members of his group from the influence of the "hard core."

COMMUNITY OF EXPERIENCE AS A COHESIVE FORCE. The factors which affect group solidarity in general were on the whole carefully manipulated by the German general staff. Although during the war Germany was more permeated by foreigners than it had ever been before in its history, the army was to a great extent carefully protected from disintegrating influences of heterogeneity of ethnic and national origin, at least in crucial military situations. German officers saw that solidarity is fostered by the recollection of jointly experienced gratifications and that accordingly the groups who had gone through a victory together should not be dissolved but should be maintained as units to the greatest degree possible.

The replacement system of the Wehrmacht operated to the same end.[13] The entire personnel of a division would be withdrawn from the front simultaneously and refitted as a unit with replacements. Since new members were added to the division while it was out of line they were thereby given the opportunity to assimilate themselves into the group; then the group as a whole was sent forward. This system continued until close to the end of the war and helped to explain the durability of the German Army in the face of the overwhelming numerical and material superiority of the Allied forces.

[13] This policy sometimes created a serious dilemma for the Wehrmacht. Increasingly, to preserve the sense of group identity and the benefits of solidarity which arose from it, regiments were allowed to become depleted in manpower by as much as 50 to 75 per cent. This, however, generated such feelings of weakness that the solidarity gains were cancelled.

Deterioration of group solidarity in the Wehrmacht which began to appear toward the very end of the war was most frequently found in hastily fabricated units. These were made up of new recruits, dragooned stragglers, air force men who had been forced into the infantry (and who felt a loss of status in the change), men transferred from the navy into the infantry to meet the emergency of manpower shortage, older factory workers, concentration camp inmates, and older married men who had been kept in reserve throughout the war and who had remained with the familial primary group until the last moment. The latter, who were the "catch" of the last "total mobilization" carried with them the resentment and bitterness which the "total mobilization" produced and which prevented the flow of affection necessary for group formation. It was clear that groups so diverse in age composition and background, and especially so mixed in their reactions to becoming infantrymen, could not very quickly become effective fighting units. They had no time to become used to one another and to develop the type of friendliness which is possible only when loyalties to outside groups have been renounced—or at least put into the background. A preview of what was to occur when units became mixed was provided by the 275th Fusilier Battalion which broke up before the First U.S. Army drive in November. Thirty-five Ps/W interrogated from this unit turned out to have been recently scraped together from fifteen different army units.

The most ineffective of all the military formations employed by the Wehrmacht during the war were the Volkssturm units. They ranged in age from boys to old men, and were not even given basic training in the weapons which they were supposed to use. Their officers were Nazi local functionaries who were already objects of hostility and who were therefore unable to release a flow of affection among equals. They had moreover not broken their family ties to the slightest extent. They still remained members of a primary group which did not fuse into the military primary group.

Finally, they had no uniforms. They had only brassards to identify them and through which to identify themselves with one another. The mutual identification function of the uniform which plays so great a role in military units was thereby lost. As soon as they were left to their own devices, they disintegrated from within, deserting in large numbers to their homes, hiding, permitting themselves to be captured, etc.

Factors Weakening Primary Group Solidarity

ISOLATION. The disintegration of a primary group depends in part on the physical and spatial variables which isolate it from the continuous pressure of face-to-face contact. The factor of spatial proximity in the maintenance of group solidarity in military situations must not be underestimated. In February and March of 1945, isolated remnants of platoons and companies were surrendering in groups with increasing frequency. The tactical situation of defensive fighting under heavy American artillery bombardment and the deployment of rear outposts forced soldiers to take refuge in cellars, trenches, and other underground shelters in small groups of three and four. This prolonged isolation from the nucleus of the primary group for several days worked to reinforce the fear of destruction of the self, and thus had a disintegrative influence on primary group relations.[14] A soldier who was isolated in a cellar or in a concrete bunker for several days and whose anxieties about physical survival were aggravated by the tactical hopelessness of his situation, was a much more easily separable member of his group than one who, though fearing physical destruction, was still bound by the continuous and vital ties of working, eating, sleeping, and being at leisure together with his fellow soldiers.

This proposition regarding the high significance of the spatial variable for primary group solidarity and the maintenance of the fighting effectiveness of an army is supported

[14] This proposition is in opposition to the frequently asserted view that social solidarity of an intense sort is positively and linearly related to fear of threat from the outside.

by the behavior of the retreating German Army in North Africa in 1943, and in France and Germany in September-October 1944 and March 1945. As long as a retreat is orderly and the structure of the component units of an army is maintained, strategic difficulties do not break up the army. An army in retreat breaks up only when the retreat is poorly organized, when command is lost over the men, so that they become separated from their units and become stragglers, or when enemy penetrations isolate larger or smaller formations from the main group.[15]

Stragglers first became a moderately serious problem in the German Army in October 1944. On October 22, 1944, General Keitel ordered that a maximum of one to three days be allowed for stragglers to reattach themselves to their units. The previous limit had been five days. The aggravation of the straggler problem was further documented by General Blaskowitz's order of March 5, 1945, according to which the category of stragglers was declared to have ceased to exist. Soldiers who lost contact with their own units were directed to attach themselves immediately to the "first troops in the line which he can contact. . . ."

FAMILIAL TIES AND PRIMARY GROUP DISINTEGRATION. Prisoners of war remarked with considerable frequency that discussions about alternative plans of action by groups of soldiers who were entirely defeatist arose not from discussions about the war in its political or strategic aspects, but rather from discussions about the soldiers' families.[16] The recollection of concrete family experiences reactivated sentiments of dependence on the family for psychological support and correspondingly weakened the hold of the military primary group. It was in such contexts that German soldiers toward the end of the war were willing to discuss group surrender.

To prevent preoccupation with family concerns, the families of German soldiers were given strict instructions to avoid references to family deprivations in letters to the front. In the winter and spring of 1945, when Allied air raids became so destructive of communal life, all telegrams to soldiers at the front had to be passed by party officials in order to insure that no distracting news reached the soldiers. On the other hand, care was taken by party and army authorities that soldiers should not be left in a state of anxiety about their families and to this end vigorous propaganda was carried on to stimulate correspondence with soldiers at the front. For those who had no families and who needed the supplementary affection which the army unit could not provide, provisions were made to obtain mail from individuals (including party officials) who would befriend unmarried or family-less soldiers, with the result that the psychic economy of the soldier was kept in equilibrium.

There was, however, a special type of situation in which the very strength of familial ties served to keep the army from further disintegration. This arose towards the end of the war, when soldiers were warned that desertion would result in severe sanctions being inflicted on the deserter's family.[17]

Toward the end of the war, soldiers tended to break away from the army more often while they were on leave and with their families, and therefore isolated from personal contact with their primary group fellows.

---

[15] The Germans in the Channel ports were able to resist so long partly because the men remained together where they were constantly in each other's presence. Thus the authority of the group over the individual was constantly in play.

[16] A 36-year-old soldier—a Berlin radioworker—who surrendered prematurely, said: "During one month in a bunker without light and without much to do, the men often discussed capture. Conversation usually started about families: who was married and what was to become of his family? The subject became more acute as the Americans approached."

[17] This threat was never actually carried out. Furthermore, the *Sicherheitsdienst* (Security Service) admitted the impossibility of taking sanctions against the deserter's family because of the difficulty of locating them in the disorder of German civilian life. As the German soldiers became aware of the impotence of the SD in this respect, the barrier against desertion weakened.

When soldiers returned to visit their families, then the conflict between contradictory primary group loyalties became acute. The hold of the military primary group became debilitated in the absence of face-to-face contacts. The prospect of facing, on return to the front, physical destruction or a prolonged loss of affection from the civilian primary group, especially the family, prompted an increasing number of desertions while on furlough.

All of these factors contributed to loosen the solidarity of the German Army, especially when the prospect of physical destruction began to weigh more heavily. Severe threats to the safety of the civilian primary group created anxiety which often weakened the hold of the military primary group. When the area of the soldier's home was occupied by the enemy or when the soldier himself was fighting in the area, there was strong disposition to desert homeward. One such soldier said: "Now I have nothing more for which to fight, because my home is occupied."

The strong pull of the civilian primary group became stronger as the coherence of the army group weakened. But sometimes, the former worked to keep the men fighting in their units, i.e., when they reasoned that the shortest way home was to keep the group intact and to avoid capture or desertion. Otherwise there would ensue a long period in an enemy P/W camp. On the other hand, in event of the defeat of a still intact army, there would be only a short period of waiting before demobilization.

DEMAND FOR PHYSICAL SURVIVAL. The individual soldier's fear of destruction ultimately pressed to weaken primary group cohesion; nevertheless it is striking to note the degree to which demands for physical survival could be exploited by Wehrmacht authority to the end of prolonging resistance. Where the social conditions were otherwise favorable, the primary bonds of group solidarity were dissolved only under the most extreme circumstances of threat to the individual organism—in situations where the tactical prospects were utterly hopeless, under devastating artillery and air bombardment, or where the basic food and medical requirements were not being met. Although aware for a long time of the high probability of German defeat in the war and of the hopelessness of the numerous individual battles, very many German soldiers continued to resist without any serious deterioration in the quality of their fighting skill. But where the most basic physiological demands of the German soldier were threatened with complete frustration, the bonds of group solidarity were broken.

Concern about food and about health always reduces the solidarity of a group. Throughout the war, and until the period just before the end, German army medical services were maintained at a high level of efficiency; the decline in their efficiency coincides with the deterioration in the morale of the men. Special care was also observed in the management of the food supply and accordingly few German soldiers felt that the food supplies were inadequate. Indeed, as late as October 1944, only 15 per cent of a sample of 92 Ps/W declared that they were at all dissatisfied with army food. By January, however, the situation changed and Ps/W reported increased preoccupation with physical survival, with food, and the shortage of clothing. Soldiers in certain units were beginning to "scrounge." The extreme cold of the winter of '44-'45 also began to tell on the men whose military self-esteem was being reduced by the raggedness of their uniforms and the failure to obtain replacements for unsatisfactory equipment.

Thus, to keep groups integral, it was necessary not only to provide positive gratifications but also to reduce to a minimum the alternative possibilities of increasing the chances for survival by leaving the unit. For this reason the Nazis sought to counteract the fear of personal physical destruction in battle by telling the men that accurate records were kept on deserters and that not only would their families and property be made to suffer in the event of their desertion, but that after the war, upon their return to Germany, they, too, would be very severely punished. They were also told by their officers that German agents were operating in American and British P/W cages in order to report on violations of security and on deserters. A Wehrmacht leaflet to German soldiers mentioned the names of two deserters of the 980th Volksgrenadiere who were alleged to have divulged information and stated that not only would their families be sent to prison and suffer the loss of their property and ration cards, but that the men themselves would also be punished after the war. In actuality, they were often punished in the P/W camps by the extreme Nazis who exercised some control in certain camps.

For the same reason, as long as the front was relatively stable, the Wehrmacht officers increased the natural hazards of war by ordering mine fields to be laid, barbed wire to be set up, and special guards to be posted to limit the freedom of movement of isolated and psychologically unattached individuals who, in situations which offered the chance of safely withdrawing from the war, would have moved over to the enemy's lines. Although the number of avowedly would-be deserters remained very small until near the end of the war, even they were frequently immobilized for fear of being killed by the devices set up to prevent their separation from the group. The danger of destruction by the Allies in event of desertion also played a part in keeping men attached to their military units. As one P/W who had thought of desertion but who never took action said, "by day our own people shoot at us, by night yours do."

Another physical narcissistic element which contributed somewhat to resistance on the Western front was fear of castration in event of the loss of the war. (This was effective only among a minority of the German soldiers.) The guilt feelings of the Nazi soldiers who had slaughtered and marauded on the Eastern front, and elsewhere in Europe, and their projection onto the enemy of their own sadistic impulses, heightened their narcissistic apprehensiveness about damage to their vital organs and to their physical organism as a whole. Rumors of

castration at the hands of the Russians circulated in the German Army throughout the last three years of the war and it is likely that they were largely the result of ruthless methods on both sides.

The Nazis perceived the function of fear of personal destruction in the event of capture as a factor in keeping a group intact after the internal bonds had been loosened. There were accordingly situations in which SS detachments deliberately committed atrocities on enemy civilians and soldiers in order to increase the anxieties of German soldiers as to what would befall them in the event of their defeat and capture. This latter policy was particularly drastically applied by the Waffen-SS in the von Rundstedt counteroffensive. It appears to have been an effort to convince German soldiers that there were no alternatives but victory or resistance to the very end and that surrender or desertion would end with slaughter of the German soldiers, as it had in the cases of the Allied soldiers. This was not effective for the mass of the German soldiers, however, who were becoming convinced that the law-abiding British and Americans would not in most situations harm them upon capture.

The dread of destruction of the self, and the demand for ₊physical survival, while breaking up the spontaneous solidarity of the military primary group in most cases, thus served under certain conditions to coerce the soldier into adherence to his group and to the execution of the orders of his superiors.

III. THE ROLE OF "SOLDIERLY HONOR"

American and British soldiers tend to consider their wartime service as a disagreeable necessity, as a task which had to be performed because there were no alternatives. For the German, being a soldier was a more than acceptable status. It was indeed honorable. The King's Regulations which govern the British Army (1940) begin with the statement that the army consists of officers and men serving for various lengths of time.

The German equivalent in the Defense Laws of 1935 opens with a declaration that "military service is a service of honor for the German people, the Wehrmacht is the armed barrier and the soldierly school of the German people."

Emphasis on the element of honor in the military profession has led in Germany to the promulgation of elaborate rules of conduct regulating the behavior of both officers and men in a great variety of specific military and extra-military situations.[18] The explicit and implicit code of soldierly honor, regulating the responsibilities of officers for their men, determined behavior in battle and established conditions under which surrender was honorable. It also provided a very comprehensive body of etiquette. This elaborate ritualization of the military profession had a significantly positive influence on group solidarity and efficiency during periods of stress. "Honor" rooted in a rigid conscience (superego) served in the German Army to keep men at their tasks better than individual reflection and evaluation could have done. When the individual was left to make decisions for himself, the whole host of contradictory impulses toward authority of officers and of the group as an entity was stimulated.

Domination by higher authority was eagerly accepted by most ordinary soldiers, who feared that if they were allowed to exercise their initiative their *innere Schweinhunde*, i.e., their own narcissistic and rebellious impulses, would come to the fore. On the other hand, rigorous suppression of these impulses constituted an appeasement of the superego which allowed the group machinery to function in an orderly manner.

The belief in the efficacy and moral worth of discipline and in the inferiority of the spontaneous, primary reactions of the personality was expressed in the jettisoning of the German Army Psychiatric Selection Services in 1942. When the manpower short-

[18] Demeter, Karl, *Das deutsche Heer und seine Offiziere*, Berlin, n.d., Ch. 3 and 5; Broch, Hermann, *The Sleepwalkers*, London, n.d.

age became stringent and superfluities had to be scrapped, the personnel selection system based on personality analyses was one of those activities which was thought to be dispensable. Apparently taking individual personality differences into account was thought to be too much of a concession to moral weakness which could and in any case *should* be overcome by hard, soldierly discipline.

STRENGTH AS AN ELEMENT IN HONOR. For persons who have deep-lying uncertainties over their own weaknesses, who fear situations which will reveal their weakness in controlling themselves and their lack of manliness, membership in an army will tend to reduce anxieties. Subjugation to discipline gives such persons support; it means that they do not have to depend on themselves, that someone stronger than themselves is guiding and protecting them. Among young males in middle and late adolescence, the challenges of love and vocation aggravate anxieties about weakness. At this stage fears about potency are considerable. When men who have passed through this stage are placed in the entirely male society of a military unit, freed from the control of adult civilian society and missing its gratifications, they tend to regress to the adolescent condition. The show of "toughness" and hardness which is regarded as a virtue among soldiers is a response to these reactivated adolescent anxieties about weakness.

In the German Army, all these tendencies were intensified by the military code, and they accounted for a considerable share of the cohesion and resistance up to the very last stages of the war. Among those at the extreme end of the scale—the "hard core" of Nazi last-ditch resisters—in whom the preoccupation with strength and weakness is to be found in most pronounced form—this attitude was manifested in unwillingness of some to acknowledge defeat even after capture.

THE HONOR OF THE OFFICER. To control the behavior of officers and to protect soldierly honor, the Court of Honor procedure of the Imperial Army was reestablished when the Nazis came into power. Its function was to adjudicate disagreements and quarrels between officers in an authoritative way, and it did succeed in minimizing disagreements and unpleasant tensions among officers in both professional and private affairs which might otherwise have endangered solidarity of the group by division among those in immediate authority. The settlement, which was arrived at in secret by officers of the same rank as those involved in the dispute, was almost always accepted without a murmur by both parties. Its minutely detailed procedural and substantive rules reduced to a minimum the possibility that an officer might feel that the collective authority which ruled over him was weak, negligible, or impotent in any sphere. The code went so far as to empower the court to recommend suspension from duty simply on the grounds of *unehrliche Gesinnung* (dishonorable attitude) derogatory to the status of the officer class. External discipline penetrated thus into even the most private sphere to give assurance that soldierly honor would be operative even in the recesses of the individual mind.[19] The officers' court of honor not only served as an "external superego," but by its continuous emphasis on "honor" and "dishonor," it heightened the sensibilities of the officers to the demands of their own superego.

One of the most elaborated aspects of soldierly honor as related to combat behavior dealt with the conditions under which surrender could be honorably performed. In this respect, great stress was laid on the oath which bound soldiers not to desert or surrender, and much casuistical effort was expended to make surrender compatible with soldierly honor. In some cases soldiers arranged circumstances in such a way as would appear to others, as well as to themselves, that they had been captured against their will. In other cases, surrender was excused as legitimate according to accepted military standards. In a few cases, fortifica-

[19] Indeed, a well known German general during the period of captivity felt so strongly the pressure of soldierly honor that he always went to sleep wearing his monocle.

tion commanders required that a token round of phosphorous shells be fired against their position in order to satisfy the requirements of their honor. Deserters often attempted to appease their conscience by ingenious arguments to the effect that the oaths which they took were signed with pencil, or that the sergeant who administered the oath turned his back on them, or that they had been forced into signing the oath which was incompatible with the "requirements of a free conscience."

The stout defense of the Channel ports, which denied vital communication centers to the Allies, was in large part the result of the determination of the commanding officers whose sense of military honor required them to carry out to the letter orders for resistance, regardless of the cost in men or of the apparent strategic futility of their operation.

Even after the extreme reverses in February and March of 1945, German colonels and generals sought to have their units captured and overrun in an approved manner. Captured German senior officers often declared that they had been aware of certain defeat in their sector but, despite this, they took little or no action to terminate hostilities. The most positive action some of them were able to take was to follow their instructions to hold fast in such a manner as to facilitate the capture of their own command posts when they were not able to retreat. But the various subterfuges to make their surrender or capture acceptable to their superego were apparently insufficient, and after capture their sense of guilt for having infringed on the moral requirements of officership usually produced regressive manifestations in the form of elaborate self-justifications for their inadequacy. In some cases it went to the extreme form of imagining how they would justify themselves in the event that Hitler were to confront them at the very moment and were to ask them why they had allowed themselves to be captured.

The reluctance of senior and general officers to enter into negotiations to surrender on their own initiative was of course not due exclusively to motivations of conscience; it was buttressed by the efficient functioning of the security system. The failure of the July 20 *Putsch* resulted in the carefully contrived isolation of senior commanding officers and their domination by Nazi secret police. The establishment of an independent chain of command for National Socialist *Führungs-offiziere* (Guidance Officers) was an additional technique established for spying on generals. Aside from their morale duties, which are described elsewhere, these fanatical Nazi Guidance Officers at higher headquarters busied themselves in reporting on German generals who appeared to be unlikely to carry out orders for final resistance.

Company grade and battalion officers on the whole behaved similarly to their superiors. The deterioration of their effectiveness which occurred was due in greater measure to the great reduction in their numbers rather than to any loss of skill or determination. At the end, the German Army suffered severely from being under-officered, rather than poorly officered. As early as January 1945, the ratio of officers to enlisted men fell to about 50 per cent of what it had been under normal conditions.

TENSION BETWEEN OFFICER'S HONOR AND SOLICITUDE OF MEN. There was, however, a difference between the behavior of junior and senior officers, which can in part be explained by the latter's closer physical proximity and more extensive contact with their men. The sense of obligation which the junior officer felt for the welfare of his men often tempered his conception of the proper relations between soldierly honor and surrender, especially when he was in a position to recognize that there was no military value in further resistance. Nonetheless, desertion by German officers was extremely rare, and only occasionally did they bring about the group surrender of their men; more typically they protected their soldierly honor by allowing themselves to be overrun.

Senior non-commissioned officers displayed a sense of military honor very similar to that of junior officers, but even closer identification with their comrades precipitated a crisis in loyalties which weighed still more heavily on their consciences. Ordinarily, soldierly honor and primary group solidarity are not only congruous with one another but actually mutually supporting. In crisis situations, however, the divergence between them begins to appear and loyalty to the larger army group (the strategically relevant unit), which is an essential component of soldierly honor, enters into contradiction to loyalty to the primary group.

Until the failure of von Rundstedt's counter-offensive, soldierly honor on the part of senior NCO's tended to outweigh primary group solidarity wherever they came into conflict with each other. As the final Allied drive against the homeland developed, they became less disposed to carry out "last-ditch" resistance, but when captured they showed signs of having experienced guilt feelings for not having done so. The recognition of the overwhelming Allied strength in their particular sectors, together with physical absence from the immediate environment of their superior officers (which was a function of the decreasing ratio of officers to men) made it possible for them to offer only token resistance or to allow themselves to be overrun. They relieved their consciences by declaring that further bloodshed would have served no further *military purpose*.

THE INFANTRY SOLDIER'S HONOR. The code of soldierly honor and its ramifications took a deep root in the personality of the German soldiers of the line—even those who were totally apolitical. Identification with the stern authority associated with the symbols of State power gave the ordinary German soldier a feeling that he became strong and morally elevated by submitting to discipline. For these people a military career was a good and noble one, enjoying high intrinsic ethical value. Even apathetic and inarticulate soldiers sometimes grew eloquent on the values of the military life.

The most defeatist soldier, who insisted that he longed to be captured and that he offered little or no resistance, was careful to point out that he was not a deserter, and showed anxiety lest the conditions under which he was captured might be interpreted as desertion. This was of course to some extent the result of the fear that German police would retaliate against his family if his company commander reported that he had deserted and that the Nazis would seek revenge against him, either in the P/W camp, or after the war in Germany. But at least of equal significance was his desire to maintain his pride in having been a good soldier who had done his duty.[20] Anti-Nazi German soldiers who went to some length to inform the interrogators of their anti-Nazi political attitudes felt no inconsistency in insisting that despite everything they were "100 per cent soldiers." Only a very small minority admitted freely that they deserted.

IV. RELATIONS WITH AUTHORITY: OFFICER-MAN RELATIONS

THE BASIS OF THE OFFICERS' STATUS. The primary group relations in modern armies, especially in the German Army, depend as much on the acceptance of the various authorities to which the soldier is subjected as on mutual respect and love between individuals of equal rank. The non-commissioned and the junior officers are the agents on whom the individual soldier depends in his relationships with the rest of the army outside his immediate group, and in his relations with the outer world (the home front and the enemy). They have charge of his safety, and they are the channels through which flow food, equipment, and other types of supplies as well as chance symbolic gratifications such as deco-

rations, promotions, leave, etc. For the German soldier, with his authoritarian background, the officer-man relation is one of submission to an overriding authority.

An exceptionally talented regular German Army officer, bred in the German military tradition, once tried to summarize to his interrogator what made the German Army "work": political indoctrination and "pep talks" were "all rot"; whether the men would follow him depended upon the personality of the officer. The leader must be a man who possesses military skill: then his men will know that he is protecting them. He must be a model to his men; he must be an all-powerful, and still benevolent, authority.

He must look after his men's needs, and be able to do all the men's duties better than they themselves in training and under combat conditions. The men must also be sure that their officer is duly considerate of their lives: they must know that he does not squander his human resources, that the losses of life which occur under his command will be minimal and justified. In the training of NCO's for officers, the German Army acted on the basis of such maxims, despite the Nazi Party's propagandistic preoccupation with such secondary aspects of morale as political ideology.

The positions of the officer and of the NCO were dependent on discipline and on the sanctions by which discipline is maintained and enforced. During training the Wehrmacht laid down the most severe disciplinary rules. In combat, even before Germany's military fortunes began to contract, life and death powers over the troops were vested in lower commanders. At the same time elaborate precautions were taken to control and even to counteract their severity in certain spheres of behavior. Officers were warned against senseless and unnecessary insults directed against their men. Special orders were issued and particular attention was paid in the training of officers to fatherly and considerate behavior in relations with their men; the combination of sternness and benevolence was strongly

[20] Frequently German soldiers who were reluctant to desert separated themselves from battle by hiding in cellars or dugouts, waiting to be overrun. Such soldiers often thought it morally necessary to volunteer the explanation for their capture that they had been found by the enemy because they had fallen asleep from exhaustion and had been taken against their will.

counseled. Numerous small indications of affection such as congratulations on birthdays and on anniversaries, and fatherly modes of address, e.g., *"Kinder"* (children), were recommended as helping to build the proper relations between officers and men.

The results of this approach to status relationships appear to have been good. Differences in privileges between officers and enlisted men in combat units almost never emerged as an object of complaint on the part of enlisted Ps/W. On the contrary, complaints of "softness" were more frequently directed against officers and enlisted men in the rear. The infantry soldier seldom attempted to attribute deficiencies in military operations to his immediate superiors. Spontaneous praise, in fact, was frequent.

German soldiers—both officers and men —greatly appreciated the ceremonial acknowledgment of hierarchical differences as expressed, for example, in the military salute. Captured Germans who saw the American Army in Great Britain before D-Day were often contemptuous of an enemy who was obviously so lax in dress and salute. Many of them said that the American Army could not be expected to fight well since the relations between officers and enlisted men were so informal. "This is no army." Such views of the value of the ceremonial aspects of discipline persisted in defeat. Ps/W taken late in the war, when they commented on American officer-man relations, often remarked with incredulous wonderment: "I don't see how it works!"

Not only was the position of German officers strengthened by their mixture of severe dominion and benevolence, but additional support for their authority came from the provision for the blameless gratification of primitive impulses and from the sanctioning of all types of aggressive social behavior outside the army group. Private personal transgressions of "civil" ethics were regarded as of slight importance, since they were outside the limits of the "manly comradeship" of the military primary group. Drunkenness and having women in the barracks were crimes which the officers overlooked; in occupied and enemy countries the latitude in personal and private transgressions was even greater. Provision was made for official houses of prostitution in which soldiers could reassure themselves about their manliness without disrupting the disciplinary structure of the Wehrmacht. This combination of practices lowered the probability of tensions in officer-man relationships.

NCO'S AND JUNIOR OFFICERS. In battle, leadership responsibility devolved in actuality on the senior NCO's (the opposite numbers of American platoon sergeants) and on the company grade officers. Only seldom did a line soldier see his battalion commander and even less frequently was he spoken to by him. Thus battalion commanders and other higher officers played a less central role in the personality system of the German soldier. They were therefore less directly related to the solidarity of the military primary group.

Nearly all non-commissioned and commissioned officers of the company grade level were regarded by the German soldier throughout the Western campaign as brave, efficient, and considerate. It was only in the very final phases of the war that Ps/W occasionally complained that they had been abandoned by their officers, and there was reason to believe that such complaints were justified not by facts but by the resurgence of uninhibited hostility against officers who, having been defeated, could now be looked upon as having shown weakness.

In addition, the slight increase in anti-officer sentiment which occurred during the last two months of the war, may be related not to the decline in competence, courage, or devotion on the part of the officers, but rather to the fact that the heavy losses of the Wehrmacht's trained junior officers had led to a large reduction in the ratio of the junior officers to men. In consequence, in order to use the available officers most economically, it was necessary to "thin" them out.[21] This resulted in a reduction in the amount of face-to-face contact between officers and men and in reduced feeling of the officers' protective function. And this, in turn, sometimes tipped the balance of the submissiveness-rebelliousness scale, in the successful manipulation of which lay the secret of the effective control of the German Army.

The junior officers of the Wehrmacht were, in general, very well selected. They were better educated than the average German, and had received extensive preliminary training. Although Nazi Party politics played a role in the general selection of officers (despite the façade of a non-political Wehrmacht) the junior officer ranks never became a field of patronage. High technical and personality requirements were made of all candidates for officership, Nazi and non-Nazi.

These facts were appreciated by many of the more intelligent enlisted Ps/W who testified that the influence of highly placed friends or of Party connections had practically no effect on an officer candidate's chances for selection, if he lacked the necessary qualifications for making a good officer.

Equally important in the provision of firm, "hard," and protective leadership, were the senior non-commissioned officers, who were everywhere appreciated as the most solid asset of the Wehrmacht. Until 1943, more than half of the NCO's who became Ps/W had belonged to the pre-1935 German Army. These men were neither very interested in politics nor very aggressive, but were thoroughly trained, solid men who were doing their job out of

[21] The absence of officers relaxed disciplinary controls. Thus soldiers who lay in bunkers and who "didn't see any officers for weeks" were more likely to desert or to allow themselves to be captured. The presence of the officer had the same function as other primary group members—he strengthened the superego by granting affection for duties performed and by threatening to withdraw it for duties disregarded.

a deeply-rooted sense of duty to the soldierly profession.

As the war progressed, their numbers declined and less well-trained men took their place. In the last stages of the war, when the speed in reforming units was increased, the top non-commissioned officers often did not have sufficient time to promote the growth of strong identifications between themselves and their men. In February 1945, for the first time, Ps/W began to complain that "they didn't even have time to learn our names." The disintegration which set in in the Wehrmacht at this time was in part due to the declining value of the NCO as a cohesive factor in the military primary group.

SENIOR OFFICERS. The High Command and the senior officers, although generally esteemed, were not directly relevant in the psychological structure of the military primary group. They were in the main less admired than the junior officers because their physical remoteness made it easier to express hostile sentiments against them; they stood between the Führer and the junior officers and NCO's. And while the latter three obtained a positive affect from the ambivalent attitude toward authority of so many of the soldiers, the general officers themselves were made to some extent into the recipients of the hostile component of the soldier's authority-attitude. The failure of the *Putsch* of July 20 served to lower the esteem in which the High Command was held, although in general there was not a very lively reaction to that incident. Stalwart Nazis viewed it as a case of treason, and for the time being the concentration of their hostility on generals whose names were announced in public increased their confidence in those generals whom the Führer left in charge. Other soldiers, less passionately political, were inclined to turn their backs on the unsuccessful plotters because of the weakness manifested in their failures. But the situation was only temporary, and in any case the officers on whom the men in the field felt they depended were but little affected. The loss of prestige of the immediate officers was too small to make any difference in battle behavior, while senior officers in whom confidence had declined to a greater extent were too remote in the soldier's mind to make much difference in his combat efficiency.

V. SECONDARY SYMBOLS

From the preceding section it is apparent that the immediately present agents and symbols of political authority—junior officers, NCO's, and conceptions of soldierly honor—were effective because of their consistency with the personality system of the individual soldier. In this section, we shall examine the effectiveness of the remoter—or secondary—agents and symbols of state authority.

STRATEGIC ASPECTS OF THE WAR For the mass of the German Army, the strategic phases of the war were viewed apathetically. The ignorance of the German troops about important military events, even on their own front, was partly a result of the poverty of information about the actual course of the war—itself a part of Nazi policy.[22] But the deliberate management of ignorance need not always result in such far-reaching indifference as the German soldiers showed. Deliberately maintained ignorance would have resulted in a flood of rumors, had the German soldiers been more eager to know about the strategic phases of the war. As it was, there were very few rumors on the subject—merely apathy. Three weeks after the fall of the city of Aachen, there were still many prisoners being taken in the adjoining area who did not know that the city had fallen. For at least a week after the beginning of von Rundstedt's counter-offensive, most of the troops on the northern hinge of the bulge did not know that the offensive was taking place and were not much interested when they were told after capture. Of 140 Ps/W taken between December 23-24, 1944, only

35 per cent had heard of the counter-offensive and only 7 per cent said that they thought it significant.[23]

Some exception to this extensive strategic indifference existed with respect to the Eastern front. Although the German soldiers were extremely ignorant of the state of affairs on that front and made little attempt to reduce their ignorance, still the question of Russians was so emotionally charged, so much the source of anxiety, that it is quite likely that fear of the Russians did play a role in strengthening resistance. National Socialist propaganda had long worked on the traditional repugnance and fear of the German towards the Russian. The experience of the German soldiers in Russia in 1941 and 1942 increased this repugnance by direct perception of the primitive life of the Russian villager. But probably more important was the projection onto the Russians of the guilt feelings generated by the ruthless brutality of the Germans in Russia during the occupation period. The shudder of horror which frequently accompanied a German soldier's remarks about Russia was a result of all of these factors. These attitudes influenced German resistance in the West through the shift of soldiers from East to West and the consequent diffusion of their attitudes among their comrades. They also took effect by making soldiers worry about what would happen to their families if the Russians entered Germany. Of course, it should also be mentioned that this fear of the Russians also made some German soldiers welcome a speedier collapse on the Western front in the hope that a larger part of Germany would fall under Anglo-American control.

Before the actual occupation, only a small minority expressed fear of the consequences of an Anglo-American occupation. The continuing monthly opinion poll

---

[22] Nazi propagandists, with their hyper-political orientation, tended to overestimate the German soldier's responsiveness to politics.

[23] The fact that the High Command made no attempt to explain away the defeat of the counter-offensive may have been due, among other things, to its conviction of the irrelevance of strategic consideration in the morale of the ordinary soldier.

conducted by the Psychological Warfare Branch, mentioned elsewhere, never showed more than 20 per cent of the prisoners answering "yes" to the question, "Do you believe that revenge will be taken against the population after the war?" Those who feared retribution were confirmed Nazis. Yet the general absence of fear of revenge did not cause a diminution of German resistance.

Neither did expectations about the outcome of the war play a great role in the integration or disintegration of the German Army. The statistics regarding German soldier opinion cited below show that pessimism as to final triumph was quite compatible with excellence in fighting behavior. The far greater effectiveness of considerations of self-preservation, and their vast preponderance over interest in the outcome of the war and the strategic situation, is shown by German prisoner recall of the contents of Allied propaganda leaflets (see Table 1). In the last two months of 1944 and the first two months of 1945, not less than 59 per cent of the sample of prisoners taken each month recalled references to the preservation of the individual, and the fig-

ure rose to 76 per cent in February of 1945. On the other hand, the proportion of prisoners recalling references to the total strategic situation of the war and the prospect of the outcome of the war seldom amounted to more than 20 per cent, while references to political subjects seldom amounted to more than 10 per cent. The general tendency was not to think about the outcome of the war unless forced to do so by direct interrogation. Even pessimism was counter-balanced by the reassurances provided by identification with a strong and benevolent Führer, by identification with good officers, and by the psychological support of a closely integrated primary group.

THE ETHICS OF WAR AND PATRIOTISM. Quite consistently, ethical aspects of the war did not trouble the German soldier much. When pressed by Allied interrogators, Ps/W said that Germany had been forced to fight for its life. There were very few German soldiers who said that Germany had been morally wrong to attack Poland, or Russia. Most of them thought that if anything had been wrong about the war, it was largely in the realm of technical decisions. The decision to extirpate the

TABLE 1

TABULATION OF ALLIED LEAFLET PROPAGANDA THEMES
REMEMBERED BY GERMAN Ps/W

	Dec. 15-31 1944	Jan. 1-15 1945	Jan. 15-31 1945	Feb. 1-15 1945
Number of Ps/W	60	83	99	135
Themes and appeals remembered:				
a. Promise of good treatment as Ps/W and self-preservation through surrender	63%	65%	59%	76%
b. Military news	15	17	19	30
c. Strategical hopelessness of Germany's position	13	12	25	26
d. Hopelessness of a local tactical situation	3	1	7	7
e. Political attacks on German leaders	7	5	4	8
f. Bombing of German cities	2	8	6	—
g. Allied Military Government	7	3	—	—
h. Appeals to civilians	5	4	2	—

(The percentages add up to more than 100% since some Ps/W remembered more than one topic. Only Ps/W remembering at least one theme were included in this tabulation.)

Jews had been too drastic not because of its immorality but because it united the world against Germany. The declaration of war against the Soviet Union was wrong only because it created a two-front war. But these were all arguments which had to be forced from the Ps/W. Left to themselves, they seldom mentioned them.

The assumption underlying these arguments was that the strong national state is a good in itself. But it was not, in fact, the highest good for any but the "hard core." In September 1944, for example, only 5 per cent of a sample of 634 Ps/W said that they were worried about anything other than personal or familial problems, while in the very same survey, more than half of the Ps/W said they believed that Germany was losing the war or that they were at best uncertain of the war's outcome. In brief, fear for Germany's future as a nation does not seem to have been very important in the ordinary soldier's outlook and in motivating his combat behavior. As a matter of fact, as the war became more and more patently a threat to the persistence of the German national state, the narcissism of the German soldier increased correspondingly, so that the idea of national survival did not become an object of widespread preoccupation even when it might have been expected to become so.[24]

Ethical-religious scruples seem to have played an equally small role. Although there were a few interesting cases of Roman Catholic deserters, Roman Catholics (except Austrians, Czechs and Polish nationals) do not seem to have deserted disproportionately. Prisoners seldom expressed remorse for Nazi atrocities, and practically

[24] The proposition often asserted during the war that the Allies' refusal to promise a "soft peace" to the Germans was prolonging the war, i.e., that German military resistance was motivated by fear of what the Allies would do to Germany in event of its defeat, scarcely finds support in the fact that in October 1944, when the German front was stiffening, 74 per cent of a sample of 345 Ps/W said they did not expect revenge to be taken against the German population after the war.

no case was noted of a desertion because of moral repugnance against Nazi atrocities.

POLITICAL IDEALS.   The significance of political ideals, of symbols of political systems, was rather pronounced in the case of the "hard core" minority of fervent Nazis in the German Army. Their desire for discipline under a strong leader made them enthusiasts for the totalitarian political system. Their passionate aggressiveness also promoted projective tendencies which facilitated their acceptance of the Nazi picture of an innocent and harmless Germany encircled by the dark, threatening cloud of Bolsheviks, Jews, Negroes, etc., and perpetually in danger from inner enemies as well. But for most of the German soldiers, the political system of National Socialism was of little interest.

The *system* was indeed of very slight concern to German civilians also, even though dissatisfaction increased to a high pitch towards the end of the war. Soldiers on the whole were out of touch with the operation of the Party on the home front. Hence the political system impinged little on their consciousness. Thus, for example, of 53 potential and actual deserters in the Mediterranean theater, only one alleged political grounds for his action. The irrelevance of party politics to effective soldiering has already been treated above: here we need only repeat the statement of a German soldier, "Nazism begins ten miles behind the front line."

Nor did the soldiers react in any noticeable way to the various attempts to Nazify the army. When the Nazi Party salute was introduced in 1944, it was accepted as just one more army order, about equal in significance to an order requiring the carrying of gas masks. The introduction of the *National Socialistische Führungsoffiziere* (Guidance, or Indoctrination Officer), usually known as the NSFO, was regarded apathetically or as a joke. The contempt for the NSFO was derived not from his Nazi connection but from his status as an "outsider" who was not a real soldier. The especially Nazified Waffen SS divisions were never the object of hostility on the part of the ordinary soldier, even when the responsibility for atrocities was attributed to them. On the contrary, the Waffen SS was highly esteemed, not as a Nazi formation, but for its excellent fighting capacity. Wehrmacht soldiers always felt safer when there was a Waffen SS unit on their flank.

DEVOTION TO HITLER. In contrast to the utterly apolitical attitude of the German infantry soldier towards almost all secondary symbols, an intense and personal devotion to Adolph Hitler was maintained in the German Army throughout the war. There could be little doubt that a high degree of identification with the Führer was an important factor in prolonging German resistance. Despite fluctuations in expectations as to the outcome of the war the trust in Hitler remained at a very high level even after the beginning of the serious reverses in France and Germany. In monthly opinion polls of German Ps/W opinion from D-Day until January 1945, in all but two samples over 60 per cent expressed confidence in Hitler,[25] and confidence in January was nearly as high as it was in the preceding June. During this same period considerably more than half of the German soldiers in seven out of eight polls said they believed that it was impossible for the German Army to defeat the Allies in France. Only when the German Army began to break up in the face of overwhelming Allied fire power and deep, communications-cutting penetrations, did confidence in Hitler fall to the unprecedentedly low level of 30 per cent. Even when defeatism was rising to the point at which only one-tenth of the prisoners taken as of March 1945 believed that the Germans had any chance of success, still a third retained confidence in Hitler.[26]

[25] See Gurfein, M. I., and Janowitz, Morris, "Trends in Wehrmacht Morale," The Public Opinion Quarterly, Vol. 10, No. 1 (1946), p. 78.

[26] Much of the reduction of trust in Hitler which occurred in this final period was simply a diminution in esteem for Hitler's technical skill as a strategist and as a diplomat.

Belief in the good intentions of the Führer, in his eminent moral qualities, in his devotion and contributions to the well-being of the German people, continued on an even higher level. This strong attachment grew in large part from the feeling of strength and protection which the German soldier got from his conception of the Führer personality.

For older men, who had lived through the unemployment of the closing years of the Weimar Republic and who experienced the joy of being reinstated in gainful employment by Nazi full-employment policies, Hitler was above all the man who had provided economic security. This attitude extended even to left wing soldiers of this generation, who denounced the National Socialist political system, but found occasion to say a good word for Hitler as a man who had restored order and work in Germany. For men of the generation between 22-35, who had first experienced Hitler's charisma in the struggles to establish their manliness during late adolescence, Hitler was the prototype of strength and masculinity. For the younger Nazi fanatics, he was a father substitute, providing the vigilant discipline and the repression of dangerous impulses both in the individual and in the social environment; for them he had the additional merit of legitimating revolt against the family and traditional restraints.

Prisoners spoke of Hitler with enthusiasm, and even those who expressed regret over the difficulties which his policies had brought on Germany by engendering a two-front war and by allowing the Jews to be persecuted so fiercely as to arouse world hatred—even these men retained their warm esteem for his good intentions. They found it necessary to exculpate him in some way by attributing his errors to dishonest advisors who kept the truth from him, or to certain technical difficulties in his strategic doctrines which did not in any way reflect on his fundamental moral greatness or nobility.

It was difficult for German soldiers, as long as they had this attitude toward Hitler, to rebel mentally against the war. Time after time, prisoners who were asked why Hitler continued the war when they themselves admitted it was so obviously lost, said he wouldn't continue the war and waste lives if he did not have a good, even though undisclosed, strategic reason for doing so, or if he didn't have the resources to realize his ends. Nazis as well as non-Nazis answered in this way. Or else they would say, "the Führer has never deceived us," or, "he must have a good reason for doing what he does."

There was obviously a fear of rendering an independent judgment of events among the German soldiers and a desire for some strong leader to assume the responsibility for determining their fate. American and British soldiers often complained that the complexity of the army organization and strategy was so great and their own particular part was so small that they could not see the role of their personal missions. Their failure to see the connection made them miserable because it reduced their sense of personal autonomy. In the German Army, on the other hand, there was no difficulty for soldiers who were used throughout their lives to having other persons determine their objectives for them.

It is also possible that the very high devotion to Hitler under conditions of great stress was in part a reaction formation growing from a hostility against lesser authorities, which emerged as the weakness of these authorities became more manifest. In the last year of the war, hostility and contempt on the part of the German soldiers toward Nazi Party functionaries and toward Nazi Party leaders below Hitler (particularly Goebbels and Goering) was increasing. After the *Putsch* of July 20, hostility toward senior Wehrmacht officers also increased somewhat, although it never reached the levels of hostility displayed by civilians against local civilian Party officials and leaders. It is possible, therefore, that guilt created in ambivalent personalities by giving expression, even though verbally, to hostility against subordinate agents of authority, had to be alleviated by reaffirmed belief in the central and highest authority.

Weakening of the Hitler symbol. As the integral pattern of defense was broken down, however, and as danger to physical survival increased, devotion to Hitler deteriorated. The tendency to attribute virtue to the strong and immorality to the weak took hold increasingly, and while it did not lead to a complete rejection of Hitler, it reached a higher point than at any other stage in the history of National Socialism. The announcement of Hitler's death met an incapacity to respond on the part of many soldiers. There seemed to be no willingness to question the truth of the report, but the great upsurge of preoccupation with physical survival as a result of disintegration of the military primary group, the loss of contact with junior officers and the greatly intensified threat of destruction, caused a deadening of the power to respond to this event. For the vast horde of dishevelled, dirty, bewildered prisoners, who were being taken in the last weeks of the war, Hitler was of slight importance alongside the problem of their own biological survival and the welfare of their families. For the small minority who still had sufficient energy to occupy themselves with "larger problems," the news of Hitler's death released a sort of amorphous resentment against the fallen leader whose weakness and immorality had been proven by the failure of his strategy. But even here, the resentment was not expressed in explicit denunciations of Hitler's character or personality. The emphasis was all on technical deficiencies and weaknesses.

The explanation of the deterioration and final—though probably only temporary—hostility toward Hitler may in part be sought in the average German soldier's ambivalence toward the symbols of authority. This psychological mechanism, which also helps to explain the lack of a significant resistance movement inside Germany, enables us to understand the curve of Hitler's fame among the German people. Hitler, the father symbol, was loved for his power and his great accomplishments and hated for his oppressiveness, but the latter sentiment was repressed. While he remained strong it was psychologically expedient—as well as politically expedient—to identify with Hitler and to displace hostility on to weaker minority groups and foreigners. But once Hitler's authority had been undermined, the German soldiers rejected it and tended to express their hostility by projecting their own weakness on to him.

Thus the only important secondary symbol in motivating the behavior of the German soldiers during the recent war also lost its efficacy when the primary group relations of comradeliness, solidarity and subordination to junior officers broke down, and with it the superego of the individual, on which the effective functioning of the primary group depends.[27]

VI. NAZI MACHINERY FOR MAINTAINING ARMY SOLIDARITY AND FIGHTING EFFECTIVENESS

ADMINISTRATIVE MACHINERY AND PERSONNEL. Even before the outbreak of the war, the Nazi Party took an active hand in the internal high policy of the Wehrmacht and in the selection of the Chief of Staff and his entourage. From September 1939 to the signing of the capitulation in May 1945 this process of Nazification continued steadily until the Wehrmacht was finally rendered powerless to make its own decisions. Nazi Party control over the Wehrmacht was designed to insure (1) that Nazi strategic intentions would be carried out (2) that capitulation would be made impossible and (3) that internal solidarity

[27] The mixture of apathy and resentment against Hitler persisted through the first part of the demobilization period following the end of the war, but as life began to reorganize and to take on new meaning and the attitudes toward authority, which sustain and are sustained by the routines of daily life, revived, esteem for Hitler also began to revive. It is likely to revive still further and to assume a prominent place in German life once more, if the new elite which is being created under the Allied occupation shows weakness and lack of decisiveness and self-confidence.

down to the lowest private would be maintained.

Most ambitious and successful of the early efforts at Nazification were the recruitment and training of the special Waffen SS (Elite) Divisions. These units initially contained only fanatically devoted Nazi volunteers and had officer staffs which were thoroughly permeated with Nazi stalwarts. They became the Nazi Party army within the Wehrmacht, and their military prowess greatly enhanced the prestige of the Nazi Party and weakened the position of the General Staff.

At the outbreak of the war, the domestic security and police services inside the Reich were completely unified under the command of Himmler. Although the Wehrmacht had its own elaborate system of security, elements of the *Sicherheitsdienst* operated in occupied areas, in conjunction with the Wehrmacht. As the fortunes of war declined, the Nazi Party accelerated the extension of its security and indoctrination services over the Wehrmacht. The security net around the German High Command was drawn most tightly in response to the 20th of July *Putsch*. In addition to those officers who were executed, a large number of doubtful loyalty were removed or put into commands where they could be closely supervised.

As the German troops retreated into Germany, SS and state police units, instead of the Wehrmacht military police, were given the normal military function of maintaining the line of demarcation between the front lines and the rear areas. A captured order, issued by the CO of the SS forces in the West on September 21, 1944, indicated that these units would have the task of preventing contact between the civilian population and the troops, as well as the arrest and execution of deserters from the army.[28] In addition to these security procedures, the Nazis made effective use of exploiting the individual German soldier's fear of physical

[28] Order of Commanding Officer of SS Forces in the West, September 21, 1944.

destruction as was described above in the section, *Demand for physical survival*.

But these measures were of a negative nature. In order to strengthen the traditional Wehrmacht indoctrination efforts, the Nazi Party appointed in the winter of 1943 political indoctrination officers, called *Nationale Socialistische Führungsoffiziere* (NS-FO), to all military formations. Later in September 1944, when the Nazis felt the need for intensifying their indoctrination efforts, the position of these officers was strengthened by the establishment of an independent chain of command which enabled them to communicate with higher headquarters without Wehrmacht interference.[29] The NSFO's were given the power, in cases of "particular political significance or where delay implies danger" to report immediately and directly to NSF officers of higher commands and upward to the highest command, irrespective of routine communication channels. To interfere with the NSFO chain of command was made a military crime. The NSFO "organization" came to publish or directly supervise most of the publications and radio stations for the troops, and to prepare the leaflets which were distributed to or dropped on the German troops. Their job also included periodic indoctrination meetings. The official publication for the indoctrination of the officers' corps, *Mitteilung für die Truppe*, which had been published throughout the war by the Wehrmacht, was also taken over by Nazi Party functionaries (*NS Führungsstab der Wehrmacht*) in November 1944.

The NSF officers, with their independent chain of command, also became security officers of the Nazi Party. They spent a great deal of time prying into the morale and political convictions of higher officers in order to warn headquarters of the need to replace men of faltering faith.[30] Captured

German generals, perhaps motivated by a desire to exculpate themselves, told how during the closing months of the war, they came to feel completely subjugated by the indoctrination officers. They reported that these Nazi junior officers maintained an independent reporting system on senior officers and often said "You're done if he gives a bad account of you."

The final step in the Nazi Party encroachment on the administration of the Wehrmacht came when the *levee en masse*, the *Volkssturm*, was raised. Here, the Nazi Party assumed complete control of training and indoctrination and units were to be turned over to the Wehrmacht only for actual deployment. No doubt the Wehrmacht was glad to be relieved of this unpopular task, as well as the even more unpopular task of organizing the Werewolf resistance, which the Nazi Party assumed for itself completely.

PROPAGANDA THEMES.   The most striking aspect of Nazi indoctrination of their own men during combat was the employment of negative appeals and counter-propaganda, which attempted less to reply directly to the substance of our claims than to explain the reasons why the Allies were using propaganda.

The Nazis frankly believed that they could employ our propaganda efforts as a point of departure for strengthening the unpolitical resolve of their men. They had the legend of the effectiveness of Allied propaganda in World War I as a warning from which to "conclude" that if the Germans failed to be tricked by propaganda this time, success was assured. A typical instance of this attitude was contained in a captured order issued by the Officer in Command of the garrison of Boulogne on

---

[29] This step was regarded as sufficiently important to be promulgated in an Order appearing over Hitler's signature.

[30] Numerous orders menaced officers who might become political dissidents. One such

document circulated in Army Group B, dated January 21, 1945, stated that Himmler had drawn up a set of instructions concerning officer offenders which were to be reviewed at least once a month. Political divergences were to be harshly dealt with, regardless of the previous military or political service of the officer in question.

September 11, 1944, in which he appealed to his men not to be misled by Allied propaganda. The German order claimed that the propaganda attack in the form of leaflets was in itself an expression of the weakness of the Allied offensive, which was in desperate need of the port for communications. During the same period, an NSF officer issued an elaborate statement in which he reminded the garrison at Le Havre that the "enemy resorts to propaganda as a weapon which he used in the last stages of the first world war," in order to point out that German victory depended on the determination of the German soldier to resist Allied propaganda.

In the fall and winter of 1944, the campaign to counteract Allied propaganda by "exposing" it was intensified and elaborated. (This method had the obvious advantage that direct refutations of Allied claims could largely be avoided.) *Mitteilung für die Truppe* (October 1944), a newspaper for officer indoctrination, reviewed the major weapons in the "poison offensive." They included: attacks against the Party and its predominant leaders ("this is not surprising as the enemy will, of course, attack those institutions which give us our greatest strength"); appeals to the Austrians to separate themselves from the Germans ("the time when we were split up in small states was the time of our greatest weakness") sympathy with the poor German women who work in hellish factories ("the institution must be a good one, otherwise the enemy would not attack it").

Other themes "exposed" in leaflets were: the enemy attempts to separate the leaders from the people ("Just as the Kaiser was blamed in 1918, it now is Hitler who is supposed to be responsible"); the enemy admits his own losses in an exaggerated way in order to obtain the reputation of veracity and to lie all the more at the opportune moment.

Even earlier in the Western campaign, the Germans followed the policy of stamping Allied leaflets with the imprint, "Hostile Propaganda," and then allowing them to circulate in limited numbers. This was being carried out at the same time that mutually contradictory orders for the complete destruction of all enemy propaganda were being issued. The explanation, in part, is that the Nazis realized that it would be impossible to suppress the flood of Allied leaflets, and therefore sought to clearly label them as such and to employ them as a point of departure for counter-propaganda.

The procedure of overstamping Allied leaflets was linked with follow-up indoctrination talks. Such indoctrination lectures, which were conducted by the Nazi NSFO's, became towards the end of the war one of the main vehicles of Nazi indoctrination of their own troops. Ps/W claimed, although it was probably not entirely correct, that they usually slept through such sessions, or at least paid little attention, until the closing *Sieg Heil* was sounded. At this late date in the war, emphasis on oral propaganda was made necessary by the marked disruption of communications. Radio listening at the front was almost non-existent due to the lack of equipment; when in reserve, troops listened more frequently. Newspapers were distributed only with great difficulty. More important were the leaflets which were either dropped by air on their own troops or distributed through command channels.

"Strength Through Fear." Major lines of the negative approach employed by these leaflets in indoctrination talks, in the rumors circulated by NSF officers, stressed "strength through fear," particularly fear of Russia and the general consequences of complete destruction that would follow defeat.

Because of the German soldier's concern about the welfare of his family living inside Germany, Nazi agencies were constantly issuing statements about the successful evacuation of German civilians to the east bank of the Rhine.

Equally stressed in the strength through fear theme were retaliation threats against the families of deserters, mistreatment of prisoners of war in Anglo-American prison camps, and the ultimate fate of prisoners. The phrase *Sieg oder Sibirien* (Victory or

Siberia) was emphasized and much material was released to prove that the Anglo-Americans planned to turn over their prisoners to the Russians. When the U.S. Army stopped shipping German Ps/W to the United States, Nazi propaganda officers spread the rumor among German soldiers "that the way to Siberia is shorter from France than from the United States."

Statements by Ps/W revealed that shortly before the Rundstedt counterattack, speeches by NSFO's were increased. One of the main subjects seems to have been weapons. In retrospect, the intent of the directives under which they were working was obvious. Attempts were made to explain the absence of the Luftwaffe, while the arrival in the near future of new and better weapons was guaranteed.

Psychological preparation for the December counter-offensive was built around the Rundstedt order of the day that "everything is at stake." Exhortations were backed up with exaggerated statements by unit commanders that large amounts of men and material were to be employed. Immediately thereafter, official statements were issued that significant penetrations had been achieved; special editions of troop papers were prepared announcing that 40,000 Americans had been killed.

Such announcements received little attention among the troops actually engaged in the counter-offensive because of the obvious difficulties in disseminating propaganda to fighting troops.

Nevertheless, after the failure of the counter-attack, the Nazis felt called upon to formulate a plausible line to explain the sum total result of that military effort, especially for those who felt that better military judgment would have resulted in a purely defensive strategy against Russia. On January 25, *Front und Heimat* announced that the December offensive had smashed the plan for a simultaneous onslaught: "The East can hold only if the West does too. . . . Every fighting man in the West knows that the Anglo-Americans are doing all they can, although belatedly, to start the assault on

the Fortress Germany. Our task in the West now is to postpone that time as long as possible and to guard the back of our Armies in the East."

Despite the obvious limitations on the efficacy of propaganda during March and April 1945, the Nazis continued to the very end to keep up their propaganda efforts. Due to the confusion within the ranks of the Wehrmacht and the resulting difficulties of dissemination, the task devolved almost wholly on the NSFO's who spent much of their time reading to the troops the most recent orders governing desertion. Leaflets called largely on the Landser's military spirit to carry on. One even demanded that he remain silent (*zu schweigen*). The Nazis taxed their fancy to create rumors as the last means of bolstering morale. Here a favorite technique for stimulating favorable rumors was for CO's to read to their men "classified" documents from official sources which contained promises of secret weapons or discussed the great losses being inflicted upon the Allies.

VII. THE IMPACT OF ALLIED PROPAGANDA ON WEHRMACHT SOLIDARITY

The system of controls which the social structure of the Wehrmacht exercised over its individual members greatly reduced those areas in which symbolic appeals of the Allies could work. But the millions of leaflets which were dropped weekly and the "round-the-clock" broadcasts to the German troops certainly did not fail to produce some reactions.

The very first German Ps/W who were interrogated directly on their reactions to Allied propaganda soon revealed a stereotyped range of answers which could be predicted from their degree of Nazification. The fanatical Nazi claimed, "No German would believe anything the enemy has to say," while an extreme attitude of acceptance was typified by a confirmed anti-Nazi who pleaded with his captors: "Now is the moment to flood the troops with leaflets. You have no idea of the effect sober and effective leaflets have on retreating troops." But these extreme reactions of soldiers were of low frequency; Nazi soldiers might admit the truth of our leaflets but usually would not accept their conclusions and implications.

The fundamentally indifferent reaction to Allied propaganda was most interestingly shown in an intensive study of 150 Ps/W captured in October 1944 of whom 65 per cent had seen our leaflets and for the most part professed that they believed their contents. This was a group which had fought very obstinately, and the number of active deserters, if any, was extremely small. Some forty of these Ps/W offered extended comments as to what they meant when they said they believed the contents of Allied leaflets.

Five stated outright that they believed the messages and that the leaflets assisted them and their comrades to surrender.

Seven declared they believed the leaflets, but were powerless to do anything about appeals to surrender.

Eight stated that they believed the contents, but nevertheless as soldiers and decent individuals would never think of deserting.

Twenty-two declared that events justified belief in the leaflets, but they clearly implied that this had been of little importance in their battle experiences.

In Normandy, where the relatively small front was blanketed with printed material, up to 90 per cent of the Ps/W reported that they had read Allied leaflets, yet this period was characterized by very high German morale and stiff resistance.

Throughout the Western campaign, with the exception of periods of extremely bad weather or when the front was fluid, the cumulative percentage of exposure ranged between 60 and 80 per cent. (This cumulative percentage of exposure was based on statements by Ps/W that they had seen leaflets sometime while fighting on the Western front after D-Day. A few samples indicated that penetration during any single month covered about 20 per cent of the prisoners.) Radio listening among combat troops was confined to a minute fraction due to the lack of equipment; rear troops listened more frequently. In the case of both leaflets and

radio it was found that there was widespread but desultory comment on the propaganda, much of which comment distorted the actual contents.

Not only was there wide penetration by Allied leaflets and newssheets, but German soldiers frequently circulated them extensively among their comrades. A readership study of *Nachrichten für die Truppe*, a daily newssheet published by the Allied Psychological Warfare Division, showed that each copy which was picked up had an average readership of between four and five soldiers —a figure which is extremely large in view of the conditions of combat life. Not only were leaflets widely circulated, but it became a widespread practice for soldiers to carry Allied leaflets on their person, especially the "safe conduct pass" leaflets which bore a statement by General Eisenhower guaranteeing the bearer swift and safe conduct through Allied lines and the protection of the Geneva convention. There is evidence that in certain sectors of the front, German soldiers even organized black-market trading in Allied propaganda materials.

It is relevant to discuss here the differences in effectiveness between tactical and strategic propaganda. By tactical propaganda, we refer to propaganda which seeks to promise immediate results in the tactical situation. The clearest example of this type of propaganda is afforded by "across the lines" loudspeaker broadcasts, which sometimes facilitated immediate capture of the prisoners of war— not by propaganda in the ordinary sense, but by giving instructions on how to surrender safely, once the wish to surrender was present.

No sufficiently accurate estimate is available of the total number of prisoners captured by the use of such techniques, but signal successes involving hundreds of isolated troops in the Normandy campaign have been credited to psychological warfare combat teams. Even more successful were the loudspeaker-carrying tanks employed in the Rhine River offensive, when the first signs of weakening resistance were encountered. For example, the Fourth Armored Division reported that its psychological warfare unit captured over 500 prisoners in a four-day dash from the Kyll River to the Rhine. Firsthand investigation of these loudspeaker missions, and interrogation of prisoners captured under such circumstances, establish that Allied propaganda was effective in describing the tactical situation to totally isolated and helpless soldiers and in arranging an Allied cease fire and thereby presenting an assurance to the German soldier of a safe surrender. The successful targets for such broadcasts were groups where solidarity and ability to function as a unit were largely destroyed. Leaflets especially written for specific sectors and dropped on pin point targets by fighter-bombs were used instead of loudspeakers where larger units were cut off. This method proved less successful, since the units to which they were addressed were usually better integrated and the necessary cease fire conditions could not be arranged.

Less spectacular, but more extensive, was strategic propaganda. Allied directives called for emphasis on four themes in this type of propaganda: (1) Ideological attacks on the Nazi Party and Germany's war aims, (2) the strategical hopelessness of Germany's military and economic position, (3) the justness of the United Nations war aims and their unity and determination to carry them out (unconditional surrender, although made known to the troops, was never stressed), (4) promises of good treatment to prisoners of war, with appeals to self-preservation through surrender.

Although it is extremely difficult, especially in view of the lack of essential data, to assess the efficacy of these various themes, some tentative clues might be seen in the answers given to the key attitude questions in the monthly Psychological Warfare opinion poll of captured German soldiers.[31] Thus, there was no significant decline in attachment to Nazi ideology until February and March 1945. In other words, propaganda attacks on Nazi ideology seem to have been of little

[31] Cf. Gurfein, M. I., and Janowitz, Morris, *op. cit.*

avail, and attachment to secondary symbols, e.g., Hitler, declined only when the smaller military units began to break up under very heavy pressure.

Since the German soldier was quite ignorant of military news on other fronts, it was believed that a great deal of printed material should contain factual reports of the military situation, stressing the strategical hopelessness of the German position. As a result, the third most frequently recalled items of our propaganda were the military news reports. It seems reasonable to believe that the emphasis on these subjects did contribute to the development of defeatist sentiment.

Despite the vast amount of space devoted to ideological attacks on German leaders, only about five per cent of the Ps/W mentioned this topic—a fact which supported the contention as to the general failure of ideological or secondary appeals. Finally, the presentation of the justness of our war aims was carried out in such a way as to avoid stressing the unconditional surrender aspects of our intentions, while emphasizing postwar peace intentions and organizational efforts; much was made of United Nations unity. All this fell on deaf ears, for of this material only a small minority of Ps/W (about 5 per cent) recalled specific statements about military government plans for the German occupation.

As has been pointed out previously, the themes which were most successful, at least in attracting attention and remaining fixed in the memory, were those promising good treatment as prisoners of war. In other words, propaganda referring to immediate concrete situations and problems seems to have been most effective in some respects.

The single leaflet most effective in communicating the promise of good treatment was the "safe conduct pass." Significantly, it was usually printed on the back of leaflets which contained no elaborate propaganda appeals except those of self-preservation. The rank and file tended to be favorably disposed to its official language and legal, document-like character. In one sector where General Eisenhower's signature was left off the leaflet, doubt was cast on its authenticity.

Belief in the veracity of this appeal was no doubt based on the attitude that the British and the Americans were respectable law-abiding soldiers who would treat their captives according to international law. As a result of this predisposition and the wide use of the safe conduct leaflets, as well as our actual practices in treating prisoners well, the German soldier came to have no fear of capture by British or American troops. The most that can be claimed for this lack of fear was that it may have decreased or undercut any tendency to fight to the death; it produced no active opposition to continued hostilities.

As an extension of the safe-conduct approach, leaflets were prepared instructing non-commissioned officers in detailed procedures by which their men could safely be removed from battle so as to avoid our fire and at the same time avoid evacuation by the German field police. If the Germans could not be induced to withdraw from combat actively, Allied propaganda appealed to them to hide in cellars. This in fact became a favorite technique of surrender, since it avoided the need of facing the conscience-twinging desertion problem.

As a result of psychological warfare research, a series of leaflets was prepared whose attack was aimed at primary group organization in the German Army, without recourse to ideological symbols. Group organization depended on the acceptance of immediate leadership and mutual trust. Therefore this series of leaflets sought to stimulate group discussion among the men and to bring into their focus of attention concerns which would loosen solidarity. One leaflet declared, "Do not take our (the Allies) word for it; ask your comrade; find out how he feels." Thereupon followed a series of questions on personal concerns, family problems, tactical consideration and supply problems. Discussion of these problems was expected to increase anxiety. It was assumed that to the degree that the soldier found that he was

not isolated in his opinion, to that degree he would be strengthened in his resolve to end hostilities, for himself at least.

CONCLUSION

At the beginning of the second world war, many publicists and specialists in propaganda attributed almost supreme importance to psychological warfare operations. The legendary successes of Allied propaganda against the German Army at the end of the first world war and the tremendous expansion of the advertising and mass communications industries in the ensuing two decades had convinced many people that human behavior could be extensively manipulated by mass communications. They tended furthermore to stress that military morale was to a great extent a function of the belief in the rightness of the "larger" cause which was at issue in the war; good soldiers were therefore those who clearly understood the political and moral implications of what was at stake. They explained the striking successes of the German Army in the early phases of the war by the "ideological possession" of the German soldiers, and they accordingly thought that propaganda attacking doctrinal conceptions would be defeating this army.

Studies of the German Army's morale and fighting effectiveness made during the last three years of the war throw considerable doubt on these hypotheses. The solidarity of the German Army was discovered by these studies—which left much to be desired from the standpoint of scientific rigor—to be based only very indirectly and very partially on political convictions or broader ethical beliefs. Where conditions were such as to allow primary group life to function smoothly, and where the primary group developed a high degree of cohesion, morale was high and resistance effective or at least very determined, regardless in the main of the political attitudes of the soldiers. The conditions of primary group life were related to spatial proximity, the capacity for intimate communication, the provision of paternal protectiveness by NCO's and junior officers, and the gratification of certain personality needs, e.g., manliness, by the military organization and its activities. The larger structure of the army served to maintain morale through the provision of the framework in which potentially individuating physical threats were kept at a minimum—through the organization of supplies and through adequate strategic dispositions.

The behavior of the German Army demonstrated that the focus of attention and concern beyond one's immediate face-to-face social circles might be slight indeed and still not interfere with the achievement of a high degree of military effectiveness. It also showed that attempts to modify behavior by means of symbols referring to events or values outside the focus of attention and concern would be given an indifferent response by the vast majority of the German soldiers. This was almost equally true under conditions of primary group integrity and under conditions of extreme primary group disintegration. In the former, primary needs were met adequately through the gratifications provided by the other members of the group; in the latter, the individual had regressed to a narcissistic state in which symbols referring to the outer world were irrelevant to his first concern—"saving his own skin."

At moments of primary group disintegration, a particular kind of propaganda less hortatory or analytical, but addressing the intensified desire to survive, and describing the precise procedures by which physical survival could be achieved, was likely to facilitate further disintegration. Furthermore, in some cases aspects of the environment towards which the soldier might hitherto have been emotionally indifferent were defined for him by prolonged exposure to propaganda under conditions of disintegration. Some of these wider aspects, e.g., particular strategic considerations, then tended to be taken into account in his motivation and he was more likely to implement his defeatist mood by surrender than he would have been without exposure to propaganda.

It seems necessary, therefore, to reconsider the potentials of propaganda in the context of all the other variables which influence behavior. The erroneous views concerning the omnipotence of propaganda must be given up and their place must be taken by much more differentiated views as to the possibilities of certain kinds of propaganda under different sets of conditions.

It must be recognized that on the moral plane most men are members of the larger society by virtue of identifications which are mediated through the human beings with whom they are in personal relationships. Many are bound into the larger society only by primary group identifications. Only a small proportion possessing special training or rather particular kinds of personalities are capable of giving a preponderant share of their attention and concern to the symbols of the larger world. The conditions under which these different groups will respond to propaganda will differ, as will also the type of propaganda to which they will respond.

·10·

Formation and Determination of Public Opinion

❧

OPINION FORMATION IN A CRISIS SITUATION

TEST-TUBE FOR PUBLIC OPINION: A RURAL COMMUNITY

THE BOSS AND THE CITY VOTE: A CASE STUDY IN CITY POLITICS

RESPONSES TO THE TELEVISED KEFAUVER HEARINGS

POLITICAL ISSUES AND THE VOTE

THE INTERACTION OF MOTIVATING FACTORS

OPINION FORMATION IN A CRISIS SITUATION

S. M. LIPSET

Studying the opinion making processes is the principal objective of public opinion research. In the main, however, such research has been forced to analyze the factors related to existing attitudes and sentiments rather than the formation of attitudes toward new problems or issues. The controversy at the University of California over the requirement that all faculty members sign an oath affirming that they were not members of the Communist Party created an opportunity to study the opinion forming process in a comparatively closed environment. Both students and faculty were faced with the necessity of making up their minds about an issue that had not previously existed.

A study was undertaken during the height of the controversy, between March 15 and April 21, 1951, to find out how the student body was reacting to this crisis situation. Ideally, such research could best have been conducted as a panel study, through which it would have been possible to see how the crisis situation actually affected the opinions of many students. Since the opportunity to do research on attitudes toward the oath did not arise until the controversy was about nine months old, the panel method, unfortunately, could not be used. It was hoped, however, that a single survey of student attitudes at that time would enable the testing of hypotheses about opinion forma-

tion that had been derived from panel studies of other situations in which the immediate crisis element and the need of the participants to form new opinions were not present. In undertaking the study, a basic assumption was made for which there was little empirical evidence, but which seemed to be logical. This assumption was that the controversy itself did not result in a change in the various factors which are treated as independent variables in the analysis. Specifically, it was assumed that a person's stand on the loyalty oath did not change his general political predisposition, significant group affiliations, newspaper reading habits, or his participation in the university community. If this assumption is made, then one can attempt retrospectively to identify the factors which would have enabled one to predict the attitudes and behavior of individuals faced with a new issue such as this one.

STUDY DESIGN

Between March 15 and April 21, 1950, a representative sample of the student body of the Berkeley campus of the University of California was interviewed concerning its opinion about the loyalty oath and the non-Communist hiring policy. Every fortieth student was selected systematically from the files of the Registrar. The study was planned

From the *Public Opinion Quarterly*, 1953, 17, 20-46. Reprinted by permission of the author and the publisher.

after February 24, when the Regents issued their ultimatum to every non-signer of the oath to sign or get out. Interviewing began on March 15 and ended on April 21, the day that the Regents lifted the ultimatum and accepted the Alumni proposal of a contract form and committee hearing.

The 480 students who were interviewed during the five weeks of the student survey represented a cross section of the student body of the Berkeley campus. Table 1 shows the relationship between the population sta-

TABLE 1

SAMPLE STATISTICS RELATED TO
POPULATION DATA

Trait	Population	Sample	Not Inter-viewed
	(N:21,903)	(N:480)	(N:56)
Males	74%	71%	82%
Females	26	29	18
	100	100	100
	(N:21,428)	(N:479)	(N:56)
Graduates	24%	24%	25%
Undergrads	76	76	75
	100	100	100

tistics and the sample. The differences between the two are within the error which could result from chance factors. There is no reason to suspect that there is any consistent biasing factor resulting from sampling. About 13 per cent of the original, 56 students, were not interviewed. Of these 31 were refusals while 25 were never reached by the interviewers. The short duration of the interviewing period, plus the fact that all the student interviewers did not show equal enthusiasm in securing their interviews, were largely responsible for the fact that the sample design was not entirely completed. The 56 students who were not interviewed did not differ from the respondents by class standing in school. There were more females interviewed than males, but sex did not differentiate on the issues.

The interview schedule was designed to obtain the students' opinions on the issue of the oath and the policy of exclusion of Communists from teaching. Information was also secured on various social background characteristics of the group, as well as on their attitudes on a variety of political subjects which were not specifically related to the issues of academic freedom and civil liberties. The attitudes of the students as a group paralleled the official position of the faculty and its supporters. That is, the students were opposed to faculty members being required to take an oath affirming that they were not members of the Communist party. They were, however, more divided on the issue of employing Communists in the university. Table 2 presents the results for the entire sample.

TABLE 2

ATTITUDE OF 480 STUDENTS TO THE
LOYALTY OATH AND THE POLICY OF
EMPLOYING COMMUNISTS*

Loyalty Oath

Approve oath requirement	26%
Disapprove oath	64.
Don't know	10
No response	0

Communist Employment

Oppose Communist employment	45%
Approve Communist employment	39
Qualified approval	
Approve if known as Communist	4
Approve if not a propagandist	4
Approve if non-controversial subject	2
Don't know	4
No response	2

* For the purpose of analysis the students were divided into nine groups on the basis of their attitudes to both the oath and the policy. Only five of these groups contained enough cases to warrant inclusion. In succeeding tables these groups will be represented by letter abbreviations: PP-PO, pro-policy of barring Communists and pro-oath requirement; PP-AO, pro-policy and anti-oath requirement; AP-PO, anti-policy and pro-oath; AP-AO, anti-policy and anti-oath; and DK for the "don't knows" in either question.

PREDISPOSITIONS

Various studies have indicated that attitude formation is related to the basic predispositions of individuals. That is, attitudes on any given issue are rarely if ever independent of the general cluster of attitudes that people bring to any situation in which

TABLE 3

PREDISPOSITION GROUPS

Attitude on Oath and Policy	Extreme Liberal (N:161)	Moderate Liberal (N:84)	Moderate Conservative (N:130)	Extreme Conservative (N:97)
PP–PO	5%	18%	25%	32%
PP–AO	25	23	18	26
AP–PO	2	6	10	8
AP–AO	58	34	29	24
Don't Know	10	19	18	10
	100	100	100	100

they participate. In the case of the loyalty oath controversy, one would expect that general political predisposition would have affected students' reactions to issues of academic freedom. In order to test this hypothesis, the respondents were asked about their past and present political preferences, and were presented with a six question attitude scale designed to rank them as conservatives or liberals. The data shown in Table 3 appear to confirm the hypothesis that attitudes on the loyalty oath and non-Communist hiring policy were not independent of general political predispositions.

A similar pattern occurred when opinions on the two issues were compared with the respondents' party identifications. As compared with Republicans, Democrats were disproportionately against the loyalty oath and the policy of barring Communists. The supporters of minority political parties were, as one would expect, even more definitely in favor of the rights of Communists than were the Democrats. The differences between the adherents of the two major parties were much less, however, when the question of liberalism or conservatism was held constant than when such partisans were compared independently (Table 4). General liberalism or conservatism appears to have been more important than party affiliation as such. Nevertheless, Democrats as a group were more prone to oppose the loyalty oath than were Republicans.

Table 5 shows that seniors and graduate students, particularly the latter, were much more liberal on the academic freedom issues than the members of the three lower classes, but this difference also decreased when liberalism and conservatism were held constant. Most of the difference between the two groups of students was contributed by the variation in the proportion of liberals, the graduate students in particular being the most liberal group in their general attitudes. While there are few data which help to account for this fact, it is possible to suggest some hypotheses. During the course of the loyalty oath controversy, students were exposed to more propaganda from the liberal or faculty side than from the conservative or Regents' side. The data indicate that senior and graduate students had more information about the controversy than lower classmen. Upper classmen and graduate students, who had closer contact with their instructors than lower classmen, may have been exposed to more discussion about the issues. Public opinion research has suggested that propaganda is more effective with people whose basic predispositions are already in line with the propaganda themes, and, moreover, that its effectiveness is increased if it is conveyed at least in part through face to face contacts. In this case, therefore, it may be suggested that seniors and graduate students received more of the preponderantly "anti-oath, anti-policy" propaganda, received it most directly and effectively in the context of personal relations, and that this propaganda influenced most those individuals with liberal predispositions.

TABLE 4

RELATION BETWEEN ATTITUDES AND ACADEMIC FREEDOM ISSUE—
PARTY HELD CONSTANT

Issue: Communists May Teach	DEMOCRATS			REPUBLICANS		
	Liberals	Moderates	Conservatives	Liberals	Moderates	Conservatives
	(N:96)	(N:90)	(N:36)	(N:18)	(N:62)	(N:66)
Yes	65%	44%	33%	50%	40%	32%
No	28	50	61	50	57	67
Don't know	7	6	6	0	3	1
	100	100	100	100	100	100

Loyalty Oath						
	(N:96)	(N:93)	(N:35)	(N:18)	(N:64)	(N:67)
Approve	3	26	34	17	39	45
Disapprove	91	60	54	72	47	49
Don't know	6	14	12	11	14	6
	100	100	100	100	100	100

The fact that the distribution of attitudes among the moderates and conservatives differed only slightly from class to class becomes understandable in terms of this hypothesis, since one would expect that those with non-liberal predispositions would not be greatly affected by the liberal propaganda of the faculty.

The pervasive influence of basic predispositions can also be seen when the students are compared by religious background. Considering religion alone, it would appear that, of the four religious preferences given, Jews were most liberal on the academic freedom issues, those with no religious preference next, followed by Protestants, with the Cath-

TABLE 5

COLLEGE CLASS AND POLITICAL ATTITUDES

Issue: Communists May Teach	FRESHMEN, SOPHOMORES AND JUNIORS			SENIORS AND GRADUATES		
	Conservative	Moderate	Liberal	Conservative	Moderate	Liberal
	(N:65)	(N:111)	(N:49)	(N:49)	(N:103)	(N:95)
Yes	39%	44%	51%	33%	48%	73%
No	58	50	39	65	48	24
Don't know	3	6	10	2	4	3
	100	100	100	100	100	100

Loyalty Oath						
	(N:66)	(N:115)	(N:49)	(N:48)	(N:104)	(N:95)
Approve	39	33	16	36	31	2
Disapprove	54	53	76	56	54	93
Don't know	7	14	8	8	15	5
	100	100	100	100	100	100

olics most conservative. Breaking down religious preference by position on the political predisposition scale indicates, however, that, with the partial exception of the Catholics, the differences among the different religious denominations were in part contributed by the varying proportions of liberals or conservatives within them. The Catholics deviate with regard to permitting Communists to teach—even liberal Catholics were opposed to this; however, a majority of liberal Catholics are opposed to the loyalty oath.

One of the most interesting findings of this study concerns the 78 students who reported having no religious beliefs of their own, but gave their parents' religious affiliation. In each case, the students answering "none" were more liberal than those students who had a religious affiliation, but the direction of the differences among the three religious groups remained the same among those who reported no religion. That is, irreligious Catholics were more conservative than irreligious Protestants, who in turn were more conservative than irreligious Jews. It is evident that the religious group into which one is born remains an effective determinant of attitudes even among those who have broken with the group.

In *The Authoritarian Personality*, R. Nevitt Sanford reports that subjects who were religious and reported the religion of their mothers were more prejudiced (ethnocentric) than those who reported a maternal religious affiliation but were irreligious themselves. If the attitudes toward the academic freedom issues are correlated with ethnocentrism, then the findings of this study also indicate that breaking with a familial religious pattern is related to liberalism.

The Authoritarian Personality materials do not discuss differences in prejudice between Catholics and Protestants, and therefore, no comparison is possible as to whether religious attitude clusters continue to affect apostates. The data of the loyalty oath study are too skimpy and the number of cases too small to support any extensive generalizations. They do suggest, however, the necessity for further work on the relationship between past and present group affiliations. Under what conditions do past membership groups continue to determine the frames of reference within which individuals operate? When does breaking with a group result in overreacting against the norms of the group? One might have expected, for example, that apostate Catholics would be more likely than apostate Protestants to reject their past group's norms.

THE PRESS

The newspapers of the San Francisco Bay Area played an important role in the entire loyalty oath dispute. All of them agreed on the policy question—that is, that no Communists be employed by the University. They divided sharply, however, on the question of the loyalty oath. The *San Francisco Chronicle* and the *San Francisco News* both vigorously supported the faculty's opposition to the non-Communist oath with many editorials and favorable news stories. The three Hearst papers in the area, the *San Francisco Examiner*, the *San Francisco Call Bulletin*, and the *Oakland Post-Enquirer*, supported the Regents in their efforts to impose a loyalty oath, and repeatedly denounced the faculty opposition as being Communist inspired. The *Oakland Tribune* took the same position as the Hearst press, but did not print as many editorials and was somewhat more objective in its news presentation. The *Berkeley Gazette* printed many objective news stories and avoided taking an editorial position. These were the papers which were being read by the student body while the controversy was on.

The students were asked which papers they had read in the last two days before being interviewed. The information obtained, shown in Table 6, gives some indication of the influence of the press on the attitudes of the student body.

There appears to have been a definite relation between the editorial opinions and news policy of the various newspapers, and the attitudes of their readers. One could not conclude from this fact alone, however, that

TABLE 6

NEWSPAPER READING HABITS*

Respondent's Attitude to Oath and Policy	Pro-Oath Hearst and Tribune (N:83)	Both Sides Chronicle, Hearst and Tribune (N:90)	Anti-Oath Chronicle, and News (N:147)
PP–PO	34%	19%	12%
PP–AO	18	21	27
AP–PO	11	7	4
AP–AO	30	41	49
Don't know	7	12	8
	100	100	100

* The other combinations contain too few cases to be meaningful.

the newspapers of the Bay area played an important factor in the development of opinion on the oath and hiring issues. It is possible that the readers of the different papers differentiated on other factors, such as class in school or political sympathies. One would have expected that liberals would have been more prone to read a liberal newspaper.

The study permits an approximation of a controlled experiment on the influence of newspapers. The newspapers all agreed on the policy of barring Communists but differed on the oath issue. If the papers had any influence on the students' attitudes, it should have been primarily on the issue of the loyalty oath rather than the policy. The data indicate that readers of the more conservative papers tended to be more conservative on the policy issue of Communist employment than did the readers of the liberal papers. This was at least in part a result of selective purchasing of newspapers, as the readers of the *Chronicle* and the *News* were in general more liberal according to the attitude scale than the readers of, the Hearst papers and the *Tribune*. Holding respondents' positions on the non-Communist hiring policy constant, readers of liberal papers were more opposed to the oath than were readers of the conservative papers. The pro-policy people who read the *Chronical* and the *News* were almost two-to-one against the oath, while the pro-policy stu-

dents reading Hearst and the *Tribune* were almost two-to-one for the oath. Over one-quarter of the students who were in favor of allowing Communists to teach and who read the pro-oath papers were for the oath, as compared to seven per cent of those who read the anti-oath papers. It is interesting that the majority of the students who answered "no opinion" to the oath question also reported that they had not read any newspapers during the two days before being interviewed.

Readers of the anti-oath papers tended to be more liberal than readers of the pro-oath papers. So far it is possible that the relationship indicated between newspaper readership and opinion is spurious—that, in other words, it is basic liberalism or conservatism which is actually being compared, not the influence of the papers. By holding political attitudes, as revealed by the pre-disposition scale, constant, it should be possible to see whether the newspapers had an effect over and above these other related attitudes.

Though the number of cases is unfortunately small, the evidence shows that, regardless of the newspaper they read, persons with similar basic political attitudes did not differ greatly on the question of the right of Communists to teach. In other words, the newspaper read did not have an independent influence on this issue. This is not surprising, since the newspapers were all agreed on the question. On the oath question, however, those reading the *Chronicle* or the *News* tended to be more pro-faculty than those reading the Hearst press or the *Oakland Tribune*, even when basic political attitudes were held constant. The newspapers which maintained a barrage of slanted stories and editorials for the duration of the conflict appear to have had a real effect on student opinion. Liberals who read both sides were similar in their attitudes on the oath to the liberals who only read the anti-oath papers, while conservatives who read both sides were similar to conservatives who read the pro-oath papers. Apparently, when exposed to the cross-pressures of conflicting newspaper reporting and editorial policy, the students were more likely to accept the point of view which fitted in best with their basic political predispositions.

Since this relationship between newspaper policy and attitude appears to contradict the findings in some other public opinion studies, it should be worthwhile to see whether any other factors, other than general political attitude, may account for the differences in the attitudes toward the oath of the readers of the various papers.

The relationship between papers read and attitude toward hiring policy, holding class in college constant, is largely related to the fact that the more liberal students tended to read the *Chronicle*, while the more conservative ones tended to read the Hearst press or the *Oakland Tribune*. It is significant, however, that the relationship between newspaper read and attitude toward the oath was greater than the one between the paper and attitude toward the policy, suggesting again the influence of the newspapers on students' attitudes toward the oath. The same pattern holds true for political party as well. Democrats and Republicans reading the *Chronicle* or the *News* were far more likely to be opposed to the oath than were those who read the papers which supported the Regents.

The data of this study suggest that the newspapers had a great influence in this controversy. They do not prove this conclusively, however, as it is possible that a

selective element other than the factors considered was present and differentiated among the readers of the various papers. Liberal *Chronicle* readers, for example, may have been basically more "liberal" than liberal Hearst readers. A panel study in which the sample's members were interviewed as the controversy proceeded, would have been necessary to evaluate definitely the influence of the newspapers. It is also necessary to remember that all of the interviewees were college students and were exposed to repeated slanted news stories and editorials about a situation which was very close to them. One would expect that they read many of the detailed stories about the University controversy.

SOCIO-ECONOMIC STATUS

Socio-economic status is one of the most important factors differentiating conservatives from liberals in the society as a whole. In general, the lower a person's socio-economic status, however defined, the more liberal that person is likely to be. It is difficult, however, to categorize a university student population in socio-economic terms. Almost all students aspire to some sort of non-manual—and usually high status—position after leaving school. The high cost of a university education means that a disproportionate number of students will come from the well-to-do sectors of the population. There are, however, certain objective and subjective indices of status in this study which

TABLE 7

OCCUPATION OF FATHER

Attitude to Oath and Policy	Professional (N:109)	Farmer (N:34)	Proprietor (N:112)	Business Executive (N:56)	Employed Worker (N:129)
PP–PO	24%	32%	14%	13%	14%
PP–AO	22	21	28	25	19
AP–PO	11	3	2	9	6
AP–AO	34	23	46	41	42
Don't know	9	21	10	12	19
	100	100	100	100	100

TABLE 8

How Financed Through School

Attitude on Issues	Work (N:64)	G.I. Bill (N:85)	G.I. Bill and Work (N:63)	Family and Work (N:97)	G.I. Bill and Family (N:48)	Family (N:93)
PP–PO	8%	18%	19%	18%	21%	26%
PP–AO	23	16	18	30	29	18
AP–PO	13	2	9	6	2	6
AP–AO	42	45	41	38	29	33
Don't know	14	19	13	8	19	17
	100	100	100	100	100	100

should enable us to analyze roughly the effect of this factor in the loyalty oath controversy.

The relation of father's occupation to student attitudes is shown in Table 7. Father's occupation, as such, does not appear to have influenced opinions on the issues. The children of professionals and of farmers were most conservative, although it is hard to see why they should have been more conservative than the children of business proprietors or executives. The lack of consistent differences related to father's occupation does not necessarily mean that socio-economic status was unrelated to these issues, since the occupational categories which were employed did not actually differentiate between high and low non-working class status.

The means that a student uses to finance his way to school should be a better clue to the socio-economic position of his family. Presumably, the more well-to-do the family, the more likely that the student will be supported by his parents. If this assumption is

true, then Table 8 confirms the relationship established between occupational position of parents and attitudes on academic freedom. Those students who relied completely on parental support were more conservative than those going through school by other means. Those working their way through school or completely dependent on the G. I. Bill contributed proportionately more to the anti-Regent group.

These data would seem to suggest that the higher the socio-economic position of the parents, the more likely the student was to be pro-Regent on the question of the oath or policy. This factor was also probably related to general conservatism-liberalism; that is, higher socio-economic status and general societal conservatism go together.

The status aspirations of the students may also have played a role in the development of their attitudes on the oath and other issues. Information was secured on the future job aspirations of the students and also on how much money they expected to

TABLE 9

Future Job Aspirations

Attitude to Oath and Policy	Teacher (N:124)	Engineer (N:41)	Independent Professional (N:78)	Salaried Professional (N:154)
PP–PO	14%	27%	18%	14%
PP–AO	22	17	21	26
AP–PO	4	5	9	7
AP–AO	47	24	40	39
Don't know	13	27	11	14
	100	100	100	100

earn ten years after leaving school. Table 9 appears to indicate that prospective teachers were more opposed to the Regents. . . . Actually, however, this relationship appears to be spurious, at least in part. Almost all of the prospective teachers were majoring in the social sciences, the humanities, or the pure physical sciences. These three disciplines were the most liberal on the issues. If major subject is held constant, there was little difference, especially on the oath issue, between the opinions of prospective teachers in these fields and those intending to go into other occupations.

CAMPUS ACTIVITIES

The students at the University of California are differentially involved in the campus life. Some of them simply attend classes and live with their parents or wives in various parts of the San Francisco Bay Area. Others spend their entire time at the University living in a fraternity house, a student cooperative, or a boarding house. These different out-of-class environments should affect student attitudes and interest in campus affairs. Students living at home should be affected more by general community opinion than those living on or near campus.

The data presented in Table 10 tend to

TABLE 10

RESIDENCE

Attitude to Oath and Policy	Lives with Family (N:195)	Lives with Schoolmates (N:275)
PP–PO	21%	16%
PP–AO	26	21
AP–PO	7	6
AP–AO	32	43
Don't know	14	14
	100	100

confirm this hypothesis. The students who lived within the University community were more prone to support the faculty in the oath controversy than those living with their families at home. One might expect such a finding on the assumption that stu-dents living away from school would have been more likely to be exposed to pro-oath sentiments than those living on campus, while the students spending their entire school life within the school community would have been subject to influence by the faculty, and to the pro-faculty activities organized by various student groups.

Holding constant class in school, political attitudes, and political party affiliation did not invalidate the finding, as in each case students living within the University community were more likely to oppose the oath than either students in the same class or students who had the same political attitudes and party affiliations but lived away from the campus. Certain interesting differences appeared, however, when the two residence groups were compared holding parental socio-economic class constant. The children of "upper-class" fathers (professionals, proprietors, and business executives) who lived with their families were more prone to be against Communists teaching and in favor of the loyalty oath than persons from the same social class background who lived within the school community. There was, however, no difference beween the children of wage workers living at home and those living at home and those living around the school, as Table 11 shows. The original finding regarding the residence groups, therefore, must be qualified in so far as it applies to the entire sample.

Looked at in another way, three of the groups in Table 11 had similar attitudes on both the oath issue and the non-Communist policy. Only one group, the children of persons with high socio-economic status who "live with the family," was deviant. This finding may be related to a number of alternative hypotheses, none of which can be evaluated on the basis of the data. It may be possible that the community as a whole differed along socio-economic lines on the communist teacher or loyalty oath issues. The differences between the two groups of students living with their families may, therefore, have reflected exposure to different community reference groups. While

TABLE 11

RESIDENCE AND OCCUPATION OF PARENTS

Communists May Teach	UPPER CLASS		WAGE EARNERS	
	Lives with Family (N:122)	Lives with Schoolmates (N:188)	Lives with Family (N:64)	Lives with Schoolmates (N:64)
Yes	37%	57%	55%	55%
No	59	41	36	40
Don't know	4	2	9	5
	100	100	100	100
Oath				
Approve	34%	22%	22%	23%
Disapprove	60	67	64	65
Don't know	6	11	14	12
	100	100	100	100

there is no evidence concerning attitudes among the people of California, it is extremely dubious that a large proportion of persons on any socio-economic level was in favor of Communists being allowed to teach; the hypothesis that different social class attitudes as such were reflected in the student body does not satisfactorily explain the differences.

A second possible hypothesis is that the classification of "upper class" was too broad, and that the students living at home with their families actually belonged to a different layer of the "upper class" than those living on campus. This hypothesis, also, does not appear likely in terms of other related data. It is true, however, that those living at home differed from those in school according to home community. Those living at school came disproportionately from the smaller cities and towns of California, although many of them were from Los Angeles and from outside of the State. The variable of community of origin did not, however, differentiate students on the issue.

There is a third hypothesis, more plausible on the basis of impressionistic evidence, which assumes that an off-campus general community and a campus community constituted two alternative reference groups toward which students could orient themselves. There is evidence that off-campus

community opinion was overwhelmingly against Communists teaching and generally unsympathetic to the faculty's position on the oath, while the campus opinion, shaped by the faculty's stand, was opposed to the loyalty oath. Moreover, a majority of students supported the right of Communists to teach.

Faced with this conflict between the two reference groups, "working-class" students, regardless of where they lived, and "upper-class" students living on the campus took the liberal position on both questions, thereby disproportionately orienting toward the campus community as the effective positive reference group on this question. The "upper-class" students living at home, however, disproportionately reacted toward off-campus opinion. This latter group was least exposed to the "climate of opinion" dominant on campus, and had least reason for taking their cues from the faculty, whose status in the non-academic community at large is not high compared with other more conservative authorities. For all of the workers' sons, including those who lived off campus, the university community was a locus and vehicle for their mobility aspirations and striving; as part of the total process of rising, they tended to assimilate the attitudes and orientations of the college community, and especially of its leaders.

This hypothesis calls for direct evidence on the effective use of positive and negative reference groups by different groups of students, and especially points up the need for additional research on the comparative influence of multiple-reference groups operating at cross-purposes. The data here suggest that the social status of different reference groups, as compared with that of the subjects being analyzed, may be one of the principal variables determining which reference group will prevail in a cross-pressure situation.

PERCEPTION OF THE SITUATION

W. I. Thomas many years ago laid down the theorem: "If men define situations as real, they are real in their consequences." It has long been apparent that perception of an external phenomenon is largely determined by the frame of reference—the supplied context—within which it is perceived. Both perception and attitude formation are heavily affected by the nature of the meanings, the frame of reference, the predispositions that individuals bring to a situation. In the controversy over the loyalty oath and the issue of Communists teaching, one would expect that people not only differed in their opinions on the issues but also in their awareness of the presence of Communists. It is to be expected that persons who feared Communists most would "see" more Communists in their environment than would those who disparaged the Communist threat.

The data set forth in Table 12 tend to confirm this hypothesis. The students who supported the oath and the Regents' policy believed that there were many more Communists in the student body than did the students who were opposed to both. Over two-fifths of the pro-Regents students thought that there were over five hundred Communist students on the campus, as compared with less than a quarter of the anti-policy anti-oath group making a similar estimate. Here one can see the operation of a perceptual self-confirming hypothesis. Those fearful of Communism saw the justi-

TABLE 12

HOW MANY STUDENTS DO YOU THINK ARE COMMUNISTS?

	Pro-Policy Pro-Oath (N:81)	Pro-Policy Anti-Oath (N:106)	Anti-Policy Anti-Oath (N:179)
Don't know	27%	18%	14%
Under 50	7	17	17
51–500	25	30	46
501 and over	41	26	23
	100	100	100

fication for such fears in their social environment, while those who were not as fearful did not see the same picture of what should have been an objective fact—the number of Communists in the student body. The question, of course, was actually a projective question; no student, unless he were a member of the Communist Party, would have had accurate information on the number of Communists on the campus. The answers, therefore, give us some insights as to the sentiments and attitudes that different groups of students brought to the situation, including perhaps varying definitions of a "Communist." Those most fearful of the Communists may have operated under broader definitions.

The variation in the students' perception of the situation also carried over to the knowledge of other facts. Some students, for example, did not know that the University had a policy barring Communists from employment. The figures are given in Table 13. Note that the supporters of the oath requirement include a large minority who, in the spring of 1950, one year after the oath controversy started and ten years

TABLE 13

UNIVERSITY POLICY ON COMMUNIST PARTY MEMBERS

	Pro-Policy Pro-Oath (N:86)	Pro-Policy Anti-Oath (N:107)	Anti-Policy Anti-Oath (N:183)
Bars Communists	77%	87%	87%
Don't know or Wrong	23	13	13
	100	100	100

after the policy was established did not know that the University bars Communists from employment. This finding is probably related to the data on the perception of Communists presented earlier. Not only do the pro-Regents students see more Communists than do other people, but they are less aware of restriction on them. In their minds the threat is great—and apparently also unchallenged.

Perceptual framework can also be analyzed from the point of view of the controversy itself. One would expect that the opposing groups of students would differ in their conception of the faculty's and public's attitude on the oath as well as on their general information on the subject. The students were asked what per cent of the faculty they thought favored the oath. Almost all the students recognized that the majority of the professors were opposed to the oath, but, as Table 14 shows, there were substantial differences in the proportions that different groups believed supported it.

The dominant view among the students was that the public supported the oath while the faculty opposed it. The pro-oath group, however, believed that a larger group of faculty members supported the oath than did the anti-oath students. The same pattern was true of estimates of the public's position; more pro-Regent than anti-Regent students believed that the public was in favor of the oath. The most interesting set of responses to these questions were the "don't knows" and those who said that the public was uninterested in the question. In this case, "don't know" and "no interest" were meaningful answers. Almost twice as many pro-oath students (17 per cent) as anti-oath students (9 per cent) said that they did not know what proportion of the faculty favored the oath. On the other hand, there were more "don't knows" among the anti-oath students (11 per cent) than among the pro-oath students (7 per cent) when it came to the question of the public's opinion about the oath. Over one-quarter of the anti-oath, anti-policy students also said that they thought the public was uninterested in the oath question.

With regard to the attitudes dominant in the two major communities of reference, disproportionate numbers in both the pro- and anti-oath groups apparently held a point of view which supported or at least did not conflict with their own position. This disproportionate ignorance and distortion of the facts is understandable in the light of the known connections between attitudes and perception. "Because perception is functionally selective, and because beliefs and attitudes play a role in determining the nature of this selectivity, new data physically available to an individual but contradictory to his beliefs and attitudes *may not even be perceived*." Moreover, "The lack of relevant facts and the frequent conflicting facts provided for us by different authorities frequently operate so as to force the creation or invention of facts that may bear no real relation to the external situation. Those pressures which work toward the formation of beliefs work in the absence of adequate data and may force the emergence of facts that support and are congruent with the beliefs."

It is not known how accessible or well

TABLE 14

WHAT PER CENT OF THE FACULTY FAVOR THE OATH?

	Pro-Policy Pro-Oath (N:86)	Pro-Policy Anti-Oath (N:108)	Anti-Policy Anti-Oath (N:183)
Don't know	17%	7%	9%
Under 1%	6	20	13
1–10%	18	30	36
10–25%	21	26	25
25–50%	23	14	10
Majority	18	3	7
	100	100	100

WHAT DO YOU THINK THE PUBLIC THINKS OF THE OATH?

	(N:85)	(N:108)	(N:183)
Don't know	7%	5%	11%
Support	51	30	44
Opposed	19	34	15
Not interested	16	23	27
Split	7	8	3
	100	100	100

disseminated were the facts regarding the attitudes held by different groups in both the campus and general communities, nor do we know the nature of the channels through which this information was communicated. These factors would have had some bearing on the actual determinants of ignorance or incorrect knowledge among the students. Moreover, within each of the two opposing groups of students, there were undoubtedly those who used the community with which it differed as a negative reference group, and others who shared their attitudes but who were not reacting against any collectively held sentiments which they could identify. Perhaps the former were more aware of the attitudes held in their negative reference group, while it was the latter, who simply did not *see* the difference in group attitudes that did exist, who appear in the tables as "don't knows" or as holding incorrect views regarding the attitudes of other groups.

The present data, however, do not permit us to do more than speculate in these directions. What can be said is that the majority of anti-oath students refused to recognize that the public was actually against them, while over one-third of the pro-oath students either regarded the faculty as on their side or said that they did not know what the faculty thought. Given the fact that the faculty repeatedly, by almost unanimous votes, voiced its opposition to the oath, it is significant that fifty-six per cent of the pro-oath students either believed that over a quarter of the faculty supported the oath, or did not know the faculty's point of view. It seems clear that attitudes entered into and distorted the perception of some proportion of each of the major groups of students in directions that would tend to support attitudes already held.

CONCLUSIONS

This study indicates anew that opinion formation tends in large part to be a product of the activation of previous experiences and attitudes. Students at the University of California reacted to a crisis situation largely according to their group affiliations and other background characteristics. It would have been worth while to have had a panel study of opinion formation on the loyalty oath to see how this activation took place. The role of the University community, specific meaningful group affiliations, and the press, could have best been analyzed by repeated interviews with a panel as different events occurred.

The "deviant cases," those students who behave different from the majority of those with the same characteristics as themselves, suggest that deviation in behavior is a result of being exposed to cross-pressures. Liberal students who read pro-oath newspapers were more likely to support the oath requirement than those reading a paper consistent with their basic political attitudes. Students who were in favor of barring Communists from University employment but who read anti-oath papers were more prone to oppose the oath. Conservative students who resided within the University community were exposed to the majority opinion of the student body against the oath and were, therefore, more likely to be liberal on the academic freedom issues than their co-thinkers politically who were not as exposed to campus opinion. Catholic graduate students were probably exposed to pressure from the liberal graduate student body and were less favorable to restrictions on Communists than their undergraduate co-religionists.

Another effect of cross-pressures on students exposed to conflicting norms or expectations appears to have been a relatively high level of ignorance regarding the issues and their background. Ignorance here may have been serving the function of reducing the clarity, and thus the intensity, of the conflict; for example, this may have accounted for the greater lack of knowledge among the pro- than among the anti-Regents students. Cross-pressures not only directly affected the distribution of attitudes and the quantity and accuracy of information among different groups and categories of students, but also apparently influenced their active behavior in the controversy. In every category, those students who were against the Regents, but who had characteristics or were exposed to pressures which made for pro-Regents attitudes, were less likely to sign an anti-oath petition than those with homogeneous anti-Regent characteristics.

It is probably impossible to generalize from an analysis of the internal evidence available within one context the weight that any given item will have in a different cross-pressure situation. The two studies of student opinion on the Berkeley and Los Angeles campuses of the University of California suggest that a much larger proportion of the students at U. C. L. A. supported the position of the Regents in requiring a non-Communist loyalty oath. It is extremely doubtful that the differences between the two campuses were a result of differing proportions of students in the categories that affected opinion on this issue. For example, there is no reason to believe that there were more conservatives or Catholics at Los Angeles. In fact, the past history of student political organization would suggest that, if anything, the U. C. L. A. campus is on the whole more liberal than Berkeley. As was indicated earlier, the differential activities of the two faculties, and the unanimous pro-Regents stand of the Los Angeles newspapers, may have meant that the variables of University community influence and press influence may have had different weights in the two situations.

These differences point up a problem that arises in many opinion studies. We know, for example, that the proportion of workers or Catholics who are Democrats varies considerably from community to community, though in most cases these variables contribute to some degree to a Democratic predisposition. The analysis of why these same factors have different weights in different contexts must involve a study of the functional interrelationships among the variables which are handled in opinion research. Most such researches, including this one, necessarily handle these various factors atomistically. One cannot determine from survey data alone the ramifications for the rest of the system of changes in any one or several factors. This suggests the necessity for comparative institutional research which would attempt to locate those aspects of the social structure that result in the same nominal variable having quite different subjective meanings and objective weights in different contexts.

The evidence presented in this paper suggests that attitudes toward academic freedom are related to the same variables which influence attitude formation in other areas of life. Though supporters of civil liberties may hope that the belief in the rights of unpopular and even dangerous minorities is shared by persons regardless of personal political belief, the evidence does not warrant maintaining that hope. In general, those individuals who are characterized by the factors which make for conservatism, or who have conservative beliefs are opposed to the civil and academic rights of Communists. Those students who stand lower in socio-economic or ethnic group status, or who are liberals politically, tend to defend the rights of Communists.

It is possible, of course, to regard these patterns from another perspective. Historically, most violations of civil and academic rights in American society have been directed against liberals, leftists, trade unions, and members of minority groups. With the exception of the restrictions on Fascists during the last war, persons who are characterized by being well-to-do, having no interest in the labor movement, conservatives, white Protestants, Republicans, have not had to fear the possibility of social discrimination, loss of economic opportunities, or imprisonment as a result of their political opinions or group characteristics. American liberals, Jews, Negroes, Orientals, trade-union supporters, even though opposed to the Communist Party and the Soviet Union, may be more prone to consider the implications of any restrictions, even those directed against a totalitarian political party, as setting dangerous precedents which may afterward react against themselves. The individual members of these groups may not consciously analyze these long-term implications, but the historic experiences of their groups may have conditioned them to react in this way.

In addition to these general factors, the legal position of the Communist Party has become a political football in American politics. Conservatives and Republicans are attempting to use the widespread American antagonism towards the Communist Party against the politics of the Democrats, liberals, and Socialists. The non-Communist left-of-center groups, therefore, have painful and recent evidence for fearing that attacks on the Communist Party may be followed by attacks on themselves.

Catholics, though members of a minority group which has frequently been persecuted in this country, belong to a church which has made anti-Communism one of its principal activities. Discrimination and persecution of Roman Catholics in Communist-controlled countries has been severe, and Catholics, therefore, may be expected to react more strongly against Communists.

In interpreting the data of this study, it is necessary to recognize the danger of generalizing these findings beyond a student population. Students operating within the intellectual atmosphere of the university may react in more rational ways than the general population. Student members of underprivileged groups may, for example, be more inclined to make rational identifications between their own group and other groups under attack, an identification which underprivileged groups outside the campus may not make.

TEST-TUBE FOR PUBLIC OPINION:
A RURAL COMMUNITY

RICHARD L. SCHANCK

In 1934 the writer described the history of a movement in a rural comunity which had as its aim the creation of a united front on the part of the community in favor of establishing a new consolidated school within the community limits. The aim was achieved. Since that time, however, a complete reorganization of the opinion of the community has permitted erection of the school in another community. The history of the movement demonstrates the psychology behind the process of reorganizing publics already formed.

As early as 1928 a study of the incipient movement in public opinion was made in the rural community mentioned. At the outset of this movement, it was obvious that a great many people had attitudes

From the *Public Opinion Quarterly*, Vol. 2, No. 1, January 1938, pp. 90-95. Reprinted by permission of the author and publisher.

concerning the local school and what ought to be done in regard to its perpetuation or abandonment. There were a certain number of people who had no attitude whatever; many of these individuals had no children. This organized opinion represented the discrete, personal, and unique opinions of a great many individuals. It was, however, the stuff from which public opinion grew.

The writer attempted to get these individuals to express their opinion upon an attitude scale. The scale seemed to allow for a possible reflection of every attitude heard in community discussion of public policy. The steps in the attitude scale were as follows:

1. Superiority of Elm Hollow over other sites is very great, and there is almost nothing to be said for the others.

2. Elm Hollow is superior in general, but there is much to be said for other sites.

3. Elm Hollow has equal merit with other sites.

4. Other sites are superior in general, but there is much to be said for Elm Hollow.

5. Superiority of other sites is very great, and there is almost nothing to be said in favor of Elm Hollow.

A sample of the attitudes of community members on this question in the year 1928 is shown in Table I.

TABLE I

ATTITUDE TOWARD THE CONSOLIDATED SCHOOL

	No.	%
1. Elm Hollow only	12	15
2. Elm Hollow first	41	62
3. Both equal	15	18
4. Other site first	1	1
5. Other site only	2	2
6. Refused to check	1	1

The chief rival for the school was a neighboring community, Green View. Analysis of the distribution obtained shows that there were many neutral individuals, people with no preference for one site or the other. Many individuals checked the scale only under pressure. The investigator was convinced that only a small proportion of the community was vitally concerned with the question, and most of these individuals were among the 15 per cent of extremists. Obviously, there is no one in a rural community who serves the function performed by the investigator in this instance. He persuaded people to funnel their attitudes into an issue, and had no motivation to influence their choice.

MANIPULATORS OF PUBLIC OPINION

Of the extremists, three or four individuals seemed to be very interested in this question. One of these individuals was the local druggist; a large part of the book business came from school children and he was concerned about a possible change in location. Another individual was a former school-board member; it was claimed that his interest in the question was motivated by a quarrel with the local school superintendent. A third individual was the local gasoline service station operator; he felt that a consolidated school would bring a good fuel trade with the school buses. A fourth interested individual was a carpenter and operator of a woodworking establishment interested in making school desks. All of these individuals were fluent talkers and expressive personalities. For a period of three years, their propaganda was heard throughout the village. They were not successful. People's attitudes of apathy, indifference, slight interest, and complete disinterest continued. Propaganda is not necessarily successful.

During the third year of this study, an extraordinary event occurred. The Department of Education condemned the local schoolhouse. This brought everybody who paid taxes into a vital relationship to this problem. They could be apathetic about a consolidated school as long as the old one worked, but now a new one was to be built whether they wanted it or not. The only questions at issue were what kind of school should be built and where it should be located.

PAST PROPAGANDA BECOMES EFFECTIVE

Instead of securing a favorable solution to this problem, such as a rapprochement with the other community or the formation of a fact-finding committee to study the best location, etc., this new crisis divided the two communities into armed camps. When the Elm Hollow people were re-checked in 1932 regarding this question, the distribution shown in Table II was obtained.

TABLE II

ATTITUDE TOWARD THE CONSOLIDATED SCHOOL (1932)

	No.	%
1. Elm Hollow only	63	77
2. Elm Hollow first	13	16
3. Both equal	5	6
4. Other site first	0	—
5. Other site only	1	1

When these results are compared with those in Table I it will be seen that the great majority now regard Elm Hollow as the *only* choice whereas formerly the majority merely voted for Elm Hollow as first choice. In other words, the attitudes of the community members had become much more extreme in one direction. Moreover, no one complained about violence being done to his feelings when asked to indicate his opinion on the scale.

Public opinion in the community is not necessarily a continuous development. It moves by jumps. There are evidently critical points in the social relationships of the community which, if crystallized, lead to complete qualitative changes. Yet this fact should not obscure the nature of the developments. Why did this crisis lead to a united front of the community as desired by the few extremists, when their propaganda alone could not have this effect? The writer believed: (1) The biased individuals who are vocal tend to create an illusion regarding community opinion that may or may not correspond with the real facts. The majority of individuals of the community may have no reason for taking a stand on the issue. Yet the continuous advocacy of a position by a minority leads them to a belief

that this stand may be fairly universal in their group. (2) A feeling of community loyalty exists that causes many individuals to feel that if they must take a stand they should espouse the opinion held by the majority of their group.

The years of the vested interests were not wasted. In fact the time interval in which they had no results may have been psychologically a contributory source of their eventual success. It gave the propaganda an impression of long standing. The community members became habituated to it as a part of the community pattern. This did two things: (1) Whereas many individuals were perfectly well aware of the vested interest of the extremists in the first years of this movement, after once recognizing the interest, habituation robbed it of its effect. Where in the early days they would have said, "Mr. X is blowing his own horn," they now said, "The community is solidly for this proposition." (2) The impression that a "great many" individuals are for the proposition became "everybody" is for it.

Once the crisis was past and a fully developed united-front opinion formed, the control of recalcitrant members by the social situation was interesting to watch. Almost no a-typicality was permitted. One family which had been sending its boy to high school in the next town for personal reasons, and which until now had felt no unpleasant consequences, was so much the center of gossip that the boy came back to the local school. A few tough-minded individuals refused to be intimidated, but they were very few as the distribution shows.[1]

Moreover, the real possibility of a new

---

[1] The writer with F. H. Allport has demonstrated the fact that complete universality is seldom found for either opinion or attitudes in even the most institutional of situations. See the writer's "The Community and Its Groups and Institutions," *Psychological Monographs*, 1932, and F. H. Allport's "The J-shaped Distribution," *Journal of Social Psychology*; also Chapter VII in *Psychology at Work*, Achilles ed. 1932, McGraw-Hill, by F. H. Allport with the cooperation of the writer and M. C. Dickens. The psychology back of such a-typicality is an interesting but irrelevant problem to the point at issue here.

school had led to the organization of a like community spirit in Green View. Actual fist fights took place between citizens of the two communities. Emotions ran high, and argument was violent. It was interesting to see how much of the argument had been originally invented in the earlier years by the extremists who had a vested interest in the problem.

Rivalry of the two communities on this issue continued for three years. Increasingly, the situation was putting one individual on the spot. That individual was a town supervisor of a township which included both communities. The rivalries were reaching a heat where it looked as if carrying one town meant necessarily losing the other. This individual went to work on the problem and succeeded in reorganizing the opinion of Elm Hollow completely.

REORGANIZATION OF A UNITED FRONT

The first step in the reorganization of this community opinion was corruption of the vested interest in the prevailing opinion. The politician came into Elm Hollow quietly. He sought out the druggist and pointed out to him the errors of his ways. True, he might be losing the sale of books. But the supervisor had intended to support him for township clerk for a long time. There was five times the salary in that office as in a few schoolbooks. He found the garage owner. Had he considered the possibility of opening an agency for school buses and selling the buses for the new school? The carpenter and owner of the woodworking factory was told that he was to become collector of school taxes. The fourth individual was ignored. A fifth individual was brought into the picture. A local Elm Hollow man had the authority to call a meeting on the school question. The politician gave him $50 to call it not at Elm Hollow but at Green View.

The second step was destruction of the feeling of universality regarding community opinion. Few people of Elm Hollow attended the meeting. They expected that the druggist, carpenter, etc., would protect the community interest, but nobody rose to defend the Elm Hollow opinion. The few individuals who attended under such circumstances and under pressure from the audience voted for union at Green View. When Elm Hollow awoke the next morning, they found themselves part of a consolidated school district which was to have a school at Green View. A few individuals were indignant. As the day went on, they found however, that there were few reasonable exponents in favor of retrying the case. Soon people began to laugh. Within a week's time, they had assumed the new opinion as reflecting the will of the community.

This technique would, of course, not work where there were genuine interests on the part of each individual in the program. But where public opinion is motivated in many individuals by (1) the impression of universality, (2) conformity to the apparent majority or illusion of the majority, (3) an illusion created by a vocal minority, such reorganization is possible.

By and large, it seems to the writer that community opinion is generally of this type. There seem to be very few issues in the rural communities with which the writer has become familiar over a long period of years in which more than a minority have an active interest. And yet the same ability to organize this opinion into a social situation compelling upon individual members often exists. Undoubtedly there may be circumstances where the issue is based upon stronger and more enduring motives. If so, the course of development and the possibilities of control may follow different principles.

THE BOSS AND THE VOTE:
A CASE STUDY IN CITY POLITICS

JEROME S. BRUNER AND SHELDON J. KORCHIN

On Tuesday, November 6, 1945, Boston went to the polls to elect a mayor. On Wednesday morning, after the election returns had been duly made official, the Boston *Herald* had this to say: "Regardless of the outcome, the election was one of the most unsatisfactory in the history of the city. There were too many candidates. The average ability of the six [candidates] was probably lower than in any previous contest. The people were so disheartened that many of them decided to register their disgust by staying away from the polls. They wondered whether it would make any difference to Boston whether this or that man came out on top." The most hopeful thing that the *Herald*'s editorialist could dredge up from the stock in trade of his profession was the remark that "the people of cities which have been in just as bad a mess [as Boston] have finally asserted themselves and rescued their cities from stagnation, confiscatory taxes, and gross waste."

The Boston *Herald*, of course, is a Republican paper, and the winner was a Democrat—if Curley, the new mayor, can be thus easily labeled by party designation. The Boston election, nevertheless, was almost as confused a spectacle as the *Herald*'s editorialist would have it.

Elements of confusion which could pro-mote indecision among voters abounded. Save for one candidate, Curley, the ability and records of the men running for office remained obscure. Curley's record was known. It had been a stormy one, marked by indictments, feuds, charges, and countercharges during his career as Mayor of the City of Boston, Governor of the Commonwealth of Massachusetts, and United States Representative of the Eleventh District of Massachusetts. For a great many voters the sole issue was Curley *versus* the field. But the "field" was at once unstructured politically and split. Opposing Curley were five candidates, two of them major threats, three of them running more for the sake of getting their names before the electorate than for any considered hope of election to office.

John Kerrigan, the Acting Mayor of the City of Boston for the year and a half between Maurice Tobin's resignation to assume the Governorship and Election Day, was a young man in his middle thirties. His rise to power had been that adventitious kind familiar enough in American city politics. Prior to induction into the Army in 1942, he had been a City Councilman and one of the lieutenants in Maurice Tobin's political train. Returning from the Army and re-entering the City Council in 1943,

From the *Public Opinion Quarterly*, 1946, 1-23. Reprinted by permission of the authors and the publisher.

he had with Tobin's backing become President of the Council, a post which is determined by the Council and not by the voters. Governor Tobin, it is said, had named Kerrigan Acting Mayor in the hope that he would be able to retain control of the Boston situation. Kerrigan's short term, though marked by no scandals, had been at the very least uninspired. The chronic problems of the city remained chronic problems during his brief tenure—a tax rate of $42.50, an impossible traffic situation, a desperately acute housing shortage, increasing obsolescence of port facilities, etc. So starved was Kerrigan for the raw material out of which to fashion boasts during his campaign that he had recourse to his achievement of cutting the cost of snow removal by 20 percent.

John Reilly, the second major opponent of Curley and also young, was relatively unknown to the city save for the dubious distinction of having been the Fire Commissioner of the city at the time of the tragic Coconut Grove disaster. The main strength in Reilly's bid for office was the support of Tobin's machine, which allegedly had been thrown behind him as a more pliable candidate when Kerrigan and Tobin had a falling out shortly before the beginning of the campaign.

The other candidates can be dismissed with brief comment. Sawtelle, virtually unknown in the city's public life, had held minor office and had been a business man, a fact which he was fond of pointing out in his campaign speeches. Veteran political writers on the city's newspapers remarked that the only substance in his political stock was his Italian background, which presumably might earn him a fairly heavy vote in Boston's Italian districts, notably the North End.[1] Feeney, who came along for the

political ride, ran what he called a "poor man's campaign" based almost exclusively on sound truck addresses around the city. Minor office-holder in the city, Feeney, like Sawtelle, helped to split the opposition vote against Curley. Finally there was Joseph Lee, Boston Brahmin and perpetual candidate for office, who, it was conceded by all who knew him, was honest, tremendously sincere, but both inept politically and without broad support in either the non-Yankee or Yankee populations of the city.

DIVIDED OPPOSITION

With such a field of candidates, it was obviously impossible for a solid anti-Curley vote to develop. We had occasion to remark to Curley during the campaign that he himself could not have planned a better campaign for gaining office than the one which was being waged against him, that if his sole opponent had been "one good Irishman" his chances of election would have been nil. Curley, who is if nothing else a realist, agreed readily.

The confusion bred by the uninspired slate of candidates had several unexpected political consequences. Most symptomatic of these, perhaps, was the negative and passive role into which the Political Action Committee of the CIO was forced. Predominantly anti-Curley, in the end it took no stand on mayoral candidates, on the ground that there was nobody really worth backing. Its efforts were concentrated on School Committee candidates. The same kind of stymie seemed to have overtaken other non-partisan groups in the city.

Still another consequence of the confused opposition to Curley was reflected in the behavior of the Boston press. The *Globe* had not taken sides in a city election for the last half-century. But both the *Herald* and the *Traveller,* which normally might back one candidate (preferably a Republican), were forced into taking a position of "a curse on all your houses." The *Herald*'s brilliant political cartoonist, Dahl, reflected the position of his paper with a cartoon the day

[1] For a picture of the degree of political tension in this critical area of Boston, the reader is referred to J. S. Bruner and J. Sayre, "Radio Listening in an Italian Community," *Public Opinion Quarterly,* 1941, 5, pp. 640-655, and J. Sayre Smith, "Broadcasting for Marginal Americans," *Public Opinion Quarterly,* 1942, 6, 588-603.

before election labelled "Here Come the Clowns," based on a story in the preceding day's paper: "Mayoralty candidates to be in on Admiral Halsey celebration (News item)." The cartoon depicts eight romping clowns in such assorted zaney activities as hand springing, squirting water in each other's ears, and so on. They dance down the street in advance of a military band, with John Citizen of Boston standing on the sidelines looking distinctly unhappy.

Other possible political symbols which might have guided voters were equally blurred. The ballot on which the names of the candidates appeared, for example, did not designate party affiliation, so that even if there had been a concerted effort to throw Republican and Democratic support behind a single "fusion" candidate, it might not have succeeded because of lack of information on the part of Boston's voters as to backing. What actually happened was that both Reilly *and* Kerrigan were receiving the support of both Democratic *and* Republican leaders. And so was Curley. Reilly, perhaps, had the strongest Republican backing, although it appeared late in the campaign, as witnessed by twenty thousand letters sent out the week before election by a prominent group of Republicans in his support. But if Reilly had the strongest Republican backing, then Kerrigan was stronger with the anti-Curley Democrats, and again the field was split.

NATURE OF THE CAMPAIGN

The nature of the campaign itself reflected the plight of the opposition candidates. Curley, who incidentally was by far the most imposing radio personality, decided at the outset not to indulge in personalities (he certainly had nothing to gain thereby). His campaign was based almost solely on two related appeals: Curley gets things done; Curley has experience. From the beginning the Curley bid was supported by all the paraphernalia of big city electioneering —radio talks, city-wide rallies, and extremely efficient face-to-face work in the

wards carried out by the well-trained Curley machine. Veteran observers were struck by the "objectivity" of the Curley speeches. Facts and figures abounded. Audiences were told what Curley had spent for schools, hospitals, playgrounds, etc., during his regime and how much had been spent by his successors since the days when Curley was in City Hall.

Curley's opponents seemed unable to decide how to conduct their campaigns. One obvious approach might have been an attack on Curley's record—he was at the very moment of the campaign under federal indictment for a charge of fraud in connection with alleged soliciting of war contracts in Washington. But for reasons which will never be clear, the anti-Curley attacks never seemed to grow to any proportion. Instead, both Reilly and Kerrigan picked up the gauntlet that Curley had thrown down and tried to justify themselves in terms of "getting things done" and experience, a situation giving rise to such dubious blossoms of oratory as Kerrigan's boast about his snow-removal record.

But most striking of all was the defensive effort of the opposition candidates to garner unto themselves the distinction of being the leading contender in the race against Curley. As Reilly put it in one of his speeches, "I am the man Curley has to watch." Curley's backers, in consequence, played an interesting game of manipulation during the race. When Kerrigan appeared to be getting too strong, several known members of the Curley entourage went out and talked publicly about placing bets on Reilly to make it seem as if he were the man most feared. When Reilly's chances began to brighten with added Republican support, Curley men concentrated on rumors that Kerrigan was the man to watch.[2]

For good measure Reilly and Kerrigan resorted to being photographed with mother and/or wife in an appeal to the feminine vote, and to raising the vast issues of housing, traffic, and port facilities without stat-

[2] The testimony of one of Curley's lieutenants.

ing any satisfactory program for solving these problems.[3]

To anybody wise in the ways of Boston politics, Curley looked like a sure winner against such a motley opposition. The result was that men who for professional or business reasons had to be on the "in" were forced to help Curley with contributions in order to be on the safe side. William E. Mullins, one of the wiser veteran writers on Boston city politics, wrote in the *Herald* the day before election, "All in all, this has been the most fruitful campaign Curley has ever conducted. There is plenty of money around, and from the start the wealthy contributors have been standing in line, influenced no doubt by the common opinion that he is home this time . . ." When reports of contributions and campaign expenditures were filed one month after election with the office of the City Clerk, contributions to the Curley cause amounted to $104,847 as compared to $80,987 for Kerrigan, the runner-up.

It was in this setting that, two weeks before election, the authors had an opportunity to conduct a city-wide poll of Boston's voters.

THE POLL, THE SAMPLE, AND THE METHOD

The pre-election survey of opinion which was conducted followed conventional lines. The size of the sample was set at 750 for various and arbitrary reasons.[4]

[3] A systematic presentation of campaign propaganda in a city election and its effectiveness in the Boston election appears in J. S. Bruner and J. Young, "Campaign Appeals in the Press and Voting Ideology in a City Election" (in preparation).

[4] Although a sample of this size guarantees confidence limits of 7.5 percent at the probability level of .95 as compared, say, with confidence limits at the same p level of 9 percent for five hundred cases and 6 percent for 1000 cases, it was felt that, both for purposes of general prediction and in order to afford enough cases for breakdown purposes, 750 cases would prove sufficient. See Wilks' graphic functions in S. S. Wilks, "Confidence limits and critical differences between percentages," *Public Opinion Quarterly*, 1940, *4*, 332-338.

The sample was controlled on four variables: region, age, sex and economic status. For regional controls, the city was divided into fifteen districts corresponding roughly to the twenty-two wards of Boston. The discrepancy between the number of wards and our districts comes from the fact that ours were the city's health and welfare districts, some of which combined two wards. For each of the fifteen areas, an age-sex distribution was worked out, and quotas assigned interviewers accordingly. In addition to age-sex quotas, interviewers were also instructed to obtain a set proportion of socio-economically above average, and below average individuals. For assignment of economic quotas in each area, the fifteen districts of the city were divided into three groups of five districts each based upon the percent of rent under twenty-five dollars per month in the area, as recorded in the 1940 Census figures.[5]

Socio-economic status quotas within wealthy, middle, and poor districts were based upon revisions of figures used by the National Opinion Research Center in setting national socio-economic quotas: 20 percent "above average," 55 percent "average," and 25 percent "below average." Using the same definitions of respondents in the three classes as used by N.O.R.C.,[6] our quotas were set as follows: in wealthy areas, 31 percent above average, 55 percent average, and 14 percent below average; in middle-class areas, 9 percent above average, 66 percent average, and 25 percent below average; in poor areas, 5 percent above average, 55 percent average, and 36 percent below average. The percentage of respondents in-

[5] "Wealthy" districts, 5.6-10.2%; "middle-class" districts, 25. 2-15.2%; "poor" districts, 69.6-81.4%. For a fuller account, see *The People of Boston and its Fifteen Health and Welfare Areas*, Greater Boston Community Council Research Bureau, 1944.

[6] Cf. Williams, D., Basic instructions for interviewers, *Public Opinion Quarterly*, 1942, *6*, 635ff., for a fuller description of the criteria used by N.O.R.C. for defining these socio-economic classes. Our "above average" corresponds to N.O.R.C.'s A and B, "average" is C, "below average" D.

terviewed in each district was, of course, determined by the representation of that district in the total population of Boston. The same can be said of the proportions of men and women and various age groups interviewed. In short, then, our sample can be said to be representative of Boston with respect to district, age, sex, and economic status.

Personal interviewing was conducted between Saturday, October 27, and Tuesday, October 30, 1945, by a staff of twenty interviewers recruited from among the staffs of national polling organizations and from among senior and graduate social science students at Harvard University and Wellesley College. The questionnaire, containing eighteen items, was introduced under the name of the "New England Research Council" with the following prefatory remarks by interviewers. "My name is ———. I am representing the New England Research Council, and we are doing a public opinion poll to find how people in Boston feel about the election for Mayor that is coming up in a week or so. We are interested in getting your opinion on the election. I don't want to know your name, we are just interested in people in general. I have some questions here I'd like to ask you."

WHO VOTED FOR WHOM

The scientific value of public opinion polls does not lie in the prediction of election results, but rather in the analysis of the motivation and structure of political behavior. Yet, when one is treating aspects of electoral behavior which cannot be validated directly against election statistics, it is comforting to have a means of checking at least the predictive accuracy of one's sample. As Table 1 indicates, the predictive value of this particular sample was considerable.

These are the bare facts. James Michael Curley, then under Federal indictment for using the mails to defraud, and since convicted, polled 111,868 votes as compared with his closest rival, who polled 60,202. Not only did Curley defeat Kerrigan and

TABLE 1

PREDICTED AND OBTAINED VOTE

Candidate	Percentage of Vote Obtained	Percentage of Vote Predicted
Curley	45.7	47.8
Kerrigan	24.7	29.6
Reilly	18.7	14.5
Sawtelle	5.3	5.4
Lee	4.2	2.4
Feeney	1.4	.3
Total	100.0	100.0

Reilly, but he actually polled more votes than the two of them combined. What is the psychological appeal of political professionals like Curley? Or to put it another way, what is there about Boston, a more or less typical big city, which makes it possible for a seventy-one-year-old machine boss with a highly dubious reputation to defeat two strongly backed young men, one a veteran of World War II?

LOWER CLASS SUPPORT

The first clue is provided by an analysis of the economic composition of Curley's supporters—predominantly lower-middle and lower class. In Table 2 the vote of the economically above average, average and below average is presented for the three major candidates, Curley, Kerrigan, and Reilly.

A word should be said here about the fact that, unlike the usual finding in opinion surveys, the lowest economic stratum in the population is least undecided about its vote. The reverse of this is, generally, found to

TABLE 2

VOTE OF THREE SOCIO-ECONOMIC GROUPS FOR MAJOR CANDIDATES

Candidate	Above-average vote	Average vote	Below-average vote
Curley	24%	46%	66%
Kerrigan	31	31	25
Reilly	34	14	5
Other	11	9	4
Total	100	100	100
Undecided	(10)	(13)	(7)
Number	119	442	190

obtain in dealing with "no opinion" vote on national and international issues.[7]

Three factors, generally, operate to affect the formation of opinion and "no opinion," whether it be on an issue or a candidate: contact with media of information, sensed self-interestedness (however induced), and familiarity with the issues or men involved. Normally the upper income group—better educated and better read—has closer contact with media of information, has a better basis for making up its mind. In a city election, this situation tends not to be true. Billboards are ubiquitous and, more important, the face-to-face canvassing of political ward workers tends to emphasize contacts with the rank and file of voters regardless of economic class almost to the exclusion of the well-to-do.

Where sensed self-interest is concerned, the city situation often differs radically from the national electoral scene. When a national candidate has the reputation of being the friend of the little man, he is still fairly remote from his constituency of little men in such matters as jobs, relief, schools, free medical care and the rest. But to the poor man, the Mayor, for all intents and purposes, is the Prime Minister. There is nothing abstract about the help one can get from the ward captain of the political machine which has just succeeded in putting its man into City Hall.

Intensive studies of city politics, particularly those of Gosnell and his students, point to the unique liaison function of the ward captain who serves as a guide to the poor and immigrant in such matters as relief, jobs, favors, and legal troubles. For many in the ranks of the poor, he is the only concrete embodiment of "government" aside from the police.[8]

Familiarity, finally, is a potent factor in a city election such as the one held in Boston. As the case evolves, it will become clear that familiarity of candidates—even on a

[7] J. S. Bruner, *Mandate from the People*, New York, 1944.

[8] See H. F. Gosnell, *Machine Politics—Chicago Model*, Chicago, 1937.

face-to-face level—was a crucial factor in the election.

Another thing to be noticed in the voting records of the three economic groups is that the lower one goes in the scale, the smaller the vote for minor candidates. Vote for minor candidates is a luxury which one dependent on a powerful ward captain for small favors can seldom afford. The poor, as far as we have been able to observe, vote "realistically" for the man with an organization.

MINORITY GROUPS

It follows that if Curley is picking up the lower and lower-middle-income vote of Boston, he is also gaining support from Boston's three principal minority groups—the Irish, the Italian, and the Jewish. This is not to say, however, that Boston's Yankee population is voting against Curley to a man. Table 3 contains the voting record of

TABLE 3

VOTE OF FOUR NATIONALITY GROUPS FOR MAJOR CANDIDATES*

Candidate	Percent Irish vote	Percent Italian vote	Percent Jewish vote	Percent Yankee vote
Curley	59	59	37	33
Kerrigan	26	25	17	36
Reilly	14	5	23	22
Others	1	11	23	9
Total	100	100	100	100
Undecided	(10)	(17)	(12)	(6)
Number	173	53	34	87

* "Irish" is defined as a person with parent or grandparent born in Ireland. It includes as well, of course, those of Irish nativity. The same criterion is used for defining "Italian." "Jewish" is defined as any person who gives as his religious preference the Jewish religion. "Yankee" is used to describe those people whose American ancestry runs back four generations or more.

the four groups. Curley's support among the city's minority groups is not simply a function of the fact that he himself is a member of one of them. The two major candidates opposing him come from the same group. In spite of it, he carried the Irish group by a more than safe margin and the Italian group with as big a lead in spite of the presence of an Italian, Sawtelle, as an opposing candidate. The Jewish vote, though not of the same landslide proportions, was safely Curley.

Curley does not leave his inter-group relations to chance. He has been careful to choose leading lieutenants from the city's Italian and Jewish groups. Names like Scolponetti, Gurvitz, and Levine are high up in the rolls of the Curley machine. Nor has Curley missed the chance to decry racial discrimination in Boston, Eighteen months before the election he delivered on the floor of the House of Representatives a speech attacking Rankin, Bilbo, and other Congressional hate-mongers. Copies of the speech were widely distributed in Wards 12 and 14, in which reside the bulk of Boston's Jewish population.

An analysis of the support obtained by the candidates from Republican and Democratic voters yields a picture of confused party loyalties. All six candidates, of course, were registered Democrats. But, obviously, Curley had the greatest hold on the Democratic rank and file, the lower and lower-middle class of the city. What happened to the Republican vote in the face of an all-Democratic slate is rather instructive. By dividing equally between the three major candidates it cancelled itself out, leaving the decision with the Democrats. The voting record of Boston's Republicans and Democrats is contained in Table 4.

AGE GROUPS

Contrary to what one might expect, particularly in a Mayoralty race in which a seventy-one-year-old, Curley, is running against a veteran of World War II, Curley did a very effective job of capturing Boston's young vote. Table 5 contains a summary of the vote of the three major age groups in Boston.

Curley's appeal to the young is probably attributable to three factors, two of them situational, the other "ideological." In the latter category is Curley's constant boast that he is the man who "gets things done"—

TABLE 4

THE VOTE OF TWO MAJOR PARTIES FOR MAJOR CANDIDATES

Candidates	Percent Democratic vote	Percent Republican vote
Curley	57	25
Kerrigan	30	28
Reilly	9	32
Other	4	15
Total	100	100
Undecided	(9)	(14)
Number	459	115

for proof of which he points to his record. The allure of such dynamism to the young voter should not be overlooked. Again and again, young voters just starting on their careers have made the point, "He's the only one among them who will make something out of Boston." A situational factor pure and simple is the slate of candidates opposing Curley. Although the slate contains some young men, by and large all the other candidates lacked color. Curley's flamboyance undoubtedly did appeal to the young in the setting of the 1945 election. A parallel, perhaps, can be drawn between Boston's election of 1945 and the presidential election of 1944 in which a young man, Dewey, campaigning on the issue of youth, lost the vote of the younger stratum to a man in his sixties but one who, for vastly different reasons, had the aura of the charismatic leader. Youthfulness, as such, is not necessarily a magnet to the young.

TABLE 5

VOTE OF THREE AGE GROUPS FOR MAJOR CANDIDATES

Candidate	Percent vote in age group 21-29	Percent vote in age group 31-39	Percent vote in age group 50 & over
Curley	58	47	43
Kerrigan	23	31	36
Reilly	11	15	16
Others	8	7	5
Total	100	100	100
Undecided	(11)	(10)	(11)
Number	157	340	250

One other factor probably accounts for the decrease in Curley's support as one goes up the age range from twenty-one to the fifties and sixties. Many of the young supporters of Curley do not know at first hand his transgressions but have only "heard about them." The older population of Boston remembers well the many scrapes and near-scrapes through which Curley has passed. These brushes with the law are not mere stories to them but hard facts which they remember vividly.

Finally, there is little difference in the support given the various candidates by men and women voters of Boston. Men are more decided as to their candidate, but the size of the undecided vote is in general greater among women on most social and political issues. The figures appear in Table 6.

TABLE 6

VOTE OF MEN AND WOMEN FOR MAJOR CANDIDATES

Candidates	Percent women's vote	Percent men's vote
Curley	46	50
Kerrigan	33	26
Reilly	15	14
Others	6	10
Total	100	100
Undecided	(14)	(8)
Number	366	385

WHY VOTERS CHOOSE CANDIDATES

Recent studies of Congressional and Presidential elections (highly structured voting situations in which two major parties contend) indicate that economic interest seems to be the chief factor in determining party allegiance. Harding, in connection with the 1942 Congressional elections, points out that two of the three main factors influencing voters were the belief among workers that they would be better off under Democratic (or Republican) party and the equally strong belief among employers that business would be better off under Republican (or Democratic) party. "*Apart from*

sentimental ties, the main reason why voters followed their traditional party allegiances was the belief that their own security and welfare would be greater if their party won."[9]

Economic self-interest was, of course, a potent factor in the Boston election of 1945. To this point we shall return. But what Harding calls "sentimental factors" were perhaps more important in the Boston race for Mayor than in most Congressional tilts in 1942. For, as we shall see, Curley's support was based upon many of those elements of sentiment that bind charismatic leaders and their followers.

As a first step in uncovering reasons for choosing candidates, voters were asked, "What do you like best about—(your chosen candidate)?" A tabular summary of replies is found in Table 7.

Before attempting to interpret these figures, it is necessary to look first at the results of a related question, one bearing on "platforms." After having asked respondents their reasons for choosing candidates, we put the following question: "Regardless of who is elected, what do you think is the most important thing the new mayor could do for Boston?" Some striking differences between supporters of various candidates were found to exist (Table 8) which when taken together with the figures of Table 7 provide a basis for discussion.

Reasons for choosing candidates seem to be classifiable most readily under three headings: economic advantage, personal appeal of the candidates, and apparent administrative effectiveness. To these we shall return shortly. Conspicuously missing from the list of factors are two, party and nationality, which are normally associated with city elections. Their absence can be explained simply. Where party is concerned, there simply was no choice save between more or less "regular" Democrats. The closest approach to party loyalty is loyalty

[9] Harding, J. S. American government and politics: the 1942 Congressional elections. *American Political Science Review*, 1944, 38, p. 49. Italics ours.

TABLE 7

REASONS FOR CHOOSING CANDIDATES

Reasons Given for Choice	Total	Curley	Supporters of: Kerrigan	Reilly	Sawtelle	Lee
Reasons of Efficiency	39%	51%	37%	28%	27%	13%
Past experience	20	15	28	27	7	—
Past accomplishments	11	18	7	1	14	5
Gives more for money	2	4	2	—	—	5
Will build up Boston	3	8	—	—	3	3
Will provide housing	1	1	—	—	3	—
Will provide jobs	2	5	—	—	—	—
Reasons of Ideology	27	22	22	33	46	78
Honesty	15	3	15	32	37	68
Progressive	2	2	3	—	3	5
Helps little man	7	14	—	1	—	—
Will help veterans	*	—	1	—	3	—
Will help needy	1	1	—	—	3	—
Will help young	2	2	3	—	—	5
Political Reasons	4	1	7	3	7	5
Not machine candidate	2	1	1	2	7	5
Party affiliation	*	*	—	—	—	—
Good backers	*	—	1	—	—	—
Candidate against Curley	2	—	5	1	—	—
Personal Characteristics	36	26	47	41	31	26
Good background	6	4	2	11	—	26
Young	6	—	18	2	—	—
Veteran	2	—	7	—	—	—
Better known	3	4	2	7	3	—
Good fellow	8	8	6	14	—	—
Know him personally	10	10	11	7	14	—
Nationality	1	*	1	—	14	—
Lesser of Evils	5	6	6	14	6	—
Miscellaneous	7	2	17	9	3	—
Best chance to win	*	1	1	—	—	—
Runs clean campaign	*	1	—	—	—	—
Deserves chance at office	7	*	16	9	3	—
Number of Cases	550	253	159	87	29	19

* Less than 0.5%.
Percentages total more than 100 since some respondents gave more than one reason for choosing candidate.

to a candidate's organization ("machine") as represented by ward workers or by the Big Men themselves. To label such loyalty "party loyalty" would be to misunderstand the meaning of the term. The matter, as voters see it, is personal—between themselves and key individuals who happen to be a certain number of steps closer to the source of political power-to-be. This type of relationship is, to be sure, the stuff of which party organization is made, but in the Boston of 1945 these loyalties were there without any clear-cut identification of parties. What would have happened to the following of the two major organizations (Tobin's, thrown behind Reilly, and Curley's personal machine) if their candidates had been brash enough to bolt from the Demo-

TABLE 8

WHAT SUPPORTERS OF CANDIDATES THINK THE NEW MAYOR SHOULD DO FOR BOSTON

		SUPPORTERS OF:				
Things to do	*Total*	*Curley*	*Kerrigan*	*Reilly*	*Sawtelle*	*Lee*
Improve traffic conditions	25%	24%	14%	15%	12%	6%
Provide housing	18	22	16	6	32	6
Help poor and needy	13	21	7	1	8	—
Improve port and airport	14	15	14	15	12	6
Build up Boston	13	14	10	17	8	22
Save money	17	13	11	34	32	17
Provide schools, etc.	10	9	15	9	—	6
Provide employment	5	6	3	5	—	—
Honest administration	11	6	10	9	44	50
Improve police	9	5	17	6	4	6
Help veterans	5	4	8	2	—	—
Introduce Plan E	1	—	1	2	—	—
Ease racial tension	*	—	—	—	—	*
Number of Cases	506	234	146	81	25	18

* Less than 0.5%.
Percentages total more than 100 since some respondents gave more than one suggestion for the improvement of Boston.

cratic Party and strong enough to take their workers with them is difficult to say. Under the circumstances which actually prevailed, such moves were never dreamed of and the issue of party remained entirely in the background, overshadowed by more primitive forms of political loyalty.

As for nationality—particularly the myth of the solid Irish vote—that too failed to operate. Too many of the candidates, first off, were Irish. In order to bring out a solid vote of such a nationality group, a single Irishman would have to be opposed by non-Irishmen. McDougall's emphasis on external threat as a solidifier of social groups is as relevant in city politics as in other spheres.[10] And, as we have pointed out, Curley, along with the other candidates, utilized lieutenants drawn from many groups, thereby clouding the issue of nationality. Sawtelle, of Italian extraction, might have turned out a heavy nationality vote, but his slim chance of election worked against him. As one highly intelligent Italian-American observer put it, "A vote for Sawtelle is a doubtful luxury for the average

[10] McDougall, W. *The Group Mind,* New York, 1920. pp. 70ff.

Italian in the North End. What does he get out of it?"

Returning to the major reasons for choosing candidates, consider first the question of personal appeal.

"I KNOW HIM PERSONALLY . . ."

Personal appeal of candidates

Table 7 indicates that, generally, all the major candidates could boast that one in ten among their supporters were backing them for directly personal reasons—"I know him personally and he's all right." The full statistical import of these figures is not grasped until one recalls that Curley polled 111,868 votes, better than 11,000 of which can be attributed in some measure to the personal appeal of the man. Undoubtedly, no man, however long in public life knows "personally'" that many voters. But that he can engender the feeling among such numbers of people demonstrates strikingly what Harding might mean by "sentimental factors" in an election.[11]

An analysis of the Curley appeal yields some interesting information. As Table 9

[11] Harding, J. S., *op. cit.*

indicates, Curley was the best known of all the candidates among members of all economic levels, and the lower one goes in the scale, the greater his edge. The question asked was, "Do you happen to know the names of all the people running for Mayor? It is perhaps superficial to place too much emphasis on the extent to which candidates remain in the forefront of the voter's consciousness, but it is of interest to note that candidates finished in the order of which they were "familiar" to voters.

TABLE 9
ECONOMIC STATUS AND KNOWLEDGE OF CANDIDATES

Candidates known	Total	Above average Voters	Average Voters	Below average Voters
Curley (45.7)*	93%	96%	93%	88%
Kerrigan (24.7)	84	93	85	77
Reilly (18.7)	71	82	74	58
Sawtelle (5.3)	55	59	58	45
Lee (4.2)	40	59	42	25
Feeney (1.4)	29	44	30	19
None known		3	5	11
Number		112	420	177

* Percent of cast vote obtained.

BEST AND LEAST LIKED

Curley, then, was the best known, and, according to the vote, the best liked of those running. Strikingly enough, he was also the *least* liked candidate. In answer to the question, "As far as you know, which of the candidates do you think is the worst?" Curley led the field by a safe margin. Figures are contained in Table 10, broken down by economic status.

Curley's position is, in a sense, the position of most contemporary charismatic leaders. In the city of Boston he is both the most preferred candidate and, as Table 10 indicates, the most disliked candidate. One either votes for him or deplores him; to be neutral towards him is a feat that few Bostonians seem able to achieve. Consider the figures in Table 11.

One quickly arrives at the crux of the

TABLE 10
ECONOMIC STATUS AND CANDIDATE DENUNCIATION

Candidate named "worst"	Total	Above average Voters	Average Voters	Below average Voters
Curley	21%	43%	21%	8%
Kerrigan	5	7	5	3
Reilly	6	7	6	5
Sawtelle	2	*	3	1
Lee	2	3	2	2
Feeney	2	3	2	2
All are bad	5	6	5	4
None are bad	12	9	12	14
Don't know	45	27	47	61
Number	703	116	409	178

Percentages total more than 100 since some respondents named more than one candidate.

problem when one inquires why many voters named Curley as their "worst" candidate. Fully three-quarters base their charges on "Curley's dishonesty," the tenor of remarks ranging from "He's a lousy crook," to "You can never be quite sure of the man's motives." In striking contrast are the accusations against Curley's leading opponents Kerrigan and Reilly. A vast majority of their critics mention not dishonesty, but inefficiency or their lack of qualifications for handling the job. To this contrast we shall return shortly but first consider the charge that Curley is dishonest.

When a substantial minority of a city's population holds the view that a man is dishonest, one may assume that the remaining majority knows about the charge. And of

TABLE 11
CURLEY AND VOTER NEUTRALITY BY ECONOMIC CLASS

	Total*	Above average Voters	Average Voters	Below average Voters
Curley supporters	48%	24%	46%	66%
Curley "worst"	21	43	21	8
Total	69	67	67	74
Remaining "neutrals"	31	33	33	26

* Survey figures.

course they did; the press and radio, word of mouth, and the grapevine had not neglected the news value of Curley's Federal indictment for fraud. How then is the imputed trait of dishonesty, a serious thing in our culture, rationalized by the vast group of Curley supporters?

The problem, essentially, is to understand how dishonesty can be incorporated into a system of beliefs about a man without at the same time diminishing the man's appeal by shadowing it with threatening qualities. Three psychological mechanisms seem to be at work. First and foremost is the Robin Hood legend built up around Curley. Again and again, respondents and informants echoed the phrase, "Curley may steal from the rich, if you want to call it that, but he gives it to the poor." That the same type of legend has surrounded leaders of the same stamp in other locales is very likely. Mayor Hague or Huey Long or any of the long line of bosses in the history of American city politics have inspired similar legend.[12] In personal habits, Curley reinforces the stereotype. Taxi drivers around the State House, bellhops at the nearby Parker House, minor workers in his machine all agree that Curley is probably the easiest "touch" in the city, always ready with a dollar bill or better in the face of a hard-luck story. And it is of more than passing interest that three of the respondents interviewed in the course of our opinion survey reported that Curley had given them amounts up to ten dollars in the darkest days of the Depression when they were completely "broke."[13] A reputation for such generosity must be understood in the context of a great city where anonymity and competition are the order of the day. It is

of such stuff that the charisma of a city boss is made.

A second element of rationalization lies in a more formal and perhaps ideological interpretation of the Robin Hood legend: "When Curley's in there, the little guy gets a break." It is said to be true that Curley during his years of office-holding has been conspicuous for building schools and hospitals, providing free clinics, and improving the plight (conspicuously if not profoundly) of the poor. That this aspect of the legend has penetrated the upper social brackets of the city is evidenced by a remark made by a distinguished university professor, nationally known for his bold adherence to liberal ideals: "When Curley did Tom Eliot out of his seat in Congress, every liberal in Massachusetts was in mourning. But when Curley started voting, the surprises began. I don't believe Curley failed to support with his vote any single liberal issue of the sort that Tom Eliot would have supported. The fact of the matter is that Curley's record in Congress has been liberal."

Finally, even Curley's critics admit that he has established an imposing record for efficiency, for "getting things done" which in the minds of a good many voters weighs in the balance to counteract his reputation for dishonesty.

A word must be said parenthetically about "middle class morality" in the domain of politics. In Table 10 is evidence for the fact that in the middle and lower classes, a majority of voters do not fall easily into a pattern of political denunciation. Majorities of both these groups are either of the opinion that no candidate is "bad" or are unable or unwilling to single out any one person for the dubious distinction of being "worst." Many of these people are supporters of Curley. Ask them about the morals of the local politicians and you get answers such as these: "Oh, they're all the same. That's what politics is. They say Curley's worse than the others but if you ask me, they all take their cut and probably always will." Another one, an intelligent voter, put it in

---

[12] See, for example, Harnett Kane's study of the Huey Long machine, *Louisiana Hayride: The American Rehearsal for Dictatorship*, 1941.

[13] Without stretching the plausibility of inferring population statistics from those of a sample, these three respondents when seen in the light of Boston's hundreds of thousands could add up to better than 1500 beneficiaries —considerable even for one who has spent his entire life in Boston and Massachusetts politics.

these terms: "In Boston, as elsewhere, politicians will get their percentage. But with Curley, politics is like R. H. Macy: big turnover and a small cut on everything. The others do nothing and take a big slice anyway."

"CURLEY GETS THINGS DONE . . ."

Apparent Administrative Effectiveness

Tables 7 and 8 are saturated with hopes and suggestions for improvement of economically deteriorating Boston: improve traffic, the airport, housing, the seaport. Boston's position is known to be desperate. Front page articles have appeared in the city's press bemoaning the fact that the city's pretentiously named Logan International Airport has the same cinder runways put in back in the '20s, incapable of supporting transoceanic aircraft. There have been protests from longshoremen about the dangerously rotten condition of the docks in the harbor. Boston, like other cities, is critically short of housing. The climate of opinion in the city is ready to accept a leader with minimum morals and maximum efficiency, one with a reputation for administrative effectiveness.

Under the circumstances it has been easy to minimize Curley's shortcomings. Very wisely, Curley's advisers told him to gear his campaign appeals to the slogan, "Curley gets things done." He did, and with telling effect.

The city's condition, taken as a background against which to judge candidates, provides an instance of a general law of social contrast. Given five candidates running for office in a city which is in sound condition financially but which is patently in need of moral uplift, the efficiency of the men will be secondary as far as voters are concerned and their moral qualities paramount. If all are regarded as equally efficient, the contrast value of moral qualities as displayed by each candidate will stand out the more strongly. In Boston, the *majority* holds that the candidates are more

or less equal in *moral virtue,* that the city is most in need of efficient and active government, that one candidate is distinguished by his record for "doing things." Curley, then, polls close to half the city's vote. That there are also present legends which help voters disregard Curley's alleged moral shortcomings undoubtedly helps his chances.[14]

ECONOMIC SELF-INTEREST

Economic Advantage

Much of what has already been said (especially in Table 8) can be translated into terms of economic self-interest. Bostonians do not want a better Boston on aesthetic grounds alone, but for reasons of sheer economic survival. We have quoted Harding[15] as saying that workers vote Democratic because they think it is that party which helps workers, employers Republican because that party is believed to be best for business. In the case of Boston, much of the vote can be summarized in the remark of a Boston journalist: "If the city is going to be kept from going to the dogs, Curley is the only one among them who can do it. So I'll vote for him even if I have to lose my breakfast doing it."

The very Robin Hood legend which surrounds Curley has its roots in the economic distress of the city's poorer population. Stealing from the rich to help the poor is a romantic virtue, but viewed from the worm's eye view of the poor, it is also an economic blessing.

CONCLUSIONS

Having thus examined in detail the nature of the support given Curley and his opponents in the 1945 Mayoralty election and

---

[14] By the same logic, a dishonest regime under Curley, should one develop, would improve the chances of a future candidate running on a "clean government" platform or of a drive to institute Plan E in Boston.

[15] Harding, J. S., *op. cit.*

having attempted to assess the reasons why people voted as they did, what can we say about the nature of Curley's grip on Boston's voters? Part of the story is, doubtless, situational. It can be said, for example, that if the opposition had not been divided, Curley might have been defeated. But that type of post-mortem is somehow fruitless. The task is to isolate those factors in the election campaign of 1945 which were not adventitious, to parcel out what it is about Curley and Boston that makes it possible for the city, three months after election, to be ruled by a man appealing a federal conviction for using the mails to defraud.[16]

1. Curley's main support comes from the lower-middle and lower income groups in Boston. His support from these groups rests in part upon the legend of his Robin Hood qualities, in part upon the inability of the lower income groups to condemn morally one of whom they regard as a protector, and upon Curley's record as a "doer" —a builder of schools, provider of jobs, etc.

2. The great bulk of Curley's support comes from the city's established minority groups—Irish, Italian, Jewish. Our figures indicate that this vote is not cast primarily on the basis of similar national background. The Irish had a chance to vote for other Irish candidates, the Italians a chance to vote for an Italian, the Jews to scatter their vote, had they wanted to.

3. Though Curley's vote was drawn largely from the ranks of his own party, he did manage to get 25% of the Republican vote. Yet political affiliation should not be rated high in considering Curley's power with the voters. Reasons of political affiliation do not loom large among voters' reasons

[16] That his conviction did not dampen the enthusiasm of some of his voters is attested to by the fact that upon his return from Washington after being sentenced, Curley was greeted at South Station by a cheering crowd estimated at between three and ten thousand people. Boston *Globe*, February 21, 1946.

for backing him. Curley, like many other charismatic leaders, is almost a party unto himself, the more so in Boston, a heavily Democratic community in which Republican strength is very much in the minority and Democrats fight it out among themselves.

4. Contrary to what might be expected, Curley continues to recruit young voters to his banner. The age group 21-29 gave him a heavier vote than any other. Younger voters, unlike their parents, do not have firsthand memories of the history of Curley's scrapes and seem to be attracted to him for his dynamism and color.

5. Curley has the great advantage of being known in all sections of the population, unlike his major opponents who, though well-known to the above-average voters, are decreasingly familiar to voters lower in the economic scale. But though he is best known and best liked, he is also the least liked of all candidates contending. Few of Boston's voters are indifferent to him. The controversiality of his position is, of course, an aid to spreading his fame.

6. Curley's appeal during the campaign was to his experience and accomplishments as a man who "gets things done." Much of his support rested upon this argument. His reputation for dishonesty, in the face of Boston's felt need for a mayor who will indeed "get things done," was thereby minimized.

7. Finally, in summing up Curley's appeal, one should end on the note of the comparative stimulus value of the personalities involved in the campaign. Rather than diminishing it, the anonymity of life in a great city has intensified the appeal of the colorful personality. Curley's is a forceful personality and that he has been exploiting it is testified to by the fact that ten percent of the 111,868 people who voted for him claimed that they knew him personally, and based their votes on their impression of him as a person.

RESPONSES TO THE TELEVISED KEFAUVER HEARINGS: SOME SOCIAL PSYCHOLOGICAL IMPLICATIONS

G. D. WIEBE

Our concern in this paper is not primarily with the Kefauver Hearings themselves. Our primary concern is with what 260 people felt about the corruption brought to light by the Hearings as compared with what they did. Public opinion studies of elections are similarly focused on how people feel as compared with what they do. But while in an election study the campaign stimuli are various and the responses to them are highly complex, the ultimate behavior—voting—is standardized, easy, and socially approved. In the present study the situation is reversed. The stimulus (the Kefauver Hearings) was single, and reactions to the stimulus were vivid, partisan and practically unanimous. But the ultimate behavior—doing something to wipe out the corruption—called for initiative and creative social action without benefit of precedent, simplicity or even the urging of general social approval.

SCOPE AND PURPOSE OF THE STUDY

The televised Kefauver Hearings, in New York City (hereafter referred to as "the Hearings") had an initial impact on the people of New York City which was probably without precedent. The routine life of the city was substantially altered as people interrupted normal pursuits to sit and watch the parade of local corruption and bribery that was unfolded on their television screens. What would become of the emotions that were mobilized and focused by the Hearings? Would their concern be translated into problem-solving behavior? The word "apathy" is often invoked in answer to such questions as these. But apathy connotes the absence of emotional involvement. The Hearings were not received with apathy. During and immediately following the Hearings, there was nearly unanimous arousal. Scale prices for police protection during illegal transactions, bribery among high municipal officials, conniving in the courts, wholesale waste of tax money—the exposure of practices such as these was not received with apathy. If the people of New York City were not apathetic, what happened to the feelings aroused in opposition to municipal corruption? This study is an attempt to throw some light on the disposition of these feelings among 260 citizens.

Because this is essentially a study of individual responses to a group problem, reference group theory appears to be a logical framework in which to examine our findings. A reference group is generally understood to be a group with which a person identifies to the extent of adopting values

* From the *Public Opinion Quarterly*, Vol. 16, Summer, 1952, pp. 179-200. Reprinted by permission of the author and the publisher.

and norms of the group as his own values and norms.

* * *

The Sample

The sample was not statistically representative of New York City. Its skewness, however, was toward male, white collar, and professional people under 36 years of age. To the extent that such people tend to be more enlightened and active than do other portions of the population, our findings tend to be conservative rather than exaggerated. That is, the rather small amount of constructive protest behavior which will be reported is probably more, rather than less, than what would have been found in a more representative sample. The age, sex, and occupational make-up of the sample is shown in Table 1. All respondents were residents of New York City. They resided in twelve different Election Districts. All had watched parts of the Hearings on television. The interviews were conducted between six and nine weeks after the close of the Hearings.

TABLE 1

MAKE-UP OF THE SAMPLE

Sample size:	260	
Age:	21–35	61%
	36–50	31
	Over 50	8
Sex:	Male	57%
	Female	43
Occupation:		
	Professional	25%
	Clerical—Office help	15
	Housewives	15
	Skilled—semi-skilled labor	13
	Retired—Student— Unemployed	12
	Sales—Store clerk	8
	Owner—Managerial	5
	Service—Protective workers	4
	Unskilled labor	2
	In Armed Forces	1

THE FINDINGS

The first question put to the 260 respondents was: "The Kefauver Hearings were about six weeks ago. As you think back to that time, how did you feel about the conditions that were brought to light?"

Responses to the question fell into three categories. Fifty-one per cent could be classed as emotional. These responses, even six to nine weeks after the Hearings, conveyed feelings of shock, anger, outrage, betrayal: for example, "A rotten business," "Terrifying, unbelievable," "I felt mad, paying taxes for graft."

Thirty-nine per cent of the sample gave favorable but unemotional responses. These showed satisfaction with the Hearings, but no surprise and little excitement: for example, "I knew that eventually things would come to light," "It was a good idea to let the public know what was going on," "Glad to see that something was being done about it."

Finally, 10 per cent gave answers best classified as cynical. These responses questioned the intentions of the investigators: for example, "Good political publicity for Kefauver," "Real conditions weren't told," "Higher ups weren't brought to light."

The respondents were not apathetic. The first group expressed clear emotional involvement. The second group seemed to express cautious satisfaction as if a chronic frustration had been somewhat diminished. The third group seemed to express a counter-emotion, as if guarding against further disillusionment. No one said, "I've forgotten about it," or "It left me cold," or "I don't remember how I felt." At this first stage, we observed that there was unanimous concern with a social problem.

The second item on the questionnaire probed a main dimension of this concern: "As you watched the Hearings, back when they were on the air, did you feel that you, personally, would like to take part in improving conditions?" To this question, 46 per cent said "yes," 12 per cent added qualifications to their "yes" answers, and 42 per cent said "no." Those who said "yes" and those who added qualifications were asked: "What did you feel like doing?"

Those who answered by saying "no" were asked: "Would you tell me why you felt that way?"

Thus all respondents were encouraged to explain how they related, in terms of their behavioral intentions, to the solution of the problem. Some who answered "no" continued with such statements as "Something ought to be done, but I don't know what." Some who answered "yes" expressed substantially the same opinion. The responses fall into the same categories regardless of an initial "yes" or "no" answer. They are reported in Table 2, which shows the per cents based on those who initially answered "yes" or "yes" qualified, the per cents based on those who initially answered "no," and per cents on the whole sample.

So much for the second stage. In the first stage, respondents indicated unanimous concern with a social problem. In the second stage when respondents were asked, and

probed as to what they "felt like" doing, only 25 per cent of the responses appeared to qualify as "problem-solving" in the sense that they might be expected to contribute to the solution of the problem.

The third item on the questionnaire moved from feeling to doing: "Did you actually do anything?" To this, 18 per cent answered "yes," and 82 per cent answered "no." Those who answered "yes" were asked: "What did you do?" Those who answered "no" were encouraged as follows: "Well, you probably talked about it, didn't you?" The responses are classified in Table 3.

Since the Hearings were, in essence, an exposure of corruption in "higher places," talking among common citizens can hardly be expected to affect significant change. If all of the behaviors reported in Table 3, except "talking to persons of approximately equal deference level" and "did nothing," are classified as problem-solving, then 19

TABLE 2

WILLINGNESS TO ACT AND BEHAVIORAL INTENTIONS

Responses	Yes or Yes qualified	No	Total
Diffuse, undirected "I know something could be done, but I don't know what." "What *could* I do?" "Don't know where to start." "There's nothing much one person can do." "I feel like fighting corruption, but I have no pull or influence."	25%	45%	33%
Power fantasies "I felt like banging a couple heads together," "Shooting them all and starting over," "Changing the form of government," "Serving on the committee and asking some questions," "Cracking down on politicians and policemen."	34	2	20
Dissociation "I haven't given it much thought," "I have no time," "Not my job," "I'm thoroughly fed up."	3	43	20
Problem Solving "I felt like joining a good government committee," "Voting more intelligently," "Getting others to vote more carefully," "Doing something in our club," "Writing my congressman," "Writing Mr. Truman."	38	6	25
No answer	2	5	3
Total	102%*	101%*	101%*

* A few respondents felt like doing things that fell into more than one of the categories.

TABLE 3

BEHAVIORAL RESPONSES TO HEARINGS

Respondent's Behavior

Talked to persons of approximately equal deference level:
Friends, acquaintances, colleagues on the job, adult members of the
family, etc.   81%

Did nothing: Didn't even talk about it   10

Talked to persons of higher deference level:
Persons considered to be influential by the respondent ("My boss," "an
acquaintance of mine who is in a position to be heard," etc.), or
members of a political hierarchy ("local politician," "a judge," etc.).   5

Wrote or wired Congressman or President   6

Talked to persons of lower deference levels
"My students," "my children," "a person who doesn't think about
these things," etc.   3

Wrote to the Mayor   1

Wrote to the Governor   1

Other   3
                                                                                   ─────
                                                                Total   110%*

*Some individuals reported more than one activity.

per cent of the responses, which were reported by 13 per cent of the sample, fall
into this category.

The fourth question related the individual's action to his judgment of its effectiveness: "Do you think what you did
made any difference?" The replies were decidedly one-sided. Only 38 respondents (14
per cent) answered "yes," 16 (6 per cent)
answered "maybe," and 10 (4 per cent)
professed not to know. As against these,
5 respondents (2 per cent) doubted that
their actions had made any difference, and
191 (74 per cent) were quite certain that
they had not.

Since an election was not held between
the Hearings and the interviews, those who
"felt like" taking action at the polls—this
was among the responses to Item 2 tabulated as "problem-solving,"—had no opportunity to actually do what they "felt
like" doing, or to judge whether it had
made a difference. The realism of action
at the polls as a corrective for widespread
corruption is open to some question unless
such action focuses on the primaries, or on

processes preceding the primaries. Of the
20 persons who "felt like" taking action at
the polls, only one mentioned the primaries.
No one mentioned such political instruments as nomination petitions. At any rate,
an additional 20 persons (8 per cent) may
actually do what they "felt like" doing at
the time of the next election, and all or
part of them might feel, at that time, that
their action has made a difference.[1]

Among the 33 persons whose actual behavior was classified as problem-solving,[2]
the responses to Item 4 were only slightly
more optimistic than those of the rest of
the sample. Six of the 33 (18 per cent)
thought that their actions had made a difference. Another 11 (33 per cent) answered
"maybe." Four (12 per cent) didn't know,
and 12 (37 per cent) answered negatively.

[1] On the other side of the ledger are the
eight individuals who "felt like" joining a good
government committee or some other citizens'
protest group (tabulated as "Problem-solving,"
Item 2). None of them had done so up to the
time of the interviews.

[2] All responses to Item 3 except "Did nothing" and "Talked on lateral deference level."

Thus, even among those who actually did things classified as "problem-solving," 82 per cent expressed varying degrees of skepticism as to the significance of what they had done.

Overall, 260 persons (100 per cent), all citizens of voting age, expressed concern with a local social problem. Sixty-five persons (25 per cent) "felt like" doing things classified as "problem-solving." Thirty-three persons (13 per cent) actually did things which, liberally interpreted, might be classified as behavior directed toward the solution of the problem. Thirty-eight persons (14 per cent) believed without reservation that what they did made a difference, but only 6 of these persons actually did things that were classified above as problem-solving.

The phenomenal impact of the Hearings dwindled to rather minor productivity insofar as it was mirrored in the reported behavior of our respondents and in their own opinions of the significance of what they did. But apart from their own behavior, and their estimate of its effectiveness, what did respondents think about the effect of the Hearings themselves as an instrument for social improvement? We asked: "Do you think the Kefauver Hearings will improve conditions in the long run, or do you think that things will settle down and be about the same as they were before?"

Only 21 per cent thought that conditions would improve. Another 21 per cent believed that they might improve. But 49 per cent thought that they would be "about the same," while 2 per cent actually thought that they would be worse. Seven per cent of the sample replied "Don't know."

The wording of the question invites one of two responses: "Conditions will improve" or "Things will be about the same." The fact that the number qualifying the first answer equalled the number giving that answer without qualification is noteworthy. The opinion that the Hearings would make things "worse" was totally unexpected, and even though this opinion was given by only 2 per cent of the respondents, it adds to a total picture of considerable skepticism.

In sum, the televised Kefauver Hearings were a new phenomenon in American life. Television itself was still new and glamorous, although approximately half of the families in the Metropolitan New York City area had sets at the time of the Hearings. The content of the Hearings combined the zest of a scandal sheet with the high purpose of righteous reform. If citizens were skeptical about the effects of these Hearings, what, one might ask, could be expected to engage their enthusiasm?

One answer seems clear. Opinion about the Hearings is separate and different from opinion about the corrective effects of the Hearings. Insofar as the Hearings themselves are concerned, there can be no reasonable doubt that they were received with phenomenal enthusiasm. Some defects of the Hearings as television programs intended to institute social reform have been discussed elsewhere. In the context of the present discussion, however, the findings add up to a disconcerting descent from vigorous arousal to a trickle of effective protest.

POLITICAL PARTIES AS REFERENCE GROUPS

The implications for representative government are obvious. One cannot be content to observe such findings as these without attempting to uncover some hint of the social dynamics involved. We have discarded "apathy" as an explanation. Citizens of New York City were not apathetic. They were aroused. We have seen that, to a large extent, rank and file citizens discharged their arousal in inconsequential fashion by talking, "griping" to acquaintances of like mind and status. Why? What conditions are conducive to such behavior?

Party Membership

In the case at hand, a case of large scale political corruption, citizens' responses might be expected to reflect their membership in political parties. Perhaps political parties are, in this case, their reference groups. The incumbent party is primarily responsible for the political status quo, and the party out of power is traditionally responsible for vigorous criticism.

* * *

Political parties do not appear to have functioned as reference groups. We do not know to which party our enrolled party members belonged, but we may safely assume that a substantial portion of them belonged to the party in power. Still, there was not a single instance of an attempt to defend that party, nor was there a single instance of threatened or actual withdrawal from the party, nor was there a single expression of intent to cooperate in removing the party leaders. There was only one respondent who reported working via his membership in an opposition party to register his protest. Finally, there was the one respondent, mentioned above, who reported talking to his committeeman about the situation. Among the remaining 258 respondents, enrolled party members and non-members appear to be indistinguishable except that party members were slightly more sophisticated and active at the verbal level.

* * *

SOCIAL IMPOTENCE

The interview responses of party members add up to what might be characterized as a social syndrome: concern with a common problem; impulses compounded of undirected energy, power fantasies, dissociation, and some impulses toward problem-solving behavior; much talking at a lateral deference level, but little actual behavior directed toward the solution of the problem; and finally, the strong tendency to reject even the problem-solving behavior as hopeless.

* * *

When many individuals who belong to a single group share both a feeling of protests regarding leadership behavior and an overriding conviction that the problem will not be solved, we may refer to this situation as social impotence. The responses from the

interviews seem to take on coherence when reviewed within this framework. The concept of social impotence, then, serves to sharpen our understanding of reference groups, for it designates a class of social situations in which an expected or plausible reference group phenomenon fails to emerge because it is overbalanced by stronger reference group forces within the same group.

We may now set down a tentative definition of social impotence: Social impotence is the characteristic absence, or near absence of constructive problem-solving behavior among the membership of a group when: (1) Rank and file members are opposed to specific leadership behavior. (2) The point of contention is not perceived by members as a threat to the perceived primary benefits of membership. (3) The perceived benefits of membership outweigh the disadvantages of the disliked behavior.

When these conditions exist, according to the present hypothesis, the traditional democratic procedures for registering effective protest within the group, through representative channels, are not exercised. The members may not only express opinions at variance with present and future group policy; they may also, having expressed these opinions, behave in such fashion as to lend tacit or even active support to the contrary policy. To characterize this disparity between expressed opinion and subsequent behavior simply as falsification of opinion is superficial moralizing. This disparity is the realistic subordination of one motive pattern in favor of another that is perceived as preferable. If an individual states that he favors going home from work at four o'clock, but continues to work until 5:30, surely his behavior doesn't give the lie to his verbalized preference. The explanation of the disparity should be sought in a primary benefit of membership in the company that employs him. One such benefit might be the full-sized pay check.

The concept of social impotence brings to mind an observation with which all of us are familiar; namely, that the leaders of every large organization, and of many that are not so large, release statements or initiate or support policies and practices in the name of the entire membership when the membership has not been consulted on the issue at hand. Although this practice is a matter of practical necessity, still it can, and does on occasion, lead to abuses. When considered in conjunction with the concept of social impotence, this practice can be stated in more meaningful terms. The leadership of a group is substantially independent of its membership in the pursuit of goals and values so long as these pursuits do not jeopardize the primary benefits of membership as perceived by the members—that is, so long as the membership is in a condition of social impotence with regard to the autonomous leadership behavior. The more important the benefits of membership as perceived by the member, the more nearly free is the leadership so long as it avoids disturbing those benefits. But the leadership must avoid, in its autonomous behavior, jeopardizing the perceived benefits that their members derive from membership *in other groups*. Jeopardy in other membership roles may cancel out the perception of benefits in the first group. But the likelihood of this situation might easily be over-estimated. Note that in no instance among our 260 respondents were the perceived benefits of membership in church, family or occupational groups felt to be jeopardized to such an extent that continued affiliation with the incumbent party seemed intolerable.

* * *

The recent history of Communist-dominated labor unions in the United States appears to illustrate social impotence. Although a very small proportion of the members of such unions were Communists, the members tolerated political activities by the leadership of a kind and to an extent that caused great perplexity among non-members. The reason, in terms of our hypothesis, would be that those unions were diligent and successful in winning improved wages and working conditions for the rank and file, and that these were the benefits of membership that the members clearly perceived. In point of fact, there is no doubt that many members clung to "good wages, hours, and grievance machinery" as personified by these unions, and dissociated themselves from their own paradoxical political positions far beyond what they would consider a reasonable point in the behavior of other citizens in other organizations. Finally, counteracting pressures via family membership, friendship groups, church membership, and similar sources diminished the relative benefits of membership in these unions, and the extremist leadership suffered the consequences. But the conclusive downfall of the errant leadership was effected not primarily by the rank and file but by the militant action of an opposed trade union leadership.

* * *

SOME IMPLICATIONS

If we may assume that social impotence has been established as a significant social psychological concept, then the question arises as to how it may be counteracted. Several possible courses of action appear to be implicit in the concept itself:

1. Teach members that there is an essential contradiction between the errant behavior of the leadership on the one hand, and the members' continued enjoyment of perceived benefits of the membership on the other. Stated differently, broaden the recognition of essential interdependence between the perceived benefits of membership and the total range of the group's policy and program.

2. Provide the opportunity for membership in a similar group where the perceived benefits of membership are largely duplicated, but where the objectionable leadership behavior is absent. Under this plan, one offers a "net increase" in perceived benefits.

3. Provide opportunity for membership in a group in which the correction of the

objectionable behavior is itself the primary benefit of membership.

The characteristics of social impotence seem to appear in a number of important instances. The concept of social impotence appears to narrow the meaning but broaden the applicability of reference group theory. Perhaps, then, social impotence merits further study as one of many social psychological entities in contemporary American culture. The implications of social impotence for public opinion research are numerous, and must be left for later consideration. It will suffice, at this point, to observe that given social impotence on a particular issue, majority opinion among the membership regarding that issue has little, if any, relevance in the determination of policy or in the application of the power derived by leaders from that membership.

POLITICAL ISSUES AND THE VOTE: NOVEMBER, 1952

ANGUS CAMPBELL, GERALD GURIN AND
WARREN E. MILLER

In March, 1952 the Carnegie Corporation made available to the Social Science Research Council a research grant to support a major study of factors influencing the popular vote in the 1952 presidential election. Under the sponsorship of the Council's Committee on Political Behavior[1] this project is currently being carried out by the Survey Research Center of the University of Michigan.

The study was developed around six major objectives:

[1] The members of the SSRC Committee on Political Behavior were V. O. Key (chairman), Conrad M. Arensberg, Angus Campbell, Alfred de Grazia, Oliver Garceau, Avery Leiserson, M. Brewster Smith, and David B. Truman. The Committee is in no way responsible for the present article.

1. To identify the voters and non-voters, Republicans and Democrats, within four major geographical areas, in regard to
   a. socio-economic characteristics;
   b. attitudes and opinions on political issues;
   c. perceptions of the parties and the candidates.
2. To compare these groups to the corresponding groups in the 1948 presidential election.
3. To trace the resolution of the vote with particular attention to the undecided and changing voters.
4. To study the impact of the activities of the major parties on the population.
5. To analyze the nature and correlates of political party identification.
6. To analyze the nature and correlates of political participation.

Data designed to meet these objectives were gathered by means of nation-wide sample surveys conducted in October and

From the *American Political Science Review*, 1953, 46, 359-385. Reprinted by permission of the authors and the publisher.

November, 1952. Two thousand and twenty-one persons, chosen by methods of probability sampling to represent all citizens of voting age living in private households in the United States, were interviewed by the Survey Research Center field staff shortly before the election; 1614 of these people were interviewed again shortly after the election.[2] The data of the present article are all based on the sample of 1614 people who were interviewed both before and after the election.

* * *

THE OBJECTIVES

Studies of political behavior and particularly sample surveys related to voting behavior have demonstrated that during recent years the followers of the two major political parties have differed substantially in their views on the pressing issues of the day.[3] In 1948, for example, the amendment of the Taft-Hartley Labor Act became an issue of such heat that it divided Republican and Democratic voters almost as clearly as the question as to who was to become president. It has recently been proposed that party identification and attitudes on partisan issues may exercise reciprocal relationships producing uniformity among party followers, some identifying with the party because of its stand on issues, others adopting positions on issues in order to conform to party position.[4]

[2] Two hundred and twenty-two of the original 2021 respondents, who constituted an extra loading of the sample in the Far West, were dropped from the November sample. An additional 185 respondents could not be reinterviewed. Statements of the sample design and sampling errors and copies of the questionnaires may be obtained from the Survey Research Center upon request.

[3] Angus Campbell and R. L. Kahn, *The People Elect a President* (Ann Arbor, 1952); Warren E. Miller, "Party Preference and Attitudes on Political Issues: 1948-1951," *American Political Science Review*, Vol. 47, pp. 45-60 (March, 1953).

[4] George Belknap and Angus Campbell, "Political Party Identification and Attitudes toward Foreign Policy," *Public Opinion Quarterly*, Vol. 15, pp. 601-23 (Winter, 1951-52).

The major purpose of the present article is to make available new data concerning the role of political issues in a presidential election campaign. Although a short appendix presents data showing the voting records of the major demographic groupings in the 1948 and 1952 elections, the primary intent of the article is to carry further than has hitherto been possible the analysis of the relationship of the voter's attitudes on partisan issues to his actual vote.

Limitations of space and the preliminary state of our analysis preclude any exhaustive treatment of the relation of issues to voting behavior in the recent election. We will concentrate, therefore, on two of the most striking characteristics of the 1952 vote—the unusually large turnout, and the shift to the Republicans after a generation of Democratic rule—and attempt to show how these phenomena were related to the issues covered in this study. The first two sections of this article, therefore, will be mainly concerned with the following two questions:

How were issues related to the movement of citizens from the passivity of non-voting into the act of voting in the 1952 presidential election?

How were issues related to changes in voting behavior whereby blocs of voters were lost by one party and gained by another party?

In addition to the study of campaign issues, another familiar method of analyzing the presidential vote has been through comparison of the voting records of various easily defined sub-groupings of the national electorate. Past research has corroborated common-sense impressions that, during the last twenty years, there has been a tendency for labor union members, college educated people, residents of large cities, farmers, Catholics, Southerners and members of other such social classifications to cast their votes rather predominantly for one or the other party. This has in fact led to the proposition put forward by Lazarsfeld and his associates that voting may be largely understood as an expression of the individual's conformance to his basic sociological environment.[5]

Although these relationships between socio-economic groupings and the vote have usually been considered separately from the relationships between campaign issues and the vote, the two analytic approaches overlap in many ways. As politicians have recognized in shifting their arguments to suit their audience, many issues have differential meaning and importance for different segments of the population. An analysis which systematically examines the differential relation between issues and the vote in different sub-groupings of the national electorate should provide added insight both into the meaning of the issues and the reasons for intergroup voting differences. Although such a systematic analysis is beyond the scope of the present report, some preliminary data bearing on this problem will be presented. The third section of this report will be mainly concerned with the following question:

Were the relationships between specified issues and voting behavior in the 1952 election essentially the same for all major sections of the electorate or were there important differences between people in different socio-economic groupings?

THE DATA

A full investigation of public attitudes on the political issues of the 1952 campaign would have required a very extensive interview devoted entirely to this objective. Because of the pressure of other interests it was decided to restrict this aspect of the present study to seven questions, three relating to domestic issues and four to foreign policy issues.[6] They were asked as part of the pre-election interview. These questions were chosen on an a priori basis as representing areas of relatively clear party difference and covering a broad range of governmental activities.

A major characteristic of the items is that they are all issues on which the Truman Administration accepted responsibility for a particular position. Adherence to this criterion means, of course, that these particular questions cannot be thought of as a representative sample of all the questions which might have been asked concerning the issues of the campaign. It will be noted, for example, that no inquiries were made regarding "corruption" or "communism in government" although these accusations were prominently featured in the oratory of the campaign.[7] The questions were selected with the following broad considerations in mind: The issues should encompass fundamental, long term party differences (e.g., governmental social welfare activity, U.S. foreign involvement), they should tap both ideological orientations and the less sophisticated "bread and butter" reactions (e.g., Taft-Hartley, FEPC, U.S. entry in the Korean war), and they should provide information on recent partisan controversies (e.g., U.S. China policy, current U.S. Korean policy).

It is possible that a different choice of questions might have yielded results different from those which are presented here. However, the questions which were used were chosen because they bore on issues which appeared to be of major significance and it is not probable that other questions bearing on these same issues would have yielded substantially different results.

Each of the seven questions was scored as to whether the respondent expressed an opinion supporting the policy of the Truman Administration or opposing it. For each question there were some respondents who did not offer a clearly pro- or anti-Democratic opinion, either because they knew nothing about the question (as in the case of the Taft-Hartley Act) or because they did not hold any clearly partisan position regarding it. In the presentations which follow, the proportions of supporting, opposing and neutral-uncertain responses to-

---

[5] P. Lazarsfeld, B. Berelson, and H. Gaudet, *The People's Choice* (New York, 1948).

[6] [Footnote omitted.]

[7] A separate analysis of the importance of these charges, based on the coding of certain open-ended questions in the interview, will be included in a later report.

tal to 100 per cent for each of the group-ings which is being represented. For the convenience of the reader, an Index of Partisanship is also included. This is ob-tained by subtracting the proportion of re-sponses opposing the Democratic position from the proportion supporting it.

Each of the respondents was asked in the November interview how he had voted on November 4th. Seventy-four per cent of the sample said they had voted.[8] The two-party division of their two-party vote was 58 per cent for Eisenhower and 42 per cent for Stevenson, indicating a slight bias "over and above the actual Eisenhower vote" but well within the sampling error of the sur-vey. When the opinions of these Democratic and Republican voters on the seven issues

[8] It must be remembered that the sample excluded the institutional population, the "floating" population, people living in military establishments, etc. Such people are estimated to total nearly ten million and it may be safely assumed that they are very largely non-voters.

are compared it is possible to see the extent to which these particular questions divided the followers of the two parties (Table 1).

The absolute values which are presented in this and the following tables are much less important for the present analysis than the relation of these values to each other. The significant conclusion to be drawn from Table I is the fact that on all of the seven questions Democrats and Republicans, taken as total groups, differ in their opinions and differ in the direction of their party posi-tion. Throughout the seven issues one finds more Democratic than Republican voters supporting Democratic policies. On four of the items there is both a preponderance of Democratic support for Democratic policies and, at the same time, a comparable bal-ance of Republican opposition to the same policies.

It will be noted that the issue of FEPC was least discriminative of all the seven is-sues in separating Democratic and Repub-lican voters. Attitudes on this issue are also

TABLE 1

THE RELATIONSHIP BETWEEN 1952 VOTE FOR PRESIDENT AND
ATTITUDES ON SEVEN 1952 CAMPAIGN ISSUES

Issue	Vote— 1952	Support Demo-cratic Position	Neutral or Un-certain	Oppose Demo-cratic Position	Total	Index of Partisan-ship
Governmental social	D	33%	62	5	100%	+28
welfare activity	R	19%	50	31	100%	−12
Taft-Hartley	D	32%	56	12	100%	+20
	R	9%	55	36	100%	−27
FEPC	D	51%	4	45	100%	+ 6
	R	40%	6	54	100%	−14
U.S. foreign	D	43%	13	44	100%	− 1
involvement	R	28%	7	65	100%	−37
U.S. China policy	D	60%	23	17	100%	+43
	R	38%	24	38	100%	0
U.S. entry in	D	52%	16	32	100%	+20
Korean war	R	34%	20	46	100%	−12
Current U.S.	D	52%	7	41	100%	+11
Korean policy	R	36%	8	56	100%	−20

Number of cases: Democratic voters—494
Republican voters—687

found to have markedly different relationships to voting patterns than do attitudes on the other six issues. Because of the unique character of this issue, possibly resulting from its strong racial and regional components, it is not included in the analysis which follows. A detailed statement of the interrelations of all the issues studied will be presented in a subsequent report.

The respondents of the survey were not only asked their 1952 vote; they were also asked how they voted in 1948.[9] When these two reports are combined for each respondent it is possible to subdivide the sample into politically meaningful groupings which have more analytical interest than the sample taken as a whole. The discussion which follows deals with five such groups:

The regular voters.

1. The regular Democrats, people who voted for the Democratic presidential nominee in both the 1948 and 1952 elections, hereafter referred to as DD's (362 cases).
2. The regular Republicans, people who voted for the Republican nominee in both 1948 and 1952, hereafter referred to as RR's (385 cases).

The new voters.

3. The new Democrats, people who did not vote in 1948, either because of age or other reasons, but who voted Democratic in 1952, hereafter referred to as ND's (104 cases).
4. The new Republicans, people who did not vote in 1948 but voted Republican in 1952, hereafter referred to as NR's (125 cases).

The switching voters.

5. The Democrats turned Republican, people who had voted Democratic in 1948 but who voted Republican in 1952, hereafter referred to as DR's (165 cases).[10]

[9] The authors are aware of the dangers of error in recalling a vote cast four years previously. Examination of the data on the reported 1948 votes shows evidence of some random error in report, but no serious systematic error. The question on 1948 vote was asked in the pre-election interview.
[10] There were also a few people who had voted Republican in 1948 but who voted Democratic in 1952. Their number was too small to warrant statistical analysis.

I. THE NEW VOTERS

The data of the survey show that those voters of 1952 who were non-voters in 1948 were composed, about one to three, of young people eligible to vote for the first time and older people who, for one reason and another, had not voted in the 1948 election. Both classes of new voters voted in very nearly the same proportions as did the rest of the population, the young people giving General Eisenhower a 57-43 majority of their two-party vote, and their older counterparts voting 53-47 for Republican electors. Inasmuch as the divisions within these two groups were not significantly different from the division within the rest of the population, it is apparent that, given no other changes, the elimination of the 1948 non-voters from the 1952 electorate would not have altered the proportionate distribution of the popular vote.

The fact that both these classes of new voters followed the national trend very closely in their choice of candidates indicates that they were not activated into the role of voters by any common point of view regarding current issues. On the contrary, it would appear that the ND's and the NR's must have differed about as much in their perceptions and attitudes as did the rest of the voters.

In order to reveal the possible relationships which may have existed in these groups between positions taken on the issues with which this study deals and preferences for one or the other candidate, it is necessary to compare the opinions expressed by the ND's and the NR's in answer to the different questions asked. This is done in Table 2, which also includes the responses given by the "regular" voters, DD's and RR's.

An overall inspection of this table makes apparent a clear polarity in partisan attitudes on each question, with a strong tendency toward a pro-Democratic position among the DD's and an anti-Democratic position among the RR's. The ND's tend to resemble the DD's and the NR's to resemble the RR's.

TABLE 2

RELATIONSHIPS BETWEEN PATTERNS OF 1948–1952 VOTING BEHAVIOR AND
ATTITUDES ON SIX 1952 CAMPAIGN ISSUES

Issue	1948–1952 Vote	Support Democratic Position	Neutral or Uncertain	Oppose Democratic Position	Total	Index of Partisanship
Governmental social welfare activity	DD	33%	64	3	100%	+30
	ND	37%	52	11	100%	+26
	NR	29%	49	22	100%	+ 7
	RR	15%	46	39	100%	−24
Taft-Hartley	DD	36%	52	12	100%	+24
	ND	27%	63	10	100%	+17
	NR	13%	63	24	100%	−11
	RR	7%	49	44	100%	−37
U.S. foreign involvement	DD	44%	11	45	100%	− 1
	ND	46%	13	41	100%	+ 5
	NR	31%	7	62	100%	−31
	RR	24%	6	70	100%	−46
U. S. China policy	DD	66%	19	15	100%	+51
	ND	51%	24	25	100%	+26
	NR	43%	24	33	100%	+10
	RR	33%	22	45	100%	−12
U.S. entry in Korean war	DD	53%	14	33	100%	+20
	ND	58%	14	28	100%	+30
	NR	36%	21	43	100%	− 7
	RR	31%	19	50	100%	−19
Current U. S. Korean policy	DD	55%	5	40	100%	+15
	ND	46%	3	51	100%	− 5
	NR	46%	4	50	100%	− 4
	RR	33%	6	61	100%	−28

It will be noted that the ND's are more consistently similar to their DD associates than the NR's are to the RR's. The distributions of the ND opinions differ only slightly from those of the DD's, in two cases appearing to be slightly more partisanly Democratic than the DD's and in the other four cases somewhat less. On the other hand, the differences between the distributions of the NR's and the RR's are generally larger and in every case the NR's tend to be less clearly Republican than the RR's.

When one considers the positions of the previously non-voting groups on individual issues, it may be seen that for the ND group four issues (governmental social welfare activity, Taft-Hartley Act, U. S. China policy,

and U. S. entry in Korean war) show a significantly larger number of pro-Democratic than anti-Democratic attitudes. On the questions of U. S. foreign involvement and current U. S. Korean policy the ND's are so evenly split as to make any statement about the relationship between *attitudes* on those questions and *behavior* in voting most tenuous.

On only one issue, U. S. foreign involvement, did the NR's show greater partisanship as a group than did members of the ND group. On most of the other issues they were clearly less homogeneous in their views. It may be concluded that except for the foreign involvement issue and, possibly, Taft-Hartley, the voting behavior of the NR's was only casually or occasionally related to their stands on those issues explored in the survey. Furthermore, the issue-vote relationships were markedly smaller for the NR's than for the ND's.

This, of course, does not preclude the possibility that for each NR voter some one or two issues, but not the remaining issues, were relevant for activating his or her Republican vote. This is a necessary reservation which applies to all such analysis conducted at this level. The absence of direct relationship between factors X and Y insofar as any *group* of individuals is concerned does not mean that the relationship does not exist for any individual within the group. It does mean, however, that in this instance the existence of a factor "X" (attitudes on an issue) is not the influence which alone produced the factor "Y" (Democratic or Republican vote) which is held in common by all members of the group.

It is possible to compare these relationships between the attitudes of "regular" voters and "new" voters in 1952 to comparable data obtained in a Survey Research Center study in 1948. In the earlier study a similar sample were asked how they had voted in the 1948 and previous elections.[11] A summary of the data from the two studies. . . . suggests that the role played by issues in activating former non-voters was different in 1952 than it had been in 1948. In the 1948 election voters who had previously been non-voters tended to take positions on issues with a degree of partisanship at least as great as that of the "regular" party voters. The plurality of ND's (individuals who usually had not voted but who voted Democratic in 1948) supporting Democratic policies in 1948 was approximately

[11] The questions about earlier voting behavior were not exactly the same in the two surveys. In 1948 the respondents were asked, "Have you voted in any presidential elections before this one? Have you usually voted Democratic or Republican?" In 1952 they were asked "In 1948, you remember that Truman ran against Dewey. Do you remember for sure whether or not you voted in that election? Which one did you vote for?"

the same as that found among members of the DD (Democratic voters in 1944 *and* 1948) group. The NR's were in even greater agreement in supporting Republican policies than were their RR cohorts.

The 1948 election was, it seems in retrospect, by and large a party election. Neither candidate was overly attractive to people who were not confirmed party followers, the campaign was hardly the exciting, arousing campaign of 1952, and the outcome may have appeared to be so certain as to discourage usual non-participants from leaving their firesides to vote. In the absence of magnetic candidates or an exciting campaign, it may be argued that those usual non-voters who did vote in 1948 must have done so because of party loyalty or out of personal concern over particular political issues. If this supposition is valid, it then follows that the ND's and NR's of 1948 were largely party followers who knew the party line on the campaign issues, or they were citizens drawn into the political conflict primarily because of the issues. In any event, the ND's and NR's in a year of abnormally low turnout proved to be well aware of the political implications of their attitudes on issues and an unmistakably high relationship between their stand on issues and the direction of their vote resulted.

When the 1952 side of the picture is examined it is seen that the degree of resemblance of the two groups of "new" voters to their "regular" counterparts is not the same as it had been in 1948. The attitudes of the ND's appear to be only slightly less Democratic in their direction than are those of the DD's. The NR's, however, who had been particularly partisan in 1948, were very near an even division in their attitudes in 1952.

The 1952 campaign differed from that of 1948 in a number of important respects. It presented two new candidates, one of whom was one of the most widely known and respected men in contemporary American life. It was featured by an intensity of campaigning and general political activity far beyond that of 1948. It was distinguished by the prominence of charges against the party in power, charges which were not issues in the sense used in this article but accusations of "corruption," "communist infiltration" and the like. It brought into focus more acutely than had been the case in 1948 the problem of over-extended one-party rule, the "time for a change" argument.

If it is surmised that the impact of these non-issue elements of the 1952 campaign was favorable to the Republican candidate, the issue positions of the ND and NR groups are not difficult to understand. It is known that the pool of 1948 non-voters, from which both the ND's and NR's came, was largely Democratic in usual party preference.[12] It was this fact that gave rise to the popular supposition before the 1952 election that an increase in turnout would be advantageous to the Democrats. If the "new" voters in 1952 had come into the ranks of voters solely on the basis of party loyalty or party-linked issues, their total vote would very likely have favored the Democratic candidate. However, the other forces at work in the campaign apparently succeeded in changing this Democratic majority into a slight Republican majority. Presumably the 1948 non-voters of a Republican inclination were joined in 1952 by enough defectors from the pool of non-voting Democrats (probably those least firmly committed to a Democratic position on issues) to create an NR group slightly larger than the remaining ND group. Considering this defection of recently, and perhaps only partially, converted Democrats in the NR ranks and the probability that irregular voters of both parties are less likely than their more regular cohorts to be sufficiently involved in politics to hold highly partisan attitudes, it is not surprising that the issue positions of the NR group should not be as partisan as those of the "regular" Republicans (RR's).

In summary, the data presented in this section appear to justify the following statements:

1. As a group Democratic voters were significantly more likely than Republican voters to support Democratic policies on all of the issues subjected to inquiry in this study.

2. The distributions of the attitudes of "new" Democrats were very similar to those of "regular" Democrats.

3. The distributions of opinions of "new" Republicans were generally less "Republican" than those of the "regular" Republicans. The general issue of extent of American involvement in world affairs was the only one on which this group was highly partisan.

4. A comparison of the voting of "new" voters in 1948 and "new" voters in 1952 suggests that differences in the electoral situations of the two years resulted in gains for the Republican party in 1952 which were not primarily associated with partisan issues as defined in this study.

II. THE "SHIFTING" VOTERS

A brief study of the reported previous voting behavior of the 1952 voters is enough to reveal that former Democrats who voted for Eisenhower held the balance of power in the 1952 election. While sizeable numbers of 1948 non-voters were coming into the ranks of 1952 voters, dividing their favors rather equally between the two presidential aspirants, smaller numbers of people who had voted in 1948 were withdrawing from the political arena to become non-voters in 1952. Although the net gain realized by the Republicans from the movement to and from active or inactive voting status was enough to jeopardize the Democrats' slim margin of 1948, the movement of changing voters away from the Democrats (offset only by a shift of one per cent in the other direction) was of crucial importance. The switching of the DR changers was not only a movement of a larger number of people, it was also a movement of double importance inasmuch as each Republican gain was also a Democratic loss.

All told, some 20 per cent of the final Republican vote came from 1948 Democrats. Given this added Republican support, only an extreme combination of pro-Democratic shifts among other parts of the total electorate could have salvaged the Democratic party hopes for victory. Conversely, if these "shift-

[12] As shown in the 1948 Survey Research Center study and in as yet unpublished data from the present study.

ing" voters had remained Democrats, DD's instead of DR's, the other shifts which took place within the groups moving into and out of the active electorate would not have been sufficient to create an Eisenhower victory.

When the attitudes of these "shifting" voters are compared to those of the "regular" voters of the two parties it will be seen that they occupy a position between the extremes on every issue (Table 3). Their disagreements with the position of the "regular" Democrats are about equally great for both domestic and foreign issues. It must be noted, however, that these former Democrats do not go all the way to the "regular" Republican position on any of these issues. In this respect they differ from the DR's of 1948 whose partisanship on the issues of that year was scarcely less Republican than that of the 1948 RR's.

The issue positions of the 1948 Democrats turned 1952 Republicans (DR's) resemble those of the 1952 Republicans who had not

voted in 1948 (NR's). It will be recalled, however, that the NR's are made up of people of both Democratic and Republican party preference. Their intermediate position on issues appears to result from combining these two unlike groups as well as from their relatively low level of political involvement (as inferred from their nonvoting in 1948). This is not the case with the DR's; they were all voting Democrats in 1948. The fact that the distributions of their attitudes digress so clearly from those of the "regular" Democrats may be explained in either of two ways:

1. The 1952 DR's may have been people whose attitudes had never been as "Democratic" as those of other Democrats, who had voted Democratic in 1948 out of a sense of party loyalty and the lack of any impelling reason to do otherwise, but who were jolted loose from the Democratic party in 1952 by some non-issue factor or combination of factors which was present in the electoral situation of that year.

TABLE 3

RELATIONSHIPS BETWEEN SHIFT OF VOTE, 1948–1952, AND ATTITUDES ON SIX 1952 CAMPAIGN ISSUES

Issue	1948–1952 Vote	Support Democratic Position	Neutral or Uncertain	Oppose Democratic Position	Total	Index of Partisanship
Governmental social welfare activity	DD	33%	64	3	100%	+30
	DR	22%	54	24	100%	− 2
	RR	15%	46	39	100%	−24
Taft-Hartley	DD	36%	52	12	100%	+24
	DR	12%	61	27	100%	−15
	RR	7%	49	44	100%	−37
U.S. foreign involvement	DD	44%	11	45	100%	− 1
	DR	35%	7	58	100%	−23
	RR	24%	6	70	100%	−46
U.S. China policy	DD	66%	19	15	100%	+51
	DR	47%	25	28	100%	+19
	RR	33%	22	45	100%	−12
U.S. entry in Korean war	DD	53%	14	33	100%	+20
	DR	41%	16	43	100%	− 2
	RR	31%	19	50	100%	−19
Current U. S. Korean policy	DD	55%	5	40	100%	+15
	DR	38%	6	56	100%	−18
	RR	33%	6	61	100%	−28

2. The 1952 DR's may have been no more or less Democratic in their views on issues in 1948 than were other Democrats. During the ensuing four years they may have been converted from their Democratic point of view to a more nearly Republican position on issues. Having made this ideological transition it was natural for them to vote Republican in 1952.

It is probably safe to assume that both these mechanisms were at work in creating the 1952 DR's. If the process had been mainly one of conversion one might have expected that the foreign policy issues might have shown greater discrepancies from the "regular" Democratic position than would the domestic issues, considering the events of the 1948-1952 period. The fact that this is not true suggests that the "switching" voters were largely people who were not sufficiently bound to the Democratic party by conviction regarding its position on issues or by simple party loyalty to withstand the pressure of other factors which were important at the time of the campaign.

This section may be summarized in the following statements:

1. The "shifting" voters fell between the "regular" voters of the two parties in their attitudes on the issues presented in this study.
2. No single issue appears to have exerted any special influence in the defection of 1948 Democrats to a 1952 Republican vote.
3. It is suggested that the "switching" voters were particularly susceptible to factors favoring the Republicans because of their comparative lack of conviction regarding the Democratic position on partisan issues.

III. SOCIO-ECONOMIC GROUPINGS WITHIN THE ELECTORATE

The two preceding sections have dealt with the relation between voting behavior and six issues of the presidential campaign, with particular emphasis on the change in voting behavior between 1948 and 1952. In this section we will be concerned with the question of whether the relations between these issues and voting behavior were essentially the same for all classes of people within the electorate, or whether there were

differential relationships for people in different socio-economic groupings. Since space does not permit a discussion of all relevant demographic groups, the discussion will center around four of the variables generally associated with the New Deal-Fair Deal coalition—occupation, union membership, education, and religion. We will compare the "regular" voters (DD's and RR's) found in these different groupings on their *overall* issue stand[13] and on their attitudes on two selected *individual* issues.

Inter-group Comparisons on Overall Issue Stands

The distributions of attitudes of the different voting groups within demographic categories are presented in Table 3. Comparing the distributions of the "regular" Democratic voters (DD's) from group to group, and examining the inter-group comparisons of the "regular" Republican voters (RR's), one finds a very high degree of similarity within the demographic groupings. This is particularly true of the Republican voters (RR's). Catholic and Protestant, union member and non-union member, businessman and farmer—all classifications of "regular" Republicans took very nearly the same overall Republican position on issues.

The "regular" Democrats show somewhat more variation from group to group. For example, there is a tendency for better educated DD's to take a more homogeneous Democratic position than their less highly educated party associates. These distributions are based on small samples, however, and the differences which appear are not large.

Although the "shifting" voters and the "new" voters are not presented in Table 4, some mention may be made of their distributions. The DR voters, shifting to the Republican candidate from a Democratic vote in 1948, take a general issue position between the "regular" Democrats and Re-

[13] By "overall issue stand" we mean a summary score based on the attitudes on all six issues, rather than the attitude on an individual issue.

TABLE 4

RELATIONSHIPS BETWEEN SUMMARY SCORES ON CAMPAIGN ISSUES AND PATTERNS
OF 1948–1952 VOTING BEHAVIOR OF DIFFERENT SOCIO-ECONOMIC GROUPS

Group	1948–1952 Vote	Support Democratic Position*	Neutral or Uncertain*	Oppose Democratic Position*	Total	Index of Partisanship*	Number of Cases
Occupation:							
Professional and	DD	56%	21	23	100%	+33	60
business	RR	28%	19	53	100%	−25	127
White collar	DD	49%	25	26	100%	+23	33
	RR	27%	22	51	100%	−24	51
Skilled and semi-	DD	48%	26	26	100%	+22	136
skilled	RR	23%	27	50	100%	−27	75
Unskilled	DD	46%	27	27	100%	+19	49
	RR	21%	27	52	100%	−31	20
Farm operator	DD	42%	28	30	100%	+12	29
	RR	21%	23	56	100%	−35	36
Union Membership:							
Union	DD	55%	22	23	100%	+32	143
	RR	24%	24	52	100%	−28	74
Non-union	DD	44%	29	27	100%	+17	219
	RR	25%	22	53	100%	−28	311
Education:							
College	DD	57%	21	22	100%	+35	33
	RR	28%	16	56	100%	−28	94
High school	DD	52%	24	24	100%	+28	171
	RR	24%	25	51	100%	−27	193
Grade school	DD	44%	29	27	100%	+17	157
	RR	22%	24	54	100%	−32	97
Religion:							
Catholic	DD	50%	28	22	100%	+28	119
	RR	26%	23	51	100%	−25	66
Protestant	DD	46%	26	28	100%	+18	207
	RR	24%	22	54	100%	−30	308

* These figures were obtained by adding the scores for all six issues and dividing by six.

publicans in nearly all of the socio-economic groupings considered. The ND's and NR's also tended to follow the ND and NR issue pattern described in the first section of this report in all of the demographic subgroups studied. The samples of these voting groups are too small to support detailed presentation.

Inter-group Comparisons on Two Individual Issues

It might be reasonably objected that the failure of these data to show any sizeable differences in attitudes between people drawn from very different circumstances of life may have resulted from the combining of scores from six separate issues. It is possible, for example, that two RR groups that are similar in their distributions of combined scores might show significant differences on individual issues, differences that cancel each other out when the issues are combined. An intensive analysis of all six issues for all demographic groups is beyond the scope of this discussion. However, to give some indication of the additional variations revealed

by an analysis of individual issues, intergroup comparisons were made for the DD's and RR's on the most general domestic and foreign issues, those pertaining to government social welfare activity and foreign involvement. The data are presented in Tables 5 and 6.

These tables show a number of variations from the pattern described in Table 4. Perhaps most striking is the fact that the dif-

TABLE 5

RELATIONSHIPS BETWEEN ATTITUDES TOWARD GOVERNMENTAL SOCIAL WELFARE
ACTIVITY AND PATTERNS OF 1948-1952 VOTING BEHAVIOR OF
DIFFERENT SOCIO-ECONOMIC GROUPS

Group	1948–1952 Vote	Support Democratic Position	Neutral or Uncertain	Oppose Democratic Position	Total	Index of Partisanship	Number of Cases
Occupation:							
Professional and	DD	51%	49	0	100%	+51	60
business	RR	15%	41	44	100%	−29	127
White collar	DD	27%	70	3	100%	+24	33
	RR	14%	47	39	100%	−25	51
Skilled and semi-	DD	34%	61	5	100%	+29	136
skilled	RR	24%	51	25	100%	−1	75
Unskilled	DD	24%	76	0	100%	+24	49
	RR	37%	53	10	100%	+27	20
Farm operator	DD	36%	61	3	100%	+33	29
	RR	8%	42	50	100%	−42	36
Union membership:							
Union	DD	36%	62	2	100%	+34	143
	RR	27%	43	30	100%	−3	74
Non-union	DD	33%	63	4	100%	+29	219
	RR	13%	45	42	100%	−29	311
Education:							
College	DD	42%	55	3	100%	+39	33
	RR	13%	35	52	100%	−39	94
High school	DD	37%	59	4	100%	+33	171
	RR	15%	48	37	100%	−22	193
Grade school	DD	29%	68	3	100%	+26	157
	RR	20%	47	33	100%	−13	97
Religion:							
Catholic	DD	28%	71	1	100%	+27	119
	RR	19%	47	34	100%	−15	66
Protestant	DD	32%	63	5	100%	+27	207
	RR	15%	44	41	100%	−26	308

ferent RR groups, which showed such similarity in their overall issue scores, differ considerably on these two individual issues. This is particularly evident when the RR's of the different occupational groups are compared. The Republican voters of higher occupational status take a more Republican position on the general domestic issue than do the lower status occupation groups, but are less Republican on the general foreign issue. "Regular" Republicans among "blue-collar" workers are as a group extremely "isolationist" in their views on foreign involvement but they do not support the Republican position on the role of the federal government in domestic welfare programs. As might be expected, the variations among the "regular" Republicans of different educa-

TABLE 6

RELATIONSHIPS BETWEEN ATTITUDES TOWARD FOREIGN INVOLVEMENT AND
PATTERNS OF 1948-1952 VOTING BEHAVIOR OF DIFFERENT
SOCIO-ECONOMIC GROUPS

Group	1948–1952 Vote	Support Democratic Position	Neutral or Uncertain	Oppose Democratic Position	Total	Index of Partisanship	Number of Cases
Occupation:							
Professional and	DD	61%	2	37	100%	+24	60
business	RR	33%	3	64	100%	−31	127
White collar	DD	41%	15	44	100%	−3	33
	RR	33%	2	65	100%	−32	51
Skilled and semi-	DD	45%	7	48	100%	−3	136
skilled	RR	22%	4	74	100%	−52	75
Unskilled	DD	42%	7	51	100%	−9	49
	RR	0	10	90	100%	−90	20
Farm operator	DD	22%	11	67	100%	−45	29
	RR	14%	9	77	100%	−63	36
Union membership:							
Union	DD	53%	8	39	100%	+14	143
	RR	19%	7	74	100%	−55	74
Non-union	DD	40%	7	53	100%	−13	219
	RR	26%	3	71	100%	−45	311
Education:							
College	DD	69%	9	22	100%	+47	33
	RR	37%	2	61	100%	−24	94
High school	DD	46%	6	48	100%	−2	171
	RR	25%	4	71	100%	−46	193
Grade school	DD	40%	8	52	100%	−12	157
	RR	11%	6	83	100%	−72	97
Religion:							
Catholic	DD	53%	8	39	100%	+14	119
	RR	24%	5	71	100%	−47	66
Protestant	DD	39%	6	55	100%	−16	207
	RR	24%	4	72	100%	−48	308

tional background follow the same pattern as those associated with occupational differences.

Following the general "cross-pressure" hypothesis,[14] one might be led to explain some of these differences among "regular" Republican voters of different educational and occupational groupings as resulting from the interaction of party position and group position in determining attitudes on issues. Thus, when the issue position dictated by one's party choice comes in conflict with the position that is congruent with one's membership in a given socio-economic grouping, one might predict that there would be a compromise between the two extremes. Conversely, when a group position coincides with a party position on an issue, the result might be expected to be a position more extreme than either would have been without the other. Accordingly, one might explain the failure of "blue-collar" Republicans as a group to support the Republican position on the government welfare activity issue as the result of a position dictated by socio-economic group interest counteracting the position associated with party choice. On the other hand, the extremely homogeneous support that the "regular" Republicans of lower education give to the Republican position on the issue of U. S. foreign involvement might be thought of as resulting from a reinforcement of the restricted world view common among people of lower education by a congruent party position.

Although this interpretation may be appropriate for these variations among the "regular" Republicans of different education and occupations, it does not explain other variations which appear in the tables. Unlike the patterns of the RR's, which are different for the two issues, the inter-group occupational and educational patterns for the "regular" Democrats are the same for both issues. On both the foreign and domestic issues there is a tendency for DD's of higher occupational status (professional people and businessmen) to take a more homogeneous

[14] P. Lazarsfeld, B. Berelson, and H. Gaudet, *The People's Choice*, cited in n. 5.

Democratic position than that taken by "blue collar" workers, and there is a similar tendency for greater support of the Democratic position to be associated with higher education. In terms of socio-economic group interest one might have expected "blue collar" Democratic voters to show more support for activity of the federal government in social welfare programs than would be shown by Democrats of professional or businessman status, whereas, as indicated in Table 5, they tend to show less.

A similar discrepancy appears when differences between the attitudes of the "regular" voters of the two main American religious groupings are examined. If one were to assume that American Catholics might have special reasons to support an internationalist position in current foreign policy, one would expect that Catholics of each party would react more favorably to the foreign involvement question than Protestants within that party. In fact Catholic Democrats do support the foreign involvement policy in somewhat larger proportion than do Protestant Democrats, but among Republicans there is no difference between Catholics and Protestants on this issue. So far as this issue is concerned, religious group position appears to have some reinforcing influence on the attitudes of Catholics who voted for the Democratic party, but no modifying influence on the attitudes of Catholics who voted for the Republican party.

It is clear that these analyses of the interaction of the influences of party and socio-economic position are hazardous in the absence of the careful control of possible "third factors." More elaborate treatment of these data is not possible in the present article.

The data presented in this section may be summarized as follows:

1. When attitudes on the six issue questions are combined into a single score, the positions of "regular" Republicans among the basic occupational, union, educational and religious classifications are seen to follow very similar distributions. This is also true of "regular" Democrats in these different categories.

2. When distributions of attitudes on two individual questions are considered, differences between demographic groupings within the two parties are apparent and significant.

3. The determination of variations between socio-economic groupings within parties in their attitudes regarding issues is too complicated to be adequately described by the simple juxtaposition of party position and socio-economic position.

CONCLUSIONS

The analysis presented in this article was intended to show how the followers of the two major parties in the 1952 presidential election divided in their views regarding prominent campaign issues. It also sought to determine the extent to which shifts in voting behavior, from non-voting to voting and from one party to the other, were associated with attitudes on issues. Finally, it compared the issue positions of people of different socio-economic groupings within each party in order to study the influence of demographic position on relations between issue positions and votes.

Although questions might be raised regarding the selection of the specific issues which were chosen for study, it is noteworthy that all of the issues presented proved to be highly partisan, in the sense that they divided the Democratic and Republican voters to a degree that cannot be attributed to factors of chance. Although other questions might have been asked which would not have divided the voters significantly into party groupings, it is apparent that Democrats and Republicans differed in 1952 in their attitudes on the important issues tapped by the questions asked in this study.

It is also clear that "regular" party followers were as a group more partisan in their views on these issues than were people who do not vote regularly or who switch from one party to the other. The irregular voters as a group held attitude positions midway between the attitudes of regular Democrats and Republicans.

Those people who had not voted in 1948 but who voted in the 1952 election divided their votes between Eisenhower and Steven-

son in about the same ratio as the rest of the population. There was a clear difference, however, in the degree to which these new Democratic or Republican voters shared the partisan position on issues of the party they supported. On the issues considered in this study, new Democrats were virtually as partisan as regular Democrats; new Republicans were significantly less partisan than regular Republicans. It is hypothesized that this discrepancy resulted from factors in the campaign situation, not associated with issues as defined in this study, which worked to the advantage of the Republican party.

In the same manner the shifting voters, those who had voted for Truman in 1948 but supported Eisenhower in 1952, were not as partisan as either the regular Republicans or Democrats in their views on the issues presented in this study. This leads to the supposition that these defectors, who made a critically important contribution to the total Eisenhower vote, were susceptible to the forces which led them to change their vote partly because they had no firm commitment to the Democratic position on foreign and domestic issues. By the same token, the fact that many of them have not accepted the Republican position on these issues implies that that party's hold on them is precarious.

Although the present article could not examine the effects of socio-economic position in great detail, the data are sufficient to indicate that they do not follow an entirely consistent pattern. Although in some cases factors associated with socio-economic position appeared to counteract party position as a determiner of attitudes, in other instances attitudes associated with party position seemed virtually unaffected by socio-economic differences. This question requires much fuller exploration before it can be adequately answered.

Finally, the reader is reminded again that the present article is a preliminary analysis taken from a study of much broader scope. It is hoped that some of the questions which are left unanswered in this presentation will be more adequately treated in the more comprehensive report which will be forthcoming.

APPENDIX I

The preceding discussion has dealt with demographic characteristics and the vote only as these characteristics related to differential commitment on a number of campaign issues. Since there may be some interest in data on the overall distribution of the 1952 vote in different demographic groupings, and a comparison with the comparable distributions in 1948, the following tables are presented. They show comparisons between the 1948 and 1952 vote of the occupational, educational, and religious groupings discussed in this report, as well as a number of others on which there are comparable data.[15]

The most striking impression gained from these tables is that the shift toward the Republicans in 1952 was a general one which affected many different classes of the population. Some components of the "Democratic coalition"—skilled and semi-skilled workers,

[15] The figures for the 1948 vote are based on the study of the 1948 election conducted by the Survey Research Center.

Catholics, young voters, union members—showed large scale defections from their Democratic preference in 1948. The shift toward the Republicans was equally marked among groups which are not usually considered to be members of this "coalition." White collar workers, for example, went from an even vote distribution in 1948 to a ratio of almost 2 to 1 in favor of the Republicans; farmers, who had favored the Democrats in 1948, swung heavily into the Republican column in 1952. Except for the Negro group, the only groups which showed no shift in favor of the Republicans were those which already had a traditionally heavy Republican majority—the high status occupational and educational groups.

The numbers of cases of the separate demographic classifications do not always add to the total sample of 1614 respondents. This results from the omission of small numbers of respondents who did not fall into the classifications represented or from whom the relevant information was not obtained.

TABLE 1

RELATION OF OCCUPATION TO VOTING BEHAVIOR IN 1948 AND 1952

| | OCCUPATION | | | | | | | | | |
| Voted for: | Professional and Managerial | | Other White Collar | | Skilled and Semi-Skilled | | Unskilled | | Farmers | |
	1948	1952	1948	1952	1948	1952	1948	1952	1948	1952
Democrat	15%	27%	38%	28%	52%	40%	33%	40%	25%	24%
Republican	57	60	39	52	15	34	12	19	13	42
Did not vote	25	12	18	19	29	26	49	41	54	33
Not ascertained, voted other, etc.	3	1	5	1	4	*	6	*	8	1
Total	100%	100%	100%	100%	100%	100%	100%	100%	100%	100%
Number of Cases	117	333	79	155	164	462	85	174	105	178

* Less than one-half of one per cent.

TABLE 2

INCOME IN RELATION TO VOTING BEHAVIOR IN 1948 AND 1952

INCOME

Voted for:	Low†		Medium†		High†	
	1948	1952	1948	1952	1948	1952
Democrat	28%	22%	36%	35%	29%	28%
Republican	16	31	24	40	46	57
Did not vote	53	47	33	24	20	14
Not ascertained, voted other, etc.	3	*	7	1	5	1
Total	100%	100%	100%	100%	100%	100%
Number of Cases	179	312	327	852	149	415

* Less than one-half of one per cent.
† Low income: 1948, $0–$1,999; 1952, $0–$1,999.
  Medium income: 1948, $2,000–$3,999; 1952, $2,000–$4,999.
  High income: 1948, $4,000 and over; 1952, $5,000 and over.

TABLE 3

RELATION OF LABOR UNION MEMBERSHIP TO VOTING BEHAVIOR IN 1948 AND 1952

"DOES RESPONDENT OR HEAD OF FAMILY BELONG
TO A LABOR UNION?"

Voted for:	Yes		No	
	1948	1952	1948	1952
Democrat	56%	42%	25%	26%
Republican	13	33	32	46
Did not vote	27	24	38	27
Not ascertained, voted other, etc.	4	1	5	1
Total	100%	100%	100%	100%
Number of Cases	150	439	493	1165

TABLE 4

RELATION OF EDUCATION TO VOTING BEHAVIOR IN 1948 AND 1952

EDUCATION

Voted for:	Grade School		High School		College	
	1948	1952	1948	1952	1948	1952
Democrat	35%	30%	34%	34%	17%	24%
Republican	16	31	29	46	55	65
Did not vote	44	38	33	20	20	10
Not ascertained, voted other, etc.	5	1	4	*	8	1
Total	100%	100%	100%	100%	100%	100%
Number of Cases	293	660	266	712	99	238

* Less than one-half of one per cent.

TABLE 5

RELATION OF RELIGION TO VOTING BEHAVIOR IN 1948 AND 1952

| Voted for: | RELIGION | | | |
| | Protestant | | Catholic | |
	1948	1952	1948	1952
Democrat	25%	26%	49%	43%
Republican	28	45	25	41
Did not vote	43	29	20	15
Not ascertained, voted other, etc.	4	*	6	1
Total	100%	100%	100%	100%
Number of Cases	461	1156	140	343

* Less than one-half of one per cent.

TABLE 6

RELATION OF TYPE OF COMMUNITY TO VOTING BEHAVIOR IN 1948 AND 1952

| Voted for: | POPULATION CLASSIFICATION | | | | | |
| | Metropolitan Areas† | | Towns and Cities | | Open Country | |
	1948	1952	1948	1952	1948	1952
Democrat	47%	33%	27%	31%	24%	25%
Republican	32	43	30	42	12	41
Did not vote	17	22	38	27	59	33
Not ascertained, voted other, etc.	4	2	5	*	5	1
Total	100%	100%	100%	100%	100%	100%
Number of Cases	181	438	354	928	127	248

* Less than one-half of one per cent.
† "Metropolitan Area" includes the suburban areas and a few rural areas surrounding the big cities. When only the actual big city dwellers are considered, the distribution of the 1952 vote shows an approximately equal Democratic-Republican division, not the 4 to 3 ratio indicated in this table.

TABLE 7

RELATION OF RACE TO VOTING BEHAVIOR IN 1948 AND 1952

| Voted for: | RACE | | | |
| | White | | Negro | |
	1948	1952	1948	1952
Democrat	33%	32%	18%	26%
Republican	29	46	10	6
Did not vote	33	21	64	67
Not ascertained, voted other, etc.	5	1	8	1
Total	100%	100%	100%	100%
Number of Cases	585	1453	61	157

TABLE 8

RELATION OF SEX TO VOTING BEHAVIOR IN 1948 AND 1952

Voted for:	SEX			
	Male		Female	
	1948	1952	1948	1952
Democrat	36%	34%	29%	28%
Republican	28	45	26	41
Did not vote	31	20	40	31
Not ascertained, voted other, etc.	5	1	5	*
Total	100%	100%	100%	100%
Number of Cases	303	738	356	876

* Less than one-half of one per cent.

TABLE 9

RELATION OF AGE TO VOTING BEHAVIOR IN 1948 AND 1952

Voted for:	AGE							
	21–34		35–44		45–54		55 and over	
	1948	1952	1948	1952	1948	1952	1948	1952
Democrat	32%	31%	38%	34%	33%	33%	27%	27%
Republican	18	37	24	41	37	45	31	48
Did not vote	44	32	33	25	25	21	36	23
Not ascertained, voted other, etc.	6	*	5	*	5	1	6	2
Total	100%	100%	100%	100%	100%	100%	100%	100%
Number	198	485	174	381	126	284	156	442

* Less than one-half of one per cent.

THE INTERACTION OF MOTIVATING FACTORS

ANGUS CAMPBELL, GERALD GURIN, AND
WARREN E. MILLER

The preceding chapters have presented and discussed three concepts which we have felt to be important to the under- standing of the motivation of voting be- havior. Each of the concepts, party identifi- cation, issue orientation, and candidate orien-

A preliminary draft of a chapter from a volume by the authors to be published during 1954 by Row, Peterson, & Co. This volume is a report of the study of the 1952 election conducted by the Survey Research Center of the University of Michigan under the sponsorship of the SSRC Committee on Political Behavior.

tation, has been considered independently of the other two. It is now time to examine first, how the variables which have been constructed to represent these constructs relate to each other, and second, how these variables taken together relate to the vote.

Three facts may be quickly summarized in answer to the first of these questions. In the first place, it is clear that all the three variables are significantly correlated with each other. People who are strongly identified with one of the parties are likely to hold a strong position on issues and on the candidates. In general these positions are consistent in direction; Democratic party identifiers are more likely to take a Democratic position on issues and to regard the Democratic candidate more favorably than the Republican. It would be remarkable if this were not true. There are, however, many exceptions to these general trends. The correlations between the three variables are not so high that they could be said to be all measures of the same thing. There is clearly sufficient independence between the variables to justify the separate consideration they have been given.

Secondly, we have seen in the preceding chapters that the three variables do not behave in the same way in regard to some of the dependent variables we have considered. This is particularly striking in the differences that appear between party identification and the other two variables in the case of ballot-splitting. It has been shown that strength of party identification is significantly and consistently related with straight-ticket voting. This is not true, however, of either issue or candidate partisanship; neither of these factors has any relationship to amount of straight-ticket voting. The same discrepancy between party identification and the other two variables is found in their relation to the time of voting decision and, less clearly, in their relation to the amount of vacillation between candidates. In other words, party identification carries with it some component which is not

present in the other two factors. Some evidence has also been presented differentiating the candidate and issue factors. Issue partisanship and candidate partisanship seem to differ in the extent to which they are potential conflict-inducers. Ambivalence in issue partisanship is associated with lower scores of political participation but ambiguity in personal reactions to the candidates has no relationship to extent of participation. This distinction, together with others to be presented in the following chapter, supports our assumption that the candidate and issue measures relate to meaningfully different constructs.

Thirdly, we find that each of the three variables is clearly related to voting behavior when the influence of the other two variables has been removed. This can be demonstrated by noting the correlation of one variable with voting within segregated brackets of the other two variables. This procedure results in very small numbers of cases in some of the final cells but the fact can be clearly shown that each of the variables correlates independently both with extent of political participation and with the direction of the vote.

Since these data support our original assumption that the three variables we have considered do represent different motivational forces it becomes meaningful to move to the second question: How do combinations of these variables relate to the vote? It was proposed first that the greater the number of congruent forces activating a person in the election situation the more likely he will be to respond to them. Secondly, we expect that when the forces motivating a person are in conflict his response will be reduced. These hypotheses are tested in Table 1 as they apply to extent of participation in the 1952 election and in Table 2 as they apply to the choice of candidate in that election.

In Table 1 people represented by different combinations of the three motivational factors we have been discussing have been combined and their participation records are

TABLE 1

RELATION OF POLITICAL PARTICIPATION TO MOTIVATIONAL PATTERNS

Extent of
Participation — *Motivational Pattern*

	DDD	DDR	DRR	RRR
Active voters	29%	29%	35%	46%
Voters	54	52	50	50
Non-voters	17	19	15	4

	DD?	D?R	RR?
Active voters	32%	20%	40%
Voters	41	49	47
Non-voters	27	31	13

	D??	R??
Active voters	16%	19%
Voters	44	49
Non-voters	40	32

	???
Active voters	10%
Voters	38
Non-voters	52

presented.[1] Thus, we find the people (DDD) who were Democratic in all three factors, party identification, issue orientation, and candidate orientation, had a relatively high participation record (29 percent active voters and only 17 percent non-voters). Their Republican counterparts (RRR) were even more active, having the highest record of participation of any of the pattern groups. If the reader will follow down the sides of the triangular matrix of Table 1, going either from DDD through DD? and D?? to ??? or from RRR through RR? and R?? to ??? he will find a decreasing amount of participation recorded. Since each of these steps represents a decrease in the number of effective motivational forces (from three to none)

[1] As described in the previous chapters, the three variables are measured on a five-point scale, which includes strong and moderate categories of pro-Democratic and pro-Republican response, and one non-partisan category. To facilitate the handling of data for this discussion, the strong and moderate categories have been combined to form scales containing the following three categories: pro-Democratic (D), pro-Republican (R) and non-partisan (?).

these findings may be seen to support our expectation that people would be found to be politically active in direct relation to the number of factors which motivated them.

The hypothesis that conflict of forces would reduce political participation can be tested by reading across the top two rows of columns in Table 1. In the top row the relevant comparisons are between the DDD and DDR groups and between the RRR and RRD groups since these patterns are similar in the number of active forces (three) but differ in the consistency of these forces. In the first of these cases the conflicted pattern does not have a lower participation record than does the non-conflicted group. In the second case, RRR as compared to RRD, the expected difference is found. In the second row the DD? and RR? patterns should be compared to the D?R pattern; in this case all three patterns have two active forces but in D?R they are in conflict. Here again the conflicted pattern has a lower participation record. We may conclude that our data incline toward support of our expectation that conflict in motivation would be associated with reduction in extent of political participation although the findings are not entirely consistent.

Two additional facts should be noted from Table 1. The reader will observe that the participation records on the Republican side of the triangular matrix are all higher than the corresponding values on the Democratic side. Our two hypotheses give us no clue as to why this should be the case. It may be conjectured that in the 1952 situation the factors we have been considering were not equally strong for Republicans and Democrats. It is possible, for example, that Republican candidate orientation may have been a stronger motivating force than Democratic candidate orientation. They have been regarded as equal in this presentation and we have no way of assigning differential values to them.

On the other hand the greater participation of the Republican pattern groups may result from other factors which are not taken account of in the three variables which we have been considering. Considering the demographic and regional differences which we have seen to exist between Republicans and Democrats it would not be surprising to find that there are additional psychological factors which differentiate the party groups and are themselves correlated with readiness to participate in politics. Some of the factors which were measured in this study but not included in the present analysis, such as sense of political efficacy or sense of civic obligation, may be found in subsequent investigation to explain part of the difference we have seen between the participation records of people with Republican and Democratic motivational patterns.

One further aspect of Table 1 supports this suggestion that additional factors must be brought into the analysis before we can consider variations in political participation to be fully accounted for. The pattern at the bottom of the matrix shown in Table 1 represents the participation record of those people who were given neutral or indifferent scores on all three of the major variables of this study. Half of these people reported

having voted. Although this is a small group, comprising approximately five percent of the total sample, we must assume that some other forces than the ones we have dealt with impelled them to go to the polls. It may be hoped that the analysis of additional data gathered in this study will tell us something of what these forces were.

Table 2 presents the preference between Eisenhower and Stevenson expressed by people in the various pattern groups. If the reader will examine this table in the same manner as he did Table 1 he will find that the same general trends appear. Clear-cut choice of one candidate over the other diminishes as one proceeds down the sides of the matrix until the bottom pattern is found to show no preference between the two candidates. Conflict between forces is reflected in ambiguity in preference for candidates, as may be seen by reading across the top two rows of pattern groups. And, just as in the previous table, the Republican-oriented patterns are in every case more consistent in their preference for the Republican candidate than are the corresponding Democratic-oriented patterns in their preference for the Democratic candidate.

The conclusions to be drawn from Table 2 are essentially similar to those we have drawn from Table 1. Preference for a candidate is strongest among people reporting the largest number of factors impelling them toward that candidate. This preference is weakened if conflict exists among these motivating factors. From a comparison of Tables 1 and 2 we may conclude that our motivational analysis has been somewhat more successful in accounting for candidate preference than it has for extent of political participation. In the "pure" positive patterns (DDD and RRR) the number of people properly classified as to candidate preference approaches 100 percent; in the "pure" negative pattern (???) the preference between candidates falls to zero. Considering the fact that actual participation in an election is undoubtedly influenced by many factors that do not affect the simple statement of a preference between candidates, i.e.,

TABLE 2

RELATION OF VOTING PREFERENCE TO MOTIVATIONAL PATTERNS

Voting Preference	Motivational Patterns			
	DDD	DDR	DRR	RRR
Stevenson	93%	69%	17%	1%
Eisenhower	7	29	81	98
Other or none	—	2	2	1
	DD?	D?R	RR?	
Stevenson	78%	48%	6%	
Eisenhower	18	50	94	
Other or none	4	2	—	
	D??	R??		
Stevenson	64%	15%		
Eisenhower	28	81		
Other or none	8	4		
	???			
Stevenson	40%			
Eisenhower	39			
Other or none	21			

weather, illness, change of address, inconvenience, conflicting obligations and the like, it is not surprising that it should be relatively more difficult to predict.

Consistency and conflict in motivational forces relate not only to political participation and preference but also to the other measures of political behavior examined in the study. In addition to its inhibitory effect on participation, we would expect conflict in motivational forces to express itself in other behavioral measures of political indecision and conflict, i.e., in late and vacillating voting decision and in split-ticket voting. In general, these expectations are supported by the data. Table 3 indicates that people whose presidential vote was supported by a consistent pattern of motivational forces voted a straight ticket more often than those with a conflicting motivational pattern. Table 4 shows a similar relationship between conflict in the three motivational variables and the tendency to have vacillated in one's voting decision and to have considered voting for the opposing presidential candidate. Finally,

Table 5 indicates that a conflicting motivational pattern tended to be associated with lateness in arriving at one's voting decision (although one unexpected reversal in this table should be noted; Stevenson voters who were Democratic on two of the motivational measures and Republican on the third reported reaching their voting decision somewhat *earlier* rather than later than those Stevenson supporters who were Democratic on all three measures.)

The data which have been presented in the foregoing tables of this chapter describe the interaction of the forces which the preceding chapters of Section II have discussed individually. Taken together, the three factors with which we have been concerned have been shown to have a very high and predictable relationship with both extent of political participation and choice of candidate. Our expectations regarding the effects of consistency and conflict in motives associated with voting behavior have been largely fulfilled.

It is important to add that while the

TABLE 3

RELATION OF MOTIVATIONAL PATTERNS TO STRAIGHT TICKET VOTING

A. AMONG STEVENSON VOTERS

	*Motivational Patterns**			
	DDD	*DDR*	*DD?*	*D?R*
Voted straight Democratic ticket	84%	75%	78%	72%
Voted split ticket	16	25	22	28
Total	100%	100%	100%	100%
Number of Cases	70	56	137	78

B. AMONG EISENHOWER VOTERS

	RRR	*DRR*	*RR?*	*D?R*
Voted straight Republican ticket	75%	44%	69%	52%
Voted split ticket	25	56	31	48
Total	100%	100%	100%	100%
Number of cases	131	75	181	91

* In order to show the influence of a conflict in forces, the number of forces should be held constant. Therefore, in this table and in Tables 4 and 5 which follow, the relevant comparisons for the Stevenson voters are the DDD's compared to the DDR's, and the DD?'s compared to the D?R's. For the Eisenhower voters, the relevant comparisons are the RRR's compared to the DRR's, and the RR?'s compared to the D?R's. Because of the small number of cases, groups with the other motivational patterns are not included in these tables.

conclusions reached in this chapter are based on data from 1952 we would expect the rationale of our analysis to apply equally well to any other presidential election in this country. The motivating factors we have conceptualized do not depend on any specific candidates, issues, or parties. The changes in candidates and issues that occur from year to year give each election a quality of its own but, as contributors to the total motivation of the voters, candidates, issues, and parties are present every year. The rela-

TABLE 4

RELATION OF MOTIVATIONAL PATTERNS TO CONSIDERATION OF
VOTING FOR OPPOSING CANDIDATE

A. AMONG STEVENSON VOTERS

	Motivational Patterns			
	DDD	*DDR*	*DD?*	*D?R*
Considered voting for Eisenhower	16%	29%	16%	35%
Did not consider voting for Eisenhower	81	69	84	64
Other or not ascertained	3	2	—	1
Total	100%	100%	100%	100%
Number of Cases	70	56	137	78

B. AMONG EISENHOWER VOTERS

	RRR	*DRR*	*RR?*	*D?R*
Considered voting for Stevenson	5%	25%	12%	23%
Did not consider voting for Stevenson	95	75	87	75
Other or not ascertained	—	—	1	2
Total	100%	100%	100%	100%
Number of cases	131	75	181	91

TABLE 5

RELATION OF MOTIVATIONAL PATTERNS TO TIME OF VOTING DECISION

A. AMONG STEVENSON VOTERS

	Motivational Patterns			
	DDD	*DDR*	*DD?*	*D?R*
Knew all along; pre-convention	32%	34%	42%	24%
Decided at Stevenson's candidacy (pre-convention)	1	—	—	—
Decided at time of convention	23	39	26	31
Decided during campaign	33	14	22	23
Decided within two weeks of election	11	9	3	12
Decided on election day	—	—	4	6
Don't know when decided or not ascertained	—	4	3	4
Total	100%	100%	100%	100%
Number of Cases	70	56	137	78

B. AMONG EISENHOWER VOTERS

	RRR	*DRR*	*RR?*	*D?R*
Knew all along; pre-convention	40%	20%	35%	23%
Decided at Eisenhower's candidacy (pre-convention)	3	13	6	7
Decided at time of convention	43	33	36	29
Decided during campaign	9	24	15	22
Decided within two weeks of election	3	7	4	15
Decided on election day	—	—	—	2
Don't know when decided or not ascertained	2	3	4	2
Total	100%	100%	100%	100%
Number of cases	131	75	181	91

tive importance of each of the three factors may well vary from one election to the next but we would assume that in any election they will account for a major share of the total motivational force affecting the public. We would also expect them to facilitate and inhibit each other in much the same way as we have observed in this report.

PART FIVE

The Identification and Measurement
of Public Opinion and Propaganda

·11·

Problems of Data Collection in the Measurement of Public Opinion: Sampling, Interviewing, Questionnaire Construction

AREA SAMPLING: SOME PRINCIPLES OF SAMPLE DESIGN

THOSE NOT AT HOME: RIDDLE FOR POLLSTERS

THE FORMULATION OF THE RESEARCH DESIGN

DUAL PURPOSE OF THE QUESTIONNAIRE

THE GENERAL PROBLEM OF QUESTIONNAIRE DESIGN

THE ART OF ASKING WHY

THE CONTROVERSY OVER DETAILED INTERVIEWS—AN OFFER FOR NEGOTIATION

THE USE OF A PROJECTIVE DEVICE IN ATTITUDE SURVEYING

AREA SAMPLING—SOME PRINCIPLES
OF SAMPLE DESIGN

MORRIS H. HANSEN AND PHILIP M. HAUSER

Considerable attention has been devoted in the past months by survey and public opinion poll organizations to problems of sampling design. In part, this is attributable to the developments and innovations in sampling techniques and procedures in the statistical work of the Federal government, particularly in the Bureau of the Census and in the Bureau of Agricultural Economics, and, in part, to the investigation of the 1944 election poll of the Institute of Public Opinion by the House Committee to Investigate Campaign Expenditures.[1] This attention, however, undoubtedly reflects the continuing interest of survey organizations in the improvement of techniques in all phases of their activities, including sampling.

In the following an attempt is made to indicate the types of situations in which one method of sampling is to be preferred over another and to describe the principles on which area sampling is based. In this discussion of sampling methods, we shall consider only the discrepancies between the results obtainable from a complete enumeration of the population under consideration and the estimates made from a sample. Errors of interviewing and other errors arising

[1] Hearings before the Committee to Investigate Campaign Expenditures, House of Representatives, 78th Congress, 2nd Session on H. Res. 551, Part 12, *U.S. Government Printing Office*, Washington, 1945.

in survey results that are present in a complete enumeration as much as in a sample enumeration may be either more or less important than sampling errors. We shall confine our remarks here to errors arising because only a sample is covered instead of taking a complete census of a finite population.

The science of sampling design involves: (1) looking at the resources available, the restrictions within which one must work, the mathematical and statistical tools available, the accumulated knowledge of certain characteristics of the populations to be sampled; and (2) putting these together to arrive at the optimum design for the purpose at hand. Ordinarily, there are many alternatives of sample designs, and an understanding of alternative designs and an analysis of their efficiency is necessary if a wise choice is to be made.

THE CRITERIA FOR SAMPLE DESIGN

The over-all criterion that should be applied in choosing a sampling design is to so design the sample that it will yield the desired information with the reliability required at a minimum cost; or, conversely, that at a fixed cost it will yield estimates of the statistics desired with the maximum reliability possible. Various restrictions and limitations may necessarily be imposed upon the design

From the *Public Opinion Quarterly*, 1945, 9, 183-193. Reprinted by permission of the authors and the publisher.

other than mere cost restrictions. In wartime those restrictions have to do with the number of interviewers with cars and with gasoline rationing, as well as with the ordinary restrictions on time, personnel, etc.

A second criterion that a sample design should meet (at least if one is to make important decisions on the basis of the sample results) is that the reliability of the sample results should be susceptible of measurement. Methods of sample selection and estimation are available for which the risk of errors in the sample estimates can be measured and controlled. If such methods are used, as the size of the sample is increased, the expected discrepancies between the estimated value from the sample and the true value (i.e., the value that would be obtained from a complete census) will decrease. With such methods one can know the risk taken that the error due to sampling will exceed a specified amount. This risk (i.e., the risk that the error will exceed a specified amount) can be made as small as desired by taking a sample of adequate size.

An essential feature of such sampling methods is that each element of the population being sampled (housewives, voters, or whoever is being interviewed) has a chance of being included in the sample and, moreover, that that chance or probability is known. The knowledge of the probability of inclusion of various elements of the population makes it possible to apply appropriate weights to the sample results so as to yield "consistent" or "unbiased" estimates, or other estimates for which the risk of error can be measured and controlled.[2]

THE "QUOTA" METHOD

On the assumption that the above criteria should govern in the selection of a sample design, we are ready to consider the relative

[2] Here the words "consistent" and "unbiased" are used technically, and have a mathematical definition. See J. Neyman, "Lectures and Conferences on Mathematical Statistics," *Graduate School of the U.S. Department of Agriculture*, Washington 25, D.C., 1938, p. 131; and R. A. Fisher, "Statistical Methods for Research Workers," 6th edition, p. 12, *Oliver and Boyd* (1936), Edinburgh.

merits of the "quota" method, which is commonly used in opinion and market surveys, and the "area sampling" method.

The quota method in its essence involves: (1) the choice of selected characteristics of the population to be sampled, which are used as "controls"; (2) the determination of the proportion of the population possessing the characteristics selected as "controls"; and (3) the fixing of quotas for enumerators who select respondents so that the population interviewed contains the proportion of each class as determined in (2).

These specifications cannot provide sample estimates for which the risk of error can be measured because they do not provide for the selection of persons in a way that permits knowing the probabilities of selection. Errors in the setting of quotas may introduce unknown differences in the probabilities of selection of persons for inclusion in the sample. Moreover, because of the latitude permitted the enumerator in selection of respondents, it is less probable, for example, that the sample will include a housewife without children who works away from home than a woman with children who does her own housework, even though each may be in the same "control" group. Because the probabilities of inclusion in the sample of various classes of elements are unknown, the estimates frequently made of sampling error of quota sample results, supposedly based on sampling theory, usually are erroneous. A fuller treatment of the difficulties and limitations of the widely known and used quota method is given elsewhere.[3]

AREA SAMPLING

Area sampling eliminates dependence on the assignment of quotas that may be more or less seriously in error, and does not permit the interviewer discretion in the choice of the individuals to be included in the sample. With appropriate methods of desig-

[3] Philip M. Hauser and Morris H. Hansen, "On Sampling in Market Surveys," *The Journal of Marketing*, July 1944; and Alfred N. Watson, "Measuring the New Market," *Printers' Ink*, June 2, 1944, vol. 207, No. 9, pp. 17-20.

nating areas for coverage in the sample, the probabilities of inclusion of the various elements of the population are known, and consequently the reliability of results from the sample can be measured and controlled. Area sampling, of course, is not the only method that produces such results, but it is frequently an effective method.

To illustrate how and why area sampling works, suppose we are interested in sampling for certain characteristics of the population in a city. For example, we may want to know the total number of persons in certain broad occupational groups, and the number within each of these occupational groups who have a particular opinion, read a specified magazine, or are in a certain income class.

To estimate the total number of persons having the various characteristics mentioned above, we might proceed by first making an up-to-date list containing the name of every person, or, at considerably less expense, identifying every address or household, in the area to be surveyed, and then selecting a sample from this listing. Through taking a random sample from such listings of individuals or of households (interviewing all persons within the selected households if households are sampled), we could, with an adequate size of sample, obtain an excellent cross-section of the people in the city for any problem. This procedure would lead to highly reliable sample results, but frequently it is not practical for a number of reasons—the principal one being that preparing a listing would cost too much. Moreover, even where a complete pre-listing is already available, it may be too costly to interview the widely scattered sample that would be obtained by sampling individuals (or households) at random from such a listing. One method of getting a reduction in cost over sampling individuals from a pre-listing is to use an area sampling method in which the individuals interviewed are clustered into a selected set of sample areas.

In "area sampling" the entire area in which the population to be covered is located is subdivided into smaller areas, and each individual in the population is associated with one and only one such small area—for example, the particular small area in which he resides. Neither the names nor numbers of persons residing in the areas need be known in advance. A sample of these small areas is drawn, and all or a sub-sample of the population residing in the selected areas is covered in the survey.

A simple illustration will show that if a complete list of areas is available and a random selection of a sample of areas is made, and if the population of these sample areas is completely enumerated, then the chances (or probabilities) of being included are the same for each individual in the population. Moreover, on the average, the population surveyed within such a sample will reveal precisely the characteristics of the entire population from which the sample was drawn. A sample can be made as reliable a cross-section as desired, for any characteristics whatever, by merely increasing the size of the sample. Thus, if the population is changing in character, a random cross-section of small areas will reveal those shifts.

Suppose, for illustration, that we wish to draw a sample out of a universe of five blocks, and that everyone living in the selected blocks will be interviewed. We shall assume certain values for each block for the total number of votes for a specified candidate, as is shown below, although the illustration will work in the same way whatever values are assumed for the total vote or for any other characteristic.

Block No.	Votes for a Specified Candidate
1	4
2	6
3	2
4	6
5	1
Total	19

Each of the possible samples that will be obtained in drawing at random a sample of two blocks is listed below, together with the estimated total number of votes for the specified candidates from each sample. In unrestricted random sampling of blocks each of these possible samples will have the same probability of being selected. The estimated totals shown are obtained by computing the average number per block from the sample, and multiplying this sample average by the known total number of blocks in the population. The results for each possible sample are as follows:

Sample Consisting of Blocks	Total Votes for the Specified Candidate Enumerated in Sample	Estimated Total Votes for the Specified Candidate
1 and 2	10	25.0
1 and 3	6	15.0
1 and 4	10	25.0
1 and 5	5	12.5
2 and 3	8	20.0
2 and 4	12	30.0
2 and 5	7	17.5
3 and 4	7	20.0
3 and 5	3	7.5
4 and 5	7	17.5
Total		190.00

Average estimate 19.00
Standard deviation
of sample estimates 6.25

Notice, first, that each block appears in four out of ten possible samples of two that can be drawn. Therefore, the probability that an individual living in Block 1 will be included in the sample is .4, and the same is true of an individual living in any one of the other blocks, even though the number of persons in each block may be different. Note, also, that on the average, the estimates from the samples of voters for the specified candidate agree exactly with the actual number of votes for the specified candidate in this population. Furthermore, it is to be observed that the standard deviation of all possible estimates from the sample is equal to 6.25, which is exactly what is given by the formula for the average error of a sample of two blocks, based on statistical theory.[4]

Of course in any real problem the num-

[4] The standard error of the estimate from the sample, $\sigma_{\bar{x}}^{-1}$, is equal to $\sigma M \sqrt{\dfrac{M-m}{(M-1)m}}$, where σ is the standard deviation between the 5 original blocks of the characteristic being estimated, M is the total number of blocks in the population, and m is the number of blocks included in the sample.

ber of blocks will be considerably larger, more efficient methods of estimation may be available, and the sampling variance formula may be considerably more complicated. However, the above example will suffice to illustrate that with area sampling the probabilities of an individual being drawn into the sample can be fixed in advance of the actual enumeration, and that when this is so, and appropriate estimating procedures are used, it is possible to measure the average or standard error of the sample estimate.

The formula for the standard error shows that as the size of the sample increases, the standard deviation of the sample estimate decreases. This fact takes on more meaning for more realistic populations where the number of blocks in the population is very large. Under such circumstances, the average error of a sample may be made very small by drawing a fairly large number of blocks, even though the number in the sample consists of a very small proportion of the blocks in the population. We have oversimplified the case here to simplify the illustration, but the principles are just as applicable to more complicated cases.

ALTERNATIVE AREA SAMPLING DESIGNS

It is to be emphasized that many modifications in the area method may be introduced that would make effective use of available information concerning the areas being sampled. A very important variation in design is the introduction of a method of subsampling, in which two or more levels of sampling are used. For example, a national population sample may involve the selection of a sample of fairly large areas such as cities or counties, and then of a sample of smaller areas within each; or a sample for a city may involve the selection of a sample of blocks, and the subsampling of addresses or dwelling units from the selected blocks. However, if the subsampling approach is to conform with the criteria of good sampling outlined earlier in this paper, purposive or judgment methods of selecting the units to be included in the sample are excluded.[5]

SAMPLING EFFICIENCY

In evaluating the alternative designs that are possible, many statistical or mathematical tools are available for guiding one to the selection of an efficient method.[6] To illustrate, suppose one is considering taking a sample of blocks in a city, and then preparing a listing of all of the people in the sampled blocks and interviewing every k-th individual on the list. The reliability of the final estimate from such a sample will depend both upon the number of blocks in the sample and the average number of interviews within each block. It is fairly obvious that if all persons were interviewed within, say, twenty selected blocks, the sample result might be highly erratic, depending on the particular twenty blocks in the sample. However, if one-tenth of the persons were interviewed in each of 200 blocks, a much better cross section of the

city would be obtained and a more reliable sample estimate could be made with the same number of interviews. But if each of 200 blocks must be completely listed before selecting the persons for interview, and if the sample is scattered over 200 instead of twenty blocks, the cost of the survey is increased both by the cost of pre-listing and of more travel. Statistical theory is available to aid in the resolution of this conflict between cost and sampling reliability, and to guide one to an efficient design for a given cost.

The efficiency of area sampling can be increased through the effective use of good maps and of the available data for small areas.[7] For reasonably large-scale survey operations, it may pay to invest in maps which make possible the clear delineation of very small clusters of households and thereby eliminate or reduce the amount of pre-listing necessary. However, if detailed maps for defining very small areas are not available and it is necessary to pre-list whole blocks or moderately large selected rural areas, the cost of pre-listing need not be particularly significant where surveys are to be taken repetitively, since the cost of designating a sample of areas and of listing the dwelling units within the sample areas can be spread over a considerable number of surveys. In some Census experiences in which pre-listing is used and sub-samples are drawn from these listings for repetitive surveys, the cost over a year's time of pre-listing actually amounts to less than ten percent of the total survey cost.

AREA SAMPLING COSTS

It has sometimes been stated that area sampling methods are practicable for the government with mass surveys and extensive

[5] For an illustration of the application of an area subsampling design to obtain a national sample see "The Labor Force Bulletin," No. 5, *Bureau of the Census*, Washington, November 1944.

[6] Morris H. Hansen and William N. Hurwitz, "A New Sample of the Population," *Bureau of the Census*, Washington, Sept. 1944; also, "On the Theory of Sampling from Finite Populations," *Annals of Mathematical Statistics*, vol. XIV (1943), pp. 333-362; and "Relative Efficiencies of Various Sampling Units in Population Inquiries," *Journal American Statistical Association*, vol. 37 (1942), pp. 89-94. J. Neyman, "On the Two Different Aspects of the Representative Method; a Method of Stratified Sampling and the Method of Purposive Selection," *Journal Royal Statistical Society*, New Series, vol. 97 (1934), pp. 558-606; also, "Contribution to the Theory of Sampling Human Populations," *Journal American Statistical Association*, vol. 35 (1938), pp. 101-116. W. G. Cochran, "The Use of Analysis of Variance in Enumeration by Sampling," *Journal American Statistical Association*, vol. 34 (1939), pp. 492-510; also, "Sampling Theory when the Sampling Units are of Unequal Sizes," *Journal American Statistical Association*, vol. 37 (1942) pp. 199-212. P. C. Mahalanobis, "A Sample Survey of the Acreage under Jute in Bengal," *Sankhyā*, vol. 4 (1940), pp. 511-530.

[7] For discussion of available data for small areas, and of detailed maps see Morris H. Hansen and W. Edwards Deming, "On Some Census Aids to Sampling," *Journal American Statistical Association*, vol. 38 (1943), pp. 353-357; and Morris H. Hansen, "Census to Sample Population Growth," *Domestic Commerce*, vol. 32, No. 11 (1944), p. 6.

resources but are not adaptable to private research organizations on a limited budget. It is clear from the above, that at least the cost of actually selecting the sample need not be a highly significant factor in the total cost of such surveys—and that if this method is more costly than other less rigorous methods it is primarily because of the cost of interviewing within the designated sample households rather than because of the cost of locating the households in which interviews are to be made. Actually, the interviewing cost may be considerably affected by the necessity for call-backs or other steps taken to insure that the pre-designated person or household is interviewed; and procedures are available for making call-backs on only a sample of those not at home on first visit that will yield unbiased sample results.[8] It is ordinarily true, however, that in practice no reasonable number of call-backs can insure an interview with *all* persons designated for interview—and that a small bias may necessarily remain in the estimate due to the non-interviews that remain. An important distinction between area sampling methods and quota sampling methods lies in the treatment of non-interviews. The quota method, by ignoring the problem, has all of the biases without pointing up the magnitude of this source of error. The area method points up this source of error and makes it possible to correct for it (through calling back to interview all or a sample of the original non-interviews) if the proportion of non-interviews is high. The maximum error attributable to this factor can be kept very small and the maximum bounds of error coming from this cause can be measured.

CHOICE OF METHODS

There should be little question that the efficiency of a sample design should be eval-

[8] "Working Plan for Annual Census of Lumber Produced in 1943" published by the *Forest Service of the Department of Agriculture* in the fall of 1943. William N. Hurwitz extended the theory of double sampling to cover this problem.

uated in terms of *reliability of results* obtained per dollar of cost, *rather than in terms of the number of interviews* obtained per dollar. Through the use of the principles of sampling described or referred to above, one is aided in the selection of a sampling method which produces results of maximum reliability per dollar expended. However, these principles lead only to choices between alternative designs that conform with the criteria of good sampling, we have assumed. Therefore, they provide a guide only in choosing between those designs for which it is possible to measure the expected sampling error and the sources of the contribution to it, and thus, through proper adjustment in design, to minimize the sampling error per dollar expended.

Since statistical theory is not available for measuring the reliability of sample results obtained by the quota method, this method is automatically excluded from consideration if the criteria of sample design outlined above are to be followed. Thus, although the facts could not be established, it could happen that a quota sampling method would in a particular situation yield more reliable results per dollar than the optimum method chosen through the application of the criteria and sampling theory we have considered. How, then is one to know which to use? A possible answer to this question is the following. If it is important that results of specified reliability be obtained, and if there is a fairly heavy loss involved if the wrong action or decision is taken as a consequence of having depended on results that actually turn out to have larger errors than are considered tolerable, then quota sampling cannot safely be employed, and area sampling or some other method for which the risk of error can be controlled should be used. On the other hand, if conditions are such that only fairly rough estimates are required from the sample, and important decisions do not hinge on the result, then only a small sample is required, or the price to be paid for using a sample whose accuracy can be measured may not be justified. Under these conditions it may be that the biases of the quota method (or of the area method used without call-backs, or of other low-cost methods) will be considerably less important than the errors resulting from the small size of the sample, and thus such methods may produce results of sufficient reliability more economically than would more rigorous alternative methods. It would, of course, be wasteful to pay for assurance of greater reliability in the results than is necessary. However, it appears reasonable to believe that in most instances in which a fairly precise estimate is desired and for which, therefore, a fairly large sample is used, that the possible biases of quota sampling may be sufficiently serious as to make that method considerably less efficient in terms of reliability of results per dollar than the appropriate area sampling methods.

We believe that the question of what criteria should be applied in determining the most appropriate sampling method for a specific purpose is deserving of more extensive attention and consideration than it has yet received.

THOSE NOT AT HOME: RIDDLE FOR POLLSTERS

ERNEST R. HILGARD AND STANLEY L. PAYNE

In both public opinion and market surveys, interviews are commonly conducted in homes. But some people are hard to find at home. Thus special precautions are necessary to prevent a bias favoring too large a proportion of stay-at-homes. If those seldom home differ in important ways from those usually at home, this bias may seriously distort survey findings which purport to be based upon a representative sample.

Two chief methods are in use for assigning the persons to be interviewed in any selected sample area. The first of these is the quota-control system; the interviewer is told to find a specified number of persons fitting given age, sex, standard of living, or other characteristics. The second method is that of specific assignment; the interviewer is told precisely where to go and whom to interview. In the method of specific assignment it is possible to insist upon repeated call-backs to assure inclusion in the sample of those hard to reach. Under the quota-control system, on the other hand, if the interviewer finds no one at home at the first house approached, he is likely to obtain an interview from a neighbor who *is* at home. Since the quota assignment cannot specify all characteristics, the sample thus tends to include too high a proportion of people who possess the non-specified characteristics of stay-at-homes.

From the *Public Opinion Quarterly*, 1944, 8, 254-261. Reprinted by permission of the authors and the publisher.

An empirical check of some of the characteristics of those hard to find at home is available from the data of a survey of consumer requirements made in November 1943 by the Special Surveys Division of the Bureau of the Census for the Office of Civilian Requirements of the War Production Board.[1] The method used was that of specific assignment, and records were kept of the number of calls which were made before each of the interviews was obtained. It is therefore possible to make a statistical characterization of the interview sample obtained on the first call, on the second call, and on later calls. Analysis of the interviews obtained on the later calls gives a picture of the kinds of people less often home, and provides a basis for estimating the distortion which would be produced if they were not reached in the survey.

A few further details regarding the conduct of the survey are needed before the results can be properly appraised. The sample design is that being followed currently in the Monthly Survey of the Labor Force. Crews of interviewers work in each of sixty-eight areas carefully chosen to give a representative national sample. Within these areas, which consist of single counties or groups of adjacent counties, smaller geographical segments are chosen for residential listing. The final sample consists of a series of designated dwelling units described specifically, e.g., "apartment 106 at 900 Cold Street," "on Highway 6, the first house south of the Ramsdell School." Told precisely where to go, the interviewer is not permitted to exercise judgment in the choice of the house at which to call. In the case of a national sample of persons, the specific individual to be interviewed is also assigned on the basis of the characteristics of

the listed households in the sample.[2] For the survey under discussion, however, the unit was the household rather than the person; the only specification was that the respondent be either the housewife or another responsible person at the stated address—a person familiar with the household purchases.[3] Every attempted interview is reported, including calls at houses found vacant. This method of sampling insures that the sample properly reflects in-migration and out-migration, a matter of considerable importance during wartime.

A national sample of 4935 completed interviews was obtained, including urban and rural interviews. Since a higher proportion of rural interviews was obtained on the first call, an analysis of interview results by calls for the total sample would result in an undue weight to farm and rural interviews. For the present analysis, only those interviews are included which were obtained in places with a population of 2,500 or more in 1940. The total sample considered consists of 3265 interviews from as many urban households. Of these, 2072 were obtained on the first call, 726 on the second call, and 467 on the third or later call. Interviewers were instructed to call back on different days and at various hours of the day. The timing of call-backs varied somewhat, according to the convenience of the interviewer, and according to local conditions such as weather and transportation.

[1] Permission to use data from the Survey of Consumer Requirements of November 1943 has been granted by the Civilian Relations Division, Office of Civilian Requirements, the agency sponsoring the survey, and by the Bureau of the Census, responsible for the field work in connection with the survey.

[2] Studies of the attitude and opinion type using this method of sampling have been done extensively by the Division of Program Surveys, Bureau of Agriculture Economics, U.S. Department of Agriculture, headed by Dr. Rensis Likert. Studies of changes in the interview sample with repeated calls, similar to the analyses presented here, were undertaken previously within the Division of Program Surveys by Mr. J. Stevens Stock. These have unfortunately not been published, but the authors take this method of acknowledging the priority of the investigations under Mr. Stock's direction.

[3] Special instructions are necessary to define single-person households, to determine when a lodger belongs in the family, when to be counted as a separate household. These details are not considered essential for the present discussion.

TABLE 1

CHARACTERISTICS OF URBAN HOUSEHOLDS INTERVIEWED ON
FIRST, SECOND, AND LATER CALLS

	Households interviewed on first call	Households interviewed on second call	Households interviewed on third or later call	All households interviewed
Number of urban interviews	2072	726	467	3265
Per cent	100.0	100.0	100.0	100.0
Respondent reporting on household purchases				
1. Responsible person, not employed outside home	78.2	57.8	46.4	69.1
2. Responsible person, employed outside home	21.8	42.2	53.6	30.9
Household composition				
1. Having children under two years of age	17.2	9.5	6.2	13.9
2. Having older children only	37.6	34.8	32.3	36.3
3. Having no children	45.2	55.7	61.5	49.8
Size of household				
1. One person	6.3	13.1	15.2	9.1
2. Two persons	24.6	29.5	34.6	27.1
3. Three persons	25.6	23.2	21.0	24.4
4. Four persons	19.9	16.5	16.5	18.7
5. Five or more persons	23.6	17.7	12.7	20.7
Average size	3.56 persons	3.11 persons	2.84 persons	3.35 persons

CHANGES IN THE INTERVIEW SAMPLE FROM CALL TO CALL

The amount of distortion which may result through relying upon accessible respondents can be determined from the differences in the samples resulting on the first call, on the second call, and on the third or later call, as shown in Table 1.

Since the survey dealt with purchases of kitchen goods, clothing, and other household articles, the "responsible person" interviewed was in most cases a woman, though there are, of course, an appreciable number of households consisting solely of men. As might be expected, housewives employed outside the home, and other employed respondents, were much harder to reach than respondents not employed outside the home. Although only 21.8 per cent

of respondents reached on the first call had employment outside the home, 53.6 per cent of respondents reached on the third and later calls were employed.

Households with young children are easier to reach than households whose children are older. These in turn are easier to reach than those with no children at all. Most difficult of all to interview is the person who lives alone; as the number of persons increases, the easier it is to find a responsible person at home.

If the survey had ended with the first interview, there would have been too many housewives not otherwise employed, too many families with young children, too few smaller households. To the extent that survey data are correlated with these family characteristics, real distortion would have occurred.

It should be noted that in the method of specific assignment followed here, the first call differs somewhat from the single calls under the quota-control system, since here the first call is restricted to assigned addresses chosen to randomize the sample. The results reported may be interpreted strictly only in relation to the method of specific assignment, although they have obvious implications for the quota-control method.

HOW RESULTS OF INTERVIEWS OBTAINED ON LATER CALLS AFFECT MARKET DATA

Because the market for household appliances and equipment is closely related to such factors as size of family, presence of young children, home ownership, and other characteristics differentiating those easier to find at home from those harder to find at home, surveys depending upon single calls will tend, in general, to overestimate the inventory of items such as washing machines which are most common among stay-at-homes. The amount of such over-estimation varies greatly from item to item, as shown in Table 2.

For the purposes of Table 2, it has been assumed that there were 23,000,000 urban households at the time of the survey. No official estimate is available, but the precise number does not matter since the figures are presented for expository purposes only. The estimates based on the first call are those which would have been made had the survey ended with the first call, and only the first-call interviews had constituted the sample. The final survey estimates are based on all interviews obtained. Accepting the final survey estimates as the figures more nearly correct, it is evident that there would have been a considerable over-estimation of home ownership, washing machines, and sewing machines, if the survey had stopped with the first call. The size of the over-estimation, around 5 per cent, is beyond the change to be expected through adding 1193 similar interviews to a sample of 2072 interviews; the additional interviews in the final survey do not change the estimates simply by increase in size of sample, but by a real change in the character of the population interviewed.

For electric irons, mechanical refrigerators, and radios, there are no appreciable differences in the estimated numbers between the households easier and harder to reach. These items are small-family appliances as well as large-family appliances, and are about as likely to be found in apartments as in separate houses.

That radios are found about equally among those interviewed on the first call and on later calls does not mean that a radio

TABLE 2

FINAL SURVEY ESTIMATES COMPARED WITH ESTIMATES BASED
ON INTERVIEWS OBTAINED ON FIRST CALL

Urban households having:	Final survey estimates (3265 interviews)	Estimates based on first call (2072 interviews)	Overestimate if Survey had ended with interviews obtained on first call	
			Number	Per cent
Owned home	9,500,000	10,000,000	500,000	5.3
Washing machine	11,200,000	11,800,000	600,000	5.4
Sewing machine	12,800,000	13,400,000	600,000	4.7
Electric iron	20,500,000	20,600,000	100,000	0.5*
Radio	21,200,000	21,300,000	100,000	0.5*
Mechanical refrigerator	14,700,000	14,600,000	−100,000	−0.7*

* Difference not statistically significant.

survey can dispense with call-backs. While no data are available within the survey, it is probable that the radio-*listening* habits of those who do not stay at home differ from the radio-*listening* habits of those more often at home, even though radio-*possession* does not differentiate between them.

The findings also suggest that radio-ownership would be a poor factor to use as a check in determining the adequacy of an obtained sample, since the proportion of radios owned by an inadequate sample (such as the first-call sample here) may not differ significantly from the proportion owned by a more adequate one. For sampling households, washing-machines or sewing machines would provide a much more sensitive check, if one accepts the results of Table 2. This follows because the first-call sample—known to differ from the complete sample—shows greater distortion for these items.

EFFECTS OF LATER CALLS ON THE RESULTS OF OPINION SURVEYS

The opinion data from the Survey of Consumer Requirements do not lend themselves well to an analysis in terms of repeated calls, because opinion-type questions were asked only of sub-groups self-selected by their buying experiences. For example, people were asked to rate the degree of inconvenience or hardship of being deprived of certain goods which they were unsuccessful in obtaining. Because only the ones who had been unsuccessful in attempts to buy were included among those questioned about inconvenience or hardship, the differences in rating between those reporting unsuccessful buying experiences on the first call and those reporting unsuccessful buying experiences on later calls were too slight to be significant.

Since opinion data are often correlated significantly with economic factors, it may be inferred that what will be true of market data will also be true to some extent of opinion data. Thus the question, "Do you and your family have more money coming in now than before the war, or not as much?" asked without elaboration, is at once an economic and an attitude question, since replies may be colored by a sense of economic well-being as well as by an actual change in money income. Replies to a question of this type conform to those previously reported, considerable difference being found between interviews on the first and on later calls, as shown in Table 3.

While among those interviewed on the first call 36.8 per cent reported more money now than before the war, the proportion answering in this way of those interviewed on later calls rose to 39.3 per cent.

In surveys in which individuals are sought out instead of households, added difficulties arise because it is so hard to reach young

TABLE 3

CHANGE IN INCOME SINCE THE WAR: REPLIES ON FIRST CALL AND LATER CALLS

	Households interviewed on first call	Households interviewed on later calls	All households interviewed
Number of urban interviews	2072	1193	3265
Per cent	100.0	100.0	100.0
More money coming in now than before the war	36.8	39.3	37.7
About the same	38.8	38.4	38.8
Not as much	23.1	20.7	22.2
Not reported	1.3	1.6	1.3

people, both married and single, and because it is so easy to reach old people. A quota assignment (*e.g.*, so many under forty years of age, so many over forty) may result in too few in their early twenties and too many sixty and over. The method of specific assignments results in proportionately too many older people on the first visit, but this disproportion is corrected through call-backs which bring in more younger people.[4] The possible effect on opinion surveys is evident, since young and old often disagree.

[4] In the studies referred to in footnote 2, Mr. Stock has shown that first calls have an undue proportion of aged people, and an under-sampling of young adults, especially of those 20-29.

THE CONCLUSION IS . . .

People easily found at home on the first call differ significantly from those found at home only after repeated calls. The latter occur in large enough proportions to make it important for repeated calls to be made in order to represent them on sample surveys. Unless such a course is followed, samples will be distorted in the direction of too large a proportion of responses from households with the characteristics of the stay-at-homes. The data here presented from a survey of consumer requirements have shown the extent of the errors to be expected if interviews made on first calls are depended upon.

THE FORMULATION OF THE RESEARCH DESIGN

DANIEL KATZ

As the results of the scouting exploration become available, the design of the final study can be worked out more exactly. There are advantages in developing the design as the scouting proceeds rather than making it a separate step in a temporal sequence. This permits of some interaction between the possible theoretical objectives and the realities of the field situation. At some point, of course, final decisions must be made about research objectives and procedures for the full-scale study, and such decisions call for a thorough consideration of

all the findings from the scouting expedition.

Roughly speaking, studies are of two major types: exploratory and hypothesis-testing. The exploratory study attempts to see what is there rather than to predict the relationships that will be found. It represents the earlier stage of a science. From its findings may come knowledge about important relationships between variables, but the more definite proof of these relationships comes from hypothesis-testing.

For example, in a field study of industrial morale we may be interested in the factors

From "Field Studies," in L. Festinger and D. Katz (eds.), *Research Methods in the Behavioral Sciences* (New York: The Dryden Press, 1953), pp. 74-77. Reprinted by permission of the author and the publisher.

related to productivity. If the study were of an exploratory type, it would not start with clearly defined notions about the relationships to be found. It would set a broad net and include measures of a wide variety of perceptual and motivational factors in the hope that some of these measures would show a relationship to productivity. If the study were of the second type—namely, hypothesis-testing—we would start with a well-formulated notion that under specified conditions productivity would vary directly with a given factor or factors—perhaps the group standards of the face-to-face members of a work section plus their involvement in the group. In this second type of study, we would develop detailed measures of these independent variables and would make exact predictions for the productivity of work groups varying in group standards and solidarity. We would also specify the conditions which have to be held constant for these predictions to be realized. Since these conditions may not be held constant directly, we would measure them to achieve some statistical control over their effects.

Ideally, the testing of hypotheses is more suited to laboratory experimentation, and exploratory discovery to field studies and surveys. This does not mean, however, that field studies should confine themselves wholly to exploratory procedures. The scouting stage can often be used as the more purely exploratory part of the investigation, and some degree of hypothesis-testing can be employed in the larger operation to follow. Moreover, there are occasions when the field approach can be used for very important hypothesis-testing, as in the "natural experiment." But it is nonetheless true that the great strength of the field type of study is its inductive procedure, its potentiality for discovering significant variables and basic relations that would never be found if we were confined to research dictated by a hypothetical-deductive model. Thus, the field study and the survey are the great protection in social science against the sterility and triviality of premature model building.

It is possible, of course, to combine both exploration and hypothesis-testing in a single field study. One major set of hypotheses can be investigated at the same time that other materials are gathered for exploratory purposes. This has the advantage of protecting the study from failure if inconclusive results are found with respect to the hypotheses. The exploratory materials then become the *safety factor*. The disadvantage of this compromise is that it attempts to combine two studies in one investigation, sometimes to the detriment of both.

Even an exploratory study should be so designed as to provide as definite information as possible for a set of research objectives. There are at least two levels of exploratory studies. At the first level is the discovery of the significant variables in the situation; at the second, the discovery of relationships between variables. Even at the first level it is important to delimit the area to be studied and to introduce controls into the data-collection process. Exploratory studies which do not set limits for themselves have limits imposed by various practical matters, some of which are not realized by the investigators.

In the second type of exploratory study, where the objective is the discovery of relationships, there is less concern with adequacy of coverage of behavior and less interest in the use of factor analysis. Thus it resembles hypothesis-testing in resting its case upon the relationships discovered rather than upon the precise use of mathematical techniques. The major difference between such an exploratory study and the hypothesis-testing investigation is that in the former there are no specific predictions of relationships based upon theoretical derivations. The researchers do have hypotheses in mind, but these are not precisely formulated. In a study of class structure in a community, for example, we may start with the general assumption that a significant motivating factor in class identification stems from the economic role which the individual plays. But we may not be prepared to specify what we mean by economic role, or what other roles may account equally well for psychological class identification. Therefore we plan our research so as to study the many possible types of economic role, including the part the individual plays in consumption, in the technical aspects of production, in the social aspects of production, etc. Within the broad frame set by our research objective, we hope to find some significant relationships. Or, in a study of industrial morale, we may be concerned with the in-plant factors which are related to worker satisfaction. We shall include all the important aspects related to the job and the plant, from wages and working conditions to type of immediate supervision and congeniality of fellow workers. Then, in analysis, we hope to find significant relationships between worker satisfaction and some of these in-plant factors.

DUAL PURPOSE OF THE QUESTIONNAIRE

CHARLES F. CANNELL AND ROBERT L. KAHN

The questionnaire, or interview schedule, serves two major purposes. First, it must translate the research objectives into specific questions, the answers to which will provide the data necessary to test the hypotheses or explore the area set by the research objectives. In order to achieve this purpose, each question must convey to the respondent the idea or group of ideas required by the research objectives, and each question must obtain a response which can be analyzed so that the results fulfill the research objective. Moreover, the question must perform these two functions with minimal distortion of the response which it elicits. That is, in asking a question of the respondent, we assume that the respondent possesses an attitude, or opinion, or piece of knowledge. Each question should, therefore, be constructed so as to elicit a response which accurately and completely reflects each respondent's position.

The second function of the questionnaire is to assist the interviewer in motivating the respondent to communicate the required information. There are many factors which determine the respondent's willingness to engage in an interview, as we have already mentioned. In motivating the respondent, the skills of the interviewer are of great importance, of course, but the questionnaire itself does much to determine the character of the interviewer-respondent relationship and, consequently, the quantity and quality of the data collected.

Since the questionnaire is constructed on the basis of the research objectives, it is clear that constructing the questionnaire cannot be the first step in undertaking a

From "The Collection of Data by Interviewing" in L. Festinger and D. Katz (eds.), *Research Methods in the Behavioral Sciences* (New York: The Dryden Press, 1953), pp. 340-341. Reprinted by permission of the authors and the publisher.

research project. The statement of the research objectives and the specification of the data required to meet those objectives must precede questionnaire construction.

Suppose that, as part of a study of how behavior is influenced by mass persuasion, we have the hypothesis that the number of government savings bonds purchased is related directly to the amount of direct personal solicitation. What data are required to test this hypothesis? What questions should be asked to elicit these data?

In the present example, the investigators decided that two approaches should be employed, one direct and one indirect. The direct approach consisted of asking recent bond purchasers what factors had led them to buy. The indirect approach during a later portion of the same interview led to inclusion of a number of questions concerning the respondent's recent exposure to such influences as newspaper advertisements, radio, other group appeals, and individual solicitation. In analyzing the obtained data, the researchers sorted those respondents who were comparable with respect to income and other demographic characteristics into groups according to the frequency and type of solicitation which they had experienced. The buying behavior of these groups was then studied, and it was found that buying behavior was closely related to the presence or absence of personal solicitation.

In this example, one can see how the questionnaire design flows logically from the specified research objectives and must anticipate the analysis of the data. Thus, construction of the questionnaire is an integrated step in getting a research project into operation.

THE GENERAL PROBLEM OF QUESTIONNAIRE DESIGN

HERBERT HYMAN

The most important problem in questionnaire design is its comprehensiveness. In election surveys the questionnaire is an attempt to translate a conception or theory of the nature of political behavior into a set of questions which will be precisely transmitted to respondents by a good interviewer, and elicit valid answers. On the basis of these answers measurements and analyses of the relevant factors can be made, leading to final predictions of political behavior. Insofar as the initial picture is inadequate and conception of voting behavior too rudimentary, the most skillful interviewing and the most perfect wording of questions are not enough to guarantee success. When the design omits something, it is necessarily omitted from the questionnaire, from the

From F. Mosteller and others, *Pre-Election Polls of 1948*, Report to the Committee on Analysis of Pre-election Polls and Forecasts (New York: Social Science Research Council), pp. 149-166. By permission of the author and the publisher.

interview, and from the final interpretation of the data. Of course, when the original conception is good, *technical errors* in interviewing or in the construction of questionnnaires can damage the results, but these are technical problems only. We shall first consider the basic problem of the design of the questionnaires that were used, and then take up some technical problems concerning the accuracy and quality of the actual questions.

COMPREHENSIVENESS OF THE DESIGN

We know relatively little about the complex problem of political behavior, but we do know that it is complex. Since many factors affect final voting behavior, successful predictions may be contingent upon the measurement of these factors. It is imperative, therefore, that the designs used should include such measurements. We shall set down a modest list of factors that ought to be considered. We can then see how well the polls actually met these specifications in their *planning*. Given factors, evaluated in detail elsewhere in this report, are treated here in terms of their inclusion in the original questionnaire designs.

Before examining the actual designs, a number of methodological points should be reviewed. First, a survey organization has more resources at its disposal in designing a study than a single questionnaire. The total design may be realized by a series of questionnaires, each of which constitutes only one part; or the design may be achieved by collateral methods other than the questions read to the respondent. For example, background reports on the community, ratings of the respondent by the interviewer, and historical trend data have all been used to fill in parts of an original research plan. Consequently, it is important in this evaluation to examine *all* the procedures before concluding that the polls did not live up to the specifications we shall set down. By the same token, the fact that a given variable or factor in the original conception of voting behavior cannot be measured by a *specific question* put to the respondent is no excuse for not measuring that factor.

Second, it is important not only to determine whether measures of important factors were available but also whether these measures were *used* properly in the final analysis and interpretation. We can have the best design and the best translation of the design into a questionnaire, but these are wasted unless the findings are used. At the stage of analysis many uncertainties arise in manipulating complex data and judgment is always involved. The polls consequently may succeed or fail at either end of the questionnaire process—in the planning of the questionnaire, or in the use of the results once they are collected. It is outside the scope of this section to examine the extent to which the available questionnaire data were actually used, and how they were used in interpretation, analysis, and prediction, but one point may be made: If the original conception is *explicit,* and the reason for the measure's inclusion is clearly understood in advance, it is much more likely that the data will be properly used. If it is sheer accident that something in the questionnaire provides information on a certain problem, it is unlikely that the results will be fully exploited. In this sense, elaborate systematic delineation of the original plan not only improves the questionnaire but also insures systematic use of the results.

One other prefatory statement is needed concerning the significance of the factors that will be listed. All of them represent *psychological measures.* They are measures of the *individual* respondent, and are not as academic and as unrelated to the real question of how he is going to vote as they may at first seem. The answer to the question is not so simple that it can be ascertained just by the asking. His voting intention is not necessarily a static permanent thing, nor does the final casting of the vote necessarily reflect the original intention. A man's final vote may be affected by campaign speeches, by the arguments of friends, by attempts of political machines to get out the vote, by the candidates' actions on issues that affect him, by sudden events like an armed attack, by new knowledge he acquires, by conflicts within himself which he finally resolves, by factors making it difficult for him to vote, and by a host of other factors. If the polling organizations are not prepared to evaluate the operation of these factors on the preferences expressed by the respondent, their predictions may err.

Since many of the factors affecting an individual's preferences are located *outside* him and since many of them appear to be sheer future contingencies which cannot be anticipated, how can the polls possibly attempt to measure their influence through the questionnaire? There are two possible answers. One is this: The *influence* they might have on the individual's vote if they were to occur cannot be measured directly through questions addressed to the individual, but can be inferred. Since outside events have no relevance to the vote unless they impinge on the person, and since their effect varies systematically depending on certain psychological characteristics of the individual, the effect of such factors is not completely unpredictable if these psychological characteristics are measured in the questionnaire design. This can be illustrated by an oversimplified example. If any one of the candidates had changed his position on the civil rights bill prior to the election, it would have been an unpredictable event that might affect the vote in an unknown way. But one would have predicted that it would have opposite effects on the vote in Alabama and New York simply because the white populations in these two states are generally known to differ in such *psychological factors as attitudes and desires* about race relations. If one had obtained a precise measure of each individual's feelings on this issue through his answers on a questionnaire, one would have been able to predict the differential effect of such a future event on the vote, much better than it could be predicted on the basis of general knowledge.

An alternative to such inferential procedures is the *direct* measurement of the impact of outside influences by continuing studies of trends. If one repeatedly interviews samples of the appropriate population, one can observe changes in behavior over time. While this procedure does not isolate the causes of shifts, it can measure their extent rather precisely. Any new contingency may require another set of measurements, and this of course makes the procedure costly and means that the polling agency has to be efficiently organized for such continuing operations. This type of trend measurement creates serious operating problems when influences need to be measured very late in an election campaign.

In evaluating the questionnaire designs that were used in the pre-election polls, we shall use the following simple set of standards for good questionnaire design:

(1) Measures of motivations that might affect preferences,
(2) Special questionnaires for contingencies,
(3) Measures of the rigidity of preferences,
(4) Measures of latent preferences,
(5) Measures of likelihood of voting,
(6) Measures of eligibility to vote.

MEASURES OF MOTIVATIONS AS AIDS IN INTERPRETING CONTINGENCIES THAT MIGHT AFFECT PREFERENCES

Merely on theoretical psychological grounds one would argue that a person's casting a ballot, his preferring one candidate, is dictated to some extent by some desire on his part. It is at least a reasonable hypothesis that the presidential vote may be affected in a complex way by such concerns as making a living, avoiding military activity in a war, receiving the same treatment as other members of society, having suitable living quarters, etc. It is also reasonable to think that a person's vote may be related to his *attitudes* on labor problems, on the United Nations, and government controls. Now if the political situation changes with respect to any of these factors, we can predict a person's voting behavior better if we know his attitudes towards them and know the correlation between manner of voting and such attitudes.

What did the polls do about including such measures? On all three of Roper's pre-election surveys, prior to his final "telegraphic" survey, he had an elaborate battery of questions on basic concerns and social and political attitudes. On the final telegraphic study there were no questions of this type.

From July through October Gallup had 11 election survey ballots in the field. By way of summary, the first three of these ballots contained a considerable amount of material on basic attitudes. However, after August, the remaining eight ballots contained no questions whatsoever on attitudes toward social or political issues (unless one considers prohibition such an issue.) It may be that Gallup felt he had an adequate picture of the distribution of social attitudes that might relate to the vote, and he may have analyzed the role of attitudes thoroughly on this early basis. Furthermore, the remaining eight ballots which were distributed regularly over the brief period of two months were designed to get at changes in preferences by the direct measurement of trends. (Our discussion of accuracy of trend measurement on pp. 165f. shows that Gallup obscured the value of some of his trend data.) On this basis the omissions may have been legitimate.

By contrast, Roper had many fewer ballots and fewer questions to measure trends, but *each* ballot permitted far more comprehensive measurement of attitudes and their relation to future voting preference.

Crossley had no questions on basic attitudes in his ballot.

SPECIAL QUESTIONNAIRES ON CONTINGENCIES

The effect of outside events on a person's preferences can sometimes be inferred if

his basic attitudes are known; and as just pointed out, the impact of such events can be measured directly by repeated questioning. Granting the possibility of a *sudden* event, a good survey design would also have at its disposal some efficient way of determining the sudden impact of such a "last minute" contingency on voting preferences, especially if basic information on individuals' attitudes was not included in the design. Despite its many limitations, the "telegraphic survey" is one such instrument.

What is the standing of the polls on this general requirement? Crossley had only two interviewing periods so that his data on trends were very limited. His second interviewing period ran from September 25 through October 18. Since he did not have a direct measure of the late trend, nor any telegraphic set-up, nor any attitudinal data for inferring the possible effect of a sudden contingency, his design was inadequate on this score. As pointed out, Gallup's eight national surveys during the last two months prior to election provided trend data on possible outside influences. His final regular ballot was in the field from October 14 to October 23 so that contingencies occurring prior to the last few days or hours were *theoretically* amenable to measurement. He also had a telegraphic set-up ready for last-minute use, but did not avail himself of it.

Roper's three major surveys were made over the period from July to September, providing a fairly good design for ascertaining trends. (The later discussion of accuracy of trend data indicates that Roper may have obscured the value of some of his data.) He had a final telegraphic survey in the field from October 25 through October 28, giving him late measure of sentiments except for possible last-minute shifts.

RIGIDITY OF PREFERENCE

On some matters people's attitudes and preferences are more rigid than on others, but there is always the possibility of change within a relatively short time. When the polls predict voting behavior on the basis of preferences expressed at a particular time, there is always the chance that the prediction will not apply in the future. While such changes in decisions are partly a product of outside forces, they are also a product of the reorganization of forces *within* the person. In addition to using direct measures of the trend of shifts and making inferences from a knowledge of the individual's basic psychological structure one can also infer whether there is likely to be a reorganization of preferences if one has some knowledge of the rigidity of the person's original feelings. Let us look at the polling organizations' approaches to the measurement of strength of preference in the questionnaire designs.

Crossley had a number of questions on his ballot which attempted to get at this factor. The answers to these questions were used as measures of probable turnout, but they were also used to determine the level of interest of the individual, and a low degree of interest might be assumed to be related to weak preferences. There were also possibilities of measuring the strength of preference from questions on how long ago the voting decision was made, and by correlating the present preference with a question on 1944 vote.

Roper asked a variety of attitudinal questions which permitted inferences about the rigidity of preference. These included such questions as how strongly the respondent liked the specific candidates, whether he thought there was much difference between the major parties, whether he would vote a straight ticket, whether he was enthusiastic about the candidates, and many questions on social attitudes which could have been analyzed to throw light on the total structure of the individual's attitudes.

Some of Gallup's questions that were used to indicate likelihood of voting may also have been used to make inferences concerning rigidity of preference, for example, interest in the election. He also had a question whose answers permitted a measure of straight-ticket voting which might have been used in the analysis. One of his ballots had

a battery of two questions dealing directly with this problem of rigidity: one on the person's feeling of certainty that he had picked the best man, and one on whether there was any likelihood that the respondent would change his mind. However, this question was dropped from all six later ballots.

The use of questions intended to measure strength or intensity of opinion is not necessarily helpful in the actual forecasting of elections. With respect to voting, a man has very few choices—he may abstain or he may vote for a candidate. He cannot indicate the intensity of his preference on the ballot; it is possible for a candidate to win by a landslide of half-hearted votes! But measures of intensity are important because of the instability of voters' intentions. If many voters are shifting their views frequently, they may be more easily swayed one way or another, and measures of rigidity can warn the poller of the existence of such a volatile situation.

MEASURES OF LATENT PREFERENCES

In any election survey there are respondents who report no definite voting intention. In the 1948 surveys this undecided group was sizable, approximating one tenth of the sample. Presumably, some of these respondents were waiting to make up their minds, but even in the final surveys close to the time of the election they reported that they *still* had not decided. The poller cannot wait longer to decide whether these numerous persons (if they vote) have some latent preference which they have not expressed, or cannot express, to the interviewer.

A second type of latent preference problem to be considered in questionnaire design is the fact that some individuals may express one attitude, but actually have a different intention which they do not reveal to the interviewer. Such individuals may definitely refuse to state their preference; or they may say they are undecided and so conceal their true feelings; or, rarely, they may say they are going to vote for a party which they actually do not intend to vote for. It is also possible that an individual may sincerely express a preference for a particular candidate, but this preference is really unstable because of other latent attitudes which conflict with it. Considering that the "don't know" group approximates 10 per cent of the total sample, while refusals to express a preference approximate 2 per cent and hidden preferences further increase this figure, this problem is of considerable magnitude in questionnaire design.

Both Roper and Gallup used secret ballot procedures, with which the "don't know" answers decline in magnitude, and the greater anonymity presumably operates to reduce evasion in responses. Gallup used secret ballots on a large scale whereas Roper used them only once. Crossley, as a matter of policy, made no use of secret ballots on the ground that the results of previous experiments showed them to be a poor tool for predicting elections. Because certain data suggest that secret ballots are affected to some extent by interviewer bias so that there may be some evasion in answers, and because we still have the problem of allocating the "don't know" answers, good questionnaire design might well include some other measures and analyses of latent preferences.

A general method would be to analyze the profile of related attitudes that would be expected for a given type of voter, and so reveal any such latent preferences of the respondent. With Crossley's data this would be possible only on a very limited scale. There are no attitude questions but the "factual" questions on 1944 vote could be used along with data on union membership, economic level, and the like, whose general correlations with real preferences are in some degree known. In Roper's and Gallup's surveys the undecided are asked a question on their leanings which could be of help in uncovering the latent preferences of those who are not evasive. In both these organizations the questionnaire designs permit some analysis or related attitudes, from which one could infer the latent preferences of other individuals who are evasive.

MEASURES OF THE LIKELIHOOD OF VOTING

One of the basic difficulties in predicting an election is the turnout problem. While a great many people have preferences for some candidate, a large number may not vote, so that their preferences have no weight in the final result. Some adjustment of the preferences reported must be made in order to take this factor into account. Otherwise, no matter how accurate the measurement of preferences or how accurate the original sample of the population, the prediction may be in error. One basic way of dealing with the turnout problem is via the questionnaire design. An alternative method involves the application of certain essentially *historical* information about voting behavior to the design of the sample or to the weighting of the results. However, there are certain *theoretical* inadequacies in the latter method that makes it important to include measures of the likelihood of voting as a requirement of good questionnaire design. Adjusting the sample so that groups, or areas, or states that have shown a low turnout in past years are undersampled can be effective only as long as this historical pattern of behavior continues. For example, the civil rights issue may have altered the traditional turnout in areas whose population includes many Negroes or persons having low incomes. Adjusting survey results by weighting the preferences of different social groups on the basis of their historical pattern of turnout is subject to the same limitations—it will fail if the pattern changes. There is no reason why new forces may not change such historical patterns. For example, the voting behavior of Negroes could be changed by new legislation; the emergence of new parties may affect the size and character of the turnout. Consequently, inclusion in the questionnaire of queries whose answers will indicate the contemporary likelihood that an individual or a group will vote is superior, if these can be devised. Such questions are also superior in measuring the most crucial aspect of turnout—the differential turnout by parties.

Before examining the questionnaire designs of the major polls for contemporary measures of turnout, it should be emphasized that all research organizations have found that asking the simple question whether a person intends to vote provides an inadequate measure of turnout. The responses to such questions generally show a great excess of persons who plan to vote over the number who actually vote. This error conceivably could be a constant and therefore not impair the use of the question for measuring the differential turnout of people who have different preferences. However, there is no assurance on this score. Therefore in evaluating the questionnaire designs, little weight should be given to handling this problem by a single direct question on intention to vote.

How well did the polls do in this respect? In the first of Roper's three regular survey questionnaires there are measures that could be used to make inferences as to the likelihood of voting, such as a projective question on interest in the election, but there are no specific measures of turnout. (However, the importance of such measures in the very early ballots is small because of the many later developments in the campaign that may affect turnout.) In the later ballots, when it was urgent that such measures be included, we find no *direct* approaches to the problem of turnout. Respondents were not even filtered by a crude question on whether they intended to vote—this answer was obtained only if volunteered and in some of the surveys it was not even given a separate answer box. Here again, an inferential measure might be based on the answer to the question on interest in the election.

Now, *implicit* in Roper's attitude questions are many possible modes of analysis of the likelihood of a respondent's voting.

Some of the questions get at the extremeness of his preference; these are graded-scale questions whose answers might be correlated with likelihood of voting. Some of the issue questions might provide indirect measures of turnout, for example, the "don't know" answers on issues could be taken as indicative of apathy. Some of the collateral questions could be regarded as measures of involvement and hence of probable turnout, such as a question on exposure to the convention speeches; and granting the errors in respondents' answers to a direct question, use of such devices to infer turnout might be very wise. However, we cannot evaluate Roper's performance on this score unless we know whether these measures were actually used during the analytic process, which is not within the scope of this chapter.

Crossley made an elaborate attempt to get at turnout via the questionnaire, which contained six directly relevant questions so that the reliability of the inference about the likelihood of a man's voting was not based on a single answer. None of these questions was as simple in structure as a verbal report on intention to vote. The information from the answers was pooled and an index of probable turnout was derived, indicating that Crossley tried to take full advantage of the potentialities of such a complex approach. Whether these questions were satisfactory technically will be discussed later; but the questionnaire design did deal with the problem of turnout in an elaborate and intelligent way.

In all of his last six ballots Gallup included three questions specifically dealing with turnout: a direct question on interest in the election, another on intention to vote, and a subquestion on the certainty of this intention. In addition, certain other questions in these six ballots could have been used to make inferences as to turnout, for example, whether the person voted in the past and whether he was undecided in his preference. In some of the ballots used prior to September there were other questions which may have been used experimentally as measures of turnout, such as whether it makes much difference who wins, whether the respondent is willing to go out and convert others to his side, and whether he knows who is running for president.

MEASURES OF ELIGIBILITY TO VOTE

Another basic difficulty in predicting elections is that many people who have preferences cannot vote because of ineligibility. This is not the same as a person's intention to vote: he may have every intention of voting, and conceivably might even go to the polling booth only to find that he is ineligible on some legal ground such as a change of residence or a technicality in registration. A person may not even know whether he is a citizen. The problem is complex because the grounds of eligibility vary so widely in different states and the questionnaire in a national survey is a gross instrument that must be standardized—48 different forms of a questionnaire are not feasible. Also, some registration laws are so complex that it would be exceedingly difficult to obtain the necessary facts in the questionnaire. Therefore, comprehending this problem in a *precise* way in the questionnaire design is difficult.

Crossley, nevertheless, attempted to deal with this problem systematically and to take account of the complexities of local differences in eligibility rules. First, since residence requirements vary widely, interviewers sent in information on the local requirements for eligibility in terms of length of residence needed in the state, county, and even precinct. All respondents were asked corresponding questions on their periods of residence in these respective areas. If the respondent was noted to be disqualified on the basis of residence, the interview was terminated. Even if the interviewer erred, those ineligible on this basis could be filtered out when the ballots were returned. To determine eligibility each respondent was also directly asked whether he was a citizen. In addition, he was asked whether he was qualified to vote and a subquestion on his

certainty of this knowledge. Finally, he was asked whether he had registered and if not registered, whether he was sure that he would register in time to vote. Crossley's design was therefore not only comprehensive in respect to eligibility, but also flexible in terms of the variations and complexities attendant on its local nature.

None of Roper's ballots contained any questions dealing with the problem of eligibility. It is true that this problem can be dealt with in two ways: by questionnaire design or by excluding from the sampled universe those who are ineligible. If the questionnaire were applied only to a sample which initially excluded this group, the lack of such questions would not be serious. Roper did two things to exclude some of the ineligibles prior to interview. Southern Negroes were not sampled because of assumptions about their ineligibility and small likelihood of voting. Also, his interviewers were instructed in the specifications accompanying the questionnaire that no non-English speaking person should be included in the returned quotas, in an attempt to exclude noncitizens. However, such measures are gravely inadequate in determining eligibility, since they do not deal at all with registration and residence requirements, and the handling of the citizenship requirement by this particular instruction to the interviewer is patently ineffective.

Gallup dealt with the problem of eligibility in part in the sample design by excluding Southern Negroes. In addition, he included two questions in his last four ballots. One asked whether the person was registered to vote or planned to register, in areas requiring registration. The other asked whether the person was eligible, in areas not requiring registration. Thus the design attempted to take the problem into account, but it is clear from examination of the answers to these questions that they are not as precise a measure as would be desirable.

We shall turn now to an evaluation of the technical aspects of the questionnaires to see whether these areas included in the design were actually handled so as to lead to accurate measurement.

TECHNICAL FEATURES AFFECTING THE ACCURACY OF MEASURES INCLUDED IN THE DESIGN

The best research design in terms of comprehensiveness will not insure accuracy of measurement unless the design is effectively translated in the questionnaire procedures. In order to determine whether this was actually the case in the election surveys we would need a large amount of empirical data. Only meager data are available, because of the committee's inability to collect and analyze the necessary information within the short time allotted for its work. In the absence of adequate data, we can suggest desirable ways of examining the problem in the future and we can investigate a variety of technical factors associated with questionnaire design, which are known to affect the accuracy of results.

* * *

VALIDITY OF QUESTIONS USED TO OBTAIN MEASURES

Questions intended to elicit answers of a type that will permit measurement of a given variable may be designed, but the degree to which the questions actually achieve the results intended is partly a function of such technical details as wording, position on the ballot, and nature of the instructions given to interviewers. However, the primary technical problem is whether a question will cause the respondent to answer in terms appropriate to obtaining the desired measure and whether all the questions combined will yield the desired series of answers. One method of determining this is by elaborate and well-organized pretesting. Although we do not have complete descriptions of the pretest experience of the major polling organizations (most organizations unfortunately do not keep careful records of their pretests), we

do have information showing that all the organizations did a considerable amount of prior testing of their questions in the field or in past elections.

Crossley had experimented with his filter questions on measuring eligibility and likelihood of voting in the 1944 election and in one gubernatorial election in 1946. He, in a sense, determined empirically the weighting to be given to the various measures of turnout by choosing the weights which gave the closest agreement with actual data on *past* turnout.

Gallup had a large amount of pretest material on which to base decisions as to the validity of his questions. He has used similar questionnaire procedures in past elections. He used also some of the New Jersey data obtained by crew interviewer trainees as a source of pretest experience. Roper, similarly, had much past experience with the type of questions he was using. No conclusions can be drawn from these facts because pretesting can be informative or not, depending on how systematic it is.

Certain kinds of analysis based on *internal* evidence within the questionnaires might show something about the validity of the questions in achieving their intended objectives. No such analyses have been made but they are suggested as a source of future evidence on validity. For example, in Crossley's ballot a series of measures, all presumably related to the same dimension of likelihood of voting, were pooled. Perhaps, empirical data on the degree to which these measures all really measured the same area could be obtained by some system of scale analysis.

A demonstration that there may possibly be some invalidity in the weights Crossley assigned in his index of interest is available from internal analysis of the Wallace voter. According to the system of weights given to these questions, the Wallace voter showed a *lower* level of interest than the voters in either of the major parties. This finding does not seem in accord with our expectation of reality and suggests that there may have been some mishandling of the weighting scheme or misinterpretation of the meaning of the questions.

Other kinds of evidence on the degree to which the questions were valid measures of the intended areas might be obtained by comparison of the survey results with external measures. Thus, for example, the question on the 1944 vote which was used by Gallup and Crossley as a measure of Democratic partisanship (and which played a considerable part in their interpretations) is known to yield a considerably higher vote for Roosevelt than he actually received in 1944. This suggests the need for some caution or correction in the way such data are interpreted.

Careful examination of interviewer report forms might show them to be a final source of evidence on the validity of the questions. These forms often yield information on the misinterpretations which respondents give to apparently unequivocal questions and reveal that the questions may actually not work as originally intended.[1]

CONSTANCY IN PROCEDURES AND ACCURACY OF TREND MEASURES

It has been pointed out that one way of dealing with the influence of events on voting preference or with the instability of preferences is through periodic measurement of sentiments, by which any trend can be observed. However, since changes in survey results have been reported when the wording or context of the questionnaire changed,[2] these factors should be constant over the series of surveys. Otherwise one cannot interpret the trend data. Sometimes other research interests dictate a change in wording or procedure, and with this there is no quarrel, but if such changes are important, one has to sacrifice the trend measures. If trend measurements are more valuable, important question changes may have to be sacrificed. Crossley, who used only one ballot, kept his questionnaire conditions constant by definition. Roper in his three postconvention surveys made certain minor changes in wording. While these changes seem to be innocuous and logical, one cannot be sure that they might not affect the validity of any interpretation of a trend in preference or obscure the existence of a trend.

Gallup's long series of ballots permitted frequent measurement of trends, but the character of the trend is obscured by the fact that the order of two alternatives, Dewey versus Truman, is switched from ballot to ballot for the last seven surveys. In one split-ballot test of Gallup's data this switch changed the Dewey and Truman figures by about 5 percentage points. About 2 percentage points of this change appeared to reflect differences between the samples to which the two forms of the question were assigned. While the order of the candidates in the question may not have produced all of the remaining 3 percentage points of change, it undoubtedly had a sufficient influence to affect the interpretation of trends. It is still true that four ballots with an identical order of alternatives permitted some trend measurements. However, by sacrificing the constancy of conditions, some of the trend points are lost and the danger of erroneous interpretations by the unwary is increased.

[1] Paul B. Sheatsley, "Some Uses of Interviewer-Report Forms," *Public Opinion Quarterly*, 11:601-611 (Winter 1947-48).

[2] Cantril and research associates, *Gauging Public Opinion*, Chapter 2, Princeton: Princeton University Press, 1944.

THE ART OF ASKING *WHY*
THREE PRINCIPLES UNDERLYING THE FORMULATION OF QUESTIONNAIRES

PAUL F. LAZARSFELD

I. ASCERTAINING WHAT A QUESTION MEANS; THE PRINCIPLE OF SPECIFICATION

Asking for reasons and giving answers are commonplace habits of everyday life. We have all had the experience of acting under certain impulses and certain influences so many times that we are sure that our fellow men have had the same experiences and reasons for their own actions. And we are seldom disappointed if we inquire. Our respondent not only has had reasons for his actions; he usually knows, also, in which reason we might be especially interested, and it is upon this assumption that he bases his answer. If a friend explains why he has come to see me, he does not start to tell me that he was once born, and that he moved to this city two years ago, although these, too, are reasons for his being here today. He is aware that most of these reasons are known as well to me as to him, and he picks out the reason which he hopes will contribute especially to a mutual understanding of the present situation.

In market research, the question-and-answer business is not so simple, and the ease of furnishing answers in everyday life may involve dangerous pitfalls. In social

intercourse, it is most likely that what is important for our respondent is important also for us who have made the inquiry. In market research interviews, we cannot rely upon this good fortune. The purpose of our *why* questions is to discover all of those factors which determine the purchases of a certain group of people; or, to put it more exactly in anticipation of a later part of this paper, we want to know all the determinants of a certain sort. Such knowledge should permit us to increase our future efficiency in this field by providing a more complete and accurate basis for anticipating demand factors of the market. We cannot leave it up to the respondents to tell us whatever they are inclined. The average consumer is not trained to survey offhand all the factors which determine his purchases and he usually has a very hazy understanding of the *why* question. On the other hand, the information we want should be exact and precise. This creates the initial problem in the art of asking *why* in market research: how can the gap between these two attitudes be bridged?

We have, in general, three possible purposes in market research in asking people questions:

From the *National Marketing Review*, Summer 1935, Vol. 1, No. 1, pp. 32-43. Reprinted by permission of the author and the publisher.

a. *Influences toward action.* We may want to know by which media people have been *influenced* to act the way they did, which is the case when we want to evaluate the role of certain advertisements, of advice of friends, etc.; or

b. *Attributes of the product.* We may want to know if it were the *attributes* of the product itself, and which of them—its taste, its color, or its use—led the customer to buy; or

c. *Impulses of the purchaser.* We may want to know certain *tendencies* by which the consumer was controlled: Whether he bought for himself, or as a gift; whether he bought under sudden impulse, or after long deliberation; whether it was an habitual or a unique proceeding, etc.

The consumer, however, is seldom aware of these varying interpretations. For example, take a simple question such as why someone bought a certain brand of coffee. One respondent might answer that he liked the taste, and another that a neighbor had told him about the brand. These two respondents interpreted our question *why* in two different ways. The one thought that we were interested mainly in the attributes of the coffee; the other, that we had in mind the outside influences which affected his choice. The answers, therefore, are not comparable. The neighbor who spoke to the one respondent may very well have mentioned the good taste of the coffee; and the man who told about the good taste may have heard about it from a neighbor in the first place. So the two cases may have had the same sequence of determinants affecting the two respondents, only the interpretation of our question *why* in different ways led to seemingly quite different answers. But it is possible, as we shall see, to ask our question in such a specific way that both of our respondents will tell the whole story.

The importance of the problem involved here becomes still more evident when we turn to the statistical treatment of answers given to a *why* question. The usual table of reasons as we find it in current market research studies would record the result of our coffee question by stating: X respondents bought their particular brand of coffee because of its taste; Y people bought it

because of some advice they had received. But these figures are apt to be completely erroneous. What the research man may really discover is: X people understood his question as pertaining to influence, and the influence they had experienced was advice; Y people understood the question as pertaining to attributes, and the decisive attribute for them was taste. This danger is illustrated by the following diagram:

Respondent has been actually determined by

Respondent understands the question to mean Pertaining to:

	Influences	Attributes	
Advice	X	N	X + N
Taste	M	Y	M + Y

Advice was the real determining factor for X+N people, and *taste* for M+Y people. But the question, improperly put, made the student lose the true reason of M and N people and his results were, therefore, unsatisfactory. (In practice, the matter would be still more complicated by two-way interpretations of the question; but we need not go into that much detail.)

From these illustrations, we can make the generalization that the innocent question *why* may contain many pitfalls and is actually only the beginning of a research questionnaire. If we want to carry out our program skillfully, we must state precisely in which of the infinite number of determinants of an action we are interested. Only when we make it clear to ourselves and to our respondents which groups of determinants are at stake will we get results which permit a sensible statistical treatment, which is, of course, the aim of every field study.

The real task, therefore, which confronts the market student every time he starts out with a *why* program is to be constantly aware of what he really means or seeks to discover by his questionnaire. What special question he will ask depends upon his decision. In the example just discussed, he will be constrained to start with two questions: "What made you buy this brand of coffee?" and "Why do you like it?" There is a probability that the wording of the first question will furnish, chiefly, reports of influences, as answers, such as radio advertising, magazine advertising, grocers' displays. However, many respondents will answer the question, "What made you start to use it?" with such an answer as, "because it is a stronger brand." Then we, as interviewers, will recognize that this answer is based on attributes, and must proceed to look for influences by asking, "How did you know that this coffee is a strong brand?" The respondent will then have to report the media, or say, "I don't know."

In order to make the basic principle of these considerations quite clear, let us take a somewhat different example. We shall assume that our program is to ask a group of individuals, "Why did you change from one brand of cigarettes to another?" Here again, if we put the question this way, the respondent must decide for himself what we mean, and he may either tell why he stopped using his old brand, or report why he chose the new one. If we then try to treat the answer statistically, we lump together the responses to two different questions. Therefore, we should ask the two questions really involved: "Why did you stop using the other brand?" and "Why did you choose this new one?" This last question, as we already know, is to be split again into two questions, one pertaining to *influences* and one to *attributes*.

The reader may be troubled by the fact that, according to the technic developed, the answers to the question *why* will not normally be recorded by one table but by several tables. There is really nothing astonishing in this; very often one word of our everyday speech becomes a group of figures in exact research. For instance, we speak about the position of a point in space and understand very well what we mean. But

when it comes to numerical treatment, this position is represented by three figures, the three co-ordinates. In the same way, the reason for an action might well be represented by several indices. The number of indices necessary depends to a great extent upon the complete purpose of the investigation, as we shall soon see.

Before proceeding, let us briefly consider what ought to happen when we are forced for one reason or another to use the general *why* question. We have already excluded one unjustifiable procedure, namely, to construct one table and to record simply every type of answer as often as it has been given. The diagram used above reveals that the figures so obtained will be misleading. Let us take the example regarding the change of cigarette brands. Since by hypothesis, the respondent has been asked only one general question, whereas he should have been asked three, he will answer this question according to his own interpretation. He will report either a *dissatisfaction* with his former brand, an *influence leading* him to the new brand, or some *attribute* of the new brand inducing him to make the change. We should, therefore, segregate these answers and present them in three separate tables. Let us suppose for the sake of simplicity that every respondent reports only one element. According to his own interpretation, the answer of one respondent will be inserted definitely in one of the three tables; if he answered, for instance, that a certain advertisement made him change, his answer will be recorded under "advertisement" in the table of influences. In the two other tables—pertaining to dissatisfaction with the previous brand and attributes of the new brand—he will contribute an entry to the columns *dissatisfaction unknown* and *attribute known*. The result will be three tables, each with the column "unknown" heavily loaded. But at least the rest of the entries will yield sensible and comparable results. We would, for instance, be able to say with some truth that, among the influences recorded, advertisement was more important than personal advice, whereas if only one tabulation were made, our conclusions would be unsound.

We might call the handling of the whole set of problems involved herein the *principle of specification*. We have elaborated on it because much of the disrepute in which the statistical treatment of reasons gathered in field studies has fallen, is due to errors connected with this principle. This, however, presents only the negative side of the question. The constructive task is to find the concrete questions which should be substituted for the general *why* program. We have already mentioned that that depends very much upon the purpose of the study. What we want to do is to pick out from the indefinite number of factors which determine a concrete action the ones which are of interest to us. To further illustrate this point, let us take the reasons for book buying. Our *program* is to find out: "Why did you buy this book?" A respondent will give, out of the same concrete experience, quite different answers, according to the particular word stressed: BUY, THIS, and BOOK. If he understood: "Why did you BUY this book?", he might answer, "Because the waiting list in the library was so long that I shouldn't have got it for two months." If he understood: "Why did you buy THIS book?" he might tell what interested him especially in the author. And if he understood: "Why did you buy this BOOK?" he might report that he at first thought of buying a concert ticket with the money but later realized that a book is a much more durable possession than a concert, and such reasoning caused him to decide upon the book. If our study is undertaken as a service to the publishing company which wants to be in a better position to compete with libraries, we will have to specify in our questions the *buying* aspect versus all other methods by which a book may be acquired. If a library wants us to find out in what books people are most interested, it is the characteristics of the book which need more specification in our questions. If the survey in which we are engaged is a leisure-time study, we will have to stress all questions which pertain to *book-reading* in comparison with other means of entertainment. There is actually no element of a concrete purchase experience which cannot be made the object of a *specified why question* for a *general why program*.

We have seen the limitations and pitfalls in the use of one question. Follow-up questions which specify definite motives are one means to correct this difficulty while more careful tabulation of answers to a single question are apt to bring more truthful conclusions. One final point on the *weight* of reasons has been made. Even after we have ascertained attributes *and* influences the question remains: Was the neighbor's authority or the vision of the coffee's taste more important? Without entering into details we mention three possibilities in getting this information. We might use the way our respondent reports immediately as our source of information. He may mention first the neighbor and the taste only upon our second question: What did the neighbor say? Then we might decide that the neighbor had more weight as a factor. Or we might use a special question; interviewing about the movie attendance we might ask: Was the theater or the show *more* important? We shall find an example in our next paragraph.

The third way, to leave the decision to the interviewer, is illustrated as follows. In interviewing about the influence of advertising, for instance, it is sometimes advisable to ask a respondent to report any example in which he bought a certain commodity under the influence of an advertisement. We will get widely varying replies, and the problem is then how to make them statistically comparable. To accomplish this, the *interviewer* must keep in mind what we want to know. We are interested in where the advertisement was seen, in order to know something about the successful medium; what the advertisement said, in order to check up on the effectiveness of the presentation; what point in the advertisements led to the purchase, in order to know what were the successful appeals. While the actual question in which we are interested is not answered directly by this method, the interviewer has an elaborate supply of facts upon which to make a decision. So we leave it to him to decide in which of the following three main classifications the respondent's answer should be placed. Has the advertisement actually aroused a *new wish*? For instance, on a hot day, a picture of an iced drink makes us enter a drugstore and ask for it. Or has it been used as a source of information about a *need of which he was already aware*? For instance, did he look in the newspaper today to see where a stocking sale is to be found? Or did the respondent see the advertisement before and did it become effective only when the corresponding *need was aroused by some other circumstances*? It is surprising to what extent these three possibilities cover, for practical purposes, the dynamic aspect of all reports regarding purchases executed under the influence of advertising. However, the problem of the weight of different determinant factors involves quite a few complicated aspects, which we cannot elaborate here. Instead, the examples cited are offered as a contribution to the *principle of specification*.

II. ENABLING THE INTERVIEWEE TO ANSWER: THE PRINCIPLE OF DIVISION

We have not yet applied our principle to the discussion of a concrete questionnaire and for a very good reason. What we have stated so far is not sufficient to lead to practical applications. Imagine, for instance, that we want to know the influences and the attributes which determine a certain purchase, and we straightway ask the housewife for them. We certainly should not get very satisfactory results. After ascertaining what we want to know, we must enable our respondent to give us the right answers. Here we touch upon the field of the psychology of interviewing, which has received much attention in this country. Bingham and Moore[1] have gathered much valuable material about the right way of keeping the respondent's attention, of avoiding leading

[1] *How to Interview*, 2nd edition, Harpers, 1934.

questions, of creating an attitude of trustworthiness, and so forth. We do not intend to repeat here material which has been successfully dealt with elsewhere. But there is one point, related to what we have said above, which needs our special attention— the *technic of fitting our questions to the experience of the respondent*. In specifying our general *why* program, we might be forced to *specify it in a different way for different types* of purchase experiences undergone by different individuals. Suppose, for instance, that we want to know why certain people prefer silk to rayon. There may be respondents who have given much thought to this topic; this one will be well able to give us her reasons directly, while another one may never have earnestly thought about the subject, and, therefore, will be unable to give immediately the reasons for her preference. After having selected the people who prefer silk to rayon, we must ask them first: "Have you any special reasons for your preference?" The one who has some may be asked directly what they are; the one who has none will have to be questioned differently. We will probably have to ask her about her general experiences with fabrics and will have to infer from her report the reason for her partiality.

Such a procedure was followed by a company which manufactured electric motors. It wanted to ascertain from individuals by means of a questionnaire the reasons *why* they bought only of that company. In the first trial questionnaire, it appeared that some respondents were able to give very definite reasons, whereas other answers were completely evasive, or stereotyped, or otherwise of no value. Therefore, the subsequent questionnaire elaborated upon the inquiry. The first question was: "Had you any special reason in this instance to buy from our company?" If the answer was "yes," the respondent was asked about the process of his deliberations and efforts which led to the purchase; and, as he was selected in this way, he was able to give satisfactory answers. The other individuals, mainly clients who habitually purchased from this company, were given another series of questions which tried to trace the origin of their habits as to influences and tendencies.

Another questionnaire which was used in a study of movie attendance will help to summarize our whole approach to the problems of specified *why* questions. The study was made to determine "Why people attend movies?" The determinants in which we were interested were: the situation which gave rise to attendance at the movie; the part played in the decision by the persons accompanying the respondent; the sources from which information was gathered; and the deciding factors of the show and the theater. There was no question inserted as to how our respondent came to the movie, although a taxicab company might have been most interested in this aspect. Possibly some reader may not at once realize how the vehicle used for conveyance to the movie can possibly be the answer to a specified *why* question. But let him consider the following case: "Why did Mary, but not John, come in time to my party yesterday?" Answer: There was a bad snowstorm. Mary came on the subway. But John used his car and got stuck. He therefore came too late *because he drove his car.* The movie attendance questionnaire follows:

Did you go primarily (1) just to go to a movie, or (II) because of a certain picture?

I_____ II_____ Both_____

If I or Both:
1. When did you decide to go to a movie?
2. Why and under what circumstances did you decide?
3. (If not yet inserted) When and how was your company chosen?
4. As to the special theater or show. (Check)
   a. Was it proposed by someone in the company?
   b. Did you have it in mind yourself?
   c. Did you look for or get special advice or information?
      If (b), how did you know about it?
      If (c), where did you look for advice or information?
5. How many pictures were taken into consideration?
6. Which was more inducive, (A) the theater_____; (B) the picture_____; (C) does not know_____. (Check.)
   Remarks for Interviewers: If B or C, ask

question 7 first. If A, ask question 8 first. But ask both questions in any case.
7. What interested you in the picture? (Please try to remember all the details.)
8. What made the theater suitable to your choice?

If II:
1a. When did you learn about this picture?
2a. How did you learn about it?
3a. What interested you in it when you heard about it? (Please try to remember all the details.)
4a. (If not yet inserted) When and how was your company chosen?

In All Cases:
1b. (If not yet inserted) When and under what circumstances was the final decision made? Why did you go at this particular time?
2b. What other uses of the time and money spent in seeing the movie were considered?

This questionnaire contains several examples of what we called the technic of fitting the question to the experience of the respondent. Take for example, the question on the media of information. If a respondent went to the movie because of a certain picture, he is very likely to remember offhand how he learned about this picture; it was the first reason which started his whole movie attendance. On the other hand, if he just went to the movie because he wanted some relaxation, he will not remember so well why he selected the special show. Therefore, in order to fit our questions to his experience, we have to proceed this way: First, we will ascertain if he went for the sake of a certain picture or not. In the former case, we might at once ask him: "How did you learn about this picture?" In the latter case, an additional question has to be inserted first. We will ask him: "When and under what circumstances did you decide to go to the movie?" This question should lead his memory back to the concrete situation in which he decided to go and then he will be more likely to remember what information he looked for in order to pick out a special picture. In a second question, we will find him prepared to give us all necessary information about influences. Another example is the way we ask about the respondent's companions in this questionnaire. If our respondent were invited to go to the movie, he will have mentioned his companion in the first question as a reason for his decision. If he were the inviting party, a special question will be necessary to find how he chose his companion. The questionnaire has to be flexible enough to cover both cases in such a way that the respondent feels at his ease in remembering the whole process of decision.

The reader is undoubtedly aware that this technic of fitting questions to the experience of the respondent is in conflict with usual procedure. Traditional opinion is that a question should be so worded as always to insure the same reaction on the part of all those interviewed. We advocate a rather loose and liberal handling of a questionnaire by an interviewer. It seems to us much more important that the question be fixed in its *meaning,* than in the *wording.* This new emphasis places the responsibility on the interviewer for knowing exactly what he is trying to discover and permits him to vary the wording in accordance with the experience of the respondent. The resulting margin of error would be much greater if a standardized question were to be interpreted in very different ways by different respondents who have their own different experiences in mind. If we get the respondent to report to us the determinants of his experience to his best knowledge and recollection, our results will be much more homogeneous than in a case where we have inflexible words but have not taken any care for ascertaining the meaning placed upon those words by our respondent.

This whole technic may be described as "The principle of division." It consists in adapting the pattern of our questionnaire to the structural pattern of the experience of the respondent from whom we are seeking our information. By this method, we find much easier access to the motives controlling his actions than if we try to compel the respondent to conform to a stereotyped questionnaire, which he may not understand in the way we intend. Our method, moreover, is supported by the most eminent authority. Plato, in his Phaedrus, speaks about the *principle of division* and points out the *wisdom of separating on the basis of the natural subdivision, as does the skillful carver, who seeks the joint rather than break the bone.*

III. ASCERTAINING WHAT THE ANSWER MEANS: THE PRINCIPLE OF TACIT ASSUMPTION

We have briefly discussed the necessity of specifying the meaning of the *why* question, and that of adapting the question to the experience of the respondent. There is a third point which deserves our consideration. Suppose we ask a man what pleased him most in the coat he bought. Why doesn't he answer that he was most pleased by the fact that the coat had just two sleeves? He would certainly never have bought it with 3 sleeves, however pleasing to him other of the attributes might have been. The reason is clear: There is a tacit assumption between interviewer and respondent that coats have only two sleeves and therefore that fact will not be mentioned in spite of its predominant importance.

Very often, however, the particular consequences of this principle of tacit assumption are omitted. Let us suppose we want to know what attributes are important in the consumption of tea. If we ask: "*Why* do you drink tea for breakfast?" we immediately get answers pertaining to the use and effect of tea: It is quickly made; it keeps one awake; it doesn't burden one's stomach in the morning; and so on. If we ask: "Why do you drink X brand tea?" we get much more specific answers concerning the tea itself; because of its nice color; because it requires less sugar; because it is economical to use; and so on. But the former group of attributes is almost completely omitted. Of course, the two series of responses are by no means contradictory; in the first group the merits of tea were judged in comparison with those of other beverages, coffee, cocoa, milk; whereas, in the second group the general qualities of tea were taken for granted in a tacit assumption, and secondary distinctions between different brands were discussed. The best results are obtained by asking both ways and interpreting the differences in the two series of answers.

Such tacit assumptions are not always easy to realize. In a study of candies, three brands of different price and quality were at stake. It was the medium brand which met most frequently the objection of being ordinary. The best brand was of high quality and nicely wrapped; the medium was also wrapped, but was of a lower quality; the cheapest brand was unwrapped. People apparently felt that the best brand and the cheapest gave just what they promised, whereas the medium brand made promises in its appearance which were not kept by its quality. Therefore, the objections of low quality were more frequent with the medium than with the cheapest brand.

The role of tacit assumptions shows up everywhere where questions are involved. Therefore, it might be worth while to quote a remark from one of Chesterton's detective stories, which brings it out in a very amusing way:

Have you ever noticed this: That people never answer what you say? They answer what you mean, or what they think you mean. Suppose one lady says to another in a country house: "Is anybody staying with you?" The lady does not answer: "Yes, the butler, the three footmen, the parlor maid," and so on, though the parlor maid may be in the room, or the butler behind her chair. She says: "There is nobody staying with us," meaning nobody of the sort you mean. But suppose a doctor inquiring into an epidemic asks, "Who is staying in the house?" then the lady will remember the butler, the parlor maid, and the rest. All language is used like that; you never get a question answered literally, even when you get it answered truly.[1]

The whole matter has, of course, immediate bearing upon the formulation of questionnaires. I quote the following questions from a questionnaire concerning shoe buying: "What is most important to you in buying shoes: color, price, durability, style, quality, fit?" Such a question and the resulting statistical tabulation have been used

[1] G. K. Chesterton, *The Invisible Man*, "Innocence of Father Brown."

over and over again, with quite contradictory results. In Germany, much discussion centered about the problem of whether customers lay more stress upon quality, or upon style, because different investigations following such procedure had brought out different results. Now, price and color and style are items which can be easily ascertained at the time of purchase. Quality and durability, on the other hand, are attributes which we can test only by wearing the shoes. While the purchase is being made, we must judge them by accessory criteria. One person might judge the quality by the style; another, by the price; still another by some feature of the leather. Therefore, the people who state that they bought according to quality have made varying assumptions as to how quality can be ascertained at the moment of purchase. Consequently, this whole group should be recorded according to the concrete criteria used, and not according to a word which implies a tacit assumption unknown to the interviewer. This can be easily done by adding another question about this ill-defined attribute: "In buying, how do you recognize quality and how do you recognize durability?"

The reader, who may recall similar cases, will readily see the benefit to be derived from a previous careful analysis by market research men of terms which they use, in order to describe attributes. They would not only obtain more reliable results; they would be more prepared to refute objections which originate from misunderstandings. Professor Donald Laird,[2] of Colgate, conducted an experiment to show of what little use it is to ask a woman about attributes of commodities and their importance to her. He took identical pairs of stockings and perfumed them slightly with different scents. Then he asked certain women to select the pair which seemed to them to be of the best quality. The women definitely preferred a certain perfume, and Laird made the point that these women thought they judged quality, whereas they actually judged scent. But what about this word *quality*?

[2] *Journal of Applied Psychology*, June, 1932.

No definition is given or presupposed. As a result, the women first exhausted the more usual criteria of quality, perhaps texture, or body of the weave, and as these did not give any clue, they finally relied upon scent as a criterion of quality, inasmuch as a definition of quality was left entirely to their own interpretation. The only thing which Laird's clever experiment shows is that scent can be used in tacit assumption as the definition of quality. No intrinsic difficulty in this kind of research is shown except that the basic problems have to be brought to light more clearly.

There is a similarity between this principle of tacit assumption and our principle of specification: Everything depends upon the purpose of the study. If we want material for writing advertising copy, then the word *quality* used by our respondent is satisfactory for us, since we intend to approach him with words anyhow. But if we want to use our interviews for guidance in shoe manufacturing, we want to know exactly what the word *quality* connotes to the consumer. It is, therefore, advisable to formulate questionnaires in such a way that the returns can be used for both copy writing and production guidance. We cite by way of example a question on book buying. The respondent was asked: "How did you learn about this book?" The problem was to ascertain: "What interested you in it?" The typical answer was: the title, or the author, or the subject matter, but in order to get more definite information, the following check list was used, which proved to be successful.[3] The respondent was first required to give his general answer, then was asked by the interviewer to specify this reply according to the following possibilities:

What interested you in it?
    Title. . . .; previous work of author. . . .;
        fame of author. . . .
    Subject matter which I understood from
        source above (the information). . . .; from

[3] No attempt is here made to discuss the problem of the checklist vs. free answer. Professor J. G. Jenkins at Cornell is now working on conclusive experiments in this field.

    glancing at the book. . . .; from the jacket.
     . . .; from the title. . . .
    Nothing in the book itself, but its reputa-
        tion. . . .; the authority of the recommenda-
        tion. . . .; reading was professionally
        required. . . .
    External features of the book (color, size,
        binding, etc.) Specify. . . .; Other reasons.

The tabulation of the results will depend upon the use which is to be made of the data. If the answers are to be used for writing advertising copy, a table according to the main groups will be most useful. If a jacket design or a store display of books is at stake, the sub-items become of chief importance. Very often in current market research, we would find that the subject matter of a book was a reason for buying. Our example shows that subject matter can mean at least four different things, and just what it means in a special case has clearly to be ascertained by the provisions of the questionnaire.

The problem of tacit assumption constitutes such a strong limitation upon the use of questionnaires alone, that it is sometimes necessary to resort to a combination of experiment and interview. In many instances it is not possible to ascertain positively what tacit assumptions the respondent is holding in mind, and an experiment is helpful in bringing out the real facts of the situation. A product experiment in market research is, from a theoretical point of view, a tool for eliminating the respondent's tacit assumption by variations of stimulus. We cannot discuss the field of experiment here, but we want to give as a final example, an experience which is just on the line between interview and experiment.

Donald Cowen offered a few hundred women two brands of the same food product; the one was the leading brand in the market, the other a new brand of his company. The subjects divided about 50-50 for the two brands. Then he added the question: "Do you prefer the product you just selected to the product you have at home?" Here the adherents of the leading product responded in general: "Not especially." The adherents of Cowen's product definitely preferred it to the brand they had at home. The inference was clear; the two products were in taste about equally popular; but the one, the leading brand, had a flavor or taste similar to that of the product already in use, whereas the Cowen product had a radically new taste. This very important difference would not have been brought to light either through the mere choice experiment or by a question: "Why do you like it?" It was a happy combination of experiment and interview which broke down a tacit assumption. It is the conviction of this writer that such a combination will prove more and more successful in the field of product improvement.[4]

IV. SUMMARY AND THEORETICAL BACKGROUND

The assumption of this paper was that the consumer we have in front of us had carried through a concrete purchase. Our problem was to record all the factors which had determined his purchase; or, better, all the factors which were important for our investigation. We have assumed that this consumer is perfectly willing to answer our questions. The main point was to formulate our questions in such a way that the different determinants really came to light. We have seen that three principles must be observed: the *principle of specification*, of *division,* and of *tacit assumption*. It is evident that our problem is a very restricted one and by no means covers the whole field of psychology in market research. It is, therefore, very important to end this paper with a short theoretical consideration which will enable us to show the connections between our problem and some others not discussed here.

Psychologists who have analyzed the structure of action, as, notably, Carl Buehler and Madison Bentley have done, agree that the determinants of an action fall into three groups: biological determinants, bio-

graphical determinants, and what we might call instantaneous or actual determinants of the first degree. These differences are easy to demonstrate in a purchase which is, of course, just a special case of action. Someone buys a book. He wants to read on the train, therefore he selects a detective story. He is especially fond of a certain author. He is in a cheerful mood, and therefore he spends more money on it than he intended. These are all determinants of the first degree. We could go on in our investigation: Why doesn't he like to read historical novels on the train? Why is he fond of this special author? What gave him his cheerful mood? The answers to these questions would be biographical determinants. They might lead us, more or less, far back into the biography of our respondents. The biological determinants are so obvious that we need not bother with them in an interview. Why does he read the book instead of eat it? Goats like to eat paper, but the biological composition of our respondent makes paper-eating uncomfortable for him.

If one wants to define explicitly the determinants of the first degree, he might put it this way: The circumstances under which the decision for purchase has been made, the purpose of the purchase, and all the factors which carry this decision on until it has actually been executed, represent the actual determinants of the first degree. It is evident that the number of different determinants can vary greatly from one purchase to another. If we buy some foods under the immediate influence of how nice they look, the number of determinants of the first degree is much smaller than if we shop around for days in order to find a certain object. That does not mean, by the way, that the number of biographical determinants is smaller in the former case. It might well be that we are led far back when we want to find out why these foods appeal so much to our respondent, whereas the shopping for the other object might have a short history as to its biographical determinants.

It is probably clear to the reader that, in this paper, we have been dealing with

[4] I refer especially to the interesting efforts of Alexis Bommaripa in connection with the Psychological Corporation.

the technics of ascertaining the determinants of the first degree which motivate a purchase. Here let us introduce a new term: *The complete motivational set-up of the first degree*. By this, we shall understand all the determinants of the first degree which are of significance for our study. This concept is of practical importance because it gives us a certain check as to the value of our questionnaire. A questionnaire is satisfactory when, and only when, it actually secures the *total* motivational set-up of the first degree. Let us suppose, for instance, that a woman gives as her reason for a purchase in a certain store that she has a charge account there. This reason is acceptable as long as she maintains a charge account only at this store. As soon as she has charge accounts in other stores also, we must demand additional reason for her selection of this store. Or, let us suppose that in a leisure-time study, reasons for time-spending are asked. Someone tells us: "I was bored, and, therefore, visited a friend." This is acceptable only if we have reason to suppose, or if the respondent tells us, that he always visits this friend when he is bored. If that is not true, we must seek an additional reason for his going to see this friend, rather than taking a walk, for instance. On the other hand, if there is only one shoe store in town, or only one which is socially "possible," we don't need to ask, in every case, why this store has been selected.

Every concrete topic of research offers new problems for getting the complete motivational set-up of the first degree. The movie questionnaire, discussed earlier in this paper, gives many examples of this sort, and the reader is asked to go back once more to it and consider it in the light of this new concept, which, in the preparation of a good questionnaire, must be taken into consideration. Further, this concept becomes a useful tool in training interviewers. In a characteristic way, even good interviewers, in the beginning, will turn in incomplete motivational set-ups. They will, for instance, report that their respondent wanted to see a certain picture and therefore, went to see it on Tuesday night. The picture, however, has been shown three consecutive days, and the respondent's interest in this picture does not explain why he went Tuesday. Such a report indicates that some determinants have escaped our interviewer. We have to train him in such a way that he realizes, on the spot, that the motivational set-up he secured was incomplete. If he understands it, he will have a very good criterion as to whether or not his interview was satisfactory. I believe that, in such training, quickest progress can be made by utilizing this concept.

The necessity for getting a complete motivational set-up may compel us to use additional tools of research beyond the mere asking why. Take for instance, the problem of ascertaining the reason why certain people did not vote in an election. It would be completely erroneous to tabulate in one straight table their reasons for not voting. Two men might report in a hasty interview that their reasons for not voting were that they were out of town. Our principle of specification quickly teaches us that not voting involves two items: amount of political interest, and the sort of hindrance that kept them away from the polls. One man might be eager to vote, but a dying relative may make it imperative for him to leave town. Another man might care so little for politics that he goes on a fishing party on election day. So if we want a complete motivational set-up, we need two sets of data, and in order to get the one we have to ascertain the amount of political interest of these two respondents. That might lead us to quite new technical problems, which we cannot discuss here. Probably an attitude scale or some other tool for measuring the amount of interest of our respondent will have been used to this end.[5] But still it will leave us in the realm of a set-up of first degree, because an interest which makes us do something is a typical example of an actual determinant of first degree.

So much for the importance of the word

[5] See "The Psychological Approach to Market Research." *Harvard Business Review*, October 1934.

complete in our concept; now to the restrictions implied in the words *first degree.* Suppose we have ascertained that a certain color appealed especially to our respondent, or that he is especially interested in one author, and so on. Do we not miss just what is essential for our study if we fail to go back to the biographical determinants and ascertain why he likes this color, or why he is interested in this author? We will not answer the question here. It would lead us not only to new technics of ascertaining biographical determinants, but it would make us face an altogether new problem: the technics of interpretation. These technics of interpretation are of enormous importance and as great a contribution of psychology to market research as the art of asking why.[6] We can only touch on this subject in this paper, in one connection, the technic of ascertaining a motivational set-up of first degree, where it impinges closely upon the content of this article. We might, for instance, find that, in a particular study, many respondents, asked why they disliked a certain commodity, might answer, "I don't know" or "I just dislike it." This answer is completely legitimate and an actual determinant of the first degree. What such a great amount of emotional dislike means is a completely different question. For example, I happened to read a market survey regarding the use of a canned beverage. A third of the respondents approved the idea because it would be inexpensive and convenient. Another third said merely that they disliked the idea, but could give no definite reason for this dislike. The research man made the point that this latter group could easily be convinced because they themselves

[6] See R. Likert, "The Technique of Attitude Measurement," *Psychological Archives,* 1932.

admitted the weakness of their point. Such a statement is, of course, preposterous. The mere fact that these respondents had an emotional dislike for this canned beverage showed that there were strong biographical roots still to be discovered. The only thing which we can do with such information is to point out that we have detected a sore spot. That is in itself a strong point. We ought not to weaken our position by going beyond our own means. We have to keep the problems of interpretation constantly in mind in order not to leave the field where the technics we discussed in this paper are located. But, on the other hand, we will not depreciate the importance of an adequate technic of asking *why* by the fact that there are other equally important things to do. It is the part of wisdom in any field, and it is consistent with the progress of methodology to develop the method step by step with the ultimate aim of integration of all of the elements into the larger pattern of methodology for the entire field. It would be indefensible to hold back simply because one step is all that could be taken at one time.

The reader who has followed our deliberations and matched them with his own experience will probably disagree with some of our statements and will feel that we overestimate the importance of others. But that is always true of discussions in a field which, at the present stage of its development, requires chiefly careful, logical, and psychological analysis. Whenever the writer of this paper has found something in his field which he believed new, he met a Mr. Smith who had already done the same thing. On the other hand, he always found scores of Mr. Joneses who did not know what Smith and he had attempted. So this paper was written for Messrs. Jones, with an apology to Smith.

THE CONTROVERSY OVER DETAILED INTERVIEWS—
AN OFFER FOR NEGOTIATION

PAUL F. LAZARSFELD

If two people vigorously disagree on whether something is blue or green, the chances are that the object is composed of both colors and that for some reason the two contestants are either unable or unwilling to see more than the one. If in methodological discussions, competent workers assume vehemently opposite positions, it is generally a good time for someone to enter the scene and suggest that the parties are both right and wrong.

A recent issue of this *Quarterly* (Summer, 1943) provides one of the many indications that such a situation has come about in the public opinion field. A representative of the Division of Program Surveys in the Department of Agriculture reports on large-scale research work, the core of which is an interviewing technique "intended to draw full intensive discussions" and using "various non-directive means of stimulating full discussion in the interviewing situation."[1] Preceding this report is an article by a well-known psychologist who dubs this technique "depth interview" and describes it in rather uncomplimentary terms. One of his conclusions is that "there is little or no evidence to support the tacit assumption that the so-called depth interview yields more valid re-

sponses from people than do other types."[2] For him, simple "yes-no" questions, used judiciously, are sufficient.

The matter is important from more than a scientific point of view, Applied social research is a new venture. Only yesterday did the government begin large-scale studies in public opinion. The market and consumer studies which are now finding acceptance in many industries are likewise all of recent date. Managers in business as well as in public administration are faced with sharply contending factions among research professionals. Should they succumb to skepticism or discouragement and fail to give this new branch of the social sciences the opportunity to prove itself, then development might be seriously retarded. It therefore seems justified to present the problem to a larger public with an earnest effort toward impartiality.

Employing a neutral terminology, we shall allude to our subject as the "open-ended interview." The term serves to describe a crucial aspect of this type of interviewing— the fact that "open-ended interviews" do not set fixed answers in terms of which a respondent must reply. Eventually a more animated expression may be desirable. (To

---

[1] Hans E. Skott, "Attitude Research in the Department of Agriculture," *Public Opinion Quarterly*, 1943, 7, 280-292.

[2] Henry C. Link, "An Experiment in Depth Interviewing," *Public Opinion Quarterly*, 1943, 7, 267-279.

From the *Public Opinion Quarterly*, 1944, 8, 38-60. Reprinted by permission of the author and the publisher.

save space we shall abbreviate the term and refer to it hereafter as OI.) Rather than asking for a definition it would be better if the reader visualizes the situation in which an OI occurs. In the interview situation the interviewer by an appropriate introduction attempts to establish the best possible rapport between himself and the respondent because he is aware that he may have to interview the respondent an hour or longer. He then proceeds to ask one of the ten or fifteen questions which have been assigned to him by the central office. Sometimes the respondent himself immediately plunges into great detail, and the interviewer simply permits him to continue. If the first answer is brief, however, the interviewer is instructed to "probe." There are quite a number of devices for eliciting detailed, free response. Mere silence will sometimes induce the respondent to elaborate. Or, the interviewer may just repeat the respondent's own words with an appropriate inflection. Asking for examples will often prove helpful. Then again questions such as the following are used: "How did you happen to notice it? What makes you think so? How did you feel about it before? Do most of your friends have the same opinion?" The trained OI field worker has the goal of his inquiry clearly imprinted in his mind, but he adapts his inquiry to the concrete situation between the interviewee and himself.

If properly conducted, such an OI will result in a detailed document which covers the whole area under investigation, including the interviewer's observations of the respondent's reactions and background.

The OI is suggested by its proponents in opposition to what one might term the "straight poll question." The latter gives the respondent the occasion to answer only "Yes," "No," "Don't know," or to make a choice among a small number of listed possible answers. Between these two extremes there are, of course, several steps. Actually there is hardly a poll where there is not some freedom left for the respondent to express himself in his own way. It is not necessary here to discuss where the straight poll ques-

tion ends and the OI begins. For all practical purposes the distinction is clear enough.

A rather thorough survey of published and unpublished studies based on the OI technique was made for the purpose of this paper. It is necessary to describe and classify these in some detail because many current misunderstandings come from an insufficient distinction among the different functions of the OI; if people disagree on its usefulness, they very often do not have the same functions in mind. It is the plan of this paper to present the main uses of the OI at their very best and to stress the advantages which are generally singled out by the advocates of this technique. Then we shall select a specific criterion for evaluation and summarize pertinent criticism. It is hoped that as a result we shall end up with a balanced view on the subject.

THE SIX MAIN FUNCTIONS OF THE OI TECHNIQUE

1. Clarifying the meaning of a respondent's answer

Before asking him whether war profits should be limited, we have to find out what the respondent thinks the word "profit" means. Some people talk of the total income of a company as profit, others believe it is the difference between wholesale and retail prices, still others are of the opinion that war profits are the difference between prewar and war earnings. By discussing the general subject matter with him we are very likely to obtain a fairly clear picture of what would be equivalent to his *private definition* of these terms. One frequently underestimates the number of terms which seem obvious to the interviewer but which are ambiguous or even unknown to the lower educated section of the population.

In other cases it is not so much the meaning of words as the *implication of an opinion* which has to be clarified. If a respondent is in favor of reducing taxes, does he know that as a result many government services will have to be reduced? If he is in favor of free speech, does he realize that such freedom must also pertain to people who may express opinions that are very distasteful to him?

If respondents are asked to voice their thoughts on a course of action, it is important to know against what *alternative possibilities* they had weighed their choice. A respondent is for the continuation of the Dies Committee: has he weighed that against the possibility that the Department of Justice can adequately handle the problem of subversive activities, or did he feel that if the Dies Committee does not do so, no one else will? Another respondent is for government regulation of business: does he prefer this to completely free enterprise, or has he considered the different ways by which an individual business man can be regulated through his own trade organizations?

Finally, the OI permits a respondent to clarify his opinion by introducing *qualifications*. He is in favor of rationing if it is administered fairly for everyone. He is in favor of married women getting defense jobs if it has been made sure that there are no unemployed men left. The respondent might not volunteer such qualifications if the interview is a too hurried one.

2. *Singling out the decisive aspects of an opinion*

If we deal with attitudes toward rather complex objects, we often want to know the *decisive aspects* by which a respondent is guided. Take the opinion on *candidates* for public office. At this moment, for example, the Republicans in some mid-western states prefer Dewey to Willkie as Presidential nominee. What does Dewey stand for in the eyes of these people? Party loyalty? Isolationism? Administrative ability? Gangbusting? Here again the OI would proceed in characteristic fashion. What has the respondent heard about the two candidates? What does he think would happen if Dewey were to become President? And so on. In the end we should be able to distinguish groups for which Dewey means quite different things, and fruitful statistical comparisons on a number of social characteristics could be carried through.

Similar possibilities can come up when people are called upon to judge *concrete situations*. They do or do not like the working conditions in their plants. If the answer is in the negative, what features do they especially dislike? In order to get a reasonable idea of people's complaints a rather detailed discussion is necessary; the OI is a good device for this purpose. Other examples of such procedure can easily be found: to what does the respondent attribute rising prices? Or the increase in juvenile delinquency?

Here belong also some recent efforts in the field of *communications* research. People like or dislike a film or a radio program. Through detailed discussions it is possible to bring out quite clearly which elements in the production make for the audience's reaction.[3]

The singling out of decisive aspects also pertains to *issues*. If respondents are against sending lend-lease supplies to Russia, it is important to know what about such a policy they dislike. Do they disapprove of Russian communism, or do they think that the Russians do not need the supplies, or do they feel that other parts of the world war panorama are more important? Here, again, the OI would not only ask for an opinion on the basic issues but would probe the respondents for further details.

Very often the decisive aspects of a candidate, a situation, a document or an issue will be elicited by starting a discussion with the words: "Why do you think so?" Or, "Why do you prefer. . . ?" But hardly ever will one such question give all the necessary information. If people prefer Dewey as the Republican nominee and are asked why they do so, they will very often say, "Because he is the better man," or, "Because a friend feels the same way." Then the interviewer must keep in mind the fact that he is looking for decisive features and must keep on asking questions. For instance: "What makes

[3] P. F. Lazarsfeld and R. K. Merton, "Studies in Radio and Film Propaganda," *Transactions of the New York Academy of Sciences*, Series II, 1943, 6, No. 2, 58-79.

him a better man?" Or, "Why do you think your friend favors him?"[4]

3. *What has influenced an opinion*

If people approve of an issue or vote for a candidate (or buy a product), it is useful to divide the determining factors of such action into three main groups: the *decisive features* of the object in question, which account for its being chosen; the *predispositions* of the respondents, which make them act one way or another; and the *influences which are brought to bear upon them*, especially those which mediate between them and the object of their choice.[5] The use of the OI to investigate the first group has just been discussed. The quest for predispositions (attitude, motives) will be dealt with under points four and five. We now consider the use of the OI in the search for *influences*.

The typical research situation here is one wherein we try to assess the importance of a certain event. Let us turn, for example, to people who bought bonds after listening to Kate Smith or who started storing potatoes after a government campaign to this effect had been started or who improved their production records after a system of music-while-you-work had been introduced in a plant. A well-conducted OI should provide enough information so that the causal role of the exposure can be appraised. The rules for such interviews have been rather well worked out.[6]

If the respondent claims that the specific

---

[4] It should be emphasized that the question "why" is useful also for the other purposes which will be discussed in the remaining four points. This is easily understood if one considers that the word has hardly any meaning in itself. It is about equivalent to saying that the respondent should talk some more. "Why" is a good start, but it seldom leads to a constructive end if it is not followed by specific questions directed toward what the interviewer really wants to know.

[5] Paul Lazarsfeld, "The Art of Asking Why," *National Marketing Review,* 1, 1935, 32-43.

[6] Paul Lazarsfeld, "Evaluating the Effectiveness of Advertising by Direct Interviews," *Journal of Consulting Psychology,* July-August, 1941.

speech had an effect on him, a sort of cross-examination is necessary along the following lines: Wasn't he ready to perform the final act before he heard the speech? Didn't something else happen after the speech which is a more likely explanation for his action? If the respondent denies being affected by the speech, then the whole interview has to be conducted as if the purpose were to break down this contention: Why didn't the respondent act before he heard the speech? Did he have any other sources of information? In other words, the technique consists of checking up on whether according to logical and psychological commonsense, the respondent would have acted otherwise than he did if he had not heard the speech or read the pamphlet. Obviously it is not possible to anticipate all the questions which have to be asked in order to bring to light the elements preceding the final act and surrounding the influence under investigation. The task of the OI is to draw out those factors so sharply that the reader of the interview can form a judgment as to whether any causal role of the influence should be assumed or not.

This technique of unearthing influences by OI's is especially pertinent to advertising problems because of the insistent use of the same "stimuli" in radio programs or magazine campaigns. With the Government turning to "campaigns" to influence the consumption or saving habits of the citizenry, however, it would deserve more attention from students of public opinion. During election campaigns similar problems come up, particularly if an effort is made to study those people who at the beginning of the campaign had not yet formulated opinions.

4. *Determining complex attitude patterns*

A fourth group of applications comes into play when we turn to the *classification of rather complex attitude patterns*. If we want to ascertain how active people are in their war participation or how disturbed they are by current food shortages, the OI actually discusses such subject matters with the respondents, getting their recent experiences and reactions. The purpose is to make an adequate classification of the material so obtained. Further assumptions come easily to mind. People can be classified according to how satisfied they are with local handling of the draft situation, according to the ways they adjust to the lack of gasoline, according to their satisfaction or dissatisfaction with the amount of information they get on the war, etc. This procedure is singularly characteristic of Rensis Likert's work in the Department of Agriculture.[7]

If it is used to assess the extent to which respondents are concerned with a certain problem and how intensely they feel about it, this approach assumes special importance. Two respondents might give the same answer to a simple opinion poll question. For the one, however, it is an important issue on which he has spent much thought, whereas the other may have formed his opinion spontaneously as the poll investigator asked him about it. The possible perfunctory nature of replies to public opinion polls has been the object of much criticism. Those who feel strongly in favor of the OI emphasize that right at this point such a danger is obviated—the danger that poll results will be misleading because they do not take into account intensity of feeling or amount of concern.

This role of the OI does not necessarily terminate with a one-dimensional rating scale of, say, intensity of feeling. The OI is suitable for more complex ratings as well. In a study of people's reactions to changes in food habits, sponsored by the National Research Council, the interviewers were instructed to "watch carefully for all offhand comments to one of the following frames of reference: Money, Health, Taste, Status."[8] The procedure was to talk with people about current food shortages, the adjustments they had made, and the points at which they experienced difficulties. From their discussion it was possible to classify them into four groups according to which of the four contexts they spontaneously stressed. The study found, for example, that high-income groups refer to health twice as often as money, whereas in low-income groups money is the frame of reference three times more frequently than is health.

Finally we have what is known as the "gratification study." In an analysis of the gratification people get from the Professor Quiz programs, for example, a variety of appeals could be distinguished. Some listeners are very much intrigued by the competitive element of the contest; others like to test their own knowledge; still others hope to learn something from the questions posed on the program.[9] We could not expect the untrained respondent to explain clearly the psychological complexities of his interest or his reaction. It is not even likely that he would classify himself accurately if we let him choose among different possibilities. Again the OI is needed to provide the necessary information for the trained analyst. Its practical use lies in the following direction: If we know what attitudes are statistically dominant we can either strengthen the "appeal" elements in the program which are likely to get an enlarged audience; or we can try to change these attitudes if, for some ulterior reason, we consider the prevailing distribution unsatisfactory.

Such studies have also been made in the public opinion field; for example, in analyzing the gratification people get out of writing letters to senators.[10]

5. Motivational interpretations

Ratings, attitude types, and gratification lists are only the beginning of a conceptual line which ends in studies based on *broad*

[7] Likert's work is mainly done for Government agencies and therefore cannot be quoted at the present time. The present paper owes much to discussions with him and some of his associates, especially Bill Gold.

[8] Kurt Lewin, "Forces Behind Food Habits and Methods of Change," *The Problem of Changing Food Habits*, Bulletin of the National Research Council, Number 108, October 1943.

[9] Herta Herzog, "On Borrowed Experience," *Studies in Philosophy and Social Science*, 1941.

[10] R. Wyant and H. Herzog, "Voting Via the Senate Mailbag," *Public Opinion Quarterly*, 1941, 5, 590-624.

motivational interpretations. We cannot hope here to present systematically the ways in which psychologists distinguish between the different kinds of "drives" according to their range, depth, or the specificity of their relations to the world of objects.[11] The picture would not be complete, nevertheless, if we were to omit a mention of the use of the OI technique for the purpose of understanding people's reactions in such broad conceptual contexts.

The OI collects a variety of impressions, experiences, and sidelines which the respondent offers when he is asked to discuss a given topic. The man who does the study then makes a kind of psychological construction. He creates a picture of some basic motivation of which all these details are, so to speak, manifestations.

Consider an example. In studying certain groups of unemployed one makes a variety of observations: they walk slowly, they lose interest in public affairs, do not keep track of their time, express opinions only with hesitation, stop looking for jobs—in short, they can best be understood as discouraged, resigned beings whose psychological living space has been severely contracted. On the basis of this conceptualization we would not expect them, e.g., to join revolutionary movements which require initiative. If, on the other hand, we are interested in retaining whatever morale they do have left, we would reject the idea of a straight dole in favor of work relief which would keep them psychologically "on the go."

There is only a rather short step from this example to the kind of OI studies which we want to discuss. For a number of reasons most of them have been done in the field of advertising.

People who talk about their shoe purchases often mention how embarrassing it is to expose one's feet in stockings, how one is virtually a prisoner in the hands of the salesman, etc. They are also likely to point out

[11] Gordon W. Allport, "Attitudes," *Handbook of Social Psychology* (ed. C. Murchison), Worcester: Clark University Press, 1935, 798-844.

that such-and-such a salesman was friendly, or that they do like stores where the customers are not seated too near each other. The study director finally forms the hypothesis that the shoe-buying situation is one likely to evoke a feeling of inferiority. To alleviate this feeling and thus lead to a larger and more satisfied patronage, a number of obvious suggestions can be made for the training of salesmen and the arrangement of the store.

Finally, take a series of OI's where women say that they like fruits in glass jars because they can see the product and also because they feel there is greater danger of food spoiling in tin cans. The conclusion is not that lots of fruits in glass jars should be shown. A motivational interpretation which takes all the pertinent remarks in the OI's into consideration will rather proceed as follows. Glass jars have something reassuring about them, whereas tin cans have a slight connotation of a dungeon in which the food and even oneself is jailed. The appropriate advertising for glass jars, therefore, would show them among flowers, in rays of sunshine, to stress the exhilarating elements in the whole complex. Visibility would then be only one of these elements.

To discuss this use of OI's in a short space is impossible, especially since its logic has not yet been thought through very well. The social scientist who tries to clarify such analysis faces a conflict between two goals to which he is equally devoted. On the one hand, these interpretations serve to integrate a host of details as well as make us aware of new ones which we might otherwise overlook; often they are very brilliant. On the other hand, they violate our need for verification because by their very nature they can never be proved but only made plausible. It is no coincidence that in the two examples given above we have added to each interpretation some practical advice derived from it. What such motivational analysis does is to see past experiences as parts of some psychological drive which can be reactivated by related material, be it propaganda or institutional devices.[12]

6. *Clarifying statistical relationships*

In the five areas outlined so far the OI was the point of departure for all subsequent analysis. Now finally we have to deal with studies where statistical results are available and where the OI serves to *interpret and refine statistical inter-relationships*. The procedure could be called the analysis of deviate cases.

When, for instance, the panic was studied which followed the famous broadcast on the "Invasion from Mars," it was found that people on a lower educational level were most likely to believe in the occurrence of the great catastrophe.[13] Yet some lower-educated people were not frightened at all. When these deviate cases were subject to an OI, many turned out to be mechanics or people who had mechanical hobbies; they were accustomed to checking up on things, a habit the "regular" people had acquired by a successful formal education. On the other hand, quite a number of well-educated people were frightened. When an OI was made with them, the following was sometimes found: During the broadcast they had been in special social situations where it was not clear who should take the initiative of checking up; the lack of social structure impeded purposeful action, and everyone got panicky.

Another example can be taken from unemployment studies. In general it is found that the more amicable the relations in a family prior to the depression, the more firmly would the family stand the impact of unemployment. Again we can inspect deviate cases. A couple fights constantly before the depression, but after the husband becomes unemployed, they get along bet-

ter. A detailed interview reveals the probability that here the husband wanted to be submissive and the wife dominant, but folkways prevented them from accepting this inverse role. Unemployment, then, enforces a social situation here which is psychologically adequate. Or, a good marriage breaks down surprisingly quickly as a result of the husband's unemployment. A specification of the case shows that the man's sexual habits are rather vulnerable and become disorganized under the blow of the loss of his job.[14]

The general pattern of these studies proceeds from an empirical correlation which is usually not very high. We take cases which do not follow the majority pattern and try to gain an impression or to account for their irregularity. The political scientist is used to such procedure.[15] He knows, for instance, that the more poor people and Catholics live in a given precinct of a big city, the more Democratic votes he can expect. But here is a precinct which qualifies on both scores, and still it went Republican. What accounts for this deviation? Is the Democratic machine inefficient? Has a special local grievance developed? Was there a recent influx of people with different political tradition? This is quite analogous to what we are trying to do when we are faced with individual cases which went statistically out of line. With the help of the OI we try to discover new factors which, if properly introduced, would improve our multiple correlation.

Usually the matter is put by saying that detailed case studies help us to understand an empirical correlation. This is quite all right as far as the psychology of the investigator goes. It would be more correct, however, to say that the OI helps to develop hypotheses as to the conditions under which you would expect our first correlation to

[12] Rhoda Metraux, "Qualitative Attitude Analysis—A Technique for the Study of Verbal Behavior," *The Problem of Changing Food Habits*, Bulletin of the National Research Council, No. 108, October 1943.

[13] Hadley Cantril, Herta Herzog, and Hazel Gaudet, *Invasion from Mars*, Princeton: Princeton University Press, 1939.

[14] Mirra Komarvosky, *The Unemployed Man and His Family*. New York: Institute of Social Research, 1940.

[15] Harold F. Gosnell, *Getting out the Vote*. Chicago: Chicago University Press, 1927.

become higher. If it were our task to formulate in general terms why the OI is so helpful to the better understanding of an attitude, our starting point would actually be here. We would have to make quite clear that the insight gained by a qualitative approach is nothing else than a hypothetical relation between a number of factors. But that would go beyond the purpose of this section, in which we intended to give no more than a vivid picture of the actual research experiences out of which the OI technique has grown. It is to the controversial aspect of the problem that we now turn.

THE ISSUE BECOMES A PROBLEM

The six areas just outlined could be looked at in two ways. For one, they represent desirable goals for public opinion research. We need more detailed knowledge as to what the answers of our respondents mean, on what specific points their opinions are based, in what larger motivational contexts they belong, etc. At the same time, the different applications of the OI also imply criticism to the effect that one straight poll question will hardly ever reach any of these goals successfully.

One can agree with this criticism without concluding that the OI technique is the only remedy. If this paper were written for a psychological journal, for instance, the course of our discussion from here on would be prescribed. We should have to compare results obtained by straight poll questions with those collected by OI's and decide which are preferable according to some adequate criteria. The present analysis, however, falls under the heading of "Research Policy." The research administrator has to make decisions as to the most desirable procedures long before we have provided all the necessary data on the comparative merits of different research methods.

What line of argument would one take in such a situation? No one can close his eyes to the shortcomings of many of the current opinion-poll practices. Having begun with the simple problem of predicting elections, they use, very often, a greatly oversimplified approach for the gauging of attitudes toward complex issues. We shall also agree that a well-conducted OI gives us a fascinating wealth of information on the attitude of a single respondent. When it comes to the statistical analysis of many OI's, the matter is already not so simple. It is in the nature of this technique that just the most valuable details of one OI become difficult to compare with the answers obtained in another interview. It can safely be said that the proponents of the OI technique have made much more progress in the conduct of the interviews than in their statistical analysis.

But even if the OI technique were not to have methodological troubles of its own, it would still be open to one very serious objection. It is necessarily an expensive and slow procedure and, as a result, studies which are made for practical purposes will always be based on a small number of cases. It is inconceivable at this moment that an agency would have the resources or the time to make many thousands of OI's on one subject. This is a decisive drawback. True, a surprisingly small number of cases is needed for a fairly correct estimate of how many Republicans there are in a community or how many people save their fat and grease. But do we want to stop here? Don't we want to know in which social groups some of those activities are more frequent than in others? Aren't we trying to account for the reasons why some people do a thing and others do not? And how can this be done except by careful cross-tabulation of one part of our data against other parts? And for this, a much larger number of cases is needed.

In other words, the OI technique, even if it were perfect in itself, places us in a dilemma. By laying all the stress on the detailed description of the single respondent's attitude, it forces us into relatively small numbers of interviews. This in turn handicaps another important progress in public opinion research: the progress which consists of comparing carefully the distribution of opinions in different sub-groups of the population and relating a given opinion to the personal characteristics and to other attitudes of the respondent.

From the standpoint of research policy, therefore, which is the standpoint taken in this paper, the whole problem comes to this. Is there not some way to use all the good ideas which the proponents of the OI technique have and still to develop methods which are more objective, more manageable on a mass basis—which, in short, give us sufficient material to do a thorough analysis of the factors which make for a given distribution of public opinion?

Under these aspects we shall go once more through the six areas discussed above. In each case we shall look for procedures which combine the administrative advantages of the straight poll question with the psychological advantages of the OI. Quite frankly we want to "eat our cake and have it, too." All folklore notwithstanding, research progress consists in the art of doing things which at first seem incompatible. As we proceed, it will turn out that these compromise techniques do not make the OI superfluous but give it a new and, as we feel, more valuable place in the whole scheme of public opinion research.

To bring out more clearly our trend of thought, we begin with a little scheme. Below are two lists: the first for our six areas, the second for the corresponding procedures which would overcome some of the shortcomings of the straight poll question and still be more formalized and manageable on a mass basis than the OI.

Current Applications of the OI Techniques
1. Clarifying the meaning of a respondent's answer
2. Singling out the decisive aspects of an opinion
3. Discerning influences
4. Determining complex attitude patterns
5. Interpreting motivation
6. Clarifying statistical relationships

Possible Objective
Alternatives for the OI
1. Interlocking system of poll questions
2. Check lists
3. None
4. Scales and typologies

5. Projective tests
6. None

It is to the short description and evaluation of the second list of the scheme that we now turn.

1. *Clarifying meaning by the use of interlocking poll questions*

In the first area we dealt with the clarification of the respondent's opinion. Did he know the significance of what he was talking about? In the course of an OI, by making the respondent elaborate in more detail, we will find out. But after all, the number of possible variations is not so great; it is often possible to get by explicit questions all the material we can use for comparative analysis of many interview returns.

Consider the following two cases. Studenski has pointed out that when people are asked whether they want lower taxes, most of them will say "yes."[16] After having asked this general question, however, he then asked a series of specific questions on whether the government should discontinue relief, work projects, expenses for national defense, expenses for schools, police, etc. Respondents who wanted taxes reduced but services maintained had obviously, to say the least, an inconsistent attitude toward the problem.[17] In a different context, Kornhauser has pointed out the shortcomings of

[16] Paul Studenski, "How Polls Can Mislead," *Harpers Magazine*, December 1939.
[17] This is the technique which Henry Link used in a more recent study ("An Experiment in Depth Interviewing," *Public Opinion Quarterly* 1943, 7, 267-279.) He first obtained a broad commitment on world participation for the post-war period from his respondents; then he asked a series of definite questions; for the sake of America's participation in world affairs, what would people be willing to accept? A standing army? Higher taxes? A lower standard of living? Etc. As a device to clarify the implications of people's opinions this is an appropriate procedure, but it is very confusing if it is suggested as a substitute for or even an improvement on the OI in all areas. It is precisely the purpose of the present paper to provide a general scheme, so that in discussing "depth interviews" *each participant can point to the specific sector of the entire field he has in mind.*

the question: Should Congress pass a law forbidding strikes in war industries or should war workers have the right to go on strike? Obviously there are other devices, such as an improved arbitration system or the endowment of union leaders with some semi-public power to keep their members from striking. By offering a whole set of such alternatives it is undoubtedly possible to get a much clearer picture of the respondent's real attitude.

In this and many similar examples the technique used consists of an *interlocking system of poll questions*, each of which is very simple but which through proper cross-tabulation permits the separation of respondents according to the extent to which they see the implications of their opinion.

Although we cannot go into details here, we have studied dozens of pertinent cases and are satisfied that for any given topic it is always possible to find an appropriate system of interlocking questions. The right procedure consists of beginning the study with a considerable number of very detailed OI's. These should come from different parts of the country and should serve to develop the structure of the problem. Experience shows that after one to three hundred such reports have been studied, very few new factors come up. At this point we can begin to develop a set of specific questions centering around the main attitude and bringing out its implications and qualifications. There is no reason why we should not ask specifically (by the use of ordinary poll questions) what knowledge and experience the respondent has in this field; what his opinions are in related fields; whether he does or does not expect certain things to happen; whether he has ever thought of the problem, or whether he cannot make up his mind about it, and so on.

Here we come across a very characteristic relationship between the OI and more formalized methods in opinion research. The OI serves as a source of observation and of ideas from which sets of precise poll questions can be derived which will be more manageable in the field and more susceptible to statistical analysis. On one occasion the

useful suggestion was made that the special job of *converter* should be developed: that people should specialize in studying OI's and seeing how they could be converted into systems of interlocking questions.

So far not enough thought has been spent in making this conversion procedure an explicit research operation for which standard examples and rules should be developed. Once this is done, it will probably turn out that in the area under discussion here the OI, although much preferable to isolated straight poll questions, is not so good as a well-structured set of straight poll questions. The proponents of the OI technique at this point usually see only the justified goal and the shortcomings of current public opinion polls. They have seldom the occasion to see in their own studies the hundreds of OI's which either do not yield really useful information or are so unique that if they are submitted to a comparative analysis, all the details which make them invaluable as a first phase of an investigation are lost when the final report is reached.

Sometimes when we want to clarify the meaning of an answer, especially in regard to qualifications, check lists can be considered an appropriate procedure. Since, however, check lists are more frequently indicated when it comes to the assessment of decisive features, they will be discussed under the next heading.

2. *Using check lists to get at the decisive aspects of an opinion*

If we want to know what people like about a candidate or what bothers them about the present rationing system, we can make a list of the probable answers and ask the respondents which answer fits their case.

The advantages and disadvantages of *check lists* have been repeatedly discussed. The minimum requirement is that they contain an exhaustive list of all the possibilities, for it is known that items not mentioned in a check list are less likely to be mentioned by the respondents. But even a good check list has certain dangers. If people are asked what wish they would make if they had a magic ring, they seldom mention "being very bright," because they do not think of intelligence as something that can be wished for. If, however, they get a check list of possible wishes which includes "intelligence," they are more likely to pick it. The less concrete the topic is, the more will the check list influence the answers.

As long as all this is not better explored by comparing the results from large-scale check lists and from the classifications of free answers, it is not possible to make a valid decision. Yet with the help of a careful analysis of OI's it seems logical to assume that exhaustive check lists can be safely constructed—ones which would be as safe as the results of open-ended interviewing. For complex topics the cautious research student will, of course, be hesitant to rely too easily on check lists. When in doubt he will prefer to rely on OI's recorded by conscientious interviewers and classified by sensitive analysts for the study of decisive features.

In studying the decisive aspects of opinion there are cases where the more formalized alternative for the OI would not be a check list, but a system of interlocking questions. This is especially true in dealing with opinions on policy issues. Suppose people have expressed themselves on the idea of married women working in war industry and are opposed to it. The open-ended question, "Why do you feel this way?" brings out a variety of comments which show that people look at the matter from a number of aspects: some feel that it is bad for the home if women stay out too much; others feel that women are not equipped for factory work or that working conditions are not adequate for them; still others do not want women to compete with men for jobs. Here are four features of the whole problem on which respondents could be asked their opinions explicitly. Do you feel that women are equipped for war jobs? Do you feel that they are a competitive danger for men? Etc. By cross-tabulating the answers to the sub-issues against the main issue of women in war work, one probably would get a better idea of the general attitude pattern than if the "reasons" were directly tabulated.

Again the OI is indispensable in preliminary studies to give one an idea as to what aspects should be considered. If, however, a large number of interviews is to be collected, the interlocking system of questions might be preferable, especially if great effort is made to get an appropriate conversion of preliminary OI's into a system of more precise questions.

3. *Are there other ways of studying what has influenced opinion?*

Whether it is possible to discern influences which are exercised upon people is a controversial question. In more extreme cases such decisions are obviously possible or impossible. If a child goes down to the grocer's "because my mother sent me down," we should consider such a statement as equivalent to a controlled experiment. Putting it rather exaggeratedly: if we set up two groups of well-matched children and had the mothers of the children in one group tell them to go to the grocer's, we should certainly expect to find more children from the "experimental" than from the control group at the grocer's. On the other hand, if a person has committed a crime and we ask him whether that is due to the fact that his parents immigrated to this country, we shall consider whatever he says not very reliable. The command of the mother is much more "discernible" as an influence than the whole background of family life.[18]

Fortunately, in public opinion research we are mostly interested in rather "discernible" influences. Whether people began to salvage paper under the influence of a government campaign or whether a specific pamphlet made them contribute blood to the Red Cross can be discovered fairly well by direct interviewing. For such studies the OI appears to be an important research tool. Thus, it becomes even more urgent to make its use as expert as possible. Sometimes it is not used wisely. Studies of the following kind have been circulated. People

[18] E. Smith and E. Suchman, "Do People Know Why They Buy?" *Journal of Applied Psychology*, 1949, 24, 673-684.

who began to can fruit were asked why they did so. Sixty per cent said "because of the campaign," 15% "because it is necessary for the war effort." Here is obviously a meaningless result—for OI or otherwise. Many of the 15% may have learned from the campaign that private canning was a patriotic duty. However, the interviewer was too easily satisfied with the first answer which came to the mind of the respondent instead of asking "Where did you learn that canning is important for the war effort?"[19]

We do not wish to discuss here under what conditions controlled experiments are possible and justified. Just for the record, we might add that the result of a controlled experiment does not necessarily indicate correctly the effectiveness of a real campaign. In a controlled experiment we expose some of the people artificially and may then find that they are strongly influenced by the campaign material. In real life people select themselves for exposure. It might well be that mainly those who are not affected by a radio speech are willing to listen to it. This is, for instance, one of the problems in educational broadcasting, where there is a wide difference between experimental and actual success of programs.

4. *Scales and typologies for the analysis of attitude patterns*

When it comes to the objective correlates for the use of the OI in the classification of complex attitude patterns, we find ourselves in a peculiar situation. The topic has been a favorite one for social-research students; we have discussed "case studies"

versus quantitative methods for a decade.[20] An appropriate instance comes from the study which this writer made during the presidential election of 1940. The task was to appraise how interested people were in the election. Had we used the OI technique, the interviewer would have talked with the respondent and by taking down what he said, by observing his participation in the discussion, he would have formed an opinion on his interest and then noted it in the form of a rating. Instead we asked the respondent three questions: whether he had tried to convince someone of his political ideas; whether he had done anything for the success of his candidate; and whether he was very anxious to see his candidate elected. Each respondent got a definite score according to how he answered the three questions.[21]

But how does such an objective scale compare with the impressionistic ratings obtained from an OI? The problems involved can best be explained by an example.

If in everyday life we call another person timid, we do so because of the way he walks or because of his hesitant speech and sometimes because of cues of which we are not precisely aware ourselves. In each case we use whatever cues the situation offers; they might be quite different from one case to the next. A "timidity rating," on the other hand, would provide us with a list of items on which an interviewer would have to get an observation for every case, if necessary by asking a direct question. The more timidity characteristics on this list applied to the respondents, the higher would

[19] We find here a mistake which corresponds to the objection we voiced above against Henry Link's paper. Because he used interlocking questions in one area, he thought that he had shown the uselessness of the OI technique in all other areas. Many of the proponents of the OI, on the other hand, do careful interviewing for the description of attitudes; but when it comes to the discerning of influences, they do bad interviewing and subject their returns to poor classification.

[20] Paul Wallin, *Case Study Methods in the Prediction of Personal Adjustment* (ed., Paul Horst). New York: Social Science Research Council, 1941.

[21] If such an interest score was used, it was found that for men the correlation between interest and voting was .20, whereas for women it was .50. Women, if they are not interested, do not vote. Men vote even if they are not interested, probably because they are more subject to social pressure. For a general theory of this score procedure see P. Lazarsfeld and W. Robinson, "Quantification of Case Studies," *Journal of Applied Psychology*, 1940, 24, 831-837.

be his timidity score. Using such a scale, the interviewer could not make use of incidental observations if they were not included in the list, even if in a special case he had a strong conviction that the respondent was much more timid than his scale value indicated.

All this can be directly applied to our problem. A good OI reproduces the full vividness of an actual observation; but if nothing characteristic happens in the interview situation or if the interviewer misses cues, then we have little on which to base our final classification. With the scale we can count on a definite amount of data, but some of them might be rather artificial and often we must forego valuable observations within our reach. *Thus, a scale because of its rigidity will hardly be as good as an OI under its best conditions but can hardly let us down as much as an OI sometimes does.*

Sometimes we classify material not in a one-dimensional order but according to *types* of attitude, types of interest, or types of gratification. The objective tools for this purpose do not present problems which go beyond what we have said about the use of scales. Suppose, for instance, we want to classify people into three groups, according to whether they look at post-war problems mainly from a domestic-economic, a foreign affairs-peace, or a civil liberties-justice point of view. We would set up a number of questions and classify people according to the pattern of the answers they give. The standard example for such procedures can be found in Allport and Vernon's Study of Values Test.[22] These psychologists took as a starting point Spranger's well-known personality types. People are characterized according to the values they are most concerned with: power, money, religion, beauty, wisdom, or personal contacts. In order to get to a formalized classification, the test asks people, for instance, what they look for first when they enter a living-room, what historical

[22] Forms of the Allport-Vernon Value Test are distributed by Psychological Corporation of New York.

person they would be most interested in meeting, and so on. A respondent who looks at the books in the room first and who would like most to meet Einstein, etc., would be classified as an intellectual type.

In deciding whether such objective tests or an impressionistic classification based on an OI is preferable, one should keep in mind the fact that it is difficult to develop good test questions of this kind. Impressionistic classifications, even if they have methodological disadvantages, are more easily made in a *new* situation. One practical solution, therefore, might be to use OI's whenever a problem comes up only once. If we deal with recurring problems such as, for instance, people's eagerness to help in the war effort or their attitude toward our allies or toward government regulation of business, more explicit and standardized criteria for classification might be desirable.

There is also the possibility of trying a combination of both approaches. Taking once more the example of interest in the election, the interviewer might first ask standard questions of the type mentioned above; then he might continue the discussion and note any additional observations which might suggest a correction of the rigid score. Such procedures are often used when it comes to classifying people according to socio-economic status. It seems useful to classify people first according to the rental area of the city in which they live. Then, after the interviewer has talked with the respondent, seen how he dresses and how his living room looks, he might make an impressionistic correction of the original score.

5. Is there an easy to way get at motivation?

When we discussed broad motivational interpretations, we stressed all the hazards involved in this method. Correspondingly, it is very difficult to find an objective or formalized method for such an approach. *Projective tests* come nearest to it. The general idea of these tests is that people are presented with unstructured material. Here is a crying girl; other children are asked to guess why she is crying. Or, an inkblot is shown to some people, as in the Rorschach test, and they are asked to state what form it signifies to them. It is then assumed that the way people interpret such material, which has no definite meaning of its own, is indicative of what the people themselves are concerned with.[23]

Applications to a public-opinion problem can only be invented because, to our knowledge, such studies have never been tried. If one wants to test people's attitudes toward public administration, one might, for instance, tell a short story of a successful public official who was suddenly dismissed. What was the reason? Was he found to be corrupt? Or was he the victim of a political intrigue? Or didn't he agree with the government's policy?

After Pearl Harbor, when so many people were concerned about the weakness of the American Navy, it would not have been easy to ask direct questions on this subject; few people would have cared to give an unpatriotic answer. One might, however, have shown them a series of pictures of battleships varying in degree of technical perfection. Which, in the opinion of the respondent, is an American and which a Japanese battleship? The proportion of people picking out the poor ship as an American model might have been a good index of the extent of concern about American armaments.

The psychological assumptions involved in a projective test have yet to be studied exhaustively. The answers are usually quite difficult to classify, and much depends upon the interpretation of the analyst. In the future such techniques may provide a very important tool for public opinion research. For the moment it can hardly be claimed that they are much better formalized than a good OI. If, therefore, one is interested in broad motivational interpretations, a well-conducted OI is probably still the best source for material.

[23] P. Symonds and W. Samuel, "Projective Methods in the Study of Personality" (Chap. VI of *Psychological Tests and Their Uses*), *Review of Educational Research*, 1941, 11, 80-93.

6. *The meaning of statistical relationships*

Nothing has to be added to our discussion of the analysis of deviate cases in the preceding section. Here the OI is in its most legitimate place.

SOME CONCLUSIONS

If we now summarize briefly this critical survey of the OI technique, we can make a number of points as to its position in the general scheme of public opinion research.

We saw that the problem is not new. Since the beginning of social research, students have tried to combine the value of detailed qualitative applications with the advantages of more formalized techniques which could be managed on a mass basis.

We saw, furthermore, that a line along which such an integration could come about emerges. The OI is indispensable at the beginning of any study where it classifies the structure of a problem in all its details. It is also invaluable at the end of a study for anyone who is not satisfied with the mere recording of the low correlations we usually obtain. Good research consists of weaving back and forth between OI's and the more cut-and-dried procedures.

The *conversion* of OI's into sets of specific poll questions has shown up a new skill in our field and one which has found much too little attention.

The stress on this problem of conversion has revealed a weakness on both sides of the controversy. The proponents of the OI have successfully denounced the shortcomings of single straight poll questions but by stressing so strongly the informality of the OI they have driven the poll managers to a defensive position, which is delaying the whole progress of opinion research. Field staffs are not equipped to make difficult decisions in the course of the interview. However, the idea of *interconnected question sets* converted from preceding OI's shifts the weight of the problem from the field staffs to the central office. The attack should be directed against the directors of polls, who do not take the time and the effort to structuralize the problem and to devise the interlocking question structure which any well-trained field staff should be able to handle.

Concerning the classification of complex attitude patterns, another point can be made. Public opinion research has grown so quickly that much of the work is handled by people who do not know the history of social research in the last thirty years. Much valuable thinking and experimenting done in universities long before election results were predicted is immediately applicable to this new field. The construction of scales and the whole tradition of the attitude measurement has developed its own logic, which can be profitably applied to the present controversy.

The same efforts have also opened up a considerable number of problems which have not yet been solved at all. The value of check lists, the use of projective tests, and the question of whether simple propaganda influences can be discerned by direct interview are characteristic examples. At all these points patient and painstaking work is needed. The solution of these problems will only be retarded if we let research administrators believe that they face different schools of research, whereas they deal only with different guesses as to what the final answers to these problems will be.

The hope might be expressed that this paper will not be regarded as an attempted judgment in the OI controversy. It tries to show that the problem consists of many different parts. For some problems the OI is indispensable; for others it is definitely wasteful. Often we do not really know the right answer. In these last cases the prudent administrator will do best to look for the *combination of methods* best adapted to the specific research task on hand.

THE USE OF A PROJECTIVE DEVICE IN ATTITUDE SURVEYING

FILLMORE H. SANFORD*

Probably every researcher who has worked with attitudes has had occasion to worry about whether the respondent was giving "real" answers or answers that were merely polite, safe, or of the top-of-the-mind variety. The problem is more knotty if the

* The present paper reports on a limited aspect of a large project on The Identification and Acceptance of Leadership. This leadership project, sponsored by the Office of Naval Research, is being carried out at the Philadelphia branch of the Institute for Research in Human Relations. John N. Patterson, Barney Korchin, Harry J. Older, Emily L. Ehle, Irwin M. Rosenstock and Doris M. Barnett were collaborators in the overall research project and direct or indirect contributors to the present paper. The opinions and assertions contained herein are not to be construed as reflecting the views of the Navy Department or the Naval Service at large.

From the *Public Opinion Quarterly,* Winter, 1950-51, 14, 697-709. Reprinted by permission of the author and the publisher.

question concerns matters that are believed to be socially or psychologically touchy to the respondents. Any respondent can be expected to have many attitudes which he will not readily express to an interviewer. He may have many others that he will not express even to himself. If we want

The projective devices now so widely in use undoubtedly do get at the responses which are censorable and hence are not to be elicited by direct questions. But most of these projective devices involve a great deal of time as well as much subtlety and subjectivity of interpretation. They obviously

Picture B-m
Male Form

to study the first kind of attitudes—the conscious but unsafe kind—we have to resort to indirection, good rapport, and inference; in dealing with attitudes with which the respondent himself is not on speaking terms, our only recourse is to such procedures as the Rorschach, the Thematic Apperception Test or perhaps the psycho-analytic couch.

are impracticable for use in gathering mass data about deep-lying attitudes. But the basic element in these projective techniques may possibly be adapted for use in a door-step interview. If the interviewee can be brought to respond to a pictorial situation that encourages projection yet keeps projection within the bounds of a fairly limited stimulus situation, then perhaps we can have some of the advantages of the freer and more elaborate projective techniques while avoiding the disadvantages involved in difficulty of administration and interpretation.

THE STUDY

During the course of an intensive interview designed to elicit respondent's attitudes toward leaders, leadership and authority, six simple drawings were presented to 963 people (a representative sample of the city of Philadelphia). Each drawing was designed to put the respondent, projectively, into a social situation to which he would respond by saying what the key person in the situaton would say. All the pictures were similar in form to that represented in the accompanying illustration. They all have much in common with what Rosenzweig has called "the picture-association" method,[1] and with Brown's adaptation of Rosenzweig.[2]

The factors involved in the use of these pictures and in the interpretation of results will be reported in detail at a later date. The present note concerns only one picture and two direct questions designed to tap the same content—what the respondent "worried about." Fairly early in this hour-long interview, the respondent was asked: "Do you think you worry more or less than most people?" This question led up to one we are immediately concerned with here: "What sort of thing do you worry about most?" After a number of unrelated questions, the respondent was shown the "worry picture." The interviewer used the following introduction: "Now here is a picture. One person is talking. The other is going to answer. What do you think the

answer would be? Give the first answer that comes to your mind." This picture was used as a lead into the succeeding questions. The first of these was "Whom did you go to the last time you wanted advice from someone?", the second, "Why did you pick him out?", and the third, another one of primary concern here, "What kind of advice did you need?"

The basic data from these three stimuli are presented in Table 1. The table gives, for each stimulus, the frequency and percentage of responses in each of the categories used to tabulate the content of worries.

There are several things in Table 1 worth at least a passing note. In the first place, there is evidence that the picture device does succeed in eliciting responses in the interview situation. While 159 people (16.5 per cent) give no answers, this does not compare too unfavorably with the 13.2 per cent who do not answer the direct question on worries or with the 13.8 per cent who fail to answer the questions on the sort of advice needed. (For four of the six pictures used in the complete study, the percentage of "no answers" runs around 4 per cent.) In terms of the technical feasibility of the pictures, there is the additional factor that most people interviewed appear to enjoy responding to the pictures, as Ehle[3] reported in a previous note on these devices. They represent, apparently, a pleasant change of pace in a long interview.

A second thing suggested in Table 1 is that the picture elicits responses that are more specific than those given to the direct question on worries. To the direct question people are somewhat more inclined to say vague things like "the future" or "many things." Allied to this tendency toward specificity is the apparent increase in the variety of responses to the picture. The system of categories used in analyzing the responses was created on the basis of pre-

[1] Rosenzweig, S. "The Picture-Association Method and its Application in a Study of Reactions to Frustration." *J. Personality*, 1945, 14, 3-23.
[2] Brown, J. F. "A Modification of the Rosenzweig Picture-Frustration Test to Study Hostile Interracial Attitudes." *J. Psychol.*, 1947, 24, 247-272.

[3] Ehle, Emily L. "Techniques for Study of Leadership." *Public Opinion Quarterly*, 1949, Vol. 13, No. 2, 235-240.

liminary responses to the direct questions. When the system was used on responses to the picture, 10.8 per cent of the responses did not fit the code. Many of these responses were highly specific and highly unique, suggesting that the picture elicited answers about more personal and more individualistic worries. This sort of tendency may be due to the fact that "real" worries, which are by nature personal and unique, are projected into the picture. Or it may simply be, whether or not projection is occurring,

that when one is face-to-face with an advisor he does not express vague worries about "many things" or "the state of the world." The picture does, however, appear to make responses more specific—and perhaps for this reason more valid.

It can also be noticed that the responses to the picture tend to be more personal, more intimate. The best example of this is that 30 people talk about sex or "love life" in response to the picture, while only one gives an answer in safer, more conventional

TABLE 1

RESPONSES TO A PROJECTIVE DEVICE AND TWO QUESTIONS RELATING
TO CONTENT OF RESPONDENT'S WORRIES

Category of Response	Picture		What Do You Worry About?		Kind of Advice Needed	
	N	%	N	%	N	%
Financial, Short term	170	17.7	189	19.6	130	13.5
Family	130	13.5	159	16.5	131	13.6
Health, general	89	9.3	91	9.5	115	11.9
Work	64	6.7	64	6.7	49	5.1
Love Life	30	3.1	1	0.1	17	1.8
Health, specific symptoms	23	2.4	14	1.5	14	1.5
Welfare of World	24	2.5	25	2.6	0	0.0
Impersonal Things not Elsewhere Codable	21	2.2	17	1.8	64	6.7
Living Conditions	20	2.1	10	1.0	20	2.1
Business Affairs	18	1.9	26	2.7	68	7.1
"Nothing"	18	1.9	44	4.6	7	0.7
Personal Things not Elsewhere Codable	16	1.7	13	1.4	29	3.0
Family's Health	12	1.2	40	4.2	19	2.0
Specific Personal Goals	11	1.1	9	0.9	29	3.0
"Personal Things"	11	1.1	8	0.8	35	3.6
Finances, Long term	10	1.0	39	4.1	6	0.6
Social Relations	10	1.0	11	1.1	9	0.9
Religious Matters	6	0.6	2	0.2	8	0.8
"The Future"	5	0.5	30	3.1	4	0.4
"Many Things"	4	0.4	12	1.2	10	1.0
Legal Matters	3	0.3	0	0.0	41	4.3
Moral Problems	2	0.2	5	0.5	0	0.0
Next War	1	0.1	4	0.4	0	0.0
Death	0	0.0	11	1.1	2	0.2
Other People's Troubles	2	0.2	12	1.2	1	0.1
Not Codable	104	10.8	0	0.0	22	2.3
Don't Know, or No Answer	159	16.5	127	13.2	133	13.8
TOTALS	963	100.0	963	100.0	963	100.0

answers. It is a very acceptable thing to worry about your family or other people's troubles. It is perhaps less safe or acceptable to worry about "love life" or specific symptoms of ill health. The data here are too meager to lead to any definite conclusion, but it is fairly easy to believe that the picture gets past the psychological censor which often operates in the standard face-to-face interview.

RELIABILITY

Approximately a month after the first interview, 201 people were reinterviewed on the complete hour-long schedule. Table 2 contains data bearing on the relative reliability of the picture and questions.

To secure these data on relative reliability, the responses on both the first and second interview were coded independently by relatively untrained coders (recent college graduates). Coding reliability was kept at a maximum by "talking out" disagreements with a more highly trained "head coder."

Then the molecular categories were combined into more general categories. Table 2 presents data for the three general categories containing the majority of the responses. The category *Material Things* includes worries about finances, about living conditions and work. The category *Family and Interpersonal Relations* includes worries about family, family health, sex and social relations. The *Health* category includes both general health and specific diseases or symptoms. Table 2 presents, for the picture and for the two questions, (a) the number of responses falling in each category on the first interview, and (b) the percentage of these responses falling in the same category on the second interview.

One might expect that the picture would prove more reliable than the worry question and at least just as reliable as the very specific historical question on the sort of advice the respondent needed the last time he went to an advisor. The reasoning behind this expectation runs as follows: if the picture works as a projective device, then responses

TABLE 2

RELATIVE RELIABILITY OF PICTURE, QUESTIONS ON CONTENT OF
WORRY AND QUESTIONS ON KIND OF ADVICE NEEDED

| | | GENERAL CATEGORIES OF RESPONSE | | |
		Material Things	Family and Interpersonal Relations	Health
Picture	No. Responding First Interview	40	37	22
	Per cent Giving Same Response Second Interview	70.2	68.5	72.7
Question on Worry	No. Responding First Interview	49	47	14
	Per cent Giving Same Response Second Interview	73.4	51.1	64.4
Question on Kind of Advice	No. Responding First Interview	48	35	24
	Per cent Giving Same Response Second Interview	60.4	65.7	70.8

to it would be due to relatively stable "inner" determiners; these "inner" determiners lead to the expression of "real" worries which do not change appreciably during a one month interval. The responses to the two questions, on the other hand, being influenced more by situational and less by "inner" determiners might be expected to vary rather widely from one interview to another.

The data in Table 2 do not clearly bear out this expectation, but there is evidence that the picture is just as reliable as either of the questions and perhaps a little more reliable than the direct question on "what you worry about most."

There is some reason to believe that the reliability of all three stimulus procedures would be higher had the coding been based on categories of a more psychological or more genotypical nature. The categories used in the study were relatively superficial ones, based on the clearly manifest content of the answers. This sort of category was judged best for use by coders who were relatively untrained in psychology. But the writer, on the basis of some soaking in the data, feels that a more professional coding based on psychologically defined categories would not only have yielded greater overall reliability, but would have increased the reliability of the picture more than that of the other procedures. The picture, if it taps "deeper" determiners, might be expected to elicit responses, upon reinterview, which are psychologically consistent even if superficially different. The use of simple and relatively molecular categories may cut across psychological variables in such a way as to obscure the real reliability. But this is a matter for further experimentation.

PSYCHOLOGICAL MEANINGFULNESS OF RESULTS

There is no direct way to examine the relative validity of the answers to the picture and to the questions. But the meaningfulness of the data, in terms of the hypothesis that led to the inclusion in the

survey of items on worry, will have a bearing on the relative usefulness of the three procedures.

One major purpose of the total survey was to investigate authoritarianism as a variable in determining attitudes toward leaders and leadership. According to the theory developed by Fromm,[4] Maslow,[5] and by Adorno, Frenkel-Brunswik, Levinson and Sanford,[6] the person who is high in authoritarianism should worry more about status-related things such as income, housing, superficial security, and about those more immediately self-related things such as personal health. The equalitarian person, however, should be concerned more with the introceptive and altruistic aspects of life. There is no point here in elaborating the theory. It is presently sufficient to know that we would expect the authoritarians to worry more about the items included in the categories "Material Things and Health," while the equalitarians should worry more about their "Families and Interpersonal Relations."

In this study authoritarianism was measured by an eight item A-E (Authoritarian-Equalitarian) scale. The scale, an adaptation of the California F scale,[7] is described in detail elsewhere,[8] but basic data on its structure are presented in Table 3. The table includes the eight items on the scale, the distribution of answers to each item, item reliabilities, item correlations with the total score and the distribution of total scores in the population.

The method of scoring the scale was as

[4] Fromm, E., Escape from Freedom. New York: Farrar and Rinehart, 1941; Fromm, E., Man for Himself. New York: Rinehart, 1947.

[5] Maslow, A. H., "The Authoritarian Personality." J. Soc. Psychol., 1943, 30, 39-48; Maslow, A. H. "Authoritarian Character Structure." J. Soc. Psychol., 1943, 18, 401-411.

[6] Adorno, W., Frenkel-Brunswik, E., Levinson, D., and Sanford, R. N., The Authoritarian Personality. New York: Harpers, 1950.

[7] Ibid.

[8] Sanford, Fillmore H., and Older, Harry J., A Short Authoritarian-Equalitarian Scale. Philadelphia: Institute for Research in Human Relations, June 1950. Series A, Report No. 6.

TABLE 3

DISTRIBUTION OF ANSWERS, ITEM RELIABILITY AND ITEM r's
WITH TOTAL SCORE FOR A-E SCALE

Distribution of Answers (N=963)

Item		Agree	Disagree	Item Reliability*	r with Total Score†
A. Human nature being what it is, there must always be war and conflict.	Very much	31.2%	31.6%		
	Pretty much	16.6	7.8	.75	.11
	A little	7.0	5.6		
B. The most important thing a child should learn is obedience to his parents.	Very much	67.4	6.5		
	Pretty much	13.1	5.4	.71	.27
	A little	3.8	3.6		
C. A few strong leaders could make this country better than all the laws.	Very much	35.2	30.0		
	Pretty much	11.3	9.9	.64	.25
	A little	6.8	6.5		
D. Most people who don't get ahead just don't have enough will power.	Very much	38.8	18.6		
	Pretty much	14.5	13.9	.56	.27
	A little	7.2	6.8		
E. Husbands should help their wives with the dishes and care for the children.	Very much	39.0	13.2		
	Pretty much	19.1	5.0	.51	.01
	A little	17.9	5.7		
F. Women should stay out of politics.	Very much	26.5	38.2		
	Pretty much	6.7	15.4	.61	.22
	A little	6.6	6.5		
G. People sometimes say that an insult to your honor should not be forgotten.	Very much	12.8	45.7		
	Pretty much	7.9	19.5	.39	.17
	A little	5.3	8.8		
H. People can be trusted.	Very much	29.8	13.6		
	Pretty much	25.6	7.3	.55	.09
	A little	17.4	6.3		

Distribution of Total Scores:	1–1.9	2–2.9	3–3.9	4–4.9	5–5.9	6
	13	128	325	396	96	1

Mean for Population=3.46:σ=.91

* Based on reinterview of 201 respondents after a one month interval.
† Corrected for overlap. The formula for this computation is from J. P. Guilford, *Fundamental Statistics in Psychology and Education* (New York, McGraw-Hill, 1942), p. 252. (Where p = part score, t = total score and q = t − p or the total with the part excluded.)

$$r_{pq} = \frac{r_{tp}\sigma t - \sigma p}{\sqrt{\sigma^2 t + \sigma^2 p \cdot 2 r_{tp}\sigma t \sigma p}}$$

follows: for items A, B, C, D, E, and G, "agree very much" was scored as six; "agree pretty much" as five; "agree a little," as four; "disagree a little," three; "disagree pretty much," two; "disagree very much" as one. On items E and H, a reverse procedure was used with "disagree very much" being scored six, and "agree very much" as one. The total score on the scale was the mean of the scores on the individual items. Thus the total scores varied from one to six.

The repeat reliability of the scale after

TABLE 4

RESPONSES TO THE PICTURE, THE WORRY QUESTION AND ADVICE
QUESTION AS RELATED TO SCORES ON THE AUTHORITARIAN-
EQUALITARIAN TEST

Category of Response	Picture		Worry Question		Advice Question	
	N	Mean A-E Score	N	Mean A-E Score	N	Mean A-E Score
Health	112	3.70	105	3.50	129	3.50
Material Things	218	3.56	264	3.44	224	3.50
Family and Social Relations	152	3.38	210	3.45	159	3.41

The Mean score on the A-E scale was 3.46 (σ– .89) with a range from 1.0 to 6.0

a one month interval is .78. Among 100 Haverford College freshmen (a very homogeneous group) the correlation between the A-E scale and the California F scale is +.67.

It is fairly safe to assume that the scale is tapping an organized syndrome of deeplying attitudes. We can then reason that if the scores on the scale meaningfully relate to another item on the interview then that item is also tapping an "inner" disposition. Thus we can study the meaningfulness of the responses to our three present items by examining the sort of psychological company they keep. Such a procedure may be called "validation by congruence."

On the basis of our hypotheses about the relation between authoritarianism and content of worries, we can say that any item or procedure that yields responses about "real" worries should be related meaningfully with data on the A-E scale. And items or procedures that elicit answers only at the "safe" or "polite" or spur-of-the-moment variety should *not* yield meaningful relations with the A-E scale.

Table 4 presents data on this sort of validation of our three present items. The table gives the number of people responding, in each of the three major categories, to the picture, to the worry question and to the advice question. And it presents the mean score on the A-E test for those re-

sponding in each category for each of the three stimulus situations. As suggested above, our theory would lead us to expect that those who worry about "Health" or "Material Things" would have higher A-E scores than those who worry about "Family and Interpersonal Relations." This theory is supported by the responses to the picture. The difference between the A-E scores of those who give answers in the "Health category" (a mean score of 3.70) and those who give answers in the "Family and Interpersonal Relations" category (a mean score of 3.38) yields a critical ratio of 2.91. The same comparison made with the answers to the question on worries yields a critical ratio of only .45. And for the advice question the critical ratio is .90. In this context, then, the picture gives meaningful results while neither of the questions does. Perhaps the most reasonable way to account for this is that the picture gets at worries that are more "real," while the answers to the questions are determined more by adventitious factors in the interviewing situation.

Related to this indirect evidence for the greater validity of the picture is another trend in the data. There is some reason to believe that the question "What sort of advice did you need?" preceded as it was in the interview by two questions about specific occasions on which the respondent sought advice, will yield "real" answers about "real" worries. Such a question, as compared with the more general one of "What sort of things do you worry about most?" is equivalent to asking "How many cans of Beeps do you *now have* on your shelf?" rather than "How often have you bought Beeps in the *last two months*?" One would expect the former question more than the latter to yield answers closely related to reality. On the basis of such reasoning we can expect that a tabulation of answers to the concrete question "What sort of advice did you need?" will tell us more about the "real" worries of our total population than will the answers to the more general question on worries. We can proceed as if the most frequent worry in the population is about the family (Table 1), the next most frequent is about short term finances, the next about health, etc. We can treat this tabulation as a criterion against which the general question on worries can be validated. And we can argue that if the picture is more valid than the general question, then the results from the picture should be more similar to the results from the advice (criterion) question than are the results from the general worry question.

We can test this hypothesis by (a) ranking, with respect to frequency, the responses to the specific question, regarding this as the "true" account of "real worries of the population," (b) creating a similar ranking for each of the other stimuli, and (c) computing rank-difference correlations. Such a procedure yields the following *rhos*:

Picture and specific advice question   .61
Worry question and specific advice question   .37

These results indicate that in giving a notion about the frequency of worries among the total population, the picture and the "criterion" agree with one another better than does the general worry question and the "criterion." Such a result suggests more validity for the picture than for the worry question. These data do not bear on whether the picture or the specific advice question has greater validity. There is, also, a potentially vitiating factor that may wipe out the tendency in the above data. It is this: the picture and the question on advice were chronologically closer together in the interview than were the question on worry and the question on advice. It is still a reasonable hypothesis, then, that temporal contiguity rather than anything inherent in the stimuli is producing the *rhos*. The factor of temporal contiguity must be controlled before making any definitive statements about an indication of validity.

A further way to examine the similarity among the three stimulus procedures is through another comparison of the relation of each of them to scores on the A-E scale. We have seen, by one procedure, that the picture yields psychologically meaningful results while neither of the other stimuli does. Now, if we assume that the specific question on advice yields the best information on what are the "real" worries among the population, and if the A-E scale is related to "real" worries, then we can assume that association, in the answers to the advice question, between A-E scores and the content of worries is a "real" association. If this is so, and if the answers to the picture also yield a relatively "real" association between A-E scores and the content of worries, then the picture and the specific question ought to yield similar associations.

We can test this hypothesis by (a) computing the mean A-E score of those giving each kind of response to each of the three stimuli (b) ranking each response to each stimulus according to the magnitude of the A-E mean of those giving it and (c) computing rank difference coefficients. There were eleven categories of response having an N greater than ten for all three stimuli; these only were used in computing the coefficients. The procedure yields the following *rhos*:

Picture and advice question   .82
Picture and worry question   .05
Worry question and advice question   .05

Though again the temporal proximity of the advice question to the picture may be an important factor, these data further suggest that both the picture and the specific question on advice are tapping "real" or "inner" determiners while the general question on worries elicits relatively superficial answers.

CONCLUSION

We have suggestive evidence that simple cartoon-like projective devices are not only technically feasible for field use but may also succeed in getting data not obtainable through the use of more conventional procedures. It is probable that simple devices, designed in accordance with the principle of "controlled projection" can elicit uncensored answers on the doorstep. Such answers may turn out to be both more reliable and more valid than answers obtained to direct questions. If so, the use of such devices can enable us to advance significantly not only in the field of attitude research but also will make possible the use of large and representative samples in testing personality hypotheses heretofore based on and tested by the study of small numbers of people drawn from the "captive" undergraduate population.

·12·

Analysis and Interpretation of Data

DETECTING COLLABORATION IN PROPAGANDA

PROBLEMS OF SURVEY ANALYSIS

A SOLUTION TO THE PROBLEM OF QUESTION "BIAS"

VALIDITY OF RESPONSES TO SURVEY QUESTIONS

THE WAUKEGAN STUDY OF VOTER TURNOUT PREDICTION

DETECTING COLLABORATION IN PROPAGANDA

BERNARD BERELSON AND SEBASTIAN DE GRAZIA

The study of mass communications can be divided into three parts—intent analysis, content analysis, and effect analysis. This order not only reflects chronology. By placing content analysis in the middle position, it also highlights the contribution of that procedure to the other two, namely, to support inferences about intent on the one hand and effect (or response) on the other. This paper reports a number of special attempts to discern the intentions of enemy propaganda during World War II by means of rigorous analysis of the manifest content of the communications under control.

Among the many other problems in the area of intent analysis is the problem of discovering whether two communications-controlling groups, formally related or not, actually collaborate in their propaganda output; and if so, under what conditions, in what ways, and to what extent. This is the general context of this study. Specifically, the subject of investigation was the nature of collaboration between the German and Italian propaganda ministries (and in some cases between them and the Japanese ministry) in their short-wave radio output beamed to North America just before and after the entry of the United States into the war. Most of the studies to be cited were done originally in late 1941 and early 1942. As rewritten in the present form, stress is placed on the methodological problems in-

volved. Procedures developed in this study might well be extended to other areas. For example, precise information about collaboration in propaganda (e.g., between a great power and an allegedly neutral buffer state) is useful intelligence for decisions on alternative political policies.

COLLABORATION VS. CORRESPONDENCE

Before presenting an account of the methods developed in the studies and the hypotheses and conclusions obtained, let us clarify the nature of the problem of detecting collaboration in propaganda.

First, a distinction must be drawn sharply between *collaboration* in propaganda and *correspondence* in propaganda. *Collaboration* refers to the interrelationships of propagandists with the intention of coordinating their separate propagandas, in one way or another, to serve the common objective. *Correspondence* is the term used for describing similarity in propaganda output, regardless of the cause for such similarity. Collaboration refers to pre-release consultation or other operations involving *intent*, whereas correspondence refers to post-release *content*.

Clearly the relationship between collaboration and correspondence need not be one-to-one. Correspondence in propaganda is

From the *Public Opinion Quarterly*, 1947, 2, 244-253. Reprinted by permission of the authors and the publisher.

neither necessary indicator nor sufficient evidence of collaboration. Two controlling groups wishing to coordinate their propaganda activities may decide that the best implementation of their objective requires the specialization and differentiation of propagandas, a division of labor rather than identity or correspondence. Thus, an overtly radical or reactionary party and its "front" organization might align their propaganda objectives without harmonizing their propaganda texts. They may agree to split the field, with one organization appealing to one group and the other to another. Rome, with its greater cultural affinity to Latin America, for instance, could have concentrated its broadcasts there, leaving the North American beam to Berlin. The tactics may have varied and yet have contributed to the same strategy, say, the neutralization of the Western Hemisphere. It is even conceivable that similar propagandas may serve different ends. If, in the hypothetical example just mentioned, Rome and Berlin had used identical scripts instead of differentiating their broadcasts, the one may have helped secure official or popular support for Italy in South American countries, while the other may have damaged this government's endeavors to get public opinion behind aid to Britain.

In short, correspondence between two simultaneous propaganda outputs does not conclusively demonstrate collaboration on the part of the propagandists, nor does lack of correspondence prove an absence of collaboration. These logical pitfalls must be kept in mind at every step in the analysis of content for collaboration in propaganda. Content analysis can deal directly with problems of propaganda correspondence, but not with problems of collaboration. At best —and sometimes this best may be good enough—content analysis can supply sound bases from which inferences about collaboration intent can be made.

The relationship between collaboration and correspondence may appear in various forms. *Specific* collaboration or correspondence treats a particular event or subject matter or theme on which detailed and concrete arrangements are necessary. *General* collaboration or correspondence refers to a long-range agreement on a whole propaganda program. Methods were devised to study both specific and general types of correspondence and collaboration.

Again, when both correspondence and collaboration are present, the latter may take the form of control (or near-control) of the one propaganda agency by the other, of consultation on a more or less equal basis between the two agencies, or of planned imitation of the one by the other. In the present case, for example, Berlin and Rome may have discussed and jointly decided propaganda policy, or Rome may have followed Berlin's lead in making its own propaganda directives. Collaboration without correspondence is specialization of propaganda. Correspondence without collaboration is parallelism, fortuitous and circumstantial.

THE MEASURES OF CORRESPONDENCE

In the studies of Berlin-Rome propaganda during the period of America's entry into the war, measures of various kinds were developed to establish the degree of correspondence between two propagandas and thus to buttress inferences about collaboration. They will now be enumerated, with illustrations from the studies in which they were used.

Attention to Specific Events

One important measure of specific correspondence between related propagandas involves the amount of attention given to particular events. The curve of attention given by the two transmitters was studied on five separate occasions—two Roosevelt speeches, one Churchill address, the Allied invasion of Timor, and the Fernando Po incident.

The results were the same in all five cases: Rome responded first, said more, and continued longer than Berlin. In every instance the Italian radio reacted to the event hours before the German radio, which delayed its response apparently in order to give more time for the formulation of high propaganda policy. Presumably, policy decisions in Berlin customarily were made higher in the hierarchy than similar decisions in Rome. At any rate, this pattern of distribution of attention by the two stations was consistent.

The matter can be illustrated by the instances of the speeches by Roosevelt (September 11, 1941) and Churchill (September 30, 1941). The first reaction from the Rome radio to the President's speech appeared about fourteen hours after the speech was delivered; the first Berlin reaction did not appear until about six hours later. An even longer interval occurred in the case of the Churchill speech, with Rome responding the evening of the day of delivery and Berlin not until the following day. In addition to replying earlier, Rome also replied at greater length. To the Roosevelt talk, for example, Rome devoted almost a third of its broadcast time, whereas Berlin gave only half as much attention. As the original report stated:

This is all the more striking since the President's speech was directed almost entirely at Germany. Presumably Berlin minimized its reply in order to lessen the importance of the event, so as to provide the United States with little opportunity for continuing the controversy by counter-propaganda. Rome, on the other hand, observed no such limitations. This is clear evidence of non-collaboration between Berlin and Rome.

The conclusion from similar evidence for the Churchill address was:

With these differences in tactics it is probable that the Axis radio did not collaborate in assigning broadcast time to comment on the speech.

Allocation of Total Broadcast Time

To what extent do international propagandists with similar (ultimate) objectives agree or diverge in the broad allocation of radio time? This problem of general collaboration was investigated for all three enemy transmitters on the basis of broad categories which day after day were used

to classify the coverage of Rome, Berlin, and Tokyo radio propaganda to North America. The main headings were: military operations, front by front; Great Britain; the United States; the Soviet Union; Axis solidarity; domestic affairs of each of the three enemy nations; and occupied areas. For a consecutive period of over three months in 1941-42, the degree of correspondence in attention given to these categories and others of less importance was computed for all three possible pairs of enemy radios, namely, Berlin-Rome, Berlin-Tokyo, Rome-Tokyo. The curves showing this degree of correspondence are based upon a series of index numbers, computed weekly, representing the "distance" between the transmitters in attention to the principal categories. This number can range from zero (or complete correspondence in attention) to 200 (or complete divergence).

The results reveal a certain consistency in correspondence among the paired transmitters. Berlin and Rome show most similarity, with Tokyo's correspondence to the European members of the Axis measuring about half again their divergence from each other. To a large extent this greater divergence arises from the simple fact of geography: Tokyo broadcasted some specifically Asiatic material which was absent from the European transmitters.

There is least correspondence before a key event and most correspondence after it. During the week ending December 4, 1941 (which is as closely as the data can be related to December 7), all three curves showed more divergence than during any other week. Then, in the first weeks following December 7, there was on the whole greater correspondence among the transmitters. This explanation, that major events force correspondence by compelling attention from each transmitter independently, is also supported by the greater degree of correspondence after the fall of Singapore (February 15, 1942) and by the fact that the three curves have the same direction of movement in every week except one. It assigns central importance to the role of events, and indicates that general correspondence in Axis propaganda is attributable to parallelism in political conditions rather than to deliberate collaboration.

Free vs. Compulsory Allocation

The role of major events in causing correspondence in the allocation of total broadcast time leads to consideration of a further breakdown. Content may be classified also into compulsory ("news") and free ("comment" or "editorial") categories, according to the presumable necessity upon the broadcaster for inclusion in his propaganda program. Important daily events, it is reasoned, cannot be omitted by any broadcaster; on the other hand, any subject may be chosen for editorializing by the propagandist, with the choice decided primarily by strategic aims. On the hypothesis that correspondence would be greater in news than in comment because of the broadcaster's inability to ignore important events, we calculated correspondence from a regrouping of the broad categories. Military operations on the Russian, Libyan, and Pacific fronts were designated as the compulsory categories since, by and large, the most important daily news in war is military action. The free categories consisted of attacks on Great Britain and the United States, which appeared most frequently in the form of commentaries.

The average divergence for the free categories was about half again as large as the average for the compulsory categories. Again, then, events seem to be more important than collaboration in explaining the correspondence of Axis propaganda. And the corollary is that correspondence in the free categories will provide a more reliable indicator of collaboration than correspondence in the compulsory categories.

Similarity of Arguments

Another major area of correspondence between propagandists, perhaps the most important of all, centers on the arguments or themes which they use. Do the propagandists take the same substantive line or not? Again, we may illustrate the use of this measure of correspondence from the studies of the Axis radios.

The distribution of the themes which Berlin and Rome used in their replies to the Churchill speech of September 30, 1941, is shown in Table 1.

TABLE 1

FREQUENCY OF THEMES USED BY BERLIN AND ROME IN REPLIES TO CHURCHILL SPEECH OF SEPTEMBER 30, 1941

	Radio Berlin	Radio Rome
1. Churchill admits that the Germans hold the military initiative; England, open to invasion, must remain on the defensive.	33%	27%
2. Churchill minimizes British shipping losses.	27	10
3. Churchill lies and is hypocritical.	15	2
4. England cannot send effective aid to Russia without sacrificing her own security.	11	28
5. England does not fight herself, but gets her allies to do her fighting.	8	19
6. Coming at this time, this speech proves that English civilian morale is low.	4	5
7. England's allies are weak.	2	9
Total number of items (approx.)	200	300

As the original report interpreted the results:

The total picture is one of divergence. Although the two official radios are almost alike in their most and least used arguments, the emphasis given other arguments varies from one transmitter to the other . . . Summarized, the differences are strikingly clear. Berlin devoted 42 per cent of its argumentation to denunciation of Churchill's lies (arguments 2 and 3), and Rome only 12 per cent. Rome devoted 56 per cent of its argumentation to the role of England's allies in the war (arguments 4, 5, and 7), and Berlin only 21 per cent. . . . Each Axis transmitter framed its reaction to the Churchill speech quite independently of the other. Presumably Berlin and Rome depend upon their parallel situations to take care of the 'united propaganda front.'

In another case, correspondence was studied in an effort to estimate the importance attached by the Axis to a military event. In January of 1942, a semi-official Spanish report accused the Free French of violating Spanish territory by seizing three Axis merchantmen in a destroyer's surprise raid on the small Spanish colonial island of Fernando Po, off the west coast of Africa. A number of protests arose immediately from Italy and Germany over this alleged violation of a neutral's territory. Since any incident, no matter how small, might have been used as a prelude to counter-moves or counter-invasion, a study of the treatment of the affair on the Berlin and Rome radios was made. The summary interpretation of the thematic analysis in the original report follows:

The absence of this note (hints of retaliatory action) from Berlin and its presence on Rome may be simply another illustration of the more rash statement of position usually made by the junior partner in the Axis. Other important differences reveal that Rome voices its own opinion, while Berlin quotes the Spanish press extensively. Berlin also stresses the violation of international law and the surprise nature of the attack, whereas Rome does not. Rome in several items claimed that the deGaullist forces were the instigators of the deed; Berlin never admitted that the Free French were involved, continually claiming that England was responsible. Berlin also skipped over the presence of Axis ships in the Spanish harbor and mentioned the harmful effect the incident would have in Latin America; Rome did neither.

These disparities in treatment indicate that the whole affair was not considered important enough to collaborate on. If there had been active collaboration, the arguments would have been much more similar. There is not even the imitation (follow-the-leader) type of collaboration. Rome, although obviously out of line with Berlin, made little effort to readjust its statements. Not being important enough to 'get together on,' the incident can hardly be construed as a precursor of large military moves.

Adoption of Arguments

If Berlin and Rome had planned an imitative form of collaboration in which one followed the argumentation of the other, that would become evident through an analysis of the adoption of arguments. Did one of the transmitters take over the "good" propaganda lines of the other? In the case of the Fernando Po incident, described above, the answer was a clear "no." Contradictions which Berlin and Rome left unresolved constitute the reverse of adoption of arguments.

The study of Roosevelt's speech of September 11, 1941, contained another analysis of the adoption of arguments. The five arguments most strongly and steadily emphasized by the Rome radio from the beginning were given little or no emphasis by Berlin for the first days following the speech. Four days later, three of them were receiving major attention on the Berlin short-wave but presumably from independent introduction (in line with Berlin's later reaction to such events). The remaining two arguments, although mentioned, never attained a rank among the five most frequent arguments on Radio Berlin. In addition, two other Rome arguments of considerable skillfulness and frequency were never taken over by Berlin at all—the arguments that Roosevelt had entered upon an undeclared war in fact and that Roosevelt's militant acts were part of a premeditated plan to get the United States into war. Berlin in its turn had three frequently appearing arguments (for example, Roosevelt's association with the Jews) to which Rome never referred.

In sum, if the weight of other studies showing strong divergence of argument (such as that of the Churchill speech cited above) were added, the conclusion is clearly suggested that there was no collaboration through the adoption of arguments.

Identification of the Self

Finally, for whom do the propagandists speak? To what extent does each speak for himself, for the other, or for both? Two examples from our studies serve to illustrate the use of this measure.

An analysis of the self-reference in whose name replies were made to the Roosevelt speech of September 11, 1941, shows a striking difference between Rome and Berlin (Table 2). As the original report put it:

The conclusion is clear. Berlin speaks for itself, disregarding Italy entirely, whereas Rome speaks in the name of the Axis and even refers

TABLE 2

PERCENTAGE OF SELF-REFERENCES BY
BERLIN AND ROME: ROOSEVELT
SPEECH, SEPTEMBER 11, 1941

Referred to:	Radio Berlin	Radio Rome
Italy	0%	1%
Germany	96	22
Axis	4	77
Total number of references	53	147

to Germany more often than to itself. . . . Although this (behavior by the Rome radio)
could be part of a collaborative plan, it seems
more likely to be simply a case of Italy's 'bask-
ing in the reflected glory' of the stronger Axis
partner.

The second study was based upon a count
of each radio's identification of the victors
in the fall of British-held Tobruk in June,
1942. The participation of both Italian
and German troops in the Libya fighting
posed a problem for Axis propagandists:
who was to get credit for the victories? If
genuine collaboration existed, two possibilities might have been expected: either both
transmitters would simply refer to "Axis
troops," or since the numerical superiority
of Italian to German forces was approximately seven to one, both transmitters might
have given an edge to the Italian contribution. However, the actual treatment of the
matter suggests that national considerations
strongly outweighed either partnership or
numerical consideration (Table 3). An even
greater degree of propaganda disunity can
be seen in the references to Generals Bastico

TABLE 3

PERCENTAGE OF REFERENCE TO AXIS
MILITARY FORCES BY BERLIN AND
ROME: FALL OF TOBRUK, JUNE, 1942

Participants in the fall of Tobruk:	Italy to North America	Germany to North America	Italian Domestic
Axis, Italy and Germany, Italo-German	79%	59%	65%
Italian	18	5	32
German	3	36	3
Total number of references (approx.)	300	200	150

TABLE 4

PERCENTAGE OF REFERENCES TO ROMMEL
AND BASTICO BY BERLIN AND ROME:
FALL OF TOBRUK, JUNE, 1942

	Radio Berlin	Radio Rome
Rommel	100%	46%
Bastico	0	31
Both	0	23
Total number of references	64	26

and Rommel (Table 4) as commanders on
the Libyan front at the time. Whereas Bastico, actually the Commander-in-Chief of
Axis forces in North Africa, figured about
as prominently as Rommel on the Italian
short-wave, he simply did not appear on
the German radio.

CONCLUSION

Before and during World War II not only
the man-on-the-street but the reporter, the
scholar, and the government official believed
firmly that the Axis countries coordinated
their foreign propaganda consciously, carefully, and cleverly. The occasional meetings
of Goebbels and Pavolini, the two propaganda chiefs, supported the notion. But every
content analysis study designed to uncover
a collaborative arrangement gave a negative
answer. There was neither general nor specific, neither directed nor imitative correspondence. The strong probability is that no
collaboration existed. Indeed, the only collaboration was apparently a common willingness to *say* that there was collaboration, to
iterate as often as possible "the Pact of
Steel" or "the spiritual cohesion and community of wills of the Axis."

From a methodological standpoint, these
studies indicate how it is possible to obtain
information about the intent and procedures of two propaganda elites when little
or no information can be derived from more
direct sources than content analysis. At a
time when the Axis was being overestimated
in the political and economic spheres, it did
not help combat defeatism to have specialists,
too, convinced for inadequate reasons that

the enemy's efficient coordination extended to the propaganda field. While these content analyses did not *prove* the existence of non-collaboration (a feat logically impossible on the basis of available data), they did make it clear that a close, operating relationship between the German and Italian propaganda ministries was extremely unlikely. In addition, the two measures of attention to specific events and adoption of arguments made it abundantly evident that Berlin was not dictating the propaganda content of the Rome radio (as some experts later contended).

PROBLEMS OF SURVEY ANALYSIS

PATRICIA L. KENDALL AND PAUL F. LAZARSFELD

* * *

In many ways the analysis of survey results can be described as the clarification of relationships between two or more variables.

There can be little doubt that we are interested primarily in relationships, rather than in the description of single variables. It may be an interesting fact that x per cent of a sample subscribed to a particular opinion or reported certain activities. But inferences of practical or theoretical significance usually emerge only from a study of the demographic characteristics, the previous experiences or attitudes to which the opinions and activities are related.

The clarification of these statistical relationships proceeds in two directions. In the first place, we want to determine how legitimate it is to draw inferences of cause and effect. Secondly, we want to examine the process through which the assumed cause is related to its effect. Both types of clarification involve a logic and a series of analytical procedures of their own. Part I of this paper is devoted to spelling these out.

SECTION I—APPROXIMATIONS OF SURVEY RESULTS TO CONTROLLED EXPERIMENTATION

Even when not explicitly stated, the presentation of a relationship between two variables suggests a causal connection between them. We do not report that combat veterans are more dissatisfied than non-veterans with certain Army policies without implying that somehow the experience of combat changes the perspectives and attitudes of soldiers.

The scientific model designed to study cause-and-effect relationships of this sort is the *controlled experiment*, in which the responses of an experimental group, exposed to the crucial stimulus, are compared with those of an exactly equivalent control group, from which the stimulus has been withheld.

Abridged from R. K. Merton and P. F. Lazarsfeld, *Continuities in Social Research: Studies in the Scope and Method of "The American Soldier"* (Glencoe, Ill.: Free Press, 1950), pp. 135-165. Reprinted by permission of the authors and the Free Press.

The difficulties of carrying out such experiments in the social sciences are well known. It is important, therefore, to consider the kinds of approximations provided by survey materials.

Sub-group Comparisons

The type of approximation most often used in survey analysis involves a comparison of the frequency with which groups *characterized in different ways* express a certain attitude or indicate a particular behavior. Thus in *The American Soldier* we find that:

There was a marked relationship between job satisfaction and chance to choose one's Army job. Those who asked for and got their Army jobs were much more satisfied than those who did not get the jobs they asked for, or who did not get a chance to ask. (I, Chap. VII, Chart II and Table I.) There was a relationship between the theater in which the soldier served and his personal adjustment. For example, men stationed overseas reported themselves in less good spirits than did men stationed in the United States. (I, 155-189. See especially Table I.)

In the first example it is the experience of having asked for and obtained the job they wanted which distinguished soldiers in the "experimental" group from those in the "control" group. In the second case the distinction is in terms of the soldier's location. To what extent can we attribute differences in job satisfaction, on the one hand, and different levels of personal adjustment, on the other hand, to these "stimuli"?

There are two main difficulties in equating the simple cross-tabulations of survey materials to real experimentation. One of these is the danger that spurious factors are present in the relationship. The second is the difficulty of establishing clearly the time sequence of the variables involved.

Spurious Factors

To illustrate the problem of spurious factors, let us consider the relationship between theater of service and answers to the question, "In general, how would you say that you feel most of the time, in good spirits or in low spirits?" We recall that men sta-tioned overseas reported themselves in less good spirits than did men stationed in the United States who had not yet been overseas. One possibility which occurs to us is that length of service might operate as a spurious factor in this relationship. It might be that men stationed overseas had, on the average, served for longer periods of time, and that men with records of long service had lower morale. If this were the case, we would not be justified in saying that personal esprit was determined by theater of service. Experimentally, this would express itself in the following way: two groups of soldiers, equated according to length of service, would show no differences in morale even when one group was shipped to an overseas theater.

In order to minimize the danger that spurious factors of this kind remain undetected, we employ analytical procedures which enable us to examine the relationship between the assumed cause and the assumed effect *when the influence of the possible spurious factor is eliminated*. We divide the sample into different groups according to length of service in the Army. Within each of the groups we examine the relationship between theater of service and personal esprit. In this way we are able to observe the original relationship when the possible spurious factor is "controlled" or "held constant."

Often it is not enough to introduce only one control. There are a number of other possible spurious factors in the relationship which we have considered. For example, the men overseas probably held higher rank and served in different branches of the Army. There might also have been educational differences between the two groups. All of these are factors which could have produced differences in the proportions saying that they were in "good spirits"; consequently, all of them must be controlled. For these reasons, it is necessary to carry out the comparison between men stationed overseas and men stationed in the United States in a large number of subclasses. But this leads to a problem. It is obvious that if we consider four controls, each divided into three classes (if we controlled branch of service we might divide our sample into Infantrymen, Air Corps men, and all others), we would end up with 81 separate comparisons. As we extend this process of controlling possible spurious factors, the number of cases in any one subclass becomes very small.

To cope with this difficulty the author uses the following technique throughout the volumes. First of all he divides his total sample (or samples) into small homogeneous sub-groups, using the relevant control factors to achieve his stratification. Within each sub-class he then makes the crucial comparison. He does not consider the size of the differences, but only their direction. His final conclusion is based on the *consistency* with which a specified relationship is found. In the example which we have been considering, the relation between overseas service and good spirits, the analyst had available 138 small but homogeneous sub-groups in which he could make his basic comparison. In 113 of these, men stationed overseas reported less good spirits than men in the United States not yet overseas; in 23 of the sub-groups the relationship was reversed; and in the remaining 2 there was no difference in the proportion of overseas and United States soldiers reporting themselves in good spirits. (I, 157, Table 1) Because the crucial relationship persists in the large majority of homogeneous sub-classes, the presumption that overseas service leads to a deterioration in morale gains some credence. This technique, combining results from many different but homogeneous sub-groups, is used at a number of points in *The American Soldier*; it is a procedure which deserves careful study.

It is possible, then, to guard against spurious factors, and thereby make our survey results approximate more closely those that would be obtained through experimentation. But these results will always remain approximations to, and never equivalents of, controlled experiments. We can never be sure that it is impossible to find another factor, not included among our controls, which would disqualify the main result.

If we want to study the relationship between overseas service and lowered morale through controlled experimentation, we would proceed in the following way. Half of a group of soldiers, selected at random, would be shipped overseas, while the other half remained in the United States. After a lapse of time the morale of both groups would be compared. If it turned out that the group randomly selected for shipment overseas showed significantly lower spirits, we would have the necessary evidence that it was overseas service which brought about a decline in morale.

As long as we can only control factors after the fact, however, our findings are always open to doubts. If we study the relationship through a statistical analysis of survey materials, rather than by experimentation, we can, at best, control four or five factors. Let us assume that we consider length of service in the Army, rank, branch of service and education to be important factors. It might be that none of these is important, and that we overlook the really relevant spurious factor. Perhaps certain soldiers were less popular than others; their lack of popularity might be reflected in low spirits, and it might also mean that their officers were more likely to put them on lists for shipment overseas. In this case, both overseas service and low spirits are the result of personality differences, and there is no causal connection between them. . . .

In actual survey analysis, the control of spurious factors requires a constant weaving back and forth between speculations as to the possible factors and examination of the data when the influence of each factor has been eliminated. There is one particularly important result in *The American Soldier* which illustrates this process very well.

The closer the contact of white with Negro soldiers, the greater the willingness of the whites to serve in mixed Negro-white companies. (I, 594, Chart XVII)

This relationship is one in which typically we might suspect that spurious factors are operating. Whenever we deal with a variable like "amount of contact" or "closeness of contact" we have a feeling that the persons who are found at various points along these continua made their way there voluntarily. That is, we suspect the presence of "self-selection" factors; those who have close contact with Negroes may do so because of initially favorable or "tolerant" attitudes. If this were the case, it would not surprise us to find that their attitudes following contacts with Negroes were also favorable.

The way in which the Army's "racial experiment" came about reduced the likelihood that these self-selective processes were at work. The Negro platoons were placed *at random* within Infantry companies needing replacements. While the Negro men had volunteered for combat service, men in the white companies were not consulted about their willingness to serve in mixed companies.

While the real-life situation seemed to meet those conditions required for controlled experimentation, the Research Branch sought additional checks. For example, the companies which had suffered the greatest casualties, and were therefore most likely to receive replacements, might have become more tolerant toward other men as a result of their combat experience. If this were the case, the men in mixed companies could be expected to have initially more favorable attitudes toward service with Negroes. In order to check this possibility, the Research Branch made use of a retrospective question: The soldiers in mixed companies were asked to recall how they had felt about serving with Negroes prior to the actual experience of doing so. The results indicated an even more *un*favorable attitude initially than was observed among men not serving in mixed companies.

Another possibility is that the persons in charge of assigning replacements put the Negro platoons in companies which they felt would receive them more favorably. There was undoubtedly some leeway in deciding which companies got which re-

placements, and the officers responsible for those decisions may not have distributed the troops at random. Again, if this were the case, we would conclude that the original relationship was a spurious one. Partial evidence that it was *not* the case is seen in the fact that there were as many Southerners serving in the mixed as in the unmixed companies.

The interweaving of speculations about possible spurious factors and actual analysis of the data emerges very clearly from this example. The original relationship was one which is typically suspect as being spurious. But the results were obtained in a situation which seemed to reproduce, in real life, the conditions required in controlled experimentation. There was more reason to believe, therefore, that the original relationship was a reasonable approximation of what might have been found through actual experimentation. But the analysts did not lose sight of the possibility that spurious factors were in operation. They introduced suitable controls and checks. Even though these did not destroy the original relationships we cannot say that the causal connection between contact with Negroes and favorable attitudes toward them has been demonstrated. The connection is more *probable* after the checks have been introduced than it was beforehand, but it is never quite certain.

The Time Order of Variables

Clearly to be distinguished from the problem of spurious factors is the second difficulty in approximation procedures. In order even to consider whether the statistical relationship between two variables is a causal one, the variables must stand in a determinate time relation, with the assumed cause *preceding* the assumed effect. (When we say that Variable A precedes Variable B in time, we mean that A was *acquired or developed* first.)

Often the time order between two variables is quite clear. If we relate formal educational level to rank in the Army, we can be quite sure that education precedes rank. Or, if we study the relation between civilian occupation and type of Army job, there is little doubt that Army job follows after civilian occupation in time.

There are some instances in which the same attribute is used as an index of different phenomena, so that its time order, rather than being fixed, is determined by the particular problem being considered. Suppose, for example, that we related each man's rank to the length of time which he had been in the Army. Now "length of time in the Army" can stand for a variety of different phenomena. We might consider it an index of the time when the soldier entered the Army; given this meaning, it would *antecede* promotion. We would then look at the relationship to see whether those who had entered the Army during early stages of the war were more likely to be promoted. But "length of time in the Army" can also indicate the amount of experience which the soldier has at the time that he is interviewed. Looked at in this way, length of service is a characteristic which follows *after* the soldier has acquired his rank. We then ask whether those with particular ranks are more experienced than others.

Finally, there are some instances in which the time sequence of two or more variables is indeterminate. One such case is the relationship between attitudes toward one's officers and willingness for combat. (II, 126, Table 7) Which of these attitudes developed or was acquired first? Does a soldier reluctant to go into combat "rationalize" his feelings by saying that his officers are not good? Or does a soldier with favorable attitudes toward his officers develop a feeling of confidence which makes him willing for combat? Because of our inability to answer these questions, because we do not know and cannot know which of the attitudes developed first, we cannot discuss whether there is a causal connection between them. (As we shall see in the next section, panel techniques often enable one to circumvent these difficulties.)

It is very difficult to answer these questions of time sequence with the materials of only one survey. But it is possible that in some cases clues to the time order will be found. In *The American Soldier,* for example, the authors are interested in the relationship between marital status and rank. They found (I, 118-20, see especially Chart V) that married men were more likely to have higher rank, even when age and length of service in the Army were controlled. But which came first, marriage or promotion? Is it that married men are more likely to be promoted, or that promotion encourages the soldier to marry? With knowledge only of marital status and rank, very little can be said. But fortunately Research Branch analysts obtained one other bit of information which provided some clue to the time sequence: they knew whether the soldier had been married prior to his entrance into the Army or whether he had married after becoming a soldier. These data enabled them to make the following observations. They noted that there was very little relationship between rank and having been married prior to entering the Army. On the other hand, there was some relationship between rank and marriage taking place after induction. This leads them to suggest that "marriage was even more likely to be a *resultant* of promotion or of expected promotion than to be a factor *predisposing promotion.*" (I, 120, authors' italics.) The clue to the sequence of the variables was the fact that where the time order was known, one kind of relationship existed; where it was unknown, another relationship, suggesting another time sequence, prevailed.

Panel Techniques

While the data of one survey may sometimes suggest the time order of variables whose sequence is apparently indeterminate, they give us nothing more than clues to be checked by other means. So-called panel techniques provide the relatively best device for establishing a time sequence of two variables. In a panel study, the same respondents are interviewed at different time periods. In those cases where the respondent changes between successive interviews, it is possible to determine when a particular attitude or behavior pattern developed.

These techniques contribute many new analytical devices.[1] While it is not possible to discuss all of these here, references to one finding in *The American Soldier,* of substantive interest as well as methodological value, may give a general idea. It was found that non-commissioned officers had more conformist attitudes toward Army discipline than did privates. This relationship could be explained in a variety of ways. The non-com might have a better understanding of the importance of discipline or he might endorse disciplinary measures in order to bolster his own position. It could also be, however, that a private with what one might call an authoritarian personality has a better chance of being promoted. One of the panel studies carried out by the Research Branch shows that this latter relationship is involved in the respondents according to their answers to a number of questions on discipline. Then a few months later they ascertained what proportion of the original respondents had become noncoms. Some of the findings are as follows: (See I, 265, Chart XI)

TABLE A

DISTRIBUTION OF CONFORMITY SCORES
AMONG PRIVATES IN NOVEMBER, 1943

	Number of cases	*Percentage of These Cases Promoted by March, 1944*
Relatively high score	68	31
Medium score	138	28
Relatively low score	112	17

Through their analysis of these panel materials, the investigators were able to establish that privates who held conformist attitudes were more likely to be promoted during a subsequent six months period than

[1] See Paul F. Lazarsfeld, "The Use of Panels in Social Research," *Proceedings of the American Philosophical Society,* 92 (1948), 405-410. The Bureau of Applied Social Research of Columbia University is currently working on a project to codify and evaluate these analytical devices.

were their relatively more rebellious barracks mates. As Table A shows, among those who had indicated a relatively high degree of conformity in the Fall of 1943, nearly one-third had been promoted by the following Spring, as compared with only one-sixth of the men who had originally received a low score on the conformity index.

* * *

Retrospective Questions

One of the main difficulties in a panel study is keeping the original sample intact. This is a problem even in studies of civilian populations: respondents move; some become ill and unable to participate further in the study; others become bored and refuse to participate. The enormity of these difficulties in studies of soldiers during a global war is obvious.

Because of these handicaps we sometimes use *retrospective questions* as a substitute for panel techniques. By asking the respondents to recall what their attitudes were at some earlier period (generally prior to a crucial experience whose effect we are trying to study), we attempt to reconstruct what would have been observed had there been a previous interview. We ask, "How did you feel about y before x took place?" We remember that the Research Branch used a question of this kind in checking the relationship between service in bi-racial companies and the willingness of whites to serve with Negroes. In addition to stating their present willingness to serve in mixed companies, the respondents were asked to recall what their attitudes had been before Negro platoons were put in their companies.

There are a number of grounds on which one might object to the use of retrospective questions as a substitute for panel techniques. First of all, it is difficult to know how accurate respondents are in their retrospection. Do they tend to remember selectively? Do they discount the extent to which they have actually changed their attitudes or habits? Secondly, there is the problem of specifying the exact time period to which the subjects should retrospect. "Before x took place" covers a wide time range.

Wherever possible, then, the accuracy of the retrospections should be checked. This was done in an interesting way at one point in *The American Soldier*. In investigating the effects of combat on the incidence of psychosomatic symptoms, the researchers used a number of different procedures. First of all, they cross-tabulated such variables as nearness to combat and length of time in combat with questions about psychosomatic symptoms. In one study of combat veterans, however, they included a retrospective question. In addition to asking, "Since you have been on active combat duty, are you ever bothered by (hand tremors, stomach disturbances, fainting spells, nightmares, shortness of breath, and pressure in the head)?" they also asked, "During your civilian and military life, but before you went on active combat duty, were you ever bothered by . . . ?" Comparison of the retrospective form of the question with the postcombat form reveals a marked increase in the proportion of men experiencing many anxiety symptoms. (II, 449, Table 17)

But how accurate were these retrospections? As a check, the analysts compared the pre-combat answers of the veterans with those given by Infantrymen in training in the United States. The close correspondence of the answers provided some assurance that the combat veterans did not distort their answers, either consciously or unconsciously, to any extent. (II, 448, Table 16)

These, then, are perhaps the major procedures through which the data obtained through surveys and utilized in secondary analyses can be made more nearly equivalent to experimental results.[2]

[2] In a recent article ("Some Observations on Study Design," *American Journal of Sociology*, LV, 1949-50, 355-361), Stouffer himself suggests a general scheme through which the interrelationships of controlled experiments, panel studies, surveys, and so on, can be shown. His paper is an elaboration of pp. 47-48 in the first volume of *The American Soldier*.

SECTION 2—INTERPRETATION AND ITS PLACE IN A GENERAL SCHEME OF ELABORATION

Once we have satisfied ourselves that a particular statistical relationship is an adequate approximation of experimental results, we raise a somewhat different series of questions. We explore the relationship further, elaborating and clarifying it.

The general process of elaboration takes a variety of specific forms. It also can be described in quite formal terms. Before discussing either of these points, however, let us outline the general argument of one type of elaboration—interpretation. When we interpret a result we try to determine the process through which the assumed cause is related to what we take to be its effect. How did the result come about? What are the "links" between the two variables? Answers to these questions are provided in the interpretation of the result.

The General Argument of an Interpretation

The interpretation of a statistical relationship between two variables involves the introduction of further variables and an examination of the resulting interrelations between all of the factors.

To illustrate the steps which one goes through in interpreting a result, and to indicate the types of material which are required, we shall start with one relationship in *The American Soldier* for which an interpretation is suggested. On one index of personal commitment, "At the time you came into the Army did you think you should have been deferred?", the analysts found a positive correlation between education and favorable responses: the higher the education of the soldier, the more likely he was to say that he had volunteered or that he should not have been deferred. (I, 124, Table 3) This finding was somewhat surprising in view of the general tendency of better educated soldiers to be more critical of the Army. The authors interpret the results in terms of the concept of "relative deprivation," which they define in the following way:

Becoming a soldier meant to many men a very real deprivation. But the felt sacrifice was greater for some than for others, *depending on their standards of comparison.* (I, 125, authors' italics.)

The analysts suggest that the lower educated soldiers, coming mainly from skilled labor occupations which accounted for many exemptions from service in the Army, compared their lot with that of their friends, many of whom had been deferred because of the importance of their jobs. On the other hand, "The great mass of professional, trade, and white-collar occupations were not deferable . . . The average high school graduate or college man was a clear-cut candidate for induction . . ." (I, 127) In other words, lower educated soldiers, coming from an environment in which deferments were relatively frequent, were more likely to experience their induction as a personal sacrifice than were the better educated soldiers, fewer of whose friends had received deferments.

How would one go about studying this interpretation? To simplify our discussion of the actual procedure, we should perhaps first restate the interpretative statement, so as to see the statistical relationships which it implies. It might read as follows:

Better educated soldiers are more likely to accept their inductions, because better-educated soldiers come from an environment in which deferments are infrequent, and coming from an environment in which deferments are infrequent leads to more willing acceptance of induction.

When we rephrase the statement in this way, we note that one characteristic of any "complete" interpretation is that the interpretative variable, the "test factor" as it might be called, is related to each of the original variables. The Research Branch interpretation implies (a) that the test factor, relative frequency of deferment in the environment from which the individual soldier comes, is negatively related to education, and (b) that the same factor is also negatively related to the dependent variable in the original relationship, the soldier's acceptance of his induction into the Army.

But this characteristic is not the only one. If we extend our reformulation of the interpretative statement, we note another aspect of "complete" interpretations.

If it is true that the relationship between education and attitudes toward one's own induction can be explained entirely by the frequency of deferments in one's civilian environment, then when soldiers are classified according to this test factor, when they are separated into different groups according to the frequency of deferments in the environments from which they come, there should no longer be any relationship between education and attitude toward induction.

Stated in somewhat more technical terms, we expect that when the population is stratified according to different values of the test factor, the partial relationship between the two original variables will vanish. If we can classify men according to whether or not they came from an environment in which deferments were frequent, we shall find, within any of the homogeneous groups thus obtained that there is no relationship between education and acceptance of induction. The well-educated soldiers who come from an environment in which deferments were common will be just as disgruntled about their inductions as are poorly educated men from similar backgrounds; the less well educated soldier from an environment in which there were few deferments will be as likely to accept his own induction as is the better educated man in the same kind of situation. In other words, if the partial relationships between education and attitudes toward induction disappeared when soldiers were classified according to the frequency of deferments in their civilian environment, we would conclude that one's previous environment completely interpreted the original relationship.

In order to test the interpretation, then, we need to know something about the rate of deferment in the civilian environment of each man. This information, apparently not available in the Research Branch study, might have been obtained from answers to a question like, "Have some of your friends or acquaintances been deferred because they are in indispensable civilian occupations?" Let us assume, for the sake of illustration, that such a question actually was asked, and that about half of the soldiers answered "yes." The next step would be to see whether this test factor actually is related to the two original characteristics, education and attitude toward induction. Again we must invent the two relationships if we want to end up with the full scheme for testing interpretations. We shall assume, finally, that, had information on this test factor been available, it would have provided a complete interpretation of the original result. Then we would have found a set of tables like those in Table B. The figures on the left represent the original relationship, taken from actual data reported in *The American Soldier*. (See I, 124, Table 3) The figures on the right are italicized because they were invented for the sake of our schematic illustration. On the left-hand side of the table, we find a relationship between education and attitudes toward induction: among the better educated men, the ratio of favorable to unfavorable attitudes toward induction is more than 7 to 1, while among the less well educated men, the ratio is less than 3 to 1. In the two partial tables on the right side of the "equals" sign, however, there is no relationship between the soldier's education and acceptance of his induction: in each table, the ratio of favorable to unfavorable replies on the attitude question is the same in both educational groups, even though

the ratio differs in the two tables. Other aspects of Table B will be discussed in the following section.

If a particular test factor actually does interpret the relationship between two variables, we shall find that the relations between all three are characterized in the following ways:

I. The test factor is related to the assumed causal variable in the original relationship.
II. The test factor is also related to the assumed effect.
III. When the sample is stratified according to the test factor the partial relationships between the original variables are smaller than the original relationship.

* * *

In interpretation the test factor lies *between x and y* in time, or, in other words, it follows *after x*. Only those factors which *precede x* in time, however, can be spurious factors. For the sake of convenience, we shall label these two time orders. A test factor which follows after x will be referred to as an *intervening variable,* while one which precedes x will be called an *antecedent variable.*

This difference is an important one, for, when it is not kept clearly in mind, we are apt to confuse the two types of elaboration despite their very different objectives. In the example of interpretation which we considered, the time relation of x and t is clear: there can be little doubt that an individual's formal education precedes in time the number of deferments among his

TABLE B

	High Educa-tion	Low Educa-tion	Total	FRIENDS OR ACQUAINTANCES DEFERRED			NO FRIENDS OR ACQUAINTANCES DEFERRED		
				High Educa-tion	Low Educa-tion	Total	High Educa-tion	Low Educa-tion	Total
Volunteered or should not have been deferred	1556	1310	2866	210	939	1149	1346	371	1717
			=				+		
Should have been deferred	205	566	771	125	545	670	80	21	101
	1761	1876	8637	335	1484	1819	1426	392	1818

friends and acquaintances. In other words, the test factor is an intervening variable. If the rate of deferment is a relevent test factor, its relevance is as an interpretative variable, providing a *link* between education and acceptance or rejection of one's induction. In contrast, when Research Branch analysts sought to make sure that the relationship between contact with Negroes and willingness to serve with them in mixed companies was not a spurious one, the factor which they introduced as a check —various measures of initially favorable attitude—was one which was clearly *antecedent* to the assumed cause.

We can thus distinguish three different types of elaboration.

I. *The M type* in which one is interested in noting whether the partial relationships become smaller than the original relationship. This can be further sub-divided according to the time relation of x and t.
A. *Interpretation* in which the test factor is an intervening variable.
B. *Explanation (or control for spurious factors)* in which the test factor is an antecedent variable.
The distinction between interpretation and explanation can be represented schematically in the following way:

Interpretation	Explanation
	↙t↘
x→t→y	x y

II. *The P type* in which interest is focused on the relative size of the partial relationships in order to specify the circumstances under which the original relation is more or less pronounced. This type of elaboration will be called *specification*.

We are now in a position to review much of our preceding discussion. In the first section of our paper, we talked of the way in which we control for spurious factors. This, as we now see, is one type of a more general system of elaboration, that type which we have called explanation. In our earlier discussion, we talked quite loosely about spurious factors. The definition which we have arrived at in the course of our discussion is as follows: a spurious factor is an antecedent variable which, in the M type of elaboration, reduces the average of the partial relationships.

In the opening parts of the second section we turned to a kind of analysis which we have called interpretation. We based our discussion on an example suggested in *The American Soldier* and, using hypothetical figures, indicated the conditions to be met if the interpretation were to be a complete one.

What remains to be discussed, then, is the type of elaboration which we have labeled specification. While we have indicated briefly the questions which one attempts to answer through the specification of a result, we have not shown the kinds of findings which are obtained through this analysis.

* * *

Specification—the P Type of Elaboration

In the final type of elaboration which we shall consider here, we focus our attention on the relative size of the partial relationships. We want to see whether the original relationship is more pronounced in one sub-group than in the other, when the total sample is divided by the test factor. Thus, we try to specify the conditions of the original result.

Because the P type of elaboration is so different from the M type, it may be instructive to give a numerical example of what is meant by specification. In studying social mobility within the Army, the Research Branch found that there was a positive relationship between formal educational level and rank among enlisted men: the better educated the soldier, the more likely he was to have higher rank. (I, 249, Table 7) This relationship is presented in the following four-fold table:

TABLE C

EDUCATIONAL LEVEL

Rank:	High School Graduate or Better	Less Than High School Graduate
Non-Com.	39	43%
Pvt., Pfc.	61%	57
Total cases	3222	3152

If we use as a crude measure of the relationship between education and rank the difference .61-.43 (which we can symbolize by "f"), the relationship here is .18.

But as is so frequently the case when one deals with relationships of this sort, it occurred to the analysts that the relationships might be more pronounced under varying conditions. The time at which one entered the Army, for example, might affect the correlation between education and rank. It might be that not even the better educated men had much chance to be promoted if they came into the Army at a late date, when tables of organization were pretty well fixed. Accordingly, length of time in the Army, indicating the time at which one had been inducted, was introduced as a test factor. The partial relationships thus obtained were then examined:

one, depending on the time at which the soldier entered the Army.

Most specific examples of statistical analysis will be described by one or more of these different kinds of elaboration. Either we try to "explain" the result, by showing that it is spurious, or we "interpret" it, or we "specify" it. In general, our analysis will follow a definite pattern. We start out with a simple association between two variables. Our first concern is whether or not the relationship is a spurious one; consequently our initial efforts of elaboration are usually of the explanatory type. Once we have gained some assurance that the original relationship is not a spurious one, we try to interpret the result or to specify it. We ask ourselves what variables might provide the links between the "cause" and the "effect," or what conditions might

TABLE D

	HAVE SERVED FOR 2 YEARS OR MORE			HAVE SERVED FOR LESS THAN 2 YEARS	
Rank:	High School Graduate or Better	Less Than High School Graduate	Rank:	High School Graduate or Better	Less Than High School Graduate
Non-Com.	23%	17%	Non-Com.	74%	53%
Pvt., Pfc.	77	83	Pvt., Pfc.	26	47
Totals	842	823	Totals	2380	2329
	f=.06			f=.21	

The f coefficients for these two partial tables are very different, indicating varying degrees of relationship between education and rank. Among late entrants into the Army, the better educated men had only slightly greater chances for promotion than did less well educated soldiers. Among those who had come into the Army at an earlier stage in the war, however, the better educated had considerably greater chances of being promoted. In other words, the relationship between education and rank is a conditional

show the original relationship to be even more pronounced than we originally saw it to be. The elaboration of a particular result can go on almost indefinitely. We are limited only by our lack of ingenuity in thinking of factors by which to elaborate the result, by the absence of data to check the relevance of factors which we have thought of, or by the difficulties of dealing with a few cases as the process of elaboration is extended.

* * *

A SOLUTION TO THE PROBLEM
OF QUESTION "BIAS"

EDWARD A. SUCHMAN AND LOUIS GUTTMAN

In the course of continuing surveys of attitudes and opinions of the men in the United States Army during the war, a perplexing problem arose that seems also to occur in civilian surveys. In a large number of cases, it was found that differently worded questions dealing with the same issue produced different percentages of the population as apparently "favorable." Slight changes in phrasing, in the order of presentation of answer categories, in the position of the question in the questionnaire, and other variations yielded apparently different polling results. Which of the results was the correct one?

The analysts of the Research Branch of the Information and Education Division of the War Department, which conducted these surveys, had considerable practical experience in the construction and analysis of questionnaire studies. Yet in any particular study, even after extensive pretest interviewing of samples of respondents, they often would not agree as to the best wording of a question. It became very apparent that judgment of what was an "unbiased" question was a rather subjective matter, and that there could be little hope for close agreement even among "experts" as long as they could rely only on intuition, regardless of whether or not this intuition were guided by pretest interviewing or any other experience.

Therefore, a way out of the impasse was sought. The desired goal was an *objective* method of dividing respondents into those *pro* and those *con* on the issue, such that this division would not vary with question wording.

At first it seemed dubious that such a method should be possible. But such a method has actually been found. The theoretical basis was worked out which predicted that certain practical procedures should do the job, and then the procedures were tested and found really to work. One analyst could make up his own questions on an issue, and another analyst could make up a different set, yet this new kind of analysis would give essentially the same answer in both cases.

The theory is based on scale analysis and its corollary, intensity analysis, as developed by one of the writers. This theory will be presented fully in the forthcoming volumes being prepared under the auspices of the Social Science Research Council on the work of the Research Branch.[1] The pur-

[1] For existing published materials, see Guttman, Louis. "A Basis for Scaling Qualitative Data," *American Sociological Review*, 1944, 9:139-150; Guttman, L. and Suchman, E. "In-

From the *Public Opinion Quarterly*, 1947, 11, 445-455. Reprinted by permission of the authors and the publisher.

pose of the present paper is to illustrate the practical consequences of this theory. We give here two examples of the technique for handling question "bias."

With the intensity technique available, the writers no longer spend time needlessly on question wording. The only requisites to be fulfilled are that the questions be clear, directly pertinent, and answerable; further considerations of form and wording are of no particular consequence. Time and energy are also saved in the tabulation and interpretation of results. And most important, the results are known to be unbiased, no matter who did the work.

OUTLINE OF THE METHOD

The procedure for eliminating the problem of question "bias" is very simple. It consists of: (1) asking a series of opinion questions on the same topic (this series need not be long—in very few cases are more than a dozen questions required in the pretest; for the final study, successful results have been obtained with only four or five questions selected on the basis of the pretest); (2) testing these questions to determine whether they all ask the respondent about the same single dimension of opinion (this is done very simply by means of any one of several scale analysis techniques that have come out of the work of the Research Branch); (3) asking "How strongly do you feel about this?" after each opinion question in order to determine intensity of feeling;[2] (4) obtaining for each respondent an opinion or content score which is the number of the opinion questions to which he gives

the *more favorable* answer;[3] and (5) plotting content scores by intensity scores to obtain a U- or J-shaped curve, the lowest point of which serves to divide the population into the desired *objective* and *invariant* favorable and unfavorable groups.

EMPIRICAL DEMONSTRATION

According to the theory of scale and intensity analysis, the same lowest point of the intensity curve (and indeed the whole curve itself) will be obtained by any sample of questions from the same scale, provided the questions are spread out enough to afford a good picture of the curve. The same people will be found to the right (and to the left) of this dividing point, no matter what variations in wording there are in a sample of questions.

How can the theory be tested? A good way is to take two series of opinion questions on the same topic, but "biased" in completely opposite directions and producing apparently widely different results, and then to see if the inclusion of the intensity measurement serves to "correct" these "biases" and produces the same final result for both sets of questions. Stated in other words, let us suppose that two different polling agencies wanted to find out how many people hold favorable or unfavorable opinions concerning a certain issue. One agency asks several questions which indicate that *less* than half of the people are "favorable" on each of the questions asked. The other agency asks several different questions which indicate, however, that *more*

---

tensity and a Zero Point for Attitude Analysis," *American Sociological Review*, February, 1947; and Guttman, Louis. "The Cornell Technique for Scale and Intensity Analysis," *Measurement of Consumer Interest*, University of Pennsylvania Press, 1947.

[2] Other techniques are also available for this step; for convenience we describe here only the "two-part" technique, where intensity is asked separately from content.

[3] For simplicity in the present discussion, we are considering each question to be dichotomized. Then, of the two categories to an opinion item, one can be regarded as the "more favorable" and the other as the "less favorable"; and of the two categories to an intensity question, one can be regarded as the "more intense" and the other as the "less intense." The scale analysis techniques indicate exactly which answer categories should be considered as the "more favorable" and "more intense."

than half of the people are "favorable" on each of the questions that it asked. Both sets of questions deal with the same issue, but apparently produce completely opposite results. Here is the problem of question "bias" stated in its most extreme terms. What kind of solution does the present method of intensity analysis offer?

The solution is illustrated here by two examples of just this nature. The first concerns an opinion survey of the attitudes of soldiers toward the Army, while the second concerns soldiers' opinions of their officers. For each example, a cross-section of enlisted men in the United States was asked two sets of six questions each. In each case, the two sets of questions produced widely opposite percentages of the population with the more favorable opinion.

The two examples, opinion of Army and opinion of officers, were obtained from two separate surveys. In each case, the two sets of six questions were spread at random in the questionnaire so that the respondent answered twelve questions in each area without knowing which six went together.

One Example

In Table 1 is shown the divergence in results obtained between the two sets of questions on enlisted men's opinion con-

TABLE 1

DISTRIBUTION OF REPLIES TO "UNFAVOR-ABLY BIASED" AND TO "FAVORABLY BIASED" SERIES OF QUESTIONS FOR ENLISTED MEN'S OPINION CONCERNING THE ARMY

Series	*Question Number*	*Per cent of Men "Favorable"*
Series A	1	8%
("Unfavorably	2	14
Biased")	3	16
	4	31
	5	33
	6	43
Series B	7	58%
("Favorably	8	65
Biased")	9	70
	10	79
	11	81
	12	90

cerning the Army. Series A is composed of questions on each of which *less* than half of the respondents expressed a "favorable" attitude, while Series B is composed of questions on each of which *more* than half of the respondents expressed a "favorable" attitude. Each series has six questions, and all twelve were tested together for scalability to assure that, from the respondents' point of view, they all concerned the same opinion dimension. The exact questions asked, together with the marginal distributions of replies, are given in List 1. Each opinion question was followed by an intensity question asking, "How strongly do you feel about this?"

From Table 1, it can be seen that, depending upon which series of six questions was used, soldiers' opinions of the Army could be characterized as "favorable" or "unfavorable." One research worker using Series A would conclude that the men "disliked" the Army, while another analyst using Series B would conclude that the men "liked" the Army. However, *were both analysts to ask intensity of feeling also and to correlate opinion scores by intensity scores, they would draw substantially the same conclusions*, regardless of which set of questions was used. The U- or J-shaped curve obtained by plotting opinion scores against intensity scores would divide the population into the same percentages with favorable and unfavorable opinions, regardless of question "bias." What do our data show in this respect?

Chart 1 shows the regression curve of intensity on content for Series A and Series B. The scattergrams on which these two regressions are based follow. Columnar medians are the averages plotted, and the percentile metric is used, for these are invariant for the sampling of questions. The technique of asking "How strongly do you feel about this?" to measure intensity is admittedly a crude one and accounts for much of the variation around the medians. For a more complete analysis of the problem of error, see the forthcoming publication on the Research Branch's work.

LIST 1

ENLISTED MEN'S OPINION CONCERNING THE ARMY

(The manner in which the answer categories were dichotomized can be seen from the weights of 0 or 1 appearing before each category. Since the answer categories represent only qualitative gradations from more or less "favorable," these weights can be given fairly arbitrarily to produce relatively high or low percentages with "favorable" opinions.)

Series A: "Unfavorably Biased" Questions

1. On the whole, do you think the Army gives a man a chance to show what he can do?

   (1) A very good chance
   (0) A fairly good chance
   (0) Not much of a chance
   (0) No chance at all
   (0) Undecided

2. In general, how well do you think the Army is run?

   (1) It is run very well
   (0) It is run pretty well
   (0) It is not run so well
   (0) It is run very poorly
   (0) Undecided

3. Do you think when you are discharged you will go back to civilian life with a *favorable* or *unfavorable* attitude toward the Army?

   (1) Very favorable
   (0) Fairly favorable
   (0) About 50-50
   (0) Fairly unfavorable
   (0) Very *unfavorable*

4. In general, do you think the Army has tried its best to see that men get as square a deal as possible?

   (1) Yes, it has tried its best
   (0) It has tried some, but not hard enough
   (0) It has hardly tried at all

5. Do too many of the things you have to do in the Army seem unnecessary?

   (1) No, *not too many* of them seem unnecessary
   (0) Yes, *too many* of them seem unnecessary

6. In the Army, some jobs are naturally harder and more dangerous than others and the Army has to put men where it thinks they are needed.
Considering everything, do you think the Army is trying its best to see that, as far as possible, no man gets more than his fair share of the hard and dangerous jobs?

   (1) Yes, it is trying its best
   (0) It is trying some, but not hard enough
   (0) It is hardly trying at all

Series B: "Favorably Biased" Questions

7. In general, how interested do you think the Army is in your welfare?

   (1) Very much
   (1) Pretty much
   (0) Not so much
   (0) Not at all

8. What do you think of the statement that *"The Army makes a man out of you"*?

   (1) There's a lot to it
   (1) There may be something to it, but I'm still doubtful
   (0) There is not much to it

9. All things considered, do you think the Army is run about as efficiently as possible, or do you think it could be run better?

   (1) It is run about as well as possible, everything considered
   (1) It could be run somewhat better
   (0) It could be run a lot better

10. Do you think the Army is trying its best to see that the men who have the hard and dangerous jobs get the special consideration and breaks they deserve?

   (1) Yes, it is trying its best
   (1) It is trying some, but not hard enough
   (0) It is hardly trying at all

11. In general, do you feel you yourself have gotten a square deal from the Army?

   (1) Yes, in most ways I have
   (1) In some ways, yes, in other ways, no
   (0) No, on the whole I haven't gotten a square deal

12. Do you feel that the Army is trying its best to look out for the welfare of enlisted men?

   (1) Yes, it is trying its best
   (1) It is trying some, but not hard enough
   (0) It is hardly trying at all

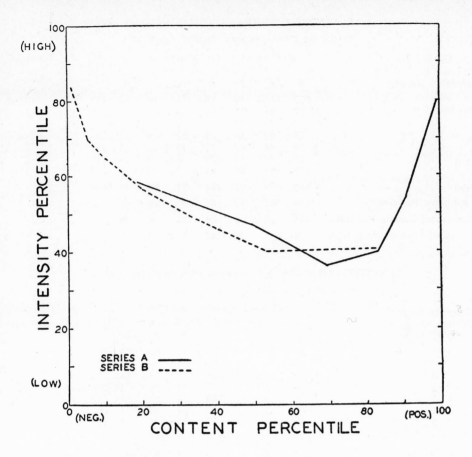

CHART 1. Approximate intensity functions of two oppositely biased sets of questions for enlisted men's opinion concerning the Army.

The research worker using the "unfavorably biased" Series A would find from its intensity curve that the low point fell at about the 70th percentile, indicating that approximately 30 per cent were favorable, and 70 per cent were unfavorable, in their opinion of the Army. The research worker using the "favorably biased" Series B would have to conclude that, despite the fact that none of his six questions showed *less* than 58 per cent "favorable," the neutral point of the curve fell between 54 per cent and 83 per cent (a crude single point estimate can be taken as halfway between, or 69 per cent); he would see that to determine this point more closely, questions showing greater "un-favorableness" toward the Army would have to be included in the series asked. Thus, both analysts would come to the conclusion that about 30 per cent of the men were favorable, and about 70 per cent were unfavorable toward the Army.

A Second Example

A similar equality of results is obtained for the area of opinion concerning officers. In Table 2 are show the marginal frequencies of two sets of six questions each. Each question in Series A shows less than 50 per cent of the men "favorable" towards their officers, whereas each question in Series B shows 50 per cent or more of the men to

ENLISTED MEN'S OPINION CONCERNING THE ARMY
SERIES A: "UNFAVORABLY BIASED" QUESTIONS

Intensity Score (Number of "Very strongly" replies)	Content Score (Number of "Favorable" Replies*)							Total	Cumulative Per cent
	0	1	2	3	4	5	6		
6	222	112	49	45	26	18	_30_	502	100
5	_112_	61	29	30	18	_21_	5	276	73
4	91	_76_	38	31	9	5	5	255	58
3	76	61	_50_	28	11	8	2	236	44
2	58	48	47	17	16	1	1	188	31
1	50	50	33	29	5	4	—	171	21
0	59	61	45	44	7	3	2	221	12
Total	668	469	291	224	92	60	45	1849	
Cumulative Per cent	36	61	77	89	95	98	100		
Midpoint of Content Percentiles	18	49	69	84	92	96	99		
Median of Intensity Percentiles	58	47	36	41	55	64	80		

* Frequencies in italics belong to the columnar medians.

ENLISTED MEN'S OPINION CONCERNING THE ARMY
SERIES B: "FAVORABLY BIASED" QUESTIONS

Intensity Score (Number of "Very strongly" replies)	Content Score (Number of "Favorable" Replies*)							Total	Cumulative Per cent
	0	1	2	3	4	5	6		
6	_35_	_45_	63	70	96	90	164	563	100
5	1	18	25	_61_	42	68	105	320	70
4	—	11	21	29	_44_	53	64	222	52
3	—	3	9	31	35	56	72	206	40
2	1	—	11	18	34	_58_	68	190	29
1	—	2	5	12	24	49	75	167	19
0	—	8	3	7	24	41	_98_	181	10
Total	37	87	137	228	299	415	646	1849	
Cumulative Per cent	2	7	14	26	43	65	100		
Midpoint of Content Percentiles	1	4	10	20	35	54	83		
Median of Intensity Percentiles	84	70	66	57	49	41	42		

* Frequencies in italics belong to the columnar medians.

be "favorable." The questions themselves are given in List 2.

A scale analysis showed that all twelve questions were part of the same scale. Therefore, despite the "biases" in the two series of questions, they must have the same approximate intensity curves, as is shown in Chart 2.[4] In each case, the men are divided by the neutral intensity point into essentially the same proportions of favorable and unfavorable. Series A has no less than 50 per cent apparently "unfavorable" on each question, and its intensity curve shows that

[4] Chart 2 is based on the two scattergrams which appear on page 737.

approximately 83 per cent actually have an unfavorable opinion of their officers. In regard to Series B, the best estimate would be between 65 and 89 per cent unfavorable (the midpoint being 77 per cent), with a clear-cut indication that additional questions showing greater unfavorableness toward officers are needed for a closer determination of the dividing point.

RECAPITULATION AND CONCLUSION

A complete discussion of the theory of this technique of handling bias is too detailed for the present paper and is reserved

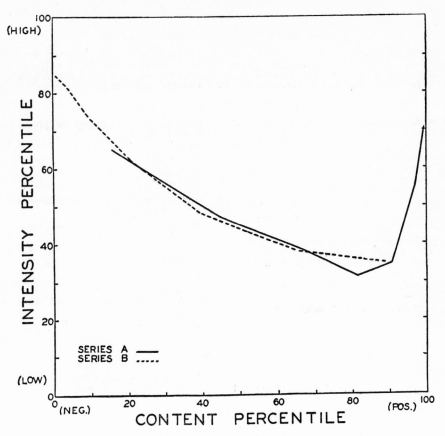

CHART 2. Approximate intensity functions of two oppositely biased sets of questions for enlisted men's opinion concerning officers.

for the forthcoming publication of the Social Science Research Council. However, the main points of the technique can be summarized briefly. Basically, there are three steps: (1) Test to see if the content has but one dimension (by using scale analysis). If there is a single dimension, the rank order of each respondent on the continuum of content is also determined, and the next steps are possible. If the content is not scalable, then there is no point to talking about "favorableness" and "unfavorableness." If there is but a single scale, then the next two steps are: (2) Determine the rank order of the respondent on a continuum which measures the *intensity of feeling* with which he holds his opinion. (3) Relate con-

TABLE 2

DISTRIBUTION OF REPLIES TO "UNFAVORABLY BIASED" AND TO "FAVORABLY BIASED" SERIES OF QUESTIONS FOR ENLISTED MEN'S OPINION CONCERNING OFFICERS

Series	Question Number	Per cent of Men "Favorable"
Series A ("Unfavorably Biased")	1	7%
	2	15
	3	23
	4	29
	5	32
	6	47
Series B ("Favorably Biased")	7	50%
	8	52
	9	68
	10	75
	11	83
	12	93

LIST 2

ENLISTED MEN'S OPINION CONCERNING OFFICERS

(The manner in which the answer categories were dichotomized can be seen from the weights of 0 or 1 appearing before each category. Since the answer categories represent only qualitative gradations from more or less "favorable," these weights can be given fairly arbitrarily to produce relatively high or low percentages with "favorable" opinions.)

Series A: "Favorably Biased" Questions

1. How much did you personally like your officers?

(1) Very much
(0) Pretty much
(0) Not so much
(0) Not at all

2. How do you feel about the privileges that officers get compared with those which enlisted men get?

(0) Officers have *far too many* privileges
(0) Officers have *a few too many* privileges
(1) Officers have *about the right number* of privileges
(1) Officers have *too few* privileges

3. How much did you personally respect your officers?

(1) Very much
(0) Pretty much
(0) Not so much
(0) Not at all

4. When you did a particularly good job did you usually get recognition or praise for it from your officers?

(1) Always
(1) Usually
(0) Rarely
(0) Never

5. How do you feel about the officers that had been selected by the Army?

(1) They were the best ones that could have been picked
(1) They were as good as any that could have been picked
(1) Undecided
(0) Somewhat better ones could have been picked
(0) Much better ones could have been picked

6. Do you think that your officers generally did what they could to help you?

(1) Yes, all the time
(1) Yes, most of the time
(0) No, they often did not
(0) No, they almost never did

Series B: "Unfavorably Biased" Questions

7. How well do you feel that your officers understood your problems and needs?

(1) They were very much aware of my problems and needs
(1) They were fairly well aware of my problems and needs
(0) They did not know very much about my real problems and needs

8. Do you feel that your officers recognized your abilities and what you were able to do?

(1) Yes, I'm sure they did
(1) Yes, I think they did, but I'm not sure
(1) Undecided
(0) No, I don't think they did

9. How many of your officers used their rank in ways that seemed unnecessary to you?

(0) Almost all of them
(0) Most of them
(1) Some of them
(1) Only a few of them
(1) None of them

10. In general, how good would you say your officers were?

(1) Very good
(1) Fairly good
(1) About average
(0) Pretty poor
(0) Very poor

11. Did your officers give you a chance to ask questions as to the *reason why* things were done the way they were?

(1) Yes, always
(1) Yes, usually
(1) Undecided
(0) No, not very often
(0) No, almost never

12. How many of your officers took a personal interest in their men?

(1) *All* of them
(1) *Most* of them
(1) *About half* of them
(0) *Few* of them
(0) *None* of them

tent of opinion with intensity of feeling. This determines the zero or neutral point for content.

The underlying theory is that, in any opinion or attitude measurement problem, there is an infinite number of questions or question wordings which could be used to get at the respondent's opinion. Depending on how the question is asked, the percentage of respondents with "favorable" opinions can conceivably vary from zero to 100 per cent. Any single question used, therefore, is just a sample of all the questions that might have been used instead. The first essential problem is one of testing the series of ques-

tions to see if they deal with the same dimension of opinion, differing only in how they express "favorableness" or "unfavorableness"; this is done by scale analysis.

The second step goes further by providing a ranking on intensity which permits one to arrange the respondents from high to low in order of the intensity of feeling with which they hold their opinions. This intensity ranking can be determined very simply in any of several ways. The technique in the examples used in this paper was to have each opinion question followed by a second part which asked, "How strongly do you feel about this?", with answer

ENLISTED MEN'S OPINION CONCERNING OFFICERS
SERIES A: "UNFAVORABLY BIASED" QUESTIONS

Intensity Score (Number of "Very strongly" replies)	Content Score (Number of "Favorable" Replies*)							Total	Cumulative Per cent
	0	1	2	3	4	5	6		
6	266	105	56	34	14	15	12	502	100
5	161	102	53	34	20	15	9	394	83
4	138	113	66	43	20	20	10	410	69
3	123	116	78	37	24	13	4	395	55
2	91	96	72	58	35	6	1	359	41
1	81	112	103	68	27	12	2	405	29
0	60	108	109	96	48	15	1	437	15
Total	920	752	537	370	188	96	39	2902	
Cumulative Per cent	32	58	76	89	95	99	100		
Midpoint of Content Percentiles	16	45	67	82	92	97	99.5		
Median of Intensity Percentiles	66	48	39	34	36	56	71		

* Frequencies in italics belong to the columnar medians.

ENLISTED MEN'S OPINION CONCERNING OFFICERS
SERIES B: "FAVORABLY BIASED" QUESTIONS

Intensity Score (Number of "Very strongly" replies)	Content Score (Number of "Favorable" Replies*)							Total	Cumulative Per cent
	0	1	2	3	4	5	6		
6	26	67	84	91	94	80	68	510	100
5	5	22	50	80	75	69	54	355	82
4	4	14	43	70	99	89	64	383	70
3	—	6	24	67	115	110	74	396	57
2	—	8	16	53	103	145	97	422	43
1	—	5	12	31	87	129	80	344	29
0	8	4	7	28	86	169	190	492	17
Total	43	126	236	420	659	791	627	2902	
Cumulative Per cent	1	6	14	28	51	78	100		
Midpoint of Content Percentiles	1	4	10	21	40	65	89		
Median of Intensity Percentiles	85	84	74	63	50	39	35		

* Frequencies in italics belong to the columnar medians.

categories of "Very strongly," "Fairly strongly," "Not so strongly," and "Not at all strongly." Each respondent is given a score depending upon the intensity of his responses.

The third step involves cross-tabulating scores on the opinion scale by scores on intensity, yielding the intensity curve. Intensity of feeling decreases as one moves toward the middle from either end until one reaches a point of least intensity. This point serves to divide the population into positive and negative. *It will stay fixed regardless of the particular opinion questions used or of the way they are worded.* No matter how badly "biased" the questions are, provided only that they deal with the same opinion dimension, the distribution of the population into pro and con will be the same. It is this invariant property of the curve formed by correlating opinion score by intensity score which provides a solution to the problem of question "bias."

If none of the questions in a sample have their frequencies near the true zero point, then the plotted curve will show that the neutral point can be located only within a crude interval provided by the sample. The interval becomes smaller as some questions hit closer and closer to the correct marginal. Thus far, in some experiments in the Research Branch, no worker has been found who could determine in advance which of several wordings of questions would hit closest to the zero point. What form of wording is most unbiased seems to vary considerably from problem to problem.

In conclusion, it should be pointed out that the intensity function also serves purposes other than providing an objective and invariant zero point for attitudes and opinions. The shape of the curve provides important additional information about the *structure* of the attitude or opinion. Are people sharply divided on the issue, or is there a large region of relative indifference? Flat U-shaped curves indicate the latter condition, and sharp V-shaped curves the former. Study of the shape of curves may provide leads in developing a theory as to when other behavior can or cannot be predicted from attitudes or opinions.

VALIDITY OF RESPONSES TO SURVEY QUESTIONS

HUGH J. PARRY AND HELEN M. CROSSLEY

Perhaps no word has been more vaguely or loosely used in all the social sciences than "validity." To some it is a matter of gradation—a continuum, so to speak—ranging from an imaginary absolute of perfection down to an equally imaginary absolute of nonvalidity. To others, more naive, it is an either-or dichotomy, chiefly useful as a weapon to hurl against personal or ideological opponents. Yet validity is basic to all

From the *Public Opinion Quarterly*, 1950, 14, 61-80. Reprinted by permission of the authors and the publisher.

research, and the concept clearly must be made more specific.

* * *

AGGREGATE AND INDIVIDUAL VALIDITY

Whether validity is considered as predictive accuracy or as interpretation, some way must still be found to measure it. Often, of course, no check is possible for the major findings which the survey was designed to uncover; validity must be established for related questions and independent characteristics. Except in test validation, the usual method has been by means of comparisons of *aggregate* results from the survey in question against actual or percentage figures from an outside source, such as election results or census figures. The concept of aggregate validation, both of sample designs and of survey results, is a familiar one in market research[1] as well as in the field of election forecasting and social research in general. On many types of surveys, given sufficient aggregate checks, results can often be assumed to have over-all validity. Yet there is always a danger that satisfactory aggregate comparisons may conceal dangerous compensating errors. Thus, the most reliable means of establishing the validity of survey results is the comparison of aggregate results with outside data accompanied by an independent check on the worth of the *individual* responses.

Validation of individual reports is extremely difficult to carry out, because of the anonymity of most respondents and the difficulty of verifying answers even when respondents are identified. Nevertheless, there have been several attempts to make such checks on a small or large scale. Some have been based on the predictive concept of validity, others on the more limited one of truthfulness. Some of the more significant of these studies are outlined briefly below

as illustrations of the difficulties involved and the results that can be achieved.

One of the earliest studies was the well-known experiment of LaPiere,[2] who between 1930 and 1932 traveled extensively with a young Chinese couple, and then obtained questionnaires from many of the hotels, auto camps, tourist homes, and eating establishments they had visited; over 90 per cent of the proprietors in each group said they would not accept Chinese as guests. His early findings did much to show that the best test of validity of measured attitudes may be something other than behavior in a hypothetical or real situation.

COMMERCIAL RESEARCH

In the commercial field, studies of individual validity, as opposed to aggregate validations, have sometimes taken the form of "pantry inventories" to see whether what is actually on the shelves agrees with housewives' reports. A similar type of study was reported in 1938 by Jenkins and Corbin,[3] who checked daily sales slips for 70 regular customers of a local grocery store in Ithaca, New York. The check covered 13 frequently purchased articles, and resulted in a range of 62 to 100 percent of respondents naming as most recent purchase the brand actually shown on the store's sales slip. The authors found that indices of validity did not exhibit uniformity from product to product, and concluded that while reliability of last-purchase questions (as measured through re-interviews) could safely be assumed, the validity of such questions should be determined individually for each product to be studied.

The Magazine Audience Group, which was sponsored originally by *Life* through the Continuing Study of Magazine Audiences and later expanded into a general advisory body on magazine research for many pub-

[1] Cf. Committee on Marketing Research Techniques, "Design, Size, and Validation of Sample for Market Research," *Journal of Marketing*, Vol. 10 (1946).

[2] LaPiere, Richard T., "Attitudes vs. Actions," *Social Forces*, Vol. 13 (1934).

[3] Jenkins, John G., and Horace H. Corbin, Jr., "Dependability of Psychological Brand Barometers—II: The Problem of Validity," *Journal of Applied Psychology*, Vol. 22 (1938).

lishers, was from its beginnings in mid-1938 especially concerned with the problem of validity. In order to eliminate invalid answers from reports of magazine readership, the committee developed a system called "Confusion Control" based on the technique used by Professor Darrell B. Lucas[4] in measuring the impact of advertisements. The basic technique involved the use of advance magazines not yet published that respondents could not possibly have seen, in order to find out the amount of false identification. At first the correction applied to readership figures on an aggregate basis only. But beginning with Report No. 4 in 1941, a method was devised to evaluate individual replies according to the number of pages identified. The amount of confusion (false identification, either deliberate or mistaken) found was generally low, well below 10 per cent.

A small study done for the Magazine Audience Group by Crossley Incorporated[5] in early 1941 was set up to check on the accuracy of education reports received from respondents on regular surveys. While done on a limited scale in a few small cities only, this experiment is particularly significant in the study of validity in view of the apparently common upward educational bias of even the most carefully designed quota or area samples. Crossley's study checked each respondent's answers on the amount of education received against three different sources: later reports from other members of the family, interviews with neighbors, and actual school records where available. As expected, results showed exaggeration of reports on the part of respondents, although the exaggeration was more evident in reports of graduation from grade, high school, or college, than it was in actual attendance at the different types of schools. On the basis of this study, Crossley con-

cluded that simple questions regarding the number of years the respondent attended school were likely to have low validity and should not be relied upon.

GOVERNMENT RESEARCH

The Federal Government has occasionally made various studies which bear on validity. In a brief but revealing article in 1944 Hyman[6] cited three surveys done for the Office of War Information which showed distortion of the truth by from 4 to 42 per cent of respondents. From these results Hyman concluded that, at least on questions concerning behavior having a prestige character, poll results should be used with the greatest caution. One of the most significant of his findings was the fact that invalidity may exist in varying amounts in different population groups.

Some work related to validity was done by the armed forces during World War II, notably the methodological studies by the Bureau of Naval Personnel and the experiments in prediction made by the Research Branch of the War Department's Information and Education Division. *The American Soldier,*[7] the impressive, recently published report of War Department research, contains a few references to the validity of individual attitudes as established by future behavior. These studies, however, are all concerned with the predictive concept of validity; there seems to have been little concern with the more vital matter of validity as representation of truth.

The most comprehensive government work on validity is that now being set up

[4] Lucas, Darrell Blaine, "Rigid Techniques for Measuring the Impression Values of Specific Magazine Advertisements," *Journal of Applied Psychology*, Vol. 24 (1940).

[5] Results of this study were never published, and the authors are indebted to Archibald M. Crossley for permission to cite them here.

[6] Hyman, Herbert, "Do They Tell the Truth?", *Public Opinion Quarterly*, Vol. 8, No. 4 (1944), p. 557.

[7] *The American Soldier,* Princeton University Press, 1949. Vol. 1: *Adjustment During Army Life,* by Samuel A. Stouffer, Edward A. Suchman, Leland C. DeVinney, Shirley A. Star, Robin M. Williams, Jr.; Vol. 2: *Combat and Its Aftermath,* by Samuel A. Stouffer, Arthur A. Lumsdaine, Marion Harper Lumsdaine, Robin M. Williams, Jr., M. Brewster Smith, Irving L. Janis, Shirley A. Star, Leonard S. Cottrell, Jr.

by the Bureau of the Census to be applied on the 1950 Census of Population. The Bureau has a Response Research Unit whose task it is to find out the kind and amount of error involved in reports obtained by enumerators. Various techniques are being used, including re-interviews and special statistical analyses. When the reports from this source are available, they should provide a wealth of hitherto unknown facts about the nature of the validity of census-type information.

* * *

MEDICAL AND RELATED RESEARCH

Medicine is generally considered as belonging to the field of the relatively exact or physical sciences, one with which social scientists have usually had little contact. But a study done in Michigan indicates that the methods of social research may soon be applied more widely in the medical field.[8] The objective of the study was the validation of a new method to determine the need for medical attention among farm families. The basic technique used was a list of symptoms which should receive medical attention, information on which was obtained by regular interviewing methods from an informant (usually the housewife) for each member of her family. The information was then validated by means of actual physical examinations of the members of about one-sixth of the families. Complete agreement between the questionnaire reports and the physician's examinations was found in 8 out of 10 cases, and indicated that the determination of the medical needs of a population by asking individuals to list their symptoms was quite feasible.

Kinsey[9] has given a great deal of attention to the problem of validity. Perhaps the most comprehensive of his techniques to

[8] Hoffer, Charles R., "Medical Needs of the Rural Population in Michigan," *Rural Sociology*, Vol. 12 (1947).

[9] Kinsey, Alfred C., Wardell B. Pomeroy, and Clyde E. Martin, *Sexual Behavior in the Human Male*. Philadelphia: W. B. Saunders Company, 1948.

establish validity is the comparison of reports from 231 pairs of spouses. For most of his items Kinsey found that between 80 and 99 per cent of this group of subjects gave replies that were later verified independently by their marriage partners. In addition to this type of check, the Kinsey investigators obtained a small number of re-takes to test the constancy of memory. They also noted such things as internal consistency of the case histories, reports from the skilled interviewers on falsification and cover-up, constancy of patterns in members of different segments of the population, checks by sexual partners other than spouses, comparisons between interviewers of results for similar groups, hundred per cent samples, and comparisons of reports from older and younger generations. Kinsey found that accuracy varies considerably with different individuals. The validity of individual histories also varies with particular items and for different segments of the population. Incidence data were found to be more accurate than frequency data, and averages of social statistics such as age, education, events concerned with marriage, etc., check closely with averages obtained by direct observations.

In spite of the author's warning that the results presented in the remainder of the book are only fair approximations of fact, the careful reader will be inclined to accept the findings as having been obtained in a most scientific manner and as having a more than satisfactory degree of validity, *so far as individual reports are concerned*. The one point at which the Kinsey Report is vulnerable to criticism is the one at which many other studies stop—*aggregate validation*. In the absence of a scientifically selected sample (a requirement which might be quite impossible for such a survey to meet on a full-scale basis), the Kinsey results and background data should be validated against all possible criteria in a regular probability sample of perhaps one or two selected areas. In this way, results which are now reasonably valid for individuals and special groups could be applied to larger, more general segments of the population.[10]

POLITICAL RESEARCH

It is only recently that election pollers have begun to recognize the need for validating individual answers. Election results were considered the acid test, and a poll which came close to the aggregate official results of an election had indeed performed a difficult task. Since elections are secret, the problem of how to validate respondent reports is almost insurmountable, the limit usually being a check against precinct records after the election to see whether each respondent voted or not, with no way of telling for whom he voted. Re-interviews with respondents after election, as were made in the 1940 Erie County survey,[11] serve somewhat the same purpose, with the added advantage of including the report of the candidate voted for—but since they are still verbal reports from the same subjects and not checks against outside data, they are as much a reliability measure as validity, and may be subject to the same kinds of inaccuracy on voting reports as the original pre-election questions.

In December 1942 the American Institute of Public Opinion[12] made a small but significant study in Ewing Township, near Trenton, New Jersey, in which 271 out of the 739 registered voters in the Seventh Precinct were interviewed and asked whether they had voted in the election a month before; their answers were then checked against precinct records. Correct answers were given by 93 per cent of the respondents. Incorrect replies included 5 per cent who said they had voted but actually had not, and 2 per cent who said they had not, but actually did. Similar results indicating high validity in some post-election studies in 1948 are not confirmed by the extensive check made in Denver six months after the election, as will be demonstrated in the following section.

The 1948 election gave rise to several post-election checks by polling agencies. Among them was the intensive panel study carried out during the campaign period in Elmira, New York, which will yield much information when it is fully analyzed. A preliminary report[13] states that the respondents' post-election reports of voting corresponded with official records in 98 per cent of the cases. These respondents, however, as members of a panel, were interviewed several times in the course of the campaign, and, because of their generally cooperative attitude, could be expected to give more truthful answers than respondents on other types of surveys.

A resurvey of 317 respondents was made by the Washington Public Opinion Laboratory in the State of Washington during the first week of December 1948. High agreement with official records was reported in this study: of the 299 respondents who reported having voted on November 2, 287 were actually found to have done so.[14] This situation may be rather unusual, however, in that the respondents had been interviewed before and may have been more inclined for this reason to give correct replies.

Re-interviews were also made in 1948 by the Survey Research Center of the University of Michigan on a national sample.[15] No check was made against official records for these respondents, however, since this study, like most others, was intended not

[10] Parry, Hugh J., "Some Contributions of the Kinsey Report to Opinion and Attitude Research," unpublished paper presented before the American Association for the Advancement of Science, New York City, December 30, 1949.

[11] Lazarsfeld, Paul F., Bernard Berelson, and Hazel Gaudet, *The People's Choice*. Second Edition, New York: Columbia University Press, 1948.

[12] The authors are indebted to William S. Gillam and the AIPO for permission to present here the results of this hitherto unpublished study.

[13] Dinerman, Helen, "1948 Votes in the Making—a Preview," *Public Opinion Quarterly*, Vol. 12, No. 4 (1948), p. 585.

[14] SSRC, *op cit.*, pp. 368-369.

[15] *Ibid.*, pp. 373-379.

as a validity check but to throw light on the problems of voting intention and turnout. In both surveys it is interesting to note that the percentage reported having voted is higher than in the population at large.

Another check was carried out in New Jersey following the 1948 elections by Carroll S. Moore, Jr. of the Trenton *Times* Poll. He did not re-interview his respondents, but checked their actual voting through precinct records. He found that 95 per cent of those who had intended to vote actually did so; but that 12 per cent of those respondents who said they were registered and eligible to vote were in fact not registered at all.

From the findings of the various studies reported above, and from others not included because of space considerations, it can be seen that the validity of individual replies can never be taken for granted, even when aggregate validity is very high. On the other hand, as is shown in studies such as the Kinsey Report and the post-election checks of voting behavior, the fact that individual replies have a great deal of validity does not automatically insure that the over-all results will therefore be valid. Before survey results can be relied on, they must be subjected to both kinds of tests—do the aggregate results check against important known data? and if so, are the individual reports sufficiently truthful? Either kind of validity without the other may be misleading.

DENVER VALIDITY STUDY

PLAN OF STUDY

In order to make a systematic attack on some of the previously outlined problems of validity, a detailed study was planned and carried out in 1949 at the University of Denver's Opinion Research Center, . . .

The study was designed to explore three areas: a substantive area of the determinants and concomitants of community satisfaction, and the methodological implications of interviewer effect and of validity. . . . This article will limit itself to a report of the design and over-all findings of the validity portion of the survey.

ITEMS OF INVESTIGATION

The subjects chosen for the check on validity of response were generally of a sort common to survey questionnaires. Wording of the questions was based on forms commonly used by other opinion research organizations. To some degree, the subjects used for investigation were supplied by the logic of necessity; that is, we had to limit our choices to items which were significant and which also could be checked against official records. The subjects finally selected for checking were:

(1) Respondent's registration and voting in the six city-wide Denver elections held between 1944 and 1948. Official precinct lists of voters are in the public domain, so each respondent's reported voting history could be checked against them. In the case of the primary election in 1948, we could also check on party affiliation.

(2) Personal contribution during the fall 1948 Community Chest drive.

(3) Possession of a valid Denver Public Library Card in respondent's name.

(4) Possession of a valid Colorado driver's license.

(5) Ownership of an automobile by respondent or spouse, and make and year of car.

(6) Respondent's age. This was checked three ways—against voting registration records, against driver's license reports, and finally, for internal consistency, against another question on the ballot.

(7) Ownership or rental of respondent's place of residence.

(8) Telephone in respondent's home.

It can be seen that the items chosen evoke varying amounts of prestige, and varying degrees of potential distortion as caused by social pressure, ease of verification, memory factors, and the like.

Perhaps the items of greatest practical interest and importance are those dealing with elections, since past performance (or the respondent's version of past performance) has often been used, deliberately or unconsciously, in an attempt to predict behavior in the future. Other items used are common ones, either in opinion and attitude research or in the more specialized field of market research. Cross-analyses are frequently made on the basis of responses to these items, and conclusions are drawn from the attitudes or past behavior of these groups; it is therefore important to know to what extent such breakdowns are based on valid information.

The results presented here, of course, will not apply automatically to any survey done on any population, although many of the findings are of importance to research in general. Their significance and application must be studied in the light of the conditions under which they were obtained. . . .

* * *

THE SAMPLE

Most fortunately, while the study was still in the planning stage, a new edition of the City Directory of Denver residents was issued. A series of informal checks on the Directory information indicated that it was sufficiently accurate and up-to-date to take the place of a costly enumeration on our part and that it could be used as the universe for this study. While there may have been some small distortions in representativeness in the Directory, they would not materially affect our results, since our purpose was to obtain a random list of individuals for the validity and interviewer effect tests rather than to make any numerical estimates.

Using a probability method of systematic selection, 1,349 names were taken from the Directory (discarding, of course, such unusable listings as business places, out-of-town addresses, and duplications of names). These 1,349 names were distributed to the 45 interviewers in assignments of 30 (one assignment was 29 names). Interviewers were allowed to make no substitutions, and were required to make at least four calls to reach their respondents. A total of 920 usable interviews was finally obtained.

* * *

INTERVIEWER SELECTION AND TRAINING

The field work was begun on April 19, 1949, and continued through May. The 45 interviewers used came from two groups: experienced professional interviewers on the staffs of national and local research organizations, and graduate and undergraduate students in opinion research and social science at the University of Denver. Each interviewer was given intensive personal training in two or more special sessions, and was assigned to a special supervisor for the duration of the field work. The result was that the interviewing staff, when it went into the field, was presumably somewhat above average in its ability and training. This point is stressed only to show that little of the invalidity of response found could have been caused by an unduly amateur or inefficient staff of interviewers. Further evidence of the quality of the field work was given by a post-interviewing check by the office staff, . . . Thus, it can be assumed on this survey, in contrast to others where such rigid control and checking of field work are not feasible, that a minimum of the invalidity uncovered is due to dishonesty or incompetence on the part of interviewers.

Another aspect of the sample design assured that differential validity among various groups could not be due to certain interviewers' interviewing more of certain types of people. The city was divided into five sectors, as equivalent as possible with respect to several factors, and within each sector respondents were stratified by sex and geographical location and assigned at random to the nine interviewers. . . . Furthermore, interviewers were allocated to the various sectors of the city so as to equalize as far as possible the effects of such factors as interviewer's sex, experience, education, age, and social introversion-extraversion.

The interviewers, it should be added, were given no indication of the real purpose of the study nor were they told that there would be a check on the respondents (although, to improve efficiency, they were, as usual, told that there might be checks on their own work). As far as they were concerned, it was a normal survey covering community satisfaction. Later checks indicated that none of the interviewers became aware of the justifiable trick being played on them.

CHECKING VALIDITY INFORMATION

To ascertain the validity of information obtained by the interviewers, a long and tedious, name-by-name, response-by-response check was carried out. Each respondent's answers to the questions cited earlier were compared with records of the City and County of Denver, the Denver Community Chest, the Denver Public Library, and the Mountain States Telephone Company. All checking, except on Community Chest records, was done by Center personnel. . . .

It is not necessary to go into the mechanical details of the validity check. Such factors as marriage and consequent change of name by female respondents between 1943 and the present, changes of address during the period, and the like all contributed to our difficulties. The official records of the City and County of Denver appear to have been in a state of much higher order and accuracy than many researchers have found in other areas, but even so occasional difficulties crept in. While it was possible to solve the great majority of problems by rechecking, digging, leg-work, and phone-work, it must be realized that some error in the base criteria was inevitable and is reflected in the measures of validity obtained.

THE RESULTS

The level of invalidity on the various items or combinations of items checked ran from nearly zero up to almost half of the responses received. As the following tables show, invalidity often follows social pressures. More respondents exaggerated their participation in elections than under-reported it. The same tendency is evident in the reports of possession of library cards and driver's licenses. Only the over-all totals are presented here. . . .

Elections

Since the largest amount of data concerns reports of voting in the various Denver elections, we shall discuss them first. Results are shown in Table 1.[16]

The cumulative amount of invalidity for the six elections is somewhat startling. While four-fifths of the respondents gave valid answers as to their registration during the period, only a third gave entirely correct answers to questions regarding all six elections. And "correct" in this check is only in terms of whether or not the respondent actually voted; if a check could be made on the truthfulness of the reports given on candidates voted for, even a larger number of errors might be uncovered.

On the questions regarding specific elections the amount of invalidity varied from a seventh to a fourth of all responses. Clearly, on the basis of these results, any of these questions would have little value as a means for checking the representativeness of a sample, for drawing assumptions on the basis of voting groups, and particularly for using this reported past voting behavior as a means of indicating future voting behavior.

The 1948 Presidential election was both nearest in time and highest in importance to respondents in general. Thus the level of invalidity here was somewhat lower than

[16] Question 14: "Here are some questions about registration and voting in Denver. Have you been *registered* to vote *in Denver* at any time since 1943?"

Question 14A (IF "YES" OR "DON'T KNOW"): "Have you voted in any election in Denver since 1943, either in person or by mailing an absentee ballot back to Denver?"

Question 15 (UNLESS "NO" TO 14 OR 14A): "We know a lot of people aren't able to vote in every election. Do you remember *for certain* whether or not you voted in any of these elections: First . . ." (ELECTIONS READ OFF, ONE AT A TIME).

TABLE 1

VALIDITY OF REGISTRATION AND VOTING REPORTS

100% = 920 Cases

A. *Whether registered or voted in Denver since 1943:*

Correct reports:		82%
Not registered since 1943	15%	
Voted or registered since 1943	67	
Exaggerated registration or voting		16
Under-reported registration or voting		2
Confused (Don't remember, No answer)		*
		100%

B. *Voting reports on combination of six elections:*

Correct in all statements	33%
Exaggerated (voted in fewer than reported)	42
Under-reported (voted in more than reported)	4
Confused (voted in same number but different elections, or Don't remember or No answer to one or more elections)	21
	100%

C. *Voting reports on six specific elections:*

(1) *November 1948 Presidential election:*

Correct reports:		86%
Did not vote	26%	
Voted	60	
Exaggerated (said voted, but did not)		13
Under-reported (said did not vote, but did)		1
Confused (Don't remember, No answer)		*
		100%

(2) *September 1948 primary election:*

Correct reports		69%
Did not vote	45%	
Voted in Republican Primary	10	
Voted in Democratic Primary	14	
Exaggerated (said voted, but did not)		21
Under-reported (said did not vote, but did)		3
Confused (Don't remember, No answer, wrong answer on party)		7
		100%

(3) *November 1947 city charter election:*

Correct reports:		60%
Did not vote	43%	
Voted	17	
Exaggerated (said voted, but did not)		28
Under-reported (said did not vote, but did)		2
Confused (Don't remember, No answer)		10
		100%

* Less than 0.5 per cent.

TABLE 1 (continued)

100% = 920 Cases

(4) *May 1947 Mayoralty election:*

Correct reports:		70%
Did not vote	35%	
Voted	35	
Exaggerated (said voted, but did not)		28
Under-reported (said did not vote, but did		1
Confused (Don't remember, No answer)		1
		100%

(5) *November 1946 Congressional election:*

Correct reports:		69%
Did not vote	42%	
Voted	27	
Exaggerated (said voted, but did not)		19
Under-reported (said did not vote, but did)		2
Confused (Don't remember, No answer)		10
		100%

(6) *November 1944 Presidential election:*

Correct reports:		73%
Did not vote	37%	
Voted	36	
Exaggerated (said voted, but did not)		23%
Under-reported (said did not vote, but did)		2
Confused (Don't remember, No answer)		2
		100%

on the other elections. However, to some extent, the lower level of invalidity is artifactual: where invalidity is basically in the direction of exaggeration and where a higher proportion vote than in most elections, there is simply a smaller group of persons who are likely to give incorrect responses.

Community Chest Contribution

Table 2 shows that the query concerning personal contributions to the 1948 Community Chest drive provided a large relative amount of invalidity.[17]

It can be seen that about a third of the respondents said that they did not contribute to the Chest; in these cases no further check was made, on the pragmatic but probably

[17] Question 25: "Did you yourself happen to contribute or pledge any money to the Community Chest during its campaign last fall?"

TABLE 2

VALIDITY OF REPORTS ON COMMUNITY
CHEST CONTRIBUTIONS

100% = 920 Cases

Reported not giving (statements assumed to be correct, but not checked against records)	31%
Reported giving, and did give	25
Reported giving, and might have given through uncheckable source	8
Reported giving, but did not give	34
Don't remember, No answer	2
	100%

reliable assumption that few if any respondents would deny contributions they had made.

About a fourth correctly said they had given, either at work or at home. Slightly over a third said they had given but were not listed as donors in the Community Chest files. About a tenth of the responses could not be classified as valid or invalid—

though the presumption is toward invalidity, since the Chest records were in very good shape and, except for certain collective donations, included a very complete list of donors.

Thus it is evident that about four out of every ten responses here were invalid. Undoubtedly social pressures and a belief that the responses would not be checked were the major factors behind the high level of invalidity. It should be noted, however, that the question created considerable ambiguity. Despite the stress on "you yourself," some respondents tended to answer in terms of pledges by other members of the family. Whatever the reason for invalidity, it can safely be said that this sort of question, whether it concerns the Community Chest or some other charitable organization, is not very helpful for survey use. Moreover, the issue tested here was only the fact of giving; if it had been necessary to find out the amounts of contributions made, even more invalidity could have been expected.

TABLE 3

VALIDITY OF REPORTS ON LIBRARY CARD

100% = 920 Cases

Correct reports:		87%
Do not have card	76%	
Have card	11	
Exaggerated (reporting having card, none on file)		9
Under-reported (reported no card, one on file)		2
Don't remember, No answer		2
		100%

Library Card

As Table 3 shows, there was a slight tendency for respondents to claim possession of a currently valid library card, when no card was actually on file.[18] About a tenth of the responses were invalid in this respect, and a negligible proportion were invalid in the direction of under-statement—probably infrequent users unaware that their cards remain in force for three years.

[18] Question 21: "Do you have a library card for the Denver public library in your own name?"

TABLE 4

VALIDITY OF REPORTS ON DRIVER'S LICENSE
AND AUTOMOBILE OWNERSHIP

100% = 920 Cases

A. *Possession of Driver's License:*

Correct reports:		88%
Do not have license	44%	
Have license	44	
Exaggerated (reported license, but none on file)		10
Under-reported (reported no license, one on file)		2
Don't know, No answer (most had licenses on file)		*
		100%

B. *Possession of Automobile, Year and Make:*

Reported no car owned (statements assumed to be correct, but not checked against records)	35%
Correct on ownership, make, and year	52
Correct on ownership and make, incorrect on year	5
Correct on ownership and year, incorrect on make	*
Correct on ownership, incorrect on make and year	2
Incorrect on ownership	3
No answer (more than half of these actually had cars registered)	3
	100%

* Less than 0.5 per cent.

Driver's License and Car Ownership

Again, as can be seen in Table 4, about a tenth of the respondents claimed possession of a valid Colorado driver's license when actually they did not have one. Less invalidity was found in items concerning ownership by respondent or spouse, of an automobile, and the make and year of such car.[19]

TABLE 5

VALIDITY OF REPORTS ON AGE

A. *Consistency check by year of birth:*
100% = 886 Cases

Age and year of birth consistent within a year	95%
Reported age more than year younger than age by year of birth	4
Reported age more than year older than age by year of birth	1
	100%

B. *Check by driver's license records:*
100% = 411 Cases

Reported age within one year of age on license record	92%
Reported age more than year younger than age on record	4
Reported age more than year older than age on record	4
	100%

C. *Check by election registration records* (Men only):[20]
100% = 297 Cases

Reported age within one year of age on registration record	83%
Reported age more than year younger than age on record	8
Reported age more than year older than age on record	9
	100%

[19] Question 22: "Do you have a Colorado driver's license that is still good?"
Question 23: "Do you happen to own an automobile at the present time? (IF "YES") Is it registered in your name alone, or in your (wife's) (husband's) name also?"
Question 23A (IF "YES" TO 23): "Does the car have Colorado plates or plates from some other state?"
Question 23B (IF "YES" TO 23): "What year and make of car is it?"
[20] In former years women in Colorado were not required to give their exact ages when registering to vote, only to swear that they

While the number of correct answers on such questions is gratifying in comparison to the answers on other types of questions, an error of as little as 3 per cent in the proportion of families owning cars might be quite serious for some purposes, such as estimating the tire needs of the country, since it is over and above any error that might be expected from sampling. If it were proved that the entire 3 per cent were actually incorrect respondent reports, and not omissions in the official files or various other types of error, a survey with direct need for valid figures on car ownership would have to examine this problem carefully. In the Denver study, a tendency was also noticed to report the car owned as newer than it actually was—a fact which might also require attention in a specialized survey.

Respondent's Age

Results on the various age checks showed a generally satisfactory level of validity, as indicated in Table 5.[21]

The correlation with age as reported on the traditional age question was highest for the information on year of birth obtained from the other end of the ballot. This result was to be expected, since the check was essentially more one of reliability than validity.

For those respondents who did not have drivers' licenses or were not registered to vote in Denver, it was, of course, not possible to check the age information against such records. The fact that those who were so checked, however, appeared more accurate when compared with drivers' license records than with registration records may mean one of several things—that the registration records are less accurate than the license records, that some respondents are motivated to give less valid reports to registration officers, or that the people for whom

were over 21. Consequently the registration check on women's ages is omitted here because the information is not sufficiently precise.
[21] Question 10: "May I ask your age?"
Question 35: "In what year were you born?"

the various checks were possible differ in their tendencies to give invalid answers to the official reporters and to interviewers. These differences emphasize the point that it is not enough merely to know that invalidity exists and the extent of it; information is also needed on its sources and on means to distinguish which of several answers is the valid one and which the invalid.

Home Ownership and Telephone[22]

These factors which are commonly used for breakdown and checking purposes in many types of surveys, were found to have a high degree of validity when checked against city property records and telephone company listings. Results of this check are given in Table 6.

CONCLUSIONS

The Denver study disclosed amounts of invalidity ranging from a twentieth to nearly

[22] Question 30: "Do you or your family rent, or own, the place where you live?"
Question 33: "Is there a telephone in your home in your family's name?"

a half of the responses received on various types of factual questions. While other situations or areas may show more or less validity depending on circumstances, the survey results demonstrate clearly the wide range of invalidity to be found in the answers to a number of factual items of types often used in survey research. They further underline the need for caution in accepting so-called "factual information" at face value; even census-type data must be considered suspect. Because of the special controls exercised in the design of the survey and the careful training and supervision of interviewers, it is believed that the invalidity found here represents close to a minimum, and that national surveys which cannot be so rigidly controlled should expect to encounter even more on many types of items. Except on certain more or less innocuous items, the range of invalidity is sufficient to cause worry, and indicates a great need for further research on the truthfulness of respondents' statements of fact.

Nevertheless, the reader should not infer from these findings that research in the social sciences is relatively hopeless. He need not feel that truth is unascertainable

TABLE 6

VALIDITY OF REPORTS ON HOME OWNERSHIP AND TELEPHONE

A. *Home Ownership:*

100% = 919 Cases

Correct reports:		96%
Home owned	53%	
Home rented	43	
Probably exaggerated ownership (place owned by someone of a different name)		3
Probably under-reported ownership (placed owned by someone of same family name)		1
		100%

B. *Telephone:*

100% = 918 Cases

Correct reports:		98%
Telephone	84%	
No telephone	14	
Exaggerated (reported telephone, but none in family name at that address)		1
Under-reported (reported no telephone, but one in family name at that address)		1
		100%

by pragmatic methods of experimental science, and that he had better turn to Yoga or Neo-Thomism. For invalidity, in the final analysis, is not inevitable. It has causes which can be found in the questionnaire, in the respondent, in the interviewer, and above

all in the interpretation of data. It varies by subject and among sub-groups. Yet it can be measured and analyzed. Once this is done, it is subject to certain pragmatic checks and controls.

* * *

THE WAUKEGAN STUDY OF VOTER TURNOUT PREDICTION

MUNGO MILLER

To be successful, a pre-election poll must determine at least two things about each respondent: first, Is he going to vote?; second, For whom will he vote? The present study was undertaken in an effort to develop techniques that might help the survey-taker to answer the first of these questions.

* * *

The Waukegan Study of Voter Turnout Prediction was undertaken with two objectives in view. The first was an attempt to discover questions that might be asked to differentiate between respondents who would vote on election day and those who would not. The secondary purpose was to define the group of non-voters who after an election falsely assert that they have voted. This second objective is really an extension of the first, inasmuch as it is known that past voting may provide some basis for predicting future voting. It would be useful in pre-election polling to know which respondents

are telling the truth when they say that they voted in the last election.

The study was conducted at the time of the 1950 Congressional elections in Waukegan, Illinois. The 13th precinct was selected as the precinct most typical of the entire city, which is predominantly Republican. Whether or not the precinct is truly representative of Waukegan or of the state or nation was not of fundamental importance, as the purpose of the study only required that it be possible to compare poll results with election results for a given political unit. A small unit was selected so that a large sample could be taken, thereby minimizing the distortion of results by any sampling bias. A house to house canvass of the precinct conducted one month before election day revealed an adult population (age 21 and over) of 796. Names were listed and a one-third probability sample selected by taking every third name. This gave a sample of 265 cases. All respondents

From the *Public Opinion Quarterly*, Vol. 16, Fall 1952, No. 3, 381-398. Reprinted by permission of the author and the publisher.

were interviewed twice—once within the three weeks before the election and once within the four weeks following. On the first wave, 225 interviews, 85 per cent of the sample, were completed. Interviewers were instructed to call at least three times and not to substitute respondents. Of these 225 cases, 91 per cent were interviewed the second time, giving a final sample of 204 cases, which is 76 per cent of the sample initially selected. Although this is a slightly lower proportion of completed interviews than is ordinarily desirable with a probability sample, it was reduced by the necessity of completing a second interview. Although the 24 per cent of the sample with whom interviews were not completed can be presumed to include a large number of non-voters, the voting record shows that 54 per cent of those interviewed voted, while 53 per cent of the adults in the precinct as a whole voted. A further indication of the representativeness of the sample is provided by the fact that of the 110 sample members who voted 57 (51.8 per cent) were women, while of the 422 voters in the precinct as a whole 214 (50.7 per cent) were women.

The data from the two interview waves were supplemented by the County Clerk's records showing which of the respondents were registered for the election and which ones voted. All data were coded and punched on I. B. M. cards. The sample was then subdivided into twelve groups, as shown in Table 1. Four additional groups were contemplated for those who voted and reported that they had not, but no respondents fell in this category. All lies came from non-voters who leaned in the prestige direction and claimed to have voted.

The ideal battery of filter questions for sorting potential voters from non-voters would consist of one question. Presumably, the best question should be "Will you vote?," or, since it is known that voters and non-voters differ in a number of significant ways, it would be ideal to find a characteristic possessed by all voters and by no non-voters. Not only is the latter approach practically impossible, but, as already discussed in connection with other studies, the "Will you vote?" question is of only limited value. Of the 147 respondents who said they would vote only 103 did, and 7 of the 57 who said they would not vote did so.

The person who votes does so for a number of complex and interdependent reasons. These reasons may be poorly integrated and in conflict with each other, and voting

TABLE 1

DISTRIBUTION OF RESPONDENTS

Group	Pre-election Statement of Voting Intent	Actual Voting Record	Post-election Self-Report of Voting Behavior	Number of Cases
A	Certain to vote	Voted	Voted	86
B	Probably will vote	Voted	Voted	17
C*	Probably won't vote	Voted	Voted	5
D*	Certain not to vote	Voted	Voted	2
E*†	Certain to vote	Did not vote	Voted	11
F*†	Probably will vote	Did not vote	Voted	6
G†	Probably won't vote	Did not vote	Voted	2
H†	Certain not to vote	Did not vote	Voted	3
I*	Certain to vote	Did not vote	Did not vote	20
J*	Probably will vote	Did not vote	Did not vote	7
K	Probably won't vote	Did not vote	Did not vote	9
L	Certain not to vote	Did not vote	Did not vote	36

N=204

* These respondents failed to carry out their expressed voting intent.
† These respondents gave a false reply when asked whether they had voted.

behavior may be more strongly influenced by factors that might otherwise be of only secondary importance. In the present study no single item was sufficiently highly related to voting to be considered a hallmark of the voter. The presence of a certain characteristic may assure that a person will vote, but its absence may be no more related to non-voting than to voting. Similarly, a negative self-report on registration assures that the respondent will not vote, but a positive report offers no assurance that he will.

As pointed out above, a number of researchers have looked on a measure of interest as an index of turnout. The present study failed to find a simple relationship. Of 42 respondents reporting high interest 13 failed to vote, and of 23 reporting a complete lack of interest 6 actually came out and voted.

Since the voter cannot be defined in terms of any single criterion, it is necessary to seek a combination of items that will give a turnout prediction with minimum error. The combination used in this study was derived from a questionnaire of 72 items. Forty of these were included on the pre-election ballot and 32 on the post-election ballot. Items were selected to tap all factors conceivably related to voter turnout. Chi squares between each item and actual voting behavior were computed, and for the purposes of the present study all items not significant at the one per cent confidence level were eliminated from further consideration.

Construction of Test Batteries

Five different batteries of questions were derived from these items. The first of these, called "B" battery, consists of the entire group of 31 items. This battery is designed for maximum utilization of data and greatest precision, although it is usually not practicable to use this many items in an actual election poll. Weights in "B" battery were assigned on the basis of mean criterion score for each category. This is the proportion of actual voters among all respondents choosing the category.

A second approach to the selection of a large, maximally sensitive battery was made by the use of the Cornell scaling technique. The same 31 items used in "B" battery were initially taken as a scale and were reduced to a scale of 28 items. This scale was called "CB" battery and had 78.2 per cent reproducibility. Taking 90 per cent as an acceptable standard, "CB" battery cannot strictly be said to represent a scalable area. Nevertheless, as is pointed out in the discussion below, the individual scores on "CB" battery are fairly good predictors of turnout. It must be borne in mind that reproducibility is computed in terms of how well the item responses match the ranking of total scale scores. These scores are not in themselves a perfect measure of turnout. It is not surprising, therefore, that "CB" battery is a usable turnout predictor even though it is only 78.2 per cent reproducible.

Batteries "B" and "CB" were designed for research purposes. Another objective of this study was to develop a battery short enough for use in large scale election polls and accurate enough to eliminate the bias of non-voter respondents. Three different methods for selecting such a battery were tried: "A" battery, "S" battery, and "CS" battery.

The first of these, "A" battery, was selected on an *a priori* basis. All items were listed in decreasing order of relationship with voting, and the battery was drawn up by taking the five highest items that did not seem to have duplicate content. This selection, quickly and easily done, was designed to test the utility of selecting a short filter battery on a judgmental basis. The other two short batteries were selected by more careful methods. Both of these proved to be more accurate than "A" battery, but not greatly different from each other.

"S" battery was constructed by plotting on a bivariate chart the following 2 x 2 table contingency coefficients for each item: (1) response to item against actual behavior (i.e., voting or non-voting); (2) response to item against score above or below median on "B" battery. The seven items showing the

TABLE 2

"S" BATTERY

Item Code	Mean Criterion Score	Weight*
5. *Where do people that live in this block cast their ballots; in other words where do you go to vote?*		
a. Correct	103/144	+1
b. Incorrect	0/2	0
c. DK	6/56	−1
d. DK, vote absentee	1/2	0
6. *On the average would you say that you vote nearly always, part of the time, or rarely?*		
a. Nearly always	97/133	+1
b. Part of the time	10/38	−1
c. Rarely	2/26	−1
d. Other	1/7	0
8. *Are you registered now so that you can vote in the next election? If yes, when did you register?*		
a. Yes, 1 year or more ago	83/111	+1
b. Yes, less than 1 year ago	8/17	0
c. Yes, DK when	17/21	+1
d. No	0/52	−8
e. DK whether registered	2/3	0
9. *Have you ever voted since you have lived at this address?*		
a. Yes	97/129	+1
b. No	13/75	−1
18. *How certain are you that you will vote in the coming election on November 7th?*		
A. I am absolutely certain that I will vote.		
B. I will most likely vote.		
C. I probably will not vote.		
D. I definitely will not be voting.		
a. A	86/117	+1
b. B	17/30	0
c. C	5/16	−1
d. D	2/41	−1
41. *Generally speaking, how much interest would you say that you have in politics?*		
a. High	29/42	+1
b Average	53/79	+1
c. Slight	22/60	0
d. None	6/23	−1
69. *In which of the groups on this card is the weekly income of the principal wage earner in your family?*		
A. $15 to $45		
B. $46 to $55		
C. $56 to $65		
D. $66 to $75		
E. $76 to $100		
F. Over $100 a. A, B, C, D	52/121	0
b. E, F	52/72	+1
c. Other	6/11	0

* Weights were assigned to mean criterion scores as follows:
+1   .67 and higher
 0   .34 to .66
−1   .33 and less
−8   numerator of zero
 0   less than 10 cases for denominator, irrespective of magnitude of ratio.

highest relationship with turnout and lowest with score on "B" battery were selected for "S" battery. The items, mean criterion scores, and weights assigned are shown in Table 2. Since "B" battery as a whole showed a high relationship with voting, and reasonably high internal consistency, none of the items highly related to voting was really low in its relationship to total score.

The final battery, called "CS" battery, was derived by the Cornell scaling technique from "CB" battery. With one exception, the six items showing highest consistency with the total scale score were selected. Although item 50, asking whether the respondent had voted at the last presidential election and for whom, was among those items individually most consistent with total score on "CB" battery, it was not included since it is not strictly comparable in presidential and non-presidential years. Since the resulting "CS" battery had 93 per cent reproducibility, it represents a truly scalable universe of items.[1]

COMPARATIVE RESULTS

On the basis of each of the five batteries, predictions of turnout and voting preference for United States senator were made and compared with actual election results. Since 110 of the 204 people in the sample voted, it was predicted that the 110 highest scor-

[1] The items used were 5, 6, 8, 9, and 18, shown in Table 2 and item 59 (Have you yourself ever taken an active part in politics? If yes, please explain).

ing respondents on each battery would vote. Slightly smaller or larger groups were taken in each case in order not to split a score group. The turnout predictions as shown in Table 3 are still far short of perfection, although a significant improvement over the "Will you vote?" question can be observed. Batteries "B," "CB," and "CS" gave equally good results.

Although the most precise batteries select groups that still contain over 15 per cent non-voters, the real objective of election prediction is not to isolate a sample of respondents who will actually vote, but rather one with voting preferences representative of actual voters. While the batteries fell somewhat short of selecting pure voter groups, they achieved high precision in selecting groups with voting preferences representative of all voters.

Predictions of the vote for United States senator were made by two methods. The first of these was based on the assumption that high score individuals represented actual voters, and the predictions are the percentages of preference for the two candidates by those of the high score group stating a preference.

The second method of predicting candidate choices consisted of weighting subgroups in proportion to their voting strength. With "B" battery, for example, respondents were divided into four equal groups at the quartiles of the range of scores. The candidate preferences of each of these four groups were multiplied by a factor propor-

TABLE 3

TURNOUT PREDICTIONS

Basis of Prediction	Number of Voters Predicted	Number of Predicted Voters Who Did Vote	Per Cent of Predicted Voters Who Did Vote
Item 18*	147	103	70.1%
B Battery	113	95	84.1
CB Battery	109	92	84.4
A Battery	107	85	79.4
S Battery	116	95	81.9
CS Battery	100	84	84.0

* "Will you vote?"

tional to the percentage of actual voters in the group.

The predictions by both methods included, of course, errors due to such factors as last minute opinion shifts and faulty allocation of the undecided vote. Since the predictions were based on percentages of voters expressing a choice, the "undecided" and "won't tell" vote was in effect prorated between the parties in proportion to the expressed preferences. The potential errors inherent in such an assumption are well known, but in the present study there was no legitimate basis for any other allocation. All predictions by the sub-group weighting method were less accurate than predictions made by the high score method. The results shown in Table 4 indicate that when turnout was accounted for, these other sources of error were minor under the conditions of this study.

The prediction was least accurate for "A" battery with a 3.6 percentage point error. "A" battery was also poorest on turnout prediction, as shown in Table 3. With an error of this magnitude it was concluded that the rough judgmental basis by which "A" battery was constructed was inadequate. Note, however, that the short batteries,

"S" and "CS," gave just as accurate preference predictions as their longer counterparts. Although groups with high scores on all batteries do include some non-voters, these non-voters match the voters not only on responses to the filter questions but also on voting preferences. Except with "A" battery a sample representative of voters has been achieved even though some of the people in the sample do not actually vote.

PREDICTORS OF TURNOUT

Analysis of the content of the filter items related to turnout throws light on the question of voter motivation. A number of factors can be discerned.

Although eligibility is the most concrete factor related to turnout, it is not the easiest to determine. Voting age was controlled by the sampling plan, and only one of the 204 respondents admitted noncitizenship. Whether or not the respondent meets the residence requirements for eligibility is also specific, but it is virtually impossible to establish from survey questions. The residence requirements vary from state to state and within a state between levels of political subdivision. Eligibility can be established if

TABLE 4

PREDICTION OF THE VOTE FOR UNITED STATES SENATOR

Actual Vote of Entire Precinct	No.	Dirksen* Per Cent	No.	Lucas† Per Cent	Votes Cast	Losses‡	Total
	279	68.2	130	31.8	409	13	422

Basis of Prediction	No.	Dirksen* Per Cent	No.	Lucas† Per Cent	Total Choices	No. Choices§	Total
Total Sample	89	59.7%	60	40.3%	149	55	204
Voters in Sample**	66	68.7	30	31.3	96	14	110
Item 18, "Will you Vote?"	80	62.5	48	37.5	128	19	147
"B" Battery	69	69.7	30	30.3	99	14	113
"CB" Battery	66	70.2	28	29.8	94	25	109
"A" Battery	62	64.6	34	35.4	96	11	107
"S" Battery	68	66.7	34	33.3	102	14	116
"CS" Battery	57	66.3	29	33.7	86	14	100

* Dirksen was the Republican candidate and winner in precinct and state.
† Lucas was the Democratic candidate and loser.
‡ This figure represents voters at the election who did not cast votes for senator.
§ These are the "undecided" and "won't tell" respondents.
** This is the actual turnout group from the sample. It is the ideal that the filter batteries tried to isolate.

the respondent reports prior voting from his current address, but no workable method for establishing ineligibility was found.

If it were practically possible to determine registration on national polls, the sample could be selected from the registration records, and all eligibility problems would be solved. But state-to-state differences in registration procedures and the volume of work involved prohibit the use of this method in a large scale survey. Self-reports of registration are subject to error both from outright lies and also from frequent honest mistakes in knowing whether or not one is registered. Twenty-two of the respondents who reported being registered were not. Of the 149 respondents claiming that they were registered, 108 (72 per cent) voted, but of the 52 reporting that they were not registered none voted. In effect then, this item is one of the best predictors of turnout with the response of not being registered giving perfect results.

Poor health undoubtedly affects turnout, but none of the items designed to evaluate health or disability yielded a significant turnout prediction. Insofar as people favoring both parties are equally susceptible to ill health, their non-voting is no obstacle to accurate forecasting. It is entirely possible, however, that the lower economic groups, generally Democratic, are more than proportionately prevented from voting due to poor health and less adequate medical care. Only two respondents said it was hard for them to vote because of old age, and both of these people did vote. The entire health problem was for present purposes considered to be of insufficient importance to justify further investigation.

Factors other than health may make a person unavailable on election day. The two items which dealt with the probability of being out of town identified only an insignificantly small group. However, the answers to a query about how much effort the respondent would make to get back or vote absentee if he were out of town, did show a relationship with turnout. Fifty-seven of the 82 who said that they would make a lot of effort did vote, whereas only 15 of the 51 who said they would make no effort voted. Of the 32 people who replied to item 10 that it was difficult for them to take time off to vote, only 8 voted. The reason given most frequently was conflict with working hours. In terms of number of people involved, availability on election day must be considered a significant but minor factor in turnout.

Several items dealt with various indices of socio-economic status. Of these, only the item asking about union affiliation failed to show a relationship to turnout. Overall, the following groups contributed more than their proportionate shares to the voter group:

persons resident over ten years at present address
college graduates
home owners
professional and semi-professional occupations, proprietors, managers, officials, skilled laborers, salesmen
families where income of principal wage earner was over $75 per week (1950)

The following groups contributed less than their proportionate shares to the voter group:

persons resident less than one year at present address
eighth grade or less education
home renters
semi-skilled and unskilled workers, persons employed in custodial, domestic, and protective service including armed forces
families where income of principal wage earner was below $75 per week (1950)

Of these measures of socio-economic status, amount of income was the best single item for turnout prediction.

A number of items dealing with specific personal characteristics were investigated. These items were thought of as representing a single factor only in the sense that they all defined the respondent on fairly objective bases. Sex, marital status, ancestral nationality, and labor union affiliation were all unrelated to turnout. The frequent finding in earlier studies that women tend to be non-voters was not verified; in the precinct as a whole women voters slightly outnumbered the men. Church affiliation, however, showed a significant relationship to turnout. Of those respondents stating a church affiliation, 60 per cent voted, whereas among non-churchgoers only 33 per cent voted.

Age was found to be a determiner of turnout. Of the 81 respondents under age 40, only 29 (36 per cent) voted, but of the 123 age 40 and over, 81 (66 per cent) voted. Even among the oldest people turnout is high; 28 of the 38 people over age 60 voted.

Although range and amount of political information are perhaps only expressions of interest, information was treated as a separate factor because of the type of item involved. Voters did not differ from non-voters on information about names of senatorial candidates, the backgrounds and qualifications of candidates, or the proposals being offered for referendum.

These items reflected the major content of the particular election. However, the people who had greater information on the date of election, the voting place, the names of lesser candidates, and the names of local political leaders did tend to vote. These items all covered information of a more local and immediate nature. The factors which can be called the voting habit may also be a reflection of interest rather than a truly independent factor. Every item that touched on regularity of past voting was significantly related to turnout at the election. It is interesting that these results were so positive, the prestige value of positive answers notwithstanding.

Party preference, loyalty, and pressure were assessed by a number of items. These items were essentially measuring interest, and it is again possible that only one factor exists. Perhaps there is little or no pure interest in voting apart from interest in a party or candidate. Answers to one question showed that party loyalty or lack of party interest was stable and that the immediate voting plans of the individual were resistant to pressure. Of 42 respondents who had been urged to vote by party workers, mail, or friends, 24 (57 per cent) did vote. Of 157 who were not subjected to such party pressure 82 (52 per cent) voted. The parties seemed to have more potency in attracting voters on a long term loyalty basis than on an immediate pressure basis. This finding might not, of course, be confirmed in a presidential year. Of the 7 items where the responses indicated a preference for a particular party, all but one showed respondents favoring the Republican party turning out in significantly higher proportions than those favoring the Democrats. The exception was a question which asked whether and for whom the respondent voted in 1948. Of the 63 who had voted for Dewey, 36 (57 per cent) voted in 1950. Of the 80 who reported voting for Truman, 59 (74 per cent) voted in 1950. This would seem to be better evidence for the phenomenon of reports swinging to the winner, as reported by Cantril and Harding, than for the higher turnout rate of Democrats.

The effect of party loyalty on turnout lies at the heart of the present study. It is because turnout by party preference is not equal that pre-election polls must predict turnout. Table 5 summarizes this party difference. Another approach to turnout control in pre-election polling might lie in developing "do vote" percentages for the two parties for each state on the basis of broad scale pre- and post-election studies.

In one sense, interest in voting or in the particular election can be expected to be the principal factor affecting turnout. In another sense interest is not a determiner of turnout but is the very thing to be predicted, turnout being merely a manifestation of interest. In our study, every question that measured intensity of interest proved to be positively related to turnout; this is illustrated in Table 6, which summarizes results on the question asking for the most direct expression of interest.

Considering all the factors discussed above it can be concluded that the voter is an older, church affiliated person of upper

TABLE 5

TURNOUT BY PARTY

Party	Preference Number	Per Cent*	I Will Vote Number	Per Cent†	Did Vote Number	Per Cent†
Republican	99	60%	80	81%	69	70%
Democrat	65	40	44	68	27	42

* Per cent of all respondents expressing a preference.
† Per cent of respondents preferring this party.

TABLE 6

INTEREST AND TURNOUT

Item 41. *Generally speaking, how much interest would you say that you have in politics?*

	High	Average	Slight	None	Total
Voted	29	53	22	6	110
Did not vote	13	26	38	17	94
	42	79	60	23	204

socio-economic status who knows about voting, votes regularly, and has an active interest in his party.

NON-VOTERS AND LIARS

All the filter batteries described above included some non-voters in the group selected as potential voters. The precision of the candidate preference predictions shows that these people were nevertheless typical voters. Most of the prediction failures were people so near the dividing point between potential voters and potential non-voters that the turnout prediction for them was made with very little confidence anyway. Nevertheless, in predicting turnout on the basis of score on one of the batteries, a yes or no prediction must be given; those for whom a yes prediction is made and who do not vote are in fact prediction failures—even though the predictions were made with the least confidence.

Of the 94 non-voters in the sample, 22 lied on the post-election survery and reported that they had voted. The 18 non-voters who were predicted voters provided 9 of the 22 liars. In other words, one half of these people who "should have voted" were unwilling to admit their delinquency.

It is as though they were somehow aware of society's expectancy that they should vote.

In comparing the high score non-voters with the high score voters, only a few items revealed noticeable differences. The high score prediction failures included fewer people with longtime residence at the same address, more people with no church affiliation, and more men. In general, the "will vote" prediction failures were people not quite as high in socio-economic status and not quite as interested in elections as those for whom the prediction was verified. The people for whom the non-voting prediction was in error seemed to be more stable socially and more familiar with elections than other low scorers.

Recognizing that nearly all failures to predict turnout were midground people for whom the prediction had a low probability of success, the general conclusion can be drawn that they are people showing a leaning away from the major characteristics of the typical voter or non-voter, except that the low score person who votes is not of significantly higher socio-economic status than his low score mates who do not.

On the post-election survey, 132 respondents reported that they had voted. Verification at the office of the County Clerk revealed that 22 of these reports were untrue. A question about prior voting activity has often been used as a rough filter to determine turnout at an election to be predicted. On almost every item that distinguished non-voters from voters, including those dealing with interest in politics, the liars differed from the honest non-voters in the direction of greater similarity to the voters. A study of the party preferences of the liars reveals that insofar as the ballots of people who lie about participation in the last election are included in a pre-election survey, the Democratic percentage will be overstated. It has been hypothesized that the liars are upper socio-economic level people for whom voting participation is recognized as a social obligation and non-voting as a violation of class standards. The lie would therefore be an effort to maintain prestige in the eyes of the interviewer. The present data do not support this hypothesis. On all indices of socio-economic status the liars were similar to the other non-voters, and consequently toward the lower end of the socio-economic scale. Although the liar is not in fact a voter and is not socially similar to the voters, it would seem that he thinks of himself as a voter. The best hypothesis about his motivation that is suggested by the present data is that he is striving for some kind of self consistency. He tends to be ego involved in politics, and the lie about voting is perhaps more nearly an ego supporting mechanism than a social response to the interviewer.

At the present time no technique for controlling untrue responses to the "Did you vote in the last election?" question can be offered. The question was included in neither the "S" nor the "CS" battery. Since the precision of these batteries is as high as it is, it is felt that this question should not be used as a turnout filter until it has been much more fully investigated.

PROBLEMS FOR FUTURE RESEARCH

It is recognized that the techniques of item selection employed in the present study have capitalized on chance variations. The extent to which this may have overstated the precision of the filter batteries should be checked in three ways. First, the same sample should be reinterviewed just before the 1952 election with the 31 items found to be significant in 1950. Second, the study should be repeated in another small political unit with a census rather than a sampling study. It would be preferable to employ a political unit with a voting record of a near 50-50 split on major party preference in order to eliminate any effects of one party being in a preferred position, as it is in Waukegan. Third, the technique should be applied in a nation-wide survey with a sample drawn according to whatever sampling method the national polling organizations have found most valuable.

Further research should also investigate the differences in turnout in presidential and non-presidential years. Probably the personalities of the candidates have a much greater effect both on turnout and on preference in a presidential year. The people who claim to have voted when they have not should be made the subject of extensive and intensive study. Specifically, it is felt that a large-scale study of these people with an ample number of subjects is much needed. In addition, a representative group of them needs to be studied by qualitative methods using open-ended questions, depth interviews, or individual clinical study. Such studies would constitute a test for the hypothesis about their motivation offered in the present study.

Index

Index

absolute government, 21-22 (*see also* totalitarianism)

academic freedom, attitudes toward, 584-598

access, to legislature, 160-176

action, resulting from opinion, 616-623 (*see also* motivation)

Adorno, T. W., 310, 312, 318, 364*n*., 707

advertising
  as propaganda, 468-469
    institutional, 478-490
  on radio, 281-282, 285-286, 478-490
  (*see also* market research)

age groups
  sampling of, 662
  voting turnout and, 758

aggressiveness, propaganda and, 498-499, 521

agitator
  in U.S.S.R., 404-413
  in United States, 470-477

Albig, William, 469*n*.

Alexander, F., 321, 336

alignment, present, in public opinion, 58-59

Allinsmith, Beverly, 151-158

Allinsmith, Wesley, 151-158

Allport, Floyd H., 51-61, 88, 600*n*.

Allport, Gordon W., 271-274, 364*n*., 366*n*., 394-404, 491*n*., 503*n*., 692*n*.

Allport-Vernon Value Test, 699

Altmark case, 492-506

American Farm Bureau Federation, 161, 162

American Institute of Public Opinion, 34*n*., 152, 742

American Jewish Committee, 34*n*.

American Legion, influence of, in legislature, 169

American Soldier, The, 718*n*., 719-728, 740

analysis
  of newspapers (*see* content analysis)
  of surveys, 666, 718-728
  (*see also* polls, public opinion)

Ann Arbor study, 532-542

antisemitism
  in German propaganda, 493, 499, 502, 504, 515, 518, 521, 549
  of German soldier, 572
  (*see also* ethnocentrism; Jews; minority groups; racial prejudice)

anxiety
  agitation and, 474
  attitude change and, 320-336
  production of, in propaganda, 520

apathy, in public opinion, 616-617

Arapesh, public opinion among, 88-89, 92

area sampling (*see* sampling)

Arensberg, Conrad M., 623*n*.

Aristotle, 30*n*., 31

Arnheim, Rudolf, 243-263

Arsenian, Seth, 296*n*.

Asch, S. E., 306, 312, 337*n*.

assimilation process, in rumor, 401-403

association
  definition of, 66-67
  in institutional advertising, 488-489

Association of Railway Executives, 163

Attitude Change Project, Yale, 508*n*.

attitudes
  of American soldier, 719-728
  changes in, 305-312, 320-336, 598-601
    education and, 435-446
    prestige and, 337-347
  definition of, 103
  formation of, 584-598

763

attitudes—*Continued*
  of German soldier, 572-573
  information and, 526-528
  measurement of, 667-668, 668-670
  in open-ended interview, 688-694, 698-
    699
  religious affiliation and, 151-158
  socioeconomic level and, 132-151
  study of, 702-710
  validating of, 739
  (*see also* opinion; public opinion)
authoritarian personality, 364, 367-380
  in army, 723
  religion and,. 588
  in urban area, 448
authoritarianism, 47
  and attitude change, 310-311
  leadership and, 706-707
  (*see also* conformity)
authority, of propaganda, 510-511

Bailey, S. K., 170, 172, 176-184
Balinese, public opinion among, 91-93
Baptists, politico-economic attitudes of,
    151-158
Barkley, Alben, 177, 178, 181
Barlow, M. F., 312
Barnett, Doris M., 446n., 702n.
Bartlett, F. C., 403, 463-470, 498-499, 528
Beaman, Middleton, 178
Beard, Charles A., 26, 67
Belknap, George, 624n.
Bendix, Reinhard, 375n.
Benoit-Smullyan, Emile, 488n.
Bentley, Madison, 684
Berelson, Bernard, 156n., 263-271, 313, 319,
    421n., 526n., 541n., 625n., 636n.,
    712-718, 742n.
Berle, A. A., 118-119
bias
  in newspapers, 105-112, 113-114
  in questionnaires, 729-738
  in radio, 113
  (*see also* ethnocentrism; prejudice; racial
    prejudice)
bigotry, 306-307
Bill of Rights, public opinion of, 41-42
Bingham, W. V., 679
Binkley, Wilfred E., 24-26
Bishop, Joseph B., 185n.
"black" propaganda, 551
Blackwood, George, 479n.
bloc, definition of, 169
Blumer, Herbert, 70-84

Bluntschli, Johann Kaspar, 50
Bolshevism (*see* communism; U.S.S.R.)
Bommaripa, Alexis, 684n.
books
  distribution of, by pressure groups, 212-
    217
  readership of, 235-236, 238, 239-242
  (*see also* bulletins; pamphlets)
Boots, Charles, 178
Borden, Neil, 478n.
Boring, E. G., 491n.
Boston, elections in, 40, 602-615
Bourne, E. G., 275n.
British Institute of Public Opinion, 232
British propaganda, *vs.* German, 491-506
broadcasting (*see* radio)
Brown, Clarence, 207, 214
Brown, Harrison, 106
Brown, J. F., 703
Bruner, Jerome S., 295n., 491-506, 602-
    615
Bruner, Katherine Frost, 491n.
Bruntz, G. G., 502n.
Bryce, James, 3-11, 50
Buchanan Committee, 206-219
Buehler, Carl, 684
bulletins, government, readership of, 237
  (*see also* books; leaflets; pamphlets)
Bureau of Applied Social Research, 106-
    112, 264, 314n., 723n.
Bureau of the Census, 741
Burgess, E. W., 100
Burke, Edmund, 466
business, economic control by, 114-126
  (*see also* corporations)

Calhoun, John C., 15-23, 26n.
campaigns
  information, 522-531
  political
    mass media of communication and,
      287-291
    municipal, 602-605
    public issues in, 623-641
  propaganda, 382-393, 499-501
  (*see also* pressure groups)
Campbell, Angus, 235-242, 287-291, 623-
    641, 641-647
Cannell, Charles F., 664-665
Cantril, Hadley, 64n., 133n., 152n., 348n.,
    488n., 493, 503n., 674n., 693n.
captive audience
  and prestige effect, 346
  propaganda and, 332

Carlson, E. R., 312
cartoons, anti-prejudice, 314-315
Cartwright, Dorwin, 226-233, 382-393
case studies, in social research, 698 (*see also* open-ended interview)
caste, definition of, 97
catharsis, 309-310
Catholics
  legislative records of, 190
  politico-economic attitudes of, 151-158
  (*see also* minority groups; religion)
cause and effect, in survey analysis, 718
censorship
  in democracy, 468
  in German propaganda, 515-516
  in mass media of communication, 42-44
  in totalitarian state, 467
Centers, Richard, 132-151, 152, 154
Chamber of Commerce, U. S., 183
Chamberlain, J. P., 177n., 181
change
  attitudes toward, 44-46
  in public opinion, propaganda and, 57-58
  (*see also* attitudes, change in; status quo)
Chapin, F. Stuart, 535n.
check lists, in questionnaires, 695-697
Chesterton, G. K., 682
Child, I. L., 491n.
Childs, H. L., 26
church (*see* religion)
Civil Rights Congress, 206, 215
Clark, K., 528
classes, social (*see* social classes; socio-economic level)
climate of opinion, 95
  in corporations, 122
  (*see also* frame of reference; reference groups)
clinical study (*see* open-ended interview)
X Cochran, John, 177, 178, 180, 181
Cochran, W. G., 655n.
Code of National Association of Broadcasters, 282-285
cognitive structure, propaganda and, 384-388, 389
collaboration, in propaganda, detection of, 712-718
colloquialism, in propaganda, 504-505, 548
combat propaganda (*see* propaganda, war)
Committee for Constitutional Government, 209-210, 212-215, 216, 217
Committee on Political Behavior, 623, 641
communication
  barriers to, 523

communication—*Continued*
  mass media of (*see* mass media of communication)
  personal, in U.S.S.R., 404-413
  (*see also* personal contact; rumor)
communism
  agitator and, 404-413
  attitudes toward, 584-598
  (*see also* totalitarianism; U.S.S.R.)
community, attitude toward, voting and, 423 (*see also* group; neighborhood)
Condon, Edward U., 105-112
conference committees, legislative, 176-184
conflict, social, 59
conformity
  in army, 723
  and attitude change, 306, 308, 312
  attitudes and, 304
  in authoritarian personality, 372-374
  prejudice and, 317
  private opinion and, 425-434
  (*see also* group membership)
Congregationalists, politico-economic attitudes of, 151-158
Congress of Industrial Organizations, 207
Congressmen (*see* legislators)
consensus, expression of, 65
consent, public opinion as, 12-14
conservatism
  education and, 436-446
  in public opinion, 44-46
  religious affiliation and, 154-157
constitutional government, 15-23
Constitutional Government, Committee for, 209-210, 212-215, 216, 217
consumers, economic control by, 129
content analysis, 106
  of Condon case, 106-112
controlled experiment, survey research and, 718-724
controls, economic, structure of, 114-131
conventions, in societal culture, 98 (*see also* morals)
Cooley, Charles Horton, 103, 556n., 557n.
Cooper, Eunice, 313-319
Corbin, Horace H., 739
corporations
  climate of opinion in, 122
  economic controls in, 118-123
  propaganda of, 478-490
correspondence, in propaganda, 702-703
Cottrell, Leonard S., Jr., 740n.
Coughlin, Charles E., 470
Cowen, Donald, 683
credibility, in propaganda, 513-514

critical thinking, 36-38
Crossley, Archibald M., 668-674, 740
Crossley, Helen M., 738-751
cross-pressures
    influence of, on attitudes, 596
    voting and, 636-637
crowd
    definition of, 62, 68
    and public, 57, 62-63
culture
    authoritarian personality and, 379-380
    definition of, 95
    group, 96, 99-101
    personal, 96, 101-102
    self, 96, 102-103
    societal, 96, 98-99
    (see also society)
Curley, James M., 602-615

Davis, A., 143
defensive propaganda, 546, 552
demigroup, 66-67
Deming, W. Edwards, 655n.
democracy
    personality structure and, 365, 368, 378
    propaganda in, 467
    public opinion in, 8-11, 26, 30-32
    public opinion of, 41
    radio and, 287
Democrats (see political parties)
denial, in war propaganda, 514-515, 545-546
dependence, feelings of, agitation and, 474
    (see also leadership)
depth interviewing, 295, 687
desertion, from army
    as social disintegration, 555-556, 557-558
    (see also propaganda, Allied; surrender)
design
    research, 662-664
    sampling, 651-657
determinants
    polling and, 675-686
    of public opinion, 94-104
    (see also motivation)
DeVinney, Leland C., 740n.
Dewey, Thomas E., 195, 198, 199, 202, 203, 204
Dicey, A. V., 51
Dickens, M. C., 600n.
Dickinson, John, 26
Dicks, Henry V., 554n.
dictatorship, public opinion and, 464 (see also Nazism; totalitarianism)

Dinerman, Helen, 742n.
direct interpretation, and attitude change, 309-310, 311-312
discipline, in German Army, 563-564, 567-570
discrimination (see Employment Act of 1946; racial prejudice)
dissolvency, in propaganda, 492-495
distortion, of samples, interviews and, 657-662
distrust, feelings of, agitation and, 474
disunification (see dissolvency)
diversionary propaganda, 522
division, in questionnaires, 679-681, 684
Dodge, Richard W., 532-542
Dollard, J., 132, 321, 333, 336, 499n.
domestic propaganda, in war propaganda, 548-549
Donovan, W., 494n.
Doob, Leonard W., 499n., 500, 508-522
Dressler-Andress, H., 492n.
drives (see campaigns)
Durr, Clifford Judkins, 278-287
dynamics, of public opinion, 26, 65-66

Ebbinghaus curve, 398
economic controls, 114-131
economic level (see socioeconomic level)
economic security, attitudes toward, 152-158
editorials, by pressure groups, 218-219 (see also newspapers)
education
    communication and, 464
    effect of, on public opinion, 5-6
    ethnocentrism and, 376
    political party membership and, 632-636, 638-639
    politico-economic attitudes and, 154-156
    prejudice and, 146-149, 151
    pressure groups and, 218
    propaganda and, 464-465, 467, 469-470
    reading and, 289
    of soldier, attitudes and, 724-728
    television viewing and, 289-291
    use of mass media of communication and, 235-240
    validating of, 740
effectiveness, of public opinion, 60-61, 73
ego defense
    and attitude change, 309-310
    in attitude formation, 306-307, 309
ego-involvement, in institutional advertising, 488

Ehle, Emily L., 446-459, 702n., 704
Eldersveld, Samuel J., 532-542
elections, 194-197
   mass media of communication and, 287-291
   municipal, 602-615
   polls and, 413-425, 606
   pressure groups and, 219
   (see also political behavior; voting)
Elmira election study, 413-425
embedding process, in rumor, 403-404
emergent theory of public opinion, 53-55
Employment Act of 1946, 170, 172, 176-184
England (see Great Britain)
envy, attitudes of, 143-145
Episcopalians, politico-economic attitudes of, 151-158
equality, public opinion of, 42 (see also democracy; minority groups; racial prejudice)
errors, in sampling, 652 (see also distortion)
ethics, of German soldier, 571-573 (see also morals)
ethnocentrism, 368
   and social status, 373-374
   and socioeconomic level, 375-377
   (see also authoritarianism; bias; racial prejudice)
ethnology, social sciences and, 87-88
eulogistic theory of public opinion, 53-55
Europe, public opinion in, 5, 6-7 (see also foreign affairs; Germany; Great Britain; U.S.S.R.)
evasion, of propaganda, 313-319
exploratory research, field surveys as, 662-664
expression, of public opinion, 73

face-to-face contact (see personal contact; primary group)
Fact Finders Associates, Inc., 264
falsehood, in war propaganda, 514, 545-546
family
   German soldier and, 561-562
   voting behavior and, 417-419
   (see also primary groups)
Farm Bureau, 161, 162, 163
farm organizations, economic control by, 128-129
fascism, agitator and, 471 (see also dictatorship; Nazism; totalitarianism)
fatalism, in propaganda, 495

fear
   agitator and, 470
   attitude change and, 320-336
   in authoritarian personality, 369
   German propaganda and, 520
   group solidarity and, 562-563
Federal Communications Commission, 278, 280
Federal Council of the Churches of Christ in America, 152n.
Fenichel, Otto, 321, 336, 369
Feshbach, Seymour, 320-336
Festinger, L., 662-664
Field, Marshall, 276n.
fifth column, and propaganda, 494-495
Fisher, R. A., 652n.
Flynn, John T., 213
folkways, in group culture, 99-101
Folsom, Joseph K., 103
Ford, Henry Jones, 28n.
foreign affairs, public opinion and, 35-36
foreign aid, attitudes toward, 46-47
foreign policy, of democracies, 31
foreigners, public opinion of, 42
Form, William H., 132
Foundation for Economic Education, 215-216, 217, 218
frame of reference
   and attitude change, 308
   group membership and, 588
   perception and, 594-596
   prejudice and, 316
   (see also climate of opinion; reference group)
Francis, Dale, 190n.
franking privilege, use of, 210-211
freedom
   academic, attitudes toward, 584-598
   of the press, 275-277 (see also newspapers)
   of speech
      public opinion of, 41, 42-44
      and radio stations, 278-287
French, T. M., 321, 336, 499n.
Frenkel-Brunswik, Else, 310, 312, 363-380, 707
Freud, Sigmund, 366-367, 377, 557n.
Friedman, Stanley, 413n.
Fromm, Erich, 364, 380, 706
frustration
   agitator and, 476-477
   reduction of, in propaganda, 520-521
Full Employment Bill (see Employment Act of 1946)

functionalism, in institutional advertising, 478-484

Galloway, George, 176n.
Gallup Poll, 34n., 43, 45, 228-229, 668-674
Garceau, Oliver, 623n.
Gardner, B. B., 143
Gardner, M. R., 143
Gaudet, Hazel, 156n., 313, 319, 421n., 526n., 541n., 625n., 636n., 693n., 742n.
general interest group, 68-69
genetic groundwork responses, in public opinion, 58-59
geographic location, polling methods and, 651-655, 658 (see also sampling)
German Army
    Allied propaganda and, 543-553, 578-582
    social organization of, 553-582
German propaganda, 491-506
    Italian and, 712-718
Germany, propaganda in, 508-522
Gibson, J. J., 403
Giddings, Franklin H., 25
Gillam, William S., 742n.
Gladstone, Arthur I., 347-362
Gleeck, L. E., 189-190
Gleicher, David B., 413-425
Glock, Charles Y., 105-112
Goebbels, Josef, 469n., 508-522, 545
Gold, Bill, 691n.
Gorden, Raymond L., 425-434
Gosnell, Harold F., 532, 534n., 541, 542, 607, 693n.
government
    absolute, 21-22
    attitudes toward, 40-41
    constitutional, 15-23
    control by, 129-131
        economic, 114-116, 117, 129-131
    public opinion and, 7-14
    in U.S.S.R., 404-413
    (see also democracy; legislature; totalitarianism)
Grandin, T., 498n.
"grass-roots" pressure, 211-219
gratification, open-ended interview and, 691
Gray, John B., 113
Grazia, Alfred de, 623n.
Grazia, Sebastian de, 712-718
Great Britain
    attitudes toward, 529-530
    propaganda from, 491-506
    public opinion polling in, 232

Grinker, R. R., 557n.
Gross, Bertram, 178, 179, 180, 181
group
    in American culture, 95
    assimilation by, 435-446
    character of, in democracy, 29-32
    communication and, 463
    definition of, 66-67, 97-98
    influence of, on individual, 427-434
    interest, 68-69
    pressure (see lobbying; pressure group)
    (see also crowd; groups; primary group; public; social organization)
group culture, 96, 99-101
group membership
    attitudes and, 585-598
    behavior patterns and, 435-446
    in German Army, 558-563
    private opinion and, 427-434
    (see also conformity)
group mind, 51-52
group opinion, 67 (see also public opinion)
group solidarity, in German Army, 558-563
    (see also conformity)
group thinking, 53-55
groups, 62-63
    leadership in, 446-459
    minority (see minority groups)
    participation in, 39
    in primitive societies, 88, 89-91
    propaganda for, 502-503
    public opinion and, 26
    in society, 72
guilt, feelings of, propaganda and, 494
Gurfein, M. I., 573n.
Gurin, Gerald, 287-291, 623-641, 641-647
Guterman, Norbert, 470-477
Guttman, Louis, 729-738

Halleck, Charles, 211-212
Hamilton, Alexander, 28, 275
Hanfmann, Eugenia, 321, 336
Hansen, Morris H., 651-657, 655n.
"hard core," in German Army, 558-559
Harding, J. S., 348n., 609, 611, 614
Hart, Albert Bushnell, 27n.
Hart, Clyde, 81
Hartmann, George W., 541n.
Harvard Laboratory of Social Relations. 295n.
Hauser, Philip M., 651-657
Hechler, Kenneth W., 185n.
Herring, E. P., 170
Herz, Martin F., 543-553

Herzog, Herta, 691n., 693n.
Hilgard, Ernest R., 657-662
Hitler, Adolf, 492-493, 496n., 500, 505, 510, 515, 547, 548, 549
  attitude of German soldier toward, 573-575
Hobbes, Thomas, 29
Hoffer, Charles R., 741n.
Hoffman, Clare, 177, 178, 181, 183
Holmes, Oliver Wendell, 160, 212
"honor," of German Army, 563-567
Horkheimer, M., 318, 319
Horst, Paul, 698n.
hostility, feelings of, rumor and, 395
House of Representatives (see legislature)
Hovland, Carl I., 320n., 336, 337-347, 348, 353, 354
humanitarianism, 46-47
humanization, in institutional advertising, 484-486
Hume, David, 50-51
Hurwitz, William N., 655n., 656n.
Hyman, Herbert H., 33-48, 522-531, 665-674, 740
hypothesis-testing, field surveys as, 662-664

Iatmul, public opinion among, 89-91, 92-93
identification, in institutional advertising, 488
ideology, in combat propaganda, 547-549
idiom, in propaganda, 548 (see also colloquialism)
impersonality, in institutional advertising, 486
income, voting turnout and, 757 (see also socioeconomic level)
individual
  feelings of futility in, 39
  society and, 474-475
  (see also personality)
individualism, religious affiliation and, 151-158
induction of behavior (see persuasion; propaganda)
influences, on opinions, 690, 697 (see also attitudes; pressure groups)
information
  campaigns of, 522-531
  intensity of opinion and, 300
  public opinion and, 36-37
  sources of, 241-242
  voting turnout and, 758
  (see also communication; persuasion; propaganda)

Inkeles, Alex, 404-413
Institute of Child Welfare, 367n.
Institute of Human Relations, 347n.
Institute of Public Opinion, 651
Institute for Research in Human Relations, 446, 702n.
institutional advertising, 478-490
intellectual traits, in institutional advertising, 485-486
intensity, of opinion, 60-61
  information and, 300
  measurement of, 81, 729-738
  minorities and, 67-68
  open-ended interview and, 691
intensity technique, in questionnaires, 729-738
interest, in public affairs, 35-36, 523-526 (see also intensity)
interest group, 68-69 (see also pressure group)
interference, of preparatory propaganda, 350, 358-362
internationalism
  agitation against, 473
  polls on, 229-230
  (see also foreign affairs; isolation; isolationism)
interpretation, in survey analysis, 724-727
interview, 687-701
  depth, 687
  obtaining of, 657-662
  open-ended, 687-701
  projective devices in, 702-710
  validating of, 738-751
  (see also personal contact; polls; questionnaire)
interview schedule (see questionnaire)
interviewers, 665
  attitudes of, 48
  selection of, 744
  training of, 685, 744-745
interviewing, techniques of, 679-681, 685
invalidity (see validity)
isolation
  democracy and, 29-32
  individual, 378
isolationism, 35 (see also internationalism)
Italian propaganda, German and, 712-718

Jaensch, E. R., 372
Jahoda, Marie, 313-319
James case, 113-114

Janis, Irving L., 320-336, 347-362, 740n.
Janowitz, Morris, 553-582
Jefferson, Thomas, 28, 30-32
Jenkins, John G., 683n., 739
Jews
  politico-economic attitudes of, 151-158
  public opinion of, 145-150
  (see also antisemitism; ethnocentrism;
      minority groups; racial prejudice)
Johnson, Claudius O., 185n.
journalist, formation of opinion by, 6-7 (see
    also newspapers)

Kahn, Robert L., 624n., 664-665
Kane, Harnett, 613n.
Kaplan, Abraham, 66-69
Kaplan, Norman, 413n.
Kardiner, Abram, 364
Katz, Daniel, 305-312, 348n., 523n., 662-
    664
Katz, Elihu, 413n.
Kefauver, Estes, 220-226
Kefauver Hearings, 616-622
Keller, A. G., 275n.
Kendall, Patricia L., 718-728
Key, V. O., 623n.
Kile, O. M., 163
Kinsey, Alfred C., 741
Kinsey Report, 43, 741, 743
Kitt, Alice S., 413-425
Klapper, Joseph T., 105-112
Klineberg, Otto, 145-147
Kluckhohn, Clyde, 364
"know-nothings," in public information,
    523-524
Koischwitz, Otto, 503, 504
Komarvosky, Mirra, 693n.
Korchin, Barney, 446n., 702n.
Korchin, Sheldon J., 602-615
Kornhauser, A. W., 143

labeling, in rumor, 400
labor organizations
  economic control by, 117, 126-128
  lobbying and, 207
  radio broadcasts by, 282-283
  (see also socioeconomic level; union af-
      filiation
La Guardia, Fiorello, 195, 197, 199
Laird, Donald, 682
La Piere, Richard T., 739
Lasswell, Harold D., 65n., 66-69, 364
latent consequences (see functionalism)

Lauritsen, Charles, 106
laws, public opinion and, 14 (see also legis-
    lature)
Lazarsfeld, P. F., 156n., 243n., 263n., 313,
    319, 413n., 421n., 526n., 532n., 541,
    624, 625n., 636n., 675-686, 687-701,
    718-728, 742n.
leader (see legislator; politician)
leadership
  attitudes toward, measurement of, 702-710
  in German Army, 567-570
  governmental, polls and, 227-228, 231,
      233
  measurement of, 82
  political, 39-41
    attitudes toward, 621-623
    social impotence and, 621-623
    in urban areas, 607, 611-612
  propaganda and, 494
  in society, 72-73
  in U.S.S.R., 406
  in urban areas, 446-459, 607, 611-612
leaflets, propaganda, Allied, 543-553, 579-
    581 (see also bulletins; pamphlets)
Lee, Alfred McClung, 94-104, 275-277
legislators
  interpersonal relationships of, 173-174
  letters to, 220-226
  lobbying and, 206-211
  pressure groups and, 166-172, 185-194,
      227
legislature
  access to, 160-176
  pressure groups and, 160-176, 177
  processes of, 176-184
  social structure of, 172-174
Leiserson, Avery, 623n.
Lerner, Max, 100
letters, to congressmen, 220-226 (see also
    mail)
leveling process, in rumor, 398-399
Levin, Jack, 220n.
Levine, J. M., 528n.
Levinson, D. J., 310, 312, 364n., 374n.,
    707
Lewin, Kurt, 500, 691n.
Lewis, H. B., 337n.
liberalism, religious affiliation and, 154-157
    (see also conservatism)
libraries, use of, 235, 240-242
Likert, Rensis, 658n., 686n., 691
Lindsay, A. D., 557n.
Link, Henry C., 687n., 695n., 698n.
Linton, Ralph, 364, 373n.
Lippmann, Walter, 27-32, 493

Lipset, S. M., 584-598
lobbying, 206-219 (*see also* pressure groups)
Lobbying Act, 212-219
local politics (*see* urban areas)
Lochner, Louis P., 508
Logan, E. B., 26*n*.
Lopez, Betty, 296*n*.
Lowell, A. Lawrence, 11-14, 27*n*.
Lowenthal, Leo, 318, 319, 470-477
lower class
  political behavior of, 606-607
  public opinions of, 5-6
  (*see also* social classes; socioeconomic
    level)
loyalty oath, attitudes toward, 584-598
Lucas, Darrell B., 740
Lumsdaine, Arthur A., 336, 337, 338,
  341*n*., 342, 345, 347-362, 740*n*.
Lumsdaine, Marion Harper, 740*n*.
Lunt, Paul S., 97, 132, 143
Lutherans, politico-economic attitudes of,
  151-158
Lynd, Helen M., 132-133, 482*n*., 483
Lynd, Robert S., 132-133, 136, 482*n*., 483

McCormick, Robert R., 276
McCown, Ada C., 176
McDougall, W., 611
Machiavelli, Niccolo di Bernardo, 29-30, 50,
  100
machine politics, 194-205 (*see also* Boston,
  elections in)
MacIver, R. M., 26*n*.
McKean, Dayton D., 167
McLean, Philip T., 508*n*.
Madison, James, 168
Magazine Audience Group, 739-740
magazines
  readership of, 236-237, 239-242, 739-740
  as substitute for newspaper, 268
  use of by pressure groups, 218-219
  (*see also* mass media of communication;
    newspapers; pamphlets)
Mahalanobis, P. C., 655*n*.
mail, use of in political propaganda, 535-
  541 (*see also* letters; pamphlets)
mail campaigns, 221-224
majority, numerical, *vs.* constitutional, 18-23
majority government (*see* democracy)
majority opinion, *vs.* public opinion, 12-13
malaise, in modern society, 474-477
management, business, economic control by,
  116-117, 120-121
Manasco, Carter, 172, 177, 178, 181

Mannon, Virginia M., 185*n*.
maps, use of, in area sampling, 655
marginal man, in propaganda, 546
marginality (*see* social marginality)
Margolies, B., 528
market controls, 115
market research
  questionnaires in, 675-686
  sampling in, 652
  (*see also* polls, public opinion; surveys)
Martin, Clyde E., 741*n*.
Maslow, A. H., 706
mass media of communication, 235-242
  censorship in, 42-44
  effectiveness of
    and source credibility, 337-347
    in warfare, 581-582
  in German Army, 577
  in Germany, 512-513
  information programs in, 522-530
  persuasion in, 382-393
  pressure groups and, 212-219
  propaganda in, 313-319
    political, 534, 535-542
    preparatory, 347-362
  public opinion in, 55
  responsibilities of, 105-106
  social groups and, 463-464
  trust in, propaganda and, 493
  (*see also* franking privilege; magazines;
    newspapers; radio; television)
masses (*see* lower class)
Mayo, Elton, 557*n*.
Mead, George H., 103
Mead, Margaret, 87-94, 364
Means, G. C., 118-119
media of communication, mass (*see* mass
  media of communication)
membership, group (*see* group membership)
Merton, Robert K., 313, 319, 478*n*., 689*n*.,
  718*n*.
Methodists, politico-economic attitudes of,
  151-158
Metraux, Rhoda, 693*n*.
Metzner, Charles A., 235-242
Meyer, Allen, 413*n*.
middle class, public opinions of, 6 (*see also*
  social classes; socioeconomic level)
middle-class morality, 613
Mill, John Stuart, 50
Miller, Mungo, 751-760
Miller, N. E., 321, 333, 336
Miller, Warren E., 287-291, 623-641, 641-
  647

Millspaugh, Martin, 113-114
minorities
  public opinion and, 12-14, 52
  in representative governments, 10-11
minority groups
  intensity of opinions in, 67-68
  leadership in, 453-455
  political behavior of, 607-611
  (see also ethnocentrism; Jews; Negroes;
    racial prejudice)
mob, definition of, 68
mobility, social (see social mobility)
monarchies, public opinion in, 7-8
monopoly
  institutional advertising and, 486-487
  in newspaper publishing, 275-277
Moore, Carroll S., Jr., 679, 743
Moos, Malcolm C., 24-26
morale
  propaganda and, 521-522
  of soldier, 719-720
  (see also group solidarity)
morals
  vs. mores, 98-99, 100
  in societal culture, 98-99
  (see also religion)
mores
  in group culture, 99-101
  vs. morals, 98-99, 100
Morrow, W. R., 373n.
Morse, Philip M., 106
Moscow, Warren, 194-205
Mosteller, F., 348n., 665n.
motion picture, in Germany, 513
motion-picture audience, composition of,
    237-238, 240-241
motivation
  and attitude change, 305-312, 320-336
  in mass persuasion, 382-393
  measurement of, 667-668
  objective interview and, 699-700
  open-ended interview and, 692-693
  in public information, 525-526
  questionnaires and, 685-686
  (see also determinants)
Mowrer, E., 494n.
Mowrer, O. H., 333, 336
municipal elections, 194-205, 602-615
Murdock, G. P., 275n.
Murphy, Gardner, 102, 528
Murphy, Lois B., 102
Murray, H. E., 368n.

Nadel, S. F., 528
National Association of Broadcasters, 282-
    285
National Association of Manufacturers, 209
  influence of, in legislature, 161
National Association of Real Estate Boards,
    207-209, 215, 216-217, 218
National Association of Retail Druggists,
    161, 163, 169
National Economic Council, 217
National Farmers Union, 172, 183
National Opinion Research Center, 34n.,
    81, 523, 525, 528, 529, 605
National Research Council, 691
National Retail Lumber Dealers Associa-
    tion, 219
National Rivers and Harbors Congress, 169
nationality (see ethnocentrism; minority
    groups; racial prejudice)
Natural Resources Committee, 114-131
Nazism
  authoritarian personality and, 372, 375-
    376, 378, 379
  influence of, in German Army, 556, 558-
    559, 566, 572, 575
  (see also fascism; German propaganda;
    Goebbels; totalitarianism)
negativism, in propaganda, 495-499
Negroes
  in army, 720-721
  attitudes toward, 306-312
  public opinion of, 145-150
  voting behavior of, 641
  (see also ethnocentrism; minority groups;
    racial prejudice)
neighborhoods, leadership in, 446-459 (see
    also community)
Nelson, Herbert U., 208, 209
Newcomb, Theodore M., 78-81, 102, 312,
    435-446
newspapers
  bias in, 113-114
  censorship of, 42-44
  circulation of, 272-274
  content analysis of, 106-112
  formation of opinion and, 3-4
  freedom of, 275-277
  German propaganda and, 499
  in Germany, 512
  headlines of, 271-274
  influence of, on attitudes, 588-590
  readership of, 236, 239, 241
  role of
    in public information, 265-266
    for reader, 236, 263-271
  use of
    in political propaganda, 534, 538-541
    by pressure groups, 218-219

Neyman, J., 652n., 655n.
nonmarket controls, 115

objective questions, in interviews, 695-697
occupational level
  attitudes and, 132-151, 152
  ethnocentrism and, 375-377
  political party membership and, 632-636, 638-639
  voting turnout and, 757
  (see also socioeconomic level)
Office of Public Opinion Research, 33, 152
Older, Harry J., 702n., 707n.
omission, in institutional advertising, 489-490
open-ended interview, 687-701
opinion
  formation of, 584-598
  private (see private opinion)
  public (see public opinion)
  questionnaires and, 688-689
  (see also attitudes)
Opinion Research Center, University of Denver, 743
optimism, in newspapers, 271-274
organizations (see groups)
overcompensation, and propaganda, 350, 358

Palyi, Melchior, 213
pamphlets
  distribution of
    to legislators, 224
    by pressure groups, 212-217
  use of, in political propaganda, 535-541
  (see also bulletins; leaflets; letters)
panel techniques, in survey analysis, 722-723
Park, Robert E., 68, 100
Parry, Hugh J., 738-751
Parsons, T., 363, 373n.
Patterson, John N., 446n., 702n.
Pauley, Edwin, 180
Payne, Stanley L., 657-662
Peak, H., 309
Pearlin, Leonard I., 478-490
Peel, Robert, 7
Pegram, George B., 106
perception, of situation, 594-596 (see also attitudes)
permissive catharsis, 309-310
personal contact
  in elections, 607
  in political propaganda, 533, 535-542
  in selling, 392-393
  (see also interviews; primary group)

personal opinions, 102 (see also individual; private opinion)
personality
  attitudes and, 443-445
  authoritarian (see authoritarian personality)
  conformity and, 431-434
  culture and, 101-102
  of German soldier, 556-575, 582
  opinions and, 301-305
  political leadership and, 611-612, 615
  prejudice and, 317-319
  social behavior and, 363-380
  (see also individual)
personality traits, in institutional advertising, 484-485
persuasion, 382-393
  in attitude change, 309, 310-312
  (see also propaganda)
petitions, 221-222
Pfeiler, William K., 556n.
political behavior, 623-641
  of German soldier, 572-573
  in municipal election, 602-615
  personality and, 363-380
  propaganda and, 532-542
  questionnaires on, 665-674
  (see also elections; voting; voting behavior)
Political Behavior Project, 532n.
political campaign (see campaign, political)
political candidates, attitudes toward, 642-647
political leadership (see leadership, political)
political parties
  access to government by, 162-163
  choice of, 609-611
  conflicts in, 187-191
  ethnocentrism and, 374
  influence of, on voting, 414-415
  legislators and, 185-194
  legislature and, 183
  machine politics and, 194-205
  membership of, 624-625, 641-647
  propaganda and, 468
  public opinion of, 37-38
  as reference groups, 620-621
  strength of, 184
  voting turnout and, 758-759
  (see also democracy; politics)
political research
  prediction in 751-760
  validation of, 742-743, 745
  (see also polls, public opinion)
political science, 27-28
  concept of public opinion in, 64

politicians
  attitudes toward, 613-614
  as community leaders, 450, 456-458
  formation of opinion by, 6-7
  in municipal election, 602-615
  (see also legislators; machine politics)
politico-economic attitude, religious affiliation and, 151-158
politics
  attitudes toward, 39-41
  machine, 194-205
  study of public opinion and, 64
  (see also elections; political parties; voting)
polling organizations (see specific organization)
polls, public opinion, 33-35, 71-84
  analysis of, 666, 718-728
  assessment of, 75-76
  democracy and, 226-233
  drawbacks of, 230
  government and, 227
  individual attitudes and, 295-305
  interpretation of, 296-305
  interviewing and, 661
  methods of, 264, 605-606
    sampling and, 651-657, 657-662
  political behavior and, 605-615, 751-760
  on public affairs, 523-526, 530
  questionnaires for, 664-665, 665-674, 675-686
  sample design for, 651-657
  social organization and, 104
  "telegraphic," 668
  wording of, 229, 729-738
  (see also interviews; market research; questionnaires; surveys)
Pomeroy, Wardell B., 741n.
Postman, Leo J., 394-404
poverty, views on, 140, 141
predisposition, attitude formation and, 585-588
prejudice
  institutional advertising and, 490
  propaganda and, 313-319
  (see also antisemitism; bias; ethnocentrism; racial prejudice)
preparatory communications, 347-362
preparatory propaganda, 347-362, 501
Presbyterians, politico-economic attitudes of, 151-158
Prescott, Frank, 225
present alignment, in public opinion, 58-59
press (see newspapers)
pressure groups, 26, 59

pressure groups—Continued
  agricultural, 161, 163
  communications from, 221-224
  democracy and, 227
  in formation of opinion, 65
  Full Employment Bill and, 176-184
  legislator and, 185-194
  legislature and, 160-176
  polls and, 82
  (see also lobbying; propaganda)
prestige
  influence of, 337-347
  in propaganda, 503, 517
primary group
  in German Army, 554, 556-563, 567, 581-582
  influence of, on attitudes, 592-594
  (see also family; reference group)
primitive societies, public opinion in, 87-94
Princeton Listening Center, 491n., 492n.
"private attitude," 56-57
private opinion, and public opinion, 425-434
  (see also individual; personal opinion)
problem-solving
  in public affairs, 616-623
  in radio serials, 247-253
profit motive, institutional advertising and, 487
progress, in government, polling and, 231-233
projective devices, 701-710
projective tests, 700
propaganda
  Allied, 543-553, 554, 576-582
  analysis of, 491-506
  attitude toward, 337
  "black," 516-517, 551
  British, 491-506
  collaboration in, detection of, 712-718
  defensive, 546
  delayed effect of, 600-601
  dissolvent, 492-495
  diversionary, 522
  and education, 464-465
  ego defense and, 307
  fear-arousing, 320-336
  German, 491-506, 508-522, 712-718
    in German Army, 576-578
  Goebbels' principles of, 508-522
  in institutional advertising, 478-490
  Italian, 712-718
  morals and, 98
  overcompensation against, 350
  political, 463-470, 604-605

propaganda—*Continued*
and prejudice, 313-319
preparatory, 501
public and, 63
public-opinion changes and, 57-58
✓—in totalitarian state, 66
war, 508-522, 543-553, 576-582
(*see also* persuasion; pressure group)
Protestants, politico-economic attitudes of, 151-158
psychoanalysis, and personality study, 365-367, 374 (*see also* psychology; psychotherapy)
psychological measures, in polls, 666-667
psychological warfare (*see* propaganda, war)
psychology, and social behavior, 363-374
psychotherapy, and attitude change, 309-310
public
conceptions of, 52-53
crowd and, 57, 62-63
definition of, 62-63
knowledge of, 228-231
public affairs, interest in, 523-526
of college students, 435-443
"public attitude," 56
public office (*see* legislators; political leadership; politicians)
public issues, voting behavior and, 623-641, 642-644
public opinion
characteristics of, 55-61, 71-74
conceptions of, 51-55
as group mind, 51-52
as product, 53-55
criteria of, 55-61
definition of, 50-51, 63, 68
government and, 3-11, 11-14
in group culture, 99-101
groups and, 67-68
information campaigns and, 522-531
knowledge and, 36-37
manipulation of, 598-601
in lobbying, 211, 217-219
(*see also* pressure groups; propaganda)
personal opinion and, 102
preparatory communications and, 347-362
in primitive societies, 87-94
private opinion and, 425-434
in societal culture, 98-99
in totalitarian state, 66
(*see also* attitudes; opinion)
Public Opinion Laboratory, Washington, 742
Public Opinion Research, Office of, 33, 152

public opinion surveys (*see* polls, public opinion; surveys)

questionnaire
design of, 665-674
formulation of, 675-686
objective, 695-697
purpose of, 664-665
rating scale in, 698-699
subjective, 687-701
wording of, 679-681, 729-738
(*see also* interviews; polls, public opinion)
"quota" method, of sampling, 652, 656-657, 658-660

racial prejudice, 145-151
agitator and, 470-477
in army, 720-721
in public opinion, 58
in rumor, 395-396, 402-403
(*see also* antisemitism; ethnocentrism; Jews; minority groups; Negroes)
radio
bias in, 113
censorship of, 42-43
FM, 286-287
foreign news on, 36
freedom of speech and, 278-287
in Germany, 513
institutional advertising on, 478-490
propaganda and, 313
German short-wave, 491-506
political, 534, 538-541
public opinion of, 232
radio audience, 237
composition of, 237, 239, 240-241
for daytime serials, 243
surveying of, 660-661
radio serials, 243-263, 285-286
radio stations, control of, 278-282
rating scale, in questionnaire, 698-699
rationality, attitudes and, 305-307, 308
rationalization, political leadership and, 613
Read, Leonard, 215-216, 219
readership (*see* mass media of communication)
reading, attitudes toward, 268-269, 270-271
Real Estate Boards, National Association of, 207-209, 215, 216-217, 218
reference group, 616-617
influence of, on attitudes, 592-594
in public affairs, 620-623
(*see also* frame of reference; primary group)

reformer, agitator vs., 470-471
Reid, Ira DeA., 446-459
reliability
  of projective device, 705-706
  in sampling, 652, 656-657
religion
  in American culture, 95-96
  attitudes and, 587-588
  in institutional advertising, 489
  leadership and, 453, 455
  political party membership and, 632-636, 638-640
  social disorganization and, 476-477
  views on, 135-136
  voting turnout and, 758
religious affiliation, attitude and, 151-158
repetition, in propaganda, 505, 518
representative government, public opinion
  in, 8-11 (see also democracy)
Republicans (see political parties)
research
  field studies in, 662-664
  market (see market research)
  public opinion (see polls, public opinion; surveys)
  questionnaire and, 664-665
  use of students in, 542
Research Branch, War Department, 719-728, 740
resistance
  in attitude change, 306-307, 309
  and prestige, 347
  in psychotherapy, 321, 332
  (see also evasion)
Response Research Unit, Bureau of the
  Census, 741
Retail Druggists, National Association of,
  161, 163, 169
retrospective questions, in survey, 723-724
reward and punishment, in attitude formation, 306-307
Rice, Stuart, 190
Riecken, Henry, 296n.
rigidity, of attitude, measurement of, 668-669
Rivers and Harbors Congress, National, 169
Robinson, W., 698n.
Roosevelt, Franklin D., 196, 198, 200, 203, 204, 205
Roper, Elmo, 34n., 264, 668-673
Rosenberg, Morris J., 312, 478-490
Rosenstock, Irwin M., 702n.
Rosenzweig, S., 303n., 703
Rousseau, Jean-Jacques, 11-12

Rugg, D., 348n.
Rumely, E. A., 210-211, 213-214, 216, 217
rumor, psychology of, 394-404
Russia (see U.S.S.R.)

Sait, E. M., 64n.
sampling, 79-80
  area, 652-657
  costs of, 655-657
  faults of, 74-75, 77-78, 79
  principles of, 651-657
  quota method of, 652, 656-657
  use of, 77
sampling survey (see polls, public opinion)
Samuel, W., 700n.
Sandusky voting study, 421
Sanford, Fillmore H., 446n., 701-710
Sanford, R. Nevitt, 310, 312, 364n., 588
Sarnoff, Irving, 305-312
Sayre, J., 603n.
scale, rating, in questionnaire, 698-699
scale analysis, in questionnaires, 730-738
Schanck, Richard L., 56, 598-601
Schneider, David, 296n.
Schramm, Wilbur, 490n.
Schreiber, Carl F., 508n.
security, economic, attitudes toward, 152-158
self-feelings, culture and, 102-103 (see also
  ego defense; personality)
Senate (see legislature)
sentiments, 103
  mores and, 102
sexuality, in authoritarian personality, 370-371
sharpening process, of rumor, 399-401
Sheatsley, Paul B., 33-48, 522-531
Sheffield, F. D., 336, 337, 338, 341n., 342, 345, 348, 353, 354
Sherif, M., 337n., 488n.
Shils, Edward A., 553-582
Simmons, Leo W., 102
Skott, Hans E., 687n.
sleeper effect, 338, 342-347
slogans, in propaganda, 518-519
Smith, E., 697n.
Smith, George Horsley, 156n.
Smith, Gerald L. K., 470
Smith, J. Sayre, 603n.
Smith, M. Brewster, 295-305, 623n., 740n.
Smith, T. V., 24n.
soap opera, 243-263, 285-286
social approval (see conformity)

social change
  agitator and, 472
  authoritarian personality and, 379-380
social classes
  definition of, 97
  ethnocentrism and, 374-377
  opinions of, 4-6
  public identification with, 45
  in radio serials, 245-247
  (*see also* lower class; middle class; social
    mobility; socioeconomic level; upper
    class
social determinants (*see* determinants; mo-
    tivation)
social disintegration, in German Army, 555
social disorganization, agitator and, 476-477
  (*see also* dissolvency)
social distance, 99
social environment, voting behavior and,
    416
social impotence, 621-623
"social lobby," 170-171, 210
social marginality, authoritarian personality
    and, 376-377, 378
social mobility, views on, 140-143
social organization
  authoritarian personality in, 379
  of German Army, 554
  propaganda and, 465-467
  in urban areas, 446-459
social problems, polls and, 231-233
social reality, agitator and, 475
Social Science Research Council, 623, 729,
    735
social status, ethnocentrism and, 373-374
society
  culture in, 96, 98-99
  primitive, public opinion in, 87-94
  public opinion and, 71-73
  structure of, and personality, 363-367,
    379-380
socioeconomic level
  attitudes and, 132, 590-591, 592-593
    politico-economic, 152-158
  ethnocentrism and, 375-377
  leadership and, 446-459
  political party membership and, 624-625,
    632-637, 638-640
  voting turnout and, 757, 760
sophistication effect, of preparatory propa-
    ganda, 351, 358
Soviet Russia (*see* U.S.S.R.)
special interest group, 68-69 (*see also* pres-
    sure groups)

specialization, in social organization, 466-
    467
specification
  in questionnaires, 675-679, 684
  in survey analysis, 727-728
speeches, 237 (*see also* personal contact)
Speier, Hans, 508
Spiegel, J. P., 557*n.*
Spranger, E., 503
spurious factors, in survey analysis, 719-721
stability
  in public opinion, 57-58
  in social organization, 466
Stanton, Frank N., 243*n.*, 263*n.*, 532*n.*
Star, Shirley A., 740*n.*
state, definition of, 25-26 (*see also* govern-
    ment)
statesman, 6-7 (*see also* legislator)
status, social (*see* social status)
status contagion, in institutional advertising,
    488-489
status quo, agitator and, 471
stereotypy, in authoritarian personality, 371
Stock, J. Stevens, 348*n.*, 658*n.*, 662*n.*
Stouffer, S. A., 724*n.*, 740*n.*
Strauss, Ulrich, 50-51
Studenski, Paul, 695
success, views on, 136-137, 138
Suchman, Edward A., 697*n.*, 729-738, 740*n.*
suffrage, 17-18 (*see also* voting)
Sumner, William Graham, 100, 275*n.*
superstition, in authoritarian personality,
    369
surrender
  attitude toward, of German Army, 564-
    567
  propaganda and, 579
  (*see also* desertion)
Survey of Consumer Requirements, 658, 661
Survey Research Center, 81, 239*n.*, 623,
    629, 630*n.*, 641, 742
surveys
  market
    questionnaires in, 675-686
    sampling in, 652
  public opinion, 33-35
    analysis of, 718-728
    (*see also* polls, public opinion)
Symonds, P., 700*n.*

tacit assumption, in questionnaires, 681-684
Taft, Robert A., 177, 178, 180, 181
Taft-Hartley Labor Relations Act, 24
Tammany Hall, 194-200

taxes, public attitude toward, 229, 231
Taylor, Edmond, 494*n.*, 495
technological progress, views on, 135-137
"telegraphic" survey, 668
television
    effect of, 616-623
    political campaigns and, 287-291
    public information and, 542
    (*see also* mass media)
Thimme, H., 502*n.*
Thomas, W. I., 594
threats, in propaganda, 552
time sequence, in survey analysis, 721-722, 723
timing, of propaganda, 517-518
Tobey, Charles, 177, 178, 180, 181
Tobin, Maurice, 602
Tonnelat, E., 502*n.*
totalitarianism
    personality structure and, 365, 368-369, 378
    propaganda and, 464-468
    public opinion and, 66
    (*see also* communism; Nazism; U.S.S.R.)
trade associations, economic control by, 124-126
trends, political, measurement of, 674 (*see also* political behavior)
"trial by newspaper," 105-112
Truman, David B., 160-176, 623*n.*
Truman, Harry S., 177, 181, 182, 183
truth, suppression of, in war propaganda, 513-514, 543-544
Turner, Julius, 185-194

union affiliation
    political party membership and, 632-636, 638-639
    voting behavior and, 420-421
    voting turnout and, 757
    (*see also* labor organizations; occupational level)
Union of Soviet Socialist Republics
    attitudes toward, 295-305, 528
        in Germany, 570
    personal oral agitation in, 404-413
    war propaganda of, 547-548
    (*see also* communism; totalitarianism)
United Nations Educational, Scientific and Cultural Organization, 522-523
U.S. Chamber of Commerce, 183
universality, of public opinion, 55, 56
upper class, public opinions of, 5-6 (*see also* social classes; socioeconomic level)

urban areas
    leadership in, 446-459
    politics in, 194-205, 602-615
Urey, Harold C., 106
U.S.S.R. (*see* Union of Soviet Socialist Republics)

validity
    of projective device, 706-708
    of questionnaire, 673-674
    of surveys, 738-751
values, cultural, institutional advertising and, 482-483, 486-488, 489
verbalization, of public opinion, 55-56
Veterans of Foreign Wars, influence of, in legislature, 169
Vinson, Fred, 177, 178, 183
voting
    eligibility for, 672-673
    participation in, 39
    prediction of, by polling, 75-76, 751-760
    as problem-solving, 619
    propaganda and, 532-542
    public issues and, 624-641
    public opinion and, 4
    (*see also* elections; political behavior)
voting behavior
    determinants of, 413-425
    questionnaires on, 665-674
    variables in, 641-647
    (*see also* political behavior)
voting turnout, measurement of, 670-672, 751-760

Wagman, M., 310, 312
Wagner, Robert F., 177
Wagner Labor Relations Act, 24
Wallas, Graham, 69
Wallin, Paul, 698*n.*
Walsh, W. B., 299*n.*
war
    propaganda during, 508-522, 543-553, 576-582
    public opinion during, 38
    rumor during, 394-396
    totalitarianism and, 467-468
War Bonds, sale of, 382-393
Warner, John C., 106
Warner, W. Lloyd, 97, 132, 143
Washington Public Opinion Laboratory, 742
Waukegan Study of Voter Turnout Prediction, 751-760
wealth, views on, 137-140
"wedge-driving," in war propaganda, 550-551

Wehrmacht (*see* German Army)
White, A. B., 499*n.*
White, M. S., 312
Whitehead, T. N., 557*n.*
Whittington, Will, 177, 178, 179, 180, 181, 183
Wiebe, G. D., 616-623
Wilks, S. S., 605*n.*
Williams, D., 605*n.*
Williams, F., 348*n.*
Williams, Robin M., Jr., 482*n.*, 740*n.*
Willoughby, W. W., 50
Wilson, A. T. M., 557*n.*
Wilson, Woodrow, 165, 174, 211
Winship, Elizabeth C., 271-274
women
   views on role of, 134-135
   voting behavior of, 421-422, 641, 757-758

Woodward, Julian, 81-83
Woolbert, A. G., 503
wording, of questionnaires, 673, 679-681, 729-738
World War II (*see* war)
Wright, Benjamin F., 26*n.*
Wulf, F., 403
Wyant, R., 691*n.*

Yale Attitude Change Project, 508*n.*
Young, J., 605*n.*
Young, Kimball, 62-66

Zander, Alvin, 296*n.*
Zuni, public opinion among, 93